gardening with light & colour

marylyn abbott

with photography by clay perry

Kyle Cathie Limited

In memory of Una Beatrice Read Abbott,
1906 – 1991, who gave me the love of gardens, and
Frederick Archibald Abbott,
1907 – 1972, who indulged this love

Gardens cannot be achieved without the dedication of those who tend them. Many hands have worked in the gardens at Kennerton Green, Mittagong NSW, and at West Green House, near Hartley Wintney, Hampshire, and to them I extend my gratitude, especially to David McKinlay whose dedication achieves the great spectacle of flowers each year at Kennerton Green, and Dominic Rendall and his father Mike, who care so well for the garden at West Green House. I remember gratefully Peter and Iris Seagar who built the seaside garden on Dangar Island and Dora Zweck who allowed me to demolish her garden at 'Yaralla' as I made my first tentative gardening attempts.

I must thank Kyle Cathie who suggested I write down my thoughts on trying to garden at either end of the world and her editors, Kirsten Abbott and Charlie Ryrie, who put an amateur's words into an accepted formula. My gratitude also to Geoff Hayes for the inspired design and to Clay Perry for the beautiful photographs of the two gardens.

Clay Perry wishes to thank Elspeth Barker for her black hollyhock, Kate Campbell of Eye Abbey for the euphorbias and tulips, the administrators of Stonecrop Gardens in New York State for the agapanthus, and Thorp Perrow Arborateum for the autumnal acer.

First published in Great Britain 1999 by
Kyle Cathie Ltd
122 Arlington Road
London NW1 7HP
general.enquiries@kyle-cathie.com
www.kylecathie.com

This paperback edition published 2007

ISBN 978 1 85626 722 9

10 9 8 7 6 5 4 3 2 1

Text © Marylyn Abbott 1999
Photography © Clay Perry 1999

Edited by Kirsten Abbott
Copy-edited by Charlie Ryrie
Design by Geoff Hayes
Production by Lorraine Baird and Sha Huxtable

Marylyn Abbott is hereby identified as the author of this work in accordance with Section 77 of the Copyright, Designs and Patents Act 1988.

A Cataloguing in Publication record for this title is available from the British Library.

Printed and bound in Singapore by Tien-Wah Press

gardening with light & colour

marylyn abbott

with photography by clay perry

contents

introduction

The phone was ringing as I dragged myself to wakefulness. I saw it was the witching hour and silently cursed the friend who had once again forgotten the world has Time Zones. So it was a rather pained 'hello' that bounced off the satellite to be answered by 'I've found your garden'. Instantly I was fully awake and all was forgiven.

The English summer of 1993 had been a cross-roads year, when realisation had come that there was probably only enough time left in my life to undertake one last grand adventure before I gave in and finally learned to play bridge. Like many of my generation I was descended from British pioneers who, although they had been Australians for four generations, still referred to 'the mother country' and were adamant that everything British was best. I had romanced for years about finding the perfect England to live in. It was a colonial's dream of a house surrounded by walls that enclosed formal gardens of some antiquity. Woodlands (bluebell carpeted, naturally), follies, lakes and fields, intersected by chalk streams. It was the Merchant Ivory image of the English countryside, where Jane Austen's Mr Bingley would find comfort and repose.

Fourteen days after that early morning awakening, red-eyed from the long Qantas flight, I pushed open a warped garden gate in Hampshire. There,

emerging from a tendril curtain of hops, was a fine old walled garden. Once formal beds of herbaceous plants now boasted only the strongest of their kind – masses of geranium tangled with waist-high weeds. Two drunken fruit cages stood like sentinels in the bare earth of a former vegetable garden. Box, wobbly with age, formed a jigsaw puzzle in patched-up parterres, and roses, their vigour unrestrained, had crushed whimsical arbours into fragments of trellis.

The crumbling remains of buildings could be glimpsed through a blanket of blackberries. What was the pineapple on top of? Heavens, that emerald green was a lake! Was that an apple tree beneath the brambles and suckers? Never have I been so consumed by desire. This was my garden, and for three long months I waited, turning away from other real estate treasures unearthed from the pages of *Country Life*, waiting for the National Trust to consider my bid to buy the ninety-nine year lease and restore this enchanted place.

Even as my heart claimed this corner of Hampshire my head was saying 'Stop', for on the other side of the world was a charming settler's cottage, surrounded by mature trees and rolling lawns. There new gardens, some still in the planning stage, were being developed alongside a garden that was already part of Australia's

heritage. My horticultural knowledge was of the mother's knee variety, learned in a land where gardeners strove just to make things grow in a climate where days of 30° heat were common-place and rain fell intermittently during the cold winter months. I knew nothing about gardening in England. Terms such as 'half-hardy plants' fascinated me. What were they? What was this curse with such an appealing name of 'ground elder'? For me, English gardening was a mixture of the Chelsea Flower Show and Rosemary Verey's book *The English Gentlewoman's Garden*.

Looking back I did not even have the sense to be terrified. All I could see was the joy of a totally new life where never would the spade be cleaned and put to rest for winter, for no sooner would one summer pass than I would emerge from a plane into another spring and begin all over again. It is now five years on from those dreaming days, and the gardens of West Green House in Hampshire are cleared, and restoration and replanting begun. At Kennerton Green near Mittagong in New South Wales the new gardens have an air of permanency. I have long since stopped being intrigued that I would garden in gardens half a world apart with 'Green' in their name, and I do not have time to consider what my life would be like if the National Trust had not said 'Yes'.

The god Bacchus, surrounded by the busts of Roman emperors, looks down from the east side of West Green House onto the lawns of the green theatre

The demands of two gardens

Climatically my two gardens are both cool temperate, but each with degrees of extremes in climate. The sometimes frozen soil and long winters of England are more intense than those in Mittagong. The dry winds and long summers in the highlands of New South Wales are foreign to England. This has allowed me the opportunity to watch many of the same plants perform in similar but different soils, climates and latitudes. It is an adventure still only at its beginning but already I am noticing that some plants look more vibrant in England than under Australian skies, and colour schemes that in Australia look clear and crisp are positively brash in England.

English friends visiting Australia laugh in amazement at the breakneck pace our plants rush from spring into summer. Within two and a half months from mid-September a range of flowers that gently open over the six months of April to August in England appear nearly all together. The first year I planted my English herbaceous border I wondered what was the matter? Had I purchased unhappy plants? Why were so few flowering? I expected my late daffodils to flower alongside the tulips, bluebells, sparaxis, ranunculus, primulas, Dutch and English iris in the bulb bed to be followed nearly immediately by lilies, forget-me-nots, delphiniums, bearded iris, alstromeria, lupins and penstemons along with the early roses together, just as they would at home.

In Australia I plan for a huge explosion of flowers in wide borders crammed with trees, shrubs and some perennials and lots of early bulbs and annuals. From September to November it is as

flamboyant a mass of flowers as possible, before the deciduous trees darken the beds in dense shade to combat the lack of water and to filter the heat. I plant this way as I simply cannot afford enough water for a midsummer perennial garden. Years ago a special bed was dug alongside a wide green hedge of *Cupressus torulosa*. Here were collected some of the hardiest perennials, asters, catmints, phlox, monarda, achilleas, aquilegias and eryngium amongst many others. They often grew riotously well in early summer, the salvias becoming a blue nightmare as they tried to strangle the entire bed.

But such displays are short lived as inevitably, just before Christmas, along comes an intense wind with searing heat, along with my anger and

frustration as broken, burnt and shrivelled plants have to be cut back before they have properly flowered. Water would allow re-growth but this is not to be for me, and I have learnt to accept that an Australian summer in the southern highlands is a time of dense green shade.

So the Hampshire borders are crammed with too many mid-summer plants from an over indulgence in too many plant catalogues. I have never before experienced such an abundance of varieties that allows for every degree of experimentation of colour and texture in leaf and flower. But the garden has told me to stop, the atmosphere of this old garden is controlling the planting now, just as the climate in Australia dictates what should be grown there.

'. . . a huge explosion of flowers in wide borders crammed with trees, shrubs and some perennials and lots of early bulbs and annuals.'

Responding to culture

The old walls at West Green House, the long green allées, the surrounding fields and woods, all seem to decide the story the garden should tell. I find I am now using colour schemes I would never have contemplated in Australia. Of course England's soft light has much to do with it, a climate that seems to soften all edges with a haze of moisture creates a magic quality of light not even contemplated in the world's driest continent, whatever the latitude.

But my bones say that the accumulated history cannot be ignored in allowing a garden to tell its story. Its civilisation cannot be subservient to fashion but begs us to consider the surrounding countryside, its soils and sky, the dictates of its climate, the colour of the fences, the style and size of the dominant buildings, the shape of the garden area. Any of these elements can suggest what could be pleasing for the garden. Dig deep into the imagination and create a garden that is right for the environment.

To hear your garden speak through all the tempting plant philosophies available is very difficult. Last summer I fell madly in love with the concept of graded colour borders that paid homage to the ideas of two great gardeners – the poet Vita Sackville West and Gertrude Jekyll the painter, both of whom became better known as gardeners. After days of visiting gardens I felt as if the colour wheel in flowers had a life of its own and was rolling across the land in a wide ribbon of yellow, blue, purple, red, orange and yellow again, never stopping to look at the passing scene, oblivious to its surroundings.

Similarly the beautiful idea of a totally white garden softened only by plants of greys and greens escaped from Sissinghurst Castle in Kent. This was a stunning concept devised particularly for a gentle landscape, but it captured the imagination of gardeners worldwide. White gardens appeared in every landscape, pristine white flowers were planted on soils of red or volcanic black. With wind and rain these soils lift and the delicate white blooms so often disappear under red or black dust or mud. It is so important to look at the land and recognise its strengths and limitations and to choose colours and plants that will enhance the existing physical landscape.

This is the story of two gardens and what I feel they have told me to do, especially as I choose the colours for my plants. Both gardens at West Green House and Kennerton Green cover about eight acres. Both are country gardens surrounded by farmland, but I fear neither will be allowed to age in peace as both are within an hour and a half from their country's principal cities, an easy trek for garden lovers. It will take wise local councils to protect both these loved and well-visited gardens for the next generation.

However, it is difficult to compare the two gardens. One is truly England: walled gardens, woodlands, lakes and follies all in a historic framework. The other embodies the traditional Australian garden's giant shade trees, too much lawn and meandering garden beds, its existence tied to the amount of water available each summer. In both gardens there have been similar sized spaces to develop. I cannot believe the different solutions I came up with for two spaces the size of a tennis court. Both gardens needed planting around ponds, vegetable gardens and beds along paths, walls and hedges.

I am sure a painter would see the stories of both my gardens in two totally different artistic styles. I wonder if he would see Kennerton Green as a Grandma Moses painting or would he see West Green House as a romantic Gainsborough. Then again would a musician tell a story with the bright sprightly music of Percy Grainger for Kennerton Green and Purcell for West Green House? Would they even remotely feel the layers of history if the gardens and their legends were unknown. By explaining a little of the gardens' histories, I hope when I divulge my ideas on mixing colours you will see where the original thoughts began.

Opposite top: A carefree mix of lavender, mauve and blue bulbs follow the rill down Cherry Walk at Kennerton Green

Opposite below: Dawn sunshine at Kennerton Green

Above: Old walls enclose the garden at West Green House trapping an atmosphere of a bygone age

Previous page: The crumbling remains of a folly in the lakefield at West Green House

West Green's story

Dominic, who is West Green's woodsman, insists he has seen the apparition, on two occasions, coming from the border alongside the allée of yew. Perhaps it is the lone piper who was once said to walk the paths at night playing a lament for Culloden. My favourite West Green story concerns General or 'Hangman' Hawley, the legendary general of the 1745 Rebellion who is said to have built West Green Manor, as it was known until the 1930s. He built the house at the end of a fine avenue of oak trees backed by dark woods, the avenue terminating at the 'Dutch House' owned by a companion in arms a quarter of a mile away. Each evening the two men dined together turnabout in each other's houses. One particular night Hawley headed home from his friend, through a windy black night, and as the horse and rider neared West Green Manor a terrifying shriek was heard. The frightened horse quickened his pace but the banshee noise rose in ever increasing decibels and the terrified animal bolted. Next morning Hawley was found in a ditch beside the road clutching a small cage similar to a lantern containing his friend's frightened parrot!

A bachelor, Hawley died childless and left the Estate to his housekeeper's second son, whose descendants remained for four generations, selling the Estate in the last years of the 19th century. Then came a succession of owners whose pleasure in the house led them to preserve the outer lines and walls of its 18th century garden, whilst creating their own gardens of unique beauty. First was Dr Playfair who, in 1898, commissioned the brilliant arts and crafts architect Robert Weir Schulz to design a beautiful series of terraces and parterres. These were infilled when Evelyn Duchess of Wellington (always addressed as 'The Duchess' even after remarriage) purchased West Green Manor in 1905 and established within the existing framework gardens that were worthy enough for praise from a *Country Life* article on 21 November 1936 'Looking back at the house…[one] confronts once more the four Roman emperors with wisteria draped over them weeping for their sins.'

About this time, into the story came Evonne FitzRoy whose remarkable life rivals that of any of the great early adventuresses. She was a voluntary nurse in Eastern Europe who was caught up in the Russian Revolution on returning home in 1916. As secretary to Lady Redding, the wife of the Viceroy of India, she met Gandhi on his first visit to the British Head of State. For good measure she motored across the width of Canada in a small car with a 'spinster' friend. To assist the financially

The notorious General Hawley who built West Green House. During his life it was rumoured that he was the son of George Lewis, son of the Elector of Hanover who was to become George I

troubled duchess she persuaded her friend Sir Victor Sassoon to purchase West Green House (the name changed from Manor in the 1930s), on the understanding that it would be home for life for the duchess and herself.

Following Miss Fitzroy's death it became the turn of the great collector Lord McAlpine to add his flourish to the old house at West Green, when he became the first tenant for the National Trust. With the neoclassical architect Quinlan Terry, McAlpine built some of the 20th century's most important garden follies, creating a landscape of innovative architecture in the field surrounding what was still in essence an 18th century garden. The Nymphaeum – a folly based on a Roman fountain – whimsical birdcages, temples and a grotto were constructed surrounding a lake which was inhabited by flamingoes and rare birds, while obscure breeds of cattle and sheep grazed the pasture. A new double avenue of lime trees was punctuated by a column with a Latin inscription that reads 'This monument was built with a large sum of money which would have otherwise fallen, sooner or later, into the hands of the tax gatherer'.

After McAlpine's tenancy the garden was left to quietly crumble into disarray beneath rampant roses to create the picturesque in gardening. But in early 1990 disaster hit the old house, for a bomb planted by the IRA exploded, some months after McAlpine, then an outspoken Conservative party treasurer, had relinquished the lease. The damage was severe and the question was asked if the house should be repaired or demolished. West Green House was saved but during its years of neglect the garden quietly slipped into a sleeping

Above: Miss Evonne FitzRoy as a young woman

Opposite: The neoclassical architect Quinlan Terry designed the impressive Nymphaeum which today forms the backdrop to a classical water garden

beauty hidden beneath weeds; and brambles became a blanket in time.

At this point of the story I enter and another chapter opens. Spectres, duchesses, visionaries, all have left their evidence of occupation of Hawley's Manor in the garden. The terraces of Dr Playfair now form the rake of the Green Theatre, the parterre filled with roses in the duchess's time is now rearranged but still entices, and although Lord McAlpine's lakefield of follies is in sad decay they are currently being restored.

Feeling the weight of what had gone before, I felt it impossible to indulge in a fashionable concept of gardening without involving the garden's story in my plans. History creates a special aura which guides me to what garden styles I should choose, which colours will express the story. I have been fortunate in stumbling upon a garden that allows the fun of the grand gesture, and its beauty will absorb fanciful plantings – but only on its own terms.

Kennnerton Green

But this is only half the tale I want to tell for 'down under' is another garden at the opposite end of the spectrum. If a child sat down with some crayons and drew a house, it would probably have a pitched roof with a chimney on top, and a plain front door would be placed in the middle with windows on either side. This simplistic style is the design of an Australian settler's cottage, the first dwellings they made as they moved inland into the bush. Kennerton Green started as such a dwelling, and my garden surrounds a simple house built by a pioneer in the 1860s. It is still basically an unpretentious settler's cottage painted pristine white, rising out of beds of frothy white cottage flowers of picture-book prettiness. The surrounding side-beds are an extension of this cloud of white flowers.

For the past thirty years the garden has been open to visitors each spring. I first came to it on a charity day to see the white flowers and stroll the tree-shaded lawns that surround the house, edging my way into the delightful small rose garden tucked away behind precisely clipped hedges, where old standard roses march in single file along the pond. Wisteria and clouds of all types of blossoms of the palest pink make this an

Right: A dense umbrella of *Wisteria sinensis* frames the colonial settler's cottage at Kennerton Green

Opposite: Every spring plantings of pure white flowers fill the cottage's front borders

Previous page: Tubs of *Azalea* 'Alba Magna' line the back verandah at Kennerton Green

idealised English garden, totally enclosed by a grey-green landscape of eucalyptus.

Australia was settled in 1788, and within twenty years the barrier of the Blue Mountains had been penetrated, and colonists had carved out small farms in the lands beyond. The cool highlands south of Sydney soon became in colonial parlance 'a hill station' where families retreated in December, January and February from the humid coastal heat. Local merchant princes came to the highlands and built grand homes surrounded by splendid gardens that were destined to become household names in polite society.

Along the same road as my cottage, a solid 1900 Federation-style house was built. By the 1950s the elderly owner endowed the main house as a children's home, and moved with his young carer to what is now my cottage. To pass the time the young man started to plant trees, and Ivan 'Snow' Hansen, one of Australia's best-known gardeners, started his career. Although much

smaller than it is today, the garden became part of Australia's gardening heritage during the thirty years that Sir Jock and Lady Pagan spent at Kennerton Green, with 'Snow' Hansen as head gardener. Their preferences set the style that must be incorporated in all I do. My mother and I purchased Kennerton Green in November 1988.

In country Australia the first battle to be fought is to protect the garden from the wind, to ensure a water supply, and to have a good line of prayers to preserve the garden from drought, flood, hot winds and from armies of snails, slugs and grasshoppers. Roses, blossom and setting fruit also need divine protection from flocks of beautiful birds: large white sulphur-crested cockatoos, sugar-pink and grey galahs, scarlet, red and blue mountain lowrys, and the spectacular Rosella parrots whose brilliance is an Australian icon, all are programmed to denude a garden. Kennerton Green answered two prayers: it had mature trees trained into windbreaks along its paddocks, it had

an area where a large dam could be made, and in an emergency, it had access to town water. Surrounding the garden were vast, empty paddocks that were crying out to be included in the planted areas.

Like most gardeners, I took twelve months to watch the original garden through the seasons to understand my land. I needed to imagine what new gardens would flow naturally from the original, and to come to terms with the spirit of the place. As in England the stage for my garden was set by the house, here it was white and simple with the aura of an older Australia. The charm of the house lay in the way it appeared to be nesting amidst its garden so I thought the garden I would plan should revolve around paths always designed to return to the centre, an inward looking garden of soft curves inviting a search around a corner gently unfolding its surprises, tall gates that open onto one scene and then another. Allées, grand vistas, and large formal plantings, would have

dwarfed the original dwelling, but I decided to use these elements in more humble form, along with simple plantings in blocks of colour, to punctuate the different images I hoped to create.

This book illustrates how I approached two incredibly different gardens at the extremes of architectural design and human aspiration. Both were gardens with their own histories, but both I feel have called to me, one to restore it from nearly terminal ruin, the other to realise its potential. Neither garden is finished and probably will never be.

The Aboriginal people tell us of a dream time when every rock, tree, river and animal, in fact every single thing, has a spirit. I do not disbelieve them. Every garden has its spirit, and it is the gardener's task to interpret this. Gardens must come from their creator's soul. The plants have also been my teachers, their colours in particular have shown me how to set the style and create what I hope is the picture that each garden needs.

'The charm of the house lay in the way it appeared to be nesting amidst its garden . . .'

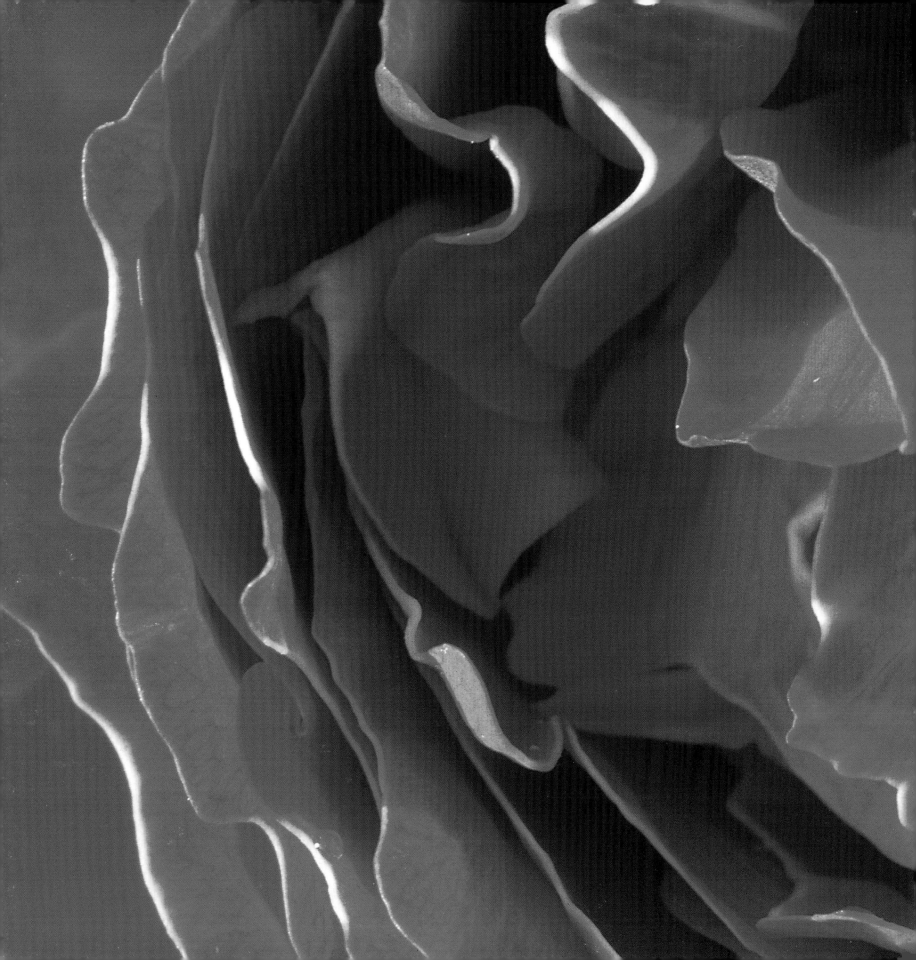

1 | shining jewels

'. . . here there would be a collection of jewel-like plants of ruby, amethyst and sapphire . . .'

Left: Crimson *Rosa* 'Cardinal Hume' with ruby *Dahlia* 'Arabian Night' glow in the 'dark' border at West Green House

Above: *Rosa* 'Charles de Mills'

The moment of truth came in late 1993 when I finally owned my long idealised English garden. I had knowingly placed myself in the epicentre of 20th century gardening, surrounded by gardens considered to be the world's best: within a two hour radius were the gardens of Hidcote, Sissinghurst, Hatfield House, Hadspen and the RHS Gardens at Wisley – to name just the tip of the iceberg. Moreover, every cool temperate plant I had ever dreamed of growing was available within an hour's drive.

All of a sudden it was indigestible, an over-indulgence in excellence, but luckily the garden saved me, it gave me time to think. It was not ready; I was not ready; I had moved too fast. Dreams on a distant shore are beautiful, but now I had to understand a new climate, landscape, light and hundreds of plants I never knew existed – plants which most of my new friends could give precise Latin names to. The garden was like a beautiful woman of a certain age: the good bones were there but a period of concentrated pampering was needed before the beautiful dress could even be considered. This gave me the breathing space I needed in which to learn.

The first summer was spent tending bonfires as years of neglect were incinerated. My restoration policy was to retain any tree or shrub that could be expected to live, to move any herbaceous plants and bulbs that were salvageable into a newly made nursery area, and to store any hard landscaping material that we found. I still smile as I remember my first summer when we not only had to clear the borders, but also an amazing area where brambles yielded up trees, follies, temples

and a leaking green lake. I allowed eighteen months for weed eradication and mulching, so when the first plants arrived in the autumn of 1995 we provided them with pampered earth attracting juicy worms, and I had a level playing field to test my skills.

My gardening years at West Green House are simply another chapter in its history, so my ideas can only be gently laid upon an already beautiful, formal structure. But as a gardener steeped in the fashionable 20th century theories of colour wheels and saturated colour, what was I to do with beds that still contained random lilacs, clumps of the magenta Rugosa rose *Rosa* 'Roseraie de l'Haÿ', a tripod of sugar pink roses and some randomly placed apple trees?

One dusk I entered the main walled garden; late sun played on the warm Hampshire brick walls but the south wall was dramatic and gloomy, a green bank of precision clipped yews, hollies and laurels towered over by cathedral high branches of limes. For a brief moment I caught sight of a flash of red, followed by crimson with an after-glimpse of black blue. It was divine inspiration, for immediately I knew what I wanted to plant in this first border: here there would be a collection of jewel-like plants of ruby, amethyst and sapphire darkly glowing as if from the depths of an open treasure box. They would be the colours from the varnished gloom of a baroque ecclesiastical painting, the magenta of a beretta, a red cloak, a purple sash. My clumps of *Rosa* 'Roseraie de l'Haÿ' had inadvertently shown me that a dark area with poor light needs points of strong, rich colour blazing from a shiny background.

Heavy colours in northern light

Conventional wisdom would I believe call for light colours to lift a dark space, but light colours can be very cold, and light clear colours have a modern crispness which was not the feeling I wanted to evoke inside West Green's historic walls, so I opted to use the colours of burgundy, maroon, cerise or magenta. I had never used them before, in fact I had never liked them at all as they are hot heavy colours that capture heat and are totally deadening under the strong white light of summer days in hotter climates. They had always pictured for me the glow in a threatening sky before a ferocious duststorm, the stuffiness of unused parlours, the harsh pink sunsets in dry years that assure us there is no rain on its way.

But in the light of northern latitudes it is so different, deep reds and purples are rich, glamorous colours adding a luxurious allure to colour schemes: all of a sudden they became new and exciting.

My plan was not for an exercise in graded or saturated colour, but to keep my picture of flashes of baroque jewels. As I searched I was intrigued to find many of these plants already had names inspired by the rich and princely church: *Rosa* 'Cardinal de Richelieu', an old Gallica rose of a rich velvety purple fading to a fine dusty purple as it ages; *Rosa* 'Cardinal Hume', a modern rose of dull crimson purple; *Rosa* 'The Prince', an English rose of the blackest scarlet, and *Rosa* 'Tuscany Superb', a burgundy-crimson velvety Gallica. These were my first choices, and it fast became a treasure hunt for the richest, darkest plants I could find from early spring to late summer. The tulips had similarly

'. . . it fast became a treasure hunt for the richest, darkest plants I could find . . .'

evocative names, there was 'Queen of Night'; a shiny purple-black 'Black Parrot', all ruffles and sexy as a black negligée; the Tyrian purple 'Negrita', and 'Arabian Mystery', another purple tulip but this time flecked with white.

Deep rich colours create their own glamour, but if you have limited space or don't want to devote an entire border to these deep hues, they are spectacular when used to lift other colours or to bring a bland colour scheme to life. Dark and poorly lit areas benefit from points of strong rich colour, but jewel colours can be equally striking when used in paler beds. There are times when a yellow border, for example, comes to look rather like a pool of melted butter, so add light and contrast with dark jewels and navy blues. The sapphire blue *Agapanthus* 'Midnight Blue', some trumpets of *Hemerocallis* 'Root Beer', the blackest red, and a few spikes of a favourite dark iris will lift a patch of yellow; add a clump or two of the bronze *Rosa* 'Just Joey' to enliven a large border.

Left: Annual *Ranunculus* 'Nearly Black' glow in the warm sunlight

Opposite top left: The shooting stars of *Allium schubertii*

Opposite top right: *Knautia macedonica* – a dark red scabious

Opposite below: Vatican-hued Gallica *Rosa* 'Cardinal de Richelieu'

Form and structure

To give the bed height and weight I planted two *Cotinus coggygria* 'Royal Purple' and five *Berberis thunbergii*, shrubs with burgundy-bronze leaves, and shaped them: the cotinus were shaped into large 1.2m (4ft) round balls and the berberis into small basket balls 90cm (3ft) high to anchor the garden. Between them the tripod – now draped with the very dark crimson climbing *Rosa* 'Guinée', plays host to star-shaped clematis, the velvet red *Clematis* 'Warszawska Nike' with 'Mrs James Mason', double violet-blue and the crimson 'Royal Velvet' with its dark central stripe.

When the short theatre of the perennial and annual border is over, clipped shapes add continued interest through their form and structure. Box, bay and yew are all ideal subjects for clipping for all year interest, but with jewel colours cotinus and berberis can be substituted as dramatic statements.

The round shapes of my balls of bronze foliage are echoed in a plant I'm literally sprinkling the garden with, the amethyst-silver balls of *Allium cristophii* which become the stars of the early summer garden, their globes joining this border to the next. The feathery *Anthriscus sylvestris* 'Ravens-wing', black cowparsley with creamy white flowers, is also an early summer plant which is later overtaken by the brighter green foliage of *Astrantia major* 'Ruby Wedding' and its nearly identical cousin *A. major* 'Hadspen Blood', sprinkled with delightful small deep crimson flowers edged in sharp points of petals, striking a slightly deeper note.

Below: An intermingling of ruby red with *Astrantia major* 'Ruby Wedding' and *Lupinus* 'My Castle'

Opposite: The colour of old crimson brocade glows from the tall pokers of *Allium sphaerocephalon*

'The sumptuous dark colours evoke a rich past, the ruby brocades on a Georgian wing chair, the deep greens and blues of old tapestry.'

Summer opulence

Irises are essential to fill the flowering gap of early summer, quite a dull time before the perennial border gets underway in earnest. There are many black irises to choose from: I've chosen the blue-black *Iris* 'Black Watch', purple-black *I.* 'Evening Silk' and the violet-blue *I.* 'Dusky Challenger', with *I.* 'Burgundy Bubbles' the exact colour of *Rosa* 'Cardinal de Richelieu'. Peonies are another salvation for this time of the year, and I have planted *Paeonia* 'Paul M. Wilde' in this border, a rich red that is rather shy in flowering. The garnet red bearded iris 'Warrior King' will look good nearby in early summer as will the Siberian iris 'Ruffled Velvet', all red-purple and black. Height is supplied by the darkest of delphiniums *D.* 'Black Knight' and the richly purple *Campanula glomerata*. The tall *Allium sphaerocephalon* is a brilliant magenta as autumn approaches, flinging up tall dramatic rods that give a zip to a tiring garden.

My summer colour dots are supplied by magenta *Knautia macedonica* and *Lychnis coronaria* 'Magenta', and my exclamation marks are *Atriplex hortensis* var. *Rubra* which grows tall between the rich red dahlia 'Arabian Knight'. It all looks like a late summer Vatican meeting, especially when the dark purple flowers of *Penstemon* 'Burgundy' hang down gently, as though asleep through a long homily on a hot afternoon.

This border is sombrely luxuriant most of the season, with melancholy plants including *Sedum atropurpureum*, murky purples and blues trying to shine through a white haze that becomes a bright mass of red-pink flowers in summer, lightening the gloom beside big clumps of the black grass *Ophiopogon planiscapus* 'Nigrescens'. *Allium karataviense* pops through as large dusty lavender tennis balls above broad grey green leaves, and to break the sombre line I've inserted splashes of the violet-purple bulb *Brodiaea* 'Queen Fabiola', which flowers in midsummer and resembles a small agapanthus whilst the small growing sapphire *Agapanthus* 'Midnight Blue' adds glamour at the close of summer. Similar in form and structure, but flowering months apart, they ensure a continuity of design in a plant grouping.

The sumptuous dark colours evoke a rich past, the ruby brocades on a Georgian wing chair, the deep greens and blues of old tapestry. They are not the bright, simple colours of Modigliani or a Conran room, but colours of an old landscape. I feel they belong to the history of a house of West Green's age.

Iris are among the most user-friendly of all plants. They perform just as well in the magic of a cool garden, or beside a hot path in Provence. The choicest iris I have ever seen were growing at Junee, outback Australia! After the flamboyance of the tulip and before the summer border really gets going, there is very little at eye-level in the herbaceous border, a gap perfectly filled with iris. Accompany dark coloured iris with deep red peonies to achieve several weeks of opulent colour. Their contrasting shapes also create a pleasing balance of lightness and stability.

The barely controlled glory of a dazzling clematis clambers over a free-standing tripod

Rich heavy colours

I felt a few brighter reds were needed in my dark bed for summer so I have put in clumps of *Lupinus* 'My Castle', an old brick red to break the overall pall. To continue this colour late in the season, I do like the deep rust red of *Sedum* 'Herbstfreude'. Sedums are excellent plants, crisp succulent leaves upright all through the dryest days in pleasing rounded clumps. Then in the last days of summer, they grow and spread flowering with great brilliance, becoming dark sculptural heads in concert with the darkening season.

I would never plant such rich colours together *en masse* at Kennerton Green. When so many of the deep red and purple perennial flowers come into flower the mercury starts to creep to nearly 30° and the plants would look tired and hot, as unsuitable as a heavy velvet robe would be to wear. A Kennerton Green garden answers the heat with deep green and crisp white which could look very stark in dark shade under the pale skies of a cool climate.

Despite their size and structure lupins are equally at home in a small garden – making a proud statement in much the same way as overstuffed furniture can sometimes make a small room look more important. If you only have room for one or two clumps of lupins, try the deep purple-magenta *Lupinus* 'Thundercloud'. Plants choose a gardener just as much as a gardener selects the plants, and lupins do not flourish in every situation, so if you don't succeed with these throw them out and plant something different.

'It all looks like a late summer Vatican meeting, especially when the dark purple flowers of *Penstemon* 'Burgundy' hang down gently, as though asleep through a long homily on a hot afternoon.'

Essential annuals

A garden class came into my garden in mid-summer and were very dismissive of my use of annuals, but I find them essential to fill midseason gaps. The huge bare spot left by late June from clearing away the luxurious *Papaver orientale* 'Patty's Plum' is appropriated by the gloss of *Salpiglossis* 'Chocolate Box', a shiny mixture of purples, dark reds and browns. The velvet *Dianthus barbatus* 'Nigrescens' – absolutely a product of the underworld – needs cutting back by mid-summer, so to have the dark leaved ruby-red *Antirrhinum majus* 'Black Prince' tucked in nearby is a bonus, as it will flower well into the autumn if sown late enough. Other bare spots are filled by the dark red-brown *Cosmos atrosanguineus* and beside the lawn I cram in the black *Viola* 'Midnight Runner'.

Some years I weave a magenta-purple *Cleome* through the centre of the bed, its tall stems of 'spider flowers' often reaching 1.75m (5ft) tall. It is a welcome fresh addition to push through rose bushes, tired after the flowering season. Repeatedly I am asked its name to be greeted by disinterest once I say it is an annual.

I do despair of the current anathema to annuals. Of course some are over large and bright, but it is a shame to dismiss all this genus, for beyond the obvious there are gems. I have been accused of being an old testament prophet in my defence of annuals, but I look at my garden in late summer, still flowering brightly, and say a silent prayer of thanks for these wonderful plants. Perhaps in time, they will be resurrected to fashion, like the now acceptable dahlia.

Annuals give enormous flexibility. They are perfect for filling gaps in spring and late summer, little fussed by climate. They are especially useful in smaller gardens planted in groups amongst earlier flowering perennials to introduce more flower as the perennials straggle and fade. In beds with roses and shrubs in the dark jewel colours I carry this colour theme into late summer by running the tall magenta cosmos and cleome through the bed and tuck in *Salpiglossis* 'Chocolate Box' at their feet for luscious deep shades. And don't be frightened of dahlias, perfect for late summer brilliance especially those of paint box colours, backed by leaves of bronze they will flower until they die back in horror when touched by the first frost.

'I have been accused of being an old testament prophet in my defence of annuals...'

The old parrot cage surrounded by trees just coming to leaf in the spring time at Kennerton Green

deep jewel-coloured favourites

Allium sphaerocephalon

Often called the drumstick allium or the round-headed leek, densely packed fluffy magenta heads appear in late summer at 60-90cm (2-3ft), on thin wiry stems. These easy-to-grow alliums seem to thrive whatever the soil, ideal for growing through low-growing denser plants to provide dramatic outbursts of colour above as autumn approaches.

Campanula glomerata 'Superba'

Also known as the clustered bellflower, the wide open bells of this erect 60cm (2ft) tall perennial are deepest violet-purple throughout the summer, providing vivid clumps of colour in the middle of a border. This bellflower will grow vigorously in both sun and shade in all but waterlogged soils and is said to be invasive, but I've never found so. If you cut stems back hard after the first flush of flowers, you are rewarded with a second display.

Dahlia 'Arabian Knight'

Largely ignored for decades, dahlias really do deserve more than a second glance, as they provide a perfect injection of colour to a late summer border. Nurseryman Nori Pope introduced me to the lovely green foliage and brilliant red flowers of 'Arabian Knight'; flowering from midsummer to the first frosts, reaching 1.5-2m (5-6ft). Plant this variety in rich well-drained soil in groups for vivid splashes of colour. All dahlia tubers are frost tender and should be lifted in autumn and replanted after the last frosts in spring, or treat as annuals and reinvest in new tubers each year.

Delphinium 'Black Knight'

If you have room for only one group of jewel-coloured spiky plants, choose this delphinium, a majestic 2-m (6-ft) tall with deep purple flowers and black-purple eyes in early summer. One of the tallest plants in the perennial border, delphiniums must be staked and like fairly rich but well-drained soil. After flowering, cut them right back to encourage a late season showing.

Dianthus barbatus 'Nigrescens'

These glossy blackish-red Sweet Williams shine out from the lower levels of a border in early summer, with foliage as dark as the flower and an intensely sweet and heady scent. Plant them in rich well-drained soil in full sun, and be ruthless and throw plants away to start again when they get straggly as Sweet Williams rarely thrive for more than three or four seasons. Despite this, and their relatively short flowering period, they deserve a place in any garden.

Lupinus 'Thundercloud'

The moody tall, about 1m (3ft), spikes of perennial lupins lift any garden, large or small, but they don't like humidity, and can be a mecca for black-flies and slugs in a damp English summer. In well-drained soils in warmer climates they start to flower in spring through to late summer, in cooler climates you may get a double showing if you cut back the spike after its first summer flowering. 'Thundercloud' is a stunning deep purple and magenta selection.

Rosa 'Cardinal de Richelieu'

No garden should be without its roses. The voluptuous purple-red flowers of this summer flowering Gallica rose fade to a divine dusty purple, perfect in any jewel-coloured planting. Compact bushes grow to around 1.2m (4ft). All roses need heavy feeding and mulching to give their best.

Rosa 'Charles de Mills'

I like to train this upright Gallica rose to a tripod or against a wall to make the most of its eager profusion of fragrant double crimson-magenta flowers and mid-green leaves. It happily grows to 1.5-2m (5-6ft) and is completely covered with blooms in early summer.

Rosa 'Guinée'

This climbing hybrid tea rose is of the deepest crimson-red and appears to be almost black in some lights. It is a sturdy, vigorous grower, with plants reaching upto 5m (15ft). Sweetly perfumed, it has a flatish flower of old-world charm and blooms profusely in summer.

Salvia nemorosa 'Ostfriesland'

Plant these dark amethyst perennials in groups of at least seven to eleven plants for a persistent presence in the centre of a sunny border. Growing to about 30cm (1ft) tall, they will provide a glowing wave of colour from midsummer into autumn. The deep blue hidden amongst the magenta is highlighted if planted beside Lavandula angustifolia 'Hidcote'.

2 | blues and mauves

No colour seems to provoke so many different images as blue; it evokes the whole spectrum of emotions. For an Australian it is the colour of our hills and horizons, for our whole land is clad in the blue-grey eucalyptus. It is a very positive image of beauty, water, shade, relief and repose. In Sydney there is even a blue month – November. Looking up from the harbour the natural blue haze of the native bush retreats before the intense blue of the Jacaranda tree, *Jacaranda mimosifolia*. The branches completely enclose whole suburbs in a blanket of tiny blossoms hanging in pyramidal clusters that fall to carpet houses and pavements. Walls are buried beneath cascades of blue *Plumbago auriculata* intertwined with the magenta-purple *Bougainvillea glabra* while mopheads of blue African lilies *Agapanthus africanus* stand sentinel at busy roundabouts, on verges, paths and drives. November is the month before the intense heat, and the sky is blue, blue, blue. It is a blue world.

The eminent horticulturist Dr Peter Valder once described a 19th century American garden planted entirely in blue. Not only were there blue trees, shrubs and flowers, but the lady wore only ravishing *toilettes* in blue. I wondered if the lady came from a hot climate where blue gets a good press as it is often seen as a cold hard colour in northern climates. For me blues are happy shades, conjuring up warm nostalgic images of childhood. Blue is never static – look for a time at the tall aconites, delphiniums, campanulas that are the stars of a blue border, there is always a feeling of movement like the light in an ever changing sky or in a restless sea. The bluebells on a woodland floor seem only a haze as we look into their depth.

Blue borders in cool climates

The colour blue ranges from grey-green blue to blue with some red pigment so it becomes purple or mauve, and these were the emotional shades that I chose to take my West Green border into the sunnier beds. Blue is such an atmospheric colour, so beautiful and mysterious, it reflects the elements that make up this garden. The range of blue flowers is immense: I decided on one blue border, it became two then three as I could not resist another wonderful blue thistle, a gentian, even a bright blue cabbage! The borders go through every emotion, shape and texture, housing giants and midgets of the garden world.

There are blues for every situation and scale of garden. If you have a small sunny corner that needs some drama, try a combination of blue such as *Cerinthe major* 'Purpurascens' and blue cabbage. The shapes as well as the colours of the plants provide good contrast, the round solid shape of the cabbage giving stability to the low branches of the cerinthe.

Cerinthe also needs a companion planting of a single dense colour. Try it behind a group of *Lavandula angustifolia* 'Hidcote', where the lavender's intense violet flower will intensify mauve highlights in the cerinthe.

Right: Each spring I remember the hot autumn of 1992 when every bluebell was planted by hand after we mattocked the ground open

Previous page: *Iris sibirica* 'Tropic Night'

'The bluebells
on a woodland
floor seem
only a haze as we
look into their
depth.'

Clear blues for spring

Spring belongs to *Brunnera macrophylla* 'Dawson's White' with cream-splashed leaves and forget-me-not blue flowers. The blue shines out under early cream flowers – the tulips *Tulipa* 'Françoise', ivory flamed with yellow, the peony style *T.* 'Mount Tacoma' and *T.* 'Maureen' which opens cream fading to white. The tulips also nod above dense clumps of *Pulmonaria* 'Roy Davidson' with its clusters of blue bells echoing watery blue sky. *Corydalis flexuosa* is a brilliant plant, easy to grow beside a dry gravel path in most climates, an intense blue flower above lacy blue-green leaves, a small necessity for an early spring border. By midsummer *Clematis* x *durandii* claims this role; although it trails it is a tidy plant, its deep indigo flowered mounds either covering spent bulbs or providing a blanket for the clear bright blue drumsticks of *Allium caeruleum* to push through.

Other early blue flowers tend to be the palest I can find such as *Veronica gentianoides* with its spikes of tiny blue flowers above a mantle of small green leaves, and *Campanula persicifolia* 'Chettle Charm', a single white flower frosted pale blue. Aquilegias seed throughout, *Aquilegia* 'Blue Bonnet' and the double pale blue *A. vulgaris* 'Blue Star' add a necessary lightness. Little clumps of the khaki green dwarf iris *I.* 'Triplicate' look smart among the blues – I love offbeat colours and look for them all the time.

Opposite: It has everything: shape, texture and wondrous colour – cabbage 'Red Drumhead'

Right: *Malva sylvestris* 'Primley Blue'

No spring garden should be without aquilegias, their delicate, iridescent heads fluttering like a cloud of butterflies above the emergent foliage of their companions. The variety is intoxicating: try *Aquilegia alpina* cultivars, the blue and white *A. caerulea* or the beautiful dark *A. vulgaris* 'Blackbird'. *Aquilegia flabellata* 'Ministar' has the brightest blue and white flowers, and as with all aquilegias their feet are clothed in leaf mounds of great beauty, branches of round scalloped leaves, welcome in their own right.

Bold summer blues

I find the bearded iris essential to carry the border towards early summer, there are so many good blues to choose from. I have planted *Iris* 'Zua' a glacial blue white, the silver-blue *I.* 'Divine Duchess', ruffled light blue and white *I.* 'Fair Dinkum' and the huge *I.* 'Sierra Grande', an absolute favourite. Further along the border is *Iris sibirica*, tall, graceful and slim with foliage that looks good all season, providing fine vertical accents after the blue flowers fade. The bright *Anchusa azurea* 'Opal' next sways beneath another sky-blue flower, *Delphinium* 'Summer Skies'. Blue and white hoods of *Aconitum* x *cammarum* 'Bicolor' follow in this patch by midsummer. The most spectacular blue *Anchusa azurea* 'Loddon Royalist' fights off the intense violet blue *Geranium* x *magnificum* that riots down the border until challenged for control by the late summer triumph *Eryngium* x *tripartitum*, a brilliant thistle that changes from green to silver blue to purple. In the driest part of the border the bright purple blues of lavender *Lavandula angustifolia* 'Hidcote' offer a frontal foil to *Cerinthe major*

'Purpurascens'. I know it's trendy, but is irresistible with its glaucous leaves an aqua-green veined with lavender, all crowned with a navy blue flower.

Every adjective is appropriate here: tall, elegant, intense, stunning, they all neatly describe the 90cm (3ft) *Iris* **'Sierra Grande' the most beautiful I think of all iris. Its standards are frozen blue white ice, its falls a midsummer blue, with ruffles as extravagant as a ballroom dancer's dress with a glimpsed underskirt of paler blue. These two tone blue iris grown in clumps will make an architectural statement of the most satisfying proportions in any garden.**

I am committed to finding more blue roses. The vigorous rambler *Rosa* 'Veilchenblau' is often called the blue rose, in fact it is not blue but its clusters of small purple-violet flowers often streaked with white are a lovely substitute. The tiny mauvey-purple buttons of the multiflora rambler *Rosa* 'Russeliana' intertwined with the small flowered *Clematis* 'Mrs Cranshaw' cover a tripod beautifully. I have placed the pinky-mauve hybrid perpetual *Rosa* 'Reine des Violettes' with the dark leaved *Penstemon digitalis* 'Husker's Red' which boasts mother of pearl flowers, a good foil for a blue bed. With some misgivings I am trying two modern roses, the large blue rose *R.* 'Charles de Gaulle' is a colour triumph for a blue border - and *R.* 'Dream Lover' is a centred lilac-pink. I think the flowers are a little big and too modern in shape for me but I am prepared to overlook this just to get the colour.

In gentler, northern light, blue and white can be too stark a contrast, so the best trick to lift a blue border that has merged with the atmosphere by midsummer is to tuck small clumps of the common annual *Lobelia erinus* **'Cambridge Blue' into all the cracks and crevices. This very light, very pale blue seems to enhance the moody blues better than white which seems just too much of a contrast. In bright sunny light, however, we can choose whether to use white or subtler colours with blue. Creamy-yellow also lifts a blue border in cooler light so plant clumps of the yellow-eyed blue daisy** *Felicia amelloides* **among purer blues.**

The crochet blue-green leaves of *Ruta graveolens* **'Jackman's Blue' makes layers of lace leaves for a host of summer flowers to perform above. Early summer pruning keeps it to a compact mound for the bare legs of the** *Lilium regale* **'Royal Gold' or the standard rose** *R.* **'Graham Thomas' to flower on high – a perfect contrast in a warm dry garden.**

'Cerinthe... irresistible with its glaucous leaves an aqua green veined with lavender, all crowned with a navy blue flower.'

Right: The deservably fashionable plant *Cerinthe major* **'Purpurascens'**

Previous page: Ridged drumsticks of *Echinops ritro* **'Veitch's Blue' in the blue border looking towards the potager at West Green House**

'…blue beds adjoin clear, bright yellow, leading the eye from one colour to the next.'

Below: The atmosphere is imbued with shades of blue at the start of the blue and yellow border at Kennerton Green

Opposite: *Echinops ritro* **'Veitch's Blue' – geometric balls of blue spikes**

Blues in warmer climates

Blue is used differently in my Australian garden, largely in blocks to tie other colours together. At Kennerton Green sky blue beds adjoin clear bright yellow, leading the eye from one colour to the next. Under a hot sky these colours are clean and bright even on the hottest days, while in cooler climates brilliant yellow needs subduing, it makes a lovely accompaniment to navy blue. I love blue spiky plants pushing up through green foliage and include the Canterbury bells, *Campanula medium*, among my all-time favourites. I have planted these along with clumps of blue cupped *Campanula persicifolia* and the stiff steel blue drumsticks of powdery blue *Echinops ritro* 'Veitch's Blue' behind banks of *Centaurea montana*, a most hardy plant.

Echinops need space and would overpower a small garden but if you fall in love with the thistle flowers try growing eryngium for the same effect. *Eryngium* **'Miss Wilmott's Ghost' will grow to about 1m (3ft) but spread no more than 30cm (1ft), producing silvery blue flowers. Or try** *E.* x *tripartitum* **which changes from green to silver to purple-blue.**

Perovskia 'Blue Spire' is a good plant for dry patches, with tall lavender-blue spikes, and monkshood *Aconitum napellus* likes the shade. I use *Allium giganteum*, tall stems with giant purple balls, to usher in a patch of bluey-mauve where treasured *Rhododendron* 'Blue Diamond' back into a cool corner. The Swan River daisy *Brachyscombe iberidifolia* accompanies the annual *Viola* 'Moody Blue', and the purple wallflower *Erysimum*

'Bowles' Mauve' flowers from winter's end till midsummer. The common foxglove *Digitalis purpurea* saturates the end of my blue border in a haze of mauve which turns back to blue with drifts of *Iris* 'China Blue' rising through *Lithospermum diffusum*, a ground hugging blue flower that responds to the driest conditions.

This blue bed then turns again to yellow, then back to the blue theme where an avenue of five large *Ceanothus* 'Blue Pacific' form huge balls of intense blue flowers in spring, perfect with the background blue of Dutch Iris, rising through the Japanese woodland plant *Epimedium*, its flowers the softest yellow. The ceanothus are surrounded by clipped balls of *Lavandula angustifolia* or *L. x allardii*, a firm favourite in Australian gardens, and blue flowers carry the story through to midsummer. Blocks of yellow and blue continue for 100m (110yds) before meeting an embankment of white to adjust the eye to the next story.

Ceanothus are much too beautiful to dismiss but I have found that, for no reason at all, they can die suddenly leaving huge gaps. *Ceanothus* 'Gloire de Versailles', with masses of powder blue flowers to match the cool blue skies of the early season, is at home given space and underplanted with pale blues and creams, but equally happy in confined spaces trained against a greyish or honey-coloured wall or fence. Or place the denser purple-blue *C.* 'Concha' against a wall for a late spring show. Lavenders are also irresistible but they too can depart suddenly, generally from too much moisture on a rich soil.

blue favourites

Aconitum 'Spark's Variety'

Like late summer fine delphiniums, they are tall spires of hooded flowers up to 1.2m (4ft) tall. This variety includes all the sombre dark blue shades that suggest the far recesses of a cloister, its hidden face providing a sense of mystery. Plants come in white and shades of blue and will flower in semi-shade or full sun in rich soil.

Anchusa azurea 'Loddon Royalist'

Although a perennial, I find in England I must treat it as an annual. Incredibly intense bright blue flowers that grow to 1.2m (4ft) on hairy stems. It is the most marvellous blue perennial I've seen, flowering from mid-spring to summer.

Campanula persicifolia 'Chettle Charm'

Has fine but strong stems up to 1m (3ft) tall, with bell-shaped flowers just tinged with blue. This perennial likes full sun and a good soil and should be grown in groups of five to seven plants to create an effect.

Cerinthe major 'Purpurascens'

I can never decide whether cerinthe or alliums are the wonder plants of today. Cerinthe is an irresistible addition, with glaucous blue-green foliage and navy blue flowers all summer. It is a bushy plant, about 60cm (2ft) tall, and is at its best when grown in generous clumps in mid-border. It thrives in full sun but will tolerate partial shade. Treat it as an annual in most cool, temperate climates, but in warmer areas you can cut it back and it will return.

Ceanothus 'Blue Pacific'

A tall, broad shrub that can grow to 2m (6ft), covered by masses of dense, intense, bright blue flowers in spring. It needs well-drained soil and an open position, and can be trained against walls. Unfortunately ceanothus tend to be shortlived but replacements grow quickly.

Clematis 'Perle d'Azur'

A beautiful, misty, pale blue-flowered climber that can go to 5m (15ft) in a mass of midsummer blooms. Clematis do not like to have their roots disturbed and in warmer areas a below-surface rock placed over their roots keeps them cool. I have allowed this clematis to grow alongside Rosa 'Veilchenblau'. I do like this combination.

Delphinium 'Pacific Giant'

Tall spikes of blue flowers up to 2m (6ft), that come in all shades of blue from near-white mauve to blue-black. Snails and slugs feast on their new shoots, but they are the superstars of any summer border. They are also the heart-breakers of a blue border if they are not well staked, for the stems are brittle and easily snapped in wind and rain.

Jacaranda mimosifolia

Although the tender jacaranda is not suitable for northern European gardens, this tall tree is a wonderful addition to any sub-tropical or frost-free Mediterranean climate garden. Covered with ferny, mid-green foliage, for three weeks in summer it is covered by large clusters of bell-shaped flowers of jacaranda-blue in large clusters. It will cope with some frost but must be covered as a small plant in frosty areas. It tends to be a 'dirty' tree in cooler districts where it will lose its foliage.

Rosa 'Veilchenblau'

A rambling rose that sends out bunches of tiny flowers of a blue-lilac colour, semi-double with a white eye. It is fragrant and vigorous growing to nearly 5m (15ft) feet. Although said to fade in the sun, I have not found this.

Syringa vulgaris (lilac)

One Sunday morning in Denmark I saw a pastor in black vestments on the steps of a white church, the entire scene surrounded by a lilac hedge in full flower. This memory is one of my most treasured mind pictures. Lilacs are large bushes that can grow to 5m (15ft) tall and varieties are available in pinks, purples, lavenders, creams and white – flowering in mid-spring with a heady perfume.

Opposite: *Delphinium* 'Black Night'

'Mauve . . . glows on dull days, is silvery under raindrops and has a luminosity I have never seen in the southern hemisphere.'

Moody mauves

In cool temperate gardens in North America, Ireland and Britain, mauve seems to shine. It glows on dull days, is silvery under raindrops and has a luminosity I have never seen in the southern hemisphere. On hot afternoons under brilliant sky mauve needs to be backed with stronger shades. Unlike lavender, it seems to bleach under intense sunlight, but when backed by blue to keep it cool mauve is strong enough to hold its own.

Dusty mauve also strengthens when backed by leaves of steel grey or polished ebony. The dark Shiraz leaves of *Geranium traversii* var. *elegans* 'Crûg Strain' forms neat spreading mounds, its small white flower, smudged with pink, takes on the mauve shades of its neighbours. Whilst the leaves create all the theatre that mauve requires.

Yellow and mauve are very fashionable but they are not two colours I like together unless there are masses of blues to divide them. Though there is a surprise element from the clash of contrary colours, I find it worrying – but this is the joy of gardening. I have taken as my motto the one inscribed over the door in the 1720s at West Green House that reads 'Do as you please'. Knowing what is said of General Hawley's character it probably actually refers to rather dubious activities but I am happy to interpret it as offering carte blanche to keen gardeners!

Raindrops enhance the shades of mauve in *Iris germanica* 'Gallant Rogue' and double blue aquilegia in the garden of West Green House

Mauve borders at West Green

Soon after my arrival in England I fell in love with a spectacular flower. It was the *Papaver orientale* 'Patty's Plum', a giant fantasy of crêpe paper blooms in dark moody mauves and purple as deep as a damson. I felt this gigantic flower would lead the eye from the colours of past times to the more subtle world of elegant mauve in my borders. It provides a dramatic enough statement to tie together the lightening mood of plants ranging from purple-mauve to pink-mauve. The colour of *P. orientale* 'Patty's Plum' comes from the last century, it looks so right in the old garden.

Papaver orientale provide a sensational splash of colour in late spring, and plants can be found in a range of reds through to pinkish-mauves. Plant them near the back of a border, never towards the front as they flower early in the season and leave a gap which needs to be filled when they are cut back in midsummer. You can use annuals but I favour clumps of tall campanulas growing up in front of the perennial poppies to take over the drama.

The mauve bed starts when my beloved mauve poppy unfurls each spring into a world of the small nodding caps of *Aquilegia vulgaris* 'Blackbird'. The aquilegia weaves right through the bed, working past the last of the lavender tulips, the crinkly petalled *Tulipa* 'Blue Parrot', the peony style *T.* 'Lilac Reflection' and the mauve-pink ruffles of the green-veined *T.* 'Webber's Parrot'. Their dominance is immediately challenged by the silver stars

of the mauve *Allium cristophii*, a metallic conductor that flows from the neighbouring bed of rich jewel colours through to the gentler world of mauve, lilac and pink. Later the foxgloves dominate, from the deep purple of the common *Digitalis purpurea*, to the more unusual *Digitalis lanata* with a throat all purple netted. These wave among a bed of *Campanula latiloba* 'Hidcote Amethyst' that flowers as the tall lilac ruffled iris *I.* 'Annabel Jane' quietly fades in early summer.

Foxgloves are part of the dream of an English cottage garden, they are such tempting plants, equally beautiful in wild open spaces and urban plots. Don't be disappointed if they keep disappearing. For although they generously self seed, seasons do come when they fail to reappear.

There are many wonderful summer flowering mauve roses; I have chosen *Rosa* 'William Lobb', the old velvet Moss rose that epitomises in its long lush growth the confidence of the Edwardian age when rich violet was a fashionable colour. The same shade is reflected nearby in the violet-magenta spikes of the *Lupinus* 'Thundercloud', making a brilliant combination. A tripod holds a modern climbing rose of the most extraordinary colour: *Rosa* 'Ash Wednesday' is truly the colour of dead ashes, and rising through it are the tall spires of *Delphinium* 'Astolat', its soft lavender-pink combining with a double clematis of grey-mauve to make this a mourning group. More dominant mauve is provided by the drumsticks of *Allium* 'Purple Sensation', and the fernlike *Thalictrum*

delavayi 'Hewitt's Double' with its grey green leaves and fluffy mauve flower heads.

With flowers like ruffled silk buttons the climbing multiflora *Rosa* 'Russeliana' trained to a pyramid becomes a mass of fragrant crimson-mauve flowers and a much needed deeper statement in a mauve border. The rose is reflected in the buds of *Salvia* x *sylvestris* 'Blauhügel', its spikes reaching up through the rose weaving towers of magenta, mauves and purpley-blue by midsummer.

When working in Japan I noticed that each morning the Japanese householder waters his garden entirely; plants, paths, objects and fences. I am told that they do this to emphasise the colour of both ground and plants. I have to resist doing this each time I pass my soft English mauves, for they too would look more glowing with a daily bath. I have often used this particular trick in Australia, especially on days when the thermometer is rising too quickly, as a quick shower will present an already dry garden in grander tones.

Papaver orientale **'Patty's Plum'**
in all her full blown glory

Strengthening mauve with pink

Mauves can disappear into the atmosphere like a faded photograph, so I have introduced a group of *Weigela florida* 'Foliis Purpureis' to strengthen the picture I am trying to create. These small bushes with their deep purplish bronze foliage and small trumpet shaped rose-pink flowers are a perfect link between shades; they reflect the mauves through their foliage and introduce the shift towards pink in the flowers. To balance the bed I have added *Papaver orientale* 'Turkish Delight', its enticing colour and shape reminiscent of a richly turbaned musical comedy Turk, with flowers a highly theatrical rich rose-pink. When I cut it back in midsummer *Campanula* 'Elizabeth' collapses into its place, its hanging bells reddish-pink spotted inside with red.

Clumps of deep rose-pink *Verbascum* 'Pink Domino' and *Sidalcea* 'Rose Queen' surround two evocative old-fashioned roses: *Rosa* 'Königin von Dänemark' is a bright pink Alba rose, squashed flat, richly quartered and delightfully perfumed, while *Rosa* 'Bourbon Queen' epitomises the story book rose with a cup of semi-double pink petals. The perfume of lavender wafts from their feet where the mauve pink *Lavandula angustifolia* 'Rosea' makes a bold curve to the end of the bed and any brown earth showing is quickly covered by *Allium schubertii*, its pale mauve flowers shaped like the sputniks of the Fifties. As the season progresses mauves are gently overtaken by plants of pinkish tones such as the moody pink *Lilium* 'Pink Perfection' and the wonderful Turk's caps of *Lilium martagon* which push their way through the roses swaying overhead.

Sidalcea 'Rose Queen' is truly a beautiful creature at the beginning of the season, however as it grows taller and taller, with floppy stems happily reaching 1m (3ft), it becomes a nightmare unless it is firmly but unobtrusively controlled by staking. If you are short of space, you could try one of the more compact cultivars such as *S.* 'Puck' which has deep pink flowers and usually grows to around 40cm (16in).

Alliums seem to grow very well in most situations, although the range of plants available is still limited in some parts of the world. If you are able to obtain them, they are well worth persevering with because of the length of flowering time they will give you, providing eye-catching spots of colour throughout the better part of the season to match most planting schemes .

'...a metallic
conductor that
flows from the
neighbouring
bed of rich
jewel colours
through
to the gentler
world of mauve,
lilac and pink.'

Opposite above: *Allium cristophii* (foreground) are the mauve balls of stars under
the old apple tree in the walled garden

Opposite below: Clumps of the bright purple
Allium giganteum are repeated throughout the garden at West Green House

Left: *Iris germanica* 'Twice Delightful' fills
the June gap in an English summer border

Dappled mauves in warm climates

While mauves have their own borders in my English garden, I haven't given them such a major role under the hot Australian sun: at Kennerton Green they make their appearance under the dappled light of my cherry tree lined bulb walk. This is the antithesis of a formal bulb walk such as the one so admired at Sissinghurst – a haphazard group of bulbs and plants that commences flowering with spring's thimble-sized mauve crocus and concludes with the faded mauve-grey *Hosta* 'Hadspen Blue' sheltering beneath the trees as the mercury soars.

I wanted the eye to travel through my cherry trees to the garden's 'showstopper' at one end of the walk, the giant parasol of *Wisteria sinensis*. Trained over the years to form a huge perfumed umbrella, this is host to the hum of a thousand bees, and its petals create a lavender carpet beneath. I did not want to plant bluebells in this bulb walk, nor daffodils and narcissus in the garden beds. I think they are like some house-guests – they give great joy at the time but take for ever to tidy up after!

When planting under blossoming trees, think of the colour of the canopy as well as the colours in the carpet you are fabricating. For example, the mauves, lilacs and blues that follow pink on the colour wheel are complementary shades, but these colours are also energetic enough to tell a story in their own right, so bulbs in these shades are ideal for planting where the light is sifted through pink blossom on high.

My bulb planting is intended to be a mixture of tones enhanced by the light reflected through oceans of pink blossom above. I first formed a dense ground-hugging mat in lavender-blue and white with huge purple violets *Viola odorata*, their clumps as old as the garden. I added sweetly smelling traditional cream freesias along with a splashy new blue hybrid, and primroses, both the small shy ones of childhood and the big bold hybrid white and blue polyanthus – attacked daily by voracious bower-birds who have shifted their fascination for Sydney's blue milk-bottle tops to my garden. The glossy bronze leaves and deep blue flowers of *Ajuga reptans* 'Jungle Beauty' trail everywhere, and I pray that the once prominent foam flower *Tiarella cordifolia* will return, its cream feathery flowers so beautiful in deep shade, but it scorches if trapped in the sun.

The tiny double white flowers of *Arabis subsp. caucasica* 'Flora Pleno' surround clumps of *Ornithogalum nutans* with strictly marked green and white leaves and silver-white flowers creating one huge pale floor-covering beneath the large pink and white blossom heads. Through this the mauves and lavenders peer, there are tulips, tulips and more tulips in every shade of lavender, mauve and white I can find, forming a swinging curve that takes the eye through the trees and beyond. Plantings of the deep purple *Tulipa* 'Queen of Night' add depth to the mauve-blue ruffles of *T.* 'Blue Parrot'. The Tyrian *T.* 'Negrita' is a powerful purple colour that makes me shudder, and it is planted here along with the oversized double-white *T.* 'White Parrot' which prevents the purple

and mauve shades of more tulips – *T.* 'Blue Beauty', *T.* 'Atilla' and *T.* 'Purple Prince' – from becoming monotonous.

The ground hugging species tulips are often overlooked in favour of more flamboyant varieties but in spring they neatly and precisely carpet beds with their tiny flowers. Try *Tulipa bakeri* 'Lilac Wonder' crammed into wide saucer pots or window boxes – a delight on city terraces where tar and cement forget to remind that spring has come.

Dutch iris, not named varieties but a good mix of blues, purples and whites from our bulb-grower, take over as tulips fade through the plague of encroaching forget-me-nots which is so atmospheric for a few weeks. The final touch is a few clumps of bearded iris, retrieved from a planting disaster: I purchased what I thought was a number of very pale blue irises for another part of the garden, on flowering they were stitched with the strongest purple-blue possible, garish in strong light. My Presbyterian blood saved them from the rubbish tip and I interred them in the deepest shade of Cherry Walk. What a wonderful thing light is, in dappled shade their purplish-mauves glow and turn quite respectable, and I'm really quite fond of them now.

A passion for shades of blue includes the blue *Clematis* 'Perle d'Azur' scrambling up a tripod to the navy hoods of *Aconitum* 'Spark's Variety' interwoven with the self-seeding pale blue annual *Nigella damascena*

Blue and mauve annual patterns

In Mittagong my garden must look beautiful very early in the spring as it opens to thousands of visitors on behalf of the local charity Tulip Festival. Originally the view across the entrance bed was spoiled by a very utilitarian-looking garage, so we brought in loads of soil and made a mini mountain with three terraces. On the top level I planted a large group of the large azalea 'Alba Magna' to make it look like Mount Fuji in spring. The second terrace had been intended for perennials but the drainage was too severe for them so it is now a grey foliage border. The bottom border had to be particularly beautiful as that is where the eye first falls. This meant it had to be planted with annuals.

To ensure there would be structure even when annuals are tiring, I planted box *Buxus semper-virens* in a zigzag design. In keeping with nearby planting I have made zigzags of blues and white, generally using blue violas with white antir-rhinums. Some years I use a pale blue viola, others a deep blue, and sometimes a mixture available in Australia called 'Moody Blues'. This bed is echoed around the corner – where it is much drier and sunnier – in a permanent zigzag bed filled with low growing lavender and rosemary, overhung with the pink rambling rose *Rosa* 'Albertine'.

Box cut into zigzag shapes or scallops and filled with annuals is a most unusual and eye catching treatment for any bed large or small. Or use a grey-leaved edging plant such as santolina or dwarf lavender, both of which are particularly effective when infilled with whites and pale blues.

mauve
favourites

Allium cristophii

A stunning addition to any garden, in early summer large flower-heads of silver-lilac balls made up of tiny star-like flowers appear, lighting up any border with their metallic glint. They grow to about 30cm (1ft) and flourish in semi-shade and full sun in well-drained soils. Leave some unpicked where they will dry in situ to a silver fawn, lasting right through autumn.

Erysimum 'Bowles' Mauve'

A perennial wallflower that is covered with small shaded mauve flat flowers above greyish foliage. In warmer areas, it flowers from late winter until midsummer spreading an understudy of stiff stems – excellent supports for later growing plants. It is shortlived in cooler temperate areas and must be replaced from cuttings. It likes full sun and grows to 50cm (20in). A must for early season colour.

Lavandula stoechas

French lavender forms a compact perennial grey-green bush about 75cm (30in) tall with dense ovoid spikes of dark purple flowers with clusters of pinkish-purple bracts on top. Sun-loving, it flowers all summer in well-drained gravelly soil, but is not reliably hardy in cold gardens.

Opposite: The precision cut hedges of box that trap spring flowering annuals at Kennerton Green illustrate the importance of structure in a garden in maintaining design after the flowers are spent

Right: The intense blue of Centaurea montana – a hardy long-flowering perennial

Papaver orientale 'Patty's Plum'

This delicious perennial poppy emerges in early spring with clusters of hairy green leaves followed by fat buds like crunched-up crêpe paper, opening in early summer to form huge mauve and dusky plum flowers on stems about 1.25m (4ft) tall. It will flower in semi-shade or in sun in well fertilised and drained soil. It spreads across the bed, so when flowering is finished and the plant cut back, it leaves a large empty space so its a good idea to plant it towards the back of the border although its ferny leaf quickly reappears.

Penstemon 'Sour Grapes'

Australian nurseryman David Glen describes this increasingly popular penstemon as 'soft green, amethyst and blue flowers like unripe grapes'. Penstemons resemble smaller growing foxgloves with bell-shaped flowers hanging down strong stems. A perennial in cool temperate climates, they are said to be able to withstand frost as long as the roots are not waterlogged, but I treat them as an annual.

Rosa 'William Lobb'

This vigorous Moss rose grows to 2m (6ft) tall, its arching stems best supported on a tripod. 'Mossy' buds open to fully double cupped highly scented flowers of magenta-purple fading to a dusky violet. All roses need sun, well manured soil and plenty of water.

Tulipa 'Blue Parrot'

A large luscious tulip on a strong stem with extravagant frilled petals in harmonious shades of lavender, blue and purple. Planted in warmer climates it will flower in part shade or full sun. In cooler areas, plant in full sun. Bulbs should be lifted after the leaves have turned brown.

Tricyrtis formosana

The toad lily produces spikes of white orchid-shaped flowers heavily spotted with pinkish-purple above shiny dark, varied leaves which are also often dotted with purple. This exotic perennial grows to about 90cm (3ft) and looks as if it should be in an equatorial jungle but it will grow in rich moist soil in sun or semi-shade. Provide it with a deep winter mulch in cooler areas.

3 | whites

Clear classic white looks beautiful, I feel, in a garden with clear strong light such as my Australian garden, but in England I find it can be too harsh on its own. It needs to be backed by the equally strong green of hedges and trees, or placed against grey walls or on trellises painted in sage green or grey. It is also elegant against brick walls where there is major planting of solid green. It is a case of an equal mixing of colour strengths, for mellow colours and lights seem to respond to half tones. Duller whites are easier to place in soft light, right against bricks slightly filmed in moss or stained with leaching lime.

White under cool skies

I had thought that during the two years we were reclaiming the West Green garden, I had come to understand its light and atmosphere, but I was wrong. The first season I cheerfully planted white plants inside the walled garden. As they flowered that first spring they looked too new, too modern for the age and ambience inherent to an old walled garden. After some seasons of tinkering, I have now barrowed most of the plants away and with spring approaching I am anxious to judge how my theories on aged white survive.

The garden will still be white but included are parchment whites, whites washed with a suggestion of pink, veined in plum and burgundy, whites with deep eyes and splashes. The tripods now await the sturdy trails of the dainty single climbing rose, *Rosa* 'Francis E. Lester', large clusters of white flowers just edged with pink, a compliant plant that will be as happy at West Green House as it is around the lake in my Australian garden.

The torn-fringed *R.* 'Frimbiata' has also come with me, it's such an unusual rose with its fringed edge and white flat face flecked with pink. A good find has been the barely white modern English shrub rose *R.* 'Jacqueline du Pré', wide faced with golden stamens. Another rose in these tones is *R.* 'Sally Holmes', joining a splash of true white in a group of the English rose, *R.* 'Winchester Cathedral'. A tiny Japanese rose *R.* 'Nozomi', a miniature white and pearl pink, is looped over canes and curves 20cm (8in) high to scollop both sides of the border.

Grey foliage is useful to soften white. By midsummer in cooler climates the soft white tufts of *Anaphalis triplinervis* smother the lower branches of tall grey-green globe artichokes that support the gooseneck white flowers of *Lysimachia clethroides*. In a smaller space combine silver and grey leaved herbs such as santolina or lavenders with stark whites, underplant white roses or edge a white bed with the soft silvery lamb's ears of *Stachys byzantina*.

The crêpe paper flowers of the oriental poppy *Papaver* 'Black and White' have a central dark blotch like tea leaves left in the bottom of a teacup, and not quite snow white petals; they will rise behind the silvery soft furry leaves of *Stachys byzantina*. Both the pure white, and pink and white varieties of the tall 1.5m (5ft) annual *Cleome* will wave through the spent roses along with the single white cosmos, equally tall above its foaming foliage. Glamorous Asiatic Lilies,

include *Lilium* 'Mont Blanc', white with deep pink tipped stamens, and 'Sterling Star', pinpoints of burgundy on white will join the Turk's caps *L. martagon* var. *album* and whitish tiger lilies.

Clouds of ethereal white *Crambe cordifolia* and *Gypsophila* will provide a bridal veil to break up dense white spires of *Campanula persicifolia alba*, *Digitalis alba*, and the tall swords of *Delphinium* 'Galahad'. *Gaura lindheimeri* proffers clouds of whitish pink butterfly flowers that will hide the leaves of *Iris germanica* 'Palamino', its flowers shell pink with white faces, whose beauty is echoed by the peony *P.* 'Miss America' in June. Gossamer flower clouds, watercolour washes across petals, and grey leaves will create old white, a gentle white for the soft light captured within the garden's tall walls.

I would love to conclude a white garden with a small tree its leaves so variegated they are nearly white falling from horizontal branches tiered to resemble a royal wedding cake. *Cornus controversa* 'Variegata' in full flower is a romatic image, a white veil of flowers, a happy ever after ending to a bed of white. They grow in cool climate gardens in Australia, but in cooler areas they appreciate a sheltered corner away from cold winds.

White alstroemeria in front of hastily planted white *Antirrhinum* – a garden saviour after a wet winter had drowned two groups of *Lavandula angustifolia* 'Alba'

Previous page: The incandescent whiteness of *Lilium* 'Casa Blanca'

'It is a case
of an equal
mixing of colour
strengths, for
mellow colours and
lights seem to
respond to half
tones.'

'. . . it is dazzling to look down on the interplay of shape, size and textures of the white on white. . .'

Opposite: A ribbon of white annual ranunculus and stock bounded by cushions of *Iberis sempervirens* in front of the cottage

Right: More white on white with flowers of miniature antirrhinum, annual iberis and ranunculus

Cool white borders for warm climates

For as long as I can remember the cottage has been framed in a snow white lace ruff of intricately planted annuals, a seasonally changing design that can include white tulips, fragrant stocks, annual iberis and ranunculi, all edged with white violas cushioned between great balls of *Iberis sempervirens*. Although white is not an easy colour for many dry countries, I am fortunate that my garden is far from the red plains where whites can turn so dusty and muddy. I have not tampered with the garden's tradition that, as spring ends, the display is changed to 'Vanilla' marigolds and white nicotiana, zinnias and antirrhinums, sometimes interwoven with the fine foliage of cosmos – a simple summer collection under garlands of the whiteish rambling rose *Rosa* 'Wedding Day'. Somehow stray white delphiniums and *Nicotiana sylvestris* have settled themselves at the back of the bed, along with the resident tree peonies.

Fashion has swung against Kennerton Green's white borders of predominantly cottage garden annuals, a remnant of elegant Edwardian style. But it is dazzling to look down on the interplay of shape, size and textures of the white on white, thousands of tiny flowers, slivers of white ice planted under a cool sun in early spring. It's breathtaking, and I hope it may awaken an interest in a dismissed range of flowers that bloom long before the summer herbaceous border – today's fashion statement – even considers taking the floor.

The simplicity of the white flowers echoes the spirit of the house. The plants are as unpretentious as the house itself, an innocent picture strayed from the pages of a Kate Greenaway illustration.

Every autumn David McKinlay and I plan, and David plants, our ribbons of annuals. For your own white border try *Iberis sempervirens* with annual *Viola*, *Lobularia maritima* and *Alyssum* at the front; annual *Ranunculus* 'Rembrandt' selection with *Matthiola incana*, annual *iberis* and *Antirrhinum majus* in the middle and at the back perennial delphinuium hybrids with annual *Nicotiana sylvestris*. In a small garden for high summer try low growing white marigolds, nicotiana, white zinnias, antirrhinums, and white annual salvia – all are good in beds but equally for attractive summer displays in troughs and tubs.

In the bed to the east of the house the white flowers are repeated under the budding spring trees like a small frill of lace on an expensive petticoat. By summer this lacy river is overtaken by a line of spreading oak-leaved *Hydrangea quercifolia*, its long clusters of white flowers repeating the white theme, covering the recently emptied bed to meet the green cushions of the trimmed *Iberis sempervirens*. It provides a spot of pure white in what has otherwise become cavernous blue-green shade.

The main perennial inhabitants of this bed are rhododendrons. The older ones are all shades of pink but those I have planted are mostly creams and white. One of my favourite shrubs is *Rhododendron* 'Frangrantissimum', its large white trumpet shaped flowers smelling of nutmeg. It is among the last of the rhododendrons to flower in spring and I plant it again and again to follow the white starry flowers of the beautiful *Magnolia stellata*, small trees planted in groups so their flowers form a dense constellation. The white borders run into a curve of green flowers, which shine out of the deep Australian summer shade.

White with pink

I am an addict for glossy garden books, I devour the latest trends, sigh over stunning combinations and mentally barrow my garden away before I have reached the final page. Occasionally the pictures of one garden become a more permanent ideal, referred to over and over again. Mrs William S. Paley's garden on Long Island near New York City was one such inspiration, a photograph showing what looked like a circular sloping bank massed in pink and white *Cornus* (dogwoods), its floor a thicket of azaleas stopping abruptly by a simple circular pool. One winter's afternoon when I was burning the autumn rubbish down beyond the old Kennerton Green vegetable plot, alongside the old buildings and the leaky dam, my mind began gradually to see that American garden taking place there. Such a vision of pink and white around a basin of water may be colonial in origin, but large plantings of a limited range of plants in a controlled palette ensure the simplicity of style that is so suitable for my country garden.

A year later a giant machine arrived to clear the dam and make a perfect oval lake, its banks to be sown to grass, the surrounds gently sloped. The plan was to capture a little of the effect of my American image, but of course the new lake filled and emptied immediately, so the machine had to return to remake it; the beautifully graded slope was pure compacted clay, and the northern end of the garden was so exposed to ferocious winds that many of my early plants died. With hindsight we should have removed all the clay from the top, but I trembled to touch the banks, so the trees and shrubs were planted by digging huge holes in the clay and filling them with compost and manure. I planted masses of the American dogwood, but the hot winds soon thinned their ranks. *Cornus florida* is the hardiest in a dryish climate, but even when regularly watered it becomes very stressed by late summer while *Cornus kousa* has flourished – I suspect its position allows it to capture more moisture. Azaleas and rhododendrons were similarly drought-susceptible so my American dream had to be adapted to Australian reality.

The desired pink canopy was achieved with the earliest flowering crab apple *Malus floribunda*, a mass of deep pink buds opening to the palest pink. *Davidia involucrata* initially struggled but has survived, its delicate flowers resemble a washing line of white handkerchiefs. All types of *Deutzia* enjoy the climate, and cushions of star-white flowers of *Deutzia crenata* var. *nakaiana* 'Nikko' are excellent in the front of a border.

Spring awakens the double flowered white lilac *Syringa vulgaris* 'Madame Lemoine', which forms a heavy mass beside the white firework-like flowers of *Cytisus* x *praecox* 'Albus'. The immense green-white flowers of *Viburnum macrocephalum* are spectacular snowballs for spring and *Hydrangea paniculata* 'Grandiflora' produces wonderful summer mounds of large white pyramidal flowers. *Viburnum opulus* 'Notcutt's Variety' has dense white flowers which are replaced by red berries in early autumn.

The tissue paper flowers of Helianthemum 'The Bride' love sun and dry feet, a small spreading plant that makes a companionable ground cover of thousands of single gold-centred white blooms above leaves of dusty green.

Opposite: Old pink azaleas and aquilegia burst into flower before the white ribbon border begins to flower in spring

Below: The elegant *Viburnum plicatum* 'Mariesii' balances white flowers along horizontal stems

A rose garden

Roses have replaced many more tender plants at Kennerton Green. Lax uncontrolled bush roses now provide clouds of pink and white in early summer – rather than my planned dogwood blossoms. There is only one David Austin rose that likes me, and the flowers of *Rosa* 'Constance Spry' are perfect for this garden, like cups of pink sugar. Another 'pink pink' is *R.* 'Königin von Dänemark', a quartered Alba rose which I have planted in clumps of threes or fives interspersed with the heavily scented dropping pink heads of the Centifolia rose *Rosa* 'Fantin-Latour'. The modern spreading shrub rose *R.* 'Raubritter' fights the winds along the edge with the small flowered fringed Rugosas *R.* 'Fimbriata' and *R.* 'Grootendorst', their petals looking as if they have been cut by pinking shears.

This part of the garden is a cheerful candyfloss palette, but it initially lacked drama. This is now supplied by a carpet of old pinks *Dianthus allwoodii* – I lifted a clump from the original garden, and it multiplied swiftly to form a plush covering of shocking pink, bleached here and there by *Cerastium tomentosum, Alyssum saxatile* and pure white verbena. Around the lake I planted a mixture of pink and white climbers and ramblers but these were a straggly mistake and now they are being replaced by the sturdy rambler *Rosa* 'Francis E. Lester'. The huge blossoms of *R.* 'Madame Grégoire Staechelin' sporadically weave through it to ensure the planting isn't too polite.

The steep bank into the lake was planned as a wall of bearded irises meeting a pale pink

Louisiana iris at the water's edge. The first year the soft ruffles of five hundred *Iris* 'Beverly Sills' were planted it was sensational, but by season's end it was a horrible sight as they were choked beneath sorrel *Rumex acetosa* which defied all recommended forms of eradication. The iris have since been removed and for now we rotate annuals, hoping the constant re-digging and spraying will allow us to replant eventually.

Pink and white roses have their own garden at Kennerton Green, surrounding a small expanse of water. A narrow path leads to 2m (6ft) high hedges of *Cupressus torulosa*. Yew is very difficult to grow in the cooler climates of the southern hemisphere but well clipped *Cypressus* makes a good substitute. The hedge opens to reveal an oblong garden with a central long narrow pond reflects predominantly pink and white standard roses on either side. On either side parallel iron arches support the modern floribunda climber *Rosa* 'Iceberg' which shades secluded seats. At the far end a partly shaded shepherdess rises above a cool cream white *Rosa* 'Valerie Swane' which I planted to commemorate the life of a friend and gardener.

The garden was originally planted by Lady Pagan with beautiful cream, pink and white hybrid teas and floribundas that the catalogues of two decades ago could supply. My mother also loved this style of rose so the garden is a mixture of their choices: the white hybrid teas *Rosa* 'Virgo' and *R.* 'Silver Jubilee', the pink *R.* 'Elizabeth Harkness', the fragrant pink-edged cream of *R.* 'Princesse de Monaco', pink tinged creamy-yellow *R.* 'Peace', pale pink *R.* 'Pink Parfait', the small white centred

pale pink flowers of *R.* 'Ballerina' and the greatest pink of all, *R.* 'Queen Elizabeth', a superb floribunda. New plantings have included *R.* 'Margaret Merril', a white floribunda with a satin pink finish; *R.* 'Seduction' a large rose of cream, its edges frills of the palest pink; the champagne roses *R.* 'Vanilla' and *R.* 'Champagne', and the pale pink to white Irish rose *R.* 'Souvenir de Saint Anne's', a semi-single sport of *R.* 'Souvenir de la Malmaison'.

There are rose types that can be slotted into any garden so even a small space can be transformed into a sensuous rose garden providing it gets enough sun. Choose from climbers reaching at least 5m (16ft), tall standards at 2.5m (8ft), half standards at 2m (6ft), bush roses from 1-2m (3-6ft) and ground hugging roses such as the generous pink *Rosa* 'Raubritter'.

Some of the most delightful are:

Rosa 'Fantin-Latour'

A tall, sturdy shrub rose growing up to 2m (6ft). This Centifolia rose flowers as a shell pink cup bursting with slightly deeper pink petals in summer. Roses like to be well fed with manure, and also like rose food in early spring. This rose reappears in every garden I grow.

Rosa 'Francis E. Lester'

Like the rose *R.* 'Wedding Day' (*see p.69*), this rambler is another trademark. It is a strong, well-leaved rose growing to 5m (15ft) in clusters of fragrant, single white flowers in midsummer, their edges touched with pink. Although (like all roses), it likes to be fed, it will still perform in dry soil.

Rosa 'Königin Von Dänemark'

This is the essence of an old rose, or Alba rose, in the softest pink with a grey-green foliage growing to 1.2m (4ft). The flowers are perfumed and large, its petals arranged in quarters.

Rosa 'Madeleine Selzer'

The double ice-lemon blooms of this rambling, but not too vigorous, rose appear only once a year, with attractive light green leaves. I have several which seem as happy growing in a gravel path as in good soil.

Opposite: An old pink rose found by an abandoned cottage now rises above *Dianthus allwoodii* in Mittagong

Left: The floribunda *Rosa* 'Saint John'

'. . . a Regency fantasy that seems to float on the waterline.'

The fashion conscious of the garden world favour heritage roses today and question this type of planting, but I love it for it represents the evolution of a garden and respect for past gardeners. The high hedges of my pink and white garden contain their own sensuous world: there are roses standing erect on grafted stems and shrub roses clutching at passing skirts, roses tumbling from arches and cascading from knarled weeping standards.

It is especially important in smaller gardens to use space effectively, with a careful choice of plants for underplanting. Roses will grow beautifully in dry climates so it is easy to forget that they need lots of nourishment and water to give their best, and underplanting must take this into account. Good low level companions for roses are *Nepeta* (catmint) and lavenders as they don't need too much water. However, these choices can become rampant and difficult to maintain, and bulbs and annuals can be a better solution. Standard roses look particularly bare in early spring but can be brought to life by underplanting with almost any bulb, the white fringed *Tulipa* 'Swan Wings' or the bells of *Allium triquetrum* could both be considered.

The hedges not only create a private world, and shield humans and roses from winds, they also capture clear light, ensuring the colours remain true and clear, less subtle than when confined amongst other plants in a herbaceous border. The underplanting of pink forget-me-nots, arabis and tulips reflects this gaiety. It would be difficult to capture similar sensations in larger rose gardens, but the confining hedges are a double-edged sword for humidity collects and stays among the glorious abundance, and the dreaded black spot takes hold by late spring.

Pink and white planting can sometimes look far too dainty so give white and pink roses an injection of exuberance by adding a few bold stripes such as those of the hybrid perpetual roses *R.* 'Ferdinand Pichard', with its brilliant stripes of crimson on soft pink, or the stylish *R.* 'Baron Girod de l'Ain' – its deep cups of crimson are edged with a white thread.

White trees with colours underfoot

I think it was the words of the 23rd Psalm 'He maketh me to lie down in green pastures, he leadeth me beside still waters, he restoreth my soul' that led me to plant a grove of white trees beside deep dark water. My Mother died at Kennerton Green in July 1991 as we were discussing a new area to plant. We both liked the idea of white birch trees and a woodland garden – my mother's last words were a request for an archway to enter this garden. Today the archway is a long cage of two parallel compartments filled with white doves, leading to a grove of three hundred slim white-trunked birch trees, a Betula Moss's selection, their lacy twigs holding tiny leaves that shimmer and talk to each other in the wind. It is a peaceful place enclosing a pond, now filled with Louisiana iris in blue and white, with white waterlilies surrounding a Chinoiserie birdcage, a Regency fantasy that seems to float on the waterline.

Opposite: The pond with its surrounding bluebell woodland was made to mark the life of my mother, Una Abbott.

Previous page: Enclosed in tall hedges of *Cypressus torulosa*, a shepherdess guards the rose garden at Kennerton Green in early November.

The woodland floor is an ever changing carpet of small bulbs. Early crocus, *Crocus chrysanthus* in soft pale blue, are followed by the nodding yellow bonnets of the hoop petticoat daffodil, *Narcissus bulbocodium*, tiny blooms naturalising at an extraordinary rate. Their faces are soon covered by thousands of blue scillas (Spanish bluebells); these were all planted by hand, mainly using a crowbar to make cracks in the earth when autumn rains were late. Beside the bluebells large patches of aromatic old-fashioned creamy white *Freesia refracta* var. *alba* add a beautiful perfume that is very special. I am fortunate to live in a warm enough climate in Australia to be able to naturalise freesias, however we do have light frosts and freesias tend every second or third year only to flower in sheltered pockets, while the hoop petticoats will flower under the most extreme conditions. The bulbs form a charming progressive tapestry of blue, yellow, blue and white, before the spikes of tall white foxglove *Digitalis alba* flower in early summer to rival the white birch trunks. Later in the year the autumn crocus (known as the autumn daffodil in England) *Sternbergia lutea* shines out a brilliant yellow among the small autumn leaves.

While freesias are not an option in northern climates, other bulbs provide a similar light touch. Nodding fritillaries and dainty *Narcissus* bring spots of light to a garden in early spring after the welcome primroses.

A woodland is not just a flat space, but an area of gullies, mounds and small embankments, so this

birch grove is shaped with hillocks, a mini range of hills, each higher than the last, covered by the tapestry of flowers. A bank behind the pond is planted with the rugosa rose *Rosa* 'Schneezwerg', white with yellow stamens; crevices in walls host *Iberis sempervirens*, the heady clove-perfumed *Dianthus* 'Mrs Sinkins', and *Cerastium tomentosum*, a mat forming ground cover that deserves its common name of 'snow in summer'.

I often sit on the bench beside the pond and

reflect on this foolhardy enterprise, for although birches will grow in well tended beds in our climate, they are not ideal for woodland plantings at Mittagong. But all gardeners have dreams of the beauty they wish to create: for me it was an intermingling of white trees, tall white flowers and a carpet of blue, white and yellow, a softening of roses and an entrance through clouds of white *Spiraea* 'Arguta' in spring with its tiniest of light green leaves, its flowers a bridal veil.

If a garden is an expression of paradise, these plans are my idea of a paradise garden. It is a garden of white trees, a minimalist approach, a simplistic use of blocks of one plant, three hundred birch trees, the floor in bold blocks of blue, white and yellow. At West Green we are also planting birch trees, *Betula jacquemontii*, as a backdrop to stiff graded hedges of dark green yew, a transition of lightness where woodland meets classical formality.

white favourites

Cleome hassleriana

This spider flower is a strong-stemmed annual that grows in full sun to 1.5m (4-5ft) tall, flowering in midsummer. Varieties come in white, light magenta or pink with spider-like petals that appear at the top of the stem.

Crambe cordifolia

Tiny scented gypsophila-like flowers cloud in clusters from 2m (6ft) tall strong stems, above a clump of large mid-green leaves. The dainty flowers appear from late spring through midsummer. *Crambe cordifolia* needs a sunny position and will tolerate dry soils but I have had difficulty establishing it in cool temperate climates.

Iberis sempervirens

Candytuft is a groundcovering perennial covered with tiny white flowers in spring, in sun or semi-shade. Old plants will develop into mounds that can be trained to hang over terraces. If candytuft is clipped after flowering, it provides a pleasing green shape all summer. There is also a sun-loving annual iberis with similar flowers but growing to around 20cm (9in) tall.

Lysimachia clethroides

In mid and late summer tall, light stems of loose-strife will soften any border. It grows to about 1m (3ft) with slender stems which curl over then straighten up slightly like goose's necks, topped with clusters of tiny white flowers. Loosestrife will grow in semi-shade or sun but prefers a reasonably moist soil.

Matthiola incana

This stock is a sweetly-smelling annual with fat spikes around 20-25cm (8-10in) tall, covered by double rosettes of flowers. It likes a well-mulched bed and flowers for around six weeks in late spring or early summer. Available in shades of lavender, pink and white. I only use white.

Ornithogalum nutans

This spring bulb has white star-like flowers with a distinctive green line. Plants grow to around 20cm (8in), often in shady patches, and they naturalise well. I like to use them to underplant tulips.

Rosa 'Wedding Day'

This rambling rose has grown and flowered for me in the subtropics, in Mediterranean and in cool temperate climate zones. Soft apricot buds open to clusters of single cream, then white fragrant flowers. In five years, these plants have grown so vigorously that two-thirds of the house at Kennerton Green is now swagged with 'Wedding Day'. Given adequate nutrients it will grow in gravel, sand and good soils with equal success. As the late Valerie Swane would say, 'Plant it and stand back'.

Viburnum plicatum 'Mariesii'

A tall spreading deciduous shrub, often growing over 3m (9ft) tall, with distinctly tiered horizontal branches, it is covered in small light green leaves in spring and small flat, white flowers. This viburnum makes an excellent specimen plant and a sensational hedge.

Opposite: The double Pheasant's Eye *Narcissus poeticus* var. *recurvus* naturalised in the lakefield at West Green House

Right: Tall Australian eucalyptus encircle the country gardens at Kennerton Green

4 | yellows, pinks and browns

Colour is a very useful tool to tie different parts of a garden together. Designers often use large groupings of one plant placed at regular intervals to carry the eye along a border. Bulb growers often favour the trick of a river of blue *Muscari* to suggest a blue river between separate groups of brightly coloured bulbs, unifying the patches of colour. I have used colour to tie the original and new gardens together at Kennerton Green, particularly where I needed to connect two different styles of gardening together.

The old garden is a typical Australian country garden with tall trees and gently curving lawns edged by flower beds, whereas my own ideas tend more to structural designs enclosed in garden rooms, divided by hedges, fences or groves of trees. My connecting device is principally large blocks of single colour, and every so often two neighbouring colours are used as contrasts. As the house, tucked into its abundant white garden, is the garden's centre and all drives and paths radiate from here, the central connecting colour is white, leading first to yellow.

The first colour bed starts at a fence covered by a yellow hedge of *Forsythia suspensa*, a blaze of yellow in early spring. Here I inherited clumps of King Alfred daffodils, simple primroses with *Alyssum saxatile* 'Compactum', and *A.* 'Gold Dust' a thick whipped butter border following the lawn line as the border widens. The whorls of yellow flowers above the furry green leaves of groups of

Phlomis russeliana are an excellent combination with the stiff sword leaves of *Sisyrinchium striatum*, its upright stems studded with small lemon-cream flowers. White flowers return in a group of twenty deliciously perfumed bushes including *Philadelphus* 'Beauclerk' and *P.* x *lemoinei* and *Choisya ternata*. Self-sown honesty and the yellow tulip *Tulipa* 'Golden Apeldoorn' struggle for room between them, mingling yellows among the predominantly white grouping before the new bed and next colour block begins.

Right: *Tulipa* 'Maureen' flowers as the long border turns to yellow

Below: The white borders in the old garden at Kennerton Green merge here to become a border of yellow

Opposite: Golden alyssum, *Tulipa* 'Maureen' and scillas in the blue and yellow border

Previous page: *Viola* 'Anitque' capture the spectrum of connecting colours – yellow, pink and brown

'My connecting
device is principally
large blocks of
single colour,
and every so
often two
neighbouring
colours are used
as contrasts.'

One way of breaking the eye from one colour to another in a garden is to insert a block of flowering shrubs such as philadelphus to provide a firm, weighty presence to change the tempo. In a dull area choose a glossy evergreen shrub such as *Choisya ternata*; its glossy green leaves and bright white flowers will provide a dramatic punctuation mark. In a small garden this blocking effect is particularly useful. If you haven't room to use groups of plants, choose one striking example, or clip evergreens into solid statements.

The bed drifts into shades of blue, but the colour here is secondary to the structure as large groups of clipped box cones, squares, balls and lollipops appear again as strong evergreen punctuation marks both in density and shapes, a foil to the soft habits of the preceding group of philadelphus. Here is not only a gentle connecting theme but formal sentinels either side of a path on its way to the geometric-shaped potager, where form is the principal statement and link, colour is secondary.

My beds in blocks of white, yellow and blue stretch halfway around the garden in a rhythmic curve using many contrasting themes, topiaries and tunnels, banks of single plants, climbers and especially trees and thousands of annuals and perennials to create unification by colour but surprises by design.

In warmer parts of the world brilliant yellow is clean and bright even on the hottest days, while in cooler climates it needs subduing. Under hot skies yellow has all the freshness of a long cool drink, and it is a bright light on cold days. It must

be the right colour for us for our bushland is host to thousands of varieties of native wattle, every shade from cream to the rich golden-yellow of the Cootamundra wattle, *A. baileyana*. I also like clear bright yellow and sky blue together, and use them in blocks, one leading to the other.

If you baulk at a vast expanse of yellow but have a small curve in a herbaceous bed, an effective tiered planting could comprise the rich dark yellow compact *Potentilla recta* 'Warrenii' in the front, the deep brownish-maroon *Hemerocallis* 'Root Beer' behind, with a little more height added by the much more lax lemon-yellow *Coreopsis verticillata* 'Moonbeam' to provide a softening effect. If you still have space at the back try one of the dark blue monkshoods such as *Aconitum* 'Bressingham Spire', and perhaps weave the deep reddish-brown annual *Cosmos atrosanguineus* through the group.

A pleasing grouping of yellow and blue is formed by matting a bed of the useful intensely blue yellow-eyed daisy *Felicia amelloides* below a standard yellow English rose, *Rosa* 'Graham Thomas'; the colours of both plants are of equal intensity but the simple daisy shape loosens the formality of standard roses. Reaching to the sun *Verbascum olympicum* looks to be covered by soft white fur from the tip of its 2m (6ft) spire to its dramatic grey leaves. It is an inpirational plant dotted with flat yellow flowers especially if a group is allowed to seed beside a path to break a view or to hide a surprise around a corner.

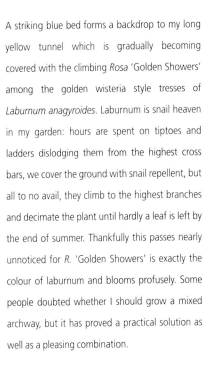

A striking blue bed forms a backdrop to my long yellow tunnel which is gradually becoming covered with the climbing *Rosa* 'Golden Showers' among the golden wisteria style tresses of *Laburnum anagyroides*. Laburnum is snail heaven in my garden: hours are spent on tiptoes and ladders dislodging them from the highest cross bars, we cover the ground with snail repellent, but all to no avail, they climb to the highest branches and decimate the plant until hardly a leaf is left by the end of summer. Thankfully this passes nearly unnoticed for *R*. 'Golden Showers' is exactly the colour of laburnum and blooms profusely. Some people doubted whether I should grow a mixed archway, but it has proved a practical solution as well as a pleasing combination.

If you have the space and the patience, laburnum tunnels are one of the great joys of late spring, but laburnum is a fleeting beauty, so to prolong the flowering period of such a major garden feature it is best interspersed with another climber such as the rose *R*. 'Golden Showers', each plant placed 1m (3ft) apart inside and either side of the arch so the matching plants join together. It will take at least eight years to achieve a covered laburnum tunnel, longer if the archway is across a driveway, but when complete it will be a brilliant display for a good month, a visual showstopper of golden light whatever the weather.

Rosa 'Golden Showers' blooms before the laburnum commences to flower in the archway at Kennerton Green

Beneath the arch the yellow faces of *Limnanthes douglasii* happily creep on to the gravel, in company of the bright blue *Lithospermum diffusum*. The tall clear sky blue bearded iris *I.* 'Portrait of Larrie' leans towards the centre of the path with a matching dwarf iris at its feet and behind the yellow tunnel the blue beds continue. These blocks of yellow and blue continue for 6m (18ft) before meeting an embankment of white to adjust the eye to the next story.

One of the visual delights that we all know and love is the image of nasturtiums creeping across the path at Monet's garden at Giverny in France. This is tremendously easy to copy but can be very rampant. Yellow *Limnanthes douglasii* and blue *Lithospermum diffusum* look very cool and clean against a white gravel path making an informal edge. *Lysimachia nummularia* 'Aurea', Creeping Jenny, and *Thymus* x *citriodorus* 'Aureus', a golden herb are brilliant shades of yellow and gold, delight in creeping across gravel and make bright edges for summer gardens.

yellow favourites

Acacia baileyana 'Cootamundra Wattle'

Although there are hundreds of 'wattle' species, this small tree with grey ferny leaves with a hint of purple is the Australian wattle for me. Covered in brilliant gold balls of flowers each spring, it will grow in well-drained soil in Southern Australia. In England, Europe and North America it will survive in the mildest of climates.

Cephalaria gigantea

This is a perennial giant scabious with slender green stems up to 2m (6ft) tall, waving pale lemon, pincushion-shaped flowers. It likes good soil and full sun.

Fritillaria imperialis 'Lutea Maxima'

These crown imperial fritillaries are bulbs that flower in mid-spring. Tall strong green stems often up to 1.5m (4ft) tall are topped by yellow bells with a topknot of green leaves. Crown imperials will not tolerate soggy soils.

Helianthus annuus

Sunflowers are perhaps the symbol of late summer with their giant yellow flowers on 2-m (6-ft) high stalks. Not quite as tall as the traditional sunflower, 'Russian Giant', 'Ruby Sunset' is rust-red and new varieties come in creams and shades of yellow, gold and tawny brown.

Laburnum x watereri 'Vossii'

A slender tree with long racemes of wisteria-type yellow flowers up to 50cm (20in) long which bloom in late spring. It is superb grown in single lines over tunnels and arches. It likes well-drained, good soil, but will not tolerate soggy feet.

Phlomis fruticosa

Jerusalem sage is a hairy blue-green leaved herbaceous shrub bearing whorls of yellow flowers at regular intervals throughout summer. It is fully hardy in cool temperate areas, but may need to be cut back in autumn to ensure survival in colder temperatures.

Rosa 'Graham Thomas'

One of David Austin's most admired roses of clear rich yellow over shiny green leaves. The flowers are cup-shaped, filled with petals, and the bush is vigorous, growing up to 1.3m (4ft). To my mind this is the very best yellow rose in summer.

Rosa 'Nevada'

A modern shrub rose that grows vigorously to around 2m (6ft) by 2m (6ft). It is covered by semi-double large creamy-white flowers with prominent stamens. It is one of the earliest roses to flower and looks very good in massed plantings along a drive.

Sisyrinchium striatum

A perennial with iris-type leaves. The small flowers are palest creamy-yellow and cluster down stems that grow to 1m (3ft) tall. It spreads well and is happiest in full sun although it will tolerate semi-shade, but not wet feet.

Sternbergia lutea

These look very similar to a spring crocus but flower in autumn. They are like brilliant yellow light bulbs under trees turning their technicolour best before the leaf carpet becomes too dense. Happy as rockery plants, they will naturalise, flowering happily in full sun or some light shade.

Opposite: *Rosa* 'Golden Showers' has proved a good rose happily confronting climatic excesses. The flower is raggedy in appearance fading gently from gold as it ages

'. . . I couldn't plant an English garden without the acknowledged presence of at least a hint of pink . . .'

Pinks at West Green

Soft English light is perfectly complemented by pink, which warms the light respectfully, providing a gentle visual glow even when the sun fails to appear. However my hand at first trembled at pink, and my plant lists at West Green House planned for rich purples, burgundy, blues and mauves. I didn't think entire beds of pink flowers could be planted so close to bricks where tones of orange and ochre dominated. But I felt I couldn't plant an English garden without the acknowledged presence of at least a hint of pink, it had to include pink roses and groups of lupins, foxgloves, peonies, lilies and pink tinged magnolias.

I looked very closely at the walls and detected a purple pigment in some of the Hampshire brick firings, so I took heart and tentatively tried to introduce a little pink to make the transition from mauve to white. The last plants of the mauve border already hint at pink: the pink-mauve *Delphinium* 'Astolat', the silver lilac balls of *Allium cristophii*, and a daylily of pinkish-mauve *Hemerocallis* 'Catherine Woodbery'. These lead into a developing cool pink bed which weaves towards flowers of white; it starts with the flourish of the striped red and white Bourbon rose *Rosa* 'Variegata di Bologna', and the pale pink and crimson striped hybrid perpetual *R.* 'Ferdinand Pichard'. I have planted groups of pink roses: my favourite soft pink *R.* 'Königin von Dänemark', the delicate pink *R.* 'Fantin-Latour', the quaint blooms of the sumptuous pink Centifolia rose *R.* 'Ispahan', and Bourbon roses *R.* 'Louise Odier' , *R.* 'Madame Isaac Pereire' and *R.* 'Reine Victoria', cups of pink petals. These are the underplanting for standard balls of *Lonicera*, honeysuckle species of cream and deep pink.

Many spreading and wayward plants are now available such as sophisticated pom pom trees, all shaped and clipped to form standard flowering balls in spring. Trees of *Lonicera*, *Weigela*, lilacs or lavenders can all add contrast in texture, colour, form and structure above waves of soft perennials. In smaller beds standards can look most effective when grown in generous containers.

All these large shapes needed a film to break down the feeling of sugar icing, so drifts of *Linaria purpurea* 'Canon Went' curtained the entire bed. This looked wonderful the first year, but soon had the denseness of a picket fence of very pale pink flowers to be severely weeded each spring. Solid pink and white lupins, *Lupinus* 'The Chatelaine', were parted by waves of *Aquilegia* 'Heidi ', pretty pink granny's bonnets, and the sturdy spires of *Verbascum chaixii* 'Pink Domino' pushed their way through the thick groups of roses. As I became more courageous, the bed became pinker, *Digitalis* x *mertonensis* arrived as did *Sidalcea* 'Rose Queen'. I loved the spikes of the wafer thin round flowers clinging to their waving spikes, but it was far too definite a pink to be tolerated by any red brick wall, so only a few strands remain, the bulk replaced with *Phlox maculata* 'Omega', white with a softish pink eye.

The beds at West Green must respect the old knee high hedges to the path so planting tends to be tall, but on the lawn side I have placed *Paeonia* 'Shirley Temple', the flowers just scoops of pink and white ice cream beside *P.* 'Lady Alexandra McDuff', deep pink frills filled with loose white petals. Clumps of the delicate hearts of pink *Dicentra spectabilis* nod above soft green foliage interspersed by the white variety. *Diascia fetcaniensis* is another prolifically flowered small pink flower, and I have planted it next to groups of *Hosta plantaginea* var. *japonica* with its sweetly smelling white flowers. The green *Zinnia elegans* 'Envy' adds zest in high summer.

The garden was reassuring, a cottage garden ambience, but it still worried me. The style of the house, the parterres, the follies, all have dramatic pretensions far removed from the spirit of unsophisticated pink. So in went leaves of burgundy, port and Shiraz to strengthen the confection.

The wine coloured leaves and stems of red mountain spinach *Atriplex hortensis* and the tall thick stems and flat burgundy red leaves of *Angelica gigas* create deep coloured backdrops to the pathside planting. Low mounds of *Heuchera* 'Palace Purple' and 'Pewter Moon', both with portwine leaves, glow richly bringing a depth and stability to the planting. *Monarda* 'Beauty of Cobham' boasts flowers in a mixture of burgundy and sugar pink, echoed in the honeysuckle which clambers over a tripod, and these tones introduce a necessary sophistication to the pinks.

Opposite: *Verbascum* 'Jackie' and *Ranunculus* 'Nearly Black' backed by flowers of black and pink at Kennerton Green

Left: Hot pink spikes of *Sidalcea* 'Rose Queen' at West Green House

pink favourites

Digitalis x mertonensis

A large, crushed strawberry foxglove growing up to 1.2m (4ft) tall. It likes a rich moist soil and will flower happily in semi-shade from late spring to early autumn.

Linaria purpurea 'Canon Went'

This toadflax is a self-seeding perennial of tall, delicate spikes, covered in small pale pink flowers to resemble a tiny snapdragon. It grows to around 1m (3ft), flowering all summer in full sun, but tolerating semi-shade and poor soils.

Malus floribunda

One of the earliest blossom trees to flower each spring, when its tight bright pink buds open to shell pink flowers, with a mass of petals attracting hundreds of bees. Trees grow to around 10m (33ft) in cool districts, with autumn colour but insignificant fruit.

Paeonia 'Sarah Bernhardt'

This is an old favourite, a large double peony, that is nearly a globe of ruffled petals of pure pink. Luscious blooms appear in midsummer on stems to around 1m (3ft) tall. Peonies like full sun in good soil.

Papaver orientale 'Turkish Delight'

The largest poppy I've grown, it's candy pink flowers are supported on strong, furry stems up to 1m (3ft). Plant it towards the back of the border as it leaves a large gap when cut back in midsummer.

Tulipa 'Webber's Parrot'

One of the prettiest pastel tulips, this ivory white Parrot tulip has very frilly edges that are a mauve-tinged pink with slashes of green. Flowering in late spring, plants may grow as tall as 50cm (20in). These tulips are overwintered at West Green House, but lifted and discarded in less temperate climates.

Wisteria floribunda 'Kuchi-beni'

Long racemes of white flowers with just a suggestion of pink may be 45cm (18in) long. In warmer areas this is a strong growing plant but in England it often takes several years to flower. Grow this wisteria in full sun.

Left: Daring pink cosmos colonise a corner in the pink border at West Green House

Opposite: *Lonicera giganten* 'Superba' and *Rosa* 'Königin von Dänemark' capture an old garden's spirit in a border of sugar pink plants

Brown

The warm tones of brown are ideal for linking all kinds of pinks and copper colours through to mellow yellows. When I first saw *Rosa* 'Julia's Rose', my love affair with brown plants began. It is a modern hybrid tea, the colour of a cappuccino, with copper-brown buds opening to a large warm parchment flower. In some lights it looks flushed with slate, in others faded copper-pink; it seemed to demand I create a bed to complement it.

I began my brown collection with the New Zealand flax *Phormium* 'Maori Sunrise', tall flat swords of brown-bronze leaves touched with pink and red, and bronze fennel, which has brown feathers exactly the colour I wanted, although it is a wilful self-seeder. Three of the most beautiful brown-toned plants are verbascums. The tall coppery *Verbascum* 'Helen Johnson', the slightly paler *V.* 'Cotswold Queen' and the small growing more branched *V.* 'Jackie', pale caramel with a darker eye. Another favourite is the rusty foxglove *Digitalis ferruginea*, its tall spikes surrounded by lesser stems covered in thousands of tiny brown bells look splendid rising behind lush low-growing leaves of *Heuchera* 'Chocolate Ruffles'.

Brown flowers are among spring's earliest. Dusty brown-tinged hellebores emerge just as winter seems to be going on for ever. *Fritillaria persica* is a mixture of wine and dark greenish-brown it's a mysterious plant, I've only been able to grow it in cooler climates, although fritillaries will grow in the coolest areas of Australia and South Africa. Iris come in all shades of rust and

Previous page: Annual pink ranunculus at Kennerton Green

browns. Iris 'Chocolate Vanilla' is warm brown and slate white, flowering in late spring upstaging everything else in the bed. The bearded iris *I.* 'Langport Duchess' is the colour of milky coffee flecked with grated nutmeg; I've planted this at West Green House but its subdued murky tones are not everyone's taste. Another favourite is the species iris *I.* 'Holden Clough', its yellow petals curving out with deep purple veins, resembling the long brownish legs of a hairy spider.

Murky browns make great conversation points in a garden bed. Just for the fun of it try a succession of them through the seasons. Begin with *Fritillaria persica* in early spring, followed by stinking hellebores *Helleborus foetidus*, black lilies – perhaps a cobra-like purple and brown striped *Arisaema triphyllum* and the dark browns and creams of *Iris tuberosa*. The naked twisting stems of *Corylus avellana* 'Contorta' provides extra mysterious presence through winter.

Brown with pinks

I thought I would try a brown garden bed in both Kennerton Green and West Green House. Groups of *R.* 'Julia's Rose', the perennials and the bronze leaved plants went into both gardens. In Australia the bed bordered the drive, so to soften the edges 'Antique' pansies with faces of gold, black, parchment, brown and old rose were tucked beneath clipped cubes of berberis – I purchased a variety known as *Berberis* 'Firecracker', very similar to *B. thunbergii* 'Rose Glow', its new shoots a brilliant mottled pink above the older dull bronze leaves.

In spring the copper and bronze tones looked shiny and very unusual grouped together, but by midsummer in Mittagong I hated the faded brown leaves above dry brown beds all edged by burnt brittle lawn. The roses were faded by the light into colourlessness, it was all utterly depressing. However I noted that where there were black or old-rose coloured violas still flowering, they reflected their colour into adjoining brown leaves, giving life to a group. So the bed was given a twelve month reprieve and the following autumn plants of black, lush raspberry and a splash of white joined the currently unpopular browns.

Left: The brown rose *R.* 'Julia's Rose'

Above: The thousands of tiny brown bells that cover *Digitalis ferruginea* by summer

The following spring *Digitalis* x *mertonensis* shot spikes through my Australian bed – its crushed strawberry bells pushing through the stiff flax, emphasising the brownish-pink on the leaves, with drifts of pink forget-me-not beneath. *Dianthus barbatus* 'Nigrescens' jostled to be seen, heads of tiny velvet flowers the colour of the dregs in a Shiraz bottle, along with the dark red pincushions of *Scabiosa atropurpurea* 'Ace of Spades', all planted in very bold clumps of seven or eleven plants. A luscious raspberry and white antirrhinum was suggested and I experimented with a new *Gaura lindheimeri*, its dark stems disguised beneath bright pink butterfly flowers.

The brilliant summer skies of hotter climates drain and dull the bronze-browns, but when they are supported by plants of rich pink to complement brown toned leaves, as well as a few good groups of blackish plants, the dark depths create a rich paisley, a brown-pink brocade. The overall effect is a border of quiet glamour. I love it all and it has become my favourite bed.

Brown grasses

There is one group of brown plants I cannot grow, grasses. They may currently be the epitome of garden chic, treasured in the cooler areas of Europe and extremely suitable climatically for most gardens in warmer areas, but I do not like to grow them – although I do make an occasional exception. Every Australian country child is warned not to walk through long brown grass in summer, not to poke around clumps of bamboo or pampas grass as they are the habitat of snakes, nasty brown or black ones with their friends and relations, copperheaded varieties and blacks with red bellies. Of course it's all in the mind, but I still associate grasses with reptiles. Additionally, long brown grass and thistles near the house are taboo in country or bushland Australia as combustible dry grass explodes when touched by fire during the dry season. Quite apart from this, I admit I do find long clumps of spiky grass foreign, intruding upon and unrelated to a classical herbaceous border where grasses seem out of style and rhythm. When I see them I have to resist a compulsive urge to pull them out. Like a bowl of daffodils proudly displayed in Singapore, I find grasses in a border out of place and unnecessary.

Left: A lively border of unusual colour combinations of brown, pinks and blacks at Kennerton Green

Brown with peach

Brown needs other colours around it to exploit its depth and in England my brown bed looked respectable but not inspiring in its first year. For two seasons I played with colour combinations. White with brown reminded me of the two-tone golf shoes, so the white was removed. Clumps of black plants were dull, then I tried the blush pink English rose R. 'Heritage', which was pretty but far too insipid. I needed a glowing colour like the cool warmth of glow worms or the pale flame in a fire, soft warm peach or a not too yellow apricot. Peach is too ethereal under hot skies, but in mellow light it is beautiful with browns.

To the tall brown foxgloves and verbascums I have added *Achillea* 'Salmon Beauty'. Its flat heads rise above feathery foliage which adds much needed bulk to a bed planted with predominantly spiky plants. These include the skyscrapers of the plant world *Eremurus robustus* with their tiny rows of pale peach flowers, and the darker *Eremurus* x *isabellinus* 'Cleopatra'. The lupin 'Peach' and the bearded peachy-pink iris *I.* 'Edward of Windsor' supply good colour, but the most important addition to the original plants are the new brown roses.

Bill le Grice Roses in Norfolk offer roses in every shade of brown from gingerbread to hot chocolate, some flushed gold, others shot with rose and slate, many worth trying to find out which colours are happiest here. *Rosa* 'Julia's Rose' is not a strong growing bush, so now I tend to crowd her, gratefully accepting the spray of blooms that appear among the perennials. This rose is a beautiful bonus rather than a main event, a rose that needs companions to reflect and enhance her colour, their choice depending on the light and latitude.

Achillea is an excellent plant, easy to grow with delightful grey-green ferny foliage which clumps beautifully and hides lots of brown earth, and flat heads of flowers rising up at different levels between spiky plants. Try mixing terracotta and orangey-brown varieties in the front of a yellow border to tone it down.

I have come quite recently to brown plants, yet some of my garden's most evocative images are brown – browns backlit by the long low beams of autumn sun, stands of seed heads, black-brown sedums, silver-brown balls of alliums, the rusty lace ruffs of *Hydrangea paniculata*. At Kennerton the ferny foliaged *Metasequoia glyptostroboides* stands like a magnificent rusty pyramid in autumn, having changed colour through the seasons from brilliant pale lime to mid-green climaxing in rust-red. Hedges of paper brown hornbeams were a cultural shock when I first came to England, they looked so untidy, but now I rejoice in their warm colour as I learn to observe and love a winter's landscape and not to buy an airline ticket as soon as the autumn leaves mess begins.

Right: Tall spires of *Verbascum* 'Helen Johnson', *Eremurus robustus* and *Digitalis ferruginea* surround the old well head at West Green House

brown favourites

Cosmos atrosanguineus

Often called the chocolate cosmos, this is said to be a perennial, but I find I treat it as an annual in cooler climates. The flower grows to 40cm (18in) tall and is a black-brown with a reddish glow and smells of chocolate. It requires a rich soil and sun and flowers from late summer into autumn.

Digitalis ferruginea

A perennial light brown foxglove that can grow to 2m (6ft) tall, covered by hundreds of light brown tiny bells. It grows happily in sun, semi-shade and shade, flowering from late spring in warm climates but midsummer in cooler areas.

Fritillaria persica

I often feel this is the most mysterious plant in the garden in spring – beautiful black-brown bells hang in pyramid shapes on slim stems up to 1.2m (4ft) high. These secretive, understated flowers have a drop dead elegance. Grow them in rich soil in a sunny spot.

Iris 'Chocolate Vanilla'

This iris often reaches 1.2m (4ft) tall, with all the delicious appeal of a two toned chocolate bar. The tops are slate white, encircled by lower petals of rich chocolate brown. Flowering in mid-spring it likes full sun and will tolerate heat.

Rosa 'Buff Beauty'

A beautiful hybrid Musk rose of yellow, its deeper buds fading to flowers of buff. I like this rose planted in groups and underplanted by Verbascum 'Jackie' – a good matching of colour. The flowers are a medium-sized semi-double and bloom profusely.

Rosa 'Edith Holden'

I am captivated by the range of brown roses now available and this is a Floribunda rose of russet-brown. It appears to be a strong growing bush worthy of a front-of-the-border position. Like all roses it needs well mulched soil to achieve abundant summer flowering.

Verbascum 'Helen Johnson'

Think of a verticle line of burnished small copper pans, this is the colour and effect of this amazingly coloured verbascum. The 1.2-m (4-ft) tall stems have a grey-green felted look, a soft foil for the flowers studded down the stem. Verbascums flower throughout summer into autumn and tolerate poorish soil.

Opposite: *Iris* 'Chocolate Vanilla' beside the croquet lawn at Kennerton Green

5 | green

Green gardens masquerade under many forms. I remember as a child my mother and grandmother returning from a midsummer visit to a country garden, languidly discussing the fine deciduous trees surrounding the homestead. It was the cool oasis of trees rather than the flowers that provided the memory of a pleasant afternoon.

The trees planted half a century ago dominate the country garden at Kennerton Green. These are a fine if haphazard collection, many planted to mark a specific occasion such as the excitement of Princess Margaret's visit, a Colonial Governor coming to lunch, a birthday. They include many contrasting shades and shapes of green such as the huge lime leaves of *Paulownia tomentosa*, the foxglove tree, an acid contrast to neighbouring darker English elms; the striking green and white *Acer negundo* 'Variegatum', and the tulip tree *Liriodendron tulipifera* with its dark green saddle-shaped leaves and green tulips edged in orange as though quickly dipped in paint. *Metasequoia glyptostroboides* is one of the garden's giants, its feathery leaves the palest green in spring and rust in autumn, while the aptly named maidenhair tree *Ginkgo biloba* is the most ancient species.

Spring is officially announced for me when the crimson buds of the *Malus floribunda* explode among young green leaves into a cloud of pearl pink blossoms overhung by thousands of humming bees, and the season departs with the last petals of *Malus Ioensis,* its sprays of cupped pink blooms succumbing to the first hot days of summer. Nyssas change from green to become the stars of autumn, with leaves like coloured ribbons, while liquidambars turn to bursts of burgundy, fire and yellow.

When I think of other green gardens I picture the giant trees so beloved by Victorian gardeners planted as exotic backdrops in English gardens. Or I see the grey-greens of an Australian native bush garden, an olive green Mediterranean landscape, the lush tropical green captured in pots in a Thai courtyard, or the leathery elephant ears of hostas in every shade of green from grey to lime as show-stoppers in a European border.

There are so many green gardens, all so different in concept and geography. For many, green gardens are symbolised by the glories of 17th century France, where the great patterns of grass, hedge and forest are viewed with awe by the tourist trudging the grounds of Vaux le Vicomte or Versailles against piercing winds, or trying to find shelter from too hot sun.

I was enchanted when I saw the small West Green House parterre. It had the design elements of the grand baroque gardens and at times of contemplation I imagine gentlemen with wigs and red heels adding colour to the green. But green gardens with topiary reach back into classical antiquity, praised by Pliny the Younger in the first century BC. He describes his villa, 'in front of the colonnade is a terrace laid out with box hedges clipped into different shapes from which a bank slopes down, also with figurines of animals...'

Above: The parterre gardens capture the spirit of another age at West Green House

Opposite: The cool allure of twin avenues of pleached Hornbeam trees rising above hedges of box at West Green House

Previous page: *Tulipa* 'Spring Green'

'. . . It was the cool oasis of trees rather than the flowers that provided the memory of a pleasant afternoon.'

Green structure

The little West Green parterre is the most romantic design of heart shapes punctuated with topiaries of lollipops, cones and standards all set in low knarled hedges of box. The area covered is a square of 19m (62ft) by 12m (40ft), enclosed by ivy-clad brick walls painted with white flowers in spring and summer. Today's design was the work of Robert Weir Schulz, around 1898. It was originally filled with roses but they are long gone and it is now simplified to small green hedges and white gravel. It is a garden that relies on its geometry of ordered calm to create a restful green picture, timeless, romantic and tranquil. Six dark green hollies like upright arrows lead the eye beyond the inner wall to a second walled parterre also of simplisitic design, twenty two sunken lead tanks outlined in neat box hedged squares of 1m (3ft) x 60cm (2ft) brimming with pads of deep green water lilies which shy white flowers peep from in the English summer.

If you plant a parterre in an enclosed area surrounded by high walls or hedges you may choose to graduate the heights of your plants to create interest and balance. In my lilypond parterre I have placed sentinels of clipped yew and lollipops of densely clipped hollies, shapes of varying height to lead the eye from the high brick walls gradually down to the small hedged ponds in the smartly raked gravel. The contrasts between the textures and different shades of green are marked by the broad shining lily pads nestling amidst the neat, miniature box.

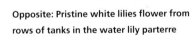

Opposite: Pristine white lilies flower from rows of tanks in the water lily parterre

Top: Parterres were popular in early American gardens. Here, one of similar style breaks the glare of white gravel

Top left: Lollipop-shaped holly trees reflect light from their shiny leaves

Below left: Midsummer *Lilium* bring polished light to the walled garden in Hampshire

Above: The gold tasselled pavilion in the water lily parterre awaits the arrival of its resident chickens

Lightening formal shapes

Walled enclosures can feel rather hard and I am trying to break the nearly too sharp feeling of the high brick walls, hard gravel and clipped lines to provide a much lighter edge in such a confined space. So I have draped the walls with all white roses, *Rosa* 'Long John Silver' a hybrid climber, and the vigorous ramblers *R.* 'Seagull' and *R.* 'Sanders' White Rambler'. Narrow border beds below the walls are now filled with all white flowers, green and white tulips in spring, followed by white herbaceous peonies and lilies for glamour.

My lilies begin with the pure white Asiatic lily *Lilium* 'Mont Blanc' in early summer, followed by white Regal lilies. *L. regale* flower until the height of summer and Oriental hybrids such as the pure white *L.* 'Casa Blanca' continue the theme throughout. From late in the season until autumn Tiger lilies such as the creamy-white *L.* 'Sweet Surrender' complete the story for summer-long flowering of these exotic flowers.

Any bare space in the beds has had *Nicotiana* 'Lime Green' tucked in, its single star shaped flowers luminous and very effective below the drama of the lilies.

My love of geometry needs still more subtle tweaking as I tend towards the severe shapes. Another softening element in this parterre are the chickens in a stylish pavilion, a romantic gesture at the end of the garden, its roof of stripes and gold tin tassels a focal point enlivened by much clucking, fluffing and strutting. Although this chicken house is fun and the parterre dramatically plain, together it is a stylish fantasy using plants and shapes always associated with classical gardens, its personality harmonising with the traditional elements throughout the gardens.

I am always most impressed on a summer's day by the sight of the glossy green shining from box, holly or tall lily leaves. They seem the perfect accessories to wax white blooms. For a small smart modern parterre try the great French couturier Chanel's signature flower, the autumn flowering white *Camellia sasanqua* with thick dark shiny leaves that can be clipped to make excellent hedges, whilst the miniature varieties like *C. sasanqua* 'Little Liane' make stunning small leaved hedges covered with compact white flowers in autumn and early winter. In frost-free climates this glossy green effect can be achieved with the bonus of the glorious perfumed flowers by planting gardenia hedges.

Contrasting parterres

The design of the Australian cottage is more in sympathy with a pre-Revolution American cottage. When constructing a parterre here I was unknowingly probably looking at the same patterns that American colonial gardeners used when they created their small cottage gardens. It uses the elements of an Anglo-Dutch garden, but in its simplest form: a plain rectangle of box hedging 8m (25ft) by 4m (12ft) with box balls and cones placed at regular intervals, dissected in quarters by a diagonally curving line. A topiary bird of unknown breed sits in a central urn; it may be a peacock or a fantail pigeon, shaped from 'Muehlenbeckia' a fine leaved fast growing creeper, only to be let loose if contained in a pot. Here it is covering a frame of the statuesque bird, providing what I think is a necessary quirky note. The parterre has proved an excellent way to provide a simple but smart green and white charm to the cottage entrance, and the dark green box absorbs the light and cuts the glare of the surrounding white gravel to an acceptable level.

Many gardeners veer away from box, thinking it slow to grow and hard to maintain, but neither is true. Box is an exceptional plant, at home climatically from subtropical to cool temperate gardens, a bold green statement that maintains its chic good looks independent of the seasons. I still find English box, *Buxus sempervirens*, with its small smooth pointed leaves, is the most compact plant for clipped edges or parterres. The Japanese box *B. microphylla* var. *japonica* grows more

quickly, a taller plant with a larger rounded leaf that is quite acid green in new growth but darkens with age. Leave this plant for taller hedges, otherwise after trimming, every leaf seems to have been clipped in half. In warmer climates dwarf box *B. sempervirens* 'Suffruticosa' is gaining in popularity as it requires minimal maintenance.

To introduce a parterre was a foreign design element in my traditional Australian garden, so the surrounding beds needed to be formalised and edged by box hedging to integrate the new idea. To one side I divided the borders with zigzag lines of box with sculptural balls of *Pittosporum tenuifolium,* hebe, santolina, *Teucrium fruticans* and rosemary in the parterre design. Espalier Granny Smith apples on free standing goblet frames repeated the idea of formality on a second side, but the third side became a long pattern of interlocking triangles and filled in zigzags of aromatic grey-green rosemary and lavender. This forms a permanent mat of mauve and blue, a decorative pattern for a dry sun baked spot.

Grey-green foliaged plants are often the most drought-tolerant, perfect for dry ridges and terraces, which need not be the Cinderella spots of the garden. By choosing a range of drought-tolerant Mediterranean shrubs and perennials, and using a small hedge trimmer, a most sophisticated garden can emerge. Plant a grouping of favourite green-grey plants, perhaps cistus, rosemary, lavender, teucrium, santolina or artemisia,

and clip them into rounded and conical shapes. Vary the heights between 50cm (18in) and 1m (3ft), with one or two slightly higher, and the result is garden sculpture, an elegant planting of shapes and textures creating harmonies of soft light and shade.

Opposite: By midsummer the old borders at West Green House are predominantly filled with green and white plants

Below: Box shaped as a corkscrew adds height, design and structure to the garden

Patterns in dull greens

Beyond the original garden at Kennerton Green was a small field slightly smaller than a bowling green but quite large enough for a grass tennis court, completely enclosed by a collection of different cypresses, all at least 7m (20ft) tall and dense enough to act as windbreaks in the winter months. I decided to make a modern parterre there, a green garden that used different textures and shapes to create a cool space. The excellent Australian nurserywoman Joan Arnold had a collection of about 80 bay trees *Laurus nobilis* that I had long coveted. Some had trunks trained as corkscrews, others straight, all about 1.5m (4½ft) tall. This idea became the basis of my Bay Tree garden.

I based my original plan on a French garden I had seen in a magazine, a courtyard of squares with each square devoted to a single plant variety. My design was a grid of eight equal oblong beds edged in box. These in turn were outlined by a grid of the 80 bay trees clipped as lollipops to a height of 1.75m (5ft) tall, their feet encircled in box rings. An established 3m (10ft) tall bay tree found behind the chicken yard was removed to become the centrepiece, its feet a circular mat of box 3m (9ft) across or 12m (36ft) round.

Unless you have plenty of help in a garden, keep a parterre simple. Some ideas, such as a clipped bay tree surrounded by a circle of box, work much better on a small scale – it's a crazy idea for 81 trees, but looks marvellous as the centrepiece of a small parterre, or a single design feature in a small garden.

Bay and box are tough plants that look immaculate all year round, ideal for busy town gardeners with limited garden maintenance time. Although a shaped plant must be trimmed from time to time, the idea of five clipped bay trees encircled in box laid out as a simple cross would be a smart solution for a town house, courtyard or basement garden. Surrounded with paving of stone, terracotta or gravel, it makes an eye-catching, low maintenance, minimalistic design. I'd enclose the perimeter with a green hedge perhaps of *Choiysa ternata* to tie the design together.

The eight beds were designed to house balls of white marguerites but the wind proved too strong and lifted them like tumbleweed. Currently I plan a seasonal progression commencing with *Tulipa* 'Maureen' which opens cream fading to white followed by white ranunculus, then white aquilegias, marguerites and *Penstemon* 'White Bedder'. The garden triumphs in midsummer when hundreds of Christmas lilies, *Lilium longiflorum*, bend their white trumpets nearly to the grass creating a medieval fantasy, their perfume overpowering. But the overall impression is the play of light on green in shapes, on leaves and on grass. It gives a precise crisp sensation by day, a moody pattern of shaped shadows by late afternoon.

The bay tree garden is made up of predominantly dull greens: the 81 round standards of bay leaves, the dull grey-green of the surrounding cypresses, so different from the shiny geometry of my parterre in England. It needs the introduction of sparkling light, and I am adding glitter to my greens with water in a long canal, a water staircase capturing the white and blue of the sky to lift the background of dull green.

You can add sparkle to dull greens in shade or sun with a ribbon or river of green leaves splashed with white, such as the ivy *Hedera helix* 'Glacier', or a covering of bright white flowers. The perennial viola, *Viola cornuta* 'Lambley White', flowers from spring to autumn, their cheerful round white faces at home in cool and less temperate climates, unfazed by midsummer sun.

Left: The many shades of atmospheric green in the Bay Tree garden at Kennerton Green

Opposite: *Echinacea purpurea* 'White Swan' stand tall in a late summer border

'. . . a moody pattern of shaped shadows by late afternoon.'

Above: Espaliered Granny Smith Apple trees filter the warm Australian light

Main picture: *Euphorbia amygdaloides*, the colour of lime, provide a welcome highlight in any bed of green on green

Opposite: Sprays of pale *Helleborus foetidus* create textured contrast in an all-green garden

Previous page: The first white flowers of winter: snow drops bravely peep through the frozen earth at West Green House

Light shades of green

A huge range of greens plants could be used as infills for a garden. Don't underestimate the stylish effect of green on green. *Helleborus augustifolius* 'Corsicus' adds stiff light green, and mounds of *Alchemilla mollis* give a froth of acid green flowers over attractive soft greyer-green leaves, wonderful for cool gardens. Climate permitting, the Pineapple lily *Eucomis bicolor* could be fun, it flowers in late summer, with its thick stems supporting lime green blooms, with leaves bunched on top just like a pineapple! Green plants alone can give tonal messages of light green, grey-green or dark green and texture images of crispness or sharpness.

The play of green on green, of foliage on grass, can be more subtle than the traditional style of green parterre enclosed by gravel. In a cool climate it is very effective to infill the beds of a parterre with huge mounds of green hostas, their shapes and textures of green emphasising a cool mood. The waxy pale green leaves and perfumed white flowers of *Hosta plantaginea* var. *japonica* would be my first choice, a very serene plant.

A story book parterre

'If you open a garden in England you must have a tea room', I was told. The idea filled me with dread, for the thought of trying to make edible cakes was my idea of a nightmare. Perhaps this conversation took place as I first viewed the top walled garden at West Green House. For behind the high walls the entire space was consumed by a swimming pool in terminal decay, its bottom filled with debris, the concrete cracks crammed with weed and filth. Beside this dank hole a roofless and rotting gardeners' bothy added the final note of depression and so for two years its gate to the old orchard through which our future garden visitors would enter remained firmly shut.

I'm not sure where the inspiration for this corner of the garden came from. Perhaps it was the nagging worry of what to do with the ugly pool area, perhaps it was the dread of serving teas, but gradually, like Alice, I came to the end of the tunnel and as all the elements of Lewis Carroll's wonderful story were remembered and I knew my new garden would be an Alice garden, a wonderful place for a Mad Hatter's Tea Party. 'There was a table set out under the tree in front of the house and the March hare and the Hatter were having tea. A dormouse was sitting between them fast asleep.'

The story inspired the transformation of the old bothy into a kitchen and the pool became a court-yard garden of strong but simple elements, a limited number of select plant species, a colour range related to the roses of the story. This created a sweet childlike statement that was planted for pure enjoyment of an impression of a very English story, the exact place to sit and partake of a traditional English afternoon tea.

As all the walled gardens at West Green House are basically formal parterres that was also the plan for this garden, the old garden once again dictating new ideas. The newest parterre is a chess board, its squares outlined in box, its base gravel, its perspective slightly sunken for tea-time visitors to sit and look down on topiary characters of the White Rabbit, the Mad Hatter, a tea pot and the hookah-smoking Caterpillar on the mushroom. These are beautifully made frames gradually filling with box or fine ivy, set in the box-framed squares.

No Alice in Wonderland garden could be complete without reference to the Queen, so the chequerboard is lined on three sides by standard roses, the good red floribunda rose *Rosa* 'Remembrance' and a bright white rose *R.* 'Saint John', both suggested by rosarian Peter Harkness. Beneath the roses box is clipped into the pawns with balls, spirals, cones, animals and birds, and the earth covered with silver plants that will cope with the dry gravel. And to soften the starkness *Dianthus* 'Devon General' matches the red roses and *D.* 'Devon Dove' the white; the annual *Senecio maritima* 'Silver Dust' has long clumps of lacy silver-grey leaves in summer, *Alyssum* 'Snow Carpet' has bedded itself into all the cracks along with large clumps of strawberries, which look inviting beside bright red tea tables. The walls are welcoming red and white roses, the brilliant deep red climber *Rosa* 'Dublin Bay' and pure white *R.* 'White Cloud'. Rose bushes crowd the gate, double blood red *R.* 'Lilli Marlene' and old white

'. . . like Alice, I came to the end of the tunnel . . .'

Left and below: Newly planted box is beginning to fill the wire shapes of the Mad Hatter and the teapot in the Alice garden at West Green House

Opposite: Nearly all the flowers in the Alice garden are red – roses, lilies, clematis, peonies and dianthus

Rugosa roses transplanted here, a simpler form of flower. Above all this stands the 2.5m (8ft) Queen, the box already filling her skirt, her finger pointing at those that enter.

To truly reflect the Alice theme I had to find a way to include many of the brilliant red flowers shining out of the catalogues in my newly created garden. So I have made a container garden around the tea tables for midsummer crammed with the darkest of red blooms including _Verbena_ 'Lawrence Johnston', _Nicotiana_ x _sanderae_ and _Pelargonium_ 'Lord Bute' placed towards the edges, with the centre containers filled to brimming with _Antirrhinum_ majus 'Black Prince', and _Dianthus barbatus_ 'Nigrescens'. These are placed alongside pots of white flowers.

When I first arrived at West Green House many cuttings were taken from the old box hedges so that we could repair the existing parterres. Within four years I had enough sturdy young plants to plant my chequerboard, so in every respect this new garden is in total harmony with our existing parterres. But the greatest bonus has been my neighbour who has relieved me of the trauma of 'The Mad Hatter's Tea Party' as she organises everything beautifully and delights our visitors with anecdotes about Alice – as her grandmother was the original Alice!

Green flowers for shafts of light

While green is largely used to create structure in the garden, the long white border at Kennerton Green eventually runs into a curve of green flowers, a new border is 150m (450ft) long, dominated by fifty year old mature trees, casting in places the densest shade, denying water to penetrate, greedy to take their share of the annual mulch. Perhaps I am stretching the imagination a trifle far, as 'green' flowers are often an amalgamation of white, green, lime and yellow, but when they are combined the effect is of shades of green limelight. In deep dry shade green flowers can look lush and liquid, and lime green will light the darkest places.

I keep trying to grow the acid green *Alchemilla mollis*, the mainstay of every English gentlewoman's garden, but it is just too hot for it in sunnier climates, so the border's edge has thankfully been taken over by *Euphorbia polychroma*, wonderful domes of intense lime green that last till autumn. Large mounds of lime green helichrysum grow all year in our shade to form a luminous ground cover, a stunning backing for *Hemerocallis* 'Missouri Beauty', its citrus yellow flowers lit with green.

Lime green is a dazzling colour in shade, its intense cool glow entices the eye. The lime-sherbert leaved shrub *Physocarpus opulifolius* 'Dart's Gold' revels in the gloomiest conditions, as does *Garrya elliptica*, perfect in any garden, its long yellowy-green catkins a particular joy above sulphur daffodils in early spring.

I like to repeat flowers and themes wherever possible around the garden, introducing special plants to different border escorts. The cream flowering *Sisyrinchium striatum* is one; clumped among bearded iris it harmonises colours and shapes, continuing the progression of flowing swords throughout spring and summer. There is no true green bearded iris but there are variants of creamy-whites with veins of greens, like *Iris* 'Celestial Ballet', or whites with acid citrus falls, or with green splashes as in the dwarf iris *I.* 'Green Spot'.

The green white story can stretch for nine months a year, beginning with winter snowdrops, varieties of *Galanthus nivalis*, and the lime green flowers of *Helleborus foetidus* which bloom from late winter into spring. These plants make huge dark architectural mounds of heavily incised leaves. Green and white bell-shaped flowers include the nodding bells of *Allium triquetrum* and the *Tulipa* 'Spring Green', a must-have in a cold spring climate. Follow these with hummocks of *Astrantia major subsp. involucrata* 'Shaggy' with its pointed ruff of green bracts and white centre, speckled green bunches of tiny flowers.

Of course I use green annuals: at the front of the border, the ice green and white *Euphorbia marginata*, a bushy plant with upper leaves of white and green stripes, the light lime stems of *Nicotiana* 'Starship' and the large flowers of *Zinnia elegans* 'Envy' for tall summer green.

The most simple of green gardens are formed from the placement of grass and trees as in the serene green theatre at West Green House

Behind them are the tall spikes of the Irish green bells of *Moluccella laevis*. Stretching a point, I have put the perennial *Echinacea purpurea* 'White Swan' at the back of the border; although white, it looks more greeny-white by autumn, its centre starts life as a green cone, turning brown with age. These spectacular daisy-shape flowers are echoed by the tall erect zinnias.

These colours are reflected again in the greeny-cream flowers of *Pieris japonica* 'Temple Bells' its bronze-green leaves polished like oriental lacquer, catching and reflecting the light in dark corners. In the deepest and coolest recess of my green border sits a colony of lush green cobra-headed arum lilies *Zantedeschia aethiopica* 'Green Goddess', stylised flowers beloved by flower arrangers. As their striking green flowers unfurl revealing generous splashes of white, their shine is another reflection of available light.

High above, the tall tree canopy forms a desired dense shade by midsummer where day after day flocks of the screeching sulphur crested cockatoos, the brilliant red and green King parrots or the multi coloured Rosellas amuse themselves with denuding a chosen branch of every leaf and twig but, when the huge jet black cockatoos hit the garden, I run for cover as cones and minor branches become missiles hurled from above.

The awning of cool shade is cast by an eclectic collection of trees which include Norfolk Island pines, *Araucaria heterophylla* and *Platanus* x *hispanica*, all reaching well over 90m (30ft) high. The spreading branches of *Magnolia denudata*, and groups of *Abies veitchii* and *Cedrus libani* subsp. *atlantica* are planted closely together,

creating a dense patchwork of green overhead. The golden elm, *Ulmus glabra* 'Lutescens', is another colourful delight but avoid planting it near a house for its lime green 'flower' invades every doorway and drain.

Two spectacular plants tolerate this awning of dry shade: *Romneya coulteri*, the Californian tree poppy, with its extraordinary white basins of papery petals around the golden centre, relishes gravelly dry soil. Flushed with success I've planted a congregation of five or six plants here, this mass of flowers the crescendo of summer. The grey leaved *Echium pininana* with an enormous tongue of blue flowers, often 1m (3ft) long, curves outwards towards the light in spring, its shape the most structural of garden statements unforgettable when planted in groups.

Winter light reflects from the polished leaf and flower of *Gordonia axillaris* (a shrub in cooler areas), its round blooms summoning images of perfectly 'poached eggs'. Away from inland frosts, in coastal city gardens, it's a small, evergreen, perfectly proportioned tree, ideal for small gardens. Camellias, too, like the dry shade: the large wax leaved and flowered 'White Nun', is espaliered to a dividing fence beneath two *Gingko biloba* and a *Liriodendron tulipifera*. Treated this way its evergreen foliage will give privacy and the flowers will turn towards the early spring light and all the blooms will look at you.

Gardens in the last months of summer in the southern hemisphere are predominantly green, the leaves often drab, dusty and tired just hanging there waiting for the first cool days to turn them into a carnival of red and golden autumn colour. So many herbaceous plants are spent, cut back and the shrubs have become monotonous green mounds in long borders. It is now I believe that clipped topiary shapes whether geometric or quirky sustain a joyous note in a garden.

Shapes made of box, holly and *Vibernum x burkwoodii* are polished features especially when holding raindrops after a summer storm, whilst *Lonicera nitida*, 'poor man's box', bay and ivy's duller leaves can act as a foil against bushes of shiny or variegated leaves.

The late season can create a middle distance gap between an earlier floral floor and the roof of leaves, so a variety of clipped plants at different heights in clusters along a border becomes a surprise when there is nothing else to exclaim over, creating furniture for the middle distance.

For me these collection of shapes hold my long border together as connecting elements as it goes from one planting and colour block to another. In winter they are the garden's chief joy, green sentinels in a bare world.

Opposite: The nodding head of *Fritillaria acmopetala* brings understated elegance to the garden at Kennerton Green

Right: *Arum maculatum*, Lords and Ladies, – a bold statement of majesty

'Striking green flowers unfurl revealing generous splashes of white, their shine is another reflection of available light.'

green favourites

Actinidia kolomitka

A wonderful oddity, this green twining climber has the occasional leaves painted in pink and white which turn to green as they age. It grows vigorously up to 4m (12ft) and needs a sunny space.

Eucalyptus

Known for the wonderful aroma emanating from their leaves, eucalyptus are also a visual delight. There are hundreds of varieties but thay all have grey-green foliage. They cover the length and breadth of Australia resulting in a landscape encased in perpetual hazy green.

Heuchera cylindrica 'Greenfinch'

Mounds of bright green leaves with stems of pale green flowers begin to appear in early summer, reaching 45-60cm (18-24in). In warmer areas this evergreen perennial likes dappled shade but is a sun-lover in cooler climates.

Physocarpus opulifolius 'Dart's Gold'

A lime-green leaved shrub that will grow easily in shade in the southern hemisphere. With creamy-white clusters of spring flowers it is said to grow to around 4m (12ft) but mine have not attained this height.

Nicotiana x sanderae 'Lime Green'

A midsummer annual with lime-green star-shaped flowers that gives a garden a cool luminous glow. Growing to 75cm (2ft) tall, they do need to be kept watered.

Ruta graveolens 'Jackman's Blue'

This herb forms a mound of deeply divided blue-green leaves in summer. It has insignificant yellow flowers and grows to over 4m (12ft) in full sun.

Santolina rosmarinifolia 'Primrose Gem'

The green santolina, a Mediterranean herb, will thrive in dry spots. Its bright green, delicate leaves look best when clipped – an excellent shrub which requires full sun.

Tulipa 'Spring Green'

This is a viridiflora tulip and absolutely my favourite bulb. It grows on a strong stem, 45cm (15in), and has pride of place in my spring borders. Its pure white petals are slashed with green and flare slightly at the edges.

Silybum marianum

This is a very prickly green thistle with leaves that look to have captured spider webs in a white and green design. It is very effective at a garden's edge producing a good mound of around 1-1.2m (3-4ft). Plant it in sun or dappled light.

Opposite: *Tulipa* 'Greenland'

Right: The giant rhubarb *Gunnera manicata* **grows prolifically in moists soils**

Previous page: The tall stems of green calyces are like bells that surround the small white flowers of *Moluccella laevis*

6 | a rainbow garden

It must be over thirty years ago that I bumped down a rather rutted road beside the Loire in France, a massive château loomed above with a 'garden to visit' sign casually put beside the road. I stopped and entered by a side door and my life changed for ever. I had stumbled on the great potager at Villandry near Tours, a grand early 20th century re-creation of a 16th century French Renaissance *jardin-potager*. Today the garden is reached down a fine road, signposted and with a huge car park, but on that first visit I was there alone. I fell in love with a style of gardening I had never seen before.

A large grid of geometrically shaped beds were immaculately planted with regimented vegetables, outer beds brimming with hot coloured flowers and espaliered fruit trees covering trellised fences and arches. The pattern centred on a square pond with cleanly raked gravel between.

This bravura display has its historical roots in the monastic gardens of medieval Europe. During the Dark Ages these gardens kept horticultural traditions alive behind high walls where monks cultivated basic fruits and vegetables and tended herb beds for flavour and medicinal needs. They were gardens shrouded in multi-layered symbolism, the eye of God looked down on beds laid out in grids to the shape of the Cross, the gardens were symbols of paradise, of man's triumph over nature, tiny oases of knowledge in a dark warring world. Physically the gardens were enclosed either by a high woven fence, a hedge or a wall to provide protection and shelter and to allow vines or espaliered fruits to be trained. A well, pond or fountain often marked the centre of the garden; water was a symbol of life as well as a convenient place to water the plants from, and for the cook's ready supply of fresh fish.

Below: From his Gothic cage the white peacock surveys espaliered peach trees, cauliflowers, bolting lettuces, white kale and strawberries

Opposite: Profusion in the potager at Kennerton Green

Previous page: Summer bounties in the potager at West Green House

From traditional to modern

Traditional monastic gardens were predominantly laid to vegetables or herbs, with a few flowers permitted as long as they had culinary, medicinal and symbolic as well as decorative uses. The iris, for example, had many virtues: its roots gave perfume and ink, its leaves were used for thatching, and its white beauty symbolised virginity. It joined the rose and lily – the flowers said to be all that was found in Mary's tomb – which became the approved Christian flowers.

The mysticism is wonderful but what first enchanted me was the realisation of just how decorative vegetables become when planted in this way, and the possibilities of plant combinations. Making a potager is like making a giant rag quilt with interlocking squares of fruit and flowers, herbs and vegetables. And this pattern can be changed twice a year in hospitable climates.

I have now made four potagers; my first was basically a herb garden at the farm at Burrumbuttock, New South Wales, a walled courtyard that trapped the blistering heat. My next was a major effort on a sub-tropical island north of Sydney, its soil pure sand, the water table only feet below the surface, and worst of all, overhung by huge gum trees that leached any nutrients out of the soil. But it was decorative and productive, its geometric beds overlooked by a hexagonal garden shed, its focal point a dovecote of great charm.

I was in high monastic fervour when the potager at Kennerton Green was laid out. It is quite large 16m x 16m (50ft x 50ft), laid out as a St George's cross intersected by St Andrew's cross, and enclosed by three 2m (6ft) walls espaliered with Red Delicious and Jonathan apples that form lines of brightly coloured fruit in autumn. The fourth side is bordered by a long low building with Gothic design windows behind which strut well loved peacocks. A second lower fence across the path is espaliered with peaches, plums and apricots enclosing the whole garden.

I modelled the Kennerton Green potager entrance on the lychgate of our neighbouring church. With subterfuge in mind, late one afternoon the gardeners departed to the church, measuring sticks in hand, to be temporarily interrupted in their work by a vicar intrigued to learn our plans for his lychgate! Its roof is wide enough for shelter with benches to sit on and its ecclesiastical design enhances our theme.

Gates or doorways leading to enclosed gardens are another interesting element in a garden. These could be solid timber doors, plain or carved wooden or metal gateways. The USA is a great source of ideas for decorative vegetable gardens and their traditional style of a simple gate in a white picket fence looks sharp and spruce around a potager. Doors with grilles are very atmospheric, but as long as your entrance can be shut to protect the crops from predators, it can be as dramatic or as simple as the design suggests.

Left: The lychgate at Kennerton Green is a replica of the entrance at St Simon and St Jude's church in neighbouring Bowral, New South Wales

Opposite: Artichokes and bean sprouts seen from the Moon Gate at West Green House

Productive parterres

Potager designs can be as simple or as intricate as desired, but a few practical design thoughts help in enabling the garden to run smoothly. Paths can be of any material, gravel, paving stones, compressed earth or sand. In wetter climates old bricks or paving stones are perhaps the best choice. Traditional cobbles are lovely but not easy to push a barrow along and paths must be wide and smooth for ease of maintenance.

If a potager is enclosed within a hedge of cypress, yew or beech, make a path inside the hedge so the roots do not rob the soil of the adjoining bed. Living walls of fruit trees, grape vines or roses are decorative and more practical as they don't rob moisture and nutrients in the same way.

Geometrically shaped beds must be big enough to contain a mixture of a few species of vegetables and flowers, edged in either evergreen perennials or annual plantings. I have had success with annual parsley and marigolds but best of all for me are low 30-cm (1-ft) high box hedges, or chives. Potagers are basically infilled parterres, so in winter and early spring the design of a box or santolina-edged parterre holds its pleasing pattern until it becomes a riotous joy later on.

Fruit cages designed by Oliver Ford provide the central vertical element in the potager at West Green House, filled with standard bushes of berry fruits with topiaried red, black and white currants and gooseberries underplanted with strawberries

Chives make excellent edging plants, and will always look good if the row is wide enough to be harvested in strips. In a large potager they can be as wide as 50cm (20in), leaving one third of the width always flowering, one third growing and one third just cut. In a smaller situation treat the border as two strips only, trimming the chives less regularly.

Height

I like to have vertical elements in a bed to give height and interest to what are generally quite level plant designs, so any bed should be big enough for a centre piece, perhaps a wigwam of beans, peas, sweet peas, a standard rose or a 'Ballerina' apple tree whose single straight trunk will be clustered with fruit in season. In France the traditional vertical element is often a model rooster on a stand made from tin or clay, guarding neatly hoed and well tended plots in grids of four or eight beds that supply much of a family's need.

Balls of lavender or rosemary, bay trees topiaried as lollipop shapes, or artichokes in pots can be used to achieve height and style in potager beds. Giant arches loaded with grapes or berry fruit make both practical and stylish high centres for larger beds. Even a clump of sunflowers or corn form excellent centre verticals. If the bed is too small, however, it will look contrived, and it is certainly not practical to have oversized elements, for potagers should be practical as well as ornamental.

Bold colours

Colour schemes for vegetable garden designs need to be bold and imaginative. Very early in the season at Kennerton Green I plant the central St George's cross with onions interplanted with tulips. One year I included the bold double raspberry and white striped *Tulipa* 'Carnaval de Nice'. Adjoining plots were planted with decorative cabbage, all frilly pink and grey-green, with 'Red Drumhead' winter cabbage behind a confection of purple and blue. Behind these I planted a five coloured heirloom silverbeet, also known as rainbow chard, with stems of red, yellow, white, pink and bicoloured for a harlequin effect.

As the season progresses tiny faces of heartsease smother my beds, hiding the bare spots left from harvested vegetables. Then the soil is prepared for late summer aubergines, another heirloom mix in whites, lavenders and pinks.

I grew up in a boarding school in Melbourne, Australia where every day from summer to winter we were fed a plate of lettuce with salad vegetables floating on top. So salads have become my least favourite menu choice, with lettuce at the very bottom of the list, but to grow lettuce and all its derivatives is an entirely different matter, for in my eyes nothing looks so beautiful as straight lines of leaves from the palest green to dark bronze-red, veined leaves, ruffled leaves, two toned leaves, long leaves, large flat leaves, miniature leaves, every leaf to make the most satisfying colour paths to delight the eye and every other person's palate.

Use all colours and shapes together to form a lettuce carpet. Some 'reds' to try are 'Cerise' with its leaves of bronze-red intricately frilled (known as oak leaf shape) from leaf edge to base. 'Lollo Rosso' is a reliable lettuce that can be planted year round – a green lettuce an extravaganza of frilled bronze red on its lacy edges.

Another year I might plant chard with bright red stems and crinkly leaves the blackest of red to back the red and white tulips. This bolt of colour adds an exciting element of surprise. I could choose to co-ordinate the ruby chard with 'Lollo Rosso' lettuce and perhaps 'Purple Ruffles' basil the reddish-purple fluted leaf variety that is much larger and more arresting than the more unusual sweet basil. The onion 'Brunswick' has the reddest of skins, and the red list continues with the almost regal-purple beetroot, the burgundy Brussels sprouts 'Falstaff', 'Aster Purple' broccoli, radishes, and in warm climates you can grow shiny red capsicums in all shades and shapes of red and cayenne to make a brilliant red vegetable garden. It is a delight to see the dashing colours of onions and beetroot emerge as the vegetables break through the surface of the soil. Add a scattering of black and red poppies and 'Scarlet' sweet peas on poles and by midsummer the vegetable bed becomes true fire.

For the fun of it I once planted at Kennerton Green a bed of the darkest colours interplanted with white, christening the garden 'The Garden of Good and Evil'. The black tulip 'Queen of Night' was interplanted with white leeks and this was backed by a planting of white and purple 'Violet Queen' cauliflowers bordered by my favourite black-red chard. As the tulips faded the black Viola 'Midnight Runner' wove between the leeks and by summer the deep burgundy sweet pea *Lathyrus odoratus* 'Beaujolais' had climbed the central poles beside the hollyhock *Alcea rosea* 'Nigra'. The black French bean 'Sutton's Purple Cream' proved an excellent choice to climb a grid of tripods. The black 'Sweet Chocolate' capsicum and 'Black Russian' tomato, with purple sage and purple basil, became fashion foils in late summer for smart white zinnias. Other fun black vegetables for warm gardens are the slate-purple sweetcorn 'Blue Popping Corn', 'Long Purple' aubergine, a dark glossy purple-black vegetable, and the flat purple podded pea.

Opposite: *Tulipa* 'Carnaval de Nice' gives a splash of colour in the potager alongside young cauliflowers and kale

Above: Pink and white kale bordered by chives

Right: The dramatic contrast of red and green in ruby chard

Giant golden pumpkins, curious gourds and long narrow squash are the knuckle dusters of the late summer vegetable patch, treasures that hide under enormous green leaves, but when grown in raised beds of woven hurdles made from pliant native saplings, these exotic shapes are at eye level, a delight to behold and easy to pick. Raised beds were features of medieval gardens and are both practical and charming additions to traditional potagers. Mine are set out in spring when seedlings of bright golden chard, the pale orange cauliflower 'Marmalade' and seeds of heirloom orange, yellow and white carrots are drilled in lines between the already flamboyant *Tulipa* 'Flaming Parrot', all feathered petals of yellow, orange and red. As summer progresses lines of polished gold and orange capsicums and trained bright yellow 'Golden Sunrise' tomatoes fight a war to try and stay above tendrils of the orangey nasturtium 'Whirlybird' It is the season for giants as runner beans like 'Crusader' with bright red flowers scale up trellises beside 2m (6ft) tall stands of golden yellow sunflowers and ears of yellow corn. The fine filigree heads of *Angelica archangelica* capture the early autumn sun in heads often 30cm (12in) across and tall red fennel becomes a giant skeleton as winter approaches.

Potagers are labour intensive and I tend to fill whole areas with one perennial plant to help save time, especially if all beds are in use. My English potager has enough space to supply a small village with produce, so to make it more manageable and to add decoration I have planted whole areas of one herb placed in a pleasing pattern. Rows of santolina cut into grey balls or maze-type designs created with two different varieties of lavender have worked well using *Lavandula angustifolia* 'Hidcote' and *L. stoechas* interplanted with rows of box. I have interwoven different sages to make an embroidery of purple, mauves and silver-greys. Carpets of thyme can imaginatively make patterns across unused beds, and mats of strawberries can cover space and smother the weeds. There are many different types of suitable strawberries to use, the tiny alpine strawberries, as well as the white flowered early fruiting 'Emily' and late strawberry 'Sophie' varieties.

One appealing story tells that in medieval times each monk's plot in the potager was identified by a specific type of rose so I like to include roses in a potager design – standards are good for height and climbers for over arches and gateways. Here I tend to favour rather brash colours, the burnt orange of the modern *Rosa* 'Belle Epoque', and the extraordinary striped orange and yellow of the modern *R.* 'Oranges and Lemons' looks dynamic among these autumn-toned vegetables and the strident marigolds – the sunniest flowers for any potager. They sometimes look out of place in the herbaceous border, but can give panache to a seasonal quilt of colour in a productive vegetable garden.

Opposite: The flame coloured tulips dress the onion patch in early spring

Above right: Late summer flowering sunflowers give a last burst of brightness

Right: Midsummer madness as nasturtium, beetroot, carrots, onions and snapdragons struggle for supremacy

rainbow favourites

Lettuces

The easiest of all vegetables to grow, there are lettuces in shapes and colours to suit most beds in a potager, and varieties that will crop in all but the coldest weather. Mix types for contrast and effect. 'Rouge d'Hiver', is dull bronze with oval leaves, 'Lollo Rosso' and 'Cerise' are frilly reds. 'Great Lakes' is a large hearted pale green butterhead, 'Susan' a stunning bright green, and 'Freckles' is pale green smudged in brown. Try cos lettuces such as large leaved mid-green 'Lobjoit' or tiny 'Little Gem' for their vertical light green leaves. Cut-and-come-again varieties include the bright light green 'Lollo Biondi'. For red-brown hues, try 'Bronze Arrowhead' with its arrow-shaped leaves. 'Deer's Tongue' has slim elegant pale green leaves with rounded ends.

Cauliflowers

You need no longer be satisfied with white curds surrounded by ruffles of blue-green leaves. Now you can grow 'Esmereldo' with its bright green curds, deep purple 'Violet Queen' or even pale orange-leaved 'Marmalade' with tiny contasting white heads.

Chard

Chard comes in a range of the most amazing colours. Rainbow chard is pure fiesta adding fun, light and drama to any vegetable garden and it is very hardy and will thrive in drier conditions. Planted in spring it will crop all summer and even if it does tend to bolt I leave it in just to enjoy its fiery colour. Stems of bright orange, lemon and gold look magical planted near lines of marigolds, trailing nasturtiums or at the feet of flame coloured dahlias and as a foreground for the round-faced sunflowers. Stems of pink, white-lemon and 'blue' produce a partytime look, and all taste good.

Beans

I like beans that look like candy canes, especially, 'Barlotta Lingua di Fuoco' with bright red splashes on a light green bean. 'Cosse Violette' is a deep purple, and 'Corono d'Oro' is pale gold and stringless, making beans a colourful vegetable to grow.

Globe artichoke

If you have a reasonable amount of space the majesty of the long silver-grey leaves makes globe artichokes among the most elegant and structural addition to a vegetable garden. Flower heads add a further bonus as giant lavender thistle heads reach for the sky but once this display is over in summer cut back immediately then by autumn the silver-grey leaves are as beautiful as ever. Artichokes like rich soil and long drinks of water which is to be expected as in three months the plant grows from a seed to a plant over 1.5m (5ft) tall.

Sage

The hairy oval grey-green leaves of sage are invaluable in any garden, and a welcome addition to any winter border. In the potager try weaving together a selection of varieties of fragrant culinary sage *Salvia officinalis. S.o.* 'Purpurascens', the purple sage is lovely when combined with the golden leaved *S.o.* 'Icterina' and *S.o.* 'Tricolor' with its variegated leaves in white, green and pink. Sage bushes tend to become spidery so prune hard after flowering, but they are hardy survivors in poor soils.

Sweet peas

Climbing up wigwams or against walls and fences, spilling over embankments, sweet peas are associated with cottage and kitchen gardens, stiff-stemmed flowers of enticing perfume. Available in white, cream, all shades of pinks, reds, lavender and purple and nearly black they are a joy to pick in early summer and last a week or so indoors. Sow old-fashioned varieties such as the purple-blue 'Matucana' or pink and white 'Painted Lady' for maximum scent. Sweet peas are easy to grow but need sunshine and watering when young. They will not grow in very hot climates. Sow into fertile well-drained soil or compost in containers, and don't go overboard with too much tender care or you'll end up with excessive leaf growth and few flowers.

Kale

From late winter to early summer the frilly leaves of the ornamental cabbage in shades of pink, mauve and white or variations of each are pure decoration in the garden or vegetable garden. Beautifully structural shapes, I use them extensively in the early spring potager. Plant out in late autumn in warmer climates, late summer for cool areas, but it is not a plant for the tropics. To keep them in the garden as long as possible cut the flowers as soon as they appear and keep cabbage moths at bay.

Opposite: Nasturtiums climb alongside the red flowered runner beans to create a tangle of rainbow colours

Above: *Coreopsis* are pure summer sunshine flowering until the autumn. I like them especially at the feet of sunflowers

Opposite: *Echeveria*, its pearly grey sheen a subtle source of light, is pure stylised beauty as a mass of it overflows in urns

Previous page: The old stable walk at West Green House was once shadowy unforgiving surfaces of old cobbles and bricks. Today pots of spring and summer flowers, climbing hydrangeas and roses capture every ray of light to create a soft and colourful walkway

I have been fortunate in gardening in several completely different environments where the local colours have impressed upon me the need to work with the demands of a landscape.

One of the most imaginative gardens I've ever seen was a Provençal hillside garden. This was a living sculpture in shades of grey-green filled with hundreds of native Mediterranean plants, the colour so soft above the white soil and rocks of Provence. These were subtle forms in a bright white light, compact plants curved against the hillside, moulded into shape by the strong winds of the Mistral. This was a garden perfectly in tune with its environment.

Mediterranean plants are now the vogue for excellent reasons: they are drought-resistant, mostly non-invasive and many are the herbs we treasure for flavour and fragrance. But before transferring the same ideas of colour and planting schemes to a different situation one has to ask whether the dull grey of Mediterranean native plants would look so pleasing under skies that are for months just shades of grey, where the soil is of a stronger colour, or in urban landscapes? Before selecting any plants one has to consider the colour of a new environment.

Look at the local landscape to find inspirational ideas for beautiful tones in the garden. In Provence the late Madame de Vesin took as her starting point the colour and form of the surrounding vegetation. Around her were soft greens and greys picked out by the whiteish stones of the rocky hills. So, by designing her memorable garden in various shades of blue, olive and white, she cleverly reflected the colours of her environment.

Tumbling from grey urns in sun drenched European courtyards like smooth shining petals carved from blue-grey stone, the perfect rosettes of pearl grey echeveria species are polished grey foliage plants that look romantic when grouped together and spilling over a sculptural shape. Being light reflective plants they add colour and light contrast in dry areas of sombre filtered shade. Echeveria are sun loving plants, that tolerate shade, yet they are also perennial succulent and evergreen subshrubs that are easy to grow in temperate to subtropical climates as long as they have good drainage. The white sheen on the grey-green leaves seems to look contented in many environments and their appearance brings to mind groups of open roses, frozen as ancient fossils in time.

Working with local colour

Nearly thirty years ago I went to live in sheep country in southern New South Wales. There the elements controlled the farmers' livelihoods. Temperatures seesawed from 30 degrees plus day after hot summer's day to bitterly cold winters. Rain, or the lack of it, was the main topic of conversation in the church yard on Sunday; grave heads noted who had received the most and commiserated with those the clouds had passed over. The soil contained red pigment, which provided a harsh canvas of bold colour quite unre- lated to the soft background colours of a garden in the cooler areas of the northern hemisphere, for the red earth captured and retained the hot sun, causing pastel shades to fade, and the colours of rich pinks to drain away. Only in pools of purple shade could they look fresh.

A local building material was a red clay that contained blue, an unforgiving colour that was nonetheless practical in withstanding the staining dust and mud. Old homesteads were often surrounded by orchards of apricots, quinces, peaches, cherries and almonds and groves of citrus trees. They were strands of polished green forming deep-shaded restful circles of dusky blue and mauve that were cool oases lit by shiny fruit of orange, yellow and lime, refreshing light and colours redolent of a climate of extremes.

Bright clear colours look designed for the reddish earth, and my first country garden was an early lesson in finding plants and colours to suit the demands of the land. Roses loved it, laid out on the red soil across a gravel ridge exposed to the winds, a sieve for water to drain through. The catalogues in those days featured mainly hybrid tea roses, heritage roses remained in old gardens loved by those that knew them but unavailable to the average gardener. The English roses were still to come. So to create my colours I turned to *Rosa* 'Sutter's Gold', a deep gold, *R.* 'Grandpa Dixon', a good yellow, cream and pink *R.* 'Peace' and the floribunda *R.* 'Apricot Nectar', sprays of soft apricot-yellow. The neon orange *R.* 'Super Star' shone as a youthful enthusiasm. I might choose none of these colours now, but in their setting they seemed entirely right.

'. . . in my memory
the sun is
always shining
there,
the bright light
dancing off water
and leaves,
a chip of
sapphire in an
azure sea.'

Daisy-style flowers grew simply by placing a cutting in the ground with a minimum of water. *Euryops pectinatus* grew into 1.2m (4ft) grey-green bushes with ferny leaves covered with golden-yellow daisies. Yellow centred white marguerites *Argyranthemum frutescens* and *Anthemis tinctoria*, the ox-eye chamomile, grew in soft mounds. *Fraxinus excelsior*, the golden ash tree, and the claret ash *Fraxinus angustifolia*, were tolerant of the dry climate and looked exciting beside beds of purple, lavender and yellow. The native mint bush *Prostanthera ovalifolia* was temperamental but covered with delightful small purple flowers, and it joined varieties of grey leaved cistus with mostly white flowers; *Lavandula dentata* and the lilac pin cushion *Scabiosa caucasica* intermingled with purple and white mealy sage *Salvia farinacea*, the toughest of plants. The twin mopsheads of white and blue South African agapanthus were the mainstay of midsummer, and brilliant birds gorged on the red, orange and yellow berries of the autumn *Crataegus*. My garden was an assembly of colours of the Mediterranean, but it was far from a Mediterranean garden.

In the dry wheat belt the Australian gums cast a shade of deep purple and blue reflected from colour deep in their grey leaves. In spring this shade is lit by the golden light of the flowers of the *Acacia baileyana*, the native Cootamundra wattle, one of the most vivid varieties. In our garden we grew *Acacia baileyana* 'Purpurea', its lacy silver-grey foliage tipped in purple providing a garden colour code for a spectacular border of plants, echoing the colour of our surrounding vegetation.

Shades of blue-purple with clear yellow and gold are strong and vibrant in any light. Among the most successful planting schemes are the dark silvery-blue sea holly *Eryngium bourgatii* 'Oxford Blue' reaching above groups of *Helichrysum italicum* clipped loosely to form silver-grey balls with tufted flowers of yellow in summer. Or try *Achillea* 'Taygetea', its flat saucers of tiny yellow flowers on stiff stems above a blue-green ferny foliage. Another crescendo suggested by bush colour could comprise mounds of *Nepeta* 'Six Hills Giant', a lavender-blue flowered perennial with lax grey leaves, with *Aster* x *frikarti* 'Mönch', a vibrant lavender Easter daisy.

Our surroundings can dictate the colours we should use around us. I once had a house on Dangar Island, a speck in the estuary of the Hawkesbury River, an hour north of Sydney. It was a tiny community where the hour of the day was judged by the putt-putt sound of the ferry echoing from the river, and the mournful call of the native mopoke brought shivers to the soul. The island is engulfed in a blue landscape, tented by blue-grey eucalyptus, surrounded by sea and sky of the clearest blue. It was there that I first grew a blue and white garden. From the verandah overlooking the water there was nothing to see but stark blue and white flowers and wistful fronds of subtropical green plants; these were the colours of the surrounding landscape. The seashore was blue and it was this blue light I aspired to reflect in my plantings.

Banks of the pale blue *Plumbago auriculata* that flowers all summer scrambled down the embankment to the beach. The hardy blue agapanthus was tucked into the meanest spots, and large bushes of *Ceanothus* 'Blue Pacific' rivalled the sea in an intensity of blue. White spider lilies grew under tree ferns, palms and rioting white and purple bougainvillea, and drifts of fragrant star jasmine. The 'floor' was a mass of the Hawkesbury River daisy (sometimes called the Swan River Daisy), *Brachyscombe multifida*, large cream gazanias and the bright blue daisy *Felicia* beside long green frangipani leaves and banks of darkly polished *Gardenia augusta*. It was the most rampant garden I've ever planted, a blue jungle creeping ever closer. The pruning knife lay beside my pillow. It was an uncomplicated happy garden, a garden for a summer's place in the summer of my life.

Eventually I sold that garden, when I fell under the spell of West Green House, and in my memory the sun is always shining there, the bright light dancing off water and leaves, a chip of sapphire in an azure sea.

Few of us can play with an entire landscape, but it is easy to light shady spots with shiny evergreens, especially those with white flowers. A dark corner in a small garden can be brought to life with a generous evergreen such as Fatsia – its sharply cut shiny leaves attracting attention into a mysterious shady area. Or plant soft white and cream flowers alongside the palest blues to bring added light to a small North European garden.

Opposite left: I cannot grow a garden without South African agapanthus in a dry Australian summer. The strappy leaves are polished green and the erect flowers in blue or white are the epitome of freshness on hot days

Opposite right: The tiny blue daisy-shaped *Felicia* will create summer blue carpets in cool and Mediterranean climate gardens

Above: It seems that no respectable rose garden is complete without *Nepata*, its aura of blue-grey the perfect foil

Using the colours of walls and buildings

I sometimes wonder how relevant gardens will become as more people live in urban communities, city centres where the environment is the colour of steel, glass, concrete and granite, the materials used to clad the buildings of the 21st century. Grey-stained contours control the movement of wind, light and shade, creating microclimates where any plant or garden must match the environment they provide, bare dark pockets of shade or sun traps of unrelenting heat. As new tall buildings arise to cope with growing urban population, changing the environment, creating new wind tunnels and areas of dense shade, town gardens are often forced to abandon traditional lawns and borders, to try new designs and styles.

Urban landscape architects contrive a myriad of stylish ideas to bring colour and pleasing life into these hard-edged landscapes, great sheets of water to capture sky, sculptured landforms to reintroduce grass, colour in man-made materials. Many are emerging that are simply paved areas interspersed with hard-edged pools, plants just narrow green boundaries. But many plants also suit urban drama, offering living shafts of light in dark corners, bold splashes of colour against the greys, soft shapes against the angles. Living walls, for example, offer welcome light and life, stylish urban boundaries include walls pleached with *Magnolia grandiflora* or espaliers of shiny leaved camellias or evergreens used as hedges, cut to the required heights.

Small urban gardens offer their own possibilities for playing with light, for example in a garden surrounded by buildings or high walls the light will be directed and trapped into quite specific areas. Try using dramatic containers as spotlights to capture and reflect this light, planting them with a striking centrepiece such as a yucca with softer shapes and colours of annual plants of your choice tumbling over the edges. Wherever they are placed the eye will be directed that way, so place containers at different heights to highlight different spots. And use obelisks, pyramids or sculptures to draw attention to different areas, and if your walls are too dark to grow climbers of your choice successfully decorate them with eyecatching lightcoloured or metallic objects. Curiously, the most striking colours for garden structures in a dark garden are often dark shades such as sage green or even black

An attractive permanent planting for long lasting colour in a container could consist of the spiky blue grass *Elymus magellanicus*, and the bright yellow woolly leaves of *Stachys byzantina* 'Primrose Heron' with *Sedum spathulifolium* 'Cape Blanco', rosettes of grey-blue with sulphur yellow flowers for summer to autumn light.

The stable walk at West Green was long and drab and used to be quite spooky, a narrow walkway overshadowed by tall buildings of mossed red bricks, and a pathway cobbled in stones of a dark hardness. It needed informal tall and broad pots planted with soft tumbling plants to add colour, light and lightness, so to achieve this I placed three pots each a quarter full with soil, one on top of another. The basepot 65cm (27in) diameter x 50cm (22in) high, the middle pot 45cm (18in) diameter x 40cm (16in) high, and the top pot 35cm (14in) diameter x 30cm (12in) tall. Each summer in soft apricot to complement the bricks,

trails of *Verbena* 'Peaches and Cream', spreading *Viola* 'Antique', *Nicotiana* 'Salmon Pink' and bushes of the bluest lavender I can find, join the powder blue *Lobelia erinus* 'Cambridge Blue', *Nepeta nederifolia variegata* and white marguerites to form a 20cm (4ft) fall of gentle profusion in white, apricot and blues.

Below: The man, his spade and his duck beside the tall obelisk have symbolically turned their back on this world. A monument to a head gardener at West Green House is a focal point of light colour amongst the green

Opposite: Against the oldest walls the pale cream, yellow and pink spidery flowers of *Lonicera* x *americana* complement the colour of the aged bricks

Colour for me is as important on the small canvas of a wall as in an entire landscape. When I arrived at West Green House only four climbing roses remained on the house, one was the buff-yellow Noisette rose *Rosa* 'Gloire de Dijon', with three plants of a rich mid-pink blossom, apparently bred by David Austin and known as the 'West Green Rose'. This was a beautiful rose, but against the warm orangey-red brick it was a violent statement, whilst the old *R.* 'Gloire de Dijon' buff touched by gold and pink softly melded into the ambience of the house.

All the roses close to the house are now different vintages of champagne: *Rosa* 'Alchymist' is a golden-yellow climber, *R.* 'Céline Forestier' is the lightest primrose on light green leaves, a Noisette rose *R.* 'Gardenia' is a Wichuriana rambler and *R.* 'Mme Jules Gravereaux' a buff-yellow climbing tea rose. Single cream and white roses with pronounced stamens, such as *R.* 'Sir Cedric Morris', a rampant mass of tiny flowers on soft grey foliage, and *R.* 'Cooperi Burmese' (*R. laevigata*) are large dramatic cream-white flowers, again with long stamens, that will climb and cover a whole wall. All are enhanced by the glow from these old walls but the rose that gives me most joy is *R.* 'Madeline Selzer', a rambler, her perfect off-white flowers touched with lemon on pale green pleated foliage, a perfect foil for the microcolour climate she now inhabits.

Grey walls can provide neutral backgrounds for experimentation with any colour. The quintessential old world image is an explosion of every shade of pink, a melody of crimson to pastel in roses, clematis and honeysuckle cascading down walls of grey. It is the imagery of the striped pink petals of *Clematis* 'Nelly Moser' intertwining through a rambling *Rosa* 'Madame de Sancy de Parabère', a blending of pinks with a smidgeon of lavender. Or it conjures up a picture of the Wichuriana rambler *R.* 'Evangeline', its clusters of delicate posies of small single white flowers, blushing pink rapturously entwined in a vigorous *Clematis montana* var. *Rubens*. This clematis will bound away from constraining supports to conquer telephone poles and wires, throughout the warmer spectrum of cool temperate areas.

On a shady wall, an alternative to roses and clematis is the strong self-suckering climber *Hydrangea petiolaris*, its flowers forming a mass of frothy lace in spring, with broad green leaves making a soft green wall carpet until autumn. In a very dark spot try one of the many ivies splashed with cream or yellow, but remember that a little ivy goes an awfully long way, and this rampant plant is generally best as a backdrop to bring some light to a very dismal corner. It is easy to tire of the bold shades of variegated ivies if they are not used subtly.

Opposite: Roses of parchment, cream and warm sunset are lit by bricks of ochre and red. Here, *Rosa* 'Glorie de Dijon' scrambles up the walls of West Green House

Above: *Clematis* 'Nellie Moser' looks beautiful intertwined with mauve-flushed roses

Below: The rich pink West Green rose – a vigorous climber looks best against walls of white or grey, or trained to be seen against the sky

Shade houses

In the new world grey walls tend to be weathered paling fences, or occasional concrete brick walls, but in old settlers' gardens there are still bush houses (shade houses) made of hundreds of grey weathered slats, the smartest ornamented with intricate fretwork. Here the harsh light is filtered through on to treasured collections of plants.

To step inside the half light of tropical shade, pushing aside cobwebs and vines into the decaying gloom of a Victorian bush house, passing tiny pools of water creating sticky humidity, brushing back palm fronds covering modest statues, is to gain a century old lesson in the beauty of filtered light a total contrast to the strongest light outside. If you gaze at an old photo of a low built verandered house, built on a ridge surrounded by sand dunes in the deserts of the far west of New South Wales, you see how the bush house alongside allows filtered shade to protect treasured plants from scorching heat and inland frosts, allowing a green plant to survive in a totally different light and climate zone to its natural habitat. Colonial bush houses contained the desired plants of the period, collections of palms, ferns, orchids and fuchsias scarcely different from those found in English conservatories of the same period. My grandmother's bush house in the desert landscape was completely crammed with ferns. On her death they came overland to us, huge baskets of maidenhair fern, *Adiantum,* plus three or four other species, always to be kept away from frost and daylight in filtered light with moist feet.

Few people are lucky enough to have shade houses these days, but a shaded conservatory or similar will do just as well. Trailing 'tassel fern' *Lygodium* forms an attractive double-fringed lace curtain hanging down from baskets. They need good drainage, as does the 'Hen and chickens' fern *Asplenium bulbiferum*, another reliable fern for indoor shade houses. Place bird's-nest ferns *Asplenium australasicum* and *A. nidus* above eye level in a decorative pedestal urn where the large light bright shiny sword leaves will look strong and architectural among the lace of other ferns and the height will hide their messy centres.

Many vines in warmer climates are so rampant that they make nonsense out of arches and decorative supports, and create shade houses all by themselves, fashioning perfect walls and ceilings out of the most basic supports to create several storey structures to show off their brilliant flowers. The heavily scented *Jasminum polyanthum* with its shell pink star flowers above pointed buds of crimson-red that can encase a small building, is gentrified when intertwined with the leather leaves of the *Hoya carnosa*, a plant often treated in cooler climates as especially tender but I've found can be quite aggressive once it becomes established. The flowers look like wax posies frozen in time under old glass domes that emerge from five sided wax packet shaped buds, the colour of ladies' corsetry. Spiders love this plant and if in a prominent

**Cool green fronds of *Adiantum*
lend soft texture and light to the
darkest and hardest sufaces**

**Previous page: A small grove of acers,
Japanese maples, are sheltered from
strong sunlight at Kennerton Green
to turn all the colours of autumn**

'. . .a century old lesson in the beauty of filtered light. . .'

position I tend to want to clear its leaves of their dust covered webs, so these climbers are best smothered in a tangle of other vines. This leads me to a story I must tell. When I arrived at West Green House, a 1720s orangery was glassless but still provided shelter for a number of camellias to survive, though they were obviously not as highly regarded as two pots deeply shrouded in frost proof cloth. I asked what they were, and whether I might look. No, I was told by the then gardener, they were special plants and would perish in England's midwinter cold. I prevailed and was eventually allowed a peep, whereupon I collapsed with laughter. For only 24 hours before in Australia I had paid a workman yet again to try and remove a row of stubborn oleanders that refused to die, whilst in England they were the treasure of the shade house!

Shade cover

By midsummer lawns in hot dry climates do not survive under a canopy of deep green shade so I have turned there to a hard landscape pattern, a grid of sandstone paths to correspond to the size of the shade cover. The squares within the grid are filled with shade-tolerant ground cover plants such as the bronze-leaved blue-flowered *Ajuga reptans* 'Jungle Beauty' and the old-fashioned sweet violet. Although these are often associated with the image of mossy banks, they are really quite adaptable and need water only on the hottest days. *Ophiopogon planiscapus* 'Nigrescens', a slow-growing grass of black-bronze looks sharp in squares juxtaposed next to its green brother *Ophiogogon japonicus*. These plants contrast in shape and texture too, the grasses both rather narrow and fine, the other plants with a more rounded leaf shape.

Rather than struggling to maintain a herbaceous bed in a shady spot, discover instead the advantages that more architectural ideas can provide, flat geometric shapes filled with different ground cover shade plants or simply with hard landscaping materials can look particularly effective – interesting in a country garden and dramatic in a townscape. A good solution for contemporary urban gardens is to make a grid of square beds that are just blocks of evergreen hedges or single plantings. I suggest blocks of the small leaved evergreen laurel *Prunus lusitanica* which are excellent in hard area. 'Lace cap' hydrangea *Hydrangea macrophylla* and *Azalea indica* 'Alba Magna' are both reliable hardy plants for dappled shade.

Coloured light

Pagodas, trellised walks, trellis across terraces or pergolas, all create pools of coloured light in a garden. Look up into a trellised ceiling of falling racemes of laburnum or wisteria and it is looking into coloured light. I grow the softest pink *Wisteria floribunda* 'Kuchi-beni', with its long waterfalls of flowers 10-45cm (4-18in) long that pale to white in stronger sun, or try *Wisteria floribunda* 'Honbeni', the better known deeper pink wisteria that's sometimes called 'Rosea' with its rosy glow. The plant is not as floriferous or reliable as 'Kuchibeni' but provides showers of pink sun in early spring light.

Aged figs trained and pruned to cover trellis cast pools of deep green shade, as do the wide leaves of grape vines in Mediterranean climates and the pruned plane trees that verandah French terraces. The Australian backyard passionfruit vine is deep shiny green with dull purple fruit, when tied high to simple wires it also provides dense cool green light in summer. A summer's day viewed from beneath an awning of green makes a bright day even more sparkling, and the last warm days of summer are unforgettable when sitting under the fiery leaves of an autumn-colouring vine such as *Vitis davidii*, creating a painted room of memorable reds and golds.

When planning a garden, if you have the space for trees don't forget the vibrant autumn colours of those such as the pistachio *Pistacia chinensis*, an autumn flame in cooler climates with leaves all crimson, orange or scarlet. A grove of acers light a row of dark crypresses like fire at Kennerton Green and the sugar maple *Acer saccharinum* is unsur-passed for colour in cooler districts. In my Australian garden *Nyssa sylvatica*, a tall pointed tree, turns the kitchen orange as the sun pours straight through it on autumn afternoons, and a waterside group at West Green House casts red light on the new lake. Although slow growing trees, nyssas are a must have if you have the temperate climate and space to grow them. Try and choose beautiful deciduous trees that do not stress and drop sad early browned leaves as summer refuses to end – *Liquidamber styraciflua* do well in many climates their leaves turning all shades from the deepest plum to red, gold and yellow, holding onto the tree while others are totally bare. Ash trees can also be relied on to perform: *Fraxinus excelsior*, the golden ash and *F. angustifolia* 'Raywood', the claret ash, individually create pools of deep gold and ruby red light.

Right: A young *Wisteria sinensis* drapes over the forecourt arcade at West Green House

Opposite: In spring simple terracotta pots hold winter violas and early flowering tulips. Small pots of green box also soften the hard surfaces

Contrasting light

In classical gardens light has often been brought to long tunnels or walls of green by objects, pale statues, urns , obelisks, columns, sculpture and ornamental fountains. The light captured in white stone is a dramatic foil for dark foliage, a shaft of light like a diamond encrusted pearl shining out from a little black dress. One special summer at West Green I filled the large urns placed in the all green theatre with a growing flower arrangement. Height came from the tall leaves of the cream and green striped leaves of *Phormium* 'Cream Delight' and transplanted pots of spiky leaved yucca, all the mature plants capped like the Matterhorn's peak with bells of white. Drooping plants of white marguerites and trailing geranium spilled over the sides, the bowl was then crammed with the Asiatic lily *Lilium* 'Apollo', grey helichrysum and fuschias completed the confection that bloomed to be a romantic centrepiece of soft white light against deep green yew hedges.

Urns in entry courts, courtyards and front gardens are often the focus of attention by night and day. Flowers of dark blues and purples 'die' under artificial light but light blue backed by clear yellow, lime or pale green looks light and inviting under hot sun, shade or lanterns. A large urn planted in simple clear yellow such as the fringed 'Maja' tulip or the tall 'West Point' lily-type tulip with masses of blue forget-me-nots, would be clear light in a still grey garden of early spring.

Each winter I place plants of box or holly clipped into interesting shapes in urns by the front door. These stylish vessels replace highlights of seasonal colour with an elegant form of shiny green. These shapes cast dramatic effect when backlit by the house lights that are nearly always on in the darker time of the year.

8 | sparkling light

On my first trip to Italy I drove from Rome through frantic traffic one hot July day to arrive at yet another car park where the dusty gravel exploded in powder puffs when I stepped on it. A garden path began immediately to descend into an underworld of green gloom where giant terraces were carved from a hillside completely encased in eiderdowns of moss. Laser shafts of sunlight pierced the green canopy above lines of playing fountains, capturing every droplet of water like thousands of glittering sequins, lighting the terraced gardens with pinpoints of tiny lights in a dark green night. The renowned gardens of the Villa d'Este gave me an unforgettable lesson in the power of water to light a garden.

When you have the chance, sit beside a clear meandering stream and see how the water dazzles in direct sunlight, but glitters in broken light. Or look at a deep still pond where water lilies decorate the surface; it will appear calm, but the serenity is broken by the life around the lilies. Their shiny leaves act as light reflectors, and the minute insects hovering and dipping around them flick the surface water to create pinpoints of broken light.

Lighting with water

Many gardens must conform to a rectangular sized general block of land. My beach cottage garden on Dangar Island was this shape. The island is a beautiful place, still well covered by stands of tall eucalyptus trees and lying in the mouth of a wide river whose high banks are virgin bush. I wanted to capture its spirit in the back garden which was heavily shaded by mature

gum trees and the lavender-blue *Jacaranda mimosifolia*. I needed to capture light on water to compete in some way with the brilliance of the sea beyond the front door. So a lazy S-shaped stream was made to meander through the garden, the water emptying into a lotus pond by the back door. The water was reticulated by a simple pump but as the stream passed over the uneven bush rocks it captured the sun's rays escaping from overhead foliage – firstly from the gums and jacaranda trees, then through citrus and then a streamside planting of spectacular Japanese iris, tall papyrus grass and a collection of spreading dwarf maples, mostly *Acer palmatum* and *A. palmatum* var. *dissectum* varieties. The water created a ribbon of silver life, at least as beguiling as the drama of the open sea beyond.

All types of iris look designed for planting near water. Above the water on dry paths or embankments the bearded iris *Iris germanica* is completely at home. The most accommodating of plants, they thrive with a few handfuls of slow release fertiliser and lime but need the sharp cold of winter for good flowers. Daylilies are even more considerate, happy from the tropics to cool climates with midsummer flowers in a continuous succession after only general garden care. Lousiana iris are true glamour for warmer climates, they are happiest in water but bloom in marginal plantings. If you can possibly grow them, do! Japanese iris seem designed for man made reticulated streams that are turned on to flow in spring and summer as this iris likes dry winter feet. In midsummer tall graceful leaves back huge blooms some as big as 30cm (12in).

'. . . the tulips nodding above a dancing light, the sparkling light reflected from the uneven water surface of the rock lined rill.'

Lifting shade with water

A subtle yet eye-catching stretch of water now lights what was originally a very predictable long bed of spring bulbs at Kennerton Green. This corner of the garden was a random collection of the usual bulbs and blossoms of spring, built up over the years and pushed out into the garden as time and money allowed. As the trees grew their canopy thickened overhead and the bulbs began to give more leaf than flower, so that the spring sunlight becoming completely captured in the huge mass of blossom. So it was time for a facelift, the garden beneath needed captured light, it required back lighting to help the bulbs to compete on equal terms with the theatre above.

The entire length of the bulb-bed was lifted and a rill 85m (275ft) long now splashes over uneven bush rocks into four ponds, reflecting and playing with the light. The bulbs rather than the rill were to be the feature, the purpose of the rill was to provide a mysterious sparkle, its source to be discovered only if visitors cared to look carefully. At the height of spring it is completely hidden by flowers – the tulips nodding above a dancing light, the sparkling light reflected from the uneven water surface of the rock-lined rill.

By midsummer the bulbs are cleared away and it becomes the time of the hostas clustered close to the rill – an eclectic collection, a sampler of all shades of green from pale green and yellow to leaves rimmed with gold and white, an admirable sight until we are outmanoeuvred in our eternal battle against the snails. The rill then changes from a lighting extra to the leading lady in this part of the garden, its ribbon of light a glittering show which emphasises the shapes and sizes of the hosta leaves, distracting from the leaves of the heat-stressed trees above.

A rill is an easy way to add sparkle to a garden of virtually any size. All that is needed is a small pond with a return tank for a reservoir, a trench lined with a black polythene membrane then covered by rocks or pebbles, a pump and a supply of water – this could be the garden hose. Before switching the pump on each spring make sure your pond and water tank are filled, then top up from time to time as the water slowly evaporates.

Hostas are five star plants forming rounded clumps of beautifully shaped and coloured leaves happy in the darkest moist corners, in filtered light, but they scorch in full sun in all but the coolest climates. *Hosta sieboldiana* has huge pleated leaves of blue making clumps often 1.5m (5ft) across. *Hosta crispula*'s oval leaves are edged in white and look particularly good as underplanting for green and white tulips in early spring, creating a river of white light under the shade of trees. *Hosta fortunei* 'Aureomarginata' has yellow-green splashed around large deep green leaves, golden highlights to echo the colour of any golden shade tree above. *Hosta* 'Gold Standard' has heart-shaped gold leaves just tipped in dark green, the best gold highlight plant of all!

Adding drama with water

Once the brambles were cleared in my English garden, I was able to walk for the first time through the beautiful 19th century Moongate, to glimpse on a rise above a large grey wall in classical style. On its crumbling façade some words of the 18th century poet Alexander Pope were carved: 'A little learning is a dangerous thing. Drink deep or taste not the Pierian spring'. From beneath these words water had once flowed from a devil's mouth into an urn that overflowed to a basin. Further away a waterless rill stopped in a pile of grey stones that had been placed to look as though they fell like water into two parallel ponds. The concept was all wonderfully allegorical but visually it was grey and disjointed.

Today it is a true water garden to complement the imposing Nymphaeum folly, with water descending down steps cut into the natural slope, catching the light and diffusing it. It is a garden of green, white and silver – a glittering display of light and water enclosed in an allée of yew trees cut at stepped heights. The water trickles from the mask to the urn, the basin and the tank, appears in the rill, then glides down wide shallow steps as a large sheet of moving mirror capturing the cool northern light, reinforcing the classical serenity of the grand design. The water reappears as smooth as glass in the ponds, then

Opposite: The new narrow rills of water bring moving light to the old steps at West Green House

Right: A fine ribbon of water pushes through old box and is an arrow light pointer in the newly planted Nymphaeum garden

cascades down beside the old uneven steps as a light filled stream inviting exploration of this sparkling garden.

Levels in even the smallest garden or courtyard create interest, a sense of space and an element of style. A change of levels means that steps can be placed in a focal point, and that their centre can be channelled out to make a small water feature which trickles down the middle. Try planting a small sharply clipped hedge against the risers of the steps; a hedge with 'blue' tones such as rosemary *Rosmarinus officinalis* will tolerate a dry position, and so too will box, *Buxus sempervirens*, or severely clipped *Lonicera nitida* for little hedges of small green leaves. The water in the tiny channel will create flickers of light depending on the lining. Marble can provide a smooth creamy-white light while pebbles give a darker broken light catching any light and diverting the eye to the garden.

Water features enthusiastically installed in gardens so often become horrible mosquito ridden bog patches when forgotten or overgrown with rampant aquatic plants, but a water feature that is a fountain will still look beautiful even if unused and abandoned. A small bronze fountain was placed in the centre of Kennerton Green's vegetable garden, of a small putti surrounded by shells, a frog and a tortoise. Water drips from these features into a pond below now blanketed in miniature bright pink water lilies, but for most of the day the putti is colonised by the fantail pigeons who have realised this is the nearest supply of fresh water to their cote. Totally unplanned, the snow white birds perched in the fountain above the pink water lilies has become one of the most enchanting spots in the garden. We made the rim of the pond a ledge wide enough to sit on to recover after hoeing a row of vegetables, and it is a favourite spot to watch water droplets catch a ray of light that breaks up into millions of sparkles as they fall into the water lilies below.

Still water and mirrored light

Light in all its forms can be captured in any still pond. In secret or enclosed parts of a garden a pool can become a charming mirror as long as the light can reach it. At Kennerton Green a long flat pond in the rose garden captures the colour of the sky from above the tall hedges and reflects the pale colours of the standard roses which run alongside. The water provides glorious reflections when the flowers bloom, but maintains style and interest in all seasons.

Modern urban gardens often include water to draw down the light. However the often angular pools are usually left unplanted, relying on the water to be the feature, although in very shaded areas water catches the most light if planted with light-reflecting waterlilies *Nymphaea* and water iris or with stylish lotus *Nelumbo* in warm climates. Shade ponds can look murky and easily become wells for wind swept debris, stagnant and unattractive if left without reticulation or plants to oxygenate the water.

Troughs

In the Bay Tree garden at Kennerton the geometric planting of dull leaved trees is now being lit by a long trough of reticulated water falling over copper cut at different lengths to capture not only facets of light but to make musical sounds. Many Australian gardens have smart pools and fountains made from water troughs placed against walls with all types of beautiful objects used to feed water to them. Easily constructed from bricks to the size required, the sides and ledge of the trough can be surfaced with Haddonstone blocks, sandstone, marble, granite or rendered cement, often to match materials used in house construction, the liners of metal inserts of the same size. Carved dolphins, lions and urns or decorative taps may be used to feed water into this increasingly favoured garden accessory. Often these troughs are features of courtyards where the sound and the light playing on the moving water creates the impression of coolness and life in areas that sometimes become hot dry suntraps.

Left: Light is captured and shines from rills, steps and ponds in a newly created space

Right: Droplets metamorphose into pure light bringing even the dullest surfaces to life

Opposite: A perfect example of still water that has become a mirrored surface reflecting all the surrounding light

'. . . a fleeting morning of white glitter, a perfect reason to set out another parterre next spring.'

Winter sparkle – water frozen as ice or snow creates garden embroideries in winter, pictures of white ice etched over dark green as the outlines of a parterre or clipped santolina become tablecloths of white lace. The light of these delicate traceries after a hard frost must be one of the most exquisite sights a gardener can plan for, a fleeting morning of white glitter, a perfect reason to set out another parterre next spring.

Reflecting light in glass and glazes

Brilliant glass mosaics and glazed ceramic tiles can capture prisms of coloured light into an arched covered walkway where light is dim and plants cannot grow. Or use mirrors for trompe l'oeil effects in a small garden to give the impression of light and distance. In my Australian garden I have introduced cheerful light into an awkward space by inserting into two niches hand painted folk tiles whose brilliant colour tells the story of St Francis and the birds. A more formal approach to attracting light appears high in the walls of West Green House where 300 years ago General Hawley had the busts of Roman emperors placed, lifting the eye to their round niches of white giving light to a plain wall and fantasy to a small house.

In enclosed courtyards a mirror placed on a wall can capture and reflect light into bleak corners. A necessarily short path can appear to lead into infinity by taking it to a wall mirror. Or follow the advice of garden designer Rosemary Alexander and create a successful illusion by placing a gate in front of a wall mirror, a beautiful gesture to attract us to continue walking into this space of light.

In town gardens problematical neighbouring walls can be turned to advantage as perfect backgrounds for all types of wall plaques. Museum shops stock excellent classical copies or do as I did, collect folk tiles whilst on holiday to make an attractive story in brightly glazed tiles, especially those with crazed finishes that break up and reflect light. I still have a shoe box of folk tiles hoarded away to insert into a path one day. The

loud sharp colours of ethnic wares are an excellent foil in a pathway of plainstone, cement, brick or terracotta. Dropped in randomly or in sequence they bring bright light, colour and conversation to very pedestrian constructions.

I must admit that in church my eyes tend to roam to the sorrowful inscriptions on the walls. Those on the brightly polished shiny brass surfaces immediately draw the eye, the bright metal attracting the eye, making the black lettering stand out. So in a garden a shiny object will capture every ray of sun, attracting us like moths

to a light. I've only used two shiny objects, a sun dial and sphere at Kennerton Green now darkening with age, and now not so brilliant, but bright enough to break up light adding captured sun to a still garden. A metal plaque with lines of treasured poetry placed on walls or in paths again captures stray beams of light. I like the idea of finding a verse when weeding a garden, it gives a pause for reflection, the light in the metal subtly illuminating the surrounding scene.

American friends had told me about the Seattle artist Dale Chihaly's glass sculptures for

gardens. Last summer his exhibition of pure vermillion glass poles was placed into the main borders of Government House, Sydney. Like tall slim poles from which Venetian gondolas moor, they were for me fantastically exciting garden objects, pure cylinders of vermillion internal light. This large assembly of poles was definitely for a major area but a small group in a contemporary garden would be magic giving perpetual coloured light against a deep green sculptural garden or providing glowing slashes of red light in the grey light of winter.

Ground light

The choice of paving in a garden can drastically effect the light and the mood. Pristine white gravel chips, for example, can bring lightness and light to heavy corners when spread along a shaded path, but sometimes this effective way to reflect light can be overwhelming. I arrived for the first time at the cottage at Kennerton Green, in February – our hottest month, and remember very clearly coming to the kitchen at midday to wash the lunch dishes. The kitchen overlooked a pristine white gravel car park that was a blindingly brilliant square, giving off an incredible glare. In the bright sunlight a calming solution was needed to create an oasis of restfulness and serenity in an area of jangling brilliance. I solved the glare by planting a small parterre to offset the light, a simple clean design of dark greens to absorb the brilliance. It showed me that dazzling effects must be controlled like a few sequins or jewels in a greater story.

Different materials react very differently to light, soft grey or sandstone paving slabs are subtle in cool northern light, allowing plants spilling over onto the surfaces to proclaim their own glory, or creating a low level light contrast when adjacent beds or pots are planted with silver or grey foliage plants. Cobbles or patterned bricks allow light to dance on their different surfaces, gravels should tone with the colour of adjacent buildings or other structures, bouncing light off each other. Intricate patterns and mosaics in ceramics and stones can provide interesting light effects in a small area; evergreens look very stylish against white gravel or marble chips.

'. . . a shiny object will capture every ray of sun, attracting us like moths to a light.'

Opposite: The marble white image of a Roman emperor lights a bare wall lifting the eye to its niche

Left: Old garden implements sprayed white are a bright statement on the old mottled pink walls in the orangery

There are a myriad of garden ideas and styles to select from. Clever books and international travel expose us to a fruit salad of stylistic impressions and plants, so it is often frightfully confusing to know what exactly is a dream garden. As we pass through life the dreams change, the ideal of a long garden with sandpits and swings becomes swimming pools and decks for smart parties. Dreams of grand gardens of classical serenity give way to quiet courtyards in sunny climates as the needs of our age change. So everyone will have different dreams. For many work will necessitate years in apartments in foreign cities, a wind swept balcony or a patch of unloved grass in a forgotten yard, the closest suggestion of green.

But some day a garden will come along, but wherever it is sit and comtemplate the sky, the countryside, the everyday culture and they will supply the clues for a beautiful garden full of light and colour.

Previous page: *Allium bulgaricum* – tall stems of greenish-white bell-shaped flowers broadly striped with red brown

IF Statement	Executes or skips a statement, depending on whether a logical expression is true or false (111)	`IF (X < 0.) X = -X/2.`
IMPORT	Imports type definitions into an interface block from the containing procedure (581)	`IMPORT :: a, b`
IMPLICIT NONE	Cancels default typing (57)	`IMPLICIT NONE`
INQUIRE	Used to learn information about a file either by name or logical unit (654)	`INQUIRE (NAME='x',EXIST=flag)`
INTEGER	Declares variables or named constants of type INTEGER (33)	`INTEGER :: i, j, k`

INTERFACE	Creates an explicit interface, a generic procedure, or a user-defined operator (578)	`INTERFACE :: sort`
		`   MODULE PROCEDURE sort_i`
		`   MODULE PROCEDURE sort_r`
		`END INTERFACE`

LOGICAL	Declares variables or named constants of type LOGICAL (90)	`LOGICAL :: test1, test2`
MODULE	Declares the start of a module (329)	`MODULE mysubs`
OPEN	Opens a file (218, 644)	`OPEN (UNIT=10,FILE='x')`
PRIVATE	Declares that the specified items in a module are not accessible outside the module (608)	`PRIVATE :: internal_data` `PRIVATE`
PROTECTED	Declares that an object in a module is protected, meaning that it can be used but not modified outside the module in which it is defined. (608)	`PROTECTED :: x`
PROGRAM	Defines the start of a program, and gives it a name (24)	`PROGRAM my_program`
PUBLIC	Declares that the specified items in a module are accessible outside the module (608)	`PUBLIC :: proc1, proc2`

READ	Read in data (49, 209, 659)	`READ (12,100) rate, time`
		`READ (unit,' (16)') count`
		`READ (*,*) nvals`

REAL	Declares variables or named constants of type REAL (33)	`REAL (KIND=sgl) :: value`
RETURN	Returns control from a procedure to the invoking routine (307)	`RETURN`
REWIND	Position file pointer at first record in a file (227)	`REWIND (UNIT=3)`
SAVE	Preserve local variables in a subprogram between calls to the subprogram (427)	`SAVE ncalls, iseed SAVE`

SELECT CASE construct	Branching among mutually exclusive choices (111)	`SELECT CASE ( ii )`
		`CASE (selector_1)`
		`   block 1`
		`CASE (selector_2)`
		`   block 2`
		`CASE DEFAULT`
		`   block 3`
		`END SELECT`

STOP	Stop program execution (26)	`STOP`
SUBROUTINE	Declares the start of a subroutine (307)	`SUBROUTINE sort (array, n)`
TYPE	Declares a derived data type (531)	`TYPE (point) :: x, y`
USE	Makes the contents of a module available to a program unit (330)	`USE mysubs`
VOLATILE	Declares that the value of a variable might be changed at any time by some source external to the program (618)	`VOLATILE :: val1`
WAIT	Wait for asynchronous I/O to complete (667)	`WAIT (UNIT=8)`

WHERE construct	Masked array assignment (389)	`WHERE (x > 0. )`
		`   x = SQRT(x)`
		`END WHERE`

WRITE	Write out data (51, 665)	`WRITE (12,100) rate, time`
		`WRITE (unit,'(1x,16)')`
		`count`
		`WRITE (*,*) nvals`

ortran 95/2003

and Engineers

Third Edition

Fortran 95/2003
for Scientists and Engineers

Third Edition

Stephen J. Chapman

BAE SYSTEMS Australia

 **Higher Education**

Boston   Burr Ridge, IL   Dubuque, IA   New York
San Francisco   St. Louis   Bangkok   Bogotá   Caracas   Kuala Lumpur
Lisbon   London   Madrid   Mexico City   Milan   Montreal   New Delhi
Santiago   Seoul   Singapore   Sydney   Taipei   Toronto

 **Higher Education**

FORTRAN 95/2003: FOR SCIENTISTS AND ENGINEERS, THIRD EDITION

Published by McGraw-Hill, a business unit of The McGraw-Hill Companies, Inc., 1221 Avenue of the Americas, New York, NY 10020. Copyright © 2008 by The McGraw-Hill Companies, Inc. All rights reserved. No part of this publication may be reproduced or distributed in any form or by any means, or stored in a database or retrieval system, without the prior written consent of The McGraw-Hill Companies, Inc., including, but not limited to, in any network or other electronic storage or transmission, or broadcast for distance learning.

Some ancillaries, including electronic and print components, may not be available to customers outside the United States.

This book is printed on acid-free paper.

2 3 4 5 6 7 8 9 0 DOC/DOC 0 9 8

ISBN 978–0–07–128578–0
MHID 0–07–128578–4

1005547530

This book is dedicated to my son Aaron on the occasion of his enrollment as an officer candidate at the Royal Australian Military College of Australia, Duntroon.

STEPHEN J. CHAPMAN received a B.S. in Electrical Engineering from Louisiana State University (1975), an M.S.E. in Electrical Engineering from the University of Central Florida (1979), and pursued further graduate studies at Rice University.

From 1975 to 1980, he served as an officer in the U.S. Navy, assigned to teach Electrical Engineering at the U.S. Naval Nuclear Power School in Orlando, Florida. From 1980 to 1982, he was affiliated with the University of Houston, where he ran the power systems program in the College of Technology.

From 1982 to 1988 and from 1991 to 1995, he served as a Member of the Technical Staff of the Massachusetts Institute of Technology's Lincoln Laboratory, both at the main facility in Lexington, Massachusetts, and at the field site on Kwajalein Atoll in the Republic of the Marshall Islands. While there, he did research in radar signal processing systems. He ultimately became the leader of four large operational range instrumentation radars at the Kwajalein field site (TRADEX, ALTAIR, ALCOR, and MMW). Each of the four radars were controlled by large (100,000+ lines) real-time programs written largely in Fortran; the trials and tribulations associated with modifying those radar systems strongly influenced his views about proper design of Fortran programs.

From 1988 to 1991, Mr. Chapman was a research engineer in Shell Development Company in Houston, Texas, where he did seismic signal processing research. The research culminated in a number of large Fortran programs used to process seismic data. He was also affiliated with the University of Houston, where he continued to teach on a part-time basis.

Mr. Chapman is currently Manager of Systems Modeling and Operational Analysis for BAE Systems Australia, in Melbourne. In this position, he uses Fortran 95 extensively to model the defense of naval ships against attacking aircraft and missiles.

Mr. Chapman is a Senior Member of the Institute of Electrical and Electronic Engineers (and several of its component societies). He is also a member of the Association for Computing Machinery and the Institution of Engineers (Australia).

TABLE OF CONTENTS

The first edition of this book was conceived as a result of my experience writing and maintaining large Fortran programs in both the defense and geophysical fields. During my time in industry, it became obvious that the strategies and techniques required to write large, *maintainable* Fortran programs were quite different from what new engineers were learning in their Fortran programming classes at school. The incredible cost of maintaining and modifying large programs once they are placed into service absolutely demands that they be written to be easily understood and modified by people other than their original programmers. My goal for this book is to teach simultaneously both the fundamentals of the Fortran language and a programming style that results in good, maintainable programs. In addition, it is intended to serve as a reference for graduates working in industry.

It is quite difficult to teach undergraduates the importance of taking extra effort during the early stages of the program design process in order to make their programs more maintainable. Class programming assignments must by their very nature be simple enough for one person to complete in a short period of time, and they do not have to be maintained for years. Because the projects are simple, a student can often "wing it" and still produce working code. A student can take a course, perform all of the programming assignments, pass all of the tests, and still not learn the habits that are really needed when working on large projects in industry.

From the very beginning, this book teaches Fortran in a style suitable for use on large projects. It emphasizes the importance of going through a detailed design process before any code is written, using a top-down design technique to break the program up into logical portions that can be implemented separately. It stresses the use of procedures to implement those individual portions, and the importance of unit testing before the procedures are combined into a finished product. Finally, it emphasizes the importance of exhaustively testing the finished program with many different input data sets before it is released for use.

In addition, this book teaches Fortran as it is actually encountered by engineers and scientists working in industry and in laboratories. One fact of life is common in all programming environments: large amounts of old legacy code that have to be maintained. The legacy code at a particular site may have been originally written in Fortran IV (or an even earlier version!), and it may use programming constructs that are no longer common today. For example, such code may use arithmetic IF statements, or computed or assigned GO TO statements. Chapter 17 is devoted to those older features of the language that are no longer commonly used, but that are encountered in legacy code. The chapter emphasizes that these features should *never* be used in a new program, but also prepares the student to handle them when he or she encounters them.

CHANGES IN THIS EDITION

This edition builds directly on the success of *Fortran 90/95 for Scientists and Engineers,* 2/e. It preserves the structure of the previous edition, while weaving the new Fortran 2003 material throughout the text. Most of the material in this book applies to both Fortran 95 and Fortran 2003. Topics that are unique to Fortran 2003 are printed in a shaded background.

Most of the additions in Fortran 2003 are logical extensions of existing capabilities in Fortran 95, and they are integrated into the text in the proper chapters. However, the object-oriented programming capabilities of Fortran 2003 are completely new, and a new Chapter 16 has been created to cover that material.

The vast majority of Fortran courses are limited to one quarter or one semester, and the student is expected to pick up both the basics of the Fortran language and the concept of how to program. Such a course would cover Chapters 1 through 7 of this text, plus selected topics in Chapters 8 and 9 if there is time. This provides a good foundation for students to build on in their own time as they use the language in practical projects.

Advanced students and practicing scientists and engineers will need the material on `COMPLEX` numbers, derived data types, and pointers found in Chapters 11 through 15. Practicing scientists and engineers will almost certainly need the material on obsolete, redundant, and deleted Fortran features found in Chapter 17. These materials are rarely taught in the classroom, but they are included here to make the book a useful reference text when the language is actually used to solve real-world problems.

FEATURES OF THIS BOOK

Many features of this book are designed to emphasize the proper way to write reliable Fortran programs. These features should serve a student well as he or she is first learning Fortran, and should also be useful to the practitioner on the job. They include:

1. *Emphasis on Modern Fortran 95/2003.*

   The book consistently teaches the best current practice in all of its examples. Many Fortran 95/2003 features duplicate and supersede older features of the Fortran language. In those cases, the proper usage of the modern language is presented. Examples of older usage are largely relegated to Chapter 17, where their old/undesirable nature is emphasized. Examples of Fortran 95/2003 features that supersede older features are the use of modules to share data instead of `COMMON` blocks, the use of `DO . . . END DO` loops instead of `DO . . . CONTINUE` loops, the use of internal procedures instead of statement functions, and the use of `CASE` constructs instead of computed `GOTO`s.

2. *Emphasis on Strong Typing.*

   The `IMPLICIT NONE` statement is used consistently throughout the book to force the explicit typing of every variable used in every program, and to catch common typographical errors at compilation time. In conjunction with the explicit declaration of every variable in a program, the book emphasizes the importance of creating a data dictionary that describes the purpose of each variable in a program unit.

3. *Emphasis on Top-Down Design Methodology.*

   The book introduces a top-down design methodology in Chapter 3, and then uses it consistently throughout the rest of the book. This methodology encourages a student to think about the proper design of a program *before* beginning to code. It emphasizes the importance of clearly defining the problem to be solved and the required inputs and outputs before any other work is begun. Once the problem is properly defined, it teaches the student to employ stepwise refinement to break the task down into successively smaller subtasks, and to implement the subtasks as separate subroutines or functions. Finally, it teaches the importance of testing at all stages of the process, both unit testing of the component routines and exhaustive testing of the final product. Several examples are given of programs that work properly for some data sets, and then fail for others. The formal design process taught by the book may be summarized as follows:

   1. *Clearly state the problem that you are trying to solve.*
   2. *Define the inputs required by the program and the outputs to be produced by the program.*
   3. *Describe the algorithm that you intend to implement in the program. This step involves top-down design and stepwise decomposition, using pseudocode or flow charts.*
   4. *Turn the algorithm into Fortran statements.*
   5. *Test the Fortran program. This step includes unit testing of specific subprograms, and also exhaustive testing of the final program with many different data sets.*

4. *Emphasis on Procedures.*

   The book emphasizes the use of subroutines and functions to logically decompose tasks into smaller subtasks. It teaches the advantages of procedures for data hiding. It also emphasizes the importance of unit testing procedures before they are combined into the final program. In addition, the book teaches about the common mistakes made with procedures, and how to avoid them (argument type mismatches, array length mismatches, etc.). It emphasizes the advantages associated with explicit interfaces to procedures, which allow the Fortran compiler to catch most common programming errors at compilation time.

5. *Emphasis on Portability and Standard Fortran 95/2003.*

The book stresses the importance of writing portable Fortran code, so that a program can easily be moved from one type of computer to another one. It teaches students to use only standard Fortran 95/2003 statements in their programs, so that they will be as portable as possible. In addition, it teaches the use of features such as the SELECTED_REAL_KIND function to avoid precision and kind differences when moving from computer to computer, and the ACHAR and IACHAR functions to avoid problems when moving from ASCII to EBCDIC computers.

The book also teaches students to isolate machine-dependent code (such as code that calls machine-dependent system libraries) into a few specific procedures, so that only those procedures will have to be rewritten when a program is ported between computers.

6. *Good Programming Practice Boxes.*

These boxes highlight good programming practices when they are introduced for the convenience of the student. In addition, the good programming practices introduced in a chapter are summarized at the end of the chapter. An example Good Programming Practice Box is shown below.

Good Programming Practice

Always indent the body of an IF structure by two or more spaces to improve the readability of the code.

7. *Programming Pitfalls Boxes.*

These boxes highlight common errors so that they can be avoided. An example Programming Pitfalls Box is shown below.

Programming Pitfalls:

Beware of integer arithmetic. Integer division often gives unexpected results.

8. *Emphasis on Pointers and Dynamic Data Structures.*

Chapter 15 contains a detailed discussion of Fortran pointers, including possible problems resulting from the incorrect use of pointers such as memory leaks and pointers to deallocated memory. Examples of dynamic data structures in the chapter include linked lists and binary trees.

Chapter 16 contains a discussion of Fortran objects and object-oriented programming, including the use of dynamic pointers to achieve polymorphic behavior.

9. *Use of Sidebars.*

A number of sidebars are scattered throughout the book. These sidebars provide additional information of potential interest to the student. Some sidebars are historical in nature. For example, one sidebar in Chapter 1 describes the IBM Model 704, the first computer to ever run Fortran. Other sidebars reinforce lessons from the main text. For example, Chapter 9 contains a sidebar reviewing and summarizing the many different types of arrays found in Fortran 95/2003.

10. *Completeness.*

Finally, the book endeavors to be a complete reference to the Fortran 95/2003 language, so that a practitioner can locate any required information quickly. Special attention has been paid to the index to make features easy to find. A special effort has also been made to cover such obscure and little understood features as passing procedure names by reference, and defaulting values in list-directed input statements.

PEDAGOGICAL FEATURES

The book includes several features designed to aid student comprehension. Each chapter begins with a list of the objectives that should be achieved in that chapter. A total of 26 quizzes appear scattered throughout the chapters, with answers to all questions included in Appendix E. These quizzes can serve as a useful self-test of comprehension. In addition, there are approximately 340 end-of-chapter exercises. Answers to selected exercises are available at the book's website, and of course answers to all exercises are included in the Instructor's Manual. Good programming practices are highlighted in all chapters with special Good Programming Practice boxes, and common errors are highlighted in Programming Pitfalls boxes. End-of-chapter materials include Summaries of Good Programming Practice and Summaries of Fortran Statements and Structures. Finally, a detailed description of every Fortran 95/2003 intrinsic procedure is included in Appendix B, and an extensive Glossary is included in Appendix D.

The book is accompanied by an Instructor's Manual, containing the solutions to all end-of-chapter exercises. Instructors can also download the solutions in the Instructor's Manual from the book's website: www.mhhe.com/chapman3e. The source code for all examples in the book, plus other supplemental materials, can be downloaded by anyone from the book's website.

A NOTE ABOUT FORTRAN COMPILERS

Three Fortran compilers were used during the preparation of this book: the Lahey/Fujitsu Fortran 95 compiler, the Intel Visual Fortran Version 9.1, and the NAGWare Fortran 95 compiler. References to all three compiler vendors may be found at this book's website (see next page).

At the time of this writing, *none* of the available Fortran compilers have implemented all of the Fortran 2003 features. As a result, some of the Fortran 2003 examples that I have included have not been "road tested" through a compiler, and there may be some undetected errors in the program source files. McGraw-Hill and I will handle this possible problem by testing all Fortran 2003 features as soon as compilers become available. If any problems are found, we will post corrections on the book's website, and we will also try to correct the listings in later printings.

I would especially like to thank Ian Hounam and the team at NAG Ltd. for allowing me to use a beta of the NAGWare Fortran 95 compiler version 5.1 during the revision of this book. NAG is way ahead of the other PC Fortran compiler vendors in implementing the object-oriented features of Fortran 2003, and its tool has been invaluable in preparing the new materials in this book.

A FINAL NOTE TO THE USER

No matter how hard I try to proofread a document like this book, it is inevitable that some typographical errors will slip through and appear in print. If you should spot any such errors, please drop me a note via the publisher, and I will do my best to get them eliminated from subsequent printings and editions. Thank you very much for your help in this matter.

I will maintain a complete list of errata and corrections at the book's website, which is www.mhhe.com/chapman3e. Please check that site for any updates and/or corrections.

ACKNOWLEDGMENTS

I would like to thank the reviewers of the text for their invaluable help. They are:

Marvin Bishop, Manhattan College
Terry Bridgman, Colorado School of Mines
Kyle V. Camarda, University of Kansas
Charlotte Coker, Mississippi State University
Keith Hohn, Kansas State University
Mark S. Hutchenreuther, California Polytechnic State University
Larry E. Johnson, Colorado School of Mines
Joseph M. Londino, Jr., Christian Brothers University
Joseph J. Wong, Worcester Polytechnic Institute

Finally, I would like to thank my wife Rosa, and our children Avi, David, Rachel, Aaron, Sarah, Naomi, Shira, and Devorah, who are always my incentive to write!

Stephen J. Chapman
Melbourne, Victoria, Australia
August 29, 2006

Introduction to Computers and the Fortran Language

OBJECTIVES

- Know the basic components of a computer.
- Understand binary, octal, and hexadecimal numbers.
- Learn about the history of the Fortran language.

The computer was probably the most important invention of the twentieth century. It affects our lives profoundly in very many ways. When we go to the grocery store, the scanners that check out our groceries are run by computers. Our bank balances are maintained by computers, and the automatic teller machines that allow us to make banking transactions at any time of the day or night are run by more computers. Computers control our telephone and electric power systems, run our microwave ovens and other appliances, and even control the engines in our cars. Almost any business in the developed world would collapse overnight if it were suddenly deprived of its computers. Considering their importance in our lives, it is almost impossible to believe that the first electronic computers were invented just about 65 years ago.

Just what is this device that has had such an impact on all of our lives? A **computer** is a special type of machine that stores information, and can perform mathematical calculations on that information at speeds much faster than human beings can think. A **program,** which is stored in the computer's memory, tells the computer what sequence of calculations is required, and which information to perform the calculations on. Most computers are very flexible. For example, the computer on which I write these words can also balance my checkbook, if I just execute a different program on it.

Computers can store huge amounts of information, and with proper programming, they can make that information instantly available when it is needed. For example, a bank's computer can hold the complete list of all the checks and deposits made by every one of its customers. On a larger scale, credit companies use their computers to hold the credit histories of every person in the United States—literally billions of pieces of information. When requested, they can search through those billions of pieces of information to recover the credit records of any single person, and present those records to the user in a matter of seconds.

It is important to realize that *computers do not think as humans understand thinking*. They merely follow the steps contained in their programs. When a computer appears to be doing something clever, it is because a clever person has written the program that it is executing. That is where we humans come into the act. It is our collective creativity that allows the computer to perform its seeming miracles. This book will help teach you how to write programs of your own, so that the computer will do what *you* want it to do.

1.1
THE COMPUTER

A block diagram of a typical computer is shown in Figure 1-1. The major components of the computer are the **central processing unit (CPU), main memory, secondary memory,** and **input** and **output devices.** These components are described in the paragraphs below.

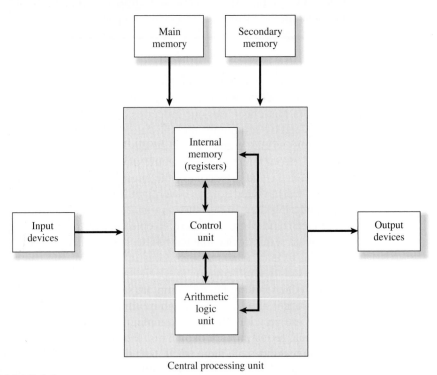

FIGURE 1-1
A block diagram of a typical computer.

1.1.1 The CPU

The central processing unit is the heart of any computer. It is divided into a *control unit,* an *arithmetic logic unit (ALU),* and internal memory. The control unit within the CPU controls all of the other parts of the computer, while the ALU performs the actual mathematical calculations. The internal memory within a CPU consists of a series of *memory registers* used for the temporary storage of intermediate results during calculations.

The control unit of the CPU interprets the instructions of the computer program. It also fetches data values from input devices or main memory and stores them in the memory registers, and sends data values from memory registers to output devices or main memory. For example, if a program says to multiply two numbers together and save the result, the control unit will fetch the two numbers from main memory and store them in registers. Then, it will present the numbers in the registers to the ALU along with directions to multiply them and store the results in another register. Finally, after the ALU multiplies the numbers, the control unit will take the result from the destination register and store it back into main memory.

Modern CPUs have become dramatically faster with the addition of multiple ALUs running in parallel, which allows more operations to be performed in a given amount of time.

1.1.2 Main and Secondary Memory

The memory of a computer is divided into two major types of memory: *main or primary memory,* and *secondary memory.* Main memory usually consists of semiconductor chips. It is very fast, and relatively expensive. Data that is stored in main memory can be fetched for use in 50 nanoseconds or less (sometimes *much* less) on a modern computer. Because it is so fast, main memory is used to temporarily store the program currently being executed by the computer, as well as the data that the program requires.

Main memory is not used for the permanent storage of programs or data. Most main memory is **volatile,** meaning that it is erased whenever the computer's power is turned off. Besides, main memory is expensive, so we only buy enough to hold the largest programs actually being executed at any given time.

Secondary memory consists of devices that are slower and cheaper than main memory. They can store much more information for much less money than main memory can. In addition, most secondary memory devices are **nonvolatile,** meaning that they retain the programs and data stored in them whenever the computer's power is turned off. Typical secondary memory devices are **hard disks, floppy disks,** USB memory sticks, CDs, and tapes. Secondary storage devices are normally used to store programs and data that are not needed at the moment, but that may be needed some time in the future.

1.1.3 Input and Output Devices

Data is entered into a computer through an input device, and is output through an output device. The most common input devices on a modern computer are the keyboard and the mouse. We can type programs or data into a computer with a keyboard. Other types of input devices found on some computers include scanners, microphones, and cameras.

Output devices permit us to use the data stored in a computer. The most common output devices on today's computers are displays and printers. Other types of output devices include plotters and speakers.

1.2
DATA REPRESENTATION IN A COMPUTER

Computer memories are composed of billions of individual switches, each of which can be ON or OFF, but not at a state in between. Each switch represents one **binary digit** (also called a **bit**); the ON state is interpreted as a binary 1, and the OFF state is interpreted as a binary 0. Taken by itself, a single switch can represent only the numbers 0 and 1. Since we obviously need to work with numbers other than 0 and 1, a number of bits are grouped together to represent each number used in a computer. When several bits are grouped together, they can be used to represent numbers in the *binary* (base 2) *number system*.

The smallest common grouping of bits is called a **byte.** *A byte is a group of 8 bits that are used together to represent a binary number.* The byte is the fundamental unit used to measure the capacity of a computer's memory. For example, the personal computer on which I am writing these words has a main memory of 1024 megabytes (1,024,000,000 bytes), and a secondary memory (disk drive) with a storage of 200 gigabytes (200,000,000,000 bytes).

The next larger grouping of bits in an computer is called a **word.** A word consists of 2, 4, or more consecutive bytes that are used to represent a single number in memory. The size of a word varies from computer to computer, so words are not a particularly good way to judge the size of computer memories. Modern CPUs tend to use words with lengths of either 32 or 64 bits.

1.2.1 The Binary Number System

In the familiar base 10 number system, the smallest (rightmost) digit of a number is the ones place (10^0). The next digit is in the tens place (10^1), and the next one is in the hundreds place (10^2), etc. Thus, the number 122_{10} is really $(1 \times 10^2) + (2 \times 10^1) + (2 \times 10^0)$. Each digit is worth a power of 10 more than the digit to the right of it in the base 10 system (see Figure 1-2a).

Similarly, in the binary number system, the smallest (rightmost) digit is the ones place (2^0). The next digit is in the twos place (2^1), and the next one is in the fours place

FIGURE 1-2
(a) The base 10 number 122 is really $(1 \times 10^2) + (2 \times 10^1) + (2 \times 10^0)$. *(b)* Similarly, the base 2 number 101_2 is really $(1 \times 2^2) + (0 \times 2^1) + (1 \times 2^0)$.

(a)

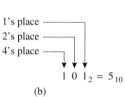

(b)

(2^2), etc. Each digit is worth a power of 2 more than the digit to the right of it in the base 2 system. For example, the binary number 101_2 is really $(1 \times 2^2) + (0 \times 2^1) + (1 \times 2^0) = 5$, and the binary number $111_2 = 7$ (see Figure 1-2b).

Note that three binary digits can be used to represent eight possible values: $0 (= 000_2)$ to $7 (= 111_2)$. In general, *if n bits are grouped together to form a binary number, then they can represent 2^n possible values*. Thus a group of 8 bits (1 byte) can represent 256 possible values, a group of 16 bits (2 bytes) can be used to represent 65,536 possible values, and a group of 32 bits (4 bytes) can be used to represent 4,294,967,296 possible values.

In a typical implementation, half of all possible values are reserved for representing negative numbers, and half of the values are reserved for representing zero plus the positive numbers. Thus, a group of 8 bits (1 byte) is usually used to represent numbers between -128 and $+127$, including 0, and a group of 16 bits (2 bytes) is usually used to represent numbers between $-32,768$ and $+32,767$, including 0.[1]

TWO'S COMPLEMENT ARITHMETIC

The most common way to represent negative numbers in the binary number system is the two's complement representation. What is two's complement, and what is so special about it? Let's find out.

The Two's Complement Representation of Negative Numbers
In the two's complement representation, the leftmost bit of a number is the *sign bit*. If that bit is 0, then the number is positive; if it is 1, then the number is negative. To change a positive number into the corresponding negative number in the two's complement system, we perform two steps:

---

[1] There are several different schemes for representing negative numbers in a computer's memory. They are described in any good computer engineering textbook. The most common scheme is the so-called *two's complement* representation, which is described in the sidebar.

1

1. Complement the number (change all 1s to 0 and all 0s to 1).
2. Add 1 to the complemented number.

Let's illustrate the process by using simple 8-bit integers. As we already know, the 8-bit binary representation of the number 3 would be 00000011. The two's complement representation of the number −3 would be found as follows:

1. Complement the positive number: 11111100
2. Add 1 to the complemented number: 11111100 + 1 = 11111101

Exactly the same process is used to convert negative numbers back to positive numbers. To convert the number −3 (11111101) back to a positive 3, we would:

1. Complement the negative number: 00000010
2. Add 1 to the complemented number: 00000010 + 1 = 00000011

Two's Complement Arithmetic

Now we know how to represent numbers in two's complement representation, and to convert between positive and two's complement negative numbers. The special advantage of two's complement arithmetic is that *positive and negative numbers may be added together according to the rules of ordinary addition without regard to the sign, and the resulting answer will be correct, including the proper sign.* Because of this fact, a computer may add any two integers together without checking to see what the signs of the two integers are. This simplifies the design of computer circuits.

Let's do a few examples to illustrate this point.

1. Add 3 + 4 in two's complement arithmetic.

$$
\begin{array}{rl}
3 & \ \ 00000011 \\
+4 & \ \ 00000100 \\
\hline
7 & \ \ 00000111
\end{array}
$$

2. Add (−3) + (−4) in two's complement arithmetic.

$$
\begin{array}{rl}
-3 & \ \ 11111101 \\
+-4 & \ \ 11111100 \\
\hline
-7 & \ \ 111111001
\end{array}
$$

In a case like this, we ignore the extra ninth bit resulting from the sum, and the answer is 11111001. The two's complement of 11111001 is 00000111 or 7, so the result of the addition is −7!

3. Add 3 + (−4) in two's complement arithmetic.

$$
\begin{array}{rl}
3 & \ \ 00000011 \\
+-4 & \ \ 11111100 \\
\hline
-1 & \ \ 11111111
\end{array}
$$

The answer is 11111111. The two's complement of 11111111 is 00000001 or 1, so the result of the addition is −1!

With two's complement numbers, binary addition comes up with the correct answer regardless of whether the numbers being added are both positive, both negative, or mixed.

1.2.2 Octal and Hexadecimal Representations of Binary Numbers

Computers work in the binary number system, but people think in the decimal number system. Fortunately, we can program the computer to accept inputs and give its outputs in the decimal system, converting them internally to binary form for processing. Most of the time, the fact that computers work with binary numbers is irrelevant to the programmer.

However, there are some cases in which a scientist or engineer has to work directly with the binary representations coded into the computer. For example, individual bits or groups of bits within a word might contain status information about the operation of some machine. If so, the programmer will have to consider the individual bits of the word, and work in the binary number system.

A scientist or engineer who has to work in the binary number system immediately faces the problem that binary numbers are unwieldy. For example, a number like 1100_{10} in the decimal system is 010001001100_2 in the binary system. It is easy to get lost working with such a number! To avoid this problem, we customarily break binary numbers down into groups of 3 or 4 bits, and represent those bits by a single base 8 (octal) or base 16 (hexadecimal) number.

To understand this idea, note that a group of 3 bits can represent any number between 0 ($= 000_2$) and 7 ($= 111_2$). These are the numbers found in an **octal** or base 8 arithmetic system. An octal number system has 7 digits: 0 through 7. We can break a binary number up into groups of 3 bits, and substitute the appropriate octal digit for each group. Let's use the number 010001001100_2 as an example. Breaking the number into groups of three digits yields $010|001|001|100_2$. If each group of 3 bits is replaced by the appropriate octal number, the value can be written as 2114_8. The octal number represents exactly the same pattern of bits as the binary number, but it is more compact.

Similarly, a group of 4 bits can represent any number between 0 ($= 0000_2$) and 15 ($= 1111_2$). These are the numbers found in a **hexadecimal,** or base 16, arithmetic system. A hexadecimal number system has 16 digits: 0 through 9 and A through F. Since the hexadecimal system needs 16 digits, we use digits 0 through 9 for the first 10 of them, and then letters A through F for the remaining 6. Thus, $9_{16} = 9_{10}$, $A_{16} = 10_{10}$, $B_{16} = 11_{10}$, and so forth. We can break a binary number up into groups of 4 bits, and substitute the appropriate hexadecimal digit for each group. Let's use the number 010001001100_2 again as an example. Breaking the number into groups of four digits yields $0100|0100|1100_2$. If each group of 4 bits is replaced by the appropriate hexadecimal number, the value can be written as $44C_{16}$. The hexadecimal number represents exactly the same pattern of bits as the binary number, but more compactly.

TABLE 1-1
Table of decimal, binary, octal, and hexadecimal numbers

Decimal	Binary	Octal	Hexadecimal
0	0000	0	0
1	0001	1	1
2	0010	2	2
3	0011	3	3
4	0100	4	4
5	0101	5	5
6	0110	6	6
7	0111	7	7
8	1000	10	8
9	1001	11	9
10	1010	12	A
11	1011	13	B
12	1100	14	C
13	1101	15	D
14	1110	16	E
15	1111	17	F

Some computer vendors prefer to use octal numbers to represent bit patterns, while other computer vendors prefer to use hexadecimal numbers to represent bit patterns. Both representations are equivalent, in that they represent the pattern of bits in a compact form. A Fortran language program can input or output numbers in any of the four formats (decimal, binary, octal, or hexadecimal). Table 1-1 lists the decimal, binary, octal, and hexadecimal forms of the numbers 1 to 15.

1.2.3 Types of Data Stored In Memory

Three common types of data are stored in a computer's memory: **character data,** **integer data,** and **real data** (numbers with a decimal point). Each type of data has different characteristics, and takes up a different amount of memory in the computer.

Character Data

The **character data** type consists of characters and symbols. A typical system for representing character data in a non-Asian language must include the following symbols:

1. The 26 uppercase letters A through Z
2. The 26 lowercase letters a through z
3. The 10 digits 0 through 9
4. Miscellaneous common symbols, such as: ", (), { }, [], !, ~, @, #, $, %, ^, &, *, etc.
5. Any special letters or symbols required by the language, such as: à ç ë, £, etc.

Since the total number of characters and symbols required to write non-Asian languages is less than 256, *it is customary to use 1 byte of memory to store each character*. Therefore, 10,000 characters would occupy 10,000 bytes of the computer's memory.

The particular bit values corresponding to each letter or symbol may vary from computer to computer, depending on the coding system used for the characters. The most important coding system is ASCII, which stands for the American Standard Code for Information Interchange (ANSI X3.4 1977). The ASCII coding system defines the values to associate with the first 128 of the 256 possible values that can be stored in a 1-byte character. The 8-bit codes corresponding to each letter and number in the ASCII coding system are given in Appendix A.

The second 128 characters that can be stored in a 1-byte character are *not* defined by the ASCII character set, and they used to be defined differently, depending on the language used in a particular country or region. These definitions are a part of the ISO-8859 standard series, and they are sometimes referred to as *code pages*. For example, the ISO-8859-1 (Latin 1) character set is the version used in Western European countries. There are similar code pages available for Eastern European Languages, Arabic, Greek, Hebrew, and so forth. Unfortunately, the use of different code pages made the output of programs and the contents of files appear different in different countries. As a result, these code pages are falling into disuse, and they are being replaced by the Unicode system described below.

A completely different 1-byte coding system is EBCDIC, which stands for Extended Binary Coded Decimal Interchange Code. EBCDIC was traditionally used by IBM on its mainframe computers. It is becoming rarer as time goes by, but can still be found in some applications. The 8-bit codes corresponding to each letter and number in the EBCDIC coding system are also given in Appendix A.

Some Asian languages, such as Chinese and Japanese, contain more than 256 characters (in fact, about 4000 characters are needed to represent each of these languages). To accommodate these languages and all of the other languages in the world, a new coding system called Unicode[2] has been developed. In the Unicode coding system, each character is stored in 2 bytes of memory, so the Unicode system can support 65,536 different characters. The first 128 Unicode characters are identical to the ASCII character set, and other blocks of characters are devoted to various languages such as Chinese, Japanese, Hebrew, Arabic, and Hindi. When the Unicode coding system is used, character data can be represented in any language.

Integer Data

The **integer data** type consists of the positive integers, the negative integers, and zero. The amount of memory devoted to storing an integer will vary from computer to computer, but will usually be 1, 2, 4, or 8 bytes. Four-byte integers are the most common type in modern computers.

Since a finite number of bits are used to store each value, only integers that fall within a certain range can be represented on a computer. Usually, the smallest number that can be stored in an n-bit integer is

---

[2] Also referred to by the corresponding standard number, ISO 10646.

$$\text{Smallest integer value} = -2^{n-1} \tag{1-1}$$

and the largest number that can be stored in an n-bit integer is

$$\text{Largest integer value} = 2^{n-1} - 1 \tag{1-2}$$

For a 4-byte integer, the smallest and largest possible values are $-2,147,483,648$ and $2,147,483,647$ respectively. Attempts to use an integer larger than the largest possible value or smaller than the smallest (most negative) possible value result in an error called an *overflow condition*.[3]

Real Data

The integer data type has two fundamental limitations:

1. It is not possible to represent numbers with fractional parts (0.25, 1.5, 3.14159, etc.) as integer data.
2. It is not possible to represent very large positive integers or very small negative integers, because there are not enough bits available to represent the value. The largest and smallest possible integers that can be stored in a given memory location are given by Equations 1-1 and 1-2.

To get around these limitations, computers include a **real** or **floating-point** data type.

The real data type stores numbers in a type of scientific notation. We all know that very large or very small numbers can be most conveniently written in scientific notation. For example, the speed of light in a vacuum is about 299,800,000 meters per second. This number is easier to work with in scientific notation: 2.998×10^8 m/s. The two parts of a number expressed in scientific notation are called the **mantissa** and the **exponent.** The mantissa of the number above is 2.998, and the exponent (in the base 10 system) is 8.

The real numbers in a computer are similar to the scientific notation above, except that a computer works in the base 2 system instead of the base 10 system. Real numbers usually occupy 32 bits (four bytes) of computer memory, divided into two components: a 24-bit mantissa and an 8-bit exponent (Figure 1-3).[4] The mantissa contains a number between -1.0 and 1.0, and the exponent contains the power of 2 required to scale the number to its actual value.

---

[3] When an overflow condition occurs, some processors will abort the program, causing the overflow condition. Other processors will "wrap around" from the most positive integer to the most negative integer without giving the user a warning that anything has happened. This behavior varies for different types of computers.

[4] This discussion is based on the IEEE Standard 754 for floating-point numbers, which is representative of most modern computers. Some computers use a slightly different division of bits (e.g., a 23-bit mantissa and a 9-bit exponent), but the basic principles are the same in any case.

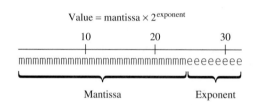

FIGURE 1-3
This floating-point number includes a 24-bit mantissa and an 8-bit exponent.

Real numbers are characterized by two quantities: **precision** and **range.** *Precision* is the number of significant digits that can be preserved in a number, and *range* is the difference between the largest and smallest numbers that can be represented. The precision of a real number depends on the number of bits in its mantissa, while the range of the number depends on the number of bits in its exponent. A 24-bit mantissa can represent approximately $\pm 2^{23}$ numbers, or about seven significant decimal digits, so the precision of real numbers is about seven significant digits. An 8-bit exponent can represent multipliers between 2^{-128} and 2^{127}, so the range of real numbers is from about 10^{-38} to 10^{38}. Note that the real data type can represent numbers much larger or much smaller than integers can, but only with seven significant digits of precision.

When a value with more than seven digits of precision is stored in a real variable, *only the most significant 7 bits of the number will be preserved.* The remaining information will be lost forever. For example, if the value 12,345,678.9 is stored in a real variable on a PC, it will be rounded off to 12,345,680.0. This difference between the original value and the number stored in the computer is known as **round-off error.**

You will use the real data type in many places throughout this book and in your programs after you finish this course. It is quite useful, but you must always remember the limitations associated with round-off error, or your programs might give you an unpleasant surprise. For example, if your program must be able to distinguish between the numbers 1,000,000.0 and 1,000,000.1, then you cannot use the standard real data type.[5] It simply does not have enough precision to tell the difference between these two numbers!

Programming Pitfalls
Always remember the precision and range of the data types that you are working with. Failure to do so can result in subtle programming errors that are very hard to find.

Quiz 1-1

This quiz provides a quick check to see if you have understood the concepts introduced in Section 1.2. If you have trouble with the quiz, reread the section, ask your instructor for help, or discuss the material with a fellow student. The answers to this quiz are found in the back of the book.

(continued)

---
[5] We will learn how to use high-precision floating-point numbers in Chapter 11.

(concluded)

1. Express the following decimal numbers as their binary equivalents:

    (*a*) 27_{10}
    (*b*) 11_{10}
    (*c*) 35_{10}
    (*d*) 127_{10}

2. Express the following binary numbers as their decimal equivalents:

    (*a*) 1110_2
    (*b*) 01010101_2
    (*c*) 1001_2

3. Express the following binary numbers as octal and hexadecimal numbers:

    (*a*) 1110010110101101_2
    (*b*) 1110111101_2
    (*c*) 1001011100111111_2

4. Is the fourth bit of the number 131_{10} a 1 or a 0?

5. Assume that the following numbers are the contents of a character variable. Find the character corresponding to each number according to the ASCII and EBCDIC encoding schemes:

    (*a*) 77_{10}
    (*b*) 01111011_2
    (*c*) 249_{10}

6. Find the maximum and minimum values that can be stored in a 2-byte integer variable.

7. Can a 4-byte variable of the real data type be used to store larger numbers than a 4-byte variable of the integer data type? Why or why not? If it can, what is given up by the real variable to make this possible?

■ 1.3

COMPUTER LANGUAGES

When a computer executes a program, it executes a string of very simple operations such as load, store, add, subtract, multiply, and so on. Each such operation has a unique binary pattern called an *operation code* (op code) to specify it. The program that a computer executes is just a string of op codes (and the data associated with the op codes[6]) in the order necessary to achieve a purpose. Op codes are collectively called **machine language,** since they are the actual language that a computer recognizes and executes.

---

[6] The data associated with op codes are called *operands*.

Unfortunately, we humans find machine language very hard to work with. We prefer to work with English-like statements and algebraic equations that are expressed in forms familiar to us, instead of arbitrary patterns of zeros and ones. We like to program computers with **high-level languages.** We write out our instructions in a high-level language, and then use special programs called **compilers** and **linkers** to convert the instructions into the machine language that the computer understands.

There are many different high-level languages, with different characteristics. Some of them are designed to work well for business problems, while others are designed for general scientific use. Still others are especially suited for applications like operating systems programming. It is important to pick a proper language to match the problem that you are trying to solve.

Some common high-level computer languages today include Ada, Basic, C++, COBOL, Fortran, and Java. Of these languages, Fortran is the preeminent language for general scientific computations. It has been around in one form or another for more than 50 years, and has been used to implement everything from computer models of nuclear power plants to aircraft design programs to seismic signal processing systems, including some projects requiring literally millions of lines of code. The language is especially useful for numerical analysis and technical calculations. In addition, Fortran is the dominant language in the world of supercomputers and massively parallel computers.

1.4

THE HISTORY OF THE FORTRAN LANGUAGE

Fortran is the grandfather of all scientific computer languages. The name Fortran is derived from FORmula TRANslation, indicating that the language was intended from the start for translating scientific equations into computer code. The first version of the FORTRAN[7] language was developed during the years 1954–1957 by IBM for use with its Type 704 computer (see Figure 1-4). Before that time, essentially all computer programs were generated by hand in machine language, which was a slow, tedious, and error-prone process. FORTRAN was a truly revolutionary product. For the first time, a programmer could write a desired algorithm as a series of standard algebraic equations, and the FORTRAN compiler would convert the statements into the machine language that the computer could recognize and execute.

THE IBM TYPE 704 COMPUTER

The IBM Type 704 computer was the first computer ever to use the FORTRAN language. It was released in 1954, and was widely used from then until about 1960, when it was replaced by the Model 709. As you can see from Figure 1-4, the computer occupied a whole room.

---

[7] Versions of the language before Fortran 90 were known as FORTRAN (written with all capital letters), while Fortran 90 and later versions are known as Fortran (with only the first letter capitalized).

FIGURE 1-4
The IBM Type 704 computer. *(Courtesy of IBM Corporation)*

What could a computer like that do in 1954? Not much, by today's standards. Any PC sitting on a desktop can run rings around it. The 704 could perform about 4000 integer multiplications and divisions per second, and an average of about 8000 floating-point operations per second. It could read data from magnetic drums (the equivalent of a disk drive) into memory at a rate of about 50,000 bytes per second. The amount of data storage available on a magnetic drum was also very small, so most programs that were not currently in use were stored as decks of punched cards.

By comparison, a typical modern personal computer (circa 2006) performs more than 20,000,000,000 integer multiplications and divisions per second, and hundreds of millions of floating-point operations per second. Some of today's workstations are small enough to sit on a desktop, and yet can perform more than 5,000,000,000 floating point operations per second! Reads from disk into memory occur at rates greater than 25,000,000 bytes per second, and a typical PC disk drive can store more than 200,000,000,000 bytes of data.

The limited resources available in the 704 and other machines of that generation placed a great premium on efficient programming. The structured programming techniques that we use today were simply not possible, because there was not enough speed or memory to support them. The earliest versions of FORTRAN were designed with those limitations in mind, which is why we find many archaic features preserved as living fossils in modern versions of Fortran.

1

FORTRAN was a wonderful idea! People began using it as soon as it was available, because it made programming so much easier than machine language did. The language was officially released in April 1957, and by the fall of 1958, more than half of all IBM 704 computer programs were being written in Fortran.

The original FORTRAN language was very small compared to our modern versions of Fortran. It contained only a limited number of statement types, and supported only the integer and real data types. There were also no subroutines in the first FORTRAN. It was a first effort at writing a high-level computer language, and naturally many deficiencies were found as people started using the language regularly. IBM addressed those problems, releasing FORTRAN II in the spring of 1958.

Further developments continued through 1962, when FORTRAN IV was released. FORTRAN IV was a great improvement, and it became the standard version of Fortran for the next 15 years. In 1966, FORTRAN IV was adopted as an ANSI standard, and it came to be known as FORTRAN 66.

The Fortran language received another major update in 1977. FORTRAN 77 included many new features designed to make structured programs easier to write and maintain, and it quickly became "the" Fortran. FORTRAN 77 introduced such structures as the block IF, and was the first version of Fortran in which character variables were truly easy to manipulate.

The next major update of Fortran was Fortran 90.[8] Fortran 90 included all of FORTRAN 77 as a subset, and extended the language in many important new directions. Among the major improvements introduced to the language in Fortran 90 were a new free source format, array sections, whole-array operations, parameterized data types, derived data types, and explicit interfaces. Fortran 90 was a dramatic improvement over earlier versions of the language.

Fortran 90 was followed in 1996 by a minor update called Fortran 95. Fortran 95 added a number of new features to the language such as the FORALL construct, pure functions, and some new intrinsic procedures. In addition, it clarified numerous ambiguities in the Fortran 90 standard.

Fortran 2003 is the latest update.[9] This is a major change from Fortran 95, including new features such as enhanced derived types, object-oriented programming support, Unicode character set support, data manipulation enhancements, procedure pointers, and interoperability with the C language.

The subjects of this book are the Fortran 95 and Fortran 2003 languages. The vast majority of the book applies to both Fortran 95 and Fortran 2003, and we will usually refer to them together as Fortran 95/2003. Where there are features that appear only in Fortran 2003, they are distinguished by a gray background and a symbol. An example of a Fortran 2003–specific comment is shown below.

F-2003 ONLY

Variable names can be up to 63 characters long in Fortran 2003.

---

[8] American National Standard Programming Language Fortran, ANSI X3.198-1992; and International Standards Organization ISO/IEC 1539: 1991, Information Technology—Programming Languages—Fortran.

[9] International Organization for Standardization ISO/IEC 1539: 2004, Information Technology—Programming Languages—Fortran.

The designers of Fortran 95 and Fortran 2003 were careful to make the language backward-compatible with FORTRAN 77 and earlier versions. Because of this backward compatibility, most of the millions of programs written in FORTRAN 77 also work with Fortran 95/2003. Unfortunately, being backward-compatible with earlier versions of Fortran required that Fortran 95/2003 retain some archaic features that should never be used in any modern program. *In this book, we will learn to program in* Fortran 95/2003 *using only its modern features.* The older features that are retained for backward compatibility are relegated to Chapter 17 of this book. They are described there in case you run into any of them in older programs, but they should never be used in any new program.

1.5
THE EVOLUTION OF FORTRAN

The Fortran language is a dynamic language that is constantly evolving to keep up with advances in programming practice and computing technology. A major new version appears about once per decade.

The responsibility for developing new versions of the Fortran language lies with the International Organization for Standardization's (ISO) Fortran Working Group, WG5. That organization has delegated authority to the X3J3 Committee of the American National Standards Institute (ANSI) to actually prepare new versions of the language. The preparation of each new version is an extended process involving first asking for suggestions for inclusion in the language, deciding which suggestions are feasible to implement, writing and circulating drafts to all interested parties throughout the world, and correcting the drafts and trying again until general agreement is reached. Eventually, a worldwide vote is held and the standard is adopted.

The designers of new versions of the Fortran language must strike a delicate balance between backward compatibility with the existing base of Fortran programs and the introduction of desirable new features. Although modern structured programming features and approaches have been introduced into the language, many undesirable features from earlier versions of Fortran have been retained for backward compatibility.

The designers have developed a mechanism for identifying undesirable and obsolete features of the Fortran language that should no longer be used, and for eventually eliminating them from the language. Those parts of the language that have been superseded by new and better methods are declared to be **obsolescent features.** *Features that have been declared obsolescent should never be used in any new programs.* As the use of these features declines in the existing Fortran code base, they will then be considered for **deletion** from the language. No feature will ever be deleted from a version of the language unless it was on the obsolescent list in at least one previous version, and unless the usage of the feature has dropped off to negligible levels. In this fashion, the language can evolve without threatening the existing Fortran code base.

The redundant, obsolescent, and deleted features of Fortran 95/2003 are described in Chapter 17 in case a programmer runs into them in existing programs, but they should never be used in any new programs.

We can get a feeling for just how much the Fortran language has evolved over the years by examining Figures 1-5 through 1-7. These three figures show programs for calculating the solutions to the quadratic equation $ax^2 + bx + c = 0$ in the styles of the original FORTRAN I, of FORTRAN 77, and of Fortran 95. It is obvious that the language has become more readable and structured over the years. Amazingly, though, Fortran 90 compilers will still compile the FORTRAN I program with just a few minor changes![10]

FIGURE 1-5

A FORTRAN I program to solve for the roots of the quadratic equation $ax^2 + bx + c = 0$.

```
C       SOLVE QUADRATIC EQUATION IN FORTRAN I
        READ 100,A,B,C
100     FORMAT(3F12.4)
        DISCR = B**2-4*A*C
        IF (DISCR) 10,20,30
10      X1=(-B)/(2.*A)
        X2=SQRTF(ABSF(DISCR))/(2.*A)
        PRINT 110,X1,X2
110     FORMAT(5H X = ,F12.3,4H +i ,F12.3)
        PRINT 120,X1,X2
120     FORMAT(5H X = ,F12.3,4H -i ,F12.3)
        GOTO 40
20      X1=(-B)/(2.*A)
        PRINT 130,X1
130     FORMAT(11H X1 = X2 = ,F12.3)
        GOTO 40
30      X1=((-B)+SQRTF(ABSF(DISCR)))/(2.*A)
        X2=((-B)-SQRTF(ABSF(DISCR)))/(2.*A)
        PRINT 140,X1
140     FORMAT(6H X1 = ,F12.3)
        PRINT 150,X2
150     FORMAT(6H X2 = ,F12.3)
40      CONTINUE
        STOP 25252
```

FIGURE 1-6

A FORTRAN 77 program to solve for the roots of the quadratic equation $ax^2 + bx + c = 0$.

```
        PROGRAM QUAD4
C
C       This program reads the coefficients of a quadratic equation of
C       the form
C           A * X**2 + B * X + C = 0,
C       and solves for the roots of the equation (FORTRAN 77 style).
C
C       Get the coefficients of the quadratic equation.
C
```

(continued)

---

[10] Change SQRTF to SQRT, ABSF to ABS, and add an END statement.

(concluded)

```
      WRITE (*,*) 'Enter the coefficients A, B and C: '
      READ (*,*) A, B, C
C
C     Echo the coefficients to make sure they are entered correctly.
C
      WRITE (*,100) 'The coefficients are : ', A, B, C
100   FORMAT (1X,A,3F10.4)
C
C     Check the discriminant and calculate its roots.
C
      DISCR = B**2 - 4.*A*C
      IF ( DISCR .LT. 0) THEN
         WRITE (*,*) ' This equation has complex roots:'
         WRITE (*,*) ' X = ', -B/(2.*A), ' +i ', SQRT(ABS(DISCR))/(2.*A)
         WRITE (*,*) ' X = ', -B/(2.*A), ' -i ', SQRT(ABS(DISCR))/(2.*A)
      ELSE IF ( (B**2 - 4.*A*C) .EQ. 0) THEN
         WRITE (*,*) ' This equation has a single repeated real root:'
         WRITE (*,*) ' X = ', -B/(2.*A)
      ELSE
         WRITE (*,*) ' This equation has two distinct real roots:'
         WRITE (*,*) ' X = ', (-B + SQRT(ABS(DISCR)))/(2.*A)
         WRITE (*,*) ' X = ', (-B - SQRT(ABS(DISCR)))/(2.*A)
      END IF
C
      END
```

FIGURE 1-7

A Fortran 95/2003 program to solve for the roots of the quadratic equation $ax^2 + bx + c = 0$.

```
PROGRAM roots

!  Purpose:
!    This program solves for the roots of a quadratic equation of the form
!    A * X**2 + B * X + C = 0.  It calculates the answers regardless of the
!    type of roots that the equation possesses (Fortran 95/2003 style).
!
IMPLICIT NONE

!  Declare the variables used in this program

REAL :: a                ! Coefficient of X**2 term of equation
REAL :: b                ! Coefficient of X term of equation
REAL :: c                ! Constant term of equation
REAL :: discriminant     ! Discriminant of the equation
REAL :: imag_part        ! Imaginary part of equation (for complex roots)
REAL :: real_part        ! Real part of equation (for complex roots)
REAL :: x1               ! First solution of equation (for real roots)
REAL :: x2               ! Second solution of equation (for real roots)
```

(continued)

(concluded)

```
!  Prompt the user for the coefficients of the equation
WRITE (*,*) 'This program solves for the roots of a quadratic '
WRITE (*,*) 'equation of the form A * X**2 + B * X + C = 0. '
WRITE (*,*) 'Enter the coefficients A, B, and C:'
READ  (*,*) a, b, c

!  Echo back coefficients
WRITE (*,*) 'The coefficients A, B, and C are: ', a, b, c

!  Calculate discriminant
discriminant = b**2 - 4. * a * c

!  Solve for the roots, depending upon the value of the discriminant

IF ( discriminant > 0. ) THEN ! there are two real roots, so...

   X1 = ( -b + sqrt(discriminant) ) / ( 2. * a )
   X2 = ( -b - sqrt(discriminant) ) / ( 2. * a )
   WRITE (*,*) 'This equation has two real roots:'
   WRITE (*,*) 'X1 = ', x1
   WRITE (*,*) 'X2 = ', x2

ELSE IF ( discriminant == 0. ) THEN ! there is one repeated root, so...

   x1 = ( -b ) / ( 2. * a )
   WRITE (*,*) 'This equation has two identical real roots:'
   WRITE (*,*) 'X1 = X2 = ', x1

ELSE ! there are complex roots, so ...

   real_part = ( -b ) / ( 2. * a )
   imag_part = sqrt ( abs ( discriminant ) ) / ( 2. * a )
   WRITE (*,*) 'This equation has complex roots:'
   WRITE (*,*) 'X1 = ', real_part, ' +i ', imag_part
   WRITE (*,*) 'X2 = ', real_part, ' -i ', imag_part

END IF

END PROGRAM roots
```

■ 1.6
SUMMARY

A computer is a special type of machine that stores information, and can perform mathematical calculations on that information at speeds much faster than human beings can think. A program, which is stored in the computer's memory, tells the computer what sequence of calculations is required, and which information to perform the calculations on.

The major components of a computer are the central processing unit (CPU), main memory, secondary memory, and input and output devices. The CPU performs all of the control and calculation functions of the computer. Main memory is fast, relatively expensive memory that is used to store the program being executed, and its associated data. Main memory is volatile, meaning that its contents are lost whenever power is turned off. Secondary memory is slower and cheaper than main memory. It is nonvolatile. Hard disks are common secondary memory devices. Input and output devices are used to read data into the computer and to output data from the computer. The most common input device is a keyboard, and the most common output device is a printer.

Computer memories are composed of millions of individual switches, each of which can be ON or OFF, but not at a state in between. These individual switches are binary devices called bits. Eight bits are grouped together to form a *byte* of memory, and 2 or more bytes (depending on the computer) are grouped together to form a *word* of memory.

Computer memories can be used to store *character, integer,* or *real* data. Each character in most character data sets occupies 1 byte of memory. The 256 possible values in the byte allow for 256 possible character codes. (Characters in the unicode character set occupy 2 bytes, allowing for 65,536 possible character codes.) Integer values occupy 1, 2, 4, or 8 bytes of memory, and store integer quantities. Real values store numbers in a kind of scientific notation. They usually occupy 4 bytes of memory. The bits are divided into a separate mantissa and exponent. The *precision* of the number depends on the number of bits in the mantissa, and the *range* of the number depends on the number of bits in the exponent.

The earliest computers were programmed in *machine language*. This process was slow, cumbersome, and error-prone. High-level languages began to appear in about 1954, and they quickly replaced machine language coding for most uses. FORTRAN was one of the first high-level languages ever created.

The FORTRAN I computer language and compiler were originally developed between 1954 and 1957. The language has since gone through many revisions, and a standard mechanism has been created to evolve the language. This book teaches good programming practices, using the Fortran 95/2003 version of the language.

1.6.1 Exercises

1-1. Express the following decimal numbers as their binary equivalents:

(*a*) 10_{10}

(*b*) 32_{10}

(*c*) 77_{10}

(*d*) 63_{10}

1-2. Express the following binary numbers as their decimal equivalents:

(*a*) 01001000_2

(*b*) 10001001_2

(c) 11111111_2

(d) 0101_2

1-3. Express the following numbers in both octal and hexadecimal forms:

(a) 1010111011110001_2

(b) 330_{10}

(c) 111_{10}

(d) 11111101101_2

1-4. Express the following numbers in binary and decimal forms:

(a) 377_8

(b) $1A8_{16}$

(c) 111_8

(d) $1FF_{16}$

1-5. Some computers (such as IBM mainframes) used to implement real data using a 23-bit mantissa and a 9-bit exponent. What precision and range can we expect from real data on these machines?

1-6. Some Cray supercomputers support 46-bit and 64-bit integer data types. What are the maximum and minimum values that we could express in a 46-bit integer? in a 64-bit integer?

1-7. Find the 16-bit two's-complement representation of the following decimal numbers:

(a) 55_{10}

(b) -5_{10}

(c) 1024_{10}

(d) -1024_{10}

1-8. Add the two's complement numbers 0010010010010010_2 and 1111110011111100_2 using binary arithmetic. Convert the two numbers to decimal form, and add them as decimals. Do the two answers agree?

1-9. The largest possible 8-bit two's complement number is 01111111_2, and the smallest possible 8-bit two's complement number is 10000000_2. Convert these numbers to decimal form. How do they compare to the results of Equations 1-1 and 1-2?

1-10. The Fortran language includes a second type of floating-point data known as *double precision*. A double precision number usually occupies 8 bytes (64 bits), instead of the 4 bytes occupied by a real number. In the most common implementation, 53 bits are used for the mantissa and 11 bits are used for the exponent. How many significant digits does a double precision value have? What is the range of double precision numbers?

Basic Elements of Fortran

OBJECTIVES

- Know which characters are legal in a Fortran statement.
- Know the basic structure of a Fortran statement and a Fortran program.
- Know the difference between executable and nonexecutable statements.
- Know the difference between constants and variables.
- Understand the differences among the INTEGER, REAL, and CHARACTER data types.
- Learn the difference between default and explicit typing, and understand why explicit typing should always be used.
- Know the structure of a Fortran assignment statement.
- Learn the differences between integer arithmetic and real arithmetic, and when each one should be used.
- Know the Fortran hierarchy of operations.
- Learn how Fortran handles mixed-mode arithmetic expressions.
- Learn what intrinsic function are, and how to use them.
- Know how to use list-directed input and output statements.
- Know why it is important to always use the IMPLICIT NONE statement.

▨ 2.1

INTRODUCTION

As engineers and scientists, we design and execute computer programs to accomplish a goal. The goal typically involves technical calculations that would be too difficult or take too long to be performed by hand. Fortran is one of the computer languages commonly used for these technical calculations.

This chapter introduces the basic elements of the Fortran language. By the end of the chapter, we will be able to write simple but functional Fortran programs.

2.2

THE FORTRAN CHARACTER SET

Every language, whether it is a natural language such as English, or a computer language such as Fortran, Java, or C++, has its own special alphabet. Only the characters in this alphabet may be used with the language.

The special alphabet used with the Fortran language is known as the **Fortran character set.** The Fortran 95 character set consists of 86 symbols, and the Fortran 2003 character set consists of 97 characters, as shown in Table 2-1.

TABLE 2-1
The Fortran character set

Number of symbols	Type	Values
26	Uppercase letters	A - Z
26	Lowercase letters	a - z
10	Digits	0 - 9
1	Underscore character	_
5	Arithmetic symbols	+ - * / **
17	Miscellaneous symbols	( ) . = , ' $: ! " % & ; < > ? and blank
11	Additional Fortran 2003 symbols	~ \ [ ] ` ^ { } | # and @

Note that the uppercase letters of the alphabet are equivalent to the lowercase ones in the Fortran character set. (For example, the uppercase letter A is equivalent to the lowercase letter a.) In other words, Fortran is *case insensitive*. This behavior is in contrast with such case sensitive languages as C++ and Java, in which A and a are two totally different things.

2.3

THE STRUCTURE OF A FORTRAN STATEMENT

A Fortran program consists of a series of *statements* designed to accomplish the goal of the programmer. There are two basic types of statements: **executable statements** and **nonexecutable statements.** Executable statements describe the actions taken by the program when it is executed (additions, subtractions, multiplications, divisions, etc.), while nonexecutable statements provide information necessary for the proper operation of the program. We will see many examples of each type of statement as we learn more about the Fortran language.

Fortran statements may be entered anywhere on a line, and each line may be up to 132 characters long. If a statement is too long to fit onto a single line, then it may be continued on the next line by ending the current line (and optionally starting the next line) with an ampersand (&) character. For example, the following three Fortran statements are identical:

```
output = input1 + input2 ! Sum the inputs
output = input1 &
        + input2         ! Sum the inputs
999 output = input1 &    ! Sum the inputs
            & + input2
```

Each of the statements specifies that the computer should add the two quantities stored in `input1` and `input2` and save the result in `output`. A Fortran 95 statement can be continued for up to 40 lines, if required. (A Fortran 2003 statement can be continued for up to 256 lines.)

**F-2003
ONLY**

The last statement shown above starts with a number, known as a **statement label.** A statement label can be any number between 1 and 99999. It is the "name" of a Fortran statement, and may be used to refer to the statement in other parts of the program. Note that a statement label has no significance other than as a "name" for the statement. It is *not* a line number, and it tells nothing about the order in which statements are executed. *Statement labels are rare in modern Fortran, and most Fortran 95/2003 statements will not have one*. If a statement label is used, it must be unique within a given program unit. For example, if `100` is used as a statement label on one line, it cannot be used again as a statement label on any other line in the same program unit.

Any characters following an exclamation point are **comments,** and are ignored by the Fortran compiler. All text from the exclamation point to the end of the line will be ignored, so comments may appear on the same line as an executable statement. Comments are very important, because they help us document the proper operation of a program. In the third example above, the comment is ignored, so the ampersand is treated by the compiler as the last character on the line.

2.4
THE STRUCTURE OF A FORTRAN PROGRAM

Each Fortran program consists of a mixture of executable and nonexecutable statements, which must occur in a specific order. An example Fortran program is shown in Figure 2-1. This program reads in two numbers, multiplies them together, and prints out the result. Let's examine the significant features of this program.

FIGURE 2-1
A simple Fortran program.

```
PROGRAM my_first_program

!  Purpose:
!    To illustrate some of the basic features of a Fortran program.
!
```

(continued)

(concluded)

```
! Declare the variables used in this program.
INTEGER :: i, j, k              ! All variables are integers

! Get two values to store in variables i and j
WRITE (*,*) 'Enter the numbers to multiply: '
READ (*,*) i, j

! Multiply the numbers together
k = i * j

!  Write out the result.
WRITE (*,*) 'Result = ', k

!  Finish up.
STOP
END PROGRAM my_first_program
```

This Fortran program, like all Fortran program units,[1] is divided into three sections:

1. *The declaration section.* This section consists of a group of nonexecutable statements at the beginning of the program that define the name of the program and the number and types of variables referenced in the program.
2. *The execution section.* This section consists of one or more statements describing the actions to be performed by the program.
3. *The termination section.* This section consists of a statement or statements stopping the execution of the program and telling the compiler that the program is complete.

Note that comments may be inserted freely anywhere within, before, or after the program.

2.4.1 The Declaration Section

The declaration section consists of the nonexecutable statements at the beginning of the program that define the name of the program and the number and types of variables referenced in the program.

The first statement in this section is the PROGRAM statement. It is a nonexecutable statement that specifies the name of the program to the Fortran compiler. Fortran 95 program names may be up to 31 characters long and contain any combination of alphabetic characters, digits, and the underscore (_) character.[2] However, the first character in a program name must always be alphabetic. If present, the PROGRAM statement must be the first line of the program. In this example, the program has been named my_first_program.

---

[1] A *program unit* is a separately compiled piece of Fortran code. We will meet several other types of program units beginning in Chapter 7.
[2] Fortran 2003 program names may be up to 63 characters long.

The next several lines in the program are comments that describe the purpose of the program. Next comes the INTEGER type declaration statement. This nonexecutable statement will be described later in this chapter. Here, it declares that three integer variables called i, j, and k will be used in this program.

2.4.2 The Execution Section

The execution section consists of one or more executable statements describing the actions to be performed by the program.

The first executable statement in this program is the WRITE statement, which writes out a message prompting the user to enter the two numbers to be multiplied together. The next executable statement is a READ statement, which reads in the two integers supplied by the user. The third executable statement instructs the computer to multiply the two numbers i and j together, and to store the result in variable k. The final WRITE statement prints out the result for the user to see. Comments may be embedded anywhere throughout the execution section.

All of these statements will be explained in detail later in this chapter.

2.4.3 The Termination Section

The termination section consists of the STOP and END PROGRAM statements. The STOP statement is a statement that tells the computer to stop running the program. The END PROGRAM statement is a statement that tells the compiler that there are no more statements to be compiled in the program.

When the STOP statement immediately precedes the END PROGRAM statement as in this example, it is optional. The compiler will automatically generate a STOP command when the END PROGRAM statement is reached. The STOP statement is therefore rarely used.[3]

2.4.4 Program Style

This example program follows a commonly used Fortran convention of capitalizing keywords such as PROGRAM, READ, and WRITE, while using lowercase for the program variables. Names are written with underscores between the words, as in my_first_program above. It also uses capital letters for named constants such as PI (π). This is *not* a Fortran requirement; the program would have worked just as well if all capital

---

[3] There is a philosophical disagreement among Fortran programmers about the use of the STOP statement. Some programming instructors believe that it should always be used, even though it is redundant when located before an END PROGRAM statement. They argue that the STOP statement makes the end of execution explicit. The author of this book is of the school that believes that a good program should only have *one* starting point and *one* ending point, with no additional stopping points anywhere along the way. In that case, a STOP is totally redundant and will never be used. Depending on the philosophy of your instructor, you may or may not be encouraged to use this statement.

letters or all lowercase letters were used. Since uppercase and lowercase letters are equivalent in Fortran, the program functions identically in either case.

Throughout this book, we will follow this convention of capitalizing Fortran keywords and constants, and using lowercase for variables, procedure names, etc.

Some programmers use other styles to write Fortran programs. For example, Java programmers who also work with Fortran might adopt a Java-like convention in which keywords and names are in lowercase, with capital letters at the beginning of each word. Such a programmer might give this program the name `myFirstProgram`. This is an equally valid way to write a Fortran program.

It is not necessary for you to follow any specific convention to write a Fortran program, but *you should always be consistent* in your programming style. Establish a standard practice, or adopt the standard practice of the organization in which you work, and then follow it consistently in all of your programs.

Good Programming Practice

Adopt a programming style, and then follow it consistently in all of your programs.

2.4.5 Compiling, Linking, and Executing the Fortran Program

Before the sample program can be run, it must be compiled into object code with a Fortran compiler, and then linked with a computer's system libraries to produce an executable program (Figure 2-2). These two steps are usually done together in response to a single programmer command. *The details of compiling and linking are different for every compiler and operating system.* You should ask your instructor or consult the appropriate manuals to determine the proper procedure for your system.

Fortran programs can be compiled, linked, and executed in one of two possible modes: **batch** and **interactive.** In batch mode, a program is executed without an input from or interaction with a user. This is the way most Fortran programs worked in the early days. A program would be submitted as a deck of punched cards or in a file, and it would be compiled, linked, and executed without any user interaction. All input data for the program had to be placed on cards or put in files before the job was started, and all output went to output files or to a line printer.

By contrast, a program that is run in interactive mode is compiled, linked, and executed while a user is waiting at an input device such as the computer screen or a terminal. Since the program executes with the human present, it can ask for input data

FIGURE 2-2
Creating an executable Fortran program involves two steps, compiling and linking.

2

from the user as it is executing, and it can display intermediate and final results as soon as they are computed.

Today, most Fortran programs are executed in interactive mode. However, some very large Fortran programs that execute for days at a time are still run in batch mode.

2.5
CONSTANTS AND VARIABLES

A **Fortran constant** is a data object that is defined before a program is executed, and that does not change value during the execution of the program. When a Fortran compiler encounters a constant, it places the value of the constant in a known location in memory, and then references that memory location whenever the constant is used in the program.

A **Fortran variable** is a data object that can change value during the execution of a program. (The value of a Fortran variable may or may not be initialized before a program is executed.) When a Fortran compiler encounters a variable, it reserves a known location in memory for the variable, and then references that memory location whenever the variable is used in the program.

Each Fortran variable in a program unit must have a unique name. The variable name is a label for a specific location in memory that is easy for humans to remember and use. Fortran 95 names may be up to 31 characters long,[4] and may contain any combination of alphabetic characters, digits, and the underscore (_) character. However, the first character in a name must always be alphabetic. The following examples are valid variable names:

```
time
distance
z123456789
I_want_to_go_home
```

The following examples are invalid variable names:

`this_is_a_very_long_variable_name`	(Illegal in Fortran 95—too long; legal in Fortran 2003.)
`this_is_a_very_very_very_very_very_very_very_very_long_variable_name`	(Name is too long for Fortran 2003.)
`3_days`	(First character is a number.)
`A$`	($ is an illegal character.)

When you are writing a program, it is important to pick meaningful names for the variables. Meaningful names make a program *much* easier to read and to maintain. Names such as day, month, and year are quite clear even to a person seeing a program for the first time. Since spaces cannot be used in Fortran variable names, underscore characters can be substituted to create meaningful names. For example, *exchange rate* might become exchange_rate.

---

[4] Fortran 2003 names can be up to 63 characters long.

Good Programming Practice
Use meaningful variable names whenever possible.

It is also important to include a **data dictionary** in the header of any program that you write. A data dictionary lists the definition each variable used in a program. The definition should include both a description of the contents of the item and the units in which it is measured. A data dictionary may seem unnecessary while the program is being written, but it is invaluable when you or another person have to go back and modify the program at a later time.

Good Programming Practice
Create a data dictionary for each program to make program maintenance easier.

There are five intrinsic or "built-in" types of Fortran constants and variables. Three of them are numeric (types INTEGER, REAL, and COMPLEX), one is logical (type LOGICAL), and one consists of strings of characters (type CHARACTER). The simplest forms of the INTEGER, REAL, and CHARACTER data types will be discussed now. The LOGICAL data type is included in Chapter 3. More advanced forms of various data types will be discussed in Chapter 11.

In addition to the intrinsic data types, Fortran permits a programmer to define **derived data types,** which are special data types intended to solve particular problems. Derived data types will also be discussed in Chapter 12.

2.5.1 Integer Constants and Variables

The integer data type consists of integer constants and variables. This data type can store only integer values—it cannot represent numbers with fractional parts.

An **integer constant** is any number that does not contain a decimal point. If a constant is positive, it may be written either with or without a + sign. No commas may be embedded within an integer constant. The following examples are valid integer constants:

```
     0
  -999
123456789
   +17
```

The following examples are *not* valid integer constants:

```
1,000,000     (Embedded commas are illegal.)
-100.         (If it has a decimal point, it is not an integer constant!)
```

An **integer variable** is a variable containing a value of the integer data type.

Constants and variables of the integer data type are usually stored in a single word on a computer. Since the length of a word varies from 16 bits up to 64 bits on different computers, the largest integer that can be stored in a computer also varies. The largest and smallest integers that can be stored in a particular computer can be determined from the word size by applying Equations 1-1 and 1-2.

Many Fortran 95/2003 compilers support integers with more than one length. For example, most PC compilers support both 16-bit integers and 32-bit integers. These different lengths of integers are known as different **kinds** of integers. Fortran 95/2003 has an explicit mechanism for choosing which kind of integer is used for a given value. This mechanism is explained in Chapter 11.

2.5.2 Real Constants and Variables

The real data type consists of numbers stored in real or floating-point format. Unlike integers, the real data type can represent numbers with fractional components.

A **real constant** is a constant written with a decimal point. It may be written with or without an exponent. If the constant is positive, it may be written either with or without a + sign. No commas may be embedded within a real constant.

Real constants may be written with or without an exponent. If used, the exponent consists of the letter E followed by a positive or negative integer, which corresponds to the power of 10 used when the number is written in scientific notation. If the exponent is positive, the + sign may be omitted. The mantissa of the number (the part of the number that precedes the exponent) should contain a decimal point. The following examples are valid real constants:

```
       10.
     -999.9
    +1.0E-3        (= 1.0 × 10⁻³, or 0.001 )
  123.45E20        (= 123.45 × 10²⁰, or 1.2345 × 10²²)
    0.12E+1        (= 0.12 × 10¹, or 1.2 )
```

The following examples are *not* valid real constants:

```
  1,000,000.       (Embedded commas are illegal.)
       111E3       (A decimal point is required in the mantissa.)
   -12.0E1.5       (Decimal points are not allowed in exponents.)
```

A **real variable** is a variable containing a value of the real data type.

A real value is stored in two parts: the **mantissa** and the **exponent.** The number of bits allocated to the mantissa determines the *precision* of the constant (that is, the number of significant digits to which the constant is known), while the number of bits allocated to the exponent determines the *range* of the constant (that is, the largest and the smallest values that can be represented). For a given word size, the more precise a real number is, the smaller its range is, and vice versa, as described in the previous chapter.

Over the last 15 years, almost all computers have switched to using floating-point numbers that conform to IEEE Standard 754. Examples include all products based on

TABLE 2-2
Precision and range of real numbers on several computers

Computer	Total number of bits	Number of bits in mantissa	Precision in decimal digits	Number of bits in exponent	Exponent range
IEEE 754 (PC, Macintosh, Sun Sparc, etc.)	32 64*	24 53	7 15	8 11	10^{-38} to 10^{38} 10^{-308} to 10^{308}
VAX	32 64*	24 56	7 15	8 8	10^{-38} to 10^{38} 10^{-38} to 10^{38}
Cray	64	49	14	15	10^{-2465} to 10^{2465}

*Indicates optional length

Intel, AMD, Sparc, and PowerPC chips, such as Windows PCs, Apple Macintoshes, and Sun Sparcstations. Table 2-2 shows the precision and the range of typical real constants and variables on IEEE Standard 754 computers, plus a couple of older non-standard computers.

All Fortran 95/2003 compilers support real numbers with more than one length. For example, PC compilers support both 32-bit real numbers and 64-bit real numbers. These different lengths of real numbers are known as different **kinds.** By selecting the proper kind, it is possible to increase the precision and range of a real constant or variable. Fortran 95/2003 has an explicit mechanism for choosing which kind of real is used for a given value. This mechanism is explained in detail in Chapter 11.

2.5.3 Character Constants and Variables

The character data type consists of strings of alphanumeric characters. A **character constant** is a string of characters enclosed in single (') or double (") quotes. The minimum number of characters in a string is 1, while the maximum number of characters in a string varies from compiler to compiler.

The characters between the two single or double quotes are said to be in a **character context.** Any characters representable on a computer are legal in a character context, not just the 86 (97) characters forming the Fortran character set.

The following are valid character constants:

```
'This is a test!'
```
```
'b'
```
(A single blank.)[5]
```
'{^}'
```
(These characters are legal in a character context even though they are not a part of the Fortran character set.)
```
"3.141593"
```
(This is a character string, *not* a number.)

---

[5] In places where the difference matters, the symbol ƀ is used to indicate a blank character, so that the student can tell the difference between a string containing *no* characters (' ') and one containing a single blank character ('ƀ').

2

The following are not valid character constants:

```
This is a test!          (No single or double quotes.)
'This is a test!"        (Mismatched quotes.)
"Try this one.'          (Unbalanced single quotes.)
```

If a character string must include an apostrophe, then that apostrophe may be represented by two consecutive single quotes. For example, the string "Man's best friend" would be written in a character constant as

```
'Man"s best friend'
```

Alternatively, the character string containing a single quote can be surrounded by double quotes. For example, the string "Man's best friend" could be written as

```
"Man"s best friend"
```

Similarly, a character string containing double quotes can be surrounded by single quotes. The character string "Who cares?" could be written in a character constant as

```
'"Who cares?"'
```

Character constants are most often used to print descriptive information, using the WRITE statement. For example, the string 'Result = ' in Figure 2-1 is a valid character constant:

```
WRITE (*,*) 'Result = ', k
```

A **character variable** is a variable containing a value of the character data type.

2.5.4 Default and Explicit Variable Typing

When we look at a constant, it is easy to see whether it is of type INTEGER, REAL, or CHARACTER. If a number does not have a decimal point, it is of type INTEGER; if it has a decimal point, it is of type REAL. If the constant is enclosed in single or double quotes, it is of type CHARACTER. With variables, the situation is not so clear. How do we (or the compiler) know if the variable junk contains an integer, real, or character value?

There are two possible ways in which the type of a variable can be defined: **default typing** and **explicit typing.** If the type of a variable is not explicitly specified in the program, then default typing is used. By default:

> Any variable names beginning with the letters I, J, K, L, M, or N are assumed to be of type INTEGER. Any variable names starting with another letter are assumed to be of type REAL.

Therefore, a variable called incr is assumed to be of type integer by default, while a variable called big is assumed to be of type REAL by default. This default typing convention goes all the way back to the original Fortran I in 1954. Note that no variable names are of type CHARACTER by default, because this data type didn't exist in Fortran I!

The type of a variable may also be explicitly defined in the declaration section at the beginning of a program. The following Fortran statements can be used to specify the type of variables[6]:

```
INTEGER :: var1 [, var2, var3, ...]
REAL ::    var1 [, var2, var3, ...]
```

where the values inside the [] are optional. In this case, the values inside the brackets show that more that two or more variables may be declared on a single line if they are separated by commas.

These nonexecutable statements are called **type declaration statements.** They should be placed after the PROGRAM statement and before the first executable statement in the program, as shown in the example below.

```
PROGRAM example
INTEGER :: day, month, year
REAL :: second
...
(Executable statements follow here...)
```

There are no default names associated with the character data type, so all character variables must be explicitly typed, using the CHARACTER type declaration statement. This statement is a bit more complicated than the previous ones, since character variables may have different lengths. Its form is:

```
CHARACTER(len=<len>) :: var1 [, var2, var3, ...]
```

where <len> is the number of characters in the variables. The (len=<len>) portion of the statement is optional. If only a number appears in the parentheses, then the character variables declared by the statement are of that length. If the parentheses are entirely absent, then the character variables declared by the statement have length 1. For example, the type declaration statements

```
CHARACTER(len=10) :: first, last
CHARACTER :: initial
CHARACTER(15) :: id
```

define two 10-character variables called first and last, a 1-character variable called initial, and a 15-character variable called id.

---

[6] The double colon : : is optional in the above statements for backward compatibility with earlier versions of Fortran. Thus the following two statements are equivalent

```
INTEGER count
INTEGER :: count
```

The form with the double colon is preferred, because the double colons are not optional in more advanced forms of the type specification statement that we will see later.

2.5.5 Keeping Constants Consistent in a Program

It is important to always keep your physical constants consistent throughout a program. For example, do not use the value 3.14 for π at one point in a program, and 3.141593 at another point in the program. Also, you should always write your constants with at least as much precision as your computer will accept. If the real data type on your computer has seven significant digits of precision, then π should be written as 3.141593, *not* as 3.14!

The best way to achieve consistency and precision throughout a program is to *assign a name to a constant, and then to use that name to refer to the constant throughout the program*. If we assign the name PI to the constant 3.141593, then we can refer to PI by name throughout the program, and be certain that we are getting the same value everywhere. Furthermore, assigning meaningful names to constants improves the overall readability of our programs, because a programmer can tell at a glance just what the constant represents.

Named constants are created by using the PARAMETER attribute of a type declaration statement. The form of a type declaration statement with a PARAMETER attribute is

```
type, PARAMETER :: name = value [, name2 = value2, ...]
```

where type is the type of the constant (integer, real, logical, or character), and name is the name assigned to constant value. More than one parameter may be declared on a single line if they are separated by commas. For example, the following statement assigns the name pi to the constant 3.141593.

```
REAL, PARAMETER :: PI = 3.141593
```

If the named constant is of type CHARACTER, then it is not necessary to declare the length of the character string. Since the named constant is being defined on the same line as its type declaration, the Fortran compiler can directly count the number of characters in the string. For example, the following statements declare a named constant error_message to be the 14-character string 'Unknown error!'.

```
CHARACTER, PARAMETER :: ERROR_MESSAGE = 'Unknown error!'
```

In languages such as C, C++, and Java, named constants are written in all capital letters. Many Fortran programmers are also familiar with these languages, and they have adopted the convention of writing named constants in capital letters in Fortran as well. We will follow that practice in this book.

Good Programming Practice

Keep your physical constants consistent and precise throughout a program. To improve the consistency and understandability of your code, assign a name to any important constants, and refer to them by name in the program.

Quiz 2-1

This quiz provides a quick check to see if you have understood the concepts introduced in Section 2.5. If you have trouble with the quiz, reread the section, ask your instructor, or discuss the material with a fellow student. The answers to this quiz are found in the back of the book.

Questions 1 to 12 contain a list of valid and invalid constants. State whether or not each constant is valid. If the constant is valid, specify its type. If it is invalid, say why it is invalid.

1. `10.0`

2. `-100,000`

3. `123E-5`

4. `'That's ok!'`

5. `-32768`

6. `3.14159`

7. `"Who are you?"`

8. `'3.14159'`

9. `'Distance =`

10. `"That's ok!"`

11. `17.877E+6`

12. `13.0^2`

Questions 13 to 16 contain two real constants each. Tell whether or not the two constants represent the same value within the computer:

13. `4650.; 4.65E+3`

14. `-12.71; -1.27E1`

15. `0.0001; 1.0E4`

16. `3.14159E0; 314.159E-3`

Questions 17 and 18 contain a list of valid and invalid Fortran 95/2003 program names. State whether or not each program name is valid. If it is invalid, say why it is invalid.

17. `PROGRAM new_program`

18. `PROGRAM 3rd`

(continued)

2

(*concluded*)

Questions 19 to 23 contain a list of valid and invalid Fortran 95/2003 variable names. State whether or not each variable name is valid. If the variable name is valid, specify its type (assume default typing). If it is invalid, say why it is invalid.

19. `length`

20. `distance`

21. `1problem`

22. `when_does_school_end`

23. `_ok`

Are the following PARAMETER declarations correct or incorrect? If a statement is incorrect, state why it is invalid.

24. `REAL, PARAMETER BEGIN = -30`

25. `CHARACTER, PARAMETER :: NAME = 'Rosa'`

■ 2.6
ASSIGNMENT STATEMENTS AND ARITHMETIC CALCULATIONS

Calculations are specified in Fortran with an **assignment statement,** whose general form is

```
variable_name = expression
```

The assignment statement calculates the value of the expression to the right of the equal sign, and *assigns* that value to the variable named on the left of the equal sign. Note that the equal sign does not mean equality in the usual sense of the word. Instead, it means: *store the value of* expression *into location* variable_name. For this reason, the equal sign is called the **assignment operator.** A statement like

```
i = i + 1
```

is complete nonsense in ordinary algebra, but makes perfect sense in Fortran. In Fortran, it means: take the current value stored in variable i, add one to it, and store the result back into variable i.

The expression to the right of the assignment operator can be any valid combination of constants, variables, parentheses, and arithmetic or logical operators. The standard arithmetic operators included in Fortran are as follows:

+   Addition
-    Subtraction
*   Multiplication
/   Division
**   Exponentiation

Note that the symbols for multiplication (*), division (/), and exponentiation (**) are not the ones used in ordinary mathematical expressions. These special symbols were chosen because they were available in 1950s-era computer character sets, and because they were different from the characters being used in variable names.

The five arithmetic operators described above are **binary operators,** which means that they should occur between and apply to two variables or constants, as shown:

```
a + b
a - b
a ** b
a * b
a / b
```

In addition, the + and - symbols can occur as **unary operators,** which means that they apply to one variable or constant, as shown:

```
+23
-a
```

The following rules apply when you are using Fortran arithmetic operators:

1. No two operators may occur side by side. Thus the expression a * -b is illegal. In Fortran, it must be written as a * (-b). Similarly, a ** -2 is illegal, and should be written as a ** (-2).
2. Implied multiplication is illegal in Fortran. An expression like $x(y + z)$ means that we should add y and z, and then multiply the result by x. The implied multiplication must be written explicitly in Fortran as x * (y + z).
3. Parentheses may be used to group terms whenever desired. When parentheses are used, the expressions inside the parentheses are evaluated before the expressions outside the parentheses. For example, the expression 2 ** ((8+2)/5) is evaluated as shown below

```
2 ** ((8+2)/5) = 2 ** (10/5)
               = 2 ** 2
               = 4
```

2.6.1 Integer Arithmetic

Integer arithmetic is arithmetic involving only integer data. Integer arithmetic always produces an integer result. This is especially important to remember when an expression involves division, since there can be no fractional part in the answer. If the division of two integers is not itself an integer, *the computer automatically truncates the fractional part of the answer.* This behavior can lead to surprising and unexpected answers. For example, integer arithmetic produces the following strange results:

$$\frac{3}{4} = 0 \qquad \frac{4}{4} = 1 \qquad \frac{5}{4} = 1 \qquad \frac{6}{4} = 1$$

$$\frac{7}{4} = 1 \qquad \frac{8}{4} = 2 \qquad \frac{9}{4} = 2$$

2

Because of this behavior, integers should *never* be used to calculate real-world quantities that vary continuously, such as distance, speed, time, etc. They should only be used for things that are intrinsically integer in nature, such as counters and indices.

Programming Pitfalls

Beware of integer arithmetic. Integer division often gives unexpected results.

2.6.2 Real Arithmetic

Real arithmetic (or **floating-point arithmetic**) is arithmetic involving real constants and variables. Real arithmetic always produces a real result that is essentially what we would expect. For example, real arithmetic produces the following results:

$$\frac{3.}{4.}=0.75 \qquad \frac{4.}{4.}=1. \qquad \frac{5.}{4.}=1.25 \qquad \frac{6.}{4.}=1.50$$

$$\frac{7.}{4.}=1.75 \qquad \frac{8.}{4.}=2. \qquad \frac{9.}{4.}=2.25 \qquad \frac{1.}{3.}=0.3333333$$

However, real numbers do have peculiarities of their own. Because of the finite word length of a computer, some real numbers cannot be represented exactly. For example, the number 1/3 is equal to 0.33333333333. . . , but since the numbers stored in the computer have limited precision, the representation of 1/3 in the computer might be 0.3333333. As a result of this limitation in precision, some quantities that are theoretically equal will not be equal when evaluated by the computer. For example, on some computers

$$3. * (1. / 3.) \neq 1.,$$

but

$$2. * (1. / 2.) = 1.$$

Tests for equality must be performed very cautiously when working with real numbers.

Programming Pitfalls

Beware of real arithmetic: Because of limited precision, two theoretically identical expressions often give slightly different results.

2.6.3 Hierarchy of Operations

Often, many arithmetic operations are combined into a single expression. For example, consider the equation for the distance traveled by an object starting from rest and subjected to a constant acceleration:

```
distance = 0.5 * accel * time ** 2
```

There are two multiplications and an exponentiation in this expression. In such an expression, it is important to know the order in which the operations are evaluated. If exponentiation is evaluated before multiplication, this expression is equivalent to

```
distance = 0.5 * accel * (time ** 2)
```

But if multiplication is evaluated before exponentiation, this expression is equivalent to

```
distance = (0.5 * accel * time) ** 2
```

These two equations have different results, and we must be able to unambiguously distinguish between them.

To make the evaluation of expressions unambiguous, Fortran has established a series of rules governing the hierarchy or order in which operations are evaluated within an expression. The Fortran rules generally follow the normal rules of algebra. The order in which the arithmetic operations are evaluated is:

1. The contents of all parentheses are evaluated first, starting from the innermost parentheses and working outward.
2. All exponentials are evaluated, working from right to left.
3. All multiplications and divisions are evaluated, working from left to right.
4. All additions and subtractions are evaluated, working from left to right.

Following these rules, we see that the first of our two possible interpretations is correct—time is squared before the multiplications are performed.

Some people use simple phrases to help them remember the order of operations. For example, try "Please excuse my dear Aunt Sally". The first letters of these words give the order of evaluation: parentheses, exponents, multiplication, division, addition, subtraction.

EXAMPLE 2-1

Variables a, b, c, d, e, f, and g have been initialized to the following values:

$$a = 3. \quad b = 2. \quad c = 5. \quad d = 4. \quad e = 10. \quad f = 2. \quad g = 3.$$

Evaluate the following Fortran assignment statements:

(*a*) `output = a*b+c*d+e/f**g`
(*b*) `output = a*(b+c)*d+(e/f)**g`
(*c*) `output = a*(b+c)*(d+e)/f**g`

2

SOLUTION

(a) Expression to evaluate: output = a*b+c*d+e/f**g
    Fill in numbers: output = 3.*2.+5.*4.+10./2.**3.
    First, evaluate 2.**3.:   output = 3.*2.+5.*4.+10./8.
    Now, evaluate multiplications
    and divisions from left to right: output = 6. +5.*4.+10./8.
                                            output = 6. +20. +10./8.
                                            output = 6. +20. + 1.25
    Now evaluate additions: output = 27.25

(b) Expression to evaluate: output = a* (b+c)*d+(e/f)**g
    Fill in numbers: output = 3.*(2.+5.)*4.+(10./2.)**3.
    First, evaluate parentheses: output = 3.*7.*4.+5.**3.
    Now, evaluate exponents: output = 3.*7.*4.+125.
    Evaluate multiplications and
    divisions from left to right: output = 21.*4.+125.
                                            output = 84. + 125.
    Evaluate additions: output = 209.

(c) Expression to evaluate: output = a*(b+c)*(d+e)/f**g
    Fill in numbers: output = 3.*(2.+5.)*(4.+10.)/2.**3.
    First, evaluate parentheses: output = 3.*7.*14./2.**3.
    Now, evaluate exponents: output = 3.*7.*14./8.
    Evaluate multiplications and
    divisions from left to right: output = 21.*14./8.
                                            output = 294./8.
                                            output = 36.75

As we saw above, the order in which operations are performed has a major effect on the final result of an algebraic expression.

EXAMPLE 2-2 Variables a, b, and c have been initialized to the following values:

a = 3.   b = 2.   c = 3.

Evaluate the following Fortran assignment statements:

(a) output = a**(b**c)
(b) output = (a**b)**c
(c) output = a**b**c

SOLUTION

(a) Expression to evaluate: `output = a**(b**c)`
    Fill in numbers: `output = 3.**(2.**3.)`
    Evaluate expression in parentheses: `output = 3.**8.`
    Evaluate remaining expression: `output = 6561.`

(b) Expression to evaluate: `output = (a**b)**c`
    Fill in numbers: `output = (3.**2.)**3.`
    Evaluate expression in parentheses: `output = 9.**3.`
    Evaluate remaining expression: `output = 729.`

(c) Expression to evaluate: `output = a**b**c`
    Fill in numbers: `output = 3.**2.**3.`
    First, evaluate rightmost exponent: `output = 3.**8.`
    Now, evaluate remaining exponent: `output = 6561.`

The results of (a) and (c) are identical, but the expression in (a) is easier to understand and less ambiguous than the expression in (c).

It is important that every expression in a program be made as clear as possible. Any program of value must not only be written but also be maintained and modified when necessary. You should always ask yourself: "Will I easily understand this expression if I come back to it in 6 months? Can another programmer look at my code and easily understand what I am doing?" If there is any doubt in your mind, use extra parentheses in the expression to make it as clear as possible.

Good Programming Practice
Use parentheses as necessary to make your equations clear and easy to understand.

If parentheses are used within an expression, then the parentheses must be balanced. That is, there must be an equal number of open parentheses and close parentheses within the expression. It is an error to have more of one type than the other. Errors of this sort are usually typographical, and the Fortran compiler catches them. For example, the expression

$$(2. + 4.) / 2.)$$

produces an error during compilation because of the mismatched parentheses.

2.6.4 Mixed-Mode Arithmetic

When an arithmetic operation is performed using two real numbers, its immediate result is of type REAL. Similarly, when an arithmetic operation is performed using two integers, the result is of type INTEGER. In general, arithmetic operations are defined only between numbers of the same type. For example, the addition of two real numbers is a valid operation, and the addition of two integers is a valid operation, but the addition of a real number and an integer is *not* a valid operation. This is true because real numbers and integers are stored in completely different forms in the computer.

What happens if an operation is between a real number and an integer? Expressions containing both real numbers and integers are called **mixed-mode expressions,** and arithmetic involving both real numbers and integers is called *mixed-mode arithmetic.* In the case of an operation between a real number and an integer, the integer is converted by the computer into a real number, and real arithmetic is used on the numbers. The result is of type real. For example, consider the following equations:

Integer expression: $\dfrac{3}{2}$ is evaluated to be 1   (integer result)

Real expression: $\dfrac{3.}{2.}$ is evaluated to be 1.5   (real result)

Mixed-mode expression: $\dfrac{3.}{2}$ is evaluated to be 1.5   (real result)

The rules governing mixed-mode arithmetic can be confusing to beginning programmers, and even experienced programmers may trip up on them from time to time. This is especially true when the mixed-mode expression involves division. Consider the following expressions:

	Expression	Result
1.	1 + 1/4	1
2.	1. + 1/4	1.
3.	1 + 1./4	1.25

Expression 1 contains only integers, so it is evaluated by integer arithmetic. In integer arithmetic, 1/4 = 0, and 1+0 = 1, so the final result is 1 (an integer). Expression 2 is a mixed-mode expression containing both real numbers and integers. However, the first operation to be performed is a division, since division comes before addition in the hierarchy of operations. The division is between integers, so the result is 1/4 = 0. Next comes an addition between a real 1. and an integer 0, so the compiler converts the integer 0 into a real number, and then performs the addition. The resulting number is 1. (a real number). Expression 3 is also a mixed-mode expression containing both real numbers and integers. The first operation to be performed is a division between a real number and an integer, so the compiler converts the integer 4 into a real number, and then performs the division. The result is a real 0.25. The next operation to be performed is an addition between an integer 1 and a real 0.25, so the compiler converts the integer 1 into a real number, and then performs the addition. The resulting number is 1.25 (a real number).

To summarize,

1. An operation between an integer and a real number is called a mixed-mode operation, and an expression containing one or more such operations is called a mixed-mode expression.
2. When a mixed-mode operation is encountered, Fortran converts the integer into a real number, and then performs the operation to get a real result.
3. The automatic mode conversion does not occur until a real number and an integer both appear in the *same* operation. Therefore, it is possible for a portion of an expression to be evaluated in integer arithmetic, followed by another portion evaluated in real arithmetic.

Automatic type conversion also occurs when the variable to which the expression is assigned is of a different type than the result of the expression. For example, consider the following assignment statement:

```
nres = 1.25 + 9 / 4
```

where nres is an integer. The expression to the right of the equal sign evaluates to 3.25, which is a real number. Since nres is an integer, the 3.25 is automatically converted into the integer number 3 before being stored in nres.

Programming Pitfalls

Mixed-mode expressions are dangerous because they are hard to understand and may produce misleading results. Avoid them whenever possible.

Fortran 95/2003 includes five type conversion functions that allow us to explicitly control the conversion between integer and real values. These functions are described in Table 2-3.

The REAL, INT, NINT, CEILING, and FLOOR functions may be used to avoid undesirable mixed-mode expressions by explicitly converting data types from one

TABLE 2-3
Type conversion functions

Function name and arguments	Argument type	Result type	Comments
INT(X)	REAL	INTEGER	Integer part of x (x is truncated)
NINT(X)	REAL	INTEGER	Nearest integer to x (x is rounded)
CEILING(X)	REAL	INTEGER	Nearest integer above or equal to the value of x
FLOOR(X)	REAL	INTEGER	Nearest integer below or equal to the value of x
REAL(I)	INTEGER	REAL	Converts integer value to real

form to another. The REAL function converts an integer into a real number, and the INT, NINT, CEILING, and FLOOR functions convert real numbers into integers. The INT function truncates the real number, while the NINT function rounds it to the nearest integer value. The CEILING function returns the nearest integer greater than or equal to the real number and the FLOOR function returns the nearest integer less than or equal to the real number.

To understand the differences amongst these four functions, let's consider the real numbers 2.9995 and −2.9995. The results of each function with these inputs is shown below:

Function	Result	Description
INT(2.9995)	2	Truncates 2.9995 to 2
NINT(2.9995)	3	Rounds 2.9995 to 3
CEILING(2.9995)	3	Selects nearest integer above 2.9995
FLOOR(2.9995)	2	Selects nearest integer below 2.9995
INT(-2.9995)	−2	Truncates −2.9995 to −2
NINT(-2.9995)	−3	Rounds −2.9995 to −3
CEILING(-2.9995)	−2	Selects nearest integer above −2.9995
FLOOR(-2.9995)	−3	Selects nearest integer below −2.9995

The NINT function is especially useful in converting back from real to integer form, since the small round-off errors occurring in real calculations will not affect the resulting integer value.

2.6.5 Mixed-Mode Arithmetic and Exponentiation

As a general rule, mixed-mode arithmetic operations are undesirable because they are hard to understand and can sometimes lead to unexpected results. However, there is one exception to this rule: exponentiation. For exponentiation, mixed-mode operation is actually *desirable*.

To understand why this is so, consider the assignment statement

$$result = y ** n$$

where result and y are real, and n is an integer. The expression y ** n is shorthand for "use y as a factor n times," and that is exactly what the computer does when it encounters this expression. Since y is a real number and the computer is multiplying y by itself, the computer is really doing real arithmetic and not mixed-mode arithmetic!

Now consider the assignment statement

$$result = y ** x$$

where result, y, and x are real. The expression y ** x is shorthand for "use y as a factor x times," but this time x is not an integer. Instead, x might be a number like 2.5. It is not physically possible to multiply a number by itself 2.5 times, so we have to rely on indirect methods to calculate y ** x in this case. The most common approach is to use the standard algebraic formula that says that

$$y^x = e^{x \ln y} \tag{2-1}$$

Using this equation, we can evaluate y ** x by taking the natural logarithm of y, multiplying by x, and then calculating e to the resulting power. While this technique certainly works, it takes longer to perform and is less accurate than an ordinary series of multiplications. Therefore, if given a choice, we should try to raise real numbers to integer powers instead of real powers.

Good Programming Practice
Use integer exponents instead of real exponents whenever possible.

Also, note that *it is not possible to raise a negative number to a negative real power*. Raising a negative number to an integer power is a perfectly legal operation. For example, (-2.0)**2 = 4. However, raising a negative number to a real power will not work, since the natural logarithm of a negative number is undefined. Therefore, the expression (-2.0)**2.0 will produce a run-time error.

Programming Pitfalls
Never raise a negative number to a real power.

Quiz 2-2

This quiz provides a quick check to see if you have understood the concepts introduced in Section 2.6. If you have trouble with the quiz, reread the section, ask your instructor, or discuss the material with a fellow student. The answers to this quiz are found in the back of the book.

1. In what order are the arithmetic and logical operations evaluated if they appear within an arithmetic expression? How do parentheses modify this order?

2. Are the following expressions legal or illegal? If they are legal, what is their result? If they are illegal, what is wrong with them?

   (*a*) 37 / 3
   (*b*) 37 + 17 / 3

(continued)

(concluded)

    (c) 28 / 3 / 4
    (d) (28 / 3) / 4
    (e) 28 / (3 / 4)
    (f) -3. ** 4. / 2.
    (g) 3. ** (-4. / 2.)
    (h) 4. ** -3

3. Evaluate the following expressions:
    (a) 2 + 5 * 2 - 5
    (b) (2 + 5) * (2 - 5)
    (c) 2 + (5 * 2) - 5
    (d) (2 + 5) * 2 - 5

4. Are the following expressions legal or illegal? If they are legal, what is their result? If they are illegal, what is wrong with them?
    (a) 2. ** 2. ** 3.
    (b) 2. ** (-2.)
    (c) (-2) ** 2
    (d) (-2.) ** (-2.2)
    (e) (-2.) ** NINT(-2.2)
    (f) (-2.) ** FLOOR(-2.2)

5. Are the following statements legal or illegal? If they are legal, what is their result? If they are illegal, what is wrong with them?

```
INTEGER :: i, j
INTEGER, PARAMETER :: K = 4
i = K ** 2
j = i / K
K = i + j
```

6. What value is stored in result after the following statements are executed?

```
REAL :: a, b, c, result
a = 10.
b = 1.5
c = 5.
result = FLOOR(a / b) + b * c ** 2
```

7. What values are stored in a, b, and n after the following statements are executed?

```
REAL :: a, b
INTEGER :: n, i, j
i = 10.
j = 3
n = i / j
a = i / j
b = REAL(i) / j
```

■ 2.7
INTRINSIC FUNCTIONS

In mathematics, a **function** is an expression that accepts one or more input values and calculates a single result from them. Scientific and technical calculations usually require functions that are more complex than the simple addition, subtraction, multiplication, division, and exponentiation operations that we have discussed so far. Some of these functions are very common, and are used in many different technical disciplines. Others are rarer and specific to a single problem or a small number of problems. Examples of very common functions are the trigonometric functions, logarithms, and square roots. Examples of rarer functions include the hyperbolic functions, Bessel functions, and so forth.

The Fortran 95/2003 language has mechanisms to support both the very common functions and the less common functions. Many of the most common ones are built directly into the Fortran language. They are called **intrinsic functions.** Less common functions are not included in the Fortran language, but the user can supply any function needed to solve a particular problem as either an **external function** or an **internal function.** External functions will be described in Chapter 7, and internal functions will be described in Chapter 9.

A Fortran function takes one or more input values, and calculates a *single* output value from them. The input values to the function are known as **arguments;** they appear in parentheses immediately after the function name. The output of a function is a single number, logical value, or character string, which can be used together with other functions, constants, and variables in Fortran expressions. When a function appears in a Fortran statement, the arguments of the function are passed to a separate routine that computes the result of the function, and then the result is used in place of the function in the original calculation (see Figure 2-3). Intrinsic functions are supplied with the Fortran compiler. For external and internal functions, the routine must be supplied by the user.

A list of some common intrinsic functions is given in Table 2-4. A complete list of Fortran 90 and Fortran 95 intrinsic functions is given in Appendix B, along with a brief description of each one.

Fortran functions are used by naming them in an expression. For example, the intrinsic function SIN can be used to calculate the sine of a number as follows:

$$y = SIN(theta)$$

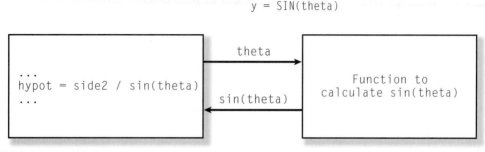

FIGURE 2-3
When a function is included in a Fortran statement, the argument(s) of the function are passed to a separate routine, which computes the result of the function, and then the result is used in place of the function in the original calculation.

TABLE 2-4
Some common intrinsic functions

Function name and arguments	Function value	Argument type	Result type	Comments
SQRT(X)	$\sqrt{x}$	R	R	Square root of x for $x \geq 0$
ABS(X)		R / I	*	Absolute value of x
ACHAR(I)		I	CHAR(1)	Returns the character at position I in the ASCII collating sequence.
SIN(X)	$\sin(x)$	R	R	Sine of x (x must be in *radians*)
COS(X)	$\cos(x)$	R	R	Cosine of x (x must be in *radians*)
TAN(X)	$\tan(x)$	R	R	Tangent of x (x must be in *radians*)
EXP(X)	e^x	R	R	e raised to the xth power
LOG(X)	$\log_e(x)$	R	R	Natural logarithm of x for $x > 0$
LOG10(X)	$\log_{10}(x)$	R	R	Base-10 logarithm of x for $x > 0$
IACHAR(C)		CHAR(1)	I	Returns the position of the character C in the ASCII collating sequence.
MOD(A,B)		R / I	*	Remainder or Modulo function
MAX(A,B)		R / I	*	Picks the larger of a and b
MIN(A,B)		R / I	*	Picks the smaller of a and b
ASIN(X)	$\sin^{-1}(x)$	R	R	Inverse sine of x for $-1 \leq x \leq 1$ (results in *radians*)
ACOS(X)	$\cos^{-1}(x)$	R	R	Inverse cosine of x for $-1 \leq x \leq 1$ (results in *radians*)
ATAN(X)	$\tan^{-1}(x)$	R	R	Inverse tangent of x (results in *radians*)

Notes:
  * = Result is of the same type as the input argument(s).
  R = REAL, I = INTEGER, CHAR(1) = CHARACTER(len = 1)

where theta is the argument of the function SIN. After this statement is executed, the variable y contains the sine of the value stored in variable theta. Note from Table 2-4 that the trigonometric functions expect their arguments to be in radians. If the variable theta is in degrees, then we must convert degrees to radians ($180° = \pi$ radians) before computing the sine. This conversion can be done in the same statement as the sine calculation:

```
y = SIN (theta*(3.141593/180.))
```

Alternatively, we could create a named constant containing the conversion factor, and refer to that constant when the function is executed:

```
INTEGER, PARAMETER :: DEG_2_RAD = 3.141593 / 180.
...
y = SIN (theta * DEG_TO_RAD)
```

The argument of a function can be a constant, a variable, an expression, or even the result of another function. All of the following statements are legal:

```
y = SIN(3.141593)          (argument is a constant)
y = SIN(x)                 (argument is a variable)
y = SIN(PI*x)              (argument is an expression)
y = SIN(SQRT(x))           (argument is the result of another function)
```

Functions may be used in expressions anywhere that a constant or variable may be used. However, functions may never appear on the left side of the assignment operator (equal sign), since they are not memory locations, and nothing can be stored in them.

The type of argument required by a function and the type of value returned by it are specified in Table 2-4 for the intrinsic functions listed there. Some of these intrinsic functions are **generic functions,** which means that they can use more than one type of input data. The absolute value function ABS is a generic function. If X is a real number, then the type of ABS(X) is real. If X is an integer, then the type of ABS(X) is integer. Some functions are called **specific functions,** because they can use only one specific type of input data, and produce only one specific type of output value. For example, the function IABS requires an integer argument and returns an integer result. A complete list of all intrinsic functions (both generic and specific) is provided in Appendix B.

2.8

LIST-DIRECTED INPUT AND OUTPUT STATEMENTS

An **input statement** reads one or more values from an input device and stores them into variables specified by the programmer. The input device could be a keyboard in an interactive environment, or an input disk file in a batch environment. An **output statement** writes one or more values to an output device. The output device could be a display screen in an interactive environment, or an output listing file in a batch environment.

We have already seen input and output statements in my_first_program, which is shown in Figure 2-1. The input statement in the figure was of the form

```
READ (*,*) input_list
```

where input_list is the list of variables into which the values being read are placed. If there is more than one variable in the list, they should be separated by commas. The parentheses (*,*) in the statement contain control information for the read. The first field in the parentheses specifies the *input/output unit* (or io unit) from which the data is to be read (the concept of an input/output unit will be explained in Chapter 5). An asterisk in this field means that the data is to be read from the standard input device for the computer—usually the keyboard when running in interactive mode. The second field in the parentheses specifies the format in which the data is to be read (formats will also be explained in Chapter 5). An asterisk in this field means that list-directed input (sometimes called free-format input) is to be used.

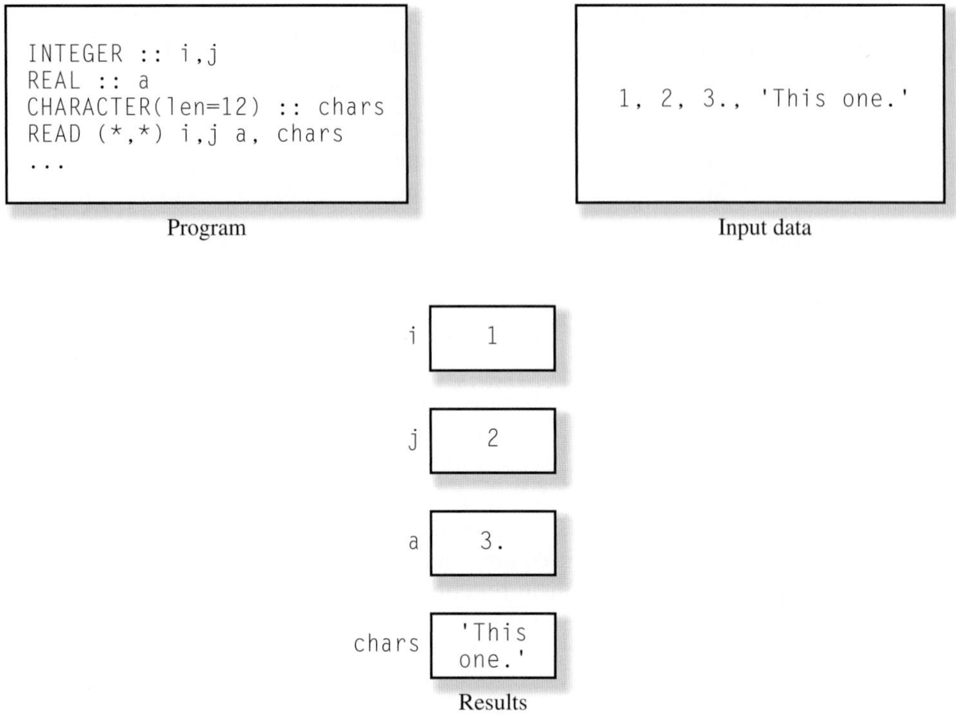

2

```
INTEGER :: i,j
REAL :: a
CHARACTER(len=12) :: chars
READ (*,*) i,j a, chars
...
```

Program

```
1, 2, 3., 'This one.'
```

Input data

i | 1

j | 2

a | 3.

chars | 'This one.'

Results

FIGURE 2-4
For list-directed input, the type and order of the input data values must match the type and order of the supplied input data.

The term **list-directed input** means that *the types of the variables in the variable list determine the required format of the input data* (Figure 2-4). For example, consider the following statements:

```
PROGRAM input_example
INTEGER :: i, j
REAL :: a
CHARACTER(len=12) :: chars
READ (*,*) i, j, a, chars
END PROGRAM input_example
```

The input data supplied to the program must consist of two integers, a real number, and a character string. Furthermore, they must be in that order. The values may be all on one line separated by commas or blanks, or they may be on separate lines. The list-directed READ statement will continue to read input data until values have been found for all of the variables in the list. If the input data supplied to the program at execution time is

```
1, 2, 3.,'This one.'
```

then the variable i will be filled with a 1, j will be filled with a 2, a will be filled with a 3.0, and chars will be filled with 'This one.   '. Since the input character string is only 9 characters long, while the variable chars has room for 12 characters, the string is *left justified* in the character variable, and three blanks are automatically added at the end of it to fill out the remaining space. Also note that for list-directed reads, input character strings must be enclosed in single or double quotes if they contain spaces.

When you are using list-directed input, the values to be read must match the variables in the input list both in order and type. If the input data had been

```
1, 2, 'This one.', 3.
```

then a run-time error would have occurred when the program tried to read the data.

Each READ statement in a program begins reading from a new line of input data. If any data was left over on the previous input line, that data is discarded. For example, consider the following program:

```
PROGRAM input_example_2
INTEGER :: i, j, k, l
READ (*,*) i, j
READ (*,*) k, l
END PROGRAM input_example_2
```

If the input data to this program is:

```
1, 2, 3, 4
5, 6, 7, 8
```

then after the READ statements, i will contain a 1, j will contain a 2, k will contain a 5, and l will contain a 6 (Figure 2-5).

It is a good idea to always *echo* any value that you read into a program from a keyboard. Echoing a value means displaying the value with a WRITE statement after it has been read. If you do not do so, a typing error in the input data might cause a wrong answer, and the user of the program would never know that anything was wrong. You may echo the data either immediately after it is read or somewhere further down in the program output, but *every input variable should be echoed somewhere in the program's output*.

Good Programming Practice

Echo any variables that a user enters into a program from a keyboard, so that the user can be certain that they were typed and processed correctly.

The *list-directed output statement* is of the form

```
WRITE (*,*) output_list
```

where *output_list* is the list of data items (variables, constants, or expressions) that are to be written. If there is more than one item in the list, then the items should be separated by commas. The parentheses (*,*) in the statement contain control

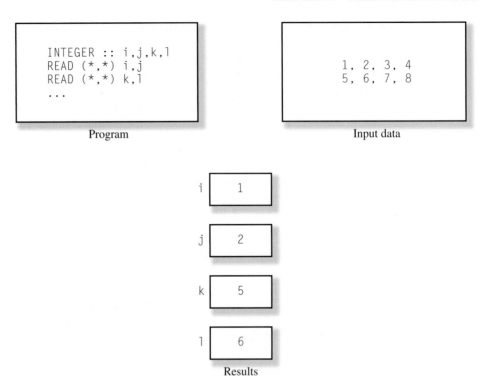

Program

Input data

```
INTEGER :: i,j,k,l
READ (*,*) i,j
READ (*,*) k,l
...
```

```
1, 2, 3, 4
5, 6, 7, 8
```

i   1

j   2

k   5

l   6

Results

FIGURE 2-5
Each list-directed READ statement begins reading from a new line of input data, and any unused
data left on the previous line is discarded. Here, the values 3 and 4 on the first line of input
data are never used.

information for the write, where the two asterisks have the same meaning as for a list-
directed read statement.[7]

The term **list-directed output** means that *the types of the values in the output list
of the write statement determine the format of the output data*. For example, consider
the following statements:

```
PROGRAM output_example
INTEGER :: ix
REAL :: theta
ix = 1
test = .TRUE.
theta = 3.141593
WRITE (*,*) ' IX =              ', ix
```

---

[7] There is another form of list-directed output statement:

```
PRINT *, output_list
```

This statement is equivalent to the list-directed WRITE statement discussed above, and is used by some
programmers. The PRINT statement is never used in this book, but it is discussed in Chapter 14 Section
14.3.7.

```
                    WRITE (*,*) ' THETA =              ', theta
                    WRITE (*,*) ' COS(THETA) =         ', COS(theta)
                    WRITE (*,*) REAL(ix), NINT(theta)
                    END PROGRAM output_example
```

The output resulting from these statements is:

```
                    IX =                      1
                    THETA =                   3.141593
                    COS(THETA) =             -1.000000
                          1.000000            3
```

This example illustrates several points about the list-directed write statement:

1. The output list may contain constants (' IX = ' is a constant), variables, functions, and expressions. In each case, the value of the constant, variable, function, or expression is output to the standard output device.
2. The format of the output data matches the type of the value being output. For example, even though theta is of type real, NINT(theta) is of type integer. Therefore, the fourth write statement produces an output of 3 (the nearest integer to 3.141593).
3. The output of list-directed write statements is not very pretty. The values printed out do not line up in neat columns, and there is no way to control the number of significant digits displayed for real numbers. We will learn how to produce neatly formatted output in Chapter 5.

Quiz 2-3

This quiz provides a quick check to see if you have understood the concepts introduced in Sections 2.7 and 2.8. If you have trouble with the quiz, reread the sections, ask your instructor, or discuss the material with a fellow student. The answers to this quiz are found in the back of the book.

Convert the following algebraic equations into Fortran assignment statements:

1. The equivalent resistance R_{eq} of four resistors R_1, R_2, R_3, and R_4 connected in series:

$$R_{eq} = R_1 + R_2 + R_3 + R_4$$

2. The equivalent resistance R_{eq} of four resistors R_1, R_2, R_3, and R_4 connected in parallel:

$$R_{eq} = \frac{1}{\dfrac{1}{R_1} + \dfrac{1}{R_2} + \dfrac{1}{R_3} + \dfrac{1}{R_4}}$$

(continued)

2

(*continued*)

   3. The period *T* of an oscillating pendulum:

$$T = 2\pi \sqrt{\frac{L}{g}}$$

      where *L* is the length of the pendulum and *g* is the acceleration due to gravity.

   4. The equation for damped sinusoidal oscillation:

$$v(t) = V_M e^{-\alpha t} \cos \omega t$$

      where V_M is the maximum value of the oscillation, α is the exponential damping factor, and ω is the angular velocity of the oscillation.

Convert the following Fortran assignment statements into algebraic equations:

   5. The motion of an object in a constant gravitational field:

```
distance = 0.5 * accel * t**2 + vel_0 * t + pos_0
```

   6. The oscillating frequency of a damped *RLC* circuit:

```
freq = 1. / (2. * PI * SQRT(1 * c))
```

      where `PI` is the constant π (3.141592 . . .).

   7. Energy storage in an inductor:

```
energy = 1.0 / 2.0 * inductance * current**2
```

   8. What values will be printed out when the following statements are executed?

```
PROGRAM quiz_1
INTEGER :: i
REAL :: a
a = 0.05
i = NINT( 2. * 3.141493 / a )
a = a * (5 / 3)
WRITE (*,*) i, a
END PROGRAM quiz_1
```

   9. If the input data is as shown, what will be printed out by the following program?

```
PROGRAM quiz_2
INTEGER :: i, j, k
```

(*continued*)

(concluded)

```
                    REAL :: a, b, c
                    READ (*,*) i, j, a
                    READ (*,*) b, k
                    c = SIN ((3.141593 / 180) * a)
                    WRITE (*,*) i, j, k, a, b, c
                    END PROGRAM quiz_2
```

The input data is :

```
                    1, 3
                    2., 45., 17.
                    30., 180, 6.
```

■ 2.9

INITIALIZATION OF VARIABLES

Consider the following program:

```
                    PROGRAM init
                    INTEGER :: i
                    WRITE (*,*) i
                    END PROGRAM init
```

What is the value stored in the variable i ? What will be printed out by the WRITE statement? The answer is: We don't know!

The variable i is an example of an **uninitialized variable.** It has been defined by the INTEGER :: i statement, but no value has been placed into it yet. The value of an uninitialized variable is not defined by the Fortran 95/2003 standard. Some compilers automatically set uninitialized variables to zero, and some set them to different arbitrary patterns. Some compilers for older version of Fortran leave whatever values previously existed at the memory location of the variables. Some compilers even produce a run-time error if a variable is used without first being initialized.

Uninitialized variables can present a serious problem. Since they are handled differently on different machines, a program that works fine on one computer may fail when transported to another one. On some machines, the same program could work sometimes and fail sometimes, depending on the data left behind by the previous program occupying the same memory. Such a situation is totally unacceptable, and we must avoid it by always initializing all of the variables in our programs.

Good Programming Practice

Always initialize all variables in a program before using them.

2

There are three techniques available to initialize variables in a Fortran program: assignment statements, READ statements, and initialization in type declaration statements.[8] An assignment statement assigns the value of the expression to the right of the equal sign to the variable on the left of the equal sign. In the following code, the variable i is initialized to 1, and we know that a 1 will be printed out by the WRITE statement.

```
PROGRAM init_1
INTEGER :: i
i = 1
WRITE (*,*) i
END PROGRAM init_1
```

A READ statement may be used to initialize variables with values input by the user. Unlike initialization with assignment statements, the user can change the value stored in the variable each time the program is run. For example, the following code will initialize variable i with whatever value the user desires, and that value will be printed out by the WRITE statement.

```
PROGRAM init_2
INTEGER :: i
READ (*,*) i
WRITE (*,*) i
END PROGRAM init_2
```

The third technique available to initialize variables in a Fortran program is to specify their initial values in the type declaration statement that defines them. This declaration specifies that *a value should be preloaded into a variable during the compilation and linking process*. Note the fundamental difference between initialization in a type declaration statement and initialization in an assignment statement: A type declaration statement initializes the variable before the program begins to run, while an assignment statement initializes the variable during execution.

The form of a type declaration statement used to initialize variables is

```
type :: var1 = value, [var2 = value, ... ]
```

Any number of variables may be declared and initialized in a single type declaration statement, provided that they are separated by commas. An example of type declaration statements used to initialize a series of variables is

```
REAL :: time = 0.0, distance = 5128.
INTEGER :: loop = 10
```

Before program execution, time is initialized to 0.0, distance is initialized to 5128., and loop is initialized to 10.

---

[8] A fourth, older, technique uses the DATA statement. This statement is kept for backward compatibility with earlier versions of Fortran, but it has been superseded by initialization in type declaration statements. DATA statements should not be used in new programs. The DATA statement is described in Chapter 17.

In the following code, the variable i is initialized by the type declaration statement, so we know that when execution starts, the variable i will contain the value 1. Therefore, the WRITE statement will print out a 1.

```
PROGRAM init_3
INTEGER :: i = 1
WRITE (*,*) i
END PROGRAM init_3
```

2.10
THE IMPLICIT NONE STATEMENT

There is another very important nonexecutable statement: the IMPLICIT NONE statement. When it is used, the IMPLICIT NONE statement disables the default typing provisions of Fortran. When the IMPLICIT NONE statement is included in a program, *any variable that does not appear in an explicit type declaration statement is considered an error*. The IMPLICIT NONE statement should appear after the PROGRAM statement and before any type declaration statements.

When the IMPLICIT NONE statement is included in a program, the programmer must explicitly declare the type of every variable in the program. On first thought, this might seem to be a disadvantage, since the programmer must do more work when he or she first writes a program. This initial impression couldn't be more wrong. In fact, there are several advantages to using this statement.

A majority of programming errors are simple typographical errors. The IMPLICIT NONE statement catches these errors at compilation time, before they can produce subtle errors during execution. For example, consider the following simple program:

```
PROGRAM test_1
REAL :: time = 10.0
WRITE (*,*) 'Time = ', tmie
END PROGRAM test_1
```

In this program, the variable time is misspelled tmie at one point. When this program is compiled with the Compaq Visual Fortran compiler and executed, the output is "Time = 0.000000E+00", which is the wrong answer! In contrast, consider the same program with the IMPLICIT NONE statement present:

```
PROGRAM test_1
IMPLICIT NONE
REAL :: time = 10.0
WRITE (*,*) 'Time = ', tmie
END PROGRAM test_1
```

When compiled with the same compiler, this program produces the following compile-time error:

Source Listing   22-Dec-2005 11:19:53 Compaq Visual Fortran 6.6-4088 Page 1

```
          22-Dec-2005 11:19:47 test1.f90

          1 PROGRAM test_1
          2 IMPLICIT NONE
          3 REAL :: time = 10.0
          4 WRITE (*,*) 'Time = ', tmie
            .....................1
(1) Error: This name does not have a type, and must have an explicit type. [TMIE]


          5 END PROGRAM test_1
```

Instead of having a wrong answer in an otherwise working program, we have an explicit error message flagging the problem at compilation time. This is an enormous advantage in working with longer programs containing many variables.

Another advantage of the IMPLICIT NONE statement is that it makes the code more maintainable. Any program using the statement must have a complete list of all variables included in the declaration section of the program. If the program must be modified, a programmer can check the list to avoid using variable names that are already defined in the program. This checking helps to eliminate a very common error, in which the modifications to the program inadvertently change the values of some variables used elsewhere in the program.

In general, the use of the IMPLICIT NONE statement becomes more and more advantageous as the size of a programming project increases. The use of IMPLICIT NONE is so important to the designing of good programs that we will use it consistently everywhere throughout this book.

Good Programming Practice

Always explicitly define every variable in your programs, and use the IMPLICIT NONE statement to help you spot and correct typographical errors before they become program execution errors.

2.11
PROGRAM EXAMPLES

In Chapter 2, we have presented the fundamental concepts required to write simple but functional Fortran programs. We will now present a few example problems in which these concepts are used.

EXAMPLE 2-3   *Temperature Conversion:*

Design a Fortran program that reads an input temperature in degrees Fahrenheit, converts it to an absolute temperature in kelvins, and writes out the result.

SOLUTION

The relationship between temperature in degrees Fahrenheit (°F) and temperature in kelvins (K) can be found in any physics textbook. It is

$$T \text{ (in kelvins)} = \left[\frac{5}{9} T \text{ (in °F)} - 32.0 \right] + 273.15 \qquad (2\text{-}2)$$

The physics books also give us sample values on both temperature scales, which we can use to check the operation of our program. Two such values are:

The boiling point of water	212° F	373.15 K
The sublimation point of dry ice	-110° F	194.26 K

Our program must perform the following steps:

1. Prompt the user to enter an input temperature in °F.
2. Read the input temperature.
3. Calculate the temperature in kelvins from Equation (2-2).
4. Write out the result, and stop.

The resulting program is shown in Figure 2-6.

FIGURE 2-6
Program to convert degrees Fahrenheit into kelvins.

```
PROGRAM temp_conversion
!  Purpose:
!    To convert an input temperature from degrees Fahrenheit to
!    an output temperature in kelvins.
!
!  Record of revisions:
!      Date          Programmer            Description of change
!      ====          ==========            =====================
!    11/03/06 -- S. J. Chapman             Original code
!
IMPLICIT NONE          ! Force explicit declaration of variables

! Data dictionary: declare variable types, definitions, & units
REAL :: temp_f         ! Temperature in degrees Fahrenheit
REAL :: temp_k         ! Temperature in kelvins

! Prompt the user for the input temperature.
WRITE (*,*) 'Enter the temperature in degrees Fahrenheit: '
READ  (*,*) temp_f

! Convert to kelvins.
temp_k = (5. / 9.) * (temp_f - 32.) + 273.15

! Write out the result.
WRITE (*,*) temp_f, ' degrees Fahrenheit = ', temp_k, ' kelvins'

! Finish up.
END PROGRAM temp_conversion
```

2

To test the completed program, we will run it with the known input values given above. Note that user inputs appear in boldface below.[9]

```
C:\book\chap2>temp_conversion
Enter the temperature in degrees Fahrenheit:
212
      212.000000 degrees Fahrenheit  =   373.150000 kelvins

C:\book\chap2>temp_conversion
Enter the temperature in degrees Fahrenheit:
-110
      -110.000000 degrees Fahrenheit =   194.261100 kelvins
```

The results of the program match the values from the physics book.

In the above program, we echoed the input values and printed the output values together with their units. The results of this program make sense only if the units (degrees Fahrenheit and kelvins) are included together with their values. As a general rule, the units associated with any input value should always be printed along with the prompt that requests the value, and the units associated with any output value should always be printed along with that value.

Good Programming Practice
Always include the appropriate units with any values that you read or write in a program.

The above program exhibits many of the good programming practices that we have described in this chapter. It uses the IMPLICIT NONE statement to force the explicit typing of all variables in the program. It includes a data dictionary as a part of the declaration section, with each variable being given a type, definition, and units. It also uses descriptive variable names. The variable temp_f is initialized by a READ statement before it is used. All input values are echoed, and appropriate units are attached to all printed values.

EXAMPLE
2-4

Electrical Engineering: Calculating Real, Reactive, and Apparent Power:

Figure 2-7 shows a sinusoidal AC voltage source with voltage V supplying a load of impedance $Z \angle \theta \ \Omega$. From simple circuit theory, the rms current I, the real power P,

---

[9] Fortran programs such as this are normally executed from a **command line.** In Windows, a Command Window can be opened by clicking the Start button, selecting the Run option, and typing "cmd" as the program to start. When the Command Window is running, the prompt shows the name of the current working directory (C:\book\chap2 in this example), and a program is executed by typing its name on the command line. Note that the prompt would look different on other operating systems such as Linux or Unix.

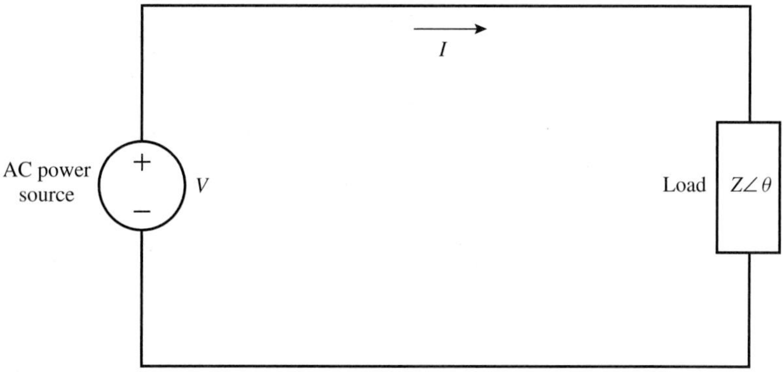

FIGURE 2-7
A sinusoidal AC voltage source with voltage V supplying a load of impedance $Z\angle\ \theta\ \Omega$.

reactive power Q, apparent power S, and power factor PF supplied to the load are given by the equations

$$I = \frac{V}{Z} \tag{2-3}$$

$$P = VI \cos\theta \tag{2-4}$$

$$Q = VI \sin\theta \tag{2-5}$$

$$S = VI \tag{2-6}$$

$$\text{PF} = \cos\theta \tag{2-7}$$

where V is the rms voltage of the power source in units of volts (V). The units of current are amperes (A), of real power are watts (W), of reactive power are volt-amperes-reactive (VAR), and of apparent power are volt-amperes (VA). The power factor has no units associated with it.

Given the rms voltage of the power source and the magnitude and angle of the impedance Z, write a program that calculates the rms current I, the real power P, reactive power Q, apparent power S, and power factor PF of the load.

SOLUTION
In this program, we need to read in the rms voltage V of the voltage source and the magnitude Z and angle θ of the impedance. The input voltage source will be measured in volts, the magnitude of the impedance Z in ohms, and the angle of the impedance θ in degrees. Once the data is read, we must convert the angle θ into radians for use with the Fortran trigonometric functions. Next, the desired values must be calculated, and the results must be printed out.

The program must perform the following steps:

1. Prompt the user to enter the source voltage in volts.
2. Read the source voltage.
3. Prompt the user to enter the magnitude and angle of the impedance in ohms and degrees.
4. Read the magnitude and angle of the impedance.
5. Calculate the current I from Equation (2-3).
6. Calculate the real power P from Equation (2-4).
7. Calculate the reactive power Q from Equation (2-5).
8. Calculate the apparent power S from Equation (2-6).
9. Calculate the power factor PF from Equation (2-7).
10. Write out the results, and stop.

The final Fortran program is shown in Figure 2-8.

FIGURE 2-8
Program to calculate the real power, reactive power, apparent power, and power factor supplied to a load.

```
PROGRAM power
!
!  Purpose:
!    To calculate the current, real, reactive, and apparent power,
!    and the power factor supplied to a load.
!
!  Record of revisions:
!     Date        Programmer           Description of change
!     ====        ==========           =====================
!   11/03/06    S. J. Chapman          Original code
!

IMPLICIT NONE

! Data dictionary: declare constants
REAL,PARAMETER :: DEG_2_RAD = 0.01745329 ! Deg to radians factor

! Data dictionary: declare variable types, definitions, & units
REAL :: amps            ! Current in the load (A)
REAL :: p               ! Real power of load (W)
REAL :: pf              ! Power factor of load (no units)
REAL :: q               ! Reactive power of the load (VAR)
REAL :: s               ! Apparent power of the load (VA)
REAL :: theta           ! Impedance angle of the load (deg)
REAL :: volts           ! Rms voltage of the power source (V)
REAL :: z               ! Magnitude of the load impedance (ohms)

! Prompt the user for the rms voltage.
WRITE (*,*) 'Enter the rms voltage of the source: '
READ  (*,*) volts
```

                                                                    (*continued*)

(concluded)

```
! Prompt the user for the magnitude and angle of the impedance.
WRITE (*,*) 'Enter the magnitude and angle of the impedance '
WRITE (*,*) 'in ohms and degrees: '
READ  (*,*) z, theta

! Perform calculations
amps = volts / z                         ! Rms current
p = volts * amps * cos (theta * DEG_2_RAD)  ! Real power
q = volts * amps * sin (theta * DEG_2_RAD)  ! Reactive power
s = volts * amps                         ! Apparent power
pf = cos ( theta * DEG_2_RAD)            ! Power factor

! Write out the results.
WRITE (*,*) 'Voltage         = ', volts, ' volts'
WRITE (*,*) 'Impedance       = ', z, ' ohms at ', theta,' degrees'
WRITE (*,*) 'Current         = ', amps, ' amps'
WRITE (*,*) 'Real Power      = ', p, ' watts'
WRITE (*,*) 'Reactive Power  = ', q, ' VAR'
WRITE (*,*) 'Apparent Power  = ', s, ' VA'
WRITE (*,*) 'Power Factor    = ', pf

! Finish up.
END PROGRAM power
```

This program also exhibits many of the good programming practices that we have described. It uses the IMPLICIT NONE statement to force the explicit typing of all variables in the program. It includes a variable dictionary defining the uses of all of the variables in the program. It also uses descriptive variable names (although the variable names are short, *P, Q,* S, and *PF* are the standard accepted abbreviations for the corresponding quantities). All variables are initialized before they are used. The program defines a named constant for the degrees-to-radians conversion factor, and then uses that name everywhere throughout the program when the conversion factor is required. All input values are echoed, and appropriate units are attached to all printed values.

To verify the operation of program power, we will do a sample calculation by hand and compare the results with the output of the program. If the rms voltage *V* is 120 V, the magnitude of the impedance *Z* is 5 Ω, and the angle θ is 30°, then the values are

$$I = \frac{V}{Z} = \frac{120 \text{ V}}{5\Omega} = 24 \text{ A} \tag{2-3}$$

$$P = VI \cos \theta = (120 \text{ V})(24 \text{ A}) \cos 30° = 2494 \text{ W} \tag{2-4}$$

$$Q = VI \sin \theta = (120 \text{ V})(24 \text{ A}) \sin 30° = 1440 \text{ VAR} \tag{2-5}$$

$$S = VI = (120 \text{ V})(24 \text{ A}) = 2880 \text{ VA} \tag{2-6}$$

$$PF = \cos \theta = \cos 30° = 0.86603 \tag{2-7}$$

When we run program power with the specified input data, the results are identical with our hand calculations:

```
C:\book\chap2>power
Enter the rms voltage of the source:
120
Enter the magnitude and angle of the impedance
in ohms and degrees:
5., 30.
Voltage          =      120.000000 volts
Impedance        =        5.000000 ohms at     30.000000 degrees
Current          =       24.000000 amps
Real Power       =     2494.153000 watts
Reactive Power   =     1440.000000 VAR
Apparent Power   =     2880.000000 VA
Power Factor     =     8.660254E-01
```

EXAMPLE   *Carbon 14 Dating:*
2-5   A radioactive isotope of an element is a form of the element that is not stable. Instead, it spontaneously decays into another element over a period of time. Radioactive decay is an exponential process. If Q_0 is the initial quantity of a radioactive substance at time $t = 0$, then the amount of that substance that will be present at any time t in the future is given by

$$Q(t) = Q_0 e^{-\lambda t} \tag{2-8}$$

where λ is the radioactive decay constant (see Figure 2-9).

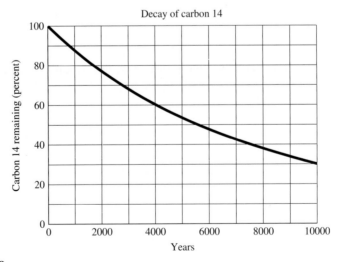

FIGURE 2-9
The radioactive decay of carbon 14 as a function of time. Notice that 50 percent of the original carbon 14 is left after about 5730 years have elapsed.

Because radioactive decay occurs at a known rate, it can be used as a clock to measure the time since the decay started. If we know the initial amount of the radioactive material Q_0 present in a sample, and the amount of the material Q left at the current time, we can solve for t in Equation (2-8) to determine how long the decay has been going on. The resulting equation is

$$t_{decay} = -\frac{1}{\lambda} \log \frac{Q}{Q_0} \qquad (2\text{-}9)$$

Equation (2-9) has practical applications in many areas of science. For example, archaeologists use a radioactive clock based on carbon 14 to determine the time that has passed since a once-living thing died. Carbon 14 is continually taken into the body while a plant or animal is living, so the amount of it present in the body at the time of death is assumed to be known. The decay constant λ of carbon 14 is well known to be 0.00012097/year, so if the amount of carbon 14 remaining now can be accurately measured, then Equation (2-9) can be used to determine how long ago the living thing died.

Write a program that reads the percentage of carbon 14 remaining in a sample, calculates the age of the sample from it, and prints out the result with proper units.

SOLUTION
Our program must perform the following steps:

1. Prompt the user to enter the percentage of carbon 14 remaining in the sample.
2. Read in the percentage.
3. Convert the percentage into the fraction Q/Q_0.
4. Calculate the age of the sample in years, using Equation (2-9).
5. Write out the result, and stop.

The resulting code is shown in Figure 2-10.

FIGURE 2-10
Program to calculate the age of a sample from the percentage of carbon 14 remaining in it.

```
PROGRAM c14_date
!
!   Purpose:
!     To calculate the age of an organic sample from the percentage
!     of the original carbon 14 remaining in the sample.
!
!   Record of revisions:
!       Date         Programmer           Description of change
!       ====         ==========           =====================
!     11/03/06      S. J. Chapman         Original code
!
IMPLICIT NONE

! Data dictionary: declare constants
REAL,PARAMETER :: LAMDA = 0.00012097 ! The radioactive decay
```

(continued)

2

(concluded)

```
                                       ! constant of carbon 14,
                                       ! in units of 1/years.

! Data dictionary: declare variable types, definitions, & units
REAL :: age        ! The age of the sample (years)
REAL :: percent    ! The percentage of carbon 14 remaining at the time
                   ! of the measurement (%)
REAL :: ratio      ! The ratio of the carbon 14 remaining at the time
                   ! of the measurement to the original amount of
                   ! carbon 14 (no units)

! Prompt the user for the percentage of C-14 remaining.
WRITE (*,*) 'Enter the percentage of carbon 14 remaining:'
READ  (*,*) percent

! Echo the user's input value.
WRITE (*,*) 'The remaining carbon 14 = ', percent, ' %.'

! Perform calculations
ratio = percent / 100.            ! Convert to fractional ratio
age = (-1.0 / LAMDA) * log(ratio) ! Get age in years

! Tell the user about the age of the sample.
WRITE (*,*) 'The age of the sample is  ', age, ' years.'

! Finish up.
END PROGRAM c14_date
```

To test the completed program, we will calculate the time it takes for half of the carbon 14 to disappear. This time is known as the *half-life* of carbon 14.

```
C:\book\chap2>c14_date
Enter the percentage of carbon 14 remaining:
50.
The remaining carbon 14 =      50.000000 %.
The age of the sample is    5729.910000 years.
```

The *CRC Handbook of Chemistry and Physics* states that the half-life of carbon 14 is 5730 years, so output of the program agrees with the reference book.

2.12

DEBUGGING FORTRAN PROGRAMS

There is an old saying that the only sure things in life are death and taxes. We can add one more certainty to that list: If you write a program of any significant size, it won't work the first time you try it! Errors in programs are known as **bugs,** and the process of locating and eliminating them is known as **debugging.** Given that we have written a program and it is not working, how do we debug it?

Three types of errors are found in Fortran programs. The first type of error is a **syntax error.** Syntax errors are errors in the Fortran statement itself, such as spelling errors or punctuation errors. These errors are detected by the compiler during

2

compilation. The second type of error is the **run-time error.** A run-time error occurs when an illegal mathematical operation is attempted during program execution (for example, attempting to divide by 0). These errors cause the program to abort during execution. The third type of error is a **logical error.** Logical errors occur when the program compiles and runs successfully but produces the wrong answer.

The most common mistakes made during programming are *typographical errors*. Some typographical errors create invalid Fortran statements. These errors produce syntax errors, which are caught by the compiler. Other typographical errors occur in variable names. For example, the letters in some variable names might have been transposed. If you have used the IMPLICIT NONE statement, then the compiler will also catch most of these errors. However, if one legal variable name is substituted for another legal variable name, the compiler cannot detect the error. This sort of substitution might occur if you have two similar variable names. For example, if variables vel1 and vel2 are both used for velocities in the program, then one of them might be inadvertently used instead of the other one at some point. This sort of typographical error will produce a logical error. You must check for that sort of error by manually inspecting the code, since the compiler cannot catch it.

Sometimes is it possible to successfully compile and link the program, but there are run-time errors or logical errors when the program is executed. In this case, there is either something wrong with the input data or something wrong with the logical structure of the program. The first step in locating this sort of bug should be to *check the input data to the program*. Your program should have been designed to echo its input data. If not, go back and add WRITE statements to verify that the input values are what you expect them to be.

If the variable names seem to be correct and the input data is correct, then you are probably dealing with a logical error. You should check each of your assignment statements.

1. If an assignment statement is very long, break it into several smaller assignment statements. Smaller statements are easier to verify.
2. Check the placement of parentheses in your assignment statements. It is a very common error to have the operations in an assignment statement evaluated in the wrong order. If you have any doubts as to the order in which the variables are being evaluated, add extra sets of parentheses to make your intentions clear.
3. Make sure that you have initialized all of your variables properly.
4. Be sure that any functions you use are in the correct units. For example, the input to trigonometric functions must be in units of radians, not degrees.
5. Check for possible errors due to integer or mixed-mode arithmetic.

If you are still getting the wrong answer, add WRITE statements at various points in your program to see the results of intermediate calculations. If you can locate the point where the calculations go bad, then you know just where to look for the problem, which is 95 percent of the battle.

If you still cannot find the problem after all of the above steps, explain what you are doing to another student or to your instructor, and let him or her look at the code. It is very common for a person to see just what he or she expects to see when they look at their own code. Another person can often quickly spot an error that you have overlooked time after time.

2

Good Programming Practice

To reduce your debugging effort, make sure that during your program design you:

1. Use the IMPLICIT NONE statement.
2. Echo all input values.
3. Initialize all variables.
4. Use parentheses to make the functions of assignment statements clear.

All modern compilers have special debugging tools called *symbolic debuggers*. A symbolic debugger is a tool that allows you to walk through the execution of your program one statement at a time, and to examine the values of any variables at each step along the way. Symbolic debuggers allow you to see all of the intermediate results without having to insert a lot of WRITE statements into your code. They are powerful and flexible, but unfortunately they are different for every type of compiler. If you will be using a symbolic debugger in your class, your instructor will introduce you to the debugger appropriate for your compiler and computer.

2.13
SUMMARY

In Chapter 2 we have presented many of the fundamental concepts required to write functional Fortran programs. We described the basic structure of Fortran programs, and introduced four data types: integer, real, logical, and character. We introduced the assignment statement, arithmetic calculations, intrinsic functions, and list-directed input / output statements. Throughout the chapter, we have emphasized those features of the language that are important for writing understandable and maintainable Fortran code.

The Fortran statements introduced in this chapter must appear in a specific order in a Fortran program. The proper order is summarized in Table 2-5.

TABLE 2-5
The order of Fortran statements in a program

1. PROGRAM Statement
2. IMPLICIT NONE Statement
3. **Type Declaration Statements:**
   REAL Statement(s)   (   )
   INTEGER Statement(s)   (Any number in any order   )
   CHARACTER Statement(s)   (   )
4. **Executable Statements:**
   Assignment Statement(s)   (   )
   READ Statement(s)   (Any number in the order   )
   WRITE Statement(s)   (required to accomplish the)
   STOP Statement(s)   (desired task.   )
5. END PROGRAM Statement

▨ **TABLE 2-6**
   Fortran hierarchy of operations

1. Operations within parentheses are evaluated first, starting with the innermost parentheses and working outward.
2. All exponential operations are evaluated next, working from *right* to *left*.
3. All multiplications and divisions are evaluated, working from left to right.
4. All additions and subtractions are evaluated, working from left to right.

The order in which Fortran expressions are evaluated follows a fixed hierarchy, with operations at a higher level evaluated before operations at lower levels. The hierarchy of operations is summarized in Table 2-6.

The Fortran language includes a number of built-in functions to help us solve problems. These functions are called intrinsic functions, since they are intrinsic to the Fortran language itself. Some common intrinsic functions are summarized in Tables 2-3 and 2-4, and a complete listing of intrinsic functions is contained in Appendix B.

There are two varieties of intrinsic functions: specific functions and generic functions. Specific functions require that their input data be of a specific type; if data of the wrong type is supplied to a specific function, the result will be meaningless. In contrast, generic functions can accept input data of more than one type and produce correct results.

2.13.1 Summary of Good Programming Practice

Every Fortran program should be designed so that another person who is familiar with Fortran can easily understand it. This is very important, since a good program may be used for a long period of time. Over that time, conditions will change, and the program will need to be modified to reflect the changes. The program modifications may be done by someone other than the original programmer. The programmer making the modifications must understand the original program well before attempting to change it.

It is much harder to design clear, understandable, and maintainable programs than it is to simply write programs. To do so, a programmer must develop the discipline to properly document his or her work. In addition, the programmer must be careful to avoid known pitfalls along the path to good programs. The following guidelines will help you to develop good programs:

1. Use meaningful variable names whenever possible. Use names which can be understood at a glance, like `day`, `month`, and `year`.
2. Always use the `IMPLICIT NONE` statement to catch typographical errors in your program at compilation time.
3. Create a data dictionary in each program that you write. The data dictionary should explicitly declare and define each variable in the program. Be sure to include the physical units associated with each variable, if applicable.
4. Use a consistent number of significant digits in constants. For example, do not use 3.14 for π in one part of your program, and 3.141593 in another part of the program. To ensure consistency, a constant may be named, and the constant may be referenced by name wherever it is needed.

5. Be sure to specify all constants with as much precision as your computer will support. For example, specify π as 3.141593, *not* 3.14.

6. Do not use integer arithmetic to calculate continuously varying real-world quantities such as distance, time, etc. Use integer arithmetic only for things that are intrinsically integer, such as counters.

7. Avoid mixed-mode arithmetic except for exponentiation. If it is necessary to mix integer and real variables in a single expression, use the intrinsic functions REAL, INT, NINT, CEILING, and FLOOR to make the type conversions explicit.

8. Use extra parentheses whenever necessary to improve the readability of your expressions.

9. Always echo any variables that you enter into a program from a keyboard to make sure that they were typed and processed correctly.

10. Initialize all variables in a program before using them. The variables may be initialized with assignment statements, with READ statements, or directly in type declaration statements.

11. Always print the physical units associated with any value being written out. The units are important for the proper interpretation of a program's results.

2.13.2 Summary of Fortran Statements

The following summary describes the Fortran statements introduced in this chapter.

Assignment Statement:

```
                    variable = expression
```

Examples:

```
        pi = 3.141593
        distance = 0.5 * acceleration * time ** 2
        side = hypot * cos(theta)
```

Description:
The left side of the assignment statement must be a variable name. The right side of the assignment statement can be any constant, variable, function, or expression. The value of the quantity on the right-hand side of the equal sign is stored into the variable named on the left-hand side of the equal sign.

CHARACTER **Statement:**

```
        CHARACTER(len=<len>) :: variable_name1[, variable_name2, ...]
        CHARACTER(<len>) :: variable_name1[, variable_name2, ...]
        CHARACTER :: variable_name1[, variable_name2, ...]
```

(continued)

(*concluded*)

Examples:

```
CHARACTER(len=10) :: first, last, middle
CHARACTER(10) :: first = 'My Name'
CHARACTER :: middle_initial
```

Description:

The CHARACTER statement is a type declaration statement that declares variables of the character data type. The length in characters of each variable is specified by the (len=<len>), or by <len>. If the length is absent, then the length of the variables defaults to 1.

The value of a CHARACTER variable may be initialized with a string when it is declared, as shown in the second example above.

END PROGRAM Statement:

```
END PROGRAM [name]
```

Description:

The END PROGRAM statement must be the last statement in a Fortran program segment. It tells the compiler that there are no further statements to process. Program execution is stopped when the END PROGRAM statement is reached. The name of the program may optionally be included in the END PROGRAM statement.

IMPLICIT NONE Statement:

```
IMPLICIT NONE
```

Description:

The IMPLICIT NONE statement turns off default typing in Fortran. When it is used in a program, every variable in the program must be explicitly declared in a type declaration statement.

INTEGER Statement:

```
INTEGER :: variable_name1[, variable_name2, ...]
```

Examples:

```
INTEGER :: i, j, count
INTEGER :: day = 4
```

(*continued*)

(*concluded*)

Description:
The INTEGER statement is a type declaration statement that declares variables of the integer data type. This statement overrides the default typing specified in Fortran. The value of an INTEGER variable may be initialized when it is declared, as shown in the second example above.

PROGRAM **Statement:**

```
PROGRAM program_name
```

Example:

```
PROGRAM my_program
```

Description:
The PROGRAM statement specifies the name of a Fortran program. It must be the first statement in the program. The name must be unique, and cannot be used as a variable name within the program. A program name may consist of one to 31 alphabetic, numeric, and underscore characters, but the first character in the program name must be alphabetic.

READ **Statement (List-Directed** READ**):**

```
READ (*,*) variable_name1[, variable_name2, ...]
```

Examples:

```
READ (*,*) stress
READ (*,*) distance, time
```

Description:
The list-directed READ statement reads one or more values from the standard input device and loads them into the variables in the list. The values are stored in the order in which the variables are listed. Data values must be separated by blanks or by commas. As many lines as necessary will be read. Each READ statement begins searching for values with a new line.

REAL **Statement:**

```
REAL :: variable_name1[, variable_name2, ...]
REAL :: variable_name = value
```

(*continued*)

2

(*concluded*)

Examples:

```
REAL :: distance, time
REAL :: distance = 100
```

Description:
The REAL statement is a type declaration statement that declares variables of the real data type. This statement overrides the default typing specified in Fortran. The value of a REAL variable may be initialized when it is declared, as shown in the second example above.

STOP Statement:

```
STOP
```

Description:
The STOP statement stops the execution of a Fortran program. There may be more than one STOP statement within a program. A STOP statement that immediately precedes an END PROGRAM statement may be omitted, since execution is also stopped when the END PROGRAM statement is reached.

WRITE Statement (List-Directed WRITE):

```
WRITE (*,*) expression1 [,expression2, etc.]
```

Examples:

```
WRITE (*,*) stress
WRITE (*,*) distance, time
WRITE (*,*) 'SIN(theta) = ', SIN(theta)
```

Description:
The list-directed WRITE statement writes the values of one or more expressions to the standard output device. The values are written in the order in which the expressions are listed.

2.13.3. Exercises

2-1. State whether or not each of the following Fortran 95/2003 constants is valid. If valid, state what type of constant it is. If not, state why it is invalid.

(*a*) 3.14159

(*b*) '.TRUE.'

(*c*) `-123,456.789`

(*d*) `+1E-12`

(*e*) `'Who's coming for dinner?'`

(*f*) `"Pass / Fail'`

(*g*) `"Enter name:"`

2-2. For each of the following pairs of numbers, state whether they represent the same value or different values within the computer.

(*a*) `123.E+0; 123`

(*b*) `1234.E-3; 1.234E3`

(*c*) `1.41421; 1.41421E0`

(*d*) `0.000005E+6; 5.`

2-3. State whether each of the following program names is valid or not. If not, state why the name is invalid.

(*a*) `junk`

(*b*) `3rd`

(*c*) `Who_are_you?`

(*d*) `time_to_intercept`

2-4. Which of the following expressions are legal in Fortran? If an expression is legal, evaluate it.

(*a*) `2.**3 / 3**2`

(*b*) `2 * 6 + 6 ** 2 / 2`

(*c*) `2 * (-10.)**-3.`

(*d*) `2 / (-10.) ** 3.`

(*e*) `23 / (4 / 8)`

2-5. Which of the following expressions are legal in Fortran? If an expression is legal, evaluate it.

(*a*) `((58/4)*(4/58))`

(*b*) `((58/4)*(4/58.))`

(*c*) `((58./4)*(4/58.))`

(*d*) `((58./4*(4/58.))`

2-6. Evaluate each of the following expressions.

(*a*) `13 / 5 * 6`

(*b*) `(13 / 5) * 6`

(*c*) `13 / (5 * 6)`

(*d*) `13. / 5 * 6`

(e) 13 / 5 * 6.

(f) INT(13. / 5) * 6

(g) NINT(13. / 5) * 6

(h) CEILING(13. / 5) * 6

(i) FLOOR(13. / 5) * 6

2-7. Evaluate each of the following expressions.

(a) 3 ** 3 ** 2

(b) (3 ** 3) ** 2

(c) 3 ** (3 ** 2)

2-8. What values will be output from the following program?

```
PROGRAM sample_1
INTEGER :: i1, i2, i3, i4
REAL :: a1 = 2.4, a2
i1 = a1
i2 = INT( -a1 * i1 )
i3 = NINT( -a1 * i1 )
i4 = FLOOR( -a1 * i1 )
a2 = a1**i1
WRITE (*,*) i1, i2, i3, i4, a1, a2
END PROGRAM sample_1
```

2-9. Figure 2-11 shows a right triangle with a hypotenuse of length C and angle θ. From elementary trigonometry, the length of sides A and B are given by

$$A = C \cos \theta$$

$$B = C \sin \theta$$

The following program is intended to calculate the lengths of sides A and B given the hypotenuse C and angle θ. Will this program run? Will it produce the correct result? Why or why not?

```
PROGRAM triangle
REAL :: a, b, c, theta
```

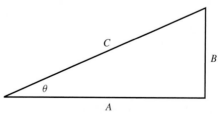

FIGURE 2-11
The right triangle of Exercise 2-9.

```
WRITE (*,*) 'Enter the length of the hypotenuse C:'
READ (*,*) c
WRITE (*,*) 'Enter the angle THETA in degrees:'
READ (*,*) theta
a = c * COS ( theta )
b = c * SIN ( theta )
WRITE (*,*) 'The length of the adjacent side is ', a
WRITE (*,*) 'The length of the opposite side is ', b
END PROGRAM triangle
```

2-10. What output will be produced by the following program?

```
PROGRAM example
REAL :: a, b, c
INTEGER :: k, l, m
READ (*,*) a, b, c, k
READ (*,*) l, m
WRITE (*,*) a, b, c, k, l, m
END PROGRAM example
```

The input data to the program is:

```
-3.141592
100, 200., 300, 400
-100, -200, -300
-400
```

2-11. Write a Fortran program that calculates an hourly employee's weekly pay. The program should ask the user for the person's pay rate and the number of hours worked during the week. It should then calculate the total pay from the formula

Total Pay = Hourly Pay Rate × Hours Worked

Finally, it should display the total weekly pay. Check your program by computing the weekly pay for a person earning $7.90 per hour and working for 42 hours.

2-12. The potential energy of an object due to its height above the surface of the Earth is given by the equation

$$PE = mgh \qquad\qquad (2\text{-}10)$$

where m is the mass of the object, g is the acceleration due to gravity, and h is the height above the surface of the Earth. The kinetic energy of a moving object is given by the equation

$$KE = \frac{1}{2}mv^2 \qquad\qquad (2\text{-}11)$$

where m is the mass of the object and v is the velocity of the object. Write a Fortran statement for the total energy (potential plus kinetic) possessed by an object in the earth's gravitational field.

2-13. If a stationary ball is released at a height h above the surface of the Earth, the velocity of the ball v when it hits the earth is given by the equation

$$v = \sqrt{2gh} \qquad (2\text{-}12)$$

where g is the acceleration due to gravity, and h is the height above the surface of the Earth (assuming no air friction). Write a Fortran equation for the velocity of the ball when it hits the Earth.

2-14. Write a Fortran program that calculates the velocity of the ball v when it hits the earth from a given height h, using Equation (2-12). Use the program to calculate the velocity for a height of (a) 1 meter; (b) 10 meters; and (c) 100 meters.

2-15. **Relativity** In Einstein's Theory of Relativity, the rest mass of matter is related to an equivalent energy by the equation

$$E = mc^2 \qquad (2\text{-}13)$$

where E is the energy in joules, m is mass in kilograms, and c is the speed of light in meters per second ($c = 2.9979 \times 10^8$ m/s). Suppose that a 400-MW (= 400 million joules per second) nuclear power generating station supplies full power to the electrical grid for a year. Write a program that calculates the amount of mass consumed in the course of the year. Use good programming practices in your program. (*Note:* Assume that the generating station is 100 percent efficient in producing electrical energy.)

2-16. Generalize the program of the previous exercise to calculate the mass consumed by a generating station with a user-specified output power for a user-specified period of months.

2-17. **Period of a Pendulum** The period of an oscillating pendulum T (in seconds) is given by the equation

$$T = 2\pi\sqrt{\frac{L}{g}} \qquad (2\text{-}14)$$

where L is the length of the pendulum in meters, and g is the acceleration due to gravity in meters per second squared. Write a Fortran program to calculate the period of a pendulum of length L. The length of the pendulum will be specified by the user when the program is run. Use good programming practices in your program. (The acceleration due to gravity at the Earth's surface is 9.81 m/s².)

2-18. Write a program to calculate the hypotenuse of a right triangle, given the lengths of its two sides. Use good programming practices in your program.

2-19. **Logarithms to an Arbitrary Base** Write a program to calculate the logarithm of a number x to an arbitrary base b ($\log_b x$). Use the following equation for the calculation

$$\log_b x = \log_{10} x / \log_{10} b \qquad (2\text{-}15)$$

Test the program by calculation the logarithm to the base e of 100. (Note that you can check your answer using the LOG(X) function, which calculates $\log_e x$.)

2

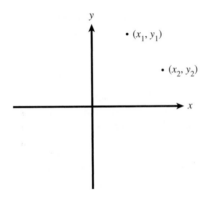

FIGURE 2-12
A Cartesian plane containing two points (x_1, y_1) and (x_2, y_2).

2-20. Write a program using the IMPLICIT NONE statement, and do not declare one of the variables in the program. What sort of error message is generated by your compiler?

2-21. The distance between two points (x_1, y_1) and (x_2, y_2) on a Cartesian coordinate plane (Figure 2-12) is given by the equation

$$d = \sqrt{(x_1 - x_2)^2 + (y_1 - y_2)^2} \qquad \qquad (2\text{-}16)$$

Write a Fortran program to calculate the distance between any two points (x_1, y_1) and (x_2, y_2) specified by the user. Use good programming practices in your program. Use the program to calculate the distance between the points $(-1,1)$ and $(6,2)$.

2-22. Decibels Engineers often measure the ratio of two power measurements in *decibels,* or dB. The equation for the ratio of two power measurements in decibels is

$$dB = 10 \log_{10} \frac{P_2}{P_1}$$

where P_2 is the power level being measured, and P_1 is some reference power level. Assume that the reference power level P_1 is 1 milliwatt, and write a program that accepts an input power P_2 and converts it into dB with respect to the 1-mW reference level.

2-23. Hyperbolic cosine The hyperbolic cosine function is defined by the equation

$$\cosh x = \frac{e^x + e^{-x}}{2}$$

Write a Fortran program to calculate the hyperbolic cosine of a user-supplied value x. Use the program to calculate the hyperbolic cosine of 3.0. Compare the answer that your program produces to the answer produced by the Fortran intrinsic function COSH(x).

2-24. Compound Interest Suppose that you deposit a sum of money P in an interest-bearing account at a local bank (P stands for *present value*). If the bank pays you interest on the money at a rate of i percent per year and compounds the interest m times a year, the amount of money that you will have in the bank after n years is given by the equation

$$F = P\left(1 + \frac{\text{APR}}{100m}\right)^{mn}$$ (2-17)

where F is the future value of the account and APR is the annual percentage rate on the account. The quantity APR/$100m$ is the fraction of interest earned in one compounding period (the extra factor of 100 in the denominator converts the rate from percentages to fractional amounts). Write a Fortran program that will read an initial amount of money P, an annual interest rate APR, the number of times m that the interest is compounded in a year, and the number of years n that the money is left in the account. The program should calculate the future value F of this account.

Use this program to calculate the future value of the bank account if $1000.00 is deposited in an account with an APR of 5 percent for a period of 1 year, and the interest is compounded (*a*) annually, (*b*) semiannually, or (*c*) monthly. How much difference does the rate of compounding make on the amount in the account?

2-25. Radio Receiver A simplified version of the front end of an AM radio receiver is shown in Figure 2-13. This receiver consists of an *RLC* tuned circuit containing a resistor, capacitor, and an inductor connected in series. The *RLC* circuit is connected to an external antenna and ground as shown in the picture.

The tuned circuit allows the radio to select a specific station out of all the stations transmitting on the AM band. At the resonant frequency of the circuit, essentially all of the signal V_0 appearing at the antenna appears across the resistor, which represents the rest of the radio. In other words, the radio receives its strongest signal at the resonant frequency. The resonant frequency of the *LC* circuit is given by the equation

$$f_0 = \frac{1}{2\pi\sqrt{LC}}$$ (2-18)

where L is inductance in henrys (H) and C is capacitance in farads (F). Write a program that calculates the resonant frequency of this radio set, given specific values of L and C.

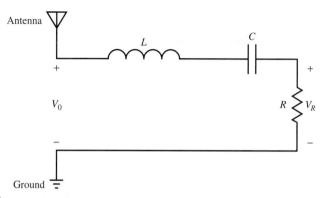

FIGURE 2-13
A simplified representation of an AM radio set.

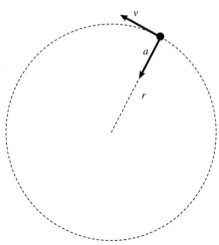

FIGURE 2-14
An object moving in uniform circular motion due to the centripetal acceleration *a*.

Test your program by calculating the frequency of the radio when $L = 0.1$ mH and $C = 0.25$ nF.

2-26. **Aircraft Turning Radius** An object moving in a circular path at a constant tangential velocity v is shown in Figure 2-14. The radial acceleration required for the object to move in the circular path is given by Equation (2-19)

$$a = \frac{v^2}{r} \tag{2-19}$$

where a is the centripetal acceleration of the object in m/s^2, v is the tangential velocity of the object in m/s, and r is the turning radius in meters. Suppose that the object is an aircraft, and write a program to answer the following questions about it:

(*a*) Suppose that the aircraft is moving at Mach 0.80, or 80 percent of the speed of sound. If the centripetal acceleration is 2.5g, what is the turning radius of the aircraft? (Note: For this problem, you may assume that Mach 1 is equal to 340 m/s and that 1$g = 9.81$ m/s^2).

(*b*) Suppose that the speed of the aircraft increases to Mach 1.5. What is the turning radius of the aircraft now?

(*c*) Suppose that the maximum acceleration that the pilot can stand is 7g. What is the minimum possible turning radius of the aircraft at Mach 1.5?

2-27. **Escape Velocity** The escape velocity from the surface of a planet or moon (ignoring the effects of atmosphere) is given by Equation (2-20)

$$v_{\text{esc}} = \sqrt{\frac{2GM}{R}} \tag{2-20}$$

where v_{esc} is the escape velocity in meters per second, G is the gravitational constant $(6.673 \times 10^{-11} \text{ N} \cdot \text{m}^{-2} \cdot \text{kg}^{-2})$, M is the mass of the planet in kilograms, and R is the radius of the planet in meters. Write a program that will calculate the escape velocity as a function of mass and radius, and use the program to calculate the escape velocity for the bodies given below.

2

Body	Mass (kg)	Radius (m)
Earth	6.0×10^{24}	6.4×10^6
Moon	7.4×10^{22}	1.7×10^6
Ceres	8.7×10^{20}	4.7×10^5
Jupiter	1.9×10^{27}	7.1×10^7

3

Program Design and Branching Structures

OBJECTIVES

- Learn the concepts of top-down design and decomposition.
- Learn about pseudocode and flowcharts, and why they should be used.
- Know how to create and use LOGICAL constants and variables.
- Learn about relational and combinational logical operators, and how they fit into the hierarchy of operations.
- Know how to use the IF construct.
- Know how to use the SELECT CASE construct.

In the previous chapter, we developed several complete working Fortran programs. However, all of the programs were very simple, consisting of a series of Fortran statements that were executed one after another in a fixed order. Such programs are called *sequential* programs. They read input data, process it to produce a desired answer, print out the answer, and quit. There is no way to repeat sections of the program more than once, and there is no way to selectively execute only certain portions of the program, depending on values of the input data.

In the next two chapters, we will introduce a number of Fortran statements that allow us to control the order in which statements are executed in a program. There are two broad categories of control statements: **branches,** which select specific sections of the code to execute, and **loops,** which cause specific sections of the code to be repeated. Branches will be introduced in this chapter, and loops will be covered in Chapter 4.

With the introduction of branches and loops, our programs are going to become more complex, and it will get easier to make mistakes. To help avoid programming errors, we will introduce a formal program design procedure based on the technique known as top-down design. We will also introduce two common algorithm development tools, flowcharts and pseudocode.

After introducing the program design process, we will introduce the logical data type and the operations that produce them. Logical expressions are used to control many branching statements, so we will learn about them before studying branches.

Finally, we will study the various types of Fortran branching statements.

3.1
INTRODUCTION TO TOP-DOWN DESIGN TECHNIQUES

Suppose that you are an engineer working in industry, and that you need to write a Fortran program to solve some problem. How do you begin?

When given a new problem, there is a natural tendency to sit down at a terminal and start programming without "wasting" a lot of time thinking about it first. It is often possible to get away with this on-the-fly approach to programming for very small problems, such as many of the examples in this book. In the real world, however, problems are larger, and a programmer attempting this approach will become hopelessly bogged down. For larger problems, it pays to completely think out the problem and the approach you are going to take to it before writing a single line of code.

We will introduce a formal program design process in this section, and then apply that process to every major application developed in the remainder of the book. For some of the simple examples that we will be doing, the design process will seem like overkill. However, as the problems that we solve get larger and larger, the process becomes more and more essential to successful programming.

When I was an undergraduate, one of my professors was fond of saying, "Programming is easy. It's knowing what to program that's hard." His point was forcefully driven home to me after I left university and began working in industry on larger-scale software projects. I found that the most difficult part of my job was to *understand the problem* I was trying to solve. Once I really understood the problem, it became easy to break the problem apart into smaller, more easily manageable pieces with well-defined functions, and then to tackle those pieces one at a time.

Top-down design is the process of starting with a large task and breaking it down into smaller, more easily understandable pieces (subtasks) that perform a portion of the desired task. Each subtask may in turn be subdivided into smaller subtasks if necessary. Once the program is divided into small pieces, each piece can be coded and tested independently. We do not attempt to combine the subtasks into a complete task until each of the subtasks has been verified to work properly by itself.

The concept of top-down design is the basis of our formal program design process. We will now introduce the details of the process, which is illustrated in Figure 3-1. The steps involved are as follows:

1. *Clearly state the problem that you are trying to solve.*

   Programs are usually written to fill some perceived need, but that need may not be articulated clearly by the person requesting the program. For example, a user may ask for a program to solve a system of simultaneous linear equations. This request is not clear enough to allow a programmer to design a program to meet the need; he or

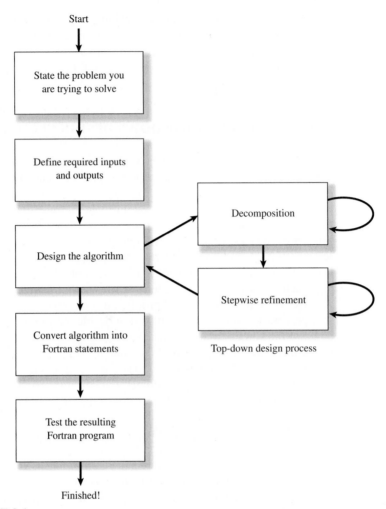

FIGURE 3-1
The program design process used in this book.

she must first know much more about the problem to be solved. Is the system of equations to be solved real or complex? What is the maximum number of equations and unknowns that the program must handle? Are there any symmetries in the equations that might be exploited to make the task easier? The program designer will have to talk with the user requesting the program, and the two of them will have to come up with a clear statement of exactly what they are trying to accomplish. A clear statement of the problem will prevent misunderstandings, and it will also help the program designer to properly organize his or her thoughts. In the example we were describing, a proper statement of the problem might have been:

Design and write a program to solve a system of simultaneous linear equations having real coefficients and with up to 20 equations in 20 unknowns.

2. *Define the inputs required by the program and the outputs to be produced by the program.*

The inputs to the program and the outputs produced by the program must be specified so that the new program will properly fit into the overall processing scheme. In the above example, the coefficients of the equations to be solved are probably in some pre-existing order, and our new program needs to be able to read them in that order. Similarly, it needs to produce the answers required by the programs that may follow it in the overall processing scheme, and to write out those answers in the format needed by the programs following it.

3. *Design the algorithm that you intend to implement in the program*

An **algorithm** is a step-by-step procedure for finding the solution to a problem. It is at this stage in the process that top-down design techniques come into play. The designer looks for logical divisions within the problem, and divides it up into subtasks along those lines. This process is called *decomposition*. If the subtasks are themselves large, the designer can break them up into even smaller sub-subtasks. This process continues until the problem has been divided into many small pieces, each of which does a simple, clearly understandable job.

After the problem has been decomposed into small pieces, each piece is further refined through a process called *stepwise refinement*. In stepwise refinement, a designer starts with a general description of what the piece of code should do, and then defines the functions of the piece in greater and greater detail until they are specific enough to be turned into Fortran statements. Stepwise refinement is usually done with **pseudocode,** which will be described in the next section.

It is often helpful to solve a simple example of the problem by hand during the algorithm development process. A designer who understands the steps that he or she went through in solving the problem by hand will be better able to apply decomposition and stepwise refinement to the problem.

4. *Turn the algorithm into Fortran statements.*

If the decomposition and refinement process was carried out properly, this step will be very simple. All the programmer will have to do is to replace pseudocode with the corresponding Fortran statements on a one-for-one basis.

5. *Test the resulting Fortran program.*

This step is the real killer. The components of the program must first be tested individually, if possible, and then the program as a whole must be tested. When testing a program, we must verify that it works correctly for *all legal input data sets*. It is very common for a program to be written, tested with some standard data set, and released for use, only to find that it produces the wrong answers (or crashes) with a different input data set. If the algorithm implemented in a program includes different branches, we must test all of the possible branches to confirm that the program operates correctly under every possible circumstance.

Large programs typically go through a series of tests before they are released for general use (see Figure 3-2). The first stage of testing is sometimes called **unit testing.** During unit testing, the individual subtasks of the program are tested separately

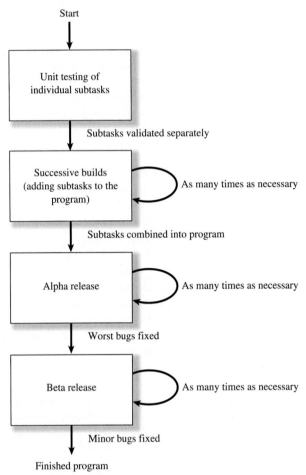

FIGURE 3-2
A typical testing process for a large program.

to confirm that they work correctly. The programmer usually writes small programs called "stubs" or "test drivers" to execute the code under test, and to see if the code is returning the proper results. This verifies the operation of the sub-tasks at a basic level before they are combined into larger groups.

After the unit testing is completed, the program goes through a series of *builds* during which the individual subtasks are combined to produce the final program. The first build of the program typically includes only a few of the subtasks. It is used to check the interactions among those subtasks and the functions performed by the combinations of the subtasks. In successive builds, more and more subtasks are added, until the entire program is complete. Testing is performed on each build, and any errors (bugs) that are detected are corrected before moving on to the next build.

Testing continues even after the program is complete. The first complete version of the program is usually called the **alpha release.** It is exercised by the programmers and others very close to them in as many different ways as possible, and the bugs discovered during the testing are corrected. When the most serious bugs have been removed from the program, a new version called the **beta release** is prepared. The beta release is normally given to "friendly" outside users who have a need for the program in their normal day-to-day jobs. These users put the program through its paces under many different conditions and with many different input data sets, and they report any bugs that they find to the programmers. When those bugs have been corrected, the program is ready to be released for general use.

Because the programs in this book are fairly small, we will not go through the sort of extensive testing described above. However, we will follow the basic principles in testing all of our programs.

The program design process may be summarized as follows:

1. Clearly state the problem that you are trying to solve.
2. Define the inputs required by the program and the outputs to be produced by the program.
3. Design the algorithm that you intend to implement in the program.
4. Turn the algorithm into Fortran statements.
5. Test the Fortran program.

Good Programming Practice

Follow the steps of the program design process to produce reliable, understandable Fortran programs.

In a large programming project, the time actually spent programming is surprisingly small. In his book *The Mythical Man-Month,*[1] Frederick P. Brooks, Jr. suggests that in a typical large software project, one-third of the time is spent planning what to do (steps 1 through 3), one-sixth of the time is spent actually writing the program (step 4), and fully half of the time is spent in testing and debugging the program! Clearly, anything that we can do to reduce the testing and debugging time will be very helpful. We can best reduce the testing and debugging time by doing a very careful job in the planning phase, and by using good programming practices. Good programming practices will reduce the number of bugs in the program, and will make the ones that do creep in easier to find.

3.2

USE OF PSEUDOCODE AND FLOWCHARTS

As a part of the design process, it is necessary to describe the algorithm that you intend to implement. The description of the algorithm should be in a standard form that is easy for both you and other people to understand, and the description should aid you in turning your concept into Fortran code. The standard forms that we use to describe algorithms are called **constructs,** and an algorithm described using these constructs is called a structured algorithm. When the algorithm is implemented in a Fortran program, the resulting program is called a **structured program.**

---

[1] *The Mythical Man-Month,* Anniversary Edition, by Frederick P. Brooks Jr., Addison-Wesley, 1995.

3

The constructs used to build algorithms can be described in two different ways: pseudocode and flowcharts. **Pseudocode** is a hybrid mixture of Fortran and English. It is structured like Fortran, with a separate line for each distinct idea or segment of code, but the descriptions on each line are in English. Each line of the pseudocode should describe its idea in plain, easily understandable English. Pseudocode is very useful for developing algorithms, since it is flexible and easy to modify. It is especially useful since pseudocode can be written and modified on the same computer terminal used to write the Fortran program—no special graphical capabilities are required.

For example, the pseudocode for the algorithm in Example 2-3 is:

```
Prompt user to enter temperature in degrees Fahrenheit
Read temperature in degrees Fahrenheit (temp_f)
temp_k in kelvins ← (5./9.) * (temp_f - 32) + 273.15
Write temperature in kelvins
```

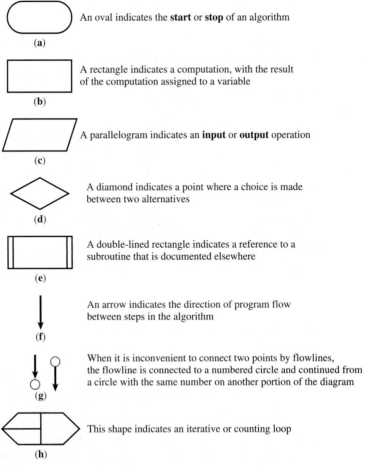

(a) An oval indicates the **start** or **stop** of an algorithm

(b) A rectangle indicates a computation, with the result of the computation assigned to a variable

(c) A parallelogram indicates an **input** or **output** operation

(d) A diamond indicates a point where a choice is made between two alternatives

(e) A double-lined rectangle indicates a reference to a subroutine that is documented elsewhere

(f) An arrow indicates the direction of program flow between steps in the algorithm

(g) When it is inconvenient to connect two points by flowlines, the flowline is connected to a numbered circle and continued from a circle with the same number on another portion of the diagram

(h) This shape indicates an iterative or counting loop

FIGURE 3-3
Common symbols used in flowcharts.

Notice that a left arrow ($\leftarrow$) is used instead of an equal sign ($=$) to indicate that a value is stored in a variable, since this avoids any confusion between assignment and equality. Pseudocode is intended to aid you in organizing your thoughts before converting them into Fortran code.

Flowcharts are a way to describe algorithms graphically. In a flowchart, different graphical symbols represent the different operations in the algorithm, and our standard constructs are made up of collections of one or more of these symbols. Flowcharts are very useful for describing the algorithm implemented in a program after it is completed. However, since they are graphical, flowcharts tend to be cumbersome to modify, and they are not very useful during the preliminary stages of algorithm definition when rapid changes are occurring. The most common graphical symbols used in flowcharts are shown in Figure 3-3, and the flowchart for the algorithm in Example 2-3 is shown in Figure 3-4.

Throughout the examples in this book, we will illustrate the use of both pseudocode and flowcharts. You are welcome to use whichever one of these tools gives you the best results in your own programming projects.

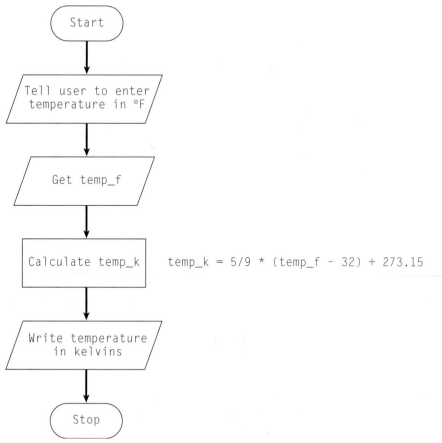

FIGURE 3-4
Flowchart for the algorithm in Example 2-3.

3

◾ 3.3

LOGICAL CONSTANTS, VARIABLES, AND OPERATORS

As we mentioned in the introduction to this chapter, most Fortran branching structures are controlled by logical values. Before studying the branching structures, we will introduce the data types that control them.

3.3.1 Logical Constants and Variables

The logical data type contains one of only two possible values: TRUE or FALSE. A **logical constant** can have one of the following values: .TRUE. or .FALSE. (note that the periods are required on either side of the values to distinguish them from variable names). Thus, the following are valid logical constants:

```
.TRUE.
.FALSE.
```

The following are not valid logical constants:

```
TRUE          (No periods—this is a variable name)
.FALSE        (Unbalanced periods)
```

Logical constants are rarely used, but logical expressions and variables are commonly used to control program execution, as we will see in this chapter and in Chapter 4.

A **logical variable** is a variable containing a value of the logical data type. A logical variable is declared using the LOGICAL statement:

```
LOGICAL :: var1 [, var2, var3, ...]
```

This type declaration statement should be placed after the PROGRAM statement and before the first executable statement in the program, as shown in the example below.

```
PROGRAM example
LOGICAL :: test1, test2
...
(Executable statements follow)
```

3.3.2 Assignment Statements and Logical Calculations

Like arithmetic calculations, logical calculations are performed with an assignment statement, whose form is

```
logical_variable_name = logical_expression
```

The expression to the right of the equal sign can be any combination of valid logical constants, logical variables, and logical operators. A **logical operator** is an operator on numeric, character, or logical data that yields a logical result. There are two basic types of logical operators: **relational operators** and **combinational operators.**

TABLE 3-1
Relational logic operators

Operation		
New style	**Older style**	**Meaning**
==	.EQ.	Equal to
/=	.NE.	Not equal to
>	.GT.	Greater than
>=	.GE.	Greater than or equal to
<	.LT.	Less than
<=	.LE.	Less than or equal to

3.3.3 Relational Operators

Relational logic operators are operators with two numerical or character operands that yield a logical result. The result depends on the *relationship* between the two values being compared, so these operators are called relational. The general form of a relational operator is

$$a_1 \text{ op } a_2$$

where a_1 and a_2 are arithmetic expressions, variables, constants, or character strings, and op is one of the relational logic operators listed in Table 3-1.

There are two forms of each relational operator. The first one is composed of symbols, and the second one is composed of characters surrounded by periods. In the second form, the periods are a part of the operator and must always be present. The first form of the operators was introduced in Fortran 90, while the second form is a holdover from earlier versions of Fortran. You may use either form of the operators in your program, but the first form is preferred in new programs.

If the relationship between a_1 and a_2 expressed by the operator is true, then the operation returns a value of .TRUE.; otherwise, the operation returns a value of .FALSE..

Some relational operations and their results are given below:

Operation	**Result**
3 < 4	.TRUE.
3 <= 4	.TRUE.
3 == 4	.FALSE.
3 > 4	.FALSE.
4 <= 4	.TRUE.
'A' < 'B'	.TRUE.

The last logical expression is .TRUE. because characters are evaluated in alphabetical order.

The equivalence relational operator is written with two equal signs, while the assignment operator is written with a single equal sign. These are very different operators that beginning programmers often confuse. The == symbol is a *comparison* operation that returns a logical result, while the = symbol *assigns* the value of the expression to the right of the equal sign to the variable on the left of the equal sign. It is a very common mistake for beginning programmers to use a single equal sign when trying to do a comparison.

Programming Pitfalls

Be careful not to confuse the equivalence relational operator (==) with the assignment operator (=).

In the hierarchy of operations, relational operators are evaluated after all arithmetic operators have been evaluated. Therefore, the following two expressions are equivalent (both are .TRUE.).

$$7 + 3 < 2 + 11$$
$$(7 + 3) < (2 + 11)$$

If the comparison is between real and integer values, then the integer value is converted to a real value before the comparison is performed. Comparisons between numerical data and character data are illegal and will cause a compile-time error:

```
4 == 4.   .TRUE.     (Integer is converted to real and comparison is made)
4 <= 'A'            (Illegal—produces a compile-time error)
```

3.3.4 Combinational Logic Operators

Combinational logic operators are operators with one or two logical operands that yield a logical result. There are four binary operators, .AND., .OR., .EQV., and .NEQV., and one unary operator, .NOT.. The general form of a binary combinational logic operation is

$$l_1 \text{ .op. } l_2$$

where l_1 and l_2 are logical expressions, variables, or constants, and .op. is one of the combinational operators listed in Table 3-2.

The periods are a part of the operator and must always be present. If the relationship between l_1 and l_2 expressed by the operator is true, then the operation returns a value of .TRUE.; otherwise, the operation returns a value of .FALSE..

The results of the operators are summarized in the **truth tables** in Tables 3-3*a* and 3-3*b*, which show the result of each operation for all possible combinations of l_1 and l_2.

■ **TABLE 3-2**
Combinational logic operators

Operator	Function	Definition
l_1 .AND. l_2	Logical AND	Result is TRUE if both l_1 and l_2 are TRUE
l_1 .OR. l_2	Logical OR	Result is TRUE if either or both of l_1 and l_2 are TRUE
l_1 .EQV. l_2	Logical equivalence	Result is TRUE if l_1 is the same as l_2 (either both TRUE or both FALSE)
l_1 .NEQV. l_2	Logical nonequivalence	Result is TRUE if one of l_1 and l_2 is TRUE and the other one is FALSE
.NOT. l_1	Logical NOT	Result is TRUE if l_1 is FALSE, and FALSE if l_1 is TRUE

3

■ **TABLE 3-3A**
Truth tables for binary combinational logic operators

l_1	l_2	l_1 .AND. l_2	l_1 .OR. l_2	l_1 .EQV. l_2	l_1 .NEQV. l_2
.FALSE.	.FALSE.	.FALSE.	.FALSE.	.TRUE.	.FALSE.
.FALSE.	.TRUE.	.FALSE.	.TRUE.	.FALSE.	.TRUE.
.TRUE.	.FALSE.	.FALSE.	.TRUE.	.FALSE.	.TRUE.
.TRUE.	.TRUE.	.TRUE.	.TRUE.	.TRUE.	.FALSE.

■ **TABLE 3-3B**
Truth table for .NOT. operator

l_1	.NOT. l_1
.FALSE.	.TRUE.
.TRUE.	.FALSE.

In the hierarchy of operations, combinational logic operators are evaluated *after all arithmetic operations and all relational operators have been evaluated.* The order in which the operators in an expression are evaluated is as follows:

1. All arithmetic operators are evaluated first in the order previously described.
2. All relational operators (==, /=, >, >=, <, <=) are evaluated, working from left to right.
3. All .NOT. operators are evaluated.
4. All .AND. operators are evaluated, working from left to right.
5. All .OR. operators are evaluated, working from left to right.
6. All .EQV. and .NEQV. operators are evaluated, working from left to right.

As with arithmetic operations, parentheses can be used to change the default order of evaluation. Examples of some combinational logic operators and their results follow.

EXAMPLE   Assume that the following variables are initialized with the values shown, and calcu-
3-1   late the result of the specified expressions:

$$log1 = .TRUE.$$
$$log2 = .TRUE.$$
$$log3 = .FALSE.$$

Logical Expression	Result
(*a*) `.NOT. log1`	`.FALSE.`
(*b*) `log1 .OR. log3`	`.TRUE.`
(*c*) `log1 .AND. log3`	`.FALSE.`
(*d*) `log2 .NEQV. log3`	`.TRUE.`
(*e*) `log1 .AND. log2 .OR. log3`	`.TRUE.`
(*f*) `log1 .OR. log2 .AND. log3`	`.TRUE.`
(*g*) `.NOT. (log1 .EQV. log2)`	`.FALSE.`

The `.NOT.` operator is evaluated before other combinational logic operators. Therefore, the parentheses in part (*g*) of the above example were required. If they had been absent, the expression in part (*g*) would have been evaluated in the order (`.NOT. log1) .EQV. log2`.

In the Fortran 95 and Fortran 2003 standards, combinational logic operations involving numerical or character data are illegal and will cause a compile-time error:

`4 .AND. 3          Error`

3.3.5 Logical Values in Input and Output Statements

If a logical variable appears in a list-directed `READ` statement, then the corresponding input value must be a character or a group of characters beginning with either a T or an F. If the first character of the input value is T, then the logical variable will be set to `.TRUE.`. If the first character of the input value is F, then the logical variable will be set to `.FALSE.`. Any input value beginning with another character will produce a run-time error.

If a logical variable or expression appears in a list-directed `WRITE` statement, then the corresponding output value will be the single character T if the value of the variable is `.TRUE.`, and F if the value of the variable is `.FALSE.`.

3.3.6 The Significance of Logical Variables and Expressions

Logical variables and expressions are rarely the final product of a Fortran program. Nevertheless, they are absolutely essential to the proper operation of most programs.

Most of the major branching and looping structures of Fortran are controlled by logical values, so you must be able to read and write logical expressions to understand and use Fortran control statements.

Quiz 3-1

This quiz provides a quick check to see if you have understood the concepts introduced in Section 3.3. If you have trouble with the quiz, reread the sections, ask your instructor, or discuss the material with a fellow student. The answers to this quiz are found in the back of the book.

1. Suppose that the real variables a, b, and c contain the values $-10.$, 0.1, and 2.1 respectively, and that the logical variable l1, l2, and l3 contain the values .TRUE., .FALSE., and .FALSE., respectively. Is each of the following expressions legal or illegal? If an expression is legal, what will its result be?

   (a)   a > b .OR. b > c

   (b)   (.NOT. a) .OR. l1

   (c)   l1 .AND. .NOT. l2

   (d)   a < b .EQV. b < c

   (e)   l1 .OR. l2 .AND. l3

   (f)   l1 .OR. (l2 .AND. l3)

   (g)   (l1 .OR. l2) .AND. l3

   (h)   a .OR. b .AND. l1

2. If the input data is as shown, what will be printed out by the following program?

   ```
   PROGRAM quiz_31
   INTEGER :: i, j, k
   LOGICAL :: l
   READ (*,*) i, j
   READ (*,*) k
   l = i + j == k
   WRITE (*,*) l
   END PROGRAM quiz_31
   ```

   The input data is:

   ```
   1, 3, 5
   2, 4, 6
   ```

3.4

CONTROL CONSTRUCTS: BRANCHES

Branches are Fortran statements that permit us to select and execute specific sections of code (called *blocks*) while skipping other sections of code. They are variations of the IF statement, plus the SELECT CASE construct.

3.4.1 The Block IF Construct

The commonest form of the IF statement is the block IF construct. This construct specifies that a block of code will be executed if and only if a certain logical expression is true. The block IF construct has the form

```
IF (logical_expr) THEN
   Statement 1
   Statement 2                 }        Code Block
   ...
END IF
```

If the logical expression is true, the program executes the statements in the block between the IF and END IF statements. If the logical expression is false, then the program skips all of the statements in the block between the IF and END IF statements, and executes the next statement after the END IF. The flowchart for a block IF construct is shown in Figure 3-5.

The IF (...) THEN is a single Fortran statement that must be written all together on the same line, and the statements to be executed must occupy separate lines below the IF (...) THEN statement. An END IF statement must follow them on a separate line. There should not be a statement number on the line containing the END IF statement. For readability, the block of code between the IF and END IF statements is usually indented by two or three spaces, but this is not actually required.

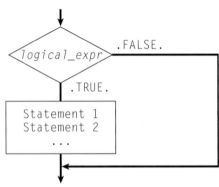

FIGURE 3-5
Flowchart for a simple block IF construct.

Good Programming Practice
Always indent the body of a block IF construct by two or more spaces to improve the readability of the code.

As an example of a block IF construct, consider the solution of a quadratic equation of the form

$$ax^2 + bx + c = 0 \qquad (3\text{-}1)$$

The solution to this equation is

$$x = \frac{-b \pm \sqrt{b^2 - 4ac}}{2a} \qquad (3\text{-}2)$$

The term $b^2 - 4ac$ is known as the *discriminant* of the equation. If $b^2 - 4ac > 0$, then there are two distinct real roots to the quadratic equation. If $b^2 - 4ac = 0$, then there is a single repeated root to the equation, and if $b^2 - 4ac < 0$, then there are two complex roots to the quadratic equation.

Suppose that we wanted to examine the discriminant of the quadratic equation and tell a user if the equation has complex roots. In pseudocode, the block IF construct to do this would take the form

```
IF (b**2 - 4.*a*c) < 0. THEN
    Write message that equation has two complex roots.
END of IF
```

In Fortran, the block IF construct is

```
IF ( (b**2 - 4.*a*c) < 0.) THEN
    WRITE (*,*) 'There are two complex roots to this equation.'
END IF
```

The flowchart for this construct is shown in Figure 3-6.

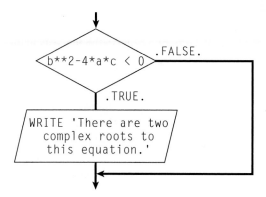

FIGURE 3-6
Flowchart showing structure to determine if a quadratic equation has two complex roots.

3.4.2 The ELSE and ELSE IF Clauses

In the simple block IF construct, a block of code is executed if the controlling logical expression is true. If the controlling logical expression is false, all of the statements in the construct are skipped.

Sometimes we may want to execute one set of statements if some condition is true, and different sets of statements if other conditions are true. If fact, there might be many different options to consider. An ELSE clause and one or more ELSE IF clauses may be added to the block IF construct for this purpose. The block IF construct with an ELSE clause and an ELSE IF clause has the form

```
IF (logical_expr_1) THEN
    Statement 1
    Statement 2              }    Block 1
    . . .

ELSE IF (logical_expr_2) THEN
    Statement 1
    Statement 2              }    Block 2
    . . .

ELSE
    Statement 1
    Statement 2              }    Block 3
    . . .

END IF
```

If *logical_expr_1* is true, then the program executes the statements in Block 1, and skips to the first executable statement following the END IF. Otherwise, the program checks for the status of *logical_expr_2*. If *logical_expr_2* is true, then the program executes the statements in Block 2, and skips to the first executable statement following the END IF. If both logical expressions are false, then the program executes the statements in Block 3.

The ELSE and ELSE IF statements must occupy lines by themselves. There should not be a statement number on a line containing an ELSE or ELSE IF statement.

There can be any number of ELSE IF clauses in a block IF construct. The logical expression in each clause will be tested only if the logical expressions in every clause above it are false. Once one of the expressions proves to be true and the corresponding code block is executed, the program skips to the first executable statement following the END IF.

The flowchart for a block IF construct with an ELSE IF and an ELSE clause is shown in Figure 3-7.

To illustrate the use of the ELSE and ELSE IF clauses, let's reconsider the quadratic equation once more. Suppose that we wanted to examine the discriminant of a quadratic equation and to tell a user whether the equation has two complex roots, two identical real roots, or two distinct real roots. In pseudocode, this construct would take the form

```
IF (b**2 - 4.*a*c) < 0.0 THEN
    Write message that equation has two complex roots.
ELSE IF (b**2 - 4.*a*c) > 0.0 THEN
    Write message that equation has two distinct real roots.
ELSE
    Write message that equation has two identical real roots.
END IF
```

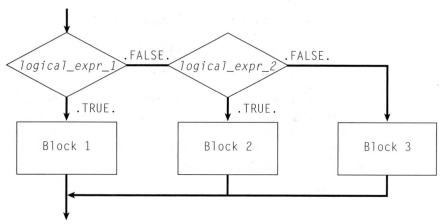

FIGURE 3-7
Flowchart for a block IF construct with an ELSE IF (...) THEN clause and an ELSE clause.

The Fortran statements to do this are

```
IF ( (b**2 - 4.*a*c) < 0.0 ) THEN
   WRITE (*,*) 'This equation has two complex roots.'
ELSE IF ( (b**2 - 4.*a*c) > 0.0 ) THEN
   WRITE (*,*) 'This equation has two distinct real roots.'
ELSE
   WRITE (*,*) 'This equation has two identical real roots.'
END IF
```

The flowchart for this construct is shown in Figure 3-8.

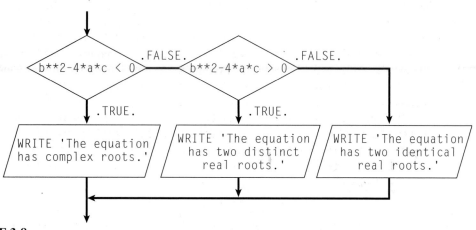

FIGURE 3-8
Flowchart showing structure to determine whether a quadratic equation has two complex roots, two identical real roots, or two distinct real roots.

3.4.3 Examples Using Block IF Constructs

We will now look at two examples that illustrate the use of block IF constructs.

EXAMPLE
3-2

The Quadratic Equation:

Design and write a program to solve for the roots of a quadratic equation, regardless of type.

SOLUTION
We will follow the design steps outlined earlier in the chapter.

1. **State the problem.**
    The problem statement for this example is very simple. We want to write a program that will solve for the roots of a quadratic equation, whether they are distinct real roots, repeated real roots, or complex roots.

2. **Define the inputs and outputs.**
    The inputs required by this program are the coefficients a, b, and c of the quadratic equation

$$ax^2 + bx + c = 0 \tag{3-1}$$

The output from the program will be the roots of the quadratic equation, whether they are distinct real roots, repeated real roots, or complex roots.

3. **Design the algorithm.**
    This task can be broken down into three major sections, whose functions are input, processing, and output:

```
Read the input data
Calculate the roots
Write out the roots
```

We will now break each of the above major sections into smaller, more detailed pieces. There are three possible ways to calculate the roots, depending on the value of the discriminant, so it is logical to implement this algorithm with a three-branched IF statement. The resulting pseudocode is:

```
Prompt the user for the coefficients a, b, and c.
    Read a, b, and c
    Echo the input coefficients
    discriminant ← b**2 - 4. * a * c

    IF discriminant > 0 THEN
        x1 ← ( -b + sqrt(discriminant) ) / ( 2. * a )
        x2 ← ( -b - sqrt(discriminant) ) / ( 2. * a )
        Write message that equation has two distinct real roots.
```

```
                    Write out the two roots.
            ELSE IF discriminant < 0 THEN
                    real_part ← -b / ( 2. * a )
                    imag_part ← sqrt ( abs ( discriminant ) ) / ( 2. * a )
                    Write message that equation has two complex roots.
                    Write out the two roots.
            ELSE
                    x1 ← -b / ( 2. * a )
                    Write message that equation has two identical real roots.
                    Write out the repeated root.
            END IF
```

The flowchart for this program is shown in Figure 3-9.

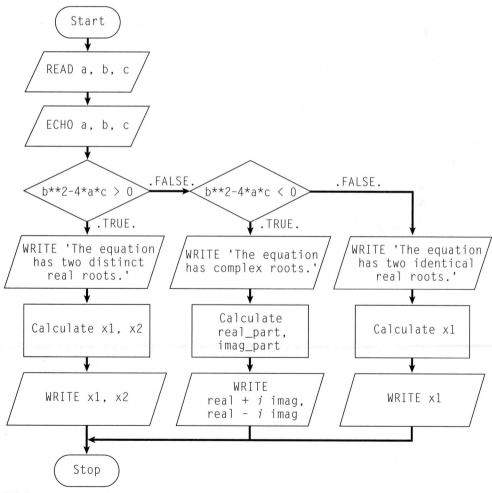

FIGURE 3-9
Flowchart of program roots.

4.   **Turn the algorithm into Fortran statements.**
     The final Fortran code is shown in Figure 3-10.

FIGURE 3-10
Program to solve for the roots of a quadratic equation.

```
PROGRAM roots
! Purpose:
!  This program solves for the roots of a quadratic equation of the
!  form a*x**2 + b*x + c = 0. It calculates the answers regardless
!  of the type of roots that the equation possesses.
!
! Record of revisions:
!   Date      Programmer          Description of change
!   ====      ==========          =====================
!  11/06/06  S. J. Chapman        Original code
!
IMPLICIT NONE

! Data dictionary: declare variable types, definitions, & units
REAL :: a               ! Coefficient of x**2 term of equation
REAL :: b               ! Coefficient of x term of equation
REAL :: c               ! Constant term of equation
REAL :: discriminant    ! Discriminant of the equation
REAL :: imag_part       ! Imaginary part of equation (for complex roots)
REAL :: real_part       ! Real part of equation (for complex roots)
REAL :: x1              ! First solution of equation (for real roots)
REAL :: x2              ! Second solution of equation (for real roots)

! Prompt the user for the coefficients of the equation
WRITE (*,*) 'This program solves for the roots of a quadratic '
WRITE (*,*) 'equation of the form A * X**2 + B * X + C = 0. '
WRITE (*,*) 'Enter the coefficients A, B, and C: '
READ (*,*) a, b, c

! Echo back coefficients
WRITE (*,*) 'The coefficients A, B, and C are: ', a, b, c

! Calculate discriminant
discriminant = b**2 - 4. * a * c

! Solve for the roots, depending upon the value of the discriminant
IF ( discriminant > 0. ) THEN ! there are two real roots, so...

   x1 = ( -b + sqrt(discriminant) ) / ( 2. * a )
   x2 = ( -b - sqrt(discriminant) ) / ( 2. * a )
   WRITE (*,*) 'This equation has two real roots:'
   WRITE (*,*) 'X1 = ', x1
   WRITE (*,*) 'X2 = ', x2

ELSE ( discriminant < 0. ) THEN ! there are complex roots, so ...

   real_part = ( -b ) / ( 2. * a )
```

(*continued*)

(concluded)

```
imag_part = sqrt ( abs ( discriminant ) ) / ( 2. * a )
WRITE (*,*) 'This equation has complex roots:'
WRITE (*,*) 'X1 = ', real_part, ' +i ', imag_part
WRITE (*,*) 'X2 = ', real_part, ' -i ', imag_part

ELSE IF ( discriminant == 0. ) THEN ! there is one repeated root, so...

x1 = ( -b ) / ( 2. * a )
WRITE (*,*) 'This equation has two identical real roots:'
WRITE (*,*) 'X1 = X2 = ', x1

END IF

END PROGRAM roots
```

3

5. Test the program.

Next, we must test the program using real input data. Since there are three possible paths through the program, we must test all three paths before we can be certain that the program is working properly. From Equation (3-2), it is possible to verify the solutions to the equations given below:

$$x^2 + 5x + 6 = 0 \qquad x = -2, \text{ and } x = -3$$
$$x^2 + 4x + 4 = 0 \qquad x = -2$$
$$x^2 + 2x + 5 = 0 \qquad x = -1 \pm i2$$

If this program is compiled, and then run three times with the above coefficients, the results are as shown below (user inputs are shown in bold face):

```
C:\book\chap3>roots
This program solves for the roots of a quadratic
equation of the form A * X**2 + B * X + C = 0.
Enter the coefficients A, B, and C:
1., 5., 6.
The coefficients A, B, and C are: 1.000000      5.000000
   6.000000
This equation has two real roots:
X1 =      -2.000000
X2 =      -3.000000

C:\book\chap3>roots
This program solves for the roots of a quadratic
equation of the form A * X**2 + B * X + C = 0.
Enter the coefficients A, B, and C:
1., 4., 4.
The coefficients A, B, and C are: 1.000000      4.000000
   4.000000
This equation has two identical real roots:
X1 = X2 =      -2.000000
```

```
C:\book\chap3>roots
This program solves for the roots of a quadratic
equation of the form A * X**2 + B * X + C = 0.
Enter the coefficients A, B, and C:
1., 2., 5.
The coefficients A, B, and C are: 1.000000        2.000000
    5.000000
This equation has complex roots:
X1 =     -1.000000 +i      2.000000
X2 =     -1.000000 -i      2.000000
```

The program gives the correct answers for our test data in all three possible cases.

EXAMPLE 3-3

Evaluating a Function of Two Variables:

Write a Fortran program to evaluate a function $f(x,y)$ for any two user-specified values x and y. The function $f(x,y)$ is defined as follows.

$$f(x,y) = \begin{cases} x+y & x \geq 0 \text{ and } y \geq 0 \\ x+y^2 & x \geq 0 \text{ and } y < 0 \\ x^2+y & x < 0 \text{ and } y \geq 0 \\ x^2+y^2 & x < 0 \text{ and } y < 0 \end{cases}$$

SOLUTION
The function $f(x,y)$ is evaluated differently, depending on the signs of the two independent variables x and y. To determine the proper equation to apply, it will be necessary to check for the signs of the x and y values supplied by the user.

1. **State the problem.**
    This problem statement is very simple: Evaluate the function $f(x,y)$ for any user-supplied values of x and y.

2. **Define the inputs and outputs.**
    The inputs required by this program are the values of the independent variables x and y. The output from the program will be the value of the function $f(x,y)$.

3. **Design the algorithm.**
    This task can be broken down into three major sections, whose functions are input, processing, and output:

```
Read the input values x and y
Calculate f(x,y)
Write out f(x,y)
```

We will now break each of the above major sections into smaller, more detailed pieces. There are four possible ways to calculate the function $f(x,y)$, depending on the values of x and y, so it is logical to implement this algorithm with a four-branched IF statement. The resulting pseudocode is:

```
Prompt the user for the values x and y.
Read x and y
Echo the input coefficients
IF x ≥ 0 and y ≥ 0 THEN
    fun ← x + y
ELSE IF x ≥ 0 and y < 0 THEN
    fun ← x + y**2
ELSE IF x < 0 and y ≥ 0 THEN
    fun ← x**2 + y
ELSE
    fun ← x**2 + y**2
END IF
Write out f(x,y)
```

The flowchart for this program is shown in Figure 3-11.

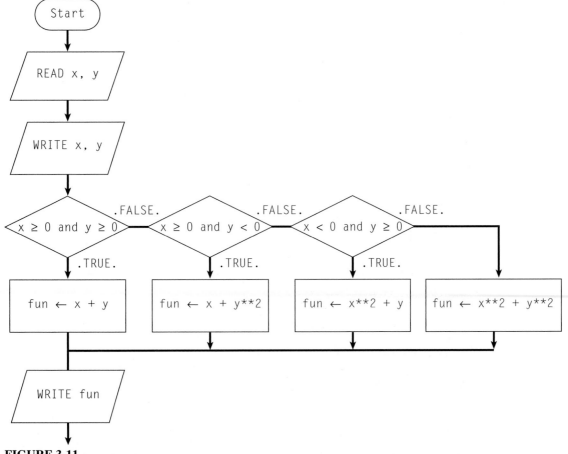

FIGURE 3-11
Flowchart of program funxy.

4. **Turn the algorithm into Fortran statements.**
   The final Fortran code is shown in Figure 3-12.

FIGURE 3-12
Program `funxy` from Example 3-3.

```
PROGRAM funxy
!
! Purpose:
!   This program solves the function f(x,y) for a user-specified x and y,
!   where f(x,y) is defined as:
!
!              _
!             |
!             |   X + Y              X >= 0 and Y >= 0
!             |   X + Y**2           X >= 0 and Y < 0
!   F(X,Y) =  |   X**2 + Y           X < 0 and Y >= 0
!             |   X**2 + Y**2        X < 0 and Y < 0
!             |
!             |_
!
! Record of revisions:
!    Date         Programmer         Description of change
!   ========     ==============      ======================
!   11/06/06     S. J. Chapman       Original code
!
IMPLICIT NONE

! Data dictionary: declare variable types, definitions, & units
REAL :: x                ! First independent variable
REAL :: y                ! Second independent variable
REAL :: fun              ! Resulting function

! Prompt the user for the values x and y
WRITE (*,*) 'Enter the coefficients x and y: '
READ (*,*) x, y

! Write the coefficients of x and y.
WRITE (*,*) 'The coefficients x and y are: ', x, y

! Calculate the function f(x,y) based upon the signs of x and y.
IF ( ( x >= 0. ) .AND. ( y >= 0. ) ) THEN
   fun = x + y
ELSE IF ( ( x >= 0. ) .AND. ( y < 0. ) ) THEN
   fun = x + y**2
ELSE IF ( ( x < 0. ) .AND. ( y >= 0. ) ) THEN
   fun = x**2 + y
ELSE
   fun = x**2 + y**2
END IF

! Write the value of the function.
WRITE (*,*) 'The value of the function is: ', fun

END PROGRAM funxy
```

5. **Test the program.**

   Next, we must test the program using real input data. Since there are four possible paths through the program, we must test all four paths before we can be certain that the program is working properly. To test all four possible paths, we will execute the program with the four sets of input values $(x,y) = (2, 3), (2,-3), (-2, 3),$ and $(-2, -3)$. Calculating by hand, we see that

$$f(2,3) = 2+3 = 5$$

$$f(-2,3) = (-2)^2 + 3 = 7$$

$$f(2,-3) = 2 + (-3)^2 = 11$$

$$f(-2,-3) = (-2)^2 + (-3)^2 = 13$$

If this program is compiled, and then run four times with the above values, the results are:

```
C:\book\chap3>funxy
Enter the coefficients X and Y:
2. 3.
The coefficients X and Y are:     2.000000     3.000000
The value of the function is:     5.000000

C:\book\chap3>funxy
Enter the coefficients X and Y:
2. -3.
The coefficients X and Y are:     2.000000    -3.000000
The value of the function is:    11.000000

C:\book\chap3>funxy
Enter the coefficients X and Y:
-2. 3.
The coefficients X and Y are:    -2.000000     3.000000
The value of the function is:     7.000000

C:\book\chap3>funxy
Enter the coefficients X and Y:
-2. -3.
The coefficients X and Y are:    -2.000000    -3.000000
The value of the function is:    13.000000
```

The program gives the correct answers for our test values in all four possible cases.

3.4.4 Named Block IF Constructs

It is possible to assign a name to a block IF construct. The general form of the construct with a name attached is

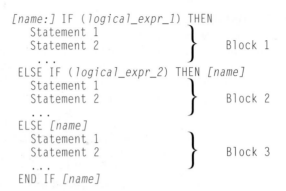

```
[name:] IF (logical_expr_1) THEN
      Statement 1
      Statement 2                        }        Block 1
         . . .
      ELSE IF (logical_expr_2) THEN [name]
      Statement 1
      Statement 2                        }        Block 2
         . . .
      ELSE [name]
      Statement 1
      Statement 2                        }        Block 3
         . . .
      END IF [name]
```

where *name* may be up to 31 alphanumeric characters long, beginning with a letter. The name given to the IF construct must be unique within each program unit, and must not be the same as any constant or variable name within the program unit. If a name is assigned to an IF, then the same name must appear on the associated END IF. Names are optional on the ELSE and ELSE IF statements of the construct, but if they are used, they must be the same as the name on the IF.

Why would we want to name an IF construct? For simple examples like the ones we have seen so far, there is no particular reason to do so. The principal reason for using names is to help us (and the compiler) keep IF constructs straight in our own minds when they get very complicated. For example, suppose that we have a complex IF construct that is hundreds of lines long, spanning many pages of listings. If we name all of the parts of such a construct, then we can tell at a glance which construct a particular ELSE or ELSE IF statement belongs to. They make a programmer's intentions explicitly clear. In addition, names on constructs can help the compiler flag the specific location of an error when one occurs.

Good Programming Practice
Assign a name to any large and complicated IF constructs in your program to help you keep the parts of the construct associated together in your own mind.

3.4.5 Notes Concerning the Use of Block IF Constructs

The block IF construct is very flexible. It must have one IF (. . .) THEN statement and one END IF statement. In between, it can have any number of ELSE IF clauses, and may also have one ELSE clause. With this combination of features, it is possible to implement any desired branching construct.

In addition, block IF constructs may be **nested.** Two block IF constructs are said to be nested if one of them lies entirely within a single code block of the other one. The following two IF constructs are properly nested.

```
outer: IF (x > 0.) THEN
    ...
    inner: IF (y < 0.) THEN
        ...
    END IF inner
    ...
END IF outer
```

It is a good idea to name IF constructs when they are being nested, since the name explicitly indicates which IF a particular END IF is associated with. If the constructs are not named, the Fortran compiler always associates a given END IF with the most recent IF statement. This works well for a properly written program, but can cause the compiler to produce confusing error messages in cases where the programmer makes an coding error. For example, suppose we have a large program containing a construct like the one shown below.

```
PROGRAM mixup
...
IF (test1) THEN
    ...
    IF (test2) THEN
        ...
        IF (test3) THEN
            ...
        END IF
        ...
    END IF
    ...
END IF
...
END PROGRAM mixup
```

This program contains three nested IF constructs that may span hundreds of lines of code. Now suppose that the first END IF statement is accidentally deleted during an editing session. When that happens, the compiler will automatically associate the second END IF with the innermost IF (test3) construct, and the third END IF with the middle IF (test2). When the compiler reaches the END PROGRAM statement, it will notice that the first IF (test1) construct was never ended, and it will generate an error message saying that there is a missing END IF. Unfortunately, it can't tell *where* the problem occurred, so we will have to go back and manually search the entire program to locate the problem.

In contrast, consider what happens if we assign names to each IF construct. The resulting program would be:

```
PROGRAM mixup_1
...
outer: IF (test1) THEN
    ...
    ...
    middle: IF (test2) THEN
        ...
        ...
```

```
inner: IF (test3) THEN
   . . .
   . . .
END IF inner
   . . .
END IF middle
   . . .
END IF outer
   . . .
END PROGRAM mixup_1
```

Suppose that the first END IF statement is again accidentally deleted during an editing session. When that happens, the compiler will notice that there is no END IF associated with the inner IF, and it will generate an error message as soon as it encounters the END IF middle statement. Furthermore, the error message will explicitly state that the problem is associated with the inner IF construct, so we know just where to go to fix it.

It is sometimes possible to implement an algorithm using either ELSE IF clauses or nested IF statements. In that case, a programmer may choose whichever style he or she prefers.

EXAMPLE 3-4

Assigning Letter Grades:

Suppose that we are writing a program that reads in a numerical grade and assigns a letter grade to it according to the following table:

```
95 < GRADE                    A
86 < GRADE ≤ 95               B
76 < GRADE ≤ 86               C
66 < GRADE ≤ 76               D
 0 < GRADE ≤ 66               F
```

Write an IF construct that will assign the grades as described above using (*a*) multiple ELSE IF clauses and (*b*) nested IF constructs.

SOLUTION

(*a*) One possible structure using ELSE IF clauses is

```
IF ( grade > 95.0 ) THEN
   WRITE (*,*) 'The grade is A.'
ELSE IF ( grade > 86.0 ) THEN
   WRITE (*,*) 'The grade is B.'
ELSE IF ( grade > 76.0 ) THEN
   WRITE (*,*) 'The grade is C.'
ELSE IF ( grade > 66.0 ) THEN
   WRITE (*,*) 'The grade is D.'
ELSE
   WRITE (*,*) 'The grade is F.'
END IF
```

(*b*) One possible structure using nested IF constructs is

```
if1: IF ( grade > 95.0 ) THEN
        WRITE (*,*) 'The grade is A.'
     ELSE
        if2: IF ( grade > 86.0 ) THEN
           WRITE (*,*) 'The grade is B.'
        ELSE
           if3: IF ( grade > 76.0 ) THEN
              WRITE (*,*) 'The grade is C.'
           ELSE
              if4: IF ( grade > 66.0 ) THEN
                 WRITE (*,*) 'The grade is D.'
              ELSE
                 WRITE (*,*) 'The grade is F.'
              END IF if4
           END IF if3
        END IF if2
     END IF if1
```

It should be clear from the above example that if there are a lot of mutually exclusive options, a single IF construct with ELSE IF clauses will be simpler than a nested IF construct.

Good Programming Practice
For branches in which there are many mutually exclusive options, use a single IF construct with ELSE IF clauses in preference to nested IF constructs.

3.4.6 The Logical IF Statement

There is an alternative form of the block IF construct described above. It is just a single statement of the form

IF (*logical_expr*) Statement

where Statement is an executable Fortran statement. If the logical expression is true, the program executes the statement on the same line with it. Otherwise, the program skips to the next executable statement in the program. This form of the logical IF is equivalent to a block IF construct with only one statement in the IF block.

3.4.7 The SELECT CASE Construct

The SELECT CASE construct is another form of branching construct. It permits a programmer to select a particular code block to execute based on the value of a single integer, character, or logical expression. The general form of a CASE construct is:

```
[name:] SELECT CASE (case_expr)
CASE (case_selector_1) [name]
   Statement 1
   Statement 2          ⎫
   . . .                ⎬          Block 1
CASE (case_selector_2) [name]
   Statement 1
   Statement 2          ⎫
   . . .                ⎬          Block 2

   . . .
CASE DEFAULT [name]
   Statement 1
   Statement 2          ⎫
   . . .                ⎬          Block n
END SELECT [name]
```

If the value of *case_expr* is in the range of values included in *case_selector_1*, then the first code block will be executed. Similarly, if the value of *case_expr* is in the range of values included in *case_selector_2*, then the second code block will be executed. The same idea applies for any other cases in the construct. The default code block is optional. If it is present, the default code block will be executed whenever the value of *case_expr* is outside the range of all of the case selectors. If it is not present and the value of *case_expr* is outside the range of all of the case selectors, then none of the code blocks will be executed. The pseudocode for the case construct looks just like its Fortran implementation; a flowchart for this construct is shown in Figure 3-13.

A name may be assigned to a CASE construct, if desired. The name must be unique within each program unit. If a name is assigned to a SELECT CASE statement, then

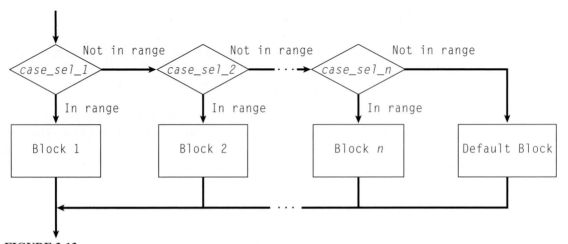

FIGURE 3-13
Flowchart for a SELECT CASE construct.

the same name must appear on the associated END SELECT. Names are optional on the CASE statements of the construct, but if they are used, they must be the same as the name on the SELECT CASE statement.

The *case_expr* may be any integer, character, or logical expression. Each case selector must be an integer, character, or logical value *or a range of values.* All case selectors must be *mutually exclusive;* no single value can appear in more than one case selector.

Let's look at a simple example of a CASE construct. This example prints out a message based on the value of an integer variable.

```
INTEGER :: temp_c          ! Temperature in degrees C
. . .
temp: SELECT CASE (temp_c)
CASE (:-1)
   WRITE (*,*) "It's below freezing today!"
CASE (0)
   WRITE (*,*) "It's exactly at the freezing point."
CASE (1:20)
   WRITE (*,*) "It's cool today."
CASE (21:33)
   WRITE (*,*) "It's warm today."
CASE (34:)
   WRITE (*,*) "It's hot today."
END SELECT temp
```

The value of temp_c controls which case is selected. If the temperature is less than 0, then the first case will be selected, and the message printed out will be "It's below freezing today!" If the temperature is exactly 0, then the second case will be selected, and so forth. Note that the cases do not overlap—a given temperature can appear in only one of the cases.

The *case_selector* can take one of four forms:

case_value	Execute block if *case_value* == *case_expr*
low_value:	Execute block if *low_value* <= *case_expr*
:*high_value*	Execute block if *case_expr* <= *high_value*
low_value:high_value	Execute block if *low_value* <= *case_expr* <= *high_value*

or it can be a list of any combination of these forms separated by commas.

The following statements determine whether an integer between 1 and 10 is even or odd, and print out an appropriate message. It illustrates the use of a list of values as case selectors, and also the use of the CASE DEFAULT block.

```
INTEGER :: value
. . .
SELECT CASE (value)
CASE (1,3,5,7,9)
   WRITE (*,*) 'The value is odd.'
CASE (2,4,6,8,10)
   WRITE (*,*) 'The value is even.'
CASE (11:)
```

```
      WRITE (*,*) 'The value is too high.'
   CASE DEFAULT
      WRITE (*,*) 'The value is negative or zero.'
   END SELECT
```

The CASE DEFAULT block is extremely important for good programming design. If an input value in a SELECT CASE statement does not match any of the cases, none of the cases will be executed. In a well-designed program, this is usually the result of an error in the logical design or an illegal input. You should always include a default case, and have that case create a warning message for the user.

Good Programming Practice

Always include a DEFAULT CASE clause in your case constructs to trap any logical errors or illegal inputs that might occur in a program.

EXAMPLE 3-5

Selecting the Day of the Week with a SELECT CASE Construct:

Write a program that reads an integer from the keyboard, and displays the day of the week corresponding to that integer. Be sure to handle the case of an illegal input value.

SOLUTION

In this example, we will prompt the user to enter an integer between 1 and 7, and then use a SELECT CASE construct to select the day of the week corresponding to that number, using the convention that Sunday is the first day of the week. The SELECT CASE construct will also include a default case to handle illegal days of the week.

The resulting program is shown in Figure 3-14.

FIGURE 3-14
Program day_of_week from Example 3-5.

```
PROGRAM day_of_week
!
! Purpose:
!   This program displays the day of week corresponding to
!   an input integer value.
!
! Record of revisions:
!    Date          Programmer        Description of change
!    ====          ==========        =====================
!  11/06/06    S. J. Chapman      Original code
!
IMPLICIT NONE

! Data dictionary: declare variable types, definitions, & units
```

```
CHARACTER(len=11) :: c_day ! Character string containing day
INTEGER :: i_day            ! Integer day of week

! Prompt the user for the numeric day of the week
WRITE (*,*) 'Enter the day of the week (1-7): '
READ (*,*) i_day

! Get the corresponding day of the week.
SELECT CASE (i_day)
CASE (1)
   c_day = 'Sunday'
CASE (2)
   c_day = 'Monday'
CASE (3)
   c_day = 'Tuesday'
CASE (4)
   c_day = 'Wednesday'
CASE (5)
   c_day = 'Thursday'
CASE (6)
   c_day = 'Friday'
CASE (7)
   c_day = 'Saturday'
CASE DEFAULT
   c_day = 'Invalid day'
END SELECT

! Write the resulting day
WRITE (*,*) 'Day = ', c_day

END PROGRAM day_of_week
```

If this program is compiled, and then executed three times with various values, the results are:

```
C:\book\chap3>day_of_week
Enter the day of the week (1-7):
1
Day = Sunday

C:\book\chap3>day_of_week
Enter the day of the week (1-7):
5
Day = Thursday

C:\book\chap3>day_of_week
Enter the day of the week (1-7):
-2
Day = Invalid day
```

Note that this program gave correct values for valid days of the week, and also displayed an error message for an invalid day.

3

EXAMPLE 3-6

Using Characters in a `SELECT CASE` *Construct:*

Write a program that reads a character string from the keyboard containing a day of the week, and displays "Weekday" if the day falls between Monday and Friday, and "weekend" if the day is Saturday or Sunday. Be sure to handle the case of an illegal input value.

SOLUTION

In this example, we will prompt the user to enter a day of the week, and then use a `SELECT CASE` construct to select whether the day is a weekday or it falls on the weekend. The `SELECT CASE` construct will also include a default case to handle illegal days of the week.

The resulting program is shown in Figure 3-15.

FIGURE 3-15

Program `weekday_weekend` from Example 3-6.

```
PROGRAM weekday_weekend
!
! Purpose:
!   This program accepts a character string containing a
!   day of the week, and responds with a message specifying
!   whether the day is a weekday or it falls on the weekend.
!
! Record of revisions:
!   Date          Programmer        Description of change
!   ====          ============      ======================
!   11/06/06   S. J. Chapman     Original code
!
IMPLICIT NONE

! Declare the variables used in this program.
CHARACTER(len=11) :: c_day  ! Character string containing day
CHARACTER(len=11) :: c_type ! Character string with day type

! Prompt the user for the day of the week
WRITE (*,*) 'Enter the name of the day: '
READ (*,*) c_day

! Get the corresponding day of the week.
SELECT CASE (c_day)
CASE ('Monday','Tuesday','Wednesday','Thursday','Friday')
   c_type = 'Weekday'
CASE ('Saturday','Sunday')
   c_type = 'Weekend'
CASE DEFAULT
   c_type = 'Invalid day'
END SELECT

! Write the resulting day type
WRITE (*,*) 'Day Type = ', c_type
END PROGRAM weekday_weekend
```

If this program is compiled, and then executed three times with various values, the results are:

```
C:\book\chap3>weekday_weekend
Enter the name of the day:
Tuesday
Day Type = Weekday

C:\book\chap3>weekday_weekend
Enter the name of the day:
Sunday
Day Type = Weekend

C:\book\chap3>weekday_weekend
Enter the name of the day:
Holiday
Day Type = Invalid day
```

3

Note that this program gave correct values for valid days of the week, and also displayed an error message for an invalid day. This program illustrates the use of a list of possible case values in each CASE clause.

Quiz 3-2

This quiz provides a quick check to see if you have understood the concepts introduced in Section 3.5. If you have trouble with the quiz, reread the section, ask your instructor, or discuss the material with a fellow student. The answers to this quiz are found in the back of the book.

Write Fortran statements that perform the functions described below.

1. If x is greater than or equal to zero, then assign the square root of x to variable sqrt_x and print out the result. Otherwise, print out an error message about the argument of the square root function, and set sqrt_x to zero.

2. A variable fun is calculated as numerator / denominator. If the absolute value of denominator is less than 1.0E-10, write "Divide by 0 error." Otherwise, calculate and print out fun.

3. The cost per mile for a rented vehicle is $0.30 for the first 100 miles, $0.20 for the next 200 miles, and $0.15 for all miles in excess of 300 miles. Write Fortran statements that determine the total cost and the average cost per mile for a given number of miles (stored in variable distance).

Examine the following Fortran statements. Are they correct or incorrect? If they are correct, what is output by them? If they are incorrect, what is wrong with them?

(continued)

(concluded)

```
4.  IF ( volts > 125. ) THEN
        WRITE (*,*) 'WARNING: High voltage on line. '
    IF ( volts < 105. ) THEN
        WRITE (*,*) 'WARNING: Low voltage on line. '
    ELSE
        WRITE (*,*) 'Line voltage is within tolerances. '
    END IF

5.  PROGRAM test
    LOGICAL :: warn
    REAL :: distance
    REAL, PARAMETER :: LIMIT = 100.
    warn = .TRUE.
    distance = 55. + 10.
    IF ( distance > LIMIT .OR. warn ) THEN
        WRITE (*,*) 'Warning: Distance exceeds limit.'
    ELSE
        WRITE (*,*) 'Distance = ', distance
    END IF

6.  REAL, PARAMETER :: PI = 3.141593
    REAL :: a = 10.
    SELECT CASE ( a * sqrt(PI) )
    CASE (0:)
        WRITE (*,*) 'a > 0'
    CASE (:0)
        WRITE (*,*) 'a < 0'
    CASE DEFAULT
        WRITE (*,*) 'a = 0'
    END SELECT

7.  CHARACTER(len=6) :: color = 'yellow'
    SELECT CASE ( color )
    CASE ('red')
        WRITE (*,*) 'Stop now!'
    CASE ('yellow')
        WRITE (*,*) 'Prepare to stop.'
    CASE ('green')
        WRITE (*,*) 'Proceed through intersection.'
    CASE DEFAULT
        WRITE (*,*) 'Illegal color encountered.'
    END SELECT

8.  IF ( temperature > 37. ) THEN
        WRITE (*,*) 'Human body temperature exceeded. '
    ELSE IF ( temperature > 100. )
        WRITE (*,*) 'Boiling point of water exceeded. '
    END IF
```

■ 3.5

MORE ON DEBUGGING FORTRAN PROGRAMS

It is much easier to make a mistake when writing a program containing branches and loops than it is when writing simple sequential programs. Even after going through the full design process, a program of any size is almost guaranteed not to be completely correct the first time it is used. Suppose that we have built the program and tested it, only to find that the output values are in error. How do we go about finding the bugs and fixing them?

The best approach to locating the error is to use a symbolic debugger, if one is supplied with your compiler. You must ask your instructor or else check with your system's manuals to determine how to use the symbolic debugger supplied with your particular compiler and computer.

An alternative approach to locating the error is to insert WRITE statements into the code to print out important variables at key points in the program. When the program is run, the WRITE statements will print out the values of the key variables. These values can be compared to the ones you expect, and the places where the actual and expected values differ will serve as a clue to help you locate the problem. For example, to verify the operation of a block IF construct:

```
WRITE (*,*) 'At if1: var1 = ', var1
if1: IF ( sqrt(var1) > 1. ) THEN
    WRITE (*,*) 'At if1: sqrt(var1) > 1.'
    . . .
ELSE IF ( sqrt(var1) < 1. ) THEN
    WRITE (*,*) 'At if1: sqrt(var1) < 1.'
    . . .
ELSE
    WRITE (*,*) 'At if1: sqrt(var1) == 1.'
    . . .
END IF if1
```

When the program is executed, its output listing will contain detailed information about the variables controlling the block IF construct and just which branch was executed.

Once you have located the portion of the code in which the error occurs, you can take a look at the specific statements in that area to locate the problem. Two common errors are described below. Be sure to check for them in your code.

1. *If the problem is in an* IF *construct, check to see if you used the proper relational operator in your logical expressions.* Did you use > when you really intended >=, etc.? Logical errors of this sort can be very hard to spot, since the compiler will not give an error message for them. Be especially careful of logical expressions that are very complex, since they will be hard to understand, and very easy to mess up. You should use extra parentheses to make them easier to understand. If the logical expressions are really large, consider breaking them down into simpler expressions that are easier to follow.

2. *Another common problem with* IF *statements occurs when real variables are tested for equality.* Because of small round-off errors during floating-point arithmetic operations, two numbers that theoretically should be equal will differ by a tiny amount, and the test for equality will fail. When you are working with real variables, it is often a good idea to replace a test for equality with a test for *near equality.* For example, instead of testing to see if x is equal to 10., you should test to see if |x - 10.| < 0.0001. Any value of x between 9.9999 and 10.0001 will satisfy the latter test, so round-off error will not cause problems. In Fortran statements,

```
IF ( x == 10. ) THEN
```

would be replaced by

```
IF ( abs(x - 10.) <= 0.0001 ) THEN
```

Good Programming Practice
Be cautious about testing for equality with real variables in an IF construct, since round-off errors may cause two variables that should be equal to fail a test for equality. Instead, test to see if the variables are nearly equal within the round-off error to be expected on the computer you are working with.

3.6
SUMMARY

In Chapter 3 we presented the top-down approach to program design, including pseudocode and flowcharts.

Next, we discussed the logical data type, and more details of the character data type, which can be used to control Fortran branching structures. This material included relational operators, which compare two numbers or character expressions to produce a logical result, and combinational logic operators, which produce a logical result from one or two logical input values.

The Fortran hierarchy of operations, expanded to include the relational and combinational logic operators, is summarized in Table 3-4.

Finally, we have presented the basic types of Fortran branches and loops. The principal type of branch is the block IF—ELSE IF—ELSE—END IF construct. This construct is very flexible. It can have as many ELSE IF clauses as needed to construct any desired test. Furthermore, block IF constructs can be nested to produce more complex tests. A second type of branch is the CASE construct. It may be used to select among mutually exclusive alternatives specified by an integer, character, or logical control expression.

◼ **TABLE 3-4**
Fortran hierarchy of operations

1. Operations within parentheses are evaluated first, starting with the innermost parentheses and working outward.
2. All exponential operations are evaluated next, working from *right* to *left*.
3. All multiplications and divisions are evaluated, working from left to right.
4. All additions and subtractions are evaluated, working from left to right.
5. All relational operators (==, /=, >, >=, <, <=) are evaluated, working from left to right.
6. All .NOT. operators are evaluated.
7. All .AND. operators are evaluated, working from left to right.
8. All .OR. operators are evaluated, working from left to right.
9. All .EQV. and .NEQV. operators are evaluated, working from left to right.

3.6.1 Summary of Good Programming Practice

The following guidelines should be adhered to in programming with branch or loop constructs. By following them consistently, your code will contain fewer bugs, will be easier to debug, and will be more understandable to others who may need to work with it in the future.

1. Always indent code blocks in block IF and CASE constructs to make them more readable.
2. Be cautious about testing for equality with real variables in an IF construct, since round-off errors may cause two variables that should be equal to fail a test for equality. Instead, test to see if the variables are nearly equal within the round-off error to be expected on the computer you are working with.
3. Always include a DEFAULT CASE clause in your case constructs to trap any logical errors or illegal inputs that might occur in a program.

3.6.2 Summary of Fortran Statements and Constructs

The following summary describes the Fortran 95/2003 statements and constructs introduced in this chapter.

Block IF Construct:

```
[name:] IF ( logical_expr_1 ) THEN
      Block 1
```

(continued)

(concluded)

```
               ELSE IF ( logical_expr_2 ) THEN [name]
                  Block 2
               ELSE [name]
                  Block 3
               END IF [name]
```

Description:

The block IF construct permits the execution of a code block based on the results of one or more logical expressions. If *logical_expr_1* is true, the first code block will be executed. If *logical_expr_1* is false and *logical_expr_2* is true, the second code block will be executed. If both logical expressions are false, the third code block will be executed. After any block is executed, control jumps the first statement after the construct.

There must be one and only one IF ( ) THEN statement in a block IF construct. There may be any number of ELSE IF clauses (zero or more), and there may be at most one ELSE clause in the construct. The name is optional, but if it is used on the IF statement, then it must be used on the END IF statement. The name is optional on the ELSE IF and ELSE statements even if it is used on the IF and END IF statements.

CASE **Construct:**

```
               [name:] SELECT CASE (case_expr)
               CASE (case_selector_1) [name]
                  Block 1
               CASE (case_selector_2) [name]
                  Block 2
               CASE DEFAULT [name]
                  Block n
               END SELECT [name]
```

Description:

The CASE construct executes a specific block of statements based on the value of the *case_expr*, which can be an integer, character, or logical value. Each case selector specifies one or more possible values for the case expression. If the *case_expr* is a value included in a given case selector, then the corresponding block of statements is executed, and control will jump to the first executable statement after the end of the construct. If no case selector is executed, then the CASE DEFAULT block will be executed if present, and control will jump to the first executable statement after the end of the construct. If CASE DEFAULT is not present, the construct does nothing.

There must be one SELECT CASE statement and one END SELECT statement in a CASE construct. There will be one or more CASE statements. At most one CASE DEFAULT statement may be included. Note that all case selectors must be *mutually exclusive*. The name is optional, but if it is used on the SELECT CASE statement, then it must also be used on the END SELECT statement. The name is optional on the CASE statements even if it is used on the SELECT CASE and END SELECT statements.

LOGICAL Statement:

```
LOGICAL :: variable_name1[, variable_name2, etc.]
```

Examples:

```
LOGICAL :: initialize, debug
LOGICAL :: debug = .false.
```

Description:

The LOGICAL statement is a type declaration statement that declares variables of the logical data type. The value of a LOGICAL variable may be initialized when it is declared, as shown in the second example above.

3

Logical IF Statement:

```
IF ( logical_expr ) statement
```

Description:

The logical IF statement is a special case of the block IF construct. If logical_expr is true, then the statement on the line with the IF is executed. Execution continues at the next line after the IF statement.

This statement may be used instead of the block IF construct if only one statement needs to be executed as a result of the logical condition.

3.6.3 Exercises

3-1. Which of the following expressions are legal in Fortran? If an expression is legal, evaluate it.

(a) `5.5 >= 5`

(b) `20 > 20`

(c) `.NOT. 6 > 5`

(d) `.TRUE. > .FALSE.`

(e) `35 / 17. > 35 / 17`

(f) `7 <= 8 .EQV. 3 / 2 == 1`

(g) `17.5 .AND. (3.3 > 2.)`

3-2. The tangent function is defined as $\tan \theta = \sin \theta / \cos \theta$. This expression can be evaluated to solve for the tangent as long as the magnitude of $\cos \theta$ is not too near to 0. (If $\cos \theta$ is 0, evaluating the equation for $\tan \theta$ will produce a divide-by-zero error.) Assume that θ is given in degrees, and write Fortran statements to evaluate $\tan\theta$ as long as the magnitude of $\cos\theta$ is greater than or equal to 10^{-20}. If the magnitude of $\cos\theta$ is less than 10^{-20}, write out an error message instead.

3-3. Write the Fortran statements required to calculate $y(t)$ from the equation

$$y(t) = \begin{cases} -3t^2 + 5 & t \geq 0 \\ 3t^2 + 5 & t < 0 \end{cases}$$

for a user-supplied value of t.

3-4. The following Fortran statements are intended to alert a user to dangerously high oral thermometer readings (values are in degrees Fahrenheit). Are they correct or incorrect? If they are incorrect, explain why and correct them.

```
IF ( temp < 97.5 ) THEN
    WRITE (*,*) 'Temperature below normal'
ELSE IF ( temp > 97.5 ) THEN
    WRITE (*,*) 'Temperature normal'
ELSE IF ( temp > 99.5 ) THEN
    WRITE (*,*) 'Temperature slightly high'
ELSE IF ( temp > 103.0 ) THEN
    WRITE (*,*) 'Temperature dangerously high'
END IF
```

3-5. The cost of sending a package by an express delivery service is $12.00 for the first 2 pounds, and $4.00 for each pound or fraction thereof over 2 pounds. If the package weighs more than 70 pounds, a $10.00 excess weight surcharge is added to the cost. No package over 100 pounds will be accepted. Write a program that accepts the weight of a package in pounds and computes the cost of mailing the package. Be sure to handle the case of overweight packages.

3-6. The inverse sine function $asin(x)$ is defined only for the range $-1.0 \leq x \leq 1.0$. If x, is outside this range, an error will occur when the function is evaluated. The following Fortran statements calculate the inverse sine of a number if it is in the proper range, and print an error message if it is not. Assume that x and $inverse\_sine$ are real. Is this code correct or incorrect? If it is incorrect, explain why and correct it:

```
test: IF ( abs(x) <= 1. ) THEN
    inverse_sine = asin(x)
ELSE test
    WRITE (*,*) x, ' is out of range!'
END IF test
```

3-7. In Example 3-3, we wrote a program to evaluate the function $f(x,y)$ for any two user-specified values x and y, where the function $f(x,y)$ was defined as follows:

$$f(x,y) = \begin{cases} x+y & x \geq 0 \text{ and } y \geq 0 \\ x+y^2 & x \geq 0 \text{ and } y < 0 \\ x^2+y & x < 0 \text{ and } y \geq 0 \\ x^2+y^2 & x < 0 \text{ and } y < 0 \end{cases}$$

The problem was solved by using a single block IF construct with four code blocks to calculate $f(x,y)$ for all possible combinations of x and y. Rewrite program $funxy$ to use nested IF constructs, where the outer construct evaluates the value of x and the inner constructs evaluate the value of y. Be sure to assign names to each of your constructs.

3-8. Suppose that a student has the option of enrolling for a single elective during a term. The student must select a course from a limited list of options: English, History, Astronomy, or Literature. Construct a fragment of Fortran code that will prompt the student for a choice, read in the choice, and use the answer as the case expression for a $SELECT\ CASE$ construct. Be sure to include a default case to handle invalid inputs.

3-9. Australia is a truly wonderful place to live, but it is also a land of high taxes. In 2002, individual citizens and residents of Australia paid the following income taxes:

Taxable Income (in A$)	Tax on This Income
$0–$6,000	Nil
$6,001–$20,000	17¢ for each $1 over $6,000
$20,001–$50,000	$2,380 plus 30¢ for each $1 over $20,000
$50,001–$60,000	$11,380 plus 42¢ for each $1 over $50,000
Over $60,000	$15,580 plus 47¢ for each $1 over $60,000

In addition, a flat 1.5 percent Medicare levy is charged on all income. Write a program to calculate how much income tax a person will owe, based on this information. The program should accept a total income figure from the user, and calculate the income tax, Medicare levy, and total tax payable by the individual. Use good programming practices in your program.

3-10. It is often hard to compare the value of two items if they are priced in different currencies. Write a program that will allow a user to enter the cost of a purchase in U.S. dollars, Australian dollars, Euros, or U.K. pounds, and then convert the cost into any of the other currencies, as specified by the user. Use the following conversion factors in your program:

$$A\$1.00 = US\$0.74$$
$$€1.00 = US\$1.21$$
$$UK£1.00 = US\$1.78$$

3-11. Decibels In Exercise 2-21, we wrote a program to calculate a power level in decibels with respect to a 1-mW reference level. The equation implemented was

$$dB = log_{10} \frac{P_2}{P_1}$$

where P_2 is the power level being measured, and P_1 is reference power level (1 milliwatt). This equation uses the logarithm to the base 10, which is undefined for negative or zero values. Modify the program to trap negative or zero input values, and inform the user of the invalid input values.

3-12. Refraction When a ray of light passes from a region with an index of refraction n_1 into a region with a different index of refraction n_2, the light ray is bent (see Figure 3-16). The angle at which the light is bent is given by *Snell's Law*

$$n_1 \sin \theta_1 = n_2 \sin \theta_2 \tag{3-20}$$

where θ_1 is the angle of incidence of the light in the first region and θ_2 is the angle of incidence of the light in the second region. Using Snell's law, it is possible to predict the angle of incidence of a light ray in Region 2 if the angle of incidence θ_1 in Region 1 and the indices of refraction n_1 and n_2 are known. The equation to perform this calculation is

$$\theta_2 = \sin^{-1}\left(\frac{n_1}{n_2} \sin \theta_1 \right) \tag{3-21}$$

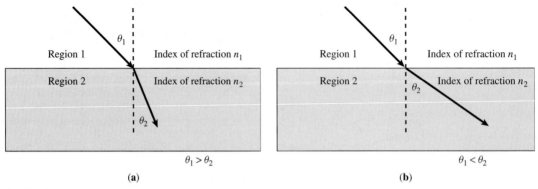

$$\theta_1 > \theta_2 \qquad\qquad\qquad\qquad\qquad\qquad \theta_1 < \theta_2$$

(a)   (b)

FIGURE 3-16
A ray of light bends as it passes from one medium into another one. (*a*) If the ray of light passes from a region with a low index of refraction into a region with a higher index of refraction, the ray of light bends more towards the vertical. (*b*) If the ray of light passes from a region with a high index of refraction into a region with a lower index of refraction, the ray of light bends away from the vertical.

Write a Fortran program to calculate the angle of incidence (in degrees) of a light ray in Region 2 given the angle of incidence θ_1 in Region 1 and the indices of refraction n_1 and n_2. (*Note*: If $n_1 > n_2$, then for some angles θ_1, Equation 3-20 will have no real solution because the absolute value of the quantity $[(n_1/n_2) \sin \theta_1]$ will be greater than 1.0. When this occurs, all light is reflected back into Region 1, and no light passes into Region 2 at all. Your program must be able to recognize and properly handle this condition.) Test your program by running it for the following two cases: (*a*) $n_1 = 1.0$, $n_2 = 1.7$, and $\theta_1 = 45°$; (*b*) $n_1 = 1.0$, $n_2 = 1.7$, and $\theta_1 = 45°$.

3

4

Loops and Character Manipulation

OBJECTIVES

- Know how to create and use while loops.
- Know how to create and use counting loops.
- Know when you should use while loops and when you should use counting loops.
- Know the purpose of the CONTINUE and EXIT statements, and how to use them.
- Understand loop names and why they are used.
- Learn about character assignments and character operators.
- Learn about substrings and string manipulations.

In the previous chapter, we introduced branching structures, which allowed a program to select and execute one of several possible sets of statements, depending on the value of some control expression. In this chapter, we will introduce **loops,** which cause specific sections of the code to be repeated.

We will also learn more about how to manipulate character variables in this chapter. Many of the manipulations will involve loops, and we will use the character manipulations as practice in using loops.

4.1
CONTROL CONSTRUCTS: LOOPS

Loops are Fortran constructs that permit us to execute a sequence of statements more than once. There are two basic forms of loop constructs: **while loops** and **iterative loops** (or **counting loops**). The major difference between these two types of loop is in how the repetition is controlled. The code in a while loop is repeated an indefinite number of times until some user-specified condition is satisfied. By contrast, the code in an iterative loop is repeated a specified number of times, and the number of repetitions is known before the loop starts.

4.1.1 The While Loop

A **while loop** is a block of statements that are repeated indefinitely as long as some condition is satisfied. The general form of a while loop in Fortran 95/2003 is

```
DO
    ...
    IF (logical_expr) EXIT        }    Code Block
    ...
END DO
```

The block of statements between the `DO` and `END DO` are repeated indefinitely until the `logical_expr` becomes true and the `EXIT` statement is executed. After the `EXIT` statement is executed, control transfers to the first statement after the `END DO`.

A while loop may contain one or more `EXIT` statements to terminate its execution. Each `EXIT` statement is usually a part of an `IF` statement or block of construct. If the `logical_expr` in the `IF` is false when the statement is executed, the loop continues to execute. If the `logical_expr` in the `IF` is true when the statement is executed, control transfers immediately to the first statement after the `END DO`. If the logical expression is true the first time we reach the while loop, the statements in the loop below the `IF` will never be executed at all!

The pseudocode corresponding to a while loop is

```
WHILE
    ...
    IF logical_expr EXIT
    ...
End of WHILE
```

and the flowchart for this construct is shown in Figure 4-1.

In a good structured program, every while loop should have a *single entry point and a single exit point*. The entry point for a while loop is the `DO` statement, and the exit point is the `EXIT` statement. Having only a single exit point from a loop helps us to confirm that the loop operates properly under all circumstances. Therefore, each while loop should have only one `EXIT` statement.

Good Programming Practice
Each while loop should contain only one `EXIT` statement.

We will now show an example statistical analysis program that is implemented by using a while loop.

EXAMPLE
4-1

Statistical Analysis:

It is very common in science and engineering to work with large sets of numbers, each of which is a measurement of some particular property that we are interested in.

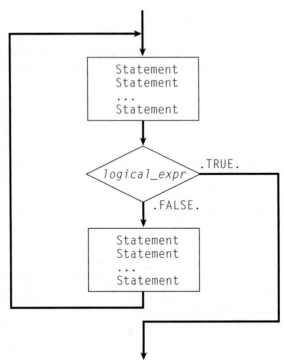

FIGURE 4-1
Flowchart for a while loop.

A simple example would be the grades on the first test in this course. Each grade would be a measurement of how much a particular student has learned in the course to date.

Much of the time, we are not interested in looking closely at every single measurement that we make. Instead, we want to summarize the results of a set of measurements with a few numbers that tell us a lot about the overall data set. Two such numbers are the *average* (or *arithmetic mean*) and the *standard deviation* of the set of measurements. The average or arithmetic mean of a set of numbers is defined as

$$\bar{x} = \frac{1}{N}\sum_{i=1}^{N} x_i \tag{4-1}$$

where x_i is sample i out of N samples. The standard deviation of a set of numbers is defined as

$$s = \sqrt{\frac{N\sum_{i=1}^{N} x_i^2 - \left(\sum_{i=1}^{N} x_i\right)^2}{N(N-1)}} \tag{4-2}$$

Standard deviation is a measure of the amount of scatter on the measurements; the greater the standard deviation, the more scattered the points in the data set are.

Implement an algorithm that reads in a set of measurements and calculates the mean and the standard deviation of the input data set.

SOLUTION

This program must be able to read in an arbitrary number of measurements, and then calculate the mean and standard deviation of those measurements. We will use a while loop to accumulate the input measurements before performing the calculations.

When all of the measurements have been read, we must have some way of telling the program that there is no more data to enter. For now, we will assume that all the input measurements are either positive or zero, and we will use a negative input value as a *flag* to indicate that there is no more data to read. If a negative value is entered, then the program will stop reading input values and will calculate the mean and standard deviation of the data set.

1. **State the problem.**

   Since we assume that the input numbers must be positive or zero, a proper statement of this problem would be: *calculate the average and the standard deviation of a set of measurements, assuming that all of the measurements are either positive or zero, and assuming that we do not know in advance how many measurements are included in the data set. A negative input value will mark the end of the set of measurements.*

2. **Define the inputs and outputs.**

   The inputs required by this program are an unknown number of positive or zero real (floating-point) numbers. The outputs from this program are a printout of the mean and the standard deviation of the input data set. In addition, we will print out the number of data points input to the program, since this is a useful check that the input data was read correctly.

3. **Design the algorithm.**

   This program can be broken down into three major steps:

   ```
   Accumulate the input data
   Calculate the mean and standard deviation
   Write out the mean, standard deviation, and number of points
   ```

   The first major step of the program is to accumulate the input data. To do this, we will have to prompt the user to enter the desired numbers. When the numbers are entered, we will have to keep track of the number of values entered, plus the sum and the sum of the squares of those values. The pseudocode for these steps is:

   ```
   Initialize n, sum_x, and sum_x2 to 0
   WHILE
       Prompt user for next number
       Read in next x
       IF x < 0. EXIT
       n ← n + 1
       sum_x ← sum_x + x
       sum_x2 ← sum_x2 + x**2
   End of WHILE
   ```

Note that we have to read in the first value before the `IF ()` `EXIT` test so that the while loop can have a value to test the first time it executes.

Next, we must calculate the mean and standard deviation. The pseudocode for this step is just the Fortran versions of Eqs. (4-1) and (4-2).

```
x_bar ← sum_x / REAL(n)
std_dev ← SQRT((REAL(n)*sum_x2 - sum_x**2) / (REAL(n)*REAL(n-1)))
```

Finally, we must write out the results.

```
Write out the mean value x_bar
Write out the standard deviation std_dev
Write out the number of input data points n
```

The flowchart for this program is shown in Figure 4-2.

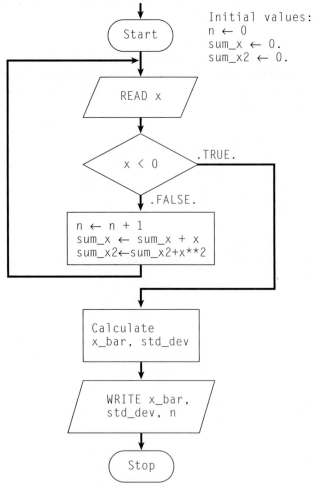

FIGURE 4-2
Flowchart for the statistical analysis program of Example 4-1.

4. **Turn the algorithm into Fortran statements.**
   The final Fortran program is shown in Figure 4-3.

FIGURE 4-3

Program to calculate the mean and standard deviation of a set of nonnegative real numbers.

```fortran
PROGRAM stats_1
!
!   Purpose:
!     To calculate mean and the standard deviation of an input
!     data set containing an arbitrary number of input values.
!
!   Record of revisions:
!      Date          Programmer         Description of change
!      ====          ==========         =====================
!    11/10/06    S. J. Chapman          Original code
!
IMPLICIT NONE

! Data dictionary: declare variable types, definitions, & units
INTEGER :: n = 0       ! The number of input samples.
REAL :: std_dev = 0.   ! The standard deviation of the input samples.
REAL :: sum_x = 0.     ! The sum of the input values.
REAL :: sum_x2 = 0.    ! The sum of the squares of the input values.
REAL :: x = 0.         ! An input data value.
REAL :: x_bar          ! The average of the input samples.

! While Loop to read input values.
DO
   ! Read in next value
   WRITE (*,*) 'Enter number: '
   READ  (*,*) x
   WRITE (*,*) 'The number is ', x

   ! Test for loop exit
   IF ( x < 0 ) EXIT

   ! Otherwise, accumulate sums.
   n      = n + 1
   sum_x  = sum_x + x
   sum_x2 = sum_x2 + x**2
END DO

! Calculate the mean and standard deviation
x_bar = sum_x / real(n)
std_dev = sqrt( (real(n) * sum_x2 - sum_x**2) / (real(n) * real(n-1)) )

! Tell user.
WRITE (*,*) 'The mean of this data set is:', x_bar
WRITE (*,*) 'The standard deviation is:   ', std_dev
WRITE (*,*) 'The number of data points is:', n

END PROGRAM stats_1
```

5. **Test the program.**

To test this program, we will calculate the answers by hand for a simple data set, and then compare the answers to the results of the program. If we used three input values: 3, 4, and 5, then the mean and standard deviation would be

$$\bar{x} = \frac{1}{N}\sum_{i=1}^{N} x_i = \frac{1}{3}12 = 4$$

$$s = \sqrt{\frac{N\sum\limits_{i=1}^{N} x_i^2 - \left(\sum\limits_{i=1}^{N} x_i\right)^2}{N(N-1)}} = 1$$

When these values are fed into the program, the results are

```
C:\book\chap4>stats_1
Enter number:
3.
The number is           3.000000
Enter number:
4.
The number is           4.000000
Enter number:
5.
The number is           5.000000
Enter number:
-1.
The number is          -1.000000
The mean of this data set is:        4.000000
The standard deviation is:           1.000000
The number of data points is:           3
```

The program gives the correct answers for our test data set.

In the preceding example, we failed to follow the design process completely. This failure has left the program with a fatal flaw! Did you spot it?

We have failed because *we did not completely test the program for all possible types of inputs.* Look at the example once again. If we enter either no numbers or only one number, then we will be dividing by zero in the above equations! The division-by-zero error will cause the program to abort. We need to modify the program to detect this problem, inform the user of it, and stop gracefully.

A modified version of the program called stats_2 is shown in Figure 4-4, with the changes shown in boldface. Here, we check to see if there are enough input values before performing the calculations. If not, the program will print out an intelligent error message and quit. Test the modified program for yourself.

FIGURE 4-4

A modified statistical analysis program that avoids the divide-by-zero problems inherent in program stats_1.

```
PROGRAM stats_2
!
!  Purpose:
!    To calculate mean and the standard deviation of an input
!    data set containing an arbitrary number of input values.
!
!  Record of revisions:
!     Date          Programmer          Description of change
!     ====          ==========          =====================
!    11/10/05    S. J. Chapman          Original code
! 1. 11/12/05    S. J. Chapman          Correct divide-by-0 error if
!                                       0 or 1 input values given.
!
IMPLICIT NONE

! Data dictionary: declare variable types, definitions, & units
INTEGER :: n = 0       ! The number of input samples.
REAL :: std_dev = 0.   ! The standard deviation of the input samples.
REAL :: sum_x = 0.     ! The sum of the input values.
REAL :: sum_x2 = 0.    ! The sum of the squares of the input values.
REAL :: x = 0.         ! An input data value.
REAL :: x_bar          ! The average of the input samples.

!  While Loop to read input values.
DO
   ! Read in next value
   WRITE (*,*) 'Enter number: '
   READ  (*,*) x
   WRITE (*,*) 'The number is ', x

   ! Test for loop exit
   IF ( x < 0 ) EXIT

   ! Otherwise, accumulate sums.
   n      = n + 1
   sum_x  = sum_x + x
   sum_x2 = sum_x2 + x**2
END DO

! Check to see if we have enough input data.
IF ( n < 2 ) THEN ! Insufficient information

   WRITE (*,*) 'At least 2 values must be entered!'

ELSE ! There is enough information, so
     ! calculate the mean and standard deviation

   x_bar = sum_x / real(n)
   std_dev = sqrt( (real(n) * sum_x2 - sum_x**2) / (real(n)*real(n-1)))

   ! Tell user.
   WRITE (*,*) 'The mean of this data set is:', x_bar
```

(continued)

(concluded)

```
    WRITE (*,*) 'The standard deviation is:   ', std_dev
    WRITE (*,*) 'The number of data points is:', n

END IF

END PROGRAM stats_2
```

4.1.2 The DO WHILE Loop

There is an alternative form of the while loop in Fortran 95/2003, called the DO WHILE loop. The DO WHILE construct has the form

```
    DO WHILE (logical_expr)                    ⎫  Statement 1
        ...                                    ⎬  Statement 2
        ...                                    ⎪     ...
        ...                                    ⎭  Statement n
    END DO
```

If the logical expression is true, statements 1 through *n* will be executed, and then control will return to the DO WHILE statement. If the logical expression is still true, the statements will be executed again. This process will be repeated until the logical expression becomes false. When control returns to the DO WHILE statement and the logical expression is false, the program will execute the first statement after the END DO.

   This construct is a special case of the more general while loop, in which the exit test must always occur at the top of the loop. There is no reason to ever use it, since the general while loop does the same job with more flexibility.

Good Programming Practice
Do not use DO WHILE loops in new programs. Use the more general while loop instead.

4.1.3 The Iterative or Counting Loop

In the Fortran language, a loop that executes a block of statements a specified number of times is called an **iterative DO loop** or a **counting loop.** The counting loop construct has the form

```
    DO index = istart, iend, incr
        Statement 1                      ⎫
        ...                              ⎬  Code Block
        Statement n                      ⎭
    END DO
```

where index is an integer variable used as the loop counter (also known as the **loop index**). The integer quantities istart, iend, and incr are the *parameters* of the counting loop; they control the values of the variable index during execution. The parameter incr is optional; if it is missing, it is assumed to be 1.

The statements between the DO statement and the END DO statement are known as the *body* of the loop. They are executed repeatedly during each pass of the DO loop.

The counting loop construct functions as follows:

1. Each of the three DO loop parameters istart, iend, and incr may be a constant, a variable, or an expression. If they are variables or expressions, then their values are calculated before the start of the loop, and the resulting values are used to control the loop.
2. At the beginning of the execution of the DO loop, the program assigns the value istart to control variable index. If index*incr ≤ iend*incr, the program executes the statements within the body of the loop.
3. After the statements in the body of the loop have been executed, the control variable is recalculated as

$$index = index + incr$$

   If index*incr is still ≤ iend*incr, the program executes the statements within the body again.
4. Step 2 is repeated over and over as long as index*incr ≤ iend*incr. When this condition is no longer true, execution skips to the first statement following the end of the DO loop.

The number of iterations to be performed by the DO loop may be calculated by the following equation

$$iter = \frac{iend - istart + incr}{incr} \qquad (4\text{-}3)$$

Let's look at a number of specific examples to make the operation of the counting loop clearer. First, consider the following example:

```
DO i = 1, 10
   Statement 1
   ...
   Statement n
END DO
```

In this case, statements 1 through *n* will be executed 10 times. The index variable i will be 1 on the first time, 2 on the second time, and so on. The index variable will be 10 on the last pass through the statements. When control is returned to the DO statement after the tenth pass, the index variable i will be increased to 11. Since 11 × 1 > 10 × 1, control will transfer to the first statement after the END DO statement.

Second, consider the following example:

```
DO i = 1, 10, 2
   Statement 1
   ...
   Statement n
END DO
```

In this case, statements 1 through *n* will be executed five times. The index variable i will be 1 on the first time, 3 on the second time, and so on. The index variable will be 9 on the fifth and last pass through the statements. When control is returned to the DO statement after the fifth pass, the index variable i will be increased to 11. Since $11 \times 2 > 10 \times 2$, control will transfer to the first statement after the END DO statement.

Third, consider the following example:

```
DO i = 1, 10, -1
    Statement 1
    ...
    Statement n
END DO
```

Here, *statements 1 through n will never be executed*, since index*incr > iend*incr on the very first time that the DO statement is reached. Instead, control will transfer to the first statement after the END DO statement.

Finally, consider the example:

```
DO i = 3, -3, -2
    Statement 1
    ...
    Statement n
END DO
```

In this case, statements 1 through *n* will be executed four times. The index variable i will be 3 on the first time, 1 on the second time, -1 on the third time, and -3 on the fourth time. When control is returned to the DO statement after the fourth pass, the index variable i will be decreased to -5. Since $-5 \times -2 > -3 \times -2$, control will transfer to the first statement after the END DO statement.

The pseudocode corresponding to a counting loop is

```
DO for index = istart to iend by incr
    Statement 1
    ...
    Statement n
End of DO
```

and the flowchart for this construct is shown in Figure 4-5.

EXAMPLE 4-2   *The Factorial Function:*

To illustrate the operation of a counting loop, we will use a DO loop to calculate the factorial function. The factorial function is defined as

$$N! = 1 \qquad\qquad N = 0$$
$$N! = N * (N-1) * (N-2) * \ldots * 3 * 2 * 1 \qquad N > 0$$

The Fortran code to calculate N factorial for positive value of N would be

```
n_factorial = 1
DO i = 1, n
    n_factorial = n_factorial * i
END DO
```

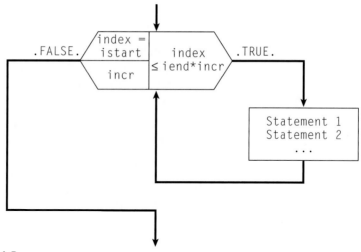

FIGURE 4-5
Flowchart for a DO loop construct.

Suppose that we wish to calculate the value of 5!. If n is 5, the DO loop parameters will be istart = 1, iend = 5, and incr = 1. This loop will be executed five times, with the variable i taking on values of 1, 2, 3, 4, and 5 in the successive loops. The resulting value of n_factorial will be 1 × 2 × 3 × 4 × 5 = 120.

EXAMPLE   *Calculating the Day of Year:*
4-3

The *day of year* is the number of days (including the current day) that have elapsed since the beginning of a given year. It is a number in the range 1 to 365 for ordinary years, and 1 to 366 for leap years. Write a Fortran program that accepts a day, month, and year, and calculates the day of year corresponding to that date.

SOLUTION
To determine the day of year, this program will need to sum up the number of days in each month preceding the current month, plus the number of elapsed days in the current month. A DO loop will be used to perform this sum. Since the number of days in each month varies, it is necessary to determine the correct number of days to add for each month. A SELECT CASE construct will be used to determine the proper number of days to add for each month.

During a leap year, an extra day must be added to the day of year for any month after February. This extra day accounts for the presence of February 29 in the leap year. Therefore, to perform the day of year calculation correctly, we must determine which years are leap years. In the Gregorian calendar, leap years are determined by the following rules:

1. Years evenly divisible by 400 are leap years.
2. Years evenly divisible by 100 but *not* by 400 are not leap years.
3. All years divisible by 4 but *not* by 100 are leap years.
4. All other years are not leap years.

We will use the MOD (for modulo) function to determine whether or not a year is evenly divisible by a given number. If the result of the MOD function is zero, then the year is evenly divisible.

A program to calculate the day of year is shown in Figure 4-6. Note that the program sums up the number of days in each month before the current month, and that it uses a SELECT CASE construct to determine the number of days in each month.

FIGURE 4-6
A program to calculate the equivalent day of year from a given day, month, and year.

```
PROGRAM doy
!  Purpose:
!    This program calculates the day of year corresponding to a
!    specified date.  It illustrates the use of counting loops
!    and the SELECT CASE construct.
!
!  Record of revisions:
!      Date        Programmer        Description of change
!      ====        ==========        =====================
!    11/13/06    S. J. Chapman       Original code
!
IMPLICIT NONE

! Data dictionary: declare variable types, definitions, & units
INTEGER :: day         ! Day (dd)
INTEGER :: day_of_year ! Day of year
INTEGER :: i           ! Index variable
INTEGER :: leap_day    ! Extra day for leap year
INTEGER :: month       ! Month (mm)
INTEGER :: year        ! Year (yyyy)

! Get day, month, and year to convert
WRITE (*,*) 'This program calculates the day of year given the '
WRITE (*,*) 'current date.  Enter current month (1-12), day(1-31),'
WRITE (*,*) 'and year in that order:  '
READ (*,*) month, day, year

! Check for leap year, and add extra day if necessary
IF ( MOD(year,400) == 0 ) THEN
   leap_day = 1            ! Years divisible by 400 are leap years
ELSE IF ( MOD(year,100) == 0 ) THEN
   leap_day = 0            ! Other centuries are not leap years
ELSE IF ( MOD(year,4) == 0 ) THEN
```

(continued)

(*concluded*)

```
    leap_day = 1           ! Otherwise every 4th year is a leap year
ELSE
    leap_day = 0           ! Other years are not leap years
END IF

! Calculate day of year
day_of_year = day
DO i = 1, month-1

    ! Add days in months from January to last month
    SELECT CASE (i)
    CASE (1,3,5,7,8,10,12)
        day_of_year = day_of_year + 31
    CASE (4,6,9,11)
        day_of_year = day_of_year + 30
    CASE (2)
        day_of_year = day_of_year + 28 + leap_day
    END SELECT

END DO

! Tell user
WRITE (*,*) 'Day         = ', day
WRITE (*,*) 'Month       = ', month
WRITE (*,*) 'Year        = ', year
WRITE (*,*) 'day of year = ', day_of_year

END PROGRAM doy
```

We will use the following known results to test the program:

1. Year 1999 is not a leap year. January 1 must be day of year 1, and December 31 must be day of year 365.
2. Year 2000 is a leap year. January 1 must be day of year 1, and December 31 must be day of year 366.
3. Year 2001 is not a leap year. March 1 must be day of year 60, since January has 31 days, February has 28 days, and this is the first day of March.

If this program is compiled, and then run five times with the above dates, the results are

```
C:\book\chap4>doy

This program calculates the day of year given the
current date.  Enter current month (1-12), day(1-31),
and year in that order:  1 1 1999

Day         =            1
Month       =            1
Year        =         1999
day of year =            1

C:\book\chap4>doy

This program calculates the day of year given the
```

(*continued*)

(concluded)

```
            current date.  Enter current month (1-12), day(1-31),
            and year in that order:  12 31 1999

            Day          =              31
            Month        =              12
            Year         =            1999
            day of year  =             365

            C:\book\chap4>doy

            This program calculates the day of year given the
            current date.  Enter current month (1-12), day(1-31),
            and year in that order:  1 1 2000

            Day          =               1
            Month        =               1
            Year         =            2000
            day of year  =               1

            C:\book\chap4>doy

            This program calculates the day of year given the
            current date.  Enter current month (1-12), day(1-31),
            and year in that order:  12 31 2000

            Day          =              31
            Month        =              12
            Year         =            2000
            day of year  =             366

            C:\book\chap4>doy

            This program calculates the day of year given the
            current date.  Enter current month (1-12), day(1-31),
            and year in that order:  3 1 2001

            Day          =               1
            Month        =               3
            Year         =            2001
            day of year  =              60
```

The program gives the correct answers for our test dates in all five test cases.

EXAMPLE 4-4

Statistical Analysis:

Implement an algorithm that reads in a set of measurements and calculates the mean and the standard deviation of the input data set, when any value in the data set can be positive, negative, or zero.

SOLUTION

This program must be able to read in an arbitrary number of measurements, and then calculate the mean and standard deviation of those measurements. Each measurement can be positive, negative, or zero.

Since we cannot use a data value as a flag this time, we will ask the user for the number of input values, and then use a DO loop to read in those values. A flowchart for this program is shown in Figure 4-7. Note that the while loop has been replaced by a

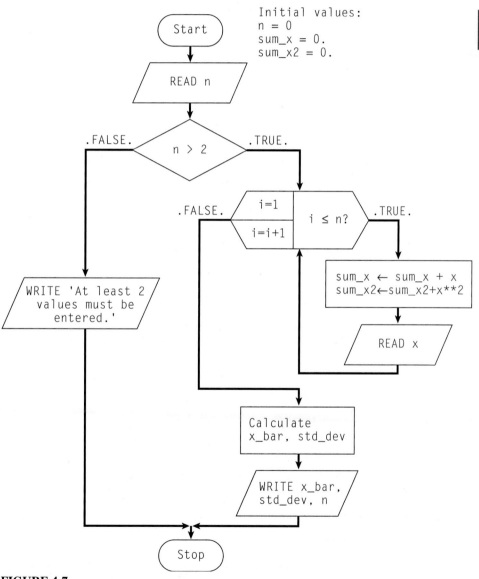

FIGURE 4-7

Flowchart for modified statistical analysis program using a DO loop.

counting loop. The modified program that permits the use of any input value is shown
in Figure 4-8. Verify its operation for yourself by finding the mean and standard deviation of the following five input values: 3., $-1.$, 0., 1., and -2.

FIGURE 4-8
Modified statistical analysis program that works with both positive and negative input values.

```
PROGRAM stats_3
!
!  Purpose:
!    To calculate mean and the standard deviation of an input
!    data set, where each input value can be positive, negative,
!    or zero.
!
!  Record of revisions:
!      Date          Programmer          Description of change
!      ====          ==========          =====================
!    11/13/06     S. J. Chapman          Original code
!
IMPLICIT NONE

! Data dictionary: declare variable types, definitions, & units
INTEGER :: i          ! Loop index
INTEGER :: n = 0      ! The number of input samples.
REAL :: std_dev       ! The standard deviation of the input samples.
REAL :: sum_x = 0.    ! The sum of the input values.
REAL :: sum_x2 = 0.   ! The sum of the squares of the input values.
REAL :: x = 0.        ! An input data value.
REAL :: x_bar         ! The average of the input samples.

! Get the number of points to input.
WRITE (*,*) 'Enter number of points: '
READ  (*,*) n

! Check to see if we have enough input data.
IF ( n < 2 ) THEN ! Insufficient data

   WRITE (*,*) 'At least 2 values must be entered.'

ELSE ! we will have enough data, so let's get it.

   ! Loop to read input values.
   DO i = 1, n

      ! Read values
      WRITE (*,*) 'Enter number: '
      READ  (*,*) x
      WRITE (*,*) 'The number is ', x

      ! Accumulate sums.
      sum_x  = sum_x + x
      sum_x2 = sum_x2 + x**2

   END DO
```

(*continued*)

(concluded)

```
! Now calculate statistics.
x_bar = sum_x / real(n)
std_dev = sqrt((real(n)*sum_x2 - sum_x**2) / (real(n)*real(n-1)))

! Tell user.
WRITE (*,*) 'The mean of this data set is:', x_bar
WRITE (*,*) 'The standard deviation is:   ', std_dev
WRITE (*,*) 'The number of data points is:', n

END IF

END PROGRAM stats_3
```

4

Details of Operation

Now that we have seen examples of a counting DO loop in operation, we will examine some of the important details required to use DO loops properly.

1. It is not necessary to indent the body of the DO loop as we have shown above. The Fortran compiler will recognize the loop even if every statement in it starts in column 1. However, the code is much more readable if the body of the DO loop is indented, so you should always indent the bodies of your DO loops.

Good Programming Practice
Always indent the body of a DO loop by two or more spaces to improve the readability of the code.

2. The index variable of a DO loop *must not be modified anywhere within the DO loop*. Since the index variable is used to control the repetitions in the DO loop, changing it could produce unexpected results. In the worst case, modifying the index variable could produce an *infinite loop* that never completes. Consider the following example:

```
PROGRAM bad_1
INTEGER :: i
DO i = 1, 4
  i = 2
END DO
END PROGRAM bad_1
```

If i is reset to 2 every time through the loop, the loop will never end, because the index variable can never be greater than 4! This loop will run forever unless the program containing it is killed. Almost all Fortran compilers will recognize this problem, and will generate a compile-time error if a program attempts to modify an index variable within a loop.

Programming Pitfalls
Never modify the value of a DO loop index variable while inside the loop.

3. If the number of iterations calculated from Equation 4-3 is less than or equal to zero, the statements within the DO loop are never executed at all. For example, the statements in the following DO loop will never be executed

```
DO i = 3, 2
    ...
END DO
```

since

$$iter = \frac{iend - istart + incr}{incr} = \frac{2 - 3 + 1}{1} = 0$$

4. It is possible to design counting DO loops that count down as well as up. The following DO loop executes three times with i being 3, 2, and 1 in the successive loops.

```
DO i = 3, 1, -1
    ...
END DO
```

5. The index variable and control parameters of a DO loop should always be of type integer. The use of real variables as DO loop indices and DO loop control parameters used to be a legal but undesirable feature of Fortran. It was declared obsolescent in Fortran 90, and has been completely deleted from Fortran 95.

6. It is possible to branch out of a DO loop at any time while the loop is executing. If program execution does branch out of a DO loop before it would otherwise finish, the loop index variable retains the value that it had when the branch occurred. Consider the following example.

```
INTEGER :: i
DO i = 1, 5
    ...
    IF (i >= 3) EXIT
    ...
END DO
WRITE (*,*) i
```

Execution will branch out of the DO loop and go to the WRITE statement on the third pass through the loop. When execution gets to the WRITE statement, variable i will contain a value of 3.

7. If a DO loop completes normally, *the value of the index variable is undefined when the loop is completed.* In the example that follows, the value written out by the WRITE statement is not defined in the Fortran standard.

```
INTEGER :: i
DO i = 1, 5
    ...
END DO
WRITE (*,*) i
```

On many computers, after the loop has completed, the index variable i will contain the first value of the index variable to fail the index*incr ≤ iend*incr test. In the above code, the result would usually contain a 6 after the loop is finished. However, don't count on it! Since the value is officially undefined in the Fortran standard, some compilers may produce a different result. If your code depends on the value of the index variable after the loop is completed, you may get different results as the program is moved between computers.

4

Good Programming Practice
Never depend on an index variable to retain a specific value after a DO loop completes normally.

4.1.4 The CYCLE and EXIT Statements

There are two additional statements that can be used to control the operation of while loops and counting DO loops: CYCLE and EXIT.

If the CYCLE statement is executed in the body of a DO loop, the execution of the *current iteration* of the loop will stop, and control will be returned to the top of the loop. The loop index will be incremented, and execution will resume again if the index has not reached its limit. An example of the CYCLE statement in a counting DO loop is shown below.

```
PROGRAM test_cycle
INTEGER :: i
DO i = 1, 5
   IF ( i == 3 ) CYCLE
   WRITE (*,*) i
END DO
WRITE (*,*) 'End of loop!'
END PROGRAM test_cycle
```

The flowchart for this loop is shown in Figure 4-9a. When this program is executed, the output is:

```
C:\book\chap4>test_cycle
          1
          2
          4
          5
End of loop!
```

Note that the CYCLE statement was executed on the iteration when i was 3, and control returned to the top of the loop without executing the WRITE statement. After control was returned to the top of the loop, the loop index was incremented and the loop continued to execute.

If the EXIT statement is executed in the body of a loop, the execution of the loop will stop and control will be transferred to the first executable statement after the loop. An example of the EXIT statement in a DO loop is shown below.

```
PROGRAM test_exit
INTEGER :: i
DO i = 1, 5
   IF ( i == 3 ) EXIT
   WRITE (*,*) i
END DO
WRITE (*,*) 'End of loop!'
END PROGRAM test_exit
```

The flowchart for this loop is shown in Figure 4-9*b*. When this program is executed, the output is:

```
C:\book\chap4>test_exit
         1
         2
End of loop!
```

Note that the EXIT statement was executed on the iteration when i was 3, and control transferred to the first executable statement after the loop without executing the WRITE statement.

Both the CYCLE and EXIT statements work with both while loops and counting DO loops.

4.1.5 Named Loops

It is possible to assign a name to a loop. The general form of a while loop with a name attached is

```
[name:] DO
   Statement
   Statement
   Statement
   IF ( logical_expr ) CYCLE [name]
   ...
   IF ( logical_expr ) EXIT [name]
END DO [name]
```

and the general form of a counting loop with a name attached is

```
[name:] DO index = istart, iend, incr
   Statement
   Statement
   IF ( logical_expr ) CYCLE [name]
   ...
END DO [name]
```

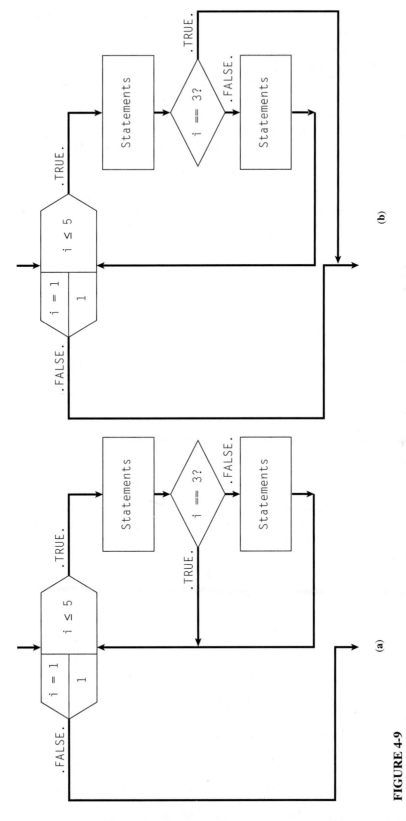

FIGURE 4-9

(*a*) Flowchart of a `DO loop` containing a `CYCLE` statement. (*b*) Flowchart of a `DO` loop containing an `EXIT` statement.

149

where *name* may be up to 31 alphanumeric characters long, beginning with a letter. The name given to the loop must be unique within each program unit. If a name is assigned to a loop, then the same name must appear on the associated END DO. Names are optional on any CYCLE and EXIT statements associated with the loop, but if they are used, they must be the same as the name on the DO statement.

Why would we want to name a loop? For simple examples like the ones we have seen so far, there is no particular reason to do so. The principal reason for using names is to help us (and the compiler) keep loops straight in our own minds when they get very complicated. For example, suppose that we have a complex loop that is hundreds of lines long, spanning many pages of listings. There may be many smaller loops inside the body of that loop. If we name all of the parts of the loop, then we can tell at a glance which construct a particular END DO, CYCLE, or EXIT statement belongs to. They make our intentions explicitly clear. In addition, names on constructs can help the compiler flag the specific location of an error when one occurs.

Good Programming Practice

Assign a name to any large and complicated loops in your program to help you keep the parts of the construct associated together in your own mind.

4.1.6 Nesting Loops and Block IF Constructs

Nesting loops

It is possible for one loop to be completely inside another loop. If one loop is completely inside another one, the two loops are called **nested loops.** The following example shows two nested DO loops used to calculate and write out the product of two integers.

```
PROGRAM nested_loops
INTEGER :: i, j, product
DO i = 1, 3
   DO j = 1, 3
      product = i * j
      WRITE (*,*) i, ' * ', j, ' = ', product
   END DO
END DO
END PROGRAM nested_loops
```

In this example, the outer DO loop will assign a value of 1 to index variable i, and then the inner DO loop will be executed. The inner DO loop will be executed three times with index variable J having values 1, 2, and 3. When the entire inner DO loop has been completed, the outer DO loop will assign a value of 2 to index variable i, and the inner DO loop will be executed again. This process repeats until the outer DO loop has executed three times, and the resulting output is

```
1 *     1 =     1
1 *     2 =     2
1 *     3 =     3
2 *     1 =     2
2 *     2 =     4
2 *     3 =     6
3 *     1 =     3
3 *     2 =     6
3 *     3 =     9
```

Note that the inner DO loop executes completely before the index variable of the outer DO loop is incremented.

When a Fortran compiler encounters an END DO *statement, it associates that statement with the innermost currently open loop.* Therefore, the first END DO statement above closes the "DO j = 1, 3 " loop, and the second END DO statement above closes the "DO i = 1, 3 " loop. This fact can produce hard-to-find errors if an END DO statement is accidentally deleted somewhere within a nested loop construct. If each of the nested loops is named, then the error will be much easier to find.

To illustrate this problem, let's "accidentally" delete the inner END DO statement in the previous example, and compile the program with the Intel Visual Fortran compiler.

```
PROGRAM bad_nested_loops_1
INTEGER :: i, j, product
DO i = 1, 3
   DO j = 1, 3
      product = i * j
      WRITE (*,*) i, ' * ', j, ' = ', product
END DO
END PROGRAM bad_nested_loops_1
```

The output of the compiler is:

```
C:\book\chap4>ifort bad_nested_loops_1.f90
Intel(R) Fortran Compiler for 32-bit applications, Version 9.1
Build 20060706 Z Package ID: W_FC_C_9.1.028
Copyright (C) 1985-2006 Intel Corporation. All rights reserved.

bad_nested_loops_1.f90(3) : Error: An unterminated block exists.
DO i = 1, 3
^

compilation aborted for bad_nested_loops_1.f90 (code 1)
```

The compiler reports that there is a problem with the loop construct, but it can not detect the problem until the END PROGRAM statement is reached, and it cannot tell where the problem occurred. If the program is very large, we would be faced with a difficult task when we tried to locate the problem.

Now let's name each loop and "accidentally" delete the inner END DO statement.

```
PROGRAM bad_nested_loops_2
INTEGER :: i, j, product
outer: DO i = 1, 3
   inner: DO j = 1, 3
      product = i * j
      WRITE (*,*) i, ' * ', j, ' = ', product
END DO outer
END PROGRAM bad_nested_loops_2
```

When we compile the program with the Intel Visual Fortran compiler, the output is:

```
C:\book\chap4>df bad_nested_loops_2.f90
Intel(R) Fortran Compiler for 32-bit applications, Version 9.1 Build
20060706
Z Package ID: W_FC_C_9.1.028

bad_nested_loops_2.f90(7) : Error: The block construct names must match,
and they do not.    [OUTER]
END DO outer
-------^
bad_nested_loops_2.f90(3) : Error: An unterminated block exists.
outer: DO i = 1, 3
^

compilation aborted for bad_nested_loops_2.f90 (code 1)
```

The compiler reports that there is a problem with the loop construct, and it reports which loops were involved in the problem. This can be a major aid in debugging the program.

Good Programming Practice
Assign names to all nested loops so that they will be easier to understand and debug.

If DO *loops are nested, they must have independent index variables*. Remember that it is not possible to change an index variable within the body of a DO loop. Therefore, it is not possible to use the same index variable for two nested DO loops, since the inner loop would be attempting to change the index variable of the outer loop within the body of the outer loop.

Also, *if two loops are to be nested, one of them must lie completely within the other one*. The following DO loops are incorrectly nested, and a compile-time error will be generated for this code.

```
outer: DO i = 1, 3
   ...
   inner: DO j = 1, 3
      ...
   END DO outer
   ...
END DO inner
```

The CYCLE and EXIT statements in nested loops

If a CYCLE or EXIT statement appears inside an *unnamed* set of nested loops, then the CYCLE or EXIT statement refers to the *innermost* of the loops containing it. For example, consider the following program

```
PROGRAM test_cycle_1
INTEGER :: i, j, product
DO i = 1, 3
   DO j = 1, 3
      IF ( j == 2) CYCLE
      product = i * j
      WRITE (*,*) i, ' * ', j, ' = ', product
   END DO
END DO
END PROGRAM test_cycle_1
```

If the inner loop counter j is equal to 2, then the CYCLE statement will be executed. This will cause the remainder of the code block of the *innermost* DO loop to be skipped, and execution of the innermost loop will start over with j increased by 1. The resulting output values are

```
1 *   1 =   1
1 *   3 =   3
2 *   1 =   2
2 *   3 =   6
3 *   1 =   3
3 *   3 =   9
```

Each time the inner loop variable had the value 2, execution of the inner loop was skipped.

It is also possible to make the CYCLE or EXIT statement refer to the *outer* loop of a nested construct of named loops by specifying a loop name in the statement. In the following example, when the inner loop counter j is equal to 2, the CYCLE outer statement will be executed. This will cause the remainder of the code block of the *outer* DO loop to be skipped, and execution of the outer loop will start over with i increased by 1.

```
PROGRAM test_cycle_2
INTEGER :: i, j, product
outer: DO i = 1, 3
   inner: DO j = 1, 3
      IF ( j == 2) CYCLE outer
      product = i * j
      WRITE (*,*) i, ' * ', j, ' = ', product
   END DO inner
END DO outer
END PROGRAM test_cycle_2
```

The resulting output values are

```
1 *   1 =   1
2 *   1 =   2
3 *   1 =   3
```

You should always use loop names with CYCLE or EXIT statements in nested loops to make sure that the proper loop is affected by the statements.

Good Programming Practice
Use loop names with CYCLE or EXIT statements in nested loops to make sure that the proper loop is affected by the statements.

4

Nesting loops within IF constructs and vice versa

It is possible to nest loops within block IF constructs or block IF constructs within loops. If a loop is nested within a block IF construct, *the loop must lie entirely within a single code block* of the IF construct. For example, the following statements are illegal since the loop stretches between the IF and the ELSE code blocks of the IF construct.

```
outer: IF ( a < b ) THEN
   ...
   inner: DO i = 1, 3
      ...
ELSE
      ...
   END DO inner
   ...
END IF outer
```

In contrast, the following statements are legal, since the loop lies entirely within a single code block of the IF construct.

```
outer: IF ( a < b ) THEN
   ...
   inner: DO i = 1, 3
      ...
   END DO inner
   ...
ELSE
   ...
END IF outer
```

Quiz 4-1

This quiz provides a quick check to see if you have understood the concepts introduced in Section 4.1. If you have trouble with the quiz, reread the section, ask your instructor, or discuss the material with a fellow student. The answers to this quiz are found in the back of the book.

Examine the following DO loops and determine how many times each loop will be executed. Assume that all of the index variables shown are of type integer.

(continued)

(continued)

1. `DO index = 5, 10`

2. `DO j = 7, 10, -1`

3. `DO index = 1, 10, 10`

4. `DO loop_counter = -2, 10, 2`

5. `DO time = -5, -10, -1`

6. `DO i = -10, -7, -3`

Examine the following loops and determine the value in ires at the end of each of the loops. Assume that ires, incr, and all index variables are integers.

7.
```
ires = 0
DO index = 1, 10
    ires = ires + 1
END DO
```

8.
```
ires = 0
DO index = 1, 10
    ires = ires + index
END DO
```

9.
```
ires = 0
DO index = 1, 10
    IF ( ires == 10 ) CYCLE
    ires = ires + index
END DO
```

10.
```
ires = 0
DO index1 = 1, 10
    DO index2 = 1, 10
        ires = ires + 1
    END DO
END DO
```

11.
```
ires = 0
DO index1 = 1, 10
    DO index2 = index1, 10
        IF ( index2 > 6 ) EXIT
        ires = ires + 1
    END DO
END DO
```

Examine the following Fortran statements and tell whether or not they are valid. If they are invalid, indicate the reason why they are invalid.

12.
```
loop1: DO i = 1, 10
    loop2: DO j = 1, 10
        loop3: DO i = i, j
            ...
        END DO loop3
```

(continued)

4

```
(concluded)
            END DO loop2
        END DO loop1
  13.  loop1: DO i = 1, 10
          loop2: DO j = i, 10
            loop3: DO k = i, j
              ...
            END DO loop3
          END DO loop2
        END DO loop1
  14.  loopx: DO i = 1, 10
          ...
          loopy: DO j = 1, 10
            ...
          END DO loopx
        END DO loopy
```

■ 4.2

CHARACTER ASSIGNMENTS AND CHARACTER MANIPULATIONS

Character data can be manipulated by using **character expressions.** A character expression can be any combination of valid character constants, character variables, character operators, and character functions. A **character operator** is an operator on character data that yields a character result. There are two basic types of character operators: **substring specifications** and **concatenation.** Character functions are functions that yield a character result.

4.2.1 Character Assignments

A character expression may be assigned to a character variable with an assignment statement. If the character expression is *shorter* than the length of the character variable to which it is assigned, then the rest of the variable is padded out with blanks. For example, the statements

```
CHARACTER(len=3) :: file_ext
file_ext = 'f'
```

store the value 'f&&' into variable file_ext (& denotes a blank character). If the character expression is *longer* than the length of the character variable to which it is assigned, then the excess portion of the character variable is discarded. For example, the statements

```
CHARACTER(len=3) :: file_ext_2
file_extent_2 = 'FILE01'
```

will store the value 'FIL' into variable file_ext_2, and the characters 'E01' are discarded.

4.2.2 Substring Specifications

A **substring specification** selects a portion of a character variable, and treats that portion as if it were an independent character variable. For example, if the variable str1 is a six-character variable containing the string '123456', then the substring str1(2:4) would be a three-character variable containing the string '234'. The substring str1(2:4) really refers to the same memory locations as characters 2 through 4 of str1, so if the contents of str1(2:4) are changed, the characters in the middle of variable str1 will also be changed.

A character substring is denoted by placing integer values representing the starting and ending character numbers separated by a colon in parentheses following the variable name. If the ending character number is less than the starting number, a zero-length character string will be produced.

The following example illustrates the use of substrings.

EXAMPLE 4-5

What will the contents of variables a, b, and c be at the end of the following program?

```
PROGRAM test_char1
CHARACTER(len=8) :: a, b, c
a = 'ABCDEFGHIJ'
b = '12345678'
c = a(5:7)
b(7:8) = a(2:6)
END PROGRAM test_char1
```

SOLUTION

The character manipulations in this program are:

1. Line 3 assigns the string 'ABCDEFGHIJ' to a, but only the first eight characters are saved, since a is only eight characters long. Therefore, a will contain 'ABCDEFGH'.
2. Line 4 statement assigns the string '12345678' to b.
3. Line 5 assigns the character substring a(5:7) to c. Since c is eight characters long, five blanks will be padded onto variable c, and c will contain 'EFGböööö'.
4. Line 6 assigns substring a(2:6) to substring b(7:8). Since b(7:8) is only two characters long, only the first two characters of a(2:6) will be used. Therefore, variable b will contain '123456BC'.

4.2.3 The Concatenation (//) Operator

It is possible to combine two or more strings or substrings into a single large string. This operation is known as **concatenation.** The concatenation operator in Fortran is a double slash with no space between the slashes (//). For example, after the following lines are executed,

```
PROGRAM test_char2
CHARACTER(len=10) :: a
CHARACTER(len=8) :: b, c
a = 'ABCDEFGHIJ'
b = '12345678'
c = a(1:3) // b(4:5) // a(6:8)
END PROGRAM test_char2
```

variable c will contain the string 'ABC45FGH'.

4.2.4 Relational Operators with Character Data

Character strings can be compared in logical expressions by using the relational operators ==, /=, <, <=, >, and >=. The result of the comparison is a logical value that is either true or false. For instance, the expression '123' == '123' is true, while the expression '123' == '1234' is false. In standard Fortran, character strings may be compared with character strings, and numbers may be compared with numbers, but *character strings may not be compared to numbers*.

How are two characters compared to determine if one is greater than the other? The comparison is based on the **collating sequence** of the characters on the computer where the program is being executed. The collating sequence of the characters is the order in which they occur within a specific character set. For example, the character 'A' is character number 65 in the ASCII character set, while the character 'B' is character number 66 in the set (see Appendix A). Therefore, the logical expression 'A' < 'B' is true in the ASCII character set. On the other hand, the character 'a' is character number 97 in the ASCII set, so 'a' < 'A' is false in the ASCII character set. Note that during character comparisons, a lowercase letter is different from the corresponding uppercase letter.

How are two strings compared to determine if one is greater than the other? The comparison begins with the first character in each string. If they are the same, then the second two characters are compared. This process continues until the first difference is found between the strings. For example, 'AAAAAB' > 'AAAAAA'.

What happens if the strings are different lengths? The comparison begins with the first letter in each string, and progresses through each letter until a difference is found. If the two strings are the same all the way to the end of one of them, then the other string is considered the larger of the two. Therefore,

'AB' > 'AAAA' and 'AAAAA' > 'AAAA'

4.2.5 Character Intrinsic Functions

A few common character intrinsic functions are listed in Table 4-1. Function IACHAR(c) accepts a single character c, and returns the integer corresponding to its position in the

TABLE 4-1
Some common character intrinsic functions

Function name and argument(s)	Argument type	Result type	Comments
ACHAR(ival)	INT	CHAR	Returns the character corresponding to ival in the ASCII collating sequence
IACHAR(char)	CHAR	INT	Returns the integer corresponding to char in the ASCII collating sequence
LEN(str1)	CHAR	INT	Returns length of str1 in characters.
LEN_TRIM(str1)	CHAR	INT	Returns length of str1, excluding any trailing blanks.
TRIM(str1)	CHAR	CHAR	Returns str1 with trailing blanks removed.

4

ASCII character set. For example, the function IACHAR('A') returns the integer 65, because 'A' is the 65th character in the ASCII character set.

Function ACHAR(i) accepts an integer value i, and returns the character at that position in the ASCII character set. For example, the function ACHAR(65) returns the character 'A', because 'A' is the 65th character in the ASCII character set.

Function LEN(str) and LEN_TRIM(str) return the length of the specified character string. Function LEN(str) returns the length, including any trailing blanks, while function LEN_TRIM(str) returns the string with any trailing blanks stripped off.

Function TRIM(str) accepts a character string, and returns the string with any trailing blanks stripped off.

Quiz 4-2

This quiz provides a quick check to see if you have understood the concepts introduced in Section 4.2. If you have trouble with the quiz, reread the sections, ask your instructor, or discuss the material with a fellow student. The answers to this quiz are found in the back of the book.

1. Assume that a computer uses the ASCII character set. Is each of the following expressions legal or illegal? If an expression is legal, what will its result be? (Note that ƀ denotes a blank character.)
   (*a*) 'AAA' >= 'aaa'
   (*b*) '1A' < 'A1'
   (*c*) 'Helloƀƀƀ' // 'there'
   (*d*) TRIM('Helloƀƀƀ') // 'there'

2. Suppose that character variables str1, str2, and str3 contain the values 'abc', 'abcd', 'ABC', respectively, and that a computer uses the ASCII

(*continued*)

(concluded)

character set. Is each of the following expressions legal or illegal? If an expression is legal, what will its result be?

(*a*) `str2(2:4)`
(*b*) `str3 // str2(4:4)`
(*c*) `str1 > str2`
(*d*) `str1 > str3`
(*e*) `str2 > 0`
(*f*) `IACHAR('C') == 67`
(*g*) `'Z' >= ACHAR(100)`

3. What is written out by each of the `WRITE` statements below?

```
PROGRAM test_char
CHARACTER(len=10) :: str1 = 'Hello'
CHARACTER(len=10) :: str2 = 'World'
CHARACTER(len=20) :: str3
str3 = str1 // str2
WRITE (*,*) LEN(str3)
WRITE (*,*) LEN_TRIM(str3)
str3 = TRIM(str1) // TRIM(str2)
WRITE (*,*) LEN(str3)
WRITE (*,*) LEN_TRIM(str3)
END PROGRAM test_char
```

EXAMPLE 4-6

Shifting Strings to Uppercase:

As we learned in this chapter, uppercase and lowercase letters are different inside strings. This difference between upper- and lowercase letters can cause a problem when we are attempting to match or compare two character strings, since `'STRING'` is not the same as `'string'` or `'String'`. If we wanted to compare two strings to see if they contained the same words, we would not get the correct answer if the capitalization of the words differed.

In making comparisons, it is often desirable to shift all characters to uppercase, so that identical strings will always match. Write a program that accepts two strings from a user, and compares them to determine if they are equal ignoring case. To do the comparison, convert a copy of each string to uppercase, and compare the copies. Tell the user whether or not the two strings are the same.

SOLUTION

We will assume that the computer executing the program uses the ASCII character set.

Appendix A shows the ASCII collating sequence. If we look at Appendix A, we can see that *there is a fixed offset of 32 characters* between an uppercase letter and the corresponding lowercase letter in each collating sequence. All letters are in order, and there are no nonalphabetic characters mixed into the middle of the alphabet.

1. **State the problem.**

Write a program that reads two character strings, converts all of the lowercase letters in a copy of each character string to uppercase, and compares the strings for equality. The conversion process should not affect numeric and special characters. The program should write out a message indicating whether the two strings are equal or not, ignoring case.

2. **Define the inputs and outputs.**

The inputs to the program are two strings str1 and str2. The output from the program is a message stating whether or not the two strings are equal ignoring case.

3. **Describe the algorithm.**

Looking at the ASCII table in Appendix A, we note that the uppercase letters begin at sequence number 65, while the lowercase letters begin at sequence number 97. There are exactly 32 numbers between each uppercase letter and its lowercase equivalent. Furthermore, there are no other symbols mixed into the middle of the alphabet.

These facts give us our basic algorithm for shifting strings to uppercase. We will determine if a character is lowercase by deciding if it is between 'a' and 'z' in the ASCII character set. If it is, then we will subtract 32 from its sequence number to convert it to uppercase, using the ACHAR and IACHAR functions. The initial pseudocode for this algorithm is

```
Prompt for str1 and str2
READ str1, str2

Make a copy of str1 and str2 in str1a and str2a
DO for each character in str1
    Determine if character is lower case. If so,
        Convert to integer form
        Subtract 32 from the integer
        Convert back to character form
    End of IF
END of DO
DO for each character in str2
    Determine if character is lower case. If so,
        Convert to integer form
        Subtract 32 from the integer
        Convert back to character form
    End of IF
END of DO

Compare shifted strings
Write out results
```

The final pseudocode for this program is

```
Prompt for str1 and str2
READ str1, str2

str1a ← str1
str2a ← str2

DO for i = 1 to LEN(str1a)
```

(continued)

(concluded)
```
            IF str1a(i:i) >= 'a' .AND. str1a(i:i) <= 'z' THEN
                str1a(i:i) ← ACHAR ( IACHAR (str1a(i:i) - 32 ) )
            END of IF
        END of DO

        DO for i = 1 to LEN(str2a)
            IF str2a(i:i) >= 'a' .AND. str2a(i:i) <= 'z' THEN
                str2a(i:i) ← ACHAR ( IACHAR (str2a(i:i) - 32 ) )
            END of IF
        END of DO

        IF str1a == str2a
            WRITE that the strings are equal
        ELSE
            WRITE that the strings are not equal
        END IF
```

where length is the length of the input character string.

4. **Turn the algorithm into Fortran statements.**
   The resulting Fortran program is shown in Figure 4-10.

FIGURE 4-10

Program compare.

```
PROGRAM compare
!
!   Purpose:
!     To compare two strings to see if they are equivalent,
!     ignoring case.
!
!   Record of revisions:
!       Date         Programmer          Description of change
!       ====         ==========          =====================
!     11/14/06     S. J. Chapman         Original code
!
IMPLICIT NONE

! Data dictionary: declare variable types, definitions, & units
INTEGER :: i                  ! Loop index
CHARACTER(len=20) :: str1     ! First string to compare
CHARACTER(len=20) :: str1a    ! Copy of first string to compare
CHARACTER(len=20) :: str2     ! Second string to compare
CHARACTER(len=20) :: str2a    ! Copy of second string to compare

! Prompt for the strings
WRITE (*,*) 'Enter first string to compare:'
READ (*,*) str1
WRITE (*,*) 'Enter second string to compare:'
READ (*,*) str2

! Make copies so that the original strings are not modified
str1a = str1
str2a = str2
```

(continued)

(concluded)

```
! Now shift lower case letters to upper case.
DO i = 1, LEN(str1a)
   IF ( str1a(i:i) >= 'a' .AND. str1a(i:i) <= 'z' ) THEN
      str1a(i:i) = ACHAR ( IACHAR ( str1a(i:i) ) - 32 )
   END IF
END DO
DO i = 1, LEN(str2a)
   IF ( str2a(i:i) >= 'a' .AND. str2a(i:i) <= 'z' ) THEN
      str2a(i:i) = ACHAR ( IACHAR ( str2a(i:i) ) - 32 )
   END IF
END DO

! Compare strings and write result
IF ( str1a == str2a ) THEN
   WRITE (*,*) "'", str1, "' = '", str2, "' ignoring case."
ELSE
   WRITE (*,*) "'", str1, "' /= '", str2, "' ignoring case."
END IF

END PROGRAM compare
```

5. **Test the resulting Fortran program.**

We will test this program by passing it two pairs of strings to compare. One pair is identical except for case, and the other pair is not. The results from the program for two sets of input strings are:

```
C:\book\chap4>compare
Enter first string to compare:
'This is a test.'
Enter second string to compare:
'THIS IS A TEST.'
'This is a test.        ' = 'THIS IS A TEST.    ' ignoring case.

C:\book\chap4>compare
Enter first string to compare:
'This is a test.'
Enter second string to compare:
'This is another test.'
'This is a test.        ' /= 'This is another test' ignoring case.
```

The program appears to be working correctly.

**EXAMPLE
4-7**   *Physics—The Flight of a Ball:*

If we assume negligible air friction and ignore the curvature of the earth, a ball that is thrown into the air from any point on the earth's surface will follow a parabolic flight path (see Figure 4-11a). The height of the ball at any time t after it is thrown is given by Equation 4-4:

$$y(t) = y_o + v_{yo}t + \frac{1}{2}gt^2 \tag{4-4}$$

where y_o is the initial height of the object above the ground, v_{yo} is the initial vertical velocity of the object, and g is the acceleration due to the earth's gravity. The horizontal distance (range) traveled by the ball as a function of time after it is thrown is given by Equation 4-5:

$$x(t) = x_o + v_{xo}t \tag{4-5}$$

where x_o is the initial horizontal position of the ball on the ground, and v_{xo} is the initial horizontal velocity of the ball.

If the ball is thrown with some initial velocity v_o at an angle of θ degrees with respect to the earth's surface, then the initial horizontal and vertical components of velocity will be

$$v_{xo} = v_o \cos \theta \tag{4-6}$$

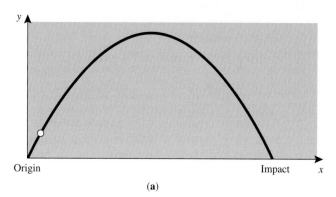

Origin   Impact x

(a)

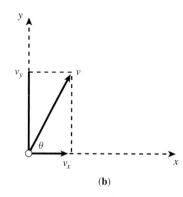

(b)

FIGURE 4-11
(a) When a ball is thrown upward, it follows a parabolic trajectory. (b) The horizontal and vertical components of a velocity vector v at an angle θ with respect to the horizontal.

$$v_{yo} = v_o \sin \theta \qquad (4\text{-}7)$$

Assume that the ball is initially thrown from position $(x_o, y_o) = (0, 0)$ with an initial velocity v of 20 meters per second at an initial angle of θ degrees. Design, write, and test a program that will determine the horizontal distance traveled by the ball from the time it was thrown until it touches the ground again. The program should do this for all angles θ from 0 to 90° in 1° steps. Determine the angle θ that maximizes the range of the ball.

SOLUTION
In order to solve this problem, we must determine an equation for the range of the thrown ball. We can do this by first finding the time that the ball remains in the air, and then finding the horizontal distance that the ball can travel during that time.

The time that the ball will remain in the air after it is thrown may be calculated from Equation 4-4. The ball will touch the ground at the time t for which $y(t) = 0$. Remembering that the ball will start from ground level ($y(0) = 0$), and solving for t, we get:

$$y(t) = y_o + v_{yo}\, t + \frac{1}{2} g t^2 \qquad (4\text{-}4)$$

$$0 = 0 + v_{yo}\, t + \frac{1}{2} g t^2$$

$$0 = \left(v_{yo} + \frac{1}{2} g t \right) t$$

so the ball will be at ground level at time $t_1 = 0$ (when we threw it), and at time

$$y_2 = -\frac{2 v_{yo}}{g}$$

The horizontal distance that the ball will travel in time t_2 is found from Equation 4-5:

$$\text{Range} = x(t_2) = x_o + x_o t_2 \qquad (4\text{-}5)$$

$$\text{Range} = 0 + v_{xo} \left(-\frac{2 v_{yo}}{g} \right)$$

$$\text{Range} = -\frac{2 v_{xo} v_{yo}}{g} \qquad (4\text{-}8)$$

We can substitute Equations 4-6 and 4-7 for v_{xo} and v_{yo} into Equation 4-8 to get an equation expressed in terms of the initial velocity v and initial angle θ:

$$\text{Range} = -\frac{2(v_o \cos \theta)(v_o \sin \theta)}{g}$$

$$\text{Range} = -\frac{2v_o^2}{g} \cos \theta \sin \theta \qquad\qquad (4\text{-}9)$$

From the problem statement, we know that the initial velocity v_o is 20 meters per second, and that the ball will be thrown at all angles from 0° to 90° in 1° steps. Finally, any elementary physics textbook will tell us that the acceleration due to the earth's gravity is −9.81 meters per second squared.

Now let's apply our design technique to this problem.

1. **State the problem.**

A proper statement of this problem would be: *Calculate the range that a ball would travel when it is thrown with an initial velocity of v_o at an initial angle θ. Calculate this range for a v_o of 20 meters per second and all angles between 0° and 90°, in 1° increments. Determine the angle θ that will result in the maximum range for the ball. Assume that there is no air friction.*

2. **Define the inputs and outputs.**

As the problem is defined above, no inputs are required. We know from the problem statement what v_o and θ will be, so there is no need to read them in. The outputs from this program will be a table showing the range of the ball for each angle θ, and the angle θ for which the range is maximum.

3. **Design the algorithm.**

This program can be broken down into the following major steps

```
DO for theta = 0 to 90 degrees
    Calculate the range of the ball for each angle theta
    Determine if this theta yields the maximum range so far
    Write out the range as a function of theta
END of DO
WRITE out the theta yielding maximum range
```

An iterative DO loop is appropriate for this algorithm, since we are calculating the range of the ball for a specified number of angles. We will calculate the range for each value of θ, and compare each range with the maximum range found so far to determine which angle yields the maximum range. Note that the trigonometric functions work in radians, so the angles in degrees must be converted to radians before the range is calculated. The detailed pseudocode for this algorithm is

```
Initialize max_range and max_degrees to 0
Initialize v0 to 20 meters/second
DO for theta = 0 to 90 degrees
    radian ← theta * degrees_2_rad        (Convert degrees to radians)
    angle ← (-2. * v0**2 / gravity ) * sin(radian) * cos(radian)
    Write out theta and range
```

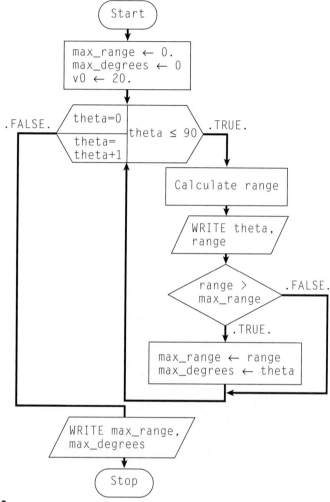

FIGURE 4-12
Flowchart for a program to determine the angle θ at which a ball thrown with an initial velocity v_o of 20 m/s will travel the farthest.

```
   IF range > max_range then
       max_range ← range
       max_degrees ← theta
   END of IF
END of DO
Write out max_degrees, max_range
```

The flowchart for this program is shown in Figure 4-12.

4. **Turn the algorithm into Fortran statements.**
   The final Fortran program is shown in Figure 4-13.

FIGURE 4-13

Program ball to determine the angle that maximizes the range of a thrown ball.

```fortran
PROGRAM ball
!
!  Purpose:
!    To calculate distance traveled by a ball thrown at a specified
!    angle THETA and at a specified velocity V0 from a point on the
!    surface of the earth, ignoring the effects of air friction and
!    the earth's curvature.
!
!  Record of revisions:
!      Date        Programmer          Description of change
!      ====        ==========          =====================
!    11/14/06    S. J. Chapman         Original code
!
IMPLICIT NONE

! Data dictionary: declare constants
REAL, PARAMETER :: DEGREES_2_RAD = 0.01745329 ! Deg ==> rad conv.
REAL, PARAMETER :: GRAVITY = -9.81             ! Accel. due to gravity (m/s)

! Data dictionary: declare variable types, definitions, & units
INTEGER :: max_degrees  ! angle at which the max rng occurs (degrees)
REAL :: max_range       ! Maximum range for the ball at vel v0 (meters)
REAL :: range           ! Range of the ball at a particular angle (meters)
REAL :: radian          ! Angle at which the ball was thrown (in radians)
INTEGER :: theta        ! Angle at which the ball was thrown (in degrees)
REAL :: v0              ! Velocity of the ball (in m/s)

! Initialize variables.
max_range = 0.
max_degrees = 0
v0 = 20.

! Loop over all specified angles.

loop: DO theta = 0, 90

   ! Get angle in radians
   radian = real(theta) * DEGREES_2_RAD

   ! Calculate range in meters.
   range = (-2. * v0**2 / GRAVITY) * SIN(radian) * COS(radian)

   ! Write out the range for this angle.
     WRITE (*,*) 'Theta = ', theta, ' degrees; Range = ', range, &
                 ' meters'

   ! Compare the range to the previous maximum range.  If this
   ! range is larger, save it and the angle at which it occurred.
   IF ( range > max_range ) THEN
      max_range = range
      max_degrees = theta
```

(continued)

(concluded)

```
   END IF

END DO loop

! Skip a line, and then write out the maximum range and the angle
! at which it occurred.
WRITE (*,*) ' '
WRITE (*,*) 'Max range = ', max_range, ' at ', max_degrees, ' degrees'

END PROGRAM ball
```

The degrees-to-radians conversion factor is always a constant, so in the program it is given a name by using the PARAMETER attribute, and all references to the constant within the program use that name. As noted above, the acceleration due to gravity at sea level can be found in any physics text. It is about 9.81 m/s², directed downward.

4

5. **Test the program.**

To test this program, we will calculate the answers by hand for a few of the angles, and compare the results with the output of the program.

$$\theta = 0°: \qquad \text{Range} = -\frac{2(20^2)}{-9.81} \cos 0 \sin 0 = 0 \text{ meters}$$

$$\theta = 5°: \qquad \text{Range} = -\frac{2(20^2)}{-9.81} \cos\left(\frac{5\pi}{180}\right) \sin\left(\frac{5\pi}{180}\right) = 7.080 \text{ meters}$$

$$\theta = 40°: \qquad \text{Range} = -\frac{2(20^2)}{-9.81} \cos\left(\frac{40\pi}{180}\right) \sin\left(\frac{40\pi}{180}\right) = 40.16 \text{ meters}$$

$$\theta = 45°: \qquad \text{Range} = -\frac{2(20^2)}{-9.81} \cos\left(\frac{45\pi}{180}\right) \sin\left(\frac{45\pi}{180}\right) = 40.77 \text{ meters}$$

When program ball is executed, a 90-line table of angles and ranges is produced. To save space, only a portion of the table is reproduced below.

```
C:\book\chap4>ball
        Theta =         0 degrees; Range =      0.000000E+00 meters
        Theta =         1 degrees; Range =          1.423017 meters
        Theta =         2 degrees; Range =          2.844300 meters
        Theta =         3 degrees; Range =          4.262118 meters
        Theta =         4 degrees; Range =          5.674743 meters
        Theta =         5 degrees; Range =          7.080455 meters
            ...
        Theta =        40 degrees; Range =         40.155260 meters
        Theta =        41 degrees; Range =         40.377900 meters
        Theta =        42 degrees; Range =         40.551350 meters
        Theta =        43 degrees; Range =         40.675390 meters
        Theta =        44 degrees; Range =         40.749880 meters
        Theta =        45 degrees; Range =         40.774720 meters
        Theta =        46 degrees; Range =         40.749880 meters
```

```
Theta =           47 degrees; Range =        40.675390 meters
Theta =           48 degrees; Range =        40.551350 meters
Theta =           49 degrees; Range =        40.377900 meters
Theta =           50 degrees; Range =        40.155260 meters
          . . .
Theta =           85 degrees; Range =         7.080470 meters
Theta =           86 degrees; Range =         5.674757 meters
Theta =           87 degrees; Range =         4.262130 meters
Theta =           88 degrees; Range =         2.844310 meters
Theta =           89 degrees; Range =         1.423035 meters
Theta =           90 degrees; Range =    1.587826E-05 meters

Max range =           40.774720 at              45 degrees
```

The program output matches our hand calculation for the angles calculated above to the 4-digit accuracy of the hand calculation. Note that the maximum range occurred at an angle of 45° .

4.3

DEBUGGING FORTRAN LOOPS

The best approach to locating an error in a program containing loops is to use a symbolic debugger, if one is supplied with your compiler. You must ask your instructor or else check with your system's manuals to determine how to use the symbolic debugger supplied with your particular compiler and computer.

An alternative approach to locating the error is to insert WRITE statements into the code to print out important variables at key points in the program. When the program is run, the WRITE statements will print out the values of the key variables. These values can be compared to the ones you expect, and the places where the actual and expected values differ will serve as a clue to help you locate the problem. For example, to verify the operation of a counting loop, the following WRITE statements could be added to the program.

```
WRITE (*,*) 'At loop1: ist, ien, inc = ', ist, ien, inc
loop1: DO i = ist, ien, inc
   WRITE (*,*) 'In loop1: i = ', i
   . . .
END DO loop1
WRITE (*,*) 'loop1 completed'
```

When the program is executed, its output listing will contain detailed information about the variables controlling the DO loop and just how many times the loop was executed.

Once you have located the portion of the code in which the error occurs, you can take a look at the specific statements in that area to locate the problem. A list of common errors follows. Be sure to check for them in your code.

1. *Most errors in counting* DO *loops involve mistakes with the loop parameters.* If you add WRITE statements to the DO loop as shown previously, the problem should be fairly clear. Did the DO loop start with the correct value? Did it end with the correct value? Did it increment at the proper step? If not, check the parameters of the DO loop closely. You will probably spot an error in the control parameters.

2. Errors in while loops are usually related to errors in the logical expression used to control their function. These errors may be detected by examining the IF (*logical_expr*) EXIT statement of the while loop with WRITE statements.

4.4
SUMMARY

In Chapter 4 we have presented the basic types of Fortran loops, plus some additional details about manipulating character data.

There are two basic types of loops in Fortran, the while loop and the iterative or counting DO loop. The while loop is used to repeat a section of code in cases where we do not know in advance how many times the loop must be repeated. The counting DO loop is used to repeat a section of code in cases where we know in advance how many times the loop should be repeated.

It is possible to exit from a loop at any time by using the EXIT statement. It is also possible to jump back to the top of a loop using the CYCLE statement. If loops are nested, an EXIT or CYCLE statement refers by default to the innermost loop.

4.4.1 Summary of Good Programming Practice

The following guidelines should be adhered to when programming with branch or loop constructs. By following them consistently, your code will contain fewer bugs, will be easier to debug, and will be more understandable to others who may need to work with it in the future.

1. Always indent code blocks in DO loops to make them more readable.
2. Use a while loop to repeat sections of code when you don't know in advance how often the loop will be executed.
3. Make sure that there is only one exit from a while loop.
4. Use a counting DO loop to repeat sections of code when you know in advance how often the loop will be executed.
5. Never attempt to modify the values of DO loop index while inside the loop.
6. Assign names to large and complicated loops or IF constructs, especially if they are nested.
7. Use loop names with CYCLE and EXIT statements in nested loops to make certain that the proper loop is affected by the action of the CYCLE or EXIT statement.

4.4.2 Summary of Fortran Statements and Constructs

The following summary describes the Fortran 95/2003 statements and constructs introduced in this chapter.

4

CYCLE Statement:

```
CYCLE [name]
```

Example:

```
CYCLE inner
```

Description:

The CYCLE statement may appear within any DO loop. When the statement is executed, all of the statements below it within the loop are skipped, and control returns to the top of the loop. In while loops, execution resumes from the top of the loop. In counting loops, the loop index is incremented, and if the index is still less than its limit, execution resumes from the top of the loop.

An unnamed CYCLE statement always causes the *innermost* loop containing the statement to cycle. A named CYCLE statement causes the named loop to cycle, even if it is not the innermost loop.

DO Loop (Iterative or Counting Loop) Construct:

```
[name:] DO index = istart, iend, incr
   ...
END DO [name]
```

Example:

```
loop: DO index = 1, last_value, 3
   ...
END DO loop
```

Description:

The iterative DO loop is used to repeat a block of code a known number of times. During the first iteration of the DO loop, the variable *index* is set to the value *istart*. *index* is incremented by *incr* in each successive loop until its *index*incr > iend*incr*, at which time the loop terminates. The loop name is optional, but if it is used on the DO statement, then it must be used on the *END DO* statement. The loop variable *index* is incremented and tested *before* each loop, so the *DO* loop code will never be executed at all if *istart*incr > iend*incr*.

EXIT Statement:

```
EXIT [name]
```

Example:

```
EXIT loop1
```

(*continued*)

(*concluded*)

Description:

The EXIT statement may appear within any DO loop. When an EXIT statement is encountered, the program stops executing the loop and jumps to the first executable statement after the END DO.

An unnamed EXIT statement always causes the *innermost* loop containing the statement to exit. A named EXIT statement causes the named loop to exit, even if it is not the innermost loop.

WHILE **Loop Construct:**

```
[name:] DO
    ...
    IF ( logical_expr ) EXIT [name]
    ...
END DO [name]
```

Example:

```
loop1: DO
    ...
    IF ( istatus /= 0 ) EXIT loop1
    ...
END DO loop1
```

Description:

The while loop is used to repeat a block of code until a specified *logical_expr* becomes true. It differs from a counting DO loop in that we do not know in advance how many times the loop will be repeated. When the IF statement of the loop is executed with the *logical_expr* true, execution skips to the next statement following the end of the loop.

The name of the loop is optional, but if a name is included on the DO statement, then the same name must appear on the END DO statement. The name on the EXIT statement is optional; it may be left out even if the DO and END DO are named.

4.4.3 Exercises

4-1. Which of the following expressions are legal in Fortran? If an expression is legal, evaluate it. Assume the ASCII collating sequence.

(*a*) '123' > 'abc'

(*b*) '9478' == 9478

(*c*) ACHAR(65) // ACHAR(95) // ACHAR(72)

(*d*) ACHAR(IACHAR('j') + 5)

4-2. Write the Fortran statements required to calculate and print out the squares of all the even integers between 0 and 50.

4-3. Write a Fortran program to evaluate the equation $y(x) = x^2 - 3x + 2$ for all values of x between -1 and 3, in steps of 0.1.

4-4. Write the Fortran statements required to calculate $y(t)$ from the equation

$$y(t) = \begin{cases} -3t^2 + 5 & t \geq 0 \\ 3t^2 + 5 & t < 0 \end{cases}$$

4-5. Write a Fortran program to calculate the factorial function, as defined in Example 4-2. Be sure to handle the special cases of 0! and of illegal input values.

4-6. What is the difference in behavior between a CYCLE statement and an EXIT statement?

4-7. Modify program stats_2 to use the DO WHILE construct instead of the while construct currently in the program.

4-8. Examine the following DO statements and determine how many times each loop will be executed. (Assume that all loop index variables are integers.)

(*a*) DO irange = -32768, 32767

(*b*) DO j = 100, 1, -10

(*c*) DO kount = 2, 3, 4

(*d*) DO index = -4, -7

(*e*) DO i = -10, 10, 10

(*f*) DO i = 10, -2, 0

(*g*) DO

4-9. Examine the following iterative DO loops and determine the value of ires at the end of each of the loops, and also the number of times each loop executes. Assume that all variables are integers.

(*a*) ires = 0
```
        DO index = -10, 10
           ires = ires + 1
        END DO
```

(*b*) ires = 0
```
        loop1: DO index1 = 1, 20, 5
            IF ( index1 <= 10 ) CYCLE
            loop2: DO index2 = index1, 20, 5
              ires = ires + index2
            END DO loop2
        END DO loop1
```

(*c*) ires = 0
```
        loop1: DO index1 = 10, 4, -2
            loop2: DO index2 = 2, index1, 2
               IF ( index2 > 6 ) EXIT loop2
               ires = ires + index2
```

```
        END DO loop2
     END DO loop1
```

(d)
```
   ires = 0
      loop1: DO index1 = 10, 4, -2
         loop2: DO index2 = 2, index1, 2
            IF ( index2 > 6 ) EXIT loop1
            ires = ires + index2
         END DO loop2
      END DO loop1
```

4-10. Examine the following while loops and determine the value of ires at the end of each of the loops, and the number of times each loop executes. Assume that all variables are integers.

(a)
```
   ires = 0
      loop1: DO
         ires = ires + 1
         IF ( (ires / 10 ) * 10 == ires ) EXIT
      END DO loop1
```

(b)
```
   ires = 2
      loop2: DO
         ires = ires**2
         IF ( ires > 200 ) EXIT
      END DO loop2
```

(c)
```
   ires = 2
      DO WHILE ( ires > 200 )
         ires = ires**2
      END DO
```

4-11. Modify program ball from Example 4-7 to read in the acceleration due to gravity at a particular location, and to calculate the maximum range of the ball for that acceleration. After modifying the program, run it with accelerations of -9.8 m/s^2, -9.7 m/s^2, and -9.6 m/s^2. What effect does the reduction in gravitational attraction have on the range of the ball? What effect does the reduction in gravitational attraction have on the best angle θ at which to throw the ball?

4-12. Modify program ball from Example 4-7 to read in the initial velocity with which the ball is thrown. After modifying the program, run it with initial velocities of 10 m/s, 20 m/s, and 30 m/s. What effect does changing the initial velocity v_o have on the range of the ball? What effect does it have on the best angle θ at which to throw the ball?

4-13. Program doy in Example 4-3 calculates the day of year associated with any given month, day, and year. As written, this program does not check to see if the data entered by the user is valid. It will accept nonsense values for months and days, and do calculations with them to produce meaningless results. Modify the program so that it checks the input values for validity before using them. If the inputs are invalid, the program should tell the user what is wrong, and quit. The year should be a number greater than zero, the month should be a number between 1 and 12, and the day should be a number between 1 and a maximum that depends on the month. Use a SELECT CASE construct to implement the bounds checking performed on the day.

4-14. Write a Fortran program to evaluate the function

$$y(x) = \ln\frac{1}{1-x}$$

for any user-specified value of x, where ln is the natural logarithm (logarithm to the base e). Write the program with a while loop, so that the program repeats the calculation for each legal value of x entered into the program. When an illegal value of x is entered, terminate the program.

4-15. Write a Fortran program to convert all uppercase characters in a user-supplied character string to lower case, without changing the uppercase and nonalphabetic characters in the string. Assume that your computer uses the ASCII collating sequence.

4-16. Calculating Orbits When a satellite orbits the Earth, the satellite's orbit will form an ellipse with the Earth located at one of the focal points of the ellipse. The satellite's orbit can be expressed in polar coordinates as

$$r = \frac{p}{1 - \varepsilon \cos\theta} \tag{4-9}$$

where r and θ are the distance and angle of the satellite from the center of the Earth, p is a parameter specifying the size of the orbit, and ε is a parameter representing the eccentricity of the orbit. A circular orbit has an eccentricity ε of 0. An elliptical orbit has an eccentricity of $0 \le \varepsilon \le 1$. If $\varepsilon > 1$, the satellite follows a hyperbolic path and escapes from the Earth's gravitational field.

Consider a satellite with a size parameter $p = 1200$ km. Write a program to calculate the distance of the satellite from the center of the earth as a function of θ if the satellite has an eccentricity of (a) $\varepsilon = 0$; (b) $\varepsilon = 0.25$; (c) $\varepsilon = 0.5$. Write a single program in which r and ε are both input values.

How close does each orbit come to the Earth? How far away does each orbit get from the Earth?

4-17. Write a program `caps` that reads in a character string, searches for all of the words within the string, and capitalizes the first letter of each word, while shifting the remainder of the word to lowercase. Assume that all nonalphabetic and nonnumeric characters can mark the boundaries of a word within the character variable (for example, periods, commas). Nonalphabetic characters should be left unchanged.

4-18. Current through a Diode The current flowing through the semiconductor diode shown in Figure 4-14 is given by the equation

$$i_D = I_o\left(e^{\frac{qv_D}{kT}} - 1\right) \tag{4-10}$$

where

v_D = the voltage across the diode, in volts

i_D = the current flow through the diode, in amperes

I_o = the leakage current of the diode, in amperes

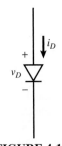

FIGURE 4-14
A semiconductor diode.

q = the charge on an electron, 1.602×10^{-19} coulombs

k = Boltzmann's constant, 1.38×10^{-23} joule/kelvin

T = temperature, in kelvins (K)

The leakage current I_o of the diode is 2.0 μA. Write a computer program to calculate the current flowing through this diode for all voltages from -1.0 V to $+0.6$ V, in 0.1-V steps. Repeat this process for the following temperatures: 75°F, 100°F, and 125°F. Use the program of Example 2-3 to convert the temperatures from °F to kelvins.

4-19. Binary to Decimal Conversion Write a program that prompts a user for a binary number, which will be entered as a string of 0s and 1s in a character variable. For example, the user might enter 01000101 as a character string. The program should then convert the input binary number into a decimal number, and display the corresponding decimal number to the user.

This program should be able to handle numbers from 0000000000 to 1111111111, converting them into the equivalent decimal values 0 to 1023. It should also test for and handle an invalid value among the input characters (a letter, symbol, or a number greater than 1). Test your program with the following binary numbers.

(*a*) 0010010010

(*b*) 1111111111

(*c*) 10000000001

(*d*) 01111111110

4-20. Decimal to Binary Conversion Write a program that prompts a user for a decimal integer in the range 0 to 1023 and converts the number into the equivalent binary number. The binary number should consist of 0s and 1s in a character string. The program should display the corresponding binary number to the user. Test your program with the following decimal numbers.

(*a*) 256

(*b*) 63

(*c*) 140

(*d*) 768

4-21. Octal to Decimal Conversion Write a program that prompts a user for an octal number, which will be entered as a string of 0s to 7s in a character variable. For example, the user might enter 377 as a character string. The program should then convert the input octal number into a decimal number, and display the corresponding decimal number to the user. Design the program to handle up to five octal digits. (*Hint:* This might be a great place for a SELECT CASE structure.) Test your program with the following binary numbers.

(*a*) 377

(*b*) 11111

(*c*) 70000

(*d*) 77777

4-22. Tension on a Cable A 200-kilogram object is to be hung from the end of a rigid 3-meter horizontal pole of negligible weight, as shown in Figure 4-15. The pole is attached to a wall by a pivot and is supported by an 3-meter cable, which is attached to the wall at a higher point. The tension on this cable is given by the equation

$$T = \frac{W \cdot l_c \cdot l_p}{d\sqrt{l_p^2 - d^2}} \tag{4-11}$$

where T is the tension on the cable, W is the weight of the object, l_c is the length of the cable, l_p is the length of the pole, and d is the distance along the pole at which the cable is attached. Write a program to determine the distance d at which to attach the cable to the pole in order to minimize the tension on the cable. To do this, the program should calculate the tension on the cable at 0.1-m intervals from $d = 0.5$ m to $d = 2.8$ m, and should locate the position d that produces the minimum tension.

4-23. If the maximum tension on the cable in the previous exercise is 700, over what range of distances d is it safe to attach the cable to the pole?

4-24. Bacterial Growth Suppose that a biologist performs an experiment in which she measures the rate at which a specific type of bacterium reproduces asexually in different culture media. The experiment shows that in Medium A the bacteria reproduce once every 90 minutes, and in Medium B the bacteria reproduce once every 120 minutes. Assume that a single bacterium is placed on each culture medium at the beginning of the experiment. Write a Fortran program that calculates and writes out the number of bacteria present in each culture at intervals of 6 hours from the beginning of the experiment until 24 hours have elapsed. How do the numbers of bacteria compare on the two media after 24 hours?

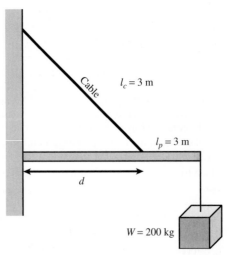

FIGURE 4-15
A 200-kilogram weight suspended from a rigid bar supported by a cable.

4-25. Decibels Engineers often measure the ratio of two power measurements in *decibels*, or dB. The equation for the ratio of two power measurements in decibels is

$$dB = \log_{10} \frac{P_2}{P_1} \qquad (4\text{-}12)$$

where P_2 is the power level being measured, and P_1 is some reference power level. Assume that the reference power level P_1 is 1 watt, and write a program that calculates the decibel level corresponding to power levels between 1 and 20 watts, in 0.5-W steps.

4-26. Infinite Series Trigonometric functions are usually calculated on computers by using a *truncated infinite series*. An *infinite series* is an infinite set of terms that together add up to the value of a particular function or expression. For example, one infinite series used to evaluate the sine of a number is

$$\sin x = x - \frac{x^3}{3!} + \frac{x^5}{5!} - \frac{x^7}{7!} + \frac{x^9}{9!} + \ldots \qquad (4\text{-}13a)$$

or

$$\sin x = \sum_{n=1}^{\infty} (-1)^{n-1} \frac{x^{2n-1}}{(2n-1)!} \qquad (4\text{-}13b)$$

where x is in units of radians.

Since a computer does not have enough time to add an infinite number of terms for every sine that is calculated, the infinite series is *truncated* after a finite number of terms. The number of terms that should be kept in the series is just enough to calculate the function to the precision of the floating point numbers on the computer on which the function is being evaluated. The truncated infinite series for $\sin x$ is

$$\sin x = \sum_{n=1}^{N} (-1)^{n-1} \frac{x^{2n-1}}{(2n-1)!} \qquad (4\text{-}14)$$

where N is the number of terms to retain in the series.

Write a Fortran program that reads in a value for x in degrees, and then calculates the sine of x using the sine intrinsic function. Next, calculate the sine of x using Equation 4-13, with $N = 1, 2, 3, \ldots, 10$. Compare the true value of $\sin x$ with the values calculated by using the truncated infinite series. How many terms are required to calculate $\sin x$ to the full accuracy of your computer?

4-27. Geometric Mean The *geometric mean* of a set of numbers x_1 through x_n is defined as the nth root of the product of the numbers:

$$\text{Geometric mean} = \sqrt[n]{x_1 x_2 x_3 \ldots x_n} \qquad (4\text{-}15)$$

Write a Fortran program that will accept an arbitrary number of positive input values and calculate both the arithmetic mean (i.e., the average) and the geometric mean of the numbers. Use a while loop to get the input values, and terminate the inputs a user enters with a negative number. Test your program by calculating the average and geometric mean of the four numbers 10, 5, 4, and 5.

4-28. RMS Average The *root-mean-square* (rms) *average* is another way of calculating a mean for a set of numbers. The rms average of a series of numbers is the square root of the arithmetic mean of the squares of the numbers:

$$\text{rms average} = \sqrt{\frac{1}{N}\sum_{i=1}^{N} x_i{}^2} \qquad (4\text{-}16)$$

Write a Fortran program that will accept an arbitrary number of positive input values and calculate the rms average of the numbers. Prompt the user for the number of values to be entered, and use a DO loop to read in the numbers. Test your program by calculating the rms average of the four numbers 10, 5, 4, and 5.

4-29. Harmonic Mean The *harmonic mean* is yet another way of calculating a mean for a set of numbers. The harmonic mean of a set of numbers is given by the equation:

$$\text{Harmonic mean} = \frac{N}{\dfrac{1}{x_1} + \dfrac{1}{x_2} + \ldots + \dfrac{1}{x_N}} \qquad (4\text{-}17)$$

Write a Fortran program that will read in an arbitrary number of positive input values and calculate the harmonic mean of the numbers. Use any method that you desire to read in the input values. Test your program by calculating the harmonic mean of the four numbers 10, 5, 4, and 5.

4-30. Write a single Fortran program that calculates the arithmetic mean (average), rms average, geometric mean, and harmonic mean for a set of positive numbers. Use any method that you desire to read in the input values. Compare these values for each of the following sets of numbers:

(*a*) 4, 4, 4, 4, 4, 4, 4

(*b*) 5, 2, 3, 6, 3, 2, 6

(*c*) 4, 1, 4, 7, 4, 1, 7

(*d*) 1, 2, 3, 4, 5, 6, 7

4-31. Mean Time Between Failure Calculations The reliability of a piece of electronic equipment is usually measured in terms of mean time between failures (MTBF), where MTBF is the average time that the piece of equipment can operate before a failure occurs in it. For large systems containing many pieces of electronic equipment, it is customary to determine the MTBFs of each component, and to calculate the overall MTBF of the system from the failure rates of the individual components. If the system is structured like the one shown in Figure 4-16, every component must work in order for the whole system to work, and the overall system MTBF can be calculated as

$$\text{MTBF}_{\text{sys}} = \frac{1}{\dfrac{1}{\text{MTBF}_1} + \dfrac{1}{\text{MTBF}_2} + \ldots + \dfrac{1}{\text{MTBF}_n}} \qquad (4\text{-}18)$$

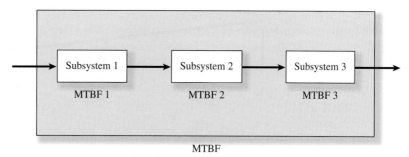

MTBF

FIGURE 4-16
An electronic system containing three subsystems with known MTBFs.

4

Write a program that reads in the number of series components in a system and the MTBFs for each component, and then calculates the overall MTBF for the system. To test your program, determine the MTBF for a radar system consisting of an antenna subsystem with an MTBF of 2000 hours, a transmitter with an MTBF of 800 hours, a receiver with an MTBF of 3000 hours, and a computer with an MTBF of 5000 hours.

4-32. Ideal Gas Law An ideal gas is one in which all collisions between molecules are perfectly elastic. It is possible to think of the molecules in an ideal gas as perfectly hard billiard balls that collide and bounce off of each other without losing kinetic energy.

Such a gas can be characterized by three quantities: absolute pressure (P), volume (V) and absolute temperature (T). The relationship among these quantities in an ideal gas is known as the ideal gas law:

$$PV = nRT \qquad (4\text{-}19)$$

where P is the pressure of the gas in kilopascals (kPa), V is the volume of the gas in liters (L), n is the number of molecules of the gas in units of moles (mol), R is the universal gas constant (8.314 L · kPa/mol · K), and T is the absolute temperature in kelvins (K). (*Note:* 1 mol = 6.02×10^{23} molecules)

Assume that a sample of an ideal gas contains 1 mol of molecules at a temperature of 273 K, and answer the following questions.

(*a*) Write a program to calculate and print out the volume of this gas as its pressure varies from 1 to 1001 kPa in steps of 100 kPa.

(*b*) Suppose that the temperature of the gas is increased to 300 K. How does the volume of this gas vary with pressure over the same range now?

4-33. Assume that the volume of 1 mol of an ideal gas has a fixed volume of 10 L, and calculate and print out the pressure of the gas as a function of temperature as the temperature is changed from 250 to 400 K.

4-34. The Lever The lever (Figure 4-17) is the simplest possible machine. It is used to lift loads that would otherwise be too heavy to lift. If there is no friction, the relationship between the force applied to the lever and the weight that can be lifted is given by the equation

$$F_{\text{APP}} \times d_1 = \text{weight} \times d_2 \qquad (4\text{-}20)$$

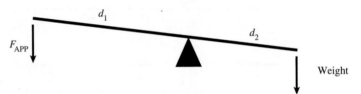

FIGURE 4-17
A lever.

where F_{APP} is the applied force in newtons, d_1 is the distance from the fulcrum to the point where the force is applied, d_2 is the distance from the fulcrum to the location of the load, and weight is the weight (downward force) of the load.

Assume that the applied force consists of weights that can be stacked onto one end of the lever. Write a program that will calculate weight required to lift a load of 600 kg if the distance d_2 from the fulcrum to the location of the load is fixed at 1 m, and the distance d_1 from the fulcrum to the point where the weights are applied varies from 0.5 to 3.0 m in 0.1-m steps. Assuming that we only have 400 kg of weights available, what is the shortest distance d_1 that could be used in this lever?

5

Basic I/O Concepts

OBJECTIVES

- Know how to use formatted WRITE statements to create neatly formatted output from a program.
- Learn how to use the I, F, E, ES, L, A, X, T, and / format descriptors.
- Know how to use formatted READ statements to read data into a program.
- Know how to open, read, write, navigate through, and close files.

In the previous chapters, we have read values into and written them out of our programs using list-directed READ and WRITE statements. List-directed I/O statements are said to be in **free format.** Free format is specified by the second asterisk in the READ (*,*) and WRITE (*,*) statements. As we saw, the results of writing out data in free format are not always pretty. There are often a large number of extra spaces in the output. In this chapter, we will learn how to write out data by using **formats** that specify the exact way in which the numbers should be printed out.

Formats may be used either when writing or when reading data. Since they are most useful during output, we will examine formatted WRITE statements first, and postpone formatted READ statements until a later section in the chapter.

The second major topic introduced in this chapter is disk file processing. We will learn the basics of how to read from and write to disk files. Advanced disk file processing will be postponed to Chapter 14.

▧ 5.1
FORMATS AND FORMATTED WRITE STATEMENTS

A **format** may be used to specify the exact manner in which variables are to be printed out by a program. In general, a format can specify both the horizontal and the vertical position of the variables on the paper, and also the number of significant digits to be printed out. A typical formatted WRITE statement for an integer i and a real variable result is shown below:

```
WRITE (*,100) i, result
100 FORMAT (' The result for iteration ', I3,' is ', F7.3)
```

The FORMAT statement contains the formatting information used by the WRITE statement. The number 100 that appears within the parentheses in the WRITE statement is the statement label of the FORMAT statement describing how the values contained in i and result are to be printed out. I3 and F7.3 are the **format descriptors** associated with variables i and result, respectively. In this case, the FORMAT statement specifies that the program should first write out the phrase ' The result for iteration ', followed by the value of variable i. The format descriptor I3 specifies that a space three characters wide should be used to print out the value of variable i. The value of i will be followed by the phrase ' is ' and then the value of the variable result. The format descriptor F7.3 specifies that a space seven characters wide should be used to print out the value of variable result, and that it should be printed with three digits to the right of the decimal point. The resulting output line is shown below, compared to the same line printed with free format.

```
The result for iteration 21 is   3.142              (formatted)
The result for iteration          21 is       3.141593   (free format)
```

Note that we are able to eliminate both extra blank spaces and undesired decimal places by using format statements. Note also that the value in variable result was rounded before it was printed out in F7.3 format. (Only the value printed out has been rounded; the contents of variable result are unchanged.) Formatted I/O will permit us to create neat output listings from our programs.

In addition to FORMAT statements, formats may be specified in character constants or variables. If a character constant or variable is used to contain the format, then the constant or the name of the variable appears within the parentheses in the WRITE statement. For example, the following three WRITE statements are equivalent:

```
WRITE (*,100) i, x                ! Format in FORMAT statement
100 FORMAT (1X,I6,F10.2)

CHARACTER(len = 20) :: string     ! Format in character variable
string = '(1X,I6,F10.2)'
WRITE (*,string) i, x
WRITE (*,'(1X,I6,F10.2)') i, x    ! Format in character constant
```

We will mix formats in FORMAT statements, character constants, and character variables in examples throughout this chapter.

In the above example, each format descriptor was separated from its neighbors by commas. With a few exceptions, *multiple format descriptors in a single format must be separated by commas.*[1]

---

[1] There is another form of formatted output statement:

```
PRINT fmt, output_list
```

This statement is equivalent to the formatted WRITE statement discussed above, where *fmt* is either the number of a format statement or a character constant or variable. The PRINT statement is never used in this book, but it is discussed in Section 14.3.7.

■ 5.2
OUTPUT DEVICES

To understand the structure of a FORMAT statement, we must know something about the **output devices** on which our data will be displayed. The output from a Fortran program is displayed on an output device. There are many types of output devices that are used with computers. Some output devices produce permanent paper copies of the data, while others just display it temporarily for us to see. Common output devices include laser printers, line printers, and flat panel displays.

The traditional way to get a paper copy of the output of a Fortran program was on a **line printer.** A line printer is a type of printer that originally got its name from the fact that it printed output data a line at a time. Since it was the first common computer output device, Fortran output specifications were designed with it in mind. Other, more modern, output devices are generally built to be compatible with the line printer, so that the same output statement can be used for any of the devices.

A line printer printed on computer paper that was divided into pages on a continuous roll. There were perforations between the pages so that it was easy to separate them. The most common size of line printer paper in the United States was 11 inches high by $14\frac{7}{8}$ inches wide. Each page was divided into a number of lines, and each line was divided into 132 columns, with one character per column. Since most line printers printed either 6 lines per vertical inch or 8 lines per vertical inch, the printers could print either 60 or 72 lines per page (note that this assumes a 0.5-inch margin at the top and the bottom of each page; if the margin is made larger, fewer lines can be printed).

Most modern printers are laser printers, which print on separate sheets of paper instead of on a connected roll of paper. The paper size is usually "letter" or "legal" in the North America, and A4 or A3 in the rest of the world. Laser printers can be set to print either 80 or 132 columns, depending on text size, so they can be compatible with line printers and respond the same way to output from Fortran programs.

The format specifies where a line is to be printed on a line printer or laser printer page (vertical position), and also where each variable is to be printed within the line (horizontal position).

The computer builds up a complete image of each line in memory before sending it to an output device. The computer memory containing the image of the line is called the **output buffer.** The output buffer for a line printer is usually 133 characters wide (Figure 5-1). In Fortran 95, the first character in the output buffer is known as

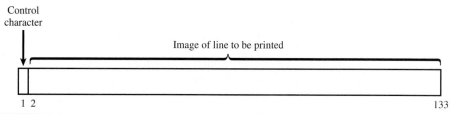

FIGURE 5-1
The output buffer is usually 133 characters long. The first character is the control character, and the next 132 characters are an image of what is to be printed on the line.

TABLE 5-1
Fortran control characters

Control character	Action
1	Skip to new page
Blank	Single spacing
0	Double spacing
+	No spacing (print over previous line)

the **control character**; it specifies the vertical spacing for the line. The remaining 132 characters in the buffer contain the data to be printed on that line.

The control character will not be printed on the page by the line printer. Instead, it provides vertical positioning control information to the printer. Table 5-1 shows the vertical spacing resulting from different control characters.

A '1' character causes the printer to skip the remainder of the current page and print the current line at the top of the next page. A blank character causes the printer to print the current line right below the previous one, while a '0' character causes the printer to skip a line before the current line is printed. A '+' character specifies no spacing; in this case, the new line will overwrite the previous line. If any other character is used as the control character, the result should be the same as for a blank.

For list-directed output [WRITE (*,*)], a blank control character is automatically inserted at the beginning of each output buffer. Therefore, list-directed output is always printed in single-spaced lines.

The following FORMAT statements illustrate the use of the control character. They will print a heading at the top of a new page, skip one line, and then print column headings for Table 5-1 below it.

```
WRITE (*,100)
100 FORMAT ('1','This heading is at the top of a new page.')
WRITE (*,110)
110 FORMAT ('0',' Control Character      Action ')
WRITE (*,120)
120 FORMAT (' ','  ==================      ====== ')
```

The results of executing these Fortran statements are shown in Figure 5-2.

You must be careful to avoid unpleasant surprises when writing output format statements. For example, the following statement will behave in an unpredictable fashion.

```
WRITE (*,'(I3)') n
```

The format descriptor I3 specifies that we want to print the value of variable n in the first three characters of the output buffer. If the value of n is 25, the three positions are filled with ƀ25 (where ƀ denotes a blank). Because the first character is interpreted as a control character, the printer will space down one line and print out 25 in the first two columns of the new line. On the other hand, if n is 125, then the first three characters of the output buffer are filled with 125. Because the first character is interpreted as a control character, the printer will *skip to a new page* and print out 25 in the first two columns of the new line. This is certainly not what we intended! You should be

```
This heading is at the top of a new page


Control Character   Action
==================  ======
```

FIGURE 5-2
Results printing Table 5-1 column headings.

5

very careful not to write any format descriptors that include column 1, since they can produce erratic printing behavior and fail to display the correct results.

Programming Pitfalls

Never write a format descriptor that includes column 1 of the output line. Erratic paging behavior and incorrectly displayed values may result if you do so, depending on the value being printed out.

To help avoid this error, it is a good idea to write out each control character separately in a format. For example, the following two formats are equivalent:

```
WRITE (*,"('1','Count = ', I3)" icount
WRITE (*, "('1Count = ', I3)" icount
```

Each of these statements produces the same output buffer, containing a 1 in the control character position followed by the string 'icount = ' and the value of the variable icount. However, the control character is more obvious in the first statement than it is in the second one.

F-2003 ONLY

The use of a control character in column 1 of the output buffer was a special mechanism designed to work with line printers. Line printers are effectively extinct, and have been for many years, so the use of the column 1 as a control character has been deleted from the Fortran 2003 standard. According to the new standard, column 1 of the output buffer has no special purpose.

However, existing Fortran programs written over the last 50 years have all assumed the control character behavior, and no compiler vendor will be able to delete this feature without risking market share. I expect that the control character behavior will be a part of all Fortran compilers for the indefinite future.

■ 5.3
FORMAT DESCRIPTORS

There are many different format descriptors. They fall into four basic categories:

1. Format descriptors that describe the *vertical position* of a line of text.
2. Format descriptors that describe the *horizontal position* of data in a line.
3. Format descriptors that describe the output format of a particular value.
4. Format descriptors that control the repetition of portions of a format.

We will deal with some common examples of format descriptors in this chapter. Other less common format descriptors will be postponed to Chapter 14. Table 5-2 contains a list of symbols used with format descriptors, together with their meanings.

■ **TABLE 5-2**
   Symbols used with format descriptors

Symbol	Meaning
c	Column number
d	Number of digits to right of decimal place for real input or output
m	Minimum number of digits to be displayed
n	Number of spaces to skip
r	**Repeat count**—the number of times to use a descriptor or group of descriptors
w	**Field width**—the number of characters to use for the input or output

5.3.1 Integer Output—The I Descriptor

The descriptor used to describe the display format of integer data is the I descriptor. It has the general form

$$r\mathrm{I}w \qquad \text{or} \qquad r\mathrm{I}w.m$$

where *r*, *w*, and *m* have the meanings given in Table 5-2. Integer values are *right justified* in their fields. This means that integers are printed out so that the last digit of the integer occupies the rightmost column of the field. If an integer is too large to fit into the field in which it is to be printed, then the field is filled with asterisks. For example, the following statements

```
INTEGER :: index = -12, junk = 4, number = -12345
WRITE (*,200) index, index+12, junk, number
WRITE (*,210) index, index+12, junk, number
WRITE (*,220) index, index+12, junk, number
200 FORMAT (' ', 2I5,    I6, I10 )
210 FORMAT (' ', 2I5.0, I6, I10.8 )
220 FORMAT (' ', 2I5.3, I6, I5 )
```

will produce the output

```
-12    0     4     -12345
-12          4 -00012345
-012  000    4*****
----|----|----|----|----|----|
    5    10   15   20   25   30
```

5.3.2 Real Output—The F Descriptor

One format descriptor used to describe the display format of real data is the F descriptor. It has the form

$$rFw.d$$

where *r*, *w*, and *d* have the meanings given in Table 5-2. Real values are printed *right justified* within their fields. If necessary, the number will be rounded off before it is displayed. For example, suppose that the variable pi contains the value 3.141593. If this variable is displayed by using the F7.3 format descriptor, the displayed value will be ƀƀ3.142. On the other hand, if the displayed number includes more significant digits than the internal representation of the number, extra zeros will be appended to the right of the decimal point. If the variable pi is displayed with an F10.8 format descriptor, the resulting value will be 3.14159300. If a real number is too large to fit into the field in which it is to be printed, then the field is filled with asterisks.

For example, the following statements

```
REAL :: a = -12.3, b = .123, c = 123.456
WRITE (*,200) a, b, c
WRITE (*,210) a, b, c
200 FORMAT (' ', 2F6.3, F8.3 )
210 FORMAT (' ', 3F10.2 )
```

will produce the output

```
****** 0.123 123.456
   -12.30      0.12    123.46
----|----|----|----|----|
    5    10   15   20   25   30
```

5.3.3 Real Output—The E Descriptor

Real data can also be printed in **exponential notation** using the E descriptor. Scientific notation is a popular way for scientists and engineers to display very large or very small numbers. It consists of expressing a number as a normalized value between 1 and 10 multiplied by 10 raised to a power.

To understand the convenience of scientific notation, let's consider the following two examples from chemistry and physics. *Avogadro's number* is the number of atoms in a mole of a substance. It can be written out as 602,000,000,000,000,000,000,000 or it can be expressed in scientific notation as 6.02×10^{23}. On the other hand, the charge on an electron is 0.0000000000000000001602 coulombs. This number can be expressed in scientific notation as 1.602×10^{-19}. Scientific notation is clearly a much more convenient way to write these numbers!

The E format descriptor has the form

$$rEw.d$$

where r, w, and d have the meanings given in Table 5-2. Unlike normal scientific notation, the real values displayed in exponential notation with the E descriptor are normalized to a range between 0.1 and 1.0. That is, they are displayed as a number between 0.1 and 1.0 multiplied by a power of 10. For example, the standard scientific notation for the number 4096.0 would be 4.096×10^3, while the computer output with the E descriptor would be 0.4096×10^4. Since it is not easy to represent exponents on a line printer, the computer output would appear on the printer as 0.4096E+04.

If a real number cannot fit into the field in which it is to be printed, then the field is filled with asterisks. You should be especially careful with field sizes when working with the E format descriptor, since many items must be considered when sizing the output field. For example, suppose that we want to print out a variable in the E format with 4 significant digits of accuracy. Then a field width of *11* characters is required, as shown below: 1 for the sign of the mantissa, 2 for the zero and decimal point, 4 for the actual mantissa, 1 for the E, 1 for the sign of the exponent, and 2 for the exponent itself.

$$\pm0.ddddE\pm ee$$

In general, the width of an E format descriptor field must satisfy the expression

$$w \geq d + 7 \qquad\qquad (5\text{-}1)$$

or the field may be filled with asterisks.[2] The 7 extra characters required are used as follows: 1 for the sign of the mantissa, 2 for the zero and decimal point, 1 for the E, 1 for the sign of the exponent, and 2 for the exponent itself.

For example, the following statements

```
REAL :: a = 1.2346E6, b = 0.001, c = -77.7E10, d = -77.7E10
WRITE (*,200) a, b, c, d
200 FORMAT (' ', 2E14.4, E13.6, E11.6 )
```

will produce the output[3]

---

[2] If the number to be displayed in the field is positive, then the field width w need only be 6 characters larger than d. If the number is negative, an extra character is needed for the minus sign. Hence, in general, w must be $\geq d + 7$. Also, note that some compilers suppress the leading zero, so that one less column is required.

[3] The presence of the leading zero in an E format descriptor is optional, and whether or not it is there will differ among compiler vendors. Some compiler displays leading zeros, while others do not. The following two lines show the output that could be produced by two different compilers for this example, and both would be considered correct.

```
    0.1235E+07   0.1000E-02-0.777000E+12***********
     .1235E+07    .1000E-02 -.777000E+12***********
----|----|----|----|----|----|----|----|----|----|
    5   10   15   20   25   30   35   40   45   50   55
```

```
    0.1235E+07    0.1000E-02-0.777000E+12**********
----|----|----|----|----|----|----|----|----|----|----|
    5   10   15   20   25   30   35   40   45   50   55
```

Notice that the fourth field is all asterisks, since the format descriptor does not satisfy Equation 5-1.

5.3.4 True Scientific Notation—The ES Descriptor

As mentioned earlier, the output of the E format descriptor doesn't exactly match conventional scientific notation. Conventional scientific notation expresses a number as a value between 1.0 and 10.0 times a power of 10, while the E format expresses the number as a value between 0.1 and 1.0 times a power of 10.

We can make the computer output match conventional scientific notation by using a slightly modified version of the E descriptor called the ES descriptor. The ES descriptor is exactly the same as the E descriptor, except that the number to be output will be displayed with a mantissa in the range between 1 and 10. The ES format descriptor has the form

$$rESw.d$$

where r, w, and d have the meanings given in Table 5-2. The formula for the minimum width of an ES format descriptor is the same as the formula for the width of an E format descriptor, but the ES descriptor can display one more significant digit in a given width because the leading zero is replaced by a significant digit. The ES field must satisfy the expression

$$w \geq d + 7 \tag{5-2}$$

or the field may be filled with asterisks. [4]

For example, the following statements

```
REAL :: a = 1.2346E6, b = 0.001, c = -77.7E10
WRITE (*,200) a, b, c
200 FORMAT (' ', 2ES14.4, ES12.6 )
```

will produce the output

```
    1.2346E+06    1.0000E-03***********
----|----|----|----|----|----|----|----|
    5   10   15   20   25   30   35   40
```

The third field is all asterisks, since the format descriptor does not satisfy Equation 5-1.

---

[4] If the number to be displayed in the field is positive, then the field width w need only be 6 characters larger than d. If the number is negative, an extra character is needed for the minus sign. Hence, in general $w \geq d + 7$.

Good Programming Practice

When displaying very large or very small numbers, use the ES format descriptor to cause them to be displayed in conventional scientific notation. This display will help a reader to quickly understand the output numbers.

5.3.5 Logical Output—The L Descriptor

The descriptor used to display logical data has the form

$$rLw$$

where r and w have the meanings given in Table 5-2. The value of a logical variable can only be .TRUE. or .FALSE.. The output of a logical variable is either a T or an F, right justified in the output field.

For example, the following statements:

```
LOGICAL :: output = .TRUE., debug = .FALSE.
WRITE (*,"(' ', 2L5 )") output, debug
```

will produce the output

```
     T    F
----|----|----|
5   10   15
```

5.3.6 Character Output—The A Descriptor

Character data is displayed by using the A format descriptor.

$$rA \ or \ rAw$$

where r and w have the meanings given in Table 5-2. The rA descriptor displays character data in a field whose width is the same as the number of characters being displayed, while the rAw descriptor displays character data in a field of fixed width w. If the width w of the field is longer than the length of the character variable, the variable is printed out *right justified* in the field. If the width of the field is shorter than the length of the character variable, only the first w characters of the variable will be printed out in the field.

For example, the following statements:

```
CHARACTER(len=17) :: string = 'This is a string.'
WRITE (*,10) string
WRITE (*,11) string
WRITE (*,12) string
10 FORMAT (' ', A)
11 FORMAT (' ', A20)
12 FORMAT (' ', A6)
```

will produce the output

```
This is a string.
   This is a string.
This i
----|----|----|----|----|
    5   10   15   20   25
```

5.3.7 Horizontal Positioning—The X and T Descriptors

Two format descriptors are available to control the spacing of data in the output buffer, and therefore on the final output line. They are the X descriptor, which inserts spaces into the buffer, and the T descriptor, which "tabs" over to a specific column in the buffer. The X descriptor has the form

$$nX$$

where *n* is the number of blanks to insert. It is used to *add one or more blanks* between two values on the output line. The T descriptor has the form

$$Tc$$

where *c* is the column number to go to. It is used to *jump directly to a specific column* in the output buffer. The T descriptor works much like a "tab" character on a type-writer, except that it is possible to jump to any position in the output line, even if we are already past that position in the FORMAT statement.

For example, the following statements:

```
CHARACTER(len=10) :: first_name = 'James      '
CHARACTER :: initial = 'R'
CHARACTER(len=16) :: last_name = 'Johnson        '
CHARACTER(len=9) :: class = 'COSC 2301'
INTEGER :: grade = 92
WRITE (*,100) first_name, initial, last_name, grade, class
100 FORMAT (1X, A10, 1X, A1, 1X, A10, 4X, I3, T51, A9)
```

will produce the output

```
James      R Johnson       92                         COSC 2301
----|----|----|----|----|----|----|----|----|----|----|----|
    5   10   15   20   25   30   35   40   45   50   55   60
```

The first 1X descriptor produces a blank control character, so this output line is printed on the next line of the printer. The first name begins in column 1, the middle initial begins in column 12, the last name begins in column 14, the grade begins in column 28, and course name begins in column 50. (The course name begins in column 51 of the buffer, but it is printed in column 50, since the first character in the output buffer is the control character.) This same output structure could have been created with the following statements.

```
WRITE (*,110) first_name, initial, last_name, class, grade
110 FORMAT (1X, A10, T13, A1, T15, A10, T51, A9, T29, I3)
```

In this example, we are actually jumping backward in the output line when we print out the grade.

Since you may freely move anywhere in the output buffer with the T descriptor, it is possible to accidentally overwrite portions of your output data before the line is printed. For example, if we change the tab descriptor for class from T51 to T17,

```
WRITE (*,120) first_name, initial, last_name, class, grade
120 FORMAT (1X, A10, T13, A1, T15, A10, T17, A9, T29, I3)
```

the program will produce the following output:

```
JAMES     R JOCOSC 2301   92
----|----|----|----|----|----|----|----|----|----|----|----|
    5   10   15   20   25   30   35   40   45   50   55   60
```

Programming Pitfalls
When using the T descriptor, be careful to make certain that your fields do not overlap.

The 1X descriptor is commonly used at the beginning of each FORMAT statement to ensure that the control character contains a blank. This action ensures that the output from each line will be printed just below the previous line. You should always do this, unless you deliberately want to skip to the next page or perform some other control action. Unless you want to perform a control action, *begin every format associated with a* WRITE *statement with the* 1X *descriptor*.

Good Programming Practice
Unless you want to perform a control action, begin every format associated with a WRITE statement with the 1X descriptor.

5.3.8 Repeating Groups of Format Descriptors

We have seen that many individual format descriptors can be repeated by preceding them with a repeat count. For example, the format descriptor 2I10 is the same as the pair of descriptors I10, I10.

It is also possible to repeat *whole groups* of format descriptors by enclosing the whole group within parentheses and placing a repetition count in front of the parentheses. For example, the following two FORMAT statements are equivalent:

```
320 FORMAT ( 1X, I6, I6, F10.2, F10.2, I6, F10.2, F10.2 )
320 FORMAT ( 1X, I6, 2(I6, 2F10.2) )
```

Groups of format descriptors may be nested if desired. For example, the following two FORMAT statements are equivalent:

```
330 FORMAT ( 1X, I6, F10.2, A, F10.2, A, I6, F10.2, A, F10.2, A )
330 FORMAT ( 1X, 2(I6, 2(F10.2,A)) )
```

However, don't go overboard with nesting. The more complicated you make your FORMAT statements, the harder it will be for you or someone else to understand and debug them.

5.3.9 Changing Output Lines—The Slash (/) Descriptor

The slash (/) descriptor causes the current output buffer to be sent to the printer, and a new output buffer to be started. With slash descriptors, a single WRITE statement can display output values on more than one line. Several slashes can be used together to skip several lines. The slash is one of the special descriptors that does not have to be separated from other descriptors by commas. However, you may use commas if you wish.

For example, suppose that we need to print out the results of an experiment in which we have measured the amplitude and phase of a signal at a certain time and depth. Assume that the integer variable index is 10 and the real variables time, depth, amplitude, and phase are 300., 330., 850.65, and 30., respectively. Then the statements

```
WRITE (*,100) index, time, depth, amplitude, phase
100 FORMAT ('1',T20,'Results for Test Number ',I3,///, &
    1X,'Time      = ',F7.0/, &
    1X,'Depth     = ',F7.1,' meters',/, &
    1X,'Amplitude = ',F8.2/ &,
    1X,'Phase     = ',F7.1)
```

generate seven separate output buffers. The first buffer contains a '1' as the control character, so it skips to a new page, and puts a title on the page. The next two output buffers are empty, so two blank lines are printed. The final four output buffers have a blank control character, so the four values for time, depth, amplitude, and phase are printed on successive lines. The resulting output is shown in Figure 5-3.

Notice the 1X descriptors after each slash. These descriptors place a blank in the control character of each output buffer to ensure that the output advances by one line between buffers. *Each slash starts a new line on the line printer*, and that new line has a control character of its own at the beginning. You must be careful to place a blank in that control character to ensure proper output. Therefore, you should *always* include a 1X descriptor after each group of 1 or more slashes, and before any other format information.

```
                      Results for Test Number 10


       Time      =   300.
       Depth     =   330.0 meters
       Amplitude =   850.65
       Phase     =    30.2
```

FIGURE 5-3
Results printing amplitude and phase.

5.3.10 How Formats are Used During WRITEs

Most Fortran compilers verify the syntax of FORMAT statements and character constants containing formats at compilation time, but do not otherwise process them. Character variables containing formats are not even checked at compilation time for valid syntax, since the format may be modified dynamically during program execution. In all cases, formats are saved unchanged as character strings within the compiled program. When the program is executed, the characters in a format are used as a template to guide the operation of the formatted WRITE.

At execution time, the list of output variables associated with the WRITE statement is processed together with the format of the statement. The program begins at the left end of the variable list and the left end of the format, and scans from left to right, associating the first variable in the output list with the first format descriptor in the format, and so forth. The variables in the output list must be of the same type and in the same order as the format descriptors in the format, or a run-time error will occur. For example, the program in Figure 5-4 will compile and link correctly, since all of the statements in it are legal Fortran statements, and the program doesn't check for correspondence between the format descriptors and the data types until it runs. However, it will abort at run time, when the check shows a logical format descriptor corresponding to a character variable.

FIGURE 5-4
A Fortran program showing a run-time error resulting from a data/format descriptor mismatch. Note that the Fortran compiler did not check for format correspondence, so it missed the error.

```
C:\book\chap5>type bad_format.f90
PROGRAM bad_format
IMPLICIT NONE
INTEGER :: i = 10
CHARACTER(len = 6) :: j = 'ABCDEF'
```

(continued)

(concluded)

```
WRITE (*,100) i, j
100 FORMAT ( I10, L10 )
END PROGRAM
```

```
C:\book\chap5>ifort bad_format.f90
Intel(R) Fortran Compiler for 32-bit applications, Version 9.1 Build 20060706
Z Package ID: W_FC_C_9.1.028
Copyright (C) 1985-2006 Intel Corporation. All rights reserved.

Microsoft (R) Incremental Linker Version 7.10.3077
Copyright (C) Microsoft Corporation. All rights reserved.

-out:bad_format.exe
-subsystem:console
bad_format.obj
```

```
C:\book\chap5>bad_format
forrtl: severe (61): format/variable-type mismatch, unit -1, file CONOUT$
```

Programming Pitfalls

Make sure that there is a one-to-one correspondence between the types of the data in a WRITE statement and the types of the format descriptors in the associated FORMAT statement, or your program will fail at execution time.

As the program moves from left to right through the variable list of a WRITE statement, it also scans from left to right through the associated format. However, the order in which the contents of a format are used may be modified by the inclusion of repetition counters and parentheses. Formats are scanned according to the following rules:

1. *Formats are scanned in order from left to right.* The first variable format descriptor in the format is associated with the first value in the output list of the WRITE statement, and so forth. The type of each format descriptor must match the type of the data being output. In the example shown below, descriptor I5 is associated with variable i, I10 with variable j, I15 with variable k, and F10.2 with variable a.

```
WRITE (*,10) i, j, k, a
10 FORMAT (1X, I5, I10, I15, F10.2)
```

2. *If a format descriptor has a repetition count associated with it, the descriptor will be used the number of times specified in the repetition count before the next descriptor will be used.* In the example shown below, descriptor I5 is associated with variable i, and again with variable j. After it has been used twice, I10 is associated with variable k, and F10.2 is associated with variable a.

```
WRITE (*,20) i, j, k, a
20 FORMAT (1X, 2I5, I10, F10.2)
```

3. *If a group of format descriptors included within parentheses has a repetition count associated with it, the entire group will be used the number of times specified in the repetition count before the next descriptor will be used.* Each descriptor within the group will be used in order from left to right during each repetition. In the example shown below, descriptor F10.2 is associated with variable a. Next, the group in parentheses is used twice, so I5 is associated with i, E14.6 is associated with b, I5 is associated with j, and E14.6 is associated with c. Finally, F10.2 is associated with d.

```
WRITE (*,30) a, i, b, j, c, d
30 FORMAT (1X, F10.2, 2(I5, E14.6), F10.2)
```

4. If the WRITE statement runs out of variables before the end of the format, *the use of the format stops at the first format descriptor without a corresponding variable, or at the end of the format, whichever comes first.* For example, the statements

```
INTEGER :: m = 1
WRITE (*,40) m
   40 FORMAT (1X, 'M = ', I3, 'N = ', I4, 'O = ', F7.2)
```

will produce the output

```
M =   1 N =
----|----|----|----|----|----|
    5   10   15   20   25   30
```

since the use of the format stops at I4, which is the first unmatched format descriptor. The statements

```
REAL :: voltage = 13800.
WRITE (*,50) voltage / 1000.
50 FORMAT (1X, 'Voltage = ', F8.1, ' kV')
```

will produce the output

```
Voltage =    13.8 kV
----|----|----|----|----|----|
    5   10   15   20   25   30
```

since there are no unmatched descriptors, and the use of the format stops at the end of the statement.

5. If the scan reaches the end of the format before the WRITE statement runs out of values, the program sends the current output buffer to the printer, and starts over *at the rightmost open parenthesis in the format that is not preceded by a repetition count.* For example, the statements

```
INTEGER :: j = 1, k = 2, l = 3, m = 4, n = 5
WRITE (*,60) j, k, l, m, n
60 FORMAT (1X,'value = ', I3)
```

will produce the output

```
value =   1
value =   2
value =   3
value =   4
value =   5
----|----|----|----|----|----|
    5   10   15   20   25   30
```

When the program reaches the end of the FORMAT statement after it prints j with the I3 descriptor, it sends that output buffer to the printer and goes back to the rightmost open parenthesis not preceded by a repetition count. In this case, the rightmost open parenthesis without a repetition count is the opening parenthesis of the statement, so the entire statement is used again to print k, l, m, and n. By contrast, the statements

```
INTEGER :: j = 1, k = 2, l = 3, m = 4, n = 5
WRITE (*,60) j, k, l, m, n
60 FORMAT (1X,'Value = ',/, (1X,'New Line',2(3X,I5)))
```

will produce the output

```
Value =
New Line        1       2
New Line        3       4
New Line        5
----|----|----|----|----|----|
    5   10   15   20   25   30
```

In this case, the entire FORMAT statement is used to print values j and k. Since the rightmost open parenthesis not preceded by a repetition count is the one just before 1X,'New Line', that part of the statement is used again to print l, m, and n. Note that the open parenthesis associated with (3X,I5) was ignored because it had a repetition count associated with it.

EXAMPLE 5-1

Generating a Table of Information:

A good way to illustrate the use of formatted WRITE statements is to generate and print out a table of data. The example program shown in Figure 5-5 generates the square roots, squares, and cubes of all integers between 1 and 10, and presents the data in a table with appropriate headings.

FIGURE 5-5

A Fortran program to generate a table of square roots, squares, and cubes.

```
PROGRAM table
!
!  Purpose:
!    To illustrate the use of formatted WRITE statements.  This
!    program generates a table containing the square roots, squares,
!    and cubes of all integers between 1 and 10.  The table includes
!    a title and column headings.
!
!  Record of revisions:
!      Date        Programmer          Description of change
!      ====        ==========          =====================
!    11/18/06    S. J. Chapman         Original code
IMPLICIT NONE

INTEGER :: cube          ! The cube of i
INTEGER :: i             ! Index variable
INTEGER :: square        ! The square of i
REAL    :: square_root   ! The square root of i

! Print the title of the table on a new page.
WRITE (*,100)
100 FORMAT ('1', T3, 'Table of Square Roots, Squares, and Cubes')

! Print the column headings after skipping one line.
WRITE (*,110)
110 FORMAT ('0',T4,'Number',T13,'Square Root',T29,'Square',T39,'Cube')
WRITE (*,120)
120 FORMAT (1X,T4,'======',T13,'===========',T29,'======',T39,'===='/)

! Generate the required values, and print them out.
DO i = 1, 10
   square_root = SQRT ( REAL(i) )
   square = i**2
   cube = i**3
   WRITE (*,130) i, square_root, square, cube
   130 FORMAT (1X, T4, I4, T13, F10.6, T27, I6, T37, I6)
END DO

END PROGRAM table
```

This program uses the tab format descriptor to set up neat columns of data for the table. When this program is compiled and executed on a PC, the result is

```
C:\book\chap5>table

Table of Square Roots, Squares, and Cubes

Number    Square Root     Square     Cube
======    ===========     ======     ====

    1       1.000000         1        1
    2       1.414214         4        8
```

(continued)

(concluded)

3	1.732051	9	27
4	2.000000	16	64
5	2.236068	25	125
6	2.449490	36	216
7	2.645751	49	343
8	2.828427	64	512
9	3.000000	81	729
10	3.162278	100	1000

5

EXAMPLE 5-2 *Charge on a Capacitor:*

A *capacitor* is an electrical device that stores electric charge. It essentially consists of two flat plates with an insulating material (the *dielectric*) between them (see Figure 5-6). The capacitance of a capacitor is defined as

$$C = \frac{Q}{V} \tag{5-3}$$

where Q is the amount of charge stored in a capacitor in units of coulombs and V is the voltage between the two plates of the capacitor in volts. The units of capacitance are farads (F), with 1 farad = 1 coulomb per volt. When a charge is present on the plates of the capacitor, there is an electric field between the two plates. The energy stored in this electric field is given by the equation

$$E = \frac{1}{2}CV^2 \tag{5-4}$$

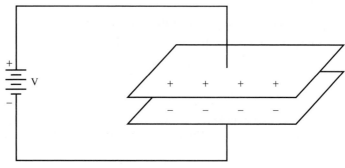

FIGURE 5-6
A capacitor consists of two metal plates separated by an insulating material.

where E is the energy in joules. Write a program that will perform one of the following calculations:

1. For a known capacitance and voltage, calculate the charge on the plates, the number of electrons on the plates, and the energy stored in the electric field.
2. For a known charge and voltage, calculate the capacitance of the capacitor, the number of electrons on the plates, and the energy stored in the electric field.

SOLUTION

This program must be able to ask the user which calculation he or she wishes to perform, read in the appropriate values for that calculation, and write out the results in a reasonable format. Note that this problem will require us to work with very small and very large numbers, so we will have to pay special attention to the FORMAT statements in the program. For example, capacitors are typically rated in microfarads (μF or 10^{-6} F) or picofarads (pF or 10^{-12} F), and there are 6.241461×10^{18} electrons per coulomb of charge.

1. **State the problem.**
   The problem may be succinctly stated as follows:

   (*a*) For a known capacitance and voltage, calculate the charge on a capacitor, the number of electrons stored, and the energy stored in its electric field.

   (*b*) For a known charge and voltage, calculate the capacitance of the capacitor, the number of electrons stored, and the energy stored in its electric field.

2. **Define the inputs and outputs.**
   There are two possible sets of input values to this program:

   (*a*) Capacitance in farads and voltage in volts.

   (*b*) Charge in coulombs and voltage in volts.

   The outputs from the program in either mode will be the capacitance of the capacitor, the voltage across the capacitor, the charge on the plates of the capacitor, and the number of electrons on the plates of the capacitor. The output must be printed out in a reasonable and understandable format.

3. **Describe the algorithm.**
   This program can be broken down into four major steps

   ```
   Decide which calculation is required
   Get the input data for that calculation
   Calculate the unknown quantities
   Write out the capacitance, voltage, charge and number of electrons
   ```

   The first major step of the program is to decide which calculation is required. There are two types of calculations: Type 1 requires capacitance and voltage, while Type 2 requires charge and voltage. We must prompt the user for the type of input data, read the user's answer, and then read in the appropriate data. The pseudocode for these steps is:

```
Prompt user for the type of calculation "type"
WHILE
    Read type
    IF type == 1 or type == 2 EXIT
    Tell user of invalid value
End of WHILE

IF type == 1 THEN
    Prompt the user for the capacitance c in farads
    Read capacitance c
    Prompt the user for the voltage v in volts
    Read voltage v
ELSE IF type == 2 THEN
    Prompt the user for the charge "charge" in coulombs
    Read "charge"
    Prompt the user for the voltage v in volts
    Read voltage v
END IF
```

Next, we must calculate unknown values. For Type 1 calculations, the unknown values are charge, the number of electrons, and the energy in the electric field, while for Type 2 calculations, the unknown values are capacitance, the number of electrons, and the energy in the electric field. The pseudocode for this step is shown below

```
IF type == 1 THEN
    charge ← c * v
ELSE
    c ← charge / v
END IF
electrons ← charge * electrons_per_coluomb
energy ← 0.5 * c * v**2
```

where `electrons_per_coluomb` is the number of electrons per coulomb of charge (6.241461×10^{18}). Finally, we must write out the results in a useful format.

```
WRITE v, c, charge, electrons, energy
```

The flowchart for this program is shown in Figure 5-7.

4. **Turn the algorithm into Fortran statements.**
   The final Fortran program is shown in Figure 5-8.

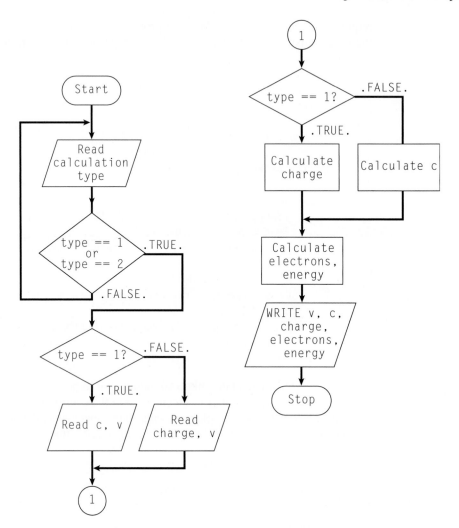

FIGURE 5-7
Flowchart for the program to calculate information about a capacitor.

FIGURE 5-8
Program to perform capacitor calculations.

```
PROGRAM capacitor
!
!   Purpose:
!      To calculate the behavior of a capacitor as follows:
!      1.   If capacitance and voltage are known, calculate
!           charge, number of electrons, and energy stored.
!      2.   If charge and voltage are known, calculate capa-
!           citance, number of electrons, and energy stored.
!
```

(*continued*)

(continued)

```
!  Record of revisions:
!       Date        Programmer          Description of change
!       ====        ==========          =====================
!     11/18/06    S. J. Chapman         Original code!
IMPLICIT NONE

! Data dictionary: declare constants
REAL, PARAMETER :: ELECTRONS_PER_COULOMB = 6.241461E18

! Data dictionary: declare variable types, definitions, & units
REAL :: c          ! Capacitance of the capacitor (farads).
REAL :: charge     ! Charge on the capacitor (coulombs).
REAL :: electrons  ! Number of electrons on the plates of the capacitor
REAL :: energy     ! Energy stored in the electric field (joules)
INTEGER :: type    ! Type of input data available for the calculation:
                   ! 1:  C and V
                   ! 2:  CHARGE and V
REAL :: v          ! Voltage on the capacitor (volts).

! Prompt user for the type of input data available.
WRITE (*, 100)
100 FORMAT (' This program calculates information about a ' &
            'capacitor.',/, ' Please specify the type of information',&
            ' available from the following list:',/,&
            '    1 -- capacitance and voltage ',/,&
            '    2 -- charge and voltage ',//,&
            ' Select options 1 or 2: ')

! Get response and validate it.
DO
   READ (*,*) type
   IF ( (type == 1) .OR. (type == 2) ) EXIT
   WRITE (*,110) type
   110 FORMAT (' Invalid response: ', I6, '.  Please enter 1 or 2:')
END DO

! Get additional data based upon the type of calculation.
input: IF ( type == 1 ) THEN

   ! Get capacitance.
   WRITE (*,' Enter capacitance in farads: ')
   READ (*,*) c

   ! Get voltage.
   WRITE (*,' Enter voltage in volts: ')
   READ (*,*) v

ELSE

   ! Get charge.
   WRITE (*,' Enter charge in coulombs: ')
   READ (*,*) charge
```

5

(continued)

(concluded)

```
    ! Get voltage.
    WRITE (*,' Enter voltage in volts: ')
    READ (*,*) v

END IF input

! Calculate the unknown quantities.
calculate: IF ( type == 1 ) THEN
    charge = c * v                              ! Charge
ELSE
    c = charge / v                              ! Capacitance
END IF calculate
electrons = charge * ELECTRONS_PER_COULOMB      ! Electrons
energy = 0.5 * c * v**2                         ! Energy

! Write out answers.
WRITE (*,120) v, c, charge, electrons, energy
120 FORMAT (' For this capacitor: ',/, &
          '    Voltage             = ', F10.2, ' V',/, &
          '    Capacitance         = ', ES10.3, ' F',/, &
          '    Total charge        = ', ES10.3, ' C',/, &
          '    Number of electrons = ', ES10.3,/, &
          '    Total energy        = ', F10.4, ' joules' )

END PROGRAM capacitor
```

5. Test the program.

To test this program, we will calculate the answers by hand for a simple data set, and then compare the answers to the results of the program. If we use a voltage of 100 V and a capacitance of 100 μF, the resulting charge on the plates of the capacitor is 0.01 C, there are 6.241×10^{16} electrons on the capacitor, and the energy stored is 0.5 joules.

Running these values through the program, using both options 1 and 2, yields the following results:

```
C:\book\chap5>capacitor

This program calculates information about a capacitor.
Please specify the type of information available from the following list:
   1 -- capacitance and voltage
   2 -- charge and voltage

Select options 1 or 2:
1
Enter capacitance in farads:
100.e-6
Enter voltage in volts:
100.
For this capacitor:
   Voltage             = 100.00 V
```

(continued)

(*concluded*)

```
Capacitance          = 1.000E-04 F
Total charge         = 1.000E-02 C
Number of electrons = 6.241E+16
Total energy         =    .5000 joules
```

C:\book\chap5>**capacitor**

```
This program calculates information about a capacitor.
Please specify the type of information available from the following list:
  1 -- capacitance and voltage
  2 -- charge and voltage

Select options 1 or 2:
2
Enter charge in coulombs:
0.01
Enter voltage in volts:
100.
For this capacitor:
  Voltage              =    100.00 V
  Capacitance          = 1.000E-04 F
  Total charge         = 1.000E-02 C
  Number of electrons = 6.241E+16
  Total energy         =    .5000 joules
```

The program gives the correct answers for our test data set.

In Example 5-2, sometimes formats appeared in FORMAT statements, and sometimes they appeared as character constants within WRITE statements. Since these two formats are equivalent, either one could be used to provide a format for any WRITE statement. If that is so, when should we use a FORMAT statement and when should we use a character constant? This author usually lets common sense be a guide: if a format is small and fits conveniently, I place it in a character constant within the WRITE statement. If the format is large and complicated, I place it in separate FORMAT statement.

Quiz 5-1

This quiz provides a quick check to see if you have understood the concepts introduced in Sections 5.1 through 5.3. If you have trouble with the quiz, reread the sections, ask your instructor, or discuss the material with a fellow student. The answers to this quiz are found in the back of the book. Unless otherwise stated, assume that variables beginning with the letters I to N are integers, and all other variables are reals.

(*continued*)

(continued)

Write Fortran statements that perform the operations described below.

1. Skip to a new page and print the title 'This is a test!' starting in column 25.

2. Skip a line, then display the values of i, j, and data_1 in fields 10 characters wide. Allow two decimal points for the real variable.

3. Beginning in column 12, write out the string 'The result is' followed by the value of result expressed to 5 significant digits in correct scientific notation.

Assume that real variables a, b, and c are initialized with -0.0001, 6.02×10^{23}, and 3.141593 respectively, and that integer variables i, j, and k are initialized with 32767, 24, and -1010101 respectively. What will be printed out by each of the following sets of statements?

4.
```
WRITE (*,10) a, b, c
10 FORMAT (1X,3F10.4)
```

5.
```
WRITE (*,20) a, b, c
20 FORMAT (1X,F10.3, 2X, E10.3, 2X, F10.5)
```

6.
```
WRITE (*,40) a, b, c
40 FORMAT (1X,ES10.4, ES11.4, F10.4)
```

7.
```
WRITE (*,'(1X,I5)') i, j, k
```

8.
```
CHARACTER(len=30) :: fmt
fmt = "(1X,I8, 2X, I8.8, 2X, I8)"
WRITE (*,fmt) i, j, k
```

Assume that string_1 is a 10-character variable initialized with the string 'ABCDEFGHIJ', and that string_2 is a five-character variable initialized with the string '12345'. What will be printed out by each of the following sets of statements?

9.
```
WRITE (*,"(1X,2A10)") string_1, string_2
```

10.
```
WRITE (*,80) string_1, string_2
80 FORMAT (T21,A10,T24,A5)
```

11.
```
WRITE (*,100) string_1, string_2
100 FORMAT (1X,A5,2X,A5)
```

Examine the following Fortran statements. Are they correct or incorrect? If they are incorrect, why are they incorrect? Assume default typing for variable names where they are not otherwise defined.

12.
```
WRITE (*,'(2I6,F10.4)') istart, istop, step
```

(continued)

(concluded)

```
13.   LOGICAL :: test
      CHARACTER(len=6) :: name
      INTEGER :: ierror
      WRITE (*,200) name, test, ierror
      200 FORMAT (1X,'Test name: ',A,/,' Completion status : ',&
      I6, ' Test results: ', L6 )
```

What output will be generated by each of the following programs? Describe the output from each of these programs, including both the horizontal and vertical position of each output item.

```
14.   INTEGER :: index1 = 1, index2 = 2
      REAL :: x1 = 1.2, y1 = 2.4, x2 = 2.4, y2 = 4.8
      WRITE (*,120) index1, x1, y1, index2, x2, y2
      120 FORMAT ('1',T11,'Output Data',/, &
                  1X, T11,'===========',//,&
                  (1X,'POINT(',I2,') = ',2F14.6))
```

5

5.4

FORMATTED READ STATEMENTS

An *input device* is a piece of equipment that can enter data into a computer. The most common input device on a modern computer is a keyboard. As data is entered into the input device, it is stored in an **input buffer** in the computer's memory. Once an entire line has been typed into the input buffer, the user hits the ENTER key on the keyboard, and the input buffer is made available for processing by the computer.

A READ statement reads one or more data values from the input buffer associated with an input device. The particular input device to read from is specified by the i/o unit number in the READ statement, as we will explain later in the chapter. It is possible to use a **formatted** READ **statement** to specify the exact manner in which the contents of an input buffer are to be interpreted.

In general, a format specifies which columns of the input buffer are to be associated with a particular variable and how those columns are to be interpreted. A typical formatted READ statement is shown below:

```
READ (*,100) increment
100 FORMAT (6X,I6)
```

This statement specifies that the first six columns of the input buffer are to be skipped, and then the contents of columns 7 through 12 are to be interpreted as an integer, with the resulting value stored in variable increment. As with WRITEs, formats may be stored in FORMAT statements, character constants, or character variables.

Formats associated with READs use many of the same format descriptors as formats associated with WRITEs. However, the interpretation of those descriptors is somewhat different. The meanings of the format descriptors commonly found with READs are described below.

5.4.1 Integer Input—The I Descriptor

The descriptor used to read integer data is the I descriptor. It has the general form

$$rIw$$

where r and w have the meanings given in Table 5-2. An integer value may be placed anywhere within its field, and it will be read and interpreted correctly.

5.4.2 Real Input—The F Descriptor

The format descriptor used to describe the input format of real data is the F descriptor. It has the form

$$rFw.d$$

where r, w, and d have the meanings given in Table 5-2. The interpretation of real data in a formatted READ statement is rather complicated. The input value in an F input field may be a real number with a decimal point, a real number in exponential notation, or a number without a decimal point. If a real number with a decimal point or a real number in exponential notation is present in the field, then the number is always interpreted correctly. For example, the consider following statement

```
READ (*,'(3F10.4)') a, b, c
```

Assume that the input data for this statement is

```
1.5          0.15E+01   15.0E-01
----|----|----|----|----|----|
   5   10   15   20   25   30
```

After the statement is executed, all three variables will contain the number 1.5.

If a number *without* a decimal point appears in the field, then a decimal point is assumed to be in the position specified by the d term of the format descriptor. For example, if the format descriptor is F10.4, then the four rightmost digits of the number are assumed to be the fractional part of the input value, and the remaining digits are assumed to be the integer part of the input value. Consider the following Fortran statements

```
READ (*,'(3F10.4)') a, b, c
```

Assume that the input data for these statements is

```
         15   150       15000
----|----|----|----|----|----|
   5   10   15   20   25   30
```

Then after these statements are executed, a will contain 0.0015, b will contain 0.0150, and c will contain 1.5000. The use of values without decimal points in a real input field is very confusing. It is a relic from an earlier version of Fortran that should never be used in your programs.

Good Programming Practice
Always include a decimal point in any real values used with a formatted READ statement.

The E and ES format descriptors are completely identical to the F descriptor for inputting data. They may be used in the place of the F descriptor, if desired.

5.4.3 Logical Input—The L Descriptor

The descriptor used to read logical data has the form

$$rLw$$

where r and w have the meanings given in Table 5-2. The value of a logical variable can only be .TRUE. or .FALSE.. The input value must be either a T or an F, appearing as the first nonblank character in the input field. If any other character is the first nonblank character in the field, a run-time error will occur. The logical input format descriptor is rarely used.

5.4.4 Character Input—The A Descriptor

Character data is read by using the A format descriptor.

$$rA \text{ or } rAw$$

where r and w have the meanings given in Table 5-2. The rA descriptor reads character data in a field whose width is the same as the length of the character variable being read, while the rAw descriptor reads character data in a field of fixed width w. If the width w of the field is larger than the length of the character variable, the data from the *rightmost* portion of the field is loaded into the character variable. If the width of the field is smaller than the length of the character variable, the characters in the field will be stored in the leftmost characters of the variable, and the remainder of the variable will be padded with blanks.

For example, the consider following statements

```
CHARACTER(len=10) :: string_1, string_2
CHARACTER(len=5)  :: string_3
CHARACTER(len=15) :: string_4, string_5
READ (*,'(A)')   string_1
READ (*,'(A10)') string_2
READ (*,'(A10)') string_3
READ (*,'(A10)') string_4
READ (*,'(A)')   string_5
```

Assume that the input data for these statements is

```
ABCDEFGHIJKLMNO
ABCDEFGHIJKLMNO
ABCDEFGHIJKLMNO
ABCDEFGHIJKLMNO
ABCDEFGHIJKLMNO
----|----|----|
    5   10   15
```

After the statements are executed, variable string_1 will contain 'ABCDEFGHIJ', since string_1 is 10 characters long, and the A descriptor will read as many characters as the length of variable. Variable string_2 will contain 'ABCDEFGHIJ', since string_2 is 10 characters long, and the A10 descriptor will read 10 characters. Variable string_3 is only 5 characters long, and the A10 descriptor is 10 characters long, so string_3 will contain the 5 rightmost of the 10 characters in the field: 'FGHIJ'. Variable string_4 will contain 'ABCDEFGHIJb̸b̸b̸b̸b̸', since string_4 is 15 characters long, and the A10 descriptor will read only 10 characters. Finally string_5 will contain 'ABCDEFGHIJKLMNO', since string_5 is 15 characters long, and the A descriptor will read as many characters as the length of variable.

5.4.5 Horizontal Positioning—The X and T Descriptors

The X and T format descriptors may be used for reading formatted input data. The chief use of the X descriptor is to skip over fields in the input data that we do not wish to read. The T descriptor may be used for the same purpose, but it may also be used to read the same data twice in two different formats. For example, the following code reads the values in characters 1 through 6 of the input buffer twice—once as an integer, and once as a character string.

```
CHARACTER(len=6) :: string
INTEGER :: input
READ (*,'(I6,T1,A6)') input, string
```

5.4.6 Vertical Positioning—The Slash (/) Descriptor

The slash (/) format descriptor causes a formatted READ statement to discard the current input buffer, get another one from the input device, and start processing from the beginning of the new input buffer. For example, the following formatted READ statement reads the values of variables a and b from the first input line, skips down two lines, and reads the values of variables c and d from the third input line.

```
REAL :: a, b, c, d
READ (*,300) a, b, c, d
300 FORMAT (2F10.2,//,2F10.2)
```

If the input data for these statements is

```
      1.0        2.0        3.0
      4.0        5.0        6.0
      7.0        8.0        9.0
---- |---- |---- |---- |---- |---- |
  5    10    15    20    25    30
```

then the contents of variables a, b, c, and d will be 1.0, 2.0, 7.0, and 8.0, respectively.

5.4.7 How Formats Are Used During READs

Most Fortran compilers verify the syntax of FORMAT statements and character constants containing formats at compilation time, but do not otherwise process them. Character variables containing formats are not even checked at compilation time for valid syntax, since the format may be modified dynamically during program execution. In all cases, formats are saved unchanged as character strings within the compiled program. When the program is executed, the characters in a format are used as a template to guide the operation of the formatted READ.

At execution time, the list of input variables associated with the READ statement is processed, together with the format of the statement. The rules for scanning a format are essentially the same for READs as they are for WRITEs. The order of scanning, the repetition counts, and the use of parentheses are identical.

When the number of variables to be read and the number of descriptors in the format differ, formatted READs behave as follows:

1. If the READ statement runs out of variables before the end of the format, the use of the format stops after the last variable has been read. The next READ statement will start with a new input buffer, and all of the other data in the original input buffer will be lost. For example, consider the following statements

```
READ (*,30) i, j
READ (*,30) k, l, m
30 FORMAT (5I5)
```

and the following input data

```
    1     2     3     4     5
    6     7     8     9    10
---- |---- |---- |---- |---- |
  5    10    15    20    25
```

After the first statement is executed, the values of i and j will be 1 and 2 respectively. The first READ ends at that point, so that input buffer is thrown away without the remainder of the buffer ever being used. The next READ uses the second input buffer, so the values of k, l, and m will be 6, 7, and 8.

2. If the scan reaches the end of the format before the READ statement runs out of variables, the program discards the current input buffer. It gets a new input buffer, and resumes in the format *at the rightmost open parenthesis that is not preceded by a repetition count*. For example, consider the statements

```
READ (*,40) i, j, k, l, m
40 FORMAT (I5,(T6,2I5))
```

and the input data

```
     1    2    3    4    5
     6    7    8    9   10
----|----|----|----|----|
     5   10   15   20   25
```

When the READ statement is executed, variables i, j, and k will be read from the first input buffer. They will contain 1, 2, and 3 respectively. The FORMAT statement ends at that point, so the first input buffer is discarded, and the next one is used. The FORMAT statement starts over at the rightmost open parenthesis not preceded by a repetition count, so variables l and m will contain 7 and 8 respectively.

Quiz 5-2

This quiz provides a quick check to see if you have understood the concepts introduced in Section 5.4. If you have trouble with the quiz, reread the section, ask your instructor, or discuss the material with a fellow student. The answers to this quiz are found in the back of the book. Unless otherwise stated, assume that variables beginning with the letters I to N are integers, and all other variables are reals.

Write Fortran statements that perform the functions described below.

1. Read the values of a real variable amplitude from columns 10 to 20, an integer variable count from columns 30 to 35, and a character variable identity from columns 60 to 72 of the current input buffer.

2. Read a 25-character variable called title from columns 10 to 34 of the first input line, and then read 5 integer variables i1 through i5 from columns 5 to 12 on each of the next 5 lines.

3. Read columns 11 to 20 from the current input line into a character variable string, skip two lines, and read columns 11 to 20 into an integer variable number. Do this with a single formatted READ statement.

What will be stored in each of the following variables?

4. READ (*,'(3F10.4)') a, b, c

    With the input data:

```
 1.65E-10    17.      -11.7
----|----|----|----|----|----|----|
     5   10   15   20   25   30   35
```

(continued)

5.
```
   READ (*,20) a, b, c
20 FORMAT (E10.2,F10.2,/,20X,F10.2)
```

With the input data:

```
-3.1415932.7182818210.1E10
      -11.        -5.      37.5532
----|----|----|----|----|----|----|----|
    5   10   15   20   25   30   35
```

6.
```
READ (*,'(3I5)') i, j, k
```

With the input data:

```
-35   67053687
----|----|----|----|----|----|----|----|
    5   10   15   20   25   30   35
```

7.
```
CHARACTER(len=5)  :: string_1
CHARACTER(len=10) :: string_2, string_4
CHARACTER(len=15) :: string_3
READ (*,'(4A10)') string_1, string_2, string_3, string_4
```

With the input data:

```
ABCDEFGHIJLKMNOPQRSTUVWXYZ0123 _TEST_ 1
----|----|----|----|----|----|----|----|
    5   10   15   20   25   30   35   40
```

Examine the following Fortran statements. Are they correct or incorrect? If they are incorrect, why are they incorrect? If they are correct, what do they do?

8.
```
   READ (*,100) nvals, time1, time2
100 FORMAT (10X,I10,F10.2,F10.4)
```

9.
```
   READ (*,220) junk, scratch
220 FORMAT ( T60,I15,/,E15.3
```

10.
```
   READ (*,220) icount, range, azimuth, elevation
220 FORMAT ( I6, 4X, F20.2)
```

5.5

AN INTRODUCTION TO FILES AND FILE PROCESSING

The programs that we have written up to now have involved relatively small amounts of input and output data. We have typed in the input data from the keyboard each time that a program has been run, and the output data has gone directly to a terminal or printer. This is acceptable for small data sets, but it rapidly becomes prohibitive when working with large volumes of data. Imagine having to type in 100,000 input values each time a program is run! Such a process would be both time-consuming and prone to typing errors. We need a convenient way to read in and write out large data sets, and to be able to use them repeatedly without retyping.

Fortunately, computers have a standard structure for holding data that we will be able to use in our programs. This structure is called a **file.** A file consists of many lines of data that are related to each other, and that can be accessed as a unit. Each line of information in a file is called a **record.** Fortran can read information from a file or write information to a file one record at a time.

The files on a computer can be stored on various types of devices, which are collectively known as *secondary memory*. (The computer's RAM is its primary memory.) Secondary memory is slower than the computer's main memory, but it still allows relatively quick access to the data. Common secondary storage devices include hard disk drives, floppy disks, USB memory sticks, CDs or DVDs, and magnetic tapes.

In the early days of computers, magnetic tapes were the most common type of secondary storage device. Computer magnetic tapes store data in a manner similar to the audiocassette tapes that were used to play music. Like them, computer magnetic tapes must be read (or "played") in order from the beginning of the tape to the end of it. When we read data in consecutive order, one record after another, in this manner, we are using **sequential access.** Other devices such as hard disks have the ability to jump from one record to another anywhere within a file. When we jump freely from one record to another following no specific order, we are using **direct access.** For historical reasons, sequential access is the default access technique in Fortran, even if we are working with devices capable of direct access.

To use files within a Fortran program, we will need some way to select the desired file and to read from or write to it. Fortunately, Fortran has a wonderfully flexible method to read from and write to files, whether they are on disk, magnetic tape, or some other device attached to the computer. This mechanism is known as the **input/ output unit** (i/o unit, sometimes called a logical unit, or simply a unit). The i/o unit corresponds to the first asterisk in the READ(*,*) and WRITE(*,*) statements. If that asterisk is replaced by an i/o unit number, then the *corresponding read or write will be to the device assigned to that unit* instead of to the standard input or output device. The statements to read or write any file or device attached to the computer are exactly the same except for the i/o unit number in the first position, so we already know most of what we need to know to use file i/o. An i/o unit number must be of type INTEGER.

Several Fortran statements may be used to control disk file input and output. The ones discussed in this chapter are summarized in Table 5-3.

I/o unit numbers are assigned to disk files or devices by using the OPEN statement, and detached from them by using the CLOSE statement. Once a file is attached to an i/o unit by using the OPEN statement, we can read and write in exactly the same manner that we have already learned. When we are through with the file, the CLOSE statement closes the file and releases the i/o unit to be assigned to some other file. The REWIND and BACKSPACE statements may be used to change the current reading or writing position in a file while it is open.

Certain unit numbers are predefined to be connected to certain input or output devices, so that we don't need an OPEN statement to use these devices. These

TABLE 5-3
Fortran control characters

I/O statement	Function
OPEN	Associate a specific disk file with a specific i/o unit number.
CLOSE	End the association of a specific disk file with a specific i/o unit number.
READ	Read data from a specified i/o unit number.
WRITE	Write data to a specified i/o unit number.
REWIND	Move to the beginning of a file.
BACKSPACE	Move back one record in a file.

predefined units vary from processor to processor.[5] Typically, i/o unit 5 is predefined to be the *standard input device* for your program (that is, the keyboard if you are running at a terminal, or the input batch file if you are running in batch mode). Similarly, i/o unit 6 is usually predefined to be the *standard output device* for your program (the screen if you are running at a terminal, or the line printer if you are running in batch mode). These assignments date back to the early days of Fortran on IBM computers, so they have been copied by most other vendors in their Fortran compilers. Another common association is i/o unit 0 for the *standard error device* for your program. This assignment goes back to the C language and Unix-based computers.

However, you cannot count on any of these associations always being true for every processor. If you need to read from and write to the standard devices, always use the asterisk instead of the standard unit number for that device. The asterisk is guaranteed to work correctly on any computer system.

Good Programming Practice
Always use asterisks instead of i/o unit numbers when referring to the standard input or standard output devices. The standard i/o unit numbers vary from processor to processor, but the asterisk works correctly on all processors.

F-2003 ONLY

Fortran 2003 has added a special mechanism to allow a user to determine the i/o units associated with the standard input device, the standard output device, and the standard error device. We will learn how to do this in Chapter 14.

If we want to access any files or devices other than the predefined standard devices, we must first use an OPEN statement to associate the file or device with a specific i/o unit number. Once the association has been established, we can use ordinary Fortran READs and WRITEs with that unit to work with the data in the file.[6]

---

[5] A processor is defined as the combination of a specific computer with a specific compiler.

[6] Some Fortran compilers attach default files to logical units that have not been opened. For example, in Compaq Fortran, a write to an unopened i/o unit 26 will automatically go into a file called fort.26. You should never use this feature, since it is nonstandard and varies from processor to processor. Your programs will be much more portable if you always use an OPEN statement before writing to a file.

5.5.1 The OPEN Statement

The OPEN statement associates a file with a given i/o unit number. Its form is

OPEN (open_list)

where *open_list* contains a series of clauses specifying the i/o unit number, the file name, and information about how to access the file. The clauses in the list are separated by commas. A discussion of the full list of possible clauses in the OPEN statement will be postponed until Chapter 14. For now, we will introduce only the six most important items from the list. They are as follows:

1. A UNIT= clause indicating the i/o unit number to associate with this file. This clause has the form

UNIT=int_expr

   where *int_expr* can be a nonnegative integer value.

2. A FILE= clause specifying the name of the file to be opened. This clause has the form

FILE=char_expr

   where *char_expr* is a character value containing the name of the file to be opened.

3. A STATUS= clause specifying the status of the file to be opened. This clause has the form

STATUS=char_expr

   where *char_expr* is one of the following: 'OLD'cc, 'NEW', 'REPLACE', 'SCRATCH', or 'UNKNOWN'.

4. An ACTION= clause specifying whether a file is to be opened for reading only, for writing only, or for both reading and writing. This clause has the form,

ACTION=char_expr

   where *char_expr* is one of the following: 'READ', 'WRITE', or 'READWRITE'. If no action is specified, the file is opened for both reading and writing.

5. An IOSTAT= clause specifying the name of an integer variable in which the status of the open operation can be returned. This clause has the form,

IOSTAT=int_var

   where *int_var* is an integer variable. If the OPEN statement is successful, a 0 will be returned in the integer variable. If it is not successful, a positive number corresponding to a system error message will be returned in the variable. The system error messages vary from processor to processor, but a zero always means success.

F-2003 ONLY

6. An IOMSG= clause specifying the name of a character variable that will contain a message if an error occurs. This clause has the form,

IOMSG=chart_var

where *char_var* is a character variable. If the OPEN statement is successful, the contents of the character variable will be unchanged. If it is not successful, a descriptive error message will be returned in this string. (Fortran 2003 only.)

The above clauses may appear in any order in the OPEN statement. Some examples of correct OPEN statements are shown below.

Case 1: Opening a File for Input

The statement below opens a file named EXAMPLE.DAT and attaches it to i/o unit 8.

```
INTEGER :: ierror
OPEN (UNIT=8, FILE='EXAMPLE.DAT', STATUS='OLD', ACTION='READ', &
      IOSTAT=ierror)
```

The STATUS='OLD' clause specifies that the file already exists; if it does not exist, then the OPEN statement will return an error code in variable ierror. This is the proper form of the OPEN statement for an *input file*. If we are opening a file to read input data from, then the file had better be present with data in it! If it is not there, something is obviously wrong. By checking the returned value in ierror, we can tell that there is a problem and take appropriate action.

The ACTION='READ' clause specifies that the file should be read-only. If an attempt is made to write to the file, and error will occur. This behavior is appropriate for an input file.

Case 2: Opening a File for Output

The statements below open a file named OUTDAT and attach it to i/o unit 25.

```
INTEGER :: unit, ierror
CHARACTER(len=6) :: filename
unit = 25
filename = 'OUTDAT'
OPEN (UNIT=unit, FILE=filename, STATUS='NEW', ACTION='WRITE', &
      IOSTAT=ierror)
```

or

```
OPEN (UNIT=unit, FILE=filename, STATUS='REPLACE', ACTION='WRITE', &
IOSTAT=ierror)
```

The STATUS='NEW' clause specifies that the file is a new file; if it already exists, then the OPEN statement will return an error code in variable ierror. This is the proper form of the OPEN statement for an *output file* if we want to make sure that we don't overwrite the data in a file that already exists.

The STATUS='REPLACE' clause specifies that a new file should be opened for output whether a file by the same name exists or not. If the file already exists, the program will delete it, create a new file, and open it for output. The old contents of the file will be lost. If it does not exist, the program will create a new file by that name and open it. This is the proper form of the OPEN statement for an output file if we want to open the file whether or not a previous file exists with the same name.

5

The `ACTION='WRITE'` clause specifies that the file should be write-only. If an attempt is made to read from the file, and error will occur. This behavior is appropriate for an output file.

Case 3: Opening a Scratch File

The statement below opens a *scratch file* and attaches it to i/o unit 12.

```
OPEN (UNIT=12, STATUS='SCRATCH', IOSTAT=ierror)
```

A scratch file is a temporary file that is created by the program, and that will be deleted automatically when the file is closed or when the program terminates. This type of file may be used for saving intermediate results while a program is running, but it may not be used to save anything that we want to keep after the program finishes. Notice that no file name is specified in the `OPEN` statement. In fact, it is an error to specify a file name with a scratch file. Since no `ACTION=` clause is included, the file has been opened for both reading and writing.

Good Programming Practice

Always be careful to specify the proper status in `OPEN` statements, depending on whether you are reading from or writing to a file. This practice will help prevent errors such as accidentally overwriting data files that you want to keep.

5.5.2 The `CLOSE` Statement

The `CLOSE` statement closes a file and releases the i/o unit number associated with it. Its form is

```
CLOSE (close_list)
```

where `close_list` must contain a clause specifying the i/o number, and may specify other options, which will be discussed with the advanced I/O material in Chapter 14. If no `CLOSE` statement is included in the program for a given file, that file will be closed automatically when the program terminates.

After a nonscratch file is closed, it may be reopened at any time using a new `OPEN` statement. When it is reopened, it may be associated with the same i/o unit or with a different i/o unit. After the file is closed, the i/o unit that was associated with it is free to be reassigned to any other file in a new `OPEN` statement.

5.5.3 `READ`s and `WRITE`s to Disk Files

Once a file has been connected to an i/o unit via the `OPEN` statement, it is possible to read from or write to the file using the same `READ` and `WRITE` statements that we have been using. For example, the statements

```
OPEN (UNIT=8, FILE='INPUT.DAT',STATUS='OLD',IOSTAT=ierror)
READ (8,*) x, y, z
```

will read the values of variables x, y, and z in free format from the file INPUT.DAT, and the statements

```
OPEN (UNIT=9, FILE='OUTPUT.DAT',STATUS='REPLACE',IOSTAT=ierror)
WRITE (9,100) x, y, z
100 FORMAT (' X = ', F10.2, ' Y = ', F10.2, ' Z = ', F10.2 )
```

will write the values of variables x, y, and z to the file OUTPUT.DAT in the specified format.

5.5.4 The IOSTAT= and IOMSG= Clauses in the READ Statement

The IOSTAT= and IOMSG= clauses are important additional features that may be added to the READ statement when you are working with disk files. The form of the IOSTAT= clause is

$$IOSTAT=int\_var$$

where *int_var* is an integer variable. If the READ statement is successful, a 0 will be returned in the integer variable. If it is not successful as a result of a file or format error, a positive number corresponding to a system error message will be returned in the variable. If it is not successful because the end of the input data file has been reached, a negative number will be returned in the variable.[7]

If an IOMSG= clause is included in a Fortran 2003 READ statement and the returned i/o status is nonzero, then the character string returned by the IOMSG= clause will explain in words what went wrong. The program should be designed to display this message to the user.

If no IOSTAT= clause is present in a READ statement, *any attempt to read a line beyond the end of a file will abort the program.* This behavior is unacceptable in a well-designed program. We often want to read all of the data from a file until the end is reached, and then perform some sort of processing on that data. This is where the IOSTAT= clause comes in: If an IOSTAT= clause is present, the program will not abort on an attempt to read a line beyond the end of a file. Instead, the READ will complete with the IOSTAT variable set to a negative number. We can then test the value of the variable, and process the data accordingly.

Good Programming Practice
Always include the IOSTAT= clause when reading from a disk file. This clause provides a graceful way to detect end-of-data conditions on the input files.

---

[7] There is an alternative method of detecting file read errors and end-of-file conditions using ERR= and END= clauses. These clauses of the READ statement will be described in Chapter 14. The IOSTAT= clause lends itself better to structured programming than the other clauses do, so they are being postponed to the later chapter.

EXAMPLE
5-3

Reading Data from a File:

It is very common to read a large data set into a program from a file, and then to process the data in some fashion. Often, the program will have no way of knowing in advance just how much data is present in the file. In that case, the program needs to read the data in a WHILE loop until the end of the data set is reached, and then must detect that there is no more data to read. Once it has read in all of the data, the program can process it in whatever manner is required.

Let's illustrate this process by writing a program that can read in an unknown number of real values from a disk file, and detect the end of the data in the disk file.

SOLUTION

This program must open the input disk file, and then read the values from it, using the IOSTAT= clause to detect problems. If the IOSTAT variable contains a negative number after a READ, then the end of the file has been reached. If the IOSTAT variable contains 0 after a READ, then everything was OK. If the IOSTAT variable contains a positive number after a READ, then a READ error occurred. In this example, the program should stop if a READ error occurs.

1. **State the problem.**

   The problem may be succinctly stated as follows:

   Write a program that can read an unknown number of real values from a user-specified input data file, detecting the end of the data file as it occurs.

2. **Define the inputs and outputs.**

   The inputs to this program consist of:

   (*a*) The name of the file to be opened.

   (*b*) The data contained in that file.

   The outputs from the program will be the input values in the data file. At the end of the file, an informative message will be written out, telling how many valid input values were found.

3. **Describe the algorithm.**

   The pseudocode for this program is

```
Initialize nvals to 0
Prompt user for file name
Get the name of the input file
OPEN the input file
Check for errors on OPEN

If no OPEN error THEN
   ! Read input data
   WHILE
      READ value
      IF status /= 0 EXIT
      nvals ← nvals + 1
      WRITE valid data to screen
   END of WHILE
```

```
      ! Check to see if the WHILE terminated due to end of file
      ! or READ error
      IF status > 0
         WRITE 'READ error occurred on line', nvals
      ELSE
         WRITE number of valid input values nvals
      END of IF ( status > 0 )
   END of IF ( no OPEN error )
   END PROGRAM
```

A flowchart for the program is shown in Figure 5-9.

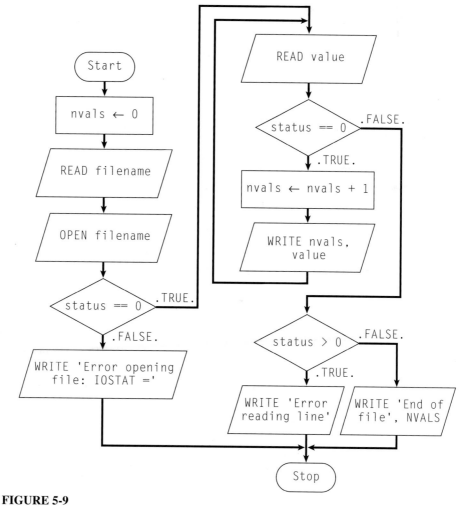

FIGURE 5-9
Flowchart for a program to read an unknown number of values
from an input data file.

4. **Turn the algorithm into Fortran statements.**

The final Fortran program is shown in Figure 5-10.

FIGURE 5-10

Program to read an unknown number of values from a user-specified input disk file.

```fortran
PROGRAM read_file
!
!   Purpose:
!     To illustrate how to read an unknown number of values from
!     an input data file, detecting both any formatting errors and
!     the end of file.
!
!   Record of revisions:
!       Date        Programmer          Description of change
!       ====        ==========          =====================
!     11/18/06    S. J. Chapman         Original code
!
IMPLICIT NONE

! Data dictionary: declare variable types, definitions, & units
CHARACTER(len=20) :: filename     ! Name of file to open
INTEGER :: nvals = 0              ! Number of values read in
INTEGER :: status                ! I/O status
REAL :: value                    ! The real value read in


! Get the file name, and echo it back to the user.
WRITE (*,*) 'Please enter input file name: '
READ  (*,*) filename
WRITE (*,1000) filename
1000 FORMAT (' ','The input file name is: ', A)

! Open the file, and check for errors on open.
OPEN (UNIT=3, FILE=filename, STATUS='OLD', ACTION='READ', &
      IOSTAT=status )
openif: IF ( status == 0 ) THEN

   ! OPEN was ok.  Read values.
   readloop: DO
      READ (3,*,IOSTAT=status) value     ! Get next value
      IF ( status /= 0 ) EXIT            ! EXIT if not valid.
      nvals = nvals + 1                  ! Valid: increase count
      WRITE (*,1010) nvals, value        ! Echo to screen
      1010 FORMAT (' ','Line ', I6, ': Value = ',F10.4 )
   END DO readloop

   ! The WHILE loop has terminated.  Was it because of a READ
   ! error or because of the end of the input file?
   readif: IF ( status > 0 ) THEN ! a READ error occurred.  Tell user.

      WRITE (*,1020) nvals + 1
      1020 FORMAT ('0','An error occurred reading line ', I6)
```

(continued)

(*concluded*)

```
  ELSE ! the end of the data was reached.  Tell user.

     WRITE (*,1030) nvals
     1030 FORMAT ('0','End of file reached.  There were ', I6, &
                       ' values in the file.')
  END IF readif

ELSE openif
   WRITE (*,1040) status
   1040 FORMAT (' ','Error opening file: IOSTAT = ', I6 )
END IF openif

! Close file
CLOSE ( UNIT=3 )

END PROGRAM read_file
```

Note that the input file is opened with STATUS='OLD', since we are reading from the file, and the input data must already exist before the program is executed.

5. **Test the program.**

To test this program, we will create two input files, one with valid data, and one with an input data error. We will run the program with both input files, and verify that it works correctly both for valid data and for data containing input errors. Also, we will run the program with an invalid file name to show that it can properly handle missing input files.

The valid input file is called READ1.DAT. It contains the following lines:

```
-17.0
30.001
1.0
12000.
-0.012
```

The invalid input file is called READ2.DAT. It contains the following lines:

```
-17.0
30.001
ABCDEF
12000.
-0.012
```

Running these files through the program yields the following results:

```
C:\book\chap5>read_file
Please enter input file name:
'read1.dat'
The input file name is: read1.dat
Line     1: Value =   -17.0000
Line     2: Value =    30.0010
Line     3: Value =     1.0000
```

```
Line      4: Value = 12000.0000
Line      5: Value =       -.0120

End of file reached. There were       5 values in the file.

C:\book\chap5>
read_file
Please enter input file name:
'read2.dat'
The input file name is: read2.dat
Line      1: Value =      -17.0000
Line      2: Value =       30.0010

An error occurred reading line        3
```

Finally, let's test the program with an invalid input file name.

```
C:\book\chap5>read
Please enter input file name:
'JUNK.DAT'
The input file name is: JUNK.DAT
Error opening file: IOSTAT = 29
```

The number of the IOSTAT error reported by this program will vary from processor to processor, but it will always be positive. You must consult a listing of the run-time error codes for your particular compiler to find the exact meaning of the error code that your computer reports. For the Fortran compiler used here, IOSTAT = 29 means "File not found."

This program correctly read all of the values in the input file, and detected the end of the data set when it occurred.

F-2003 ONLY

If the compiler used to compile this program supports Fortran 2003, then the program could be modified to use the IOMSG= clause as follows:

```
...
CHARACTER(len=80) :: msg                ! Status message
...
! Open the file, and check for errors on open.
OPEN (UNIT=3, FILE=filename, STATUS='OLD', ACTION='READ', &
        IOSTAT=status,IOMSG=msg )
openif: IF ( status == 0 ) THEN

...

ELSE openif
    WRITE (*,*) TRIM(msg)
END IF openif
```

In this case, an open error will produce an understandable error message instead of an error number.

5.5.5 File Positioning

As we stated previously, ordinary Fortran files are sequential—they are read in order from the first record in the file to the last record in the file. However, we sometimes need to read a piece of data more than once, or to process a whole file more than once during a program. How can we skip around within a sequential file?

Fortran provides two statements to help us move around within a sequential file. They are the BACKSPACE statement, which moves back one record each time it is called, and the REWIND statement, which restarts the file at its beginning. The forms of these statements are

BACKSPACE (UNIT=unit)

and

REWIND (UNIT=unit)

where unit is the i/o unit number associated with the file that we want to work with.[8]

Both statements can also include IOSTAT= clauses to detect errors during the backspace or rewind operation without causing the program to abort.

**EXAMPLE
5-4**

Using File Positioning Commands:

We will now illustrate the use of scratch files and file positioning commands in a simple example problem. Write a program that accepts a series of nonnegative real values and stores them in a scratch file. After the data is input, the program should ask the user what data record he or she is interested in, and then recover and display that value from the disk file.

SOLUTION
Since the program is expected to read only positive or zero values, we can use a negative value as a flag to terminate the input to the program. A Fortran program that does this is shown in Figure 5-11. This program opens a scratch file, and then reads input values from the user. If a value is nonnegative, is it written to the scratch file. When a negative value is encountered, the program asks the user for the record to display. It checks to see if a valid record number was entered. If the record number is valid, it rewinds the file and reads forward to that record number. Finally, it displays the contents of that record to the user.

FIGURE 5-11
Sample program illustrating the use of file positioning commands.

```
PROGRAM scratch_file
!
!  Purpose:
!    To illustrate the use of a scratch file and positioning
```

(continued)

---

[8] Alternative forms of these statements are described in Chapter 14.

(continued)

```
!    commands as follows:
!    1.   Read in an arbitrary number of positive or zero
!         values, saving them in a scratch file.  Stop
!         reading when a negative value is encountered.
!    2.   Ask the user for a record number to display.
!    3.   Rewind the file, get that value, and display it.
!
!  Record of revisions:
!      Date        Programmer          Description of change
!      ====        ==========          =====================
!    11/19/06     S. J. Chapman        Original code
!
IMPLICIT NONE

! Data dictionary: declare constants
INTEGER, PARAMETER :: LU = 8  ! i/o unit for scratch file

! Data dictionary: declare variable types, definitions, & units
REAL :: data              ! Data value stored in a disk file
INTEGER :: icount = 0     ! The number of input data records
INTEGER :: irec           ! Record number to recover and display
INTEGER :: j              ! Loop index

! Open the scratch file
OPEN (UNIT=LU, STATUS='SCRATCH' )

! Prompt user and get input data.
WRITE (*, 100)
100 FORMAT (1X,'Enter positive or zero input values. ',/, &
            1X,'A negative value terminates input.' )

! Get the input values, and write them to the scratch file
DO
    WRITE (*, 110) icount + 1      ! Prompt for next value
    110 FORMAT (1X,'Enter sample ',I4,':' )
    READ (*,*) data                ! Read value
    IF ( data < 0. ) EXIT          ! Exit on negative numbers
    icount = icount + 1            ! Valid value: bump count
    WRITE (LU,120) data            ! Write data to scratch file
    120 FORMAT (1X, ES16.6)
END DO

! Now we have all of the records.  Ask which record to see.
! icount records are in the file.
WRITE (*,130) icount
130 FORMAT (1X,'Which record do you want to see (1 to ',I4, ')? ')
READ (*,*) irec

! Do we have a legal record number?  If so, get the record.
! If not, tell the user and stop.
IF ( (irec >= 1) .AND. (irec <= icount) ) THEN
```

(continued)

(concluded)

```
    ! This is a legal record.  Rewind the scratch file.
    REWIND (UNIT=LU)

    ! Read forward to the desired record.
    DO j = 1, irec
        READ (LU,*) data
    END DO

    ! Tell user.
    WRITE (*,140) irec, data
    140 FORMAT (1X,'The value of record ', I4, ' is ', ES14.5 )

ELSE

    ! We have an illegal record number.  Tell user.
    WRITE (*,150) irec
    150 FORMAT (1X,'Illegal record number entered: ', I8)

END IF

! Close file
CLOSE(LU)

END PROGRAM scratch_file
```

5

Let us test the program with valid data:

```
C:\book\chap5>scratch_file

Enter positive or zero input values.
A negative input value terminates input.

Enter sample      1:
234.
Enter sample      2:
12.34
Enter sample      3:
0.
Enter sample      4:
16.
Enter sample      5:
11.235
Enter sample      6:
2.
Enter sample      7:
-1
Which record do you want to see (1 to 6)?
5
The value of record 5 is 1.12350E+01
```

Next, we should test the program with an invalid record number to see that the error condition is handled properly.

```
C:\book\chap5>scratch_file

Enter positive or zero input values.
A negative input value terminates input.
Enter sample     1:
234.
Enter sample     2:
12.34
Enter sample     3:
0.
Enter sample     4:
16.
Enter sample     5:
11.235
Enter sample     6:
2.
Enter sample     7:
-1
Which record do you want to see (1 to 6):
7
Illegal record number entered: 7
```

The program appears to be functioning correctly.

**EXAMPLE
5-5**

Fitting a Line to a Set of Noisy Measurements:

The velocity of a falling object in the presence of a constant gravitational field is given by the equation

$$v(t) = at + v_o \tag{5-4}$$

where $v(t)$ is the velocity at any time t, a is the acceleration due to gravity, and v_o is the velocity at time 0. This equation is derived from elementary physics—it is known to every freshman physics student. If we plot velocity versus time for the falling object, our (v, t) measurement points should fall along a straight line. However, the same freshman physics student also knows that if we go out into the laboratory and attempt to *measure* the velocity versus time of an object, our measurements will *not* fall along a straight line. They may come close, but they will never line up perfectly. Why not? Because we can never make perfect measurements. There is always some *noise* included in the measurements, which distorts them.

There are many cases in science and engineering where there are noisy sets of data such as this, and we wish to estimate the straight line that "best fits" the data. This problem is called the *linear regression* problem. Given a noisy set of measurements

(x, y) that appear to fall along a straight line, how can we find the equation of the line

$$y = mx + b \qquad (5\text{-}5)$$

that best fits the measurements? If we can determine the regression coefficients m and b, then we can use this equation to predict the value of y at any given x by evaluating Equation 5-5 for that value of x.

A standard method for finding the regression coefficients m and b is the *method of least squares*. This method is named least squares because it produces the line $y = mx + b$ for which the sum of the squares of the differences between the observed y values and the predicted y values is as small as possible. The slope of the least squares line is given by

$$m = \frac{(\Sigma xy) - (\Sigma x)\bar{y}}{(\Sigma x^2) - (\Sigma x)\bar{x}} \qquad (5\text{-}6)$$

and the intercept of the least squares line is given by

$$b = \bar{y} - m\bar{x} \qquad (5\text{-}7)$$

where

Σx is the sum of the x values
Σx^2 is the sum of the squares of the x values
Σxy is the sum of the products of the corresponding x and y values
$\bar{x}$ is the mean (average) of the x values
$\bar{y}$ is the mean (average) of the y values

Write a program that will calculate the least-squares slope m and y-axis intercept b for a given set of noisy measured data points (x, y) that are found in an input data file.

SOLUTION

1. **State the problem.**
   Calculate the slope m and intercept b of a least-squares line that best fits an input data set consisting of an arbitrary number of (x, y) pairs. The input (x, y) data resides in a user-specified input file.

2. **Define the inputs and outputs.**
   The inputs required by this program are pairs of points (x, y), where x and y are real quantities. Each pair of points will be located on a separate line in the input disk file. The number of points in the disk file is not known in advance.
   The outputs from this program are the slope and intercept of the least-squares fitted line, plus the number of points going into the fit.

3. **Describe the algorithm.**
   This program can be broken down into four major steps

```
Get the name of the input file and open it
Accumulate the input statistics
Calculate the slope and intercept
Write out the slope and intercept
```

The first major step of the program is to get the name of the input file and to open the file. To do this, we will have to prompt the user to enter the name of the input file. After the file is opened, we must check to see that the open was successful. Next, we must read the file and keep track of the number of values entered, plus the sums Σx, Σy, Σx^2, and Σxy. The pseudocode for these steps is:

```
Initialize n, sum_x, sum_x2, sum_y, and sum_xy to 0
Prompt user for input file name
Open file "filename"
Check for error on OPEN

WHILE
   READ x, y from file "filename"
   IF ( end of file ) EXIT
   n ← n + 1
   sum_x ← sum_x + x
   sum_y ← sum_y + y
   sum_x2 ← sum_x2 + x**2
   sum_xy ← sum_xy + x*y
End of WHILE
```

Next, we must calculate the slope and intercept of the least-squares line. The pseudocode for this step is just the Fortran versions of Equations 5-5 and 5-6.

```
x_bar ← sum_x / real(n)
y_bar ← sum_y / real(n)
slope ← (sum_xy - sum_x * y_bar) / ( sum_x2 - sum_x * x_bar)
y_int ← y_bar - slope * x_bar
```

Finally, we must write out the results.

```
Write out slope "slope" and intercept "y_int".
```

4. **Turn the algorithm into Fortran statements.**
   The final Fortran program is shown in Figure 5-12.

FIGURE 5-12
The least-squares fit program of Example 5-5.

```
PROGRAM least_squares_fit
!
! Purpose:
!   To perform a least-squares fit of an input data set
```

(continued)

(continued)

```
!    to a straight line, and print out the resulting slope
!    and intercept values.  The input data for this fit
!    comes from a user-specified input data file.
!
!  Record of revisions:
!     Date       Programmer          Description of change
!     ====       ==========          =====================
!    11/19/06    S. J. Chapman       Original code
!
IMPLICIT NONE

! Data dictionary: declare constants
INTEGER, PARAMETER :: LU = 18 ! I/o unit for disk I/O

! Data dictionary: declare variable types, definitions, & units
! Note that cumulative variables are all initialized to zero.
CHARACTER(len=24) :: filename ! Input file name (<= 24 chars)
INTEGER :: ierror             ! Status flag from I/O statements
INTEGER :: n = 0              ! Number of input data pairs (x,y)
REAL :: slope                 ! Slope of the line
REAL :: sum_x = 0.            ! Sum of all input X values
REAL :: sum_x2 = 0.           ! Sum of all input X values squared
REAL :: sum_xy = 0.           ! Sum of all input X*Y values
REAL :: sum_y = 0.            ! Sum of all input Y values
REAL :: x                     ! An input X value
REAL :: x_bar                 ! Average X value
REAL :: y                     ! An input Y value
REAL :: y_bar                 ! Average Y value
REAL :: y_int                 ! Y-axis intercept of the line

! Prompt user and get the name of the input file.
WRITE (*,1000)
1000 FORMAT (1X,'This program performs a least-squares fit of an ',/, &
             1X,'input data set to a straight line. Enter the name',/ &
             1X,'of the file containing the input (x,y) pairs: ' )
READ (*,1010) filename
1010 FORMAT (A)

! Open the input file
OPEN (UNIT=LU, FILE=filename, STATUS='OLD', IOSTAT=ierror )

! Check to see of the OPEN failed.
errorcheck: IF ( ierror > 0 ) THEN

   WRITE (*,1020) filename
   1020 FORMAT (1X,'ERROR: File ',A,' does not exist!')

ELSE

   ! File opened successfully. Read the (x,y) pairs from
   ! the input file.
   DO
      READ (LU,*,IOSTAT=ierror) x, y    ! Get pair
```

(continued)

(concluded)

```
      IF ( ierror /= 0 ) EXIT
      n       = n + 1                        !
      sum_x   = sum_x + x                    ! Calculate
      sum_y   = sum_y + y                    !   statistics
      sum_x2  = sum_x2 + x**2                !
      sum_xy  = sum_xy + x * y               !
   END DO

   ! Now calculate the slope and intercept.
   x_bar = sum_x / real(n)
   y_bar = sum_y / real(n)
   slope = (sum_xy - sum_x * y_bar) / ( sum_x2 - sum_x * x_bar)
   y_int = y_bar - slope * x_bar

   ! Tell user.
   WRITE (*, 1030 ) slope, y_int, N
   1030 FORMAT ('0','Regression coefficients for the least-squares line:',&
          /,1X,'  slope (m)     = ', F12.3,&
          /,1X,'  Intercept (b) = ', F12.3,&
          /,1X,'  No of points  = ', I12 )

   ! Close input file, and quit.
   CLOSE (UNIT=LU)

END IF errorcheck

END PROGRAM least_squares_fit
```

5. **Test the program.**

 To test this program, we will try a simple data set. For example, if every point in the input data set actually falls along a line, then the resulting slope and intercept should be exactly the slope and intercept of that line. Thus the data set

```
1.1, 1.1
2.2, 2.2
3.3, 3.3
4.4, 4.4
5.5, 5.5
6.6, 6.6
7.7, 7.7
```

should produce a slope of 1.0 and an intercept of 0.0. If we place these values in a file called INPUT, and run the program, the results are:

```
C:\book\chap5>least_squares_fit

This program performs a least-squares fit of an
input data set to a straight line. Enter the name
of the file containing the input (x,y) pairs:
INPUT
Regression coefficients for the least-squares line:
```

```
slope (m)       =           1.000
Intercept (b)   =            .000
No of points    =              7
```

Now let's add some noise to the measurements. The data set becomes

```
1.1, 1.01
2.2, 2.30
3.3, 3.05
4.4, 4.28
5.5, 5.75
6.6, 6.48
7.7, 7.84
```

If these values are placed in a file called INPUT1, and the program is run on that file, the results are:

```
C:\book\chap5>least_squares_fit

This program performs a least-squares fit of an
input data set to a straight line. Enter the name
of the file containing the input (x,y) pairs:
INPUT1
Regression coefficients for the least-squares line:
   slope (m)      = 1.024
   Intercept (b) = -.120
   No of points  =    7
```

If we calculate the answer by hand, it is easy to show that the program gives the correct answers for our two test data sets. The noisy input data set and the resulting least-squares fitted line are shown in Figure 5-13.

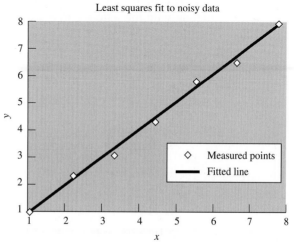

FIGURE 5-13
A noisy input data set and the resulting least-squares fitted line.

The program in this example has a problem—it cannot distinguish between the end of an input file and a read error (such as character data instead of real data) in the input file. How would you modify the program to distinguish between these two possible cases?

Quiz 5-3

This quiz provides a quick check to see if you have understood the concepts introduced in Section 5.5. If you have trouble with the quiz, reread the section, ask your instructor, or discuss the material with a fellow student. The answers to this quiz are found in the back of the book.

Write Fortran statements that perform the functions described below. Unless otherwise stated, assume that variables beginning with the letters I to N are integers, and all other variables are reals.

1. Open an existing file named IN052691 on i/o unit 25 for read-only input, and check the status to see if the OPEN was successful.

2. Open a new output file, making sure that you do not overwrite any existing file by the same name. The name of the output file is stored in character variable out_name.

3. Close the file attached to unit 24.

4. Read variables first and last from i/o unit 8 in free format, checking for end of data during the READ.

5. Backspace eight lines in the file attached to i/o unit 13.

Examine the following Fortran statements. Are they correct or incorrect? If they are incorrect, why are they incorrect? Unless otherwise stated, assume that variables beginning with the letters I to N are integers, and all other variables are reals.

6.  ```
    OPEN (UNIT=35, FILE='DATA1', STATUS='REPLACE',IOSTAT=ierror)
    READ (35,*) n, data1, data2
    ```

7.  ```
    CHARACTER(len=80) :: str
    OPEN (UNIT=11, FILE='DATA1', STATUS='SCRATCH',IOSTAT=ierror, &
    IOMSG=str)
    ```

8.  ```
    OPEN (UNIT=15,STATUS='SCRATCH',ACTION='READ', IOSTAT=ierror)
    ```

9.  ```
    OPEN (UNIT=x, FILE='JUNK', STATUS='NEW',IOSTAT=ierror)
    ```

10. ```
    OPEN (UNIT=9, FILE='TEMP.DAT', STATUS='OLD', ACTION='READ', &
            IOSTAT=ierror)
    READ (9,*) x, y
    ```
    ```

▪ 5.6

SUMMARY

In Chapter 5, we presented a basic introduction to formatted WRITE and READ statements, and to the use of disk files for input and output of data.

In a formatted WRITE statement, the second asterisk of the unformatted WRITE statement (WRITE (*,*)) is replaced by a FORMAT statement number or a character constant or variable containing the format. The format describes how the output data is to be displayed. It consists of format descriptors, which describe the vertical and horizontal position of the data on a page, as well as the display format for INTEGER, REAL, LOGICAL, and CHARACTER data types.

The format descriptors discussed in this chapter are summarized in Table 5-4.

Formatted READ statements use a format to describe how the input data is to be interpreted. All of the above format descriptors are also legal in formatted READ statements.

A disk file is opened by using the OPEN statement, read and written by using READ and WRITE statements, and closed by using the CLOSE statement. The OPEN statement associates a file with an i/o unit number, and that i/o unit number is used by the READ statements and WRITE statements in the program to access the file. When the file is closed, the association is broken.

It is possible to move around within a sequential disk file, using the BACKSPACE and REWIND statements. The BACKSPACE statement moves the current position in the file backward by one record whenever it is executed, and the REWIND statement moves the current position back to the first record in the file.

▪ **TABLE 5-4**

Fortran 95/2003 format descriptors discussed in chapter 5

FORMAT descriptors		Usage
A	Aw	Character data
E$w.d$		Real data in exponential notation
ES$w.d$		Real data in scientific notation
F$w.d$		Real data in decimal notation
Iw	I$w.m$	Integer data
Lw		Logical data
Tc		TAB: move to column c of current line
nX		Horizontal spacing: skip n spaces
/		Vertical spacing: move down 1 line

where:
c column number
d number of digits to right of decimal place
m minimum number of digits to be displayed
n number of spaces to skip
w field width in characters

5.6.1 Summary of Good Programming Practice

The following guidelines should be adhered to when programming with formatted output statements or with disk I/O. By following them consistently, your code will contain fewer bugs, will be easier to debug, and will be more understandable to others who may need to work with it in the future.

1. The first column of any output line is reserved for a control character. Never put anything in the first column except for the control character. Be especially careful to not to write a format descriptor that includes column 1, since the program could behave erratically depending upon the value of the data begin written out.
2. Always be careful to match the type of data in a WRITE statement to the type of descriptors in the corresponding format. Integers should be associated with I format descriptors, reals with E, ES, or F format descriptors, logicals with L descriptors, and characters with A descriptors. A mismatch between data types and format descriptors will result in an error at execution time.
3. Use the ES format descriptor instead of the E descriptor when displaying data in exponential format to make the output data appear to be in conventional scientific notation.
4. Use an asterisk instead of an i/o unit number when reading from the standard input device or writing to the standard output device. This makes your code more portable, since the asterisk is the same on all systems, while the actual unit numbers assigned to standard input and standard output devices may vary from system to system.
5. Always open input files with STATUS='OLD'. By definition, an input file must already exist if we are to read data from it. If the file does not exist, this is an error, and the STATUS='OLD' will catch that error. Input files should also be opened with ACTION='READ' to prevent accidental overwriting of the input data.
6. Open output files with STATUS='NEW' or STATUS='REPLACE', depending on whether or not you want to preserve the existing contents of the output file. If the file is opened with STATUS='NEW', it should be impossible to overwrite an existing file, so the program cannot accidentally destroy data. If you don't care about the existing data in the output file, open the file with STATUS='REPLACE', and the file will be overwritten if it exists. Open scratch files with STATUS='SCRATCH', so that they will be automatically deleted upon closing.
7. Always include the IOSTAT= clause when reading from disk files to detect an end-of-file or error condition.

5.6.2 Summary of Fortran Statements and Structures

The following summary describes the Fortran statements and structures introduced in this chapter.

BACKSPACE Statement:

```
BACKSPACE (UNIT=unit)
```

Example:

```
BACKSPACE (UNIT=8)
```

Description:
The BACKSPACE statement moves the current position of a file back by one record.

CLOSE Statement:

```
CLOSE (close_list)
```

Example:

```
CLOSE (UNIT=8)
```

Description:
The CLOSE statement closes the file associated with a i/o unit number.

5

FORMAT Statement:

```
label FORMAT (format descriptor, ... )
```

Example:

```
100 FORMAT (' This is a test: ', I6 )
```

Description:
The FORMAT statement describes the position and format of the data being read or written.

Formatted READ Statement:

```
READ (unit, format) input_list
```

Example:

```
READ (1,100) time, speed
100 FORMAT ( F10.4, F18.4 )
READ (1,'(I6)') index
```

Description:
The formatted READ statement reads data from an input buffer according to the format descriptors specified in the format. The format is a character string that may be specified in a FORMAT statement, a character constant, or a character variable.

Formatted WRITE Statement:

```
            WRITE (unit, format) output_list
```

Example:

```
            WRITE (*,100) i, j, slope
            100 FORMAT ( 1X, 2I10, F10.2 )
            WRITE (*,'( 1X, 2I10, F10.2 )') i, j, slope
```

Description:
The formatted WRITE statement outputs the data in the output list according to the format descriptors specified in the format. The format is a character string that may be specified in a FORMAT statement, a character constant, or a character variable.

5

OPEN Statement:

```
            OPEN (open_list)
```

Example:

F-2003 ONLY

```
            OPEN (UNIT=8, FILE='IN', STATUS='OLD' ACTION='READ', &
                  IOSTAT=ierror,IOMSG=msg)
```

Description:
The OPEN statement associates a file with an i/o unit number, so that it can be accessed by READ or WRITE statements.

REWIND Statement:

```
            REWIND (UNIT=lu)
```

Example:

```
            REWIND (UNIT=8)
```

Description:
The REWIND statement moves the current position of a file back to the beginning.

5.6.3 Exercises

5-1. What is the purpose of a format? In what three ways can formats be specified?

5-2. What is the effect of each of the following characters when it appears in the control character of the Fortran output buffer? (*a*) '1' , (*b*) ' ' , (*c*) '0' , (*d*) '+' , (*e*) '2'

5-3. What is printed out by the following Fortran statements?

(*a*)
```
INTEGER :: i
CHARACTER(len=20) :: fmt
fmt = "('1','i = ', I6.5)"
i = -123
WRITE (*, fmt) i
```

(*b*)
```
REAL :: a, b, sum, difference
a = 1.0020E6
b = 1.0001E6
sum = a + b
difference = a - b
WRITE (*,101) a, b, sum, difference
101 FORMAT (1X,'A = ',ES14.6,' B = ', E14.6, &
' Sum = ',E14.6,' Diff = ', F14.6)
```

(*c*)
```
INTEGER :: i1, i2
i1 = 10
i2 = 4**2
WRITE (*, 300) i1 > i2
300 FORMAT (' ','Result = ', L6)
```

5-4. What is printed out by the following Fortran statements?

```
REAL :: a = 1.602E-19, b = 57.2957795, c = -1.
WRITE (*,'(1X,ES14.7,2(1X,E13.7))') a, b, c
```

5-5. For the Fortran statements and input data given below, state what the values of each variable will be when the READ statement has been completed.

Statements:

```
CHARACTER(5)  :: a
CHARACTER(10) :: b
CHARACTER(15) :: c
READ (*,'(3A10)') a, b, c
```

Input Data:

```
This is a test of reading characters.
----|----|----|----|----|----|----|----|----|
    5   10   15   20   25   30   35   40   45
```

5-6. For the Fortran statements and input data given below, state what the values of each variable will be when the READ statements has completed.

(*a*) Statements:

```
INTEGER :: item1, item2, item3, item4, item5
INTEGER :: item6, item7, item8, item9, item10
```

```
READ (*,*) item1, item2, item3, item4, item5, item6
READ (*,*) item7, item8, item9, item10
```

Input Data:

-300	-250	-210	-160	-135
-105	-70	-55	-28	-11
17	55	102	165	225

```
----|----|----|----|----|----|----|----|----|----|
    5   10   15   20   25   30   35   40   45   50
```

(b) Statements:

```
INTEGER :: item1, item2, item3, item4, item5
INTEGER :: item6, item7, item8, item9, item10
READ (*,8) item1, item2, item3, item4, item5, item6
READ (*,8) item7, item8, item9, item10
8 FORMAT (4I10)
```

Input Data:Same as for (a) above.

5-7. Table of Logarithms Write a Fortran program to generate a table of the base-10 logarithms between 1 and 10 in steps of 0.1. The table should start in a new page, and it should include a title describing the table and row and column headings. This table should be organized as shown below:

	X.0	X.1	X.2	X.3	X.4	X.5	X.6	X.7	X.8	X.9
1.0	0.000	0.041	0.079	0.114	...					
2.0	0.301	0.322	0.342	0.362	...					
3.0	...									
4.0	...									
5.0	...									
6.0	...									
7.0	...									
8.0	...									
9.0	...									
10.0	...									

5-8. Example 5-3 illustrates the technique of reading an arbitrary amount of real data from an input data file. Modify that program to read in the data from an input data file and to calculate the mean and standard deviation of the samples in the file.

5-9. A real number length is to be displayed in Fw.d format with four digits to the right of the decimal point (d = 4). If the number is known to lie within the range $-10000.0 \le$

length ≤ 10000.0, what is the minimum field width *w* that will always be able to display the value of length ?

5-10. In what columns will the following characters be printed? Why?

```
WRITE (*,'(T30,A)') 'Rubbish!'
```

5-11. Write Fortran statements to perform the functions described below. Assume that variables beginning with I to N are integers, and all other variables are reals.

(*a*) Skip to a new page and print the title 'INPUT DATA' starting in column 40.

(*b*) Skip a line, and then display the data point number ipoint in columns 6 to 10, and the data point value data_1 in columns 15 to 26. Display the data value in scientific notation with seven significant digits.

5-12. What is the minimum field width necessary to display any real data value in E or ES format with six significant bits of accuracy?

5-13. Write a Fortran program that reads in a time in seconds since the start of the day (this value will be somewhere between 0. and 86400.), and writes out the time in the form HH:MM:SS, using the 24-hour-clock convention. Use the I*w.m* format descriptor to ensure that leading zeros are preserved in the MM and SS fields. Also, be sure to check the input number of seconds for validity, and write an appropriate error message if an invalid number is entered.

5-14. Gravitational Acceleration The acceleration due to the Earth's gravity at any height *h* above the surface of the Earth is given by the equation

$$g = -G\frac{M}{(R+h)^2} \tag{5-8}$$

where *G* is the gravitational constant (6.672×10^{-11} N m^2 / kg^2), *M* is the mass of the earth (5.98×10^{24} kg), *R* is the mean radius of the Earth (6371 km), and *h* is the height above the Earth's surface. If *M* is measured in kilograms and *R* and *h* in meters, then the resulting acceleration will be in units of meters per second squared. Write a program to calculate the acceleration due to the Earth's gravity in 500-km increments at heights from 0 km to 40,000 km above the surface of the Earth. Print out the results in a table of height versus acceleration with appropriate labels, including the units of the output values.

5-15. What is the proper STATUS to use in opening a file for reading input data? What is the proper STATUS to use in opening a file for writing output data? What is the proper STATUS to use in opening a temporary storage file?

5-16. What is the proper ACTION to use in opening a file for reading input data? What is the proper ACTION to use in opening a file for writing output data? What is the proper ACTION to use in opening a temporary storage file?

5-17. Is a CLOSE statement always required in a Fortran program that uses disk files? Why or why not?

5-18. Write Fortran statements to perform the functions described below. Assume that file INPUT.DAT contains a series of real values organized with one value per record.

(*a*) Open an existing file named INPUT.DAT on i/o unit 98 for input, and a new file named NEWOUT.DAT on i/o unit 99 for output.

(*b*) Read data values from file INPUT.DAT until the end-of-file is reached. Write all positive data values to the output file.

(c) Close the input and output data files.

5-19. Write a program that reads an arbitrary number of real values from a user-specified input data file, rounds the values to the nearest integer, and writes the integers out to a user-specified output file. Open the input and output files with the appropriate status, and be sure to handle end-of-file and error conditions properly.

5-20. Write a program that opens a scratch file and writes the integers 1 through 10 in the first 10 records. Next, move back six records in the file, and read the value stored in that record. Save that value in variable x. Next, move back three records in the file, and read the value stored in that record. Save that value in variable y. Multiply the two values x and y together. What is their product?

5-21. Examine the following Fortran statements. Are they correct or incorrect? If they are incorrect, why are they incorrect? (Unless otherwise indicated, assume that variables beginning with I to N are integers, and all other variables are reals.)

(*a*)
```
OPEN (UNIT=1, FILE='INFO.DAT',STATUS='NEW', IOSTAT=ierror)
READ (1,*) i, j, k
```

(*b*)
```
OPEN (UNIT=17, FILE='TEMP.DAT',STATUS='SCRATCH', IOSTAT=ierror)
```

(*c*)
```
OPEN (UNIT = 99, FILE = 'INFO.DAT',STATUS = 'NEW', &
      ACTION = 'READWRITE', IOSTAT = ierror)
WRITE (99,*) i, j, k
```

(*d*)
```
INTEGER :: unit = 8
OPEN (UNIT=unit, FILE='INFO.DAT', STATUS='OLD',IOSTAT=ierror)
READ (8,*) unit
CLOSE (UNIT = unit)
```

(*e*)
```
OPEN (UNIT=9, FILE='OUTPUT.DAT', STATUS='NEW', ACTION='WRITE', &
IOSTAT = ierror)
WRITE (9,*) mydat1, mydat2
WRITE (9,*) mydat3, mydat4
CLOSE (U\NIT = 9)
```

5-22. **Table of Sines and Cosines** Write a program to generate a table containing the sine and cosine of θ for θ between 0° and 90°, in 1° increments. The program should properly label each of the columns in the table.

5-23. **Table of Speed versus Height** The velocity of an initially stationary ball can be calculated as a function of the distance it has fallen from the equation

$$v = \sqrt{2g\Delta h} \qquad (5\text{-}9)$$

where g is the acceleration due to gravity and Δh is the distance that the ball has fallen. If g is in units of m/s^2 and Δh is in units of meters, then the velocity will be in units of m/s. Write a program to create a table of the velocity of the ball as a function of how far it has fallen for distances from 0 to 200 m in steps of 10 m. The program should properly label each of the columns in the table.

5-24. **Potential versus Kinetic Energy** The potential energy of a ball due to its height above ground is given by the equation

$$PE = mgh \qquad (5\text{-}10)$$

where m is the mass of the ball in kilograms, g is the acceleration due to gravity in m/s^2, and h is the height of the ball above the surface of the earth in meters. The kinetic energy of a ball due to its speed is given by the equation

$$KE = \frac{1}{2}mv^2 \qquad (5\text{-}11)$$

where m is the mass of the ball in kilograms and v is the velocity of the ball in m/s. Assume that a ball, with a mass of 1 kg, is initially stationary at a height of 100 m. When this ball is released, it will start to fall. Calculate the potential energy and the kinetic energy of the ball at 10-m increments as it falls from the initial height of 100 m to the ground, and create a table containing height, PE, KE, and the total energy (PE + KE) of the ball at each step. The program should properly label each of the columns in the table. What happens to the total energy as the ball falls? (*Note:* You can use Equation (5-9) to calculate the velocity at a given height, and then use that velocity to calculate the KE.)

5-25. **Interest Calculations** Suppose that you have a sum of money P in an interest-bearing account at a local bank (P stands for *present value*). If the bank pays you interest on the money at a rate of i percent per year and compounds the interest monthly, the amount of money that you will have in the bank after n months is given by the equation

$$F = P\left(1 + \frac{i}{1200}\right)^n \qquad (5\text{-}12)$$

where F is the future value of the account and $i/12$ is the monthly percentage interest rate (the extra factor of 100 in the denominator converts the interest rate from percentages to fractional amounts). Write a Fortran program that will read an initial amount of money P and an annual interest rate i, and will calculate and write out a table showing the future value of the account every month for the next 4 years. The table should be written to an output file called 'interest'. Be sure to properly label the columns of your table.

5-26. Write a program to read a set of integers from an input data file, and locate the largest and smallest values within the data file. Print out the largest and smallest values, together with the lines on which they were found. Assume that you do not know the number of values in the file before the file is read.

5-27. Means In Exercise 4-29, we wrote a Fortran program that calculated the arithmetic mean (average), rms average, geometric mean, and harmonic mean for a set of numbers. Modify that program to read an arbitrary number of values from an input data file, and calculate the means of those numbers. To test the program, place the following values into an input data file and run the program on that file: 1.0, 2.0, 5.0, 4.0, 3.0, 2.1, 4.7, 3.0.

5-28. Converting Radians to Degrees/Minutes/Seconds Angles are often measured in degrees (°), minutes ('), and seconds ("), with 360 degrees in a circle, 60 minutes in a degree, and 60 seconds in a minute. Write a program that reads angles in radians from an input disk file, and converts them into degrees, minutes, and seconds. Test your program by placing the following four angles expressed in radians into an input file, and reading that file into the program: 0.0, 1.0, 3.141593, 6.0.

5-29. There is a logical error in program least_squares_fit from Example 5-5. The error can cause the program to abort with a divide-by-zero error. It slipped through the example because we did not test the program exhaustively for all possible inputs. Find the error, and rewrite the program to eliminate it.

5-30. Ideal Gas Law Modify the ideal gas law programs in Exercise 4-32 to print their output in neat columns, with appropriate column headings.

5-31. Antenna Gain Pattern The gain G of a certain microwave dish antenna can be expressed as a function of angle by the equation

$$G(\theta) = \left| \text{sinc } 6\theta \right| \quad \text{for } -\frac{\pi}{2} \leq \theta \leq \frac{\pi}{2} \tag{5-13}$$

where θ is measured in radians from the boresite of the dish, and the sinc function is defined as follows:

$$\text{sinc } x = \begin{cases} \dfrac{\sin x}{x} & x \neq 0 \\ 1 & x = 0 \end{cases}$$

Calculate a table of gain versus the angle off boresite *in degrees* for this antenna for the range $0° \leq 0 \leq 90°$ in 1° steps. Label this table with the title "Antenna Gain vs Angle (deg)," and include column headings on the output.

5-32. Output Power from a Motor The output power produced by a rotating motor is given by the equation

$$P = \tau_{\text{IND}} \, \omega_m \tag{5-14}$$

where τ_{IND} is the induced torque on the shaft in newton-meters, ω_m is the rotational speed of the shaft in radians per second, and P is in watts. Assume that the rotational speed of a particular motor shaft is given by the equation

$$\omega_m = 377\left(1 - e^{-0.25t}\right) \text{ rad/s}$$

and the induced torque on the shaft is given by

$$\tau_{\text{IND}} = 10e^{-0.25t} \text{ N} \cdot \text{m}$$

Calculate the torque, speed, and power supplied by this shaft versus time for $0 \leq t \leq 10$ s at intervals of 0.25 s, and display the results in a table. Be sure to label your table and provide column headings.

5-33. **Calculating Orbits** When a satellite orbits the Earth, the satellite's orbit will form an ellipse with the Earth located at one of the focal points of the ellipse. The satellite's orbit can be expressed in polar coordinates as

$$r = \frac{p}{1 - \varepsilon \cos \theta} \tag{5-15}$$

where r and θ are the distance and angle of the satellite from the center of the Earth, p is a parameter specifying the size of the size the orbit, and ε is a parameter representing the eccentricity of the orbit. A circular orbit has an eccentricity ε of 0. An elliptical orbit has an eccentricity of $0 \leq \varepsilon \leq 1$. If $\varepsilon > 1$, the satellite follows a hyperbolic path and escapes from the Earth's gravitational field.

Consider a satellite with a size parameter $p = 10{,}000$ km. Calculate and create a table of the height of this satellite versus θ if (a) $\varepsilon = 0$; (b) $\varepsilon = 0.25$; (c) $\varepsilon = 0.5$. How close does each orbit come to the center of the Earth? How far away does each orbit get from the center of the Earth?

5-34. **Apogee and Perigee** The term r in Equation (5-15) refers to the range from a satellite to the *center of the Earth*. If the radius of the Earth $R = 6.371 \times 10^6$ m, then we can calculate the satellite height above the Earth from the equation

$$h = r - R \tag{5-16}$$

where h is the height in meters and r is the range to the center of the Earth calculated from Equation (5-15).

The *apogee* of an orbit is the maximum height of the orbit above the surface of the Earth, and the *perigee* of an orbit is the minimum height of the orbit above the surface of the Earth. We can use Equations (5-15) and (5-16) to calculate the apogee and perigee of an orbit.

Consider a satellite with a size parameter $p = 10{,}000$ km. Calculate and create a table of the apogee and perigee of this satellite versus eccentricity for $0 \leq \varepsilon \leq 0.5$, in steps of 0.05.

5-35. **Dynamically Modifying Format Descriptors** Write a program to read a set of four real values in free format from each line of an input data file, and print them out on the standard output device. Each value should be printed in F14.6 format if it is exactly zero or if it lies in the range $0.01 \le |value| < 1000.0$, and in $\text{ES}14.6$ format otherwise. (*Hint:* Define the output format in a character variable, and modify it to match each line of data as it is printed.) Test your program on the following data set:

```
0.00012        -250.      6.02E23       -0.012
     0.0    12345.6       1.6E-19      -1000.
----|----|----|----|----|----|----|----|----|----|
 5    10   15   20   25   30   35   40   45   50
```

5-36. Correlation Coefficient The method of least squares is used to fit a straight line to a noisy input data set consisting of pairs of values *(x, y)*. As we saw in Example 5-5, the best fit to equation

$$y = mx + b \qquad \qquad (5\text{-}5)$$

is given by

$$m = \frac{(\Sigma xy) - (\Sigma x)\bar{y}}{(\Sigma x^2) - (\Sigma x)\bar{x}} \qquad \qquad (5\text{-}6)$$

and

$$b = \bar{y} - m\bar{x} \qquad \qquad (5\text{-}7)$$

where

Σx is the sum of the *x* values

Σx^2 is the sum of the squares of the *x* values

Σxy is the sum of the products of the corresponding *x* and *y* values

$\bar{x}$ is the mean (average) of the *x* values

$\bar{y}$ is the mean (average) of the *y* values

Figure 5-14 shows two data sets and the least-squares fits associated with each one. As you can see, the low-noise data fits the least-squares line much better than the noisy data does. It would be useful to have some quantitative way to describe how well the data fits the least-squares line given by Equations 5-5 through 5-7.

There is a standard statistical measure of the "goodness of fit" of a data set to a least-squares line. It is called a *correlation coefficient*. The correlation coefficient is equal to 1.0 when there is a perfect positive linear relationship between data *x* and *y*, and it is equal to -1.0 when there is a perfect negative linear relationship between data *x* and *y*. The correlation coefficient is 0.0 when there is no linear relationship between *x* and *y* at all. The correlation coefficient is given by the equation

$$r = \frac{n(\Sigma xy) - (\Sigma x)(\Sigma y)}{\sqrt{\left[\left(n\Sigma x^2\right) - (\Sigma x)^2\right]\left[\left(n\Sigma y^2\right) - (\Sigma y)^2\right]}} \qquad \qquad (5\text{-}17)$$

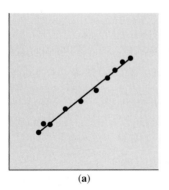
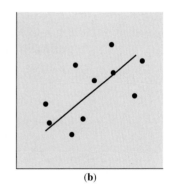

(a)   (b)

FIGURE 5-14
Two different least-squares fits: (*a*) with good, low-noise data; (*b*) with very noisy data.

5

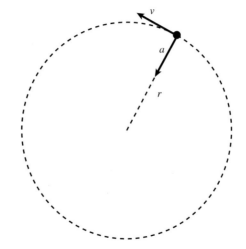

FIGURE 5-15
An object moving in uniform circular motion due to the centripetal acceleration *a*.

where *r* is the correlation coefficient and *n* is the number of data points included in the fit.

Write a program to read an arbitrary number of *(x, y)* data pairs from an input data file, and to calculate and print out both the least squares fit to the data and the correlation coefficient for the fit. If the correlation coefficient is small ($|r| < 0.3$), write out a warning message to the user.

5-37. Aircraft Turning Radius An object moving in a circular path at a constant tangential velocity *v* is shown in Figure 5-15. The radial acceleration required for the object to move in the circular path is given by Equation (5-18)

$$a = \frac{v^2}{r} \qquad\qquad (5\text{-}18)$$

where a is the centripetal acceleration of the object in m/s^2, v is the tangential velocity of the object in m/s, and r is the turning radius in m. Suppose that the object is an aircraft, and write a program to answer the following questions about it:

(a) Print a table of the aircraft turning radius as a function of aircraft speed for speeds between Mach 0.5 and Mach 2.0 in Mach 0.1 steps, assuming that the acceleration remains 2g. Be sure to include proper labels on your table.

(b) Print a table of the aircraft turning radius as a function of centripetal acceleration for accelerations between 2g and 8g in 0.5g steps, assuming a constant speed of Mach 0.85. Be sure to include proper labels on your table.

5

6

Introduction to Arrays

OBJECTIVES

- Know how to define, initialize, and use arrays.
- Know how to use whole array operations to operate on entire arrays of data in a single statement.
- Know how to use array sections.
- Learn how read and write arrays and array sections.

An **array** is a group of variables or constants, all of the same type, that are referred to by a single name. The values in the group occupy consecutive locations in the computer's memory (see Figure 6-1). An individual value within the array is called an **array element;** it is identified by the name of the array together with a **subscript** pointing to the particular location within the array. For example, the first variable shown in Figure 6-1 is referred to as $a(1)$, and the fifth variable shown in the figure is referred to as $a(5)$. The subscript of an array is of type INTEGER. Either constants or variables may be used for array subscripts.

As we shall see, arrays can be extremely powerful tools. They permit us to apply the same algorithm over and over again to many different data items with a simple DO loop. For example, suppose that we need to take the square root of 100 different real numbers. If the numbers are stored as elements of an array a consisting of 100 real values, then the code

```
DO i = 1, 100
   a(i) = SQRT(a(i))
END DO
```

will take the square root of each real number, and store it back into the memory location that it came from. If we wanted to take the square root of 100 real numbers without using arrays, we would have to write out

```
a1   = SQRT(a1)
a2   = SQRT(a2)
     . . .
a100 = SQRT(a100)
```

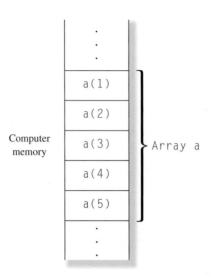

FIGURE 6-1
The elements of an array occupy successive locations in a computer's memory.

as 100 separate statements! Arrays are obviously a *much* cleaner and shorter way to handle repeated similar operations.

Arrays are very powerful tools for manipulating data in Fortran. As we shall see, it is possible to manipulate and perform calculations with individual elements of arrays one by one, with whole arrays at once, or with various subsets of arrays. We will first learn how to declare arrays in Fortran programs. Then, we will learn how to use individual array elements in Fortran statements, and afterward we will learn to use whole arrays or array subsets in Fortran statements.

6.1

DECLARING ARRAYS

Before an array can be used, its type and the number of elements it contains must be declared to the compiler in a type declaration statement, so that the compiler will know what sort of data is to be stored in the array, and how much memory is required to hold it. For example, a real array `voltage` containing 16 elements could be declared as follows.[1]

```
REAL, DIMENSION(16) :: voltage
```

The `DIMENSION` **attribute** in the type declaration statement declares the size of the array being defined. The elements in array `voltage` would be addressed as `voltage(1)`,

---

[1] An alternative way to declare an array is to attach the dimension information directly to the array name:

```
REAL :: voltage(16)
```

This declaration style is provided for backward compatibility with earlier versions of Fortran. It is fully equivalent to the array declaration shown above.

voltage(2), etc., up to voltage(16). Similarly, an array of fifty 20-character-long variables could be declared as follows:

CHARACTER(len = 20), DIMENSION(50) :: last_name

Each of the elements in array last_name would be a 20-character-long variable, and the elements would be addressed as last_name(1), last_name(2), etc.

Arrays may be declared with more than one subscript, so they may be organized into two or more dimensions. These arrays are convenient for representing data that is normally organized into multiple dimensions, such as map information, temperature measurements on a flat surface, and so forth. The number of subscripts declared for a given array is called the **rank** of the array. Both array voltage and array last_name are rank 1 arrays, since they have only one subscript. We will see more complex arrays later in Chapter 8.

The number of elements in a given dimension of an array is called the **extent** of the array in that dimension. The extent of the first (and only) subscript of array voltage is 20, and the extent of the first (and only) subscript of array last_name is 50. The **shape** of an array is defined as the combination of its rank and the extent of the array in each dimension. Thus, two arrays have the same shape if they have the same rank and the same extent in each dimension. Finally, the **size** of an array is the total number of elements declared in that array. For simple rank 1 arrays, the size of the array is the same as the extent of its single subscript. Therefore, the size of array voltage is 20, and the size of array last_name is 50.

Array constants may also be defined. An array constant is an array consisting entirely of constants. It is defined by placing the constant values between special delimiters, called **array constructors.** The starting delimiter of a Fortran 95 array constructor is (/, and the ending delimiter of an array constructor is /). For example, the expression shown below defines an array constant containing five integer elements:

(/ 1, 2, 3, 4, 5 /)

F-2003 ONLY

In Fortran 2003, square brackets ([]) can also be used as array constructors. For example, the expression shown below defines a Fortran 2003 array constant containing five integer elements:

[1, 2, 3, 4, 5]

6.2

USING ARRAY ELEMENTS IN FORTRAN STATEMENTS

This section contains some of the practical details involved in using arrays in Fortran programs.

6.2.1 Array Elements Are Just Ordinary Variables

Each element of an array is a variable just like any other variable, and *an array element may be used in any place where an ordinary variable of the same type may be used*. Array elements may be included in arithmetic and logical expressions, and the results of an expression may be assigned to an array element. For example, assume that arrays `index` and `temp` are declared as:

```
INTEGER, DIMENSION(10) :: index
REAL, DIMENSION(3) :: temp
```

Then the following Fortran statements are perfectly valid:

```
index(1) = 5
temp(3) = REAL(index(1)) / 4.
WRITE (*,*) ' index(1) = ', index(1)
```

Under certain circumstances, entire arrays or subsets of arrays can be used in expressions and assignment statements. These circumstances will be explained in Section 6.3 below.

6.2.2 Initialization of Array Elements

Just as with ordinary variables, the values in an array must be initialized before use. If an array is not initialized, the contents of the array elements are undefined. In the following Fortran statements, array `j` is an example of an **uninitialized array.**

```
INTEGER, DIMENSION(10) :: j
WRITE (*,*) ' j(1) = ', j(1)
```

The array `j` has been declared by the type declaration statement, but no values have been placed into it yet. Since the contents of an uninitialized array are unknown and can vary from computer to computer, *the elements of the array should never be used until they are initialized to known values.*

Good Programming Practice
Always initialize the elements in an array before they are used.

The elements in an array may be initialized by one of three techniques:

1. Arrays may be initialized by using assignment statements.
2. Arrays may be initialized in type declaration statements at compilation time.
3. Arrays may be initialized by using `READ` statements.

Initializing arrays with assignment statements
Initial values may be assigned to the array by using assignment statements, either element by element in a `DO` loop or all at once with an array constructor. For example, the following `DO` loop will initialize the elements of array `array1` to 0.0, 2.0, 3.0, etc. one element at a time:

```
REAL, DIMENSION(10) :: array1
DO i = 1, 10
```

```
                        array1(i) = REAL(i)
                   END DO
```

The following assignment statement accomplishes the same function all at once, using an array constructor:

```
REAL, DIMENSION(10) :: array1
array1 = (/1.,2.,3.,4.,5.,6.,7.,8.,9.,10./)
```

It is also possible to initialize all of the elements of a array to a single value with a simple assignment statement. For example, the following statement initializes all of the elements of array1 to zero:

```
REAL, DIMENSION(10) :: array1
array1 = 0.
```

The simple program shown in Figure 6-2 calculates the squares of the numbers in array number, and then prints out the numbers and their squares. Note that the values in array number are initialized element by element with a DO loop.

FIGURE 6-2
A program to calculate the squares of the integers from 1 to 10, using assignment statements to initialize the values in array number.

```
PROGRAM squares

IMPLICIT NONE

INTEGER :: i
INTEGER, DIMENSION(10) :: number, square

! Initialize number and calculate square.
DO i = 1, 10
   number(i) = i                 ! Initialize number
   square(i) = number(i)**2      ! Calculate square
END DO

! Write out each number and its square.
DO i = 1, 10
   WRITE (*,100) number(i), square(i)
   100 FORMAT (1X,'Number = ',I6,' Square = ',I6)
END DO

END PROGRAM squares
```

Initializing arrays in type declaration statements

Initial values may be loaded into an array at compilation time by declaring their values in a type declaration statement. To initialize an array in a type declaration statement, we use an array constructor to declare its initial values in that statement. For example, the following statement declares a five-element integer array array2, and initializes the elements of array2 to 1, 2, 3, 4, and 5:

```
INTEGER, DIMENSION(5) :: array2 = (/ 1, 2, 3, 4, 5 /)
```

The five-element array constant (/ 1, 2, 3, 4, 5 /) was used to initialize the five-element array array2. In general, *the number of elements in the constant must match the number of elements in the array being initialized.* Either too few or too many elements will result in a compiler error.

This method works well to initialize small arrays, but what do we do if the array has 100 (or even 1000) elements? Writing out the initial values for a 100-element array would be very tedious and repetitive. To initialize larger arrays, we can use an **implied** DO **loop.** An implied DO loop has the general form

$$(arg1, arg2, \ldots, index = istart, iend, incr)$$

where $arg1$, $arg2$, etc., are values evaluated each time the loop is executed, and $index$, $istart$, $iend$, and $incr$ function in exactly the same way as they do for ordinary counting DO loops. For example, the $array2$ declaration above could be written by using an implied DO loop as:

```
INTEGER, DIMENSION(5) :: array2 = (/ (i, i = 1, 5) /)
```

and a 1000-element array could be initialized to have the values 1, 2, . . . , 1000, using an implied DO loop as follows:

```
INTEGER, DIMENSION(1000) :: array3 = (/ (i, i = 1, 1000) /)
```

Implied DO loops can nested or mixed with constants to produce complex patterns. For example, the following statements initialize the elements of $array4$ to zero if they are not divisible by 5, and to the element number if they are divisible by 5.

```
INTEGER, DIMENSION(25) :: array4 = (/ ((0,i=1,4),5*j, j=1,5) /)
```

The inner DO loop $(0,i=1,4)$ executes completely for each step of the outer DO loop, so for each value of the outer loop index j, we will have four zeros (from the inner loop) followed by the number $5*j$. The resulting pattern of values produced by these nested loops is:

```
0, 0, 0, 0, 5, 0, 0, 0, 0, 10, 0, 0, 0, 0, 15, ...
```

Finally, all of the elements of an array can be initialized to a single constant value by simply including the constant in the type declaration statement. In the following example, all of the elements of $array5$ are initialized to 1.0:

```
REAL, DIMENSION(100) :: array5 = 1.0
```

The program in Figure 6-3 illustrates the use of type declaration statements to initialize the values in an array. It calculates the square roots of the numbers in array $value$, and then prints out the numbers and their square roots.

FIGURE 6-3
A program to calculate the square roots of the integers from 1 to 10, using a type declaration statement to initialize the values in array $value$.

```
PROGRAM square_roots

IMPLICIT NONE

INTEGER :: i
```

(continued)

(concluded)

```
REAL, DIMENSION(10) :: value = (/ (i, i=1,10) /)
REAL, DIMENSION(10) :: square_root

! Calculate the square roots of the numbers.
DO i = 1, 10
   square_root(i) = SQRT(value(i))
END DO

! Write out each number and its square root.
DO i = 1, 10
   WRITE (*,100) value(i), square_root(i)
   100 FORMAT (1X,'Value = ',F5.1,' Square Root = ',F10.4)
END DO

END PROGRAM square_roots
```

Initializing arrays with READ statements

Arrays may also be initialized with READ statements. The use of arrays in I/O statements will be described in detail in Section 6.4.

6.2.3 Changing the Subscript Range of an Array

The elements of an *N*-element array are normally addressed using the subscripts 1, 2, ..., *N*. Thus the elements of array arr declared with the statement

```
REAL, DIMENSION(5) :: arr
```

would be addressed as arr(1), arr(2), arr(3), arr(4), and arr(5). In some problems, however, it is more convenient to address the array elements with other subscripts. For example, the possible grades on an exam might range from 0 to 100. If we wished to accumulate statistics on the number of people scoring any given grade, it would be convenient to have a 101-element array whose subscripts ranged from 0 to 100 instead of 1 to 101. If the subscripts ranged from 0 to 100, each student's exam grade could be used directly as an index into the array.

For such problems, Fortran provides a way to specify the range of numbers that will be used to address the elements of an array. To specify the subscript range, we include the starting and ending subscript numbers in the declaration statement, with the two numbers separated by a colon.

```
REAL, DIMENSION(lower_bound:upper_bound) :: array
```

For example, the following three arrays all consist of five elements:

```
REAL, DIMENSION(5) :: a1
REAL, DIMENSION(-2:2) :: b1
REAL, DIMENSION(5:9) :: c1
```

Array a1 is addressed with subscripts 1 through 5, array b1 is addressed with subscripts –2 through 2, and array c1 is addressed with subscripts 5 through 9. *All three arrays have the same shape,* since they have the same number of dimensions and the same extent in each dimension.

In general, the number of elements in a given dimension of an array can be found from the equation

$$\text{extent} = \text{upper\_bound} - \text{lower\_bound} + 1 \qquad (6\text{-}1)$$

The simple program squares_2 shown in Figure 6-4 calculates the squares of the numbers in array number, and then prints out the numbers and their squares. The arrays in this example contain 11 elements, addressed by the subscripts -5, $-4, \ldots, 0, \ldots, 4, 5$.

FIGURE 6-4
A program to calculate the squares of the integers from -5 to 5, using array elements addressed by subscripts -5 through 5.

```
PROGRAM squares_2

IMPLICIT NONE

INTEGER :: i
INTEGER, DIMENSION(-5:5) :: number, square

! Initialize number and calculate square.
DO i = -5, 5
   number(i) = i              ! Initialize number
   square(i) = number(i)**2   ! Calculate square
END DO

! Write out each number and its square.
DO i = -5, 5
   WRITE (*,100) number(i), square(i)
   100 FORMAT (1X,'Number = ',I6,' Square = ',I6)
END DO

END PROGRAM squares_2
```

When program squares_2 is executed, the results are

```
C:\book\chap6>squares_2
Number =       -5 Square =      25
Number =       -4 Square =      16
Number =       -3 Square =       9
Number =       -2 Square =       4
Number =       -1 Square =       1
Number =        0 Square =       0
Number =        1 Square =       1
Number =        2 Square =       4
Number =        3 Square =       9
Number =        4 Square =      16
Number =        5 Square =      25
```

6.2.4 Out-of-Bounds Array Subscripts

Each element of an array is addressed by using an integer subscript. The range of integers that can be used to address array elements depends on the declared extent of the array. For a real array declared as

```
REAL, DIMENSION(5) :: a
```

the integer subscripts 1 through 5 address elements in the array. *Any other integers* (less than 1 or greater than 5) *could not be used as subscripts, since they do not correspond to allocated memory locations*. Such integer subscripts are said to be **out of bounds** for the array. But what would happen if we make a mistake and try to access the out-of-bounds element a(6) in a program?

The answer to this question is very complicated, since it varies from processor to processor. On some processors, a running Fortran program will check every subscript used to reference an array to see if it is in bounds. If an out-of-bounds subscript is detected, the program will issue an informative error message and stop. Unfortunately, such **bounds checking** requires a lot of computer time, and the program will run slowly. To make programs run faster, most Fortran compilers make bounds checking optional. If it is turned on, programs run slower, but they are protected from out-of-bounds references. If it is turned off, programs will run much faster, but out-of-bounds references will not be checked. If your Fortran compiler has a bounds-checking option, you should always turn it on during debugging to help detect programming errors. Once the program has been debugged, bounds checking can be turned off if necessary to increase the execution speed of the final program.

Good Programming Practice

Always turn on the bounds checking option on your Fortran compiler during program development and debugging to help you catch programming errors producing out-of-bounds references. The bounds-checking option may be turned off if necessary for greater speed in the final program.

What happens in a program if an out-of-bounds reference occurs and the bounds checking option is not turned on? Sometimes, the program will abort. Much of the time, though, the computer will simply go to the location in memory *at which the referenced array element would have been if it had been allocated*, and use that memory location (see Figure 6-5). For example, the array a declared above has five elements in it. If a(6) were used in a program, the computer would access the first word beyond the end of array a. Since that memory location will be allocated for a totally different purpose, the program can fail in subtle and bizarre ways that can be almost impossible to track down. Be careful with your array subscripts, and always use the bounds checker when you are debugging!

The program shown in Figure 6-6 illustrates the behavior of a Fortran program containing incorrect array references with and without bounds checking turned on. This simple program declares a five-element real array a and a five-element real array b. The array a is initialized with the values 1., 2., 3., 4., and 5., and array b is initialized with the values 10., 20., 30., 40., and 50. Many Fortran compilers will allocate the memory for array b immediately after the memory for array a, as shown in Figure 6-5.

The program in Figure 6-6 uses a DO loop to write out the values in the elements 1 through 6 of array a, despite the fact that array a only has five elements. Therefore, it will attempt to access the out-of-bounds array element a(6).

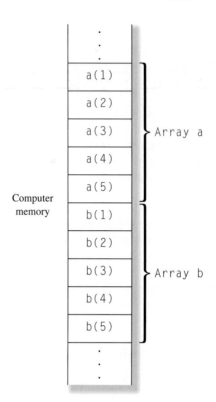

FIGURE 6-5
A computer memory showing a five-element array a immediately followed by a five-element array b. If bounds checking is turned off, some processors may not recognize the end of array a, and may treat the memory location after the end of a as a(6).

FIGURE 6-6
A simple program to illustrate the effect of out-of-bounds array references with and without bounds checking turned on.

```
PROGRAM bounds
!
! Purpose:
!   To illustrate the effect of accessing an out-of-bounds
!   array element.
!
! Record of revisions:
!    Date         Programmer          Description of change
!    ====         ==========          =====================
!   11/15/06    S. J. Chapman         Original code
!
IMPLICIT NONE
```

(continued)

(concluded)

```
! Declare and initialize the variables used in this program.
INTEGER :: i                    ! Loop index
REAL, DIMENSION(5) :: a = (/ 1., 2., 3., 4., 5./)
REAL, DIMENSION(5) :: b = (/10.,20.,30.,40.,50./)

! Write out the values of array a
DO i = 1, 6
   WRITE (*,100) i, a(i)
   100 FORMAT ( 1X,'a(', I1, '} = ', F6.2 )
END DO

END PROGRAM bounds
```

If this program is compiled with the Lahey Fortran 90 compiler on a PC-compatible computer with bounds checking turned *on,* the result is

```
C:\book\chap6>bounds

a(1) =  1.00
a(2) =  2.00
a(3) =  3.00
a(4) =  4.00
a(5) =  5.00
a(6
Array subscript exceeds allocated area (see "Arrays" in the Lahey
 Fortran 90 Language Reference).
 Error occurred in bounds.f90 at line 26.
```

The program checked each array reference, and aborted when an out-of-bounds expression was encountered. Note that the error message tells us what is wrong, and even the line number at which it occurred. If bounds checking is turned *off,* the result is

```
C:\book\chap6>bounds

a(1) =    1.00
a(2) =    2.00
a(3) =    3.00
a(4) =    4.00
a(5) =    5.00
a(6) =   10.00
```

When the program tried to write out `a(6)`, it wrote out the contents of the first memory location after the end of the array. This location just happened to be the first element of array `b`.

6.2.5 The Use of Named Constants with Array Declarations

In many Fortran programs, arrays are used to store large amounts of information. The amount of information that a program can process depends on the size of the arrays it contains. If the arrays are relatively small, the program will be small and will not require much memory to run, but it will be able to handle only a small amount of data. On the other hand, if the arrays are large, the program will be able to handle a lot of information, but it will require a lot of memory to run. The array sizes in such a program are frequently changed to make it run better for different problems or on different processors.

It is good practice to always declare the array sizes by using named constants. Named constants make it easy to resize the arrays in a Fortran program. In the following code, the sizes of all arrays can be changed by simply changing the single named constant MAX_SIZE.

```
INTEGER, PARAMETER :: MAX_SIZE = 1000
REAL :: array1(MAX_SIZE)
REAL :: array2(MAX_SIZE)
REAL :: array3(2*MAX_SIZE)
```

This may seem like a small point, but it is *very* important to the proper maintenance of large Fortran programs. If all related array sizes in a program are declared by using named constants, and if those same named constants are used in any size tests in the program, then it will be much simpler to modify the program later. Imagine what it would be like if you had to locate and change every reference to array sizes within a 50,000-line program! The process could take weeks to complete and debug. By contrast, the size of a well-designed program could be modified in 5 minutes by changing only one statement in the code.

Good Programming Practice

Always declare the sizes of arrays in a Fortran program by using parameters to make them easy to change.

EXAMPLE 6-1

Finding the Largest and Smallest Values in a Data Set:

To illustrate the use of arrays, we will write a simple program that reads in data values, and finds the largest and smallest numbers in the data set. The program will then write out the values, with the word 'LARGEST' printed by the largest value and the word 'SMALLEST' printed by the smallest value in the data set.

SOLUTION

This program must ask the user for the number of values to read, and then read the input values into an array. Once the values are all read, it must go through the data to find the largest and smallest values in the data set. Finally, it must print out the values, with the appropriate annotations beside the largest and smallest values in the data set.

1. **State the problem.**

We have not yet specified the type of data to be processed. If we are processing integer data, then the problem may be stated as follows:

> Develop a program to read a user-specified number of integer values from the standard input device, locate the largest and smallest values in the data set, and write out all of the values with the words 'LARGEST' and 'SMALLEST' printed by the largest and smallest values in the data set.

2. **Define the inputs and outputs.**

There are two types of inputs to this program:

(*a*) An integer containing the number of integer values to read. This value will come from the standard input device.

(*b*) The integer values in the data set. These values will also come from the standard input device.

The outputs from this program are the values in the data set, with the word 'LARGEST' printed by the largest value, and the word 'SMALLEST' printed by the smallest value.

3. **Describe the algorithm.**

The program can be broken down into four major steps

```
Get the number of values to read
Read the input values into an array
Find the largest and smallest values in the array
Write out the data with the words 'LARGEST' and 'SMALLEST' at the
    appropriate places
```

The first two major steps of the program are to get the number of values to read in and to read the values into an input array. We must prompt the user for the number of values to read. If that number is less than or equal to the size of the input array, then we should read in the data values. Otherwise, we should warn the user and quit. The detailed pseudocode for these steps is:

```
Prompt user for the number of input values nvals
Read in nvals
IF nvals <= max_size then
   DO for j = 1 to nvals
      Read in input values
   End of DO
   . . .
   . . .  (Further processing here)
   . . .
ELSE
   Tell user that there are too many values for array size
End of IF
END PROGRAM
```

Next we must locate the largest and smallest values in the data set. We will use variables `ilarge` and `ismall` as pointers to the array elements having the largest and smallest values. The pseudocode to find the largest and smallest values is:

```
! Find largest value
temp ← input(1)
ilarge ← 1
DO for j = 2 to nvals
   IF input(j) > temp then
      temp ← input(j)
      ilarge ← j
   End of IF
End of DO

! Find smallest value
temp ← input(1)
ismall ← 1
DO for j = 2 to nvals
   IF input(j) < temp then
      temp ← input(j)
      ismall ← j
   End of IF
End of DO
```

The final step is writing out the values with the largest and smallest numbers labeled:

```
DO for j = 1 to nvals
   IF ismall == j then
      Write input(j) and 'SMALLEST'
   ELSE IF ilarge == j then
      Write input(j) and 'LARGEST'
   ELSE
      Write input(j)
   End of IF
End of DO
```

4. **Turn the algorithm into Fortran statements.**
   The resulting Fortran program is shown in Figure 6-7.

FIGURE 6-7
A program to read in a data set from the standard input device, find the largest and smallest values, and print the values with the largest and smallest values labeled.

```
PROGRAM extremes
!
!  Purpose:
!    To find the largest and smallest values in a data set,
!    and to print out the data set with the largest and smallest
!    values labeled.
!
!  Record of revisions:
!     Date          Programmer          Description of change
!     ====          ==========          =====================
!     11/15/06   S. J. Chapman          Original code
!
```

(continued)

(continued)

```
IMPLICIT NONE

! Data dictionary: declare constants
INTEGER, PARAMETER :: MAX_SIZE = 10     ! Max size of data set

! Data dictionary: declare variable types, definitions, & units
INTEGER, DIMENSION(MAX_SIZE) :: input  ! Input values
INTEGER :: ilarge                      ! Pointer to largest value
INTEGER :: ismall                      ! Pointer to smallest value
INTEGER :: j                           ! DO loop index
INTEGER :: nvals                       ! Number of vals in data set
INTEGER :: temp                        ! Temporary variable

! Get number of values in data set
WRITE (*,*) 'Enter number of values in data set:'
READ (*,*) nvals

! Is the number <=  MAX_SIZE?
size: IF ( nvals <=  MAX_SIZE ) THEN

   ! Get input values.
   in: DO J = 1, nvals
      WRITE (*,100) 'Enter value ', j
      100 FORMAT (' ',A,I3,': ')
      READ (*,*) input(j)
   END DO in

   ! Find the largest value.
   temp = input(1)
   ilarge = 1
   large: DO j = 2, nvals
      IF ( input(j) > temp ) THEN
         temp = input(j)
         ilarge = j
      END IF
   END DO large

   ! Find the smallest value.
   temp = input(1)
   ismall = 1
   small: DO j = 2, nvals
      IF ( input(j) < temp ) THEN
         temp = input(j)
         ismall = j
      END IF
   END DO small

   ! Write out list.
   WRITE (*,110)
   110 FORMAT ('0','The values are:')
   out: DO j = 1, nvals
      IF ( j == ilarge ) THEN
         WRITE (*,'(1X,I6,2X,A)') input(j), 'LARGEST'
```

(continued)

6

(concluded)

```
      ELSE IF ( J == ismall ) THEN
         WRITE (*,'(1X,I6,2X,A)') input(j), 'SMALLEST'
      ELSE
         WRITE (*,'(1X,I6)') input(j)
      END IF
   END DO out

ELSE size

   ! nvals > max_size. Tell user and quit.
   WRITE (*,120) nvals, MAX_SIZE
   120 FORMAT (1X,'Too many input values: ', I6, ' > ', I6)

END IF size

END PROGRAM extremes
```

5. **Test the program.**
   To test this program, we will use two data sets, one with 6 values and one with 12 values. Running this program with 6 values yields the following result:

```
C:\book\chap6>extremes
Enter number of values in data set:
6
Enter value 1:
-6
Enter value 2:
5
Enter value 3:
-11
Enter value 4:
16
Enter value 5:
9
Enter value 6:
0

The values are:
    -6
     5
   -11   SMALLEST
    16   LARGEST
     9
     0
```

The program correctly labeled the largest and smallest values in the data set. Running this program with 12 values yields the following result:

```
C:\book\chap6>extremes
Enter number of values in data set:
12
Too many input values:      12 >      10
```

The program recognized that there were too many input values, and quit. Thus, the program gives the correct answers for both of our test data sets.

This program used the named constant MAX_SIZE to declare the size of the array, and also in all comparisons related to the array. As a result, we could change this program to process up to 1000 values by simply changing the value of MAX_SIZE from 10 to 1000.

6.3
USING WHOLE ARRAYS AND ARRAY SUBSETS IN FORTRAN STATEMENTS

Both whole arrays and array subsets may be used in Fortran statements. When they are, the operations are performed on all of the specified array elements simultaneously. This section teaches us how to use whole arrays and array subsets in Fortran statements.

6.3.1 Whole Array Operations

Under certain circumstances, **whole arrays** may be used in arithmetic calculations as though they were ordinary variables. If two arrays are the same **shape,** then they can be used in ordinary arithmetic operations, and the operation will be applied on an element-by-element basis (see Figure 6-8). Consider the example program in Figure 6-9. Here, arrays a, b, c, and d are all four elements long. Each element in array c is calculated as the sum of the corresponding elements in arrays a and b, using a DO loop. Array d is calculated as the sum of arrays a and b in a single assignment statement.

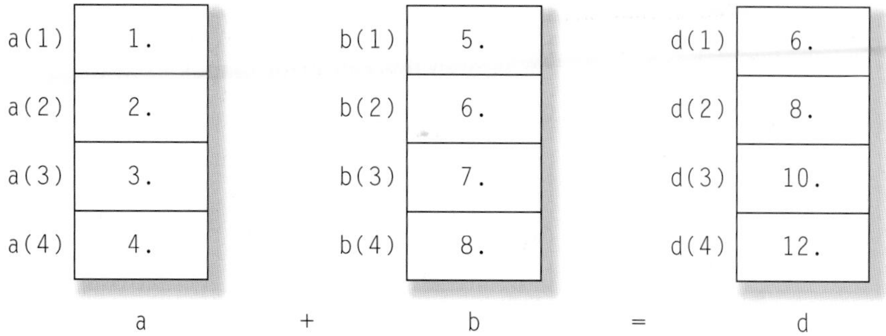

FIGURE 6-8
When an operation is applied to two arrays of the same shape, the operation is performed on the arrays on an element-by-element basis.

FIGURE 6-9
A program illustrating both element-by-element addition and whole array addition.

```
PROGRAM add_arrays

IMPLICIT NONE

INTEGER :: i
REAL, DIMENSION(4) :: a = (/ 1., 2., 3., 4./)
REAL, DIMENSION(4) :: b = (/ 5., 6., 7., 8./)
REAL, DIMENSION(4) :: c, d

! Element by element addition
DO i = 1, 4
   c(i) = a(i) + b(i)
END DO

! Whole array addition
d = a + b

! Write out results
WRITE (*,100) 'c', c
WRITE (*,100) 'd', d
100 FORMAT (' ',A,' = ',5(F6.1,1X))

END PROGRAM add_arrays
```

When this program is executed, the results are exactly the same for both calculations:

```
C:\book\chap6>add_arrays
c =    6.0    8.0   10.0   12.0
d =    6.0    8.0   10.0   12.0
```

Two arrays can be used as operands in an intrinsic operation (addition etc.) if and only if they have the *same shape*. This means that they must have the *same number of dimensions* (the same **rank**), and *the same number of elements in each dimension* (the same **extent**). Two arrays of the same shape are said to be **conformable.** Note that although the two arrays must be the same shape, they do *not* have to have the same subscript range in each dimension. The following arrays can be added freely, even though the subscript ranges used to address their elements are different.

```
REAL, DIMENSION(1:4) :: a = (/ 1., 2., 3., 4./)
REAL, DIMENSION(5:8) :: b = (/ 5., 6., 7., 8./)
REAL, DIMENSION(101:104) :: c
c = a + b
```

🔴 If two arrays are not conformable, then any attempt to perform arithmetic operations with them will produce a compile-time error.

Scalar values are also conformable with arrays. In that case, the scalar value is applied equally to every element of the array. For example, after the following piece of code is executed, array c will contain the values [10., 20., 30., 40.].

```
REAL, DIMENSION(4) :: a = (/ 1., 2., 3., 4./), c
REAL :: b = 10
c = a * b
```

Many Fortran 95/2003 intrinsic functions that are used with scalar values will also accept arrays as input arguments, and return arrays as results. The returned arrays will contain the result of applying the function to the input array on an element-by-element basis. These functions are called **elemental intrinsic functions,** since they operate on arrays on a element-by-element basis. Most common functions are elemental, including ABS, SIN, COS, EXP, LOG, etc. A complete list of elemental functions is contained in Appendix B. For example, consider an array a defined as

```
REAL, DIMENSION(4) :: a = (/ -1., 2., -3., 4./)
```

Then the function ABS(a) would return [1., 2., 3., 4.].

6.3.2 Array Subsets

We have already seen that it is possible to use either array elements or entire arrays in calculations. In addition, it is possible to use subsets of arrays in calculations. A subset of an array is called an **array section.** It is specified by replacing an array subscript with a **subscript triplet** or **vector subscript.**

A subscript triplet has the general form

```
subscript_1 : subscript_2 : stride
```

where *subscript_1* is the first subscript to be included in the array subset, *subscript_2* is the last subscript to be included in the array subset, and *stride* is the subscript increment through the data set. It works much like an implied DO loop. A subscript triplet specifies the ordered set of all array subscripts starting with *subscript_1* and ending with *subscript_2*, advancing at a rate of *stride* between values. For example, let's define an array array as

```
INTEGER, DIMENSION(10) :: array = (/1,2,3,4,5,6,7,8,9,10/)
```

Then the array subset array(1:10:2) would be an array containing only elements array(1), array(3), array(5), array(7), and array(9).

Any or all of the components of a subscript triplet may be defaulted. If *subscript_1* is missing from the triplet, it defaults to the subscript of the first element in the array. If *subscript_2* is missing from the triplet, it defaults to the subscript of the last element in the array. If *stride* is missing from the triplet, it defaults to one. All of the following possibilities are examples of legal triplets:

```
subscript_1 : subscript_2 : stride
subscript_1 : subscript_2
subscript_1 :
subscript_1 : : stride
: subscript_2
: subscript_2 : stride
: : stride
:
```

EXAMPLE   *Specifying Array Sections with Subscript Triplets:*
6-2

Assume the following type declaration statements:

```
INTEGER :: i = 3, j = 7
REAL, DIMENSION(10) :: a = (/1.,-2.,3.,-4.,5.,-6.,7.,-8.,9.,-10./)
```

Determine the number of elements in and the contents of the array sections specified by each of the following subscript triplets:

    (*a*) `a(:)`
    (*b*) `a(i:j)`
    (*c*) `a(i:j:i)`
    (*d*) `a(i:j:j)`
    (*e*) `a(i:)`
    (*f*) `a(:j)`
    (*g*) `a(::i)`

SOLUTION

    (*a*) `a(:)` is identical to the original array: [1., – 2.,3., – 4.,5., – 6.,7., – 8.,9., – 10.]
    (*b*) `a(i:j)` is the array subset starting at element 3 and ending at element 7, with a default stride of 1: [3., –4., 5., –6.,7.]
    (*c*) `a(i:j:i)` is the array subset starting at element 3 and ending at element 7, with a stride of 3: [3., –6.]
    (*d*) `a(i:j:j)` is the array subset starting at element 3 and ending at element 7, with a stride of 7: [3.]
    (*e*) `a(i:)` is the array subset starting at element 3 and by default ending at element 10 (the end of the array), with a default stride of 1: [3., –4.,5., –6.,7., –8.,9., –10.]
    (*f*) `a(:j)` is the array subset starting by default at element 1 and ending at element 7, with a default stride of 1: [1., –2., 3., –4., 5., –6., 7.]
    (*g*) `a(::i)` is the array subset starting by default at element 1 and ending by default at element 10, with a stride of 3: [1., –4., 7., –10.]

Subscript triplets select ordered subsets of array elements for use in calculations. In contrast, **vector subscripts** allow arbitrary combinations of array elements to be selected for use in an operation. *A vector subscript is a one-dimensional integer array specifying the array elements to be used in a calculation.* The array elements may be specified in any order, and array elements may be specified more than once. The resulting array will contain one element for each subscript specified in the vector. For example, consider the following type declaration statements:

```
INTEGER, DIMENSION(5) :: vec = (/1, 6, 4, 1, 9 /)
REAL, DIMENSION(10) :: a = (/1., -2., 3., -4., 5., -6., 7., -8., 9., -10./)
```

With these definitions, a(vec) would be the array [1., –6., –4., 1., 9.].

If a vector subscript includes any array element more than once, then the resulting array section is called a **many-one array section.** Such an array section *cannot be used on the left side of an assignment statement,* because it would specify that two or more different values should be assigned to the same array element at the same time! For example, consider the following Fortran statements:

```
INTEGER, DIMENSION(5) :: vec = (/1, 2, 1 /)
REAL, DIMENSION(10) :: a = (/10.,20.,30./)
REAL, DIMENSION(2) :: b
b(vec) = a
```

The assignment statement attempts to assign both the value 10. and the value 30. to array element b(1), which is impossible.

■ 6.4
INPUT AND OUTPUT

6

It is possible to perform I/O operations on either individual array elements or entire arrays. Both types of I/O operations are described in this section.

6.4.1 Input and Output of Array Elements

We previously stated that an *array element* is a variable just like any other variable, and that an array element may be used in any place where an ordinary variable of the same type may be used. Therefore, READ and WRITE statements containing array elements are just like READ and WRITE statements for any other variables. To write out specific elements from an array, just name them in the argument list of the WRITE statement. For example, the following code writes out the first five elements of the real array a.

```
WRITE (*,100) a(1), a(2), a(3), a(4), a(5)
100 FORMAT (1X,'a = ', 5F10.2)
```

6.4.2 The Implied DO Loop

The implied DO loop is also permitted in I/O statements. It allows an argument list to be written many times as a function of an index variable. Every argument in the argument list is written once for each value of the index variable in the implied DO loop. With an implied DO loop, the previous statement becomes:

```
WRITE (*,100) ( a(i), i = 1, 5 )
100 FORMAT (1X,'a = ', 5F10.2)
```

The argument list in this case contains only one item: a(i). This list is repeated once for each value of the index variable i. Since i takes on the values from 1 to 5, the array elements a(1), a(2), a(3), a(4), and a(5) will be written.

The general form of a WRITE or READ statement with an implied DO loop is:

```
WRITE (unit,format) (arg1, arg2, ... , index = istart, iend, incr)
READ  (unit,format) (arg1, arg2, ... , index = istart, iend, incr)
```

where *arg1, arg2*, etc., are the values to be written or read. The variable *index* is the DO loop index, and *istart, iend,* and *incr* are respectively the starting value, ending value, and increment of the loop index variable. The index and all of the loop control parameters should be of type INTEGER.

For a WRITE statement containing an implied DO loop, each argument in the argument list is written once each time the loop is executed. Therefore, a statement like

```
WRITE (*,1000) (i, 2*i, 3*i, i = 1, 3)
1000 FORMAT (1X,9I6)
```

will write out nine values on a single line:

```
        1   2   3   2   4   6   3   6   9
```

Now let's look at a slightly more complicated example using arrays with an implied DO loop. Figure 6-10 shows a program that calculates the square root and cube root of a set of numbers, and prints out a table of square and cube roots. The program computes square roots and cube roots for all numbers between 1 and MAX_SIZE, where MAX_SIZE is a parameter. What will the output of this program look like?

FIGURE 6-10
A program that computes the square and cube roots of a set of number, and writes them out, using an implied DO loop.

```
PROGRAM square_and_cube_roots
!
!   Purpose:
!     To calculate a table of numbers, square roots, and cube roots
!     using an implied DO loop to output the table.
!
!   Record of revisions:
!       Date          Programmer        Description of change
!       ====          ==========        =========================
!     11/15/06      S. J. Chapman       Original code
!
IMPLICIT NONE

! Data dictionary: declare constants
INTEGER, PARAMETER :: MAX_SIZE = 10      ! Max values in array

! Data dictionary: declare variable types, definitions, & units
INTEGER :: j                             ! Loop index
REAL, DIMENSION(MAX_SIZE) :: value       ! Array of numbers
REAL, DIMENSION(MAX_SIZE) :: square_root ! Array of square roots
REAL, DIMENSION(MAX_SIZE) :: cube_root   ! Array of cube roots
```

(continued)

(*concluded*)

```
! Calculate the square roots & cube roots of the numbers.
DO j = 1, MAX_SIZE
   value(j) = real(j)
   square_root(j) = sqrt(value(j))
   cube_root(j) = value(j)**(1.0/3.0)
END DO

! Write out each number, its square root, and its cube root.
WRITE (*,100)
100 FORMAT ('0',20X,'Table of Square and Cube Roots',/, &
             4X,' Number      Square Root  Cube Root', &
             3X,' Number      Square Root  Cube Root',/, &
             4X,' =======     ===========  =========', &
             3X,' =======     ===========  =========')
WRITE (*,110) (value(j), square_root(j), cube_root(j), j = 1, MAX_SIZE)
110 FORMAT (2(4X,F6.0,9X,F6.4,6X,F6.4))

END PROGRAM square_and_cube_roots
```

The implied DO loop in this example will be executed 10 times, with j taking on every value between 1 and 10 (the loop increment is defaulted to 1 here). During each iteration of the loop, the entire argument list will be written out. Therefore, this WRITE statement will write out 30 values, six per line. The resulting output is

```
                      Table of Square and Cube Roots
        Number    Square Root    Cube Root      Number    Square Root    Cube Root
        ======    ===========    =========      ======    ===========    =========
          1.        1.0000        1.0000          2.        1.4142        1.2599
          3.        1.7321        1.4422          4.        2.0000        1.5874
          5.        2.2361        1.7100          6.        2.4495        1.8171
          7.        2.6458        1.9129          8.        2.8284        2.0000
          9.        3.0000        2.0801         10.        3.1623        2.1544
```

Nested implied DO loops

Like ordinary DO loops, implied DO loops may be *nested*. If they are nested, the inner loop will execute completely for each step in the outer loop. As a simple example, consider the following statements

```
WRITE (*,100) ((i, j, j = 1, 3), i = 1, 2)
100 FORMAT (1X,I5,1X,I5)
```

There are two implicit DO loops in this WRITE statement. The index variable of the inner loop is j, and the index variable of the outer loop is i. When the WRITE statement is executed, variable j will take on values 1, 2, and 3 while i is 1, and then 1, 2, and 3 while i is 2. The output from this statement will be

```
1    1
1    2
1    3
2    1
2    2
2    3
```

Nested implied DO loops are important in working with arrays having two or more dimensions, as we will see later in Chapter 8.

The difference between I/O with standard DO loops and I/O with implied DO loops

Array input and output can be performed either with a standard DO loop containing I/O statements or with an implied DO loop. However, *there are subtle differences between the two types of loops.* To better understand those differences, let's compare the same output statement written with both types of loops. We will assume that integer array arr is initialized as follows

```
INTEGER, DIMENSION(5) :: arr = (/ 1, 2, 3, 4, 5 /)
```

and compare output for a regular DO loop with output for an implied DO loop. An output statement using an ordinary DO loop is shown below.

```
DO i = 1, 5
   WRITE (*,1000) arr(i), 2.*arr(i). 3*arr(i)
   1000 FORMAT (1X,6I6)
END DO
```

In this loop, the WRITE statement is executed *five times.* In fact, this loop is equivalent to the following statements:

```
WRITE (*,1000) arr(1), 2.*arr(1). 3*arr(1)
WRITE (*,1000) arr(2), 2.*arr(2). 3*arr(2)
WRITE (*,1000) arr(3), 2.*arr(3). 3*arr(3)
WRITE (*,1000) arr(4), 2.*arr(4). 3*arr(4)
WRITE (*,1000) arr(5), 2.*arr(5). 3*arr(5)
1000 FORMAT (1X,6I6)
```

An output statement using an implied DO loop is shown below.

```
WRITE (*,1000) (arr(i), 2.*arr(i). 3*arr(i), i = 1, 5)
1000 FORMAT (1X,6I6)
```

Here, there is only *one* WRITE statement, but the WRITE statement has 15 arguments. In fact, the WRITE statement with the implied DO loop is equivalent to

```
WRITE (*,1000) arr(1), 2.*arr(1). 3*arr(1), &
               arr(2), 2.*arr(2). 3*arr(2), &
               arr(3), 2.*arr(3). 3*arr(3), &
               arr(4), 2.*arr(4). 3*arr(4), &
               arr(5), 2.*arr(5). 3*arr(5)
1000 FORMAT (1X,6I6)
```

The main difference between having many WRITE statements with few arguments and one WRITE statement with many arguments is in the behavior of its associated format. Remember that each WRITE statement starts at the beginning of the format. Therefore, each of the five WRITE statements in the standard DO loop will start over at the beginning of the FORMAT statement, and only the first three of the six I6 descriptors will be used. The output of the standard DO loop will be

```
      1     2     3
      2     4     6
      3     6     9
      4     8    12
      5    10    15
```

On the other hand, the implied DO loop produces a single WRITE statement with 15 arguments, so the associated format will be used completely 2½ times. The output of the implied DO loop will be

```
      1     2     3     2     4     6
      3     6     9     4     8    12
      5    10    15
```

The same concept applies to a comparison of READ statements using standard DO loops with READ statements using implied DO loops. (See Exercise 6-9 at the end of the chapter.)

6.4.3 Input and Output of Whole Arrays and Array Sections

Entire arrays or array sections may also be read or written with READ and WRITE statements. If an array name is mentioned without subscripts in a Fortran I/O statement, then the compiler assumes that every element in the array is to be read in or written out. If an array section is mentioned in a Fortran I/O statement, then the compiler assumes that the entire section is to be read in or written out. Figure 6-11 shows a simple example of using an array and two array sections in I/O statements.

FIGURE 6-11
An example program illustrating array I/O.

```
PROGRAM array_io
!
! Purpose:
!   To illustrate array I/O.
!
! Record of revisions:
!    Date         Programmer          Description of change
!    ====         ==========          =====================
!   11/16/06    S. J. Chapman         Original code
!
IMPLICIT NONE

! Data dictionary: declare variable types & definitions
REAL, DIMENSION(5) :: a = (/1.,2.,3.,20.,10./) ! 5-element test array
INTEGER, DIMENSION(4) :: vec = (/4,3,4,5/)      ! vector subscript

! Output entire array.
WRITE (*,100) a
100 FORMAT ( 2X, 5F8.3 )
```

(*continued*)

(concluded)

```
! Output array section selected by a triplet.
WRITE (*,100) a(2::2)

! Output array section selected by a vector subscript.
WRITE (*,100) a(vec)

END PROGRAM array_io
```

The output from this program is:

```
     1.000     2.000     3.000      20.000     10.000
     2.000    20.000
    20.000     3.000    20.000      10.000
```

Quiz 6-1

This quiz provides a quick check to see if you have understood the concepts introduced in Sections 6.1 through 6.4. If you have trouble with the quiz, reread the sections, ask your instructor, or discuss the material with a fellow student. The answers to this quiz are found in the back of the book.

For questions 1 to 3, determine the length of the array specified by each of the following declaration statements and the valid subscript range for each array.

1. `INTEGER :: itemp(15)`

2. `LOGICAL :: test(0:255)`

3. ```
   INTEGER, PARAMETER :: I1 = -20
   INTEGER, PARAMETER :: I2 = -1
   REAL, DIMENSION(I1:I1*I2) :: a
   ```

Determine which of the following Fortran statements are valid. For each valid statement, specify what will happen in the program. Assume default typing for any variable not explicitly typed.

4. ```
   REAL :: phase(0:11) = (/ 0., 1., 2., 3., 3., 3., &
                            3., 3., 3., 2., 1., 0. /)
   ```

5. `REAL, DIMENSION(10) :: phase = 0.`

6. ```
   INTEGER :: data1(256)
   data1 = 0
   data1(10:256:10) = 1000
   WRITE (*,'(1X,10I8)') data1
   ```

7. ```
   REAL, DIMENSION(21:31) :: array1 = 10.
   REAL, DIMENSION(10) :: array2 = 3.
   WRITE (*,'(1X,10I8)') array1 + array2
   ```

8. ```
   INTEGER :: i, j
   INTEGER, DIMENSION(10) :: sub1
   INTEGER, DIMENSION(0:9) :: sub2
   ```

(continued)
   ```

(concluded)

```
      INTEGER, DIMENSION(100) :: in = &
            (/((0,i=1,9),j*10,j=1,10)/)
      sub1 = in(10:100:10)
      sub2 = sub1 / 10
      WRITE (*,100) sub1 * sub2
  100 FORMAT (1X,10I8)
```

9.
```
   REAL, DIMENSION(-3:0) :: error
   error(-3) = 0.00012
   error(-2) = 0.0152
   error(-1) = 0.0
   WRITE (*,500) error
500 FORMAT (T6,error = ,/,(3X,I6))
```

10.
```
    INTEGER, PARAMETER :: MAX = 10
    INTEGER :: i
    INTEGER, DIMENSION(MAX) :: ivec1 = (/(i,i=1,10)/)
    INTEGER, DIMENSION(MAX) :: ivec2 = (/(i,i=10,1,-1)/)
    REAL, DIMENSION(MAX) :: data1
    data1 = real(ivec1)**2
    WRITE (*,500) data1(ivec2)
500 FORMAT (1X,'Output = ',/,5(3X,F7.1))
```

11.
```
    INTEGER, PARAMETER :: NPOINT = 10
    REAL, DIMENSION(NPOINT) :: mydata
    DO i=1, NPOINT
       READ (*,*) mydata
    END DO
```

▦ 6.5
EXAMPLE PROBLEMS

Now we will examine two example problems that illustrate the use of arrays.

EXAMPLE 6-3

Sorting Data:

In many scientific and engineering applications, it is necessary to take a random input data set and to sort it so that the numbers in the data set are either all in *ascending order* (lowest to highest) or all in *descending order* (highest to lowest). For example, suppose that you were a zoologist studying a large population of animals, and that you wanted to identify the largest 5 percent of the animals in the population. The most straightforward way to approach this problem would be to sort the sizes of all of the animals in the population into ascending order, and take the top 5 percent of the values.

Sorting data into ascending or descending order seems to be an easy job. After all, we do it all the time. It is a simple matter for us to sort the data (10, 3, 6, 4, 9) into the order (3, 4, 6, 9, 10). How do we do it? We first scan the input data list (10, 3, 6, 4, 9) to find the smallest value in the list (3), and then scan the remaining input data (10, 6, 4, 9) to find the next smallest value (4), etc., until the complete list is sorted.

In fact, sorting can be a very difficult job. As the number of values to be sorted increases, the time required to perform the simple sort described above increases rapidly, since we must scan the input data set once for each value sorted. For very large data sets, this technique just takes too long to be practical. Even worse, how would we sort the data if there were too many numbers to fit into the main memory of the computer? The development of efficient sorting techniques for large data sets is an active area of research, and is the subject of whole courses all by itself.

In this example, we will confine ourselves to the simplest possible algorithm to illustrate the concept of sorting. This simplest algorithm is called the **selection sort.** It is just a computer implementation of the mental math described above. The basic algorithm for the selection sort is:

1. Scan the list of numbers to be sorted to locate the smallest value in the list. Place that value at the front of the list by swapping it with the value currently at the front of the list. If the value at the front of the list is already the smallest value, then do nothing.

2. Scan the list of numbers from position 2 to the end to locate the next smallest value in the list. Place that value in position 2 of the list by swapping it with the value currently at that position. If the value in position 2 is already the next smallest value, then do nothing.

3. Scan the list of numbers from position 3 to the end to locate the third smallest value in the list. Place that value in position 3 of the list by swapping it with the value currently at that position. If the value in position 3 is already the third smallest value, then do nothing.

4. Repeat this process until the next-to-last position in the list is reached. After the next-to-last position in the list has been processed, the sort is complete.

Note that if we are sorting N values, this sorting algorithm requires $N - 1$ scans through the data to accomplish the sort.

This process is illustrated in Figure 6-12. Since there are five values in the data set to be sorted, we will make four scans through the data. During the first pass through the entire data set, the minimum value is three, so the three is swapped with the ten that was in position one. Pass two searches for the minimum value in positions two through five. That minimum is four, so the four is swapped with the ten in position two. Pass three searches for the minimum value in positions three through five. That minimum is six, which is already in position three, so no swapping is required. Finally, pass four searches for the minimum value in positions four through five. That minimum is nine, so the nine is swapped with the ten in position four, and the sort is completed.

Programming Pitfalls

The selection sort algorithm is the easiest sorting algorithm to understand, but it is computationally inefficient. *It should never be applied to sort really large data sets* (say, sets with more than 1000 elements). Over the years, computer scientists have developed much more efficient sorting algorithms. We will encounter one such algorithm (the *heapsort algorithm*) in Exercise 7-35.

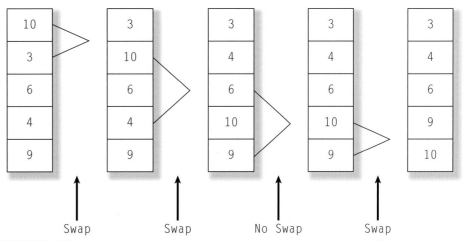

Swap   Swap   No Swap   Swap

FIGURE 6-12
An example problem demonstrating the selection sort algorithm.

6

We will now develop a program to read in a data set from a file, sort it into ascending order, and display the sorted data set.

SOLUTION
This program must be able to ask the user for the name of the file to be sorted, open that file, read the input data, sort the data, and write out the sorted data. The design process for this problem is given below.

1. **State the problem.**
   We have not yet specified the type of data to be sorted. If the data is real, then the problem may be stated as follows:

   > Develop a program to read an arbitrary number of real input data values from a user-supplied file, sort the data into ascending order, and write the sorted data to the standard output device.

2. **Define the inputs and outputs.**
   There are two types of inputs to this program:
   (*a*) A character string containing the file name of the input data file. This string will come from the standard input device.
   (*b*) The real data values in the file.
   The outputs from this program are the sorted real data values written to the standard output device.

3. **Describe the algorithm.**
   This program can be broken down into five major steps

   ```
   Get the input file name
   Open the input file
   Read the input data into an array
   Sort the data in ascending order
   Write the sorted data
   ```

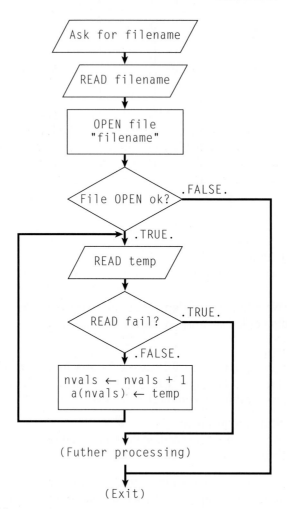

FIGURE 6-13
Flowchart for reading values to sort from an input file.

    The first three major steps of the program are to get the name of the input file, to open the file, and to read in the data. We must prompt the user for the input file name, read in the name, and open the file. If the file open is successful, we must read in the data, keeping track of the number of values that have been read. Since we don't know how many data values to expect, a while loop is appropriate for the READ. A flowchart for these steps is shown in Figure 6-13, and the detailed pseudocode is shown below:

```
Prompt user for the input file name "filename"
Read the file name "filename"
OPEN file "filename"
IF OPEN is successful THEN
    WHILE
        Read value into temp
        IF read not successful EXIT
        nvals ← nvals + 1
```

```
          a(nvals) ← temp
        End of WHILE
        . . .
        . . .                          (Insert sorting step here)
        . . .                          (Insert writing step here)
        End of IF
```

Next we have to sort the data. We will need to make `nvals-1` passes through the data, finding the smallest remaining value each time. We will use a pointer to locate the smallest value in each pass. Once the smallest value is found, it will be swapped to the top of the list of it is not already there. A flowchart for these steps is shown in Figure 6-14, and the detailed pseudocode is shown below:

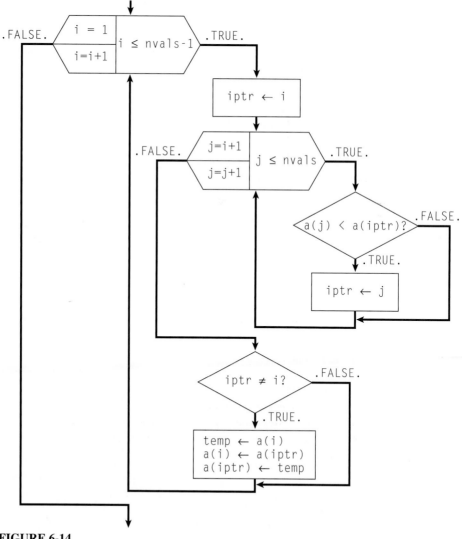

FIGURE 6-14
Flowchart for sorting values with a selection sort.

6

```
DO for i = 1 to nvals-1

    ! Find the minimum value in a(i) through a(nvals)
    iptr ← i
    DO for j == i+1 to nvals
        IF a(j) < a(iptr) THEN
            iptr ← j
        END of IF
    END of DO
    ! iptr now points to the min value, so swap a(iptr) with
    ! a(i) if iptr /= i.
    IF i /= iptr THEN
        temp ← a(i)
        a(i) ← a(iptr)
        a(iptr) ← temp
    END of IF
END of DO
```

The final step is writing out the sorted values. No refinement of the pseudocode is required for that step. The final pseudocode is the combination of the reading, sorting and writing steps.

4. **Turn the algorithm into Fortran statements.**

The resulting Fortran program is shown in Figure 6-15.

FIGURE 6-15
A program to read values from an input data file, and to sort them into ascending order.

```
PROGRAM sort1
!
!  Purpose:
!    To read in a real input data set, sort it into ascending order
!    using the selection sort algorithm, and to write the sorted
!    data to the standard output device.
!
!  Record of revisions:
!      Date        Programmer          Description of change
!      ====        ==========          =====================
!    11/15/06    S. J. Chapman         Original code
!
IMPLICIT NONE

! Data dictionary: declare constants
INTEGER, PARAMETER :: MAX_SIZE = 10   ! Maximum input data set size

! Data dictionary: declare variable types & definitions
REAL, DIMENSION(MAX_SIZE) :: a   ! Data array to sort
CHARACTER(len=20) :: filename    ! Input data file name
INTEGER :: i                     ! Loop index
INTEGER :: iptr                  ! Pointer to smallest value
INTEGER :: j                     ! Loop index
INTEGER :: nvals = 0             ! Number of data values to sort
INTEGER :: status                ! I/O status: 0 for success
```

(continued)

(continued)

```
REAL :: temp                       ! Temporary variable for swapping

! Get the name of the file containing the input data.
WRITE (*,1000)
1000 FORMAT (1X,'Enter the file name with the data to be sorted: ')
READ (*,'(A20)') filename

! Open input data file. Status is OLD because the input data must
! already exist.
OPEN ( UNIT=9, FILE=filename, STATUS='OLD', ACTION='READ', &
       IOSTAT=status )

! Was the OPEN successful?
fileopen: IF ( status == 0 ) THEN    ! Open successful

   ! The file was opened successfully, so read the data to sort
   ! from it, sort the data, and write out the results.
   ! First read in data.
   DO
      READ (9, *, IOSTAT=status) temp     ! Get value
      IF ( status /= 0 ) EXIT             ! Exit on end of data
      nvals = nvals + 1                   ! Bump count
      a(nvals) = temp                     ! Save value in array
   END DO

   ! Now, sort the data.
   outer: DO i = 1, nvals-1

      ! Find the minimum value in a(i) through a(nvals)
      iptr = i
      inner: DO j = i+1, nvals
         minval: IF ( a(j) < a(iptr) ) THEN
            iptr = j
         END IF minval
      END DO inner

      ! iptr now points to the minimum value, so swap a(iptr) with
      ! a(i) if i /= iptr.
      swap: IF ( i /= iptr ) THEN
         temp = a(i)
         a(i) = a(iptr)
         a(iptr) = temp
      END IF swap

   END DO outer

   ! Now write out the sorted data.
   WRITE (*,'(1X,A)') 'The sorted output data values are: '
   WRITE (*,'(4X,F10.4)') ( a(i), i = 1, nvals )

ELSE fileopen
```

(continued)

(concluded)

```
    ! Else file open failed. Tell user.
    WRITE (*,1050) status
    1050 FORMAT (1X,'File open failed--status = ', I6)
```

```
END IF fileopen
```

```
END PROGRAM sort1
```

5. **Test the program.**

To test this program, we will create an input data file and run the program with it. The data set will contain a mixture of positive and negative numbers as well as at least one duplicated value to see if the program works properly under those conditions. The following data set will be placed in file INPUT2:

```
    13.3
    12.
    -3.0
     0.
     4.0
     6.6
     4.
    -6.
```

Running this file through the program yields the following result:

```
C:\book\chap6>sort1
Enter the file name containing the data to be sorted:
input2
The sorted output data values are:
     -6.0000
     -3.0000
       .0000
      4.0000
      4.0000
      6.6000
     12.0000
     13.3000
```

The program gives the correct answers for our test data set. Note that it works for both positive and negative numbers as well as for repeated numbers.

To be certain that our program works properly, we must test it for every possible type of input data. This program worked properly for the test input data set, but will it work for *all* input data sets? Study the code now and see if you can spot any flaws before continuing to the next paragraph.

The program has a major flaw that must be corrected. If there are more than 10 values in the input data file, this program will attempt to store input data in memory locations a(11), a(12), etc., which have not been allocated in the program (this is an out-of-bounds or **array overflow** condition). If bounds checking is turned on, the program will abort when we try to write to a(11). If bounds checking is not turned on, the results are unpredictable and vary from computer to computer. This program must be rewritten to prevent it from attempting to write into locations beyond the end of the allocated array. This can be done by checking to see if the number of values exceeds max_size before storing each number into array a. The corrected flowchart for reading in the data is shown in Figure 6-16, and the corrected program is shown in Figure 6-17.

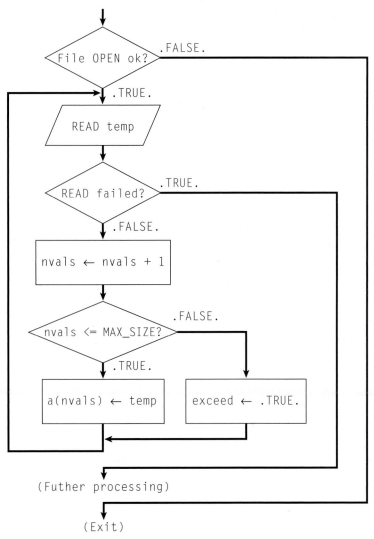

FIGURE 6-16
Corrected flowchart for reading the values to sort from an input file without causing an array overflow.

FIGURE 6-17
A corrected version of the sort program that detects array overflows.

```
PROGRAM sort2
!
! Purpose:
!   To read in a real input data set, sort it into ascending order
!   using the selection sort algorithm, and to write the sorted
!   data to the standard output device.
!
! Record of revisions:
!     Date        Programmer       Description of change
!     ====        ==========       =====================
!   11/15/06    S. J. Chapman    Original code
! 1. 11/16/06   S. J. Chapman    Modified to protect against
!                                array overflow.
!
IMPLICIT NONE

! Data dictionary: declare constants
INTEGER, PARAMETER :: MAX_SIZE = 10 ! Maximum input data set size

! Data dictionary: declare variable types & definitions
REAL, DIMENSION(MAX_SIZE) :: a       ! Data array to sort
LOGICAL :: exceed = .FALSE.          ! Logical indicating that array
                                     ! limits are exceeded.
CHARACTER(len=20) :: filename        ! Input data file name
INTEGER :: i                         ! Loop index
INTEGER :: iptr                      ! Pointer to smallest value
INTEGER :: j                         ! Loop index
INTEGER :: nvals = 0                 ! Number of data values to sort
INTEGER :: status                    ! I/O status: 0 for success
REAL :: temp                         ! Temporary variable for swapping

! Get the name of the file containing the input data.
WRITE (*,1000)
1000 FORMAT (1X,'Enter the file name with the data to be sorted: ')
READ (*,'(A20)') filename

! Open input data file. Status is OLD because the input data must
! already exist.
OPEN ( UNIT=9, FILE=filename, STATUS='OLD', ACTION='READ', &
       IOSTAT=status )

! Was the OPEN successful?
fileopen: IF ( status ==  0 ) THEN       ! Open successful

   ! The file was opened successfully, so read the data to sort
   ! from it, sort the data, and write out the results.
   ! First read in data.
   DO
       READ (9, *, IOSTAT=status) temp           ! Get value
```

(continued)

(concluded)

```
    IF ( status /= 0 ) EXIT                    ! Exit on end of data
    nvals = nvals + 1                          ! Bump count
    size: IF ( nvals <=  MAX_SIZE ) THEN       ! Too many values?
       a(nvals) = temp                         ! No: Save value in array
    ELSE
       exceed = .TRUE.                          ! Yes: Array overflow
    END IF size
END DO

! Was the array size exceeded? If so, tell user and quit.
toobig: IF ( exceed ) THEN
    WRITE (*,1010) nvals, MAX_SIZE
    1010 FORMAT (' Maximum array size exceeded: ', I6, ' > ', I6 )
ELSE toobig

    ! Limit not exceeded: sort the data.
    outer: DO i = 1, nvals-1

        ! Find the minimum value in a(i) through a(nvals)
        iptr = i
        inner: DO j = i+1, nvals
           minval: IF ( a(j) < a(iptr) ) THEN
              iptr = j
           END IF minval
        END DO inner

        ! iptr now points to the minimum value, so swap a(iptr) with
        ! a(i) if i /= iptr.
        swap: IF ( i /= iptr ) THEN
           temp     = a(i)
           a(i)     = a(iptr)
           a(iptr) = temp
        END IF swap

    END DO outer

    ! Now write out the sorted data.
    WRITE (*,'(A)') ' The sorted output data values are: '
    WRITE (*,'(4X,F10.4)') ( a(i), i = 1, nvals )

  END IF toobig

ELSE fileopen

    ! Else file open failed. Tell user.
    WRITE (*,1050) status
    1050 FORMAT (1X,'File open failed--status = ', I6)

END IF fileopen

END PROGRAM sort2
```

6

In the test for array overflow conditions, we have used a logical variable `exceed`. If the next value to be read into the array would result on an array overflow, then `exceed` is set to true, and the value is not stored. When all values have been read from the input file, the program checks to see if the array size would have been exceeded. If so, it writes out an error message and quits. If not, it reads in and sorts the numbers.

This program also illustrates the proper use of named constants to allow the size of a program to be changed easily. The size of array `a` is set by parameter `MAX_SIZE`, and the test for array overflow within the code also uses parameter `MAX_SIZE`. The maximum sorting capacity of this program could be changed from 10 to 1000 by simply modifying the definition of the named constant `MAX_SIZE` at the top of the program.

EXAMPLE 6-4   *The Median:*

In Chapter 4 we examined two common statistical measures of data: averages (or means) and standard deviations. Another common statistical measure of data is the median. The median of a data set is the value such that half of the numbers in the data set are larger than the value and half of the numbers in the data set are smaller than the value. If there are an even number of values in the data set, then there cannot be a value exactly in the middle. In that case, the median is usually defined as the average of the two elements in the middle. The median value of a data set is often close to the average value of the data set, but not always. For example, consider the following data set:

```
  1
  2
  3
  4
100
```

The average or mean of this data set is 22, while the median of this data set is 3!

An easy way to compute the median of a data set is to sort it into ascending order, and then to select the value in the middle of the data set as the median. If there are an even number of values in the data set, then average the two middle values to get the median.

Write a program to calculate the mean, median, and standard deviation of an input data set that is read from a user-specified file.

SOLUTION
This program must be able to read in an arbitrary number of measurements from a file, and then calculate the mean and standard deviation of those measurements.

1. **State the problem.**

    Calculate the average, median, and standard deviation of a set of measurements that are read from a user-specified input file, and write those values out on the standard output device.

2. **Define the inputs and outputs.**

    There are two types of inputs to this program:

    (*a*) A character string containing the file name of the input data file. This string will come from the standard input device.
    (*b*) The real data values in the file.

    The outputs from this program are the average, median, and standard deviation of the input data set. They are written to the standard output device.

3. **Describe the algorithm.**

    This program can be broken down into six major steps:

    ```
    Get the input file name
    Open the input file
    Read the input data into an array
    Sort the data in ascending order
    Calculate the average, mean, and standard deviation
    Write average, median, and standard deviation
    ```

    The detailed pseudocode for the first four steps is similar to that of the previous example:

    ```
    Initialize variables.
    Prompt user for the input file name "filename"
    Read the file name "filename"
    OPEN file "filename"
    IF OPEN is successful THEN
        WHILE
            Read value into temp
            IF read not successful EXIT
            nvals ← nvals + 1
            IF nvals <=  max_size then
                a(nvals) ← temp
            ELSE
              exceed ← .TRUE.
        End of IF
    End of WHILE

    ! Notify user if array size exceeded.
    IF array size exceeded then
        Write out message to user
    ELSE
        ! Sort the data
        DO for i = 1 to nvals-1

            ! Find the minimum value in a(i) through a(nvals)
            iptr ← i
    ```

6

```
         DO for j = i+1 to nvals
            IF a(j) < a(iptr) THEN
               iptr ← j
            END of IF
         END of DO (for j = i+1 to nvals)

         ! iptr now points to the min value, so swap A(iptr)
         ! with a(i) if iptr /= i.
         IF i /= iptr THEN
            temp ← a(i)
            a(i) ← a(iptr)
            a(iptr) ← temp
         END of IF
      END of DO (for i = 1 to nvals-1)

      (Add code here)

   End of IF (array size exceeded ... )

   End of IF (open successful ... )
```

The fifth step is to calculate the required average, median, and standard deviation. To do this, we must first accumulate some statistics on the data (Σx and Σx^2), and then apply the definitions of average, median, and standard deviation given previously. The pseudocode for this step is:

```
DO for i = 1 to nvals
   sum_x ← sum_x + a(i)
   sum_x2 ← sum_x2 + a(i)**2
End of DO
IF nvals >=  2 THEN
   x_bar ← sum_x / real(nvals)
   std_dev ← sqrt((real(nvals)*sum_x2-
            sum_x**2)/(real(nvals)*real(nvals-1)))
   IF nvals is an even number THEN
      median ← (a(nvals/2) + a(nvals/2+1)) / 2.
   ELSE
      median ← a(nvals/2+1)
   END of IF
END of IF
```

We will decide if nvals is an even number by using the modulo function mod(nvals,2). If nvals is even, this function will return a 0; if nvals is odd, it will return a 1. Finally, we must write out the results.

```
   Write out average, median, standard deviation, and no. of points
```

4. **Turn the algorithm into Fortran statements.**
   The resulting Fortran program is shown in Figure 6-18.

FIGURE 6-18

A program to read in values from an input data file, and to calculate their mean, median, and standard deviation.

```
PROGRAM stats_4
!
!    Purpose:
!      To calculate mean, median, and standard deviation of an input
!      data set read from a file.
!
!    Record of revisions:
!        Date         Programmer          Description of change
!        ====         ==========          =====================
!      11/17/06     S. J. Chapman         Original code
!
IMPLICIT NONE

! Data dictionary: declare constants
INTEGER, PARAMETER :: MAX_SIZE = 100 ! Max data size

! Data dictionary: declare variable types & definitions
REAL, DIMENSION(MAX_SIZE) :: a        ! Data array to sort
LOGICAL :: exceed = .FALSE.           ! Logical indicating that array
                                      ! limits are exceeded.
CHARACTER(len=20) :: filename         ! Input data file name
INTEGER :: i                          ! Loop index
INTEGER :: iptr                       ! Pointer to smallest value
INTEGER :: j                          ! Loop index
REAL :: median                        ! The median of the input samples
INTEGER :: nvals = 0                  ! Number of data values to sort
INTEGER :: status                     ! I/O status: 0 for success
REAL :: std_dev                       ! Standard deviation of input samples
REAL :: sum_x = 0.                    ! Sum of input values
REAL :: sum_x2 = 0.                   ! Sum of input values squared
REAL :: temp                          ! Temporary variable for swapping
REAL :: x_bar                         ! Average of input values

! Get the name of the file containing the input data.
WRITE (*,1000)
1000 FORMAT (1X,'Enter the file name with the data to be sorted: ')
READ (*,'(A20)') filename

! Open input data file. Status is OLD because the input data must
! already exist.
OPEN ( UNIT=9, FILE=filename, STATUS='OLD', ACTION='READ', &
       IOSTAT=status )

! Was the OPEN successful?
fileopen: IF ( status == 0 ) THEN      ! Open successful
```

(continued)

(continued)

```
    ! The file was opened successfully, so read the data to sort
    ! from it, sort the data, and write out the results.
    ! First read in data.
    DO
        READ (9, *, IOSTAT=status) temp         ! Get value
        IF ( status /= 0 ) EXIT                 ! Exit on end of data
        nvals = nvals + 1                       ! Bump count
        size: IF ( nvals <=  MAX_SIZE ) THEN    ! Too many values?
            a(nvals) = temp                     ! No: Save value in array
        ELSE
            exceed = .TRUE.                     ! Yes: Array overflow
        END IF size
    END DO

    ! Was the array size exceeded? If so, tell user and quit.
    toobig: IF ( exceed ) THEN
        WRITE (*,1010) nvals, MAX_SIZE
        1010 FORMAT (' Maximum array size exceeded: ', I6, ' > ', I6 )
    ELSE

        ! Limit not exceeded: sort the data.
        outer: DO i = 1, nvals-1

            ! Find the minimum value in a(i) through a(nvals)
            iptr = i
            inner: DO j = i+1, nvals
                minval: IF ( a(j) < a(iptr) ) THEN
                    iptr = j
                END IF minval
            END DO inner

            ! iptr now points to the minimum value, so swap A(iptr)
            ! with a(i) if i /= iptr.
            swap: IF ( i /= iptr ) THEN
                temp = a(i)
                a(i) = a(iptr)
                a(iptr) = temp
            END IF swap

        END DO outer

        ! The data is now sorted. Accumulate sums to calculate
        ! statistics.
        sums: DO i = 1, nvals
        sum_x = sum_x + a(i)
        sum_x2 = sum_x2 + a(i)**2
    END DO sums

    ! Check to see if we have enough input data.
```

(continued)

(concluded)

```
         enough: IF ( nvals < 2 ) THEN

            ! Insufficient data.
            WRITE (*,*) ' At least 2 values must be entered.'
         ELSE

            ! Calculate the mean, median, and standard deviation
            x_bar   = sum_x / real(nvals)
            std_dev = sqrt( (real(nvals) * sum_x2 - sum_x**2) &
                     / (real(nvals) * real(nvals-1)) )
            even: IF ( mod(nvals,2) == 0 ) THEN
               median = ( a(nvals/2) + a(nvals/2+1) ) / 2.
            ELSE
               median = a(nvals/2+1)
            END IF even

            ! Tell user.
            WRITE (*,*) 'The mean of this data set is:   ', x_bar
            WRITE (*,*) 'The median of this data set is: ', median
            WRITE (*,*) 'The standard deviation is:      ', std_dev
            WRITE (*,*) 'The number of data points is:   ', nvals

         END IF enough

      END IF toobig

   ELSE fileopen

      ! Else file open failed. Tell user.
      WRITE (*,1050) status
      1050 FORMAT (1X,'File open failed--status = ', I6)

   END IF fileopen

   END PROGRAM stats_4
```

5. Test the program.

To test this program, we will calculate the answers by hand for a simple data set, and then compare the answers to the results of the program. If we use five input values: 5, 3, 4, 1, and 9, then the mean and standard deviation would be

$$\bar{x} = \frac{1}{N} \sum_{i=1}^{N} x_i = \frac{1}{5} 22 = 4.4$$

$$s = \sqrt{\frac{N \sum_{i=1}^{N} x_i^2 - \left(\sum_{i=1}^{N} x_i \right)^2}{N(N-1)}} = 2.966$$

Median = 4

If these values are placed in the file INPUT4 and the program is run with that file as an input, the results are

```
C:\book\chap6>stats_4
Enter the file name containing the input data:
input4
 The mean of this data set is:        4.400000
 The median of this data set is:      4.000000
 The standard deviation is:           2.966479
 The number of data points is:            5
```

The program gives the correct answers for our test data set.

Note the use of names on loops and branches in the above program. These names help us to keep the loops and branches straight. This becomes more and more important as programs get larger. Even in this simple program, loops and branches are nested four deep at some points!

6.6
WHEN SHOULD YOU USE AN ARRAY?

We have now learned *how* to use arrays in our Fortran programs, but we have not yet learned *when* to use them. At this point in a typical Fortran course, many students are tempted to use arrays to solve problems whether they are needed or not, just because they know how to do so. How can we decide whether or not it makes sense to use an array in a particular problem?

In general, *if much or all of the input data must be in memory at the same time in order to solve a problem efficiently, then the use of arrays to hold that data is appropriate for that problem.* Otherwise, arrays are not needed. For example, let's contrast the statistics programs that we have written in Examples 4-1 and 6-4. Example 4-1 calculated the mean and standard deviation of a data set, while Example 6-4 calculated the mean, median, and standard deviation of a data set.

Recall that the equations for the mean and standard deviation of a data set are

$$\bar{x} = \frac{1}{N} \sum_{i=1}^{N} x_i \tag{4-1}$$

and

$$s = \sqrt{\frac{N \sum_{i=1}^{N} x_i^2 - \left(\sum_{i=1}^{N} x_i \right)^2}{N(N-1)}} \tag{4-2}$$

The sums in Equations 4-1 and 4-2 that are required to find the mean and standard deviation can be formed easily as data values are read in one by one. There is no need to wait until all of the data is read before starting to build the sums. Therefore, a program to calculate the mean and standard deviation of a data set does not need to use arrays. You *could* use an array to hold all of the input values before calculating the mean and standard deviation, but since the array is not necessary, you should not do so. Example 4-1 works fine, and is built entirely without arrays.

On the other hand, finding the median of a data set requires that the data be sorted into ascending order. Since sorting requires all data to be in memory, a program that calculates the median must use an array to hold all of the input data before the calculations start. Therefore, Example 6-4 uses an array to hold its input data.

What's wrong with using an array within a program even if it is not needed? There are two major problems associated with using unnecessary arrays:

1. *Unnecessary arrays waste memory.* Unnecessary arrays can eat up a lot of memory, making a program larger than it needs to be. A large program requires more memory to run it, which makes the computer that it runs on more expensive. In some cases, the extra size may make it impossible to run on a particular computer at all.

2. *Unnecessary arrays restrict program capabilities.* To understand this point, let's consider an example program that calculates the mean and standard deviation of a data set. If the program is designed with a 1000-element static input array, then it will work only for data sets with up to 1000 elements. If we encounter a data set with more than 1000 elements, the program would have to be recompiled and relinked with a larger array size. On the other hand, a program that calculates the mean and standard deviation of a data set as the values are input has no upper limit on data set size.

Good Programming Practice
Do not use arrays to solve a problem unless they are actually needed.

6.7
SUMMARY

In Chapter 6, we presented an introduction to arrays and to their use in Fortran programs. An array is a group of variables, all of the same type, that are referred to by a single name. An individual variable within the array is called an array element. Individual array elements are addressed by means of one or more (up to seven) subscripts.

Arrays with one subscript (rank-1 arrays) were discussed in this chapter. Arrays with more than one subscript will be discussed in Chapter 8.

An array is declared with a type declaration statement by naming the array and specifying the maximum (and, optionally, the minimum) subscript values with the `DIMENSION` attribute. The compiler uses the declared subscript ranges to reserve space in the computer's memory to hold the array.

As with any variable, an array must be initialized before use. An array may be initialized at compile time using array constructors in the type declaration statements, or at run time using array constructors, `DO` loops, or Fortran `READ`s.

Individual array elements may be used freely in a Fortran program just like any other variable. They may appear in assignment statements on either side of the equal sign. Entire arrays and array sections may also be used in calculations and assignment statements as long as the arrays are conformable with each other. Arrays are conformable if they have the same number of dimensions (rank) and the same extent in each dimension. A scalar is also conformable with any array. An operation between two conformable arrays is performed on an element-by-element basis. Scalar values are also conformable with arrays.

Arrays are especially useful for storing data values that change as a function of some variable (time, location, etc.). Once the data values are stored in an array, they can be easily manipulated to derive statistics or other information that may be desired.

6.7.1 Summary of Good Programming Practice

The following guidelines should be adhered to when working with arrays.

1. Before writing a program that uses arrays, you should decide whether an array is really needed to solve the problem or not. If arrays are not needed, don't use them!

2. All array sizes should be declared by using named constants. If the sizes are declared by using named constants, and if those same named constants are used in any size tests within the program, then it will be very easy to modify the maximum capacity of the program at a later time.

3. All arrays should be initialized before use. The results of using an uninitialized array are unpredictable and vary from processor to processor.

4. The most common problem in programming with arrays is attempting to read from or write to locations outside the bounds of the array. To detect these problems, the bounds checking option of your compiler should always be turned on during program testing and debugging. Because bounds checking slows down the execution of a program, the bounds checking option may be turned off once debugging is completed.

6.7.2 Summary of Fortran Statements and Constructs

Type Declaration Statements with Arrays:

```
type, DIMENSION( [i1:]i2 ) :: array1, ...
```

Examples:

```
REAL, DIMENSION(100) :: array
INTEGER, DIMENSION(-5:5) :: i
```

Description:
These type declaration statements declare both type and the size of an array.

6

Implied DO loop structure:

```
READ  (unit, format) (arg1, arg2, ... , index = istart, iend, incr)
WRITE (unit, format) (arg1, arg2, ... , index = istart, iend, incr)
(/ (arg1, arg2, ... , index = istart, iend, incr) /)
```

Examples:

```
WRITE (*,*) ( array(i), i = 1, 10 )
INTEGER, DIMENSION(100) :: values
values = (/ (i, i=1, 100) /)
```

Description:
The implied DO loop is used to repeat the values in an argument list a known number of times. The values in the argument list may be functions of the DO loop index variable. During the first iteration of the DO loop, the variable *index* is set to the value *istart*. *index* is incremented by *incr* in each successive loop until its value exceeds *iend*, at which time the loop terminates.

6.7.3 Exercises

6-1. How may arrays be declared?

6-2. What is the difference between an array and an array element?

6-3. Execute the following Fortran program on your computer with both bounds checking turned on and bounds checking turned off. What happens in each case?

```fortran
PROGRAM bounds
IMPLICIT NONE
REAL, DIMENSION(5) :: test = (/ 1., 2., 3., 4., 5. /)
REAL, DIMENSION(5) :: test1
INTEGER :: i
DO i = 1, 6
    test1(i) = SQRT(test(i))
    WRITE (*,100) 'SQRT(',test(i), ') = ', test1(i)
    100 FORMAT (1X,A,F6.3,A,F14.4)
END DO
END PROGRAM bounds
```

6-4. Determine the shape and size of the arrays specified by the following declaration statements, and the valid subscript range for each dimension of each array.

(*a*) `CHARACTER(len=80), DIMENSION(60) :: line`

(*b*)
```fortran
INTEGER, PARAMETER :: ISTART = 32
INTEGER, PARAMETER :: ISTOP = 256
INTEGER, DIMENSION(ISTART:ISTOP) :: char
```

(*c*)
```fortran
INTEGER, PARAMETER :: NUM_CLASS = 3
INTEGER, PARAMETER :: NUM_STUDENT = 35
LOGICAL, DIMENSION(NUM_STUDENT,NUM_CLASS) :: passfail
```

6-5. Determine which of the following Fortran program fragments are valid. For each valid statement, specify what will happen in the program. (Assume default typing for any variables that are not explicitly typed within the program fragments.)

(*a*)
```fortran
INTEGER, DIMENSION(100) :: icount, jcount
. . .
icount = (/ (i, i=1, 100) /)
jcount = icount + 1
```

(*b*)
```fortran
REAL, DIMENSION(10) :: value
value(1:10:2) = (/ 5., 4., 3., 2., 1. /)
value(2:11:2) = (/ 10., 9., 8., 7., 6. /)
WRITE (*,100) value
100 FORMAT ('1','Value = ',/,(F10.2))
```

(*c*)
```fortran
INTEGER, DIMENSION(6) :: a
INTEGER, DIMENSION(6) :: b
a = (/1,-3,0,-5,-9,3/)
b = (/-6,6,0,5,2,-1/)
WRITE (*,*) a > b
```

6-6. What is meant by each of the following array terms? (*a*) size, (*b*) shape, (*c*) extent, (*d*) rank, (*e*) conformable.

6-7. Given an array `my_array` defined as and containing the values shown below, determine whether each of the following array sections is valid. Specify the shape and contents of each valid array section.

```
REAL,DIMENSION(-2:7) :: my_array = [-3 -2 -1 0 1 2 3 4 5 6]
```

(*a*) `my_array(-3,3)`

(*b*) `my_array(-2:2)`

(*c*) `my_array(1:5:2)`

(*d*) `INTEGER, DIMENSION(5) :: list = (/ -2, 1, 2, 4, 2 /)`
`my_array(list)`

6-8. What will be the output from each of the `WRITE` statements in the following program? Why is the output of the two statements different?

```
PROGRAM test_output
IMPLICIT NONE
INTEGER, DIMENSION(0:7) :: my_data
INTEGER :: i, j
my_data = (/ 1, 2, 3, 4, 5, 6, 7, 8 /)

DO i = 0,1
    WRITE (*,100) (my_data(4*i+j), j=0,3)
    100 FORMAT (6(1X,I4))
END DO
WRITE (*,100) ((my_data(4*i+j), j=0,3), i=0,1)
END PROGRAM test_output
```

6-9. An input data file `INPUT1` contains the following values:

```
27   17   10    8    6
11   13  -11   12  -21
-1    0    0    6   14
-16  11   21   26  -16
04   99  -99   17    2
```

Assume that file `INPUT1` has been opened on i/o unit 8, and that array `values` is a 16-element integer array, all of whose elements have been initialized to zero. What will be the contents of array `values` after each of the following `READ` statements has been executed?

(*a*) `DO i = 1, 4`
`READ (8,*) (values(4*(i-1)+j), j = 1, 4)`
`END DO`

(*b*) `READ (8,*) ((values(4*(i-1)+j), j = 1, 4), i = 1, 4)`

(*c*) `READ (8,'(4I6)') ((values(4*(i-1)+j), j = 1, 4), i = 1, 4)`

6-10. Polar to Rectangular Conversion A *scalar quantity* is a quantity that can be represented by a single number. For example, the temperature at a given location is a scalar. In contrast, a *vector* is a quantity that has both a magnitude and a direction associated with it. For example, the velocity of an automobile is a vector, since it has both a magnitude and a direction.

Vectors can be defined either by a magnitude and a direction, or by the components of the vector projected along the axes of a rectangular coordinate system. The two representations are equivalent. For two-dimensional vectors, we can convert back and forth between the representations using the following equations.

$$\mathbf{V} = V\angle\theta = V_x\mathbf{i} + V_y\mathbf{j}$$
$$V_x = V\,\cos\theta$$
$$V_y = V\,\sin\theta$$
$$V = \sqrt{V_x^2 + V_y^2}$$
$$\theta = \tan^{-1}\frac{V_y}{V_x}$$

where $\mathbf{i}$ and $\mathbf{j}$ are the unit vectors in the x and y directions respectively. The representation of the vector in Figure 6-19 in terms of magnitude and angle is known as *polar coordinates*, and the representation of the vector in terms of components along the axes is know as *rectangular coordinates*.

Write a program that reads the polar coordinates (magnitude and angle) of a two-dimensional vector into a rank-1 array polar (polar(1) will contain the magnitude V and polar(2) will contain the angle θ in degrees), and converts the vector from polar to rectangular form, storing the result in a rank-1 array rect. The first element of rect should contain the x component of the vector, and the second element should contain the y component of the vector. After the conversion, display the

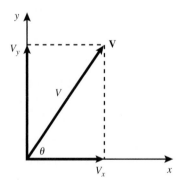

FIGURE 6-19
Representations of a vector.

contents of array `rect`. Test your program by converting the following polar vectors to rectangular form:

(a) $5\angle -36.87°$

(b) $10\angle 45°$

(c) $25\angle 233.13°$

6-11. Rectangular to Polar Conversion Write a program that reads the rectangular components of a two-dimensional vector into a rank-1 array `rect` (`rect(1)` will contain the component V_x and `rect(2)` will contain the component V_y), and converts the vector from rectangular to polar form, storing the result in a rank-1 array `polar`. The first element of `polar` should contain the magnitude of the vector, and the second element should contain the angle of the vector in degrees. After the conversion, display the contents of array `polar`. (*Hint:* Look up function ATAN2 in Appendix B.) Test your program by converting the following rectangular vectors to polar form:

(a) $3\mathbf{i} - 4\mathbf{j}$

(b) $5\mathbf{i} + 5\mathbf{j}$

(c) $-5\mathbf{i} + 12\mathbf{j}$

6-12. Assume that `values` is a 101-element array containing a list of measurements from a scientific experiment, which has been declared by the statement

```
REAL, DIMENSION(-50:50) :: values
```

Write the Fortran statements that would count the number of positive values, negative values, and zero values in the array, and write out a message summarizing how many values of each type were found.

6-13. Write Fortran statements that would print out every fifth value in the array `values` described in Exercise 6-12. The output should take the form

```
values(-50) = xxx.xxxx
values(-45) = xxx.xxxx
. . .
values( 50) = xxx.xxxx
```

6-14. Dot Product A three-dimensional vector can be represented in rectangular coordinates as

$$\mathbf{V} = V_x\mathbf{i} + V_y\mathbf{j} + V_z\mathbf{k}$$

where V_x is the component of vector $\mathbf{V}$ in the x direction, V_y is the component of vector $\mathbf{V}$ in the y direction, and V_z is the component of vector $\mathbf{V}$ in the z direction. Such a vector can be stored in a rank-1 array containing three elements, since there are three dimensions in the coordinate system. The same idea applies to an n-dimensional vector. An n-dimensional vector can be stored in a rank-1 array containing n elements. This is the reason why rank-1 arrays are sometimes called vectors.

One common mathematical operation between two vectors is the *dot product*. The dot product of two vectors $\mathbf{V}_1 = V_{x1}\,\mathbf{i} + V_{y1}\,\mathbf{j} + V_{z1}\,\mathbf{k}$ and $\mathbf{V}_2 = V_{x2}\,\mathbf{i} + V_{y2}\,\mathbf{j} + V_{z2}\,\mathbf{k}$ is a scalar quantity defined by the equation

$$\mathbf{V}_1 \bullet \mathbf{V}_2 = V_{x1}V_{x2} + V_{y1}V_{y2} + V_{z1}V_{z2}$$

Write a Fortran program that will read two vectors $\mathbf{V}_1$ and $\mathbf{V}_2$ into two one-dimensional arrays in computer memory, and then calculate their dot product according to the equation given above. Test your program by calculating the dot product of vectors $\mathbf{V}_1 = 5\mathbf{i} - 3\mathbf{j} + 2\mathbf{k}$ and $\mathbf{V}_2 = 2\mathbf{i} + 3\mathbf{j} + 4\mathbf{k}$.

6-15. Power Supplied to an Object If an object is being pushed by a force $\mathbf{F}$ at a velocity $\mathbf{v}$ (Figure 6-20), then the power supplied to the object by the force is given by the equation

$$P = \mathbf{F} \bullet \mathbf{v}$$

where the force $\mathbf{F}$ is measured in newtons, the velocity $\mathbf{v}$ is measured in meters per second, and the power P is measured in watts. Use the Fortran program written in Exercise 6-14 to calculate the power supplied by a force of $\mathbf{F} = 4\mathbf{i} + 3\mathbf{j} - 2\mathbf{k}$ newtons to an object moving with a velocity of $\mathbf{v} = 4\mathbf{i} - 2\mathbf{j} + 1\mathbf{k}$ meters per second.

6-16. Cross Product Another common mathematical operation between two vectors is the *cross product*. The cross product of two vectors $\mathbf{V}_1 = V_{x1}\,\mathbf{i} + V_{y1}\,\mathbf{j} + V_{z1}\,\mathbf{k}$ and $\mathbf{V}_2 = V_{x2}\,\mathbf{i} + V_{y2}\,\mathbf{j} + V_{z2}\,\mathbf{k}$ is a vector quantity defined by the equation

$$\mathbf{V}_1 \times \mathbf{V}_2 = (V_{y1}V_{z2} - V_{y2}V_{z1})\mathbf{i} + (V_{z1}V_{x2} - V_{z2}V_{x1})\mathbf{j} + (V_{x1}V_{y2} - V_{x2}V_{y1})\mathbf{k}$$

Write a Fortran program that will read two vectors $\mathbf{V}_1$ and $\mathbf{V}_2$ into arrays in computer memory, and then calculate their cross product according to the equation given above. Test your program by calculating the cross product of vectors $\mathbf{V}_1 = 5\mathbf{i} - 3\mathbf{j} + 2\mathbf{k}$ and $\mathbf{V}_2 = 2\mathbf{i} + 3\mathbf{j} + 4\mathbf{k}$.

6-17. Velocity of an Orbiting Object The vector angular velocity ω of an object moving with a velocity $\mathbf{v}$ at a distance $\mathbf{r}$ from the origin of the coordinate system (Figure 6-21) is given by the equation

$$\mathbf{v} = \mathbf{r} \times \omega$$

where $\mathbf{r}$ is the distance in meters, ω is the angular velocity in radians per second, and $\mathbf{v}$ is the velocity in meters per second. If the distance from the center of the earth to an orbiting satellite is $\mathbf{r} = 300{,}000\mathbf{i} + 400{,}000\mathbf{j} + 50{,}000\mathbf{k}$ meters, and the angular velocity of

FIGURE 6-20
A force $\mathbf{F}$ applied to an object moving with velocity $\mathbf{v}$.

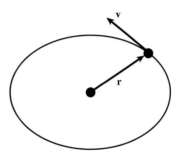

FIGURE 6-21
Velocity of an orbiting object.

the satellite is $\omega = -6 \times 10^{-3}\mathbf{i} + 2 \times 10^{-3}\mathbf{j} - 9 \times 10^{-4}\mathbf{k}$ radians per second, what is the velocity of the satellite in meters per second? Use the program written in the previous exercise to calculate the answer.

6-18. Program stat_4 in Example 6-4 will behave incorrectly if a user enters an invalid value in the input data set. For example, if the user enters the characters 1.o instead of 1.0 on a line, then the READ statement will return a nonzero status for that line. This nonzero status will be misinterpreted as the end of the data set, and only a portion of the input data will be processed. Modify the program to protect against invalid values in the input data file. If a bad value is encountered in the input data file, the program should display the line number containing the bad value, and skip it. The program should process all of the good values in the file, even those after a bad value.

6-19. In set theory, the union of two sets is the list of all elements that appear in *either* (or both) of the sets, and the intersection of the two sets is the list of all elements that appear in *both* sets only. For example, if one set A consists of the elements

$$A \in \{1\ 3\ 7\ 6\ 2\ 5\}$$

and a second set B consists of the elements

$$B \in \{-1\ 2\ 0\ 5\ 8\ 9\}$$

then the union of the two sets would be

$$A \cup B \in \{-1\ \ 0\ \ 1\ \ 2\ \ 3\ \ 5\ \ 6\ \ 7\ \ 8\ \ 9\}$$

and the intersection of the two sets would be

$$A \cap B \in \{2\ \ 5\}$$

Write a program that will read in two arrays of integers representing the elements of two sets from two different user-specified input files, and calculate both the union and the intersection of the two sets. Use arrays to contain the input sets, and also to build both the union and the intersection. Note that the input sets may not be sorted in order, so your algorithm must work regardless of the order in which set elements are entered.

Test your program on two files named inputA.dat and inputB.dat, containing the following two sets:

File inputA.dat: 0, 1, –3, 5, –11, 6, 8, 11, 17, 15

File inputB.dat: 0, –1, 3, 7, –6, 16, 5, 12, 21

6-20. The location of any point P in a three-dimensional space can be represented by a set of three values (x, y, z), where x is the distance along the x axis to the point, y is the distance along the y axis to the point, and z is the distance along the z axis to the point. Thus a point can be represented by a three-element vector containing the values x, y, and z. If two points P_1 and P_2 are represented by the values (x_1, y_1, z_1) and (x_2, y_2, z_2), then the distance between the points P_1 and P_2 can be calculated from the equation

$$\text{distance} = \sqrt{(x_1 - x_2)^2 + (y_1 - y_2)^2 + (z_1 - z_2)^2}$$

Write a Fortran program to read in two points (x_1, y_1, z_1) and (x_2, y_2, z_2), and to calculate the distance between them. Test your program by calculating the distance between the points $(-1, 4, 6)$ and $(1, 5, -2)$.

6

Introduction to Procedures

OBJECTIVES

- Learn how Fortran procedures help with good program design.
- Know the difference between a subroutine and a function.
- Be able to create and call subroutines.
- Understand and be able to use the `INTENT` attribute.
- Understand the pass-by-reference scheme for variable passing.
- Understand the differences among explicit-shape dummy arrays, assumed-shape dummy arrays, and assumed-size dummy arrays.
- Understand why assumed-size dummy arrays should never be used.
- Know how to share data between procedures by using modules.
- Understand explicit interfaces and why it is good to define procedures within modules.
- Be able to create and invoke user-defined functions.
- Know how to pass Fortran procedures as calling arguments to other procedures.

In Chapter 3, we learned the importance of good program design. The basic technique that we employed is **top-down design.** In top-down design, the programmer starts with a statement of the problem to be solved and the required inputs and outputs. Next, he or she describes the algorithm to be implemented by the program in broad outline, and applies *decomposition* to break the algorithm down into logical subdivisions called subtasks. Then, the programmer breaks down each subtask until he or she winds up with many small pieces, each of which does a simple, clearly understandable job. Finally, the individual pieces are turned into Fortran code.

Although we have followed this design process in our examples, the results have been somewhat restricted, because we have had to combine the final Fortran code generated for each subtask into a single large program. There has been no way to code, verify, and test each subtask independently before combining them into the final program.

Fortunately, Fortran has a special mechanism designed to make subtasks easy to develop and debug independently before building the final program. It is possible to code each subtask as a separate **program unit**[1] called an **external procedure,** and each external procedure can be compiled, tested, and debugged independently of all of the other subtasks (procedures) in the program.[2]

There are two kinds of external procedures in Fortran: **subroutines** and **function subprograms** (or just **functions**). Subroutines are procedures that are invoked by naming them in a separate CALL statement, and that can return multiple results through calling arguments. Function subprograms are procedures that are invoked by naming them in an expression, and whose result is a *single value* that is used in the evaluation of the expression. Both types of procedures will be described in this chapter.

Well-designed procedures enormously reduce the effort required on a large programming project. Their benefits include:

1. **Independent testing of subtasks.** Each subtask can be coded and compiled as an independent unit. The subtask can be tested separately to ensure that it performs properly by itself before combining it into the larger program. This step is known as **unit testing.** It eliminates a major source of problems before the final program is even built.

2. **Reusable code.** In many cases, the same basic subtask is needed in many parts of a program. For example, it may be necessary to sort a list of values into ascending order many different times within a program, or even in other programs. It is possible to design, code, test, and debug a *single* procedure to do the sorting, and then to reuse that procedure whenever sorting is required. This reusable code has two major advantages: it reduces the total programming effort required, and it simplifies debugging, since the sorting function needs to be debugged only once.

3. **Isolation from unintended side effects.** Subprograms communicate with the main programs that invoke them through a list of variables called an **argument list.** *The only variables in the main program that can be changed by the procedure are those in the argument list.* This is very important, since accidental programming mistakes can affect only the variables in the procedure in which the mistake occurred.

Once a large program is written and released, it has to be *maintained.* Program maintenance involves fixing bugs and modifying the program to handle new and unforeseen circumstances. The programmer who modifies a program during maintenance is often not the person who originally wrote it. In poorly written programs, it is common for the programmer modifying the program to make a change in one region of the code, and to have that change cause unintended side effects in a totally different part of the program. This happens because variable names are reused in different portions of the program. When the programmer changes the values left behind in some of the variables, those values are accidentally picked up and used in other portions of the code.

---

[1] A program unit is a *separately compiled* portion of a Fortran program. Main programs, subroutines, and function subprograms are all program units.

[2] Fortran also supports **internal procedures,** which are procedures entirely contained within another program unit. Internal procedures will be described in Chapter 9. Unless otherwise indicated, the references in this chapter to procedures, subroutines, and functions refer to external procedures, external subroutines, and external functions.

The use of well-designed procedures minimizes this problem by **data hiding.** All of the variables in the procedure except for those in the argument list are not visible to the main program, and therefore mistakes or changes in those variables cannot accidentally cause unintended side effects in the other parts of the program.

Good Programming Practice
Break large program tasks into procedures whenever practical to achieve the important benefits of independent component testing, reusability, and isolation from undesired side effects.

We will now examine the two different types of Fortran 95/2003 procedures: subroutines and functions.

■ 7.1
SUBROUTINES

A **subroutine** is a Fortran procedure that is invoked by naming it in a CALL statement and that receives its input values and returns its results through an **argument list.** The general form of a subroutine is

```
SUBROUTINE subroutine_name ( argument_list )
    . . .
        (Declaration section)
    . . .
        (Execution section)
    . . .
    RETURN
    END SUBROUTINE [name]
```

The SUBROUTINE statement marks the beginning of a subroutine. It specifies the name of the subroutine and the argument list associated with it. The subroutine name must follow standard Fortran conventions: it may be up to 31 characters long[3] and contain both alphabetic characters and digits, but the first character must be alphabetic. The argument list contains a list of the variables and/or arrays that are being passed from the calling program to the subroutine. These variables are called **dummy arguments,** since the subroutine does not actually allocate any memory for them. They are just placeholders for actual arguments that will be passed from the calling program unit when the subroutine is invoked.

Note that, like any Fortran program, a subroutine must have a declaration section and an execution section. When a program calls the subroutine, the execution of the calling program is suspended, and the execution section of the subroutine is run. When a RETURN or END SUBROUTINE statement is reached in the subroutine, the calling program starts running again at the line following the subroutine call.

F-2003 ONLY

---
[3] Up to 63 characters in Fortran 2003.

Each subroutine is an independent program unit, beginning with a SUBROUTINE statement and terminated by an END SUBROUTINE statement. It is compiled separately from the main program and from any other procedures. Because each program unit in a program is compiled separately, local variable names and statement labels may be reused in different routines without causing an error.

Any executable program unit may call a subroutine, including another subroutine. (However, a subroutine may not call itself unless it is declared to be **recursive;** recursion will be explained in Chapter 13.) To call a subroutine, the calling program uses a CALL statement. The form of a CALL statement is

CALL *subroutine_name (argument_list)*

where the order and type of the **actual arguments** in the argument list must match the order and type of the dummy arguments declared in the subroutine.

A simple example subroutine is shown in Figure 7-1. This subroutine calculates the hypotenuse of a right triangle from the lengths of the other two sides.

FIGURE 7-1

A simple subroutine to calculate the hypotenuse of a right triangle.

```
SUBROUTINE calc_hypotenuse ( side_1, side_2, hypotenuse )
!
!   Purpose:
!     To calculate the hypotenuse of a right triangle from the two
!     other sides.
!
!   Record of revisions:
!       Date          Programmer          Description of change
!       ====          ==========          =====================
!     11/18/06     S. J. Chapman         Original code
!
IMPLICIT NONE

! Data dictionary: declare calling parameter types & definitions
REAL, INTENT(IN) :: side_1          ! Length of side 1
REAL, INTENT(IN) :: side_2          ! Length of side 2
REAL, INTENT(OUT) :: hypotenuse     ! Length of hypotenuse

! Data dictionary: declare local variable types & definitions
REAL :: temp                        ! Temporary variable

! Calculate hypotenuse
temp = side_1**2 + side_2**2
hypotenuse = SQRT ( temp )

END SUBROUTINE calc_hypotenuse
```

This subroutine has three arguments in its dummy argument list. Arguments side_1 and side_2 are placeholders for real values containing the lengths of sides 1 and 2 of the triangle. These dummy arguments are used to pass data to the subroutine but are not changed inside the subroutine, so they are declared to be input values with the INTENT(IN) attribute. Dummy argument hypotenuse is a placeholder for a real variable that will receive the length of the hypotenuse of the triangle. The value of hypotenuse is set in the subroutine, so it is declared to be an output variable with the INTENT(OUT) attribute.

The variable temp is actually defined within the subroutine. It is used in the subroutine, but it is not accessible to any calling program. Variables that are used within a subroutine and that are not accessible by calling programs are called **local variables.**

Finally, the RETURN statement in the subroutine is optional. Execution automatically returns to the calling program when the END SUBROUTINE statement is reached. A RETURN statement is necessary only when we wish to return to the calling program before the end of the subroutine is reached. As a result, the RETURN statement is rarely used.

To test a subroutine, it is necessary to write a program called a **test driver program.** The test driver program is a small program that calls the subroutine with a sample data set for the specific purpose of testing it. A test driver program for subroutine calc_hypotenuse is shown in Figure 7-2.

FIGURE 7-2
A test driver program for subroutine calc_hypotenuse.

```
PROGRAM test_hypotenuse
!
!  Purpose:
!    Program to test the operation of subroutine calc_hypotenuse.
!
!  Record of revisions:
!    Date        Programmer          Description of change
!    ====        ==========          =====================
!    11/18/06    S. J. Chapman       Original code
!
IMPLICIT NONE

! Data dictionary: declare variable types & definitions
REAL :: s1              ! Length of side 1
REAL :: s2              ! Length of side 2
REAL :: hypot           ! Hypotenuse

! Get the lengths of the two sides.
WRITE (*,*) 'Program to test subroutine calc_hypotenuse: '
WRITE (*,*) 'Enter the length of side 1: '
READ (*,*) s1
WRITE (*,*) 'Enter the length of side 2: '
READ (*,*) s2

! Call calc_hypotenuse.
CALL calc_hypotenuse ( s1, s2, hypot )

! Write out hypotenuse.
WRITE (*,1000) hypot
```

(continued)

(*concluded*)

```
1000 FORMAT (1X,'The length of the hypotenuse is: ', F10.4 )
END PROGRAM test_hypotenuse
```

This program calls subroutine `calc_hypotenuse` with an actual argument list of variables `s1`, `s2`, and `hypot`. Therefore, wherever the dummy argument `side_1` appears in the subroutine, variable `s1` is really used instead. Similarly, the hypotenuse is really written into variable `hypot`.

7.1.1 Example Problem—Sorting

Let us now reexamine the sorting problem of Example 6-3, using subroutines where appropriate.

EXAMPLE 7-1

Sorting Data:

Develop a program to read in a data set from a file, sort it into ascending order, and display the sorted data set. Use subroutines where appropriate.

SOLUTION

The program in Example 6-3 read an arbitrary number of real input data values from a user-supplied file, sorted the data into ascending order, and wrote the sorted data to the standard output device. The sorting process would make a good candidate for a subroutine, since only the array `a` and its length `nvals` are in common between the sorting process and the rest of the program. The rewritten program using a sorting subroutine is shown in Figure 7-3.

FIGURE 7-3
Program to sort real data values into ascending order using a `sort` subroutine.

```
PROGRAM sort3
!
!  Purpose:
!    To read in a real input data set, sort it into ascending order
!    using the selection sort algorithm, and to write the sorted
!    data to the standard output device.  This program calls subroutine
!    "sort" to do the actual sorting.
!
!  Record of revisions:
!      Date          Programmer          Description of change
!      ====          ==========          =====================
!    11/18/06     S. J. Chapman          Original code
!
IMPLICIT NONE
```

(*continued*)

(continued)

```fortran
! Data dictionary: declare constants
INTEGER, PARAMETER :: MAX_SIZE = 10   ! Max input data size

! Data dictionary: declare variable types & definitions
REAL, DIMENSION(MAX_SIZE) :: a       ! Data array to sort
LOGICAL :: exceed = .FALSE.          ! Logical indicating that array
                                     !   limits are exceeded.
CHARACTER(len=20) :: filename        ! Input data file name
INTEGER :: i                         ! Loop index
INTEGER :: nvals = 0                 ! Number of data values to sort
INTEGER :: status                    ! I/O status: 0 for success
REAL :: temp                         ! Temporary variable for reading

! Get the name of the file containing the input data.
WRITE (*,*) 'Enter the file name with the data to be sorted: '
READ (*,1000) filename
1000 FORMAT ( A20 )

! Open input data file.  Status is OLD because the input data must
! already exist.
OPEN ( UNIT=9, FILE=filename, STATUS='OLD', ACTION='READ', &
       IOSTAT=status )

! Was the OPEN successful?
fileopen: IF ( status == 0 ) THEN        ! Open successful

   ! The file was opened successfully, so read the data to sort
   ! from it, sort the data, and write out the results.
   ! First read in data.
   DO
      READ (9, *, IOSTAT=status) temp     ! Get value
      IF ( status /= 0 ) EXIT             ! Exit on end of data
      nvals = nvals + 1                   ! Bump count
      size: IF ( nvals <= MAX_SIZE ) THEN ! Too many values?
         a(nvals) = temp                  ! No: Save value in array
      ELSE
         exceed = .TRUE.                  ! Yes: Array overflow
      END IF size
   END DO

   ! Was the array size exceeded?  If so, tell user and quit.
   toobig: IF ( exceed ) THEN
      WRITE (*,1010) nvals, MAX_SIZE
      1010 FORMAT (' Maximum array size exceeded: ', I6, ' > ', I6 )
   ELSE

      ! Limit not exceeded: sort the data.
      CALL sort (a, nvals)

      ! Now write out the sorted data.
      WRITE (*,1020) ' The sorted output data values are: '
      1020 FORMAT (A)
```

(continued)

(continued)

```
      WRITE (*,1030) ( a(i), i = 1, nvals )
      1030 FORMAT (4X,F10.4)

   END IF toobig

ELSE fileopen

   ! Else file open failed.  Tell user.
   WRITE (*,1040) status
   1040 FORMAT (1X,'File open failed--status = ', I6)

END IF fileopen

END PROGRAM sort3

!*****************************************************************
!*****************************************************************

SUBROUTINE sort (arr, n)
!
!  Purpose:
!    To sort real array "arr" into ascending order using a selection
!    sort.
!
IMPLICIT NONE

! Data dictionary: declare calling parameter types & definitions
INTEGER, INTENT(IN) :: n                     ! Number of values
REAL, DIMENSION(n), INTENT(INOUT) :: arr  ! Array to be sorted

! Data dictionary: declare local variable types & definitions
INTEGER :: i              ! Loop index
INTEGER :: iptr           ! Pointer to smallest value
INTEGER :: j              ! Loop index
REAL :: temp              ! Temp variable for swaps

! Sort the array
outer: DO i = 1, n-1

        ! Find the minimum value in arr(I) through arr(N)
        iptr = i
        inner: DO j = i+1, n
           minval: IF ( arr(j) < arr(iptr) ) THEN
               iptr = j
           END IF minval
        END DO inner

        ! iptr now points to the minimum value, so swap arr(iptr)
        ! with arr(i) if i /= iptr.
        swap: IF ( i /= iptr ) THEN
           temp      = arr(i)
           arr(i)    = arr(iptr)
```

(continued)

(concluded)

```
            arr(iptr) = temp
        END IF swap

END DO outer

END SUBROUTINE sort
```

This new program can be tested just as the original program was, with identical results. If the following data set is placed in file `INPUT2`:

```
13.3
12.
-3.0
 0.
 4.0
 6.6
 4.
-6.
```

then the results of the test run will be:

```
C:\book\chap7>sort3
Enter the file name containing the data to be sorted:
input2
The sorted output data values are:
-6.0000
-3.0000
  .0000
 4.0000
 4.0000
 6.6000
12.0000
13.3000
```

The program gives the correct answers for our test data set, as before.

Subroutine `sort` performs the same function as the sorting code in the original example, but now `sort` is an independent subroutine that we can reuse unchanged whenever we need to sort any array of real numbers.

Note that the array was declared in the sort subroutine as

```
REAL, DIMENSION(n), INTENT(INOUT) :: arr ! Array to be sorted
```

The statement tells the Fortran compiler that dummy argument `arr` is an array whose length is `n`, where `n` is also a calling argument. The dummy argument `arr` is only a placeholder for whatever array is passed as an argument when the subroutine is called. The actual size of the array will be the size of the array that is passed from the calling program.

Also, note that `n` was declared to be an input parameter *before* it was used to define `arr`. Most compilers will require `n` to be declared first, so that its meaning is known before it is used in the array declaration. If the order of the declarations were reversed, most compilers will generate an error saying that n is undefined when arr is declared.

Finally, note that the dummy argument arr was used both to pass the data to subroutine sort and to return the sorted data to the calling program. Since it is used for both input and output, it is declared with the INTENT(INOUT) attribute.

7.1.2 The INTENT Attribute

Dummy subroutine arguments can have an INTENT attribute associated with them. The INTENT attribute is associated with the type declaration statement that declares each dummy argument. The attribute can take one of three forms:

INTENT(IN)	Dummy argument is used only to pass input data to the subroutine.
INTENT(OUT)	Dummy argument is used only to return results to the calling program.
INTENT(INOUT) or INTENT(IN OUT)	Dummy argument is used both to pass input data to the subroutine and to return results to the calling program.

The purpose of the INTENT attribute is to tell the compiler how the programmer intends each dummy argument to be used. Some arguments may be intended only to provide input data to the subroutine, and some may be intended only to return results from the subroutine. Finally, some may be intended both to provide data and return results. The appropriate INTENT attribute should *always* be declared for each argument.[4]

Once the compiler knows what we intend to do with each dummy argument, it can use that information to help catch programming errors at compile time. For example, suppose that a subroutine accidentally modifies an input argument. Changing that input argument will cause the value of the corresponding variable in the calling program to be changed, and the changed value will be used in all subsequent processing. This type of programming error can be very hard to locate, since it is caused by the interaction between procedures.

A simple example is shown below. Here subroutine sub1 calculates an output value, but also accidentally modifies its input value.

```
SUBROUTINE sub1(input,output)
IMPLICIT NONE
REAL, INTENT(IN) :: input
REAL, INTENT(OUT) :: output

output = 2. * input
input = -1.    ! This line is an error!
END SUBROUTINE sub1
```

---

[4] The intent of a dummy argument may also be declared in a separate INTENT statement of the form

```
INTENT(IN) :: arg1, arg2,...
```

. By declaring our intent for each dummy argument, the compiler can spot this error for us at compilation time. When this subroutine is compiled with the Compaq Visual Fortran compiler, the results are

```
C:\book\chap4>df /list:CON /nolink sub1.f90
Compaq Visual Fortran Optimizing Compiler Version 6.6
Copyright 2001 Compaq Computer Corp. All rights reserved.

SUB1  Source Listing 14-Jul-2002 15:11:50 Compaq Visual Fortran 6.6 Page 1
                   25-Oct-1995 05:42:42 sub1.f90

        1 SUBROUTINE sub1(input,output)
        2
        3 REAL, INTENT(IN) :: input
        4 REAL, INTENT(OUT) :: output
        5
        6 output = 2. * input
        7 input = -1.
          1
(1) Error: There is an assignment to a dummy symbol with the explicit INTENT(IN)
    attribute [INPUT]

        8 END SUBROUTINE sub1
```

The INTENT attribute is valid only for dummy procedure arguments. It is an error to declare the intent of local variables in a subroutine, or of variables in a main program.

As we will see later, declaring the intent of each dummy argument will also help us spot errors that occur in the calling sequence *between* procedures. You should always declare the intent of every dummy argument in every procedure.

Good Programming Practice

Always declare the intent of every dummy argument in every procedure.

7.1.3 Variable Passing in Fortran: The Pass-by-Reference Scheme

Fortran programs communicate with their subroutines using a **pass-by-reference** scheme. When a subroutine call occurs, the main program passes a pointer to the location in memory of each argument in the actual argument list. The subroutine looks at the memory locations pointed to by the calling program to get the values of the dummy arguments it needs. This process is illustrated in Figure 7-4.

The figure shows a main program test calling a subroutine sub1. There are three actual arguments being passed to the subroutine: a real variable a, a four-element real array b, and an integer variable next. These variables occupy memory addresses 001, 002–005, and 006 respectively in some computers. Three dummy arguments are

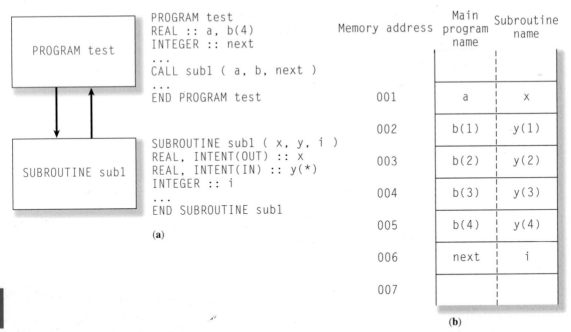

FIGURE 7-4
The pass-by-reference memory scheme. Note that only pointers to the memory addresses of the actual arguments
are passed to the subroutine.

declared in sub1: a real variable x, a real array y, and an integer variable i. When the
main program calls sub1, *what is passed to the subroutine are the pointers to the mem-*
ory locations containing the calling arguments: 001, 002, and 006. Whenever variable
x is referred to in the subroutine, the contents of memory location 001 are accessed,
etc. This parameter passing scheme is called pass-by-reference, since only pointers to
the values are passed to the subroutine, not the actual values themselves.

There are some possible pitfalls associated with the pass-by-reference scheme. *The
programmer must ensure that the values in the calling argument list match the subroutine's calling parameters in number, type, and order.* If there is a mismatch, the Fortran
program will not be able to recognize that fact, and it will misuse the parameters
without informing you of the problem. *This is the most common error made by programmers when using Fortran subroutines.* For example, consider the program shown
in Figure 7-5.

FIGURE 7-5
Example illustrating the effects of a type mismatch when calling a subroutine.

```
PROGRAM bad_call
!
!  Purpose:
!    To illustrate misinterpreted calling arguments.
```

                                                                                          (*continued*)

(concluded)

```
!
IMPLICIT NONE
REAL :: x = 1.                  ! Declare real variable x.
CALL bad_argument ( x )         ! Call subroutine.
END PROGRAM bac_call

SUBROUTINE bad_argument ( i )
IMPLICIT NONE
INTEGER :: i                    ! Declare argument as integer.
WRITE (*,*) 'i = ', i           ! Write out i.
END SUBROUTINE bad_argument
```

The argument in the call to subroutine `bad_argument` is real, but the corresponding dummy argument is type integer. Fortran will pass the address of the real variable x to the subroutine, which will then treat it as an integer. The results are quite bad. When the program is compiled with the Intel Visual Fortran compiler, we get:

```
C:\book\chap7>bad_call
I =  1065353216
```

Another serious problem can occur if a variable is placed in the calling argument list in a position at which an array is expected. The subroutine cannot tell the difference between a variable and an array, so it will treat the variable and the variables following it in memory as though they were all part of one big array! This behavior can produce a world of problems. A subroutine containing a variable named x in its calling sequence could wind up modifying another variable y that wasn't even passed to the subroutine, just because y happens to be allocated after x in the computer's memory. Problems like that can be *extremely* difficult to find and debug.

In Section 7.3, we will learn how to get a Fortran 95/2003 compiler to automatically check the number, type, intent, and order of each argument in each subroutine call, so that the compiler can catch these errors for us at compilation time.

Programming Pitfalls

Make sure that the values in the argument list of a subroutine call match the subroutine's declared parameters in number, type, and order. Very bad results may occur if you do not ensure that the arguments match properly.

7.1.4 Passing Arrays to Subroutines

A calling argument is passed to a subroutine by passing a pointer to the memory location of the argument. If the argument happens to be an array, then the pointer points to the first value in the array. However, the subroutine needs to know both the location and the size of the array to ensure that it stays within the boundaries of the array, and in order to perform array operations. How can we supply this information to the subroutine?

There are three possible approaches to specifying the length of a dummy array in a subroutine. One approach is to pass the bounds of each dimension of the array to the subroutine as arguments in the subroutine call, and to declare the corresponding dummy array to be that length. The dummy array is thus an **explicit-shape dummy array,** since each of its bounds is explicitly specified. If this is done, the subroutine will know the shape of each dummy array when it is executed. Since the shape of the array is known, the bounds checkers on most Fortran compilers will be able to detect and report out-of-bounds memory references. For example, the following code declares two arrays data1 and data2 to be of extent n, and then processes nvals values in the arrays. If an out-of-bounds reference occurs in this subroutine, it can be detected and reported.

```
SUBROUTINE process ( data1, data2, n, nvals )
INTEGER, INTENT(IN) :: n, nvals
REAL, INTENT(IN),  DIMENSION(n) :: data1 ! Explicit shape
REAL, INTENT(OUT), DIMENSION(n) :: data2 ! Explicit shape

DO i = 1, nvals
   data2(i) = 3. * data1(i)
END DO
END SUBROUTINE process
```

When explicit-shape dummy arrays are used, the size and shape of each dummy array is known to the compiler. Since the size and shape of each array is known, it is possible to use array operations and array sections with the dummy arrays. The following subroutine uses array sections; it will work because the dummy arrays are explicit-shape arrays.

```
SUBROUTINE process2 ( data1, data2, n, nvals )
INTEGER, INTENT(IN) :: nvals
REAL, INTENT(IN),  DIMENSION(n) :: data1 ! Explicit shape
REAL, INTENT(OUT), DIMENSION(n) :: data2 ! Explicit shape

data2(1:nvals) = 3. * data1(1:nvals)
END SUBROUTINE process2
```

A second approach is to declare all dummy arrays in a subroutine as **assumed-shape dummy arrays** and to create an explicit interface to the subroutine. This approach will be explained in Section 7.3.

The third (and oldest) approach is to declare the length of each dummy array with an asterisk as an **assumed-size dummy array.** In this case, the compiler knows nothing about the length of the actual array passed to the subroutine. Bounds checking, whole array operations, and array sections will not work for assumed-size dummy arrays, because the compiler does not know the actual size and shape of the array. For example, the following code declares two assumed-size dummy arrays data1 and data2 then processes nvals values in the arrays.

```
SUBROUTINE process3 ( data1, data2, nvals )
REAL, INTENT(IN),  DIMENSION(*) :: data1 ! Assumed size
REAL, INTENT(OUT), DIMENSION(*) :: data2 ! Assumed size
INTEGER, INTENT(IN) :: nvals
```

```
      DO i = 1, nvals
         data2(i) = 3. * data1(i)
      END DO
      END SUBROUTINE process3
```

Arrays data1 and data2 had better be at least nvals values long. If they are not, the Fortran code will either abort with an error at run time, or else overwrite other locations in memory. Subroutines written like this are hard to debug, since the bounds-checking option of most compilers will not work for unknown-length arrays. They also cannot use whole array operations or array sections.

⁂ Assumed-size dummy arrays are a holdover from earlier versions of Fortran. *They should never be used in any new programs.*

Good Programming Practice
Use explicit-shape or assumed-shape dummy arrays in all new procedures. This permits whole array operations to be used within the procedure. It also allows for easier debugging, since out-of-bounds references can be detected. *Assumed-size dummy arrays should never be used.* They are undesirable, and are likely to be eliminated from a future version of the Fortran language.

7

EXAMPLE 7-2   *Bounds Checking in Subroutines:*

Write a simple Fortran program containing a subroutine that oversteps the limits of an array in its argument list. Compile and execute the program both with bounds checking turned off and with bounds checking turned on.

SOLUTION
The program in Figure 7-6 allocates a five-element array a. It initializes all the elements of a to zero, and then calls subroutine sub1. Subroutine sub1 modifies six elements of array a, despite the fact that a has only five elements.

FIGURE 7-6
A program illustrating the effect of exceeding the boundaries of an array in a subroutine.

```
PROGRAM array2
!
! Purpose:
!   To illustrate the effect of accessing an out-of-bounds
!   array element.
!
! Record of revisions:
!    Date        Programmer          Description of change
!    ====        ==========          =====================
!   11/19/06   S. J. Chapman        Original code
!
```

(continued)

(concluded)

```
IMPLICIT NONE

! Declare and initialize the variables used in this program.
INTEGER :: i                              ! Loop index
REAL, DIMENSION(5) :: a = 0.              ! Array

! Call subroutine sub1.
CALL sub1( a, 5, 6 )

! Write out the values of array a
DO i = 1, 6
   WRITE (*,100) i, a(i)
   100 FORMAT ( 1X,'A(', I1, ') = ', F6.2 )
END DO

!*****************************************************************
!*****************************************************************
!

END PROGRAM array2

SUBROUTINE sub1 ( a, ndim, n )
IMPLICIT NONE

INTEGER, INTENT(IN) :: ndim               ! size of array
REAL, INTENT(OUT), DIMENSION(ndim) :: a   ! Dummy argument
INTEGER, INTENT(IN) :: n                  ! # elements to process
INTEGER :: i                              ! Loop index

DO i = 1, n
 a(i) = i
END DO

END SUBROUTINE sub1
```

When this program is compiled with the Intel Visual Fortran compiler with bounds checking turned *off*, the result is

```
C:\book\chap7>array2
a(1) = 1.00
a(2) = 2.00
a(3) = 3.00
a(4) = 4.00
a(5) = 5.00
a(6) = 6.00
```

In this case, the subroutine has written beyond the end of array a, into memory that was allocated for some other purpose. If this memory were allocated to another variable, then the contents of that variable would have been changed without the user knowing that anything can happen. This can produce a very subtle and hard to find bug!

If the program is recompiled with the Intel Visual Fortran compiler with bounds checking turned *on*, the result is

```
C:\book\chap7>array2

forrtl: severe (408): fort: (2): Subscript #1 of the array A
has value 6 which is greater than the upper bound of 5

Image           PC          Routine         Line        Source
x.exe           00440E6A    Unknown         Unknown     Unknown
x.exe           0043E0E8    Unknown         Unknown     Unknown
x.exe           00403896    Unknown         Unknown     Unknown
x.exe           00403A58    Unknown         Unknown     Unknown
x.exe           0040114A    _SUB1                38     array2.f90
x.exe           0040103C    _MAIN__              19     array2.f90
x.exe           00443DA0    Unknown         Unknown     Unknown
x.exe           00435145    Unknown         Unknown     Unknown
kernel32.dll    7C816D4F    Unknown         Unknown     Unknown
```

Here the program detected the out-of-bounds reference and shut down after telling the user where the problem occurred.

7.1.5 Passing Character Variables to Subroutines

When a character variable is used as a dummy subroutine argument, the length of the character variable is declared with an asterisk. Since no memory is actually allocated for dummy arguments, it is not necessary to know the length of the character argument when the subroutine is compiled. A typical dummy character argument is shown below:

```
SUBROUTINE sample ( string )
CHARACTER(len = *), INTENT(IN) :: string
. . .
```

When the subroutine is called, the length of the dummy character argument will be the length of the actual argument passed from the calling program. If we need to know the length of the character string passed to the subroutine during execution, we can use the intrinsic function LEN() to determine it. For example, the following simple subroutine displays the length of any character argument passed to it.

```
SUBROUTINE sample ( string )
CHARACTER(len = *), INTENT(IN) :: string
WRITE (*,'(1X,A,I3)') 'Length of variable = ', LEN(string)
END SUBROUTINE sample
```

7.1.6 Error Handling in Subroutines

What happens if a program calls a subroutine with insufficient or invalid data for proper processing? For example, suppose that we are writing a subroutine that subtracts two input variables and takes the square root of the result. What should we do if the difference of the two variables is a negative number?

```
SUBROUTINE process (a, b, result)
IMPLICIT NONE
REAL, INTENT(IN) :: a, b
REAL, INTENT(OUT) :: result
REAL :: temp
temp = a - b
result = SQRT ( temp )
END SUBROUTINE process
```

For example, suppose that a is 1 and b is 2. If we just process the values in the subroutine, a run-time error will occur when we attempt to take the square root of a negative number, and the program will abort. This is clearly not an acceptable result.

An alternative version of the subroutine is shown below. In this version, we test for a negative number, and if one is present, we print out an informative error message and stop.

```
SUBROUTINE process (a, b, result)
IMPLICIT NONE
REAL, INTENT(IN) :: a, b
REAL, INTENT(OUT) :: result
REAL :: temp
temp = a - b
IF ( temp > = 0. ) THEN
   result = SQRT ( temp )
ELSE
   WRITE (*,*) 'Square root of negative value in subroutine
PROCESS!'
   STOP
END IF
END SUBROUTINE process
```

While better than the previous example, this design is also bad. If temp is ever negative, the program will just stop without ever returning from subroutine process. If this happens, the user will lose all of the data and processing that has occurred up to that point in the program.

   A much better way to design the subroutine is to detect the possible error condition, and to report it to the calling program by setting a value into an **error flag.** The calling program can then take appropriate actions about the error. For example, it can be designed to recover from the error if possible. If not, it can at least write out an informative error message, save the partial results calculated so far, and then shut down gracefully.

In the example shown below, a zero returned in the error flag means successful completion, and a 1 means that the square-root-of-a-negative-number error occurred.

```
SUBROUTINE process (a, b, result, error)
IMPLICIT NONE
REAL, INTENT(IN) :: a, b
REAL, INTENT(OUT) :: result
INTEGER, INTENT(OUT) :: error
```

```
REAL :: temp
temp = a - b
IF ( temp >=  0. ) THEN
   result = SQRT ( temp )
   error = 0
ELSE
   result = 0
   error = 1
END IF
END SUBROUTINE process
```

Programming Pitfalls

Never include STOP statements in any of your subroutines. If you do, you might create a working program and release it to users, only to find that it mysteriously halts from time to time on certain unusual data sets.

Good Programming Practice

If there are possible error conditions within a subroutine, you should test for them and set an error flag to be returned to the calling program. The calling program should test for the error conditions after a subroutine call and take appropriate actions.

7

Quiz 7-1

This quiz provides a quick check to see if you have understood the concepts introduced in Section 7.1. If you have trouble with the quiz, reread the section, ask your instructor, or discuss the material with a fellow student. The answers to this quiz are found in the back of the book.

For questions 1 through 3, determine whether the subroutine calls are correct or not. If they are in error, specify what is wrong with them.

```
1.  PROGRAM test1
    REAL, DIMENSION(120) :: a
    REAL :: average, sd
    INTEGER :: n
    ...
    CALL ave_sd ( a, 120, n, average, sd )
    ...
    END PROGRAM test1
```

(continued)

(concluded)

```
      SUBROUTINE ave_sd( array, nvals, n, average, sd )
      REAL, INTENT(IN) :: nvals, n
      REAL, INTENT(IN), DIMENSION(nvals) :: array
      REAL, INTENT(OUT) :: average, sd

      . . .
      END SUBROUTINE ave_sd
  2.  PROGRAM test2
      CHARACTER(len=12) :: str1, str2
      str1 = 'ABCDEFGHIJ'
      CALL swap_str (str1, str2)
      WRITE (*,*) str1, str2
      END PROGRAM test2
      SUBROUTINE swap_str (string1, string2)
      CHARACTER(len=*),INTENT(IN) :: string1
      CHARACTER(len=*),INTENT(OUT) :: string2
      INTEGER :: i, length
      length = LEN(string1)
      DO i = 1, length
         string2(length-i+1:length-i+1)=string1(i:i)
      END DO
      END SUBROUTINE swap_str
  3.  PROGRAM test3
      INTEGER, DIMENSION(25) :: idata
      REAL :: sum

      . . .
      CALL sub3 ( idata, sum )

      . . .
      END PROGRAM test3
      SUBROUTINE sub3( iarray, sum )
      INTEGER, INTENT(IN), DIMENSION(*) :: iarray
      REAL, INTENT(OUT) :: sum
      INTEGER :: i
      sum = 0.
      DO i = 1, 30
         sum = sum + iarray(i)
      END DO
      END SUBROUTINE sub3
```

7.1.7 Examples

EXAMPLE 7-3

Statistics Subroutines:

Develop a set of reusable subroutines capable of determining the statistical properties of a data set of real numbers in an array. The set of subroutines should include:

1. A subroutine to determine the maximum value in a data set, and the sample number containing that value.
2. A subroutine to determine the minimum value in a data set, and the sample number containing that value.
3. A subroutine to determine the average (mean) and standard deviation of the data set.
4. A subroutine to determine the median of the data set.

SOLUTION

We will be generating four different subroutines, each of which works on a common input data set consisting of an array of real numbers.

1. **State the problem.**

   The problem is clearly stated above. We will write four different subroutines: `rmax` to find the maximum value and the location of that value in a real array, `rmin` to find the minimum value and the location of that value in a real array, `ave_sd` to find the average and standard deviation of a real array, and `median` to find the median of a real array.

2. **Define the inputs and outputs.**

   The input to each subroutine will be an array of values, plus the number of values in the array. The outputs will be as follows:

   1. The output of subroutine `rmax` will be a real variable containing the maximum value in the input array, and an integer variable containing the offset in the array at which the maximum value occurred.
   2. The output of subroutine `rmin` will be a real variable containing the minimum value in the input array, and an integer variable containing the offset in the array at which the minimum value occurred.
   3. The output of subroutine `ave_sd` will be two real variables containing the average and standard deviation of the input array.
   4. The output of subroutine `median` will be a real variable containing the median value of the input array.

3. **Describe the algorithm.**

   The pseudocode for the `rmax` routine is:

   ```
   ! Initialize "real_max" to the first value in the array
   ! and "imax" to 1.
   real_max ← a(1)
   imax ← 1

   ! Find the maximum value in a(1) through a(n)
   DO for i = 2 to n
      IF a(i) > real_max THEN
         real_max ← a(i)
         imax ← i
      END of IF
   END of DO
   ```

   The pseudocode for the `rmin` routine is:

   ```
   ! Initialize "real_min" to the first value in the array
   ! and "imin" to 1.
   ```

```
real_min ← a(1)
imin ← 1

! Find the maximum value in a(1) through a(n)
DO for i = 2 to n
   IF a(i) < real_min THEN
      real_min ← a(i)
      imin ← i
   END of IF
END of DO
```

The pseudocode for the `ave_sd` routine is essentially the same as that in Example 6-4. It will not be repeated here. For the `median` calculation, we will be able to take advantage of the `sort` subroutine that we have already written. (Here is an example of reusable code saving us time and effort.) The pseudocode for the `median` subroutine is:

```
CALL sort ( n, a )
IF n is an even number THEN
   med ← (a(n/2) + a(n/2 + 1)) / 2.
ELSE
   med ← a(n/2 + 1)
END of IF
```

4. **Turn the algorithm into Fortran statements.**

   The resulting Fortran subroutines are shown in Figure 7-7.

FIGURE 7-7
The subroutines `rmin`, `rmax`, `ave_sd`, and `median`.

```
SUBROUTINE rmax ( a, n, real_max, imax )
!  Purpose:
!    To find the maximum value in an array, and the location
!    of that value in the array.
!
IMPLICIT NONE

! Data dictionary: declare calling parameter types & definitions
INTEGER, INTENT(IN) :: n                 ! No. of vals in array a.
REAL, INTENT(IN), DIMENSION(n) :: a      ! Input data.
REAL, INTENT(OUT) :: real_max            ! Maximum value in a.
INTEGER, INTENT(OUT) :: imax             ! Location of max value.

! Data dictionary: declare local variable types & definitions
INTEGER :: i                             ! Index variable

! Initialize the maximum value to first value in array.
real_max = a(1)
imax = 1

! Find the maximum value.
DO i = 2, n
   IF ( a(i) > real_max ) THEN
      real_max = a(i)
      imax = i
   END IF
END DO
```

(*continued*)

(continued)

```
END SUBROUTINE rmax

!******************************************************************
!******************************************************************

SUBROUTINE rmin ( a, n, real_min, imin )
!
!   Purpose:
!     To find the minimum value in an array, and the location
!     of that value in the array.
!
IMPLICIT NONE

! Data dictionary: declare calling parameter types & definitions
INTEGER, INTENT(IN) :: n                  ! No. of vals in array a.
REAL, INTENT(IN), DIMENSION(n) :: a       ! Input data.
REAL, INTENT(OUT) :: real_min             ! Minimum value in a.
INTEGER, INTENT(OUT) :: imin              ! Location of min value.

! Data dictionary: declare local variable types & definitions
INTEGER :: i                              ! Index variable

! Initialize the minimum value to first value in array.
real_min = a(1)
imin = 1

! Find the minimum value.
DO I = 2, n
   IF ( a(i) < real_min ) THEN
      real_min = a(i)
      imin = i
   END IF
END DO

END SUBROUTINE rmin

!******************************************************************
!******************************************************************

SUBROUTINE ave_sd ( a, n, ave, std_dev, error )
!
!   Purpose:
!     To calculate the average and standard deviation of an array.
!
IMPLICIT NONE

! Data dictionary: declare calling parameter types & definitions
INTEGER, INTENT(IN) :: n                  ! No. of vals in array a.
REAL, INTENT(IN), DIMENSION(n) :: a       ! Input data.
REAL, INTENT(OUT) :: ave                  ! Average of a.
REAL, INTENT(OUT) :: std_dev              ! Standard deviation.
INTEGER, INTENT(OUT) :: error             ! Flag: 0 — no error
                                          !       1 — sd invalid
                                          !       2 — ave & sd invalid
```

(continued)

(*continued*)

```
! Data dictionary: declare local variable types & definitions
INTEGER :: i                      ! Loop index
REAL :: sum_x                     ! Sum of input values
REAL :: sum_x2                    ! Sum of input values squared

! Initialize the sums to zero.
sum_x = 0.
sum_x2 = 0.

! Accumulate sums.
DO I = 1, n
   sum_x = sum_x + a(i)
   sum_x2 = sum_x2 + a(i)**2
END DO

! Check to see if we have enough input data.
IF ( n >= 2 ) THEN ! we have enough data

   ! Calculate the mean and standard deviation
   ave = sum_x / REAL(n)
   std_dev = SQRT( (REAL(n) * sum_x2 - sum_x**2) &
           / (REAL(n) * REAL(n - 1)) )
   error = 0

ELSE IF ( n == 1 ) THEN ! no valid std_dev

   ave = sum_x
   std_dev = 0.                    ! std_dev invalid
   error = 1

ELSE

   ave = 0.                        ! ave invalid
   std_dev = 0.                    ! std_dev invalid
   error = 2

END IF
END SUBROUTINE ave_sd

!*****************************************************************
!*****************************************************************

SUBROUTINE median ( a, n, med )
!
!  Purpose:
!    To calculate the median value of an array.
!
IMPLICIT NONE

! Data dictionary: declare calling parameter types & definitions
```

(*continued*)

(concluded)

```
INTEGER, INTENT(IN) :: n                ! No. of vals in array a.
REAL, INTENT(IN), DIMENSION(n) :: a     ! Input data.
REAL, INTENT(OUT) :: med                ! Median value of a.

! Sort the data into ascending order.
CALL sort ( a, n )

! Get median.
IF ( MOD(n,2) == 0 ) THEN
    med = ( a(n/2) + a(n/2+1) ) / 2.
ELSE
    med = a(n/2+1)
END IF
END SUBROUTINE median
```

5. **Test the resulting Fortran programs.**

   To test these subroutines, it is necessary to write a driver program to read the input data, call the subroutines, and write out the results. This test is left as an exercise to the student (see Exercise 7-13 at the end of the chapter.)

7

■ 7.2

SHARING DATA USING MODULES

We have seen that programs exchange data with the subroutines they call through an argument list. Each item in the argument list of the program's CALL statement must be matched by a dummy argument in the argument list of the subroutine being invoked. A pointer to the location of each argument is passed from the calling program to the subroutine for use in accessing the arguments.

In addition to the argument list, Fortran programs, subroutines, and functions can also exchange data through modules. A **module** is a separately compiled program unit that contains the definitions and initial values of the data that we wish to share between program units.[5] If the module's name is included in a USE statement within a program unit, then the data values declared in the module may be used to within that program unit. Each program unit that uses a module will have access to the same data values, so *modules provide a way to share data between program units*.

A module begins with a MODULE statement, which assigns a name to the module. The name may be up to 31 characters long,[6] and must follow the standard Fortran naming conventions. The module ends with an END MODULE statement, which may optionally include the module's name. The declarations of the data to be shared are placed between these two statements. An example module is shown in Figure 7-8.

---

[5] Modules also have other functions, as we shall see in Section 7.3 and in Chapter 13.
[6] Up to 63 characters in Fortran 2003.

FIGURE 7-8
A simple module used to share data among program units.

```
MODULE shared_data
!
!  Purpose:
!    To declare data to share between two routines.

IMPLICIT NONE
SAVE
INTEGER, PARAMETER :: num_vals = 5        ! Max number of values in array
REAL, DIMENSION(num_vals) :: values       ! Data values

END MODULE shared_data
```

The SAVE statement guarantees that all data values declared in the module will be preserved between references in different procedures. It should always be included in any module that declares sharable data. SAVE statements will be discussed in detail in Chapter 9.

To use the values in this module, a program unit must declare the module name in a USE statement. The form of a USE statement is

```
        USE module_name
```

USE statements must appear before any other statements in a program unit (except for the PROGRAM or SUBROUTINE statement, and except for comments, which may appear anywhere). The process of accessing information in a module with a USE statement is known as USE **association.**

An example that uses module shared_data to share data between a main program and a subroutine is shown in Figure 7-9.

FIGURE 7-9
An example program using a module to share data between a main program and a subroutine.

```
PROGRAM test_module
!
!  Purpose:
!    To illustrate sharing data via a module.
!
USE shared_data                    ! Make data in module "test" visible
IMPLICIT NONE

REAL, PARAMETER :: PI = 3.141592 ! Pi

values = PI * (/ 1., 2., 3., 4., 5. /)

CALL sub1                          ! Call subroutine

END PROGRAM test_module
!*******************************************************************
!*******************************************************************
SUBROUTINE sub1
```

                                                                    (*continued*)

(concluded)

```
!
!  Purpose:
!    To illustrate sharing data via a module.
!
USE shared_data                   ! Make data in module "test" visible
IMPLICIT NONE

WRITE (*,*) values

END SUBROUTINE sub1
```

The contents of module shared_data are being shared between the main program and subroutine sub1. Any other subroutines or functions within the program could also have access to the data by including the appropriate USE statements.

Note that the array values is defined in the module, and used in both program test_module and subroutine sub1. However, the array values does *not* have a type declaration in either the program or the subroutine; the definition is inherited through USE association. In fact, it is an error to declare a variable within a procedure that has the same name as one inherited through USE association.

7

Programming Pitfalls

Do not declare local variables with the same name as variables inherited through USE association. This redefinition of a variable name will produce a compilation error.

Modules are especially useful for sharing large volumes of data among many program units, and for sharing data among a group of related procedures while keeping it invisible from the invoking program unit.

Good Programming Practice

You may use modules to pass large amounts of data between procedures within a program. If you do so, always include the SAVE statement within the module to ensure that the contents of the module remain unchanged between uses. To access the data in a particular program unit, include a USE statement as the *first noncomment statement* after the PROGRAM, SUBROUTINE, or FUNCTION statement within the program unit.

EXAMPLE 7-4   *Random Number Generator:*

It is always impossible to make perfect measurements in the real world. There will always be some *measurement noise* associated with each measurement. This fact is an important consideration in the design of systems to control the operation of such real-world devices as airplanes, refineries, and telecommunication networks. A good engineering design must take these measurement errors into account, so that the noise in the measurements will not lead to unstable behavior (no plane crashes or refinery explosions!).

Most engineering designs are tested by running *simulations* of the operation of the system before it is ever built. These simulations involve creating mathematical models of the behavior of the system, and feeding the models a realistic string of input data. If the models respond correctly to the simulated input data, then we can have reasonable confidence that the real-world system will respond correctly to the real-world input data.

The simulated input data supplied to the models must be corrupted by a simulated measurement noise, which is just a string of random numbers added to the ideal input data. The simulated noise is usually produced by a *random number generator*.

A random number generator is a procedure that will return a different and apparently random number each time it is called. Since the numbers are in fact generated by a deterministic algorithm, they only appear to be random.[7] However, if the algorithm used to generate them is complex enough, the numbers will be random enough to use in the simulation.

One simple random number generator algorithm is shown below.[8] It relies on the unpredictability of the modulo function when applied to large numbers. Consider the following equation:

$$n_{i+1} = \text{MOD}(8121n_i + 28411, 134456) \qquad (7\text{-}1)$$

Assume that n_i is a nonnegative integer. Then, because of the modulo function, n_{i+1} will be a number between 0 and 134455 inclusive. Next, n_{i+1} can be fed into the equation to produce a number n_{i+2} that is also between 0 and 134455. This process can be repeated forever to produce a series of numbers in the range [0,134455]. If we didn't know the numbers 8121, 28411, and 134456 in advance, it would be impossible to guess the order in which the values of n would be produced. Furthermore, it turns out that there is an equal (or uniform) probability that any given number will appear in the sequence. Because of these properties, Equation 7-1 can serve as the basis for a simple random number generator with a uniform distribution.

We will now use Equation 7-1 to design a random number generator whose output is a real number in the range [0.0, 1.0).[9]

SOLUTION
We will write a subroutine that generates one random number in the range $0 \le \text{ran} < 1.0$ each time that it is called. The random number will be based on the equation

$$\text{ran}_i = \frac{n_i}{134456} \qquad (7\text{-}2)$$

where n_i is a number in the range 0 to 134455 produced by Equation 7-1.

---

[7] For this reason, some people refer to these procedures as *pseudorandom number generators*.
[8] This algorithm is adapted from the discussion found in Chapter 7 of *Numerical Recipes: The Art of Scientific Programming,* by Press, Flannery, Teukolsky, and Vetterling, Cambridge University Press, 1986.
[9] The notation [0.0,1.0) implies that the range of the random numbers is between 0.0 and 1.0, including the number 0.0, but excluding the number 1.0.

The particular sequence produced by Equations 7-1 and 7-2 will depend on the initial value of n_o (called the *seed*) of the sequence. We must provide a way for the user to specify n_o so that the sequence may be varied from run to run.

1. **State the problem.**

   Write a subroutine random0 that will generate and return a single number ran with a uniform probability distribution in the range $0 \leq$ ran < 1.0, based on the sequence specified by Equations 7-1 and 7-2. The initial value of the seed n_o will be specified by a call to a subroutine called seed.

2. **Define the inputs and outputs.**

   There are two subroutines in this problem: seed and random0. The input to subroutine seed is an integer to serve as the starting point of the sequence. There is no output from this subroutine. There is no input to subroutine random0, and the output from the subroutine is a single real value in the range [0.0, 1.0).

3. **Describe the algorithm.**

   The pseudocode for subroutine random0 is very simple:

   ```
   SUBROUTINE random0 ( ran )
   n ← MOD (8121 * n + 28411, 134456 )
   ran ← REAL(n) / 134456.
   END SUBROUTINE random0
   ```

   where the value of n is saved between calls to the subroutine. The pseudocode for subroutine seed is also trivial:

   ```
   SUBROUTINE seed ( iseed )
   n ← ABS ( iseed )
   END SUBROUTINE seed
   ```

   The absolute value function is used so that the user can enter any integer as the starting point. The user will not have to know in advance that only positive integers are legal seeds.

   The variable n will be placed in a module so that it may be accessed by both subroutines. In addition, we will initialize n to a reasonable value so that we will get good results even if subroutine seed is not called to set the seed before the first call to random0.

4. **Turn the algorithm into Fortran statements.**

   The resulting Fortran subroutines are shown in Figure 7-10.

FIGURE 7-10

Subroutines to generate a random number sequence, and to set the seed of the sequence.

```
MODULE ran001
!
! Purpose:
!    To declare data shared between subs random0 and seed.
!
```

(*continued*)

(*continued*)

```
!   Record of revisions:
!       Date        Programmer          Description of change
!       ====        ==========          =======================
!     11/22/06      S. J. Chapman       Original code
!
IMPLICIT NONE
SAVE
INTEGER :: n = 9876
END MODULE ran001


!*******************************************************************
!*******************************************************************

SUBROUTINE random0 ( ran )
!
!   Purpose:
!     Subroutine to generate a pseudorandom number with a uniform
!     distribution in the range 0. <= ran < 1.0.
!
!   Record of revisions:
!       Date        Programmer          Description of change
!       ====        ==========          =======================
!     11/22/06      S. J. Chapman       Original code
!
USE ran001                         ! Shared seed
IMPLICIT NONE

! Data dictionary: declare calling parameter types & definitions
REAL, INTENT(OUT) :: ran           ! Random number

! Calculate next number
n = MOD (8121 * n + 28411, 134456 )

! Generate random value from this number
ran = REAL(n) / 134456.

END SUBROUTINE random0

!*******************************************************************
!*******************************************************************

SUBROUTINE seed ( iseed )
!
!   Purpose:
!     To set the seed for random number generator random0.
!
!   Record of revisions:
!       Date        Programmer          Description of change
!       ====        ==========          =======================
!     11/22/06      S. J. Chapman       Original code
!
USE ran001                         ! Shared seed
```

(*continued*)

(continued)

```
IMPLICIT NONE

! Data dictionary: declare calling parameter types & definitions
INTEGER, INTENT(IN) :: iseed    ! Value to initialize sequence

! Set seed
n = ABS ( iseed )

END SUBROUTINE seed
```

5. **Test the resulting Fortran programs.**

If the numbers generated by these routines are truly uniformly distributed random numbers in the range $0 \leq ran < 1.0$, then the average of many numbers should be close to 0.5. To test the results, we will write a test program that prints out the first 10 values produced by random0 to see if they are indeed in the range $0 \leq ran < 1.0$. Then, the program will average five consecutive 1000-sample intervals to see how close the averages come to 0.5. The test code to call subroutines seed and random0 is shown in Figure 7-11.

FIGURE 7-11

Test driver program for subroutines seed and random0.

```
PROGRAM test_random0
!
!   Purpose:
!     Subroutine to test the random number generator random0.
!
!   Record of revisions:
!      Date         Programmer          Description of change
!      ====         ==========          =====================
!     11/22/06    S. J. Chapman         Original code
!
IMPLICIT NONE

! Data dictionary: declare variable types & definitions
REAL :: ave          ! Average of random numbers
INTEGER :: i         ! DO loop index
INTEGER :: iseed     ! Seed for random number sequence
INTEGER :: iseq      ! DO loop index
REAL :: ran          ! A random number
REAL :: sum          ! Sum of random numbers

! Get seed.
WRITE (*,*) 'Enter seed: '
READ (*,*) iseed

! Set seed.
CALL SEED ( iseed )

! Print out 10 random numbers.
```

(continued)

(concluded)

```
WRITE (*,*) '10 random numbers: '
DO i = 1, 10
   CALL random0 ( ran )
   WRITE (*,'(3X,F16.6)') ran
END DO

! Average 5 consecutive 1000-value sequences.
WRITE (*,*) 'Averages of 5 consecutive 1000-sample sequences:'
DO iseq = 1, 5
   sum = 0.
   DO i = 1, 1000
      CALL random0 ( ran )
      sum = sum + ran
   END DO
   ave = sum / 1000.
   WRITE (*,'(3X,F16.6)') ave
END DO

END PROGRAM test_random0
```

The results of compiling and running the test program are shown below:

```
C:\book\chap7>test_random0
Enter seed:
12
10 random numbers:
          .936091
          .203204
          .431167
          .719105
          .064103
          .789775
          .974839
          .881686
          .384951
          .400086
Averages of 5 consecutive 1000-sample sequences:
          .504282
          .512665
          .496927
          .491514
          .498117
```

The numbers do appear to be between 0.0 and 1.0, and the averages of long sets of these numbers are nearly 0.5, so these subroutines appear to be functioning correctly. You should try them again, using different seeds to see if they behave consistently.

Fortran 95/2003 includes an intrinsic subroutine RANDOM_NUMBER to generate sequences of random numbers. That subroutine will typically produce more nearly random results than the simple subroutine developed in this example. The full details of how to use subroutine RANDOM_NUMBER are found in Appendix B.

■ 7.3

MODULE PROCEDURES

In addition to data, modules may also contain complete subroutines and functions, which are known as **module procedures.** These procedures are compiled as a part of the module, and are made available to a program unit by including a USE statement containing the module name in the program unit. Procedures that are included within a module must follow any data objects declared in the module, and must be preceded by a CONTAINS statement. The CONTAINS statement tells the compiler that the following statements are included procedures.

A simple example of a module procedure is shown below. Subroutine sub1 is contained within module my_subs.

```
          MODULE my_subs
 ──▶IMPLICIT NONE

          (Declare shared data here)

          CONTAINS
             SUBROUTINE sub1 ( a, b, c, x, error )
 ──▶IMPLICIT NONE
             REAL, DIMENSION(3), INTENT(IN) :: a
             REAL, INTENT(IN) :: b, c
             REAL, INTENT(OUT) :: x
             LOGICAL, INTENT(OUT) :: error
             ...
             END SUBROUTINE sub1
          END MODULE my_subs
```

Subroutine sub1 is made available for use in a calling program unit if the statement USE my_subs is included as the first noncomment statement within the program unit. The subroutine can be called with a standard CALL statement as shown below.

```
          PROGRAM main_prog
          USE my_subs
          IMPLICIT NONE
             ...
          CALL sub1 ( a, b, c, x, error )
             ...
          END PROGRAM main_prog
```

7.3.1 Using Modules to Create Explicit Interfaces

Why would we bother to include a procedure in a module? We already know that it is possible to separately compile a subroutine and to call it from another program unit, so why go through the extra steps of including the subroutine in a module, compiling the module, declaring the module in a USE statement, and then calling the subroutine?

The answer is that *when a procedure is compiled within a module and the module is used by a calling program, all of the details of the procedure's interface are made available to the compiler.* When the calling program is compiled, the compiler can automatically check the number of arguments in the procedure call, the type of each argument, whether or not each argument is an array, and the INTENT of each argument. In short, the compiler can catch most of the common errors that a programmer might make when using procedures!

A procedure compiled within a module and accessed by USE association is said to have an **explicit interface,** since all of the details about every argument in the procedure are explicitly known to the Fortran compiler whenever the procedure is used, and the compiler checks the interface to ensure that it is being used properly.

In contrast, procedures not in a module are said to have an **implicit interface.** A Fortran compiler has no information about these procedures when it is compiling a program unit that invokes them, so it just *assumes* that the programmer got the number, type, intent, etc. of the arguments right. If the programmer actually got the calling sequence wrong, then the program will fail in strange and hard-to-find ways.

To illustrate this point, let's reexamine the program in Figure 7-5. In that program, there was an implicit interface between program bad_call and subroutine bad_argument. A real value was passed to the subroutine when an integer argument was expected, and the number was misinterpreted by the subroutine. As we saw from that example, the Fortran compiler did not catch the error in the calling arguments.

Figure 7-12 shows the program rewritten to include the subroutine within a module.

FIGURE 7-12
Example illustrating the effects of a type mismatch when a subroutine included within a module is called.

```
MODULE my_subs
CONTAINS
   SUBROUTINE bad_argument ( i )
   IMPLICIT NONE
   INTEGER, INTENT(IN) :: i      ! Declare argument as integer.
   WRITE (*,*) ' i = ', i        ! Write out i.
   END SUBROUTINE
END MODULE my_subs

!******************************************************************
!******************************************************************

PROGRAM bad_call2
!
!  Purpose:
!     To illustrate misinterpreted calling arguments.
!
USE my_subs
IMPLICIT NONE
REAL :: x = 1.                    ! Declare real variable x.
```

(*continued*)

```
(concluded)
CALL bad_argument ( x )        ! Call subroutine.
END PROGRAM bad_call2
```

When this program is compiled, the Fortran compiler will catch the argument mismatch for us.

```
C:\book\chap7>ifort bad_call2.f90
Intel(R) Fortran Compiler for 32-bit applications, Version 9.0 Build
 20051130
Z Package ID: W_FC_C_9.0.028
Copyright (C) 1985-2005 Intel Corporation. All rights reserved.

x.f90(18) : Error: The type of the actual argument differs from the type
 of the dummy argument. [X]
CALL bad_argument ( x )        ! Call subroutine.
--------------------^
compilation aborted for x.f90 (code 1)
```

There is also another way to allow a Fortran compiler to explicitly check procedure interfaces—the INTERFACE block. We will learn more about it in Chapter 13.

7

Good Programming Practice

Use either assumed-shape arrays or explicit-shape arrays as dummy array arguments in procedures. If assumed-shape arrays are used, an explicit interface is required. Whole array operations, array sections, and array intrinsic functions may be used with the dummy array arguments in either case. *Never use assumed-size arrays in any new program.*

Quiz 7-2

This quiz provides a quick check to see if you have understood the concepts introduced in Sections 7.2 through 7.3. If you have trouble with the quiz, reread the sections, ask your instructor, or discuss the material with a fellow student. The answers to this quiz are found in the back of the book.

1. How can we share data between two or more procedures without passing it through a calling interface? Why would we want to do this?

2. Why should you gather up the procedures in a program and place them into a module?

For questions 3 and 4, determine whether there are any errors in these programs. If possible, tell what the output from each program will be.

(continued)

(concluded)

```
3. MODULE mydata
   IMPLICIT NONE
   REAL, SAVE, DIMENSION(8) :: a
   REAL, SAVE :: b
   END MODULE mydata

   PROGRAM test1
   USE mydata
   IMPLICIT NONE
   a = (/ 1.,2.,3.,4.,5.,6.,7.,8. /)
   b = 37.
   CALL sub2
   END PROGRAM test1

   SUBROUTINE sub1
   USE mydata
   IMPLICIT NONE
   WRITE (*,*) 'a(5) = ', a(5)
   END SUBROUTINE sub1

4. MODULE mysubs
   CONTAINS
      SUBROUTINE sub2(x,y)
      REAL, INTENT(IN) :: x
      REAL, INTENT(OUT) :: y
      y = 3. * x - 1.
      END SUBROUTINE sub2
   END MODULE

   PROGRAM test2
   USE mysubs
   IMPLICIT NONE
   REAL :: a = 5.
   CALL sub2 (a, -3.)
   END PROGRAM test2
```

7.4
FORTRAN FUNCTIONS

A Fortran **function** is a procedure whose result is a single number, logical value, character string, or array. The result of a function is a single value or single array that can be combined with variables and constants to form Fortran expressions. These expressions may appear on the right side of an assignment statement in the calling program. There are two different types of functions: **intrinsic functions** and **user-defined functions** (or **function subprograms**).

Intrinsic functions are those functions built into the Fortran language, such as SIN(X), LOG(X), etc. Some of these functions were described in Chapter 2; all of them are detailed in Appendix B. User-defined functions or function subprograms are functions defined by individual programmers to meet a specific need not addressed by the standard intrinsic functions. They are used just like intrinsic functions in expressions. The general form of a user-defined Fortran function is:

```
FUNCTION name ( argument_list )
    . . .
    (Declaration section must declare type of name)
    . . .
    (Execution section)
    . . .
    name = expr
    RETURN
END FUNCTION [name]
```

The function must begin with a FUNCTION statement and end with an END FUNCTION statement. The name of the function may be up to 31 alphabetic, numeric, and under-score characters long, but the first letter must be alphabetic. The name must be specified in the FUNCTION statement, and is optional on the END FUNCTION statement.

A function is invoked by naming it in an expression. When a function is invoked, execution begins at the top of the function, and ends when either a RETURN statement or the END FUNCTION statement is reached. Because execution ends at the END FUNCTION statement anyway, the RETURN statement is not actually required in most functions, and is rarely used. When the function returns, the returned value is used to continue evaluating the Fortran expression that it was named in.

The name of the function must appear on the left side of a least one assignment statement in the function. The value assigned to name when the function returns to the invoking program unit will be the value of the function.

The argument list of the function may be blank if the function can perform all of its calculations with no input arguments. The parentheses around the argument list are required even if the list is blank.

Since a function returns a value, it is necessary to assign a type to the function. If IMPLICIT NONE is used, the type of the function must be declared both in the function procedure and in the calling programs. If IMPLICIT NONE is not used, the default type of the function will follow the standard rules of Fortran unless they are overridden by a type declaration statement. The type declaration of a user-defined Fortran function can take one of two equivalent forms:

```
INTEGER FUNCTION my_function ( i, j )
```

or

```
FUNCTION my_function ( i, j )
INTEGER :: my_function
```

An example of a user-defined function is shown in Figure 7-13. Function quadf evaluates a quadratic expression of the form $f(x) = ax^2 + bx + c$ with user-specified coefficients a, b, and c at a user-specified value x.

FIGURE 7-13
A function to evaluate a quadratic polynomial of the form $f(x) = ax^2 + bx + c$.

```
REAL FUNCTION quadf ( x, a, b, c )
!
!  Purpose:
!    To evaluate a quadratic polynomial of the form
!    quadf = a * x**2 + b * x + c
!
!  Record of revisions:
!     Date        Programmer          Description of change
!     ====        ==========          =====================
!    11/22/06    S. J. Chapman        Original code
!
IMPLICIT NONE

! Data dictionary: declare calling parameter types & definitions
REAL, INTENT(IN) :: x       ! Value to evaluate expression for
REAL, INTENT(IN) :: a       ! Coefficient of X**2 term
REAL, INTENT(IN) :: b       ! Coefficient of X term
REAL, INTENT(IN) :: c       ! Coefficient of constant term

! Evaluate expression.
quadf = a * x**2 + b * x + c

END FUNCTION quadf
```

This function produces a result of type REAL. Note that the INTENT attribute is not used with the declaration of the function name quadf, since it must always be used for output only. A simple test program using the function is shown in Figure 7-14.

FIGURE 7-14
A test driver program for function quadf.

```
PROGRAM test_quadf
!
!  Purpose:
!    Program to test function quadf.
!
IMPLICIT NONE

! Data dictionary: declare variable types & definitions
REAL :: quadf               ! Declare function
REAL :: a, b, c, x          ! Declare local variables

! Get input data.
WRITE (*,*) 'Enter quadratic coefficients a, b, and c: '
READ (*,*) a, b, c
WRITE (*,*) 'Enter location at which to evaluate equation: '
READ (*,*) x

! Write out result.
WRITE (*,100) ' quadf(', x, ') = ', quadf(x,a,b,c)
100 FORMAT (A,F10.4,A,F12.4)

END PROGRAM test_quadf
```

Notice that function `quadf` is declared as type `REAL` both in the function itself and in the test program. In this example, function `quadf` was used in the argument list of a `WRITE` statement. It could also have been used in assignment statements or wherever a Fortran expression is permissible.

Good Programming Practice

Be sure to declare the type of any user-defined functions both in the function itself and in any routines that call the function.

7.4.1 Unintended Side Effects in Functions

Input values are passed to a function through its argument list. Functions use the same argument-passing scheme as subroutines. A function receives pointers to the locations of its arguments, and it can deliberately or accidentally modify the contents of those memory locations. Therefore, *it is possible for a function subprogram to modify its own input arguments*. If any of the function's dummy arguments appear on the left side of an assignment statement within the function, then the values of the input variables corresponding to those arguments will be changed. A function that modifies the values in its argument list is said to have **side effects.**

By definition, a function should produce a *single output value* using one or more input values, and it should have no side effects. The function should never modify its own input arguments. If a programmer needs to produce more than one output value from a procedure, then the procedure should be written as a subroutine and not as a function. To ensure that a function's arguments are not accidentally modified, they should always be declared with the `INTENT(IN)` attribute.

Good Programming Practice

A well-designed Fortran function should produce a single output value from one or more input values. It should never modify its own input arguments. To ensure that a function does not accidentally modify its input arguments, always declare the arguments with the `INTENT(IN)` attribute.

Quiz 7-3

This quiz provides a quick check to see if you have understood the concepts introduced in Section 7-4. If you have trouble with the quiz, reread the section, ask your instructor, or discuss the material with a fellow student. The answers to this quiz are found in the back of the book.

(continued)

(concluded)

Write a user-defined function to perform the following calculations:

1. $f(x) = \dfrac{x-1}{x+1}$

2. The hyperbolic tangent function $\tanh(x) = \dfrac{e^x - e^{-x}}{e^x + e^{-x}}$

3. The factorial function $n! = (n)(n-1)(n-2)\ldots(2)(1)$
4. Write a logical function that has two input arguments, $-x$ and $-y$. The function should return a true value if $x^2 + y^2 > 1.0$, and a false value otherwise.

For questions 5 to 7, determine whether there are any errors in these functions. If so, show how to correct them.

5.
```
REAL FUNCTION average ( x, n )
IMPLICIT NONE
INTEGER, INTENT(IN) :: n
REAL, DIMENSION(n), INTENT(IN) :: x
INTEGER :: j
REAL :: sum
DO j = 1, n
   sum = sum + x(j)
END DO
average = sum / n
END FUNCTION average
```

6.
```
FUNCTION fun_2 ( a, b, c )
IMPLICIT NONE
REAL, INTENT(IN) :: a, b, c
a = 3. * a
fun_2 = a**2 - b + c
END FUNCTION fun_2
```

7.
```
LOGICAL FUNCTION badval ( x, y )
IMPLICIT NONE
REAL, INTENT(IN) :: x, y
badval = x > y
END FUNCTION badval
```

**EXAMPLE
7-5**

The Sinc Function:

The sinc function is defined by the equation

$$\text{sinc}(x) = \frac{\sin(x)}{x} \qquad\qquad (7\text{-}3)$$

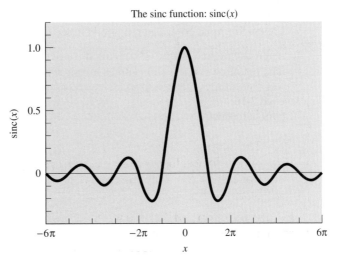

FIGURE 7-15
Plot of sinc(x) versus x.

This function occurs in many different types of engineering analysis problems. For example, the sinc function describes the frequency spectrum of a rectangular time pulse. A plot of the function sinc(x) versus x is shown in Figure 7-15. Write a user-defined Fortran function to calculate the sinc function.

SOLUTION
The sinc function looks easy to implement, but there is a calculation problem when $x = 0$. The value of sinc(0) = 1, since

$$\text{sinc}(0) = \lim_{x \to 0} \left[\frac{\sin(x)}{x} \right] = 1$$

Unfortunately, a computer program would blow up on the division by 0. We must include a logical IF construct in the function to handle the special case where x is nearly 0.

1. **State the problem.**
   Write a Fortran function that calculates sinc(x).

2. **Define the inputs and outputs.**
   The input to the function is the real argument x. The function is of type REAL, and its output is the value of sinc(x).

3. **Describe the algorithm.**
   The pseudocode for this function is

```
IF |x| > epsilon THEN
    sinc ← SIN(x) / x
ELSE
    sinc ← 1.
END IF
```

where epsilon is chosen to ensure that the division does not cause divide-by-zero errors. For most computers, a good choice for epsilon might be 1.0E - 30.

4. **Turn the algorithm into Fortran statements.**

The resulting Fortran subroutines are shown in Figure 7-16.

FIGURE 7-16
The Fortran function sinc(x).

```
FUNCTION sinc ( x )
!
!  Purpose:
!    To calculate the sinc function
!       sinc(x) = sin(x) / x
!
! Record of revisions:
!    Date        Programmer          Description of change
!    ====        ==========          =====================
!  11/23/06   S. J. Chapman          Original code
!
IMPLICIT NONE

! Data dictionary: declare calling parameter types & definitions
REAL, INTENT(IN) :: x          ! Value for which to evaluate sinc
REAL :: sinc                   ! Output value sinc(x)

! Data dictionary: declare local constants
REAL, PARAMETER :: EPSILON = 1.0E-30  ! the smallest value for which
                                      ! to calculate SIN(x)/x

! Check to see of ABS(x) > EPSILON.
IF ( ABS(x) > EPSILON ) THEN
   sinc = SIN(x) / x
ELSE
   sinc = 1.
END IF

END FUNCTION sinc
```

5. **Test the resulting Fortran program.**

To test this function, it is necessary to write a driver program to read an input value, call the function, and write out the results. We will calculate several values of sinc(x) on a hand calculator and compare them with the results of the test program. Note that we must verify the function of the program for input values both greater than and less than epsilon.

A test driver program is shown in Figure 7-17.

FIGURE 7-17
A test driver program for the function sinc(x).

```
PROGRAM test_sinc
!
!  Purpose:
!    To test the sinc function sinc(x)
```

(continued)

(*concluded*)
```
!
IMPLICIT NONE

! Data dictionary: declare function types
REAL :: sinc                  ! sinc function

! Data dictionary: declare variable types & definitions
REAL :: x                     ! Input value to evaluate

! Get value to evaluate
WRITE (*,*) 'Enter x: '
READ (*,*) x

! Write answer.
WRITE (*,'(1X,A,F8.5)') 'sinc(x) = ', sinc(x)

END PROGRAM test_sinc
```

Hand calculations yield the following values for sinc(*x*):

x	sinc(*x*)
0	1.00000
10^{-29}	1.00000
$\dfrac{\pi}{2}$	0.63662
π	0.00000

The results from the test program for these input values are:

```
C:\book\chap7>test_sinc
Enter x:
0
sinc(x) = 1.0000

C:\book\chap7>test_sinc
Enter x:
1.E-29
sinc(x) = 1.0000

C:\book\chap7>test_sinc
Enter x:
1.570796
sinc(x) = 0.63662

C:\book\chap7>test_sinc
Enter x:
3.141593
sinc(x) = 0.0000
```

The function appears to be working correctly.

▪ 7.5

PASSING PROCEDURES AS ARGUMENTS TO OTHER PROCEDURES

When a procedure is invoked, the actual argument list is passed to the procedure as a series of pointers to specific memory locations. How the memory at each location is interpreted depends on the type and size of the dummy arguments declared in the procedure.

This pass-by-reference approach can be extended to permit us to pass a pointer to a *procedure* instead of a memory location. Both functions and subroutines can be passed as calling arguments. For simplicity, we will first discuss passing user-defined functions to procedures, and afterward discuss passing subroutines to procedures.

7.5.1 Passing User-Defined Functions as Arguments

If a user-defined function is named as an actual argument in a procedure call, then a *pointer to that function* is passed to the procedure. If the corresponding formal argument in the procedure is used as a function, then when the procedure is executed, the function in the calling argument list will be used in place of the dummy function name in the procedure. Consider the following example:

```
PROGRAM :: test
REAL, EXTERNAL :: fun_1, fun_2
REAL :: x, y, output

. . .
CALL evaluate ( fun_1, x, y, output )
CALL evaluate ( fun_2, x, y, output )
. . .
END PROGRAM test

SUBROUTINE evaluate ( fun, a, b, result )
REAL, EXTERNAL :: fun
REAL, INTENT(IN) :: a, b
REAL, INTENT(OUT) :: result
result = b * fun(a)
END SUBROUTINE evaluate
```

Assume that fun_1 and fun_2 are two user-supplied functions. Then a pointer to function fun_1 is passed to subroutine evaluate on the first occasion that it is called, and function fun_1 is used in place of the dummy formal argument fun in the subroutine. A pointer to function fun_2 is passed to subroutine evaluate the second time that it is called, and function fun_2 is used in place of the dummy formal argument fun in the subroutine.

User-supplied functions may be passed as calling arguments only if they are declared to be *external* in the calling and the called procedures. When a name in an argument list is declared to be external, this tells the compiler that a separately compiled function is being passed in the argument list instead of a variable. A function may be declared to be external either with an EXTERNAL attribute or in an EXTERNAL statement. The EXTERNAL attribute is included in a type declaration statement, just like any other attribute. An example is

```
REAL, EXTERNAL :: fun_1, fun_2
```

The EXTERNAL statement is a specification statement of the form

```
EXTERNAL fun_1, fun_2
```

Either of the above forms state that fun_1, fun_2, etc., are names of procedures that are defined outside of the current routine. If used, the EXTERNAL statement must appear in the declaration section, before the first executable statement.

EXAMPLE 7-6

Passing Functions to Procedures in an Argument List:

The function ave_value in Figure 7-18 determines the average amplitude of a function between user-specified limits first_value and last_value by sampling the function at n evenly spaced points, and calculating the average amplitude between those points. The function to be evaluated is passed to function ave_value as the dummy argument func.

FIGURE 7-18

Function ave_value calculates the average amplitude of a function between two points first_value and last_value. The function is passed to function ave_value as a calling argument.

```
REAL FUNCTION ave_value ( func, first_value, last_value, n )
!
!   Purpose:
!     To calculate the average value of function "func" over the
!     range [first_value, last_value] by taking n evenly spaced
!     samples over the range, and averaging the results. Function
!     "func" is passed to this routine via a dummy argument.
!
!   Record of revisions:
!      Date       Programmer          Description of change
!      ====       ==========          =====================
!     11/24/06    S. J. Chapman       Original code
!
IMPLICIT NONE

! Data dictionary: declare calling parameter types & definitions
REAL, EXTERNAL :: func              ! Function to be evaluated
REAL, INTENT(IN) :: first_value     ! First value in range
REAL, INTENT(IN) :: last_value      ! Last value in rnage
INTEGER, INTENT(IN) :: n            ! Number of samples to average

! Data dictionary: declare local variable types & definitions
REAL :: delta                       ! Step size between samples
INTEGER :: i                        ! Index variable
```

(*continued*)

(concluded)

```
REAL :: sum                         ! Sum of values to average

! Get step size.
delta = ( last_value - first_value ) / REAL(n-1)

! Accumulate sum.
sum = 0.
DO i = 1, n
   sum = sum + func ( REAL(i-1) * delta )
END DO

! Get average.
ave_value = sum / REAL(n)

END FUNCTION ave_value
```

A test driver program to test function `ave_value` is shown in Figure 7-19. In that program, function `ave_value` is called with the user-defined function `my_function` as a calling argument. Note that `my_function` is declared as `EXTERNAL` in the test driver program `test_ave_value`. The function `my_function` is averaged over 101 samples in the interval [0, 1], and the results are printed out.

FIGURE 7-19
Test driver program for function `ave_value`, illustrating how to pass a user-defined function as a calling argument.

```
PROGRAM test_ave_value
!
! Purpose:
! To test function ave_value by calling it with a user-defined
! function my_func.
!
! Record of revisions:
!    Date        Programmer          Description of change
!    ====        ==========          =====================
!    11/24/06    S. J. Chapman       Original code
!
IMPLICIT NONE

! Data dictionary: declare function types
REAL :: ave_value              ! Average value of function
REAL, EXTERNAL :: my_function ! Function to evaluate

! Data dictionary: declare local variable types & definitions
REAL :: ave                    ! Average of my_function

! Call function with func=my_function.
ave = ave_value ( my_function, 0., 1., 101 )
WRITE (*,1000) 'my_function', ave
1000 FORMAT (1X,'The average value of ',A,' between 0. and 1. is ', &
             F16.6,'.')

END PROGRAM test_ave_value

REAL FUNCTION my_function( x )
```

(continued)

(concluded)
```
IMPLICIT NONE
REAL, INTENT(IN) :: x
my_function = 3. * x
END FUNCTION my_function
```

When program `test_ave_value` is executed, the results are

```
C:\book\chap7>test_ave_value
The average value of my_function between 0. and 1. is 1.500000.
```

Since for this case `my_function` is a straight line between (0,0) and (1,3), it is obvious that the average value was correctly calculated as 1.5.

7.5.2 Passing Subroutines as Arguments

Subroutines may also be passed to procedures as calling arguments. If a subroutine is to be passed as a calling argument, it must be declared in an `EXTERNAL` statement. The corresponding dummy argument should appear in a `CALL` statement in the procedure.

EXAMPLE *Passing Subroutines to Procedures in an Argument List:*
7-7

The function `subs_as_arguments` in Figure 7-20 accepts two input arguments `x` and `y`, and passes them to a subroutine for calculations. The name of the subroutine to execute is also passed as a command line argument.

FIGURE 7-20
Subroutine `subs_as_arguments` calls a subroutine to perform an operation on values `x` and `y`. The name of the subroutine to execute is also passed as a command line argument.

```
SUBROUTINE subs_as_arguments(x, y, sub, result )
!
!  Purpose:
!    To test passing subroutine names as arguments.
!
IMPLICIT NONE

! Data dictionary: declare calling parameter types & definitions
EXTERNAL :: sub                  ! Dummy subroutine  name
REAL, INTENT(IN) :: x            ! First value
REAL, INTENT(IN) :: y            ! Last value
REAL, INTENT(OUT) :: result      ! Result

CALL sub(x, y, result)

END SUBROUTINE subs_as_arguments
```

A test driver program to test subroutine `test_subs_as_arguments` is shown in Figure 7-21. In that program, subroutine `subs_as_arguments` is called twice with the user-defined subroutines `prod` and `sum` passed as calling arguments. Note that the dummy argument `sub` is declared as `EXTERNAL` in subroutine `subs_as_arguments`, and that the actual subroutines `prod` and `sum` are declared external in the main program.

FIGURE 7-21
Test driver program for subroutine `subs_as_arguments`, illustrating how to pass a user-defined subroutine as a calling argument.

```
PROGRAM test_subs_as_arguments
!
!  Purpose:
!    To test passing subroutine names as arguments.
!
IMPLICIT NONE

! Data dictionary: declare calling parameter types & definitions
EXTERNAL :: sum, prod              ! Name of subroutines to call
REAL :: x                          ! First value
REAL :: y                          ! Last value
REAL :: result                     ! Result

! Get the x and y values
WRITE (*,*) 'Enter x:'
READ (*,*) x
WRITE (*,*) 'Enter y:'
READ (*,*) y

! Calculate product
CALL subs_as_arguments(x, y, prod, result)
WRITE (*,*) 'The product is ', result

! Calculate product and sum
CALL subs_as_arguments(x, y, sum, result)
WRITE (*,*) 'The sum is ', result

END PROGRAM test_subs_as_arguments

!******************************************************************
!******************************************************************

SUBROUTINE prod ( x, y, result )
!
! Purpose:
! To calculate product of two real numbers.
!
IMPLICIT NONE

! Data dictionary: declare calling parameter types & definitions
REAL, INTENT(IN) :: x              ! First value
```

(continued)

(*concluded*)
```
REAL, INTENT(IN) :: y              ! Last value
REAL, INTENT(OUT) :: result        ! Result

! Calculate value.
result = x * y

END SUBROUTINE prod

!*****************************************************************
!*****************************************************************

SUBROUTINE sum ( x, y, result )
!
!  Purpose:
!    To calculate sum of two real numbers.
!
IMPLICIT NONE

! Data dictionary: declare calling parameter types & definitions
REAL, INTENT(IN) :: x              ! First value
REAL, INTENT(IN) :: y              ! Last value
REAL, INTENT(OUT) :: result        ! Result

! Calculate value.
result = x + y

END SUBROUTINE sum
```

When program `test_subs_as_arguments` is executed, the results are

```
C:\book\chap7>test_subs_as_arguments
Enter x:
4
Enter y:
5
The product is    20.00000
The sum is    9.000000
```

Here subroutine `subs_as_arguments` is being executed twice, once with subroutine `prod` and once with subroutine `sum`.

▩ 7.6

SUMMARY

In Chapter 7, we presented an introduction to Fortran procedures. Procedures are independently compiled program units with their own declaration sections, execution sections, and termination sections. They are extremely important to the design, coding, and maintenance of large programs. Procedures permit the independent testing of subtasks as a project is being built, allow time savings through reusable code, and improve reliability through variable hiding.

There are two types of procedures: subroutines and functions. Subroutines are procedures whose results include one or more values. A subroutine is defined by using a SUBROUTINE statement, and is executed by using a CALL statement. Input data is passed to a subroutine and results are returned from the subroutine through argument lists on the SUBROUTINE statement and CALL statement. When a subroutine is called, pointers are passed to the subroutine pointing to the locations of each argument in the argument list. The subroutine reads from and writes to those locations.

The use of each argument in a subroutine's argument list can be controlled by specifying an INTENT attribute in the argument's type declaration statement. Each argument can be specified as either input only (IN), output only (OUT), or both input and output (INOUT). The Fortran compiler checks to see that each argument is used properly, and so can catch many programming errors at compile time.

Data can also be passed to subroutines through modules. A module is a separately compiled program unit that can contain data declarations, procedures, or both. The data and procedures declared in the module are available to any procedure that includes the module with a USE statement. Thus, two procedures can share data by placing the data and a module, and having both procedures USE the module.

If procedures are placed in a module and that module is used in a program, then the procedures have an explicit interface. The compiler will automatically check to ensure that number, type, and use of all arguments in each procedure call match the argument list specified for the procedure. This feature can catch many common errors.

Fortran functions are procedures whose results are a single number, logical value, character string, or array. There are two types of Fortran functions: intrinsic (built-in) functions, and user-defined functions. Some intrinsic functions were discussed in Chapter 2, and all intrinsic functions are included in Appendix B. User-defined functions are declared by using the FUNCTION statement, and are executed by naming the function as a part of a Fortran expression. Data may be passed to a user-defined function through calling arguments or via modules. A properly designed Fortran function should not change its input arguments. It should *only* change the single output value.

It is possible to pass a function or subroutine to a procedure via a calling argument, provided that the function or subroutine is declared EXTERNAL in the calling program.

7.6.1 Summary of Good Programming Practice

The following guidelines should be adhered to in working with subroutines and functions.

1. Break large program tasks into smaller, more understandable procedures whenever possible.

2. Always specify the INTENT of every dummy argument in every procedure to help catch programming errors.
3. Make sure that the actual argument list in each procedure invocation matches the dummy argument list in *number, type, intent,* and *order.* Placing procedures in a module and then accessing the procedures by USE association will create an explicit interface, which will allow the compiler to automatically check that the argument lists are correct.
4. Test for possible error conditions within a subroutine, and set an error flag to be returned to the calling program unit. The calling program unit should test for error conditions after the subroutine call, and take appropriate actions if an error occurs.
5. Always use either explicit-shape dummy arrays or assumed-shape dummy arrays for dummy array arguments. Never use assumed-size dummy arrays in any new program.
6. Modules may be used to pass large amounts of data between procedures within a program. The data values are declared only once in the module, and all procedures needing access to that data use that module. Be sure to include a SAVE statement in the module to guarantee that the data is preserved between accesses by different procedures.
7. Collect the procedures that you use in a program and place them in a module. When they are a module, the Fortran compiler will automatically verify the calling argument list each time that they are used.
8. Be sure to declare the type of any function both in the function itself and in any program units that invoke the function.
9. A well-designed Fortran function should produce a single output value from one or more input values. It should never modify its own input arguments. To ensure that a function does not accidentally modify its input arguments, always declare the arguments with the INTENT(IN) attribute.

7.6.2 Summary of Fortran Statements and Structures

CALL **Statement:**

```
CALL subname( arg1, arg2, ... )
```

Example:

```
CALL sort ( number, data1 )
```

Description:
This statement transfers execution from the current program unit to the subroutine, passing pointers to the calling arguments. The subroutine executes until either a RETURN or an END SUBROUTINE statement is encountered, and then execution will continue in the calling program unit at the next executable statement following the CALL statement.

CONTAINS Statement:

```
                              CONTAINS
```

Examples:

```
            MODULE test
            . . .
            CONTAINS
            SUBROUTINE sub1(x, y)
            . . .
            END SUBROUTINE sub1
            END MODULE test
```

Description:
The CONTAINS statement specifies that the following statements are separate procedures within a module. The CONTAINS statement and the module procedures following it must appear after any type and data definitions within the module.

END Statements:

```
            END FUNCTION [name]
            END MODULE [name]
            END SUBROUTINE [name]
```

Example:

```
            END FUNCTION my_function
            END MODULE my_mod
            END SUBROUTINE my_sub
```

Description:
These statements end user-defined Fortran functions, modules, and subroutines respectively. The name of the function, module, or subroutine may optionally be included, but it is not required.

EXTERNAL Attribute:

```
            type, EXTERNAL :: name1, name2, ...
```
Example:
```
            REAL, EXTERNAL :: my_function
```
Description:
This attribute declares that a particular name is an externally defined function. It is equivalent to naming the function in an EXTERNAL statement.

EXTERNAL Statement:

           EXTERNAL name1, name2, ...

Example:

           EXTERNAL my_function

Description:
This statement declares that a particular name is an externally defined procedure. Either it or the EXTER-NAL attribute must be used in the calling program unit and in the called procedure if the procedure specified in the EXTERNAL statement is to be passed as an actual argument.

FUNCTION Statement:

           [type] FUNCTION name(arg1, arg2, ...)

Examples:

           INTEGER FUNCTION max_value (num, iarray)
           FUNCTION gamma(x)

Description:
This statement declares a user-defined Fortran function. The type of the function may be declared in the FUNCTION statement, or it may be declared in a separate type declaration statement. The function is executed by naming it in an expression in the calling program. The dummy arguments are placeholders for the calling arguments passed when the function is executed. If a function has no arguments, then it must be declared with an empty pair of parentheses [name( )].

INTENT Attribute:

           type, INTENT(intent_type) :: name1, name2, ...

Example:

           REAL, INTENT(IN) :: value
           INTEGER, INTENT(OUT) :: count

Description:
This attribute declares the intended use of a particular dummy procedure argument. Possible values of intent_type are IN, OUT, and INOUT. The INTENT attribute allows the Fortran compiler to know the intended use of the argument, and to check that it is used in the way intended. This attribute may only appear on dummy arguments in procedures.

INTENT Statement:

$$\text{INTENT}(\textit{intent\_type}) :: \textit{name1}, \textit{name2}, \ldots$$

Example:

```
INTENT(IN) :: a, b
INTENT(OUT) :: result
```

Description:

This statement declares the intended use of a particular dummy procedure argument. Possible values of *intent_type* are IN, OUT, and INOUT. The INTENT statement allows the Fortran compiler to know the intended use of the argument, and to check that it is used in the way intended. Only dummy arguments may appear in INTENT statements. **Do not use this statement; use the INTENT attribute instead.**

MODULE Statement:

```
MODULE name
```

Example:

```
MODULE my_data_and_subs
```

Description:

This statement declares a module. The module may contain data, procedures, or both. The data and procedures are made available for use in a program unit by declaring the module name in a USE statement (USE association).

RETURN Statement:

```
RETURN
```

Example:

```
RETURN
```

Description:

When this statement is executed in a procedure, control returns to the program unit that invoked the procedure. This statement is optional at the end of a subroutine or function, since execution will automatically return to the calling routine whenever an END SUBROUTINE or END FUNCTION statement is reached.

SUBROUTINE Statement:

```
SUBROUTINE name( arg1, arg2, ... )
```

(continued)

(concluded)

Example:

```
SUBROUTINE sort ( num, data1 )
```

Description:
This statement declares a Fortran subroutine. The subroutine is executed with a `CALL` statement. The dummy arguments are placeholders for the calling arguments passed when the subroutine is executed.

`USE` **Statement:**

```
USE module1, module2, ...
```

Example:

```
USE my_data
```

Description:
This statement makes the contents of one or more modules available for use in a program unit. `USE` statements must be the first noncomment statements within the program unit after the `PROGRAM`, `SUBROUTINE`, or `FUNCTION` statement.

7

7.6.3 Exercises

7-1. What is the difference between a subroutine and a function?

7-2. When a subroutine is called, how is data passed from the calling program to the subroutine, and how are the results of the subroutine returned to the calling program?

7-3. What are the advantages and disadvantages of the pass-by-reference scheme used in Fortran?

7-4. What are the advantages and disadvantages of using explicit-shape dummy arrays in procedures? What are the advantages and disadvantages of using assumed-shape dummy arrays? Why should assumed-size dummy arrays never be used?

7-5. Suppose that a 15-element array `a` is passed to a subroutine as a calling argument. What will happen if the subroutine attempts to write to element `a(16)`?

7-6. Suppose that a real value is passed to a subroutine in an argument that is declared to be an integer in the subroutine. Is there any way for the subroutine to tell that the argument type is mismatched? What happens on your computer when the following code is executed?

```
PROGRAM main
IMPLICIT NONE
REAL :: x
x = -5.
```

```
CALL sub1 ( x )
END PROGRAM main

SUBROUTINE sub1 ( i )
IMPLICIT NONE
INTEGER, INTENT(IN) :: i
WRITE (*,*) ' I = ', i
END SUBROUTINE sub1
```

7-7. How could the program in Exercise 7-6 be modified to ensure that the Fortran compiler catches the argument mismatch between the actual argument in the main program and the dummy argument in subroutine sub1?

7-8. What is the purpose of the INTENT attribute? Where can it be used? Why should it be used?

7-9. Determine whether the following subroutine calls are correct or not. If they are in error, specify what is wrong with them.

    (*a*)
```
PROGRAM sum_sqrt
IMPLICIT NONE
INTEGER, PARAMETER :: LENGTH = 20
INTEGER :: result
REAL :: test(LENGTH) = &
      (/ 1., 2., 3., 4., 5., 6., 7., 8., 9.,10., &
        11.,12.,13.,14.,15.,16.,17.,18.,19.,20. /)
. . .
CALL test_sub ( LENGTH, test, result )
. . .
END PROGRAM sum_sqrt

SUBROUTINE test_sub ( length, array, res )
IMPLICIT NONE
INTEGER, INTENT(IN) :: length
REAL, INTENT(OUT) :: res
INTEGER, DIMENSION(length), INTENT(IN) :: array
INTEGER, INTENT(INOUT) :: i
DO i = 1, length
   res = res + SQRT(array(i))
END DO
END SUBROUTINE test_sub
```

    (*b*)
```
PROGRAM test
IMPLICIT NONE
CHARACTER(len=8) :: str = '1AbHz05Z'
CHARACTER :: largest
CALL max_char (str, largest)
```

```
      WRITE (*,100) str, largest
100 FORMAT (' The largest character in ', A, ' is ', A)
      END PROGRAM test

      SUBROUTINE max_char(string, big)
      IMPLICIT NONE
      CHARACTER(len=10), INTENT(IN) :: string
      CHARACTER, INTENT(OUT) :: big
      INTEGER :: i
      big = string(1:1)
      DO i = 2, 10
         IF ( string(i:i) > big ) THEN
            big = string(i:i)
         END IF
      END DO
      END SUBROUTINE max_char
```

7-10. Is the following program correct or incorrect? If it is incorrect, what is wrong with it? If it is correct, what values will be printed out by the following program?

```
MODULE my_constants
IMPLICIT NONE
REAL, PARAMETER :: PI = 3.141593  ! Pi
REAL, PARAMETER :: G = 9.81        ! Accel. due to gravity
END MODULE my_constants

PROGRAM main
IMPLICIT NONE
USE my_constants
WRITE (*,*) 'SIN(2*PI) = ' SIN(2.*PI)
G = 17.
END PROGRAM main
```

7-11. Modify the selection sort subroutine developed in this chapter so that it sorts real values in *descending* order.

7-12. Write a subroutine ucase that accepts a character string, and converts any lowercase letter in the string to uppercase without affecting any nonalphabetic characters in the string.

7-13. Write a driver program to test the statistical subroutines developed in Example 7-3. Be sure to test the routines with a variety of input data sets. Did you discover any problems with the subroutines?

7-14. Write a subroutine that uses subroutine random0 to generate a random number in the range $[-1.0, 1.0)$.

7-15. Dice Simulation It is often useful to be able to simulate the throw of a fair die. Write a Fortran function `dice()` that simulates the throw of a fair die by returning some random integer between 1 and 6 every time that it is called. (*Hint:* Call `random0` to generate a random number. Divide the possible values out of `random0` into six equal intervals, and return the number of the interval that a given random number falls into.)

7-16. Road Traffic Density Subroutine `random0` produces a number with a *uniform* probability distribution in the range [0.0, 1.0). This subroutine is suitable for simulating random events if each outcome has an equal probability of occurring. However, in many events, the probability of occurrence is *not* equal for every event, and a uniform probability distribution is not suitable for simulating such events.

For example, when traffic engineers studied the number of cars passing a given location in a time interval of length t, they discovered that the probability of k cars passing during the interval is given by the equation

$$P(k,t) = e^{-\lambda t} \frac{(\lambda t)^k}{k!} \text{ for } t \geq 0, \lambda > 0, \text{ and } k = 0, 1, 2, \dots \tag{7-4}$$

This probability distribution is known as the *Poisson distribution*; it occurs in many applications in science and engineering. For example, the number of calls k to a telephone switchboard in time interval t, the number of bacteria k in a specified volume t of liquid, and the number of failures k of a complicated system in time interval t all have Poisson distributions. Write a function to evaluate the Poisson distribution for any k, t, and λ. Test your function by calculating the probability of 0, 1, 2, ..., 5 cars passing a particular point on a highway in 1 minute, given that λ is 1.6 per minute for that highway.

7-17. What are two purposes of a module? What are the special advantages of placing procedures within modules?

7-18. Write three Fortran functions to calculate the hyperbolic sine, cosine, and tangent functions:

$$\sinh(x) = \frac{e^x - e^{-x}}{2} \qquad \cosh(x) = \frac{e^x + e^{-x}}{2} \qquad \tanh(x) = \frac{e^x - e^{-x}}{e^x + e^{-x}}$$

Use your functions to calculate the hyperbolic sines, cosines, and tangents of the following values: -2, -1.5, -1.0, -0.5, -0.25, 0.0, 0.25, 0.5, 1.0, 1.5, and 2.0. Sketch the shapes of the hyperbolic sine, cosine, and tangent functions.

7-19. Cross Product Write a function to calculate the cross product of two vectors $\mathbf{V}_1$ and $\mathbf{V}_2$:

$$\mathbf{V}_1 \times \mathbf{V}_2 = (V_{y1}V_{z2} - V_{y2}V_{z1})\mathbf{i} + (V_{z1}V_{x2} - V_{z2}V_{x1})\mathbf{j} + (V_{x1}V_{y2} - V_{x2}V_{y1})\mathbf{k}$$

where $\mathbf{V}_1 = V_{x1}\mathbf{i} + V_{y1}\mathbf{j} + V_{z1}\mathbf{k}$ and $\mathbf{V}_2 = V_{x2}\mathbf{i} + V_{y2}\mathbf{j} + V_{z2}\mathbf{k}$. Note that this function will return a real array as its result. Use the function to calculate the cross product of the two vectors $\mathbf{V}_1 = [-2, 4, 0.5]$ and $\mathbf{V}_2 = [0.5, 3, 2]$.

7-20. Sort with Carry It is often useful to sort an array `arr1` into ascending order, while simultaneously carrying along a second array `arr2`. In such a sort, each time an element of array `arr1` is exchanged with another element of `arr1`, the corresponding elements of array `arr2` are also swapped. When the sort is over, the elements of array `arr1` are in ascending order, while the elements of array `arr2` that were associated with particular elements of array `arr1` are still associated with them. For example, suppose we have the following two arrays:

Element	arr1	arr2
1.	6.	1.
2.	1.	0.
3.	2.	10.

After sorting array `arr1` while carrying along array `arr2`, the contents of the two arrays will be:

Element	arr1	arr2
1.	1.	0.
2.	2.	10.
3.	6.	1.

Write a subroutine to sort one real array into ascending order while carrying along a second one. Test the subroutine with the following two 9-element arrays:

```
REAL, DIMENSION(9) :: &
  a = (/ 1., 11., -6., 17.,-23., 0., 5., 1., -1. /)
REAL, DIMENSION(9) :: &
  b = (/ 31.,101., 36.,-17., 0., 10., -8., -1., -1. /)
```

7-21. Minima and Maxima of a Function Write a subroutine that attempts to locate the maximum and minimum values of an arbitrary function $f(x)$ over a certain range. The function being evaluated should be passed to the subroutine as a calling argument. The subroutine should have the following input arguments:

`first_value`	— The first value of x to search
`last_value`	— The last value of x to search
`num_steps`	— The number of steps to include in the search
`func`	— The name of the function to search

The subroutine should have the following output arguments:

`xmin`	— The value of x at which the minimum was found
`min_value`	— The minimum value of $f(x)$ found
`xmax`	— The value of x at which the maximum was found
`max_value`	— The maximum value $f(x)$ found

7-22. Write a test driver program for the subroutine generated in the previous problem. The test driver program should pass to the subroutine the user-defined function $f(x) = x^3 - 5x^2 + 5x + 2$, and search for the minimum and maximum in 200 steps over the range $-1 \le x \le 3$. It should print out the resulting minimum and maximum values.

7-23. Derivative of a Function The *derivative* of a continuous function $f(x)$ is defined by the equation

$$\frac{d}{dx}f(x) = \lim_{\Delta x \to 0} \frac{f(x + \Delta x) - f(x)}{\Delta x} \qquad (7\text{-}5)$$

In a sampled function, this definition becomes

$$f'(x_i) = \frac{f(x_{i+1}) - f(x_i)}{\Delta x} \qquad (7\text{-}6)$$

where $\Delta x = x_{i+1} - x_i$. Assume that a vector vect contains nsamp samples of a function taken at a spacing of dx per sample. Write a subroutine that will calculate the derivative of this vector from Equation 7-6. The subroutine should check to make sure that dx is greater than zero to prevent divide-by-zero errors in the subroutine.

To check your subroutine, you should generate a data set whose derivative is known, and compare the result of the subroutine with the known correct answer. A good choice for a test function is sin x. From elementary calculus, we know that

$$\frac{d}{dx}(\sin x) = \cos x$$

Generate an input vector containing 100 values of the function sin x starting at $x = 0$ and using a step size Δx of 0.05. Take the derivative of the vector with your subroutine, and then compare the resulting answers to the known correct answer. How close did your routine come to calculating the correct value for the derivative?

7-24. Derivative in the Presence of Noise We will now explore the effects of input noise on the quality of a numerical derivative (Figure 7-22). First, generate an input vector containing 100 values of the function sin x starting at $x = 0$, and using a step size Δx of 0.05, just as you did in the previous problem. Next, use subroutine random0 to generate a small amount of random noise with a maximum amplitude of ± 0.02, and add that random noise to the samples in your input vector. Note that the peak amplitude of the noise is only 2 percent of the peak amplitude of your signal, since the maximum value of sin x is 1. Now take the derivative of the function using the derivative subroutine that you developed in the last problem. How close to the theoretical value of the derivative did you come?

7-25. Two's Complement Arithmetic As we learned in Chapter 1, an 8-bit integer in two's complement format can represent all the numbers between -128 and $+127$, including 0. The sidebar in Chapter 1 also showed us how to add and subtract binary numbers in two's complement format. Assume that a two's complement binary number is supplied in an 8-character variable containing 0s and 1s, and perform the following instructions:

(*a*) Write a subroutine or function that adds 2 two's complement binary numbers stored in character variables, and returns the result in a third character variable.

(*b*) Write a subroutine or function that subtracts 2 two's complement binary numbers stored in character variables, and returns the result in a third character variable.

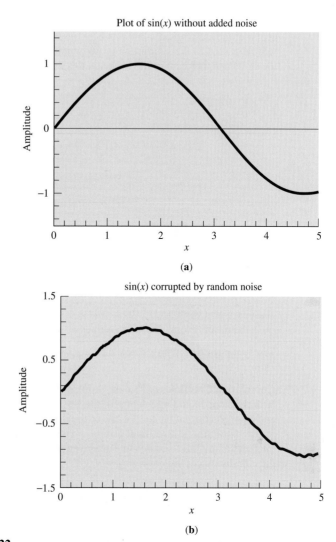

FIGURE 7-22
(*a*) A plot of sin *x* as a function of *x* with no noise added to the data. (*b*) A plot of sin *x* as a function of *x* with a 2 percent peak amplitude uniform random noise added to the data.

(*c*) Write a subroutine or function that converts a two's complement binary number stored in a character variable into a decimal integer stored in an INTEGER variable, and returns the result.

(*d*) Write a subroutine or function that converts a decimal integer stored in an INTEGER variable into a two's complement binary number stored in a character variable, and returns the result.

(*e*) Write a program that uses the four procedures created above to implement a two's complement calculator, in which the user can enter numbers in either decimal or binary form, and perform addition and subtraction on them. The results of any operation should be displayed in both decimal and binary form.

7-26. Linear Least-Squares Fit Develop a subroutine that will calculate slope m and intercept b of the least-squares line that best fits an input data set. The input data points (x, y) will be passed to the subroutine in two input arrays, X and Y. The equations describing the slope and intercept of the least-squares line are

$$y = mx + b \qquad (5\text{-}5)$$

$$m = \frac{(\Sigma xy) - (\Sigma x)\bar{y}}{(\Sigma x^2) - (\Sigma x)\bar{x}} \qquad (5\text{-}6)$$

and

$$b = \bar{y} - m\bar{x} \qquad (5\text{-}7)$$

where

Σx is the sum of the x values
Σx^2 is the sum of the squares of the x values
Σxy is the sum of the products of the corresponding x and y values
$\bar{x}$ is the mean (average) of the x values
$\bar{y}$ is the mean (average) of the y values

Test your routine using a test driver program and the 20-point input data set in Table 7-1.

7-27. Correlation Coefficient of Least-Squares Fit Develop a subroutine that will calculate both the slope m and intercept b of the least-squares line that best fits an input data set, and also the correlation coefficient of the fit. The input data points (x, y) will be passed to the subroutine in two input arrays, X and Y. The equations describing the slope and intercept of the least-squares line are given in the previous problem, and the equation for the correlation coefficient is

$$r = \frac{n(\Sigma xy) - (\Sigma x)(\Sigma y)}{\sqrt{\left[(n\Sigma x^2) - (\Sigma x)^2\right]\left[(n\Sigma y^2) - (\Sigma y)^2\right]}} \qquad (5\text{-}17)$$

TABLE 7-1
Sample data to test least squares fit routine

No.	x	y	No.	x	y
1	−4.91	−8.18	11	−0.94	0.21
2	−3.84	−7.49	12	0.59	1.73
3	−2.41	−7.11	13	0.69	3.96
4	−2.62	−6.15	14	3.04	4.26
5	−3.78	−5.62	15	1.01	5.75
6	−0.52	−3.30	16	3.60	6.67
7	−1.83	−2.05	17	4.53	7.70
8	−2.01	−2.83	18	5.13	7.31
9	0.28	−1.16	19	4.43	9.05
10	1.08	0.52	20	4.12	10.95

where

Σx is the sum of the x values

Σy is the sum of the y values

Σx^2 is the sum of the squares of the x values

Σy^2 is the sum of the squares of the y values

Σxy is the sum of the products of the corresponding x and y values

n is the number of points included in the fit

Test your routine using a test driver program and the 20-point input data set given in the previous problem.

7-28. The Birthday Problem The Birthday Problem is: If there are a group of n people in a room, what is the probability that two or more of them have the same birthday? It is possible to determine the answer to this question by simulation. Write a function that calculates the probability that two or more of n people will have the same birthday, where n is a calling argument. (*Hint:* To do this, the function should create an array of size n and generate n birthdays in the range 1 to 365 randomly. It should then check to see if any of the n birthdays are identical. The function should perform this experiment at least 10,000 times, and calculate the fraction of those times in which two or more people had the same birthday.) Write a main program that calculates and prints out the probability that two or more of n people will have the same birthday for $n = 2, 3, \ldots, 40$.

7-29. Elapsed Time Measurement In testing the operation of procedures, it is very useful to have a set of *elapsed time subroutines*. By starting a timer running before a procedure executes, and then checking the time after the execution is completed, we can see how fast or slow the procedure is. In this manner, a programmer can identify the time-consuming portions of a program, and rewrite them if necessary to make them faster.

Write a pair of subroutines named `set_timer` and `elapsed_time` to calculate the elapsed time in seconds between the last time that subroutine `set_timer` was called and the time that subroutine `elapsed_time` is being called. When subroutine `set_timer` is called, it should get the current time and store it into a variable in a module. When subroutine `elapsed_time` is called, it should get the current time, and then calculate the difference between the current time and the stored time in the module. The elapsed time in seconds between the two calls should be returned to the calling program unit in an argument of subroutine `elapsed_time`. (*Note*: The intrinsic subroutine to read the current time is called `DATE_AND_TIME`; see Appendix B.)

7-30. Use subroutine `random0` to generate a set of three arrays of random numbers. The three arrays should be 100, 1000, and 10000 elements long. Then, use your elapsed time subroutines to determine the time that it takes subroutine `sort` to sort each array. How does the elapsed time to sort increase as a function of the number of elements being sorted? (*Hint:* On a fast computer, you will need to sort each array many times and calculate the average sorting time in order to overcome the quantization error of the system clock.)

7-31. Evaluating Infinite Series The value of the exponential function e^x can be calculated by evaluating the following infinite series:

$$e^x = \sum_{n=0}^{\infty} \frac{x^n}{n!}$$

Write a Fortran function that calculates e^x using the first 12 terms of the infinite series. Compare the result of your function with the result of the intrinsic function EXP(x) for $x = -10., -5., -1., 0., 1., 5., 10.,$ and 15.

7-32. Use subroutine random0 to generate an array containing 10,000 random numbers between 0.0 and 1.0. Then, use the statistics subroutines developed in this chapter to calculate the average and standard deviation of values in the array. The theoretical average of a uniform random distribution in the range [0,1) is 0.5, and the theoretical standard deviation of the uniform random distribution is $1/\sqrt{12}$. How close does the random array generated by random0 come to behaving like the theoretical distribution?

7-33. Gaussian (Normal) Distribution Subroutine random0 returns a uniformly distributed random variable in the range [0,1), which means that there is an equal probability of any given number in the range occurring on a given call to the subroutine. Another type of random distribution is the Gaussian distribution, in which the random value takes on the classic bell-shaped curve shown in Figure 7-23. A Gaussian Distribution with an average of 0.0 and a standard deviation of 1.0 is called a *standardized normal distribution,* and the probability of any given value occurring in the standardized normal distribution is given by the equation

$$p(x) = \frac{1}{\sqrt{2\pi}} e^{-x^2/2} \tag{7-7}$$

It is possible to generate a random variable with a standardized normal distribution starting from a random variable with a uniform distribution in the range [−1,1) as follows:

1. Select two uniform random variables x_1 and x_2 from the range [−1,1) such that $x_1^2 + x_2^2 < 1$. To do this, generate two uniform random variables in the range [−1,1), and see if the sum of their squares happens to be less than 1. If so, use them. If not, try again.

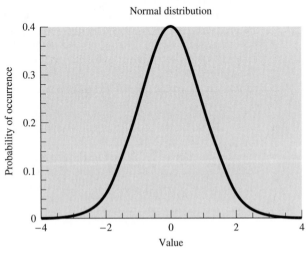

FIGURE 7-23
A normal probability distribution.

2. Then each of the values y_1 and y_2 in the equations below will be a normally distributed random variable.

$$y_1 = \sqrt{\frac{-2\log_e r}{r}}\, x_1 \qquad (7\text{-}8)$$

$$y_2 = \sqrt{\frac{-2\log_e r}{r}}\, x_2 \qquad (7\text{-}9)$$

where

$$r = x_1^2 + x_2^2 \qquad (7\text{-}10)$$

Write a subroutine that returns a normally distributed random value each time that it is called. Test your subroutine by getting 1000 random values and calculating the standard deviation. How close to 1.0 was the result?

7-34. **Gravitational Force** The gravitational force F between two bodies of masses m_1 and m_2 is given by the equation

$$F = \frac{Gm_1 m_2}{r^2} \qquad (7\text{-}11)$$

where G is the gravitation constant (6.672×10^{-11} N · m²/kg²), m_1 and m_2 are the masses of the bodies in kilograms, and r is the distance between the two bodies. Write a function to calculate the gravitation force between two bodies given their masses and the distance between them. Test your function by determining the force on a 1000-kg satellite in orbit 38,000 km above the Earth. (The mass of the Earth is 5.98×10^{24} kg.)

7-35. **Heapsort** The selection sort subroutine that was introduced in this chapter is by no means the only type of sorting algorithm available. One alternative possibility is the *heapsort* algorithm, the description of which is beyond the scope of this book. However, an implementation of the heapsort algorithm is included in file `heapsort.f90`, which is available among the Chapter 7 files at the book's website.

If you have not done so previously, write a set of elapsed time subroutines for your computer, as described in Exercise 7-29. Generate an array containing 10,000 random values. Use the elapsed time subroutines to compare the time required to sort these 10,000 values, using the selection sort and the heapsort algorithms. Which algorithm is faster? (*Note*: Be sure that you are sorting the same array each time. The best way to do this is to make a copy of the original array before sorting, and then sort the two arrays with the different subroutines.)

Additional Features of Arrays

OBJECTIVES

- Know how to declare and use two-dimensional or rank-2 arrays.
- Know how to declare and use multidimensional or rank-*n* arrays.
- Know how and when to use the WHERE construct.
- Know how and when to use the FORALL construct.
- Understand how to allocate, use, and deallocate allocatable arrays.

In Chapter 6, we learned how to use simple one-dimensional (rank-1) arrays. This chapter picks up where Chapter 6 left off, covering advanced topics such as multidimensional arrays, array functions, and allocatable arrays.

8.1

TWO-DIMENSIONAL OR RANK-2 ARRAYS

The arrays that we have worked with so far in Chapter 6 are **one-dimensional arrays** or **rank-1 arrays** (also known as **vectors**). These arrays can be visualized as a series of values laid out in a column, with a single subscript used to select the individual array elements (Figure 8-1*a*). Such arrays are useful to describe data that is a function of one independent variable, such as a series of temperature measurements made at fixed intervals of time.

Some types of data are functions of more than one independent variable. For example, we might wish to measure the temperature at five different locations at four different times. In this case, our 20 measurements could logically be grouped into five different columns of four measurements each, with a separate column for each location (Figure 8-1*b*). Fortran has a mechanism especially designed to hold this sort of data—a **two-dimensional** or **rank-2 array** (also called a **matrix**).

Rank-2 arrays are arrays whose elements are addressed with two subscripts, and any particular element in the array is selected by simultaneously choosing values for both of them. For example, Figure 8-2*a* shows a set of four generators whose power output has been measured at six different times. Figure 8-2*b* shows an array consisting of the six different power measurements for each of the four different generators.

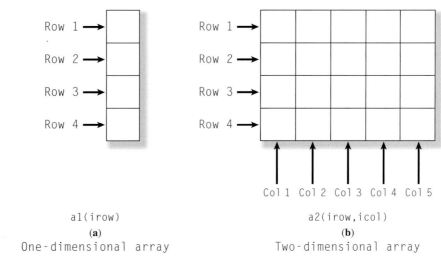

al(irow)

(a)

One-dimensional array

a2(irow,icol)

(b)

Two-dimensional array

FIGURE 8-1

Representations of one- and two-dimensional arrays.

In this example, each row specifies a measurement time, and each column specifies a generator number. The array element containing the power supplied by generator 3 at time 4 would be power(4,3); its value is 41.1 MW.

8.1.1 Declaring Rank-2 Arrays

The type and size of a rank-2 array must be declared to the compiler by using a type declaration statement. Some example array declarations are shown below:

1. REAL, DIMENSION(3,6) :: sum

   This type statement declares a real array consisting of 3 rows and 6 columns, for a total of 18 elements. The legal values of the first subscript are 1 to 3, and the

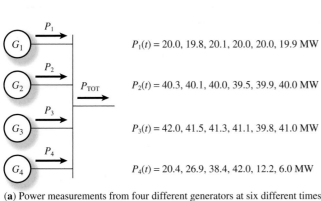

$P_1(t) = 20.0, 19.8, 20.1, 20.0, 20.0, 19.9$ MW

$P_2(t) = 40.3, 40.1, 40.0, 39.5, 39.9, 40.0$ MW

$P_3(t) = 42.0, 41.5, 41.3, 41.1, 39.8, 41.0$ MW

$P_4(t) = 20.4, 26.9, 38.4, 42.0, 12.2, 6.0$ MW

	G_1	G_2	G_3	G_4
Time 1	20.0	40.3	42.0	20.4
Time 2	19.8	40.1	41.5	26.9
Time 3	20.1	40.0	41.3	38.4
Time 4	20.0	39.5	41.1	42.0
Time 5	20.0	39.9	39.8	12.2
Time 6	19.9	40.0	41.0	6.0

(a) Power measurements from four different generators at six different times

(b) Two-dimensional matrix of power measurements

FIGURE 8-2

(*a*) A power generating station consisting of four different generators. The power output of each generator is measured at six different times. (*b*) Two-dimensional matrix of power measurements.

legal values of the second subscript are 1 to 6. Any other subscript values are out of bounds.

2. `INTEGER, DIMENSION(0:100,0:20) :: hist`

   This type statement declares an integer array consisting of 101 rows and 21 columns, for a total of 2121 elements. The legal values of the first subscript are 0 to 100, and the legal values of the second subscript are 0 to 20. Any other subscript values are out of bounds.

3. `CHARACTER(len=6), DIMENSION(-3:3,10) :: counts`

   This type statement declares an array consisting of 7 rows and 10 columns, for a total of 70 elements. Its type is `CHARACTER`, with each array element capable of holding 6 characters. The legal values of the first subscript are -3 to 3, and the legal values of the second subscript are 1 to 10. Any other subscript values are out of bounds.

8.1.2 Rank-2 Array Storage

We have already learned that a rank-1 array of length N occupies N successive locations in the computer's memory. Similarly, a rank-2 array of size M by N occupies $M \times N$ successive locations in the computer's memory. How are the elements of the array arranged in the computer's memory? Fortran always allocates array elements in **column major order.** That is, Fortran allocates the first column in memory, then the second one, then the third one, etc. until all columns have been allocated. Figure 8-3

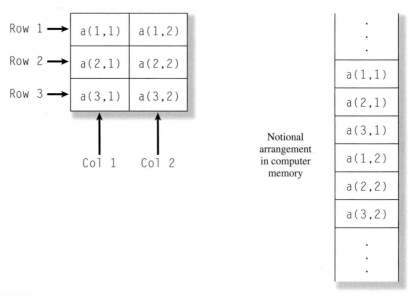

FIGURE 8-3

Notional memory allocation for a 3×2 rank 2 array a.

illustrates this memory allocation scheme for a 3 × 2 array a. As we can see from the picture, the array element a(2,2) is really the fifth location reserved in memory. The order of memory allocation will become important when we discuss data initialization and I/O statements later in this section.[1]

8.1.3 Initializing Rank-2 Arrays

Rank-2 arrays may be initialized with assignment statements, type declaration statements, or Fortran READ statements.

Initializing rank-2 arrays with assignment statements

Initial values may be assigned to an array on an element-by-element basis, using assignment statements in a nested DO loop, or all at once with an array constructor. For example, suppose we have a 4 × 3 integer array istat that we wish to initialize with the values shown in Figure 8-4. This array could be initialized at run time on an element-by-element with DO loops, as shown below:

```
INTEGER, DIMENSION(4,3) :: istat
DO i = 1, 4
    DO j = 1, 3
        istat(i,j) = j
    END DO
END DO
```

The array could also be initialized in a single statement with an array constructor. However, this is not as simple as it might seem. The notional data pattern in memory that would initialize the array is shown in Figure 8-4b. It consists of four 1s, followed by four 2s, followed by four 3s. The array constructor that would produce this pattern in memory is

$$(/ 1,1,1,1,2,2,2,2,3,3,3,3 /)$$

so it would seem that the array could be initialized with the assignment statement

$$istat = (/ 1,1,1,1,2,2,2,2,3,3,3,3 /)$$

Unfortunately, *this assignment statement will not work*. The array constructor produces a 1 × 12 array, while array istat is a 4 × 3 array. Although they both have the

---

[1] The Fortran 95 and Fortran 2003 standards do not actually *require* that the elements of an array occupy successive locations in memory. They only require that they *appear* to be successive when addressed with appropriate subscripts or when used in operations such as I/O statements. To keep this distinction clear, we will refer to the *notional order* of the elements in memory, with the understanding that the actual order implemented by the processor could be anything. (As a practical matter, though, every Fortran compiler that the author has ever seen allocates the elements of an array in successive memory locations.) The allocation of array elements in memory was deliberately not constrained by the standard to make it easier to implement Fortran on massively parallel computers, where different memory models might be appropriate.

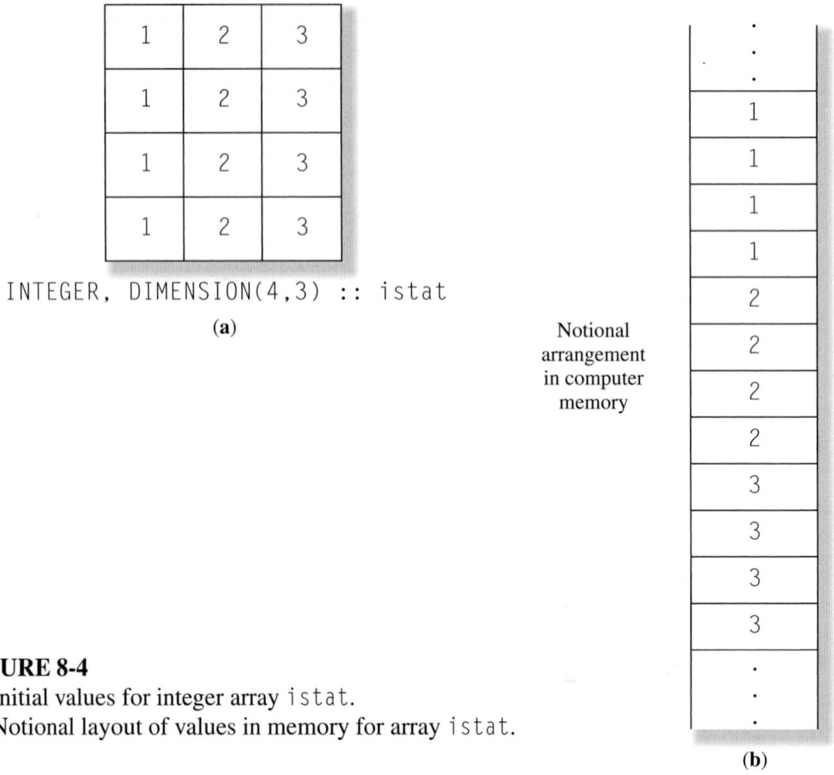

1	2	3
1	2	3
1	2	3
1	2	3

```
INTEGER, DIMENSION(4,3) :: istat
```

(a)

Notional
arrangement
in computer
memory

·
·
·
1
1
1
1
2
2
2
2
3
3
3
3
·
·
·

(b)

FIGURE 8-4
(a) Initial values for integer array istat.
(b) Notional layout of values in memory for array istat.

same number of elements, the two arrays are not **conformable** because they have different shapes, and so cannot be used in the same operation. This assignment statement will produce a compile-time error on a Fortran 95/2003 compiler.

Array constructors always produce rank-1 arrays. So how can we overcome this limitation to use array constructors to initialize rank-2 arrays? Fortran 95/2003 provides a special intrinsic function, called RESHAPE, which changes the shape of an array without changing the number of elements in it. The form of the RESHAPE function is

```
output = RESHAPE ( array1, array2 )
```

where array1 contains the data to reshape, and array2 is a rank-1 array describing the new shape. The number of elements in array2 is the number of dimensions in the output array, and the value of each element in array2 is the extent of each dimension. *The number of elements in array1 must be the same as the number of elements in the shape specified in array2*, or the RESHAPE function will fail. The assignment statement to initialize array istat becomes:

```
istat = RESHAPE ( (/ 1,1,1,1,2,2,2,2,3,3,3,3 /), (/4,3/) )
```

The RESHAPE function converts the 1×12 array constructor into a 4×3 array that can be assigned to istat.

Note that when RESHAPE changes the shape of an array, it maps the elements from the old shape to the new shape in column major order. Thus the first element in the array constructor becomes istat(1,1), the second one becomes istat(2,1), etc.

Good Programming Practice

Use the RESHAPE function to change the shape of an array. This is especially useful when used with an array constructor to create array constants of any desired shape.

Initializing rank-2 arrays with type declaration statements

Initial values may also be loaded into the array at compilation time by using type declaration statements. When a type declaration statement is used to initialize a rank-2 array, the data values are loaded into the array in the order in which memory is notionally allocated by the Fortran compiler. *Since arrays are allocated in column order, the values listed in the type declaration statement must be in column order.* That is, all of the elements in column 1 must be listed in the statement first, and then all of the elements in column 2, etc. Array istat contains 4 rows and 3 columns, so to initialize the array with a type declaration statement, the four values of column 1 must be listed first, then the four values for column 2, and finally the four values for column 3.

The values used to initialize the array must have the same shape as the array, so the RESHAPE function must be used as well. Therefore, array istat could be initialized at compilation time with the following statement:

```
INTEGER, DIMENSION(4,3) :: istat(4,3) = &
            RESHAPE ( (/ 1,1,1,1,2,2,2,2,3,3,3,3 /), (/4,3/) )
```

Initializing rank-2 arrays with READ statements

Arrays may be initialized with Fortran READ statements. If an array name appears without subscripts in the argument list of a READ statement, the program will attempt to read values for all of the elements in the array, and the values will be assigned to the array elements in the order in which they are notionally stored in the computer's memory. Therefore, if file INITIAL.DAT contains the values

```
1  1  1  1  2  2  2  2  3  3  3  3
```

then the following code will initialize array istat to have the values shown in Figure 8-4:

```
INTEGER, DIMENSION(4,3) :: istat
OPEN (7, FILE='initial.dat', STATUS='OLD', ACTION='READ')
READ (7,*) istat
```

Implied DO loops may be used in READ statements to change the order in which array elements are initialized, or to initialize only a portion of an array. For example, if file INITIAL1.DAT contains the values

```
1  2  3  1  2  3  1  2  3  1  2  3
```

then the following code will initialize array istat to have the values shown in Figure 8-4.

```
INTEGER :: i, j
INTEGER, DIMENSION(4,3) :: istat
OPEN (7, FILE='initial1.dat', STATUS='OLD', ACTION='READ')
READ (7,*) ((istat(i,j), j=1,3), i=1,4)
```

The values would have been read from file INITIAL1.DAT in a different order than in the previous example, but the implied DO loops would ensure that the proper input values went into the proper array elements.

8.1.4 Example Problem

EXAMPLE 8-1

Electric Power Generation:

Figure 8-2 shows a series of electrical output power measurements at six different times for four different generators at the Acme Electric Power generating station. Write a program to read these values from a disk file, and to calculate the average power supplied by each generator over the measurement period, and the total power supplied by all of the generators at each time in the measurement period.

SOLUTION

1. **State the problem.**
   Calculate the average power supplied by each generator in the station over the measurement period, and calculate the total instantaneous power supplied by the generating station at each time within the measurement period. Write those values out on the standard output device.

2. **Define the inputs and outputs.**
   There are two types of inputs to this program:

   (a) A character string containing the file name of the input data file. This string will come from the standard input device.
   (b) The 24 real data values in the file, representing the power supplied by each of the four generators at each of six different times. The data in the input file must be organized so that the six values associated with generator G_1 appear first, followed by the six values associated with generator G_2, etc.

The outputs from this program are the average power supplied by each generator in the station over the measurement period, and the total instantaneous power supplied by the generating station at each time within the measurement period.

3. **Describe the algorithm.**

This program can be broken down into six major steps

```
Get the input file name
Open the input file
Read the input data into an array
Calculate the total instantaneous output power at each time
Calculate the average output power of each generator
Write the output values
```

The detailed pseudocode for the problem is given below:

```
Prompt user for the input file name "filename"
Read file name "filename"
OPEN file "filename"
IF OPEN is successful THEN
   Read array power

   ! Calculate the instantaneous output power of the station
   DO for itime = 1 to 6
      DO for igen = 1 to 4
         power_sum(itime) ← power(itime,igen) + power_sum(itime)
      END of DO
   END of DO

   ! Calculate the average output power of each generator
   DO for igen = 1 to 4
      DO for itime = 1 to 6
         power_ave(igen) ← power(itime,igen) + power_ave(igen)
      END of DO
      power_ave(igen) ← power_ave(igen) / 6
   END of DO

   ! Write out the total instantaneous power at each time
   Write out power_sum for itime = 1 to 6

   ! Write out the average output power of each generator
   Write out power_ave for igen = 1 to 4

End of IF
```

4. **Turn the algorithm into Fortran statements.**

The resulting Fortran program is shown in Figure 8-5.

FIGURE 8-5

Program to calculate the instantaneous power produced by a generating station, and the average power produced by each generator within the station.

```
PROGRAM generate
!
!  Purpose:
```

(continued)

(*continued*)

```
!     To calculate total instantaneous power supplied by a generating
!     station at each instant of time, and to calculate the average
!     power supplied by each generator over the period of measurement.
!
!   Record of revisions:
!      Date        Programmer           Description of change
!      ====        ==========           =====================
!    11/19/06    S. J. Chapman          Original code
!
IMPLICIT NONE

! Data dictionary: declare constants
INTEGER, PARAMETER :: MAX_GEN = 4      ! Max number of generators
INTEGER, PARAMETER :: MAX_TIME = 6     ! Max number of times

! Data dictionary: declare variable types, definitions, & units
CHARACTER(len=20) :: filename          ! Input data file name
INTEGER :: igen                        ! Loop index: generators
INTEGER :: itime                       ! Loop index: time
REAL, DIMENSION(MAX_TIME,MAX_GEN) :: power
                                       ! Pwr of each gen at each time (MW)
REAL, DIMENSION(MAX_GEN) :: power_ave  ! Ave power of each gen (MW)
REAL, DIMENSION(MAX_TIME) :: power_sum ! Total power at each time (MW)
INTEGER :: status                      ! I/O status: 0 = success

! Initialize sums to zero.
power_ave = 0.
power_sum = 0.

! Get the name of the file containing the input data.
WRITE (*,1000)
1000 FORMAT (' Enter the file name containing the input data: ')
READ (*,'(A20)') filename

! Open input data file. Status is OLD because the input data must
! already exist.
OPEN ( UNIT=9, FILE=filename, STATUS='OLD', ACTION='READ', &
       IOSTAT=status )

! Was the OPEN successful?
fileopen: IF ( status == 0 ) THEN

   ! The file was opened successfully, so read the data to process.
   READ (9, *, IOSTAT=status) power

   ! Calculate the instantaneous output power of the station at
   ! each time.
   sum1: DO itime = 1, MAX_TIME
      sum2: DO igen = 1, MAX_GEN
```

(*continued*)

(concluded)

```
            power_sum(itime) = power(itime,igen) + power_sum(itime)
      END DO sum2
END DO sum1

! Calculate the average output power of each generator over the
! time being measured.
ave1: DO igen = 1, MAX_GEN
   ave2: DO itime = 1, MAX_TIME
      power_ave(igen) = power(itime,igen) + power_ave(igen)
   END DO ave2
   power_ave(igen) = power_ave(igen) / REAL(MAX_TIME)
END DO ave1

! Tell user.
out1: DO itime = 1, MAX_TIME
   WRITE (*,1010) itime, power_sum(itime)
   1010 FORMAT (' The instantaneous power at time ', I1, ' is ', &
                  F7.2, ' MW.')
   END DO out1

   out2: DO igen = 1, MAX_GEN
      WRITE (*,1020) igen, power_ave(igen)
      1020 FORMAT (' The average power of generator ', I1, ' is ', &
                     F7.2, ' MW.')
   END DO out2

ELSE fileopen

   ! Else file open failed. Tell user.
   WRITE (*,1030) status
   1030 FORMAT (1X,'File open failed--status = ', I6)

END IF fileopen

END PROGRAM generate
```

5. Test the program.

To test this program, we will place the data from Figure 8-2 into a file called GENDAT. The contents of file GENDAT are shown below:

```
20.0   19.8   20.1   20.0   20.0   19.9
40.3   40.1   40.0   39.5   39.9   40.0
42.0   41.5   41.3   41.1   39.8   41.0
20.4   26.9   38.4   42.0   12.2    6.0
```

Note that each row of the file corresponds to a specific generator, and each column corresponds to a specific time. Next, we will calculate the answers by hand for one generator and one time, and compare the results with those from the program. At time 3, the total instantaneous power being supplied by all of the generators is

$$P_{\text{TOT}} = 20.1 \text{ MW} + 40.0 \text{ MW} + 41.3 \text{ MW} + 38.4 \text{ MW} = 139.8 \text{ MW}$$

The average power for Generator 1

$$P_{G_1, \text{AVE}} = \frac{(20.1 + 19.8 + 20.1 + 20.0 + 20.0 + 19.9)}{6} = 19.98 \text{ MW}$$

The output from the program is

```
C:\book\chap8>generate
Enter the file name containing the input data:
gendat
The instantaneous power at time 1 is 122.70 MW.
The instantaneous power at time 2 is 128.30 MW.
The instantaneous power at time 3 is 139.80 MW.
The instantaneous power at time 4 is 142.60 MW.
The instantaneous power at time 5 is 111.90 MW.
The instantaneous power at time 6 is 106.90 MW.
The average power of generator  1 is   19.97 MW.
The average power of generator  2 is   39.97 MW.
The average power of generator  3 is   41.12 MW.
The average power of generator  4 is   24.32 MW.
```

The numbers match, and the program appears to be working correctly.

Note that in this problem the raw data array power was organized as a 6 × 4 matrix (6 times by 4 generators) but the input data file was organized as a 4 × 6 matrix (4 generators by 6 times). This reversal is caused by the fact that Fortran stores array data in columns, but reads in data along lines. In order for the columns to be filled correctly in memory, the data had be transposed in the input file! Needless to say, this can be very confusing for people having to work with the program and its input data.

It would be much better if we could eliminate this source of confusion by making the organization of the data in the input file match the organization of the data within the computer. How can we do this? With implied DO loops. If we were to replace the statement

```
READ (9,*,IOSTAT=status) power
```

with the statement

```
READ (9,*,IOSTAT=status) ((power(itime,igen), igen=1,max_gen), itime=1, max_time)
```

then the data along a row in the input file would go into the corresponding row of the matrix in the computer's memory. With the new READ statement, the input data file could be structured as follows

```
20.0  40.3  42.0  20.4
19.8  40.1  41.5  26.9
20.1  40.0  41.3  38.4
20.0  39.5  41.1  42.0
20.0  39.9  39.8  12.2
19.9  40.0  41.0   6.0
```

and after the READ statement, the contents of array power would be

$$
power = \begin{bmatrix}
20.0 & 40.3 & 42.0 & 20.4 \\
19.8 & 40.1 & 41.5 & 26.9 \\
20.1 & 40.0 & 41.3 & 38.4 \\
20.0 & 39.5 & 41.1 & 42.0 \\
20.0 & 39.9 & 39.8 & 12.2 \\
19.9 & 40.0 & 41.0 & 6.0
\end{bmatrix}
$$

Good Programming Practice

Use DO loops and/or implied DO loops when reading or writing rank 2 arrays in order to keep the structure of the matrix in the file the same as the structure of the matrix within the program. This correspondence makes the programs easier to understand.

8

8.1.5 Whole Array Operations and Array Subsets

Two arrays may be used together in arithmetic operations and assignment statements as long as they are conformable (that is, as long as they either have the same shape or one of them is a scalar). If they are conformable, then the corresponding operation will be performed on an element-by-element basis.

Array subsets may be selected from rank-2 arrays by using subscript triplets or vector subscripts. A separate subscript triplet or vector subscript is used for each dimension in the array. For example, consider the following 5 × 5 array.

$$
a = \begin{bmatrix}
1 & 2 & 3 & 4 & 5 \\
6 & 7 & 8 & 9 & 10 \\
11 & 12 & 13 & 14 & 15 \\
16 & 17 & 18 & 19 & 20 \\
21 & 22 & 23 & 24 & 25
\end{bmatrix}
$$

The array subset corresponding to the first column of this array is selected as a(:,1):

$$a(:,1) = \begin{bmatrix} 1 \\ 6 \\ 11 \\ 16 \\ 21 \end{bmatrix}$$

and the array subset corresponding to the first row is selected as a(1,:):

$$a(1,:) = \begin{bmatrix} 1 & 2 & 3 & 4 & 5 \end{bmatrix}$$

Array subscripts may be used independently in each dimension. For example, the array subset a(1:3,1:5:2) selects rows 1 through 3 and columns 1, 3, and 5 from array a. This array subset is:

$$a(1:3,1:5:2) = \begin{bmatrix} 1 & 3 & 5 \\ 6 & 8 & 10 \\ 11 & 13 & 15 \end{bmatrix}$$

Similar combinations of subscripts can be used to select any rows or columns out of a rank-2 array.

8.2

MULTIDIMENSIONAL OR RANK-*n* ARRAYS

Fortran supports more complex arrays with up to seven different subscripts. These larger arrays are declared, initialized, and used in the same manner as the rank-2 arrays described in the previous section.

Rank-*n* arrays are notionally allocated in memory in a manner that is an extension of the column order used for rank-2 arrays. Memory allocation for a $2 \times 2 \times 2$ rank-3 array is illustrated in Figure 8-6. Note that the first subscript runs through its complete range before the second subscript is incremented, and the second subscript runs through its complete range before the third subscript is incremented. This process repeats for whatever number of subscripts are declared for the array, with the first subscript always changing most rapidly, and the last subscript always changing most slowly. We must keep this allocation structure in mind if we wish initialize or perform I/O operations with rank-*n* arrays.

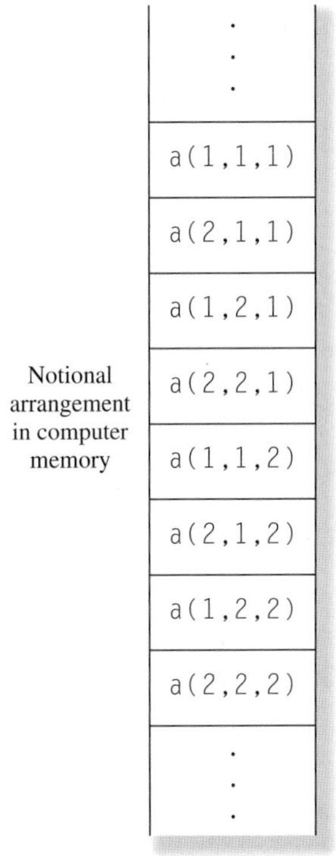

FIGURE 8-6

Notional memory allocation for a $2 \times 2 \times 2$ array a. Array elements are allocated so that the first subscript changes most rapidly, the second subscript the next most rapidly, and the third subscript the least rapidly.

· · ·
a(1,1,1)
a(2,1,1)
a(1,2,1)
a(2,2,1)
a(1,1,2)
a(2,1,2)
a(1,2,2)
a(2,2,2)
· · ·

Notional arrangement in computer memory

8

Quiz 8-1

This quiz provides a quick check to see if you have understood the concepts introduced in Sections 8.1 and 8.2. If you have trouble with the quiz, reread the sections, ask your instructor, or discuss the material with a fellow student. The answers to this quiz are found in the back of the book.

For questions 1 to 3, determine the number of elements in the array specified by the declaration statements and the valid subscript range(s) for each array.

1. `REAL, DIMENSION(-64:64,0:4) :: data_input`

2. `INTEGER, PARAMETER :: MIN_U = 0, MAX_U = 70`
   `INTEGER, PARAMETER :: MAXFIL = 3`
   `CHARACTER(len=24), DIMENSION(MAXFIL,MIN_U:MAX_U) :: filenm`

3. `INTEGER, DIMENSION(-3:3,-3:3,6) :: in`

(continued)

(continued)

Determine which of the following Fortran statements are valid. For each valid statement, specify what will happen in the program. Assume default typing for any variables that are not explicitly typed.

4.
```
REAL, DIMENSION(0:11,2) :: dist
dist = (/ 0.00,  0.25,  1.00,  2.25,  4.00,  6.25, &
          9.00, 12.25, 16.00, 20.25, 25.00, 30.25, &
         -0.00, -0.25, -1.00, -2.25, -4.00, -6.25, &
         -9.00,-12.25,-16.00,-20.25,-25.00,-30.25/)
```

5.
```
REAL, DIMENSION(0:11,2) :: dist
dist = RESHAPE((/0.00, 0.25,  1.00,  2.25,  4.00,  6.25, &
                 9.00,12.25, 16.00, 20.25, 25.00, 30.25, &
                 0.00, 0.25,  1.00,  2.25,  4.00,  6.25, &
                 9.00,12.25, 16.00, 20.25, 25.00,30.25/) &
               , (/12,2/))
```

6.
```
REAL, DIMENSION(-2:2,-1:0) :: data1 = &
       RESHAPE ( (/ 1.0, 2.0, 3.0, 4.0, 5.0, &
                    6.0, 7.0, 8.0, 9.0, 0.0 /), &
                (/ 5, 2 /) )
REAL, DIMENSION(0:4,2) :: data2 = &
       RESHAPE ( (/ 0.0, 9.0, 8.0, 7.0, 6.0, &
                    5.0, 4.0, 3.0, 2.0, 1.0 /), &
                (/ 5, 2 /) )
REAL, DIMENSION(5,2) :: data_out
data_out = data1 + data2
WRITE (*,*) data_out(:,1)
WRITE (*,*) data_out(3,:)
```

7.
```
INTEGER, DIMENSION(4) :: list1 = (/1,4,2,2/)
INTEGER, DIMENSION(3) :: list2 = (/1,2,3/)
INTEGER, DIMENSION(5,5) :: array
DO i = 1,5
   DO j = 1,5
      array(i,j) = i + 10 * j
   END DO
END DO
WRITE (*,*) array(list1, list2)
```

8.
```
INTEGER, DIMENSION(4) :: list = (/2,3,2,1/)
INTEGER, DIMENSION(10) :: vector = (/ (10*k, k = -4,5) /)
vector(list) = (/ 1, 2, 3, 4 /)
WRITE (*,*) vector
```

Suppose that a file INPUT is opened on i/o unit 2, and contains the following data:

(continued)

(*concluded*)

11.2	16.5	31.3	3.1414	16.0	12.0
1.1	9.0	17.1	11.	15.0	-1.3
10.0	11.0	12.0	13.0	14.0	5.0
15.1	16.7	18.9	21.1	24.0	-22.2

What data would be read from file INPUT by each of the following statements?
What would the value of mydata(2,4) be in each case?

9. ```
   REAL, DIMENSION(3,5) :: mydata
   READ (2,*) mydata
   ```

10. ```
    REAL, DIMENSION(0:2,2:6) :: mydata
    READ (2,*) mydata
    ```

11. ```
    REAL, DIMENSION(3,5) :: mydata
    READ (2,*) ((mydata(i,j), j=1,5), i=1,3)
    ```

12. ```
    REAL, DIMENSION(3,5) :: mydata
    DO i = 1, 3
       READ (2,*) (mydata(i,j), j=1,5)
    END DO
    ```

Answer the following questions.

13. What is the value of dist(6,2) in Question 5 of this quiz?

14. What is the rank of mydata in Question 10 of this quiz?

15. What is the shape of mydata in Question 10 of this quiz?

16. What is the extent of the first dimension of data_input in Question 1 of this quiz?

17. What is the maximum number of dimensions that an array can have in Fortran 95/2003?

■ 8.3
USING FORTRAN INTRINSIC FUNCTIONS WITH ARRAYS

There are three classes of Fortran 95/2003 intrinsic functions: **elemental functions,**
inquiry functions, and **transformational functions.** Some of the functions from each
of these classes are designed for use with array arguments. We will now examine a few
of them. A complete description of all Fortran intrinsic functions and subroutines is
found in Appendix B.

8.3.1 Elemental Intrinsic Functions

Elemental intrinsic functions are ones that are specified for scalar arguments, but
that may also be applied to array arguments. If the argument of an elemental function

is a scalar, then the result of the function will be a scalar. If the argument of the function is an array, then the result of the function will be an array of the same shape as the input array. Note that if there is more than one input argument, all of the arguments must have the same shape. If an elemental function is applied to an array, the result will be the same as if the function were applied to each element of the array on an element-by-element basis. Thus, the following two sets of statements are equivalent:

```
REAL, DIMENSION(4) :: x = (/ 0., 3.141592, 1., 2. /)
REAL, DIMENSION(4) :: y
INTEGER :: i

y = SIN(x)                      ! Whole array at once

DO i = 1,4
   y(i) = SIN(x(i))             ! Element by element
END DO
```

Most of the Fortran intrinsic functions that accept scalar arguments are elemental, and so can be used with arrays. This includes such common functions as ABS, SIN, COS, TAN, EXP, LOG, LOG10, MOD, and SQRT.

8.3.2 Inquiry Intrinsic Functions

Inquiry intrinsic functions are functions whose value depends on the properties of an object being investigated. For example, the function UBOUND(arr) is an inquiry function that returns the largest subscript(s) of array arr. A list of some of the common array inquiry functions is shown in Table 8-1. Any function arguments shown in italics are optional; they may or may not be present when the function is invoked.

These functions are useful for determining the properties of an array, such as its size, shape, extent, and the legal subscript range in each extent. They will be especially important once we begin passing arrays to procedures in Chapter 9.

TABLE 8-1
Some common array inquiry functions

Function name and calling sequence	Purpose
ALLOCATED(ARRAY)	Determines allocation status of an allocatable array (see Section 8.6)
LBOUND(ARRAY, *DIM*)	Returns all of the lower bounds of ARRAY if *DIM* is absent, or a specified lower bound of ARRAY if *DIM* is present. The result is a rank-1 array if *DIM* is absent, or a scalar if *DIM* is present.
SHAPE(SOURCE)	Returns the shape of array SOURCE.
SIZE(ARRAY, *DIM*)	Returns either the extent of ARRAY along a particular dimension if *DIM* is present; otherwise, it returns the total number of elements in the array.
UBOUND(ARRAY, *DIM*)	Returns all of the upper bounds of ARRAY if *DIM* is absent, or a specified upper bound of ARRAY if *DIM* is present. The result is a rank-1 array if *DIM* is absent, or a scalar if *DIM* is present.

**EXAMPLE
8-2**

Determining the Properties of an Array:

To illustrate the use of the array inquiry functions, we will declare a rank-2 array a, and use the functions to determine its properties.

SOLUTION

The program in Figure 8-7 invokes the functions SHAPE, SIZE, LBOUND, and UBOUND to determine the properties of the array.

FIGURE 8-7
Program to determine the properties of an array.

```
PROGRAM check_array
!
!  Purpose:
!     To illustrate the use of array inquiry functions.
!
!  Record of revisions:
!     Date          Programmer             Description of change
!     ====          ==========             =====================
!     11/19/06     S. J. Chapman           Original code!
!
IMPLICIT NONE

! List of variables:
REAL,DIMENSION(-5:5,0:3) :: a = 0. ! Array to examine

! Get the shape, size, and bounds of the array.
WRITE (*,100) SHAPE(a)
100 FORMAT (1X,'The shape of the array is:          ',7I6)

WRITE (*,110) SIZE(a)
110 FORMAT (1X,'The size of the array is:           ',I6)

WRITE (*,120) LBOUND(a)
120 FORMAT (1X,'The lower bounds of the array are: ',7I6)

WRITE (*,130) UBOUND(a)
130 FORMAT (1X,'The upper bounds of the array are: ',7I6)

END PROGRAM check_array
```

When the program is executed, the results are:

```
C:\book\chap8>check_array
The shape of the array is:          11      4
The size of the array is:           44
The lower bounds of the array are:  -5      0
The upper bounds of the array are:   5      3
```

These are obviously the correct answers for array a.

8.3.3 Transformational Intrinsic Functions

Transformational intrinsic functions are functions that have one or more array-valued arguments or an array-valued result. Unlike elemental functions, which operate on an element-by-element basis, transformational functions operate on arrays as a whole. The output of a transformational function will often not have the same shape as the input arguments. For example, the function DOT_PRODUCT has two vector input arguments of the same size, and produces a scalar output.

There are *many* transformational intrinsic functions in Fortran. Some of the more common ones are summarized in Table 8-2 below. Some of the functions listed in the table have additional optional arguments that are not mentioned. The complete details of each function, including any additional arguments, are found in Appendix B. Any function arguments shown in italics are optional; they may or may not be present when the function is invoked.

We have already seen the RESHAPE function used to initialize arrays. A number of other transformational functions will appear in the exercises at the end of this chapter.

TABLE 8-2
Some common transformational functions

Function name and calling sequence	Purpose
ALL(MASK)	Logical function that returns TRUE if *all* of the values in array MASK are true.
ANY(MASK)	Logical function that returns TRUE if *any* of the values in array MASK are true.
COUNT(MASK)	Returns the number of TRUE elements in array MASK.
DOT_PRODUCT(VECTOR_A, VECTOR_B)	Calculates the dot product of two equal-sized vectors.
MATMUL(MATRIX_A, MATRIX_B)	Performs matrix multiplication on two conformable matrices.
MAXLOC(ARRAY, *MASK*)	Returns the *location* of the maximum value in ARRAY among those elements for which *MASK* was true. The result is a rank-1 array with one element for each subscript in ARRAY. (*MASK* is optional.)
MAXVAL(ARRAY, *MASK*)[1]	Returns the maximum value in ARRAY among those elements for which *MASK* was true. (*MASK* is optional.)
MINLOC(ARRAY, *MASK*)	Returns the *location* of the minimum value in ARRAY among those elements for which *MASK* was true. The result is a rank-1 array with one element for each subscript in ARRAY. (*MASK* is optional.)
MINVAL(ARRAY, *MASK*)[1]	Returns the minimum value in ARRAY among those elements for which *MASK* was true. (*MASK* is optional.)
PRODUCT(ARRAY, *MASK*)[1]	Calculates the product of the elements in ARRAY for which the *MASK* is true. *MASK* is optional; if not present, it calculates the product of all of the elements in the array.
RESHAPE(SOURCE,SHAPE)	Constructs an array of the specified shape from the elements of array SOURCE. SHAPE is a rank-1 array containing the extents of each dimension in the array to be built.
SUM(ARRAY, *MASK*)[1]	Calculates the sum of the elements in ARRAY for which the *MASK* is true. *MASK* is optional; if not present, it calculates the sum of all of the elements in the array.
TRANSPOSE(MATRIX)	Returns the transpose of a rank-2 array.

[1] If a MASK is specified in these functions, it must be specified in the form MASK = *mask_expr*, where *mask_expr* is the logical array specifying the mask. The reason for this form is explained in Chapter 9 and Appendix B.

8.4

MASKED ARRAY ASSIGNMENT: THE WHERE CONSTRUCT

We have already seen that Fortran permits us to use either array elements or entire arrays in array assignment statements. For example, we could take the logarithm of the elements in a rank-2 array `value` in either of the following ways:

```
DO i = 1, ndim1
   DO j = 1, ndim2
      logval(i,j) = LOG(value(i,j))          logval = LOG ( value )
   END DO
END DO
```

Both of the above examples take the logarithm of all of the elements in array `value` and store the result in array `logval`.

Suppose that we would like to take the logarithm of *some* of the elements of array `value`, but not all of them. For example, suppose that we only want to take the logarithm of *positive* elements, since the logarithms of zero and negative numbers are not defined and produce run-time errors. How could we do this? One way would be to do it on an element-by-element basis, using a combination of DO loops and an IF construct. For example,

```
DO i = 1, ndim1
   DO j = 1, ndim2
      IF ( value(i,j) > 0. ) THEN
         logval(i,j) = LOG(value(i,j))
      ELSE
         logval(i,j) = -99999.
      END IF
   END DO
END DO
```

We can also perform this calculation all at once, using a special form of array assignment statement known as **masked array assignment.** A masked array assignment statement is an assignment statement whose operation is controlled by a logical array of the *same shape* as the array in the assignment. The assignment operation is performed *only* for the elements of the array that correspond to TRUE values in the mask. In Fortran 95/2003, masked array assignments are implemented using the WHERE construct or statement.

8.4.1 The WHERE Construct

The general form of a WHERE construct is

```
[name:] WHERE (mask_expr1)
   Array Assignment Statement(s)    ! Block 1
ELSEWHERE (mask_expr2) [name]
   Array Assignment Statement(s)    ! Block 2
ELSEWHERE [name]
```

```
      Array Assignment Statement(s)    ! Block 3
   END WHERE [name]
```

where each *mask_expr1* is a logical array of the same shape as the arrays being manipulated in the array assignment statements. This construct applies the operation or set of operations in Block 1 to all of the elements of the array for which *mask_expr1* is TRUE. It applies the operation or set of operations in Block 2 to all of the elements of the array for which *mask_expr1* is FALSE and mask_expr2 is TRUE. Finally, it applies the operation or set of operations in Block 3 to all of the elements of the array for which both *mask_expr1* and *mask_expr2* are FALSE. There can be as many masked ELSEWHERE clauses as desired in a Fortran 95/2003 WHERE construct.[2]

Note that *at most one block of statements will be executed for any given element in the array.*

A name may be assigned to a WHERE construct, if desired. If the WHERE statement at the beginning of a construct is named, then the associated END WHERE statement must also have the same name. The name is optional on an ELSEWHERE statement even if it is used on the corresponding WHERE and END WHERE statements.

The example given above could be implemented with a WHERE construct as:

```
WHERE ( value > 0. )
   logval = LOG(value)
ELSEWHERE
   logval = -99999.
END WHERE
```

The expression value > 0. produces a logical array whose elements are TRUE where the corresponding elements of value are greater than zero, and FALSE where the corresponding elements of value are less than or equal zero. This logical array then serves as a mask to control the operation of the array assignment statement.

The WHERE construct is generally more elegant than element-by-element operations, especially for multidimensional arrays.

Good Programming Practice

Use WHERE constructs to modify and assign array elements when you want to modify and assign only those elements that pass some test.

8.4.2 The WHERE Statement

Fortran 95/2003 also includes a single-line WHERE statement:

```
WHERE (mask_expr) Array Assignment Statement
```

The assignment statement is applied to those elements of the array for which the mask expression is true.

---

[2] Fortran 90 did not allow masked ELSEWHERE clauses in a WHERE construct.

EXAMPLE
8-3

Limiting the Maximum and Minimum Values in an Array:

Suppose that we are writing a program to analyze an input data set whose values should be in the range [−1000, 1000]. If numbers greater than 1000 or less than −1000 would cause problems with our processing algorithm, it might be desirable to put in a test limiting all data values to the acceptable range. Write such a test for a 10,000-element rank-1 real array input using both DO and IF constructs and a WHERE construct.

SOLUTION
The test using DO and IF constructs is

```
DO i = 1, 10000
    IF ( input(i) > 1000. ) THEN
        input(i) = 1000.
    ELSE IF ( input(i) < -1000. ) THEN
        input(i) = -1000.
    END IF
END DO
```

The test using a WHERE construct is

```
WHERE ( input > 1000. )
    input = 1000.
ELSEWHERE ( input < -1000. )
    input = -1000.
END WHERE
```

The WHERE construct is simpler than the DO and IF constructs for this example.

■ 8.5
THE FORALL CONSTRUCT

Fortran 95/2003 also includes a construct that is designed to permit a set of operations to be applied on an element-by-element basis to a subset of the elements in an array. The elements to be operated on may be chosen *both* by subscript index *and* by a logical condition. The operations will be applied only to those elements of the array that satisfy both the index constraints and the logical condition. This construct is called the FORALL construct.

8.5.1 The Form of the FORALL Construct

The general form of the FORALL construct is

```
[name:] FORALL (in1=triplet1[, in2=triplet2, ... , logical_expr])
    Statement 1
    Statement 2
    . . .
```

```
        Statement n
    END FORALL [name]
```

Each index in the FORALL statement is specified by a subscript triplet of the form

$$subscript\_1 : subscript\_2 : stride$$

where *subscript_1* is the starting value of the index, *subscript_2* is the ending value, and *stride* is the index step. Statements 1 through *n* in the body of the construct are assignment statements that manipulate the elements of arrays having the selected indices and satisfying the logical expression on an element-by-element basis.

A name may be assigned to a FORALL construct, if desired. If the FORALL statement at the beginning of a construct is named, then the associated END FORALL statement must also have the same name.

A simple example of a FORALL construct is shown below. These statements create a 10×10 identity matrix, which has ones along the diagonal and zeros everywhere else.

```
    REAL, DIMENSION(10,10) :: i_matrix = 0.
    . . .
    FORALL ( i=1:10 )
        i_matrix(i,i) = 1.0
    END FORALL
```

As a more complex example, let's suppose that we would like to take the reciprocal of all of the elements in an n × m array work. We might do this with the simple assignment statement

```
    work = 1. / work
```

but this statement would cause a run-time error and abort the program if any of the elements of work happened to be zero. A FORALL construct that avoids this problem is

```
    FORALL ( i=1:n, j=1:m, work(i,j) /= 0. )
        work(i,j) = 1. / work(i,j)
    END FORALL
```

8.5.2 The Significance of the FORALL Construct

In general, any expression that can be written in a FORALL construct could also be written as a set of nested DO loops combined with a block IF construct. For example, the previous FORALL example could be written as

```
    DO i = 1, n
        DO j = 1, m
            IF ( work(i,j) /= 0. ) THEN
                work(i,j) = 1. / work(i,j)
            END IF
        END DO
    END DO
```

What is the difference between these two sets of statements, and why is the FORALL construct included in the Fortran language at all?

The answer is that *the statements in the DO loop structure must be executed in a strict order, while the statements in the FORALL construct may be executed in any order*. In the DO loops, the elements of array work are processed in the following strict order:

```
work(1,1)
work(1,2)
 . . .
work(1,m)
work(2,1)
work(2,2)
 . . .
work(2,m)
 . . .
work(n,m)
```

In contrast, the FORALL construct processes the same set of elements *in any order selected by the processor*. This freedom means that massively parallel computers can optimize the program for maximum speed by parceling out each element to a separate processor, and the processors can finish their work in any order without affecting the final answer.

If the body of a FORALL construct contains more than one statement, then the processor completely finishes all of the selected elements of the first statement before starting any of the elements of the second statement. In the example below, the values for a(i,j) that are calculated in the first statement are used to calculate b(i,j) in the second statement. All of the a values are calculated before the first b value is calculated.

```
FORALL (i=2:n-1, j=2:n-1)
   a(i,j) = SQRT(a(i,j))
   b(i,j) = 1.0 / a(i,j)
END FORALL
```

Because each element must be capable of being processed independently, the body of a FORALL construct cannot contain transformational functions whose results depend on the values in the entire array. However, the body can contain nested FORALL and WHERE constructs.

8.5.3 The FORALL Statement

Fortran 95/2003 also includes a single-line FORALL statement:

```
FORALL (ind1=triplet1[, ... , logical_expr]) Assignment Statement
```

The assignment statement is executed for those indices and logical expressions that satisfy the FORALL control parameters. This simpler form is the same as a FORALL construct with only one statement.

8.6

ALLOCATABLE ARRAYS

In all of the examples that we have seen so far, the size of each array was declared in a type declaration statement at the beginning of the program. This type of array declaration is called **static memory allocation,** since the size of each array is set at compilation time and never changes. *The size of each array must be made large enough to hold the largest problem that a particular program will ever have to solve*, which can be a very serious limitation. If we declare the array sizes to be large enough to handle the largest problem that we will ever need to solve, then the program will waste memory 99 percent of the time that it is run. In addition, the program might not run at all on small computers that don't have enough memory to hold it. If the arrays are made small, then the program cannot solve large problems at all.

What can a programmer do about this problem? If the program is well designed, then the array limitations could be modified by just changing one or two array size parameters in the source code and recompiling it. This process will work for in-house programs for which the source code is available, but it is not very elegant. It won't work at all for programs whose source code is unavailable, such as those programs that you buy from someone else.

A much better solution is to design a program that uses **dynamic memory allocation;** it dynamically sets the sizes of the arrays each time it is executed to be just large enough to solve the current problem. This approach does not waste computer memory, and will allow the same program to run on both small and large computers.

8.6.1 Fortran 95 Allocatable Arrays

A Fortran 95 array using dynamic memory is declared by using the ALLOCATABLE attribute in the type declaration statement, and is actually allocated with an ALLOCATE statement. When the program is through with using the memory, it should free it up for other uses with a DEALLOCATE statement. The structure of a typical array declaration with the ALLOCATABLE attribute[3] is

```
REAL, ALLOCATABLE, DIMENSION(:,:) :: arr1
```

Note that colons are used as placeholders in the declaration, since we do not know how big the array will actually be. The *rank* of the array is declared in the type declaration statement, but not the *size* of the array.

---

[3] An array may also be declared to be allocatable in a separate ALLOCATABLE statement of the form

```
ALLOCATABLE :: arr1
```

It is preferable *not* to use this statement, since it is always possible to specify the ALLOCATABLE attribute in a type declaration statement, and the array will appear in a type declaration statement anyway. The only time when a separate ALLOCATABLE statement is necessary is when default typing is used and there is no type declaration statement. Since we should *never* use default typing in any program, there is never a need for this statement.

An array declared with colons for dimensions is known as a **deferred-shape array,** because the actual shape of the array is deferred until the memory for the array is allocated. (In contrast, an array whose size is explicitly declared in a type declaration statement is known as an **explicit-shape array.**)

When the program executes, the actual size of the array will be specified with an ALLOCATE statement. The form of an ALLOCATE statement is

ALLOCATE (list of arrays to allocate, STAT=status)

A typical example is

ALLOCATE (arr1(100,0:10), STAT=status)

This statement allocates a 100 × 11 array arr1 at execution time. The STAT= clause is optional. If it is present, it returns an integer status. The status will be 0 for successful allocation, and a compiler-dependent positive number if the allocation process fails. The most common source of failure is not having enough free memory to allocate the array. If the allocation fails and the STAT= clause is not present, then the program will abort. You should always use the STAT= clause so that the program can terminate gracefully if there is not enough memory available to allocate the array.

Good Programming Practice
Always include the STAT= clause in any ALLOCATE statement, and always check the returned status, so that a program can be shut down gracefully if there is insufficient memory to allocate the necessary arrays.

8

An allocatable array *may not be used in any way* in a program until memory is allocated for it. Any attempt to use an allocatable array that is not currently allocated will produce a run-time error and cause the program to abort. Fortran includes the logical intrinsic function ALLOCATED() to allow a program to test the allocation status of an array before attempting to use it. For example, the following code tests the status of allocatable array input_data before attempting to reference it:

```
REAL, ALLOCATABLE, DIMENSION(:) :: input_data
...
IF ( ALLOCATED(input_data) ) THEN
   READ (8,*) input_data
ELSE
   WRITE (*,*) 'Warning: Array not allocated!'
END IF
```

This function can be very helpful in large programs involving many procedures, in which memory is allocated in one procedure and used in a different one.

At the end of the program or procedure in which an allocatable array is used, you should *deallocate* the memory to make it available for reuse. This is done with a DEALLOCATE statement. The structure of a DEALLOCATE statement is

DEALLOCATE (list of arrays to deallocate, STAT=status)

A typical example is

```
DEALLOCATE (arr1, STAT=status)
```

where the status clause has the same meaning as in the ALLOCATE statement. After a DEALLOCATE statement is executed, the data in the deallocated arrays is no longer available for use.

You should always deallocate any allocatable arrays once you are finished with them. This frees up the memory to be used elsewhere in the program, or in other programs running on the same computer.

Good Programming Practice
Always deallocate allocatable arrays with a DEALLOCATE statement as soon as you are through using them.

EXAMPLE 8-4

Using Allocatable Arrays:

To illustrate the use of allocatable arrays, we will rewrite the statistical analysis program of Example 6-4 to dynamically allocate only the amount of memory needed to solve the problem. To determine how much memory to allocate, the program will read the input data file and count the number of values. It will then allocate the array, rewind the file, read in the values, and calculate the statistics.

SOLUTION
The modified program with allocatable arrays is shown in Figure 8-8.

FIGURE 8-8
A modified form of the statistics program that uses allocatable arrays.

```
PROGRAM stats_5
!
!  Purpose:
!    To calculate mean, median, and standard deviation of an input
!    data set read from a file.  This program uses allocatable arrays
!    to use only the memory required to solve each problem.
!
!  Record of revisions:
!      Date         Programmer          Description of change
!      ====         ==========          =====================
!    11/17/06    S. J. Chapman        Original code
! 1. 11/19/06    S. J. Chapman        Modified for dynamic memory
!
IMPLICIT NONE
```

(continued)

(continued)

```
! Data dictionary: declare variable types & definitions
REAL,ALLOCATABLE,DIMENSION(:) :: a ! Data array to sort
CHARACTER(len=20) :: filename    ! Input data file name
INTEGER :: i                     ! Loop index
INTEGER :: iptr                  ! Pointer to smallest value
INTEGER :: j                     ! Loop index
REAL :: median                   ! The median of the input samples
INTEGER :: nvals = 0             ! Number of values to process
INTEGER :: status                ! Status: 0 for success
REAL :: std_dev                  ! Standard deviation of input samples
REAL :: sum_x = 0.               ! Sum of input values
REAL :: sum_x2 = 0.              ! Sum of input values squared
REAL :: temp                     ! Temporary variable for swapping
REAL :: x_bar                    ! Average of input values

! Get the name of the file containing the input data.
WRITE (*,1000)
1000 FORMAT (1X,'Enter the file name with the data to be sorted:')
READ (*,'(A20)') filename

! Open input data file.  Status is OLD because the input data must
! already exist.
OPEN ( UNIT=9, FILE=filename, STATUS='OLD', ACTION='READ', &
       IOSTAT=status )

! Was the OPEN successful?
fileopen: IF ( status == 0 ) THEN        ! Open successful

   ! The file was opened successfully, so read the data to find
   ! out how many values are in the file, and allocate the
   ! required space.
   DO
      READ (9, *, IOSTAT=status) temp     ! Get value
      IF ( status /= 0 ) EXIT             ! Exit on end of data
      nvals = nvals + 1                   ! Bump count
   END DO

   ! Allocate memory
   WRITE (*,*) ' Allocating a: size = ', nvals
   ALLOCATE ( a(nvals), STAT=status)      ! Allocate memory

   ! Was allocation successful? If so, rewind file, read in
   ! data, and process it.
   allocate_ok: IF ( status == 0 ) THEN

      REWIND ( UNIT=9 )                   ! Rewind file

      ! Now read in the data.  We know that there are enough
      ! values to fill the array.
      READ (9, *) a                       ! Get value

      ! Sort the data.
      outer: DO i = 1, nvals-1
```

(continued)

(continued)

```
            ! Find the minimum value in a(i) through a(nvals)
            iptr = i
            inner: DO j = i+1, nvals
               minval: IF ( a(j) < a(iptr) ) THEN
                   iptr = j
               END IF minval
            END DO inner

            ! iptr now points to the minimum value, so swap a(iptr)
            ! with a(i) if i /= iptr.
            swap: IF ( i /= iptr ) THEN
               temp     = a(i)
               a(i)     = a(iptr)
               a(iptr) = temp
            END IF swap

         END DO outer

         ! The data is now sorted.  Accumulate sums to calculate
         ! statistics.
         sums: DO i = 1, nvals
            sum_x  = sum_x + a(i)
            sum_x2 = sum_x2 + a(i)**2
         END DO sums

         ! Check to see if we have enough input data.
         enough: IF ( nvals < 2 ) THEN

            ! Insufficient data.
            WRITE (*,*) ' At least 2 values must be entered.'

         ELSE

            ! Calculate the mean, median, and standard deviation
            x_bar   = sum_x / real(nvals)
            std_dev = sqrt( (real(nvals) * sum_x2 - sum_x**2) &
                     / (real(nvals) * real(nvals-1)) )
            even: IF ( mod(nvals,2) == 0 ) THEN
               median = ( a(nvals/2) + a(nvals/2+1) ) / 2.
            ELSE
               median = a(nvals/2+1)
            END IF even

            ! Tell user.
            WRITE (*,*) ' The mean of this data set is:   ', x_bar
            WRITE (*,*) ' The median of this data set is:', median
            WRITE (*,*) ' The standard deviation is:      ', std_dev
            WRITE (*,*) ' The number of data points is:  ', nvals

         END IF enough

         ! Deallocate the array now that we are done.
         DEALLOCATE ( a, STAT=status )
```

(continued)

(concluded)

```
    END IF allocate_ok

ELSE fileopen

    ! Else file open failed.  Tell user.
    WRITE (*,1050) status
    1050 FORMAT (1X,'File open failed--status = ', I6)

END IF fileopen

END PROGRAM stats_5
```

To test this program, we will run it with the same data set as Example 6-4.

```
C:\book\chap8>stats_5
Enter the file name containing the input data:
input4
    Allocating a: size =              5
    The mean of this data set is:          4.400000
    The median of this data set is:        4.000000
    The standard deviation is:             2.966479
    The number of data points is:          5
```

The program gives the correct answers for our test data set.

8

F-2003 ONLY

8.6.2 Fortran 2003 Allocatable Arrays

The forms of a Fortran 2003 ALLOCATE statement are

```
ALLOCATE (list of arrays, STAT=status, ERRMSG=err_msg)
ALLOCATE (array to allocate, SOURCE=source_expr, STAT=status, ERRMSG=string)
```

The first form of the ALLOCATE statement is similar to a Fortran 95 allocation statement, except that it includes an ERRMSG= clause. If the allocation is successful, the integer value returned by the STAT= clause will be 0, and the character variable in the ERRMSG= clause will not be changed. If the allocation is unsuccessful, the integer value returned by the STAT= clause will be a nonzero code indicating the type of the error, and the character variable in the ERRMSG= clause will contain a descriptive message indicating what the problem is for display to the user.

An example of the second form of the ALLOCATE statement is shown below:

```
ALLOCATE (arr1, SOURCE=arr2, STAT=status, ERRMSG=err_msg)
```

This statement allocates array arr1 to be the same size and shape as array arr2, and initializes the content of arr1 to be identical to arr2. This form of the ALLOCATE statement can allocate only one array at a time, and the array being allocated must be conformable with (have the same rank and shape as) the source array or expression. The status and error message clauses in this case are the same as for the other form of the ALLOCATE statement.

The following code is valid, because the array being allocated is conformable with the source expression:

```
REAL, DIMENSION(:,:), ALLOCATABLE :: arr1
REAL, DIMENSION(2,2), :: arr2 = RESHAPE ( (/ 1,2,3,4 /), (/2,2/) )
INTEGER :: istat
CHARACTER(len=80) :: err_msg
...
ALLOCATE (arr1, SOURCE=arr2+2, STAT=istat, ERRMSG=err_msg)
```

The expression `arr2+2` is a 2 × 2 array whose value is

$$\begin{bmatrix} 3 & 5 \\ 4 & 6 \end{bmatrix}$$

so `arr1` is allocated as a 2 × 2 array, and is initialized to these values.

On the other hand, the following code is *invalid*, because the rank of the array being allocated is different than the rank of the source expression:

```
REAL, DIMENSION(:), ALLOCATABLE :: arr1
REAL, DIMENSION(2,2), :: arr2 = RESHAPE ( (/ 1,2,3,4 /), (/2,2/) )
INTEGER :: istat
CHARACTER(len=80) :: err_msg
...
ALLOCATE (arr1, SOURCE=arr2+2, STAT=istat, ERRMSG=err_msg)   ! Error
```

A Fortran 2003 `DEALLOCATE` statement is similar to a Fortran 95 `DEALLOCATE` statement, except that the statement can include an `ERRMSG=` clause:

```
DEALLOCATE (list of arrays, STAT=status, ERRMSG=err_msg)
```

Good Programming Practice

Always include the `ERRMSG=` clause in any Fortran 2003 `ALLOCATE` or `DEALLOCATE` statement to return a user-readable error message in case of an allocation failure.

8.6.3 Using Fortran 2003 Allocatable Arrays in Assignment Statements

Fortran 2003 allocatable arrays are *much* more flexible and useful than in earlier versions of Fortran, because they can be allocated and deallocated automatically during normal program assignments.

If an expression is assigned to a Fortran 2003 allocatable array of the same rank, then the array is *automatically allocated* to the correct shape if it is unallocated, or it is *automatically deallocated and reallocated* to the correct shape if it was previously allocated with an incompatible shape. This means that the arrays can be used seamlessly in calculations.

For example, consider the following statements.

```
REAL, DIMENSION(:), ALLOCATABLE :: arr1
REAL, DIMENSION(8), :: arr2 = (/ 1., 2., 3., 4., 5., 6., 7., 8. /)
REAL, DIMENSION(3), :: arr3 = (/ 1., -2., 3. /)
...
arr1 = 2. * arr3
WRITE (*,*) arr1
arr1 = arr2(1:8:2)
WRITE (*,*) arr1
arr1 = 2. * arr2(1:4)
WRITE (*,*) arr1
```

When the first assignment statement is executed, arr1 is unallocated, so it is auto-matically allocated as a 3-element array, and the values [2. -4. 6.] are stored in it. When the second assignment statement is executed, arr1 is allocated as a 3-element array, which is the wrong size, so the array is automatically deallocated and reallo-cated with 4 elements, and the values [1. 3. 5. 7.] are stored in it. When the third assignment statement is executed, arr1 is allocated as a 4-element array, which is the correct size, so the array is *not* reallocated, and the values [2. 4. 6. 8.] are stored in the existing allocation.

Note that this automatic allocation and deallocation works only if the allocatable variable is the same rank as the expression being assigned to it. If the ranks differ, the assignment will produce a compile-time error:

```
REAL, DIMENSION(:), ALLOCATABLE :: arr1
REAL, DIMENSION(2,2), :: arr2 = RESHAPE ( (/ 1,2,3,4 /), (/2,2/) )
...
arr1 = arr2        ! Error
```

8

Quiz 8-2

This quiz provides a quick check to see if you have understood the concepts in-troduced in Sections 8.3 through 8.6. If you have trouble with the quiz, reread the sections, ask your instructor, or discuss the material with a fellow student. The answers to this quiz are found in the back of the book.

For questions 1 to 5, determine what will be printed out by the WRITE state-ments.

```
1.  REAL, DIMENSION(-3:3,0:50) :: values
    WRITE (*,*) LBOUND(values,1)
    WRITE (*,*) UBOUND(values,2)
    WRITE (*,*) SIZE(values,1)
    WRITE (*,*) SIZE(values)
    WRITE (*,*) SHAPE(values)
```

(continued)

2. ```
REAL, ALLOCATABLE, DIMENSION(:,:,:) :: values
 . . .
ALLOCATE(values(3,4,5), STAT=istat)
WRITE (*,*) UBOUND(values,2)
WRITE (*,*) SIZE(values)
WRITE (*,*) SHAPE(values)
```

3. ```
REAL, DIMENSION(5,5) :: input1
DO i = 1, 5
   DO j = 1, 5
      input1(i,j) = i+j-1
   END DO
END DO
WRITE (*,*) MAXVAL(input1)
WRITE (*,*) MAXLOC(input1)
```

4. ```
REAL, DIMENSION(2,2) :: arr1
arr1 = RESHAPE((/3.,0.,-3.,5./), (/2,2/))
WRITE (*,*) SUM(arr1)
WRITE (*,*) PRODUCT(arr1)
WRITE (*,*) PRODUCT(arr1, MASK=arr1 /= 0.)
WRITE (*,*) ANY(arr1 > 0.)
WRITE (*,*) ALL(arr1 > 0.)
```

5. ```
INTEGER, DIMENSION(2,3) :: arr2
arr2 = RESHAPE( (/3,0,-3,5,-8,2/), (/2,3/) )
WHERE ( arr2 > 0 )
   arr2 = 2 * arr2
END WHERE
WRITE (*,*) SUM( arr2, MASK=arr2 > 0. )
```

6. Rewrite Question 3 of this quiz using a `FORALL` construct to initialize `input1`.

Determine which of the following sets of Fortran statements are valid. For each set of valid statements, specify what will happen in the program. For each set of invalid statements, specify what is wrong. Assume default typing for any variables that are not explicitly typed.

7. ```
REAL, DIMENSION(6) :: dist1
REAL, DIMENSION(5) :: time
dist1 = (/ 0.00, 0.25, 1.00, 2.25, 4.00, 6.25 /)
time = (/ 0.0, 1.0, 2.0, 3.0, 4.0 /)
WHERE (time > 0.)
   dist1 = SQRT(dist1)
END WHERE
```

*(continued)*
```

(concluded)

```
8.  REAL, DIMENSION(:), ALLOCATABLE :: time
    time = (/ 0.00,  0.25,  1.00,  2.25,  4.00,  6.25, &
                9.00, 12.25, 16.00, 20.25/)
    WRITE (*,*) time

9.  INTEGER, DIMENSION(5,5) :: data1 = 0.
    FORALL (i=1:5:2, j=1:5, i-j>=0 )
       data1(i,j) = i - j + 1
    END FORALL
    WRITE (*,100) ((data1(i,j), j=1,5), i=1,5)
100 FORMAT (1X,5I6)

10. REAL, DIMENSION(:,:), ALLOCATABLE :: test
    WRITE (*,*) ALLOCATED(test)
```

■ 8.7

SUMMARY

In Chapter 8, we presented two-dimensional (rank-2) and multidimensional (rank-*n*) arrays. Fortran allows up to seven dimensions in an array.

A multidimensional array is declared by using a type declaration statement by naming the array and specifying the maximum (and, optionally, the minimum) subscript values with the DIMENSION attribute. The compiler uses the declared subscript ranges to reserve space in the computer's memory to hold the array. The array elements are allocated in the computer's memory in an order such that the first subscript of the array changes most rapidly, and the last subscript of the array changes most slowly.

As with any variable, an array must be initialized before use. An array may be initialized at compile time using array constructors in the type declaration statements, or at run time using array constructors, DO loops, or Fortran READs.

Individual array elements may be used freely in a Fortran program just like any other variable. They may appear in assignment statements on either side of the equal sign. Entire arrays and array sections may also be used in calculations and assignment statements as long as the arrays are conformable with each other. Arrays are conformable if they have the same number of dimensions (rank) and the same extent in each dimension. A scalar is also conformable with any array. An operation between two conformable arrays is performed on an element-by-element basis. Scalar values are also conformable with arrays.

Fortran 95/2003 contains three basic types of intrinsic functions: elemental functions, inquiry functions, and transformational functions. Elemental functions are defined for a scalar input and produce a scalar output. When applied to an array, an elemental function produces an output that is the result of applying the operation separately to each element of the input array. Inquiry functions return information about an array, such as its size or bounds. Transformational functions operate on entire arrays and produce an output that is based on all of the elements of the array.

The WHERE construct permits an array assignment statement to be performed on only those elements of an array that meet specified criteria. It is useful for preventing errors caused by out-of-range data values in the array.

The FORALL construct is a method of applying an operation to many elements of an array without specifying the order in which the operation must be applied to the individual elements.

Arrays may be either static or allocatable. The size of static arrays are declared at compilation time, and they may only be modified by recompiling the program. The size of dynamic arrays may be declared a execution time, allowing a program to adjust its memory requirements to fit the size of the problem to be solved. Allocatable arrays are declared by using the ALLOCATABLE attribute, are allocated during program execution by using the ALLOCATE statement, and are deallocated by using the DEALLOCATE statement.

F-2003 ONLY

In Fortran 2003, allocatable arrays can also be automatically allocated and deallocated using assignment statements.

8.7.1 Summary of Good Programming Practice

The following guidelines should be adhered to when working with arrays.

1. Use the RESHAPE function to change the shape of an array. This is especially useful when used with an array constructor to create array constants of any desired shape.
2. Use implicit DO loops to read in or write out rank-2 arrays so that each row of the array appears as a row of the input or output file. This correspondence makes it easier for a programmer to relate the data in the file to the data present within the program.
3. Use WHERE constructs to modify and assign array elements when you want to modify and assign only those elements that pass some test.
4. Use allocatable arrays to produce programs that automatically adjust their memory requirements to the size of the problem being solved. Declare allocatable arrays with the ALLOCATABLE attribute, allocate memory to them with the ALLOCATE statement, and deallocate memory with the DEALLOCATE statement.
5. Always include the STAT= clause in any ALLOCATE statement, and always check the returned status, so that a program can be shut down gracefully if there is insufficient memory to allocate the necessary arrays.

F-2003 ONLY

6. Always include the ERRMSG= clause in any Fortran 2003 ALLOCATE or DEALLOCATE statement to return a user-readable error message in case of an allocation failure.

7. Always deallocate allocatable arrays with a DEALLOCATE statement as soon as you are through using them.

8.7.2 Summary of Fortran Statements and Constructs

ALLOCATABLE **Attribute:**

      `type, ALLOCATABLE, DIMENSION(:,[:, ...]) :: array1, ...`

Examples:

      `REAL, ALLOCATABLE, DIMENSION(:) :: array1`
      `INTEGER, ALLOCATABLE, DIMENSION(:,:,:) :: indices`

Description:

The `ALLOCATABLE` attribute declares that the size of an array is dynamic. The size will be specified in an `ALLOCATE` statement at run time. The type declaration statement must specify the rank of the array, but not the extent in each dimension. Each dimension is specified using a colon as a placeholder.

ALLOCATABLE **Statement:**

      `ALLOCATABLE :: array1, ...`

Example:

      `ALLOCATABLE :: array1`

Description:

The `ALLOCATABLE` statement declares that the size of an array is dynamic. It duplicates the function of the `ALLOCATABLE` attribute associated with a type declaration statement. **Do not use this statement.** Use the `ALLOCATABLE` attribute instead.

8

ALLOCATE **Statement:**

      `ALLOCATE (array1( [i1:]i2, [j1:]j2, ... ), ... , STAT=status)`

F-2003 ONLY

      `ALLOCATE (array1( [i1:]i2, [j1:]j2, ... ), ... , STAT=status, ERRMSG=msg)`
      `ALLOCATE (array1, SOURCE=expr, STAT=status, ERRMSG=msg)`

Examples:

      `ALLOCATE (array1(10000), STAT=istat)`
      `ALLOCATE (indices(-10:10,-10:10,5), STAT=allocate_status)`

Description:

The `ALLOCATE` statement dynamically allocates memory to an array that was previously declared allocatable. The extent of each dimension is specified in the `ALLOCATE` statement. The returned status will be zero for successful completion, and will be a machine-dependent positive number in the case of an error.

F-2003 ONLY

    The `SOURCE=` clause and the `ERRMSG=` clause are only supported in Fortran 2003.

DEALLOCATE Statement:

```
DEALLOCATE (array1, ... , STAT=status)
DEALLOCATE (array1, ... , STAT=status, ERRMSG=msg)
```

Example:

```
DEALLOCATE (array1, indices, STAT=status)
```

Description:

The DEALLOCATE statement dynamically deallocates the memory that was assigned by an ALLOCATE statement to one or more allocatable arrays. After the statement executes, the memory associated with those
arrays is no longer accessible. The returned status will be zero for successful completion, and will be a
machine-dependent positive number in the case of an error.

The ERRMSG= clause is supported only in Fortran 2003.

FORALL Construct:

```
[name: ] FORALL (index1=triplet1 [, ... , logical_expr])
    Assignment Statement(s)
END FORALL [name]
```

Example:

```
FORALL (i=1:3, j=1:3, i > j)
    arr1(i,j) = ABS(i-j) + 3
END FORALL
```

Description:

The FORALL construct permits assignment statements to be executed for those indices that meet the triplet
specifications and the optional logical expression, but it does not specify the order in which they are executed. There may be as many indices as desired, and each index will be specified by a subscript triplet.
The logical expression is applied as a mask to the indices, and those combinations of specified indices for
which the logical expression is TRUE will be executed.

FORALL Statement:

```
FORALL (index1=triplet1 [, ... , logical_expr]) Assignment Statement
```

Description:

The FORALL statement is a simplified version of the FORALL construct in which there is only one assignment statement.

WHERE **Construct:**

```
[name:] WHERE ( mask_expr1 )
   Block 1
ELSEWHERE ( mask_expr2 ) [name]
   Block 2
ELSEWHERE [name]
   Block 3
END WHERE [name]
```

Description:

The WHERE construct permits operations to be applied to the elements of an array that match a given criterion. A different set of operations may be applied to the elements that do not match. Each *mask_expr* must be a logical array of the same shape as the arrays being manipulated within the code blocks. If a given element of the *mask_expr1* is true, then the array assignment statements in Block 1 will be applied to the corresponding element in the arrays being operated on. If an element of the *mask_expr1* is false and the corresponding element of the *mask_expr2* is true, then the array assignment statements in Block 2 will be applied to the corresponding element in the arrays being operated on. If both mask expressions are false, then the array assignment statements in Block 3 will be applied to the corresponding element in the arrays being operated on.

The ELSEWHERE clauses are optional in this construct. There can be as many masked ELSEWHERE clauses are desired, and up to one plain ELSEWHERE.

8

WHERE **Statement:**

```
WHERE ( mask expression ) array_assignment_statement
```

Description:

The WHERE statement is a simplified version of the WHERE construct in which there is only one array assignment statement and no ELSEWHERE clause.

8.7.3 Exercises

8-1. Determine the shape and size of the arrays specified by the following declaration statements, and the valid subscript range for each dimension of each array.

(*a*) CHARACTER(len=80), DIMENSION(3,60) :: line

(*b*) INTEGER, DIMENSION(-10:10,0:20) :: char

(*c*) REAL, DIMENSION(-5:5,-5:5,-5:5,-5:5,-5:5) :: range

8-2. Determine which of the following Fortran program fragments are valid. For each valid statement, specify what will happen in the program. (Assume default typing for any variables that are not explicitly typed within the program fragments.)

(*a*)
```
REAL, DIMENSION(6,4) :: b
. . .
DO i = 1, 6
   DO j = 1, 4
      temp    = b(i,j)
      b(i,j) = b(j,i)
      b(j,i) = temp
   END DO
END DO
```

(*b*)
```
INTEGER, DIMENSION(9) :: info
info = (/1,-3,0,-5,-9,3,0,1,7/)
WHERE ( info > 0 )
   info = -info
ELSEWHERE
   info = -3 * info
END WHERE
WRITE (*,*) info
```

(*c*)
```
INTEGER, DIMENSION(8) :: info
info = (/1,-3,0,-5,-9,3,0,7/)
WRITE (*,*) info <=  0
```

(*d*)
```
REAL, DIMENSION(4,4) :: z = 0.
. . .
FORALL ( i=1:4, j=1:4 )
   z(i,j) = ABS(i-j)
END FORALL
```

8-3 Given a 5 × 5 array my_array containing the values shown below, determine the shape and contents of each of the following array sections.

$$
my\_array = \begin{bmatrix}
1 & 2 & 3 & 4 & 5 \\
6 & 7 & 8 & 9 & 10 \\
11 & 12 & 13 & 14 & 15 \\
16 & 17 & 18 & 19 & 20 \\
21 & 22 & 23 & 24 & 25
\end{bmatrix}
$$

(*a*) my_array(3,:)
(*b*) my_array(:,2)
(*c*) my_array(1:5:2,:)
(*d*) my_array(:,2:5:2)
(*e*) my_array(1:5:2,1:5:2)
(*f*) INTEGER, DIMENSION(3) :: list = (/ 1, 2, 4 /)
      my_array(:,list)

8-4. What will be the output from each of the WRITE statements in the following program? Why is the output of the two statements different?

```
PROGRAM test_output1
IMPLICIT NONE
INTEGER, DIMENSION(0:1,0:3) :: my_data
INTEGER :: i, j
my_data(0,:) = (/ 1, 2, 3, 4 /)
my_data(1,:) = (/ 5, 6, 7, 8 /)
!
DO i = 0,1
   WRITE (*,100) (my_data(i,j), j=0,3)
   100 FORMAT (6(1X,I4))
END DO
WRITE (*,100) ((my_data(i,j), j=0,3), i=0,1)
END PROGRAM test_output1
```

8-5. An input data file INPUT1 contains the following values:

27	17	10	8	6
11	13	-11	12	-21
-1	0	0	6	14
-16	11	21	26	-16
04	99	-99	17	2

Assume that file INPUT1 has been opened on i/o unit 8, and that array values is a 4 × 4 integer array, all of whose elements have been initialized to zero. What will be the contents of array values after each of the following READ statements has been executed?

(*a*) ```
DO i = 1, 4
    READ (8,*) (values(i,j), j = 1, 4)
END DO
```

(*b*) ```
READ (8,*) ((values(i,j), j = 1, 4), i=1,4)
```

(*c*) ```
DO i = 1, 4
    READ (8,*) values(i,:)
END DO
```

(*d*) ```
READ (8,*) values
```

8-6. What will be printed out by the following program?

```
PROGRAM test
IMPLICIT NONE
INTEGER, PARAMETER :: N = 5, M = 10
INTEGER, DIMENSION(N:M,M-N:M+N) :: info

WRITE (*,100) SHAPE(info)
100 FORMAT (1X,'The shape of the array is:       ',2I6)
WRITE (*,110) SIZE(info)
110 FORMAT (1X,'The size of the array is:        ',I6)
WRITE (*,120) LBOUND(info)
120 FORMAT (1X,'The lower bounds of the array are: ',2I6)
```

```
WRITE (*,130) UBOUND(info)
130 FORMAT (1X,'The upper bounds of the array are: ',2I6)
END PROGRAM test
```

8-7. Assume that `values` is a 10,201-element array containing a list of measurements from a scientific experiment, which has been declared by the statement

$$\text{REAL, DIMENSION}(-50:50,0:100) :: \text{values}$$

(*a*) Create a set of Fortran statements that would count the number of positive values, negative values, and zero values in the array, and write out a message summarizing how many values of each type were found. Do not use any intrinsic functions in your code.

(*b*) Use the transformational intrinsic function `COUNT` to create a set of Fortran statements that would count the number of positive values, negative values, and zero values in the array, and write out a message summarizing how many values of each type were found. Compare the complexity of this code to the complexity of the code in (*a*).

8-8. Write a program that can read in a rank-2 array from an input disk file, and calculate the sums of all of the data in each row and each column in the array. The size of the array to read in will be specified by two numbers on the first line in the input file, and the elements in each row of the array will be found on a single line of the input file. Size the program to handle arrays of up to 100 rows and 100 columns. An example of an input data file containing a 2 row × 4 column array is shown below:

```
    2         4
-24.0    -1121.     812.1      11.1
 35.6     8.1E3    135.23     -17.3
```

Write out the results in the form:

```
Sum of row 1 =
Sum of row 2 =
     . . .
Sum of col 1 =
     . . .
```

8-9. Test the program that you wrote in Exercise 8-8 by running it on the following array:

$$\text{array} = \begin{bmatrix} 33. & -12. & 16. & 0.5 & -1.9 \\ -6. & -14. & 3.5 & 11. & 2.1 \\ 4.4 & 1.1 & -7.1 & 9.3 & -16.1 \\ 0.3 & 6.2 & -9.9 & -12. & 6.8 \end{bmatrix}$$

8-10. Modify the program you wrote in Exercise 8-8 to use allocatable arrays that are adjusted to match the number of rows and columns in the problem each time the program is run.

8-11. Write a program that demonstrates the use of Fortran 2003 allocatable arrays.

8-12. Write a set of Fortran statements that would search a rank-3 array `arr` and limit the maximum value of any array element to be less than or equal to 1000. If any element exceeds 1000, its value should be set to 1000. Assume that array `arr` has dimensions 1000 × 10 × 30. Write two sets of statements, one checking the array elements one at a time using `DO` loops, and one using the `WHERE` construct. Which of the two approaches is easier?

8-13. Average Annual Temperature As a part of a meteorological experiment, average annual temperature measurements were collected at 36 locations specified by latitude and longitude as shown in the chart below.

	90.0° W long	90.5° W long	91.0° W long	91.5° W long	92.0° W long	92.5° W long
30.0° N lat	68.2	72.1	72.5	74.1	74.4	74.2
30.5° N lat	69.4	71.1	71.9	73.1	73.6	73.7
31.0° N lat	68.9	70.5	70.9	71.5	72.8	73.0
31.5° N lat	68.6	69.9	70.4	70.8	71.5	72.2
32.0° N lat	68.1	69.3	69.8	70.2	70.9	71.2
32.5° N lat	68.3	68.8	69.6	70.0	70.5	70.9

Write a Fortran program that calculates the average annual temperature along each latitude included in the experiment, and the average annual temperature along each longitude included in the experiment. Finally, calculate the average annual temperature for all of the locations in the experiment. Take advantage of intrinsic functions where appropriate to make your program simpler.

8-14. Matrix Multiplication Matrix multiplication is only defined for two matrices in which *the number of columns in the first matrix is equal to the number of rows in the second matrix.* If matrix A is an $N \times L$ matrix, and matrix B is an $L \times M$ matrix, then the product $C = A \times B$ is an $N \times M$ matrix whose elements are given by the equation

$$c_{ik} = \sum_{j=1}^{L} a_{ij} b_{jk}$$

For example, if matrices A and B are 2×2 matrices

$$A = \begin{bmatrix} 3.0 & -1.0 \\ 1.0 & 2.0 \end{bmatrix} \quad \text{and} \quad B = \begin{bmatrix} 1.0 & 4.0 \\ 2.0 & -3.0 \end{bmatrix}$$

then the elements of matrix C will be

$$c_{11} = a_{11}b_{11} + a_{12}b_{21} = (3.0)(1.0) + (-1.0)(2.0) = 1.0$$
$$c_{12} = a_{11}b_{12} + a_{12}b_{22} = (3.0)(4.0) + (-1.0)(-3.0) = 15.0$$
$$c_{21} = a_{21}b_{11} + a_{22}b_{21} = (1.0)(1.0) + (2.0)(2.0) = 5.0$$
$$c_{22} = a_{21}b_{12} + a_{22}b_{22} = (1.0)(4.0) + (2.0)(-3.0) = -2.0$$

Write a program that can read two matrices of arbitrary size from two input disk files, and multiply them if they are of compatible sizes. If they are of incompatible sizes, an appropriate error message should be printed. The number of rows and columns in each matrix will be specified by two integers on the first line in each file, and the elements in each row of the matrix will be found on a single line of the input file. Use allocatable arrays to hold both the input matrices and the resulting output matrix. Verify your program by creating two input data files containing matrices of the compatible sizes, calculating the resulting values, and checking the answers by hand. Also, verify the proper behavior of the program if it is given two matrices of incompatible sizes.

8-15. Use the program produced in Exercise 8-14 to calculate $C = A \times B$ where:

$$A = \begin{bmatrix} 1. & -5. & 4. & 2. \\ -6. & -4. & 2. & 2. \end{bmatrix} \quad \text{and} \quad B = \begin{bmatrix} 1. & -2. & -1. \\ 2. & 3. & 4. \\ 0. & -1. & 2. \\ 0. & -3. & 1. \end{bmatrix}$$

How many rows and how many columns are present in the resulting matrix C?

8-16. Fortran 95/2003 includes an intrinsic function MATMUL to perform matrix multiplication. Rewrite the program of Exercise 8-14 to use function MATMUL to multiply the matrices together.

8-17. Relative Maxima A point in a rank-2 array is said to be a *relative maximum* if it is higher than any of the 8 points surrounding it. For example, the element at position (2, 2) in the array shown below is a relative maximum, since it is larger than any of the surrounding points.

$$\begin{bmatrix} 11 & 7 & -2 \\ -7 & 14 & 3 \\ 2 & -3 & 5 \end{bmatrix}$$

Write a program to read a matrix A from an input disk file, and to scan for all relative maxima within the matrix. The first line in the disk file should contain the number of rows and the number of columns in the matrix, and then the next lines should contain the values in the matrix, with all of the values in a given row on a single line of the input disk file. (Be sure to use the proper form of implied DO statements to read in the data correctly.) Use allocatable arrays. The program should only consider interior points within the matrix, since any point along an edge of the matrix cannot be completely surrounded by points lower than itself. Test your program by finding all of the relative maxima the following matrix, which can be found in file FINDPEAK:

$$A = \begin{bmatrix} 2. & -1. & -2. & 1. & 3. & -5. & 2. & 1. \\ -2. & 0. & -2.5 & 5. & -2. & 2. & 1. & 0. \\ -3. & -3. & -3. & 3. & 0. & 0. & -1. & -2. \\ -4.5 & -4. & -7. & 6. & 1. & -3. & 0. & 5. \\ -3.5 & -3. & -5. & 0. & 4. & 17. & 11. & 5. \\ -9. & -6. & -5. & -3. & 1. & 2. & 0. & 0.5 \\ -7. & -4. & -5. & -3. & 2. & 4. & 3. & -1. \\ -6. & -5. & -5. & -2. & 0. & 1. & 2. & 5. \end{bmatrix}$$

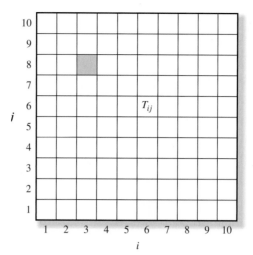

FIGURE 8-9
A metallic plate divided into 100 small segments.

8-18. **Temperature Distribution on a Metallic Plate** Under steady-state conditions, the temperature at any point on the surface of a metallic plate will be the average of the temperatures of all points surrounding it. This fact can be used in an iterative procedure to calculate the temperature distribution at all points on the plate.

Figure 8-9 shows a square plate divided in 100 squares or nodes by a grid. The temperatures of the nodes form a two-dimensional array T. The temperature in all nodes at the edges of the plate is constrained to be $20°$ C by a cooling system, and the temperature of the node (3, 8) is fixed at $100°$ C by exposure to boiling water.

A new estimate of the temperature $T_{i,j}$ in any given node can be calculated from the average of the temperatures in all segments surrounding it:

$$T_{ij,\text{new}} = \frac{1}{4}\left(T_{i+1,j} + T_{i-1,j} + T_{i,j+1} + T_{i,j-1}\right) \tag{8-1}$$

To determine the temperature distribution on the surface of a plate, an initial assumption must be made about the temperatures in each node. Then Equation 8-1 is applied to each node whose temperature is not fixed to calculate a new estimate of the temperature in that node. These updated temperature estimates are used to calculate newer estimates, and the process is repeated until the new temperature estimates in each node differ from the old ones by only a small amount. At that point, a steady-state solution has been found.

Write a program to calculate the steady-state temperature distribution throughout the plate, making an initial assumption that all interior segments are at a temperature of $50°$ C. Remember that all outside segments are fixed at a temperature of $20°$ C and segment (3, 8) is fixed at a temperature of $100°$ C. The program should apply Equation 8-1 iteratively until the maximum temperature change between iterations in any node is less than $0.01°$. What will be the steady-state temperature of segment (5, 5)?

Additional Features of Procedures

OBJECTIVES

- Learn how to use multidimensional arrays in Fortran procedures.
- Understand how and when to use the SAVE attribute or statement.
- Understand the difference between allocatable and automatic arrays, and when to use each in a procedure.
- Understand pure and elemental procedures.
- Learn how to declare and use internal subroutines and functions.

In Chapter 7, we learned the basics of using Fortran subroutines, function subprograms, and modules. This chapter describes more advanced features of procedures, including multidimensional arrays in procedures and the use of internal procedures.

9.1

PASSING MULTIDIMENSIONAL ARRAYS TO SUBROUTINES AND FUNCTIONS

Multidimensional arrays can be passed to subroutines or functions in a manner similar to that for one-dimensional arrays. However, the subroutine or function will need to know *both the number of dimensions and the extent of each dimension* in order to use the array properly. There are three possible ways to pass this information to the subprogram.

9.1.1 Explicit-Shape Dummy Arrays

The first approach is to use **explicit-shape dummy arrays.** In this case, we pass the array and the extent of each dimension of the array to the subroutine. The extent values are used to declare the size of the array in the subroutine, and thus the subroutine knows all about the array. An example subroutine using explicit-shape dummy arrays is shown below.

```
SUBROUTINE process1 ( data1, data2, n, m )
INTEGER, INTENT(IN) :: n, m
REAL, INTENT(IN),  DIMENSION(n,m) :: data1  ! Explicit shape
REAL, INTENT(OUT), DIMENSION(n,m) :: data2  ! Explicit shape

data2 = 3. * data1

END SUBROUTINE process1
```

When explicit-shape dummy arrays are used, the size and shape of each dummy array in the subprogram is known to the compiler. Since the size and shape of each array is known, it is possible to use array operations and array sections with the dummy arrays.

9.1.2 Assumed-Shape Dummy Arrays

The second approach is to declare all dummy arrays in a subroutine as **assumed-shape dummy arrays.** Assumed-shape arrays are declared by using colons as placeholders for each subscript of the array. These arrays work only if the subroutine or function has an explicit interface, so that the calling program knows everything about the subroutine interface. This is normally accomplished by placing the subprogram into a module, and then USEing the module in the calling program.

Whole array operations, array sections, and array intrinsic functions can all be used with assumed-shape dummy arrays, because the compiler can determine the size and shape of each array from the information in the interface. If needed, the actual size and extent of an assumed-shape array can be determined by using the array inquiry functions in Table 8-1. However, the upper and lower bounds of each dimension cannot be determined, since only the *shape* of the actual array but not the *bounds* are passed to the procedure. If the actual bounds are needed for some reason in a particular procedure, then an explicit-shape dummy array must be used.

Assumed-shape dummy arrays are generally better than explicit-shape dummy arrays in that we don't have to pass every bound from the calling program unit to a procedure. However, assumed-shape arrays only work if a procedure has an explicit interface.

An example subroutine using assumed-shape dummy arrays is shown below.

```
MODULE test_module
CONTAINS

   SUBROUTINE process2 ( data1, data2 )
   REAL, INTENT(IN),  DIMENSION(:,:) :: data1  ! Explicit shape
   REAL, INTENT(OUT), DIMENSION(:,:) :: data2  ! Explicit shape

   data2 = 3. * data1

   END SUBROUTINE process2

END MODULE test_module
```

9.1.3 Assumed-Size Dummy Arrays

The third (and oldest) approach is to use an **assumed-size dummy array.** These are arrays in which the lengths of the all but the last dimension are declared explicity, and the length of the last array dimension is an asterisk. Assumed-size dummy arrays are a holdover from earlier versions of Fortran. *They should never be used in any new programs,* so we will not discuss them here.

Good Programming Practice
Use either assumed-shape arrays or explicit-shape arrays as dummy array arguments in procedures. If assumed-shape arrays are used, an explicit interface is required. Whole array operations, array sections, and array intrinsic functions may be used with the dummy array arguments in either case. *Never use assumed-size arrays in any new program.*

EXAMPLE   *Gauss-Jordan Elimination:*
9-1

Many important problems in science and engineering require the solution of a system of N simultaneous linear equations in N unknowns. Some of these problems require the solution of small systems of equations, say 3×3 or 4×4. Such problems are relatively easy to solve. Other problems might require the solution of really large sets of simultaneous equations, like 1000 equations in 1000 unknowns. Those problems are *much* harder to solve, and the solution requires a variety of special iterative techniques. A whole branch of the science of numerical methods is devoted to different ways to solve systems of simultaneous linear equations.

We will now develop a subroutine to solve a system of simultaneous linear equations using the straightforward approach known as Gauss-Jordan elimination. The subroutine that we develop should work fine for systems of up to about 20 equations in 20 unknowns.

Gauss-Jordan elimination depends on the fact that you can multiply one equation in a system of equations by a constant and add it to another equation, and the new system of equations will still be equivalent to the original one. In fact, it works in exactly the same way that we solve systems of simultaneous equations by hand.

To understand the technique, consider the 3×3 system of equations shown below.

$$\begin{aligned}
1.0\ x1 + 1.0\ x2 + 1.0\ x3 &= 1.0 \\
2.0\ x1 + 1.0\ x2 + 1.0\ x3 &= 2.0 \\
1.0\ x1 + 3.0\ x2 + 2.0\ x3 &= 4.0
\end{aligned} \tag{9-1}$$

We would like to manipulate this set of equations by multiplying one of the equations by a constant and adding it to another one until we eventually wind up with a set of equations of the form

$$
\begin{aligned}
1.0 \ x1 + 0.0 \ x2 + 0.0 \ x3 &= b1 \\
0.0 \ x1 + 1.0 \ x2 + 0.0 \ x3 &= b2 \\
0.0 \ x1 + 0.0 \ x2 + 1.0 \ x3 &= b3
\end{aligned}
\qquad (9\text{-}2)
$$

When we get to this form, the solution to the system will be obvious: $x1 = b1$, $x2 = b2$, and $x3 = b3$.

To get from Equations 9-1 to Equations 9-2, we must go through three steps:

1. Eliminate all coefficients of $x1$ except in the first equation.
2. Eliminate all coefficients of $x2$ except in the second equation.
3. Eliminate all coefficients of $x3$ except in the third equation.

First, we will eliminate all coefficients of $x1$ except that in the first equation. If we multiply the first equation by -2 and add it to the second equation, and multiply the first equation by -1 and add it to the third equation, the results are:

$$
\begin{aligned}
1.0 \ x1 + 1.0 \ x2 + 1.0 \ x3 &= 1.0 \\
0.0 \ x1 - 1.0 \ x2 - 1.0 \ x3 &= 0.0 \\
0.0 \ x1 + 2.0 \ x2 + 1.0 \ x3 &= 3.0
\end{aligned}
\qquad (9\text{-}3)
$$

Next, we will eliminate all coefficients of $x2$ except in the second equation. If we add the second equation as it is to the first equation, and multiply the second equation by 2 and add it to the third equation, the results are:

$$
\begin{aligned}
1.0 \ x1 + 0.0 \ x2 + 0.0 \ x3 &= 1.0 \\
0.0 \ x1 - 1.0 \ x2 - 1.0 \ x3 &= 0.0 \\
0.0 \ x1 + 0.0 \ x2 - 1.0 \ x3 &= 3.0
\end{aligned}
\qquad (9\text{-}4)
$$

9

Finally, we will eliminate all coefficients of $x3$ except in the third equation. In this case, there is no coefficient of $x3$ in the first equation, so we don't have to do anything there. If we multiply the third equation by -1 and add it to the second equation, the results are:

$$
\begin{aligned}
1.0 \ x1 + 0.0 \ x2 + 0.0 \ x3 &= \ \ \ 1.0 \\
0.0 \ x1 - 1.0 \ x2 + 0.0 \ x3 &= -3.0 \\
0.0 \ x1 + 0.0 \ x2 - 1.0 \ x3 &= \ \ \ 3.0
\end{aligned}
\qquad (9\text{-}5)
$$

The last step is almost trivial. If we divide the first equation by the coefficient of $x1$, the second equation by the coefficient of $x2$, and the third equation by the coefficient of $x3$, then the solution to the equations will appear on the right-hand side of the equations.

$$
\begin{aligned}
1.0 \ x1 + 0.0 \ x2 + 0.0 \ x3 &= \ \ \ 1.0 \\
0.0 \ x1 + 1.0 \ x2 + 0.0 \ x3 &= \ \ \ 3.0 \\
0.0 \ x1 + 0.0 \ x2 + 1.0 \ x3 &= -3.0
\end{aligned}
\qquad (9\text{-}6)
$$

The final answer is $x1 = 1$, $x2 = 3$, and $x3 = -3$.

Sometimes the technique shown above does not produce a solution. This happens when the set of equations being solved are not all *independent*. For example, consider the following 2×2 system of simultaneous equations:

$$2.0\ x1 + 3.0\ x2 = 4.0 \tag{9-7}$$
$$4.0\ x1 + 6.0\ x2 = 8.0$$

If the first equation is multiplied by -2 and added to the first equation, we get

$$2.0\ x1 + 3.0\ x2 = 4.0 \tag{9-8}$$
$$0.0\ x1 + 0.0\ x2 = 0.0$$

There is no way to solve this system for a unique solution, since there are infinitely many values of $x1$ and $x2$ that satisfy Equations 9-8. These conditions can be recognized by the fact that the coefficient of $x2$ in the second equation is 0. The solution to this system of equations is said to be nonunique. Our computer program will have to test for problems like this, and report them with an error code.

SOLUTION

We will now write a subroutine to solve a system of N simultaneous equations in N unknowns. The computer program will work in exactly the manner shown above, except that at each step in the process, we will reorder the equations. In the first step, we will reorder the N equations such that the first equation is the one with the largest coefficient (absolute value) of the first variable. In the second step, we will reorder the second equation through the Nth equation such that the second equation is the one with the largest coefficient (absolute value) of the second variable. This process is repeated for each step in the solution. Reordering the equations is important, because it reduces roundoff errors in large systems of equations, and also avoids divide-by-zero errors. (This reordering of equations is called the *maximum pivot* technique in the literature of numerical methods.)

1. **State the problem.**

    Write a subroutine to solve a system of N simultaneous equations in N unknowns using Gauss-Jordan elimination and the maximum pivot technique to avoid roundoff errors. The subroutine must be able to detect singular sets of equations, and set an error flag if they occur. Use explicit-shape dummy arrays in the subroutine.

2. **Define the inputs and outputs.**

    The input to the subroutine consists of an ndim $\times$ ndim matrix a, containing an n $\times$ n set of coefficients for the simultaneous equations, and an ndim vector b, with the contents of the right-hand sides of the equations. The size of the matrix ndim must be greater than or equal to the size of the set of simultaneous equations n. Since the subroutine is to have explicit-shape dummy arrays, we will also have to pass ndim to the subroutine, and use it to declare the dummy array sizes. The outputs from the subroutine are the solutions to the set of equations (in vector b), and an error flag. Note that the matrix of coefficients a will be destroyed during the solution process.

3. **Describe the algorithm.**

The pseudocode for this subroutine is:

```
DO for irow = 1 to n

   ! Find peak pivot for column irow in rows i to n
   ipeak ← irow
   DO for jrow = irow+1 to n
      IF |a(jrow,irow)| > |a(ipeak,irow)| then
         ipeak ← jrow
      END of IF
   END of DO

   ! Check for singular equations
   IF |a(ipeak,irow)| < EPSILON THEN
      Equations are singular; set error code & exit
   END of IF

   ! Otherwise, if ipeak /= irow, swap equations irow & peak
   IF ipeak <> irow
      DO for kcol = 1 to n
         temp ← a(ipeak,kcol)
         a(ipeak,kcol) ← a(irow,kcol)
         a(irow,kcol) ← temp
      END of DO
      temp ← b(ipeak)
      b(ipeak) ← b(irow)
      b(irow) ← temp
   END of IF

   ! Multiply equation irow by -a(jrow,irow)/a(irow,irow),
   ! and add it to Eqn jrow
   DO for jrow = 1 to n except for irow
      factor ← -a(jrow,irow)/a(irow,irow)
      DO for kcol = 1 to n
         a(jrow,kcol) ← a(irow,kcol) * factor + a(jrow,kcol)
      END of DO
      b(jrow) ← b(irow) * factor + b(jrow)
   END of DO
END of DO

! End of main loop over all equations. All off-diagonal
! terms are now zero. To get the final answer, we must
! divide each equation by the coefficient of its on-diagonal
! term.
DO for irow = 1 to n
   b(irow) ← b(irow) / a(irow,irow)
   a(irow,irow) ← 1.
END of DO
```

4. **Turn the algorithm into Fortran statements.**

The resulting Fortran subroutine is shown in Figure 9-1. Note that the sizes of arrays a and b are passed explicitly to the subroutine as a(ndim,ndim) and b(ndim).

By doing so, we can use the compiler's bounds checker while we are debugging the subroutine. Note also that the subroutine's large outer loops and IF structures are all named to make it easier for us to understand and keep track of them.

FIGURE 9-1
Subroutine simul.

```
SUBROUTINE simul ( a, b, ndim, n, error )
!
!   Purpose:
!     Subroutine to solve a set of n linear equations in n
!     unknowns using Gaussian elimination and the maximum
!     pivot technique.
!
!   Record of revisions:
!       Date        Programmer          Description of change
!       ====        ==========          =====================
!     11/23/06    S. J. Chapman         Original code
!
IMPLICIT NONE

! Data dictionary: declare calling parameter types & definitions
INTEGER, INTENT(IN) :: ndim            ! Dimension of arrays a and b
REAL, INTENT(INOUT), DIMENSION(ndim,ndim) :: a
                                       ! Array of coefficients (n × n).
                                       ! This array is of size ndim ×
                                       ! ndim, but only n × n of the
                                       ! coefficients are being used.
                                       ! The declared dimension ndim
                                       ! must be passed to the sub, or
                                       ! it won't be able to interpret
                                       ! subscripts correctly.  (This
                                       ! array is destroyed during
                                       ! processing.)
REAL, INTENT(INOUT), DIMENSION(ndim) :: b
                                       ! Input: Right-hand side of eqns.
                                       ! Output: Solution vector.
INTEGER, INTENT(IN) :: n               ! Number of equations to solve.
INTEGER, INTENT(OUT) :: error          ! Error flag:
                                       !   0 -- No error
                                       !   1 -- Singular equations

! Data dictionary: declare constants
REAL, PARAMETER :: EPSILON = 1.0E-6    ! A "small" number for comparison
                                       ! when determining singular eqns

! Data dictionary: declare local variable types & definitions
REAL :: factor                         ! Factor to multiply eqn irow by
                                       ! before adding to eqn jrow
INTEGER :: irow                        ! Number of the equation currently
                                       ! being processed
```

(*continued*)

(continued)

```fortran
INTEGER :: ipeak                       ! Pointer to equation containing
                                       ! maximum pivot value
INTEGER :: jrow                        ! Number of the equation compared
                                       ! to the current equation
INTEGER :: kcol                        ! Index over all columns of eqn
REAL :: temp                           ! Scratch value

! Process n times to get all equations...
mainloop: DO irow = 1, n

   ! Find peak pivot for column irow in rows irow to n
   ipeak = irow
   max_pivot: DO jrow = irow+1, n
      IF (ABS(a(jrow,irow)) > ABS(a(ipeak,irow))) THEN
         ipeak = jrow
      END IF
   END DO max_pivot

   ! Check for singular equations.
   singular: IF ( ABS(a(ipeak,irow)) < EPSILON ) THEN
      error = 1
      RETURN
   END IF singular

   ! Otherwise, if ipeak /= irow, swap equations irow & ipeak
   swap_eqn: IF ( ipeak /= irow ) THEN
      DO kcol = 1, n
         temp        = a(ipeak,kcol)
         a(ipeak,kcol) = a(irow,kcol)
         a(irow,kcol)  = temp
      END DO
      temp      = b(ipeak)
      b(ipeak) = b(irow)
      b(irow)  = temp
   END IF swap_eqn

   ! Multiply equation irow by -a(jrow,irow)/a(irow,irow),
   ! and add it to Eqn jrow (for all eqns except irow itself).
   eliminate: DO jrow = 1, n
      IF ( jrow /= irow ) THEN
         factor = -a(jrow,irow)/a(irow,irow)
         DO kcol = 1, n
            a(jrow,kcol) = a(irow,kcol)*factor + a(jrow,kcol)
         END DO
         b(jrow) = b(irow)*factor + b(jrow)
      END IF
   END DO eliminate
END DO mainloop
```

9

(continued)

CHAPTER 9: Additional Features of Procedures

(concluded)

```
! End of main loop over all equations.  All off-diagonal
! terms are now zero.  To get the final answer, we must
! divide each equation by the coefficient of its on-diagonal
! term.
divide: DO irow = 1, n
   b(irow)       = b(irow) / a(irow,irow)
   a(irow,irow) = 1.
END DO divide

! Set error flag to 0 and return.
error = 0
END SUBROUTINE simul
```

5. **Test the resulting Fortran programs.**

To test this subroutine, it is necessary to write a driver program. The driver program will open an input data file to read the equations to be solved. The first line of the file will contain the number of equations n in the system, and each of the next n lines will contain the coefficients of one of the equations. To show that the simultaneous equation subroutine is working correctly, we will display the contents of arrays a and b both before and after the call to simul.

The test driver program for subroutine simul is shown in Figure 9-2.

FIGURE 9-2
Test driver routine for subroutine simul.

```
PROGRAM test_simul
!
!  Purpose:
!    To test subroutine simul, which solves a set of N linear
!    equations in N unknowns.
!
!  Record of revisions:
!      Date       Programmer          Description of change
!      ====       ==========          =====================
!    11/23/06    S. J. Chapman        Original code
!
IMPLICIT NONE

! Data dictionary: declare constants
INTEGER, PARAMETER :: MAX_SIZE = 10     ! Max number of eqns

! Data dictionary: declare local variable types & definitions
REAL, DIMENSION(MAX_SIZE,MAX_SIZE) :: a
                            ! Array of coefficients (n × n).
                            ! This array is of size ndim ×
                            ! ndim, but only n × n of the
                            ! coefficients are being used.
                            ! The declared dimension ndim
                            ! must be passed to the sub, or
```

(continued)

(continued)

```
                                          ! it won't be able to interpret
                                          ! subscripts correctly.  (This
                                          ! array is destroyed during
                                          ! processing.)
REAL, DIMENSION(MAX_SIZE) :: b            ! Input: Right-hand side of eqns.
                                          ! Output: Solution vector.
INTEGER :: error                          ! Error flag:
                                          !   0 -- No error
                                          !   1 -- Singular equations
CHARACTER(len=20) :: file_name            ! Name of file with eqns
INTEGER :: i                              ! Loop index
INTEGER :: j                              ! Loop index
INTEGER :: n                              ! Number of simul eqns (<= MAX_SIZE)
INTEGER :: istat                          ! I/O status

! Get the name of the disk file containing the equations.
WRITE (*,"(' Enter the file name containing the eqns: ')")
READ (*,'(A20)') file_name

! Open input data file.  Status is OLD because the input data must
! already exist.
OPEN ( UNIT=1, FILE=file_name, STATUS='OLD', ACTION='READ', &
       IOSTAT=istat )

! Was the OPEN successful?
fileopen: IF ( istat == 0 ) THEN
   ! The file was opened successfully, so read the number of
   ! equations in the system.
   READ (1,*) n

   ! If the number of equations is <= MAX_SIZE, read them in
   ! and process them.
   size_ok: IF ( n <= MAX_SIZE ) THEN
      DO i = 1, n
         READ (1,*) (a(i,j), j=1,n), b(i)
      END DO

      ! Display coefficients.
      WRITE (*,"(/,1X,'Coefficients before call:')")
      DO i = 1, n
         WRITE (*,"(1X,7F11.4)") (a(i,j), j=1,n), b(i)
      END DO

      ! Solve equations.
      CALL simul (a, b, MAX_SIZE, n, error )

      ! Check for error.
      error_check: IF ( error /= 0 ) THEN

         WRITE (*,1010)
```

9

(continued)

(concluded)

```
      1010 FORMAT (/1X,'Zero pivot encountered!', &
                    //1X,'There is no unique solution to this system.')

   ELSE error_check

      ! No errors. Display coefficients.
      WRITE (*,"(/,1X,'Coefficients after call:')")
      DO  i = 1, n
          WRITE (*,"(1X,7F11.4)") (a(i,j), j=1,n), b(i)
      END DO

      ! Write final answer.
      WRITE (*,"(/,1X,'The solutions are:')")
      DO i = 1, n
          WRITE (*,"(3X,'X(',I2,') = ',F16.6)") i, b(i)
      END DO

   END IF error_check
  END IF size_ok
ELSE fileopen

   ! Else file open failed.  Tell user.
   WRITE (*,1020) istat
   1020 FORMAT (1X,'File open failed--status = ', I6)

END IF fileopen
END PROGRAM test_simul
```

To test the subroutine, we need to call it with two different data sets. One of them should have a unique solution, and the other one should be singular. We will test the system with two sets of equations. The original equations that we solved by hand will be placed in file INPUTS1.

$$1.0 \ X1 + 1.0 \ X2 + 1.0 \ X3 = 1.0$$
$$2.0 \ X1 + 1.0 \ X2 + 1.0 \ X3 = 2.0 \qquad\qquad (9\text{-}1)$$
$$1.0 \ X1 + 3.0 \ X2 + 2.0 \ X3 = 4.0$$

and the following set of equations will be placed in file INPUTS2.

$$1.0 \ X1 + 1.0 \ X2 + 1.0 \ X3 = 1.0$$
$$2.0 \ X1 + 6.0 \ X2 + 4.0 \ X3 = 8.0$$
$$1.0 \ X1 + 3.0 \ X2 + 2.0 \ X3 = 4.0$$

The second equation of this set is a multiple of the third equation, so the second set of equations is singular. When we run program test_simul with these data sets, the results are:

```
C:\book\chap9>test_simul
Enter the file name containing the eqns:
inputs1
```

```
Coefficients before call:
    1.0000      1.0000      1.0000      1.0000
    2.0000      1.0000      1.0000      2.0000
    1.0000      3.0000      2.0000      4.0000

Coefficients after call:
    1.0000       .0000       .0000      1.0000
     .0000      1.0000       .0000      3.0000
     .0000       .0000      1.0000     -3.0000

The solutions are:
  X( 1) =         1.000000
  X( 2) =         3.000000
  X( 3) =        -3.000000

C:\book\chap9>test_simul
Enter the file name containing the eqns:
inputs2

Coefficients before call:
    1.0000      1.0000      1.0000      1.0000
    2.0000      6.0000      4.0000      8.0000
    1.0000      3.0000      2.0000      4.0000

Zero pivot encountered!

There is no unique solution to this system.
```

The subroutine appears to be working correctly for both unique and singular sets of simultaneous equations.

You will be asked to modify this subroutine to use assumed-shape dummy arrays in an end-of-chapter exercise.

**EXAMPLE
9-2**

Using Assumed-Shape Dummy Arrays:

A simple procedure using an assumed-shape dummy array is shown in Figure 9-3. This procedure declares an assumed-shape dummy array "array", and then determines its size, shape, and bounds using array intrinsic functions. Note that the subroutine is contained in a module, so it has an explicit interface.

FIGURE 9-3
Subroutine to illustrate the use of assumed-shape arrays.

```
MODULE test_module
!  Purpose:
!    To illustrate the use of assumed-shape arrays.
!
```

(*continued*)

(concluded)

```
CONTAINS
   SUBROUTINE test_array(array)
   IMPLICIT NONE
   REAL, DIMENSION(:,:) :: array       ! Assumed-shape array
   INTEGER :: i1, i2                   ! Bounds of first dimension
   INTEGER :: j1, j2                   ! Bounds of second dimension

   ! Get details about array.
   i1 = LBOUND(array,1)
   i2 = UBOUND(array,1)
   j1 = LBOUND(array,2)
   j2 = UBOUND(array,2)
   WRITE (*,100) i1, i2, j1, j2
   100 FORMAT (1X,'The bounds are: (',I2,':',I2,',',I2,':',I2,')')
   WRITE (*,110) SHAPE(array)
   110 FORMAT (1X,'The shape is: ',2I4)
   WRITE (*,120) SIZE(array)
   120 FORMAT (1X,'The size is: ',I4)
   END SUBROUTINE test_array

END MODULE test_module

PROGRAM assumed_shape
!
!  Purpose:
!    To illustrate the use of assumed-shape arrays.
!
USE test_module
IMPLICIT NONE

! Declare local variables
REAL, DIMENSION(-5:5, -5:5) :: a = 0. ! Array a
REAL, DIMENSION(10,2) :: b = 1.       ! Array b

! Call test_array with array a.
WRITE (*,*) 'Calling test_array with array a:'
CALL test_array(a)

! Call test_array with array b.
WRITE (*,*) 'Calling test_array with array b:'
CALL test_array(b)

END PROGRAM assumed_shape
```

When program `assumed_shape` is executed, the results are:

```
C:\book\chap9>assumed_shape
Calling test_array with array a:
The bounds are: ( 1:11, 1:11)
The shape is:     11  11
The size is:     121
Calling test_array with array b:
The bounds are: ( 1:10, 1: 2)
```

```
The shape is:      10    2
The size is:       20
```

Note that the subroutine has complete information about the rank, shape, and size of each array passed to it, but not about the bounds used for the array in the calling program.

9.2

THE SAVE ATTRIBUTE AND STATEMENT

According to the Fortran 95 and 2003 standards, *the values of all the local variables and arrays in a procedure become undefined whenever we exit the procedure*. The next time that the procedure is invoked, the values of the local variables and arrays may or may not be the same as they were the last time we left it, depending on the behavior of the particular compiler being used. If we write a procedure that depends on having its local variables undisturbed between calls, the procedure will work fine on some computers and fail miserably on other ones!

Fortran provides a way to guarantee that local variables and arrays are saved unchanged between calls to a procedure: the SAVE attribute. The SAVE attribute appears in a type declaration statement like any other attribute. *Any local variables declared with the SAVE attribute will be saved unchanged between calls to the procedure*. For example, a local variable sums could be declared with the SAVE attribute as

```
REAL, SAVE :: sums
```

In addition, *any local variable that is initialized in a type declaration statement is automatically saved*. The SAVE attribute may be specified explicitly, if desired, but the value of the variable will be saved whether or not the attribute is explicitly included. Thus the following two variables are both saved between invocations of the procedure containing them.

```
REAL, SAVE :: sum_x = 0.
REAL :: sum_x2 = 0.
```

Fortran also includes a SAVE statement. It is a nonexecutable statement that goes into the declaration portion of the procedure along with the type declaration statements. Any local variables listed in the SAVE statement will be saved unchanged between calls to the procedure. If no variables are listed in the SAVE statement, then *all* of the local variables will be saved unchanged. The format of the SAVE statement is

```
SAVE :: var1, var2, ...
```

or simply

```
SAVE
```

✳ The SAVE attribute may not appear associated with dummy arguments, or with data items declared with the PARAMETER attribute. Similarly, neither of these items may appear in a SAVE statement.

  The SAVE statement should appear in any module used to share data, to ensure that the values in the module remain intact between calls to procedures that USE the module. Figure 7-8 showed a sample module that included a SAVE statement.

Good Programming Practice

If a procedure requires that the value of a local variable not change between successive invocations, include the SAVE attribute in the variable's type declaration statement, include the variable in a SAVE statement, or initialize the variable in its type declaration statement. If you do not do so, the subroutine will work correctly on some processors but will fail on others.

EXAMPLE 9-3

Running Averages:

It is sometimes desirable to keep running statistics on a data set as the values are being entered. The subroutine running_average shown in Figure 9-4 accumulates running averages and standard deviations for use in problems where we would like to keep statistics on data as it is coming in to the program. As each new data value is added, the running averages and standard deviations of all data up to that point are updated. The running sums used to derive the statistics are reset when the subroutine is called with the logical argument reset set to true. Note that the sums n, sum_x, and sum_x2 are being accumulated in local variables in this subroutine. To ensure that they remain unchanged between subroutine calls, *those local variables must appear in a SAVE statement or with a SAVE attribute.*

FIGURE 9-4

A subroutine to calculate the running mean and standard deviation of an input data set.

```
SUBROUTINE running_average ( x, ave, std_dev, nvals, reset )
!
!  Purpose:
!    To calculate the running average, standard deviation,
!    and number of data points as data values x are received.
!    If "reset" is .TRUE., clear running sums and exit.
!
!  Record of revisions:
!     Date       Programmer          Description of change
!     ====       ==========          =====================
!   06/26/06    S. J. Chapman        Original code
```

(*continued*)

(concluded)

```
!
IMPLICIT NONE

! Data dictionary: declare calling parameter types & definitions
REAL, INTENT(IN) :: x              ! Input data value.
REAL, INTENT(OUT) :: ave           ! Running average.
REAL, INTENT(OUT) :: std_dev       ! Running standard deviation.
INTEGER, INTENT(OUT) :: nvals      ! Current number of points.
LOGICAL, INTENT(IN) :: reset       ! Reset flag: clear sums if true

! Data dictionary: declare local variable types & definitions
INTEGER, SAVE :: n                 ! Number of input values.
REAL, SAVE :: sum_x                ! Sum of input values.
REAL, SAVE :: sum_x2               ! Sum of input values squared.

! If the reset flag is set, clear the running sums at this time.
calc_sums: IF ( reset ) THEN

   n       = 0
   sum_x   = 0.
   sum_x2  = 0.
   ave     = 0.
   std_dev = 0.
   nvals   = 0

ELSE

   ! Accumulate sums.
   n      = n + 1
   sum_x  = sum_x + x
   sum_x2 = sum_x2 + x**2

   ! Calculate average.
   ave = sum_x / REAL(n)

   ! Calculate standard deviation.
   IF ( n >= 2 ) THEN
      std_dev = SQRT( (REAL(n) * sum_x2 - sum_x**2) &
              / (REAL(n) * REAL(n-1)) )
   ELSE
      std_dev = 0.
   END IF

   ! Number of data points.
   nvals = n

END IF calc_sums

END SUBROUTINE running_average
```

9

A test driver for this subroutine is shown in Figure 9-5.

FIGURE 9-5
A test driver program to test subroutine running_average.

```
PROGRAM test_running_average
!
!   Purpose:
!     To test running average subroutine.
!
IMPLICIT NONE

! Declare variables:
INTEGER :: istat            ! I/O status
REAL :: ave                 ! Average
REAL :: std_dev             ! Standard deviation
INTEGER :: nvals            ! Number of values
REAL :: x                   ! Input data value
CHARACTER(len=20) file_name ! Input data file name

! Clear the running sums.
CALL running_average ( 0., ave, std_dev, nvals, .TRUE. )

! Get the name of the file containing the input data.
WRITE (*,*) ' Enter the file name containing the data: '
READ (*,'(A20)') file_name

! Open input data file. Status is OLD because the input data must
! already exist.
OPEN ( UNIT=21, FILE=file_name, STATUS='OLD', ACTION='READ', &
       IOSTAT=istat )

! Was the OPEN successful?
openok: IF ( istat == 0 ) THEN

   ! The file was opened successfully, so read the data to calculate
   ! running averages for.
   calc: DO
      READ (21,*,IOSTAT=istat) x       ! Get next value
      IF ( istat /= 0 ) EXIT           ! EXIT if not valid.

      ! Get running average & standard deviation
      CALL running_average ( x, ave, std_dev, nvals, .FALSE. )

      ! Now write out the running statistics.
      WRITE (*,1020) 'Value = ', x, ' Ave = ', ave, &
                     ' Std_dev = ', std_dev, &
                     ' Nvals = ', nvals
      1020 FORMAT (1X,3(A,F10.4),A,I6)
   END DO calc

ELSE openok
```

(continued)

(concluded)

```
    ! Else file open failed. Tell user.
    WRITE (*,1030) istat
    1030 FORMAT (1X,'File open failed--status = ', I6)

END IF openok

END PROGRAM test_running_average
```

To test this subroutine, we will calculate running statistics by hand for a set of five numbers, and compare the hand calculations to the results from the computer program. Recall that the average and standard deviation are defined as

$$\bar{x} = \frac{1}{N} \sum_{i=1}^{N} x_i \tag{4-1}$$

and

$$s = \sqrt{\frac{N \sum_{i=1}^{N} x_i^2 - \left(\sum_{i=1}^{N} x_i \right)^2}{N(N-1)}} \tag{4-2}$$

where x_i is sample i out of N samples. If the five values are:

3., 2., 3., 4., 2.8

then the running statistics calculated by hand would be:

Value	n	Σx	Σx^2	Average	Std_dev
3.0	1	3.0	9.0	3.00	0.000
2.0	2	5.0	13.0	2.50	0.707
3.0	3	8.0	22.0	2.67	0.577
4.0	4	12.0	38.0	3.00	0.816
2.8	5	14.8	45.84	2.96	0.713

The output of the test program for the same data set is:

```
C:\book\chap9>test_running_average
Enter the file name containing the data:
input6
Value =    3.0000  Ave =    3.0000  Std_dev =    0.0000  Nvals =    1
Value =    2.0000  Ave =    2.5000  Std_dev =    0.7071  Nvals =    2
Value =    3.0000  Ave =    2.6667  Std_dev =    0.5774  Nvals =    3
Value =    4.0000  Ave =    3.0000  Std_dev =    0.8165  Nvals =    4
Value =    2.8000  Ave =    2.9600  Std_dev =    0.7127  Nvals =    5
```

so the results check to the accuracy shown in the hand calculations.

■ 9.3

ALLOCATABLE ARRAYS IN PROCEDURES

In Chapter 7, we learned how to declare and allocate memory for **allocatable arrays.** Allocatable arrays could be adjusted to exactly the size required by the particular problem being solved.

 An allocatable array that is used in a procedure must be declared as a local variable in that procedure. If the allocatable array is declared with the SAVE attribute or appears in a SAVE statement, then the array would be allocated once by using an ALLOCATE statement the first time the procedure is called. That array would be used in the calculations, and then its contents would be preserved intact between calls to the procedure.

If the allocatable array is declared *without* the SAVE attribute, then the array must be allocated using an ALLOCATE statement[1] *every time* the procedure is called. That array would be used in the calculations, and then its contents would be automatically deallocated when execution returns to the calling program.

■ 9.4

AUTOMATIC ARRAYS IN PROCEDURES

Fortran 95/2003 provides another, simpler way to *automatically* create temporary arrays while a procedure is executing and to automatically destroy them when execution returns from the procedure. These arrays are called **automatic arrays.** An automatic array is *a local explicit-shape array with non-constant bounds.* (The bounds are specified either by dummy arguments or through data from modules.)

For example, array temp in the following code is an automatic array. Whenever subroutine sub1 is executed, dummy arguments n and m are passed to the subroutine. Note that arrays x and y are explicit-shape dummy arrays of size n × m that have been *passed to* the subroutine, while array temp is an automatic array that is *created* within the subroutine. When the subroutine starts to execute, an array temp of size n × m is automatically created, and when the subroutine ends, the array is automatically destroyed.

```
SUBROUTINE sub1 ( x, y, n, m )
IMPLICIT NONE
INTEGER, INTENT(IN) :: n, m
REAL, INTENT(IN), DIMENSION(n,m) :: x  ! Dummy array
REAL, INTENT(OUT), DIMENSION(n,m) :: y ! Dummy array
REAL, DIMENSION(n,m) :: temp               ! Automatic array
temp = 0.
...
END SUBROUTINE sub1
```

Automatic arrays may not be initialized in their type declaration statements, but they may be initialized by assignment statements at the beginning of the procedure in

F-2003 ONLY

---

[1] Or by direct assignment in the case of a Fortran 2003 program.

which they are created. They may be passed as calling arguments to other procedures invoked by the procedure in which they are created. However, they cease to exist when the procedure in which they are created executes a RETURN or END statement. It is illegal to specify the SAVE attribute for an automatic array.

9.4.1 Comparing Automatic Arrays and Allocatable Arrays

Both automatic arrays and allocatable arrays can be used to create temporary working arrays in a program. What is the difference between them, and when should we choose one type of array or another for a particular application? The major differences between the two types of arrays are as follows:

1. *Automatic arrays are allocated automatically whenever a procedure containing them is entered, while allocatable arrays must be allocated and deallocated manually.* This feature favors the use of automatic arrays when the temporary memory is needed only within a single procedure and any procedures that may be invoked by it.
2. *Allocatable arrays are more general and flexible,* since they may be created and destroyed in separate procedures. For example, in a large program we might create a special subroutine to allocate all arrays to be just the proper size to solve the current problem, and we might create a different subroutine to deallocate them after they have been used. Also, allocatable arrays may be used in a main program, while automatic arrays may not.
3. *Allocatable arrays can be resized during a calculation.* A programmer can change the size of an allocatable array during execution using DEALLOCATE and ALLOCATE statements,[2] so a single array can serve multiple purposes requiring different shapes within a single procedure. In contrast, an automatic array is automatically allocated to the specified size at the beginning of the procedure execution, and the size cannot be changed during that particular execution.

Automatic arrays should normally be used to create temporary working arrays within a single procedure, while allocatable arrays should be used to create arrays in main programs, or arrays that will be created and destroyed in different procedures, or arrays that must be able to change size within a given procedure.

Good Programming Practice
Use automatic arrays to create local temporary working arrays in procedures. Use allocatable arrays to create arrays in main programs, or arrays that will be created and destroyed in different procedures, or arrays that must be able to change size within a given procedure.

F-2003 ONLY

[2] Or by direct assignment in the case of a Fortran 2003 program.

9.4.2 Example Program

EXAMPLE   *Using Automatic Arrays in a Procedure:*
9-4

As an example of using automatic arrays in a procedure, we will write a new version of subroutine `simul` that does not destroy its input data while calculating the solution.

To avoid destroying the data, it will be necessary to add a new dummy argument to return the solution to the system of equations. This argument will be called `soln`, and will have `INTENT(OUT)`, since it will be used only for output. Dummy arguments `a` and `b` will now have `INTENT(IN)`, since they will not be modified at all in the subroutine. In addition, we will take advantages of array sections to simplify the nested `DO` loops found in the original subroutine `simul`.

The resulting subroutine is shown in Figure 9-6. Note that arrays `a1` and `temp1` are automatic arrays, since they are local to the subroutine but their bounds are passed to the subroutine as dummy arguments. Arrays `a`, `b`, and `soln` are explicit-shape dummy arrays, because they appear in the argument list of the subroutine.

FIGURE 9-6

A rewritten version of subroutine `simul` using allocatable arrays. This version does not destroy its input arrays. The declarations of automatic arrays `a1` and `temp1` and the use of array sections are shown in bold face.

```
SUBROUTINE simul2 ( a, b, soln, ndim, n, error )
!
!   Purpose:
!     Subroutine to solve a set of N linear equations in N
!     unknowns using Gaussian elimination and the maximum
!     pivot technique.  This version of simul has been
!     modified to use array sections and allocatable arrays
!     It DOES NOT DESTROY the original input values.
!
!   Record of revisions:
!       Date          Programmer          Description of change
!       ====          ==========          =====================
!     11/23/06      S. J. Chapman         Original code
! 1.  11/24/06      S. J. Chapman         Add automatic arrays
!
IMPLICIT NONE

! Data dictionary: declare calling parameter types & definitions
INTEGER, INTENT(IN) :: ndim            ! Dimension of arrays a and b
REAL, INTENT(IN), DIMENSION(ndim,ndim) :: a
                                       ! Array of coefficients (N × N).
                                       ! This array is of size ndim ×
                                       ! ndim, but only N × N of the
                                       ! coefficients are being used.
```

(continued)

(continued)

```
REAL, INTENT(IN), DIMENSION(ndim) :: b
                                    ! Input: Right-hand side of eqns.
REAL, INTENT(OUT), DIMENSION(ndim) :: soln
                                    ! Output: Solution vector.
INTEGER, INTENT(IN) :: n            ! Number of equations to solve.
INTEGER, INTENT(OUT) :: error       ! Error flag:
                                    !    0 -- No error
                                    !    1 -- Singular equations

! Data dictionary: declare constants
REAL, PARAMETER :: EPSILON = 1.0E-6 ! A "small" number for comparison
                                    ! when determining singular eqns

! Data dictionary: declare local variable types & definitions
REAL, DIMENSION(n,n) :: a1          ! Copy of "a" which will be
                                    ! destroyed during the solution
REAL :: factor                      ! Factor to multiply eqn irow by
                                    ! before adding to eqn jrow
INTEGER :: irow                     ! Number of the equation currently
                                    ! being processed
INTEGER :: ipeak                    ! Pointer to equation containing
                                    ! maximum pivot value
INTEGER :: jrow                     ! Number of the equation compared
                                    ! to the current equation
REAL :: temp                        ! Scratch value
REAL, DIMENSION(n) :: temp1         ! Scratch array

! Make copies of arrays "a" and "b" for local use
a1 = a(1:n,1:n)
soln = b(1:n)

! Process N times to get all equations...
mainloop: DO irow = 1, n

   ! Find peak pivot for column irow in rows irow to N
   ipeak = irow
   max_pivot: DO jrow = irow+1, n
      IF (ABS(a1(jrow,irow)) > ABS(a1(ipeak,irow))) THEN
         ipeak = jrow
      END IF
   END DO max_pivot

   ! Check for singular equations.
   singular: IF ( ABS(a1(ipeak,irow)) < EPSILON ) THEN
      error = 1
      RETURN
   END IF singular

   ! Otherwise, if ipeak /= irow, swap equations irow & ipeak
   swap_eqn: IF ( ipeak /= irow ) THEN
      temp1 = a1(ipeak,1:n)
```

(continued)

(concluded)

```
        al(ipeak,1:n) = al(irow,1:n)   ! Swap rows in a
        al(irow,1:n) = temp1
        temp = soln(ipeak)
        soln(ipeak) = soln(irow)       ! Swap rows in b
        soln(irow)  = temp
     END IF swap_eqn

     ! Multiply equation irow by -al(jrow,irow)/al(irow,irow),
     ! and add it to Eqn jrow (for all eqns except irow itself).
     eliminate: DO jrow = 1, n
        IF ( jrow /= irow ) THEN
           factor = -al(jrow,irow)/al(irow,irow)
           al(jrow,:) = al(irow,1:n)*factor + al(jrow,1:n)
           soln(jrow) = soln(irow)*factor + soln(jrow)
        END IF
     END DO eliminate
  END DO mainloop

  ! End of main loop over all equations.  All off-diagonal terms
  ! are now zero.  To get the final answer, we must divide
  ! each equation by the coefficient of its on-diagonal term.
  divide: DO irow = 1, n
     soln(irow) = soln(irow) / al(irow,irow)
     al(irow,irow) = 1.
  END DO divide

  ! Set error flag to 0 and return.
  error = 0

END SUBROUTINE simul2
```

Testing this subroutine is left as an exercise to the student (see Exercise 9-9).

A PROFUSION (AND CONFUSION!) OF FORTRAN ARRAY TYPES

We have now seen many different types of Fortran arrays, and no doubt produced a little confusion along the way. Let's step back and review the different array types, seeing just where each type is used and how they relate to each other.

1. Explicit-Shape Arrays with Constant Bounds

Explicit-shape arrays with constant bounds are nondummy arrays whose shape is explicitly specified in their type declaration statements. They may be declared either in main programs or in procedures, but they *do not appear* in the dummy argument list of a procedure. Explicit-shape arrays with constant bounds allocate fixed, permanent arrays for use in a program. They may be initialized in their type declaration statements.

If an explicit-shape array with constant bounds is allocated in a procedure, the data stored in it is guaranteed to be intact from invocation to invocation only if the array is declared with the SAVE attribute, or if the array is initialized in the type declaration statement.

Two examples of explicit-shape arrays with constant bounds are

```
INTEGER, PARAMETER :: NDIM = 100
REAL, DIMENSION(NDIM,NDIM) :: input_data = 1.
REAL, DIMENSION(-3:3) :: scratch = 0.
```

2. Dummy Arrays

Dummy arrays are arrays that appear in the dummy argument list of procedures. They are placeholders for the actual arrays passed to the procedure when it is invoked. No actual memory is allocated for dummy arrays. There are three types of dummy arrays: *explicit-shape dummy arrays, assumed-shape dummy arrays,* and *assumed-size dummy arrays.*

a. Explicit-Shape Dummy Arrays

Explicit-shape dummy arrays are arrays that appear in the dummy argument list of a procedure, and whose dimensions are explicitly declared by arguments in the procedure's argument list. All of the advanced features of Fortran arrays can be used with explicit-shape dummy arrays, including whole array operations, array sections, and array intrinsic functions. An example of an explicit-shape dummy array is

```
SUBROUTINE test ( array, n, m1, m2 )
INTEGER, INTENT(IN) :: n, m1, m2
REAL, DIMENSION(n,m1:m2) :: array
```

b. Assumed-Shape Dummy Arrays

Assumed-shape dummy arrays are arrays that appear in the dummy argument list of a procedure, and whose dimensions are declared by colons. The type declaration statement specifies the type and rank of the array, but not the extent of each dimension. *An assumed-shape dummy array is usable only in a procedure with an explicit interface.* These arrays assume the shape of whatever actual array is passed to the procedure when it is invoked. All of the advanced features of Fortran arrays can be used with assumed-shape dummy arrays, including whole array operations, array sections, and array intrinsic functions. An example of an assumed-shape dummy array is

```
SUBROUTINE test ( array )
REAL, DIMENSION(:,:) :: array
```

c. Assumed-Size Dummy Arrays

Assumed-size dummy arrays are arrays that appear in the dummy argument list of a procedure, and whose last dimension is declared with an asterisk. The size of all dimensions except for the last must be explicitly specified so that the procedure can determine how to locate specific array elements in memory. An assumed-size dummy array cannot be used with whole array operations or with many of the array intrinsic functions, because the shape of the actual array is unknown. Assumed-size dummy arrays are a holdover from earlier versions of Fortran; *they should never be used in any new programs*. An example of an assumed-size dummy array is

```
SUBROUTINE test ( array )
REAL, DIMENSION(10,*) :: array
```

3. Automatic Arrays

Automatic arrays are explicit-shape arrays with nonconstant bounds that appear in procedures. They do *not* appear in the procedure's argument list, but the *bounds of the array* are either passed via the argument list or by shared data in a module.

When the procedure is invoked, an array of the shape and size specified by the nonconstant bounds is *automatically* created. When the procedure ends, the array is automatically destroyed. If the procedure is invoked again, a new array will be created that could be either the same shape as or a different shape from the previous one. Data is *not* preserved in automatic arrays between invocations of the procedure, and it is illegal to specify either a SAVE attribute or a default initialization for an automatic array. An example of an automatic array is:

```
SUBROUTINE test ( n, m )
INTEGER, INTENT(IN) :: n, m
REAL, DIMENSION(n,m) :: array    ! Bounds in argument list, but not array
```

4. Deferred-Shape Arrays

Deferred-shape arrays are allocatable arrays or pointer arrays (pointer arrays are covered in Chapter 15). A deferred-shape array is declared in a type declaration statement with an ALLOCATABLE (or POINTER) attribute, and with the dimensions declared by colons. It may appear in either main programs or procedures. The array may not be used in any fashion (except as an argument to the ALLOCATED function) until memory is actually allocated for it. Memory is allocated by using an ALLOCATE statement and deallocated by using a DEALLOCATE statement. (In Fortran 2003, memory can also be allocated automatically by an assignment statement.) A deferred-shape array may not be initialized in its type declaration statement.

If an allocatable array is declared and allocated in a procedure, and if it is desired to keep the array between invocations of the procedure, it must be declared with the SAVE attribute. If the array is not needed, it should *not* be declared with the SAVE attribute. In that case, the allocatable array will be automatically deallocated at the end of the procedure. An unneeded pointer array (defined later) should be explicitly deallocated to avoid possible problems with "memory leaks."

An example of a deferred-shape allocatable array is:

```
INTEGER, ALLOCATABLE :: array(:,:)
ALLOCATE ( array(1000,1000), STATUS=istat)
...
DEALLOCATE ( array, STATUS=istat)
```

Quiz 9-1

This quiz provides a quick check to see if you have understood the concepts introduced in Sections 9.1 through 9.4. If you have trouble with the quiz, reread the sections, ask your instructor, or discuss the material with a fellow student. The answers to this quiz are found in the back of the book.

1. When should a SAVE statement or attribute be used in a program or procedure? Why should it be used?
2. What is the difference between an automatic and an allocatable array? When should each of them be used?
3. What are the advantages and disadvantages of assumed-shape dummy arrays?

For questions 4 through 6, determine whether there are any errors in these programs. If possible, tell what the output from each program will be.

4.
```
PROGRAM test1
IMPLICIT NONE
INTEGER, DIMENSION(10) :: i
INTEGER :: j
DO j = 1, 10
   CALL sub1 ( i(j) )
   WRITE (*,*) ' i = ', i(j)
END DO
END PROGRAM test1

SUBROUTINE sub1 ( ival )
IMPLICIT NONE
INTEGER, INTENT(INOUT) :: ival
INTEGER :: isum
isum = isum + 1
ival = isum
END SUBROUTINE sub1
```

5.
```
PROGRAM test2
IMPLICIT NONE
REAL, DIMENSION(3,3) :: a
a(1,:) = (/ 1., 2., 3. /)
a(2,:) = (/ 4., 5., 6. /)
a(3,:) = (/ 7., 8., 9. /)
CALL sub2 (a, b, 3)
WRITE (*,*) b
END PROGRAM test2
```

(continued)

(concluded)

```
      SUBROUTINE sub2(x, y, nvals)
      IMPLICIT NONE
      REAL, DIMENSION(nvals), INTENT(IN) :: x
      REAL, DIMENSION(nvals), INTENT(OUT) :: y
      REAL, DIMENSION(nvals) :: temp
      temp = 2.0 * x**2
      y = SQRT(x)
      END SUBROUTINE sub2
```

6.
```
   PROGRAM test3
   IMPLICIT NONE
   REAL, DIMENSION(2,2) :: a = 1., b = 2.
   CALL sub3(a, b)
   WRITE (*,*) a
   END PROGRAM test3

   SUBROUTINE sub3(a,b)
   REAL, DIMENSION(:,:), INTENT(INOUT) :: a
   REAL, DIMENSION(:,:), INTENT(IN) :: b
   a = a + b
   END SUBROUTINE sub3
```

9

F-2003
ONLY

■ **9.5**

ALLOCATABLE ARRAYS IN FORTRAN 2003 PROCEDURES

Allocatable arrays have been made more flexible in Fortran 2003. Two of the changes in allocatable arrays affect procedures:

1. It is now possible to have allocatable dummy arguments.
2. It is now possible for a function to return an allocatable value.

9.5.1 Allocatable Dummy Arguments

If a Fortran 2003 subroutine has an explicit interface, it is possible for subroutine dummy arguments to be allocatable. If a dummy argument is declared to be allocatable, then the corresponding actual arguments used to call the subroutine must be allocatable as well.

Allocatable dummy arguments are allowed to have an INTENT attribute. The INTENT affects the operation of the subroutine as follows:

1. If an allocatable argument has the INTENT(IN) attribute, then the array is not permitted to be allocated or deallocated in the subroutine, and the values in the array cannot be modified.

2. If the allocatable argument has the INTENT(INOUT) attribute, then the status (allocated or not) and the data of the corresponding actual argument will be passed to the subroutine when it is called. The array may be deallocated, reallocated, or modified in any way in the subroutine, and the final status (allocated or not) and the data of the dummy argument will be passed back to the calling program in the actual argument.

3. If the allocatable argument has the INTENT(OUT) attribute, *then the actual argument in the calling program will be automatically deallocated on entry,* so any data in the actual array will be lost. The subroutine can then use the unallocated argument in any way, and the final status (allocated or not) and the data of the dummy argument will be passed back to the calling program in the actual argument.

A program that illustrates the use of allocatable array dummy arguments is shown in Figure 9-7. This program allocates and initializes an allocatable array and passes it to subroutine test_alloc. The data in the array on entry to test_alloc is the same as the originally initialized values. The array is deallocated, reallocated, and initialized in the subroutine, and that data is present in the main program when the subroutine returns.

FIGURE 9-7
Program illustrating the use of allocatable array dummy arguments.

```
MODULE test_module
!  Purpose:
!    To illustrate the use of allocatable arguments.
!
CONTAINS

   SUBROUTINE test_alloc(array)
   IMPLICIT NONE
   REAL,DIMENSION(:),ALLOCATABLE,INTENT(INOUT) :: array
                                     ! Test array

   ! Local variables
   INTEGER :: i              ! Loop index
   INTEGER :: istat          ! Allocate status

   ! Get the status of this array
   IF ( ALLOCATED(array) ) THEN
      WRITE (*,'(A)') 'Sub: the array is allocated'
      WRITE (*,'(A,6F4.1)') 'Sub: Array on entry = ', array
   ELSE
      WRITE (*,*) 'In sub: the array is not allocated'
   END IF
```

(continued)

(concluded)

```fortran
    ! Deallocate the array
    IF ( ALLOCATED(array) ) THEN
       DEALLOCATE( array, STAT=istat )
    END IF

    ! Reallocate as a 5 element vector
    ALLOCATE(array(5), STAT=istat )

    ! Save data
    DO i = 1, 5
       array(i) = 6 - i
    END DO

    ! Display contents of array a on exit
    WRITE (*,'(A,6F4.1)') 'Sub: Array on exit = ', array

    ! Return to caller
    END SUBROUTINE test_alloc

END MODULE test_module


PROGRAM allocatable_arguments
!
!  Purpose:
!     To illustrate the use of allocatable arguments.
!
USE test_module
IMPLICIT NONE

! Declare local variables
REAL,ALLOCATABLE,DIMENSION(:) :: a
INTEGER :: istat                 ! Allocate status

! Allocate array
ALLOCATE( a(6), STAT=istat )

! Initialize array
a = (/ 1., 2., 3., 4., 5., 6. /)

! Display a before call
WRITE (*,'(A,6F4.1)') 'Main: Array a before call = ', a

! Call subroutine
CALL test_alloc(a)

! Display a after call
WRITE (*,'(A,6F4.1)') 'Main: Array a after call = ', a

END PROGRAM allocatable_arguments
```

When this program executes, the results are as shown below:

```
C:\book\chap9>allocatable_arguments
Main: Array a before call = 1.0 2.0 3.0 4.0 5.0 6.0
Sub: the array is allocated
Sub: Array on entry = 1.0 2.0 3.0 4.0 5.0 6.0
Sub: Array on exit = 5.0 4.0 3.0 2.0 1.0
Main: Array a after call = 5.0 4.0 3.0 2.0 1.0
```

F-2003
ONLY

9.5.2 Allocatable Functions

A Fortran 2003 function result is permitted to have the ALLOCATABLE attribute. The return variable will not be allocated on entry to the function. The variable can be allocated and deallocated as often as desired inside the function, but it must be allocated and contain a value before the function returns.

A program that illustrates the use of allocatable functions is shown in Figure 9-8. This program calls function test_alloc_fun with a parameter specifying the number of values to return in the allocatable array. The function allocates the result variable, saves data into it, and returns to the main program for display.

FIGURE 9-8
Program illustrating the use of allocatable functions.

```
MODULE test_module
!  Purpose:
!    To illustrate the use of allocatable arguments.
!
CONTAINS

   FUNCTION test_alloc_fun(n)
   IMPLICIT NONE
   INTEGER,INTENT(IN) :: n  ! Number of elements to return
   REAL,ALLOCATABLE,DIMENSION(:) :: test_alloc_fun

   ! Local variables
   INTEGER :: i             ! Loop index
   INTEGER :: istat         ! Allocate status

   ! Get the status of the array
   IF ( ALLOCATED(test_alloc_fun) ) THEN
      WRITE (*,'(A)') 'Array is allocated'
   ELSE
      WRITE (*,'(A)') 'Array is NOT allocated'
   END IF
```

9

(continued)

(concluded)

```
    ! Allocate as an n element vector
    ALLOCATE(test_alloc_fun(n), STAT=istat )

    ! Initialize data
    DO i = 1, n
        test_alloc_fun(i) = i
    END DO

    ! Display contents of array a on exit
    WRITE (*,'(A,20F4.1)') 'Array on exit = ', test_alloc_fun

    ! Return to caller
    END FUNCTION test_alloc_fun

END MODULE test_module


PROGRAM allocatable_function
!
!   Purpose:
!     To illustrate the use of allocatable arguments.
!
USE test_module
IMPLICIT NONE

! Declare local variables
INTEGER :: n = 5            ! Number of elements to allocate

! Call function and display results
WRITE (*,'(A,20F4.1)') 'Function return = ', test_alloc_fun(n)

END PROGRAM allocatable_function
```

When this program executes, the results are as shown below:

```
C:\book\chap9>allocatable_function
Array is NOT allocated
Array on exit = 1.0 2.0 3.0 4.0 5.0
Function return = 1.0 2.0 3.0 4.0 5.0
```

9.6

PURE AND ELEMENTAL PROCEDURES

As we mentioned in previous chapters, the Fortran language has been evolving in ways to make it easier to execute on massively parallel processors. As a part of this evolution, Fortran 95 introduced two new classifications of procedures: **pure procedures** and **elemental procedures.**

Pure Function.

9.6.1 Pure Procedures

Pure functions *are functions that do not have side effects.* That is, they do not modify their input arguments, and they do not modify any other data (such as data in modules) that is visible outside the function. In addition, local variables may not have the SAVE attribute, and may not be initialized in type declaration statements (since such initialization implies the SAVE attribute). Any procedures invoked by a pure function must also be pure.

Because pure functions do not have side effects, it is safe to invoke them in a FORALL construct, where they might be executed in any order. This is very helpful on massively parallel processors, because each processor can take one combination of control indices from the FORALL construct, and execute it in parallel with all of the others.

Every argument in a pure function must be declared with INTENT(IN), and any subroutine or functions invoked by the function must itself be pure. In addition, the function must not do any external file I/O operations, and must not contain a STOP statement. These constraints are easy to abide by—all of the functions that we have created so far are pure.

A pure function is declared by adding a PURE prefix to the function statement. For example, the following function is pure:

```
PURE FUNCTION length(x, y)
IMPLICIT NONE
REAL, INTENT(IN) :: x, y
REAL :: length
length = SQRT(x**2 + y**2)
END FUNCTION length
```

Pure subroutines *are subroutines that do not have side effects.* Their constraints are exactly the same as those on pure functions, except that they are permitted to modify arguments declared with INTENT(OUT) or INTENT(INOUT). Pure subroutines are declared by adding the PURE prefix to the SUBROUTINE statement.

9.6.2 Elemental Procedures

Elemental functions are functions that are specified for scalar arguments, but that may also be applied to array arguments. If the arguments of an elemental function are scalars, then the result of the function will be a scalar. If the arguments of the function are arrays, then the result of the function will be an array of the same shape as the input arguments.

User-defined elemental functions must be PURE functions, and must satisfy the following additional constraints:

1. All dummy arguments must be scalars, and must not have the POINTER attribute. (We will learn about pointers in Chapter 15.)
2. The function result must be a scalar, and must not have the POINTER attribute.
3. Dummy arguments must not be used in type declaration statements except as arguments of certain intrinsic functions. This constraint prohibits the use of automatic arrays in elemental functions.

A user-defined elemental function is declared by adding an ELEMENTAL prefix to the function statement. For example, the function sinc(x) from Figure 7-16 is elemental, so in Fortran 95/2003 it would be declared as:

```
ELEMENTAL FUNCTION sinc( x )
```

Elemental subroutines are subroutines that are specified for scalar arguments, but that may also be applied to array arguments. They must meet the same constraints as elemental functions. An elemental subroutine is declared by adding an ELEMENTAL prefix to the subroutine statement. For example,

```
ELEMENTAL SUBROUTINE convert(x, y, z)
```

■ 9.7
INTERNAL PROCEDURES

In Chapter 7, we learned about **external procedures** and **module procedures.** There is also a third type of procedure—the **internal procedure.** An internal procedure is a procedure that is entirely contained within another program unit, called the **host program unit,** or just the **host.** The internal procedure is compiled together with the host, and it can only be invoked from the host program unit. Like module procedures, internal procedures are introduced by a CONTAINS statement. *An internal procedure must follow all of the executable statements within the host procedure,* and must be introduced by a CONTAINS statement.

Why would we want to use internal procedures? In some problems, there are low-level manipulations that must be performed repeatedly as a part of the solution. These low-level manipulations can be simplified by defining an internal procedure to perform them.

A simple example of an internal procedure is shown in Figure 9-9. This program accepts an input value in degrees and uses an internal procedure to calculate the secant of that value. Although the internal procedure secant is invoked only once in this simple example, it could have been invoked repeatedly in a larger problem to calculate secants of many different angles.

FIGURE 9-9
Program to calculate the secant of an angle in degrees by using an internal procedure.

```
PROGRAM test_internal
!
!  Purpose:
!    To illustrate the use of an internal procedure.
!
!  Record of revisions:
!    Date          Programmer           Description of change
!    ====          ==========           =====================
!    07/03/06     S. J. Chapman         Original code
!
```

(*continued*)

(concluded)

```
IMPLICIT NONE

! Data dictionary: declare constants
REAL, PARAMETER :: PI = 3.141592        ! PI

! Data dictionary: declare variable types & definitions
REAL :: theta                           ! Angle in degrees

! Get desired angle
WRITE (*,*) 'Enter desired angle in degrees: '
READ (*,*) theta

! Calculate and display the result.
WRITE (*,'(A,F10.4)') ' The secant is ', secant(theta)

! Note that the WRITE above was the last executable statement.
! Now, declare internal procedure secant:
CONTAINS
   REAL FUNCTION secant(angle_in_degrees)
   !
   !  Purpose:
   !    To calculate the secant of an angle in degrees.
   !
   REAL :: angle_in_degrees

   ! Calculate secant
   secant = 1. / cos( angle_in_degrees * pi / 180. )

   END FUNCTION secant

END PROGRAM test_internal
```

Note that the internal function secant appears after the last executable statement in program test. It is not a part of the executable code of the host program. When program test is executed, the user is prompted for an angle, and the internal function secant is called to calculate the secant of the angle as a part of the final WRITE statement. When this program is executed, the results are:

```
C:\book\chap9>test
Enter desired angle in degrees:
45
The secant is     1.4142
```

An internal procedure functions exactly like an external procedure, with the following three exceptions:

1. The internal procedure can be invoked *only* from the host procedure. No other procedure within the program can access it.

2. The name of an internal procedure may not be passed as a command line argument to another procedure.

3. An internal procedure inherits all of the data entities (parameters and variables) of its host program unit by **host association.**

The last point requires more explanation. When an internal procedure is defined within a host program unit, all of the parameters and variables within the host program unit are also usable within the internal procedure. Look at Figure 9-9 again. Note that there is no IMPLICIT NONE statement within the internal procedure, because the one in the host program applies to the internal procedure as well. Note also that the named constant PI, which is defined in the host program, is used in the internal procedure.

The only time that an internal procedure cannot access a data entity defined in its host is *when the internal procedure defines a different data entity with the same name.* In that case, the data entity defined in the host is not accessible in the procedure, and the data entity in the host will be totally unaffected by any manipulations that occur within the internal procedure.

Good Programming Practice

Use internal procedures to perform low-level manipulations that must be performed repeatedly, but are needed by only one program unit.

9.8
SUMMARY

Multidimensional arrays can be passed to a subroutine or function subprogram either as explicit-shape dummy arrays or as assumed-shape dummy arrays. If multidimensional arrays are passed as explicit-shape dummy arrays, then the extent of each array dimension must also be passed to the subroutine as a calling argument, and must be used to declare the array. If multidimensional arrays are passed as assumed-shape dummy arrays, then the procedure must have an explicit interface, and the dimensions of the arrays are declared with colons as placeholders.

When a procedure finishes executing, the Fortran 95 and Fortran 2003 Standards say that the local variables in the procedure become undefined. When the procedure is called again, the local variables might or might not have the same values as they did during the previous call, depending on the compiler and compiler options you are using. If a procedure needs for some local variables to be preserved between calls, the variables must be declared with the SAVE attribute or in a SAVE statement.

Automatic arrays are automatically created when a procedure starts executing, and are automatically destroyed when the procedure finishes executing. Automatic arrays are local arrays whose dimensions are set by calling arguments, so they can have different sizes each time that the procedure is called. Automatic arrays are used as temporary work areas within a procedure.

F-2003 ONLY Allocatable arrays may be used as dummy arguments and function return values in Fortran 2003, as long as the subroutine or function has an explicit interface.

An internal procedure is a procedure defined entirely within another program unit, which is called the host program unit. It is only accessible from the host program unit. Internal procedures are included in the host program unit after all of the executable statements of the program unit, and are preceded by a CONTAINS statement. An internal procedure has access to all of the data items defined in its host program unit by host association, unless the internal procedure contains a data item of the same name as a data item in the host. In that case, the data item in the host is not accessible to the internal procedure.

9.8.1 Summary of Good Programming Practice

The following guidelines should be adhered to when working with subroutines and functions.

1. Always use either explicit-shape dummy arrays or assumed-shape dummy arrays for dummy array arguments. Never use assumed-size dummy arrays in any new program.
2. If a procedure requires that the value of a local variable not change between successive invocations of the procedure, specify the SAVE attribute in the variable's type declaration statement, include the variable in a SAVE statement, or initialize the variable in its type declaration statement.
3. Use automatic arrays to create local temporary working arrays in procedures. Use allocatable arrays to create arrays in main programs, or arrays that will be created and destroyed in different procedures, or arrays that must be able to change size within a given procedure.
4. Use internal procedures to perform low-level manipulations that must be performed repeatedly, but are needed by only one program unit.

9

9.8.2 Summary of Fortran Statements and Structures

CONTAINS **Statement:**

```
                CONTAINS
```

Example:

```
                PROGRAM main
                . . .
                CONTAINS
                   SUBROUTINE sub1(x, y)
                   . . .
                   END SUBROUTINE sub1
                END PROGRAM
```

Description:
The CONTAINS statement is a statement that specifies that the following statements are one or more separate procedures within the host unit. When used within a module, the CONTAINS statement marks the beginning of one or more module procedures. When used within a main program or an external procedure, the CONTAINS statement marks the beginning of one or more internal procedures. The CONTAINS statement must appear after any type, interface, and data definitions within a module, and must follow the last executable statement within a main program or an external procedure.

ELEMENTAL **Prefix:**

```
ELEMENTAL FUNCTION name(arg1, ...)
ELEMENTAL SUBROUTINE name(arg1, ...)
```

Example:

```
ELEMENTAL FUNCTION my_fun (a, b, c)
```

Description:
This prefix declares that a procedure is ELEMENTAL, which means that it is defined with scalar inputs and outputs, but can be used with array inputs and outputs. When it is used with arrays, the operation defined by the elemental procedure is applied on an element-by-element basis to every element in the input array.

PURE **Prefix:**

```
PURE FUNCTION name(arg1, ...)
PURE SUBROUTINE name(arg1, ...)
```

Example:

```
PURE FUNCTION my_fun (a, b, c)
```

Description:
This prefix declares that a procedure is PURE, which means that it has no side effects.

SAVE **Attribute:**

```
type, SAVE :: name1, name2, ...
```

Example:

```
REAL, SAVE :: sum
```

Description:
This attribute declares that the value of a *local variable* in a procedure must remain unchanged between successive invocations of the procedure. It is equivalent to the naming the variable in a SAVE statement.

SAVE **Statement:**

```
SAVE [var1, var2, ...]
```

Examples:

```
SAVE count, index
SAVE
```

Description:
This statement declares that the value of a *local variable* in a procedure must remain unchanged between successive invocations of the procedure. If a list of variables is included, only those variables will be saved. If no list is included, every local variable in the procedure or module will be saved.

9.8.3 Exercises

9-1. What are the advantages and disadvantages of using explicit-shape dummy arrays in procedures? What are the advantages and disadvantages of using assumed-shape dummy arrays? Why should assumed-size dummy arrays never be used?

9-2. What are the differences between internal procedures and external procedures? When should an internal procedure be used instead of an external procedure?

9-3. What is the purpose of the SAVE statement and attribute? When should they be used?

9-4. Is the following program correct or not? If it is correct, what is printed out when it executes? If not, what is wrong with it?

```
PROGRAM junk
IMPLICIT NONE
REAL :: a = 3, b = 4, output
INTEGER :: i = 0
call sub1(a, i, output)
WRITE (*,*) 'The output is ', output

CONTAINS

    SUBROUTINE sub1(x, j, junk)
    REAL, INTENT(IN) :: x
    INTEGER, INTENT(IN) :: j
    REAL, INTENT(OUT) :: junk
    junk = (x - j) / b
    END SUBROUTINE sub1

END PROGRAM junk
```

9-5. What is printed out when the following code is executed? What are the values of x, y, i, and j at each point in the program? If a value changes during the course of execution, explain why it changes.

```
PROGRAM exercise9_5
IMPLICIT NONE
REAL :: x = 12., y = -3., result
INTEGER :: i = 6, j = 4
WRITE (*,100) ' Before call: x, y, i, j = ', x, y, i, j
100 FORMAT (A,2F6.1,2I6)
result = exec(y,i)
WRITE (*,*) 'The result is ', result
WRITE (*,100) ' After call: x, y, i, j = ', x, y, i, j
CONTAINS

    REAL FUNCTION exec(x,i)
    REAL, INTENT(IN) :: x
    INTEGER, INTENT(IN) :: i
    WRITE (*,100) ' In exec: x, y, i, j = ', x, y, i, j
    100 FORMAT (A,2F6.1,2I6)
    exec = ( x + y ) / REAL ( i + j )
    j = i
    END FUNCTION exec

END PROGRAM exercise9_5
```

9

9-6. Matrix Multiplication Write a subroutine to calculate the product of two matrices if they are of compatible sizes, and if the output array is large enough to hold the result. If the matrices are not of compatible sizes, or if the output array is too small, set an error flag and return to the calling program. The dimensions of all three arrays a, b, and c should be passed to the subroutines from the calling program so that explicit-shape dummy arrays can be used and size checking can be done. (*Note:* The definition of matrix multiplication may be found in Exercise 8-14.) Check your subroutine by multiplying the following two pairs of arrays both with the subroutine and with the intrinsic subroutine MATMUL.

$$(a) \qquad a = \begin{bmatrix} 2 & -1 & 2 \\ -1 & -3 & 4 \\ 2 & 4 & 2 \end{bmatrix} \qquad b = \begin{bmatrix} 1 & 2 & 3 \\ 2 & 1 & 2 \\ 3 & 2 & 1 \end{bmatrix}$$

$$(b) \qquad a = \begin{bmatrix} 1 & -1 & -2 \\ 2 & 2 & 0 \\ 3 & 3 & 3 \\ 5 & 4 & 4 \end{bmatrix} \qquad b = \begin{bmatrix} -2 \\ 5 \\ 2 \end{bmatrix}$$

9-7. Write a new version of the matrix multiplication subroutine from Exercise 9-6 that uses an explicit interface and assumed-shape arrays. Before multiplying the matrices, this version should check to ensure that the input arrays are compatible, and that the output array is large enough to hold the product of the two matrices. It can check for compatibility by using the inquiry intrinsic functions found in Table 8-1. If these conditions are not satisfied, the subroutine should set an error flag and return.

9-8. Modify subroutine simul from Example 9-1 to use assumed-shape arrays. Use the two data sets in Example 9-1 to test the subroutine.

9-9. Write a test driver program to test subroutine simul2 in Figure 9-6. Use the two data sets in Example 9-1 to test the subroutine.

9-10. Why should the data in a module be declared with the SAVE attribute?

F-2003 ONLY

9-11. Modify program test_alloc in Figure 9-7 so that the allocatable dummy argument has an INTENT(IN) attribute. Does this program work now? If so, what does it do? If not, why not?

9-12. Modify program test_alloc in Figure 9-7 so that the allocatable dummy argument has an INTENT(OUT) attribute. Does this program work now? If so, what does it do? If not, why not?

9-13. Simulating Dice Throws Assume that a programmer is writing a game program. As a part of the program, it is necessary to simulate the throw of a pair of dice. Write a subroutine called throw to return two random values from 1 to 6 each time that it is called. The subroutine should contain an internal function called die to actually calculate the result of each toss of a die, and that function should be called twice by the subroutine to get the two results to return to the calling routine. (*Note:* It is possible to generate a random die result by using the intrinsic subroutine RANDOM_NUMBER.)

9-14. Create a set of ELEMENTAL functions to calculate the sine, cosine, tangent, of an angle θ, where θ is measured in degrees. Create a set of ELEMENTAL functions to calculate the arcsine, arccosine, and arctangent functions, returning the results in degrees. Test your functions by attempting to calculate the sine, cosine, and tangent of the 2 × 3 array `arr1`, and then inverting the calculations with the inverse functions. Array `arr1` is defined as follows:

$$arr1 = \begin{bmatrix} 10.0 & 20.0 & 30.0 \\ 40.0 & 50.0 & 60.0 \end{bmatrix}$$

You should attempt to apply each function to the entire array in a single statement. Did your functions work properly with an array input?

9-15. Convert the ELEMENTAL functions of the previous exercise into PURE functions and try the problem again. What results do you get with PURE functions?

9-16. Second-Order Least-Squares Fits Sometimes, it makes no sense to fit a set of data points to a straight line. For example, consider a thrown ball. We know from basic physics that the height of the ball versus time will follow a parabolic shape, not a linear shape. How do we fit noisy data to a shape that is not a straight line?

It is possible to extend the idea of least-squares fits to find the best (in a least-squares sense) fit to a polynomial more complicated than a straight line. Any polynomial may be represented by an equation of the form

$$y(x) = c_0 + c_1 x + c_2 x^2 + c_3 x^3 + c_4 x^4 + \dots \tag{9-9}$$

where the order of the polynomial corresponds to the highest power of x appearing in the polynomial. To perform a least-squares fit to a polynomial of order n, we must solve for the coefficients $c_0, c_1, \dots, c_n$ that minimize the error between the polynomial and the data points being fit.

The polynomial being fitted to the data may be of any order as long as there are at least as many distinct data points as there are coefficients to solve for. For example, the data may be fitted to a first order polynomial of the form

$$y(x) = c_0 + c_1 x$$

as long as there are at least two distinct data points in the fit. This is a straight line, where c_0 is the intercept of the line and c_1 is the slope of the line. Similarly, the data may be fitted to a second order polynomial of the form

$$y(x) = c_0 + c_1 x + c_2 x^2$$

as long as there are at least three distinct data points in the fit. This is a quadratic expression whose shape is parabolic.

It can be shown[3] that the coefficients of a linear least squares fit to the polynomial $y(x) = c_0 + c_1 x$ are the solutions of the following system of equations

$$N c_0 + (\Sigma x) c_1 = \Sigma y \tag{9-10}$$

$$(\Sigma x) c_0 + (\Sigma x^2) c_1 = \Sigma xy$$

---

[3] *Probability and Statistics,* by Athanasios Papoulis, Prentice-Hall, 1990, pp. 392–393.

where

  (x_i, y_i) is the ith sample measurement
  N is the number of sample measurements included in the fit
  Σx is the sum of the x_i values of all measurements
  Σx^2 is the sum of the squares of the x_i values of all measurements
  Σxy is the sum of the products of the corresponding x_i and y_i values

Any number of sample measurements (x_i, y_i) may be used in the fit, as long as the number of measurements is greater than or equal to 2.

The formulation shown above can be extended to fits of higher-order polynomials. For example, it can be shown that the coefficients of a least squares fit to the second order polynomial $y(x) = c_0 + c_1 x + c_2 x^2$ are the solutions of the following system of equations

$$
\begin{aligned}
Nc_0 \quad + (\Sigma x)c_1 \; + (\Sigma x^2)c_2 &= \Sigma y \\
(\Sigma x)c_0 \; + (\Sigma x^2)c_1 + (\Sigma x^3)c_2 &= \Sigma xy \\
(\Sigma x^2)c_0 + (\Sigma x^3)c_1 + (\Sigma x^4)c_2 &= \Sigma x^2 y
\end{aligned}
\tag{9-11}
$$

where the various terms have meanings similar to the ones described above. Any number of sample measurements (x_i, y_i) may be used in the fit, as long as the number of distinct measurements is greater than or equal to 3. The least-squares fit of the data to a parabola can be found by solving Equations 9-11 for c_0, c_1, and c_2.

Create a subroutine to perform a least-squares fit to a second order polynomial (a parabola), and use that subroutine to fit a parabola to the position data contained in Table 9-1. Use an internal subroutine to solve the system of simultaneous equations given in Equations 9-11.

9

TABLE 9-1
Measured position and velocity of a ball versus time

Time (s)	Position (m)	Velocity (m/s)
0.167	49.9	−5.1
0.333	52.2	−12.9
0.500	50.6	−15.1
0.667	47.0	−6.8
0.833	47.7	−12.3
1.000	42.3	−18.0
1.167	37.9	−5.7
1.333	38.2	−6.3
1.500	38.0	−12.7
1.667	33.8	−13.7
1.833	26.7	−26.7
2.000	24.8	−31.3
2.167	22.0	−22.9
2.333	16.5	−25.6
2.500	14.0	−25.7
2.667	5.6	−25.2
2.833	2.9	−35.0
3.000	0.8	−27.9

9-17. Create a test data set by calculating points (x_i, y_i) along the curve $y(x) = x^2 - 4x + 3$ for $x_i = 0, 0.1, 0.2, \ldots, 5.0$. Next, use the intrinsic subroutine RANDOM_NUMBER to add random noise to each of the y_i values. Then, use the subroutine created in Exercise 9-16 to try to estimate the coefficients of the original function that generated the data set. Try this when the added random noise has the range:

(a) 0.0 (no added noise)

(b) $[-0.1, 0.1]$

(c) $[-0.5, 0.5]$

(d) $[-1.0, 1.0]$

How did the quality of the fit change as the amount of noise in the data increased?

9-18. Higher-Order Least-Squares Fits It can be shown that the coefficients of a least squares fit to the nth order polynomial $y(x) = c_0 + c_1 x + c_2 x^2 + \ldots + c_n x^n$ are the solutions of the following system of n equations in n unknowns:

$$
\begin{aligned}
N c_0 &+ (\Sigma x) c_1 &+ (\Sigma x^2) c_2 &+ \cdots &+ (\Sigma x^n) c_n &= \Sigma y \\
(\Sigma x) c_0 &+ (\Sigma x^2) c_1 &+ (\Sigma x^3) c_2 &+ \cdots &+ (\Sigma x^{n+1}) c_n &= \Sigma xy \\
(\Sigma x^2) c_0 &+ (\Sigma x^3) c_1 &+ (\Sigma x^4) c_2 &+ \cdots &+ (\Sigma x^{n+2}) c_n &= \Sigma x^2 y \qquad (9\text{-}12) \\
&\vdots \\
(\Sigma x^n) c_0 &+ (\Sigma x^{n+1}) c_1 &+ (\Sigma x^{n+2}) c_2 &+ \cdots &+ (\Sigma x^{2n}) c_n &= \Sigma x^n y
\end{aligned}
$$

9

Write a subroutine that implements a least-squares fit to any polynomial of any order. (*Note:* Use dynamic memory allocation to create arrays of the proper size for the problem being solved.)

9-19. Create a test data set by calculating points (x_i, y_i) along the curve $y(x) = x^4 - 3x^3 - 4x^2 + 2x + 3$ for $x_i = 0, 0.1, 0.2, \ldots, 5.0$. Next, use the intrinsic subroutine RANDOM_NUMBER to add random noise to each of the y_i values. Then, use the higher-order least-squares fit subroutine created in Exercise 9-18 to try to estimate the coefficients of the original function that generated the data set. Try this when the added random noise has the range:

(a) 0.0 (no added noise)

(b) $[-0.1, 0.1]$

(c) $[-0.5, 0.5]$

(d) $[-1.0, 1.0]$

How did the quality of the fit change as the amount of noise in the data increased? How does the quality of the higher-order fit for a given amount of noise compare to the quality of a quadratic fit (Exercise 9-17) for the same amount of noise?

9-20. Interpolation A least-squares fit of order n calculates the nth order polynomial that "best fits" an (x, y) data set in a least-squares sense. Once this polynomial has been calculated, it can be used to estimate the expected value y_0 associated with any location x_0

within the data set. This process is called *interpolation*. Write a program that calculates a quadratic least-squares fit to the data set given below, and then uses that fit to estimate the expected value y_0 at $x_0 = 3.5$.

Noisy Measurements

x	y
0.00	−23.22
1.00	−13.54
2.00	−4.14
3.00	−0.04
4.00	3.92
5.00	4.97
6.00	3.96
7.00	−0.07
8.00	−5.67
9.00	−12.29
10.00	−20.25

9-21. Extrapolation Once a least-squares fit has been calculated, the resulting polynomial can also be used to estimate the values of the function *beyond the limits of the original input data set*. This process is called *extrapolation*. Write a program that calculates a linear least-squares fit to the data set given below, and then uses that fit to estimate the expected value y_0 at $x_0 = 14.0$.

Noisy Measurements

x	y
0.00	−14.22
1.00	−10.54
2.00	−5.09
3.00	−3.12
4.00	0.92
5.00	3.79
6.00	6.99
7.00	8.95
8.00	11.33
9.00	14.71
10.00	18.75

10

More about Character Variables

OBJECTIVES

- Understand the kinds of characters available in Fortran compilers, including the Unicode support available in Fortran 2003.
- Understand how relational operations work with character data.
- Understand the lexical functions `LLT`, `LLE`, `LGT`, and `LGE` and why they are safer to use than the corresponding relational operators.
- Know how to use the character intrinsic functions `CHAR`, `ICHAR`, `ACHAR`, `IACHAR`, `LEN`, `LEN_TRIM`, `TRIM`, and `INDEX`.
- Know how to use internal files to convert numeric data to character form, and vice versa.

A **character variable** is a variable that contains character information. In this context, a "character" is any symbol found in a **character set.** There are three basic character sets in common use in the United States: ASCII (American Standard Code for Information Interchange, ANSI X3.4 1977), EBCDIC, and Unicode (ISO 10646).

The ASCII character set is a system in which each character is stored in 1 byte (8 bits). Such a system allows for 256 possible characters, and the ASCII standard defines the first 128 of these possible values. The 8-bit codes corresponding to each letter and number in the ASCII coding system are given in Appendix A. The remaining 128 possible values that can be stored in a 1-byte character have different definitions in different countries, depending on the "code page" used in that particular country. These characters are defined in the ISO-8859 standard series.

The EBCDIC character set is another 1-byte character set used in older IBM mainframes. It is largely irrelevant today, except that you might run into it if you work with legacy IBM systems. The complete EBCDIC character set is also given in Appendix A.

The Unicode character set uses *two bytes* to represent each character, allowing a maximum of 65,536 possible characters. The Unicode character set includes the characters required to represent almost every language on Earth.

Every Fortran compiler supports a 1-byte character set called the *default charac-ter set.* This will be either ASCII or EBCDIC, depending on the computer the compiler is executing on. In addition, most Fortran 2003 compilers support the Unicode character set. We will learn in the next chapter how to select which character set is used in a particular program.

F-2003 ONLY

Fortran generally does not care about the difference between default (ASCII or EBCDIC) character sets. It takes each symbol and stores it in 1 byte of computer memory, whether that symbol is from an ASCII or an EBCDIC character set. All reads, writes, and assignments are the same regardless of character set. However, *some character comparisons and manipulations are character-set dependent.* If not handled properly, these dependencies could cause trouble when we try to move programs from one processor to another one. We will point out these dependencies and how to avoid them as they arise.

■ 10.1

CHARACTER COMPARISON OPERATIONS

Character strings may be compared to each other by using either relational operators or special character comparison functions called lexical functions. Lexical functions have an advantage over the relational operators when program portability is considered.

10.1.1 The Relational Operators with Character Data

Character strings can be compared in logical expressions by using the **relational operators** ==,/ -,<,<=,>, and >=. The result of the comparison is a logical value that is either true or false. For instance, the expression '123' == '123' is true, while the expression '123' == '1234' is false.

How are two characters compared to determine if one is greater than the other? The comparison is based on the **collating sequence** of the characters. The collating sequence of the characters is the order in which they occur within a specific character set. For example, the character 'A' is character number 65 in the ASCII character set, while the character 'B' is character number 66 in the set (see Appendix A). Therefore, the logical expression 'A' < 'B' is true in the ASCII character set. On the other hand, the character 'a' is character number 97 in the ASCII set, so 'a' is greater than 'A'.

Comparisons based on collating sequence are inherently dangerous, since different character sets have different collating sequences. For example, in the EBCDIC character set, 'a' is less than 'A', just the opposite of the ASCII character set. Code that depends on collating sequence is likely to fail when moved between processors!

We can make some comparisons safely regardless of character set. The letters 'A' to 'Z' are always in alphabetical order, the numbers '0' to '9' are always in numerical sequence, and the letters and numbers are not intermingled in the collating sequence. Beyond that, however, all bets are off. The relationships among the special symbols and the relationship between the uppercase and lowercase letters may differ for different character sets. We must be very careful in comparing strings with relational operators.

How are two strings compared to determine if one is greater than the other? The comparison begins with the first character in each string. If they are the same, then the second two characters are compared. This process continues until the first difference is found between the strings. For example, `'AAAAAB'` > `'AAAAAA'`.

What happens if the strings are different lengths? The comparison begins with the first letter in each string, and progresses through each letter until a difference is found. If the two strings are the same all the way to the end of one of them, then the other string is considered the larger of the two. Therefore,

`'AB'` > `'AAAA'` and `'AAAAA'` > `'AAAA'`

**EXAMPLE
10-1**

Alphabetizing Words:

It is often necessary to alphabetize lists of character strings (names, places, etc.). Write a subroutine that will accept a character array and alphabetize the data in the array.

SOLUTION

Since relational operators work for character strings the same way that they work for real values, it is easy to modify the sorting subroutine that we developed in Chapter 7 to alphabetize an array of character variables. All we have to do is to substitute character array declarations for the real declarations in the sorting routines. The rewritten program is shown in Figure 10-1.

FIGURE 10-1
A program to alphabetize character strings using a version of the selection sort algorithm adapted for character strings.

```
PROGRAM sort4
!
!   Purpose:
!     To read in a character input data set, sort it into ascending
!     order using the selection sort algorithm, and to write the
!     sorted data to the standard output device. This program calls
!     subroutine "sortc" to do the actual sorting.
!
!   Record of revisions:
!     Date          Programmer          Description of change
!     ====          ==========          =====================
!     06/28/06     S. J. Chapman        Original code
!
IMPLICIT NONE

! Data dictionary: declare constants
INTEGER, PARAMETER :: MAX_SIZE = 10     ! Max number to sort
```

(continued)

(continued)

```
! Data dictionary: declare variable types & definitions
CHARACTER(len=20), DIMENSION(MAX_SIZE) :: a
                              ! Data array to sort
LOGICAL :: exceed = .FALSE.   ! Logical indicating that array
                              !   limits are exceeded.
CHARACTER(len=20) :: filename ! Input data file name
INTEGER :: i                  ! Loop index
INTEGER :: nvals = 0          ! Number of data values to sort
INTEGER :: status             ! I/O status: 0 for success
CHARACTER(len=20) :: temp     ! Temporary variable for reading

! Get the name of the file containing the input data.
WRITE (*,*) 'Enter the file name with the data to be sorted: '
READ (*,'(A20)') filename

! Open input data file. Status is OLD because the input data must
! already exist.
OPEN ( UNIT=9, FILE=filename, STATUS='OLD', ACTION='READ', &
       IOSTAT=status )

! Was the OPEN successful?
fileopen: IF ( status == 0 ) THEN      ! Open successful

   ! The file was opened successfully, so read the data to sort
   ! from it, sort the data, and write out the results.
   ! First read in data.
   DO
      READ (9, *, IOSTAT=status) temp      ! Get value
      IF ( status /= 0 ) EXIT              ! Exit on end of data
      nvals = nvals + 1                    ! Bump count
      size: IF ( nvals <= MAX_SIZE ) THEN  ! Too many values?
         a(nvals) = temp                   ! No: Save value in array
      ELSE
         exceed = .TRUE.                   ! Yes: Array overflow
      END IF size
   END DO

   ! Was the array size exceeded? If so, tell user and quit.
   toobig: IF ( exceed ) THEN
      WRITE (*,1010) nvals, MAX_SIZE
      1010 FORMAT (' Maximum array size exceeded: ', I6, ' < ', I6 )
   ELSE

      ! Limit not exceeded: sort the data.
      CALL sortc (a, nvals)

      ! Now write out the sorted data.
      WRITE (*,*) 'The sorted output data values are: '
      WRITE (*,'(4X,A)') ( a(i), i = 1, nvals )

   END IF toobig

ELSE fileopen
```

(continued)

(concluded)

```
      ! Else file open failed. Tell user.
      WRITE (*,1020) status
      1020 FORMAT (1X,'File open failed--status = ', I6)

   END IF fileopen

END PROGRAM sort4


SUBROUTINE sortc (array, n )
!
!   Purpose:
!     To sort a character array into ascending order using a
!     selection sort.
!
!   Record of revisions:
!       Date        Programmer          Description of change
!       ====        ==========          =====================
!     11/25/06    S. J. Chapman         Original code
!
IMPLICIT NONE

! Data dictionary: declare calling parameter types & definitions
INTEGER, INTENT(IN) :: n                    ! Number of values
CHARACTER(len=20), DIMENSION(n), INTENT(INOUT) :: array
                                            ! Array to be sorted

! Data dictionary: declare local variable types & definitions
INTEGER :: i                  ! Loop index
INTEGER :: iptr               ! Pointer to smallest value
INTEGER :: j                  ! Loop index
CHARACTER(len=20) :: temp     ! Temp variable for swaps

! Sort the array
outer: DO i = 1, n-1

   ! Find the minimum value in array(i) through array(n)
   iptr = i
   inner: DO j = i+1, n
      minval: IF ( array(j) < array(iptr) ) THEN
         iptr = j
      END IF minval
   END DO inner

   ! iptr now points to the minimum value, so swap array(iptr)
   ! with array(i) if i /= iptr.
   swap: IF ( i /= iptr ) THEN
      temp       = array(i)
      array(i)   = array(iptr)
      array(iptr) = temp
   END IF swap

END DO outer

END SUBROUTINE sortc
```

10

To test this program, we will place the following character values in file `INPUTC`:

```
Fortran
fortran
ABCD
ABC
XYZZY
9.0
A9IDL
```

If we compile and execute the program on a computer with an ASCII collating sequence, the results of the test run will be:

```
C:\book\chap10>sort4
Enter the file name containing the data to be sorted:
inputc
The sorted output data values are:
    9.0
    A9IDL
    ABC
    ABCD
    Fortran
    XYZZY
    fortran
```

Note that the number 9 was placed before any of the letters, and that the lowercase letters were placed after the uppercase letters. These locations are in accordance with the ASCII table in Appendix A.

If this program were executed on a computer with the EBCDIC character set and collating sequence, the answer would have been different from the one given above. In Exercise 10-3, you will be asked to work out the expected output of this program if it were executed on an EBCDIC computer.

10.1.2 The Lexical Functions `LLT`, `LLE`, `LGT`, and `LGE`

The result of the sort subroutine in the previous example depended on the character set and on the characters used by the processor on which it was executed. This dependence is bad, since it makes our Fortran program less portable between processors. We need some way to ensure that programs produce the *same answer* regardless of the computer on which they are compiled and executed.

Fortunately, the Fortran language includes a set of four logical intrinsic functions for just this purpose: `LLT` (lexically less than), `LLE` (lexically less than or equal to), `LGT` (lexically greater than), and `LGE` (lexically greater than or equal to). These functions are the exact equivalent of the relational operators $<$, $<=$, $>$, and $>=$, except that *they always compare characters according to the ASCII collating sequence, regardless of the computer they are running on.* If these **lexical functions** are used instead of the relational operators to compare character strings, the results will be the same on every computer!

A simple example using the `LLT` function follows. Here, character variables `string1` and `string2` are being compared by using the relational operator $<$ and the logical function `LLT`. The value of `result1` will vary from processor to processor, but the value of `result2` will always be true on any processor.

```
LOGICAL :: result1, result2
CHARACTER(len=6) :: string1, string2
string1 = 'A1'
string2 = 'a1'
result1 = string1 < string2
result2 = LLT( string1, string2 )
```

Good Programming Practice

If there is any chance that your program will have to run on computers with both ASCII and EBCDIC character sets, use the logical functions LLT, LLE, LGT, and LGE to test for inequality between two character strings. Do not use the relational operators <, <=, >, and >= with character strings, since their results may vary from computer to computer.

10.2

INTRINSIC CHARACTER FUNCTIONS

The Fortran language contains several additional intrinsic functions that are important for manipulating character data (Table 10-1). Eight of these functions are CHAR, ICHAR, ACHAR, IACHAR, LEN, LEN_TRIM, TRIM, and INDEX. We will now discuss these functions and describe their use.

TABLE 10-1
Some common character intrinsic functions

10

Function name and arguments	Argument types	Result type	Comments
ACHAR(ival)	INT	CHAR	Returns the character corresponding to ival in the ASCII collating sequence
CHAR(ival)	INT	CHAR	Returns the character corresponding to ival in the processor's collating sequence
IACHAR(char)	CHAR	INT	Returns the integer corresponding to char in the ASCII collating sequence
ICHAR(char)	CHAR	INT	Returns the integer corresponding to char in the processor's collating sequence
INDEX(str1, str2,back)	CHAR, LOG	INT	Returns the character number of the first location in str1 to contain the pattern in str2 (0 = no match). Argument back is optional; if present and true, then the search starts from the end of str1 instead of the beginning
LEN(str1)	CHAR	INT	Returns length of str1
LEN_TRIM(str1)	CHAR	INT	Returns length of str1, excluding any trailing blanks.
LLT(str1,str2)	CHAR	LOG	True if str1 < str2 according to the ASCII collating sequence
LLE(str1,str2)	CHAR	LOG	True if str1 <= str2 according to the ASCII collating sequence
LGT(str1,str2)	CHAR	LOG	True if str1 > str2 according to the ASCII collating sequence
LGE(str1,str2)	CHAR	LOG	True if str1 >= str2 according to the ASCII collating sequence
TRIM(str1)	CHAR	CHAR	Returns str1 with trailing blanks removed

The CHAR function converts an input integer value into a corresponding output character. An example of the CHAR function is shown below:

```
CHARACTER :: out
INTEGER :: input = 65
out = CHAR(input)
```

The input to the CHAR function is a single integer argument, and the output from the function is *the character whose collating sequence number matches the input argument* for the particular processor. For example, if a processor uses the ASCII collating sequence, then CHAR(65) is the character 'A'.

The ICHAR function converts an input character into a corresponding output integer. An example of the ICHAR function is shown below:

```
CHARACTER :: input = 'A'
INTEGER :: out
out = ICHAR(input)
```

The input to the ICHAR function is a single character, and the output from the function is *the integer whose collating sequence number matches the input character* for the particular processor. For example, if a processor uses the ASCII collating sequence, then ICHAR('A') is the integer 65.

The functions ACHAR and IACHAR are exactly the same as the functions CHAR and ICHAR, except that they work with the ASCII collating sequence *regardless of the character set used by a particular processor.* Therefore, the results of the functions ACHAR and IACHAR will be the same on any computer. They should be used instead of the previous functions to improve the portability of the programs that you write.

Good Programming Practice

Use functions ACHAR and IACHAR instead of CHAR and ICHAR, since the results of the first set of functions are independent of the processor on which they are executed, while the results of the second set of functions vary, depending on the collating sequence of the particular processor on which they are executed.

Function LEN returns the declared length of a character string. The input to LEN is a character string str1, and the output from it is an integer containing the number of characters in str1. An example of the LEN function is shown below:

```
CHARACTER(len=20) :: str1
INTEGER :: out
str1 = 'ABC XYZ'
out = LEN(str1)
```

The output from LEN is 20. Note that the output of LEN is the declared size of the string, and not the number of nonblank characters in the string.

Function `LEN_TRIM` returns the length of a character string without trailing blanks. The input to `LEN_TRIM` is a character string `str1`, and the output from it is an integer containing the number of characters in `str1`, excluding trailing blanks. If `str1` is entirely blank, then function `LEN_TRIM` returns a 0. An example of the `LEN_TRIM` function is shown below:

```
CHARACTER(len=20) :: str1
INTEGER :: out
str1 = 'ABC XYZ'
out = LEN_TRIM(str1)
```

The output from `LEN_TRIM` is 7

Function `TRIM` returns a character string without trailing blanks. The input to `TRIM` is a character string `str1`, and the output from it is the same string, excluding trailing blanks. If `str1` is entirely blank, then function `TRIM` returns a blank string. An example of the `LEN_TRIM` function is shown below:

```
CHARACTER(len=20) :: str1
str1 = 'ABC XYZ'
WRITE (*,*) '"', TRIM(str1), '"'
```

The output from `TRIM` is a 7-character string containing `'ABC XYZ'`.

The `INDEX` function searches for a pattern in a character string. The inputs to the function are two strings: `str1` containing the string to search, and `str2` containing the pattern that we are looking for. The output from the function is an integer containing the first position in the character string `str1` at which the pattern was found. If no match is found, `INDEX` returns a 0. An example of the `INDEX` function is shown below:

```
CHARACTER(len=20) :: str1 = 'THIS IS A TEST!'
CHARACTER(len=20) :: str2 = 'TEST'
INTEGER :: out
out = INDEX(str1,str2)
```

10

The output of this function is the integer 11, since `TEST` begins at character 11 in the input character string.

If `str2` were `'IS'`, then what would the value of `INDEX(str1,str2)` be? The answer is 3, since `'IS'` occurs within the word `'THIS'`. The `INDEX` function will never see the word `'IS'` because it stops searching at the first occurrence of the search pattern in the string.

The `INDEX` function can also have an optional third argument, *back*. If present, the argument *back* must be a logical value. If *back* is present and true, then the search starts from the end of string `str1` instead of from the beginning. An example of the `INDEX` function with the optional third argument is shown below:

```
CHARACTER(len=20) :: str1 = 'THIS IS A TEST!'
CHARACTER(len=20) :: str2 = 'IS'
INTEGER :: out
OUT = INDEX(str1,str2,.TRUE.)
```

The output of this function is the integer 6, since the last occurrence of `IS` begins at character 6 in the input character string.

■ 10.3

PASSING CHARACTER VARIABLES TO SUBROUTINES AND FUNCTIONS

In Example 10-1, we created a subroutine to alphabetize an array of character variables. The character array in that subroutine was declared as

```
INTEGER, INTENT(IN) :: n
CHARACTER(len=20), DIMENSION(n), INTENT(INOUT) :: array
```

This subroutine will sort characters in an array with any number of elements, but it will sort the array *only* when each element in the array is 20 characters long. If we wanted to sort data in an array whose elements were a different length, we would need a whole new subroutine to do it! This behavior is unreasonable. It should be possible to write a single subroutine to process character data in a given fashion regardless of the number of characters in each element.

Fortran contains a feature to support this. The language allows a special form of the character type declaration for dummy character arguments in procedures. This special declaration takes the form

```
CHARACTER(len=*) :: char_var
```

where *char_var* is the name of a dummy character argument. This declaration says that dummy argument *char_var* is a character variable, but the length of the character variable is not explicitly known at compilation time. If the procedure using *char_var* needs to know its length, it can call function LEN to get that information. The dummy arguments in subroutine sortc could have been declared as

```
INTEGER, INTENT(IN) :: n
CHARACTER(len=*), DIMENSION(n), INTENT(INOUT) :: array
```

If they were declared in this manner, the subroutine would work equally well for arrays of character variables containing elements of any length.

Good Programming Practice

Use the CHARACTER(len=*) type statement to declare dummy character arguments in procedures. This feature allows the procedure to work with strings of arbitrary lengths. If the procedure needs to know the actual length of a particular variable, it may call the LEN function with that variable as a calling argument.

Remember that dummy arguments are just placeholders for the variables that will be passed to the procedure when it is invoked. No actual memory is allocated for the dummy arguments. Since no memory is being allocated, the Fortran compiler does not need to know the length of the character variables that will be passed to the procedure in advance. Therefore, we can use the `CHARACTER(len=*)` type declaration statement for dummy character arguments in a procedure.

On the other hand, any character variables that are local to the procedure must be declared with explicit lengths. Memory will be allocated in the procedure for these local variables, and we must explicitly specify the length of each one for the compiler to know how much memory to allocate for it. This creates a problem for local variables that must be the same length as a dummy argument passed to the procedure. For example, in subroutine `sortc`, the variable `temp` was used for swapping, and must be the same length as an element of the dummy argument `array`.

How can we adjust the size of a temporary variable to fit the size of a dummy array whenever the subroutine is called? *If we declare the length of the variable to be the length of a dummy subroutine argument, then when the subroutine is executed, an* **automatic character variable** *of that size will be allocated.* (This is very similar to the behavior of automatic arrays described in the last chapter.) When the subroutine execution ends, that automatic variable will be destroyed. Like automatic arrays, this automatic character variable may not be initialized in its type declaration statement.

For example, the following statements create an automatic character variable `temp` of the same length as the dummy argument `string`:

```
SUBROUTINE sample ( string )
CHARACTER(len=*) :: string
CHARACTER(len=LEN(string)) :: temp
```

A version of the character sort subroutine that will work for character arrays of any length, with any number of elements, and on any processor is shown in Figure 10-2.

FIGURE 10-2
A modified version of subroutine `sortc` that will work for arrays of any size and array elements of any length.

10

```
SUBROUTINE sortc (array, n)
!
!  Purpose:
!    To sort character array "array" into ascending order using
!    a selection sort. This version of the subroutine sorts
!    according to the ASCII collating sequence. It works for
!    character arrays with any number of elements, with array
!    elements of any length, and on processors regardless of
!    character set.
!
!  Record of revisions:
!    Date         Programmer        Description of change
!    ====         ==========        =====================
!    11/25/06     S. J. Chapman     Original code
! 1. 11/25/06     S. J. Chapman     Modified to work with lexical
!                                   fns and arbitrary element
!                                   lengths
IMPLICIT NONE
```

(*continued*)

(concluded)

```
! Declare calling parameters:
INTEGER, INTENT(IN) :: n               ! Number of values
CHARACTER(len=*), DIMENSION(n), INTENT(INOUT) :: array
                                       ! Array to be sorted
! Declare local variables:
INTEGER :: i                  ! Loop index
INTEGER :: iptr               ! Pointer to smallest value
INTEGER :: j                  ! Loop index
CHARACTER(len=LEN(array)) :: temp   ! Temp variable for swaps

! Sort the array
outer: DO i = 1, n-1

   ! Find the minimum value in array(i) through array(n)
   iptr = i
   inner: DO j = i+1, n
      minval: IF ( LLT(array(j),array(iptr)) ) THEN
         iptr = j
      END IF minval
   END DO inner

   ! iptr now points to the minimum value, so swap array(iptr)
   ! with array(i) if i /= iptr.
   swap: IF ( i /= iptr ) THEN
      temp       = array(i)
      array(i)   = array(iptr)
      array(iptr) = temp
   END IF swap

END DO outer

END SUBROUTINE sortc
```

10

**EXAMPLE
10-2**

Shifting Strings to Uppercase:

We saw in Example 10-1 that lowercase character strings were not alphabetized properly with uppercase strings, since the collating sequence positions of the lowercase letters were different from the collating sequence numbers of the corresponding uppercase letters. The difference between upper- and lowercase letters also causes a problem when we are attempting to match a pattern within a character variable, since `'STRING'` is not the same as `'string'` or `'String'`. It is often desirable to shift all character variables to uppercase to make matching and sorting easier. Write a subroutine to convert all of the lowercase letters in a character string to uppercase, while leaving any other characters in the string unaffected.

SOLUTION

This problem is made more complicated by the fact that we don't know which collating sequence is used by the computer that the subroutine will be running on. Appendix A shows the two common collating sequences, ASCII and EBCDIC. If we look at

Appendix A, we can see that *there is a fixed offset* between an uppercase letter and the corresponding lowercase letter in each collating sequence. However, that offset is different for the two sequences. Furthermore, the EBCDIC sequence complicates matters by inserting some nonalphabetic characters into the middle of the alphabet. These characters should not be affected by the uppercase shift. The ASCII character set is much simpler, since all letters are in order, and there are no nonalphabetic characters mixed into the middle of the alphabet.

Fortunately, if we use the lexical functions for comparisons and the ACHAR and IACHAR functions for conversions, then we can act as though the processor were ASCII and be assured of correct results regardless of the collating sequence of the actual machine.

1. **State the problem.**

Write a subroutine to convert all of the lower case letters in a character string to uppercase, while not affecting numeric and special characters. Design the subroutine to work properly on any processor by using functions that are independent of collating sequence.

2. **Define the inputs and outputs.**

The input to the subroutine is the character argument string. The output from the subroutine is also in string. string can be of arbitrary length.

3. **Describe the algorithm.**

Looking at the ASCII table in Appendix A, we note that the uppercase letters begin at sequence number 65, while the lowercase letters begin at sequence number 97. There are exactly 32 numbers between each uppercase letter and its lowercase equivalent. Furthermore, there are no other symbols mixed into the middle of the alphabet.

These facts give us our basic algorithm for shifting strings to uppercase. We will determine if a character is lowercase by deciding if it is between 'a' and 'z' in the ASCII character set. If it is, then we will subtract 32 from its sequence number to convert it to upper case using the ACHAR and IACHAR functions. The initial pseudocode for this algorithm is

```
Determine if character is lowercase. If so,
   Convert to integer form
   Subtract 32 from the integer
   Convert back to character form
End of IF
```

The final pseudocode for this subroutine is

```
! Get length of string
length ← LEN(string)

DO for i = 1 to length
   IF LGE(string(i:i),'a') .AND. LLE(string(i:i),'z') THEN
      string(i:i) ← ACHAR ( IACHAR (string(i:i) - 32 ) )
   END of IF
END of DO
```

where length is the length of the input character string.

4. **Turn the algorithm into Fortran statements.**

The resulting Fortran subroutines are shown in Figure 10-3.

FIGURE 10-3
Subroutine ucase.

```
SUBROUTINE ucase ( string )
!
!  Purpose:
!    To shift a character string to uppercase on any processor,
!    regardless of collating sequence.
!
!  Record of revisions:
!     Date        Programmer          Description of change
!     ====        ==========          =====================
!    11/25/06    S. J. Chapman        Original code
!
IMPLICIT NONE

! Declare calling parameters:
CHARACTER(len=*), INTENT(INOUT) :: string

! Declare local variables:
INTEGER :: i                    ! Loop index
INTEGER :: length               ! Length of input string

! Get length of string
length = LEN ( string )

! Now shift lowercase letters to uppercase.
DO i = 1, length
   IF ( LGE(string(i:i),'a') .AND. LLE(string(i:i),'z') ) THEN
      string(i:i) = ACHAR ( IACHAR ( string(i:i) ) - 32 )
   END IF
END DO

END SUBROUTINE ucase
```

5. **Test the resulting Fortran program.**

To test this subroutine, it is necessary to write a driver program to read a character string, call the subroutine, and write out the results. A test driver program is shown in Figure 10-4.

FIGURE 10-4
Test driver program for subroutine ucase.

```
PROGRAM test_ucase
!
!  Purpose:
!    To test subroutine ucase.
!
```

(continued)

(concluded)

```
IMPLICIT NONE
CHARACTER(len=20) string
WRITE (*,*) 'Enter test string (up to 20 characters): '
READ (*,'(A20)') string
CALL ucase(string)
WRITE (*,*) 'The shifted string is: ', string
END PROGRAM test_ucase
```

The results from the test program for two input strings are:

```
C:\book\chap10>test_ucase
 Enter test string (up to 20 characters):
This is a test! ...
 The shifted string is: THIS IS A TEST! ...

C:\book\chap10>test_ucase
 Enter test string (up to 20 characters):
abcf1234^&*$po()-
 The shifted string is: ABCF1234^&*$PO()-
```

The subroutine is shifting all lowercase letters to uppercase, while leaving everything else alone. It appears to be working correctly.

10.4

VARIABLE-LENGTH CHARACTER FUNCTIONS

We have already seen that subroutines can work with strings of variable lengths by declaring them with the CHARACTER(len=*) declaration. Is there a way to write a character function that can return a string of arbitrary length?

The answer is yes. We can create an **automatic length character function,** where the length returned by the function is specified by a calling argument. Figure 10-5 shows a simple example. Function abc returns the first n characters of the alphabet, where n is specified in the call to the function.

FIGURE 10-5
A sample function that returns a variable-length character string.

```
MODULE character_subs

CONTAINS
   FUNCTION abc( n )
   !
   ! Purpose:
   !   To return a string containing the first N characters
   !   of the alphabet.
   !
```

(continued)

(concluded)

```
!   Record of revisions:
!      Date        Programmer       Description of change
!      ====        ==========       =====================
!    06/29/06    S. J. Chapman      Original code
!
IMPLICIT NONE

! Declare calling parameters:
INTEGER, INTENT(IN) :: n           ! Length of string to return
CHARACTER(len=n) abc               ! Returned string

! Declare local variables:
character(len=26) :: alphabet = 'abcdefghijklmnopqrstuvwxyz'

! Get string to return
abc = alphabet(1:n)

END FUNCTION abc

END MODULE character
```

A test driver program for this function is shown in Figure 10-6. The module containing the function must be named in a USE statement in the calling program.

FIGURE 10-6
Program to test function abc.

```
PROGRAM test_abc
!
!   Purpose:
!      To test function abc.
!
USE character_subs
IMPLICIT NONE

INTEGER :: n                              ! String length

WRITE(*,*) 'Enter string length:'        ! Get string length
READ (*,*) n

WRITE (*,*) 'The string is: ', abc(n)    ! Tell user

END PROGRAM test_abc
```

When this program is executed, the results are:

```
C:\book\chap10>test_abc
Enter string length:
10
The string is: abcdefghij

C:\book\chap10>test_abc
Enter string length:
3
The string is: abc
```

The length of the character function `abc` could also be declared with an asterisk instead of a passed length:

```
CHARACTER(len=*) abc            ! Returned string
```

This declaration would have created an **assumed length character function.** The behavior of the resulting function is exactly the same as in the example above. However, assumed character length functions have been declared obsolescent as of Fortran 95, and are candidates for deletion in future versions of the language. Do not use them in any of your programs.

Quiz 10-1

This quiz provides a quick check to see if you have understood the concepts introduced in Sections 10.1 through 10.4. If you have trouble with the quiz, reread the sections, ask your instructor, or discuss the material with a fellow student. The answers to this quiz are found in the back of the book.

For questions 1 to 3, state the result of the following expressions. If the result depends on the character set used, state the result for both the ASCII and EBCDIC character sets.

1. `'abcde' < 'ABCDE'`

2. `LLT ('abcde','ABCDE')`

3. `'1234' == '1234 '`

For questions 4 and 5, state whether each of the following statements is legal or not. If the statement is legal, tell what it does. If it is not legal, state why it is not legal.

4.
```
FUNCTION day(iday)
IMPLICIT NONE
INTEGER, INTENT(IN) :: iday
CHARACTER(len=3) :: day
CHARACTER(len=3), DIMENSION(7) :: days = &
    (/'SUN', 'MON', 'TUE', 'WED', 'THU', 'FRI', 'SAT'/)
IF ( ( iday >= 1 ) .AND. ( iday <= 7 ) ) THEN
   day = days(iday)
END IF
END FUNCTION day
```

5.
```
FUNCTION swap_string(string)
IMPLICIT NONE
CHARACTER(len=*), INTENT(IN) :: string
CHARACTER(len=len(string)) :: swap_string
INTEGER :: length, i
```

(continued)

10

(concluded)

```
      length = LEN(string)
      DO i = 1, length
         swap_string(length-i+1:length-i+1) = string(i:i)
      END DO
      END FUNCTION swap_string
```

For questions 6 to 8, state the contents of each variable after the code has been executed.

6.
```
CHARACTER(len=20) :: last = 'JOHNSON'
CHARACTER(len=20) :: first = 'JAMES'
CHARACTER :: middle_initial = 'R'
CHARACTER(len=42) name
name = last // ',' // first // middle_initial
```

7.
```
CHARACTER(len=4) :: a = '123'
CHARACTER(len=12) :: b
b = 'ABCDEFGHIJKLMNOPQRSTUVWXYZ'
b(5:8) = a(2:3)
```

8.
```
CHARACTER(len=80) :: line
INTEGER :: ipos1, ipos2, ipos3, ipos4
line = 'This is a test line containing some input data!'
ipos1 = INDEX (LINE, 'in')
ipos2 = INDEX (LINE, 'Test')
ipos3 = INDEX (LINE, 't l')
ipos4 = INDEX (LINE, 'in', .TRUE.)
```

10.5

INTERNAL FILES

We learned how to manipulate numeric data in the previous chapters of this book. In this chapter, we have learned how to manipulate character data. What we have *not* learned yet is how to convert numeric data into character data, and vice versa. There is a special mechanism in Fortran for such conversions, known as **internal files.**

Internal files are a special extension of the Fortran I/O system in which the READs and WRITEs occur to internal character buffers (internal files) instead of disk files (external files). Anything that can be written to an external file can also be written to an internal file, where it will be available for further manipulation. Likewise, anything that can be read from an external file can be read from an internal file.

The general form of a READ from an internal file is

```
READ (buffer,format) arg1, arg2, ...
```

where *buffer* is the input character buffer, *format* is the format for the READ, and *arg1, arg2*, etc. are the variables whose values are to be read from the buffer. The general form of a WRITE to an internal file is

```
WRITE (buffer,format) arg1, arg2, ...
```

where *buffer* is the output character buffer, *format* is the format for the WRITE, and *arg1, arg2*, etc. are the values to be written to the buffer.

A common use of internal files is to convert character data into numeric data, and vice versa. For example, if the character variable input contains the string '135.4', then the following code will convert the character data into a real value:

```
CHARACTER(len=5) :: input = '135.4'
REAL :: value
READ (input,*) value
```

Certain I/O features are not available with internal files. For example, the OPEN, CLOSE, BACKSPACE, and REWIND statements may not be used with them.

Good Programming Practice
Use internal files to convert data from character format to numeric format, and vice versa.

▦ 10.6
EXAMPLE PROBLEM

10

EXAMPLE 10-3

Varying a Format to Match the Data to be Output:

So far, we have seen three format descriptors to write real data values. The F*w.d* format descriptor displays the data in a format with a fixed decimal point, and the E*w.d* and ES*w.d* format descriptors display the data in exponential notation. The F format descriptor displays data in a way that is easier for a person to understand quickly, but it will fail to display the number correctly if the absolute value of the number is either too small or too large. The E and ES format descriptors will display the number correctly regardless of size, but it is harder for a person to read at a glance.

Write a Fortran function that converts a real number into characters for display in a 12-character-wide field. The function should check the size of the number to be printed out, and modify the format statement to display the data in F12.4 format for as long as possible until the absolute value of the number either gets too big or too small. When the number is out of range for the F format, the function should switch to ES format.

SOLUTION

In the F12.4 format, the function displays four digits to the right of the decimal place. One additional digit is required for the decimal point, and another one is required for the minus sign, if the number is negative. After subtracting those characters, there are seven characters left over for positive numbers, and six characters left over for negative numbers. Therefore, we must convert the number to exponential notation for any positive number larger than 9,999,999, and any negative number smaller than −999,999.

If the absolute value of the number to be displayed is smaller than 0.01, then the display should shift to ES format, because there will not be enough significant digits displayed by the F12.4 format. However, an exact zero value should be displayed in normal F format rather than exponential format.

When it is necessary to switch to exponential format, we will use the ES12.5 format, since the number appears in ordinary scientific notation.

1. **State the problem.**

Write a function to convert a real number into 12 characters for display in a 12-character-wide field. Display the number in F12.4 format if possible, unless the number overflows the format descriptor or gets too small to display with enough precision in an F12.4 field. When it is not possible to display the number in F12.4 format, switch to the ES12.5 format. However, display an exact zero in F12.4 format.

2. **Define the inputs and outputs.**

The input to the function is a real number passed through the argument list. The function returns a 12-character expression containing the number in a form suitable for displaying.

3. **Describe the algorithm.**

The basic requirements for this function were discussed above. The pseudocode to implement these requirements is shown below:

```
IF value > 9999999. THEN
    Use ES12.5 format
ELSE IF value < -999999. THEN
    Use ES12.5 format
ELSE IF value == 0. THEN
    Use F12.4 format
ELSE IF ABS(value) < 0.01
    Use ES12.5 format
ELSE
    USE F12.4 format
END of IF
WRITE value to buffer using specified format
```

4. **Turn the algorithm into Fortran statements.**

The resulting Fortran function is shown in Figure 10-7. Function real_to_char illustrates both how to use internal files and how to use a character variable to contain format descriptors. The proper format descriptor for the real-to-character conversion is stored in variable fmt, and an internal WRITE operation is used to write the character string into buffer string.

FIGURE 10-7
Character function real_to_char.

```
FUNCTION real_to_char ( value )
!
!  Purpose:
!    To convert a real value into a 12-character string, with the
!    number printed in as readable a format as possible considering
!    its range. This routine prints out the number according to the
!    following rules:
!       1.  value > 9999999.              ES12.5
!       2.  value < -999999.              ES12.5
!       3.  0.    < ABS(value) < 0.01     ES12.5
!       4.  value = 0.0                   F12.4
!       5.  Otherwise                     F12.4
!
!  Record of revisions:
!      Date       Programmer          Description of change
!      ====       ==========          =====================
!    11/25/06    S. J. Chapman        Original code
!
IMPLICIT NONE

! Data dictionary: declare calling parameter types & definitions
REAL, INTENT(IN) :: value            ! value to convert to char form
CHARACTER (len=12) :: real_to_char   ! Output character string

! Data dictionary: declare local variable types & definitions
CHARACTER(len=9) :: fmt              ! Format descriptor
CHARACTER(len=12) :: string          ! Output string

! Clear string before use
string = ' '

! Select proper format
IF ( value > 9999999. ) THEN
   fmt = '(ES12.5)'
ELSE IF ( value < -999999. ) THEN
   fmt = '(ES12.5)'
ELSE IF ( value == 0. ) THEN
   fmt = '(F12.4)'
ELSE IF ( ABS(value) < 0.01 ) THEN
   fmt = '(ES12.5)'
ELSE
   fmt = '(F12.4)'
END IF

! Convert to character form.
WRITE (string,fmt) value
real_to_char = string

END FUNCTION real_to_char
```

10

5. **Test the resulting Fortran program.**

To test this function, it is necessary to write a driver program to read a real number, call the subroutine, and write out the results. A test driver program is shown in Figure 10-8.

FIGURE 10-8
Test driver program for function `real_to_char`.

```fortran
PROGRAM test_real_to_char
!
!   Purpose:
!     To test function real_to_char.
!
!   Record of revisions:
!       Date       Programmer          Description of change
!       ====       ==========          =====================
!     11/25/06    S. J. Chapman        Original code
!
!   External routines:
!     real_to_char -- Convert real to character string
!     ucase         -- Shift string to upper case
!
IMPLICIT NONE

! Declare external functions:
CHARACTER(len=12), EXTERNAL :: real_to_char

! Data dictionary: declare variable types & definitions
CHARACTER :: ch                ! Character to hold Y/N response.
CHARACTER(len=12) :: result ! Character output
REAL :: value                  ! Value to be converted

while_loop: DO

   ! Prompt for input value.
   WRITE (*,'(1X,A)') 'Enter value to convert:'
   READ (*,*) value

   ! Write converted value, and see if we want another.
   result = real_to_char(value)
   WRITE (*,'(1X,A,A,A)') 'The result is ', result, &
                          ': Convert another one? (Y/N) [N]'

   ! Get answer.
   READ (*,'(A)') ch

   ! Convert answer to uppercase to make match.
   CALL ucase ( ch )

   ! Do another?
     IF ( ch /= 'Y' ) EXIT

   END DO while_loop

END PROGRAM test_real_to_char
```

To verify that this function is working correctly for all cases, we must supply test values that fall within each of the ranges that it is designed to work for. Therefore, we will test it with the following numbers:

```
       0.
       0.001234567
    1234.567
12345678.
 -123456.7
-1234567.
```

The results from the test program for the six input values are:

```
C:\book\chap10>test_real_to_char
Enter value to convert:
0.
The result is .0000: Convert another one? (Y/N) [N]
y
Enter value to convert:
0.001234567
The result is 1.23457E-03: Convert another one? (Y/N) [N]
Y
Enter value to convert:
1234.567
The result is 1234.5670: Convert another one? (Y/N) [N]
Y
Enter value to convert:
12345678.
The result is 1.23457E+07: Convert another one? (Y/N) [N]
y
Enter value to convert:
-123456.7
The result is -123456.7000: Convert another one? (Y/N) [N]
y
Enter value to convert:
-1234567.
The result is -1.23457E+06: Convert another one? (Y/N) [N]
n
```

The function appears to be working correctly for all possible input values.

The test program test_real_to_char also contains a few interesting features. Since we would normally use the program to test more than one value, it is structured as a WHILE loop. The user is prompted by the program to determine whether or not to repeat the loop. The first character of the user's response is stored in variable ch, and is compared to the character 'Y'. If the user responded with a 'Y', the loop is repeated; otherwise, it is terminated. Note that subroutine ucase is called to shift the contents of ch to uppercase, so that both 'y' and 'Y' will be interpreted as "yes" answers. This form of repetition control is very useful in interactive Fortran programs.

Quiz 10-2

This quiz provides a quick check to see if you have understood the concepts introduced in Sections 10.5 and 10.6. If you have trouble with the quiz, reread the sections, ask your instructor, or discuss the material with a fellow student. The answers to this quiz are found in the back of the book.

For questions 1 to 3, state whether each of the following groups of statements is correct or not. If correct, describe the results of the statements.

```
1.  CHARACTER(len=12) :: buff
    CHARACTER(len=12) :: buff1 = 'ABCDEFGHIJKL'
    INTEGER :: i = -1234
    IF ( buff1(10:10) == 'K' ) THEN
       buff = "(1X,I10.8)"
    ELSE
       buff = "(1X,I10)"
    END IF
    WRITE (*,buff) i

2.  CHARACTER(len=80) :: outbuf
    INTEGER :: i = 123, j, k = -11
    j = 1023 / 1024
    WRITE (outbuf,*) i, j, k

3.  CHARACTER(len=30) :: line = &
            '123456789012345678901234567890'
    CHARACTER(len=30) :: fmt = &
            '(3X,I6,12X,I3,F6.2)'
    INTEGER :: ival1, ival2
    REAL :: rval3
    READ (line,fmt) ival1, ival2, rval3
```

10.7
SUMMARY

A character variable is a variable that contains character information. Two character strings may be compared by using the relational operators. However, the result of the comparison may differ, depending on the collating sequence of the characters on a particular processor. It is safer to test character strings for inequality by using the lexical functions, which always return the same value on any computer regardless of collating sequence.

It is possible to declare automatic character variables in procedures. The length of an automatic character variable is specified by either a dummy argument or by a value passed in a module. Each time the procedure is run, a character variable of the specified length is automatically generated, and the variable is automatically destroyed when the execution of the procedure ends.

It is possible to generate character functions that can return character strings of variable length, provided that there is an explicit interface between the function and any invoking program units. The easiest way to generate an explicit interface is to package the function within a module, and then to use that module in the calling procedure.

Internal files provide a means to convert data from character form to numeric form and vice versa within a Fortran program. They involve writes to and reads from a character variable within the program.

10.7.1 Summary of Good Programming Practice

The following guidelines should be adhered to when you are working with character variables:

1. Use the lexical functions rather than the relational operators to compare two character strings for inequality. This action avoids potential problems when a program is moved from a processor with an ASCII character set to a processor with an EBCDIC character set.
2. Use functions ACHAR and IACHAR instead of functions CHAR and ICHAR, since the results of the first set of functions are independent of the processor on which they are executed, while the results of the second set of functions vary depending on the collating sequence of the particular processor that they are executed on.
3. Use the CHARACTER(len=*) type statement to declare dummy character arguments in procedures. This feature allows the procedure to work with strings of arbitrary lengths. If the subroutine or function needs to know the actual length of a particular variable, it may call the LEN function with that variable as a calling argument.
4. Use internal files to convert data from character format to numeric format, and vice versa.

10

10.7.2 Summary of Fortran Statements and Structures

Internal READ Statement:

```
READ (buffer,fmt) input_list
```

Example:

```
READ (line,'(1X, I10, F10.2)') i, slope
```

Description:
The internal READ statement reads the data in the input list according to the formats specified in *fmt*, which can be a character string, a character variable, the label of a FORMAT statement, or *. The data is read from the internal character variable *buffer*.

Internal WRITE **Statement:**

```
WRITE (buffer,fmt) output_list
```

Example:

```
WRITE (line,'(2I10,F10.2)') i, j, slope
```

Description:
The internal WRITE statement writes the data in the output list according to the formats specified in *fmt*,
which can be a character string, a character variable, the label of a FORMAT statement, or *. The data is
written to the internal character variable *buffer*.

10.7.3 Exercises

10-1. Determine the contents of each variable in the following code fragment after the code
has been executed:

```
CHARACTER(len=16) :: a = '1234567890123456'
CHARACTER(len=16) :: b = 'ABCDEFGHIJKLMNOP', c
IF ( a > b ) THEN
   c = a(1:6) // b(7:12) // a(13:16)
ELSE
   c = b(7:12) // a(1:6) // a(13:16)
END IF
a(7:9) = '='
```

10-2. Determine the contents of each variable in the following code fragment after the code
has been executed. How does the behavior of this code fragment differ from the behavior
of the one in Exercise 10-1?

```
CHARACTER(len=16) :: a = '1234567890123456'
CHARACTER(len=16) :: b = 'ABCDEFGHIJKLMNOP', c
IF ( LGT(a,b) ) THEN
   c = a(1:6) // b(7:12) // a(13:16)
ELSE
   c = b(7:12) // a(1:6) // a(13:16)
END IF
a(7:9) = '='
```

10-3. Determine the order in which the character strings in Example 10-1 would be sorted by
the subroutine sortc, if executed in a computer using the EBCDIC collating sequence.

10-4. Rewrite subroutine ucase as a character function. Note that this function must return a
variable-length character string.

10-5. Write a subroutine `lcase` that properly converts a string to lowercase regardless of collating sequence.

10-6. Determine the order in which the following character strings will be sorted by the subroutine `sortc` of Example 10-1 (*a*) according to the ASCII collating sequence, and (*b*) according to the EBCDIC collating sequence.

```
'This is a test!'
'?well?'
'AbCd'
'aBcD'
'1DAY'
'2nite'
'/DATA/'
'quit'
```

10-7. Determine the contents of each variable in the following code fragment after the code has been executed:

```
CHARACTER(len=132) :: buffer
REAL :: a, b
INTEGER :: i = 1700, j = 2400
a = REAL(1700 / 2400)
b = REAL(1700) / 2400
WRITE (buffer,100) i, j, a, b
100 FORMAT (T11,I10,T31,I10,T51,F10.4,T28,F10.4)
```

10-8. Write a subroutine `caps` that searches for all of the words within a character variable, and capitalizes the first letter of each word, while shifting the remainder of the word to lowercase. Assume that all nonalphabetic and nonnumeric characters can mark the boundaries of a word within the character variable (for example, periods, commas, forward slash). Nonalphabetic characters should be left unchanged. Test your routine on the following character variables:

```
CHARACTER(len=40) :: a = 'this is a test--does it work?'
CHARACTER(len=40) :: b = 'this iS the 2nd test!'
CHARACTER(len=40) :: c = '123 WHAT NOW?!? xxxoooxxx.'
```

10-9. Rewrite subroutine `caps` as a variable-length character function, and test the function using the same data as in the previous exercise.

10-10. The intrinsic function `LEN` returns the number of characters that a character variable can store, *not* the number of characters actually stored in the variable. Write a function `len_used` that returns the number of characters actually used within a variable. The function should determine the number of characters actually used by determining the positions of the first and last nonblank characters in the variable, and performing the appropriate math. Test your function with the following variables. Compare the results of function `len_used` with the results returned by `LEN` and `LEN_TRIM` for each of the values given.

10

```
CHARACTER(len=30) :: a(3)
a(1) = 'How many characters are used?'
a(2) = '   ... and how about this one?'
a(3) = '  !   ! '
```

10-11. When a relatively short character string is assigned to a longer character variable, the extra space in the variable is filled with blanks. In many circumstances, we would like to use a substring consisting of only the *nonblank* portions of the character variable. To do so, we need to know where the nonblank portions are within the variable. Write a subroutine that will accept a character string of arbitrary length, and return two integers containing the numbers of the first and last nonblank characters in the variable. Test your subroutine with several character variables of different lengths and with different contents.

10-12. Input Parameter File A common feature of large programs is an *input parameter file* in which the user can specify certain values to be used during the execution of the program. In simple programs, the values in the file must be listed in a specific order, and none of them may be skipped. These values may be read with a series of consecutive READ statements. If a value is left out of the input file or an extra value is added to the input file, all subsequent READ statements are misaligned, and the numbers will go into the wrong locations in the program.

In more sophisticated programs, default values are defined for the input parameters in the file. In such a system, *only the input parameters whose defaults need to be modified need to be included in the input file*. Furthermore, the values that do appear in the input file may occur in any order. Each parameter in the input file is recognized by a corresponding *keyword* indicating what that parameter is for.

For example, a numerical integration program might include default values for the starting time of the integration, the ending time of the integration, the step size to use, and whether or not to plot the output. These values could be overridden by lines in the input file. An input parameter file for this program might contain the following items:

```
start = 0.0
stop = 10.0
dt = 0.2
plot off
```

These values could be listed in any order, and some of them could be omitted if the default values are acceptable. In addition, the keywords might appear in uppercase, lowercase, or mixed case. The program will read this input file a line at a time, and update the variable specified by the keyword with the value on the line.

Write a subroutine that accepts a character argument containing a line from the input parameter file, and has the following output arguments:

```
REAL :: start, stop, dt
LOGICAL :: plot
```

The subroutine should check for a keyword in the line, and update the variable that matches that keyword. It should recognize the keywords 'START', 'STOP', 'DT', and 'PLOT'. If the keyword 'START' is recognized, the subroutine should check for an equal sign, and use the value to the right of the equal sign to update variable START. It should behave similarly for the other keywords with real values. If the keyword 'PLOT' is recognized, the subroutine should check for `'ON'` or `'OFF'`, and update the logical accordingly. (*Hint:* Shift each line to uppercase for easy recognition. Then, use function `INDEX` to identify keywords.)

10-13. Histograms A *histogram* is a plot that shows how many times a particular measurement falls within a certain range of values. For example, consider the students in a class. Suppose that there are 30 students in the class, and that their scores on the last exam fell within the following ranges:

Range	Number of Students
100–95	3
94–90	6
89–85	9
84–80	7
79–75	4
74–70	2
69–65	1

A plot of the number of students scoring in each range of numbers is a histogram (Figure 10-9).

To create this histogram, we started with a set of data consisting of 30 student grades. We divided the range of possible grades on the test (0 to 100) into 20 bins, and then counted how many student scores fell within each bin. Then we plotted the number of grades in each bin. (Since no one scored below 65 on the exam, we didn't bother to plot all of the empty bins between 0 and 64 in Figure 10-9.)

Write a subroutine that will accept an array of real input data values, divide them into a user-specified number of bins over a user-specified range, and accumulate the number of samples that fall within each bin. Create a simple plot of the histogram, using asterisks to represent the levels in each bin.

10

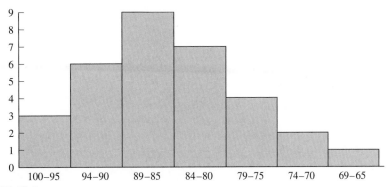

FIGURE 10-9
Histogram of student scores on last test.

10-14. Use the random-number subroutine `random0` that was developed in Chapter 7 to generate an array of 20,000 random numbers in the range [0,1). Use the histogram subroutine developed in the previous exercise to divide the range between 0 and 1 into 20 bins, and to calculate a histogram of the 20,000 random numbers. How uniform was the distribution of the numbers generated by the random number generator?

10-15. Write a program that opens a user-specified disk file containing the source code for a Fortran program. The program should copy the source code from the input file to a user-specified output file, stripping out any comments during the copying process. Assume that the Fortran source file is in free format, so that the ! character marks the beginning of a comment.

10

Additional Intrinsic Data Types

- Understand what is meant by different KINDs of a given data type.
- Understand how to select a specific kind of REAL, INTEGER, or CHARACTER data.
- Know how to select the precision and range of a real variable in a computer-independent manner.
- Know how to allocate and use variables of the COMPLEX data type.

In this chapter, we will examine alternative kinds of the REAL, INTEGER, and CHARACTER data types, and explain how to select the desired kind for a particular problem. Then, we will turn our attention to an additional data type that is built into the Fortran language: the COMPLEX data type. The COMPLEX data type is used to store and manipulate complex numbers, which have both real and imaginary components.

11.1

ALTERNATIVE KINDS OF THE REAL DATA TYPE

The REAL (or floating-point) data type is used to represent numbers containing decimal points. On most computers, a **default real** variable is 4 bytes (or 32 bits) long. It is divided into two parts, a **mantissa** and an **exponent.** Most modern computers use the IEEE 754 Standard for floating point variables to implement real numbers. In this implementation, 24 bits of the number are devoted to the mantissa, and 8 bits are devoted to the exponent. The 24 bits devoted to the mantissa are enough to represent 6 to 7 significant decimal digits, so a real number can have up to about 7 significant digits.[1]

---

[1] One bit is used to represent the sign of the number, and 23 bits are used to represent the magnitude of the mantissa. Since $2^{23} = 8,388,608$, it is possible to represent between 6 and 7 significant digits with a real number. Similarly, the 8 bits of the exponent are enough to represent numbers as large as 10^{38} and as small as 10^{-38}.

There are times when a 4-byte floating-point number cannot adequately express a value that we need to solve a problem. Scientists and engineers sometimes need to express a number to more than 7 significant digits of precision, or to work with numbers larger than 10^{38} or smaller than 10^{-38}. In either case, we cannot use a 32-bit variable to represent the number. Fortran 95/2003 includes a longer version of the REAL data type for use in these circumstances.

The longer version of the REAL data type is usually 8 bytes (or 64 bits) long. In a typical implementation,[2] 53 bits of the number are devoted to the mantissa, and 11 bits are devoted to the exponent. The 53 bits devoted to the mantissa are enough to represent 15 to 16 significant decimal digits. Similarly, the 11 bits of the exponent are enough to represent numbers as large as 10^{308} and as small as 10^{-308}.

The Fortran 95 and 2003 Standards guarantee that a Fortran compiler will support *at least* two sizes of real numbers. However, they do *not* specify how many bits must be used for each size. For traditional reasons, the shorter version of the REAL data type on any particular computer is known as **single precision,** and the longer version of the REAL data type on any particular computer is known as **double precision.** On most computers, a single-precision real value is stored in 32 bits, and a double-precision real value is stored in 64 bits. However, some 64-bit processors use 64 bits for single precision and 128 bits for double precision. There is no guarantee that a "single-precision" variable will be the same length on different processors. This variability makes the terms "single precision" and "double precision" poor choices for describing the accuracy of a floating-point value. We will introduce a better way to specify the accuracy of a floating-point value in Section 11.1.3.

11.1.1 Kinds of REAL Constants and Variables

Since Fortran compilers have at least two different kinds of real variables, there must be some way to declare which of the types we want to use in a particular problem. This is done by using a **kind type parameter.** Single-precision reals and double-precision reals are different **kinds** of the REAL data type, each with its own unique kind number. Examples of a REAL type declaration statement with a kind type parameter are shown below:

```
REAL(KIND=1) :: value_1
REAL(KIND=4) :: value_2
REAL(KIND=8), DIMENSION(20) :: array
REAL(4) :: temp
```

The kind of a real value is specified in parentheses after the REAL, either with or without the phrase KIND=. A variable declared with a kind type parameter is called a

---

[2] This statement refers to the IEEE Standard 754 for double-precision numbers. Almost all new computer systems conform to this standard, but some older systems allocate their bits in a different fashion. For example, older VAX computers allocated 56 bits to the mantissa and 8 bits to the exponent of their double-precision numbers, giving them a range of 10^{-38} to 10^{38}, and 16 to 17 significant digits of accuracy.

TABLE 11-1
KIND **Numbers for real values in some fortran 95 compilers**

Computer/compiler	32-bit real	64-bit real	128-bit real
Cray supercomputer/CF90	N/A	4, 8*	16
PC/Intel Visual Fortran 95	4*	8	16
PC/Lahey Fortran 95	4*	8	N/A
PC/NAGWare f95	1*	2	N/A

* Denotes the **default real** type for a particular processor.

parameterizedvariable. If no kind is specified, then the default kind of real value is used. *The default kind may vary among different processors*, but is usually 32 bits long.

What do the kind numbers mean? Unfortunately, we do not know. Each compiler vendor is free to assign any kind number to any size of variable. For example, on some compilers, a 32-bit real value might be KIND=1 and a 64-bit real value might be KIND=2. On other compilers, a 32-bit real value might be KIND=4 and a 64-bit real value might be KIND=8. Table 11-1 shows examples of kind numbers for some representative computer/compiler combinations.

Therefore, to make your programs portable between computers, you should always assign kind numbers to a named constant, and then use that named constant in all type declaration statements. It will then be possible to modify the program to run on different processors by changing only the value of the named constant. For example,

```
INTEGER, PARAMETER :: SINGLE = 4   ! Compiler dependent value
INTEGER, PARAMETER :: DOUBLE = 8   ! Compiler dependent value
REAL(KIND=SINGLE) :: value_1
REAL(KIND=DOUBLE), DIMENSION(20) :: array
REAL(SINGLE) :: temp
```

An even better approach for a large program would be to define the kind parameters within a module, and to use that module in each procedure within the program. Then it is possible to change the kind numbers for the entire program by editing a single file.

It is also possible to declare the kind of a real constant. The kind of a real constant is declared by appending an underscore and the kind number to the constant. The following are examples of valid real constants:

```
34.                    ! Default kind
34._4                  ! Only valid if 4 is a legal kind of real
34.E3                  ! Single precision
1234.56789_DBL         ! Only valid if "DBL" is an integer named constant
```

The first example produces a constant of the *default kind* for the particular processor where the program is being executed. The second example is valid only if KIND=4 is a valid kind of real on the particular processor where the program is being executed. The third example produces a constant of the single-precision kind for the particular processor. The fourth example is only valid if DBL is a valid previously defined integer named constant, whose value is a valid kind number.

11

In addition to the previous examples, a double-precision constant in exponential notation can be declared by using a D instead of an E to declare the exponent of the constant. For example,

         3.0E0   is a single-precision constant
         3.0D0   is a double-precision constant

Good Programming Practice

Always assign kind numbers to a named constant, and then use that named constant in all type declaration statements and constant declarations. This practice will make it easier to port the program to different computers, which may use different kind numbers. For large programs, place the named constants containing the kind parameters in a single module, and then use that module in every procedure within the program.

11.1.2   Determining the KIND of a Variable

Fortran 95/2003 includes an intrinsic function KIND, which returns the kind number of a given constant or variable. This function can be used to determine the kind numbers in use by your compiler. For example, the program in Figure 11-1 determines the kind numbers associated with single and double-precision variables on a particular processor.

FIGURE 11-1
Program to determine the kind numbers associated with single- and double-precision real variables on a particular computer system.

```
PROGRAM kinds
!
!  Purpose:
!    To determine the kinds of single and double precision real
!    values on a particular computer.
!
IMPLICIT NONE

! Write out the kinds of single & double precision values
WRITE (*,'(" The KIND for single precision is",I2)') KIND(0.0)
WRITE (*,'(" The KIND for double precision is",I2)') KIND(0.0D0)

END PROGRAM kinds
```

When this program is executed on a Pentium 4–based PC using the Intel Visual Fortran 95 compiler, the results are:

```
C:\book\chap11>kinds
The KIND for single precision is 4
The KIND for double precision is 8
```

When the program is executed on a Pentium 4–based PC using the NAGWare Fortran 95 compiler, the results are:

```
C:\book\chap11>kinds
The KIND for single precision is 1
The KIND for double precision is 2
```

As you can see, the kind numbers will vary from processor to processor. Try the program on your own computer/compiler and see what values you get.

11.1.3 Selecting Precision in a Processor-Independent Manner

A major problem encountered in porting a Fortran program from one computer to another one is the fact that the terms "single precision" and "double precision" are not precisely defined. Double-precision values have approximately twice the precision of single-precision values, but the number of bits associated with each kind of real is entirely up to the computer vendor. On most computers, a single-precision value is 32 bits long and a double-precision value is 64 bits long. However, on some computers, such as Cray supercomputers and those based on the 64-bit Intel® Itanium® chip, single precision is 64 bits long and double precision is 128 bits long. Thus a program that runs properly in single precision on a Cray might need double precision to run properly when it is migrated to a 32-bit computer, and a program that requires double precision for proper operation on a 32-bit computer will need only single precision on a computer based on the 64-bit Itanium® chip.

How can we write programs so that they can be easily ported between processors with different word sizes and still function correctly? We can use an intrinsic function to *automatically select the proper kind of real value to use* as the program is moved between computers. This function is called SELECTED_REAL_KIND. When it is executed, it returns the kind number of the *smallest* type of real value that meets or exceeds the specified range and precision on that particular processor. The general form of this function is

$$kind\_number = SELECTED\_REAL\_KIND(p=precision, r=range)$$

where *precision* is the number of decimal digits of precision required, and *range* is the range of the exponent required in powers of 10. The two arguments *precision* and *range* are called optional arguments; either one or both may be supplied to specify the desired characteristics of the real value. The function returns the kind number of the smallest real kind satisfying the specified requirements. It returns a -1 if the specified precision is not available from any REAL data type on the processor, a -2 if the specified range is not available from any REAL data type on the processor, and a -3 if neither is available.

All of the following are legal uses of this function

```
kind_number = SELECTED_REAL_KIND(p=6,r=37)
kind_number = SELECTED_REAL_KIND(p=12)
kind_number = SELECTED_REAL_KIND(r=100)
```

```
kind_number = SELECTED_REAL_KIND(13,200)
kind_number = SELECTED_REAL_KIND(13)
kind_number = SELECTED_REAL_KIND(p=17)
```

On a Pentium 4–based computer using the Intel Visual Fortran compiler, the first of the functions will return a 4 (the kind number for single precision) and the next four will return an 8 (the kind number for double precision). The last function will return a 16, since Intel Visual Fortran supports a 16-byte real that supplies 17 decimal digits of precision.

On a Pentium 4–based computer using the NAGWare Fortran compiler, the first of the functions will return a 1 (the kind number for single precision) and the next four will return a 2 (the kind number for double precision). The last function will return a −1, since no kind of supported REAL supply 17 decimal digits of precision.

Notice from the above example that the p= and r= are optional as long as *precision* and *range* are specified in that order, and the p= is optional if only the precision is specified. These are general characteristics of optional arguments, which we will learn more about in Chapter 13.

The function SELECTED_REAL_KIND should be used with a certain amount of caution, since over-specifying your program's requirements can increase the program's size and slow down execution. For example, 32-bit computers have between 6 and 7 decimal digits of precision in their single-precision variables. If you specify a REAL data type as SELECTED_REAL_KIND(6), then you will get single precision on those machines. However, if you specify a REAL data type as SELECTED_REAL_KIND(7), then you will get double precision, and the program will be both larger and slower. Make sure that you really need that seventh decimal place before you ask for it!

11

Good Programming Practice

Use the function SELECTED_REAL_KIND to determine the kind numbers of the real variables needed to solve a problem. The function will return the proper kind numbers on any computer, making your programs more portable.

Three other intrinsic functions are available that can be used to determine kind of a real value and the precision and range of the real value on a particular computer. These functions are summarized in Table 11-2. The integer function KIND() returns the kind number of a specified value. The integer function PRECISION() returns the number of decimal digits that can be stored in the real value, and the integer function RANGE() returns the exponent range that can be supported by the real value. The use of these functions is illustrated in the program in Figure 11-2.

▮ **TABLE 11-2**
Common KIND-related intrinsic functions

Function	Description
SELECTED_REAL_KIND(p,r)	Return smallest kind of real value with a minimum of p decimal digits of precision and maximum range $\geq 10^r$.
SELECTED_INT_KIND(r)	Return smallest kind of integer value with a maximum range $\geq 10^r$.
KIND(X)	Return kind number of X, where X is a variable or constant of any intrinsic type.
PRECISION(X)	Return decimal precision of X, where X is a real or complex value.
RANGE(X)	Return the decimal exponent range for X, where X is an integer, real, or complex value.

FIGURE 11-2
Program to illustrate the use of function SELECTED_REAL_KIND() to select desired kinds of real variables in a processor-independent manner, and the use of functions KIND(), PRECISION(), and RANGE() to get information about real values.

```
PROGRAM select_kinds
!
!   Purpose:
!     To illustrate the use of SELECTED_REAL_KIND to select
!     desired kinds of real variables in a processor-independent
!     manner.
!
!   Record of revisions:
!      Date        Programmer         Description of change
!      ====        ==========         =====================
!    11/27/06    S. J. Chapman        Original code
!
IMPLICIT NONE

! Declare parameters:
INTEGER, PARAMETER :: SGL = SELECTED_REAL_KIND(p=6,r=37)
INTEGER, PARAMETER :: DBL = SELECTED_REAL_KIND(p=13,r=200)

! Declare variables of each type:
REAL(kind=SGL) :: var1 = 0.
REAL(kind=DBL) :: var2 = 0._DBL

! Write characteristics of selected variables.
WRITE (*,100) 'var1', KIND(var1), PRECISION(var1), RANGE(var1)
WRITE (*,100) 'var2', KIND(var2), PRECISION(var2), RANGE(var2)
100 FORMAT(1X,A,': kind = ',I2,', Precision = ',I2,', Range = ',I3)

END PROGRAM select_kinds
```

11

When this program is executed on a Pentium-based PC using the Intel Visual Fortran compiler, the results are:

```
C:\book\chap11>select_kinds
var1: kind = 4, Precision =  6, Range =  37
var2: kind = 8, Precision = 15, Range = 307
```

Note that the program requested 13 decimal digits of precision and a range of 200 powers of 10 for the second variable, but the variable actually assigned by the processor has 15 digits of precision and a range of 308 powers of 10. This type of real variable was the smallest size available on the processor that met or exceeded the request. Try this program on your own computer and see what values you get.

11.1.4 Mixed-Mode Arithmetic

When an arithmetic operation is performed between a double-precision real value and another real or integer value, Fortran converts the other value to double precision, and performs the operation in double precision with a double-precision result. However, the automatic mode conversion *does not occur* until the double-precision number and the other number both appear in the same operation. Therefore, it is possible for a portion of an expression to be evaluated in integer or single-precision real arithmetic, followed by another portion evaluated in double-precision real arithmetic.

For example, suppose that a particular processor uses 32 bits to represent single-precision real values, and 64 bits to represent double-precision real values. Then suppose that we want to add ⅓ to ⅓, and get the answer to 15 significant digits. We might try to calculate the answer with any of the following expressions:

	Expression	Result
1.	1.D0/3. + 1/3	3.333333333333333E-001
2.	1./3. + 1.D0/3.	6.666666333333333E-001
3.	1.D0/3. + 1./3.D0	6.666666666666666E-001

1. In the first expression, the single-precision constant 3. is converted to double precision before it is divided into the double-precision constant 1.D0, producing the result 3.333333333333333E-001. Next, the integer constant 1 is divided by the integer constant 3, producing an integer 0. Finally, the integer 0 is converted into double precision and added to the first number, producing the final value of 3.333333333333333E-001.
2. In the second expression, 1./3. is evaluated in single precision, producing the result 3.333333E-01, and 1./3.D0 is evaluated in double precision, producing the result 3.333333333333333E-001. Then, the single-precision result is converted to double precision and added to the double-precision result to produce the final value of 6.666666333333333E-001.
3. In the third expression, both terms are evaluated in double precision, leading to a final value of 6.666666666666666E-001.

As we can see, adding $\frac{1}{3} + \frac{1}{3}$ produces significantly different answers, depending on the type of numbers used in each part of the expression. The third expression shown above yields the answer that we really wanted, while the first two are inaccurate to a greater or lesser degree. This result should serve as a warning: if you really need double-precision arithmetic, you should be very careful to ensure that *all* intermediate portions of a calculation are performed with double-precision arithmetic, and that all intermediate results are stored in double-precision variables.

A special case of mixed-mode arithmetic occurs during the initialization of double-precision real variables in type declaration statements and DATA statements. *If the constant used to initialize the variable is written in single-precision form, then the variable will only be initialized to single-precision accuracy*, regardless of the number of significant digits written in the constant.[3] For example, the variable a1 in the following program is initialized to only 7 significant digits even though it is double precision:

```
PROGRAM test_initial
INTEGER, PARAMETER :: DBL = SELECTED_REAL_KIND(p=13)
REAL(KIND=DBL) :: a1 = 6.666666666666666
REAL(KIND=DBL) :: a2 = 6.666666666666666_DBL
WRITE (*,*) a1, a2
END PROGRAM test_initial
```

When this program is executed, the value of a1 is valid to only 7 significant digits:

```
C:\book\chap11>test_initial
      6.666666507720947        6.666666666666666
```

Programming Pitfalls

Always be careful to initialize double-precision real variables with double-precision real constants so that the full precision of the constant is preserved.

11.1.5 Higher Precision Intrinsic Functions

All generic functions that support single-precision real values will also support double-precision real values. If the input value is single precision, then the function will be calculated with a single-precision result. If the input value is double precision, then the function will be calculated with a double-precision result.

One important intrinsic function is DBLE. This function converts any numeric input argument to double precision on the particular processor where it is executed.

---

[3] FORTRAN 77 behaved differently here—it would permit all of the digits of a constant to be used in an initialization statement, even if there were more digits than a single-precision value could support. This difference could cause problems when a FORTRAN 77 program is transported to Fortran 95/2003.

11.1.6 When to Use High-Precision Real Values

We have seen that 64-bit real numbers are better than 32-bit real numbers, offering more precision and greater range. If they are so good, why bother with 32-bit real numbers at all? Why don't we just use 64-bit real numbers all the time?

There are a couple of good reasons for not using 64-bit real numbers all the time. For one thing, every 64-bit real number requires twice as much memory as a 32-bit real number. This extra size makes programs using them much larger, and computers with more memory are required to run the programs. Another important consideration is speed. Higher-precision calculations are normally slower than lower-precision calculations, so computer programs using higher-precision calculations run more slowly than computer programs using lower-precision calculations.[4] Because of these disadvantages, we should only use higher-precision numbers when they are actually needed.

When are 64-bit numbers actually needed? There are three general cases:

1. *When the dynamic range of the calculation requires numbers whose absolute values are smaller than* 10^{-39} *or larger than* 10^{39}. In this case, either the problem must be rescaled or 64-bit variables must be used.

2. *When the problem requires numbers of very different sizes to be added to or subtracted from one another.* If two numbers of very different sizes must be added or subtracted from one another, the resulting calculation will lose a great deal of precision. For example, suppose we wanted to add the number 3.25 to the number 1000000.0. With 32-bit numbers, the result would be 1000003.0. With 64-bit numbers, the result would be 1000003.25.

3. *When the problem requires two numbers of very nearly equal size to be subtracted from one another.* When two numbers of very nearly equal size must be subtracted from each other, small errors in the last digits of the two numbers become greatly exaggerated. For example, consider two nearly equal numbers that are the result of a series of single-precision calculations. Because of the round-off error in the calculations, each of the numbers is accurate to 0.0001%. The first number a1 should be 1.0000000, but through round-off errors in previous calculations is actually 1.0000010, while the second number a2 should be 1.0000005, but through round-off errors in previous calculations is actually 1.0000000. The difference between these numbers should be

$$\text{true\_result} = a1 - a2 = -0.0000005$$

but the actual difference between them is

$$\text{actual\_result} = a1 - a2 = 0.0000010$$

---

[4] Intel-based PCs are an exception to this general rule. The math processor performs hardware calculations with 80-bit accuracy regardless of the precision of the data being processed. As a result, there is little speed penalty for double-precision operations on a PC.

Therefore, the error in the subtracted number is

$$\% \text{ error} = \frac{\text{actual\_result} - \text{true\_result}}{\text{true\_result}} \times 100\%$$

$$\% \text{ error} = \frac{0.0000010 - (-0.0000005)}{-0.0000005} \times 100\% = -300\%$$

The single-precision math created a 0.0001% error in a1 and a2, and then the subtraction blew that error up into a 300% error in the final answer! When two nearly equal numbers must be subtracted as a part of a calculation, then the entire calculation should be performed in higher precision to avoid round-off error problems.

EXAMPLE   *Numerical Calculation of Derivatives:*
11-1

The derivative of a function is defined mathematically as

$$\frac{d}{dx} f(x) = \lim_{\Delta x \to 0} \frac{f(x + \Delta x) - f(x)}{\Delta x} \tag{11-1}$$

The derivative of a function is a measure of the instantaneous slope of the function at the point being examined. In theory, the smaller Δx, the better the estimate of the derivative is. However, the calculation can go bad if there is not enough precision to avoid round-off errors. Note that as Δx gets small, we will be subtracting two numbers that are very nearly equal, and the effects of round-off errors will be multiplied.

To test the effects of precision on our calculations, we will calculate the derivative of the function

$$f(x) = \frac{1}{x} \tag{11-2}$$

for the location $x = 0.15$. This function is shown in Figure 11-3.

SOLUTION
From elementary calculus, the derivative of $f(x)$ is

$$\frac{d}{dx} f(x) = \frac{d}{dx} \frac{1}{x} = -\frac{1}{x^2}$$

For $x = 0.15$,

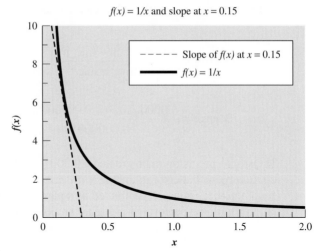

FIGURE 11-3
Plot of the function $f(x) = 1/x$, showing the slope at $x = 0.15$.

$$\frac{d}{dx}f(x) = -\frac{1}{x^2} = -44.44444444444\ldots$$

We will now attempt to evaluate the derivative of Equation 11-2 for sizes of Δx from 10^{-1} to 10^{-10}, using both 32- and 64-bit mathematics on a computer that has a 32-bit single-precision and a 64-bit double-precision real data type. We will print out the results for each case, together with the true analytical solution and the resulting error.

A Fortran program to evaluate the derivative of Equation 11-2 is shown in Figure 11-4.

FIGURE 11-4
Program to evaluate the derivative of the function $f(x) = 1/x$ at $x = 0.15$, using both single-precision and double-precision arithmetic.

```
PROGRAM diff
!
!   Purpose:
!     To test the effects of finite precision by differentiating
!     a function with 10 different step sizes, with both single
!     precision and double precision. The test will be based on
!     the function F(X) = 1./X.
!
!   Record of revisions:
!       Date       Programmer          Description of change
!       ====       ==========          =====================
!     11/27/06    S. J. Chapman         Original code
```

(continued)

(continued)

```
!
IMPLICIT NONE

! Data dictionary: declare constants
INTEGER, PARAMETER :: SGL = SELECTED_REAL_KIND(p=6,r=37)
INTEGER, PARAMETER :: DBL = SELECTED_REAL_KIND(p=13)

! List of local variables:
REAL(KIND=DBL) :: ans              ! True (analytic) answer
REAL(KIND=DBL) :: d_ans            ! Double precision answer
REAL(KIND=DBL) :: d_error          ! Double precision percent error
REAL(KIND=DBL) :: d_fx             ! Double precision F(x)
REAL(KIND=DBL) :: d_fxdx           ! Double precision F(x+dx)
REAL(KIND=DBL) :: d_dx             ! Step size
REAL(KIND=DBL) :: d_x = 0.15_DBL   ! Location to evaluate dF(x)/dx
INTEGER :: i                       ! Index variable
REAL(KIND=SGL) :: s_ans            ! Single precision answer
REAL(KIND=SGL) :: s_error          ! Single precision percent error
REAL(KIND=SGL) :: s_fx             ! Single precision F(x)
REAL(KIND=SGL) :: s_fxdx           ! Single precision F(x+dx)
REAL(KIND=SGL) :: s_dx             ! Step size
REAL(KIND=SGL) :: s_x = 0.15_SGL   ! Location to evaluate dF(x)/dx

! Print headings.
WRITE (*,1)
1 FORMAT (1X,'   DX        TRUE ANS     SP ANS        DP ANS ', &
          '             SP ERR   DP ERR   ')

! Calculate analytic solution at x=0.15.
ans = - ( 1.0_DBL / d_x**2 )

! Calculate answer from definition of differentiation
step_size: DO i = 1, 10

   ! Get delta x.
   s_dx = 1.0 / 10.0**i
   d_dx = 1.0_DBL / 10.0_DBL**i

   ! Calculate single precision answer.
   s_fxdx = 1. / ( s_x + s_dx )
   s_fx = 1. / s_x
   s_ans = ( s_fxdx - s_fx ) / s_dx

   ! Calculate single precision error, in percent.
   s_error = ( s_ans - REAL(ans) ) / REAL(ans) * 100.

   ! Calculate double precision answer.
   d_fxdx = 1.0_DBL / ( d_x + d_dx )
   d_fx = 1.0_DBL / d_x
   d_ans = ( d_fxdx - d_fx ) / d_dx

   ! Calculate double precision error, in percent.
   d_error = ( d_ans - ans ) / ans * 100.
```

11

(continued)

(concluded)

```
    ! Tell user.
    WRITE (*,100) d_dx, ans, s_ans, d_ans, s_error, d_error
    100 FORMAT (1X, ES10.3, F12.7, F12.7, ES22.14, F9.3, F9.3)

END DO step_size

END PROGRAM diff
```

When this program is compiled and executed by using Intel Visual Fortran on a PC, the following results are obtained.[5]

```
C:\book\chap11>diff
     DX        TRUE ANS      SP ANS           DP ANS              SP ERR   DP ERR
 1.000E-01 -44.4444444 -26.6666641 -2.66666666666667E+01    -40.000 -40.000
 1.000E-02 -44.4444444 -41.6666527 -4.16666666666667E+01     -6.250  -6.250
 1.000E-03 -44.4444444 -44.1503487 -4.41501103752762E+01     -0.662  -0.662
 1.000E-04 -44.4444444 -44.4173813 -4.44148345547379E+01     -0.061  -0.067
 1.000E-05 -44.4444444 -44.4412231 -4.44414816790584E+01     -0.007  -0.007
 1.000E-06 -44.4444444 -44.3458557 -4.44441481501912E+01     -0.222  -0.001
 1.000E-07 -44.4444444 -47.6837158 -4.44444148151035E+01      7.288   0.000
 1.000E-08 -44.4444444 -47.6837158 -4.44444414604561E+01      7.288   0.000
 1.000E-09 -44.4444444   0.0000000 -4.44444445690806E+01   -100.000   0.000
 1.000E-10 -44.4444444   0.0000000 -4.44444481217943E+01   -100.000   0.000
```

When Δx was fairly large, both the single-precision and double-precision results gave essentially the same answer. In that range, the accuracy of the result is limited only by the step size. As Δx gets smaller and smaller, the single-precision answer gets better and better until $\Delta x \approx 10^{-5}$. For step sizes smaller than 10^{-5}, round-off errors start to dominate the solution. The double-precision answer gets better and better until $\Delta x \approx 10^{-9}$. For step sizes smaller than 10^{-9}, double-precision round-off errors start to get progressively worse.

In this problem, the use of double precision allowed us to improve the quality of our answer from four correct significant digits to eight correct significant digits. The problem also points out the critical importance of a proper Δx size in producing a right answer. Such concerns occur in all computer programs performing scientific and engineering calculations. In all such programs, there are parameters that *must* be chosen correctly, or round-off errors will result in bad answers. The design of proper algorithms for use on computers is a whole discipline in itself, known as *numerical analysis*.

---

[5] To reproduce these results with the Intel Visual Fortran Compiler Version 9.0, it is necessary to compile the program with the "/Od" option, which turns off all optimizations. To reproduce these results with the Lahey Fortran compiler, it is necessary to compile the program with the "-o0" option, which turns off all optimizations. In both cases, if the optimizer is used, the compiler stores intermediate single-precision results as double-precision values in CPU registers, and the calculation is effectively performed in double precision. This practice makes single-precision arithmetic look misleadingly good.

11.1.7 Solving Large Systems of Simultaneous Linear Equations

In Chapter 9, we introduced the method of Gauss-Jordan elimination to solve systems of simultaneous linear equations of the form

$$
\begin{aligned}
a_{11}x_1 + a_{12}x_2 + \cdots + a_{1n}x_n &= b_1 \\
a_{21}x_1 + a_{22}x_2 + \cdots + a_{2n}x_n &= b_2 \\
&\cdots \\
a_{n1}x_1 + a_{n2}x_2 + \cdots + a_{nn}x_n &= b_n
\end{aligned}
\tag{11-3}
$$

In the Gauss-Jordan method, the first equation in the set is multiplied by a constant and added to all of the other equations in the set to eliminate x_1, and then the process is repeated with the second equation in the set multiplied by a constant and added to all of the other equations in the set to eliminate x_2, and so forth for all of the equations. *This type of solution is subject to cumulative round-off errors that eventually make the answers unusable.* Any round-off errors in eliminating the coefficients of x_1 are propagated into even bigger errors by eliminating the coefficients of x_2, which are propagated into even bigger errors by eliminating the coefficients of x_3, etc. For a large enough system of equations, the cumulative round-off errors will produce unacceptably bad solutions.

How big must a system of equations be before round-off error makes it impossible to solve them by using Gauss-Jordan elimination? There is no easy answer to this question. Some systems of equations are more sensitive to slight round-off errors than others are. To understand why this is so, let's look at the two simple sets of simultaneous equations shown in Figure 11-5. Figure 11-5a shows a plot of the two simultaneous equations.

$$
\begin{aligned}
3.0x - 2.0y &= 3.0 \\
5.0x + 3.0y &= 5.0
\end{aligned}
\tag{11-4}
$$

The solution to this set of equations is $x = 1.0$ and $y = 0.0$. The point $(1.0, 0.0)$ is the intersection of the two lines on the plot in Figure 11-5a. Figure 11-5b shows a plot of the two simultaneous equations

$$
\begin{aligned}
1.00x - 1.00y &= -2.00 \\
1.03x - 0.97y &= -2.03
\end{aligned}
\tag{11-5}
$$

The solution to this set of equations is $x = -1.5$ and $y = 0.5$. The point $(-1.5, 0.5)$ is the intersection of the two lines on the plot in Figure 11-5b.

Now let's compare the sensitivity of Equations 11-4 and 11-5 to slight errors in the coefficients of the equations. (A slight error in the coefficients of the equations is similar to the effect of round-off errors on the equations.) Assume that coefficient a_{11} of Equations 11-4 is in error 1 percent, so that a_{11} is really 3.03 instead of 3.00. Then the solution to the equations becomes $x = 0.995$ and $y = 0.008$, which is almost the

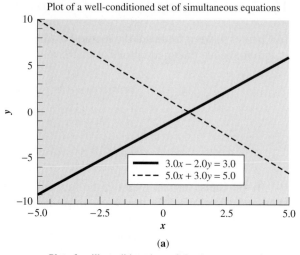

(a)

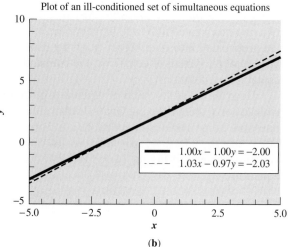

(b)

FIGURE 11-5
(a) Plot of a well-conditioned 2 × 2 set of equations. (b) Plot of an ill-conditioned 2 × 2 set of
equations.

same as the solution to the original equations. Now, let's assume that coefficient a_{11} of
Equations 11-5 is in error by 1 percent, so that a_{11} is really 1.01 instead of 1.00. Then
the solution to the equations becomes $x = 1.789$ and $y = 0.193$, which is a major shift
compared to the previous answer. Equations 11-4 are relatively insensitive to small
coefficient errors, while Equations 11-5 are *very* sensitive to small coefficient errors.

If we examine Figure 11-5b closely, it will be obvious why Equations 11-5 are
so sensitive to small changes in coefficients. The lines representing the two equations
are almost parallel to each other, so a tiny change in one of the equations moves their
intersection point by a very large distance. If the two lines had been exactly parallel
to each other, then the system of equations would have had either no solutions or an

infinite number of solutions. In the case where the lines are nearly parallel, there is a single unique solution, but its location is very sensitive to slight changes in the coefficients. Therefore, systems like Equations 11-5 will be very sensitive to accumulated round-off noise during Gauss-Jordan elimination.

Systems of simultaneous equations that behave well like Equations 11-4 are called **well-conditioned systems,** and systems of simultaneous equations that behave poorly like Equations 11-5 are called **ill-conditioned systems.** Well-conditioned systems of equations are relatively immune to round-off error, while ill-conditioned systems are very sensitive to round-off error.

In working with very large systems of equations or ill-conditioned systems of equations, it is helpful to work in double-precision arithmetic. Double-precision arithmetic dramatically reduces round-off errors, allowing Gauss-Jordan elimination to produce correct answers even for difficult systems of equations.

EXAMPLE 11-2

Solving Large Systems of Linear Equations:

For large and/or ill-conditioned systems of equations, Gauss-Jordan elimination will produce a correct answer only if double-precision arithmetic is used to reduce round-off error. Write a subroutine that uses double-precision arithmetic to solve a system of simultaneous linear equations. Test your subroutine by comparing it to the single-precision subroutine `simul` created in Chapter 9. Compare the two subroutines on both well-defined and ill-defined systems of equations.

SOLUTION

The double-precision subroutine `dsimul` will be essentially the same as the single-precision subroutine `simul2` in Figure 9-6 that we developed in Chapter 9. Subroutine `simul2`, which is renamed `simul` here, is used as the starting point because that version includes the use of both array operations and automatic arrays for simplicity and flexibility, and because it does not destroy its input data.

11

1. **State the problem.**

   Write a subroutine to solve a system of N simultaneous equations in N unknowns, using Gauss-Jordan elimination, double-precision arithmetic, and the maximum pivot technique to avoid round-off errors. The subroutine must be able to detect singular sets of equations, and set an error flag if they occur.

2. **Define the inputs and outputs.**

   The input to the subroutine consists of an $N \times N$ double-precision matrix `a` with the coefficients of the variables in the simultaneous equations, and a double-precision vector `b` with the contents of the right-hand sides of the equations. The outputs from the subroutine are the solutions to the set of equations (in vector `soln`), and an error flag.

3. **Describe the algorithm.**

   The pseudocode for this subroutine is the same as the pseudocode for subroutine `simul2` in Chapter 9, and is not repeated here.

4. **Turn the algorithm into Fortran statements.**

The resulting Fortran subroutine is shown in Figure 11-6.

FIGURE 11-6

Subroutine to solve a system of simultaneous equations in double precision.

```
SUBROUTINE dsimul ( a, b, soln, ndim, n, error )
!
!   Purpose:
!     Subroutine to solve a set of N linear equations in N
!     unknowns using Gaussian elimination and the maximum
!     pivot technique. This version of simul has been
!     modified to use array sections and automatic arrays.
!     It uses double precision arithmetic to avoid
!     cumulative roundoff errors. It DOES NOT DESTROY the
!     original input values.
!
!   Record of revisions:
!       Date        Programmer        Description of change
!       ====        ==========        =====================
!     11/23/06    S. J. Chapman       Original code
! 1.  11/24/06    S. J. Chapman       Add automatic arrays
! 2.  11/27/06    S. J. Chapman       Double precision
!
IMPLICIT NONE

! Data dictionary: declare constants
INTEGER, PARAMETER :: DBL = SELECTED_REAL_KIND(p=13)
                                        ! Double kind number
REAL(KIND=DBL), PARAMETER :: EPSILON = 1.0E-12
                                        ! A "small" number for comparison
                                        ! when determining singular eqns

! Data dictionary: declare calling parameter types & definitions
INTEGER, INTENT(IN) :: ndim             ! Dimension of arrays a and b
REAL(KIND=DBL), INTENT(IN), DIMENSION(ndim,ndim) :: a
                                        ! Array of coefficients (N x N).
                                        ! This array is of size ndim x
                                        ! ndim, but only N x N of the
                                        ! coefficients are being used.
REAL(KIND=DBL), INTENT(IN), DIMENSION(ndim) :: b
                                        ! Input: Right-hand side of eqns.
REAL(KIND=DBL), INTENT(OUT), DIMENSION(ndim) :: soln
                                        ! Output: Solution vector.
INTEGER, INTENT(IN) :: n                ! Number of equations to solve.
INTEGER, INTENT(OUT) :: error           ! Error flag:
                                        !   0 -- No error
                                        !   1 -- Singular equations

! Data dictionary: declare local variable types & definitions
REAL(KIND=DBL), DIMENSION(n,n) :: a1 ! Copy of "a" that will be
                                        ! destroyed during the solution
REAL(KIND=DBL) :: factor                ! Factor to multiply eqn irow by
                                        ! before adding to eqn jrow
```

(continued)

(*continued*)

```
INTEGER :: irow                          ! Number of the equation currently
                                         ! being processed
INTEGER :: ipeak                         ! Pointer to equation containing
                                         ! maximum pivot value
INTEGER :: jrow                          ! Number of the equation compared
                                         ! to the current equation
REAL(KIND=DBL) :: temp                   ! Scratch value
REAL(KIND=DBL),DIMENSION(n) :: temp1     ! Scratch array

! Make copies of arrays "a" and "b" for local use
a1 = a(1:n,1:n)
soln = b(1:n)

! Process N times to get all equations...
mainloop: DO irow = 1, n

   ! Find peak pivot for column irow in rows irow to N
   ipeak = irow
   max_pivot: DO jrow = irow+1, n
      IF (ABS(a1(jrow,irow)) > ABS(a1(ipeak,irow))) THEN
         ipeak = jrow
      END IF
   END DO max_pivot

   ! Check for singular equations.
   singular: IF ( ABS(a1(ipeak,irow)) < EPSILON ) THEN
      error = 1
      RETURN
   END IF singular

   ! Otherwise, if ipeak /= irow, swap equations irow & ipeak
   swap_eqn: IF ( ipeak /= irow ) THEN
      temp1 = a1(ipeak,1:n)
      a1(ipeak,1:n) = a1(irow,1:n)    ! Swap rows in a
      a1(irow,1:n) = temp1
      temp = soln(ipeak)
      soln(ipeak) = soln(irow)        ! Swap rows in b
      soln(irow) = temp
   END IF swap_eqn

   ! Multiply equation irow by -a1(jrow,irow)/a1(irow,irow),
   ! and add it to Eqn jrow (for all eqns except irow itself).
   eliminate: DO jrow = 1, n
      IF ( jrow /= irow ) THEN
         factor = -a1(jrow,irow)/a1(irow,irow)
         a1(jrow,1:n) = a1(irow,1:n)*factor + a1(jrow,1:n)
         soln(jrow) = soln(irow)*factor + soln(jrow)
      END IF
   END DO eliminate
END DO mainloop

! End of main loop over all equations. All off-diagonal
! terms are now zero. To get the final answer, we must
! divide each equation by the coefficient of its on-diagonal
! term.
```

(*continued*)

(concluded)

```
divide: DO irow = 1, n
   soln(irow) = soln(irow) / a1(irow,irow)
END DO divide

! Set error flag to 0 and return.
error = 0

END SUBROUTINE dsimul
```

5. **Test the resulting Fortran programs.**

To test this subroutine, it is necessary to write a driver program. The driver program will open an input data file to read the equations to be solved. The first line of the file will contain the number of equations N in the system, and each of the next N lines will contain the coefficients of one of the equations. The coefficients will be stored in a single-precision array and sent to subroutine simul for solution, and will also be stored in a double-precision array and sent to subroutine dsimul for solution. To verify that the solutions are correct, they will be plugged back into the original equations, and the resulting errors will be calculated. The solutions and errors for single-precision and double-precision arithmetic will be displayed in a summary table.

The test driver program for subroutine dsimul is shown in Figure 11-7. Note that it uses allocatable arrays throughout, so it will work with input data sets of any size.

FIGURE 11-7

Test driver program for subroutine dsimul.

```
PROGRAM test_dsimul
!
!  Purpose:
!    To test subroutine dsimul, which solves a set of N linear
!    equations in N unknowns. This test driver calls subroutine
!    simul to solve the problem in single precision, and subrou-
!    tine dsimul to solve the problem in double precision. The
!    results of the two solutions together with their errors are
!    displayed in a summary table.
!
!  Record of revisions:
!     Date        Programmer          Description of change
!     ====        ==========          =====================
!    11/27/06    S. J. Chapman        Original code
!
IMPLICIT NONE

! Declare parameters
INTEGER, PARAMETER :: SGL = SELECTED_REAL_KIND(p=6)   ! Single
INTEGER, PARAMETER :: DBL = SELECTED_REAL_KIND(p=13)  ! Double

! List of local variables
REAL(KIND=SGL), ALLOCATABLE, DIMENSION(:,:) :: a
                          ! Single-precision coefficients
REAL(KIND=SGL), ALLOCATABLE, DIMENSION(:) :: b
                          ! Single-precision constant values
```

(continued)

(continued)

```
REAL(KIND=SGL), ALLOCATABLE, DIMENSION(:) :: soln
                                 ! Single-precision solution
REAL(KIND=SGL), ALLOCATABLE, DIMENSION(:) :: serror
                                 ! Array of single-precision errors
REAL(KIND=SGL) :: serror_max     ! Max single precision error
REAL(KIND=DBL), ALLOCATABLE, DIMENSION(:,:) :: da
                                 ! Double-precision coefficients
REAL(KIND=DBL), ALLOCATABLE, DIMENSION(:) :: db
                                 ! Double-precision constant values
REAL(KIND=DBL), ALLOCATABLE, DIMENSION(:) :: dsoln
                                 ! Double-precision solution
REAL(KIND=DBL), ALLOCATABLE, DIMENSION(:) :: derror
                                 ! Array of double-precision errors
REAL(KIND=DBL) :: derror_max     ! Max double precision error
INTEGER :: error_flag            ! Error flag from subroutines
INTEGER :: i, j                  ! Loop index
INTEGER :: istat                 ! I/O status
INTEGER :: n                     ! Size of system of eqns to solve
CHARACTER(len=20) :: filename    ! Input data file name

! Get the name of the disk file containing the equations.
WRITE (*,*) 'Enter the file name containing the eqns: '
READ (*,'(A20)') filename

! Open input data file. Status is OLD because the input data must
! already exist.
OPEN ( UNIT=1, FILE=filename, STATUS='OLD', ACTION='READ', &
    IOSTAT=istat )

! Was the OPEN successful?
open_ok: IF ( istat == 0 ) THEN

   ! The file was opened successfully, so read the number of
   ! equations in the system.
   READ (1,*) n

   ! Allocate memory for that number of equations
   ALLOCATE ( a(n,n), b(n), soln(n), serror(n), &
            da(n,n), db(n), dsoln(n), derror(n), STAT=istat )

   ! If the memory is available, read in equations and
   ! process them.
   solve: IF ( istat == 0 ) THEN

      DO i = 1, n
         READ (1,*) (da(i,j), j=1,n), db(i)
      END DO

      ! Copy the coefficients in single precision for the
      ! single precision solution.
      a = da
      b = db

      ! Display coefficients.
      WRITE (*,1010)
```

(continued)

(*continued*)

```
1010 FORMAT (/,1X,'Coefficients:')
DO i = 1, n
   WRITE (*,'(1X,7F11.4)') (a(i,j), j=1,n), b(i)
END DO

! Solve equations.
CALL simul (a, b, soln, n, n, error_flag )
CALL dsimul (da, db, dsoln, n, n, error_flag )

! Check for error.
error_check: IF ( error_flag /= 0 ) THEN
   WRITE (*,1020)
   1020 FORMAT (/1X,'Zero pivot encountered!', &
        //1X,'There is no unique solution to this system.')

ELSE error_check

   ! No errors. Check for roundoff by substituting into
   ! the original equations, and calculate the differences.
   serror_max = 0.
   derror_max = 0._DBL
   serror = 0.
   derror = 0._DBL
   DO i = 1, n
      serror(i) = SUM ( a(i,:)  * soln(:)  ) - b(i)
      derror(i) = SUM ( da(i,:) * dsoln(:) ) - db(i)
   END DO
   serror_max = MAXVAL ( ABS ( serror ) )
   derror_max = MAXVAL ( ABS ( derror ) )

   ! Tell user about it.
   WRITE (*,1030)
   1030 FORMAT (/1X,'  i      SP x(i)         DP x(i)       ', &
        '      SP Err         DP Err ')
   WRITE (*,1040)
   1040 FORMAT ( 1X,' ===   =========     =========      ', &
        '   ========      ======== ')
   DO i = 1, n
      WRITE (*,1050) i, soln(i), dsoln(i), serror(i), derror(i)
      1050 FORMAT (1X, I3, 2X, G15.6, G15.6, F15.8, F15.8)
   END DO

   ! Write maximum errors.
   WRITE (*,1060) serror_max, derror_max
   1060 FORMAT (/,1X,'Max single-precision error:',F15.8, &
        /,1X,'Max double-precision error:',F15.8)

   END IF error_check
END IF solve

! Deallocate dynamic memory
DEALLOCATE ( a, b, soln, serror, da, db, dsoln, derror )
```

(*continued*)

(*concluded*)

```
ELSE open_ok
   ! Else file open failed. Tell user.
   WRITE (*,1070) istat
   1070 FORMAT (1X,'File open failed--status = ', I6)
END IF open_ok

END PROGRAM
```

To test the subroutine, we will call it with three different data sets. The first of them should be a well-conditioned system of equations, the second one should be an ill-conditioned system of equations, and the third should have no unique solution. The first system of equations that we will use to test the subroutine is the 6×6 system of equations shown below:

$$
\begin{aligned}
-2.0\ X_1 + 5.0\ X_2 + 1.0\ X_3 + 3.0\ X_4 + 4.0\ X_5 - 1.0\ X_6 &= 0.0 \\
2.0\ X_1 - 1.0\ X_2 - 5.0\ X_3 - 2.0\ X_4 + 6.0\ X_5 + 4.0\ X_6 &= 1.0 \\
-1.0\ X_1 + 6.0\ X_2 - 4.0\ X_3 - 5.0\ X_4 + 3.0\ X_5 - 1.0\ X_6 &= -6.0 \\
4.0\ X_1 + 3.0\ X_2 - 6.0\ X_3 - 5.0\ X_4 - 2.0\ X_5 - 2.0\ X_6 &= 10.0 \\
-3.0\ X_1 + 6.0\ X_2 + 4.0\ X_3 + 2.0\ X_4 - 6.0\ X_5 + 4.0\ X_6 &= -6.0 \\
2.0\ X_1 + 4.0\ X_2 + 4.0\ X_3 + 4.0\ X_4 + 5.0\ X_5 - 4.0\ X_6 &= -2.0
\end{aligned}
\tag{11-6}
$$

If this system of equations is placed in a file called SYS6.WEL, and program test_dsimul is run on this file, the results are:

```
C:\book\chap11>test_dsimul
Enter the file name containing the eqns:
sys6.wel
Coefficients:
   -2.0000    5.0000    1.0000    3.0000    4.0000   -1.0000    0.0000
    2.0000   -1.0000   -5.0000   -2.0000    6.0000    4.0000    1.0000
   -1.0000    6.0000   -4.0000   -5.0000    3.0000   -1.0000   -6.0000
    4.0000    3.0000   -6.0000   -5.0000   -2.0000   -2.0000   10.0000
   -3.0000    6.0000    4.0000    2.0000   -6.0000    4.0000   -6.0000
    2.0000    4.0000    4.0000    4.0000    5.0000   -4.0000   -2.0000

 i     SP x(i)        DP x(i)            SP Err        DP Err
===   =========      =========         ========      ========
 1    0.662556       0.662556         0.00000125    0.00000000
 2   -0.132567      -0.132567         0.00000072    0.00000000
 3   -3.01373       -3.01373          0.00000238    0.00000000
 4    2.83548        2.83548          0.00000095    0.00000000
 5   -1.08520       -1.08520         -0.00000095    0.00000000
 6   -0.836043      -0.836043        -0.00000119    0.00000000

Max single-precision error:    0.00000238
Max double-precision error:    0.00000000
```

For this well-conditioned system, the results of single-precision and double-precision calculations were essentially identical. The second system of equations that we will use to test the subroutine is the 6 × 6 system of equations shown below. Note that the second and sixth equations are almost identical, so this system is ill-conditioned.

$$
\begin{aligned}
-2.0\ X_1 + 5.0\ X_2 && + 1.0\ X_3 + 3.0\ X_4 + 4.0\ X_5 - 1.0\ X_6 &= 0.0 \\
2.0\ X_1 - 1.0\ X_2 && - 5.0\ X_3 - 2.0\ X_4 + 6.0\ X_5 + 4.0\ X_6 &= 1.0 \\
-1.0\ X_1 + 6.0\ X_2 && - 4.0\ X_3 - 5.0\ X_4 + 3.0\ X_5 - 1.0\ X_6 &= -6.0 \\
4.0\ X_1 + 3.0\ X_2 && - 6.0\ X_3 - 5.0\ X_4 - 2.0\ X_5 - 2.0\ X_6 &= 10.0 \\
-3.0\ X_1 + 6.0\ X_2 && + 4.0\ X_3 + 2.0\ X_4 - 6.0\ X_5 + 4.0\ X_6 &= -6.0 \\
2.0\ X_1 - 1.00001\ X_2 && - 5.0\ X_3 - 2.0\ X_4 + 6.0\ X_5 + 4.0\ X_6 &= 1.0001
\end{aligned}
\qquad (11\text{-}7)
$$

If this system of equations is placed in a file called SYS6.ILL, and program test_dsimul is run on this file, the results are[6]

```
C:\book\chap11>test_dsimul
Enter the file name containing the eqns:
sys6.ill

Coefficients:
    -2.0000     5.0000     1.0000     3.0000     4.0000    -1.0000     0.0000
     2.0000    -1.0000    -5.0000    -2.0000     6.0000     4.0000     1.0000
    -1.0000     6.0000    -4.0000    -5.0000     3.0000    -1.0000    -6.0000
     4.0000     3.0000    -6.0000    -5.0000    -2.0000    -2.0000    10.0000
    -3.0000     6.0000     4.0000     2.0000    -6.0000     4.0000    -6.0000
     2.0000    -1.0000    -5.0000    -2.0000     6.0000     4.0000     1.0001

   i      SP x(i)         DP x(i)              SP Err          DP Err
  ===    =========       =========           =========       =========
   1     -44.1711        -38.5295            2.83737278      0.00000000
   2     -11.1934        -10.0000           -3.96770477      0.00000000
   3     -52.9274        -47.1554           -2.92593479      0.00000000
   4      29.8776         26.1372           -4.72321892      0.00000000
   5     -17.9852        -15.8502            4.52078247      0.00000000
   6      -5.69733        -5.08561          -3.96769810      0.00000000

Max single-precision error:    4.72321892
Max double-precision error:    0.00000000
```

For this ill-conditioned system, the results of the single-precision and double-precision calculations were dramatically different. The single-precision numbers x(i) differ from the true answers by almost 20%, while the double-precision answers are almost exactly correct. Double-precision calculations are essential for a correct answer to this

---

[6] To reproduce these results with the Intel Visual Fortran Compiler Version 9.0, it is necessary to compile the program with the "/Od" option, which turns off all optimizations. To reproduce these results with the Lahey Fortran compiler, it is necessary to compile the program with the "-o0" option, which turns off all optimizations. In both cases, if the optimizer is used, the compiler stores intermediate single-precision results as double-precision values in CPU registers, and the calculation is effectively performed in double precision. This practice makes single-precision arithmetic look misleadingly good.

problem! The third system of equations that we will use to test the subroutine is the 6×6 system of equations shown below:

$$
\begin{aligned}
-2.0\ X_1 + 5.0\ X_2 + 1.0\ X_3 + 3.0\ X_4 + 4.0\ X_5 - 1.0\ X_6 &= 0.0 \\
2.0\ X_1 - 1.0\ X_2 - 5.0\ X_3 - 2.0\ X_4 + 6.0\ X_5 + 4.0\ X_6 &= 1.0 \\
-1.0\ X_1 + 6.0\ X_2 - 4.0\ X_3 - 5.0\ X_4 + 3.0\ X_5 - 1.0\ X_6 &= -6.0 \\
4.0\ X_1 + 3.0\ X_2 - 6.0\ X_3 - 5.0\ X_4 - 2.0\ X_5 - 2.0\ X_6 &= 10.0 \\
-3.0\ X_1 + 6.0\ X_2 + 4.0\ X_3 + 2.0\ X_4 - 6.0\ X_5 + 4.0\ X_6 &= -6.0 \\
2.0\ X_1 - 1.0\ X_2 - 5.0\ X_3 - 2.0\ X_4 + 6.0\ X_5 + 4.0\ X_6 &= 1.0
\end{aligned}
\tag{11-8}
$$

If this system of equations is placed in a file called SYS6.SNG, and program test_dsimul is run on this file, the results are:

```
C:\book\chap11>test_dsimul
Enter the file name containing the eqns:
sys6.sng
Coefficients before calls:
  -2.0000     5.0000     1.0000     3.0000     4.0000    -1.0000      .0000
   2.0000    -1.0000    -5.0000    -2.0000     6.0000     4.0000     1.0000
  -1.0000     6.0000    -4.0000    -5.0000     3.0000    -1.0000    -6.0000
   4.0000     3.0000    -6.0000    -5.0000    -2.0000    -2.0000    10.0000
  -3.0000     6.0000     4.0000     2.0000    -6.0000     4.0000    -6.0000
   2.0000    -1.0000    -5.0000    -2.0000     6.0000     4.0000     1.0000

Zero pivot encountered!

There is no unique solution to this system.
```

Since the second and sixth equations of this set are identical, there is no unique solution to this system of equations. The subroutine correctly identified and flagged this situation.

Subroutine dsimul seems to be working correctly for all three cases: well-conditioned systems, ill-conditioned systems, and singular systems. Furthermore, these tests showed the clear advantage of the double-precision subroutine over the single-precision subroutine for ill-conditioned systems.

11.2

ALTERNATE LENGTHS OF THE INTEGER DATA TYPE

The Fortran 95/2003 standard also allows (but does not require) a Fortran compiler to support integers of multiple lengths. The idea of having integers of different lengths is that shorter integers could be used for variables that have a restricted range in order to reduce the size of a program, while longer integers could be used for variables that needed the extra range.

The lengths of supported integers will vary from processor to processor, and the kind type parameters associated with a given length will also vary. You will have

TABLE 11-3
KIND numbers for integer values in some Fortran 95/2003 compilers

Computer/Compiler	int8	int16	int32	int48	int64
Cray supercomputer/CF90	N/A	N/A	1, 2, 4	6*	8
PC/Intel Visual Fortran 95	1	2	4*	N/A	8
PC/Lahey Fortran 95	1	2	4*	N/A	N/A
PC/NAGWare f95	1	2	3*	N/A	4

* Denotes the **default integer** type for a particular processor

to check with your particular compiler vendor to see what lengths are supported by your compiler. The lengths and kind type parameters of integers supported by several processors is shown in Table 11-3. (In the table, int8 is an 8-bit integer, int16 is a 16-bit integer, etc.) Both the lengths of integers supported and the kind type parameters assigned to them differ from processor to processor. This variation creates a problem when we want to write programs that are portable across different types of processors.

How can we write programs so that they can be easily ported between processors with different kind numbers and still function correctly? The best approach is to use a Fortran 95/2003 intrinsic function to *automatically select the proper kind of integer to use* as the program is moved from processor to processor. This function is called SELECTED_INT_KIND. When it is executed, it returns the kind type parameter of the smallest kind of integer value that meets the specified range on that particular computer. The general form of this function is

```
kind_number = SELECTED_INT_KIND(range)
```

where *range* is the required range of the integer in powers of 10. The function returns the kind number of the smallest integer kind satisfying the specified requirements. It returns a -1 if the specified range is not available from any integer data type on the processor.

The following examples are legal uses of this function

```
kind_number = SELECTED_INT_KIND(3)
kind_number = SELECTED_INT_KIND(9)
kind_number = SELECTED_INT_KIND(12)
kind_number = SELECTED_INT_KIND(20)
```

On a Pentium 4–based computer using the Intel Visual Fortran compiler, the first of the functions will return a 2 (the kind number for 2-byte integers), since the specified range is -10^3 to $+10^3$, and a 2-byte integer can hold any number in the range $-32,768$ to 32,767. Similarly, the next function will return a 4 (the kind number for 4-byte integers), since the specified range is -10^9 to $+10^9$, and a 4-byte integer can hold any number in the range $-2,147,483,648$ to 2,147,483,647. The third function will return an 8 (the kind number for 8-byte integers), since the specified range is -10^{12} to $+10^{12}$, and an 8-byte integer can hold any number in the range $-9,223,372,036,854,775,808$ to 9,223,372,036,854,775,807. The last function will return a -1, since no integer data type has a range of -10^{20} to $+10^{20}$. Different results will be returned on other processors; try it on yours and see what you get.

The following code sample illustrates the use of integer kinds in a processor-independent fashion. It declares two integer variables i1 and i2. Integer i1 is guaranteed to be able to hold integer values between $-1,000$ and $1,000$, while integer i2 is guaranteed to be able to hold integer values between $-1,000,000,000$ and $1,000,000,000$. The actual capacity of each integer may vary from computer to computer, but it will always satisfy this minimum guarantee.

```
INTEGER, PARAMETER :: SHORT = SELECTED_INT_KIND(3)
INTEGER, PARAMETER :: LONG  = SELECTED_INT_KIND(9)
INTEGER(KIND=SHORT) :: i1
INTEGER(KIND=LONG) :: i2
```

It is also possible to declare the kind of an integer constant. The kind of an integer constant is declared by appending an underscore and the kind number to the constant. The following are examples of valid integer constants:

```
34           ! Default integer kind
34_4         ! Only valid if 4 is a legal kind of integer
24_LONG      ! Only valid if "LONG" is an integer named constant
```

The first example produces an integer constant of the *default kind* for the particular processor where the program is being executed. The second example is valid only if KIND=4 is a valid kind of integer on the particular processor where the program is being executed. The third example is valid only if LONG is a valid previously defined integer named constant, whose value is a valid kind number.

Good Programming Practice

Use the function SELECTED_INT_KIND to determine the kind numbers of the integer variables needed to solve a problem. The function will return the proper kind numbers on any processor, making your programs more portable.

11

11.3

ALTERNATIVE KINDS OF THE CHARACTER DATA TYPE

Fortran 95/2003 includes a provision for supporting multiple kinds of character sets. Support for multiple character sets is optional, and may not be implemented on your processor. If present, this feature allows the Fortran language to support different character sets for the many different languages found around the world, or even special "languages" such as musical notation.

The general form of a character declaration with a kind parameter is

```
CHARACTER(kind=kind_num,len=length) :: string
```

where *kind_num* is the kind number of the desired character set.

Fortran 2003 includes a new function called SELECTED_CHAR_KIND to return the kind number for a specific character set. When it is executed, it returns the kind type parameter matching a particular character set. The general form of this function is

```
kind_number = SELECTED_CHAR_KIND(name)
```

where *name* is a character expression of the default type containing one of the following values: 'DEFAULT', 'ASCII', or 'ISO_10646'. The function returns the kind number of the corresponding character set if it is supported and a −1 if it is not supported.

The following examples are legal uses of this function

```
kind_number = SELECTED_CHAR_KIND('DEFAULT')
kind_number = SELECTED_CHAR_KIND('ISO_10646')
```

The Fortran 2003 standard does not *require* a compiler to support the Unicode character set, but it provides the support functions required to use Unicode characters if they are present.

11.4

THE COMPLEX DATA TYPE

Complex numbers occur in many problems in science and engineering. For example, complex numbers are used in electrical engineering to represent alternating current voltages, currents, and impedances. The differential equations that describe the behavior of most electrical and mechanical systems also give rise to complex numbers. Because they are so ubiquitous, it is impossible to work as an engineer without a good understanding of the use and manipulation of complex numbers.

A complex number has the general form

$$c = a + bi \tag{11-9}$$

where c is a complex number, a and b are both real numbers, and i is $\sqrt{-1}$. The number a is called the *real part* and b is called the *imaginary part* of the complex number c. Since a complex number has two components, it can be plotted as a point on a plane (see Figure 11-8). The horizontal axis of the plane is the real axis, and the vertical axis of the plane is the imaginary axis, so that any complex number $a + bi$ can be represented as a single point a units along the real axis and b units along the imaginary axis. A complex number represented this way is said to be in *rectangular coordinates,* since the real and imaginary axes define the sides of a rectangle.

A complex number can also be represented as a vector of length z and angle θ pointing from the origin of the plane to the point P (see Figure 11-9). A complex number represented this way is said to be in *polar coordinates.*

$$c = a + bi = z \angle \theta$$

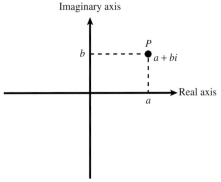

FIGURE 11-8
Representing a complex number in rectangular coordinates.

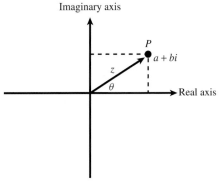

FIGURE 11-9
Representing a complex number in polar coordinates.

The relationships among the rectangular and polar coordinate terms a, b, z, and θ are:

$$a = z \cos \theta \qquad (11\text{-}10)$$

$$b = z \sin \theta \qquad (11\text{-}11)$$

$$z = |c| = \sqrt{a^2 + b^2} \qquad (11\text{-}12)$$

$$\theta = tan^{-1} \frac{b}{a} \qquad (11\text{-}13)$$

Fortran uses rectangular coordinates to represent complex numbers. Each complex number consists of a pair of real numbers (a, b) occupying successive locations in memory. The first number (a) is the real part of the complex number, and the second number (b) is the imaginary part of the complex number.

If complex numbers c_1 and c_2 are defined as $c_1 = a_1 + b_1 i$ and $c_2 = a_2 + b_2 i$, then the addition, subtraction, multiplication, and division of c_1 and c_2 are defined as:

$$c_1 + c_2 = (a_1 + a_2) + (b_1 + b_2)i \qquad (11\text{-}14)$$

$$c_1 - c_2 = (a_1 - a_2) + (b_1 - b_2)i \qquad (11\text{-}15)$$

$$c_1 \times c_2 = (a_1 a_2 - b_1 b_2) + (a_1 b_2 + b_1 a_2)i \qquad (11\text{-}16)$$

$$\frac{c_1}{c_2} = \frac{a_1 a_2 + b_1 b_2}{a_2^2 + b_2^2} + \frac{b_1 a_2 - a_1 b_2}{a_2^2 + b_2^2} i \qquad (11\text{-}17)$$

When two complex numbers appear in a binary operation, Fortran performs the required additions, subtractions, multiplications, or divisions between the two complex numbers, using the above formulas.

11.4.1 Complex Constants and Variables

A **complex constant** consists of two numeric constants separated by commas and enclosed in parentheses. The first constant is the real part of the complex number, and the second constant is the imaginary part of the complex number. For example, the following complex constants are equivalent to the complex numbers shown next to them:

```
(1., 0.)                 1 + 0i
(0.7071,0.7071)          0.7071 + 0.7071i
(0., -1.)                −i
(1.01E6, 0.5E2)          1010000 + 50i
(1.12_DBL, 0.1_DBL)      1.12 + 0.1i   (Kind is DBL)
```

The last constant will only be valid if `DBL` is a named constant that has been set to a valid kind number for real data on the particular processor where the constant is used.

In Fortran 2003, a named constant may be used to specify either the real or imaginary part of a complex constant. Thus, if `PI` is a named constant, then the following is a valid Fortran 2003 complex constant:

```
             (PI,-PI)                 π + πi
```

A complex variable is declared by using a `COMPLEX` type declaration statement. The form of this statement is

```
COMPLEX(KIND=kind_num) :: :: variable_name1 [,variable_name2, ...]
```

The kind of the complex variable is optional; if it is left out the default kind will be used. For example, the following statement declares a 256 element complex array. Remember that we are actually allocating 512 default-length values, since two real values are required for each complex number.

```
COMPLEX, DIMENSION(256) :: array
```

There are at least two kinds of complex values on any processor, corresponding to the single-precision and double-precision kinds of real data. The single-precision version of the complex data type will have the same kind number as the single-precision version of the real data type, and the double-precision version of the complex data type will have the same kind number as the double-precision version of the real data type. Therefore, the intrinsic function SELECTED_REAL_KIND can also be used to specify the size of complex data in a processor-independent manner.

The **default complex** kind will always be the same as the default real kind on any given processor.

11.4.2 Initializing Complex Variables

Like other variables, complex variables may be initialized by assignment statements, in type declaration statements, or by READ statements. The following code initializes all of the elements of array array1 to (0.,0.), using an assignment statement.

```
COMPLEX, DIMENSION(256) :: array1
array1 = (0.,0.)
```

A complex number may also be initialized in a type declaration statement by using a complex constant. The following code declares and initializes variable a1 to (3.141592,-3.141592), using a type declaration statement.

```
COMPLEX :: a1 = (3.141592, -3.141592)
```

When a complex number is read or written with a formatted I/O statement, the first format descriptor encountered is used for the real part of the complex number, and the second format descriptor encountered is used for the imaginary part of the complex number. The following code initializes variable a1, using a formatted READ statement.

```
COMPLEX :: a1
READ (*,'(2F10.2)') a1
```

The value in the first 10 characters of the input line will be placed in the real part of variable a1, and the value in the second 10 characters of the input line will be placed in the imaginary part of variable a1. Note that no parentheses are included on the input line when we read a complex number by using formatted I/O. In contrast, when we read a complex number with a *list-directed* I/O statement, the complex number must be typed exactly like a complex constant, parentheses and all. The following READ statement

```
COMPLEX :: a1
READ (*,*) a1
```

requires that the input value be typed as shown: (1.0,0.25). When a complex number is written with a free-format WRITE statement, it is output as a complex value complete with parentheses. For example, the statements

```
COMPLEX :: a1 = (1.0,0.25)
WRITE (*,*) a1
```

produce the result:

```
(1.000000,2.500000E-01)
```

11.4.3 Mixed-Mode Arithmetic

When an arithmetic operation is performed between a complex number and another number (any kind of real or integer), Fortran converts the other number into a complex number, and then performs the operation, with a complex result. For example, the following code will produce an output of (300.,-300.):

```
COMPLEX :: c1 = (100.,-100.), c2
INTEGER :: i = 3
c2 = c1 * i
WRITE (*,*) c2
```

Initially, c1 is a complex variable containing the value (100.,-100.), and i is an integer containing the value 3. When the fourth line is executed, the integer i is converted into the complex number (3.,0.), and that number is multiplied by c1 to give the result (300.,-300.).

When an arithmetic operation is performed between two complex or real numbers of different kinds, *both numbers are converted into the kind having the higher decimal precision* before the operation, and the resulting value will have the higher precision.

If a real expression is assigned to a complex variable, the value of the expression is placed in the real part of the complex variable, and the imaginary part of the complex variable is set to zero. If two real values need to be assigned to the real and imaginary parts of a complex variable, then the CMPLX function (described below) must be used. When a complex value is assigned to a real or integer variable, *the real part of the complex number is placed in the variable, and the imaginary part is discarded.*

11.4.4 Using Complex Numbers with Relational Operators

It is possible to compare two complex numbers with the == relational operator to see if they are equal to each other, and to compare them with the /= operator to see if they are not equal to each other. However, they *cannot be compared with the >, <, >=, or <= operators*. The reason for this is that complex numbers consist of two separate parts. Suppose that we have two complex numbers $c_1 = a_1 + b_1 i$ and $c_2 = a_2 + b_2 i$, with $a_1 > a_2$ and $b_1 < b_2$. How can we possibly say which of these numbers is larger?

On the other hand, it is possible to compare the *magnitudes* of two complex numbers. The magnitude of a complex number can be calculated with the CABS intrinsic function (see below), or directly from Equation 11-12.

$$|c| = \sqrt{a^2 + b^2} \qquad\qquad (11\text{-}12)$$

Since the magnitude of a complex number is a real value, two magnitudes can be compared with any of the relational operators.

11.4.5 COMPLEX **Intrinsic Functions**

Fortran includes many specific and generic functions that support complex calculations. These functions fall into three general categories:

1. **Type conversion functions.** These functions convert data to and from the complex data type. Function CMPLX(a,b,*kind*) is a generic function that converts real or integer numbers a and b into a complex number whose real part has value a and whose imaginary part has value b. The kind parameter is optional; if it is specified, then the resulting complex number will be of the specified kind. Functions REAL() and INT() convert the *real part* of a complex number into the corresponding real or integer data type, and throw away the imaginary part of the complex number. Function AIMAG() converts the *imaginary part* of a complex number into a real number.

2. **Absolute value function.** This function calculates the absolute value of a number. Function CABS(c) is a specific function that calculates the absolute value of a complex number, using the equation

$$CABS(c) = \sqrt{a^2 + b^2}$$

where $c = a + bi$.

3. **Mathematical functions.** These functions include exponential functions, logarithms, trigonometric functions, and square roots. The generic functions SIN, COS, LOG10, SQRT, etc. will work as well with complex data as they will with real data.

Some of the intrinsic functions that support complex numbers are listed in Table 11-4.

It is important to be careful when converting a complex number to a real number. If we use the REAL() or DBLE() functions to do the conversion, only the *real* portion of the complex number is translated. In many cases, what we really want is the *magnitude* of the complex number. If so, we must use ABS() instead of REAL() to do the conversion.

Programming Pitfalls
Be careful when converting a complex number into a real number. Find out whether the real part of the number or the magnitude of the number is needed, and use the proper function to do the conversion.

Also, it is important to be careful in using double-precision variables with the function CMPLX. The Fortran standard states that *the function* CMPLX *returns a result*

■ **TABLE 11-4**
Some intrinsic functions that support complex numbers

Generic function	Specific function	Function value	Comments
ABS(c)	CABS(c)	$\sqrt{a^2+b^2}$	Calculate magnitude of a complex number (result is a real value of the same kind as c)
CMPLX(a,b,*kind*)			Combines a and b into a complex number $a + bi$ (a, b may be integer, real, or double precision). *kind* is an optional integer. If present, it specifies the kind of the resulting complex number. If not specified, the kind will be default complex.
	CONJG(c)	c^*	Calculate the complex conjugate of c. If $c = a + bi$, then $c^* = a - bi$.
DBLE(c)			Convert real part of c into a double-precision real number.
INT(c)			Convert real part of c into an integer.
REAL(c,*kind*)			Convert real part of c into a real number. *kind* is an optional integer. If present, it specifies the kind of the resulting real number.

of the default complex kind regardless of its input arguments, unless another kind is explicitly specified. This can lead to a trap in which a programmer accidentally loses precision without being aware of it. Consider the following code as an example. In it we declare two double-precision real variables and a double-precision complex variable, and try to assign the contents of the two real variables to the complex variable. Because the kind is not specified in the CMPLX function, the accuracy of the information in the complex variable is reduced to single precision.

```
PROGRAM test_complex
INTEGER, PARAMETER :: DBL = SELECTED_REAL_KIND(p=13)
COMPLEX(KIND=DBL) :: c1 = (0.,0.)
REAL(KIND=DBL) :: a1 = 3.333333333333333_DBL
REAL(KIND=DBL) :: b1 = 6.666666666666666_DBL
c1 = CMPLX(a1,b1)
WRITE (*,*) c1
END PROGRAM test_complex
```

When this program is executed, the result is accurate only to single precision:

```
C:\book\chap11>test_complex
              (3.333333253860474,6.666666507720947)
```

To get the desired result, the CMPLX function must be rewritten as with the kind of the result specified:

```
c1 = CMPLX(a1,b1,DBL)
```

Programming Pitfalls
Be careful to specify the output kind type parameter when using the CMPLX function with double-precision values. Failure to do so can produce mysterious losses of precision within a program.

EXAMPLE   *The Quadratic Equation (Revisited):*
11-3

Write a general program to solve for the roots of a quadratic equation, regardless of type. Use complex variables so that no branches based on the value of the discriminant will be required.

SOLUTION

1. **State the problem.**
    Write a program that will solve for the roots of a quadratic equation, whether they are distinct real roots, repeated real roots, or complex roots, without requiring tests on the value of the discriminant.

2. **Define the inputs and outputs.**
    The inputs required by this program are the coefficients *a, b,* and *c* of the quadratic equation

$$ax^2 + bx + c = 0 \tag{3-1}$$

The output from the program will be the roots of the quadratic equation, whether they are real, repeated, or complex.

3. **Describe the algorithm.**
    This task can be broken down into three major sections, whose functions are input, processing, and output:

```
Read the input data
Calculate the roots
Write out the roots
```

We will now break each of the above major sections into smaller, more detailed pieces. In this algorithm, the value of the discriminant is unimportant in determining how to proceed. The resulting pseudocode is:

```
Write 'Enter the coefficients A, B, and C: '
Read in a, b, c
discriminant ← CMPLX( b**2 - 4.*a*c, 0. )
x1 ← ( -b + SQRT(discriminant) ) / ( 2. * a )
x2 ← ( -b - SQRT(discriminant) ) / ( 2. * a )
Write 'The roots of this equation are: '
Write 'x1 = ', REAL(x1), ' +i ', AIMAG(x1)
Write 'x2 = ', REAL(x2), ' +i ', AIMAG(x2)
```

11

4. **Turn the algorithm into Fortran statements.**

The final Fortran code is shown in Figure 11-10.

FIGURE 11-10

A program to solve the quadratic equation using complex numbers.

```
PROGRAM roots_2
!
!   Purpose:
!     To find the roots of a quadratic equation
!        A * X**2 + B * X + C = 0.
!     using complex numbers to eliminate the need to branch
!     based on the value of the discriminant.
!
!   Record of revisions:
!        Date        Programmer          Description of change
!        ====        ==========          =====================
!     12/01/06     S. J. Chapman         Original code
!
IMPLICIT NONE

! Data dictionary: declare variable types & definitions
REAL :: a                   ! The coefficient of X**2
REAL :: b                   ! The coefficient of X
REAL :: c                   ! The constant coefficient
REAL :: discriminant        ! The discriminant of the quadratic eqn
COMPLEX :: x1               ! First solution to the equation
COMPLEX :: x2               ! Second solution to the equation

! Get the coefficients.
WRITE (*,1000)
1000 FORMAT (' Program to solve for the roots of a quadratic', &
            /,' equation of the form A * X**2 + B * X + C = 0. ' )
WRITE (*,1010)
1010 FORMAT (' Enter the coefficients A, B, and C: ')
READ (*,*) a, b, c

! Calculate the discriminant
discriminant = b**2 - 4. * a * c

! Calculate the roots of the equation
x1 = ( -b + SQRT( CMPLX(discriminant,0.) ) ) ) / (2. * a)
x2 = ( -b - SQRT( CMPLX(discriminant,0.) ) ) ) / (2. * a)

! Tell user.
WRITE (*,*) 'The roots are: '
WRITE (*,1020) ' x1 = ', REAL(x1), ' + i ', AIMAG(x1)
WRITE (*,1020) ' x2 = ', REAL(x2), ' + i ', AIMAG(x2)
1020 FORMAT (A,F10.4,A,F10.4)

END PROGRAM roots_2
```

5. **Test the program.**

Next, we must test the program using real input data. We will test cases in which the discriminant is greater than, less than, and equal to 0 to be certain that the program is working properly under all circumstances. From Equation (3-1), it is possible to verify the solutions to the equations given below:

$$x^2 + 5x + 6 = 0 \qquad\qquad x = -2 \text{ and } x = -3$$
$$x^2 + 4x + 4 = 0 \qquad\qquad x = -2$$
$$x^2 + 2x + 5 = 0 \qquad\qquad x = -1 \pm 2i$$

When the above coefficients are fed into the program, the results are

```
C:\book\chap11>roots_2
Program to solve for the roots of a quadratic
equation of the form A * X**2 + B * X + C.
Enter the coefficients A, B, and C:
1,5,6
The roots are:
   X1 =    -2.0000 + i       .0000
   X2 =    -3.0000 + i       .0000

C:\book\chap11>roots_2
Program to solve for the roots of a quadratic
equation of the form A * X**2 + B * X + C.
Enter the coefficients A, B, and C:
1,4,4
The roots are:
   X1 =    -2.0000 + i       .0000
   X2 =    -2.0000 + i       .0000

C:\book\chap11>roots_2
Program to solve for the roots of a quadratic
equation of the form A * X**2 + B * X + C.
Enter the coefficients A, B, and C:
1,2,5
The roots are:
   X1 =    -1.0000 + i      2.0000
   X2 =    -1.0000 + i     -2.0000
```

The program gives the correct answers for our test data in all three possible cases. Note how much simpler this program is compared to the quadratic root solver found in Example 3-1. The use of the complex data type has greatly simplified our program.

Quiz 11-1:

This quiz provides a quick check to see if you have understood the concepts introduced in Sections 11.1 through 11.4. If you have trouble with the quiz, reread the sections, ask your instructor, or discuss the material with a fellow student. The answers to this quiz are found in the back of the book.

(continued)

(concluded)

1. What kinds of real numbers and integers are supported by your compiler? What are the kind numbers associated with each one?
2. What will be written out by the code shown below?

```
COMPLEX :: a, b, c, d
a = ( 1., -1. )
b = ( -1., -1. )
c = ( 10., 1. )
d = ( a + b ) / c
WRITE (*,*) d
```

3. Use the definitions in Equations 11-14 through 11-17 to write a computer program that evaluates d in the problem above *without using complex numbers*. How much harder is it to evaluate this expression without the benefit of complex numbers?

11.5

SUMMARY

In this chapter, we introduced the concept of kinds and kind type parameters. Kinds are versions of the same basic data type, each differing in size, precision, range, etc.

All Fortran compilers support at least two kinds of real data, which are usually known as single precision and double precision. Double-precision data occupies twice the memory of single-precision data on most computers. Double-precision variables have both a greater range and more significant digits than single-precision variables.

The choice of precision for a particular real value is specified by the kind type parameter in the type declaration statement. Unfortunately, the numbers associated with each kind of real value vary among different processors. They can be determined by using the KIND intrinsic function on a particular processor, or the desired precision can be specified in a processor-independent manner by using the SELECTED_REAL_ KIND intrinsic function.

Double-precision real numbers take up more space and require more computer time to calculate than single-precision real numbers, so they should not be used indiscriminately. In general, they should be used when:

1. A problem requires many significant digits or a large range of numbers.
2. Numbers of dramatically different sizes must be added or subtracted.
3. Two nearly equal numbers must be subtracted, and the result used in further calculations.

Fortran 95/2003 permits (but does not require) a compiler to support multiple kinds of integers. Not all compilers will support multiple kinds of integers. The kind numbers associated with particular integer lengths vary from processor to processor. Fortran includes an intrinsic function SELECTED_INT_KIND to help programmers select the kind of integer required for a particular application in a processor-independent manner.

Fortran 95/2003 also allows a compiler to support multiple kinds of character sets. If your compiler implements this feature, you can use it to write out character data in different languages. Fortran 2003 also includes an intrinsic function SELECTED_CHAR_KIND to help programmers select the kind number of the ASCII or Unicode character set in a processor-independent manner.

F-2003 ONLY

Complex numbers consist of two real numbers in successive locations in memory. These two numbers are treated as though they were the real and imaginary parts of a complex number expressed in rectangular coordinates. They are processed according to the rules for complex addition, subtraction, multiplication, division, etc. There is a kind of complex number corresponding to each kind of real number available on a particular processor. The kind numbers are identical for real and complex data, so the desired precision of a complex value may be selected by using the SELECTED_REAL_KIND intrinsic function.

Complex constants are written as two numbers in parentheses, separated by commas [for example: (1.,-1.)]. Complex variables are declared by using a COMPLEX type declaration statement. They may be read and written by using any type of real format descriptor (E, ES, F, etc.). When complex numbers are read or written, the real and imaginary parts of the number are processed separately. The first value read will become the real part, and the next value will become the imaginary part. If list-directed input is used with complex numbers, the input value must be typed as a complex constant, complete with parentheses.

In a binary operation involving a complex number and an integer or real number, the other number is first converted to complex, and then the operation is performed by using complex arithmetic. All arithmetic is performed at the highest precision of any number in the calculation.

11.5.1 Summary of Good Programming Practice

The following guidelines should be adhered to when you are working with parameterized variables, complex numbers, and derived data types:

1. Always assign kind numbers to a named constant, and then use that named constant in all type declaration statements and constant declarations. For large programs with many procedures, place the kind parameters in a single module, and then use that module in every procedure within the program.
2. Use the function SELECTED_REAL_KIND to determine the kind numbers of the real values needed to solve a problem. The function will return the proper kind numbers on any processor, making your programs more portable.

3. Use the function SELECTED_INT_KIND to determine the kind numbers of the integer variables needed to solve a problem.

4. Use double-precision real numbers instead of single-precision real numbers whenever:

   (*a*) A problem requires many significant digits or a large range of numbers.

   (*b*) Numbers of dramatically different sizes must be added or subtracted.

   (*c*) Two nearly equal numbers must be subtracted, and the result used in further calculations.

5. Be careful when you are converting a complex number to a real or double-precision number. If you use the REAL() or DBLE() functions, only the *real* portion of the complex number is translated. In many cases, what we really want is the *magnitude* of the complex number. If so, we must use CABS() instead of REAL() to do the conversion.

6. Be careful when you are converting a pair of double-precision real numbers into a complex number, using function CMPLX. If you do not explicitly specify that the kind of the function result is double precision, the result will be of type default complex, and precision will be lost.

11.5.2 Summary of Fortran Statements and Structures

COMPLEX **Statement:**

```
COMPLEX(KIND=kind_no) :: variable_name1 [,variable_name2, ...]
```

Examples:

```
COMPLEX(KIND=single) :: volts, amps
```

Description:
The COMPLEX statement declares variables of the complex data type. The kind number is optional and machine dependent. If it is not present, the kind is the default complex kind for the particular machine (usually single precision).

REAL **Statement with** KIND **parameter:**

```
REAL(KIND=kind_no) :: variable_name1 [,variable_name2,...]
```

Examples:

```
REAL(KIND=single), DIMENSION(100) :: points
```

(continued)

11

(concluded)

Description:
The REAL statement is a type declaration statement that declares variables of the real data type. The kind number is optional and machine dependent. If it is not present, the kind is the default real kind for the particular machine (usually single precision).

   To specify double-precision real values, the kind must be set to the appropriate number for the particular machine. The kind number may be found by using the function KIND(0.0D0) or by using the function SELECTED_REAL_KIND.

11.5.3 Exercises

11-1. What are kinds of the REAL data type? How many kinds of real data must be supported by a compiler according to the Fortran 95/2003 standard?

11-2. What kind numbers are associated with the different types of real variables available on your compiler/computer? Determine the precision and range associated with each type of real data.

11-3. What are the advantages and disadvantages of double-precision real numbers compared to single-precision real numbers? When should double-precision real numbers be used instead of single-precision real numbers?

11-4. What is an ill-conditioned system of equations? Why is it hard to find the solution to an ill-conditioned set of equations?

11-5. State whether each of the following sets of Fortran statements are legal or illegal. If they are illegal, what is wrong with them? If they are legal, what do they do?

   (*a*) Statements:
```
INTEGER, PARAMETER :: SGL = KIND(0.0)
INTEGER, PARAMETER :: DBL = KIND(0.0D0)
REAL(KIND=SGL) :: a
REAL(KIND=DBL) :: b
READ (*,'(F18.2)') a, b
WRITE (*,*) a, b
```

   Input data:
```
11111111111111111111111111111111111111111
22222222222222222222222222222222222222222
----|----|----|----|----|----|----|----|
    5   10   15   20   25   30   35   40
```

   (*b*) Statements:
```
INTEGER, PARAMETER :: SINGLE = SELECTED_REAL_KIND(p=6)
COMPLEX(kind=SINGLE), DIMENSION(5) :: a1
INTEGER :: i
```

11

```
DO i = 1, 5
   a1(i) = CMPLX ( i, -2*i )
END DO
IF (a1(5) > a1(3)) THEN
   WRITE (*,100) (i, a1(i), i = 1, 5)
   100 FORMAT (3X,'a1(',I2,') = (',F10.4,',',F10.4,')')
END IF
```

11-6. Derivative of a Function Write a subroutine to calculate the derivative of a double-precision real function $f(x)$ at position $x = x_0$. The calling arguments to the subroutine should be the function $f(x)$, the location x_0 at which to evaluate the function, and the step size Δx to use in the evaluation. The output from the subroutine will be the derivative of the function at point $x = x_0$. To make your subroutine machine independent, define double precision as the kind of real value having at least 13 digits of precision. Note that the function to be evaluated should be passed to the subroutine as a calling argument. Test your subroutine by evaluating the function $f(x) = 10 \sin 20x$ at position $x = 0$.

11-7. If you have not done so previously, write a set of elapsed-time subroutines for your computer, as described in Exercise 7-29. Use the elapsed-time subroutines to compare the time required to solve a 10×10 system of simultaneous equations in single precision and in double precision. To do this, you will need to write two test driver programs (one single precision and one double precision) that read the coefficients of the equations, start the timer running, solve the equations, and then calculate the elapsed time. How much slower is the double-precision solution than the single-precision solution on your computer? (*Hint*: If you have a very fast computer, you might have to create an inner loop and solve the system of equations 10 or more times in order to get a meaningful elapsed time.)

Test your program on the system of equations shown below (this set of equations is contained in file SYS10 in directory chap11 at the book's website.):

$$
\begin{aligned}
-2x_1 + 5x_2 + x_3 + 3x_4 + 4x_5 - x_6 + 2x_7 - x_8 - 5x_9 - 2x_{10} &= -5 \\
6x_1 + 4x_2 - x_3 + 6x_4 - 4x_5 - 5x_6 + 3x_7 - x_8 + 4x_9 + 3x_{10} &= -6 \\
-6x_1 - 5x_2 - 2x_3 - 2x_4 - 3x_5 + 6x_6 + 4x_7 + 2x_8 - 6x_9 + 4x_{10} &= -7 \\
2x_1 + 4x_2 + 4x_3 + 4x_4 + 5x_5 - 4x_6 + 0x_7 + 0x_8 - 4x_9 + 6x_{10} &= 0 \\
-4x_1 - x_2 + 3x_3 - 3x_4 - 4x_5 - 4x_6 - 4x_7 + 4x_8 + 3x_9 - 3x_{10} &= 5 \\
4x_1 + 3x_2 + 5x_3 + x_4 + x_5 + x_6 + 0x_7 + 3x_8 + 3x_9 + 6x_{10} &= -8 \\
x_1 + 2x_2 - 2x_3 + 0x_4 + 3x_5 - 5x_6 + 5x_7 + 0x_8 + x_9 - 4x_{10} &= 1 \\
-3x_1 - 4x_2 + 2x_3 - x_4 - 2x_5 + 5x_6 - x_7 - x_8 - 4x_9 + x_{10} &= -4 \\
5x_1 + 5x_2 - 2x_3 - 5x_4 + x_5 - 4x_6 - x_7 + 0x_8 - 2x_9 - 3x_{10} &= -7 \\
-5x_1 - 2x_2 - 5x_3 + 2x_4 + x_5 - 3x_6 + 4x_7 - x_8 - 4x_9 + 4x_{10} &= 6
\end{aligned}
$$

11-8. Write a program to determine the kinds of integers supported by your particular compiler. The program should use the function SELECTED_INT_KIND with various input ranges to determine all legal kind numbers. What are the kind numbers and ranges associated with each kind of integer?

11-9. Simultaneous Equations with Complex Coefficients Create a subroutine csimul to solve for the unknowns in a system of simultaneous linear equations that have complex coefficients. Test your subroutine by solving the system of equations shown below.

$$(-2+i5)x_1 + \quad (1+i3)x_2 + (4-i1)x_3 = (7+i5)$$
$$(2-i1)x_1 + (-5-i2)x_2 + (6+i4)x_3 = (-10-i8)$$
$$(-1+i6)x_1 + (-4-i5)x_2 + (3-i1)x_3 = (-3-i3)$$

11-10. Amplitude and Phase of a Complex Number Write a subroutine that will accept a complex number $c = a + ib$ stored in a variable of type `COMPLEX`, and return the amplitude `amp` and the phase `theta` (in degrees) of the complex number in two real variables. (*Hint:* Use intrinsic function `ATAN2` to help calculate the phase.)

11-11. Euler's Equation Euler's equation defines e raised to an imaginary power in terms of sinusoidal functions as follows:

$$e^{i\theta} \quad = \cos\theta + i\sin\theta \qquad\qquad (11\text{-}18)$$

Write a function to evaluate $e^{i\theta}$ for any θ using Euler's equation. Also, evaluate $e^{i\theta}$ using the intrinsic complex exponential function `CEXP`. Compare the answers that you get by the two methods for the cases where $\theta = 0$, $\pi/2$, and π.

11

Derived Data Types

OBJECTIVES

- Learn how to declare a derived data type.
- Learn how to create and use variables of a derived data type.

- Learn how to create parameterized versions of a derived data type (Fortran 2003 only).
- Learn how to create derived data types that are extensions of other data types (Fortran 2003 only).
- Learn how to create and use type-bound procedures (Fortran 2003 only).
- Learn how to use the ASSOCIATE construct (Fortran 2003 only).

In this chapter, we will introduce derived data types. The derived data type is a mechanism for users to create special new data types to suit the needs of a particular problem that they may be trying to solve.

The features of derived data types have been expanded dramatically in Fortran 2003, and many sections of this chapter deal with Fortran 2003–only features.

■ 12.1

INTRODUCTION TO DERIVED DATA TYPES

So far, we have studied Fortran's **intrinsic data types:** integer, real, complex, logical, and character. In addition to these data types, the Fortran language permits us to create our own data types to add new features to the language, or to make it easier to solve specific types of problems. A user-defined data type may have any number and combination of components, but each component must be either an intrinsic data type or a user-defined data type, which was previously defined. Because user-defined data types must be ultimately derived from intrinsic data types, they are called **derived data types.**

Basically, a derived data type is a convenient way to group together all of the information about a particular item. In some ways, it is like an array. Like an array, a single derived data type can have many components. Unlike an array, the components of a derived data type may have different types. One component may be an integer, while the next component is a real, the next a character string, and so forth. Furthermore, each component is known by a name instead of a number.

A derived data type is defined by a sequence of type declaration statements beginning with a TYPE statement and ending with an END TYPE statement. Between these two statements are the definitions of the components in the derived data type. The form of a derived data type is

```
TYPE [::] type_name
   component definitions
   . . .
END TYPE [type_name]
```

where the double colons and the name on the END TYPE statement are optional. There may be as many component definitions in a derived data type as desired.

To illustrate the use of a derived data type, let's suppose that we were writing a grading program. The program would contain information about the students in a class—such as name, social security number, age, sex, etc. We could define a special data type called person to contain all of the personal information about each person in the program:

```
TYPE :: person
   CHARACTER(len=14) :: first_name
   CHARACTER :: middle_initial
   CHARACTER(len=14) :: last_name
   CHARACTER(len=14) :: phone
   INTEGER :: age
   CHARACTER :: sex
   CHARACTER(len=11) :: ssn
END TYPE person
```

Once the derived type person is defined, variables of that type may be declared as shown:

```
TYPE (person) :: john, jane
TYPE (person), DIMENSION(100) :: people
```

The latter statement declares an array of 100 variables of type person. Each item of a derived data type is known as a **structure.**

It is also possible to create unnamed constants of a derived data type. To do so, we use a **structure constructor.** A structure constructor consists of the name of the type followed by the components of the derived data type in parentheses. The components appear in the order in which they were declared in the definition of the derived type. For example, the variables john and jane could be initialized by constants of type person as follows:

```
john = person('John','R','Jones','323-6439',21,'M','123-45-6789')
jane = person('Jane','C','Bass','332-3060',17,'F','999-99-9999')
```

A derived data type may be used as a component within another derived data type. For example, a grading program could include a derived data type called grade_info containing a component of the type `person` defined above to contain personal information about the students in the class. The example below defines the derived type `grade_info`, and declares an array `class` to be 30 variables of this type.

```
TYPE :: grade_info
   TYPE (person) :: student
   INTEGER :: num_quizzes
   REAL, DIMENSION(10) :: quiz_grades
   INTEGER :: num_exams
   REAL, DIMENSION(10) :: exam_grades
   INTEGER :: final_exam_grade
   REAL :: average
END TYPE
TYPE (grade_info), DIMENSION(30) :: class
```

12.2

WORKING WITH DERIVED DATA TYPES

Each component in a variable of a derived data type can be addressed independently, and can be used just like any other variable of the same type; if the component is an integer, then it can be used just like any other integer, etc. A component is specified by a **component selector,** which consists of the name of the variable followed by a percent sign (%) and then followed by the component name. For example, the following statement sets the component `age` of variable `john` to 35:

```
john%age = 35
```

To address a component within an array of a derived data type, *place the array subscript after the array name and before the percent sign.* For example, to set the final exam grade for student 5 in array `class` above, we would write:

```
class(5)%final_exam_grade = 95
```

To address a component of a derived data type that is included within another derived data type, we simply concatenate their names separated by percent signs. Thus, we could set the age of student 5 within the class with the statement:

```
class(5)%student%age = 23
```

As you can see, it is easy to work with the components of a variable of a derived data type. However, it is *not* easy to work with variables of derived data types as a whole. It is legal to assign one variable of a given derived data type to another variable of the same type, but that is almost the only operation that is defined. Other intrinsic operations such as addition, subtraction, multiplication, division, and comparison are not defined by default for these variables. We will learn how to extend these operations to work properly with derived data types in Chapter 13.

12.3

INPUT AND OUTPUT OF DERIVED DATA TYPES

If a variable of a derived data type is included in a WRITE statement, then by default each of the components of the variable are written out in the order in which they are declared in the type definition. If the WRITE statement uses formatted I/O, then the format descriptors must match the type and order of the components in the variable.[1]

Similarly, if a variable of a derived data type is included in a READ statement, then the input data must be supplied in the order in which each of the components is declared in the type definition. If the READ statement uses formatted I/O, then the format descriptors must match the type and order of the components in the variable.

The program shown in Figure 12-1 illustrates the output of a variable of type person using both formatted and free format I/O.

FIGURE 12-1
A program to illustrate output of variables of derived data types.

```
PROGRAM test_io
!
!  Purpose:
!    To illustrate I/O of variables of derived data types.
!
!  Record of revisions:
!      Date          Programmer          Description of change
!      ====          ==========          =====================
!    12/04/06     S. J. Chapman          Original code
!
IMPLICIT NONE

! Declare type person
TYPE :: person
   CHARACTER(len=14) :: first_name
   CHARACTER :: middle_initial
   CHARACTER(len=14) :: last_name
   CHARACTER(len=14) :: phone
   INTEGER :: age
   CHARACTER :: sex
   CHARACTER(len=11) :: ssn
END TYPE person

! Declare a variable of type person:
TYPE (person) :: john

! Initialize variable
john = person('John','R','Jones','323-6439',21,'M','123-45-6789')

! Output variable using free format I/O
WRITE (*,*) 'Free format: ', john
```

(continued)

[1] There is a way to modify this behavior in Fortran 2003, as we will see in Chapter 16.

(concluded)

```
! Output variable using formatted I/O
WRITE (*,1000) john
1000 FORMAT (' Formatted I/O:',/,4(1X,A,/),1X,I4,/,1X,A,/,1X,A)

END PROGRAM test_io
```

When this program is executed, the results are:

```
C:\book\chap12>test_io
Free format:       John        RJones       323-6439       21M123-45-6789

Formatted I/O:
John
R
Jones
323-6439
  21
M
123-45-6789
```

12.4

DECLARING DERIVED DATA TYPES IN MODULES

As we have seen, the definition of a derived data type can be fairly bulky. This definition must be included in every procedure that uses variables or constants of the derived type, which can present a painful maintenance problem in large programs. To avoid this problem, it is customary to define all derived data types in a program in a single module, and then to use that module in all procedures needing to use the data type. This practice is illustrated in Example 12-1 below.

Good Programming Practice

For large programs using derived data types, declare the definitions of each data type in a module, and then use that module in each procedure of the program that needs to access the derived data type.

12

MEMORY ALLOCATION FOR DERIVED DATA TYPES

When a Fortran compiler allocates memory for a variable of a derived data type, the compiler is *not* required to allocate the elements of the derived data type in successive memory locations. Instead, it is free to place them anywhere it wants, as long as the proper element order is preserved during I/O operations. This freedom was deliberately built into the Fortran 95 and Fortran 2003 standards to allow compilers on massively parallel computers to optimize memory allocations for the fastest possible performance.

However, there are times when a strict order of memory allocations is important. For example, if we want to pass a variable of a derived data type to a procedure written in another language, it is necessary for the elements of that variable to be in strict order.

If the elements of a derived data type must be allocated in consecutive memory locations for some reason, a special SEQUENCE statement must be included in the type definition. An example of a derived data type whose elements will always be declared in consecutive locations in memory is:

```
TYPE :: vector
    SEQUENCE
    REAL :: a
    REAL :: b
    REAL :: c
END TYPE
```

EXAMPLE 12-1

Sorting Derived Data Types by Components:

To illustrate the use of derived data types, we will create a small customer database program that permits us to read in a database of customer names and addresses, and to sort and display the addresses by either last name, city, or zip code.

SOLUTION
To solve this problem, we will create a simple derived data type containing the personal information about each customer in the database, and initialize the customer database from a disk file. Once the database is initialized, we will prompt the user for the desired display order and sort the data into that order.

1. **State the problem.**
   Write a program to create a database of customers from a data file, and to sort and display that database in alphabetical order by either last name, city, or zip code.

2. **Define the inputs and outputs.**
   The inputs to the program are the name of the customer database file, the customer database file itself, and an input value from the user, specifying the order in which the data is to be sorted. The output from the program is the customer list, sorted in alphabetical order by the selected field.

3. **Describe the algorithm.**
   The first step in writing this program will be to create a derived data type to hold all of the information about each customer. This data type will need to be placed in a module so that it can be used by each procedure in the program. An appropriate data type definition is shown below:

```
TYPE :: personal_info
    CHARACTER(len=12) :: first          ! First name
```

```
        CHARACTER            :: mi         ! Middle Initial
        CHARACTER(len=12) :: last          ! Last name
        CHARACTER(len=26) :: street        ! Street Address
        CHARACTER(len=12) :: city          ! City
        CHARACTER(len=2)  :: state         ! State
        INTEGER              :: zip         ! Zip code
     END TYPE personal_info
```

The program can logically be broken up into two sections: a main program that reads and writes the customer database and a separate procedure that sorts the data into the selected order. The top-level pseudocode for the main program is

```
Get name of customer data file
Read customer data file
Prompt for sort order
Sort data in specified order
Write out sorted customer data
```

Now we must expand and refine the pseudocode for the main program. We must describe in more detail how the data will be read in, how the sort order is selected, and how the sorting is done. A detailed version of the pseudocode for the main program is shown below.

```
Prompt user for the input file name "filename"
Read the file name "filename"
OPEN file "filename"
IF OPEN is successful THEN
   WHILE
      Read value into temp
      IF read not successful EXIT
      nvals ← nvals + 1
      customers(nvals) ← temp
   End of WHILE

   Prompt user for type of sort (1=last name;2=city;3=zip)
   Read choice
   SELECT CASE (choice)
   CASE (1)
      Call sort_database with last_name comparison function
   CASE (2)
      Call sort_database with city comparison function
   CASE (3)
      Call sort_database with zip code comparison function
   CASE DEFAULT
      Tell user of illegal choice
   END of SELECT CASE

   Write out sorted customer data
END of IF
```

The sorting procedure will be a selection sort similar to any of the sorting routines that we have already encountered in Chapters 6, 7, and 10. The one tricky thing about this particular sorting process is that *we do not know in advance what component of the data type we will be sorting on.* Sometimes we will be sorting on the last name, while other times we will be sorting on the city or zip code. We must do something to make the sort procedure work properly regardless of the component of the data that we are sorting on.

The easiest way to get around this problem is to write a series of functions that compare individual components of two different variables of the data type to determine which is the lesser of the two. One function will compare two last names to determine which is the lesser (lower in alphabetical order), while another function will compare two city names to determine which is the lesser (lower in alphabetical order), and a third will compare two zip codes to determine which is the lesser (lower in numerical sequence). Once the comparison functions are written, we will be able to sort the data in any order by passing the appropriate comparison function to the sorting subroutine as a command line argument.

The pseudocode for the last name comparison routine is

```
LOGICAL FUNCTION lt_last (a, b)
lt_lastname ← LLT(a%last, b%last)
```

Note that the routine uses the LLT function to ensure that the sorting order is the same on all computers regardless of collating sequence. The pseudocode for the city comparison routine is

```
LOGICAL FUNCTION lt_city (a, b)
lt_city ← LLT(a%city, b%city)
```

Finally, the pseudocode for the zip code comparison routine is

```
LOGICAL FUNCTION lt_zip (a, b)
lt_zip ← a%zip < b%zip
```

The pseudocode for the sorting routine will be the same as the pseudocode for subroutine sort in Chapter 7, except that the comparison function will be passed as a command line argument. It is not reproduced here.

4. **Turn the algorithm into Fortran statements.**

The resulting Fortran subroutine is shown in Figure 12-2.

FIGURE 12-2
Program to sort a customer database according to a user-specified field.

```
MODULE types
!
!  Purpose:
!    To define the derived data type used for the customer
!    database.
!
!  Record of revisions:
!      Date        Programmer          Description of change
!      ====        ==========          =====================
!    12/04/06    S. J. Chapman         Original code
!
IMPLICIT NONE

! Declare type personal_info
```

12

(*continued*)

(continued)

```
TYPE :: personal_info
   CHARACTER(len=12) :: first          ! First name
   CHARACTER         :: mi             ! Middle Initial
   CHARACTER(len=12) :: last           ! Last name
   CHARACTER(len=26) :: street         ! Street Address
   CHARACTER(len=12) :: city           ! City
   CHARACTER(len=2)  :: state          ! State
   INTEGER           :: zip            ! Zip code
END TYPE personal_info

END MODULE types

PROGRAM customer_database
!
!   Purpose:
!     To read in a character input data set, sort it into ascending
!     order using the selection sort algorithm, and to write the
!     sorted data to the standard output device.  This program calls
!     subroutine "sort_database" to do the actual sorting.
!
!   Record of revisions:
!       Date          Programmer          Description of change
!       ====          ==========          =====================
!     12/04/06      S. J. Chapman         Original code
!
USE types                          ! Declare the module types
IMPLICIT NONE

! Data dictionary: declare constants
INTEGER, PARAMETER :: MAX_SIZE = 100   ! Max addresses in database

! Data dictionary: declare external functions
LOGICAL, EXTERNAL :: lt_last       ! Comparison fn for last names
LOGICAL, EXTERNAL :: lt_city       ! Comparison fn for cities
LOGICAL, EXTERNAL :: lt_zip        ! Comparison fn for zip codes

! Data dictionary: declare variable types & definitions
TYPE(personal_info), DIMENSION(MAX_SIZE) :: customers
                                   ! Data array to sort
INTEGER :: choice                  ! Choice of how to sort database
LOGICAL :: exceed = .FALSE.        ! Logical indicating that array
                                   !   limits are exceeded.
CHARACTER(len=20) :: filename      ! Input data file name
INTEGER :: i                       ! Loop index
INTEGER :: nvals = 0               ! Number of data values to sort
INTEGER :: status                  ! I/O status: 0 for success
TYPE(personal_info) :: temp        ! Temporary variable for reading

! Get the name of the file containing the input data.
WRITE (*,*) 'Enter the file name with customer database: '
READ (*,'(A20)') filename

! Open input data file.  Status is OLD because the input data must
! already exist.
```

(continued)

(continued)

```
OPEN ( UNIT=9, FILE=filename, STATUS='OLD', IOSTAT=status )

! Was the OPEN successful?
fileopen: IF ( status == 0 ) THEN          ! Open successful

   ! The file was opened successfully, so read the customer
   ! database from it.
   DO
      READ (9, 1010, IOSTAT=status) temp    ! Get value
      1010 FORMAT (A12,1X,A1,1X,A12,1X,A26,1X,A12,1X,A2,1X,I5)
      IF ( status /= 0 ) EXIT              ! Exit on end of data
      nvals = nvals + 1                    ! Bump count
      size: IF ( nvals <= MAX_SIZE ) THEN  ! Too many values?
         customers(nvals) = temp           ! No: Save value in array
      ELSE
         exceed = .TRUE.                   ! Yes: Array overflow
      END IF size
   END DO

   ! Was the array size exceeded?  If so, tell user and quit.
   toobig: IF ( exceed ) THEN
      WRITE (*,1020) nvals, MAX_SIZE
      1020 FORMAT (' Maximum array size exceeded: ', I6, ' > ', I6 )
   ELSE

      ! Limit not exceeded: find out how to sort data.
      WRITE (*,1030)
      1030 FORMAT (1X,'Enter way to sort database:',/, &
                   1X,'  1 -- By last name ',/, &
                   1X,'  2 -- By city ',/, &
                   1X,'  3 -- By zip code ')
      READ (*,*) choice

      ! Sort database
      SELECT CASE ( choice)
      CASE (1)
         CALL sort_database (customers, nvals, lt_last )
      CASE (2)
         CALL sort_database (customers, nvals, lt_city )
      CASE (3)
         CALL sort_database (customers, nvals, lt_zip )
      CASE DEFAULT
         WRITE (*,*) 'Invalid choice entered!'
      END SELECT

      ! Now write out the sorted data.
      WRITE (*,'(A)') ' The sorted database values are: '
      WRITE (*,1040) ( customers(i), i = 1, nvals )
      1040 FORMAT (1X,A12,1X,A1,1X,A12,1X,A26,1X,A12,1X,A2,1X,I5)

   END IF toobig

ELSE fileopen

   ! Status /= 0, so an open error occurred.
```

(continued)

(continued)
```
    WRITE (*,'(A,I6)') ' File open error: IOSTAT = ', status
END IF fileopen

END PROGRAM customer_database

SUBROUTINE sort_database (array, n, lt_fun )
!
!   Purpose:
!     To sort array "array" into ascending order using a selection
!     sort, where "array" is an array of the derived data type
!     "personal_info".  The sort is based on the external
!     comparison function "lt_fun", which will differ depending on
!     which component of the derived type array is used for
!     comparison.
!
!   Record of revisions:
!       Date        Programmer          Description of change
!       ====        ==========          =====================
!     12/04/06    S. J. Chapman         Original code
!
USE types                         ! Declare the module types
IMPLICIT NONE

! Data dictionary: declare calling parameter types & definitions
INTEGER, INTENT(IN) :: n                      ! Number of values
TYPE(personal_info), DIMENSION(n), INTENT(INOUT) :: array
                                              ! Array to be sorted
LOGICAL, EXTERNAL :: lt_fun                   ! Comparison function

! Data dictionary: declare local variable types & definitions
INTEGER :: i                      ! Loop index
INTEGER :: iptr                   ! Pointer to smallest value
INTEGER :: j                      ! Loop index
TYPE(personal_info) :: temp       ! Temp variable for swaps

! Sort the array
outer: DO i = 1, n-1

   ! Find the minimum value in array(i) through array(n)
   iptr = i
   inner: DO j = i+1, n
     minval: IF ( lt_fun(array(J),array(iptr)) ) THEN
         iptr = j
     END IF minval
   END DO inner

   ! iptr now points to the minimum value, so swap array(iptr)
   ! with array(i) if i /= iptr.
   swap: IF ( i /= iptr ) THEN
      temp       = array(i)
      array(i)   = array(iptr)
      array(iptr) = temp
   END IF swap

END DO outer
```

(continued)

(concluded)

```
END SUBROUTINE sort_database

LOGICAL FUNCTION lt_last (a, b)
!
!  Purpose:
!    To compare variables "a" and "b" and determine which
!    has the smaller last name (lower alphabetical order).
!
USE types                      ! Declare the module types
IMPLICIT NONE

! Data dictionary: declare calling parameter types & definitions
TYPE (personal_info), INTENT(IN) :: a, b

! Make comparison.
lt_last = LLT ( a%last, b%last )

END FUNCTION lt_last

LOGICAL FUNCTION lt_city (a, b)
!
!  Purpose:
!    To compare variables "a" and "b" and determine which
!    has the smaller city (lower alphabetical order).
!
USE types                      ! Declare the module types
IMPLICIT NONE

! Data dictionary: declare calling parameter types & definitions
TYPE (personal_info), INTENT(IN) :: a, b

! Make comparison.
lt_city = LLT ( a%city, b%city )

END FUNCTION lt_city

LOGICAL FUNCTION lt_zip (a, b)
!
!  Purpose:
!    To compare variables "a" and "b" and determine which
!    has the smaller zip code (lower numerical value).
!
USE types                      ! Declare the module types
IMPLICIT NONE

! Data dictionary: declare calling parameter types & definitions
TYPE (personal_info), INTENT(IN) :: a, b

! Make comparison.
lt_zip = a%zip < b%zip

END FUNCTION lt_zip
```

5. **Test the resulting Fortran programs.**

To test this program, it is necessary to create a sample customer database. A simple customer database is shown in Figure 12-3; it is stored in the disk in a file called database.

FIGURE 12-3
Sample customer database used to test the program of Example 12-1.

```
John       Q Public      123 Sesame Street    Anywhere       NY 10035
James      R Johnson     Rt. 5 Box 207C       West Monroe    LA 71291
Joseph     P Ziskend     P. O. Box 433        APO            AP 96555
Andrew     D Jackson     Jackson Square       New Orleans    LA 70003
Jane       X Doe         12 Lakeside Drive    Glenview       IL 60025
Colin      A Jeffries    11 Main Street       Chicago        IL 60003
```

To test the program, we will execute it three times, using this database once with each possible sorting option.

```
C:\book\chap12>customer_database
Enter the file name with customer database:
database
Enter way to sort database:
  1 -- By last name
  2 -- By city
  3 -- By zip code
1
The sorted database values are:
Jane       X Doe         12 Lakeside Drive    Glenview       IL 60025
Andrew     D Jackson     Jackson Square       New Orleans    LA 70003
Colin      A Jeffries    11 Main Street       Chicago        IL 60003
James      R Johnson     Rt. 5 Box 207C       West Monroe    LA 71291
John       Q Public      123 Sesame Street    Anywhere       NY 10035
Joseph     P Ziskend     P. O. Box 433        APO            AP 96555

C:\book\chap12>customer_database
Enter the file name with customer database:
database
Enter way to sort database:
  1 -- By last name
  2 -- By city
  3 -- By zip code
2
The sorted database values are:
Joseph     P Ziskend     P. O. Box 433        APO            AP 96555
John       Q Public      123 Sesame Street    Anywhere       NY 10035
Colin      A Jeffries    11 Main Street       Chicago        IL 60003
Jane       X Doe         12 Lakeside Drive    Glenview       IL 60025
Andrew     D Jackson     Jackson Square       New Orleans    LA 70003
James      R Johnson     Rt. 5 Box 207C       West Monroe    LA 71291

C:\book\chap12>customer_database
Enter the file name with customer database:
database
Enter way to sort database:
  1 -- By last name
  2 -- By city
  3 -- By zip code
```

```
3
The sorted database values are:
John        Q Public       123 Sesame Street    Anywhere     NY 10035
Colin       A Jeffries     11 Main Street       Chicago      IL 60003
Jane        X Doe          12 Lakeside Drive    Glenview     IL 60025
Andrew      D Jackson      Jackson Square       New Orleans  LA 70003
James       R Johnson      Rt. 5 Box 207C       West Monroe  LA 71291
Joseph      P Ziskend      P. O. Box 433        APO          AP 96555
```

Note that the program is working correctly with one minor exception. When it sorted the data by city, it got "APO" and "Anywhere" out of order. Can you tell why this happened? You will be asked to rewrite this program to eliminate the problem in Exercise 12-1.

12.5
RETURNING DERIVED TYPES FROM FUNCTIONS

It is possible to create a function of a derived data type *if and only if the function has an explicit interface*. The easiest way to create such an interface is to place the function within a module, and to access that module by using a USE statement. Example 12-2 creates two sample functions that return a derived data type.

EXAMPLE
12-2

Adding and Subtracting Vectors:

To illustrate the use of functions with derived data types, create a derived data type containing a two-dimensional vector, plus two functions to add and subtract them. Also, create a test driver program to test the vector functions.

SOLUTION

1. **State the problem.**
   Create a module containing a two-dimensional vector data type, plus functions to add and subtract vectors. Create a test driver program that prompts the user for two input vectors, and then adds and subtracts them using the functions.

2. **Define the inputs and outputs.**
   The inputs to the program are two vectors v1 and v2. The outputs are the sum and differences of the two vectors.

3. **Describe the algorithm.**
   The first step in writing this program will be to create a derived data type to hold a 2D vector. This type can be defined as follows:

```
TYPE :: vector
   REAL :: x                          ! X value
   REAL :: y                          ! Y value
END TYPE vector
```

12

We must also define two functions `vector_add` and `vector_sub` that add and subtract 2D vectors, respectively. The pseudocode for the `vector_add` function is

```
TYPE(vector) FUNCTION vector_add (v1, v2)
vector_add.x ← v1%x + v2%x
vector_add.y ← v1%y + v2%y
```

and the pseudocode for the `vector_sub` function is

```
TYPE(vector) FUNCTION vector_sub (v1, v2)
vector_sub.x ← v1%x - v2%x
vector_sub.y ← v1%y - v2%y
```

The top-level pseudocode for the main program is

```
Prompt user for the vector v1
Read v1
Prompt user for the vector v2
Read v2
Write the sum of the two vectors
Write the difference of the two vectors
```

4. **Turn the algorithm into Fortran statements.**
   The resulting Fortran vector module is shown in Figure 12-4.

FIGURE 12-4
Two-dimensional vector module.

```
MODULE vector_module
!
!  Purpose:
!    To define the derived data type for 2D vectors,
!    plus addition and subtraction operations.
!
!  Record of revisions:
!      Date          Programmer          Description of change
!      ====          ==========          =====================
!    12/04/06     S. J. Chapman          Original code
!
IMPLICIT NONE

! Declare type vector
TYPE :: vector
   REAL :: x                              ! X value
   REAL :: y                              ! Y value
END TYPE vector

! Add procedures
CONTAINS

   TYPE (vector) FUNCTION vector_add ( v1, v2 )
   !
   !  Purpose:
   !    To add two vectors.
   !
   !  Record of revisions:
```

(*continued*)

(concluded)

```
!         Date        Programmer          Description of change
!         ====        =========           =====================
!      12/04/06    S. J. Chapman        Original code
!
IMPLICIT NONE

! Data dictionary: declare calling parameter types & definitions
TYPE (vector), INTENT(IN) :: v1          ! First vector
TYPE (vector), INTENT(IN) :: v2          ! Second vector

! Add the vectors
vector_add%x = v1%x + v2%x
vector_add%y = v1%y + v2%y

END FUNCTION vector_add

TYPE (vector) FUNCTION vector_sub ( v1, v2 )
!
!  Purpose:
!    To subtract two vectors.
!
!  Record of revisions:
!        Date        Programmer          Description of change
!        ====        =========           =====================
!      12/04/06    S. J. Chapman        Original code
!
IMPLICIT NONE

! Data dictionary: declare calling parameter types & definitions
TYPE (vector), INTENT(IN) :: v1          ! First point
TYPE (vector), INTENT(IN) :: v2          ! Second point

! Add the points
vector_sub%x = v1%x - v2%x
vector_sub%y = v1%y - v2%y

END FUNCTION vector_sub
END MODULE vector_module
```

The test driver program is shown in Figure 12-5.

FIGURE 12-5
Test driver program for the vector module.

```
PROGRAM test_vectors
!
!  Purpose:
!    To test adding and subtracting 2D vectors.
!
!  Record of revisions:
!        Date        Programmer          Description of change
!        ====        =========           =====================
!      12/04/06    S. J. Chapman        Original code
!
USE vector_module
```

(continued)

(*concluded*)

```
IMPLICIT NONE

! Enter first point
TYPE (vector) :: v1              ! First point
TYPE (vector) :: v2              ! Second point

! Get the first vector
WRITE (*,*) 'Enter the first vector (x,y):'
READ (*,*) v1.x, v1.y

! Get the second point
WRITE (*,*) 'Enter the second vector (x,y):'
READ (*,*) v2.x, v2.y

! Add the points
WRITE (*,1000) vector_add(v1,v2)
1000 FORMAT(1X,'The sum of the points is (',F8.2,',',F8.2,')')

! Subtract the points
WRITE (*,1010) vector_sub(v1,v2)
1010 FORMAT(1X,'The difference of the points is (',F8.2,',',F8.2,')')

END PROGRAM test_vectors
```

5. **Test the resulting Fortran programs.**

    We will test this program entering two vectors, and manually checking the result-ing answer. If vector v1 is $(-2, 2)$ and vector v2 is $(4, 3)$, then the sum of the vectors will be v1 + v2 = $(2, 5)$ and the difference of the vectors will be v1 - v2 = $(-6, -1)$.

```
C:\book\chap12>test_vectors
 Enter the first vector (x,y):
-2. 2.
 Enter the second vector (x,y):
4. 3.
 The sum of the points is (    2.00,     5.00)
 The difference of the points is (    -6.00,    -1.00)
```

The functions appear to be working correctly.

Good Programming Practice

To create functions of a derived data type, declare them within a module, and access the module by using a USE statement.

Quiz 12-1

This quiz provides a quick check to see if you have understood the concepts in-troduced in Sections 12.1 through 12.5. If you have trouble with the quiz, reread the sections, ask your instructor, or discuss the material with a fellow student. The answers to this quiz are found in the back of the book.

(*continued*)

(concluded)

For questions 1 to 7, assume the derived data types defined below:

```
TYPE :: position
   REAL :: x
   REAL :: y
   REAL :: z
END TYPE position
TYPE :: time
   INTEGER :: second
   INTEGER :: minute
   INTEGER :: hour
   INTEGER :: day
   INTEGER :: month
   INTEGER :: year
END TYPE time
TYPE :: plot
   TYPE (time) :: plot_time
   TYPE (position) :: plot_position
END TYPE
TYPE (plot), DIMENSION(10) :: points
```

1. Write the Fortran statements to print out the date associated with the seventh plot point in format DD/MM/YYYY HH:MM:SS.
2. Write the Fortran statements to print out the position associated with the seventh plot point.
3. Write the Fortran statements required to calculate the rate of motion between the second and third plot points. To do this, you will have to calculate the difference in position and the difference in time between the two points. The rate of motion will be Δ position/Δ time.

For questions 4 to 6, state whether each of the following statements is valid. If the statements are valid, describe what they do.

4. `WRITE (*,*) points(1)`

5. `WRITE (*,1000) points(4)`
   `1000 FORMAT (1X, 3ES12.6, 6I6 )`

6. `dpos = points(2).plot_position - points(1).plot_position`

12

12.6

DYNAMIC ALLOCATION OF DERIVED DATA TYPES (FORTRAN 2003 ONLY)

F-2003 ONLY

In Fortran 2003, a variable or array of a derived data type can be declared with the `ALLOCATABLE` attribute, and can be dynamically allocated and deallocated. For example, suppose that a derived data type is defined as follows:

```
TYPE :: personal_info
   CHARACTER(len=12) :: first          ! First name
   CHARACTER :: mi                     ! Middle Initial
   CHARACTER(len=12) :: last           ! Last name
   CHARACTER(len=26) :: street         ! Street Address
   CHARACTER(len=12) :: city           ! City
   CHARACTER(len=2)  :: state          ! State
   INTEGER           :: zip            ! Zip code
END TYPE personal_info
```

Then an allocatable variable of this type can be declared as

```
TYPE(personal_info),ALLOCATABLE :: person
```

and can be allocated with the statement

```
ALLOCATE( person, STAT=istat )
```

Similarly, an allocatable array of this type can be declared as

```
TYPE(personal_info),DIMENSION(:),ALLOCATABLE :: people
```

and can be allocated with the statement

```
ALLOCATE( people(1000), STAT=istat )
```

This was not possible in Fortran 95 and earlier versions.

12.7

PARAMETERIZED DERIVED DATA TYPES (FORTRAN 2003 ONLY)

Just as Fortran allows multiple KINDs of integer or real data types, Fortran 2003 allows a user to a define derived data type with elements having different KIND numbers and different element lengths. Dummy values representing the KIND numbers and element lengths are specified in parentheses after the type name, and these dummy values are then used to define the actual kinds and lengths of the elements in the derived type. If no dummy values are specified, then the derived data type will be created by using default values that are specified in the type definition.

For example, the following lines declare a vector data type with KIND and length parameters.

```
TYPE :: vector(kind,n)
   INTEGER, KIND :: kind = KIND(0.)    ! Defaults to single precision
   INTEGER, n = 3                      ! Defaults to three elements
   REAL(kind),DIMENSION(n) :: v        ! Parameterized vector
END TYPE vector
```

The following type declarations will produce a derived data type containing a three-element single-precision vector.

```
TYPE (vector(KIND(0.),3)) :: v1        ! Kind and length specified
TYPE (vector) :: v2                    ! Kind and length defaulted
```

Similarly, the following type declaration produces a derived data type containing a 20-element double-precision vector:

```
TYPE (vector(KIND(0.D0),20)) :: v3      ! Kind and length specified
```

The next type declaration produces an array of 100 items of a derived data type, each containing a 20-element double-precision vector:

```
TYPE (vector(KIND(0.D0),20)),DIMENSION(100) :: v4
```

In Fortran 2005, derived data types can be declared allocatable, with the length of the individual elements deferred until allocation time. The following type declaration creates an allocatable structure whose length is deferred until the actual ALLOCATE statement is executed:

```
TYPE (vector(KIND(0.),:)),ALLOCATABLE :: v5
```

12.8

TYPE EXTENSION (FORTRAN 2003 ONLY)

F-2003 ONLY

In Fortran 2003, a derived type that does not have the SEQUENCE or BIND(C)[2] attribute is *extensible*. This means that an existing user-defined type can be used as the basis of a larger, more comprehensive type definition. For example, suppose the a two-dimensional point data type is defined as:

```
TYPE :: point
   REAL :: x
   REAL :: y
END TYPE
```

Then three-dimensional point data can be defined as an extension of the existing two-dimensional point data type as follows:

```
TYPE, EXTENDS(point) :: point3d
   REAL :: z
END TYPE
```

This new data type contains three elements x, y, and z. Elements x and y were defined in type point and *inherited* by type point3d, while element z is unique to type point3d. Data type point is referred to as the *parent* of data type point3d.

The components of an extended data type can be used just like the components of any other data type. For example, suppose that we declare a variable of type point3d as follows:

```
TYPE(point3d) :: p
```

Then p will contain three components, which are usually addressed as p%x, p%y, and p%z. These components can be used in any calculations required.

---

[2] The BIND(C) attribute makes a Fortran 2005 type interoperable with C. It is not discussed in this text.

12

The inherited components of a derived data type can also be addressed by reference to the parent data type. For example, the x and y components of the item can also be addressed as p%parent%x and p%parent%y. Here, parent refers to the data type from which point3d was derived. This alternative form of address is used when we want to pass only the inherited values to a procedure.

The program shown below illustrates the use of extended data types. It declares a point data type, and then extends it to a point3d data type.

```
PROGRAM test_type_extension
!
!   Purpose:
!     To illustrate type extension of derived data types.
!
!   Record of revisions:
!       Date        Programmer .        Description of change
!       ====        ==========          ======================
!     12/04/06    S. J. Chapman        Original code
!
IMPLICIT NONE

! Declare type point
TYPE :: point
   REAL :: x
   REAL :: y
END TYPE

! Declare type point3d
TYPE, EXTENDS(point) :: point3d
   REAL :: z
END TYPE

! Declare a variable of type person:
TYPE (point3d) :: my_point

! Initialize variable
my_point%x = 1.
my_point%y = 2.
my_point%z = 3.

! Output variable using free format I/O
WRITE (*,*) 'my_point = ', my_point

END PROGRAM test_type_extension
```

When this program is executed, the results are:

```
C:\book\chap12> test_type_extension
   my_point =    1.0000000   2.0000000    3.0000000
```

12.9

TYPE-BOUND PROCEDURES

Fortran 2003 allows procedures to be specifically associated ("bound") to a derived data type. These procedures can be invoked by reference to the derived data type in a syntax similar to that used to access a data element.

Type-bound Fortran procedures are created by adding a CONTAINS statement to the type definition, and declaring the bindings in that statement. For example, suppose that we wanted to include a function to add two items of type point together. Then we would declare the type definition as follows:

```
TYPE :: point
   REAL :: x
   REAL :: y
CONTAINS
   PROCEDURE,PASS :: add
END TYPE
```

This definition would declare that a procedure called add is associated with (bound to) this data type. If p is a variable of type point, then the add procedure would be referenced as p%add(...), just as element x would be referenced as p%x. The attribute PASS indicates that the variable of type point used to invoke the procedure is automatically passed to this procedure as the first calling argument whenever it is called.

The procedure add would then need to be defined in the same module as the type definition statement. An example of a module declaring type point and including a procedure add is shown below:

```
MODULE point_module
IMPLICIT NONE

! Type definition
TYPE :: point
   REAL :: x
   REAL :: y
CONTAINS
   PROCEDURE,PASS :: add
END TYPE

CONTAINS

   TYPE(point) FUNCTION add(this, another_point)
   CLASS(point) :: this, another_point
   add%x = this%x + another_point%x
   add%y = this%y + another_point%y
   END FUNCTION add

END MODULE point_module
```

The function add has two arguments, this and another_point. Argument this is the variable that was used to invoke the procedure. It is automatically passed to the procedure when it is invoked without it being explicit in the call, while argument another_point will show up in the list of calling arguments.

Note that the derived data types are declared in the bound procedure by using the CLASS keyword. CLASS is a special version of the TYPE keyword with additional properties; it will be discussed in Chapter 16.

Three objects of this type could be declared as follows:

```
TYPE(point) :: a, b, c
a%x = -10.
a%y = 5.
b%x = 4.
b%y = 2.
```

12

With this definition, the following statement adds points a and b together and stores the result in point c.

```
c = a%add(b)
```

This statement calls function add, automatically passing it a as its first argument and b as its second argument. The function returns a result of type point, which is stored in variable c. After the function call, c%x will contain the value -6 and c%y will contain the value 7.

If the procedure binding contains the attribute NOPASS instead of PASS, then the bound procedure will *not* automatically get the variable used to invoke it as a calling argument. If the data type were declared as follows:

```
TYPE :: point
    REAL :: x
    REAL :: y
CONTAINS
    PROCEDURE,NOPASS :: add
END TYPE
```

then the bound function would have to be called with the first argument explicitly shown in the call:

```
c = a%add(a,b)
```

If no attribute is given in a binding, the default attribute is PASS. As we shall see in Chapter 16, this feature is useful in object-oriented programming.

**EXAMPLE
12-3**

Using Bound Procedures:

Convert the vector module of Example 12-2 so that it uses bound procedures.

SOLUTION
If a derived data type uses bound procedures, then the procedures will be addressed by using variable name followed by the component selector (%), and the variable used to invoke the procedures will be automatically passed as the first calling argument. The modified vector module is shown in Figure 12-6.

FIGURE 12-6
Two-dimensional vector module with bound procedures.

```
MODULE vector_module
!
!  Purpose:
!    To define the derived data type for 2D vectors,
!    plus addition and subtraction operations.
!
!  Record of revisions:
!      Date       Programmer          Description of change
!      ====       ==========          =====================
!    12/04/06   S. J. Chapman        Original code
! 1. 12/22/06   S. J. Chapman        Use bound procedures
```

(continued)

(continued)

```
!
IMPLICIT NONE

! Declare type vector
TYPE :: vector
   REAL :: x                              ! X value
   REAL :: y                              ! Y value
CONTAINS
   PROCEDURE,PASS :: vector_add
   PROCEDURE,PASS :: vector_sub
END TYPE vector

! Add procedures
CONTAINS

   TYPE (vector) FUNCTION vector_add ( this, v2 )
   !
   !  Purpose:
   !    To add two vectors.
   !
   !  Record of revisions:
   !      Date          Programmer          Description of change
   !      ====          ==========          =====================
   !    12/04/06      S. J. Chapman        Original code
   ! 1. 12/22/06      S. J. Chapman        Use bound procedures
   !
   IMPLICIT NONE

   ! Data dictionary: declare calling parameter types & definitions
   CLASS(vector),INTENT(IN) :: this           ! First vector
   CLASS(vector),INTENT(IN) :: v2             ! Second vector

   ! Add the vectors
   vector_add%x = this%x + v2%x
   vector_add%y = this%y + v2%y

   END FUNCTION vector_add

   TYPE (vector) FUNCTION vector_sub ( this, v2 )
   !
   !  Purpose:
   !    To subtract two vectors.
   !
   !  Record of revisions:
   !      Date          Programmer          Description of change
   !      ====          ==========          =====================
   !    12/04/06      S. J. Chapman        Original code
   ! 1. 12/22/06      S. J. Chapman        Use bound procedures
   !
   IMPLICIT NONE

   ! Data dictionary: declare calling parameter types & definitions
   CLASS(vector),INTENT(IN) :: this           ! First vector
   CLASS(vector),INTENT(IN) :: v2             ! Second vector

   ! Add the points
   vector_sub%x = this%x - v2%x
   vector_sub%y = this%y - v2%y
```

12

(continued)

(concluded)

```
   END FUNCTION vector_sub

END MODULE vector_module
```

The test driver program is shown in Figure 12-7

FIGURE 12-7
Test driver program for the vector module with bound procedures.

```
PROGRAM test_vectors
!
!  Purpose:
!    To test adding and subtracting 2D vectors.
!
!  Record of revisions:
!      Date        Programmer          Description of change
!      ====        ==========          =====================
!     12/04/06    S. J. Chapman        Original code
! 1.  12/22/06    S. J. Chapman        Use bound procedures
!
USE vector_module
IMPLICIT NONE

! Enter first point
TYPE(vector) :: v1                ! First point
TYPE(vector) :: v2                ! Second point

! Get the first vector
WRITE (*,*) 'Enter the first vector (x,y):'
READ (*,*) v1%x, v1%y

! Get the second point
WRITE (*,*) 'Enter the second vector (x,y):'
READ (*,*) v2%x, v2%y

! Add the points
WRITE (*,1000) v1%vector_add(v2)
1000 FORMAT(1X,'The sum of the points is (',F8.2,',',F8.2,')')

! Subtract the points
WRITE (*,1010) v1%vector_sub(v2)
1010 FORMAT(1X,'The difference of the points is (',F8.2,',',F8.2,')')

END PROGRAM test_vectors
```

We will test this program, using the same data as in the previous example.

```
    C:\book\chap12>test_vectors
     Enter the first vector (x,y):
    -2. 2.
     Enter the second vector (x,y):
    4. 3.
     The sum of the points is (    2.00,    5.00)
     The difference of the points is (   -6.00,   -1.00)
```

The functions appear to be working correctly.

12.10

THE ASSOCIATE CONSTRUCT (FORTRAN 2003 ONLY)

The ASSOCIATE construct allows a programmer to temporarily associate a name with a variable or expression during the execution of a code block. This construct is useful for simplifying multiple references to variables or expressions with long names and/or many subscripts.

The form of an associate construct is

```
[name:] ASSOCIATE (association_list)
    Statement 1
    Statement 2
    ...
    Statement n
END ASSOCIATE [name]
```

The *association_list* is a set of one or more associations of the form

```
assoc_name => variable, array element or expression
```

If more than one association appears in the list, they are separated by commas.

To get a better understanding of the ASSOCIATE construct, let's examine a practical case. Suppose that a radar is tracking a series of objects, and each object's position is stored in a data structure of the form:

```
TYPE :: trackfile
    REAL :: x          ! X position (m)
    REAL :: y          ! Y position (m)
    REAL :: dist       ! Distance to target (m)
    REAL :: bearing    ! Bearing to target (rad)
END TYPE trackfile
TYPE(trackfile),DIMENSION(1000) :: active_tracks
```

Suppose that the location of the radar itself is stored in a data structure of the form:

```
TYPE :: radar_loc
    REAL :: x          ! X position (m)
    REAL :: y          ! Y position (m)
END TYPE radar_loc
TYPE(radar_loc) :: my_radar
```

We would like to calculate the range and bearing to all of the tracks. This can be done with the following statements:

```
DO i = 1, n_tracks
   active_tracks(i)%dist    = SQRT( (my_radar%x - active_tracks(i)%x) ** 2 &
                             + (my_radar%y - active_tracks(i)%y) ** 2 )
   active_tracks(i)%bearing = ATAN2( (my_radar%y - active_tracks(i)%y), &
                             (my_radar%x - active_tracks(i)%x) )
END DO
```

12

These statements are legal, but they are *not* very readable because of the long names involved. If instead we use the ASSOCIATE construct, the fundamental equations are much clearer:

```
DO itf = 1, n_tracks
   ASSOCIATE ( x => active_tracks(i)%x, &
               y => active_tracks(i)%y, &
               dist => active_tracks(i)%dist, &
               bearing => active_tracks(i)%bearing )
      dist    = SQRT( (my_radar%x - x) ** 2 + (my_radar%y - y) ** 2 )
      bearing = ATAN2( (my_radar%y - y), (my_radar%x - x) )
   END ASSOCIATE
END DO
```

The ASSOCIATE construct is never required, but it can be useful to simplify and emphasize the algorithm being used.

12.11
SUMMARY

Derived data types are data types defined by the programmer for use in solving a particular problem. They may contain any number of components, and each component may be of any intrinsic data type or any previously defined derived data type. Derived data types are defined by using a TYPE . . . END TYPE construct, and variables of that type are declared by using a TYPE statement. Constants of a derived data type may be constructed by using structure constructors. A variable or constant of a derived data type is called a structure.

The components of a variable of a derived data type may be used in a program just like any other variables of the same type. They are addressed by naming both the variable and the component separated by a percent sign (e.g., student%age). Variables of a derived data type may not be used with any Fortran intrinsic operations except for assignment. Addition, subtraction, multiplication, division, etc. are undefined for these variables. They may be used in I/O statements.

We will learn how to extend intrinsic operations to variables of a derived data type in Chapter 13.

12.11.1 Summary of Good Programming Practice

The following guideline should be adhered to when you are working with parameterized variables, complex numbers, and derived data types:

- For large programs using derived data types, declare the definitions of each data type in a module, and then use that module in each procedure of the program that needs to access the derived data type.

12.11.2 Summary of Fortran Statements and Structures

ASSOCIATE **Construct:**

F-2003 ONLY

```
[name:] ASSOCIATE (association_list)
   Statement 1
   ...
   Statement n
END ASSOCIATE [name]
```

Example:

```
ASSOCIATE (x => target(i)%state_vector%x, &
           y => target(i)%state_vector%y )
   dist(i) = SQRT(x**2 + y**2)
END ASSOCIATE
```

Description:

The ASSOCIATE construct allows a programmer to address one or more variables with very long names by a shorter name within the body of the construct. The equations within the ASSOCIATE construct can be much more compact, because the individual variable names are not too cumbersome.

Derived Data Type:

```
TYPE [::] type_name
   component 1
   ...
   component n
CONTAINS
   PROCEDURE[,(NO)PASS] :: proc_name1[, proc_name2, ...]
END TYPE [type_name]
TYPE (type_name) :: var1 (, var2, ...)
```

F-2003 ONLY

Example:

```
TYPE :: state_vector
   LOGICAL :: valid              ! Valid data flag
   REAL(kind=single) :: x        ! x position
   REAL(kind=single) :: y        ! y position
   REAL(kind=double) :: time     ! time of validity
   CHARACTER(len=12) :: id       ! Target ID
END TYPE state_vector
TYPE (state_vector), DIMENSION(50) :: objects
```

Description:

The derived data type is a structure containing a combination of intrinsic and previously defined derived data types. The type is defined by a TYPE ... END TYPE construct, and variables of that type are declared with a TYPE() statement.

F-2003 ONLY   Bound procedures in derived data types are only available in Fortran 2003.

12

NOPASS Attribute:

F-2003
ONLY

```
TYPE :: name
    variable definitions
CONTAINS
    PROCEDURE,NOPASS :: proc_name
END TYPE
```

Example:

```
TYPE :: point
    REAL :: x
    REAL :: y
CONTAINS
    PROCEDURE,NOPASS :: add
END TYPE
```

Description:
The NOPASS attribute means that the variable used to invoke a bound procedure will *not* be automatically passed to the procedure as its first calling argument.

PASS Attribute:

F-2003
ONLY

```
TYPE :: name
    variable definitions
CONTAINS
    PROCEDURE,PASS :: proc_name
END TYPE
```

Example:

```
TYPE :: point
    REAL :: x
    REAL :: y
CONTAINS
    PROCEDURE,PASS :: add
END TYPE
```

Description:
The PASS attribute means that the variable used to invoke a bound procedure will be automatically passed to the procedure as its first calling argument. This is the default case for bound procedures

12.11.3 Exercises

12-1. When the database was sorted by city in Example 12-1, "APO" was placed ahead of "Anywhere". Why did this happen? Rewrite the program in this example to eliminate this problem.

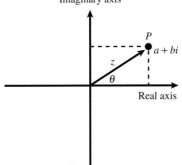

Imaginary axis

Real axis

FIGURE 12-8
Representing a complex number in polar coordinates.

12-2. Create a derived data type called POLAR to hold a complex number expressed in polar (z, θ) format as shown in Figure 12-8. The derived data type will contain two components, a magnitude z and an angle θ, with the angle expressed in degrees. Write two functions that convert an ordinary complex number into a polar number, and that convert a polar number into an ordinary complex number.

12-3. If two complex numbers are expressed polar form, the two numbers may be multiplied by multiplying their magnitudes and adding their angles. That is, if $P_1 = z_1 \angle \theta_1$ and $P_2 = z_2 \angle \theta_2$, then $P_1 \cdot P_2 = z_1 z_2 \angle \theta_1 + \theta_2$. Write a function that multiplies two variables of type POLAR together, using this expression, and returns a result in polar form. Note that the resulting angle θ should be in the range $-180° < \theta \le 180°$.

12-4. If two complex numbers are expressed polar form, the two numbers may be divided by dividing their magnitudes and subtracting their angles. That is, if $P_1 = z_1 \angle \theta_1$ and $P_2 = z_2 \angle \theta_2$, then

$$\frac{P_1}{P_2} = \frac{z_1}{z_2} \angle \theta_1 - \theta_2$$

Write a function that divides two variables of type POLAR together by using this expression, and returns a result in polar form. Note that the resulting angle θ should be in the range $-180° < \theta \le 180°$.

F-2003 ONLY

12-5. Create a version of the polar data type with the functions defined in Exercises 12-2 through 12-4 as bound procedures. Write a test driver program to illustrate the operation of the data type.

12-6. A point can be located in a Cartesian plane by two coordinates (x, y), where x is the displacement of the point along the x axis from the origin and y is the displacement of the point along the y axis from the origin. Create a derived data type called POINT whose components are x and y. A line can be represented in a Cartesian plane by the equation

$$y = mx + b \tag{12-1}$$

where m is the slope of the line and b is the y-axis intercept of the line. Create a derived data type called LINE whose components are m and b.

12

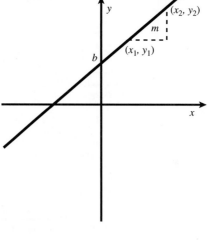

FIGURE 12-9
The slope and intercept of a line can be determined from two points (x_1, y_1) and (x_2, y_2)
that lie along the line.

12-7. The distance between two points (x_1, y_1) and (x_2, y_2) is given by the equation

$$\text{distance} = \sqrt{(x_2 - x_1)^2 + (y_2 - y_1)^2} \tag{12-2}$$

Write a function that calculates the distance between two values of type `POINT` as defined in Exercise 12-6 above. The inputs should be two points, and the output should be
the distance between the two points expressed as a real number.

12-8. From elementary geometry, we know that two points uniquely determine a line as long as
they are not coincident. Write a function that accepts two values of type `POINT`, and returns
a value of type `LINE` containing the slope and y-intercept of the line. If the two points are
identical, the function should return zeros for both the slope and the intercept. From Figure
12-9, we can see that the slope of the line can be calculated from the equation

$$m = \frac{y_2 - y_1}{x_2 - x_1} \tag{12-3}$$

and the intercept can be calculated from the equation

$$b = y_1 - mx_1 \tag{12-4}$$

12-9. **Tracking Radar Targets** Many surveillance radars have antennas that rotate at a fixed
rate, scanning the surrounding airspace. The targets detected by such radars are usually
displayed on *plan position indicator* (PPI) displays, such as the one shown in Figure 12-10.
As the antenna sweeps around the circle, a bright line sweeps around the PPI display.
Each target detected shows up on the display as a bright spot at a particular range r and
angle θ, where θ is measured in compass degrees relative to North.

Each target will be detected at a different position every time that the radar
sweeps around the circle, both because the target moves and because of inherent noise
in the range and angle measurement process. The radar system needs to track detected

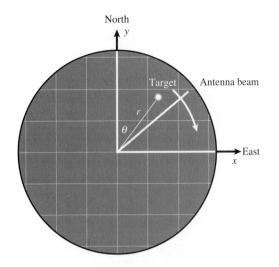

FIGURE 12-10
The PPI display of a track-while-scan radar. Target detections show up as bright spots on the display. Each detection is characterized by a range, compass azimuth, and detection time (r, θ, T_n).

targets through successive sweeps, and to estimate target position and velocity from the successive detected positions. Radar systems that accomplish such tracking automatically are known as *track while scan* (TWS) radars. They work by measuring the position of the target each time it is detected, and passing that position to a *tracking algorithm*.

One of the simplest tracking algorithms is known as the α-β tracker. The α-β tracker works in Cartesian coordinates, so the first step in using the tracker is to convert each target detection from polar coordinates (r, θ) into rectangular coordinates (x, y). The tracker then computes a smoothed target position (x_n, y_n) and velocity $(\bar{x}_n, \bar{y}_n)$ from the equations:

Smoothed position: $\bar{x}_n = x_{pn} + \alpha(x_n - x_{pn})$ (12-5a)

$\bar{y}_n = y_{pn} + \alpha(y_n - y_{pn})$ (12-5b)

Smoothed velocity: $\bar{\dot{x}}_n = \bar{\dot{x}}_{n-1} + \dfrac{\beta}{T_s}(x_n - x_{pn})$ (12-6a)

$\bar{\dot{y}}_n = \bar{\dot{y}}_{n-1} + \dfrac{\beta}{T_s}(y_n - y_{pn})$ (12-6b)

Predicted position: $x_{pn} = \bar{x}_{n-1} + \bar{\dot{x}}_{n-1}T_s$ (12-7a)

$y_{pn} = \bar{y}_{n-1} + \bar{\dot{y}}_{n-1}T_s$ (12-7b)

where (x_n, y_n) is the *measured* target position at time n, (x_{pn}, y_{pn}) is the *predicted* target position at time n, $(\bar{\dot{x}}_n, \bar{\dot{y}}_n)$ is the smoothed target velocity at time n, $(\bar{x}_{n-1}, \bar{y}_{n-1})$ and $(\bar{\dot{x}}_{n-1}, \bar{\dot{y}}_{n-1})$ are the smoothed positions and velocity from time $n - 1$, α is the position smoothing parameter, β is the velocity smoothing parameter, and T_s is the time between observations.

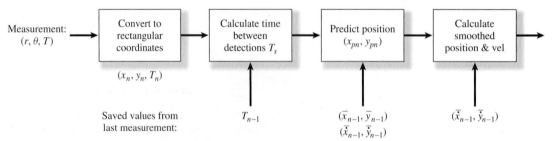

FIGURE 12-11
Block diagram of the operation of an $\alpha-\beta$ tracker. Note that the smoothed position, velocity, and time from the last update must be saved for use in the current tracker cycle.

Design a Fortran program that acts as a radar tracker. The input to the program will be a series of radar target detections (r, θ, T), where r is range in meters, θ is azimuth in compass degrees, and T is the time of the detection in seconds. The program should convert the observations to rectangular coordinates on an East-North grid, and use them to update the tracker as follows:

(a) Calculate the time difference T_s since the last detection.

(b) Predict the position of the target at the time of the new detection, using Equations 12-7.

(c) Update the smoothed position of the target using Equations 12-5. Assume that the position smoothing parameter $\alpha = 0.7$.

(d) Update the smoothed velocity of the target, using Equations 12-6. Assume that the velocity smoothing parameter $\beta = 0.38$.

A block diagram illustrating the operation of the tracker is shown in Figure 12-11.
The program should print out a table containing the observed position of the target, predicted position of the target, and smoothed position of the target each time that the target is measured. Finally, it should produce line printer plots of the estimated x and y velocity components of the target.
The program should include separate derived data types to hold the detections in polar coordinates (r_n, θ_n, T_n), the detections in rectangular coordinates (x_n, y_n, T_n), and the smoothed state vectors $(\bar{x}_n, \bar{y}_n, \dot{x}_n, \dot{y}_n, T_n)$. It should include separate procedures to perform the polar-to-rectangular conversion, target predictions, and target updates. (Be careful of the polar-to-rectangular conversion—since it uses compass angles, the equations to convert to rectangular coordinates will be different from what we saw earlier!)
Test your program by supplying it both a noise-free and a noisy input data set. Both data sets are from a plane flying in a straight line, making a turn, and flying in a straight line again. The noisy data is corrupted by a Gaussian noise with a standard deviation of 200 meters in range and 1.1° in azimuth. (The noise-free data can be found in file `track1.dat` and the noisy data can be found in file `track2.dat` on the disk accompanying the Instructor's Manual, or at the website for this book.) How well does the tracker work at smoothing out errors? How well does the tracker handle the turn?

Advanced Features of
Procedures and Modules

OBJECTIVES

- Understand the three types of scope available in Fortran, and when each one applies.
- Learn how to create recursive subroutines and functions.
- Learn how to create and use keyword arguments.
- Learn how to create and use optional arguments.
- Learn how to create explicit interfaces with Interface Blocks.
- Learn how to create user-defined generic procedures.
- Learn how to create bound generic procedures (Fortran 2003 only).
- Learn how to create user-defined operators.
- Learn how to create assignments and operators that are bound to a specific derived data type (Fortran 2003 only).
- Learn how to restrict access to entities defined within a Fortran module.
- Learn how to create and use type-bound procedures (Fortran 2003 only).
- Learn about the standard Fortran 2003 intrinsic modules.
- Learn the standard procedures for accessing command line arguments and environment variables (Fortran 2003 only).

This chapter introduces some more advanced features of Fortran 95/2003 procedures and modules. These features permit us to have better control over access to the information contained in procedures and modules, allow us to write more flexible procedures that support optional arguments and varying data types, and allow us to extend the Fortran language to support new operations on both intrinsic and derived data types.

■ 13.1

SCOPE AND SCOPING UNITS

In Chapter 7, we learned that the main program and each external subroutine and function in a program are compiled independently, and are then associated together by a linker. Because they were compiled independently, variable names, constant names, loop names, statement labels, etc. could be reused in the different procedures without interfering with each other. For example, the name `my_data` could be declared and used as a character variable in one procedure and declared and used as an integer array in another procedure without causing a conflict. There was no conflict because the **scope** of each name or label was restricted to a single procedure.

The scope of an object (a variable, named constant, procedure name, statement label, etc.) is the portion of a Fortran program over which it is defined. There are three levels of scope in a Fortran 95/2003 program. They are:

1. **Global.** Global objects are objects that are defined throughout an entire program. The names of these objects must be unique within a program. The only global objects that we have encountered so far are the names of programs, external procedures, and modules. Each of these names must be unique within the entire program.[1]
2. **Local.** Local objects are objects that are defined and must be unique within a single **scoping unit.** Examples of scoping units are programs, external procedures, and modules. A local object within a scoping unit must be unique within that unit, but the object name, statement label, etc. may be reused in another scoping unit without causing a conflict.
3. **Statement.** The scope of certain objects may be restricted to a single statement within a program unit. The only examples that we have seen of objects whose scope is restricted to a single statement are the implied `DO` variable in an array constructor and the index variables in a `FORALL` statement. An example array constructor is

$$\text{array} = (/\ (2*i,\ i=1,10,2)\ /)$$

Here the variable `i` is used to define the array values using an implied `DO` loop. This use of variable `i` should not interfere with the use of `i` in the surrounding program, because the scope of this variable is limited to this single statement.

Just what is a scoping unit? It is the portion of a Fortran program over which a local object is defined. The scoping units in a Fortran 95/2003 program are:

1. A main program, internal or external procedure, or module, excluding any derived type definitions or procedures contained within it.
2. A derived type definition.
3. An interface, which we will meet later in this chapter.

---

[1] In some circumstances, there can be local objects with the same names as some global objects. For example, if a program contains an external subroutine called `sort`, then no other global object in the program can have the name `sort`. However, a *different subroutine* within the program could contain a local variable called `sort` without causing a conflict. Since the local variable is not visible outside the subroutine, it does not conflict with the global object of the same name.

Local objects within each of these scoping units must be unique, but they may be reused between scoping units. The fact that a derived type definition is a scoping unit means that we can have a variable named x as a component of the derived type definition, and also have a variable named x within the program containing the derived type definition, without the two variables conflicting with each other.

If one scoping unit completely surrounds another scoping unit, then it is called the **host scoping unit,** or just the **host,** of the inner scoping unit. The inner scoping unit automatically inherits the object definitions declared in the host scoping unit, unless the inner scoping unit explicitly redefines the objects. This inheritance is called **host association.** Thus, an internal procedure inherits all of the variable names and values defined in the host procedure unless the internal procedure explicitly redefines a variable name for its own use. If the internal procedure uses a variable name defined in the host unit without redefining it, then changes to that variable in the internal procedure, it will also change the variable in the host unit. In contrast, if the internal procedure redefines a variable name used in the host unit, then modifications to that local variable will not affect the value of the variable with the same name in the host unit.

Finally, objects defined in a module normally have the scope of that module, but their scope may be extended by USE **association.** If the module name appears in a USE statement in a program unit, then all of the objects defined in the module become objects defined in the program unit using the module, and the names of those objects must be unique. If an object named x is declared within a module and that module is used in a procedure, then no other object may be named x within the procedure.

**EXAMPLE
13-1**

Scope and Scoping Units:

When you are dealing with a subject as complex as scope and scoping units, it is helpful to look at an example. Figure 13-1 shows a Fortran program written specifically to explore the concept of scope. If we can answer the following questions about that program, then we will have a pretty good understanding of scope.

1. What are the scoping units within this program?
2. Which scoping units are hosts to other units?
3. Which objects in this program have global scope?
4. Which objects in this program have statement scope?
5. Which objects in this program have local scope?
6. Which objects in this program are inherited by host association?
7. Which objects in this program are made available by USE association?
8. Explain what will happen in this program as it is executed.

FIGURE 13-1
Program to illustrate the concept of scope and scoping units.

```
MODULE module_example
IMPLICIT NONE
REAL :: x = 100.
REAL :: y = 200.
END MODULE
```

(*continued*)

(concluded)

```
PROGRAM scoping_test
USE module_example
IMPLICIT NONE
INTEGER :: i = 1, j = 2
WRITE (*,'(A25,2I7,2F7.1)') ' Beginning:', i, j, x, y
CALL sub1 ( i, j )
WRITE (*,'(A25,2I7,2F7.1)') ' After sub1:', i, j, x, y
CALL sub2
WRITE (*,'(A25,2I7,2F7.1)') ' After sub2:', i, j, x, y
CONTAINS
    SUBROUTINE sub2
    REAL :: x
    x = 1000.
    y = 2000.
    WRITE (*,'(A25,2F7.1)') ' In sub2:', x, y
    END SUBROUTINE sub2
END PROGRAM scoping_test

SUBROUTINE sub1 (i,j)
IMPLICIT NONE
INTEGER, INTENT(INOUT) :: i, j
INTEGER, DIMENSION(5) :: array
WRITE (*,'(A25,2I7)') ' In sub1 before sub2:', i, j
CALL sub2
WRITE (*,'(A25,2I7)') ' In sub1 after sub2:', i, j
array = (/ (1000*i, i=1,5) /)
WRITE (*,'(A25,7I7)') ' After array def in sub2:', i, j, array
CONTAINS
    SUBROUTINE sub2
    INTEGER :: i
    i = 1000
    j = 2000
    WRITE (*,'(A25,2I7)') 'In sub1 in sub2:', i, j
    END SUBROUTINE sub2
END SUBROUTINE sub1
```

SOLUTION
The answers to the questions are given below.

1. *What are the scoping units within this program?*
   Each module, main program, internal procedure, and external procedure is a scoping unit, so the scoping units are module `module_example`, main program `scoping_test`, external subroutine `sub1`, and the two internal subroutines `sub2`. If there had been any derived data types within the program, their definitions would also have been scoping units. Figure 13-2 illustrates the relationships among the five scoping units in this program.

2. *Which scoping units are hosts to other units?*
   The main program `scoping_test` is the host scoping unit for the internal subroutine `sub2` contained within it, and the external subroutine `sub1` is the host

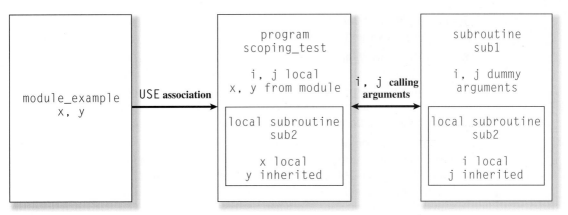

FIGURE 13-2
A block diagram illustrating the relationships among the various scoping units in program `scoping_test`.

scoping unit for the internal subroutine `sub2` contained within it. Note that the two internal subroutines are different, even though they have the same name!

3. *Which objects in this program have global scope?*
   The objects within this program that have global scope are the names of the module `module_example`, the main program `scoping_test`, and the external subroutine `sub1`. These names must be unique throughout the program. For example, there cannot be two external subroutines both named `sub1` in a single program. In contrast, the names of the internal subroutines `sub2` have local scope only, so it is legal to have two different local subroutines of the same name in two different scoping units.

4. *Which objects in this program have statement scope?*
   The only object within this program that has statement scope is the variable `i` within the array definition in subroutine `sub1`. Because that variable has statement scope, the value of variable `i` in subroutine `sub1` will be unchanged by the use of `i` to define the array.

5. *Which objects in this program have local scope?*
   All other objects within this program have local scope, including the names of the internal subroutines `sub2`. Because each internal subroutine is local to its host scoping unit, there is no conflict involved in having two subroutines with the same name. Each of the internal subroutines is defined only within and callable only from its host scoping unit.

6. *Which objects in this program are inherited by host association?*
   All objects in the two internal subroutines are inherited from their host scoping units by host association with the exception of those objects explicitly redefined within the internal subroutines. Thus, variable `x` is local to the first internal subroutine, while variable `y` is inherited from the main program, which is the host scoping unit. Similarly, variable `i` is local to the second internal subroutine, while variable `j` is inherited from the subroutine `sub1`, which is the host scoping unit.

13

7. *Which objects in this program are made available by* USE *association?*

Variables x and y are made available to the main program by USE association.

8. *Explain what will happen in this program as it is executed.*

When this program begins execution, variables x and y are initialized to 100. and 200. respectively in module module_example, and variables i and j are initialized to 1 and 2 respectively in the main program. Variables x and y are visible in the main program by USE association.

When subroutine sub1 is called, variables i and j are passed to sub1 as calling arguments. Subroutine sub1 then calls its local subroutine sub2, which sets i to 1000 and j to 2000. However, variable i is local to sub2, so changing it has no effect on variable i in sub1. Variable j is the same variable in sub1 and sub2 through host association, so when sub2 sets a new value for j, the value of j in sub1 is changed to 2000.

Next a value is assigned to the array, using variable i as an array constructor. Variable i takes on values from 1 to 5 as a part of the implied DO loop, but the scope of that variable is statement only, so in the next line of the subroutine the value of variable i remains 1 as it was before the array assignment.

When execution returns from sub1 to the main program, i is still 1 and j is 2000. Next, the main program calls its own local subroutine sub2. Subroutine sub2 sets x to 1000. and y to 2000. However, variable x is local to sub2, so changing it has no effect on variable x in the main program. Variable y is the same variable in the main program and in sub2 through host association, so when sub2 sets a new value for y, the value of y in the main program is changed to 2000.

After the call to sub2, the values of i, j, x, and y in the main program are 1, 2000, 100., and 2000. respectively.

We can verify our analysis of the operation of this program by executing it and examining the results:

```
C:\book\chap13>scoping_test
            Beginning:      1       2   100.0   200.0
     In sub1 before sub2:   1       2
       In sub1 in sub2:  1000    2000
     In sub1 after sub2:    1    2000
   After array def in sub2:  1    2000   1000    2000    3000    4000    5000
            After sub1:      1    2000   100.0   200.0
          In sub2: 1000.0  2000.0
          After sub2:        1    2000   100.0  2000.0
```

The output of this program matches our analysis.

It is possible to reuse a local object name for different purposes in nested scoping units. For example, the integer i was defined in subroutine sub1 and would normally have been available to internal subroutine sub2 by host association. However, sub2 defined its own integer i, so in fact the integer i is different in the two scoping units. This sort of double definition is a recipe for confusion, and should be avoided in your code. Instead, just create a new variable name in the internal subroutine that does not conflict with any in the host.

Good Programming Practice

When working with nested scoping units, avoid redefining the meaning of objects that have the same name in both the inner and outer scoping units. This applies especially to internal procedures. You can avoid confusion about the behavior of variables in the internal procedure by simply giving them different names from the variables in the host procedure.

■ 13.2
RECURSIVE PROCEDURES

An ordinary Fortran 95/2003 procedure may not invoke itself either directly or indirectly (that is, by either invoking itself or by invoking another procedure that then invokes the original procedure). In other words, ordinary Fortran 95/2003 procedures are not **recursive.** However, there are certain classes of problems that are most easily solved recursively. For example, the factorial function can be defined as

$$N! = \begin{cases} N(N-1)! & N \geq 1 \\ 1 & N = 0 \end{cases} \qquad (13\text{-}1)$$

This definition can most easily be implemented recursively, with the procedure that calculates $N!$ calling itself to calculate $(N - 1)!$, and that procedure calling itself to calculate $(N - 2)!$, etc. until finally the procedure is called to calculate 0!.

To accommodate such problems, Fortran allows subroutines and functions to be declared recursive. If a procedure is declared recursive, then the Fortran compiler will implement it in such a way that it can invoke itself either directly or indirectly as often as desired.

A subroutine is declared recursive by adding the keyword RECURSIVE to the SUBROUTINE statement. Figure 13-3 shows an example subroutine that calculates the factorial function directly from Equation 13-1. It looks just like any other subroutine except that it is declared to be recursive. You will be asked to verify the proper operation of this subroutine in Exercise 13-2.

FIGURE 13-3

A subroutine to recursively implement the factorial function.

```
RECURSIVE SUBROUTINE factorial ( n, result )
!
!  Purpose:
!    To calculate the factorial function
!            | n(n-1)!    n >= 1
!    n ! =   |
!            | 1          n = 0
!
```

13

(continued)

(concluded)

```
!  Record of revisions:
!      Date         Programmer          Description of change
!      ====         ==========          =====================
!    12/07/06      S. J. Chapman        Original code
!
IMPLICIT NONE

! Data dictionary: declare calling parameter types & definitions
INTEGER, INTENT(IN) :: n           ! Value to calculate
INTEGER, INTENT(OUT) :: result     ! Result

! Data dictionary: declare local variable types & definitions
INTEGER :: temp                    ! Temporary variable

IF ( n >= 1 ) THEN
   CALL factorial ( n-1, temp )
   result = n * temp
ELSE
   result = 1
END IF

END SUBROUTINE factorial
```

It is also possible to define recursive Fortran functions. However, there is an extra complication when you are working with recursive functions. Remember that a function is invoked by naming the function in an expression, while the value to be returned from the function is specified by assigning it to the function name. Thus, if a function were to invoke itself, the function's name *would appear on the left-hand side of an assignment statement when its return value is being set, and on the right-hand side of an assignment statement when it invoking itself recursively.* This double use of the function name could certainly cause confusion.

To avoid confusion between the two uses of the function name in a recursive function, *Fortran allows us to specify two different names for invoking the function recursively and for returning its result.* The actual name of the function is used whenever we want the function to invoke itself, and a special dummy argument is used whenever we want to specify a value to return. The name of this special dummy argument is specified in a RESULT clause in the FUNCTION statement. For example, the following line declares a recursive function fact that uses the dummy argument answer for the value returned to the invoking program unit:

```
RECURSIVE FUNCTION fact(n) RESULT(answer)
```

If a RESULT clause is included in a function, then the function name *may not* appear in a type declaration statement in the function. The name of the dummy result variable is declared instead. For example, Figure 13-4 shows a recursive function that calculates the factorial function directly from Equation 13-1. Note that the type of the result variable answer is declared, not the type of the function name fact. You will be asked to verify the proper operation of this function in Exercise 13-2.

FIGURE 13-4
A function to recursively implement the factorial function.

```
RECURSIVE FUNCTION fact(n) RESULT(answer)
!
!  Purpose:
!    To calculate the factorial function
!                | n(n-1)!     n >= 1
!        n ! =   |
!                | 1           n = 0
!
!  Record of revisions:
!      Date        Programmer           Description of change
!      ====        ==========           =====================
!    12/07/06    S. J. Chapman          Original code
!
IMPLICIT NONE

! Data dictionary: declare calling parameter types & definitions
INTEGER, INTENT(IN) :: n              ! Value to calculate
INTEGER :: answer                     ! Result variable

IF ( n >= 1 ) THEN
   answer = n * fact(n-1)
ELSE
   answer = 1
END IF

END FUNCTION fact
```

User-defined elemental functions, which are present only in Fortran 95, may not be recursive.

13.3

KEYWORD ARGUMENTS AND OPTIONAL ARGUMENTS

In Chapter 7, we stated that when we invoke a procedure, *the actual argument list used to invoke the procedure must match the dummy argument list exactly in number, type, and order*. If the first dummy argument is a real array, then the first actual argument must also be a real array, etc. If the procedure has four dummy arguments, then the procedure invocation must have four actual arguments.

This statement is usually true in Fortran. However, it is possible to change the order of the calling arguments in the list, or to specify actual arguments for only some of the procedure's dummy arguments *provided that the interface to the procedure is explicit*. A procedure interface can be made explicit by placing the procedure in a module, and accessing that module in the invoking program by USE association. (A procedure interface can also be made explicit by using an interface block, as we will explain in the next section.)

If a procedure's interface is explicit, then it is possible to use **keyword arguments** in the calling program to provide increased flexibility. A keyword argument is an argument of the form

```
keyword = actual_argument
```

where `keyword` is the name of the dummy argument that is being associated with the actual argument. If the procedure invocation uses keyword arguments, then the calling arguments can be arranged in any order, because the keywords allow the compiler to sort out which actual argument goes with which dummy argument.

Let's illustrate this idea with an example. Figure 13-5 shows a function `calc` that takes three real arguments: `first`, `second`, and `third`. The function is contained inside a module to make its interface explicit. The main program invokes this function in four different ways, using the same arguments. The first time that the function is invoked, it is done the conventional way, in which the actual arguments match the dummy arguments in type, number, and order.

```
WRITE (*,*) calc ( 3., 1., 2. )
```

The next two times that the function is invoked, we use keyword arguments.

```
WRITE (*,*) calc ( first=3.,second=1.,third=2. )
WRITE (*,*) calc ( second=1.,third=2.,first=3. )
```

The final time that the function is called, we use a mixture of conventional arguments and keyword arguments. The first argument is conventional, and so it is associated with the first dummy argument. The later arguments are keyword arguments, so they are associated with dummy arguments by their keywords. In general, it is legal to mix conventional calling arguments and keyword arguments, but *once a keyword argument appears in the list, all of the remaining arguments must also be keyword arguments.*

```
WRITE (*,*) calc ( 3., third=2.,second=1.)
```

FIGURE 13-5
Program to illustrate the use of keyword arguments.

```
MODULE procs
CONTAINS
    REAL FUNCTION calc ( first, second, third )
    IMPLICIT NONE
    REAL, INTENT(IN) :: first, second, third
    calc = ( first - second ) / third
    END FUNCTION calc
END MODULE procs

PROGRAM test_keywords

USE procs
IMPLICIT NONE

WRITE (*,*) calc ( 3., 1., 2. )
WRITE (*,*) calc ( first=3.,second=1.,third=2. )
WRITE (*,*) calc ( second=1.,third=2.,first=3. )
WRITE (*,*) calc ( 3., third=2.,second=1.)

END PROGRAM test_keywords
```

When the program in Figure 13-5 is executed, the results are

```
C:\book\chap13>test_keywords
        1.000000
        1.000000
        1.000000
        1.000000
```

The function calculated the same value every time regardless of the order in which the arguments were presented.

Keyword arguments allow us to change the order in which actual arguments are presented to a procedure, but by itself that is not very useful. It appears that all we are doing here is creating extra typing to accomplish the same goal! However, keyword arguments are useful when used with optional arguments.

An **optional argument** is a dummy procedure argument that does not always have to be present when the procedure is invoked. If it is present, then the procedure will use it. If not, then the procedure will function without it. Optional arguments are possible only in procedures with explicit interfaces. They are specified by including the OPTIONAL attribute in the declaration of a dummy argument:

```
INTEGER, INTENT(IN), OPTIONAL :: upper_limit
```

The procedure containing an optional argument must have some way to determine if the optional argument is present when the procedure is executed. This is accomplished by a logical intrinsic function PRESENT, which returns a true value if the optional argument is present and a false value if it is not present. For example, a procedure could take some action based on the presence or absence of an optional argument upper_limit as follows:

```
IF ( PRESENT(upper_limit) ) THEN
   . . .
ELSE
   . . .
END IF
```

Keywords are very useful for procedures with optional arguments. If the optional arguments are present and in order in the calling sequence, then no keywords are required. If only some of the optional arguments are present, but the ones that are present are in order, then no keywords are required. However, if optional arguments are out of order, or if some of the earlier optional arguments are missing while later ones are supplied, then keywords must be supplied, and the compiler will use the keywords to sort out which optional arguments are present and which ones are absent.

Incidentally, we have already met an intrinsic function that uses keywords and optional arguments. Recall that the function SELECTED_REAL_KIND accepts two arguments for the desired precision p and the desired range r of the real number. The default order for the two arguments is (p,r), so if the arguments are specified in that order, no keywords are necessary. If they are specified out of order, or if only the range is specified, then the keywords must be used. Examples of legal uses of the function include:

```
kind_num = SELECTED_REAL_KIND(13,100)
kind_num = SELECTED_REAL_KIND(13)
kind_num = SELECTED_REAL_KIND(r=100,p=13)
kind_num = SELECTED_REAL_KIND(r=100)
```

13

EXAMPLE
13-2

Finding the Extreme Values in a Data Set:

Suppose that we would like to write a subroutine that searches through a real array to locate the minimum and/or maximum values in the array, and the locations where the minimum and/or maximum values occur. This subroutine could be used in many different applications. On some occasions, we might be looking for only the maximum value in the array. At other times, we might care only about the minimum value. On still other occasions we might be interested in both values (for example, if we were setting the limits on a plotting program). Sometimes we will care where the extreme values occur within an array, and other times it will not matter.

To accommodate all of these possibilities in a single subroutine, we will write a subroutine that has four optional output arguments: the maximum value, the location of the maximum value, the minimum value, and the location of the minimum value. The values returned will depend on the arguments specified by the user in the subroutine call.

Solution

The subroutine is shown in Figure 13-6. The subroutine can return from one to four optional results in any possible combination. Note that the subroutine must have an explicit interface in order to support optional arguments, so it is placed inside a module.

FIGURE 13-6

A subroutine to locate the extreme values in a real array. The subroutine is embedded in a module to make its interface explicit.

```
MODULE procs
CONTAINS
    SUBROUTINE extremes(a, n, maxval, pos_maxval, minval, pos_minval)
    !
    !   Purpose:
    !     To find the maximum and minimum values in an array, and
    !     the location of those values in the array.  This subroutine
    !     returns its output values in optional arguments.
    !
    !   Record of revisions:
    !       Date         Programmer          Description of change
    !       ====         ==========          =====================
    !     12/08/06     S. J. Chapman         Original code
    !
    IMPLICIT NONE

    ! Data dictionary: declare calling parameter types & definitions
    INTEGER, INTENT(IN) :: n                   ! # vals in array a
    REAL, INTENT(IN), DIMENSION(n) :: a        ! Input data.
    REAL, INTENT(OUT), OPTIONAL :: maxval      ! Maximum value.
    INTEGER, INTENT(OUT), OPTIONAL :: pos_maxval ! Pos of maxval
    REAL, INTENT(OUT), OPTIONAL :: minval      ! Minimum value.
    INTEGER, INTENT(OUT), OPTIONAL :: pos_minval ! Pos of minval

    ! Data dictionary: declare local variable types & definitions
    INTEGER :: i                               ! Index
```

(continued)

(concluded)

```
REAL :: real_max                ! Max value
INTEGER :: pos_max              ! Pos of max value
REAL :: real_min                ! Min value
INTEGER :: pos_min              ! Pos of min value

! Initialize the values to first value in array.
real_max = a(1)
pos_max = 1
real_min = a(1)
pos_min = 1

! Find the extreme values in a(2) through a(n).
DO i = 2, n
   max: IF ( a(i) > real_max ) THEN
      real_max = a(i)
      pos_max = i
   END IF max
   min: IF ( a(i) < real_min ) THEN
      real_min = a(i)
      pos_min = i
   END IF min
END DO

! Report the results
IF ( PRESENT(maxval) ) THEN
   maxval = real_max
END IF
IF ( PRESENT(pos_maxval) ) THEN
   pos_maxval = pos_max
END IF
IF ( PRESENT(minval) ) THEN
   minval=real_min
END IF
IF ( PRESENT(pos_minval) ) THEN
   pos_minval=pos_min
END IF

END SUBROUTINE extremes
END MODULE procs
```

You will be asked to verify the proper operation of this subroutine in Exercise 13-3 at the end of this chapter.

13

Quiz 13-1

This quiz provides a quick check to see if you have understood the concepts introduced in Sections 13.1 through 13.3. If you have trouble with the quiz, reread the sections, ask your instructor, or discuss the material with a fellow student. The answers to this quiz are found in the back of the book.

(continued)

(*continued*)

1. What is the scope of an object in Fortran? What are the three levels of scope in Fortran?

2. What is host association? Explain how variables and constants are inherited by host association.

3. What is the value of z that is written out after the following code is executed? Explain how the value is produced.

```
PROGRAM x
REAL :: z = 10.
TYPE position
    REAL :: x
    REAL :: y
    REAL :: z
END TYPE position
TYPE (position) :: xyz
xyz = position(1., 2., 3.)
z = fun1( z )
WRITE (*,*) z
CONTAINS
    REAL FUNCTION fun1(x)
    REAL, INTENT(IN) :: x
    fun1 = (x + xyz%x) / xyz%z
    END FUNCTION fun1
END PROGRAM x
```

4. What is the value of i after the following code is executed?

```
PROGRAM xyz
INTEGER :: i = 0
INTEGER, DIMENSION(6) :: count
i = i + 27
count = (/ (2*i, i=6,1,-1) /)
i = i - 7
WRITE (*,*) i
END PROGRAM xyz
```

5. Is the following program legal or illegal? Why or why not?

```
PROGRAM abc
REAL :: abc = 10.
WRITE (*,*) abc
END PROGRAM abc
```

6. What are recursive procedures? How are they declared?

7. Is the following function legal or illegal? Why or why not?

(*continued*)

(concluded)

```
RECURSIVE FUNCTION sum_1_n(n) RESULT(sum)
IMPLICIT NONE
INTEGER, INTENT(IN) :: n
INTEGER :: sum_1_n
IF ( n > 1 ) THEN
    sum = n + sum_1_n(n-1)
ELSE
    sum = 1
END IF
END FUNCTION sum_1_n
```

8. What are keyword arguments? What requirement(s) must be met before they can be used? Why would you want to use a keyword argument?

9. What are optional arguments? What requirement(s) must be met before they can be used? Why would you want to use an optional argument?

13.4

PROCEDURE INTERFACES AND INTERFACE BLOCKS

As we have seen, a calling program unit must have an *explicit interface* to a procedure if it is to use advanced Fortran features such as keyword arguments and optional arguments. In addition, an explicit interface allows the compiler to catch many errors that occur in the calling sequences between procedures. These errors might otherwise produce subtle and hard-to-find bugs.

The easiest way to create an explicit interface is to place procedures in a module, and then use that module in the calling program unit. Any procedures placed in a module will always have an explicit interface.

Unfortunately, it is sometimes inconvenient or even impossible to place the procedures in a module. For example, suppose that a technical organization has a large library of hundreds of subroutines and functions written in an earlier version of Fortran that are used both in old, still used programs and in new programs. This is a very common occurrence because various versions of Fortran have been in general use since the late 1950s. Rewriting all of these subroutines and functions to place them into modules and add explicit interface characteristics such as the INTENT attribute would create a major problem. If the procedures were modified in this way, then the older programs would no longer be able to use them. Most organizations would not want to make two versions of each procedure, one with an explicit interface and one without, because this would create a significant configuration control problem whenever one of the library procedures is modified. Both versions of the procedure would have to be modified separately, and each one would have to be independently verified to be working properly.

13

The problem can be even worse, since the external library of procedures could be written in another language such as C. In that case, it is completely impossible to place the procedures in a module.

13.4.1 Creating Interface Blocks

How do we take advantage of the features of an explicit interface when it is impossible or impractical to place procedures into a module? In these cases, Fortran allows us to define an **interface block** in the invoking program unit. The interface block specifies all of the interface characteristics of an external procedure, and the Fortran compiler uses the information in the interface block to perform its consistency checks and to apply such advanced features as keyword arguments.[2]

An interface block is created by duplicating the calling argument information of a procedure within the interface. The general form of an interface is

```
INTERFACE
    interface_body_1
    interface_body_2
    . . .
END INTERFACE
```

Each `interface_body` consists of the initial SUBROUTINE or FUNCTION statement of the corresponding external procedure, the type specification statements associated with its arguments, and an END SUBROUTINE or END FUNCTION statement. These statements provide enough information for the compiler to check the consistency of the interface between the calling program and the external procedure.

When an interface is used, it is placed in the header section of the invoking program unit along with all of the type declaration statements.

EXAMPLE 13-3

Creating an Interface to an External Subroutine:

In Example 7-1 we created a subroutine `sort` to sort an array of real values into ascending order. Assume that it is impossible to place that subroutine into a module, and create an interface block to explicitly define the interface between the subroutine and a calling program unit. Use that interface to allow a program to call subroutine `sort` while using keyword arguments.

SOLUTION
First, we must create an interface for subroutine `sort`. The interface will consist of the SUBROUTINE statement, the type declaration statements of the subroutine's dummy arguments, and the END SUBROUTINE statement. It is

```
INTERFACE
    SUBROUTINE sort (array, n)
    IMPLICIT NONE
    REAL, DIMENSION(:), INTENT(INOUT) :: array
```

---

[2] Fortran interface blocks are essentially equivalent to prototypes in the C language.

```
           INTEGER, INTENT(IN) :: n
           END SUBROUTINE sort
        END INTERFACE
```

Next, we will use this interface in the calling program's header to explicitly define the interface to subroutine `sort`. Figure 13-7 shows a calling program that uses the interface block to create an explicit interface to subroutine `sort`.

FIGURE 13-7
A simple program illustrating the use of interface blocks.

```
PROGRAM interface_example
!
!   Purpose:
!     To illustrate the use of interface blocks to create explicit
!     interfaces. This program uses an interface block to create
!     an explicit interface to subroutine "sort", and then takes
!     advantage of that interface to use keyword arguments.
!
!   Record of revisions:
!      Date          Programmer          Description of change
!      ====          ==========          =====================
!    12/04/06      S. J. Chapman        Original code
!
IMPLICIT NONE

! Declare interface to subroutine "sort"
INTERFACE
    SUBROUTINE sort(a,n)
    IMPLICIT NONE
    REAL, DIMENSION(:), INTENT(INOUT) :: a
    INTEGER, INTENT(IN) :: n
    END SUBROUTINE sort
END INTERFACE

! Data dictionary: declare local variable types & definitions
REAL, DIMENSION(6) :: array = (/ 1., 5., 3., 2., 6., 4. /)
INTEGER :: nvals = 6

! Call "sort" to sort data into ascending order.
CALL sort (N=nvals,A=array)

! Write out sorted array.
WRITE (*,*) array

END PROGRAM interface_example
```

When this program is compiled together with subroutine `sort` and executed, the results are:

```
C:\book\chap13>interface_example
      1.000000      2.000000      3.000000      4.000000
      5.000000      6.000000
```

The compiler used the interface block to correctly sort out the keyword arguments in the call to subroutine `sort`, and the program produced the correct answer.

13.4.2 Notes on the Use of Interface Blocks

How and when should interface blocks be used to best advantage in a program? When we look at the structure of an interface block, it seems that we are just creating extra work for ourselves by duplicating some of the statements from the original procedure in the interface block. When should we create an interface block, and why? The following notes provide guidance on the use of interface blocks in Fortran.

1. Whenever possible, *avoid interface blocks by simply placing all of your procedures in modules*, and access the appropriate modules by USE association.

Good Programming Practice
Avoid interface blocks by placing your procedures in modules whenever possible.

2. An interface block must not specify the interface of a procedure already in a module available by USE association. This constitutes a double definition of the explicit interface, which is illegal and will cause a compiler error.
3. A common use of interface blocks is to provide explicit interfaces to separately compiled procedures written in earlier versions of Fortran or in other languages such as C. In this case, writing an interface block allows modern Fortran programs to have an explicit interface with full argument checking, while allowing older or non-Fortran programs to continue to use the procedures unchanged.
4. An easy way to make the interfaces for a large library of old subroutines or functions available to all calling program units is to place them in a module, and then to USE that module in each calling program unit. For example, the interface to subroutine sort could be placed in a module as follows:

```
MODULE interface_definitions
    INTERFACE
        SUBROUTINE sort (array, n)
        IMPLICIT NONE
        REAL, DIMENSION(:), INTENT(INOUT) :: array
        INTEGER, INTENT(IN) :: n
        END SUBROUTINE sort
        . . .
        (insert other procedure interfaces here)
        . . .
    END INTERFACE
END MODULE interface_definitions
```

- Unlike module procedures, there is no CONTAINS statement when interfaces are included in a module.

Good Programming Practice
If you must create interfaces to many procedures, place all of the interfaces in a module so that they will be easily accessible to many program units by USE association.

13

5. Each interface is a separate scoping unit, so the same variable name may appear in an interface and in a program including that interface without causing a conflict.

6. The names used for dummy arguments in an interface block do not have to be the same as the names used for the dummy arguments in the corresponding procedures. The dummy arguments in the interface block must match the dummy arguments in the corresponding procedures in type, intent, array size, etc., but the names themselves do not have to match. However, there is no reason for you to ever rename the arguments in an interface. Even though it is legal to do so, it adds extra confusion and increases the possibility for error.

7. An interface block is an independent scoping unit, so any dummy variables used in the interface block *must be declared separately within the block*, even if they were declared in the surrounding scoping unit.

```
PROGRAM test_interface

! Declare variables
REAL,DIMENSION(10) :: x, y          ! x, y declared in main
INTEGER :: n                        ! n declared in main
...
INTERFACE
   SUBROUTINE proc (x, y, n)
   IMPLICIT NONE
   REAL, DIMENSION(:), INTENT(INOUT) :: x ! Declared in interface block
   REAL, DIMENSION(:), INTENT(INOUT) :: y ! Declared in interface block
   INTEGER, INTENT(IN) :: n               ! Declared in interface block
   END SUBROUTINE proc
END INTERFACE
...
CALL proc(x,y,n)
...
END PROGRAM test_interface
```

F-2003 ONLY

Fortran 2003 includes an IMPORT statement that can modify this behavior. If an IMPORT statement appears in an interface definition, then the variables specified in the IMPORT statement will be imported from the host scoping unit. If the IMPORT statement appears without a list of variables, then all of the variables in the host scoping unit will be imported. Examples of IMPORT statements are shown below:

```
IMPORT :: a, b    ! Import variables a and b only
IMPORT            ! Import all variables in host scoping unit
```

13

13.5

GENERIC PROCEDURES

The Fortran 95/2003 language includes both generic and specific intrinsic functions. A **generic function** is a function that can operate properly with many different types of input data, while a **specific function** is a function that requires one specific type of input data. For example, Fortran includes a generic function ABS() to take the absolute value of a number. It can function with integer data, single-precision real data, double-precision real data, or complex data. The language also includes the specific functions IABS(), which requires an integer input value; ABS(), which requires a single-precision real input value; DABS(), which requires a double-precision real input value; and CABS(), which requires a complex input value.

Now for a little secret: the generic function ABS() does not actually exist anywhere within a Fortran compiler. Instead, whenever the compiler encounters the generic function, it examines the arguments of the function and invokes the appropriate specific function for those arguments. For example, if the compiler detects the generic function ABS(-34) in a program, it will generate a call to the specific function IABS() because the calling argument of the function is an integer. When we use generic functions, we are allowing the compiler to do some of the detail work for us.

13.5.1 User-Defined Generic Procedures

Fortran 95/2003 allows us to define our own generic procedures in addition to the standard ones built into the compiler. For example, we might wish to define a generic subroutine sort that is capable of sorting integer data, single-precision real data, double-precision real data, or character data, depending on the arguments supplied to it. We could use that generic subroutine in our programs instead of worrying about the specific details of the calling arguments each time that we want to sort a data set.

How is this accomplished? It is done with a special version of the interface block called a **generic interface block.** If we add a generic name to the INTERFACE statement, then every procedure interface defined within the interface block will be assumed to be a specific version of that generic procedure. The general form of an interface block used to declare a generic procedure is

```
INTERFACE generic_name
   specific_interface_body_1
   specific_interface_body_2
   . . .
END INTERFACE
```

When the compiler encounters the generic procedure name in a program unit containing this generic interface block, it will examine the arguments associated with the call to the generic procedure to decide which of the specific procedures it should use.

In order for the compiler to determine which specific procedure to use, each of the specific procedures in the block must be *unambiguously* distinguished from the others. For example, one specific procedure might have real input data while another one has integer input data, etc. The compiler can then compare the generic procedure's calling sequence to the calling sequences of each specific procedure to decide which one to use. The following rules apply to the specific procedures in a generic interface block:

1. Either all of the procedures in a generic interface block must be subroutines, or all of the procedures in the block must be functions. They cannot be mixed, because the generic procedure being defined must either be a subroutine or a function—it cannot be both.

13

2. Every procedure in the block must be distinguishable from all of the other procedures in the block by the type, number, and position of its nonoptional arguments. As long as each procedure is distinguishable from all of the other procedures in the block, the compiler will be able to decide which procedure to use by comparing the type, number, and position of the generic procedure's calling arguments with the type, number, and position of each specific procedure's dummy arguments.

Generic interface blocks may be placed either in the header of a program unit that invokes the generic procedure or in a module and that module may be used in the program unit that invokes the generic procedure.

Good Programming Practice

Use generic interface blocks to define procedures that can function with different types of input data. Generic procedures will add to the flexibility of your programs, making it easier for them to handle different types of data.

As an example, suppose that a programmer has written the following four subroutines to sort data into ascending order.

Subroutine	Function
SUBROUTINE sorti (array, nvals)	Sorts integer data
SUBROUTINE sortr (array, nvals)	Sorts single-precision real data
SUBROUTINE sortd (array, nvals)	Sorts double-precision real data
SUBROUTINE sortc (array, nvals)	Sorts character data

Now the programmer wishes to create a generic subroutine sort to sort any of these types of data into ascending order. This can be done with the following generic interface block (parameters single and double will have to be previously defined):

```
INTERFACE sort
   SUBROUTINE sorti (array, nvals)
   IMPLICIT NONE
   INTEGER, INTENT(IN) :: nvals
   INTEGER, INTENT(INOUT), DIMENSION(nvals) :: array
   END SUBROUTINE sorti

   SUBROUTINE sortr (array, nvals)
   IMPLICIT NONE
   INTEGER, INTENT(IN) :: nvals
   REAL(KIND=single), INTENT(INOUT), DIMENSION(nvals) :: array
   END SUBROUTINE sortr

   SUBROUTINE sortd (array, nvals)
   IMPLICIT NONE
   INTEGER, INTENT(IN) :: nvals
   REAL(KIND=double), INTENT(INOUT), DIMENSION(nvals) :: array
   END SUBROUTINE sortd
```

13

```
      SUBROUTINE sortc (array, nvals)
      IMPLICIT NONE
      INTEGER, INTENT(IN) :: nvals
      CHARACTER(len=*), INTENT(INOUT), DIMENSION(nvals) :: array
      END SUBROUTINE sortc
   END INTERFACE sort
```

This generic interface block satisfies the requirements stated above because all of the procedures are subroutines, and they can be distinguished from one another by the type of the array in their calling sequences.

13.5.2 Generic Interfaces for Procedures in Modules

In the above example, an explicit interface was given for each specific subroutine in the generic interface block defining the generic subroutine sort. This arrangement would be appropriate if each of the specific subroutines were separately compiled and did not have an explicit interface. But what happens if the individual subroutines are in a module, and so they already have explicit interfaces?

We learned in Section 13.4.2 that it is illegal to explicitly declare an interface for a procedure that already has an explicit interface by being in a module. If that is so, then how can we include procedures defined in modules in a generic interface block? To get around this problem, Fortran includes a special MODULE PROCEDURE statement that can be used in a generic interface block. The form of this statement is

```
   MODULE PROCEDURE module_procedure_1 (, module_procedure_2, ...)
```

where *module_procedure_1* etc. are the names of procedures whose interfaces are defined in a module that is available by USE association.

If the four sorting subroutines had been defined in a module instead of being separately compiled, then the generic interface for subroutine sort would become:

```
      INTERFACE sort
         MODULE PROCEDURE sorti
         MODULE PROCEDURE sortr
         MODULE PROCEDURE sortd
         MODULE PROCEDURE sortc
      END INTERFACE sort
```

This interface block should be placed in the module in which the procedures are defined.

EXAMPLE   *Creating a Generic Subroutine:*
13-4

Create a subroutine maxval that returns the maximum value in an array, and optionally the location of that maximum value. This subroutine should work correctly for integer, single-precision real, double-precision real, single-precision complex, or double-precision complex data. Since relational comparisons of complex data values are meaningless, the complex versions of the subroutine should look for the maximum absolute value in the array.

SOLUTION

We will be producing a generic subroutine that can work with five different types of input data, so in fact we create five different subroutines and relate them together by using a generic interface block. Note that the subroutines must have an explicit interface in order to support optional arguments, so they will all be placed in a module.

1. **State the problem.**

Write a generic subroutine to find the maximum value in an array and optionally the location of that maximum value. The subroutine should work for integer, single-precision real, double-precision real, single-precision complex, or double-precision complex data. For complex data, the comparisons should be based on the magnitude of the values in the array.

2. **Define the inputs and outputs.**

There are five different subroutines in this problem. The input to each subroutine will be an array of values of the appropriate type, plus the number of values in the array. The outputs will be as follows:

(*a*) A variable containing the maximum value in the input array.

(*b*) An optional integer variable containing the offset in the array at which the maximum value occurred.

The types of the input and output arguments for each of the five subroutines are specified in Table 13-1.

3. **Describe the algorithm.**

The pseudocode for the first three specific subroutines is identical. It is:

```
! Initialize "value_max" to a(1) and "pos_max" to 1.
value_max ← a(1)
pos_max ← 1

! Find the maximum values in a(2) through a(nvals)
DO for i = 2 to nvals
    IF a(i) > value_max THEN
        value_max ← a(i)
```

TABLE 13-1
Arguments for the subroutines

Specific Name	Input Array Type	Array Length Type	Output Maximum Value	Optional Location of Max Value
maxval_i	Integer	Integer	Integer	Integer
maxval_r	Single-precision real	Integer	Single-precision real	Integer
maxval_d	Double-precision real	Integer	Double-precision real	Integer
maxval_c	Single-precision complex	Integer	Single-precision real	Integer
maxval_dc	Double-precision complex	Integer	Double-precision real	Integer

13

```
                pos_max ← i
            END of IF
        END of DO

        ! Report results
        IF argument pos_maxval is present THEN
            pos_maxval ← pos_max
        END of IF
```

The pseudocode for the two complex subroutines is slightly different, because comparisons must be with the absolute values. It is:

```
        ! Initialize "value_max" to ABS(a(1)) and "pos_max" to 1.
        value_max ← ABS(a(1))
        pos_max ← 1

        ! Find the maximum values in a(2) through a(nvals)
        DO for i = 2 to nvals
            IF ABS(a(i)) > value_max THEN
                value_max ← ABS(a(i))
                pos_max ← i
            END of IF
        END of DO

        ! Report results
        IF argument pos_maxval is present THEN
            pos_maxval ← pos_max
        END of IF
```

4. **Turn the algorithm into Fortran statements.**
   The resulting Fortran subroutine is shown in Figure 13-8.

FIGURE 13-8
A generic subroutine maxval that finds the maximum value in an array and optionally the location of that maximum value.

```
MODULE generic_maxval
!
!   Purpose:
!     To produce a generic procedure maxval that returns the
!     maximum value in an array and optionally the location
!     of that maximum value for the following input data types:
!     integer, single precision real, double precision real,
!     single precision complex, and double precision complex.
!     Complex comparisons are done on the absolute values of
!     values in the input array.
!
!   Record of revisions:
!       Date        Programmer          Description of change
!       ====        ==========          =====================
!     12/15/06     S. J. Chapman        Original code
!
IMPLICIT NONE

! Declare parameters:
```

(continued)

(continued)

```
INTEGER, PARAMETER :: SGL = SELECTED_REAL_KIND(p=6)
INTEGER, PARAMETER :: DBL = SELECTED_REAL_KIND(p=13)

! Declare generic interface.
INTERFACE maxval
   MODULE PROCEDURE maxval_i
   MODULE PROCEDURE maxval_r
   MODULE PROCEDURE maxval_d
   MODULE PROCEDURE maxval_c
   MODULE PROCEDURE maxval_dc
END INTERFACE

CONTAINS
   SUBROUTINE maxval_i ( array, nvals, value_max, pos_maxval )
   IMPLICIT NONE

   ! List of calling arguments:
   INTEGER, INTENT(IN) :: nvals                             ! # vals.
   INTEGER, INTENT(IN), DIMENSION(nvals) :: array    ! Input data.
   INTEGER, INTENT(OUT) :: value_max                        ! Max value.
   INTEGER, INTENT(OUT), OPTIONAL :: pos_maxval      ! Position

   ! List of local variables:
   INTEGER :: i                              ! Index
   INTEGER :: pos_max                        ! Pos of max value

   ! Initialize the values to first value in array.
   value_max = array(1)
   pos_max = 1

   ! Find the extreme values in array(2) through array(nvals).
   DO i = 2, nvals
      IF ( array(i) > value_max ) THEN
         value_max = array(i)
         pos_max = i
      END IF
   END DO

   ! Report the results
   IF ( PRESENT(pos_maxval) ) THEN
      pos_maxval = pos_max
   END IF

   END SUBROUTINE maxval_i

   SUBROUTINE maxval_r ( array, nvals, value_max, pos_maxval )
   IMPLICIT NONE

   ! List of calling arguments:
   INTEGER, INTENT(IN) :: nvals
   REAL(KIND=SGL), INTENT(IN), DIMENSION(nvals) :: array
   REAL(KIND=SGL), INTENT(OUT) :: value_max
   INTEGER, INTENT(OUT), OPTIONAL :: pos_maxval

   ! List of local variables:
   INTEGER :: i                              ! Index
   INTEGER :: pos_max                        ! Pos of max value
```

13

(continued)

(continued)

```fortran
! Initialize the values to first value in array.
value_max = array(1)
pos_max = 1

! Find the extreme values in array(2) through array(nvals).
DO i = 2, nvals
   IF ( array(i) > value_max ) THEN
      value_max = array(i)
      pos_max = i
   END IF
END DO

! Report the results
IF ( PRESENT(pos_maxval) ) THEN
   pos_maxval = pos_max
END IF

END SUBROUTINE maxval_r

SUBROUTINE maxval_d ( array, nvals, value_max, pos_maxval )
IMPLICIT NONE

! List of calling arguments:
INTEGER, INTENT(IN) :: nvals
REAL(KIND=DBL), INTENT(IN), DIMENSION(nvals) :: array
REAL(KIND=DBL), INTENT(OUT) :: value_max
INTEGER, INTENT(OUT), OPTIONAL :: pos_maxval

! List of local variables:
INTEGER :: i                             ! Index
INTEGER :: pos_max                       ! Pos of max value

! Initialize the values to first value in array.
value_max = array(1)
pos_max = 1

! Find the extreme values in array(2) through array(nvals).
DO i = 2, nvals
   IF ( array(i) > value_max ) THEN
      value_max = array(i)
      pos_max = i
   END IF
END DO

! Report the results
IF ( PRESENT(pos_maxval) ) THEN
   pos_maxval = pos_max
END IF

END SUBROUTINE maxval_d

SUBROUTINE maxval_c ( array, nvals, value_max, pos_maxval )
IMPLICIT NONE

! List of calling arguments:
INTEGER, INTENT(IN) :: nvals
COMPLEX(KIND=SGL), INTENT(IN), DIMENSION(nvals) :: array
```

(continued)

(concluded)

```fortran
      REAL(KIND=SGL), INTENT(OUT) :: value_max
      INTEGER, INTENT(OUT), OPTIONAL :: pos_maxval

      ! List of local variables:
      INTEGER :: i                          ! Index
      INTEGER :: pos_max                    ! Pos of max value

      ! Initialize the values to first value in array.
      value_max = ABS(array(1))
      pos_max = 1

      ! Find the extreme values in array(2) through array(nvals).
      DO i = 2, nvals
         IF ( ABS(array(i)) > value_max ) THEN
            value_max = ABS(array(i))
            pos_max = i
         END IF
      END DO

      ! Report the results
      IF ( PRESENT(pos_maxval) ) THEN
         pos_maxval = pos_max
      END IF

      END SUBROUTINE maxval_c

      SUBROUTINE maxval_dc ( array, nvals, value_max, pos_maxval )
      IMPLICIT NONE

      ! List of calling arguments:
      INTEGER, INTENT(IN) :: nvals
      COMPLEX(KIND=DBL), INTENT(IN), DIMENSION(nvals) :: array
      REAL(KIND=DBL), INTENT(OUT) :: value_max
      INTEGER, INTENT(OUT), OPTIONAL :: pos_maxval

      ! List of local variables:
      INTEGER :: i                          ! Index
      INTEGER :: pos_max                    ! Pos of max value

      ! Initialize the values to first value in array.
      value_max = ABS(array(1))
      pos_max = 1

      ! Find the extreme values in array(2) through array(nvals).
      DO i = 2, nvals
         IF ( ABS(array(i)) > value_max ) THEN
            value_max = ABS(array(i))
            pos_max = i
         END IF
      END DO

      ! Report the results
      IF ( PRESENT(pos_maxval) ) THEN
         pos_maxval = pos_max
      END IF

      END SUBROUTINE maxval_dc

   END MODULE generic_maxval
```

13

5. **Test the resulting Fortran programs.**

To test this generic subroutine, it is necessary to write a test driver program to call the subroutine with the five different types of data which it supports, and display the results. The test driver program will also illustrate the use of keyword and optional arguments, by calling the subroutine with different combinations and orders of arguments. Figure 13-9 shows an appropriate test driver program.

FIGURE 13-9

Test driver program for generic subroutine `maxval`.

```
PROGRAM test_maxval
!
!  Purpose:
!    To test the generic subroutine maxval with five different types
!    of input data sets.
!
!  Record of revisions:
!      Date          Programmer           Description of change
!      ====          ==========           =====================
!    12/15/06    S. J. Chapman            Original code
!
USE generic_maxval
IMPLICIT NONE

! Data dictionary: declare variable types & definitions
INTEGER, DIMENSION(6) :: array_i                  ! Integer array
REAL(KIND=SGL), DIMENSION(6) :: array_r           ! Sng prec real arr
REAL(KIND=DBL), DIMENSION(6) :: array_d           ! Dbl prec real arr
COMPLEX(KIND=SGL), DIMENSION(6) :: array_c        ! Sing. prec. cx arr
COMPLEX(KIND=DBL), DIMENSION(6) :: array_dc       ! Sing. prec. cx arr
INTEGER :: value_max_i                            ! Max value
REAL(KIND=SGL) :: value_max_r                     ! Max value
REAL(KIND=DBL) :: value_max_d                     ! Max value
INTEGER :: pos_maxval                             ! Pos of max value

! Initialize arrays
array_i = (/ -13, 3, 2, 0, 25, -2 /)
array_r = (/ -13., 3., 2., 0., 25., -2. /)
array_d = (/ -13._DBL, 3._DBL, 2._DBL, 0._DBL, &
              25._DBL, -2._DBL /)
array_c = (/ (1.,2.), (-4.,-6.), (4.,-7), (3.,4.), &
             (0.,1.), (6.,-8.) /)
array_dc = (/ (1._DBL,2._DBL), (-4._DBL,-6._DBL), &
              (4._DBL,-7._DBL), (3._DBL,4._DBL), &
              (0._DBL,1._DBL), (6._DBL,-8._DBL) /)

! Test integer subroutine. Include optional argument.
CALL maxval ( array_i, 6, value_max_i, pos_maxval )
WRITE (*,1000) value_max_i, pos_maxval
1000 FORMAT (' Integer args: max value = ',I3, &
             '; position = ', I3 )

! Test single prec real subroutine. Leave out optional arg.
CALL maxval ( array_r, 6, value_max_r )
```

(continued)

(concluded)

```
WRITE (*,1010) value_max_r
1010 FORMAT (' Single prec real args: max value = ',F7.3)

! Test double prec real subroutine. Use keywords.
CALL maxval (ARRAY=array_d,NVALS=6,VALUE_MAX=value_max_d)
WRITE (*,1020) value_max_d
1020 FORMAT (' Double prec real args: max value = ',F7.3)

! Test single prec cmplx subroutine. Use scrambled keywords.
CALL maxval ( NVALS=6, ARRAY=array_c, VALUE_MAX=value_max_r, &
              POS_MAXVAL=pos_maxval)
WRITE (*,1030) value_max_r, pos_maxval
1030 FORMAT (' Single precision complex args:' &
             ' max abs value = ',F7.3, &
             '; position = ', I3 )

! Test double prec cmplx subroutine. Leave out optional arg.
CALL maxval ( array_dc, 6, value_max_d )
WRITE (*,1040) value_max_r
1040 FORMAT (' Double precision complex args:' &
             ' max abs value = ',F7.3 )

END PROGRAM test_maxval
```

When the test driver program is executed, the results are:

```
C:\book\chap13>test_maxval
Integer arguments: max value =  25; position =   5
Single precison real arguments: max value = 25.000
Double precison real arguments: max value = 25.000
Single precision complex arguments: max abs value =  10.000; position =  6
Double precision complex arguments: max abs value = 10.000
```

It is obvious from inspection that the subroutine picked out the proper maximum values and locations for each data type.

13.5.3 Generic Bound Procedures

Fortran 2003 procedures bound to derived data types can also be generic. These procedures are declared by using the GENERIC statement, as shown below.

```
TYPE :: point
   REAL :: x
   REAL :: y
CONTAINS
   GENERIC :: add => point_plus_point, point_plus_scalar
END TYPE point
```

This binding declares that the two procedures point_plus_point and point_plus_scalar will both be known by the generic procedure add, and will both be accessed using the component operator: p%add().

13

As with other generic interfaces, every procedure in the generic binding must be distinguishable from all of the other procedures in the binding by the type, number, and position of its non-optional arguments. As long as each procedure is distinguishable from all of the other procedures in the binding, the compiler will be able to decide which procedure to use by comparing the type, number, and position of the generic procedure's calling arguments with the type, number, and position of each specific procedure's dummy arguments.

EXAMPLE 13-5

Using Generic Bound Procedures:

Create a vector data type with a bound generic procedure add. There should be two specific procedures associated with the generic procedure: one to add two vectors and one to add a vector to a scalar.

SOLUTION

A module using bound generic procedures to add either a vector or a scalar to another vector is shown in Figure 13-10.

FIGURE 13-10
Two-dimensional vector module with bound generic procedures.

```
MODULE generic_procedure_module
!
!   Purpose:
!     To define the derived data type for 2D vectors,
!     plus two generic bound procedures.
!
!   Record of revisions:
!       Date          Programmer            Description of change
!       ====          ==========            =====================
!     12/27/06      S. J. Chapman           Original code
!
IMPLICIT NONE

! Declare type vector
TYPE :: vector
   REAL :: x                              ! X value
   REAL :: y                              ! Y value
CONTAINS
   GENERIC :: add => vector_plus_vector, vector_plus_scalar
   PROCEDURE,PASS :: vector_plus_vector
   PROCEDURE,PASS :: vector_plus_scalar
END TYPE vector

! Add procedures
CONTAINS

   TYPE (vector) FUNCTION vector_plus_vector ( this, v2 )
   !
   !   Purpose:
   !     To add two vectors.
```

(continued)

(concluded)

```
!   Record of revisions:
!       Date         Programmer          Description of change
!       ====         ==========          =====================
!     12/27/06     S. J. Chapman         Original code
!
IMPLICIT NONE

! Data dictionary: declare calling parameter types & definitions
CLASS(vector),INTENT(IN) :: this          ! First vector
CLASS(vector),INTENT(IN) :: v2            ! Second vector

! Add the vectors
vector_plus_vector%x=this%x + v2%x
vector_plus_vector%y=this%y + v2%y

END FUNCTION vector_plus_vector

TYPE (vector) FUNCTION vector_plus_scalar ( this, s )
!
! Purpose:
!    To add a vector and a scalar.
!
!   Record of revisions:
!       Date         Programmer          Description of change
!       ====         ==========          =====================
!     12/27/06     S. J. Chapman         Original code
!
IMPLICIT NONE

! Data dictionary: declare calling parameter types & definitions
CLASS(vector),INTENT(IN) :: this          ! First vector
REAL,INTENT(IN) :: s                      ! Scalar

! Add the points
vector_plus_scalar%x=this%x + s
vector_plus_scalar%y=this%y + s

END FUNCTION vector_plus_scalar
END MODULE generic_procedure_module
```

The test driver program is shown in Figure 13-11.

FIGURE 13-11

Test driver program for the vector module with bound generic procedures.

```
PROGRAM test_generic_procedures
!
! Purpose:
!    To test generic bound procedures.
!
! Record of revisions:
!       Date         Programmer          Description of change
!       ====         ==========          =====================
!     12/27/06     S. J. Chapman         Original code
```

13

(continued)

(concluded)

```
!
USE generic_procedure_module
IMPLICIT NONE

! Enter first point
TYPE(vector) :: v1                    ! First vector
TYPE(vector) :: v2                    ! Second vector
REAL :: s                             ! Scalar

! Get the first vector
WRITE (*,*) 'Enter the first vector (x,y):'
READ (*,*) v1%x, v1%y

! Get the second vector
WRITE (*,*) 'Enter the second vector (x,y):'
READ (*,*) v2%x, v2%y

! Get a scalar
WRITE (*,*) 'Enter a scalar:'
READ (*,*) s

! Add the vectors
WRITE (*,1000) v1%add(v2)
1000 FORMAT(1X,'The sum of the vectors is (',F8.2,',',F8.2,')')

! Subtract the points
WRITE (*,1010) v1%add(s)
1010 FORMAT(1X,'The sum of the vector and scalar is (',F8.2,',',F8.2,')')
END PROGRAM test_generic_procedures
```

We will test this program using the same data as in the previous example.

```
C:\book\chap12>test_generic_procedures
  Enter the first vector (x,y):
  -2, 2.
  Enter the second vector (x,y):
  4., 3.
  Enter a scalar:
  2
  The sum of the vectors is (    2.00,    5.00)
  The sum of the vector and scalar is (    0.00,    4.00)
```

The functions appear to be working correctly.

◼ 13.6

EXTENDING FORTRAN WITH USER-DEFINED OPERATORS AND ASSIGNMENTS

When we were introduced to derived data types in Chapter 12, we learned that none of the intrinsic unary and binary operators are defined for derived data types. In fact, the only operation that was defined for derived data types was the assignment of one item of a derived data type to another variable of the same type. We were able to work freely with the *components* of derived data types, but not with the derived data types themselves. This is a serious limitation that reduces the usefulness of derived data types.

Fortunately, there is a way around this limitation. Fortran 95/2003 is an *extensible* language, which means that an individual programmer can add new features to it to accommodate special types of problems. The first examples of this extensibility were derived data types themselves. In addition, Fortran permits the programmer to define new unary and binary operators for both intrinsic and derived data types, and to define new extensions to standard operators for derived data types. With appropriate definitions, the Fortran language can be made to add, subtract, multiply, divide, compare, etc. two operands of a derived data type.

How can we define new operators or extend existing ones? The first step is to write a function that performs the desired task and place it into a module. For example, if we wanted to add two values of a derived data type, we would first create a function whose arguments are the two values to be added, and whose result is the sum of the two values. The function will implement the instructions required to perform the addition. The next step is to associate the function with a user-defined or intrinsic operator using an **interface operator block.** The form of an interface operator block is

```
INTERFACE OPERATOR (operator_symbol)
    MODULE PROCEDURE function_1
    . . .
END INTERFACE
```

where *operator_symbol* is any standard intrinsic operator $(+, -, *, /, >, <, \text{etc.})$, or any user-defined operator. A user-defined operator is a sequence of up to 31 letters surrounded by periods (numbers and underscore characters are not allowed in an operator name). For example, a user-defined operator might be named .INVERSE.. Each interface body can either be a complete description of the interface to the function if the function is not in a module, or a MODULE PROCEDURE statement if the function is in a module. In either case, the function *must* have an explicit interface.

More than one function can be associated with the same operator symbol, but the functions must be distinguishable from one another by having different types of dummy arguments. When the compiler encounters the operator symbol in a program, it invokes the function whose dummy arguments match the operands associated with the operator symbol. If no associated function has dummy arguments that match the operands, then a compilation error results.

If the function associated with an operator has two dummy arguments, then the resulting operator will be a binary operator. If the function has only one dummy argument, then the operator will be a unary operator. Once defined, the operator will be treated as a reference to the function. For binary operations, the left-hand operand will become the first argument of the function and the right-hand operand will become the second argument of the function. The function must not modify its calling arguments. To ensure this, it is customary to declare all function arguments with INTENT(IN).

13

If the operator being defined by the interface is one of Fortran's intrinsic operators $(+, -, *, /, >, \text{etc.})$, then there are three additional constraints to consider:

1. It is not possible to change the meaning of an intrinsic operator for predefined intrinsic data types. For example, it is not possible to change the meaning of the addition operator $(+)$ when it is applied to two integers. It is only possible to *extend* the meaning of the operator by defining the actions to perform when the operator is applied to derived data types, or combinations of derived data types and intrinsic data types.
2. The number of arguments in a function must be consistent with the normal use of the operator. For example, multiplication $(*)$ is a binary operator, so any function extending its meaning must have two arguments.
3. If a relational operator is extended, then the same extension applies regardless of which way the operator is written. For example, if the relational operator "greater than" is given an additional meaning, then the extension applies whether "greater than" is written as $>$ or .GT..

It is possible to extend the meaning of the assignment operator $(=)$ in a similar fashion. To define extended meanings for the assignment operator, we use an **interface assignment block:**

```
INTERFACE ASSIGNMENT (=)
    MODULE PROCEDURE subroutine_1
      . . .
    END INTERFACE
```

For an assignment operator, the interface body must refer to a *subroutine* instead of a function. The subroutine must have two arguments. The first argument is the output of the assignment statement, and must have INTENT(OUT). The second dummy argument is the input to the assignment statement, and must have INTENT(IN). The first argument corresponds to the left-hand side of the assignment statement, and the second argument corresponds to the right-hand side of the assignment statement.

More than one subroutine can be associated with the assignment symbol, but the subroutines must be distinguishable from one another by having different types of dummy arguments. When the compiler encounters the assignment symbol in a program, it invokes the subroutine whose dummy arguments match the types of the values on either side of the equal sign. If no associated subroutine has dummy arguments that match the values, then a compilation error results.

Good Programming Practice
Use interface operator blocks and interface assignment blocks to create new operators and to extend the meanings of existing operators to work with derived data types. Once proper operators are defined, working with derived data types can be very easy.

The best way to explain the use of user-defined operators and assignments is by an example. We will now define a new derived data type and create appropriate user-defined operations and assignments for it.

**EXAMPLE
13-6**

Vectors:

The study of the dynamics of objects in motion in three dimensions is an important area of engineering. In the study of dynamics, the position and velocity of objects, forces, torques, and so forth are usually represented by three-component vectors $\mathbf{v} = x\hat{\mathbf{i}} + y\hat{\mathbf{j}} + z\hat{\mathbf{k}}$, where the three components (x, y, z) represent the projection of the vector $\mathbf{v}$ along the x, y, and z axes respectively, and $\hat{\mathbf{i}}$, $\hat{\mathbf{j}}$, and $\hat{\mathbf{k}}$ are the unit vectors along the x, y, and z axes (see Figure 13-12). The solutions of many mechanical problems involve manipulating these vectors in specific ways.

The most common operations performed on these vectors are:

1. **Addition.** Two vectors are added together by separately adding their x, y, and z components. If $\mathbf{v}_1 = x_1\hat{\mathbf{i}} + y_1\hat{\mathbf{j}} + z_1\hat{\mathbf{k}}$ and $\mathbf{v}_2 = x_2\hat{\mathbf{i}} + y_2\hat{\mathbf{j}} + z_2\hat{\mathbf{k}}$, then
    $\mathbf{v}_1 + \mathbf{v}_2 = (x_1 + x_2)\hat{\mathbf{i}} + (y_1 + y_2)\hat{\mathbf{j}} + (z_1 + z_2)\hat{\mathbf{k}}$.
2. **Subtraction.** Two vectors are subtracted by separately subtracting their x, y, and z components. If $\mathbf{v}_1 = x_1\hat{\mathbf{i}} + y_1\hat{\mathbf{j}} + z_1\hat{\mathbf{k}}$ and $\mathbf{v}_2 = x_2\hat{\mathbf{i}} + y_2\hat{\mathbf{j}} + z_2\hat{\mathbf{k}}$, then
    $\mathbf{v}_1 - \mathbf{v}_2 = (x_1 - x_2)\hat{\mathbf{i}} + (y_1 - y_2)\hat{\mathbf{j}} + (z_1 - z_2)\hat{\mathbf{k}}$.

FIGURE 13-12
A three-dimensional vector.

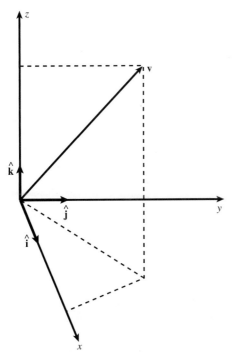

3. **Multiplication by a Scalar.** A vector is multiplied by a scalar by separately multiplying each component by the scalar. If $\mathbf{v} = x\hat{\mathbf{i}} + y\hat{\mathbf{j}} + z\hat{\mathbf{k}}$, then $a\mathbf{v} = ax\hat{\mathbf{i}} + ay\hat{\mathbf{j}} + az\hat{\mathbf{k}}$.

4. **Division by a Scalar.** A vector is divided by a scalar by separately dividing each component by the scalar. If $\mathbf{v} = x\hat{\mathbf{i}} + y\hat{\mathbf{j}} + z\hat{\mathbf{k}}$, then

$$\frac{\mathbf{v}}{a} = \frac{x}{a}\hat{\mathbf{i}} + \frac{y}{a}\hat{\mathbf{j}} + \frac{z}{a}\hat{\mathbf{k}}$$

5. **The Dot Product.** The dot product of two vectors is one form of multiplication operation performed on vectors. It produces a scalar that is the sum of the products of the vector's components. If $\mathbf{v}_1 = x_1\hat{\mathbf{i}} + y_1\hat{\mathbf{j}} + z_1\hat{\mathbf{k}}$ and $\mathbf{v}_2 = x_2\hat{\mathbf{i}} + y_2\hat{\mathbf{j}} + z_2\hat{\mathbf{k}}$, then the dot product of the vectors is $\mathbf{v}_1 \cdot \mathbf{v}_2 = x_1 x_2 + y_1 y_2 + z_1 z_2$.

6. **The Cross Product.** The cross product is another multiplication operation that appears frequently between vectors. The cross product of two vectors is another vector whose direction is perpendicular to the plane formed by the two input vectors. If $\mathbf{v}_1 = x_1\hat{\mathbf{i}} + y_1\hat{\mathbf{j}} + z_1\hat{\mathbf{k}}$ and $\mathbf{v}_2 = x_2\hat{\mathbf{i}} + y_2\hat{\mathbf{j}} + z_2\hat{\mathbf{k}}$, then the cross product of the two vectors is defined as $\mathbf{v}_1 \times \mathbf{v}_2 = (y_1 z_2 - y_2 z_1)\hat{\mathbf{i}} + (z_1 x_2 - z_2 x_1)\hat{\mathbf{j}} + (x_1 y_2 - x_2 y_1)\hat{\mathbf{k}}$.

Create a derived data type called `vector`, having three components x, y, and z. Define functions to create vectors from arrays, to convert vectors to arrays, and to perform the six vector operations defined above. Extend the intrinsic operators +, −, *, and / to have valid meanings when you are working with vectors, and create a new operator .DOT. for the dot product of two vectors. Finally, extend the assignment operator (=) to allow 3-element arrays to be assigned to vectors, and vectors to 3-element arrays.

SOLUTION

To make it easy to work with vectors, we should place the definition of the data type, the manipulating functions, and the operator definitions all in a single module. That one module can then be used by any programs wanting to manipulate vectors.

Note that six operations were defined for vectors, but *more than six functions must be written to implement them*. For example, the multiplication of a vector by a scalar could occur in either order: vector times scalar or scalar times vector. Both orders produce the same result, but the order of command line arguments for an implementing function is different in either case. Also, a scalar could be either an integer or a single-precision real number. To allow for all four possibilities (either order and either type of scalar) we actually have to write four functions!

1. **State the problem.**

Create a derived data type called `vector`, having three single precision real components x, y, and z. Write the following functions and subroutines for manipulating vectors:

(a) Create a vector from a three-element single-precision real array.
(b) Convert a vector into a three-element single-precision real array.

(c) Add two vectors.
(d) Subtract two vectors.
(e) Multiply a single precision real scalar by a vector.
(f) Multiply a vector by a single precision real scalar.
(g) Multiply an integer scalar by a vector.
(h) Multiply a vector by an integer scalar.
(i) Divide a vector by a single precision real scalar.
(j) Divide a vector by an integer scalar.
(k) Calculate the dot product of two vectors.
(l) Calculate the cross product of two vectors.

Associate these functions and subroutines with the appropriate operators using the interface operator constructs and interface assignment constructs.

2. **Define the inputs and outputs.**
   Each of the procedures described above has its own inputs and outputs. The types of the input and output arguments for each function are specified in Table 13-2.

3. **Describe the algorithm.**
   The following definitions apply in the pseudocode for all of the above routines:

   (a) `vec_1`   First input argument (vector)
   (b) `vec_2`   Second input argument (vector)
   (c) `real_1`   First input argument (single-precision real)

TABLE 13-2
Subroutines for Manipulating Vectors

Specific Function/ Subroutine Name	Input Argument 1 Type	Input Argument 2 Type	Output Type
`array_to_vector` (subroutine)	Three-element single-precision real array	N/A	Vector
`vector_to_array` (subroutine)	Vector	N/A	Three-element single-precision real array
`vector_add`	Vector	Vector	Vector
`vector_subtract`	Vector	Vector	Vector
`vector_times_real`	Vector	Single-precision real	Vector
`real_times_vector`	Single-precision real	Vector	Vector
`vector_times_int`	Vector	Integer	Vector
`int_times_vector`	Integer	Vector	Vector
`vector_div_real`	Vector	Single-precision real	Vector
`vector_div_int`	Vector	Integer	Vector
`dot_product`	Vector	Vector	Single-precision real
`cross_product`	Vector	Vector	Vector

(*d*) `real_2`   Second input argument (single-precision real)
(*e*) `int_1`   First input argument (integer)
(*f*) `int_2`   Second input argument (integer)
(*g*) `array`   Input argument (single-precision real array)
(*h*) `vec_result`   Function result (vector)
(*i*) `real_result`   Function result (single-precision real)
(*j*) `array_result`   Function result (single-precision real array)

Given these definitions, the pseudocode for the `array_to_vector` subroutine is:

```
vec_result%x ← array(1)
vec_result%y ← array(2)
vec_result%z ← array(3)
```

The pseudocode for the `vector_to_array` subroutine is:

```
array_result(1) ← vec_1%x
array_result(2) ← vec_1%y
array_result(3) ← vec_1%z
```

The pseudocode for the `vector_add` function is:

```
vec_result%x ← vec_1%x + vec_2%x
vec_result%y ← vec_1%y + vec_2%y
vec_result%z ← vec_1%z + vec_2%z
```

The pseudocode for the `vector_subtract` function is:

```
vec_result%x ← vec_1%x - vec_2%x
vec_result%y ← vec_1%y - vec_2%y
vec_result%z ← vec_1%z - vec_2%z
```

The pseudocode for the `vector_times_real` function is:

```
vec_result%x ← vec_1%x * real_2
vec_result%y ← vec_1%y * real_2
vec_result%z ← vec_1%z * real_2
```

The pseudocode for the `real_times_vector` function is:

```
vec_result%x ← real_1 * vec_2%x
vec_result%y ← real_1 * vec_2%y
vec_result%z ← real_1 * vec_2%z
```

The pseudocode for the `vector_times_int` function is:

```
vec_result%x ← vec_1%x * REAL(int_2)
vec_result%y ← vec_1%y * REAL(int_2)
vec_result%z ← vec_1%z * REAL(int_2)
```

The pseudocode for the `int_times_vector` function is:

```
vec_result%x ← REAL(int_1) * vec_2%x
vec_result%y ← REAL(int_1) * vec_2%y
vec_result%z ← REAL(int_1) * vec_2%z
```

The pseudocode for the `vector_div_real` function is:

```
vec_result%x ← vec_1%x / real_2
vec_result%y ← vec_1%y / real_2
vec_result%z ← vec_1%z / real_2
```

The pseudocode for the `vector_div_int` function is:

```
vec_result%x ← vec_1%x / REAL(int_2)
vec_result%y ← vec_1%y / REAL(int_2)
vec_result%z ← vec_1%z / REAL(int_2)
```

The pseudocode for the `dot_product` function is:

```
real_result ← vec_1%x*vec_2%x + vec_1%y*vec_2%y + vec_1%z*vec_2%z
```

The pseudocode for the `cross_product` function is:

```
vec_result%x ← vec_1%y*vec_2%z - vec_1%z*vec_2%y
vec_result%y ← vec_1%z*vec_2%x - vec_1%x*vec_2%z
vec_result%z ← vec_1%x*vec_2%y - vec_1%y*vec_2%x
```

These 12 functions will be assigned to operators in interface operator and interface assignment blocks as follows:

Function	Operator
array_to_vector	=
vector_to_array	=
vector_add	+
vector_subtract	-
vector_times_real	*
real_times_vector	*
vector_times_int	*
int_times_vector	*
vector_div_real	/
vector_div_int	/
dot_product	.DOT.
cross_product	*

4. **Turn the algorithm into Fortran statements.**
   The resulting Fortran module is shown in Figure 13-13.

FIGURE 13-13
A module to create a derived data type `vector`, and to define mathematical operations that can be performed on values of type `vector`.

```
MODULE vectors
!
! Purpose:
!   To define a derived data type called vector, and the
```

(continued)

(continued)

```
!    operations that can be performed on it. The module
!    defines 8 operations that can be performed on vectors:
!
!                    Operation                      Operator
!                    =========                      ========
!         1.   Creation from a real array               =
!         2.   Conversion to real array                 =
!         3.   Vector addition                          +
!         4.   Vector subtraction                       -
!         5.   Vector-scalar multiplication (4 cases)   *
!         6.   Vector-scalar division (2 cases)         /
!         7.   Dot product                           .DOT.
!         8.   Cross product                             *
!
!    It contains a total of 12 procedures to implement those
!    operations: array_to_vector, vector_to_array, vector_add,
!    vector_subtract, vector_times_real, real_times_vector,
!    vector_times_int, int_times_vector, vector_div_real,
!    vector_div_int, dot_product, and cross_product.
!
!    Record of revisions:
!        Date        Programmer         Description of change
!        ====        ==========         =====================
!      12/15/06    S. J. Chapman        Original code
!
IMPLICIT NONE

! Declare vector data type:
TYPE :: vector
    REAL :: x
    REAL :: y
    REAL :: z
END TYPE

! Declare interface operators
INTERFACE ASSIGNMENT (=)
    MODULE PROCEDURE array_to_vector
    MODULE PROCEDURE vector_to_array
END INTERFACE

INTERFACE OPERATOR (+)
    MODULE PROCEDURE vector_add
END INTERFACE

INTERFACE OPERATOR (-)
    MODULE PROCEDURE vector_subtract
END INTERFACE

INTERFACE OPERATOR (*)
    MODULE PROCEDURE vector_times_real
    MODULE PROCEDURE real_times_vector
    MODULE PROCEDURE vector_times_int
```

(continued)

(*continued*)

```fortran
    MODULE PROCEDURE int_times_vector
    MODULE PROCEDURE cross_product
END INTERFACE

INTERFACE OPERATOR (/)
    MODULE PROCEDURE vector_div_real
    MODULE PROCEDURE vector_div_int
END INTERFACE

INTERFACE OPERATOR (.DOT.)
    MODULE PROCEDURE dot_product
END INTERFACE

! Now define the implementing functions.
CONTAINS
    SUBROUTINE array_to_vector(vec_result, array)
        TYPE (vector), INTENT(OUT) :: vec_result
        REAL, DIMENSION(3), INTENT(IN) :: array
        vec_result%x = array(1)
        vec_result%y = array(2)
        vec_result%z = array(3)
    END SUBROUTINE array_to_vector

    SUBROUTINE vector_to_array(array_result, vec_1)
        REAL, DIMENSION(3), INTENT(OUT) :: array_result
        TYPE (vector), INTENT(IN) :: vec_1
        array_result(1) = vec_1%x
        array_result(2) = vec_1%y
        array_result(3) = vec_1%z
    END SUBROUTINE vector_to_array

    FUNCTION vector_add(vec_1, vec_2)
        TYPE (vector) :: vector_add
        TYPE (vector), INTENT(IN) :: vec_1, vec_2
        vector_add%x = vec_1%x + vec_2%x
        vector_add%y = vec_1%y + vec_2%y
        vector_add%z = vec_1%z + vec_2%z
    END FUNCTION vector_add

    FUNCTION vector_subtract(vec_1, vec_2)
        TYPE (vector) :: vector_subtract
        TYPE (vector), INTENT(IN) :: vec_1, vec_2
        vector_subtract%x = vec_1%x - vec_2%x
        vector_subtract%y = vec_1%y - vec_2%y
        vector_subtract%z = vec_1%z - vec_2%z
    END FUNCTION vector_subtract

    FUNCTION vector_times_real(vec_1, real_2)
        TYPE (vector) :: vector_times_real
        TYPE (vector), INTENT(IN) :: vec_1
        REAL, INTENT(IN) :: real_2
```

13

(*continued*)

(continued)

```
      vector_times_real%x = vec_1%x * real_2
      vector_times_real%y = vec_1%y * real_2
      vector_times_real%z = vec_1%z * real_2
   END FUNCTION vector_times_real

   FUNCTION real_times_vector(real_1, vec_2)
      TYPE (vector) :: real_times_vector
      REAL, INTENT(IN) :: real_1
      TYPE (vector), INTENT(IN) :: vec_2
      real_times_vector%x = real_1 * vec_2%x
      real_times_vector%y = real_1 * vec_2%y
      real_times_vector%z = real_1 * vec_2%z
   END FUNCTION real_times_vector

   FUNCTION vector_times_int(vec_1, int_2)
      TYPE (vector) :: vector_times_int
      TYPE (vector), INTENT(IN) :: vec_1
      INTEGER, INTENT(IN) :: int_2
      vector_times_int%x = vec_1%x * REAL(int_2)
      vector_times_int%y = vec_1%y * REAL(int_2)
      vector_times_int%z = vec_1%z * REAL(int_2)
   END FUNCTION vector_times_int

   FUNCTION int_times_vector(int_1, vec_2)
      TYPE (vector) :: int_times_vector
      INTEGER, INTENT(IN) :: int_1
      TYPE (vector), INTENT(IN) :: vec_2
      int_times_vector%x = REAL(int_1) * vec_2%x
      int_times_vector%y = REAL(int_1) * vec_2%y
      int_times_vector%z = REAL(int_1) * vec_2%z
   END FUNCTION int_times_vector

   FUNCTION vector_div_real(vec_1, real_2)
      TYPE (vector) :: vector_div_real
      TYPE (vector), INTENT(IN) :: vec_1
      REAL, INTENT(IN) :: real_2
      vector_div_real%x = vec_1%x / real_2
      vector_div_real%y = vec_1%y / real_2
      vector_div_real%z = vec_1%z / real_2
   END FUNCTION vector_div_real

   FUNCTION vector_div_int(vec_1, int_2)
      TYPE (vector) :: vector_div_int
      TYPE (vector), INTENT(IN) :: vec_1
      INTEGER, INTENT(IN) :: int_2
      vector_div_int%x = vec_1%x / REAL(int_2)
      vector_div_int%y = vec_1%y / REAL(int_2)
      vector_div_int%z = vec_1%z / REAL(int_2)
   END FUNCTION vector_div_int

   FUNCTION dot_product(vec_1, vec_2)
      REAL :: dot_product
      TYPE (vector), INTENT(IN) :: vec_1, vec_2
      dot_product = vec_1%x*vec_2%x + vec_1%y*vec_2%y &
                  + vec_1%z*vec_2%z
```

(continued)

(concluded)

```
   END FUNCTION dot_product

   FUNCTION cross_product(vec_1, vec_2)
      TYPE (vector) :: cross_product
      TYPE (vector), INTENT(IN) :: vec_1, vec_2
      cross_product%x = vec_1%y*vec_2%z - vec_1%z*vec_2%y
      cross_product%y = vec_1%z*vec_2%x - vec_1%x*vec_2%z
      cross_product%z = vec_1%x*vec_2%y - vec_1%y*vec_2%x
   END FUNCTION cross_product
END MODULE vectors
```

5. **Test the resulting Fortran programs.**

   To test this data type and its associated operations, it is necessary to write a test driver program that defines and manipulates vectors, and prints out the results. The program should exercise every operation defined for vectors in the module. Figure 13-14 shows an appropriate test driver program.

FIGURE 13-14

Test driver program to test the vector data type and associated operations.

```
PROGRAM test_vectors
!
!   Purpose:
!     To test the definitions, operations, and assignments
!     associated with the vector data type.
!
!   Record of revisions:
!      Date        Programmer          Description of change
!      ====        ==========          =====================
!    12/15/06    S. J. Chapman         Original code
!
USE vectors
IMPLICIT NONE

! Data dictionary: declare variable types & definitions
REAL, DIMENSION(3) :: array_out        ! Output array
TYPE (vector) :: vec_1, vec_2          ! Test vectors

! Test assignments by assigning an array to vec_1 and
! assigning vec_1 to array_out.
vec_1 = (/ 1., 2., 3. /)
array_out = vec_1
WRITE (*,1000) vec_1, array_out
1000 FORMAT (' Test assignments: ',/, &
             ' vec_1 =      ', 3F8.2,/, &
             ' array_out = ', 3F8.2)

! Test addition and subtraction.
vec_1 = (/ 10., 20., 30. /)
vec_2 = (/ 1., 2., 3. /)
WRITE (*,1010) vec_1, vec_2, vec_1 + vec_2, vec_1 - vec_2
1010 FORMAT (/' Test addition and subtraction: ',/, &
```

13

(continued)

(concluded)

```
                     ' vec_1 =               ', 3F8.2,/, &
                     ' vec_2 =               ', 3F8.2,/, &
                     ' vec_1 + vec_2 = ',  3F8.2,/, &
                     ' vec_1 - vec_2 = ',  3F8.2)

! Test multiplication by a scalar.
vec_1 = (/ 1., 2., 3. /)
WRITE (*,1020) vec_1, 2.*vec_1, vec_1*2., 2*vec_1, vec_1*2
1020 FORMAT (/' Test multiplication by a scalar: ',/, &
                     ' vec_1 =               ', 3F8.2,/, &
                     ' 2. * vec_1 =          ', 3F8.2,/, &
                     ' vec_1 * 2. =          ', 3F8.2,/, &
                     ' 2 * vec_1  =          ', 3F8.2,/, &
                     ' vec_1 * 2  =          ', 3F8.2)

! Test division by a scalar.
vec_1 = (/ 10., 20., 30. /)
WRITE (*,1030) vec_1, vec_1/5., vec_1/5
1030 FORMAT (/' Test division by a scalar: ',/, &
                     ' vec_1 =               ', 3F8.2,/, &
                     ' vec_1 / 5. =          ', 3F8.2,/, &
                     ' vec_1 / 5 =           ', 3F8.2)

! Test dot product.
vec_1 = (/ 1., 2., 3. /)
vec_2 = (/ 1., 2., 3. /)
WRITE (*,1040) vec_1, vec_2, vec_1 .DOT. vec_2
1040 FORMAT (/' Test dot product: ',/, &
                     ' vec_1 =               ', 3F8.2,/, &
                     ' vec_2 =               ', 3F8.2,/, &
                     ' vec_1 .DOT. vec_2 = ', 3F8.2)

! Test cross product.
vec_1 = (/ 1., -1., 1. /)
vec_2 = (/ -1., 1., 1. /)
WRITE (*,1050) vec_1, vec_2, vec_1*vec_2
1050 FORMAT (/' Test cross product: ',/, &
                     ' vec_1 =               ', 3F8.2,/, &
                     ' vec_2 =               ', 3F8.2,/, &
                     ' vec_1 * vec_2 = ', 3F8.2)

END PROGRAM test_vectors
```

When the test driver program is executed, the results are:

```
C:\book\chap13>test_vectors
Test assignments:
vec_1 =         1.00    2.00    3.00
array_out =     1.00    2.00    3.00

Test addition and subtraction:
vec_1 =            10.00   20.00   30.00
vec_2 =             1.00    2.00    3.00
vec_1 + vec_2 =    11.00   22.00   33.00
vec_1 - vec_2 =     9.00   18.00   27.00
```

```
Test multiplication by a scalar:
vec_1 =            1.00    2.00    3.00
2. * vec_1 =       2.00    4.00    6.00
vec_1 * 2. =       2.00    4.00    6.00
2 * vec_1 =        2.00    4.00    6.00
vec_1 * 2 =        2.00    4.00    6.00

Test division by a scalar:
vec_1 =           10.00   20.00   30.00
vec_1 / 5. =       2.00    4.00    6.00
vec_1 / 5 =        2.00    4.00    6.00

Test dot product:
vec_1 =                    1.00    2.00    3.00
vec_2 =                    1.00    2.00    3.00
vec_1 .DOT. vec_2 =       14.00

Test cross product:
vec_1 =            1.00   -1.00    1.00
vec_2 =           -1.00    1.00    1.00
vec_1 * vec_2 =   -2.00   -2.00     .00
```

The results of the program are correct, and we can verify them by calculating the answers from the definitions of the operations.

What would happen in a program if we tried to perform an operation with vectors that was not defined in the module? For example, what would happen if we tried to multiply a vector by a double-precision real scalar? A compilation error would result, because the compiler does not know how to perform the operation. When defining a new data type and its operations, be careful to define *every* combination of operations that you might wish to use.

13.7

BOUND ASSIGNMENTS AND OPERATORS

In Fortran 2003, assignments and operators can be bound to derived data types using the GENERIC statement. These procedures are declared by using the GENERIC statement, as shown below.

```
TYPE :: point
   REAL :: x
   REAL :: y
CONTAINS
   GENERIC :: ASSIGNMENT(=) => assign1
   GENERIC :: OPERATOR(+) => plus1, plus2, plus3
END TYPE point
```

The bodies of the procedures implementing the operators must be declared in the same way as the generic assignments and operators defined in the previous section.

13

13.8
RESTRICTING ACCESS TO THE CONTENTS OF A MODULE

When a module is accessed by USE association, by default all of the entities defined within that module become available for use in the program unit containing the USE statement. In the past, we have used this fact to share data between program units, to make procedures with explicit interfaces available to program units, to create new operators, and to extend the meanings of existing operators.

In Example 13-6, we created a module called vectors to extend the Fortran language. Any program unit that accesses module vectors can define its own vectors, and can manipulate them using the binary operators $+, -, *, /,$ and .DOT.. Unfortunately, the program will also be able to invoke such functions as vector_add, vector_subtract, etc., even though it should be using them only indirectly through the use of the defined operators. These procedure names are not needed in any program unit, but they are declared, and they might conflict with a procedure name defined in the program. A similar problem could occur when many data items are defined within a module, but only a few of them are needed by a particular program unit. All of the unnecessary data items will also be available in the program unit, making it possible for a programmer to modify them by mistake.

In general, *it is a good idea to restrict access to any procedures or data entities in a module to only those program units that must know about them.* This process is known as **data hiding.** The more access is restricted, the less chance there is of a programmer using or modifying an item by mistake. Restricting access makes programs more modular and easier to understand and maintain.

How can we restrict access to the entities in a module? Fortran provides a way to control the access to a particular item in a module by program units *outside* that module: the PUBLIC, PRIVATE, and PROTECTED attributes and statements.[3] If the PUBLIC attribute or statement is specified for an item, then the item will be available to program units outside the module. If the PRIVATE attribute or statement is specified, then the item will not be available to program units outside the module, although procedures inside the module still have access to it. If the PROTECTED attribute or statement is specified, then the item will be available on a *read-only* basis to program units outside the module. Any attempt to modify the value of a PROTECTED variable outside the module in which it is defined will produce a compile-time error. The default attribute for all data and procedures in a module is PUBLIC, so by default any program unit that uses a module can have access to every data item and procedure within it.

The PUBLIC, PRIVATE, or PROTECTED status of a data item or procedure can be declared in one of two ways. It is possible to specify the status as an attribute in a type definition statement, or in an independent Fortran statement. Examples in which the attributes are declared as a part of a type definition statement are:

```
INTEGER, PRIVATE :: count
REAL, PUBLIC :: voltage
REAL, PROTECTED :: my_data
TYPE (vector), PRIVATE :: scratch_vector
```

F-2003
ONLY

13

---

[3] The PROTECTED attribute and statement are available in Fortran 2003 only.

This type of declaration can be used for data items and for functions, but not for subroutines.

A PUBLIC, PRIVATE, or PROTECTED statement can also be used to specify the status of data items, functions, and subroutines. The form of a PUBLIC, PRIVATE, or PROTECTED statement is:

```
PUBLIC :: list of public items
PRIVATE :: list of private items
PROTECTED :: list of private items
```

If a module contains a PRIVATE statement without a list of private items, *then by default every data item and procedure in the module is private*. Any items that should be public must be explicitly listed in a separate PUBLIC statement. This is the preferred way to design modules, since only the items that are actually required by programs are exposed to them.

Good Programming Practice

It is good programming practice to hide any module data items or procedures that do not need to be directly accessed by external program units. The best way to do this is to include a PRIVATE statement in each module, and then list the specific items that you wish to expose in a separate PUBLIC statement.

As an example of the proper use of data hiding, let's reexamine module vectors from Example 13-6. Programs accessing this module need to define variables of type vector, and need to perform operations involving vectors. However, the programs do *not* need direct access to any of the subroutines or functions in the module. The proper declarations for this circumstance are shown in Figure 13-15.

FIGURE 13-15

The first part of module vector, modified to hide all nonessential items from external program units. Changes to the module are shown in bold type.

```
MODULE vectors
!
!  Purpose:
!    To define a derived data type called vector, and the
!    operations that can be performed on it. The module
!    defines 8 operations that can be performed on vectors:
!
!                  Operation                        Operator
!                  =========                        ========
!        1.  Creation from a real array                =
!        2.  Conversion to real array                  =
!        3.  Vector addition                            +
!        4.  Vector subtraction                         -
!        5.  Vector-scalar multiplication (4 cases)     *
!        6.  Vector-scalar division (2 cases)           /
!        7.  Dot product                              .DOT.
!        8.  Cross product                              *
```

13

(continued)

(concluded)

```
!
!      It contains a total of 12 procedures to implement those
!      operations: array_to_vector, vector_to_array, vector_add,
!      vector_subtract, vector_times_real, real_times_vector,
!      vector_times_int, int_times_vector, vector_div_real,
!      vector_div_int, dot_product, and cross_product. These
!      procedures are private to the module; they can only be
!      accessed from the outside via the defined operators.
!
!   Record of revisions:
!        Date        Programmer            Description of change
!        ====        ==========            =====================
!     12/15/06    S. J. Chapman         Original code
! 1.  12/16/06    S. J. Chapman         Modified to hide non-
!                                          essential items.
!
IMPLICIT NONE

! Declare all items to be private except for type vector and
! the operators defined for it.
PRIVATE
PUBLIC :: vector, assignment(=), operator(+), operator(-), &
          operator(*), operator(/), operator(.DOT.)

! Declare vector data type:
TYPE :: vector
   REAL :: x
   REAL :: y
   REAL :: z
END TYPE
```

The following notes apply to PUBLIC and PRIVATE declarations for derived data types in modules.

1. The components of a derived data type declared in a module can be made inaccessible to program units outside of the module by including a PRIVATE statement *within* the derived data type. Note that *the derived data type as a whole is still available to outside program units, but its components cannot be accessed separately.* Outside program units may freely declare variables of the derived data type, but they may not work with individual components of those variables. An example of a derived data type with private components is:

```
        TYPE vector
            PRIVATE
            REAL :: x
            REAL :: y
        END TYPE
```

2. In contrast to the situation above, an entire derived data type can be declared to be private. An example is:

```
        TYPE, PRIVATE :: vector
            REAL :: x
            REAL :: y
        END TYPE
```

In this case, the data type `vector` is not accessible by any program units that use the module. This differs from the previous case, in which the data type was available but its components could not be accessed separately. Such a derived data type can be used only for internal calculations within the module.

F-2003 ONLY

3. In Fortran 2003, *individual components* of a derived data type can be declared to be public or private. An example is:

```
TYPE :: vector
   REAL,PUBLIC :: x
   REAL,PRIVATE :: y
END TYPE
```

In this case, outside program units may freely declare variables of type `vector`, and may freely access component `x`, but component `y` cannot be accessed outside the module in which the derived data type is defined.

4. Finally, it is possible to declare private variables of a derived data type even though the type itself is public. For example,

```
TYPE :: vector
   REAL :: x
   REAL :: y
END TYPE
TYPE (vector), PRIVATE :: vec_1
```

In this case, the derived data type `vector` is public and available in program units that use the module, but the variable `vec_1` may be used only within the module. This type of declaration might be used for variables in internal calculations within the module.

13.9

ADVANCED OPTIONS OF THE USE STATEMENT

When a program unit accesses a module by USE association, by default it gets access to every data item, interface, and procedure in the module. It is possible for the module to restrict access to some items by declaring them to be PRIVATE. In addition to this control, it is possible for a program unit using the module to further restrict the list of items being used, and to modify the names of those items.

Why would we want to further restrict the list of items from a module that is accessed by USE association in a program unit? If a data item from a module is not needed in the program unit, then it is good defensive programming to make that item unavailable. This action will prevent the program unit from using or modifying the item *by mistake*, and will reduce the chance of developing hard-to-find bugs. A common problem of this sort would be to make a typographical error in a local variable name and not know it because the new name just accidentally happens to be declared in the module. Most typographical errors are caught by the compiler because the IMPLICIT NONE statement makes undeclared variables illegal. However, if the new name happens to be defined in the module, then using it will not be an error. Furthermore, since the contents of the module do not appear in the program unit listing, the programmer may

13

not realize that a variable of that name was defined in the module. Problems like this can be hard to find.

To restrict access to certain specific items in a module, an ONLY clause may be added to the USE statement. The form of the statement is

```
USE module_name, ONLY: only_list
```

where module_name is the module name, and only_list is the list of items from the module to be used, with items in the list separated by commas. As an example, we could further restrict access to operations in module vectors by using the statement

```
USE vectors, ONLY: vector, assignment(=)
```

In a procedure containing this statement, it would be legal to declare a variable of type vector and to assign a three-element array to it, but it would not be legal to add two vectors together.

It is also possible to rename a data item or procedure in the USE statement. There are two reasons why we might wish to rename a data item or procedure when it is used by a program unit. One reason is that the item might have a name that is the same as a local data item or an item from another module also used by the program unit. In this case, renaming the item avoids a clash between the two definitions of the name.

The second reason to rename a module data item or procedure is that we might wish to shorten a name declared in a module when it is used very frequently in a program unit. For example, a module called data_fit might contain a procedure with the name sp_real_least_squares_fit to distinguish it from a double-precision version sp_real_least_squares_fit. When this module is used in a program unit, the programmer might wish to refer to the procedure by a less unwieldy name. He or she might wish to call the procedure simply lsqfit or something similar.

The forms of the USE statement that permit a programmer to rename a data item or procedure are

```
USE module_name, rename_list
USE module_name, ONLY: rename_list
```

where each item in the rename_list takes the form

```
local_name => module_name
```

In the first case, all public items in the module will be available to the program unit, but the ones in the rename list will be renamed. In the second case, only the items listed would be available, and they would be renamed. For example, the USE statement to rename the least squares fit routine mentioned above while simultaneously restricting access to all other items in module data_fits would be

```
USE data_fit, ONLY: lsqfit => sp_real_least_squares_fit
```

A few complications can arise when multiple USE statements in a single program unit refer to the same module. It makes no sense to use more than one USE statement in a single routine to refer to a given module, so you should never have this problem in well-written code. However, if you do have more than one USE statement referring to the same module, the following rules apply.

1. If none of the USE statements have rename lists or ONLY clauses, then the statements are just duplicates of each other, which is legal but has no effect on the program.
2. If all of the USE statements include rename lists but no ONLY clauses, then the effect is the same as if all of the renamed items were listed in a single USE statement.
3. If all of the USE statements include ONLY clauses, then the effect is the same as if all of the lists were listed in a single USE statement.
4. If some USE statements have an ONLY clause and some do not, then the ONLY clauses have no effect on the program at all. This happens because the USE statements without ONLY clauses allow all public items in the module to be visible in the program unit.

Quiz 13-2

This quiz provides a quick check to see if you have understood the concepts introduced in Sections 13.4 to 13.9. If you have trouble with the quiz, reread the sections, ask your instructor, or discuss the material with a fellow student. The answers to this quiz are found in the back of the book.

1. What is an interface block? What are the two possible locations for interface blocks in a Fortran program?
2. Why would a programmer choose to create an interface block to a procedure instead of including the procedure in a module?
3. What items must appear in the interface body of an interface block?
4. Is the following program valid? Why or why not? If it is legal, what does it do?

```
PROGRAM test
IMPLICIT NONE
TYPE :: data
    REAL :: x1
    REAL :: x2
END TYPE
CHARACTER(len=20) :: x1 = 'This is a test.'
TYPE (data) :: x2
x2%x1 = 613.
x2%x2 = 248.
WRITE (*,*) x1, x2
END PROGRAM test
```

5. How is a generic procedure defined?
6. How is a generic bound procedure defined?
7. Is the following code valid? Why or why not? If it is legal, what does it do?

(continued)

F-2003 ONLY

13

(continued)

```
INTERFACE fit
   SUBROUTINE least_squares_fit (array, nvals, slope, intercept)
   IMPLICIT NONE
   INTEGER, INTENT(IN) :: nvals
   REAL, INTENT(IN), DIMENSION(nvals) :: array
   REAL, INTENT(OUT) :: slope
   REAL, INTENT(OUT) :: intercept
   END SUBROUTINE least_squares_fit

   SUBROUTINE median_fit (data1, n, slope, intercept)
   IMPLICIT NONE
   INTEGER, INTENT(IN) :: n
   REAL, INTENT(IN), DIMENSION(n) :: data1
   REAL, INTENT(OUT) :: slope
   REAL, INTENT(OUT) :: intercept
   END SUBROUTINE median_fit
END INTERFACE fit
```

8. What is a `MODULE PROCEDURE` statement? What is its purpose?
9. What is the difference in structure between a user-defined operator and a user-defined assignment? How are they implemented?
10. How can access to the contents of a module be controlled? Why would we wish to limit the access to some data items or procedures in a module?
11. What is the default type of access for items in a module?
12. How can a program unit accessing a module by `USE` association control which items in the module it sees? Why would a programmer wish to do this?
13. How can a program unit accessing a module by `USE` association rename data items or procedures in the module? Why would a programmer wish to do this?

F-2003 ONLY

14. Is the following code valid? Why or why not? If it is legal, what does it do?

```
MODULE test_module
TYPE :: test_type
   REAL :: x, y, z
   PROTECTED :: z
END TYPE test_type
END MODULE test_module

PROGRAM test
USE test_module
TYPE(test_type) :: t1, t2
```

(continued)

(concluded)

```
      t1%x = 10.
      t1%y = -5.
      t2%x = -2.
      t2%y = 7.
      t1%z = t1%x * t2%y
      END PROGRAM test
```

13.10

F-2003 ONLY

INTRINSIC MODULES

Fortran 2003 defines a new concept called an **intrinsic module**. An intrinsic module is just like an ordinary Fortran module, except that it is predefined and coded by the creator of the Fortran compiler. Like ordinary modules, we access procedures and data in intrinsic modules via a USE statement.

There are three standard intrinsic modules in Fortran 2003:

1. Module ISO_FORTRAN_ENV, which contains constants describing the characteristics of storage in a particular computer (how many bits in a standard integer, how many bits in a standard character, etc.), and also constants defining I/O units for the particular computer. (We will use this module in Chapter 14.)
2. Module ISO_C_BINDING, which contains data necessary for a Fortran compiler to interoperate with C on a given processor.
3. The IEEE modules, which describe the characteristics of IEEE 754 floating-point calculations on a particular processor.

The Fortran 2003 standard requires compiler vendors to implement certain procedures in these intrinsic modules, but it allows them to add additional procedures, and also to define their own intrinsic modules. In the future, this should be a common way to ship special features with a compiler.

13.11

F-2003 ONLY

ACCESS TO COMMAND LINE ARGUMENTS AND ENVIRONMENT VARIABLES

13

Fortran 2003 includes standard procedures to allow a Fortran program to retrieve the command line that started the program, and to recover data from the program's environment. These mechanisms allow the user to pass parameters to the program at start-up by typing them on the command line after the program name, or by including them as environment variables.

Fortran compiler vendors have allowed Fortran programs get access command line arguments and environment variables for many years, but since there was no *standard* way to do this; each vendor created its own special subroutines and functions. Since these procedures differed from vendor to vendor, Fortran programs tended to be less portable. Fortran 2003 has solved this problem by creating standard intrinsic procedures for how to retrieve command line parameters.

13.11.1 Access to Command Line Arguments

There are three standard intrinsic procedures for getting variables from the command line.

1. **Function** `COMMAND_ARGUMENT_COUNT( )`. This function returns the number of command line arguments present when the program started in an integer of the default type. It has no arguments.
2. **Subroutine** `GET_COMMAND(COMMAND,LENGTH,STATUS)`. This subroutine returns the entire set of command line arguments in the character variable `COMMAND`, the length of the argument string in integer `LENGTH`, and the success or failure of the operation in integer `STATUS`. If the retrieval is successful, the `STATUS` will be zero. If the character variable `COMMAND` is too short to hold the argument, the `STATUS` will be -1. Any other error will cause a nonzero number to be returned. Note that all of these arguments are optional, so a user can include only some of them, using keyword syntax to specify which ones are present.
3. **Subroutine** `GET_COMMAND_ARGUMENT(NUMBER,VALUE,LENGTH,STATUS)` This subroutine returns a specified command argument. The integer value `NUMBER` specifies which argument to return. The number must be in the range 0 to `COMMAND_ARGUMENT_COUNT( )`. The argument is returned in character variable `VALUE`, the length of the argument string in integer `LENGTH`, and the success or failure of the operation in integer `STATUS`. If the retrieval is successful, the `STATUS` will be zero. If the character variable `VALUE` is too short to hold the argument, the `STATUS` will be -1. Any other error will cause a nonzero number to be returned. Note that all of these arguments except `NUMBER` are optional, so a user can include only some of them, using keyword syntax to specify which ones are present.

A sample program that illustrates the use of these procedures is shown in Figure 13-16. This program recovers and displays the command line arguments used to start the program.

FIGURE 13-16
Program illustrating the use of intrinsic procedures to get command line arguments.

```
PROGRAM get_command_line

! Declare local variables
INTEGER :: i                    ! Loop index
CHARACTER(len=128) :: command   ! Command line
CHARACTER(len=80) :: arg        ! Single argument

! Get the program name
CALL get_command_argument(0, command)
WRITE (*,'(A,A)') 'Program name is: ', TRIM(command)
```

(continued)

(*concluded*)

```
! Now get the individual arguments
DO i = 1, command_argument_count()
   CALL get_command_argument(i, arg)
   WRITE (*,'(A,I2,A,A)') 'Argument ', i, ' is ', TRIM(arg)
END DO

END PROGRAM get_command_line
```

When this program is executed, the results are:

```
C:\book\chap13>get_command_line 1 sdf 4 er4
Program name is: get_command_line
Argument 1 is 1
Argument 2 is sdf
Argument 3 is 4
Argument 4 is er4
```

13.11.2 Retrieving Environment Variables

The value of an environment variable can be retrieved by using subroutine GET_ ENVIRONMENT_VARIABLE. The arguments for this subroutine are:

```
CALL GET_ENVIRONMENT_VARIABLE(NAME,VALUE,LENGTH,STATUS,TRIM_NAME)
```

The argument NAME is a character expression supplied by the user, containing the name of the environment variable whose value is desired. The environment variable is returned in character variable VALUE, the length of the environment variable in integer LENGTH, and the success or failure of the operation in integer STATUS. If the retrieval is successful, the STATUS will be zero. If the character variable VALUE is too short to hold the argument, the STATUS will be −1. If the environment variable does not exist, the STATUS will be 1. If the processor does not support environment variables, the STATUS will be 2. If another error occurs, the status will be greater than 2. TRIM_NAME is a logical input argument. If it is true, then the command will ignore trailing blanks when matching the environment variable. If it is false, it will include the trailing blanks in the comparison.

Note that VALUE, LENGTH, STATUS, and TRIM_NAME are all optional arguments, so they can be included or left out, as desired.

A sample program that illustrates the use of GET_ENVIRONMENT_VARIABLE is shown in Figure 13-17. This program recovers and displays the value of the "windir" environment variable, which is defined on the computer where this text is being written.

FIGURE 13-17
Program illustrating the use of GET_ENVIRONMENT_VARIABLE.

```
PROGRAM get_env

! Declare local variables
INTEGER :: length            ! Length
```

(*continued*)

(concluded)

```
INTEGER :: status              ! Status
CHARACTER(len=80) :: value     ! Environment variable value

! Get the value of the "windir" environment variable
CALL get_environment_variable('windir',value,length,status)

! Tell user
WRITE (*,*) 'Get "windir" environment variable:'
WRITE (*,'(A,I6)') 'Status = ', status
IF ( status <= 0 ) THEN
   WRITE (*,'(A,A)') 'Value = ', TRIM(value)
END IF

END PROGRAM get_env
```

When this program is executed, the results are:

```
C:\book\chap13>get_env
 Get 'windir' environment variable:
 Status =      0
 Value = C:\WINDOWS
```

Good Programming Practice

Use the standard Fortran 2003 intrinsic procedures to retrieve the command line arguments used to start a program and the values of environment variables instead of the nonstandard procedures supplied by individual vendors.

F-2003 ONLY

▪ 13.12

F-2003 ONLY

THE VOLATILE ATTRIBUTE AND STATEMENT

When a Fortran compiler compiles a program for release, it usually runs an optimizer to increase the program's speed. The optimizer performs many techniques to increase the program's speed, but one very common approach is to hold the value of a variable in a CPU register between uses, since the access to registers is much faster than the access to main memory. This is commonly done for variables that are modified a lot in DO loops, provided that there are free registers to hold the data.

This optimization can cause serious problems if the variable being used is also accessed or modified by other processes outside the Fortran program. In that case, the external process might modify the value of the variable while the Fortran program is using a different value that was previously stored in a register.

To avoid incompatible values, there must always be one and only one location where the data is stored. The Fortran compiler must know not to hold a copy of the variable in a register, and must know to update main memory as soon as any change happens to the value of the variable. This is accomplished by declaring a variable to be volatile. If a variable is volatile, the compiler does not apply any optimizations to it, and the program works directly with the location of the variable in main memory.

A variable is declared to be volatile with a VOLATILE attribute or statement. A volatile attribute takes the form

```
REAL,VOLATILE :: x        ! Volatile variable
REAL,VOLATILE :: y        ! Volatile variable
```

and a volatile statement takes the form

```
REAL :: x, y              ! Declarations
VOLATILE :: x, y          ! Volatile declaration
```

The VOLATILE attribute or statement is commonly used with massively parallel processing packages, which have methods to asynchronously transfer data between processes.

▦ 13.13
SUMMARY

This chapter introduced several advanced features in procedures and modules in Fortran 95/2003. None of these features were available in earlier versions of Fortran.

Fortran supports three levels of scope: global, local, and statement. Global-scope objects include program, external procedure, and module names. The only statement-scope objects that we have seen so far are the variables in an implied DO loop in an array constructor, and the index variables in a FORALL statement. Local-scope objects have a scope restricted to a single scoping unit. A scoping unit is a main program, a procedure, a module, a derived data type, or an interface. If one scoping unit is defined entirely inside another scoping unit, then the inner scoping unit inherits all of the data items defined in the host scoping unit by host association.

Ordinarily, Fortran 95/2003 subroutines and functions are not recursive—they cannot call themselves either directly or indirectly. However, they can be made recursive if they are declared to be recursive in the corresponding SUBROUTINE or FUNCTION statement. A recursive function declaration includes a RESULT clause specifying the name to be used to return the function result.

If a procedure has an explicit interface, then keyword arguments may be used to change the order in which calling arguments are specified. A keyword argument consists of the dummy argument's name followed by an equal sign and the value of the argument. Keyword arguments are very useful in supporting optional arguments.

If a procedure has an explicit interface, then optional arguments may be declared and used. An optional argument is an argument that may or may not be present in the procedure's calling sequence. An intrinsic function PRESENT() is provided to determine whether or not a particular optional argument is present when the procedure gets called. Keyword arguments are commonly used with optional arguments because optional arguments often appear out of sequence in the calling procedure.

Interface blocks are used to provide an explicit interface for procedures that are not contained in a module. They are often used to provide Fortran 95/2003 interfaces to older pre–Fortran 90 code without rewriting all of the code. The body of an interface block must contain either a complete description of the calling sequence to a procedure, including the type and position of every argument in the calling sequence, or else a MODULE PROCEDURE statement to refer to a procedure already defined in a module.

13

Generic procedures are procedures that can function properly with different types of input data. A generic procedure is declared by using a generic interface block, which looks like an ordinary interface block with the addition of a generic procedure name. One or more specific procedures may be declared within the body of the generic interface block. Each specific procedure must be distinguishable from all other specific procedures by the type and sequence of its nonoptional dummy arguments. When a generic procedure is referenced in a program, the compiler uses the sequence of calling arguments associated with the reference to decide which of the specific procedures to execute.

F-2003 ONLY

In Fortran 2003, generic bound procedures can be declared by using the `GENERIC` statement in a derived data type.

New operators may be defined and intrinsic operators may be extended to have new meanings in Fortran 95/2003. A new operator may have a name consisting of up to 31 characters surrounded by periods. New operators and extended meanings of intrinsic operators are defined by using an interface operator block. The first line of the interface operator block specifies the name of the operator to be defined or extended, and its body specifies the Fortran functions that are invoked to define the extended meaning. For binary operators, each function must have two input arguments; for unary operators, each function must have a single input argument. If several functions are present in the interface body, then they must be distinguishable from one another by the type and/or order of their dummy arguments. When the Fortran compiler encounters a new or extended operator, it uses the type and order of the operands to decide which of the functions to execute. This feature is commonly used to extend operators to support derived data types.

F-2003 ONLY

In Fortran 2003, generic bound operators can be declared by using the `GENERIC` statement in a derived data type.

The assignment statement ($=$) may also be extended to work with derived data types. This extension is done by using an interface assignment block. The body of the interface assignment block must refer to one or more subroutines. Each subroutine must have exactly two dummy arguments, with the first argument having `INTENT(OUT)` and the second argument having `INTENT(IN)`. The first argument corresponds to the left-hand side of the equal sign, and the second argument corresponds to the right-hand side of the equal sign. All subroutines in the body of an interface assignment block must be distinguishable from one another by the type and order of their dummy arguments.

F-2003 ONLY

It is possible to control access to the data items, operators, and procedures in a module by using the `PUBLIC`, `PRIVATE`, and `PROTECTED` statements or attributes. If an entity in a module is declared `PUBLIC`, then it will be available to any program unit that accesses the module by `USE` association. If an entity is declared `PRIVATE`, then it will not be available to any program unit that accesses the module by `USE` association. However, it will remain available to any procedures defined within the module.

F-2003 ONLY

If an entity is declared `PROTECTED`, then it will be read-only in any program unit that accesses the module by `USE` association.

The contents of a derived data type may be declared PRIVATE. If they are declared PRIVATE, then the components of the derived data type will not be separately accessible in any program unit that accesses the type by USE association. The data type as a whole will be available to the program unit, but its components will not be separately addressable. In addition, an entire derived data type may be declared PRIVATE. In that case, neither the data type nor its components are accessible.

The USE statement has two options. The statement may be used to rename specific data items or procedures accessed from a module, which can prevent name conflicts or provide simplified names for local use. Alternatively, the ONLY clause may be used to restrict a program unit's access to only those items that appear in the list. Both options may be combined in a single USE statement.

F-2003 ONLY

Fortran 2003 includes intrinsic procedures to retrieve the command line arguments used to start a program and the values of environment variables. These new procedures replace nonstandard procedures that have varied from vendor to vendor. Use the new procedures instead of the nonstandard ones as soon as they become available to you.

13.13.1 Summary of Good Programming Practice

The following guidelines should be adhered to when you are working with the advanced features of procedures and modules:

1. When working with nested scoping units, avoid redefining the meaning of objects that have the same name in both the inner and outer scoping units. This applies especially to internal procedures. You can avoid confusion about the behavior of variables in the internal procedure by simply giving them different names from the variables in the host procedure.
2. Avoid interface blocks by placing your procedures in modules whenever possible.
3. If you must create interfaces to many procedures, place all of the interfaces in a module so that they will be easily accessible to program units by USE association.
4. Use user-defined generic procedures to define procedures that can function with different types of input data.
5. Use interface operator blocks and interface assignment blocks to create new operators and to extend the meanings of existing operators to work with derived data types. Once proper operators are defined, working with derived data types can be very easy.
6. It is good programming practice to hide any module data items or procedures that do not need to be directly accessed by external program units. This best way to do this is to include a PRIVATE statement in each module, and then list the specific items that you wish to expose in a separate PUBLIC statement.

F-2003 ONLY

7. Use the standard Fortran 2003 intrinsic procedures to retrieve the command line arguments used to start a program and the values of environment variables instead of the nonstandard procedures supplied by individual vendors.

13

13.13.2 Summary of Fortran Statements and Structures

CONTAINS **Statement:**

```
        CONTAINS
```

Example:

```
        PROGRAM main
        . . .
        CONTAINS
            SUBROUTINE sub1(x, y)
            . . .
            END SUBROUTINE sub1
        END PROGRAM
```

Description:

The CONTAINS statement is a statement that specifies that the following statements are one or more separate procedures within the host unit. When used within a module, the CONTAINS statement marks the beginning of one or more module procedures. When used within a main program or an external procedure, the CONTAINS statement marks the beginning of one or more internal procedures. The CONTAINS statement must appear after any type, interface, and data definitions within a module, and must follow the last executable statement within a main program or an external procedure.

GENERIC **Statement:**

F-2003 ONLY

```
        TYPE [::] type_name
            component 1
            . . .
            component n
        CONTAINS
            GENERIC :: generic_name => proc_name1[, proc_name2, ...]
        END TYPE [type_name]
```

Example:

```
        TYPE :: point
            REAL :: x
            REAL :: y
        CONTAINS
            GENERIC :: add => point_plus_point, point_plus_scalar
        END TYPE point
```

Description:

The GENERIC statement defines a generic binding to a derived data type. The specific procedures associated with the generic procedure are listed after the => operator.

Generic Interface Block:

```
INTERFACE generic_name
   interface_body_1
   interface_body_2
   . . .
END INTERFACE
```

Examples:

```
INTERFACE sort
   MODULE PROCEDURE sorti
   MODULE PROCEDURE sortr
END INTERFACE
```

Description:

A generic procedure is declared by using a generic interface block. A generic interface block declares the name of the generic procedure on the first line, and then lists the explicit interfaces of the specific procedures associated with the generic procedure in the interface body. The explicit interface must be fully defined for any specific procedures not appearing in a module. Procedures appearing in a module are referred to with a MODULE PROCEDURE statement, since their interfaces are already known.

F-2003 ONLY

IMPORT **Statement:**

```
IMPORT :: var_name1 [, var_name2, ...]
```

Example:

```
IMPORT :: x, y
```

Description:

The IMPORT statement imports type definitions into an interface definition from the encompassing procedure.

Interface Assignment Block:

```
INTERFACE ASSIGNMENT (=)
   interface_body
END INTERFACE
```

Example:

```
INTERFACE ASSIGNMENT (=)
   MODULE PROCEDURE vector_to_array
   MODULE PROCEDURE array_to_vector
END INTERFACE
```

13

(continued)

(concluded)

Description:
An interface assignment block is used to extend the meaning of the assignment statement to support assignment operations between two different derived data types or between derived data types and intrinsic data types. Each procedure in the interface body must be a subroutine with two arguments. The first argument must have INTENT(OUT) and the second one must have INTENT(IN). All subroutines in the interface body must be distinguishable from each other by the order and type of their arguments.

Interface Block:

```
            INTERFACE
                interface_body_1
                . . .
            END INTERFACE
```

Examples:

```
            INTERFACE
                SUBROUTINE sort(array,n)
                INTEGER, INTENT(IN) :: n
                REAL, INTENT(INOUT), DIMENSION(n) :: array
                END SUBROUTINE
            END INTERFACE
```

Description:
An interface block is used to declare an explicit interface for a separately compiled procedure. It may appear in the header of a procedure that wishes to invoke the separately compiled procedure, or it may appear in a module, and the module may be used by the procedure that wishes to invoke the separately compiled procedure.

Interface Operator Block:

```
            INTERFACE OPERATOR (operator_symbol)
                interface_body
            END INTERFACE
```

Example:

```
            INTERFACE OPERATOR (*)
                MODULE PROCEDURE real_times_vector
                MODULE PROCEDURE vector_times_real
            END INTERFACE
```

Description:
An interface operator block is used to define a new operator, or to extend the meaning of an intrinsic operator to support derived data types. Each procedure in the interface must be a function whose arguments are INTENT(IN). If the operator is a binary operator, then the function must have two arguments. If the operator is a unary operator, then the function must have only one argument. All functions in the interface body must be distinguishable from each other by the order and type of their arguments.

MODULE PROCEDURE Statement:

```
MODULE PROCEDURE module_procedure_1 [, module_procedure_2, ... ]
```

Examples:

```
INTERFACE sort
   MODULE PROCEDURE sorti
   MODULE PROCEDURE sortr
END INTERFACE
```

Description:

The MODULE PROCEDURE statement is used in interface blocks to specify that a procedure contained in a module is to be associated with the generic procedure, operator, or assignment defined by the interface.

F-2003 ONLY

PROTECTED Attribute:

```
type, PROTECTED :: name1[, name2, ... ]
```

Examples:

```
INTEGER,PROTECTED :: i_count
REAL,PROTECTED :: result
```

Description:

The PROTECTED attribute declares that the value of a variable is read-only outside of the module in which it is declared. The value may be used but not modified in any procedure that accesses the defining module by USE access.

F-2003 ONLY

PROTECTED Statement:

```
PROTECTED :: name1[, name2, ... ]
```

Example:

```
PROTECTED :: i_count
```

Description:

The PROTECTED statement declares that the value of a variable is read-only outside of the module in which it is declared. The value may be used but not modified in any procedure that accesses the defining module by USE access.

13

Recursive FUNCTION Statement:

         RECURSIVE [*type*] FUNCTION *name*(*arg1*[, *arg2, ...*]) RESULT (*res*)

Example:

         RECURSIVE FUNCTION fact(n) RESULT (answer)
         INTEGER :: answer

Description:
This statement declares a recursive Fortran function. A recursive function is one that can invoke itself. The type of the function may either be declared in the FUNCTION statement or in a separate type declaration statement. (The type of the result variable res is declared, not the type of the function name.) The value returned by the function call is the value assigned to res within the body of the function.

USE Statement:

         USE *module_name* [, *rename_list*, ONLY: *only_list*]

Examples:

         USE my_procs
         USE my_procs, process_vector_input => input
         USE my_procs, ONLY: input => process_vector_input

Description:
The USE statement makes the contents of the named module available to the program unit in which the statement appears. In addition to its basic function, the USE statement permits module objects to be renamed as they are made available. The ONLY clause permits the programmer to specify that only certain objects from the module will be made available to the program unit.

VOLATILE Attribute:

         type, VOLATILE :: *name1*[, *name2, ...*]

Examples:

F-2003 ONLY

         INTEGER,VOLATILE :: I_count
         REAL,VOLATILE :: result

Description:
The VOLATILE attribute declares that the value of a variable might be changed at any time by some source external to the program, so all reads of the value in the variable must come directly from main memory, and all writes to the variable must go directly to main memory, not to a cached copy.

F-2003 ONLY

VOLATILE **Statement:**

    VOLATILE :: name1[, name2, ...]

Examples:

    VOLATILE :: x, y

Description:
The VOLATILE statement declares that the value of a variable might be changed at any time by some source external to the program, so all reads of the value in the variable must come directly from main memory, and all writes to the variable must go directly to main memory, not to a cached copy.

13.13.3 Exercises

13-1. In Example 12-1, the logical function lt_city failed to sort "APO" and "Anywhere" in proper order because all capital letters appear before all lowercase letters in the ASCII collating sequence. Add an internal procedure to function lt_city to avoid this problem by shifting both city names to uppercase before the comparison. Note that this procedure should *not* shift the names in the database to uppercase. It should only shift the names to uppercase temporarily as they are being used for the comparison.

13-2. Write test driver programs for the recursive subroutine factorial and the recursive function fact, which were introduced in Section 13-2. Test both procedures by calculating 5! and 10! with each one.

13-3. Write a test driver program to verify the proper operation of subroutine extremes in Example 13-2.

13-4. What is printed out when the following code is executed? What are the values of x, y, i, and j at each point in the program? If a value changes during the course of execution, explain why it changes.

```
PROGRAM exercise13_4
IMPLICIT NONE
REAL :: x = 12., y = -3., result
INTEGER :: i = 6, j = 4
WRITE (*,100) ' Before call: x, y, i, j = ', x, y, i, j
100 FORMAT (A,2F6.1,2I6)
result = exec(y,i)
WRITE (*,*) 'The result is ', result
WRITE (*,100) ' After call: x, y, i, j = ', x, y, i, j
CONTAINS
    REAL FUNCTION exec(x,i)
    REAL, INTENT(IN) :: x
    INTEGER, INTENT(IN) :: i
    WRITE (*,100) ' In exec: x, y, i, j = ', x, y, i, j
    100 FORMAT (A,2F6.1,2I6)
    exec = ( x + y ) / REAL ( i + j )
```

13

```
        j = i
      END FUNCTION exec
    END PROGRAM exercise13_4
```

13-5. Is the following program correct or not? If it is correct, what is printed out when it executes? If not, what is wrong with it?

```
PROGRAM junk
IMPLICIT NONE
REAL :: a = 3, b = 4, output
INTEGER :: i = 0
call sub1(a, i, output)
WRITE (*,*) 'The output is ', output

CONTAINS
    SUBROUTINE sub1(x, j, junk)
    REAL, INTENT(IN) :: x
    INTEGER, INTENT(IN) :: j
    REAL, INTENT(OUT) :: junk
    junk = (x - j) / b
    END SUBROUTINE sub1
END PROGRAM junk
```

13-6. What are the three levels of scope in Fortran? Give examples of objects of each type.

13-7. What are scoping units in Fortran? Name the different types of scoping units.

13-8. What is a keyword argument? Under what circumstances can keyword arguments be used?

13-9. In the subroutine definition shown below, are the following calls legal or illegal? Assume that all calling arguments are of type REAL, and assume that the subroutine interface is explicit. Explain why each illegal call is illegal.

```
SUBROUTINE my_sub (a, b, c, d, e )
REAL, INTENT(IN) :: a, d
REAL, INTENT(OUT) :: b
REAL, INTENT(IN), OPTIONAL :: c, e
IF ( PRESENT(c) ) THEN
   b = (a - c) / d
ELSE
   b = a / d
END IF
IF ( PRESENT(e) ) b = b - e
END SUBROUTINE my_sub
```

(*a*) CALL my_sub (1., x, y, 2., z)
(*b*) CALL my_sub (10., 21., x, y, z)
(*c*) CALL my_sub (x, y, 25.)
(*d*) CALL my_sub (p, q, d=r)
(*e*) CALL my_sub (a=p, q, d=r,e=s)
(*f*) CALL my_sub (b=q,a=p,c=t,d=r,e=s)

13-10. What is an interface block? When would interface blocks be needed in a Fortran program?

13-11. In Example 9-1, we created a subroutine `simul` to solve a system of N simultaneous equations in N unknowns. Assuming that the subroutine is independently compiled, it will not have an explicit interface. Write an interface block to define an explicit interface for this subroutine.

13-12. What is a generic procedure? How can a generic procedure be defined?

13-13. How are generic procedures defined for bound procedures?

13-14. In Example 9-4, we created an improved version of the single-precision subroutine `simul2` to solve a system of N simultaneous equations in N unknowns. In Example 11-2, we created a double-precision subroutine `dsimul` to solve a double-precision system of N simultaneous equations in N unknowns. In Exercise 11-9, we created a complex subroutine `csimul` to solve a complex system of N simultaneous equations in N unknowns. Write a generic interface block for these three procedures.

13-15. Are the following generic interface blocks legal or illegal? Why?

(*a*)
```
INTERFACE my_procedure
    SUBROUTINE proc_1 (a, b, c)
    REAL, INTENT(IN) ::a
    REAL, INTENT(IN) ::b
    REAL, INTENT(OUT) ::c
    END SUBROUTINE proc_1
    SUBROUTINE proc_2 (x, y, out1, out2)
    REAL, INTENT(IN) ::x
    REAL, INTENT(IN) ::y
    REAL, INTENT(OUT) ::out1
    REAL, INTENT(OUT), OPTIONAL ::out2
    END SUBROUTINE proc_2
END INTERFACE my_procedure
```

(*b*)
```
INTERFACE my_procedure
    SUBROUTINE proc_1 (a, b, c)
    REAL, INTENT(IN) ::a
    REAL, INTENT(IN) ::b
    REAL, INTENT(OUT) ::c
    END SUBROUTINE proc_1
    SUBROUTINE proc_2 (x, y, z)
    INTEGER, INTENT(IN) ::x
    INTEGER, INTENT(IN) ::y
    INTEGER, INTENT(OUT) :: z
    END SUBROUTINE proc_2
END INTERFACE my_procedure
```

13-16. How can a new Fortran operator be defined? What rules apply to the procedures in the body of an interface operator block?

13-17. How can an intrinsic Fortran operator be extended to have new meanings? What special rules apply to procedures in an interface operator block if an intrinsic operator is being extended?

13-18. How can the assignment operator be extended? What rules apply to the procedures in the body of an interface assignment block?

13

13-19. Polar Complex Numbers A complex number may represented in one of two ways: rectangular or polar. The rectangular representation takes the form $c = a + bi$, where a is the real component and b is the imaginary component of the complex number. The polar representation is of the form $z\angle\theta$, where z is the magnitude of the complex number and θ is the angle of the number (Figure 13-18). The relationship between these two representations of complex numbers is:

$$a = z\cos\theta \tag{11-10}$$

$$b = z\sin\theta \tag{11-11}$$

$$z = \sqrt{a^2 + b^2} \tag{11-12}$$

$$\theta = \tan^{-1}\frac{b}{a} \tag{11-13}$$

The COMPLEX data type represents a complex number in rectangular form. Define a new data type called POLAR that represents a complex number in polar form. Then, write a module containing an interface assignment block and the supporting procedures to allow complex numbers to be assigned to polar numbers, and vice versa.

13-20. If two complex numbers $P_1 = z_1\angle\theta_1$ and $P_2 = z_2\angle\theta_2$ are expressed in polar form, then the product of the numbers is $P_1 \cdot P_2 = z_1 z_2 \angle\theta_1 + \theta_2$. Similarly, P_1 divided by P_2 is

$$\frac{P_1}{P_2} = \frac{z_1}{z_2}\angle\theta_1 - \theta_2$$

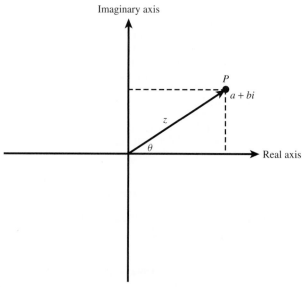

FIGURE 13-18
Representing a complex number in both rectangular and polar coordinates.

Extend the module created in Exercise 13-19 to add an interface operator block and the supporting procedures to allow two POLAR numbers to be multiplied and divided.

13-21. How can the access to data items and procedures in a module be controlled?

13-22. Are the following programs legal or illegal? Why?

(a)
```
MODULE my_module
IMPLICIT NONE
PRIVATE
REAL, PARAMETER :: PI = 3.141592
REAL, PARAMETER :: TWO_PI = 2 * PI
END MODULE my_module

PROGRAM test
USE my_module
IMPLICIT NONE
WRITE (*,*) 'Pi/2 =', PI / 2.
END PROGRAM test
```

(b)
```
MODULE my_module
IMPLICIT NONE
PUBLIC
REAL, PARAMETER :: PI = 3.141592
REAL, PARAMETER :: TWO_PI = 2 * PI
END MODULE my_module

PROGRAM test
USE my_module
IMPLICIT NONE
REAL :: TWO_PI
WRITE (*,*) 'Pi/2 =', PI / 2.
TWO_PI = 2. * PI
END PROGRAM test
```

13-23. Modify the module in Exercise 13-19 to allow access only to the definition of the POLAR type, to the assignment operator, and to the multiplication and division operators. Restrict access to the functions that implement the operator definitions.

13-24. In each of the cases shown below, indicate which of the items defined in the module will be available in the program that accesses it.

(a)
```
MODULE module_1
IMPLICIT NONE
PRIVATE
PUBLIC pi, two_pi, name
REAL, PARAMETER :: PI = 3.141592
REAL, PARAMETER :: TWO_PI = 2 * PI
TYPE :: name
   CHARACTER(len=12) :: first
   CHARACTER :: mi
   CHARACTER(len=12) :: last
END TYPE name
TYPE (name), PUBLIC :: name1 = name("John","Q","Doe")
TYPE (name) :: name2 = name("Jane","R","Public")
END MODULE module_1
```

13

```
PROGRAM test
USE module_1, sample_name => name1
...
END PROGRAM test
```

(*b*)
```
MODULE module_2
IMPLICIT NONE
REAL, PARAMETER :: PI = 3.141592
REAL, PARAMETER :: TWO_PI = 2 * PI
TYPE, PRIVATE :: name
   CHARACTER(len=12) :: first
   CHARACTER :: mi
   CHARACTER(len=12) :: last
END TYPE name
TYPE (name), PRIVATE :: name1 = name("John","Q","Doe")
TYPE (name), PRIVATE :: name2 = name("Jane","R","Public")
END MODULE module_2

PROGRAM test
USE module_2, ONLY: PI
...
END PROGRAM test
```

13

Advanced I/O Concepts

OBJECTIVES

- Learn about all of the types of format descriptors available in Fortran.
- Learn additional options available for the OPEN, CLOSE, READ, and WRITE statements.
- Understand how to maneuver through a file, using the REWIND, BACKSPACE, and ENDFILE statements.
- Understand how to check on file parameters, using the INQUIRE statement.
- Know how to flush the output data to be written to disk, using the FLUSH statement (Fortran 2003 only).
- Understand the differences between formatted and unformatted files, and between sequential and random access files. Learn when you should use each type of file.
- Learn about asynchronous I/O (Fortran 2003 only).

Chapter 5 introduced the basics of Fortran input and output statements. We learned how to read data by using the formatted READ statement and to write data by using the formatted WRITE statement. We also learned about the most common format descriptors: A, E, ES, F, I, L, T, X, and /. Finally, we learned how to open, close, read, write, and position sequential disk files.

This chapter deals with the more advanced features of the Fortran I/O system. It includes a description of the additional format descriptors not yet mentioned, and provides more details about the operation of list-directed I/O statements. Next, it provides more details about the proper use of the various Fortran I/O statements, and introduces namelist I/O. Finally, the chapter explains the difference between formatted and unformatted disk files, and between sequential access and direct access disk files. We will learn when and how to properly use each type of file.

▉ 14.1

ADDITIONAL FORMAT DESCRIPTORS

A complete list of all Fortran 95/2003 format descriptors is shown in Table 14-1. Twelve of the format descriptors describe input/output data types: E, ES, EN, F, and D for single- and double-precision real values; I for integer values; B, 0, and Z for either integer or real values; L for logical values; A for character values; and finally G for any type of value. There is an additional DT format descriptor (in Fortran 2003 only) for specifying the output format of derived data types. Five of the format descriptors control the horizontal and vertical position of data: X, /, T, TL, and TR. The ':' character controls the way that formats associated with WRITE statements are scanned after the last variable in the WRITE statement has been output. Six of the format descriptors control the rounding of floating point data (in Fortran 2003 only): RU, RD, RN, RZ, RC, and RP. Two of them control the type of separator used between the integer and fractional parts of a number (in Fortran 2003 only): DC and DP. Finally, a number of undesirable and/or obsolete format descriptors are briefly mentioned. The Fortran 2003–only descriptors appear shaded and the undesirable and/or obsolete format descriptors appear in darker shading in Table 14-1.

We will now discuss those format descriptors not previously described.

TABLE 14-1
Complete list of Fortran 95/2003 format descriptors

FORMAT Descriptors		Usage
		Real data I/O descriptors
D$w.d$		Double-precision data in exponential notation
E$w.d$	E$w.dE e$	Real data in exponential notation
EN$w.d$	EN$w.dE e$	Real data in engineering notation
ES$w.d$	ES$w.dE e$	Real data in scientific notation
F$w.d$		Real data in decimal notation
		Integer data I/O descriptor
Iw	I$w.m$	Integer data in decimal format
		Real or Integer data I/O descriptors
Bw	B$w.m$	Data in binary format
Ow	O$w.m$	Data in octal format
Zw	Z$w.m$	Data in hexadecimal format
		Logical data I/O descriptor
Lw		Logical data
		Character data I/O descriptors
A	Aw	Character data
'$x...x$'	nH$x...x$	Character constants (the nH$x...x$ form is *deleted* as of
"$x...x$"		Fortran 95)
		Generalized I/O descriptor
G$w.d$	G$w.dE e$	Generalized edit descriptor for any type of data

(continued)

14

(concluded)

Derived type I/O descriptor (Fortran 2005 only)	
`DT 'string' (vals)`	Derived type edit descriptor

Rounding Descriptors (Fortran 2005 only)	
`RU`	Specify rounding up values for all descriptors following this descriptor in the current I/O statement
`RD`	Specify rounding down values for all descriptors following this descriptor in the current I/O statement
`RZ`	Specify rounding toward zero for all descriptors following this descriptor in the current I/O statement
`RN`	Specify rounding to nearest values for all descriptors following this descriptor in the current I/O statement
`RC`	Specify compatible rounding for all descriptors following this descriptor in the current I/O statement
`RP`	Specify processor-dependent rounding for all descriptors following this descriptor in the current I/O statement

Decimal descriptors (Fortran 2005 only)	
`DC`	Use a comma as the character that separates the parts of a decimal for all descriptors following this descriptor in the current I/O statement
`DP`	Use a point as the character that separates the parts of a decimal for all descriptors following this descriptor in the current I/O statement

Positioning descriptors	
nX	Horizontal Spacing: skip n spaces
/	Vertical Spacing: move down 1 line
Tc	TAB: move to column c of current line
TLn	TAB: move left n columns in current line
TRn	TAB: move right n columns in current line

Scanning control descriptor	
:	Format scanning control character

Miscellaneous descriptors (undesirable)	
kP	Scale factor for display of real data
BN	Blank Null: ignore blanks in numeric input fields
BZ	Blank Zero: interpret blanks in a numeric input field as zeros
S	Sign control: Use default system convention
SP	Sign control: Display "+" before positive numbers
SS	Sign control: Suppress "+" before pos numbers

Where:

c column number
d number of digits to right of decimal place
e number of digits in exponent
k scale factor (number of places to shift decimal point)
m minimum number of digits to be displayed
r repetition count
w field width in characters

14

14.1.1 Additional Forms of the E and ES Format Descriptors

The E, ES, and F format descriptors were described in Chapter 5. In addition to the information presented there, there are optional forms of the E and ES descriptors that allow a programmer to specify the number of digits to display in the exponent of the real number. These forms are

$$rEw.dEe \quad \text{or} \quad rESw.dEe$$

where *w*, *d*, *e*, and *r* have the meanings given in Table 14-1. They function exactly as described in Chapter 5 except that the number of digits in the exponent is specified.

14.1.2 Engineering Notation—The EN Descriptor

Engineering notation is a modified version of scientific notation in which a real number is expressed as a value between 1.0 and 1000.0 times a power of 10, where the power of 10 is always a multiple of three. This form of notation is very convenient in the engineering world, because 10^{-6}, 10^{-3}, 10^3, 10^6, etc., all have standard, universally recognized prefixes. For example, 10^{-6} is known by the prefix *micro*, 10^{-3} is known by the prefix *milli*, and so forth. Engineers will commonly speak of 250 kΩ resistors and 50 nF capacitors instead of 2.5×10^5 Ω resistors and 5×10^{-8} F capacitors.

Fortran can print out numbers in engineering notation with the EN descriptor. When writing data, the EN descriptor displays a floating-point number with a mantissa in the range between 1 and 1000, while the exponent is always a power of 10 divisible by 3. The EN format descriptor has the form

$$rENw.d \quad \text{or} \quad rENw.dEe$$

where *w*, *d*, *e*, and *r* have the meanings given in Table 14-1.

For example, the following statements

```
a = 1.2346E7; b = 0.0001; c = -77.7E10
WRITE (*,'(1X,3EN15.4)') a, b, c
```

will produce the output

```
    12.3460E+06    100.000E-06  -777.0000E+09
----|----|----|----|----|----|----|----|----|
    5    10   15   20   25   30   35   40   45
```

Note that all of the exponents are powers of 3. When reading data, the EN descriptor behaves exactly like the E, ES, and F descriptors.

14.1.3 Double-Precision Data—The D Descriptor

There is an obsolete format descriptor for use with double-precision data: the D format descriptor. The D format descriptor has the form

$$rDw.d$$

It is functionally identical to the E format descriptor, except that the exponent indicator is sometimes a D instead of an E. This descriptor is preserved only for backward compatibility with earlier versions of Fortran. *You should never use the D format descriptor in any new program.*

14.1.4 The Generalized (G) Format Descriptor

The F format descriptor is used to display real values in a fixed format. For example, the descriptor F7.3 will display a real value in the format ddd.ddd for positive numbers, or -dd.ddd for negative numbers. The F descriptor produces output data in a very easy-to-read format. Unfortunately, if the number to be displayed with an F7.3 descriptor is ≥ 1000 or ≤ -100, then the output data will be replaced by a field of asterisks: *******. In contrast, the E format descriptor will display a number regardless of its range. However, numbers displayed in the E format are not as easy to interpret as numbers displayed in the F format. Although the following two numbers are identical, the one displayed in the F format is easier to understand:

225.671   0.225671E+03

Because the F format is easier to read, it would be really nice to have a format descriptor that displays numbers in the F format whenever possible, but then switches to the E format when they become too big or too small. The G (generalized) format descriptor behaves in just this fashion when used with real data.

The G format descriptor has the form

*r*G*w.d*   or   *r*G*w.dEe*

where *w*, *d*, *e*, and *r* have the meanings given in Table 14-1. A real value displayed with a G format descriptor will be displayed in either F or E format, depending on the exponent of the number. If the real value to be displayed is represented as $\pm 0.dddddd \times 10^{k}$ and the format descriptor to be used for the display is G*w.d*, then the relationship between *d* and *k* will determine how the data is to be displayed. If $0 \leq k \leq d$, the value will be output in F format with a field width of *w* − 4 characters followed by four blanks. *The decimal point will be adjusted* (within the *w* − 4 characters) *as necessary to display as many significant digits as possible.* If the exponent is negative or is greater than *d*, the value will be output in E format. In either case, a total of *d* significant digits will be displayed.

The operation of the G format descriptor with real data is illustrated in the table below. In the first example, *k* is −1, so the output comes out in E format. For the last example, *k* is 6 and *d* is 5, so the output again comes out in E format. For all of the examples in between, $0 \leq k \leq d$, so the output comes out in F format with the decimal point adjusted to display as many significant digits as possible.

Value	Exponent	G Descriptor	Output
0.012345	−1	G11.5	0.12345E-01
0.123450	0	G11.5	0.12345ЬЬЬЬ
1.234500	1	G11.5	1.23450ЬЬЬЬ
12.34500	2	G11.5	12.3450ЬЬЬЬ
123.4500	3	G11.5	123.450ЬЬЬЬ
1234.5600	4	G11.5	1234.50ЬЬЬЬ
12345.600	5	G11.5	12345.0ЬЬЬЬ
123456.00	6	G11.5	0.12345E+06

14

The generalized format descriptor can also be used with integer, logical, and character data. When it is used with integer data, it behaves like the I format descriptor. When it is used with logical data, it behaves like the L format descriptor. When it is used with character data, it behaves like the A format descriptor.

14.1.5 The Binary, Octal, and Hexadecimal (B, O, and Z) Descriptors

The binary (B), octal (O), and hexadecimal (Z) descriptors can be used to read or write data in binary, octal, and hexadecimal formats. They work for both integer and real data. The general forms of these descriptors are

rBw	or	rBw.m
rOw	or	rOw.m
rZw	or	rZw.m

where w, m, and r have the meanings given in Table 14-1. The format descriptors must be large enough to display all of the digits in the appropriate notation, or the field will be filled with asterisks. For example, the statements

```
a = 16
b = -1
WRITE (*,'(1X,A,B16,1X,B16)')      'Binary: ', a, b
WRITE (*,'(1X,A,O11.4,1X,O11.4)') 'Octal:  ', a, b
WRITE (*,'(1X,A,Z8,1X,Z8)')        'Hex:    ', a, b
```

will produce the output

```
Binary:          10000 ****************
Octal:            0020 37777777777
Hex:              10 FFFFFFFF
----|----|----|----|----|----|----|----|----|
    5   10   15   20   25   30   35   40   45
```

Since numbers are stored in 2's complement format on this computer, a −1 will be 32 bits set to 1. Therefore, the binary representation of b will consist of 32 ones. Since the B16 field is too small to display this number, it is filled with asterisks.

14.1.6 The TAB Descriptors

There are three TAB format descriptors: Tc, TLn, and TRn. We met the Tc descriptor in Chapter 5. In a formatted WRITE statement, it makes the output of the following descriptor begin at column c in the output buffer. In a formatted READ statement, it makes the field of the following descriptor begin at column c in the input buffer. For example, the following code will print the letter 'Z' in column 30 of the output line (remember that column 1 is used for carriage control and is not printed).

```
WRITE (*,'(T31,A)') 'Z'
```

The Tc descriptor performs an *absolute* tab function, in the sense that the output moves to column c regardless of where the previous output was. By contrast, the TLn and TR*n* descriptors are *relative* tab functions. TL*n* moves the output left by *n* columns, and TR*n* moves the output right by *n* columns. Where the next output will occur depends on the location of the previous output on the line. For example, the following code prints a 100 in columns 10 to 12 and a 200 in columns 17 to 19:

```
WRITE (*,'(T11,I3,TR4,I3)') 100, 200
```

14.1.7 The Colon (:) Descriptor

We have learned that if a WRITE statement runs out of variables before the end of its corresponding format, the use of the format continues until the first format descriptor without a corresponding variable, or until the end of the format, whichever comes first. For example, consider the statements

```
m = 1
voltage = 13800.
WRITE (*,40) m
40 FORMAT (1X, 'M = ', I3, ' N = ', I4, ' O = ', F7.2)
WRITE (*,50) voltage / 1000.
50 FORMAT (1X, 'Voltage = ', F8.1, ' kV')
```

These statements will produce the output

```
        M =    1 N =
Voltage =      13.8 kV
----|----|----|----|----|
    5   10   15   20   25
```

The use of the first FORMAT statement stops at I4, which is the first unmatched format descriptor. The use of the second FORMAT statement stops at the end of the statement, since there are no unmatched descriptors before that.

The colon descriptor (:) permits a user to modify the normal behavior of format descriptors during writes. The colon descriptor serves as a *conditional stopping point* for the WRITE statement. If there are more values to print out, the colon is ignored, and the execution of the formatted WRITE statement continues according to the normal rules for using formats. However, if a colon is encountered in the format and there are no more values to write out, execution of the WRITE statement stops at the colon.

To help understand the use of the colon, let's examine the simple program shown in Figure 14-1.

FIGURE 14-1
Program illustrating the use of the colon format descriptor.

```
PROGRAM test_colon
IMPLICIT NONE
REAL, DIMENSION(8) :: x
INTEGER :: i
x = (/ 1.1, 2.2, 3.3, 4.4, 5.5, 6.6, 7.7, 8.8 /)
```

(continued)

14

```
(concluded)
WRITE (*,100) (i, x(i), i = 1, 8)
100 FORMAT (/,1X,'The output values are: '/, &
          3(5X,'X(',I2,') = ',F10.4))

WRITE (*,200) (i, x(i), i = 1, 8)
200 FORMAT (/,1X,'The output values are: '/,
          3(:,5X,'X(',I2,') = ',F10.4))

END PROGRAM test_colon
```

This program contains an eight-element array whose values we wish to print out three abreast across the page. Note that the portion of the format descriptors inside the parentheses has a repeat count of three, so each line will contain three values printed in identical format before the program advances to the next line. If the program is compiled and executed, the result is

```
C:\book\chap14>test

The output values are:
    X( 1) =      1.1000      X( 2) =      2.2000      X( 3) =      3.3000
    X( 4) =      4.4000      X( 5) =      5.5000      X( 6) =      6.6000
    X( 7) =      7.7000      X( 8) =      8.8000      X(

The output values are:
    X( 1) =      1.1000      X( 2) =      2.2000      X( 3) =      3.3000
    X( 4) =      4.4000      X( 5) =      5.5000      X( 6) =      6.6000
    X( 7) =      7.7000      X( 8) =      8.8000
```

The first WRITE statement and FORMAT statement run out of values to output after x(8) is written, but since it is in the middle of a format, the WRITE continues to execute until it comes to the first output descriptor without a corresponding variable. As a result, an extra 'X(' is printed out. The second WRITE statement and FORMAT are identical to the first pair, except that there is a colon at the beginning of the repeated portion of the FORMAT statement. This pair also runs out of values to output after x(8) is written. Since it is in the middle of a format, the WRITE continues to execute, but immediately bumps into the colon, and stops. In this case, the extra 'X(' is not printed out.

The colon descriptor is most commonly used to terminate output cleanly in the middle of a line, as it was in the example above.

14.1.8 Scale Factors—The P Descriptor

The P descriptor adds a scale factor to any real values printed out with the E and F format descriptors. A scale factor has the form

$$nP$$

where n is the number of places by which to shift the decimal point. The P scale factor may precede either E or F format descriptors. The general form of the descriptors with a scale factor are

$$nPrFw.d \qquad \text{and} \qquad nPrEw.d$$

With the F format descriptor, the P scale factor causes the displayed number to be multiplied by 10^n. With the E format descriptor, the P scale factor causes the fractional part of the displayed number to be multiplied by 10^n, and the exponent to be decreased by n.

The P scale factor has been made redundant by the introduction of the ES and EN format descriptors in Fortran 90. *It should never be used in any new program.*

14.1.9 The SIGN Descriptors

The SIGN format descriptors control the display of positive signs before positive numbers in an output line. There are three SIGN format descriptors: S, SP, and SS. The SP descriptor causes positive signs to be displayed before all positive numerical values following it in the same format statement, while the SS descriptor suppresses positive signs before all positive numerical values following it in the same format statement. The S descriptor restores the system default behavior for all positive numerical values following it. These format descriptors are almost never needed, and so are little used.

14.1.10 Blank Interpretation: The BN and BZ Descriptors

The BN (blank null) and BZ (blank zero) descriptors control the way in which blanks are interpreted in input data fields. If the BN descriptor is in effect, then blanks are ignored. If the BZ descriptor is in effect, then blanks are treated as zeros. In either case, if an entire input data field is blank, then the field is interpreted as 0. *The BN and BZ descriptors are never needed in any modern program.* They are present only for backward compatibility with the I/O behavior of FORTRAN 66.

14.1.11 Rounding Control: The RU, RD, RZ, RN, RC, and RP Descriptors (Fortran 2003 only)

The RU (round up), RD (round down), RZ (round toward zero), RN (round nearest), RC (round compatible), and RP (round processor defined) descriptors control the way that data is rounded as it is read in or written out. Values such as 0.1 have no exact representation in the binary floating-point arithmetic used on IEEE 754 processors, so a number such as this must be *rounded* as it is saved into memory. Similarly, the binary representation of numbers inside the computer will not exactly match the decimal data written out in formatted files, so rounding must occur on output too. These descriptors control how the rounding works for a given input statement or output statement.

The RU descriptor specifies that all numeric values following it in the same READ or WRITE statement will be rounded up (toward positive infinity) during the conversion process. The RD descriptor specifies that all numeric values following it in the same READ or WRITE statement will be rounded down (toward negative infinity) during the conversion process. The RZ descriptor specifies that all numeric values following it in

14

the same READ or WRITE statement will be rounded toward zero during the conversion process. The RN descriptor specifies that all numeric values following it in the same READ or WRITE statement will be rounded to the nearest representable value during the conversion process. If two representable values are equally distant, then the direction of rounding is not defined. The RC descriptor specifies that all numeric values following it in the same READ or WRITE statement will be rounded to the nearest representable value during the conversion process. If two representable values are equally distant, then the direction of rounding is away from zero. The RP descriptor specifies that all floating-point values following it in the same WRITE statement will be rounded in a processor-dependent manner.

14.1.12 Decimal Specifier: The DC and DP Descriptors (Fortran 2003 only)

The DC (decimal comma) and DP (decimal point) descriptors control the character used to divide the integer part of an expression from the fractional part. If the DC descriptor is used, then all floating-point values following it in the same READ or WRITE statement will use a comma as the separator. If the DP descriptor is used, then all floating-point values following it in the same READ or WRITE statement will use a decimal point as the separator. Note that the default separator behavior for a given file is set by the DECIMAL= clause in the OPEN statement. The DC and DP descriptors are used only if we wish to temporarily override the choice made when the file was opened.

14.2
DEFAULTING VALUES IN LIST-DIRECTED INPUT

List-directed input has the advantage of being very simple to use, since no FORMAT statements need be written for it. A list-directed READ statement is very useful for getting input information from a user at a terminal. The user may type the input data in any column, and the READ statement will still interpret it properly.

In addition, list-directed READ statements support *null values*. If an input data line contains two consecutive commas, then the corresponding variable in the input list will be left unchanged. This behavior permits a user to default one or more input data values to their previously defined values. Consider the following example

```
PROGRAM test_read
INTEGER :: i = 1, j = 2, k = 3
WRITE (*,*) 'Enter i, j, and k: '
READ (*,*) i, j, k
WRITE (*,*) 'i, j, k = ', i, j, k
END PROGRAM test_read
```

When this program is compiled and executed, the results are

```
C:\book\chap14>test_read
Enter i, j, and k:
1000,,-2002
i, j, k =          1000          2          -2002
```

Note that the value of j was defaulted to 2, while new values were assigned to i and k. It is also possible to default all of the remaining variables on a line by concluding it with a slash.

```
C:\book\chap14>test_read
Enter i, j, and k:
1000 /
i, j, k =              1000           2             3
```

Quiz 14-1

This quiz provides a quick check to see if you have understood the concepts introduced in Sections 14.1 and 14.2. If you have trouble with the quiz, reread the sections, ask your instructor, or discuss the material with a fellow student. The answers to this quiz are found in the back of the book.

For questions 1 to 4, determine what will be written out when the statements are executed.

1. ```
   REAL :: a = 4096.07
   WRITE (*,1) a, a, a, a, a
   1 FORMAT (1X, F10.1, F9.2, E12.5, G12.5, G11.4)
   ```

2. ```
   INTEGER :: i
   REAL, DIMENSION(5) :: data1 = (/ -17.2,4.,4.,.3,-2.22 /)
   WRITE (*,1) (i, data1(i), i=1, 5)
   1 FORMAT (2(5X,'Data1(',I3,') = ',F8.4,:,','))
   ```

3. ```
   REAL :: x = 0.0000122, y = 123456.E2
   WRITE (*,'(1X,2EN14.6,/,1X,2ES14.6)') x, y, x, y
   ```

4. ```
   INTEGER :: i = -2002, j = 1776, k = -3
   WRITE (*,*) 'Enter i, j, and k: '
   READ (*,*) i, j, k
   WRITE (*,1) i, j, k
   1 FORMAT (' i = ',I10,' j = ',I10,' k = ',I10)
   ```

   where the input line is,

   ```
   ,         -1001/
   ---------|---------|
        10        20
   ```

▪ 14.3

DETAILED DESCRIPTION OF FORTRAN I/O STATEMENTS

A summary of Fortran I/O statements is shown in Table 14-2, with the statements and clauses unique to Fortran 2003 shown shaded. These statements permit us to open and

TABLE 14-2
Fortran 95/2003 I/O statements

Statement	Function
OPEN	Open a file (connect it to an i/o unit)
CLOSE	Close a file (disconnect it from an i/o unit)
INQUIRE	Check on properties of a file
READ	Read data from a file (via an i/o unit)
PRINT	Write data to the standard output device
WRITE	Write data to a file (via an i/o unit)
REWIND	Rewind a sequential file to the beginning
BACKSPACE	Move back one record in a sequential file
ENDFILE	Move to the end of a sequential file
FLUSH	Flush output buffers to disk
WAIT	Wait for asynchronous I/O to complete

F-2003 ONLY

close files, check the status of files, go to a specific position within a file, and to read from or write to a file. In this section, we will learn about all of the statements found in the table. Some of them were introduced in simplified form in Chapter 5, but even the statements that we are already familiar with have many additional options for us to learn about.

The discussion of each i/o statement includes a table listing all of the possible clauses that can be used with the statement. Those clauses that should not be used in modern Fortran programs are shown with a dark shaded background.

14.3.1 The OPEN Statement

A disk file must be connected to an i/o unit before data can be read from or written to the file. Depending on the particular implementation of your compiler, a few files may be pre-connected to some of the i/o units when execution begins. If preconnected files exist, it is possible to write data to them without opening them first. For example, Intel Visual Fortran automatically preconnects a file called 'fort.21' to i/o unit 21, and so forth. The preconnected file is automatically created the first time that a Fortran program writes to it.

Unfortunately, the number and the names of preconnected files (if any) differ from processor to processor, so if you use this feature in your programs, they will be much less portable. You should always explicitly open any file that you use to improve the portability of your programs, and to allow you to choose your own name for each file.

14

Good Programming Practice
Do not rely on preconnected files in your Fortran programs (except for the standard input and output devices). The number and the names of preconnected files vary from processor to processor, so using them will reduce the portability of your programs.

An i/o unit is explicitly connected to a disk file using the OPEN statement. Once we are through using a file, we should disconnect the file from the i/o unit by using the CLOSE statement. After the CLOSE statement has been executed, the i/o unit will no longer be connected to the file, and it may be connected to some other file by using another OPEN statement.

The OPEN statement has the general form

$$OPEN \ (open\_list)$$

where *open_list* consists of two or more clauses separated by commas. The possible clauses in an OPEN statement are summarized in Table 14-3. These clauses may be included in the OPEN statement in any order. Not all of the clauses will be included in every statement. Some of them are meaningful only for specific types of files. For example, the RECL= clause is meaningful only for direct access files. Also, some combinations of clauses have contradictory meanings, and will produce errors at compile time. We will point out some examples of these contradictions as we discuss the details of the clauses below.

Note that the shaded items in Table 14-3 are Fortran 2003–only features.

F-2003 ONLY

TABLE 14-3
Clauses allowed in the OPEN statement

Clause	Input or output	Purpose	Possible values
[UNIT=]int_expr	Input	Denotes i/o unit to attach file to. The "UNIT=" phrase is optional.	Processor-dependent integer
FILE=char_expr	Input	Name of file to open.[1]	Character string
STATUS=char_expr	Input	Specifies status for file to be opened.	'OLD', 'NEW', 'SCRATCH', 'REPLACE', 'UNKNOWN'
IOSTAT=int_var	Output	I/O status at end of operation.	Processor-dependent integer int_var. 0 = success; positive = open failure
IOMSG=char_var	Output	Character string describing any error that occurred during operation.	Character string
ACCESS=char_expr	Input	Specifies sequential, direct, or stream access.	'SEQUENTIAL', 'DIRECT', 'STREAM'
ASYNCHRONOUS=char_expr	Input	Specifies whether or not to use asynchronous I/O.[2]	'YES', 'NO'
DECIMAL=char_expr	Input	Specifies the separator to use between the integer and fractional parts of a number. (Default 'POINT')	'COMMA', 'POINT'
ENCODING=char_expr	Input	Specifies the type of character data to read / write from a file. 'UTF-8' specifies a Unicode file.[3]	'UTF-8', 'DEFAULT'
ROUND=char_expr	Input	Specifies the type of rounding to perform during formatted I/O operations. (Default 'PROCESSOR DEFINED'.)	'UP', 'DOWN', 'ZERO', 'NEAREST', 'COMPATIBLE', 'PROCESSOR DEFINED'

F-2003 ONLY

F-2003 ONLY

F-2003 ONLY

14

(continued)

(concluded)

SIGN=*char_expr*	Input	Specifies whether to display plus signs on positive output values during formatted write operations.	'PLUS', 'SUPPRESS', 'PROCESSOR DEFINED'
FORM=*char_expr*	Input	Specifies formatted or unformatted data.	'FORMATTED', 'UNFORMATTED'
ACTION=*char_expr*	Input	Specifies whether file is read only, write only, or read/write.	'READ', 'WRITE', 'READWRITE'
RECL=*int_expr*	Input	For a formatted direct access file, the number of characters in each record. For an unformatted direct access file, the number of processor-dependent units in each record.[4]	Processor-dependent positive integer
POSITION=*char_expr*	Input	Specifies the position of the file pointer after the file is opened.	'REWIND', 'APPEND', 'ASIS'
DELIM=*char_expr*	Input	Specifies whether list-directed character output is to be delimited by apostrophes, by quotation marks, or by nothing.[5] (Default 'NONE'.)	'APOSTROPHE', 'QUOTE', 'NONE'
PAD=*variable*	Input	Specifies whether formatted input records are padded with blanks. (Default 'YES'.)	'YES', 'NO'
BLANK=*char_expr*	Input	Specifies whether blanks are to be treated as nulls or zeros. Nulls are the default case.[6]	'NULL', 'ZERO'
ERR=*label*	Input	Statement label to transfer control to if open fails.[7]	Statement labels in current scoping unit.

[1] The FILE= clause is not allowed for scratch files.
[2] The ASYNCHRONOUS= clause allows asynchronous I/O statements for this file. The default value is 'NO'.
[3] The ENCODING= clause is defined only for files connected for formatted I/O. The default value is 'DEFAULT', which is processor dependent, but normally with 1-byte characters.
[4] The RECL= clause is defined only for files connected for direct access.
[5] The DELIM= clause is defined only for files connected for formatted I/O.
[6] The BLANK= clause is defined only for files connected for formatted I/O. This clause is never needed in a modern Fortran program.
[7] The ERR= clause is never needed in a modern Fortran program. Use the IOSTAT= clause instead.

The UNIT= clause

This clause specifies the **i/o unit** number to be associated with the file. *The* UNIT= *clause must be present in any* OPEN *statement.* The i/o unit number specified here will be used in later READ and WRITE statements to access the file. The UNIT=io_unit clause may be abbreviated to just the io_unit number if it appears as the first clause in an OPEN statement. This feature is included in Fortran 95/2003 for backward compatibility with earlier versions of Fortran. Therefore, the following two statements are equivalent:

```
OPEN ( UNIT=10, ... )
OPEN ( 10, ... )
```

The FILE= clause

This clause specifies the name of the file to connect to the specified i/o unit. *A file name must be supplied for all files* except for scratch files.

The STATUS= **clause**

This clause specifies the status of the file to connect to the specified i/o unit. There are five possible file statuses: 'OLD', 'NEW', 'REPLACE', 'SCRATCH', and 'UNKNOWN'.

If the file status is 'OLD', then the file must already exist on the system when the OPEN statement is executed, or the OPEN will fail with an error. If the file status is 'NEW', then the file must *not* already exist on the system when the OPEN statement is executed, or the OPEN will fail with an error. If the file status is STATUS='REPLACE', then a new file will be opened whether it exists or not. If the file already exists, the program will delete it, create a new file, and then open it for output. The old contents of the file will be lost. If it does not exist, the program will create a new file by that name and open it.

If the file status is 'SCRATCH', then a **scratch file** will be created on the computer and attached to the i/o unit. A scratch file is a temporary file created by the computer that the program can use for temporary data storage while it is running. When a scratch file is closed or when the program ends, the file is automatically deleted from the system. Note that *the* FILE= *clause is not used with a scratch file*, since no permanent file is created. It is an error to specify a file name for a scratch file.

If the file status is 'UNKNOWN', then the behavior of the program will vary from processor to processor—the Fortran standard does not specify the behavior of this option. The most common behavior is for the program to first look for an existing file with the specified name, and open it if it exists. The contents of the file are not destroyed by the act of opening it with unknown status, but the original contents can be destroyed if we later write to the file. If the file does not exist, then the computer creates a new file with that name and opens it. Unknown status should be avoided in a program because the behavior of the OPEN statement is processor dependent, which could reduce the portability of the program.

If there is no STATUS= clause in an OPEN statement, then the default status is 'UNKNOWN'.

The IOSTAT= **clause**

This clause specifies an integer variable that will contain the i/o status after the OPEN statement is executed. If the file is opened successfully, then the status variable will contain a zero. If the open failed, then the status variable will contain a processor-dependent positive value corresponding to the type of error that occurred.

F-2003 ONLY

The IOMSG= **clause**

This clause specifies a character variable that will contain the i/o status after the OPEN statement is executed. If the file is opened successfully, then the contents of this variable will be unchanged. If the open failed, then this variable will contain a message describing the problem that occurred.

14

The ACCESS= **clause**

This clause specifies the access method to be used with the file. There are three types of access methods: 'SEQUENTIAL', 'DIRECT', and 'STREAM'. **Sequential access** involves opening a file and reading or writing its records in order from beginning to end. Sequential access is the default access mode in Fortran, and all files that we have seen so far have been sequential files. The records in a file opened with sequential access do not have to be any particular length.

If a file is opened with **direct access**, it is possible to jump directly from one record to another within the file at any time without having to read any of the records in between. Every record in a file opened with direct access must be of the same length.

If a file is opened with **stream access**, data is written to the file or read from the file in "file storage units" (normally bytes). This mode differs from sequential access in that sequential access is record oriented, with end-of-record (new line) characters automatically inserted at the end of each record. In contrast, stream access just writes or reads the specified bytes with no extra processing for the ends of lines. Stream access is similar to the file I/O in the C language.

The ASYNCHRONOUS= **clause**

This clause specifies whether or not asynchronous I/O is possible to or from this file. The default (compatible with Fortran 95 and earlier) is 'NO'.

The DECIMAL= **clause**

This clause specifies whether the separator between the integer and fraction values in a real number is a decimal point or a comma. The default is a decimal point, which is compatible with Fortran 95 and earlier versions of Fortran.

The value in this clause can be overridden for a particular READ or WRITE statement by the DC and DP format descriptors

The ENCODING= **clause**

This clause specifies whether the character encoding in this file is standard ASCII or Unicode. If this value is 'UTF-8', then the character encoding is 2-byte Unicode. If this value is 'DEFAULT', then the character encoding is processor dependent, which for practical purposes means that it will be 1-byte ASCII characters.

The ROUND= **clause**

This clause specifies how rounding occurs when data is written to or read from formatted files. The options are 'UP', 'DOWN', 'ZERO', 'NEAREST', 'COMPATIBLE', and 'PROCESSOR DEFINED'. Values such as 0.1 have no exact representation in the binary floating-point arithmetic used on IEEE 754 processors, so a number such as this must be *rounded* as it is saved into memory. Similarly, the binary representation of numbers inside the computer will not exactly match the decimal data written out in formatted files, so rounding must occur on output too. This clause controls how the rounding works for a given file.

The 'UP' option specifies that all numeric values will be rounded up (toward positive infinity) during the conversion process. The 'DOWN' option specifies that all

14

numeric values will be rounded down (toward negative infinity) during the conversion process. The 'ZERO' option specifies that all numeric values will be rounded toward zero during the conversion process. The 'NEAREST' option specifies that all numeric values will be rounded to the nearest representable value during the conversion process. If two representable values are equally distant, then the direction of rounding is not defined. The 'COMPATIBLE' option is the same as the 'NEAREST' option, except that if two representable values are equally distant, then the direction of rounding is away from zero. The PROCESSOR DEFINED specifies that all floating-point values will be rounded in a processor-dependent manner.

The value in this clause can be overridden for a particular READ or WRITE statement by the RU, RD, RZ, RN, RC, and RP format descriptors

**F-2003
ONLY**

The SIGN= clause

This clause controls the display of positive signs before positive numbers in an output line. The options are 'PLUS', 'SUPPRESS', and 'PROCESSOR DEFINED'. The 'PLUS' option causes positive signs to be displayed before all positive numerical values, while the 'SUPPRESS' option suppresses positive signs before all positive numerical values. The 'PROCESSOR DEFINED' option allows the computer to use the system default behavior for all positive numerical values. This is the default behavior.

The value in this clause can be overridden for a particular READ or WRITE statement by the S, SP, and SS format descriptors.

The FORM= clause

This clause specifies the format status of the file. There are two file formats: 'FORMATTED' and 'UNFORMATTED'. The data in **formatted files** consists of recognizable characters, numbers, etc. These files are called formatted because we use format descriptors (or list-directed I/O statements) to convert their data into a form usable by the computer whenever we read or write them. When we write to a formatted file, the bit patterns stored in the computer's memory are translated into a series of characters that humans can read, and those characters are written to the file. The instructions for the translation process are included in the format descriptors. All of the disk files that we have used so far have been formatted files.

In contrast, **unformatted files** contain data that is an exact copy of the data stored in the computer's memory. When we write to an unformatted file, the exact bit patterns in the computer's memory are copied into the file. Unformatted files are much smaller than the corresponding formatted files, but the information in an unformatted file is coded in bit patterns that cannot be easily examined or used by people. Furthermore, the bit patterns corresponding to particular values vary among different types of computer systems, so unformatted files cannot easily be moved from one type of computer to another one.

If a file uses sequential access, the default file format is 'FORMATTED'. If the file uses direct access, the default file format is 'UNFORMATTED'.

14

The ACTION= clause

This clause specifies whether a file is to be opened for reading only, for writing only, or for both reading and writing. Possible values are 'READ', 'WRITE', or 'READWRITE'. The default action is 'READWRITE'.

The RECL= clause

This clause specifies the length of each record in a direct access file. For formatted files opened with direct access, this clause contains the length of each record in characters. For unformatted files, this clause contains the length of each record in processor-dependent units.

The POSITION= clause

This clause specifies the position of the file pointer after the file is opened. The possible values are 'REWIND', 'APPEND', or 'ASIS'. If the expression is 'REWIND', then the file pointer points to the first record in the file. If the expression is 'APPEND', then the file pointer points just after the last record in the file, and just before the end-of-file marker. If the expression is 'ASIS', then the position of the file pointer is unspecified and processor dependent. The default position is 'ASIS'.

The DELIM= clause

This clause specifies which characters are to be used to delimit character strings in list-directed output and namelist output statements. The possible values are 'QUOTE', 'APOSTROPHE', or 'NONE'. If the expression is 'QUOTE', then the character strings will be delimited by quotation marks, and any quotation marks in the string will be doubled. If the expression is 'APOSTROPHE', then the character strings will be delimited by apostrophes, and any apostrophes in the string will be doubled. If the expression is 'NONE', then the character strings have no delimiters.

The PAD= clause

This clause has the possible values 'YES' or 'NO'. If this clause is 'YES', then the processor will pad out input data lines with blanks as required to match the length of the record specified in a READ format descriptor. If it is 'NO', then the input data line must be at least as long as the record specified in the format descriptor, or an error will occur. The default value is 'YES'.

The BLANK= clause

This clause specifies whether blank columns in numeric fields are to be treated as blanks or zeros. The possible values are 'ZERO' or 'NULL'. It is the equivalent of the BN and BZ format descriptors, except that the value specified here applies to the entire file. This clause provides backward compatibility with FORTRAN 66; it should never be needed in any new Fortran program.

The ERR= clause

This clause specifies the label of a statement to jump to if the file open fails. The ERR= clause provides a way to add special code to handle file open errors. (This clause should not be used in new programs; use the IOSTAT= and IOMSG= clauses instead.)

The importance of using the IOSTAT= and IOMSG= clauses

If a file open fails and there is no IOSTAT= clause or ERR= clause in the OPEN statement, then the Fortran program will print out an error message and abort. This behavior is very inconvenient in a large program that runs for a long period of time, since large amounts of work can be lost if the program aborts. It is *much* better to trap such errors, and let the user tell the program what to do about the problem. The user could specify a new disk file, or let the program shut down gracefully, saving all the work done so far.

If either the IOSTAT= clause or ERR= clause are present in the OPEN statement, then the Fortran program will not abort when an open error occurs. If an error occurs and the IOSTAT= clause is present, then a positive i/o status will be returned specifying the type of error that occurred. If the IOMSG= clause is also present, then a user-readable character string describing the problem is also returned. The program can check for an error, and provide the user with options for continuing or shutting down gracefully. For example,

```
OPEN ( UNIT=8,FILE='test.dat',STATUS='OLD',IOSTAT=istat)

! Check for OPEN error
in_ok: IF ( istat /= 0 ) THEN
    WRITE (*,*) 'Input file OPEN failed: istat = ', istat
    WRITE (*,*) 'Shutting down ... '
    . . .
ELSE
    normal processing
    . . .
END IF in_ok
```

In general, the IOSTAT= clause should be used instead of the ERR= clause in all new programs, since the IOSTAT= clause allows more flexibility and is better suited to modern structured programming. The use of the ERR= clause encourages "spaghetti code." in which execution jumps around in a fashion that is hard to follow and hard to maintain.

Good Programming Practice

Always use the IOSTAT= clause in OPEN statements to trap file open errors. When an error is detected, tell the user all about the problem before shutting down gracefully or requesting an alternative file.

14

Examples

Some example OPEN statements are shown below:

1. OPEN (UNIT=9, FILE='x.dat', STATUS='OLD', POSITION='APPEND', &
       ACTION='WRITE')
   This statement opens a file named x.dat and attaches it to i/o unit 9. The status of the file is 'OLD', so the file must already exist. The position is 'APPEND', so the file pointer will be positioned after the last record in the file, and just before the end-of-file marker. The file is a formatted file opened for sequential access, and is write-only. Since there is no IOSTAT= or ERR= clause, an open error would abort the program containing this statement.

2. OPEN (22, STATUS='SCRATCH')
   This statement creates a scratch file and attaches it to i/o unit 22. The scratch file is automatically given some unique name by the system, and is automatically deleted when the file is closed or the program ends. It is a formatted file and is opened for sequential access. Since there is no IOSTAT= or ERR= clause, an open error would abort the program containing this statement.

3. OPEN (FILE='input',UNIT=lu,STATUS='OLD',ACTION='READ',IOSTAT=istat)
   This statement opens an existing file named input, and attaches it to the i/o unit corresponding to the value of variable lu. The status of the file is 'OLD', so this OPEN statement will fail if the file does not already exist. The file is a formatted file opened for sequential access, and is opened for reading only. A status code is returned in variable istat. It will be 0 for a successful file open, and positive for an unsuccessful file open. Since the IOSTAT= clause is present in this statement, an open error would not abort the program containing this statement.

14.3.2 The CLOSE Statement

Once a file is no longer needed, it should be disconnected from its i/o unit by the CLOSE statement. After the CLOSE statement has been executed, the i/o unit will no longer be connected to the file, and it may be connected to some other file by another OPEN statement.

A Fortran program will automatically update and close any open files whenever the program ends. Therefore, a CLOSE statement is not actually required unless we want to attach more than one file to the same i/o unit. However, it is good practice to close any file with a CLOSE statement just as soon as the program is finished using it. When a file has been opened by one program, no other program may have access to it at the same time. By closing the file as soon as possible, the file is made available for other programs to use. This is especially important for files that are shared by many people.

Good Programming Practice

Always explicitly close each disk file with a CLOSE statement as soon as possible after a program is finished using it, so that it may be available for use by others.

The CLOSE statement has the general form

```
CLOSE (close_list)
```

where *close_list* consists of one or more clauses separated by commas. The possible clauses in the CLOSE statement are summarized in Table 14-4. They may be included in the CLOSE statement in any order. Note that the shaded item in Table 14-4 is a Fortran 2003–only feature.

The UNIT= clause

This clause is exactly the same as the UNIT= clause in the OPEN statement. *The UNIT= clause must be present in any CLOSE statement.*

The STATUS= clause

This clause specifies the status of the file connected to the specified i/o unit. There are two possible types of file status: 'KEEP' and 'DELETE'. If the file status is 'KEEP', then the file is kept on the file system after it is closed. If the file status is 'DELETE', then the file is deleted after it is closed. A scratch file is always deleted when it is closed; it is not legal to specify keep status for a scratch file. For any other type of file, the default status is 'KEEP'.

TABLE 14-4
Clauses allowed in the CLOSE statement

Clause	Input or output	Purpose	Possible values
[UNIT=]*int_expr*	Input	I/o unit to close. The "UNIT=" phrase is optional.	Processor-dependent integer.
STATUS=*char_expr*	Input	Specifies whether file is to be kept or deleted after closing.	'KEEP', 'DELETE'
IOSTAT=*int_var*	Output	I/O status at end of operation.	Processor-dependent integer *int_var*. 0 = success; positive = close failure.
IOMSG=*char_var*	Output	Character string describing any error that occurred during operation.	Character string.
ERR=*label*	Input	Statement label to transfer control to if open fails.[1]	Statement labels in current scoping unit.

[1] The ERR= clause is never needed in a modern Fortran program. Use the IOSTAT= clause instead.

14

The IOSTAT= clause

This clause specifies an integer variable that will contain the i/o status after the CLOSE statement is executed. If the file is closed successfully, then the status variable will contain a zero. If the close failed, then the status variable will contain a processor-dependent positive value corresponding to the type of error that occurred.

The IOMSG= clause

This clause specifies a character variable that will contain the i/o status after the CLOSE statement is executed. If the file is closed successfully, then the contents of this variable will be unchanged. If the close failed, then this variable will contain a message describing the problem that occurred.

The ERR= clause

This clause specifies the label of a statement to jump to if the file close fails. The ERR= clause provides a way to add special code to handle file close errors. (This clause should not be used in new programs; use the IOSTAT= clause instead.)

Examples

Some example CLOSE statements are shown below:

1. CLOSE (9)
   This statement closes the file attached to i/o unit 9. If the file is a scratch file, it will be deleted; otherwise, it will be kept. Since there is no IOSTAT= or ERR= clause, an error would abort the program containing this statement.

2. CLOSE (UNIT=22,STATUS='DELETE',IOSTAT=istat,IOMSG=err_str)
   This statement closes and deletes the file attached to i/o unit 22. An operation status code is returned in variable istat. It will be 0 for success, and positive for failure. Since the IOSTAT= clause is present in this statement, a close error will not abort the program containing this statement. If an error occurs, character variable err_str will contain a descriptive error message.

14.3.3 The INQUIRE Statement

It is often necessary to check on the status or properties of a file that we want to use in a Fortran program. The INQUIRE statement is used for this purpose. It is designed to provide detailed information about a file, either before or after the file has been opened.

There are three different versions of the INQUIRE statement. The first two versions of the statement are similar, except for the manner in which the file is looked up. The file can be found by either specifying the FILE= clause or the UNIT= clause (but not both simultaneously!). If a file has not yet been opened, it must be identified by name. If the file is already open, it may be identified by either name or i/o unit. There are many possible output clauses in the INQUIRE statement. To find out a particular piece of information about a file, just include the appropriate clause in the statement. A complete list of all clauses is given in Table 14-5.

F-2003 ONLY

Note that the shaded items in Table 14-5 are Fortran 2003-only features.

TABLE 14-5
Clauses allowed in the INQUIRE **statement**

Clause	Input or output	Purpose	Possible values
[UNIT=]int_expr	Input	I/O unit of file to check.[1]	Processor-dependent integer.
FILE=char_expr	Input	Name of file to check.[1]	Processor-dependent character string.
IOSTAT=int_var	Output	I/O status	Returns 0 for success; processor-dependent positive number for failure.
IOMSG=char_var	Output	I/O error message	If a failure occurs, this variable will contain a descriptive error message
EXIST=log_var	Output	Does the file exist?	.TRUE., .FALSE.
OPENED=log_var	Output	Is the file opened?	.TRUE., .FALSE.
NUMBER=int_var	Output	I/O unit number of file, if opened. If file is not opened, this value is undefined.	Processor-dependent positive number.
NAMED=log_var	Output	Does the file have a name? (Scratch files are unnamed.)	.TRUE., .FALSE.
NAME=char_var	Output	Name of file if file is named; undefined otherwise.	File name
ACCESS=char_var	Output	Specifies type of access if the file is currently open.[2]	'SEQUENTIAL', 'DIRECT', 'STREAM'
SEQUENTIAL=char_var	Output	Specifies if file *can be opened* for sequential access.	'YES', 'NO', 'UNKNOWN'
DIRECT=char_var	Output	Specifies if file *can be opened* for direct access.	'YES', 'NO', 'UNKNOWN'
STREAM=char_var	Output	Specifies if file *can be opened* for stream access.[2]	'YES', 'NO', 'UNKNOWN'
FORM=char_var	Output	Specifies type of formatting for a file if the file is open.[3]	'FORMATTED', 'UNFORMATTED'
FORMATTED=char_var	Output	Specifies if file *can be* connected for formatted I/O.[3]	'YES', 'NO', 'UNKNOWN'
UNFORMATTED=char_var	Output	Specifies if file *can be* connected for unformatted I/O.[3]	'YES', 'NO', 'UNKNOWN'
RECL=int_var	Output	Specifies the record length of a direct access file; undefined for sequential files.	Record length is in processor-dependent units.
NEXTREC=int_var	Output	For a direct access file, one more than the number of the last record read from or written to the file; undefined for sequential files.	

F-2003 ONLY

F-2003 ONLY

F-2003 ONLY

14

(continued)

(*continued*)

BLANK=*char_var*	Output	Specifies whether blanks in numeric fields are treated as nulls or zeros.[4]	'ZERO', 'NULL'
POSITION=*char_var*	Output	Specifies location of file pointer when the file is first opened. This value is undefined for unopened files, or for files opened for direct access.	'REWIND', 'APPEND', 'ASIS', 'UNDEFINED'
ACTION=*char_var*	Output	Specifies read, write, or read-write status for opened files. This value is undefined for unopened files.[5]	'READ', 'WRITE', 'READWRITE', 'UNDEFINED'
READ=*char_var*	Output	Specifies whether file *can be* opened for read-only access.[5]	'YES', 'NO', 'UNKNOWN'
WRITE=*char_var*	Output	Specifies whether file *can be* opened for write-only access.[5]	'YES', 'NO', 'UNKNOWN'
READWRITE=*char_var*	Output	Specifies whether file *can be* opened for readwrite access.[5]	'YES', 'NO', 'UNKNOWN'
DELIM=*char_var*	Output	Specifies type of character delimiter used with list-directed and namelist I/O to this file.	'APOSTROPHE', 'QUOTE', 'NONE', 'UNKNOWN'
PAD=*char_var*	Output	Specifies whether or not input lines are to be padded with blanks. This value is always yes unless a file is explicitly opened with PAD='NO'.	'YES', 'NO'
IOLENGTH=*int_var*	Output	Returns the length of an unformatted record, in processor dependent units. This clause is special to the third type of INQUIRE statement (see text).	
ASYNCHRONOUS=*char_var*	Output	Specifies whether or not asynchronous I/O is permitted for this file.	'YES', 'NO'
ENCODING=*char_var*	Output	Specifies type of character encoding for the file.[6]	'UTF-8', 'UNDEFINED' 'UNKNOWN'
ID=*int_expr*	Input	The ID number of a pending asynchronous data transfer. Results are returned in the ID= clause.	
PENDING=*log_var*	Output	Returns the status of the asynchronous I/O operation specified in the ID= clause.	.TRUE., .FALSE.
POS=*int_var*	Output	Returns the position in the file for the next read or write.	
ROUND=*char_var*	Output	Returns the type of rounding in use.	'UP', 'DOWN', 'ZERO', 'NEAREST', 'COMPATIBLE', 'PROCESSOR DEFINED'

F-2003 ONLY (ASYNCHRONOUS)

F-2003 ONLY (ENCODING)

F-2003 ONLY (ID)

F-2003 ONLY (PENDING)

F-2003 ONLY (POS)

F-2003 ONLY (ROUND)

14

(*continued*)

(*concluded*)

SIGN=*char_var*	Output	Returns the option for printing + sign.	'PLUS', 'SUPPRESS', 'PROCESSOR' 'DEFINED'
ERR=*statementlabel*	Input	Statement to branch to if statement fails.[7]	Statement label in current program unit.

[1] One and only one of the FILE= and UNIT= clauses may be included in any INQUIRE statement.
[2] The difference between the ACCESS= clause and the SEQUENTIAL=, DIRECT=, and STREAM= clauses is that the ACCESS= clause tells what sort of access *is being used*, while the other three clauses tell what sort of access *can be used*.
[3] The difference between the FORM= clause and the FORMATTED= and UNFORMATTED= clauses is that the FORM= clause tells what sort of I/O *is being used*, while the other two clauses tell what sort of I/O *can be used*.
[4] The BLANK= clause is only defined for files connected for formatted I/O.
[5] The difference between the ACTION= clause and the READ=, WRITE=, and READWRITE= clauses is that the ACTION= clause specifies the action for which the file *is* opened, while the other clauses specify the action for which the file *can be* opened.
[6] The value 'UTF-8' is returned for Unicode files; the value 'UNDEFINED' is returned for unformatted files.
[7] The ERR= clause is never needed in a modern Fortran program. Use the IOSTAT= clause instead.

The third form of the INQUIRE statement is the inquire-by-output-list statement. This statement takes the form

```
INQUIRE (IOLENGTH=int_var) output_list
```

where *int_var* is an integer variable and *output_list* is a list of variables, constants, and expressions like the ones that would appear in a WRITE statement. The purpose of this statement is to return the length of the unformatted record that can contain the entities in the output list. As we will see later in this chapter, unformatted direct access files have a fixed record length that is measured in processor-dependent units, and so the length changes from processor to processor. Furthermore, this record length must be specified when the file is opened. This form of the INQUIRE statement provides us with a processor-independent way to specify the length of records in direct access files. An example of this form of INQUIRE statement will be shown when we introduce direct access files in Section 14.6.

EXAMPLE
14-1

Preventing Output Files from Overwriting Existing Data:

In many programs, the user is asked to specify an output file into which the results of the program will be written. It is good programming practice to check to see if the output file already exists before opening it and writing into it. If it already exists, the user should be asked if he or she *really* wants to destroy the data in the file before the program overwrites it. If so, the program can open the file and write into it. If not, the program should get a new output file name and try again. Write a program that demonstrates a technique for protection against overwriting existing files.

14

SOLUTION
The resulting Fortran program is shown in Figure 14-2.

FIGURE 14-2
Program illustrating how to prevent an output file from accidentally overwriting data.

```fortran
PROGRAM open_file
!
!   Purpose:
!     To illustrate the process of checking before overwriting an
!     output file.
!
IMPLICIT NONE

! Data dictionary: declare variable types & definitions
CHARACTER(len=20) ::name           ! File name
CHARACTER :: yn                    ! Yes / No flag
LOGICAL :: lexist                  ! True if file exists
LOGICAL :: lopen = .FALSE.         ! True if file is open

! Do until file is open
openfile: DO

    ! Get output file name.
    WRITE (*,*) 'Enter output file name: '
    READ (*,'(A)') file_name

    ! Does file already exist?
    INQUIRE ( FILE=file_name,EXIST=lexist )
    exists: IF ( .NOT. lexist ) THEN
       ! It's OK, the file didn't already exist. Open file.
       OPEN (UNIT=9,FILE=name,STATUS='NEW',ACTION='WRITE')
       lopen = .TRUE.

    ELSE
       ! File exists. Should we replace it?
       WRITE (*,*) 'Output file exists. Overwrite it? (Y/N) '
       READ (*,'(A)') yn
       CALL ucase ( yn )                  ! Shift to upper case

       replace: IF ( yn == 'Y' ) THEN
          ! It's OK. Open file.
          OPEN (UNIT=9,FILE=name,STATUS='REPLACE',ACTION='WRITE')
          lopen = .TRUE.
       END IF replace

    END IF exists
    IF ( lopen ) EXIT
END DO openfile

! Now write output data, and close and save file.
WRITE (9,*) 'This is the output file!'
CLOSE (9,STATUS='KEEP')

END PROGRAM open_file
```

14

Test this program for yourself. Can you suggest additional improvements to make this program work better? (*Hint*: What about the OPEN statements?)

Good Programming Practice
Check to see if your output file is overwriting an existing data file. If it is, make sure that the user really wants to do that before destroying the data in the file.

14.3.4 The READ statement

The READ statement reads data from the file associated with a specified i/o unit, converts its format according to the specified FORMAT descriptors, and stores it into the variables in the I/O list. A READ statement keeps reading input lines until all of the variables in *io_list* have been filled, the end of the input file is reached, or an error occurs. A READ statement has the general form

        READ (*control_list*) *io_list*

where *control_list* consists of one or more clauses separated by commas. The possible clauses in a READ statement are summarized in Table 14-6. The clauses may be included in the READ statement in any order. Not all of the clauses will be included in any given READ statement.

F-2003 ONLY

Note that the shaded items in Table 14-6 are Fortran 2003–only features.

■ **TABLE 14-6**
Clauses allowed in the READ statement

Clause	Input or output	Purpose	Possible values
[UNIT=]*int_expr*	Input	I/O unit to read from.	Processor-dependent integer.
[FMT=]*statement_label* [FMT=]*char_expr* [FMT=]*	Input	Specifies the format to use when reading formatted data.	
IOSTAT=*int_var*	Output	I/O status at end of operation.	Processor-dependent integer *int_var*: 0 = success positive = READ failure −1 = end of file −2 = end of record
IOMSG=*char_var*	Output	I/O error message	If a failure occurs, this variable will contain a descriptive error message

F-2003 ONLY

14

(continued)

(*continued*)

	REC=*int_expr*	Input	Specifies the record number to read in a direct access file.	
	NML=*namelist*	Input	Specifies namelist of I/O entities to read.	Namelists defined in the current scoping unit, or accessed through use or host association.
	ADVANCE=*char_expr*	Input	Specifies whether to perform advancing or nonadvancing I/O. Valid for sequential files only.	'YES', 'NO'
	SIZE=*int_var*	Output	Specifies number of characters read during nonadvancing I/O. Valid for nonadvancing I/O only.	
DANGER DO NOT USE	EOR=*label*	Input	Statement label to transfer control to if end of record is reached during nonadvancing I/O. Valid for nonadvancing I/O only.	Statement labels in current scoping unit.
F-2003 ONLY	ASYNCHRONOUS=*char_expr*	Input	Specifies whether or not asynchronous I/O is used for this statement.[1] (Default= 'NO')	'YES', 'NO'
F-2003 ONLY	DECIMAL=*char_expr*	Input	Temporarily overrides the separator specification specified in the OPEN statement.	'COMMA', 'POINT'
	DELIM=*char_expr*	Input	Temporarily overrides the delimiter specification specified in the OPEN statement.	'APOSTROPHE', 'QUOTE', 'NONE'
F-2003 ONLY	ID=*int_var*	Output	Returns a unique ID associated with an asynchronous I/O transfer.[2]	
F-2003 ONLY	POS=*int_var*	Input	Specifies the read position in a file opened for STREAM access.[3]	
F-2003 ONLY	ROUND=*char_var*	Input	Temporarily overrides the rounding specification specified in the OPEN statement.	'UP', 'DOWN', 'ZERO', 'NEAREST', 'COMPATIBLE' 'PROCESSOR DEFINED'
F-2003 ONLY	SIGN=*char_var*	Input	Temporarily overrides the sign specification specified in the OPEN statement.	'PLUS', 'SUPPRESS' 'PROCESS OR 'DEFINED'
DANGER DO NOT USE	END=*statement_label*	Input	Statement label to transfer control to if end of file is reached[4].	Statement labels in current scoping unit.

(*continued*)

ERR=*statement_label*	Input	Statement label to transfer control to if an error occurs.[4]	Statement labels in current scoping unit.

[1] The ASYNCHRONOUS= clause can only be 'YES' if the file was opened to allow asynchronous I/O.
[2] The ID= clause can only be used if an asynchronous data transfer is specified.
[3] The POS= clause can only be used with a file opened for stream access.
[4] The END=, ERR= and EOR= clauses are never needed in a modern Fortran program. Use the IOSTAT= clause instead.

The UNIT= clause

This clause specifies the i/o unit number from which to read the data. An * indicates reading data from the standard input device. *The UNIT= clause must be present in any READ statement.*

The i/o unit may also be specified by just naming it in the READ statement without the UNIT= keyword. This feature is included in Fortran 95/2003 for backward compatibility with earlier versions of Fortran. If the i/o unit is specified in this alternative form, then it must be the first clause in the READ statement. The following two statements are equivalent:

```
READ ( UNIT=10, ... )
READ ( 10, ... )
```

The FMT= clause

This clause has the form

[FMT=] *statement_label* or [FMT=] *char_expr* or [FMT=] *

where *statement_label* is the label of a FORMAT statement, *char_expr* is a character string containing the format information, or * indicates list-directed I/O. An FMT= clause must be supplied for all formatted READ statements.

If the FMT= clause is *second* clause in a READ statement, and if the first clause is an abbreviated unit number without the UNIT= keyword, then the format clause may be abbreviated by just naming the statement number, character variable, or * containing the format. This feature is included in Fortran 95/2003 for backward compatibility with earlier versions of Fortran. Therefore, the following two statements are equivalent:

```
READ ( UNIT=10,FMT=100 ) data1
READ ( 10, 100 ) data1
```

The IOSTAT= clause

This clause specifies an integer variable that will contain the status after the READ statement is executed. If the read is successful, then the status variable will contain a zero. If an end-of-file condition is detected, then the status variable will contain a -1. If an end-of-record condition is encountered during nonadvancing i/o, the status variable will contain a -2. If the read fails, then the status variable will contain a positive value corresponding to the type of error that occurred.

14

The `IOMSG=` clause

This clause specifies a character variable that will contain the i/o status after the READ statement is executed. If the read is successful, then the contents of this variable will be unchanged. If the read failed, then this variable will contain a message describing the problem that occurred.

The `REC=` clause

This clause specifies the number of the record to read in a direct access file. It is valid only for direct access files.

The `NML=` clause

This clause specifies a named list of values to read in. The details of namelist I/O will be described in Section 14.4.

The `ADVANCE=` clause

This clause specifies whether or not the current input buffer should be discarded at the end of the READ. The possible values are 'YES' or 'NO'. If the value is 'YES', then any remaining data in the current input buffer will be discarded when the READ statement is completed. If the value is 'NO', then the remaining data in the current input buffer will be saved and used to satisfy the next READ statement. The default value is 'YES'. This clause is valid only for sequential files.

The `SIZE=` clause

This clause specifies the name of an integer variable to contain the number of characters that have been read from the input buffer during a nonadvancing I/O operation. It may be specified only if the ADVANCE='NO' clause is specified.

The `EOR=` clause

This clause specifies the label of an executable statement to jump to if the end of the current record is detected during a nonadvancing READ operation. If the end of the input record is reached during a nonadvancing I/O operation, then the program will jump to the statement specified and execute it. This clause may be specified only if the ADVANCE='NO' clause is specified. If the ADVANCE='YES' clause is specified, then the read will continue on successive input lines until all of the input data is read.

The `ASYNCHRONOUS=` clause

This clause specifies whether or not a particular read is to be asynchronous. This value can be 'YES' only if the file was opened for asynchronous I/O.

The `DECIMAL=` clause

This clause temporarily overrides the specification of the decimal separator in the OPEN statement.

The value in this clause can be overridden for a particular READ or WRITE statement by the DC and DP format descriptors

The DELIM= clause

This clause temporarily overrides the specification of the delimiter in the OPEN statement.

The ID= clause

This clause returns a unique ID associated with an asynchronous I/O transfer. This ID can be used later in the INQUIRE statement to determine if the I/O transfer has completed.

The POS= clause

This clause specifies the position for the read from a stream file.

The ROUND= clause

This clause temporarily overrides the value of the ROUND clause specified in the OPEN statement. The value in this clause can be overridden for a particular value by the RU, RD, RZ, RN, RC, and RP format descriptors.

The SIGN= clause

This clause temporarily overrides the value of the SIGN clause specified in the OPEN statement. The value in this clause can be overridden for a particular value by the S, SP, and SS format descriptors.

The END= clause

This clause specifies the label of an executable statement to jump to if the end of the input file is detected. The END= clause provides a way to handle unexpected end-of-file conditions. This clause should not be used in modern programs; use the more general and flexible IOSTAT= clause instead.

The ERR= clause

This clause specifies the label of an executable statement to jump to if a read error occurs. The most common read error is a mismatch between the type of the input data in a field and the format descriptors used to read it. For example, if the characters 'A123' appeared by mistake in a field read with the I4 descriptor, an error would be generated. This clause should not be used in modern programs; use the more general and flexible IOSTAT= clause instead.

14

The importance of using IOSTAT= and IOMSG= clauses

If a read fails and there is no IOSTAT= clause or ERR= clause in the READ statement, the Fortran program will print out an error message and abort. If the end of the input file is reached and there is no IOSTAT= clause or END= clause, the Fortran program will abort. Finally, if the end of an input record is reached during nonadvancing i/o and there is no IOSTAT= clause or EOR= clause, the Fortran program will abort. If either the IOSTAT= clause or the ERR=, END=, and EOR= clauses are present in the READ statement, then the Fortran program will not abort when read errors, end-of-file conditions, or end-of-record conditions occur. If the IOMSG= clause is also present, then a user-readable character string describing the problem is also returned. The programmer can do something to handle those conditions and allow the program to continue running.

F-2003 ONLY

The following code fragment shows how to use the IOSTAT= message to read an unknown number of input values without aborting when the end of the input file is reached. It uses a while loop to read data until the end of the input file is reached.

```
OPEN ( UNIT=8, FILE='test.dat', STATUS='OLD' )

! Read input data
nvals = 0
DO
    READ (8,100,IOSTAT=istat) temp
    ! Check for end of data
    IF ( istat < 0 ) EXIT
    nvals = nvals + 1
    array(nvals) = temp
END DO
```

The IOSTAT= clause should be used instead of the END=, ERR=, and EOR= clauses in all new programs, since the IOSTAT= clause allows more flexibility and is better suited to modern structured programming. The use of the other clauses encourages "spaghetti code," in which execution jumps around in a fashion that is hard to follow and hard to maintain.

Good Programming Practice
Use the IOSTAT= and IOMSG= clauses in READ statements to prevent programs from aborting on errors, end-of-file conditions, or end-of-record conditions. When one of these conditions is detected, the program can take appropriate actions to continue processing or to shut down gracefully.

14.3.5 Alternative Form of the READ Statement

There is an alternative form of the READ statement that works only for formatted reads or list-directed reads from the standard input device. This statement has the form

```
READ fmt, io_list
```

where *fmt* is the format specification to use when reading the list of variables in the *io_list*. The format may be the number of a FORMAT statement, the name of a character variable containing the formatting information, a character string containing the formatting information, or an asterisk. Examples of this version of the READ statement include:

```
READ 100, x, y
100 FORMAT (2F10.2)

READ '(2F10.2)', x, y
```

This version of the READ statement is much less flexible than the standard READ statement, since it can work only with the standard input device and cannot support any of the optional clauses. It is a holdover from an earlier versions of FORTRAN. There is no need to ever use it in a modern program.

14.3.6 The WRITE Statement

The WRITE statement takes data from the variables in the I/O list, converts it according to the specified FORMAT descriptors, and writes it out to the file associated with the specified i/o unit. The WRITE statement has the general form

```
WRITE (control_list) io_list
```

where control_list consists of one or more clauses separated by commas. The possible clauses in a WRITE statement are the same as those in the READ statement, except that there are no END=, SIZE=, or EOR= clauses.

14.3.7 The PRINT Statement

There is an alternative output statement called the PRINT statement that works only for formatted writes or list-directed writes to the standard output device. This statement has the form

```
PRINT fmt, io_list
```

where fmt is the format specification to use for reading the list of variables in the io_list. The format may be the number of a FORMAT statement, the name of a character variable containing the formatting information, a character string containing the formatting information, or an asterisk. Examples of the PRINT statement include:

```
PRINT 100, x, y
100 FORMAT (2F10.2)

string = '(2F10.2)'
PRINT string, x, y
```

The PRINT statement is much less flexible than the standard WRITE statement, since it can work only with the standard output device and cannot support any of the optional clauses. It is a holdover from earlier versions of FORTRAN. There is no need to ever use it in a modern program. However, many Fortran programmers are stylistically committed to using this statement through long years of habit. It does work, and programs using the PRINT statement will continue to be supported indefinitely in the future. You should recognize the statement when you see it, but in the opinion of this author it is better not to use it in your own programs.

14

14.3.8 File Positioning Statements

There are two file positioning statements in Fortran: REWIND and BACKSPACE. The REWIND statement positions the file so that the next READ statement will read the first line in the file. The BACKSPACE statement moves the file back by one line. These statements are valid only for sequential files. The statements have the general form

```
REWIND (control_list)
BACKSPACE (control_list)
```

where control_list consists of one or more clauses separated by commas. The possible clauses in a file positioning statement are summarized in Table 14-7. The meanings of these clauses are the same as in the other I/O statements described above.

The i/o unit may be specified without the UNIT= keyword if it is in the first position of the control list. The following statements are examples of legal file positioning statements:

```
REWIND (unit_in)
BACKSPACE (UNIT=12,IOSTAT=istat)
```

For compatibility with earlier versions of FORTRAN, a file positioning statement containing only an i/o unit number can also be specified without parentheses:

```
REWIND 6
BACKSPACE unit_in
```

The IOSTAT= clause should be used instead of the ERR= clause in modern Fortran programs. It is better suited to modern structured programming techniques.

14.3.9 The ENDFILE Statement

The ENDFILE statement writes an end-of-file record at the current position in a sequential file, and then positions the file after the end-of-file record. After an ENDFILE

TABLE 14-7
Clauses allowed in the REWIND, BACKSPACE, or ENDFILE statements

Clause	Input or output	Purpose	Possible values
[UNIT=]int_expr	Input	i/o unit to operate on. The UNIT= phrase is optional.	Processor-dependent integer.
IOSTAT=int_var	Output	I/O status at end of operation.	Processor-dependent integer int_var. 0=success Positive=failure
IOMSG=char_var	Output	Character string containing an error message if an error occurs.	
ERR=statement_label	Input	Statement label to transfer control to if an error occurs.[1]	Statement labels in current scoping unit.

F-2003 ONLY

DANGER DO NOT USE

[1] The ERR= clause is never needed in a modern Fortran program. Use the IOSTAT= clause instead.

statement has been executed on a file, no further READs or WRITEs are possible until either a BACKSPACE or a REWIND statement is executed. Until then, any further READ or WRITE statements will produce an error. This statement has the general form

        ENDFILE (*control_list*)

where *control_list* consists of one or more clauses separated by commas. The possible clauses in an ENDFILE statement are summarized in Table 14-7. The meanings of these clauses are the same as in the other I/O statements described above. The i/o unit may be specified without the UNIT= keyword if it is the first position of the control list.

For compatibility with earlier versions of Fortran, an ENDFILE statement containing only an i/o unit number can also be specified without parentheses. The following statements are examples of legal ENDFILE statements:

        ENDFILE (UNIT=12,IOSTAT=istat)
        ENDFILE 6

The IOSTAT= clause should be used instead of the ERR= clause in modern Fortran programs. It is better suited to modern structured programming techniques.

14.3.10 The WAIT Statement

When an asynchronous I/O transfer starts, execution returns to the program immediately before the I/O operation is completed. This allows the program to continue running in parallel with the I/O operation. It is possible that at some later point the program may need to guarantee that the operation is complete before progressing further. For example, the program may need to read back data that was being written during an asynchronous write.

If this is so, the program can use the WAIT statement to guarantee that the operation is complete before continuing. The form of this statement is

        WAIT (*unit*)

where *unit* is the I/O unit to wait for. Control will return from this statement only when all pending I/O operations to that unit are complete.

14.3.11 The FLUSH Statement

F-2003 ONLY

14

The FLUSH statement causes all data being written to a file to be posted or otherwise available for use before the statement returns. It has the effect of forceably writing any data stored in temporary output buffers to disk. The form of this statement is

        FLUSH (*unit*)

where *unit* is the I/O unit to flush. Control will return from this statement only when all data has been written to disk.

■ 14.4

NAMELIST I/O

Namelist I/O is a convenient way to write out a fixed list of variable names and values, or to read in a fixed list of variable names and values. A **namelist** is just a list of variable names that are always read or written as a group. The form of a namelist is

```
NAMELIST / nl_group_name / var1 [, var2, ...]
```

where nl_group_name is the name of the namelist, and $var1$, $var2$, etc. are the variables in the list. The NAMELIST is a specification statement, and must appear before the first executable statement in a program. If there is more than one NAMELIST statement with the same name, then the variables in all statements are concatenated and treated as though they were in a single large statement. The variables listed in a NAMELIST may be read or written as a unit by using namelist-directed I/O statements.

A NAMELIST I/O statement looks like a formatted I/O statement, except that the FMT= clause is replaced by a NML= clause. The form of a namelist-directed WRITE statement is

```
WRITE (UNIT=unit, NML=nl_group_name,[...])
```

where $unit$ is the i/o unit to which the data will be written, and nl_group_name is the name of the namelist to be written. (Unlike most other clauses in I/O statements, the nl_group_name is not enclosed in apostrophes or quotes.) When a namelist-directed WRITE statement is executed, the names of all of the variables in the namelist are printed out together with their values in a special order. The first item to be printed is an ampersand (&) followed by the namelist name. Next comes a series of output values in the form "NAME=value". These output values may either appear on a single line separated by commas or appear on separate lines, depending on the way a particular processor implements the namelist. Finally, the list is terminated by a slash (/).

For example, consider the program shown in Figure 14-3.

FIGURE 14-3
A simple program using a NAMELIST-directed WRITE statement.

```
PROGRAM write_namelist
!  Purpose:
!    To illustrate a NAMELIST-directed WRITE statement.
!
IMPLICIT NONE

! Data dictionary: declare variable types & definitions
INTEGER :: i = 1, j = 2                         ! Integer variables
REAL :: a = -999., b = 0.                       ! Real variables
CHARACTER(len=12) :: string = 'Test string.'    ! Char variables
NAMELIST / mylist / i, j, string, a, b          ! Declare namelist

OPEN (8,FILE='output.nml',DELIM='APOSTROPHE')   ! Open output file
WRITE (UNIT=8,NML=mylist)                       ! Write namelist
CLOSE (8)                                       ! Close file
END PROGRAM write_namelist
```

14

After this program is executed, the file `output.nml` contains the lines:

```
&MYLIST
I =              1
J =              2
STRING = 'Test string.'
A =       -999.000000
B =        0.000000E + 00
/
```

The namelist output begins with an ampersand and the list name, and concludes with a slash. Note that the character string is surrounded by apostrophes, because the file was opened with the clause `DELIM='APOSTROPHE'`.

The general form of a `NAMELIST`-directed `READ` statement is

```
READ (UNIT=unit,NML=nl_group_name,[...])
```

where *unit* is the i/o unit from which the data will be read, and *nl_group_name* is the name of the namelist to be read. When a namelist-directed `READ` statement is executed, the program searches the input file for the marker *&nl_group_name*, which indicates the beginning of the name-list. It then reads all of the values in the name-list until a slash character (`/`) is encountered to terminate the `READ`. The values in the input list may appear on any line within the input file, as long as they are between the markers *&nl_group_name* and `/`. The values are assigned to the namelist variables according to the names given in the input list. The namelist `READ` statement does not have to set a value for every variable in the namelist. If some namelist variables are not included in the input file list, then their values will remain unchanged after the name-list `READ` executes.

Namelist-directed `READ` statements are *very* useful. Suppose that you are writing a program containing 100 input variables. The variables will be initialized to their usual values by default in the program. During any particular run of the program, anywhere from 1 to 10 of these values may need to be changed, but the others would remain at their default values. In this case, you could include all 100 values in a namelist and include a `NAMELIST`-directed `READ` statement in the program. Whenever a user runs the program, he or she can just list the few values to be changed in the namelist input file, and all of the other input variables will remain unchanged. This approach is much better than using an ordinary `READ` statement, because all 100 values would need to be listed in the ordinary `READ`'s input file, even if they were not being changed during a particular run.

Consider the example in Figure 14-4, which illustrates how a namelist `READ` can update selected values in the namelist.

FIGURE 14-4

A simple program using a `NAMELIST`-directed `READ` statement.

```
PROGRAM read_namelist
!  Purpose:
!     To illustrate a NAMELIST-directed READ statement.
```

(continued)

14

(concluded)

```
!
IMPLICIT NONE

! Data dictionary: declare variable types & definitions
INTEGER :: i = 1, j = 2                      ! Integer variables
REAL :: a = -999., b = 0.                    ! Real variables
CHARACTER(len=12) :: string = 'Test string.' ! Char variables
NAMELIST / mylist / i, j, string, a, b       ! Declare namelist

OPEN (7,FILE='input.nml',DELIM='APOSTROPHE') ! Open input file.

! Write NAMELIST before update
WRITE (*,'(1X,A)') 'Namelist file before update: '
WRITE (UNIT=*,NML=mylist)

READ (UNIT=7,NML=mylist)                            ! Read namelist file.

! Write NAMELIST after update
WRITE (*,'(1X,A)') 'Namelist file after update: '
WRITE (UNIT=*,NML=mylist)

END PROGRAM read_namelist
```

If the file `input.nml` contains the following data,

```
&MYLIST
I =            -111
STRING = 'Test 1.'
STRING = 'Different!'
B =        123456.
/
```

then variable b will be assigned the value 123456., variable i will be assigned the value −111, and variable `string` will be assigned a value of `'Different!'`. Note that if more than one input value exists for the same variable, the last one in the name-list is the one that is used. The values of all variables other than b, i, and `string` will not be changed. The result of executing this program will be:

```
C:\book\chap14>namelist_read
Namelist file before update:
&MYLIST
I =               1
J =               2
STRING =   Test string.
A =        -999.000000
B =        0.000000E+00
/
Namelist file after update:
&MYLIST
I =            -111
J =               2
STRING =   Different!
A =        -999.000000
B =       123456.000000
/
```

If a namelist output file is opened with the character delimiter set to 'APOSTROPHE' or 'QUOTE', then the output file written by a namelist WRITE statement is in a form that can be directly read by a namelist READ statement. This fact makes the namelist a great way to exchange a lot of data between separate programs or between different runs of the same program.

Good Programming Practice

Use NAMELIST I/O to save data to be exchanged between programs or between different runs of a single program. Also, you may use NAMELIST READ statements to update selected input parameters when a program begins executing.

Array names, array sections, and array elements may all appear in a NAMELIST statement. If an array name appears in a namelist, then when a namelist WRITE is executed, every element of the array is printed out in the output namelist one at a time, such as $a(1) = 3.$, $a(2) = -1.$, etc. When a namelist READ is executed, each element of the array may be set separately, and only the elements whose values are to be changed need to be supplied in the input file.

Dummy arguments and variables that are created dynamically may not appear in a NAMELIST. This includes array dummy arguments with nonconstant bounds, character variables with nonconstant lengths, automatic variables, and pointers.

■ 14.5

UNFORMATTED FILES

All of the files that we have seen so far in this book have been **formatted files.** A formatted file contains recognizable characters, numbers, etc. stored in a standard coding scheme such as ASCII or EBCDIC. These files are easy to distinguish, because we can see the characters and numbers in the file when we display them on the screen or print them on a printer. However, to use data in a formatted file, a program must translate the characters in the file into the internal integer or real format used by the particular processor that the program is running on. The instructions for this translation are provided by format descriptors.

Formatted files have the advantage that we can readily see what sort of data they contain. However, they also have disadvantages. A processor must do a good deal of work to convert a number between the processor's internal representation and the characters contained in the file. All of this work is just wasted effort if we are going to be reading the data back into another program on the same processor. Also, the internal representation of a number usually requires much less space than the corresponding ASCII or EBCDIC representation of the number found in a formatted file. For example, the internal representation of a 32-bit real value requires 4 bytes of space. The ASCII representation of the same value would be $\pm.dddddddE\pm ee$, which requires 13 bytes of space (1 byte per character). Thus, storing data in ASCII or EBCDIC format is inefficient and wasteful of disk space.

14

Unformatted files overcome these disadvantages by copying the information from the processor's memory directly to the disk file with no conversions at all. Since no conversions occur, no processor time is wasted formatting the data. Furthermore, the data occupies a much smaller amount of disk space. On the other hand, unformatted data cannot be examined and interpreted directly by humans. In addition, it usually cannot be moved between different types of processors, because those types of processors have different internal ways to represent integers and real values.

Formatted and unformatted files are compared in Table 14-8. In general, formatted files are best for data that people must examine, or data that may have to be moved between different types of processors. Unformatted files are best for storing information that will not need to be examined by human beings, and that will be created and used on the same type of processor. Under those circumstances, unformatted files are both faster and occupy less disk space.

Unformatted I/O statements look just like formatted I/O statements, except that the FMT= clause is left out of the control list in the READ and WRITE statements. For example, the following two statements perform formatted and unformatted writes of array arr:

```
WRITE (UNIT=10,FMT=100,IOSTAT=istat) (arr(i), i = 1, 1000)
100 FORMAT ( 1X, 5E13.6 )

WRITE (UNIT=10,IOSTAT=istat) (arr(i), i = 1, 1000)
```

A file may be either FORMATTED or UNFORMATTED, but not both. Therefore, we cannot mix formatted and unformatted I/O statements within a single file. The INQUIRE statement can be used to determine the formatting status of a file.

Good Programming Practice

Use formatted files to create data that must be readable by humans, or that must be transferable between processors of different types. Use unformatted files to efficiently store large quantities of data that does not have to be directly examined, and that will remain on only one type of processor. Also, use unformatted files when I/O speed is critical.

TABLE 14-8
Comparison of formatted and unformatted files

Formatted files	Unformatted files
Can display data on output devices.	Cannot display data on output devices.
Can easily transport data between different computers.	Cannot easily transport data between computers with different internal data representations.
Requires a relatively large amount of disk space.	Requires relatively little disk space.
Slow: requires a lot of computer time.	Fast: requires little computer time.
Truncation or rounding errors possible in formatting.	No truncation or rounding errors.

▓ 14.6

DIRECT ACCESS FILES

Direct access files are files that are written and read by using the direct access mode. The records in a sequential access file must be read in order from beginning to end. By contrast, the records in a direct access file may be read in arbitrary order. Direct access files are especially useful for information that may need to be accessed in any order, such as database files.

The key to the operation of a direct access file is that *every record in a direct access file must be of the same length*. If each record is the same length, then it is a simple matter to calculate exactly how far the *i*th record is into the disk file, and to read the disk sector containing that record directly without reading all of the sectors before it in the file. For example, suppose that we want to read the 120th record in a direct access file with 100-byte records. The 120th record will be located between bytes 11,901 and 12,000 of the file. The computer can calculate the disk sector containing those bytes, and read it directly.

A direct access file is opened by specifying `ACCESS='DIRECT'` in the `OPEN` statement. The length of each record in a direct access file must be specified in the `OPEN` statement using the `RECL=` clause. A typical `OPEN` statement for a direct access formatted file is shown below.

```
OPEN ( UNIT=8,FILE='dirio.fmt',ACCESS='DIRECT',FORM='FORMATTED', &
       RECL=40 )
```

The `FORM=` clause had to be specified here, because the default form for direct access is `'UNFORMATTED'`.

For formatted files, the length of each record in the `RECL=` clause is specified in units of characters. Therefore, each record in file `dirio.fmt` above is 40 characters long. For unformatted files, the length specified in the `RECL=` clause may be in units of bytes, words, or some other machine dependent quantity. You can use the `INQUIRE` statement to determine the record length required for an unformatted direct access file in a processor-independent fashion.

`READ` and `WRITE` statements for direct access files look like ones for sequential access files, except that the `REC=` clause may be included to specify the particular record to read or write (if the `REC=` clause is left out, then the next record in the file will be read or written). A typical `READ` statement for a direct access formatted file is shown below.

```
READ ( 8, '(I6)', REC=irec ) ival
```

Direct access, unformatted files whose record length is a multiple of the sector size of a particular computer are the most efficient Fortran files possible on that computer. Because they are direct access, it is possible to read any record in such a file directly. Because they are unformatted, no computer time is wasted in format conversions during reads or writes. Finally, because each record is exactly one disk sector long, only one disk sector will need to be read or written for each record. (Shorter records which are not multiples of the disk sector size might stretch across two disk

14

sectors, forcing the computer to read both sectors in order to recover the information in the record.) Because these files are so efficient, many large programs written in Fortran are designed to use them.

A simple example program using a direct access, formatted file is shown in Figure 14-5. This program creates a direct access, formatted file named `dirio.fmt` with 40 characters per record. It fills the first 100 records with information, and then directly recovers whichever record the user specifies.

FIGURE 14-5

An example program using a direct access, formatted file.

```
PROGRAM direct_access_formatted
!
!   Purpose:
!     To illustrate the use of direct access Fortran files.
!
!   Record of revisions:
!       Date        Programmer         Description of change
!       ====        ==========         =====================
!     12/11/06    S. J. Chapman        Original code
!
IMPLICIT NONE

! Data dictionary: declare variable types & definitions
INTEGER :: i                    ! Index variable
INTEGER :: irec                 ! Number of record in file
CHARACTER(len=40) :: line       ! String containing current line.

! Open a direct access formatted file with 40 characters per record.
OPEN ( UNIT=8,FILE='dirio.fmt',ACCESS='DIRECT', &
       FORM='FORMATTED',STATUS='REPLACE',RECL=40 )

! Insert 100 records into this file.
DO i = 1, 100
   WRITE ( 8, '(A,I3,A)', REC=i ) 'This is record ', i, '.'
END DO

! Find out which record the user wants to retrieve.
WRITE (*,'(A)',ADVANCE='NO') ' Which record would you like to see? '
READ (*,'(I3)') irec

! Retrieve the desired record.
READ ( 8, '(A)', REC=irec ) line

! Display the record.
WRITE (*, '(A,/,5X,A)' ) ' The record is: ', line

END PROGRAM direct_access_formatted
```

When the program is compiled and executed, the results are:

```
C:\book\chap14>direct_access_formatted
Which record would you like to see? 34
The record is:
     This is record 34.
```

This program also illustrates the use of the ADVANCE='NO' clause in a WRITE statement to allow a response to be entered on the same line that the prompt is printed on. The cursor did not advance to a new line when the WRITE statement was executed.

EXAMPLE 14-2

Comparing Direct Access Formatted and Unformatted Files:

To compare the operation of formatted and unformatted direct access files, create two files containing 20,000 records, each with four double-precision real values per line. One file should be formatted and the other one should be unformatted. Compare the sizes to the two files, and then compare the time that it takes to recover 50,000 records in random order from each file. Use subroutine random0 from Chapter 7 to generate the values placed in the files, and also the order in which the values are to be recovered. Use subroutine elapsed_time from Exercise 7-29 to determine how long it takes to read each of the files.

SOLUTION
A program to generate the files and then the access to them is shown in Figure 14-6. Note that the program uses the INQUIRE statement to determine how long each record in the unformatted file should be.

FIGURE 14-6
An example program comparing direct access, unformatted files to direct access, formatted files.

```
PROGRAM direct_access
!
!   Purpose:
!     To compare direct access formatted and unformatted files.
!
!   Record of revisions:
!       Date        Programmer          Description of change
!       ====        ==========          =====================
!     12/11/06    S. J. Chapman         Original code
!
IMPLICIT NONE

! List of parameters:
INTEGER, PARAMETER :: SINGLE = SELECTED_REAL_KIND(p=6)
INTEGER, PARAMETER :: DOUBLE = SELECTED_REAL_KIND(p=14)
INTEGER, PARAMETER :: MAX_RECORDS = 20000      ! Max # of records
INTEGER, PARAMETER :: NUMBER_OF_READS = 50000 ! # of reads

! Data dictionary: declare variable types & definitions
INTEGER :: i, j               ! Index variable
INTEGER :: length_fmt = 80    ! Length of each record in
                              !   formatted file
```

(continued)

14

(concluded)

```fortran
INTEGER :: length_unf           ! Length of each record in
                                !   unformatted file
INTEGER :: irec                 ! Number of record in file
REAL(KIND=SINGLE) :: time_fmt   ! Time for formatted reads
REAL(KIND=SINGLE) :: time_unf   ! Time for unformatted reads
REAL(KIND=SINGLE) :: value      ! Value returned from random0
REAL(KIND=DOUBLE), DIMENSION(4) :: values ! Values in record

! Get the length of each record in the unformatted file.
INQUIRE (IOLENGTH=length_unf) values
WRITE (*,'(A,I2)') ' The unformatted record length is ', &
                   length_unf
WRITE (*,'(A,I2)') ' The formatted record length is ', &
                   length_fmt

! Open a direct access unformatted file.
OPEN ( UNIT=8,FILE='dirio.unf',ACCESS='DIRECT', &
       FORM='UNFORMATTED',STATUS='REPLACE',RECL=length_unf)

! Open a direct access formatted file.
OPEN (UNIT=9,FILE='dirio.fmt',ACCESS='DIRECT', &
      FORM='FORMATTED',STATUS='REPLACE',RECL=length_fmt )

! Generate records and insert into each file.
DO i = 1, MAX_RECORDS
   DO j = 1, 4
      CALL random0(value)               ! Generate records
      values(j) = 30._double * value
   END DO
   WRITE (8,REC=i) values               ! Write unformatted
   WRITE (9,'(4ES20.14)',REC=i) values  ! Write formatted
END DO

! Measure the time to recover random records from the
! unformatted file.
CALL set_timer
DO i = 1, NUMBER_OF_READS
   CALL random0(value)
   irec = (MAX_RECORDS-1) * value + 1
   READ (8,REC=irec) values
END DO
CALL elapsed_time (time_unf)

! Measure the time to recover random records from the
! formatted file.
CALL set_timer
DO i = 1, NUMBER_OF_READS
   CALL random0(value)
   irec = (MAX_RECORDS-1) * value + 1
   READ (9,'(4ES20.14)',REC=irec) values
END DO
CALL elapsed_time (time_fmt)

! Tell user.
WRITE (*,'(A,F6.2)') ' Time for unformatted file = ', time_unf
WRITE (*,'(A,F6.2)') ' Time for formatted file =   ', time_fmt

END PROGRAM direct_access
```

14

When the program is compiled with the Intel Visual Fortran compiler and executed on a 1.6-MHz Pentium 4 personal computer, the results are:

```
C:\book\chap14>direct_access
 The unformatted record length is 8
 The formatted record length is 80
 Time for unformatted file =    0.19
 Time for formatted file =      0.33
```

The length of each record in the unformatted file is 32 bytes, since each record contains four double-precision (64-bit or 8-byte) values. Since the Intel Visual Fortran compiler happens to measure record lengths in 4-byte units, the record length is reported as 8. On other processors or with other compilers, the length might come out in different, processor-dependent units. If we examine the files after the program executes, we see that the formatted file is much larger than the unformatted file, even though they both store the same information.

```
C:\book\chap14>dir dirio.*

Volume in drive C is SYSTEM
Volume Serial Number is 6462-A133

Directory of C:\book\chap14

12/20/2005 11:17 AM           1,600,000 dirio.fmt
12/20/2005 11:17 AM             640,000 dirio.unf
               2 File(s)     2,240,000 bytes
               0 Dir(s) 14,396,612,608 bytes free
```

Unformatted direct access files are both smaller and faster than formatted direct access files, but they are not portable between different kinds of processors.

F-2003 ONLY

■ 14.7
STREAM ACCESS MODE

The **stream access** mode reads or writes a file byte by byte, without processing special characters such as carriage returns, line feeds, and so forth. This differs from sequential access in that sequential access reads data a record at a time, using the carriage return and/or line feed data to mark the end of the record to process. Stream access mode is similar to the C language I/O functions getc and putc, which can read or write data a byte at time, and which treat control characters just like any others in the file.

A file is opened in stream access mode by specifying ACCESS='STREAM' in the OPEN statement. A typical OPEN statement for a stream access is shown below.

```
OPEN ( UNIT=8,FILE='infile.dat',ACCESS='STREAM',FORM='FORMATTED', &
       IOSTAT=istat )
```

Data can be written out to the file in a series of WRITE statements. When the programmer wishes to complete a line he or she should output a "newline" character

14

(similar to outputting \n in C). Fortran 2005 include a new intrinsic function new_line(a) that returns a newline character of the same KIND as the input character a. For example, the following statements would open a file and write two lines to it.

```
OPEN (UNIT=8,FILE='x.dat',ACCESS='STREAM',FORM='FORMATTED',IOSTAT=istat)
WRITE (8, '(A)') 'Text on first line'
WRITE (8, '(A)') new_line(' ')
WRITE (8, '(A)') 'Text on second line'
WRITE (8, '(A)') new_line(' ')
CLOSE (8, IOSTAT=istat)
```

Good Programming Practice

Use sequential access files for data that is normally read and processed sequentially. Use direct access files for data that must be read and written in any arbitrary order.

Good Programming Practice

Use direct access, unformatted files for applications where large quantities of data must be manipulated quickly. If possible, make the record length of the files a multiple of the basic disk sector size for your computer.

F-2003 ONLY

■ 14.8
NONDEFAULT I/O FOR DERIVED TYPES (FORTRAN 2003 ONLY)

We learned in Chapter 12 that, by default, derived data types are read in and written out in the order in which they are defined in the type definition statement, and the sequence of Fortran descriptors must match the order of the individual elements in the derived data type.

In Fortran 2003, it is possible to create a nondefault *user-defined* way to read or write data for derived data types. This is done by binding procedures to the data type to handle the input and output. There can be four types of procedures, for formatted input, formatted output, unformatted input, and unformatted output respectively. One or more of them can be declared and bound to the data type as shown below:

```
TYPE :: point
   REAL :: x
   REAL: :: y
CONTAINS
   GENERIC :: READ(FORMATTED) => read_fmt
   GENERIC :: READ(UNFORMATTED) => read_unfmt
   GENERIC :: WRITE(FORMATTED) => write_fmt
   GENERIC :: WRITE(UNFORMATTED) => write_unfmt
END TYPE
```

The procedure names specified on the generic READ(FORMATTED) line are called to perform formatted read output and so forth for the other types of I/O.

14

The bound procedures are accessed by specifying the `DT` format descriptor in an I/O statement. The format of this descriptor is:

```
DT 'string' (10, -4, 2)
```

where the character string and the list of parameters are passed to the procedure that will perform the I/O function. The character string is optional, and may be deleted if it is not needed for a particular user-defined I/O operation.

The procedures that perform the I/O function must have the following interfaces:

```
SUBROUTINE formatted_io (dtv,unit,iotype,v_list,iostat,iomsg)
SUBROUTINE unformatted_io(dtv,unit,               iostat,iomsg)
```

where the calling arguments are as follows:

1. `dtv` is the derived data type to read or write. For `WRITE` statements, this value must be declared with `INTENT(IN)` and not modified. For `READ` statements, this value must be declared with `INTENT(INOUT)` and the data read in must be stored in it.
2. `unit` is the I/O unit number to read from or write to. It must be declared as an integer with `INTENT(IN)`.
3. `iotype` is a `CHARACTER(len=*)` variable with `INTENT(IN)`. It will contain one of three possible strings: `'LISTDIRECTED'` if this is a list-directed I/O operation, `'NAMELIST'` if this is a namelist I/O operation, `'DT'` // `string` (where `string` is the string in the `DT` format descriptor) if this is ordinary formatted I/O.
4. `v_list` is an array of integers with `INTENT(IN)` that contains the set of integers in parentheses in the `DT` format descriptor.
5. `iostat` is the I/O status variable, set by the procedures when they complete their operations.
6. `iomsg` is a `CHARACTER(len=*)` variable with `INTENT(OUT)`. If `iostat` is nonzero, a message must be placed in this variable. Otherwise, it must not be changed.

Each subroutine will perform the specified type and direction of I/O in any way that the programmer desires. As long as the interface is honored, the nondefault I/O will function seamlessly with other Fortran I/O features.

Quiz 14-2

This quiz provides a quick check to see if you have understood the concepts introduced in Sections 14.3 to 14.8. If you have trouble with the quiz, reread the sections, ask your instructor, or discuss the material with a fellow student. The answers to this quiz are found in the back of the book.

14

1. What is the difference between a formatted and an unformatted file? What are the advantages and disadvantages of each type of file?

2. What is the difference between a direct access file and a sequential file? What are the advantages and disadvantages of each type of file?

(continued)

(concluded)

3. What is the purpose of the INQUIRE statement? In what three ways can it be used?

For questions 4 to 9, determine whether the following statements are valid. If not, specify what is wrong with them. If they are valid, what do they do?

4.
```
INTEGER :: i = 29
OPEN (UNIT=i,FILE='temp.dat',STATUS='SCRATCH')
WRITE (FMT='(1X,'The unit is',I3)',UNIT=i) i
```

5.
```
INTEGER :: i = 7
OPEN (i,STATUS='SCRATCH',ACCESS='DIRECT')
WRITE (FMT='(1X,'The unit is ',I3)',UNIT=i) i
```

6.
```
INTEGER :: i = 7, j = 0
OPEN (UNIT=i,STATUS='SCRATCH',ACCESS='DIRECT',RECL=80)
WRITE (FMT='(I10)',UNIT=i) j
CLOSE (i)
```

7.
```
INTEGER :: i
REAL,DIMENSION(9) :: a = (/ (-100,i=1,5),(100,i=6,9) /)
OPEN (8,FILE='mydata',STATUS='REPLACE',IOSTAT=istat)
WRITE (8,'(1X,3EN14.7)') (a(i), i = 1, 3)
WRITE (8,*) (a(i), i = 4, 6)
WRITE (UNIT=8) (a(i), I = 7, 9)
CLOSE (8)
```

8.
```
LOGICAL :: exists
INTEGER :: lu = 11, istat
INQUIRE (FILE='mydata.dat',EXIST=exists,UNIT=lu,IOSTAT=istat)
```

9. What is the data file out.dat after the following statements are executed?

```
INTEGER :: i, istat
REAL, DIMENSION(5) :: a = (/ (100.*i, i=-2,2) /)
REAL :: b = -37, c = 0
NAMELIST / local_data / a, b, c
OPEN(UNIT=3,FILE='in.dat',ACTION='READ',STATUS='OLD',IOSTAT=istat)
OPEN(UNIT=4,FILE='out.dat',ACTION='WRITE',IOSTAT=istat)
READ(3,NML=local_data,IOSTAT=istat)
WRITE(4,NML=local_data,IOSTAT=istat)
```

Assume that the file in.dat contains the following information:

```
                &local_data A(2) = -17., A(5) = 30. /
```

**EXAMPLE
14-3**

Spare Parts Inventory:

Any engineering organization that maintains computers or test equipment needs to keep a supply of spare parts and consumable supplies on hand for use when equipment breaks, printers run out of paper, etc. The organization needs to keep track of these supplies to determine how many of each type are being used in a given period of time, how many are in stock, and when to order more of a particular item. In actual practice, these functions are usually implemented with a database program. Here, we will write a simple Fortran program to keep track of stockroom supplies.

SOLUTION

A program to keep track of stockroom supplies needs to maintain a database of all available supplies, their descriptions, and their quantities. A typical database record might consist of:

1. **Stock Number** A unique number by which the item is known. Stock numbers start at 1 and go up to however many items are carried in the stockroom. (6 characters on disk; 1 integer in memory)
2. **Description** Description of item (30 characters)
3. **Vendor** The company that makes or sells the item (10 characters)
4. **Vendor Number** The number by which the item is known to the vendor (20 characters)
5. **Number in stock** (6 characters on disk; 1 integer in memory)
6. **Minimum quantity** If less than this number of the item is in stock, it should be reordered. (6 characters on disk; 1 integer in memory)

We will create a database file on disk in which the number of each record corresponds to the stock number of the item in the record. There will be as many records as there are items in stock, and each record will be 78 bytes long to hold the 78 characters of a database record. Furthermore, it may be necessary to withdraw items from stock in any order, so we should have direct access to any record in the database. We will implement the database using a *direct access, formatted* Fortran file with a record length of 78 bytes.

   In addition, we will need a file containing information about the withdrawals from stock of various parts and supplies, and their replenishment by purchases from vendors. This *transaction file* will consist of stock numbers and quantities purchased or withdrawn (purchases of supplies are indicated by positive numbers, and withdrawals from stock are indicated by negative numbers). Since the transactions in the transaction file will be read in chronological sequence, it will be OK to use a sequential file for the transaction file.

   Finally, we will need a file for reorders and error messages. This output file will contain reordering messages whenever the quantity of a stock item falls below the minimum quantity. It will also contain error messages if someone tries to withdraw an item that is not currently in stock.

14

1. **State the problem.**

Write a program to maintain a database of stockroom supplies for a small company. The program will accept inputs describing the issues from the stockroom and replenishments of the stock, and will constantly update the database of stockroom supplies. It will also generate reorder messages whenever the supply of an item gets too low.

2. **Define the inputs and outputs.**

The input to the program will be a sequential transaction file describing the issues from the stockroom and replenishments of the stocks. Each purchase or issue will be a separate line in the transaction file. Each record will consist of a *stock number* and *quantity* in free format.

There are two outputs from the program. One will be the database itself, and the other will be a message file containing reordering and error messages. The database file will consist of 78-byte records structured as described above.

3. **Describe the algorithm.**

When the program starts, it will open the database file, transaction file, and message file. It will then process each transaction in the transaction file, updating the database as necessary and generating required messages. The high-level pseudocode for this program is

```
Open the three files
WHILE transactions file is not at end-of-file DO
   Read transaction
   Apply to database
   IF error or limit exceeded THEN
      Generate error / reorder message
   END of IF
End of WHILE
Close the three files
```

The detailed pseudocode for this program is

```
! Open files
Open database file for DIRECT access
Open transaction file for SEQUENTIAL access
Open message file for SEQUENTIAL access

! Process transactions
WHILE
   Read transaction
   IF end-of-file EXIT
   Add / subtract quantities from database
   IF quantity < 0 THEN
      Generate error message
   END of IF
   IF quantity < minimum THEN
      Generate reorder message
   END of IF
End of WHILE
```

14

```
                    ! Close files
                    Close database file
                    Close transaction file
                    Close message file
```

4. **Turn the algorithm into Fortran statements.**
   The resulting Fortran subroutines are shown in Figure 14-7.

FIGURE 14-7
Program stock.

```
PROGRAM stock
!
!   Purpose:
!     To maintain an inventory of stockroom supplies, and generate
!     warning messages when supplies get low.
!
!   Record of revisions:
!       Date          Programmer            Description of change
!       ====          ==========            =====================
!     12/17/06    S. J. Chapman          Original code
!
IMPLICIT NONE

! Data dictionary: declare constants
INTEGER, PARAMETER :: LU_DB = 7          ! Unit for db file
INTEGER, PARAMETER :: LU_M = 8           ! Unit for message file
INTEGER, PARAMETER :: LU_T = 9           ! Unit for trans file

! Declare derived data type for a database item
TYPE :: database_record
   INTEGER :: stock_number               ! Item number
   CHARACTER(len=30) :: description       ! Description of item
   CHARACTER(len=10) :: vendor            ! Vendor of item
   CHARACTER(len=20) :: vendor_number     ! Vendor stock number
   INTEGER :: number_in_stock             ! Number in stock
   INTEGER :: minimum_quanitity           ! Minimum quantity
END TYPE

! Declare derived data type for transaction
TYPE :: transaction_record
   INTEGER :: stock_number                ! Item number
   INTEGER :: number_in_transaction       ! Number in transaction
END TYPE

! Data dictionary: declare variable types & definitions
TYPE (database_record) :: item            ! Database item
TYPE (transaction_record) :: trans        ! Transaction item
CHARACTER(len=3) :: file_stat             ! File status
INTEGER :: istat                          ! I/O status
LOGICAL :: exist                          ! True if file exists
```

(continued)

14

(continued)

```
CHARACTER(len=24) :: db_file = 'stock.db'    ! Database file
CHARACTER(len=24) :: msg_file = 'stock.msg'  ! Message file
CHARACTER(len=24) :: trn_file = 'stock.trn'  ! Trans. file

! Begin execution: open database file, and check for error.
OPEN (LU_DB, FILE=db_file, STATUS='OLD', ACCESS='DIRECT', &
      FORM='FORMATTED', RECL=78, IOSTAT=istat )
IF ( istat /= 0 ) THEN
   WRITE (*,100) db_file, istat
   100 FORMAT (' Open failed on file ',A,'. IOSTAT = ',I6)
   STOP
END IF

! Open transaction file, and check for error.
OPEN (LU_T, FILE=trn_file, STATUS='OLD', ACCESS='SEQUENTIAL', &
      IOSTAT=istat )
IF ( istat /= 0 ) THEN
   WRITE (*,100) trn_file, istat
   STOP
END IF

! Open message file, and position file pointer at end of file.
! Check for error.
INQUIRE (FILE=msg_file,EXIST=exist)  ! Does the msg file exist?
IF ( exist ) THEN
   file_stat = 'OLD'                     ! Yes, append to it.
ELSE
   file_stat = 'NEW'                     ! No, create it.
END IF
OPEN (LU_M, FILE=msg_file, STATUS=file_stat, POSITION='APPEND', &
      ACCESS='SEQUENTIAL', IOSTAT=istat )
IF ( istat /= 0 ) THEN
   WRITE (*,100) msg_file, istat
   STOP
END IF

! Now begin processing loop for as long as transactions exist.
process: DO
   ! Read transaction.
   READ (LU_T,*,IOSTAT=istat) trans

   ! If we are at the end of the data, exit now.
   IF ( istat /= 0 ) EXIT

   ! Get database record, and check for error.
   READ (LU_DB,'(A6,A30,A10,A20,I6,I6)',REC=trans%stock_number, &
        IOSTAT=istat) item

   IF ( istat /= 0 ) THEN
      WRITE (*,'(A,I6,A,I6)') &
          ' Read failed on database file record ', &
          trans%stock_number, ' IOSTAT = ', istat
```

(continued)

(concluded)

```
      STOP
    END IF

    ! Read ok, so update record.
    item%number_in_stock = item%number_in_stock &
                        + trans%number_in_transaction

    ! Check for errors.
    IF ( item%number_in_stock < 0 ) THEN
        ! Write error message & reset quantity to zero.
        WRITE (LU_M,'(A,I6,A)') ' ERROR: Stock number ', &
              trans%stock_number, ' has quantity < 0! '
        item%number_in_stock = 0
    END IF

    ! Check for quantities < minimum.
    IF ( item%number_in_stock < item%minimum_quanitity ) THEN
        ! Write reorder message to message file.
        WRITE (LU_M,110) ' Reorder stock number ', &
              trans%stock_number, ' from vendor ', &
              item%vendor, '   Description:  ', &
              item%description
    110 FORMAT (A,I6,A,A,/,A,A)
    END IF

    ! Update database record
    WRITE (LU_DB,'(A6,A30,A10,A20,I6,I6)',REC=trans%stock_number, &
          IOSTAT=istat) item

END DO process

! End of updates.  Close files and exit.
CLOSE ( LU_DB )
CLOSE ( LU_T )
CLOSE ( LU_M )

END PROGRAM stock
```

5. Test the resulting Fortran program.

To test this subroutine, it is necessary to create a sample database file and transaction file. The following simple database file has only four stock items:

```
1Paper, 8.5 × 11", 500 sheets  MYNEWCO   111-345               12      5
2Toner, Laserjet IIP           HP        92275A                 2      2
3Disks, 3.5 in Floppy, 1.44 MB MYNEWCO   54242                 10     10
4Cable, Parallel Printer       MYNEWCO   11-32-J6               1      1
----|----|----|----|----|----|----|----|----|----|----|----|----|----|----|
    10   20   30   40   50   60   70   80
```

The following transaction file contains records of the dispensing of three reams of paper and five floppy disks. In addition, two new toner cartridges arrive and are placed in stock.

```
1    -3
3    -5
2     2
```

If the program is run against this transaction file, the new database becomes:

```
1Paper, 8.5 × 11", 500 sheets  MYNEWCO    111-345                      9     5
2Toner, Laserjet IIP                      HP         92275A            4     2
3Disks, 3.5 in Floppy, 1.44 MB MYNEWCO    54242                        5    10
4Cable, Parallel Printer       MYNEWCO    11-32-J6                     1     1
----|----|----|----|----|----|----|----|----|----|----|----|----|----|----|----|
     10        20        30        40        50        60        70        80
```

and the message file contains the following lines:

```
Reorder stock number        3 from vendor MYNEWCO
    Description:  Disks, 3.5 in Floppy, 1.44 MB
```

By comparing the before and after values in the database, we can see that the program is functioning correctly.

This example illustrated several advanced I/O features. The files that must exist for the program to work are opened with the 'OLD' status. The output message file may or may not previously exist, so is opened with the proper status 'OLD' or 'NEW', depending on the results of an INQUIRE statement. The example uses both direct access and sequential access files. The direct access file was used in the database, where it is necessary to be able to access any record in any order. The sequential files were used for simple input and output lists that were processed in sequential order. The message file was opened with the 'APPEND' option so that new messages could be written at the end of any existing messages.

The program also exhibits a few undesirable features. The principal one is the use of STOP statements whenever an error occurs. This was done here to keep the example simple for classroom purposes. However, in a real program we should either close all files and shut down gracefully when an error occurs, or else offer the chance for the user to fix whatever problem is detected.

A real database would have probably used direct access *unformatted* files, instead of formatted files. We used formatted files here to make it easy to see the before-and-after effects on the database.

14

F-2003
ONLY

14.9

ASYNCHRONOUS I/O

Fortran 2003 has defined a new I/O mode called **asynchronous I/O.** In normal Fortran I/O operations, if a program writes data to a file with a WRITE statement, program execution halts at the WRITE statement until the data is completely written out, and then the program continues to run. Similarly, if a program reads data to a file with a READ statement, program execution halts at the READ statement until the data is completely read, and then the program continues to run. This is referred to a **synchronous I/O,** since the I/O operations are synchronized with the execution of the program.

In contrast, asynchronous I/O operations occur *in parallel* with the running of the program. If an asynchronous WRITE statement is executed, the data to be written is copied into some internal buffer, the write process is started, and control returns instantly to the calling program. In that fashion, the calling program can continue running at full speed while the write operation is going on.

The situation is a little more complex for an asynchronous read operation. If an asynchronous READ statement is executed, the read process is started, and control returns instantly to the calling program. At the time execution is returned to the calling program, *the variables being read are undefined.* They may have the old values, they may have the new values, or they may be in the middle of being updated, so the values must not be used until the read operation completes. The computer can go ahead and perform other calculations, but it must not use the variables in the asynchronous READ statement until the operation is complete.

How can a program using asynchronous reads know when the operation is complete? When it starts the I/O operation, it can get an ID for the operation by using the ID= clause, and it can query the status of the operation by using the INQUIRE statement. Alternatively, the program can execute a WAIT or a file positioning statement (REWIND, BACKSPACE) on the I/O unit. In either case, control will not return to the calling program until all I/O operations on that unit are complete, so the program can safely use the new data after the execution resumes.

A typical way to use asynchronous I/O would be to start a read operation, do some other calculations in the meantime, and then call WAIT to ensure that the I/O operation has completed before using the data from the read. If programs are structured properly, it should be possible to keep running most of the time instead of being blocked by I/O operations.

Note that Fortran 2003 compilers are *allowed but not required* to implement asynchronous I/O. It is most likely to be found on systems designed to support many CPUs, where the I/O operations could proceed independently of the calculations on different CPUs. Massively parallel computers (hypercubes and so forth) should always support asynchronous I/O operations.

14.9.1 Performing Asynchronous I/O

To use asynchronous I/O operations, a file must first be opened with the option to allow asynchronous I/O, and then each individual READ or WRITE statement must select the asynchronous I/O option. If an asynchronous WRITE is performed, no special actions need to be taken by the program. If an asynchronous READ is performed, then the program must wait for the READ to complete before using the variable.

An asynchronous WRITE operation is set up as shown below. Note that the ASYNCHRONOUS= clause must be in both the OPEN and the WRITE statement.

```
REAL,DIMENSION(5000,5000) :: data1
...
OPEN( UNIT=8,FILE='x.dat',ASYNCHRONOUS='yes',STATUS='NEW', &
```

14

```
                        ACTION='WRITE',IOSTAT=istat)
        ...
        ! Write data to file
        WRITE(8, 1000, ASYNCHRONOUS='yes',IOSTAT=istat) data1
        1000 FORMAT( 10F10.6 )

        (continue processing ...)
```

An asynchronous READ operation is set up as shown below. Note that the ASYNCHRONOUS= clause must be in both the OPEN and the READ statement.

```
        REAL,DIMENSION(5000,5000) :: data2
        ...
        OPEN( UNIT=8,FILE='y.dat',ASYNCHRONOUS='yes',STATUS='OLD', &
              ACTION='READ',IOSTAT=istat)
        ...
        ! Read data from file
        READ(8, 1000, ASYNCHRONOUS='yes',IOSTAT=istat) data2
        1000 FORMAT( 10F10.6 )

        (continue processing but DO NOT USE data2 ...)

        ! Now wait for I/O completion
        WAIT(8)

        (Now it is safe to use data2 ...)
```

14.9.2 Problems with Asynchronous I/O

F-2003 ONLY

A major problem with asynchronous I/O operations can occur when Fortran compilers try to optimize execution speed. Modern optimizing compilers often move the order of actions around and do things in parallel to increase the overall speed of a program. This usually works fine, but it could cause a real problem if the compiler moved a statement using the data in an asynchronous READ from a point after to a point before a WAIT statement on that unit. In that case, the data being used might be the old information, the new information, of some combination of the two!

Fortran 2003 has defined a new attribute to warn a compiler of this sort of problem with asynchronous I/O. The ASYNCHRONOUS attribute or statement provides this warning. For example, the following array is declared with the ASYNCHRONOUS attribute:

```
        REAL,DIMENSION(1000),ASYNCHRONOUS :: data1
```

And the following statement declares that several variables have the ASYNCHRONOUS attribute:

```
        ASYNCHRONOUS :: x, y, z
```

The ASYNCHRONOUS attribute is automatically assigned to a variable if it (or a component of it), appears in an input/output list or a namelist associated with an asynchronous I/O statement. There is no need to declare the variable ASYNCHRONOUS in that case, so as a practical matter you may not see this attribute explicitly declared very often.

14.10
ACCESS TO PROCESSOR-SPECIFIC I/O SYSTEM INFORMATION

Fortran 2003 includes a new intrinsic module that provides a processor-independent way to get information about the I/O system for that processor. This module is called ISO_FORTRAN_ENV. It defines the constants shown in Table 14-9.

If you use these constants in a Fortran program instead of hard-coding the corresponding values, your program will be more portable. If the program is moved to another processor, the implementation of ISO_FORTRAN_ENV on that processor will contain the correct values for the new environment, and the code itself will not need to be modified.

To access the constants stored in this module, just include a USE statement in the corresponding program unit, and then access the constants by name:

```
USE ISO_FORTRAN_ENV
. . .
WRITE (OUTPUT_UNIT,*) 'This is a test'
```

TABLE 14-9
Constants defined in Module ISO_FORTRAN_ENV

Constant	Value/Description
INPUT_UNIT	This is an integer containing the unit number of the **standard input stream,** which is the unit accessed by a READ(*,*) statement.
OUTPUT_UNIT	This is an integer containing the unit number of the **standard output stream,** which is the unit accessed by a WRITE(*,*) statement.
ERROR_UNIT	This is an integer containing the unit number of the **standard error stream.**
IOSTAT_END	This is an integer containing the value returned by a READ statement in the IOSTAT= clause if the end of file is reached.
IOSTAT_EOR	This is an integer containing the value returned by a READ statement in the IOSTAT= clause if the end of record is reached.
NUMERIC_STORAGE_SIZE	This is an integer containing the number of bits in a default numeric value.
CHARACTER_STORAGE_SIZE	This is an integer containing the number of bits in a default character value.
FILE_STORAGE_SIZE	This is an integer containing the number of bits in a default file storage unit.

14

■ 14.11
SUMMARY

F-2003 ONLY

In this chapter, we introduced the additional Fortran 95/2003 format descriptors EN, D, G, B, O, Z, P, TL, TR, S, SP, SN, BN, BZ, and :. We also introduced the following Fortran 2003–only descriptors: RU, RD, RN, RZ, RC, RP, DC, and DP. The EN descriptor provides a way to display data in engineering notation. The G descriptor provides a way to display any form of data. The B, O, and Z descriptors display integer or real data in binary, octal, and hexadecimal format, respectively. The TL*n* and TR*n* descriptors shift the position of data in the current line left and right by *n* characters. The colon descriptor (:) serves as a conditional stopping point for a WRITE statement. The D, P, S, SP, SN, BN, and BZ descriptors should not be used in new programs.

Then, we covered advanced features of Fortran I/O statements. The INQUIRE, PRINT, and ENDFILE statements were introduced, and all options were explained for all Fortran I/O statements. We introduced NAMELIST I/O, and explained the advantages of namelists for exchanging data between two programs or between two runs of the same program.

Fortran includes two file forms: *formatted* and *unformatted*. Formatted files contain data in the form of ASCII or EBCDIC characters, while unformatted files contain data that is a direct copy of the bits stored in the computer's memory. Formatted I/O requires a relatively large amount of processor time, since the data must be translated every time a read or write occurs. However, formatted files can be easily moved between processors of different types. Unformatted I/O is very quick, since no translation occurs. However, unformatted files cannot be easily inspected by humans, and cannot be easily moved between processors of different types.

F-2003 ONLY

Fortran 95 includes three access methods: *sequential* and *direct*. Fortran 2003 adds a *stream* access mode. Sequential access files are files intended to be read or written in sequential order. There is a limited ability to move around within a sequential file by using the REWIND and BACKSPACE commands, but the records in these files must basically be read one after another. Direct access files are files intended to be read or written in any arbitrary order. To make this possible, each record in a direct access file must be of a fixed length. If the length of each record is known, then it is possible to directly calculate where to find any specific record in the disk file, and to read or write only that record. Direct access files are especially useful for large blocks of identical records that might need to be accessed in any order. A common application for them is in databases.

F-2003 ONLY

The stream access mode reads or writes a file byte by byte, without processing special characters such as carriage returns, line feeds, and so forth. This differs from sequential access in that sequential access reads data a record at a time, using the carriage return and/or line feed data to mark the end of the record to process. Stream access mode is similar to the C language I/O functions getc and putc, which can read or write data a byte at time, and which treat control characters just like any others in the file.

14

14.11.1 Summary of Good Programming Practice

The following guidelines should be adhered to when working with Fortran I/O:

1. Never use the D, P, BN, BZ, S, SP, or SS format descriptors in new programs.
2. Do not rely on preconnected files in your Fortran programs (except for the standard input and output files). The number and the names of preconnected files vary from processor to processor, so using them will reduce the portability of your programs. Instead, always explicitly open each file that you use with an OPEN statement.
3. Always use the IOSTAT= and IOMSG= clauses in OPEN statements to trap errors. When an error is detected, tell the user all about the problem before shutting down gracefully or requesting an alternative file.
4. Always explicitly close each disk file with a CLOSE statement as soon as possible after a program is finished using it, so that it may be available for use by others in a multitasking environment.
5. Check to see if your output file is overwriting an existing data file. If it is, make sure that the user really wants to do that before destroying the data in the file.
6. Use the IOSTAT= and IOMSG= clauses in READ statements to prevent programs from aborting on errors, end-of-file conditions, or end-of-record conditions. When an error or end-of-file condition is detected, the program can take appropriate actions to continue processing or to shut down gracefully.
7. Use NAMELIST I/O to save data to be exchanged between programs or between different runs of a single program. Also, you may use NAMELIST READ statements to update selected input parameters when a program begins executing.
8. Use formatted files to create data that must be readable by humans, or that must be transferable between different types of computers. Use unformatted files to efficiently store large quantities of data that do not have to be directly examined, and that will remain on only one type of computer. Also, use unformatted files when I/O speed is critical.
9. Use sequential access files for data that is normally read and processed sequentially. Use direct access files for data that must be read and written in any arbitrary order.
10. Use direct access, unformatted files for applications where large quantities of data must be manipulated quickly. If possible, make the record length of the files a multiple of the basic disk sector size for your computer.

14.11.2 Summary of Fortran Statements and Structures

BACKSPACE **Statement:**

```
          BACKSPACE (control_list)
or        BACKSPACE (unit)
or        BACKSPACE unit
```

(continued)

14

(concluded)

Example:

```
BACKSPACE (lu,IOSTAT=istat)
BACKSPACE (8)
```

Description:

The BACKSPACE statement moves the current position of a file back by one record. Possible clauses in the control list are UNIT=, IOSTAT=, and ERR=.

ENDFILE Statement:

```
                  ENDFILE (control_list)
or                ENDFILE (unit)
or                ENDFILE unit
```

Examples:

```
ENDFILE (UNIT=lu,IOSTAT=istat)
ENDFILE (8)
```

Description:

The ENDFILE statement writes an end-of-file record to a file, and positions the file pointer beyond the end-of-file record. Possible clauses in the control list are UNIT=, IOSTAT=, and ERR=.

FLUSH Statement:

F-2003 ONLY

```
FLUSH (control_list)
```

Examples:

```
FLUSH (8)
```

Description:

The FLUSH statement forces any output data still in memory buffers to be written to the disk.

INQUIRE Statement:

```
INQUIRE (control_list)
```

(continued)

(*concluded*)

Example:

```
LOGICAL :: lnamed
CHARACTER(len=12) :: filename, access
INQUIRE (UNIT=22,NAMED=lnamed,NAME=filename,ACCESS=access)
```

Description:

The INQUIRE statement permits a user to determine the properties of a file. The file may be specified either by its file name or (after the file is opened) by its i/o unit number. The possible clauses in the INQUIRE statement are described in Table 14-5.

NAMELIST Statement:

```
NAMELIST / nl_group_name / var1 [, var2, ...]
```

Examples:

```
NAMELIST / control_data / page_size, rows, columns
WRITE (8,NML=control_data)
```

Description:

The NAMELIST statement is a specification statement that associates a group of variables in a name-list. All of the variables in the namelist may be written or read as a unit using the namelist version of the WRITE and READ statements. When a namelist is read, only the values that appear in the input list will be modified by the READ. The values appear in the input list in a keyword format, and individual values may appear in any order.

PRINT Statement:

```
PRINT fmt, output_list
```

Examples:

```
PRINT *, intercept
PRINT '(2I6)', i, j
```

14

Description:

The PRINT statement outputs the data in the output list *to the standard output device* according to the formats specified in the format descriptors. The format descriptors may be in a FORMAT statement or a character string, or the format might be defaulted to list-directed I/O with an asterisk.

REWIND Statement:

```
                    REWIND (control_list)
or                  REWIND (lu)
or                  REWIND lu
```

Example:

```
                    REWIND (8)
                    REWIND (lu,IOSTAT=istat)
                    REWIND 12
```

Description:

The REWIND statement moves the current position of a file back to the beginning of the file. Possible clauses in the control list are UNIT=, IOSTAT=, and ERR=.

WAIT Statement:

F-2003 ONLY

```
                    WAIT (control_list)
```

Examples:

```
                    WAIT (8)
```

Description:

The WAIT statement waits for any pending asynchronous I/O operations to complete before returning to the calling program.

14.11.3 Exercises

14-1. What is the difference between the ES and the EN format descriptor? How would the number 12345.67 be displayed by each of these descriptors?

14-2. What types of data may be displayed with the B, O, Z descriptors? What do these descriptors do?

14-3. Write the form of the G format descriptor that will display 7 significant digits of a number. What is the minimum width of this descriptor?

14

14-4. Write the following integers with the I8 and I8.8 format descriptors. How do the outputs compare?

(a) 1024

(b) -128

(c) 30,000

14-5. Write the integers from the previous exercise with the B16 (binary), O11 (octal), and Z8 (hexadecimal) format descriptors.

14-6. Use subroutine random0 developed in Chapter 7 to generate nine random numbers in the range [−100000, 100000). Display the numbers with the G11.5 format descriptor.

14-7. Suppose that you wanted to display the nine random numbers generated in the previous exercise in the following format:

```
VALUE(1) = ±xxxxxx.xx    VALUE(2) = ±xxxxxx.xx
VALUE(3) = ±xxxxxx.xx    VALUE(4) = ±xxxxxx.xx
VALUE(5) = ±xxxxxx.xx    VALUE(5) = ±xxxxxx.xx
VALUE(7) = ±xxxxxx.xx    VALUE(8) = ±xxxxxx.xx
VALUE(9) = ±xxxxxx.xx
----|----|----|----|----|----|----|----|----|----|----|----|
    10        20        30        40        50        60
```

Write a single format descriptor that would generate this output. Use the colon descriptor appropriately in the format statement.

14-8. Suppose that the following values were to be displayed with a G10.4 format descriptor. What would each output look like?

(a) -6.38765×10^{10}

(b) -6.38765×10^{2}

(c) -6.38765×10^{-1}

(d) 2345.6

(e) .TRUE.

(f) 'String!'

14-9. Suppose that the first four values from the previous exercise were to be displayed with an EN15.6 format descriptor. What would each output look like?

14-10. Explain the operation of NAMELIST I/O. Why is it especially suitable for initializing a program or sharing data between programs?

14-11. What will be written out by the statements shown below?

```
INTEGER :: i, j
REAL, DIMENSION(3,3) :: array
NAMELIST / io / array
array = RESHAPE( (/ ((10.*i*j, j=1,3), i=0,2) /), (/3,3/) )
WRITE (*,NML=io)
```

14-12. What will be written out by the statements shown below?

```
INTEGER :: i, j
REAL, DIMENSION(3,3) :: a
NAMELIST / io / a
a = RESHAPE( (/ ((10.*i*j, j=1,3), i=0,2) /), (/3,3/) )
READ (8,NML=io)
WRITE (*,NML=io)
```

14

Input data on unit 8:

```
&io a(1,1) = -100.
a(3,1) = 6., a(1,3) = -6. /
a(2,2) = 1000. /
```

14-13. What is the difference between using the TR*n* format descriptor and the *n*X format descriptor to move 10 characters to the right in an output format statement?

14-14. What is printed out by the following sets of Fortran statements?

(*a*)
```
REAL:: value = 356.248
INTEGER :: i
WRITE (*,200) 'Value = ', (value, i=1,5)
200 FORMAT ('0',A,F10.4,G10.2,G11.5,G11.6,ES10.3)
```

(*b*)
```
INTEGER, DIMENSION(5) :: i
INTEGER :: j
DO j = 1, 5
   i(j) = j**2
END DO
READ (*,*) i
WRITE (*,500) i.
500 FORMAT (3(10X,I5))
```

Input data:

```
  -101      ,,      17                /
     20              71                     ,,
```

14-15. Assume that a file is opened with the following statement:

```
OPEN (UNIT=71,FILE='myfile')
```

What is the status of the file when it is opened this way? Will the file be opened for sequential or direct access? Where will the file pointer be? Will it be formatted or unformatted? Will the file be opened for reading, writing, or both? How long will each record be? How will list-directed character strings that are written to the file be delimited? What will happen if the file is not found? What will happen if an error occurs during the open process?

14-16. Answer the questions of the previous exercise for the following files.

(*a*)
```
OPEN (UNIT=21,FILE='myfile',ACCESS='DIRECT', &
      FORM='FORMATTED',RECL=80,IOSTAT=istat)
```

(*b*)
```
OPEN (UNIT=10,FILE='yourfile',ACCESS='DIRECT',ACTION='WRITE', &
      STATUS='REPLACE',RECL=80,IOSTAT=istat)
```

(*c*)
```
OPEN (5, FILE='file_5',ACCESS='SEQUENTIAL', &
      STATUS='OLD',DELIM='QUOTE',ACTION='READWRITE', &
      POSITION='APPEND', IOSTAT = istat)
```

(*d*)
```
OPEN (UNIT=1,STATUS='SCRATCH',IOSTAT=istat)
```

14-17. The `IOSTAT=` clause in a `READ` statement can return positive, negative, or zero values. What do positive values mean? Negative values? Zero values?

14-18. File Copy While Trimming Trailing Blanks Write a Fortran program that prompts the user for an input file name and an output file name, and then copies the input file to the output file, trimming trailing blanks off of the end of each line before writing it out. The program should use the `STATUS=` and `IOSTAT=` clauses in the `OPEN` statement to confirm that the input file already exists, and use the `STATUS=` and `IOSTAT=` clauses in the `OPEN` statement to confirm that the output file does not already exist. Be sure to use the proper `ACTION=` clause for each file. If the output file is already present, then prompt the user to see if it should be overwritten. If so, overwrite it, and if not, stop the program. After the copy process is completed, the program should ask the user whether or not to delete the original file. The program should set the proper status in the input file's `CLOSE` statement if the file is to be deleted.

14-19. Determine whether or not each of the following sets of Fortran statements is valid. If not, explain why not. If so, describe the output from the statements.

(*a*) Statements:
```
CHARACTER(len=10) :: acc, fmt, act, delim
INTEGER :: unit = 35
LOGICAL :: lexist, lnamed, lopen
INQUIRE (FILE='input',EXIST=lexist)
IF ( lexist ) THEN
   OPEN (unit, FILE='input',STATUS='OLD')
   INQUIRE (UNIT=unit,OPENED=lopen,EXIST=lexist, &
           NAMED=lnamed,ACCESS=acc,FORM=fmt, &
           ACTION=act,DELIM=delim)
   WRITE (*,100) lexist, lopen, lnamed, acc, fmt, &
           act, delim
   100 FORMAT (1X,'File status: Exists = ',L1, &
             ' Opened = ', L1, ' Named = ',L1, &
             ' Access = ', A,/,' Format = ',A, &
             ' Action = ', A,/,' Delims = ',A)
END IF
```

(*b*) Statements:
```
INTEGER :: i1 = 10
OPEN (9, FILE='file1',ACCESS='DIRECT',FORM='FORMATTED', &
      STATUS='NEW')
WRITE (9,'(I6)') i1
```

14-20. Copying a File in Reverse Order Write a Fortran program that prompts the user for an input file name and an output file name, and then copies the input file to the output file *in reverse order*. That is, the last record of the input file is the first record of the output file. The program should use the `INQUIRE` statement to confirm that the input file already exists, and that the output file does not already exist. If the output file is already present, then prompt the user to see if it should be overwritten before proceeding. (*Hint:* Read all of the lines in the input file to count them, and then use `BACKSPACE` statements to work backward through the file. Be careful of the `IOSTAT` values!)

14

14-21. Comparing Formatted and Unformatted Files Write a Fortran program containing a real array with 10,000 random values in the range $[-10^6, 10^6)$. Then perform the following actions:

(a) Open a formatted sequential file and write the values to the file preserving the full seven significant digits of the numbers. (Use the ES format so that numbers of any size will be properly represented.) Write 10 values per line to the file, so that there are 100 lines in the file. How big is the resulting file?

(b) Open an unformatted sequential file and write the values to the file. Write 10 values per line to the file, so that there are 100 lines in the file. How big is the resulting file?

(c) Which file was smaller, the formatted file or the unformatted file?

(d) Use the subroutines set_timer and elapsed_time created in Exercise 7-29 to time the formatted and unformatted writes. Which one is faster?

14-22. Comparing Sequential and Direct Access Files Write a Fortran program containing a real array with 1000 random values in the range $[-10^5, 10^5)$. Then perform the following actions:

(a) Open a *formatted sequential file*, and write the values to the file, preserving the full seven significant digits of the numbers. (Use the ES14.7 format so that numbers of any size will be properly represented.) How big is the resulting file?

(b) Open a *formatted direct access file* with 14 characters per record, and write the values to the file preserving the full seven significant digits of the numbers. (Again, use the ES14.7 format.) How big is the resulting file?

(c) Open an *unformatted direct access file* and write the values to the file. Make the length of each record large enough to hold one number. (This parameter is computer dependent; use the INQUIRE statement to determine the length to use for the RECL= clause.) How big is the resulting file?

(d) Which file was smaller, the formatted direct access file or the unformatted direct access file?

(e) Now, retrieve 100 records from each of the three files in the following order: Record 1, Record 1000, Record 2, Record 999, Record 3, Record 998, etc. Use the subroutines set_timer and elapsed_time created in Exercise 7-29 to time the reads from each of the files. Which one is fastest?

(f) How did the sequential access file compare to the random access files when reading data in this order?

14

Pointers and Dynamic Data Structures

OBJECTIVES

- Understand dynamic memory allocation using pointers.
- Be able to explain what a target is, and why targets must be declared explicitly in Fortran.
- Understand the difference between a pointer assignment statement and a conventional assignment statement.
- Understand how to use pointers with array subsets.
- Know how to dynamically allocate and deallocate memory using pointers.
- Now how to create dynamic data structures such as linked lists using pointers.

In earlier chapters, we have created and used variables of the five intrinsic Fortran data types and of derived data types. These variables all had two characteristics in common: they all stored some form of data, and they were almost all **static,** meaning that the number and types of variables in a program were declared before program execution, and remained the same throughout program execution.[1]

Fortran 95/2003 includes another type of variable that contains no data at all. Instead, it contains the *address in memory* of another variable where the data is actually stored. Because this type of variable points to another variable, it is called a **pointer.** The difference between a pointer and an ordinary variable is illustrated in Figure 15-1.

p1	Address of variable	var1	Data value
	(a)		(b)

FIGURE 15-1
The difference between a pointer and an ordinary variable: (*a*) A pointer stores the *address* of an ordinary variable in its memory location. (*b*) An ordinary variable stores a data value.

---

[1] Allocatable arrays, automatic arrays, and automatic character variables were the limited exceptions to this rule.

Both pointers and ordinary variables have names, but pointers store the addresses of ordinary variables, while ordinary variables store data values.

Pointers are primarily used in situations where variables and arrays must be created and destroyed dynamically during the execution of a program, and where it is not known before the program executes just how many of any given type of variable will be needed during a run. For example, suppose that a mailing list program must read in an unknown number of names and addresses, sort them into a user-specified order, and then print mailing labels in that order. The names and addresses will be stored in variables of a derived data type. If this program is implemented with static arrays, then the arrays must be as large as the largest possible mailing list ever to be processed. Most of the time the mailing lists will be much smaller, and this will produce a terrible waste of computer memory. If the program is implemented with allocatable arrays, then we can allocate just the required amount of memory, but we must still know in advance how many addresses there will be before the first one is read. By contrast, we will now learn how to *dynamically allocate a variable for each address as it is read in,* and how to use pointers to manipulate those addresses in any desired fashion. This flexibility will produce a much more efficient program.

We will first learn the basics of creating and using pointers, and then see several examples of how they can be used to write flexible and powerful programs.

■ 15.1
POINTERS AND TARGETS

A Fortran variable is declared to be a pointer by either including the `POINTER` attribute in its type definition statement (the preferred choice), or listing it in a separate `POINTER` statement. For example, each of the following statements declares a pointer `p1`, which must point to a real variable.

```
REAL, POINTER :: p1
```

or

```
REAL :: p1
POINTER :: p1
```

Note that the *type* of a pointer must be declared, even though the pointer does not contain any data of that type. Instead, it contains the *address* of a variable of the declared type. A pointer is allowed to point only to variables of its declared type. Any attempt to point to a variable of a different type will produce a compilation error.

Pointers to variables of derived data types may also be declared. For example,

```
TYPE (vector), POINTER :: vector_pointer
```

declares a pointer to a variable of derived data type `vector`. Pointers may also point to an array. A pointer to an array is declared with a **deferred-shape array specification,** meaning that the rank of the array is specified, but the actual extent of the array in each dimension is indicated by colons. Two pointers to arrays are:

```
INTEGER, DIMENSION(:), POINTER :: ptr1
REAL, DIMENSION(:,:), POINTER :: ptr2
```

The first pointer can point to any one-dimensional integer array, while the second pointer can point to any two-dimensional real array.

A pointer can point to any variable or array of the pointer's type as long as the variable or array has been declared to be a **target.** A target is a data object whose address has been made available for use with pointers. A Fortran variable or array is declared to be a target by either including the TARGET attribute in its type definition statement (the preferred choice), or by listing it in a separate TARGET statement. For example, each of the following sets of statements declares two targets to which pointers may point.

```
REAL, TARGET :: a1 = 7
INTEGER, DIMENSION(10), TARGET :: int_array
```

or

```
REAL :: a1 = 7
INTEGER, DIMENSION(10) :: int_array
TARGET :: a1, int_array
```

They declare a real scalar value a1 and a rank 1 integer array int_array. Variable a1 may be pointed to by any real scalar pointer (such as the pointer p1 declared above), and int_array may be pointed to by any integer rank 1 pointer (such as pointer ptr1 above).

THE SIGNIFICANCE OF THE TARGET ATTRIBUTE

A pointer is a variable that contains the memory location of another variable, which is called the target. The target itself is just an ordinary variable of the same type as the pointer. Given that the target is just an ordinary variable, why is it necessary to attach a special TARGET attribute to the variable before a pointer can point to it? Other computer languages such as C have no such requirement.

The reason that the TARGET attribute is required has to do with the way Fortran compilers work. Fortran is normally used for large, numerically intensive mathematical problems, and most Fortran compilers are designed to produce output programs that are as fast as possible. These compilers include an *optimizer* as a part of the compilation process. The optimizer examines the code and rearranges it, unwraps loops, eliminates common subexpressions, etc. in order to increase the final execution speed. As a part of this optimization process, some of the variables in the original program can actually disappear, having been combined out of existence or replaced by temporary values in registers. So, what would happen if the variable that we wish to point to is optimized out of existence? There would be a problem pointing to it!

It is possible for a compiler to analyze a program and determine whether or not each individual variable is ever used as the target of a pointer, but that process is tedious. The TARGET attribute was added to the language to make it easier for the compiler writers. The attribute tells a compiler that a particular variable *could* be pointed to by a pointer, and therefore it must not be optimized out of existence.

15

15.1.1 Pointer Assignment Statements

A pointer can be **associated** with a given target by means of a **pointer assignment statement.** A pointer assignment statement takes the form

```
pointer => target
```

where `pointer` is the name of a pointer, and `target` is the name of a variable or array of the same type as the pointer. The pointer assignment operator consists of an equal sign followed by a greater than sign with no space in between.[2] When this statement is executed, the memory address of the target is stored in the pointer. After the pointer assignment statement, any reference to the pointer will actually be a reference to the data stored in the target.

If a pointer is already associated with a target, and another pointer assignment statement is executed by using the same pointer, then the association with the first target is lost, and the pointer now points to the second target. Any reference to the pointer after the second pointer assignment statement will actually be a reference to the data stored in the second target.

For example, the program in Figure 15-2 defines a real pointer p and two target variables t1 and t2. The pointer is first associated with variable t1 by a pointer assignment statement, and p is written out by a WRITE statement. Then the pointer is associated with variable t2 by another pointer assignment statement, and p is written out by a second WRITE statement.

FIGURE 15-2
Program to illustrate pointer assignment statements.

```
PROGRAM test_ptr
IMPLICIT NONE
REAL, POINTER :: p
REAL, TARGET :: t1 = 10., t2 = - 17.
p => t1
WRITE (*,*) 'p, t1, t2 = ', p, t1, t2
p => t2
WRITE (*,*) 'p, t1, t2 = ', p, t1, t2
END PROGRAM test_ptr
```

When this program is executed, the results are:

```
C:\book\chap15>test_ptr
p, t1, t2 =      10.000000      10.000000     -17.000000
p, t1, t2 =     -17.000000      10.000000     -17.000000
```

It is important to note that p never contains either 10. or −17. Instead, it contains the addresses of the variables in which those values were stored, and the Fortran compiler treats a reference to the pointer as a reference to those addresses. Also, note that a value could be accessed either through a pointer to a variable or through the variable's

---

[2] This sign is identical in form to the rename sign in the USE statement (see Chapter 13), but it has a different meaning.

name, and the two forms of access can be mixed even within a single statement (see Figure 15-3).

It is also possible to assign the value of one pointer to another pointer in a pointer assignment statement.

```
pointer1 => pointer2
```

After such a statement, *both pointers point directly and independently to the same target.* If either pointer is changed in a later assignment, the other one will be unaffected and will continue to point to the original target. If `pointer2` is disassociated (does not point to a target) at the time the statement is executed, then `pointer1` also becomes disassociated. For example, the program in Figure 15-4 defines two real pointers p1 and p2, and two target variables t1 and t2. The pointer p1 is first associated with variable t1 by a pointer assignment statement, and then pointer p2 is assigned the value of pointer p1 by another pointer assignment statement. After these statements, both pointers p1 and p2 are independently associated with variable t1. When pointer p1 is later associated with variable t2, pointer p2 remains associated with t1.

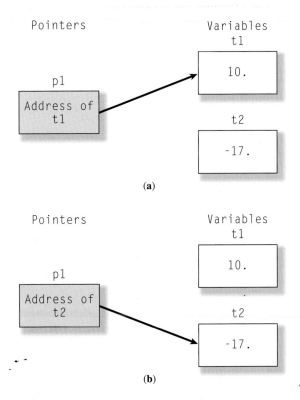

FIGURE 15-3
The relationship between the pointer and the variables in program `test_ptr`. (*a*) The situation after the first executable statement: p1 contains the address of variable t1, and a reference to p1 is the same as a reference to t1. (*b*) The situation after the third executable statement: p1 contains the address of variable t2, and a reference to p1 is the same as a reference to t2.

15

FIGURE 15-4
Program to illustrate pointer assignment between two pointers.

```
PROGRAM test_ptr2
IMPLICIT NONE
REAL, POINTER :: p1, p2
REAL, TARGET :: t1 = 10., t2 = - 17.
p1 => t1
p2 => p1
WRITE (*,'(A,4F8.2)') ' p1, p2, t1, t2 = ', p1, p2, t1, t2
p1 => t2
WRITE (*,'(A,4F8.2)') ' p1, p2, t1, t2 = ', p1, p2, t1, t2
END PROGRAM test_ptr2
```

When this program is executed, the results are (see Figure 15-5)

```
C:\book\chap15>test_ptr2
p1, p2, t1, t2 =     10.00    10.00    10.00    -17.00
p1, p2, t1, t2 =    -17.00    10.00    10.00    -17.00
```

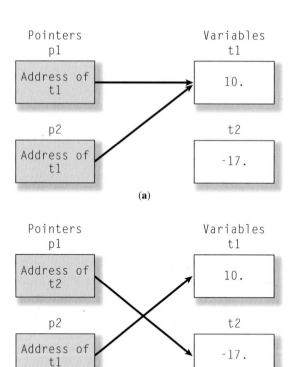

FIGURE 15-5
The relationship between the pointer and the variables in program test_ptr2. (*a*) The situation after the second executable statement: p1 and p2 both contain the address of variable t1, and a reference to either one is the same as a reference to t1. (*b*) The situation after the fourth executable statement: p1 contains the address of variable t2, and p2 contains the address of variable t1. Note that p2 was unaffected by the reassignment of pointer p1.

15.1.2 Pointer Association Status

The **association status** of a pointer indicates whether or not the pointer currently points to a valid target. There are three possible statuses: **undefined, associated,** and **disassociated.** When a pointer is first declared in a type declaration statement, its pointer association status is *undefined.* Once a pointer has been associated with a target by a pointer assignment statement, its association status becomes *associated.* If a pointer is later disassociated from its target and is not associated with any new target, then its association status becomes *disassociated.*

How can a pointer be disassociated from its target? It can be disassociated from one target and simultaneously associated with another target by executing a pointer assignment statement. In addition, a pointer can be disassociated from all targets by executing a NULLIFY statement. A NULLIFY statement has the form

```
NULLIFY ( ptr1 [,ptr2, ...] )
```

where *ptr1, ptr2*, etc. are pointers. After the statement is executed, the pointers listed in the statement are disassociated from all targets.

A pointer can be used to reference a target only when it is associated with that target. Any attempt to use a pointer when it is not associated with a target will result in an error, and the program containing the error will abort. Therefore, we must be able to tell whether or not a particular pointer is associated with a particular target, or with any target at all. This can be done by using the logical intrinsic function ASSOCIATED. The function comes in two forms, one containing a pointer as its only argument and one containing both a pointer and a target. The first form is

```
status = ASSOCIATED ( pointer )
```

This function returns a true value *if the pointer is associated with any target,* and a false value if it is not associated with any target. The second form is

```
status = ASSOCIATED ( pointer, target )
```

This function returns a true value *if the pointer is associated with the particular target included in the function,* and a false value otherwise.

A pointer's association status can be undefined only from the time that it is declared until it is first used. Thereafter, the pointer's status will always be either associated or disassociated. Because the undefined status is ambiguous, it is recommended that every pointer's status be clarified as soon as it is created by either assigning it to a target or nullifying it. For example, pointers could be declared and nullified in a program as follows:

```
REAL, POINTER :: p1, p2
INTEGER, POINTER :: i1
...
(additional specification statements)
...
NULLIFY (p1, p2, i1)
```

15

Good Programming Practice

Always nullify or assign all pointers in a program unit as soon as they are created. This eliminates any possible ambiguities associated with the undefined state.

Fortran also provides an intrinsic function NULL() that can be used to nullify a pointer at the time it is declared (or at any time during the execution of a program). Thus, pointers can be declared and nullified as follows:

```
REAL, POINTER :: p1 = NULL(), p2 = NULL()
INTEGER, POINTER :: i1 = NULL()
...
(additional specification statements)
```

The details of the NULL() function are described in Appendix B.

The simple program shown in Figure 15-6 illustrates the use of the NULLIFY statement and the ASSOCIATED intrinsic function.

FIGURE 15-6
Program to illustrate the use of the NULLIFY statement and the ASSOCIATED function.

```
PROGRAM test_ptr3
IMPLICIT NONE
REAL, POINTER :: p1, p2, p3
REAL, TARGET :: a = 11., b = 12.5, c = 3.141592
NULLIFY ( p1, p2, p3) ! Nullify pointers
WRITE (*,*) ASSOCIATED(p1)
p1 => a                    ! p1 points to a
p2 => b                    ! p2 points to b
p3 => c                    ! p3 points to c
WRITE (*,*) ASSOCIATED(p1)
WRITE (*,*) ASSOCIATED(p1,b)
END PROGRAM test_ptr3
```

The pointers p1, p2, and p3 will be nullified as soon as program execution begins. Thus the result of the first ASSOCIATED(p1) function will be false. Then the pointers are associated with targets a, b, and c. When the second ASSOCIATED(p1) function is executed, the pointer will be associated, so the result of the function will be true. The third ASSOCIATED(p1,b) function checks to see if pointer p1 points to variable b. It doesn't, so the function returns false.

■ 15.2

USING POINTERS IN ASSIGNMENT STATEMENTS

Whenever a pointer appears in a Fortran expression where a value is expected, *the value of the target pointed to is used* instead of the pointer itself. This process is known as **dereferencing** the pointer. We have already seen an example of dereferencing in the previous section: whenever a pointer appeared in a WRITE statement, the value of the target pointed to was printed out instead. As another example, consider two pointers p1 and p2 that are associated with variables a and b, respectively. In the ordinary assignment statement

```
p2 = p1
```

both p1 and p2 appear in places where variables are expected, so they are dereferenced, and this statement is exactly identical to the statement

```
b = a
```

By contrast, in the pointer assignment statement

```
p2 => p1
```

p2 appears in a place where a pointer is expected, while p1 appears in a place where a target (an ordinary variable) is expected. As a result, p1 is dereferenced, while p2 refers to the pointer itself. The result is that the target pointed to by p1 is assigned to the pointer p2.

The program shown in Figure 15-7 provides another example of using pointers in place of variables:

FIGURE 15-7
Program to illustrate the use of pointers in place of variables in assignment statements.

```
PROGRAM test_ptr4
IMPLICIT NONE
REAL, POINTER :: p1, p2, p3
REAL, TARGET :: a = 11., b = 12.5, c
NULLIFY (p1, p2, p3)          ! Nullify pointers
p1 => a                      ! p1 points to a
p2 => b                      ! p2 points to b
p3 => c                      ! p3 points to c
p3 = p1 + p2                 ! Same as c = a + b
WRITE (*,*) 'p3 = ', p3
p2 => p1                     ! p2 points to a
p3 = p1 + p2                 ! Same as c = a + a
WRITE (*,*) 'p3 = ', p3
p3 = p1                      ! Same as c = a
p3 => p1                     ! p3 points to a
WRITE (*,*) 'p3 = ', p3
WRITE (*,*) 'a, b, c = ', a, b, c
END PROGRAM test_ptr4
```

In this example, the first assignment statement p3 = p1 + p2 is equivalent to the statement c = a + b, since the pointers p1, p2, and p3 point to variables a, b, and c respectively, and since ordinary variables are expected in the assignment statement. The pointer assignment statement p2 => p1 causes pointer p1 to point to a, so the second assignment statement p3 = p1 + p2 is equivalent to the statement c = a + a. Finally, the assignment statement p3 = p1 is equivalent to the statement c = a, while the pointer assignment statement p3 => p1 causes pointer p3 to point to a. The output of this program is:

15

```
C:\book\chap15>test_ptr4
p3 =      23.500000
p3 =      22.000000
p3 =      11.000000
a, b, c =       11.000000       12.500000       11.000000
```

We will now show one way that pointers can improve the efficiency of a program. Suppose that it is necessary to swap two 100 × 100 element real arrays `array1` and `array2` in a program. To swap these arrays, we would normally use the following code:

```
REAL, DIMENSION(100,100) :: array1, array2, temp
. . .
temp = array1
array1 = array2
array2 = temp
```

The code is simple enough, but note that we are moving 10,000 real values in each assignment statement! All of that moving requires a lot of time. By contrast, we could perform the same manipulation with pointers and exchange only the *addresses* of the target arrays:

```
REAL, DIMENSION(100,100), TARGET :: array1, array2
REAL, DIMENSION(:,:), POINTER :: p1, p2, temp
p1 => array1
p2 => array2
. . .
temp => p1
p1 => p2
p2 => temp
```

In the latter case, we have swapped only the addresses, and not the entire 10,000 element arrays! This is enormously more efficient than the previous example.

Good Programming Practice

In sorting or swapping large arrays or derived data types, it is more efficient to exchange pointers to the data than it is to manipulate the data itself.

■ 15.3

USING POINTERS WITH ARRAYS

A pointer can point to an array as well as a scalar. A pointer to an array must declare the type and the rank of the array that it will point to, but does *not* declare the extent in each dimension. Thus the following statements are legal:

```
REAL, DIMENSION(100,1000), TARGET :: mydata
REAL, DIMENSION(:,:), POINTER :: pointer
pointer => array
```

A pointer can point not only to an array but also to a *subset* of an array (an array section). Any array section that can be defined by a subscript triplet can be used as the target of a pointer. For example, the program in Figure 15-8 declares a 16-element integer array info, and fills the array with the values 1 through 16. This array serves as the target for a series of pointers. The first pointer ptr1 points to the entire array, while the second one points to the array section defined by the subscript triplet ptr1(2::2). This will consist of the even subscripts 2, 4, 6, 8, 10, 12, 14, and 16 from the original array. The third pointer also uses the subscript triplet 2::2, and it points the even elements from the list pointed to by the second pointer. This will consist of the subscripts 4, 8, 12, and 16 from the original array. This process of selection continues with the remaining pointers.

FIGURE 15-8
Program to illustrate the use of pointers with array sections defined by subscript triplets.

```
PROGRAM array_ptr
IMPLICIT NONE
INTEGER :: i
INTEGER, DIMENSION(16), TARGET :: info = (/ (i, i = 1,16) /)
INTEGER, DIMENSION(:), POINTER :: ptr1, ptr2, ptr3, ptr4, ptr5
ptr1 => info
ptr2 => ptr1(2::2)
ptr3 => ptr2(2::2)
ptr4 => ptr3(2::2)
ptr5 => ptr4(2::2)
WRITE (*,'(A,16I3)') ' ptr1 = ', ptr1
WRITE (*,'(A,16I3)') ' ptr2 = ', ptr2
WRITE (*,'(A,16I3)') ' ptr3 = ', ptr3
WRITE (*,'(A,16I3)') ' ptr4 = ', ptr4
WRITE (*,'(A,16I3)') ' ptr5 = ', ptr5
END PROGRAM array_ptr
```

When this program is executed, the results are:

```
C:\book\chap15>array_ptr
ptr1 =  1  2  3  4  5  6  7  8  9  10  11  12  13  14  15  16
ptr2 =  2  4  6  8 10 12 14 16
ptr3 =  4  8 12 16
ptr4 =  8 16
ptr5 = 16
```

Although pointers work with array sections defined by subscript triplets, *they do not work with array sections defined by vector subscripts*. Thus, the code in Figure 15-9 is illegal and will produce a compilation error.

FIGURE 15-9
Program to illustrate invalid pointer assignments to array sections defined with vector subscripts.

```
PROGRAM bad
IMPLICIT NONE
INTEGER :: i
INTEGER, DIMENSION(3) :: subs = (/ 1, 8, 11 /)
```

(continued)

(concluded)

```
INTEGER, DIMENSION(16), TARGET :: info = (/ (i, i=1,16) /)
INTEGER, DIMENSION(:), POINTER :: ptr1
ptr1 => info(subs)
WRITE (*,'(A,16I3)') ' ptr1 = ', ptr1
END PROGRAM bad
```

15.4

DYNAMIC MEMORY ALLOCATION WITH POINTERS

One of the most powerful features of pointers is that they can be used to dynamically create variables or arrays whenever required, and then to release the space used by the dynamic variables or arrays once they are no longer needed. The procedure for doing this is similar to that used to create allocatable arrays. Memory is allocated using an ALLOCATE statement, and it is deallocated by using a DEALLOCATE statement. The ALLOCATE statement has the same form as the ALLOCATE statement for an allocatable array. The statement takes the form

```
ALLOCATE (pointer(size),[ ...,] STAT=status)
```

where *pointer* is the name of a pointer to the variable or array being created, *size* is the dimension specification if the object being created is an array, and *status* is the result of the operation. If the allocation is successful, then the status will be 0. If it fails, a processor-dependent positive integer will be returned in the status variable. The STAT= clause is optional but should always be used, since a failed allocation statement without a STAT= clause will cause a program to abort.

This statement creates an unnamed data object of the specified size and the pointer's type, and sets the pointer to point to the object. Because the new data object is unnamed, it can be accessed only by using the pointer. After the statement is executed, the association status of the pointer will become *associated.* If the pointer was associated with another data object before the ALLOCATE statement is executed, then that association is lost.

The data object created by using the pointer ALLOCATE statement is unnamed, and so can be accessed only by the pointer. *If all pointers to that memory are either nullified or reassociated with other targets, then the data object will no longer be accessible by the program.* The object will still be present in memory, but it will no longer be possible to use it. Thus careless programming with pointers can result in memory being filled with unusable space. This unusable memory is commonly referred to as a "memory leak." One symptom of this problem is that a program seems to grow larger and larger as it continues to execute, until it either fills the entire computer or uses all available memory. An example of a program with a memory leak is shown in Figure 15-10. In this program, 10-element arrays are allocated using both ptr1 and ptr2. The two arrays are initialized to different values, and those values are printed out. Then ptr2 is assigned to point to the same memory as ptr1 in a pointer assignment statement. *After that statement, the memory that was assigned to* ptr2 *is no longer accessible to the program.* That memory has been "lost" and will not be recovered until the program stops executing.

15

FIGURE 15-10
Program to illustrate memory leaks in a program.

```
PROGRAM mem_leak
IMPLICIT NONE
INTEGER :: i, istat
INTEGER, DIMENSION(:), POINTER :: ptr1, ptr2

! Check associated status of ptrs.
WRITE (*,'(A,2L5)') ' Are ptr1, ptr2 associated? ', &
     ASSOCIATED(ptr1), ASSOCIATED(ptr2)

! Allocate and initialize memory
ALLOCATE (ptr1(1:10), STAT=istat)
ALLOCATE (ptr2(1:10), STAT=istat)
ptr1 = (/ (i, i = 1,10 ) /)
ptr2 = (/ (i, i = 11,20 ) /)

! Check associated status of ptrs.
WRITE (*,'(A,2L5)') ' Are ptr1, ptr2 associated? ', &
     ASSOCIATED(ptr1), ASSOCIATED(ptr2)

WRITE (*,'(A,10I3)') ' ptr1 = ', ptr1    ! Write out data
WRITE (*,'(A,10I3)') ' ptr2 = ', ptr2

ptr2 =>ptr1                              ! Reassignptr2

WRITE (*,'(A,10I3)') ' ptr1 = ', ptr1    ! Write out data
WRITE (*,'(A,10I3)') ' ptr2 = ', ptr2

NULLIFY(ptr1)                            ! Nullify pointer
DEALLOCATE(ptr2, STAT=istat)             ! Deallocate memory

END PROGRAM mem_leak
```

When program mem_leak executes, the results are:

```
C:\book\chap15>mem_leak
Are ptr1, ptr2 associated?      F    F
Are ptr1, ptr2 associated?      T    T
ptr1 =   1  2  3  4  5  6  7  8  9 10
ptr2 =  11 12 13 14 15 16 17 18 19 20
ptr1 =   1  2  3  4  5  6  7  8  9 10
ptr2 =   1  2  3  4  5  6  7  8  9 10
```

Memory that has been allocated with an ALLOCATE statement should be deallocated with a DEALLOCATE statement when the program is finished using it. If it is not
deallocated, then that memory will be unavailable for any other use until the program
finishes executing. When memory is deallocated in a pointer DEALLOCATE statement,
the pointer to that memory is nullified at the same time. Thus the statement,

```
DEALLOCATE(ptr2, STAT=istat)
```

both deallocates the memory pointed to and nullifies the pointer ptr2.

15

The pointer DEALLOCATE statement can only deallocate memory that was created by an ALLOCATE statement. It is important to remember this fact. If the pointer in the statement happens to point to a target that was not created with an ALLOCATE statement, then the DEALLOCATE statement will fail, and the program will abort unless the STAT= clause was specified. The association between such pointers and their targets can be broken by the use of the NULLIFY statement.

A potentially serious problem can occur in deallocating memory. Suppose that two pointers ptr1 and ptr2 both point to the same allocated array. If pointer ptr1 is used in a DEALLOCATE statement to deallocate the array, then that pointer is nullified. However, ptr2 will *not* be nullified. *It will continue to point to the memory location where the array used to be,* even if that memory location is reused for some other purpose by the program. If that pointer is used to either read data from or write data to the memory location, it will be either reading unpredictable values or overwriting memory used for some other purpose. In either case, using that pointer is a recipe for disaster! If a piece of allocated memory is deallocated, then *all* of the pointers to that memory should be nullified or reassigned. One of them will be automatically nullified by the DEALLOCATE statement, and any others should be nullified in NULLIFY statements.

Good Programming Practice

Always nullify or reassign *all* pointers to a memory location when that memory is deallocated. One of them will be automatically nullified by the DEALLOCATE statement, and any others should be manually nullified in NULLIFY statements or reassigned in pointer assignment statements.

Figure 15-11 illustrates the effect of using a pointer after the memory to which it points has been deallocated. In this example, two pointers ptr1 and ptr2 both point to the same 10-element allocatable array. When that array is deallocated with ptr1, that pointer becomes disassociated. Pointer ptr2 remains associated, but now points to a piece of memory that can be freely reused by the program for other purposes. When ptr2 is accessed in the next WRITE statement, it points to an unallocated part of memory that could contain anything. Then, a new two-element array is allocated by using ptr1. Depending on the behavior of the compiler, this array could be allocated over the freed memory from the previous array, or it could be allocated somewhere else in memory.

FIGURE 15-11
Program to illustrate the effect of using a pointer after the memory to which it points has been deallocated.

```
PROGRAM bad_ptr
IMPLICIT NONE
INTEGER :: i, istat
INTEGER, DIMENSION(:), POINTER :: ptr1, ptr2
```

(*continued*)

(*concluded*)

```
! Allocate and initialize memory
ALLOCATE (ptr1(1:10), STAT=istat)        ! Allocate ptr1
ptr1 = (/ (i, i = 1, 10) /)              ! Initizlize ptr1
ptr2 => ptr1                             ! Assign ptr2

! Check associated status of ptrs.
WRITE (*,'(A,2L5)') ' Are ptr1, ptr2 associated? ', &
        ASSOCIATED(ptr1), ASSOCIATED(ptr2)

WRITE (*,'(A,10I3)') ' ptr1 = ', ptr1    ! Write out data
WRITE (*,'(A,10I3)') ' ptr2 = ', ptr2

! Now deallocate memory associated with ptr1
DEALLOCATE(ptr1, STAT=istat)             ! Deallocate memory

! Check associated status of ptrs.
WRITE (*,'(A,2L5)') ' Are ptr1, ptr2 associated? ', &
        ASSOCIATED(ptr1), ASSOCIATED(ptr2)

! Write out memory associated with ptr2
WRITE(*,'(A,10I3)')'ptr2 = ',ptr2

ALLOCATE (ptr1(1:2), STAT=istat)         ! Reallocate ptr1
ptr1 = (/21,22/)

WRITE (*,'(A,10I3)') ' ptr1 = ', ptr1    ! Write out data
WRITE (*,'(A,10I3)') ' ptr2 = ', ptr2

END PROGRAM bad_ptr
```

These results of this program will vary from compiler to compiler, since deallocated memory may be treated differently on different processors. When this program is executed on the Lahey Fortran compiler, the results are:

```
C:\book\chap15>bad_ptr
Are ptr1, ptr2 associated?     T    T
ptr1 =   1   2   3   4   5   6   7   8   9  10
ptr2 =   1   2   3   4   5   6   7   8   9  10
Are ptr1, ptr2 associated?     F    T
ptr2 =   1   2   3   4   5   6   7   8   9  10
ptr1 =  21  22
ptr2 =  21  22   3   4   5   6   7   8   9  10
```

After `ptr1` was used to deallocate the memory, its pointer status changed to *disassociated,* while the status of `ptr2` remained *associated*. When `ptr2` was then used to examine memory, it pointed to the memory location *where the array used to be,* and saw the old values because the memory had not yet been reused. Finally, when `ptr1` was used to allocate a new two-element array, some of the freed-up memory was reused.

It is possible to mix pointers and allocatable arrays in a single `ALLOCATE` statement or `DEALLOCATE` statement, if desired.

15

15.5

USING POINTERS AS COMPONENTS OF DERIVED DATA TYPES

Pointers may appear as components of derived data types. Pointers in derived data types may even point to the derived data type being defined. This feature is very useful, since it permits us to construct various types of dynamic data structures linked together by successive pointers during the execution of a program. The simplest such structure is a **linked list,** which is a list of values linked together in a linear fashion by pointers. For example, the following derived data type contains a real number and a pointer to another variable of the same type:

```
TYPE :: real_value
   REAL :: value
   TYPE (real_value), POINTER :: p
END TYPE
```

A linked list is a series of variables of a derived data type, with the pointer from each variable pointing to the next variable in the list. The pointer in the last variable is nullified, since there is no variable after it in the list. Two pointers (say, head and tail) are also defined to point to the first and last variables in the list. Figure 15-12 illustrates this structure for variables of type real_value.

Linked lists are much more flexible than arrays. Recall that a static array must be declared with a fixed size when a program is compiled. As a result, we must size each such array to be large enough to handle the *largest problem* that a program will ever be required to solve. This large memory requirement can result in a program being too large to run on some computers, and also results in a waste of memory most of the time that the program is executed. Even allocatable arrays don't completely solve the problem. Allocatable arrays prevent memory waste by allowing us to allocate only the amount of memory needed for a specific problem, but we must know before we allocate the memory just how many values will be present during a particular run. In contrast, *linked lists permit us to add elements one at a time,* and we do not have to know in advance how many elements will ultimately be in the list.

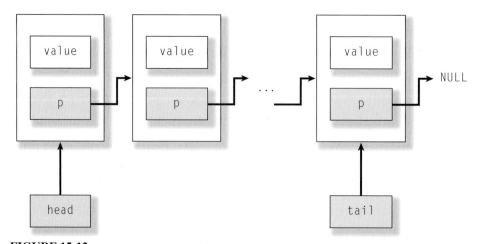

FIGURE 15-12
A typical linked list. Note that pointer in each variable points to the next variable in the list.

When a program containing a linked list first starts to execute, there are no values in the list. In that case, the head and tail pointers have nothing to point to, so they are both nullified (see Figure 15-13a). When the first value is read, a variable of the

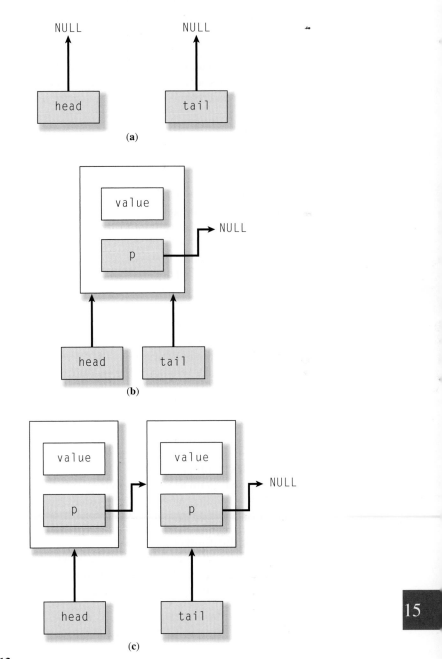

FIGURE 15-13
Building a linked list: (a) The initial situation with an empty list. (b) After adding one value to the list. (c) After adding a second value to the list.

derived data type is created, and the value is stored in that variable. The `head` and `tail` pointers are set to point to the variable, and the pointer in the variable is nullified (Figure 15-13*b*).

When the next value is read, a new variable of the derived data type is created, the value is stored in that variable, and the pointer in the variable is nullified. The pointer in the previous variable is set to point to the new variable, and the `tail` pointer is set to point to the new variable. The `head` pointer does not change (Figure 15-13*c*). This process is repeated as each new value is added to the list.

Once all of the values are read, the program can process them by starting at the `head` pointer and following the pointers in the list until the `tail` pointer is reached.

EXAMPLE 15-1

Creating a Linked List:

In this example, we will write a simple program that reads in a list of real numbers and then writes them out again. The number of values that the program can handle should be limited only by the amount of memory in the computer. This program doesn't do anything interesting by itself, but building a linked list in memory is a necessary first step in many practical problems. We will learn how to create the list in this example, and then start using lists to do useful work in later examples.

SOLUTION
We will use a linked list to hold the input values, since the size of a linked list can keep growing as long as additional memory can be allocated for new values. Each input value will be stored in a variable of the following derived data type, where the element p points to the next item in the list and the element `value` stores the input real value.

```
TYPE :: real_value
   REAL :: value
      TYPE (real_value), POINTER :: p
END TYPE
```

1. **State the problem.**
   Write a program to read an arbitrary number of real values from a file and to store them in a linked list. After all of the values have been read, the program should write them to the standard output device.

2. **Define the inputs and outputs.**
   The input to the program will be a file name, and a list of real values arranged one value per line in that file. The output from the program will be the real values in the file listed to the standard output device.

3. **Describe the algorithm.**
   This program can be broken down into four major steps

```
Get the input file name
Open the input file
```

```
Read the input data into a linked list
Write the data to the standard output device
```

The first three major steps of the program are to get the name of the input file, to open the file, and to read in the data. We must prompt the user for the input file name, read in the name, and open the file. If the file open is successful, we must read in the data, keeping track of the number of values read. Since we don't know how many data values to expect, a WHILE loop is appropriate for the READ. The pseudocode for these steps is shown below:

```
Prompt user for the input file name "filename"
Read the file name "filename"
OPEN file "filename"
IF OPEN is successful THEN
   WHILE
      Read value into temp
      IF read not successful EXIT
      nvals ← nvals + 1
      (ALLOCATE new list item & store value)
   End of WHILE
   ...                        (Insert writing step here)
End of IF
```

The step of adding a new item to the linked list needs to be examined more carefully. When a new variable is added to the list, there are two possibilities: either there is nothing in the list yet, or else there are already values in the list. If there is nothing in the list yet, then the head and tail pointers are nullified, so we will allocate the new variable using the head pointer, and point the tail pointer to the same place. The pointer p within the new variable must be nullified because there is nothing to point to yet, and the real value will be stored in the element value of the variable.

If there are already values in the list, then the tail pointer points to the last variable in the list. In that case, we will allocate the new variable, using the pointer p within the last variable in the list, and then point the tail pointer to the new variable. The pointer p within the new variable must be nullified because there is nothing to point to, and the real value will be stored in the element value of the new variable. The pseudocode for the steps is:

```
Read value into temp
IF read not successful EXIT
nvals ← nvals + 1
IF  head is not associated THEN
   ! The list is empty
   ALLOCATE head
   tail => head          ! Tail points to first value
   NULLIFY tail%p        ! Nullify p within 1st value
   tail%value ← temp     ! Store new number
ELSE
   ! The list already has values
   ALLOCATE tail%p
   tail => tail%p        ! Tail now points to new last value
   NULLIFY tail%p        ! Nullify p within new last value
   tail%value ← temp     ! Store new number
END of IF
```

15

The final step is to write the values in the linked list. To do this, we must go back to the head of the list and follow the pointers in it to the end of the list. We will define a local pointer `ptr` to point to the value currently being printed out. The pseudocode for this step is:

```
ptr => head
WHILE ptr is associated
    WRITE ptr%value
    ptr => ptr%p
END of WHILE
```

4. **Turn the algorithm into Fortran statements.**
   The resulting Fortran subroutine is shown in Figure 15-14.

FIGURE 15-14
Program to read in a series of real values and store them in a linked list.

```
PROGRAM linked_list
!
!   Purpose:
!     To read in a series of real values from an input data file
!     and store them in a linked list. After the list is read in
!     it will be written back to the standard output device.
!
!   Record of revisions:
!       Date        Programmer         Description of change
!       ====        ==========         =====================
!     12/23/06    S. J. Chapman        Original code
!
IMPLICIT NONE

! Derived data type to store real values in
TYPE :: real_value
   REAL :: value
   TYPE (real_value), POINTER :: p
END TYPE

! Data dictionary: declare variable types & definitions
TYPE (real_value), POINTER :: head   ! Pointer to head of list
CHARACTER(len=20) :: filename         ! Input data file name
INTEGER :: nvals = 0                   ! Number of data read
TYPE (real_value), POINTER :: ptr    ! Temporary pointer
TYPE (real_value), POINTER :: tail   ! Pointer to tail of list
INTEGER :: istat                       ! Status: 0 for success
REAL :: temp                           ! Temporary variable

! Get the name of the file containing the input data.
WRITE (*,*) 'Enter the file name with the data to be read: '
READ (*,'(A20)') filename

! Open input data file.
```

(continued)

(concluded)

```
OPEN ( UNIT=9, FILE=filename, STATUS='OLD', ACTION='READ', &
       IOSTAT=istat )

! Was the OPEN successful?
fileopen: IF ( istat == 0 ) THEN              ! Open successful

   ! The file was opened successfully, so read the data from
   ! it, and store it in the linked list.
   input: DO
      READ (9, *, IOSTAT=istat) temp          ! Get value
      IF ( istat /= 0 ) EXIT                   ! Exit on end of data
      nvals = nvals + 1                        ! Bump count

      IF (.NOT. ASSOCIATED(head)) THEN         ! No values in list
         ALLOCATE(head,STAT=istat)             ! Allocate new value
         tail => head                          ! Tail pts to new value
         NULLIFY (tail%p)                       ! Nullify p in new value
         tail%value = temp                     ! Store number
      ELSE                                     ! Values already in list
         ALLOCATE(tail%p,STAT=istat)           ! Allocate new value
         tail => tail%p                        ! Tail pts to new value
         NULLIFY (tail%p)                       ! Nullify p in new value
         tail%value = temp                     ! Store number
      END IF
   END DO input

   ! Now, write out the data.
   ptr =>head
   output: DO
      IF ( .NOT. ASSOCIATED(ptr) ) EXIT        ! Pointer valid?
      WRITE (*,'(1X,F10.4)') ptr%value         ! Yes: Write value
      ptr =>ptr%p                              ! Get next pointer
   END DO output

ELSE fileopen

   ! Else file open failed. Tell user.
   WRITE (*,'(1X,A,I6)') 'File open failed--status = ', istat

END IF fileopen

END PROGRAM linked_list
```

5. Test the resulting Fortran programs.

To test this program, we must generate a file of input data. If the following 10 real values are placed in a file called input.dat, then we can use that file to test the program: 1.0, 3.0, −4.4, 5., 2., 9.0, 10.1, −111.1, 0.0, −111.1. When the program is executed with this file, the results are:

```
C:\book\chap15>linked_list
Enter the file name with the data to be read:
```

```
input.dat
   1.0000
   3.0000
  -4.4000
   5.0000
   2.0000
   9.0000
  10.1000
-111.1000
    .0000
-111.1000
```

The program appears to be working properly. Note that the program does not check the status of the ALLOCATE statements. This was done deliberately to make the manipulations of the linked list as clear as possible. In any real program, these statuses should be checked to detect memory problems so that the program can shut down gracefully.

EXAMPLE 15-2

The Insertion Sort:

We introduced the selection sort in Chapter 6. That algorithm sorted a list by searching for the smallest value in the list and placing it at the top. Then it searched for the smallest value in the remaining portion of the list, and placed it in the second position, and so forth until all of the values were sorted.

Another possible sorting algorithm is the *insertion sort*. The insertion sort works by placing each value in its proper position in the list as it is read in. If the value is smaller than any previous value in the list, then it is placed at the top. If the value is larger than any previous value in the list, then it is placed at the bottom. If the value is in between, then the number is inserted at the appropriate place in the middle of the list.

An insertion sort of the values 7, 2, 11, −1, and 3 is shown in Figure 15-15. The first value read is a 7. Since there are no other values in the list, it is placed at the top. The next value read is a 2. Since it is smaller than the 7, it is placed above the 7 in the list. The third value read is an 11. Since it is larger than any other value in the list, it is placed at the bottom. The fourth value read is a −1. Since it is smaller than any other value in the list, it is placed at the top. The fifth value read is a 3. Since it is larger than 2 and smaller than 7, it is placed between them in the list. In the insertion sort, the list is always kept sorted as each value is read.

Linked lists are ideally suited for implementing an insertion sort, since new values can be added at the front, at the end, or anywhere in the middle of the list by simply changing pointers. Use a linked list to implement an insertion sort algorithm to sort an arbitrary number of integer values.

SOLUTION

We will use a linked list to hold the input values, since it is easy to insert new values anywhere in the linked list by simply changing pointers. Each input value will be

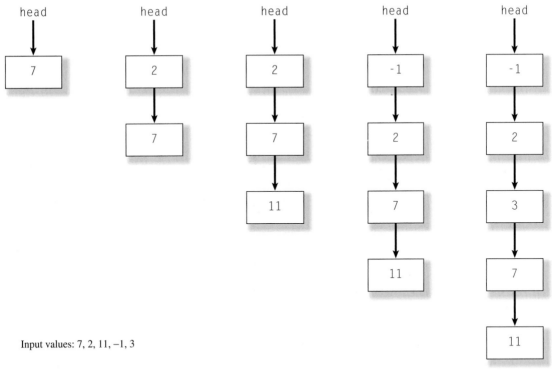

Input values: 7, 2, 11, −1, 3

FIGURE 15-15
Sorting the values 7, 2, 11, −1, and 3 with the insertion sort.

read and stored in a variable of the following derived data type, where the pointer
`next_value` points to the next item in the list and the element `value` stores the input
integer value.

```
TYPE :: int_value
    INTEGER :: value
    TYPE (int_value), POINTER :: next_value
END TYPE
```

Each value will be read, compared to all previous values, and inserted at the proper
point in the list.

1. **State the problem.**
   Write a program to read an arbitrary number of integer values from a file and to
   sort them, using an insertion sort. After all of the values have been read and sorted, the
   program should write the sorted list out to the standard output device.

2. **Define the inputs and outputs.**
   The input to the program will be a file name, and a list of integer values arranged
   one value per line in that file. The output from the program will be the sorted integer
   values listed to the standard output device.

15

3. **Describe the algorithm.**

The pseudocode for this program is shown below:

```
Prompt user for the input file name "filename"
Read the file name "filename"
OPEN file "filename"
IF OPEN is successful THEN
    WHILE
        Read value into temp
        IF read not successful EXIT
        nvals ← nvals + 1
        ALLOCATE new data item & store value
        Insert item at proper point in list
    End of WHILE
    Write the data to the standard output device
End of IF
```

The step of adding a new item to the linked list needs to be examined in more detail. When we add a new variable to the list, there are two possibilities: either there is nothing in the list yet, or else there are already values in the list. If there is nothing in the list yet, then the head and tail pointers are nullified, so we will allocate the new variable by using the head pointer, and point the tail pointer to the same place. The pointer next_value within the new variable must be nullified because there is nothing to point to yet, and the integer will be stored in the element value of the variable.

If there are already values in the list, then we must search to find the proper place to insert the new value into the list. There are three possibilities here. If the number is smaller than the first number in the list (pointed to by the head pointer), then we will add the value at the front of the list. If the number is greater than or equal to the last number in the list (pointed to by the tail pointer), then we will add the value at the end of the list. If the number is between those values, we will search until we locate the two values that it lies between, and insert the new value there. Note that we must allow for the possibility that the new value is equal to one of numbers already in the list. The pseudocode for these steps is:

```
Read value into temp
IF read not successful EXIT
nvals ← nvals + 1
ALLOCATE ptr
ptr%value ← temp
IF head is not associated THEN
    ! The list is empty
    head => ptr
    tail => head
    NULLIFY tail%next_value
ELSE
    ! The list already has values. Check for
    ! location for new value.
    IF ptr%value < head%value THEN
        ! Add at front
        ptr%next_value => head
        head => ptr
```

```
        ELSE IF ptr%value >= tail%value THEN
            ! Add at rear
            tail%next_value => ptr
            tail => ptr
            NULLIFY tail%next_value
        ELSE
            ! Find place to add value
            ptr1 => head
            ptr2 => ptr1%next_value
            DO
                IF ptr%value >= ptr1%value AND
                   ptr%value < ptr2%value THEN
                   ! Insert value here
                   ptr%next_value => ptr2
                   ptr1%next_value => ptr
                   EXIT
                END of IF
                ptr1 => ptr2
                ptr2 => ptr2%next_value
            END of DO
        END of IF
    END of IF
```

The final step is to write the values in the linked list. To do this, we must go back to the head of the list and follow the pointers to the end of the list. We will use pointer ptr to point to the value currently being printed out. The pseudocode for this step is:

```
ptr => head
WHILE ptr is associated
    WRITE ptr%value
    ptr => ptr%next_value
END of WHILE
```

4. **Turn the algorithm into Fortran statements.**
   The resulting Fortran subroutine is shown in Figure 15-16.

FIGURE 15-16

Program to read in a series of integer values and sort them, using the insertion sort.

```
PROGRAM insertion_sort
!
!  Purpose:
!    To read a series of integer values from an input data file
!    and sort them using an insertion sort. After the values
!    are sorted, they will be written back to the standard
!    output device.
!
!  Record of revisions:
!      Date        Programmer           Description of change
!      ====        ==========           =====================
!    12/23/06    S. J. Chapman          Original code
!
IMPLICIT NONE
```

15

(continued)

(*continued*)

```fortran
! Derived data type to store integer values in
TYPE :: int_value
   INTEGER :: value
   TYPE (int_value), POINTER :: next_value
END TYPE

! Data dictionary: declare variable types & definitions
TYPE (int_value), POINTER :: head    ! Pointer to head of list
CHARACTER(len=20) :: filename         ! Input data file name
INTEGER :: istat                      ! Status: 0 for success
INTEGER :: nvals = 0                   ! Number of data read
TYPE (int_value), POINTER :: ptr     ! Ptr to new value
TYPE (int_value), POINTER :: ptr1    ! Temp ptr for search
TYPE (int_value), POINTER :: ptr2    ! Temp ptr for search
TYPE (int_value), POINTER :: tail    ! Pointer to tail of list
INTEGER :: temp                       ! Temporary variable

! Get the name of the file containing the input data.
WRITE (*,*) 'Enter the file name with the data to be sorted: '
READ (*,'(A20)') filename

! Open input data file.
OPEN ( UNIT=9, FILE=filename, STATUS='OLD', ACTION='READ', &
       IOSTAT=istat )

! Was the OPEN successful?
fileopen: IF ( istat == 0 ) THEN              ! Open successful

   ! The file was opened successfully, so read the data value
   ! to sort, allocate a variable for it, and locate the proper
   ! point to insert the new value into the list.
   input: DO
      READ (9, *, IOSTAT=istat) temp           ! Get value
      IF ( istat /= 0 ) EXIT input             ! Exit on end of data
      nvals = nvals + 1                         ! Bump count

      ALLOCATE (ptr,STAT=istat)                 ! Allocate space
      ptr%value = temp                          ! Store number

      ! Now find out where to put it in the list.
      new: IF (.NOT. ASSOCIATED(head)) THEN   ! No values in list
         head => ptr                           ! Place at front
         tail => head                          ! Tail pts to new value
         NULLIFY (ptr%next_value)              ! Nullify next ptr
      ELSE
         ! Values already in list. Check for location.
         front: IF(ptr%value < head%value)THEN
            ! Add at front of list
            ptr%next_value => head
            head => ptr
         ELSE IF (ptr%value >= tail%value)THEN
            ! Add at end of list
            tail%next_value => ptr
```

(*continued*)

(concluded)

```
                    tail => ptr
                    NULLIFY ( tail%next_value )
                 ELSE
                    ! Find place to add value
                    ptr1 => head
                    ptr2 => ptr1%next_value
                    search: DO
                        IF ( (ptr%value >= ptr1%value) .AND. &
                             (ptr%value < ptr2%value) ) THEN
                           ! Insert value here
                           ptr%next_value => ptr2
                           ptr1%next_value => ptr
                           EXIT search
                        END IF
                        ptr1 => ptr2
                        ptr2 => ptr2%next_value
                    END DO search
                 END IF front
           END IF new
      END DO input

      ! Now, write out the data.
      ptr => head
      output: DO
         IF ( .NOT. ASSOCIATED(ptr) ) EXIT   ! Pointer valid?
         WRITE (*,'(1X,I10)') ptr%value      ! Yes: Write value
         ptr => ptr%next_value               ! Get next pointer
      END DO output

ELSE fileopen

   ! Else file open failed. Tell user.
   WRITE (*,'(1X,A,I6)') 'File open failed--status = ', istat

END IF fileopen

END PROGRAM insertion_sort
```

5. Test the resulting Fortran programs.

To test this program, we must generate a file of input data. If the following seven integer values are placed in a file called 'input1.dat', then we can use that file to test the program: 7, 2, 11, −1, 3, 2, and 0. When the program is executed with this file, the results are:

```
C:\book\chap15>insertion_sort
Enter the file name with the data to be sorted:
input1.dat
        -1
         0
         2
         2
         3
         7
        11
```

15

The program appears to be working properly. Note that this program also does not check the status of the ALLOCATE statements. This was done deliberately to make the manipulations as clear as possible. (At one point in the program, the DO and IF structures are nested six deep!) In any real program, these statuses should be checked to detect memory problems so that the program can shut down gracefully.

15.6
ARRAYS OF POINTERS

It is not possible to declare an array of pointers in Fortran. In a pointer declaration, the DIMENSION attribute *refers to the dimension of the pointer's target,* not to the dimension of the pointer itself. The dimension must be declared with a deferred-shape specification, and the actual size will be the size of the target with which the pointer is associated. In the example shown below, the subscript on the pointer refers the corresponding position in the target array, so the value of ptr(4) is 6.

```
REAL, DIMENSION(:), POINTER :: ptr
REAL, DIMENSION(5), TARGET :: tgt = (/ -2, 5., 0., 6., 1 /)
ptr => tgt
WRITE (*,*) ptr(4)
```

There are many applications in which *arrays of pointers* are useful. Fortunately, we can create an array of pointers for those applications by using derived data types. It is illegal to have an array of pointers in Fortran, but it is perfectly legal to have an array of any derived data type. Therefore, we can declare a derived data type containing only a pointer, and then create an array of that data type! For example, the program in Figure 15-17 declares an array of a derived data type containing real pointers, each of which points to a real array.

FIGURE 15-17
Program illustrating how to create an array of pointers by using a derived data type.

```
PROGRAM ptr_array
IMPLICIT NONE
TYPE :: ptr
   REAL, DIMENSION(:), POINTER :: p
END TYPE
TYPE (ptr), DIMENSION(3) :: p1
REAL, DIMENSION(4), TARGET :: a = (/ 1.,  2.,  3.,  4. /)
REAL, DIMENSION(4), TARGET :: b = (/ 5.,  6.,  7.,  8. /)
REAL, DIMENSION(4), TARGET :: c = (/ 9., 10., 11., 12. /)
p1(1)%p => a
p1(2)%p => b
p1(3)%p => c
WRITE (*,*) p1(3)%p
WRITE (*,*) p1(2)%p(3)
END PROGRAM ptr_array
```

With the declarations in program `ptr_array`, the expression `p1(3)%p` refers to the *third* array (array c), so the first WRITE statement should print out 9., 10., 11., and 12. The expression `p1(2)%p(3)` refers to the *third* value of the *second* array (array b), so the second WRITE statement prints out the value 7. When this program is compiled and executed with the Compaq Visual Fortran compiler, the results are:

```
C:\book\chap15>ptr_array
     9.000000        10.000000        11.000000        12.000000
     7.000000
```

Quiz 15-1

This quiz provides a quick check to see if you have understood the concepts introduced in Sections 15.1 through 15.6. If you have trouble with the quiz, reread the sections, ask your instructor, or discuss the material with a fellow student. The answers to this quiz are found in the back of the book.

1. What is a pointer? What is a target? What is the difference between a pointer and an ordinary variable?

2. What is a pointer assignment statement? What is the difference between a pointer assignment statement and an ordinary assignment statement?

3. What are the possible association statuses of a pointer? How can the association status be changed?

4. What is dereferencing?

5. How can memory be dynamically allocated with pointers? How can it be deallocated?

Is each of the following code segments valid or invalid? If a code segment is valid, explain what it does. If it is invalid, explain why.

6.
```
REAL, TARGET :: value = 35.2
REAL, POINTER :: ptr2
ptr2 = value
```

7.
```
REAL, TARGET :: value = 35.2
REAL, POINTER :: ptr2
ptr2 => value
```

8.
```
INTEGER, DIMENSION(10,10), TARGET :: array
REAL, DIMENSION(:,:), POINTER :: ptr3
ptr3 => array
```

9.
```
REAL, DIMENSION(10,10) :: array
REAL, DIMENSION(:,:) :: ptr4
POINTER :: ptr4
```

(continued)

15

(concluded)

```
        TARGET :: array
        ptr4 => array

    10. INTEGER, POINTER :: ptr
        WRITE (*,*) ASSOCIATED(ptr)
        ALLOCATE (ptr)
        ptr = 137
        WRITE (*,*) ASSOCIATED(ptr), ptr
        NULLIFY (ptr)

    11. INTEGER, DIMENSION(:), POINTER :: ptr1, ptr2
        INTEGER :: istat
        ALLOCATE (ptr1(10), STAT=istat)
        ptr1 = 0
        ptr1(3) = 17
        ptr2 => ptr1
        DEALLOCATE (ptr1)
        WRITE (*,*) ptr2

    12. TYPE mytype
            INTEGER, DIMENSION(:), POINTER :: array
        END TYPE
        TYPE (mytype), DIMENSION(10) :: p
        INTEGER :: i, istat
        DO i = 1, 10
            ALLOCATE (p(i).array(10), STAT=istat)
            DO j = 1, 10
                p(i)%array(j) = 10*(i-1) + j
            END DO
        END DO
        WRITE (*,'(1X,10I4)') p(4).array
        WRITE (*,'(1X,10I4)') p(7).array(1)
```

15.7

USING POINTERS IN PROCEDURES

Pointers may be used as dummy arguments in procedures and may be passed as actual arguments to procedures. In addition, a function result can be a pointer. The following restrictions apply if pointers are used in procedures:

1. If a procedure has dummy arguments with either the POINTER or TARGET attributes, then the procedure must have an explicit interface.

2. If a dummy argument is a pointer, then the actual argument passed to the procedure must be a pointer of the same type, kind, and rank.

3. In Fortran 95, a pointer dummy argument cannot have an INTENT attribute.

4. A pointer dummy argument cannot appear in an ELEMENTAL procedure.

It is important to be careful in passing pointers to procedures. As programs get larger and more flexible, we will often get to a situation where pointers are allocated in one procedure, used in others, and finally deallocated and nullified in yet another. In such a complex program, it is *very* easy to make errors such as attempting to work with disassociated pointers, or allocating new arrays with pointers that are already in use. It is very important that the status results be checked for all ALLOCATE and DEALLOCATE statements, and that the status of pointers be checked by using the ASSOCIATED function.

When a pointer is used to pass data to a procedure, we automatically know the type of the data associated with the pointer from the type of the pointer itself. If the pointer points to an array, we will know the rank of the array, but not its extent or size. If we need to know the extent or size of the array, then we can use the intrinsic functions LBOUND and UBOUND to determine the bounds of each dimension of the array.

EXAMPLE 15-3

Extracting the Diagonal Elements from a Matrix:

To illustrate the proper use of pointers, we will write a subroutine that accepts a pointer to a square matrix, and returns a pointer to an array containing the diagonal elements of the matrix.

SOLUTION

A subroutine with appropriate error checking is shown in Figure 15-18. This example subroutine accepts a pointer to a two-dimensional square array, and returns the diagonal elements of the array in a one-dimensional array that it allocates on a separate pointer. The subroutine checks the association status of the input pointer to ensure that it is currently associated, checks the array to make sure that it is square, and checks the association status of the output pointer to ensure that it is *not* currently associated. (The last test ensures that we don't accidentally reuse a pointer that is currently in use. Reusing the pointer might leave the original data inaccessible if there were no other pointer to it.) If any of the conditions fail, then an appropriate error flag is set and the subroutine returns to the calling program unit.

FIGURE 15-18
Subroutine to extract the diagonal elements from a square array. This subroutine illustrates the proper technique for working with pointers passed as calling arguments.

```
SUBROUTINE get_diagonal ( ptr_a, ptr_b, error )
!
!  Purpose:
!    To extract the diagonal elements from the rank 2
!    square array pointed to by ptr_a, and store them in
!    a rank 1 array allocated on ptr_b. The following
!    error conditions are defined:
!      0 -- No error.
!      1 -- ptr_a not associated on input
```

15

(continued)

(concluded)

```
!      2 -- ptr_b already associated on input
!      3 -- Array on ptr_a not suqare
!      4 -- Unable to allocate memory for ptr_b
!
!   Record of revisions:
!      Date        Programmer            Description of change
!      ====        ==========            =====================
!      12/23/06    S. J. Chapman         Original code
!
IMPLICIT NONE

! Data dictionary: declare calling parameter types & definitions
INTEGER, DIMENSION(:,:), POINTER :: ptr_a ! Ptr to square array
INTEGER, DIMENSION(:), POINTER :: ptr_b   ! Ptr to output array
INTEGER, INTENT(OUT) :: error             ! Errors flag

! Data dictionary: declare variable types & definitions
INTEGER :: i                   ! Loop counter
INTEGER :: istat               ! Allocate status
INTEGER, DIMENSION(2) :: l_bound    ! Lower bounds on ptr_a
INTEGER, DIMENSION(2) :: u_bound    ! Upper bounds on ptr_a
INTEGER, DIMENSION(2) :: extent     ! Extent of array on ptr_a

! Check error conditions
error_1: IF ( .NOT. ASSOCIATED ( ptr_a ) ) THEN
    error = 1
ELSE IF ( ASSOCIATED ( ptr_b ) ) THEN
    error = 2
ELSE
   ! Check for square array
   l_bound = LBOUND ( ptr_a )
   u_bound = UBOUND ( ptr_a )
   extent = u_bound - l_bound + 1
   error_3: IF ( extent(1) /= extent(2) ) THEN
      error = 3
   ELSE
      ! Everything is ok so far, allocate ptr_b.
      ALLOCATE ( ptr_b(extent(1)), STAT=istat )
      error_4: IF ( istat /= 0 ) THEN
         error = 4
      ELSE
         ! Everything is ok, extract diagonal.
         ok: DO i =1, extent(1)
            ptr_b(i) =ptr_a(l_bound(1)+i-1,l_bound(2)+i-1)
         END DO ok

         ! Reset error flag.
         error = 0
      END IF error_4
   END IF error_3
END IF error_1

END SUBROUTINE get_diagonal
```

A test driver program for this subroutine is shown in Figure 15-19. This program tests the first three possible error conditions, and also the proper operation of the subroutine when no error occurs. There is no easy way to get the memory allocation of ptr_b to fail, so there is no explicit test in the driver for that.

FIGURE 15-19

Test driver program for subroutine get_diagonal.

```
PROGRAM test_diagonal
!
!   Purpose:
!     To test the diagonal extraction subroutine.
!
!   Record of revisions:
!      Date        Programmer          Description of change
!      ====        ==========          =====================
!     12/23/06     S. J. Chapman       Original code
!
IMPLICIT NONE

! Declare interface to subroutine diagonal:
INTERFACE
    SUBROUTINE get_diagonal ( ptr_a, ptr_b, error )
    INTEGER, DIMENSION(:,:), POINTER :: ptr_a
    INTEGER, DIMENSION(:), POINTER :: ptr_b
    INTEGER, INTENT(OUT) :: error
    END SUBROUTINE get_diagonal
END INTERFACE

! Data dictionary: declare variable types & definitions
INTEGER :: i, j, k                         ! Loop counter
INTEGER :: istat                           ! Allocate status
INTEGER, DIMENSION(:,:), POINTER :: ptr_a  ! Ptr to square array
INTEGER, DIMENSION(:), POINTER :: ptr_b    ! Ptr to output array
INTEGER :: error                           ! Errors flag

! Call diagonal with nothing defined to see what happens.
CALL get_diagonal ( ptr_a, ptr_b, error )
WRITE (*,*) 'No pointers allocated: '
WRITE (*,*) ' Error = ', error

! Allocate both pointers, and call the subroutine.
ALLOCATE (ptr_a(10,10), STAT=istat )
ALLOCATE (ptr_b(10), STAT=istat )
CALL get_diagonal ( ptr_a, ptr_b, error )
WRITE (*,*) 'Both pointers allocated: '
WRITE (*,*) ' Error = ', error

! Allocate ptr_a only, but with unequal extents.
DEALLOCATE (ptr_a, STAT=istat)
DEALLOCATE (ptr_b, STAT=istat)
ALLOCATE (ptr_a(-5:5,10), STAT=istat )
```

(continued)

15

(concluded)

```
CALL get_diagonal ( ptr_a, ptr_b, error )
WRITE (*,*) 'Array on ptr_a not square: '
WRITE (*,*) ' Error = ', error

! Allocate ptr_a only, initialize, and get results.
DEALLOCATE (ptr_a, STAT=istat)
ALLOCATE (ptr_a(-2:2,0:4), STAT=istat )
k = 0
DO j = 0, 4
   DO i = -2, 2
      k = k + 1                    ! Store the numbers 1 .. 25
      ptr_a(i,j) = k               ! in row order in the array
   END DO
END DO
CALL get_diagonal ( ptr_a, ptr_b, error )
WRITE (*,*) 'ptr_a allocated & square; ptr_b not allocated: '
WRITE (*,*) ' Error = ', error
WRITE (*,*) ' Diag = ', ptr_b

END PROGRAM test_diagonal
```

When the test driver program is executed, the results are:

```
C:\book\chap15>test_diagonal
No pointers allocated:
   Error =           1
Both pointers allocated:
   Error =           2
Array on ptr_a not square:
   Error =           3
ptr_a allocated & square; ptr_b not allocated:
   Error =           0
   Diag  =           1       7      13      19      25
```

All error were flagged properly, and the diagonal values are correct, so the subroutine appears to be working properly.

Good Programming Practice

Always test the association status of any pointers passed to a procedure as calling arguments. It is easy to make mistakes in a large program that result in an attempt to use an unassociated pointer or an attempt to reallocate an already associated pointer (the latter case will produce a memory leak).

15

F-2003 ONLY

15.7.1 Using the INTENT Attribute with Pointers

In Fortran 95, a pointer dummy argument may not have an INTENT attribute, because of the confusion as to whether the INTENT information applied to the pointer or to the pointer's target.

This issue has been resolved in Fortran 2003, and the INTENT attribute is now allowed. If the INTENT attribute appears on a pointer dummy argument, it refers to the *pointer* and not to its target. Thus, if a subroutine has the following declaration

```
SUBROUTINE test(xval)
REAL,POINTER,DIMENSION(:),INTENT(IN) :: xval
. . .
```

then the pointer xval cannot be allocated, deallocated, or reassigned within the subroutine. However, the contents of the pointer's *target* can be changed. Therefore, the statement

```
xval(90:100) = -2.
```

would be legal within this subroutine if the target of the pointer has at least 100 elements.

15.7.2 Pointer-Valued Functions

It is also possible for a function to return a pointer value. If a function is to return a pointer, then the RESULT clause must be used in the function definition, and the RESULT variable must be declared to be a pointer. For example, the function in Figure 15-20 accepts a pointer to a rank 1 array, and returns a pointer to every fifth value in the array.

FIGURE 15-20
A pointer-valued function.

```
FUNCTION every_fifth (ptr_array) RESULT (ptr_fifth)
!
!  Purpose:
!    To produce a pointer to every fifth element in an
!    input rank 1 array.
!
!  Record of revisions:
!     Date        Programmer       Description of change
!     ====        ==========       =====================
!   12/24/06   S. J. Chapman       Original code
!
IMPLICIT NONE

! Data dictionary: declare calling parameter types & definitions
INTEGER, DIMENSION(:), POINTER :: ptr_array
INTEGER, DIMENSION(:), POINTER :: ptr_fifth

! Data dictionary: declare local variable types & definitions
INTEGER :: low         ! Array lower bound
INTEGER :: high        ! Array upper bound

low = LBOUND(ptr_array,1)
high = UBOUND(ptr_array,1)
ptr_fifth => ptr_array(low:high:5)

END FUNCTION every_fifth
```

15

A pointer-valued function must always have an explicit interface in any procedure that uses it. The explicit interface may be specified by an interface or by placing the function in a module and then using the module in the procedure. Once the function is defined, it can be used any place that a pointer expression can be used. For example, it can be used on the right-hand side of a pointer assignment statement as follows:

```
ptr_2 => every_fifth( ptr_1 )
```

The function can also be used in a location where an integer array is expected. In that case, the pointer returned by the function will automatically be dereferenced, and the values pointed to will be used. Thus, the following statement is legal, and will print out the values pointed to by the pointer returned from the function.

```
WRITE (*,*) every_fifth( ptr_1 )
```

As with any function, a pointer-valued function can *not* be used on the left-hand side of an assignment statement.

F-2003
ONLY

15.8
PROCEDURE POINTERS

It is also possible for a Fortran 2003 pointer to refer to a *procedure* instead of a variable or array. A procedure pointer is declared by the statement:

```
PROCEDURE (proc), POINTER :: p => NULL()
```

This statement declares a pointer to a procedure that has the *same calling sequence* as procedure proc, which must have an explicit interface.

Once a procedure pointer is declared, a procedure can be assigned to it in the same fashion as for variables or arrays. For example, suppose that subroutine sub1 has an explicit interface. Then a pointer to sub1 could be declared as

```
PROCEDURE (sub1), POINTER :: p => NULL()
```

and the following assignment would be legal

```
p => sub1
```

After such an assignment, the following two subroutine calls are identical, producing exactly the same results.

```
CALL sub1(a, b, c)
CALL p(a, b, c)
```

Note that this pointer will work for *any* subroutine that has the same interface as sub1. For example, suppose that subroutines sub1 and sub2 both have the same interface (number, sequence, type, and intent of calling parameters). Then the first call to p below would call sub1 and the second one would call sub2.

```
p => sub1
CALL p(a, b, c)
p => sub2
CALL p(a, b, c)
```

Procedure pointers are very useful in Fortran programs, because a user can associate a specific procedure with a defined data type. For example, the following type declaration includes a pointer to a procedure that can invert the matrix declared in the derived data type.

```
TYPE matrix(m)
    INTEGER, LEN :: m
    REAL :: element(m,m)
    PROCEDURE (lu), POINTER :: invert
END TYPE
:
TYPE(m=10) :: a
:
CALL a%invert(....
```

Note that this is different from binding the procedure to the data type in that binding is permanent, while the procedure pointed to by the function pointer can change during the course of program execution.

15.9

BINARY TREE STRUCTURES

We have already seen one example of a dynamic data structure: the linked list. Another very important dynamic data structure is the **binary tree.** A binary tree consists of repeated components (or **nodes**) arranged in an inverted tree structure. Each component or node is a variable of a derived data type that stores some sort of data plus *two* pointers to other variables of the same data type. A sample derived data type might be:

```
TYPE :: person
    CHARACTER(len=10) :: last
    CHARACTER(len=10) :: first
    CHARACTER :: mi
    TYPE (person), POINTER :: before
    TYPE (person), POINTER :: after
END TYPE
```

This data type is illustrated in Figure 15-21. It could be extended to included further information about each person such as address, phone number, social security number, and so forth.

An important requirement for binary trees is that *the components must be sortable according to some known criterion.* For our example, the components may be sortable alphabetically by last name, first name, and middle initial. If the pointers in a

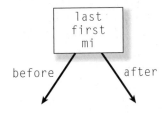

FIGURE 15-21
A typical component of a binary tree.

component are associated, then the pointer `before` must point to another component that falls before the current component in the sorting order, and the pointer `after` must point to another component that falls after the current component in the sorting order.

Binary trees start from a single node (the *root node*), which is the first value read into the program. When the first value is read, a variable is created to hold it, and the two pointers in the variable are nullified. When the next value is read, a new node is created to hold it, and it is compared to the value in the root node. If the new value is less than the value in the root node, then the `before` pointer of the root node is set to point to the new variable. If the new value is greater than the value in the root node, then the `after` pointer of the root node is set to point to the new variable. If a value is greater than the value in the root node but the `after` pointer is already in use, then we compare the new value to the value in the node pointed to by the `after` pointer, and insert the new node in the proper position below that node. This process is repeated as new values are added, producing nodes arranged in an inverted tree structure, with their values in order.

This process is best illustrated by an example. Let's add the following names to a binary tree structure consisting of variables of the type defined above.

```
Jackson, Andrew D
Johnson, James R
Johnson, Jessie R
Johnson, Andrew C
Chapman, Stephen J
Gomez, Jose A
Chapman, Rosa P
```

The first name read in is "Jackson, Andrew D". Because there is no other data yet, this name is stored in node 1, which becomes the root node of the tree, and both of the pointers in the variable are nullified (see Figure 15-22*a*). The next name read in is "Johnson, James R". This name is stored in node 2, and both pointers in the new variable are nullified. Next, the new value is compared to the root node. Because it is greater than the value in the root node, the pointer `after` of the root node is set to point to the new variable (see Figure 15-22*b*).

The third name read in is "Johnson, Jessie R". This name is stored in node 3, and both pointers in the new variable are nullified. Next, the new value is compared to the root node. It is greater than the value in the root node, but the `after` point of the root node already points to node 2, so we compare the new variable with the value in node 2. That value is "Johnson, James R". Because the new value is greater than that value, the new variable is attached below node 2, and the `after` pointer of node 2 is set to point to it (see Figure 15-22*c*).

The fourth name read in is "Johnson, Andrew C". This name is stored in node 4, and both pointers in the new variable are nullified. Next, the new value is compared to the root node. It is greater than the value in the root node, but the `after` point of the root node already points to node 2, so we compare the new variable with the value in node 2. That value is "Johnson, James R". Because the new value is less than that value, the new variable is attached below node 2, and the `before` pointer of node 2 is set to point to it (see Figure 15-22*d*).

The fifth name read in is "Chapman, Stephen J". This name is stored in node 5, and both pointers in the new variable are nullified. Next, the new value is compared to the root node. Because the new value is less than that value, the new variable is attached below the root node, and the `before` pointer of the root node is set to point to it (see Figure 15-22e).

The sixth name read in is "Gomez, Jose A". This name is stored in node 6, and both pointers in the new variable are nullified. Next, the new value is compared to the root node. It is less than the value in the root node, but the `before` point of the root

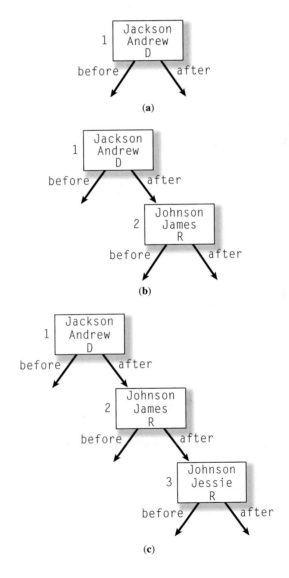

FIGURE 15-22
The development of a binary tree structure.

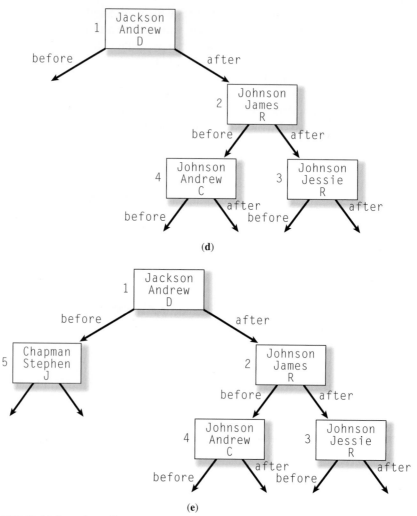

FIGURE 15-22 (*continued*)
The development of a binary tree structure.

node already points to node 5, so we compare the new variable with the value in node 5. That value is "Chapman, Stephen J". Because the new value is greater than that value, the new variable is attached below node 5, and the `after` pointer of node 5 is set to point to it (see Figure 15-22*f*).

The seventh name read in is "Chapman, Rosa P". This name is stored in node 7, and both pointers in the new variable are nullified. Next, the new value is compared to the root node. It is less than the value in the root node, but the `before` point of the root node already points to node 5, so we compare the new variable with the value in node 5. That value is "Chapman, Stephen J". Because the new value is less than that value, the new variable is attached below node 5, and the `before` pointer of node 5 is set to point to it (see Figure 15-22*g*).

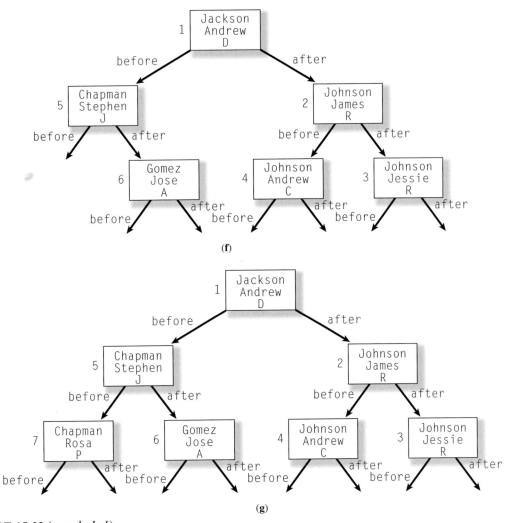

FIGURE 15-22 (*concluded*)
The development of a binary tree structure.

This process can be repeated indefinitely as more data values are added to the tree.

15.9.1 The Significance of Binary Tree Structures

Now let's examine the completed structure in Figure 15-22g. Notice that when the tree is finished, the values are arranged in *sorted order from left to right across the structure*. This fact means that the binary tree can be used as a way to sort a data set (see Figure 15-23). (In this application, it is similar to the insertion sort described earlier in the chapter.)

15

However, there is something far more important about this data structure than the fact that it is sorted. Suppose that we wanted to search for a particular name in the original list of names. Depending on where the name appears in the list, we would have to check from one to seven names before locating the one we wanted. On the average, we would have to search 3½ names before spotting the desired one. In contrast, if the names are arranged a binary tree structure, then, starting from the root node, *no more than three checks would be required to locate any particular name.* A binary tree is a very efficient way to search for and retrieve data values.

This advantage increases rapidly as the size of the database to be searched increases. For example, suppose that we have 32,767 values in a database. If we search through the linear list to try to find a particular value, from 1 to 32,767 values would have to be searched, and the average search length would be 16,384. In contrast, 32,767 values can be stored in a binary tree structure consisting of only 15 layers, so the maximum number of values to search to find any particular value would be 15! Binary trees are a *very* efficient way to store data for easy retrieval.

In practice, binary trees may not be quite this efficient. Since the arrangement of the nodes in a binary tree depends on the order in which data was read in, it is possible that there may be more layers of nodes in some parts of the tree than in others. In that case there may be a few extra layers to search to find some of the values. However, the efficiency of a binary tree is so much greater than that of a linear list that binary trees are still better for data storage and retrieval.

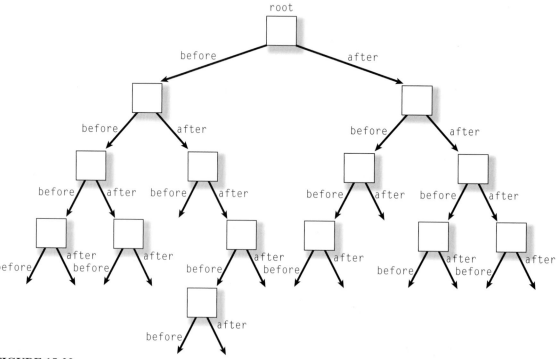

FIGURE 15-23
A binary tree structure whose lowest branches are not completely filled in.

The worst sort of data to store in a binary tree is sorted data. If sorted data is read, then each value is larger than the previous one, and so each new node is placed after the previous one. In the end, we wind up with a binary tree consisting of only one branch, which just reproduces the structure of the original list (see Figure 15-24). The best sort of data to store in a binary tree is random data, since random values will fill in all branches of the tree roughly equally.

Many databases are structured as binary trees. These databases often include special techniques called *hashing techniques* to partially randomize the order of the data stored in the database, and so avoid the situation shown in Figure 15-24. They also often include special procedures to even out the bottom branches of the binary tree in order to make searching for data in the tree faster.

15.9.2 Building a Binary Tree Structure

Because each node of a binary tree looks and behaves just like any other node, binary trees are perfectly suited to recursive procedures. For example, suppose that we would like to add a value to a binary tree. A program could read the new value, create a new node for it, and call a subroutine named insert_node to insert the node into the tree. The subroutine will first be called with a pointer to the root node. The root node

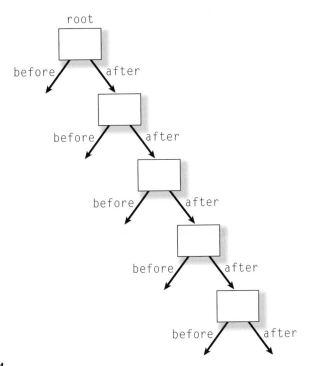

FIGURE 15-24
A binary tree resulting from sorted input data. Note that the tree just becomes a list, and all of the advantages of the binary tree structure have been lost.

15

becomes the "current node" for the subroutine. If the current node doesn't exist, then it will add the new node at that location. If the current node does exist, then it will compare the value in the current node to the value in the new node. If the value in the new node is less than the value in the current node, then the subroutine will call itself recursively using the `before` pointer from the current node. If the value in the new node is greater than the value in the current node, then the subroutine will call itself recursively, using the `after` pointer from the current node. Subroutine `insert_node` will continue to call itself recursively until it reaches the bottom of the tree and locates the proper place to insert the new node.

Similar recursive subroutines can be written to retrieve specific values from the binary tree, or to write out all of the values in the tree in sorted order. The following example will illustrate the construction of a binary tree.

EXAMPLE   *Storing and Retrieving Data in a Binary Tree:*
15-4

Suppose that we would like to create a database containing the names and telephone numbers of a group of people. (This structure could easily accommodate more information about each person, but we will keep it simple for the purposes of this example.) Write a program to read the names and phone numbers, and store them in a binary tree. After reading all of the names, the program should be able to print out all of the names and phone numbers in alphabetical order. In addition, it should be able to recover the phone number of any individual, given his or her name. Use recursive subroutines to implement the binary tree functions.

SOLUTION
The information about each person will be stored in a binary tree. We must create a derived data type to hold the information contained in each node: name, telephone number, and pointers to two other nodes. An appropriate derived data type is:

```
TYPE :: node
   CHARACTER(len=10) :: last
   CHARACTER(len=10) :: first
   CHARACTER :: mi
   CHARACTER(len=16) :: phone
   TYPE (node), POINTER :: before
   TYPE (node), POINTER :: after
END TYPE
```

The main program will read names and phone numbers from an input data file, and create nodes to hold them. When each node is created, it will call a recursive subroutine `insert_node` to locate the proper place in the tree to put the new node. Once all of the names and phone numbers are read in, the main program will call recursive subroutine `write_node` to list out all names and phone numbers in alphabetical order. Finally, the program will prompt the user to provide a name, and it will call recursive subroutine `find_node` to get the phone number associated with that name.

Note that for a binary tree to work, *there must be a way to compare two values of the derived data type representing each node.* In our case, we wish to sort and compare the data by last name, first name, and middle initial. Therefore, we will create extended definitions for the operators $>$, $<$, and $==$ so that they can work with the derived data type.

1. **State the problem.**

Write a program that reads a list of names and phone numbers from an input file, and stores them in a binary tree structure. After reading in all of the names, the program will print out all of the names and phone numbers in alphabetical order. Then, it will prompt the user for a specific name, and retrieve the phone number associated with that name. It will use recursive subroutines to implement the binary tree functions.

2. **Define the inputs and outputs.**

The inputs to the program are a file name, and a list of names and phone numbers within the file. The names and phone numbers will be in the order: last, first, middle initial, phone number.

The outputs from the program will be a list of all names and phone numbers in alphabetical order and the phone number associated with a user-specified name.

3. **Describe the algorithm.**

The basic pseudocode for the main program is

```
Get input file name
Read input data and store in binary tree
Write out data in alphabetical order
Get specific name from user
Recover and display phone number associated with that name
```

The data to be stored in the binary tree will be read from the input file by using a WHILE loop, and stored by using recursive subroutine add_node. Once all of the data has been read, the sorted data will be written out to the standard output device by using subroutine write_node, and then the user will be prompted to input the name of the record to find. Subroutine find_node will be used to search for the record. If the record is found, it will be displayed. The detailed pseudocode for the main program is:

```
Prompt user for the input file name "filename"
Read the file name "filename"
OPEN file "filename"
IF OPEN is successful THEN
    WHILE
        Create new node using pointer "temp"
        Read value into temp
        IF read not successful EXIT
        CALL add_node(root, temp) to put item in tree
    End of WHILE
    Call write_node(root) to write out sorted data
    Prompt user for name to recover; store in "temp"
    CALL find_node(root, temp, error)
    Write the data to the standard output device
End of IF
```

15

It is necessary to create a module containing the definition of the derived data type and the three recursive subroutines required to manipulate the binary tree structure. To add a node to the tree, we should start by looking at the root node. If the root node does not exist, then the new node will become the root node. If the root node exists, then we should compare the name in the new node to the name in the root node to determine if the new node is alphabetically less than or greater than the root node. If it is less, then we should check the `before` pointer of the root node. If that pointer is null, then we will add the new node there. Otherwise, we will check the node pointed to by the `before` pointer, and repeat the process. If the new node is alphabetically greater than or equal to the root node, then we should check the `after` pointer of the root node. If that pointer is null, then we will add the new node there. Otherwise, we will check the node pointed to by the `after` pointer, and repeat the process.

For each node we examine, we perform the same steps:

1. Determine whether the new node is $<$ or $>=$ the current node.
2. If it is less than the current node and the `before` pointer is null, add the new node there.
3. If it is less than the current node and the `before` pointer is not null, examine the node pointed to.
4. If the new node is greater than or equal to the current node and the `after` pointer is null, add the new node there.
5. If it is greater than or equal to the current node and the `after` pointer is not null, examine the node pointed to.

Because the same pattern repeats over and over again, we can implement `add_node` as a recursive subroutine.

```
IF ptr is not associated THEN
   ! There is no tree yet. Add the node right here.
   ptr => new_node
ELSE IF new_node < ptr THEN
   ! Check to see if we can attach new node here.
   IF ptr%before is associated THEN
      ! Node in use, so call add_node recursively
      CALL add_node ( ptr%before, new_node )
   ELSE
      ! Pointer not in use. Add node here.
      ptr%before => new_node
   END of IF
ELSE
   ! Check to see if we can attach new node to after ptr.
   IF ptr%after is associated THEN
      ! Node in use, so call add_node recursively
      CALL add_node ( ptr%after, new_node )
   ELSE
      ! Pointer not in use. Add node here.
      ptr%after => new_node
   END of IF
END of IF
```

Subroutine `write_node` is a recursive subroutine to write out the values in the tree in alphabetical order. To do this, it starts at the root node and works its way down to the leftmost branch in the tree. Then, it works its way along from left to right through the structure. The pseudocode is shown below:

```
IF pointer "before" is associated THEN
   CALL write_node ( ptr%before )
END of IF
WRITE contents of current node
IF pointer "after" is associated THEN
   CALL write_node ( ptr%after )
END of IF
```

Subroutine `find_node` is a recursive subroutine to locate a particular node in the tree. To find a node in the tree, we start by looking at the root node. We should compare the name we are searching for to the name in the root node to determine if the name we want is alphabetically less than or greater than the root node. If it is less, then we should check the `before` pointer of the root node. If that pointer is null, then the desired node does not exist. Otherwise, we will check the node pointed to by the `before` pointer, and repeat the process. If the name we are searching for is alphabetically greater than or equal to the root node, then we should check the `after` pointer of the root node. If that pointer is null, then the desired node does not exist. Otherwise, we will check the node pointed to by the `after` pointer, and repeat the process. If the name we are searching for is equal to the root node, then the root node contains the data we want, and we will return it. This process is repeated recursively for each node called until either the desired data is found or a null pointer is reached. The pseudocode is shown below:

```
IF search_value < ptr THEN
   IF ptr%before is associated THEN
      CALL find_node ( ptr%before, search_value, error )
   ELSE ! not found
      error ← 1
   END of IF
ELSE IF search_value == ptr THEN
   search_value = ptr
   error ← 0
ELSE
   IF ptr%after is associated THEN
      CALL find_node ( ptr%after, search_value, error )
   ELSE ! not found
      error ← 1
   END of IF
END of IF
```

It is necessary to include in the module the definition of the derived data type and the definitions of the $>$, $<$, and == operators for that data type. To do this, we will include three INTERFACE OPERATOR blocks in the module. In addition, we must write the three private functions that implement the operators. The first function is called `greater_than`, the second one is called `less_than`, and the third one is called `equal_to`. These functions must compare the two last names to decide whether the first is greater than, less than, or the same as the second. If they are the same, then the functions must compare the two first names and middle initials. Note that all names should be shifted to uppercase to avoid mixing upper- and lowercase during the comparisons. This will be done by using a subroutine called `ushift`, which in turn calls

15

the subroutine `ucase` that we developed in Chapter 10. The pseudocode for function `greater_than` is:

```
IF last1 > last2 THEN
   greater_than = .TRUE.
ELSE IF last1 < last2 THEN
   greater_than = .FALSE.
ELSE ! Last names match
   IF first1 > first2 THEN
      greater_than = .TRUE.
   ELSE IF first1 < first2 THEN
      greater_than = .FALSE.
   ELSE ! First names match
      IF mi1 > mi2 THEN
         greater_than = .TRUE.
      ELSE
         greater_than = .FALSE.
      END of IF
   END of IF
END of IF
```

The pseudocode for function `less_than` is:

```
IF last1 < last2 THEN
   less_than = .TRUE.
ELSE IF last1 > last2 THEN
   less_than = .FALSE.
ELSE ! Last names match
   IF first1 < first2 THEN
      less_than = .TRUE.
   ELSE IF first1 > first2 THEN
      less_than = .FALSE.
   ELSE ! First names match
      IF mi1 < mi2 THEN
         less_than = .TRUE.
      ELSE
         less_than = .FALSE.
      END of IF
   END of IF
END of IF
```

The pseudocode for function `equal_to` is:

```
IF last1 == last2 .AND. first1 == first2 .AND. mi1 == mi2 THEN
   equal_to = .TRUE.
ELSE
   equal_to = .FALSE.
END of IF
```

4. **Turn the algorithm into Fortran statements.**

The resulting Fortran program is shown in Figure 15-25. Module `btree` contains the definition of the derived data type and all of the supporting subroutines and functions, as well as defining the operators >, <, and == for the derived data type. Note that only the essential procedures in the module are `PUBLIC`. The main program accesses the procedures in the module by `USE` association, so the procedures have an explicit interface.

FIGURE 15-25
A program to store a database of names and phone numbers in a binary tree structure, and to retrieve a selected item from that tree.

```
MODULE btree
!
!  Purpose:
!    To define the derived data type used as a node in the
!    binary tree, and to define the operations >, <. and ==
!    for this data type. This module also contains the
!    subroutines to add a node to the tree, write out the
!    values in the tree, and find a value in the tree.
!
!  Record of revisions:
!     Date        Programmer          Description of change
!     ====        ==========          =====================
!    12/24/06    S. J. Chapman        Original code
!
IMPLICIT NONE

! Restrict access to module contents.
PRIVATE
PUBLIC :: node, OPERATOR(>), OPERATOR(<), OPERATOR(==)
PUBLIC :: add_node, write_node, find_node

! Declare type for a node of the binary tree.
TYPE :: node
   CHARACTER(len=10) :: last
   CHARACTER(len=10) :: first
   CHARACTER :: mi
   CHARACTER(len=16) :: phone
   TYPE (node), POINTER :: before
   TYPE (node), POINTER :: after
END TYPE

INTERFACE OPERATOR (>)
   MODULE PROCEDURE greater_than
END INTERFACE

INTERFACE OPERATOR (<)
   MODULE PROCEDURE less_than
END INTERFACE

INTERFACE OPERATOR (==)
   MODULE PROCEDURE equal_to
END INTERFACE

CONTAINS
   RECURSIVE SUBROUTINE add_node (ptr, new_node)
   !
   !  Purpose:
   !    To add a new node to the binary tree structure.
   !
   TYPE (node), POINTER :: ptr      ! Pointer to current pos. in tree
   TYPE (node), POINTER :: new_node ! Pointer to new node
```

15

(continued)

(continued)

```
IF ( .NOT. ASSOCIATED(ptr) ) THEN
   ! There is no tree yet. Add the node right here.
   ptr => new_node
ELSE IF ( new_node < ptr ) THEN
   IF ( ASSOCIATED(ptr%before) ) THEN
      CALL add_node ( ptr%before, new_node )
   ELSE
      ptr%before => new_node
   END IF
ELSE
   IF ( ASSOCIATED(ptr%after) ) THEN
      CALL add_node ( ptr%after, new_node )
   ELSE
      ptr%after => new_node
   END IF
END IF
END SUBROUTINE add_node

RECURSIVE SUBROUTINE write_node (ptr)
!
!  Purpose:
!    To write out the contents of the binary tree
!    structure in order.
!
TYPE (node), POINTER :: ptr ! Pointer to current pos. in tree

! Write contents of previous node.
IF ( ASSOCIATED(ptr%before) ) THEN
   CALL write_node ( ptr%before )
END IF

! Write contents of current node.
WRITE (*,"(1X,A,', ',A,1X,A)") ptr%last, ptr%first, ptr%mi

! Write contents of next node.
IF ( ASSOCIATED(ptr%after) ) THEN
   CALL write_node ( ptr%after )
END IF
END SUBROUTINE write_node

RECURSIVE SUBROUTINE find_node (ptr, search, error)
!
!  Purpose:
!    To find a particular node in the binary tree structure.
!    "Search" is a pointer to the name to find, and will
!    also contain the results when the subroutine finishes
!    if the node is found.
!
TYPE (node), POINTER :: ptr    ! Pointer to curr pos. in tree
TYPE (node), POINTER :: search ! Pointer to value to find.
INTEGER :: error                ! Error: 0 = ok, 1 = not found
```

(continued)

(continued)

```
          IF ( search < ptr ) THEN
             IF ( ASSOCIATED(ptr%before) ) THEN
                CALL find_node (ptr%before, search, error)
             ELSE
                error = 1
             END IF
          ELSE IF ( search == ptr ) THEN
             search = ptr
             error = 0
          ELSE
             IF ( ASSOCIATED(ptr%after) ) THEN
                CALL find_node (ptr%after, search, error)
             ELSE
                error = 1
             END IF
          END IF
          END SUBROUTINE find_node

          LOGICAL FUNCTION greater_than (op1, op2)
          !
          !  Purpose:
          !     To test to see if operand 1 is > operand 2
          !     in alphabetical order.
          !
          TYPE (node), INTENT(IN) :: op1, op2
          CHARACTER(len=10) :: last1, last2, first1, first2
          CHARACTER :: mi1, mi2

          CALL ushift (op1, last1, first1, mi1 )
          CALL ushift (op2, last2, first2, mi2 )

          IF (last1 > last2) THEN
             greater_than = .TRUE.
          ELSE IF (last1 < last2) THEN
             greater_than = .FALSE.
          ELSE ! Last names match
             IF (first1 > first2) THEN
                greater_than = .TRUE.
             ELSE IF (first1 < first2) THEN
                greater_than = .FALSE.
             ELSE ! First names match
                IF (mi1 > mi2) THEN
                   greater_than = .TRUE.
                ELSE
                   greater_than = .FALSE.
                END IF
             END IF
          END IF
          END FUNCTION greater_than
```

15

(continued)

(continued)

```
LOGICAL FUNCTION less_than (op1, op2)
!
!  Purpose:
!    To test to see if operand 1 is < operand 2
!    in alphabetical order.
!
TYPE (node), INTENT(IN) :: op1, op2
CHARACTER(len=10) :: last1, last2, first1, first2
CHARACTER :: mi1, mi2

CALL ushift (op1, last1, first1, mi1 )
CALL ushift (op2, last2, first2, mi2 )

IF (last1 < last2) THEN
   less_than = .TRUE.
ELSE IF (last1 > last2) THEN
   less_than = .FALSE.
ELSE ! Last names match
   IF (first1 < first2) THEN
      less_than = .TRUE.
   ELSE IF (first1 > first2) THEN
      less_than = .FALSE.
   ELSE ! First names match
      IF (mi1 < mi2) THEN
         less_than = .TRUE.
      ELSE
         less_than = .FALSE.
      END IF
   END IF
END IF
END FUNCTION less_than

LOGICAL FUNCTION equal_to (op1, op2)
!
!  Purpose:
!    To test to see if operand 1 is equal to operand 2
!    alphabetically.
!
TYPE (node), INTENT(IN) :: op1, op2

CHARACTER(len=10) :: last1, last2, first1, first2
CHARACTER :: mi1, mi2

CALL ushift (op1, last1, first1, mi1 )
CALL ushift (op2, last2, first2, mi2 )

IF ( (last1 == last2) .AND. (first1 == first2) .AND. &
     (mi1 == mi2 ) ) THEN
   equal_to = .TRUE.
```

(continued)

(continued)

```
ELSE
   equal_to = .FALSE.
END IF
END FUNCTION equal_to

SUBROUTINE ushift( op, last, first, mi )
!
!  Purpose:
!    To create upshifted versions of all strings for
!    comparison.
!
TYPE (node), INTENT(IN) :: op
CHARACTER(len=10), INTENT(INOUT) :: last, first
CHARACTER, INTENT(INOUT) :: mi

last = op%last
first = op%first
mi = op%mi
CALL ucase (last)
CALL ucase (first)
CALL ucase (mi)
END SUBROUTINE ushift

SUBROUTINE ucase ( string )
!
!  Purpose:
!    To shift a character string to uppercase on any processor,
!    regardless of collating sequence.
!
!  Record of revisions:
!     Date        Programmer         Description of change
!     ====        ==========         =====================
!    12/24/06   S. J. Chapman        Original code
!
IMPLICIT NONE

! Declare calling parameters:
CHARACTER(len=*), INTENT(INOUT) :: string

! Declare local variables:
INTEGER :: i                    ! Loop index
INTEGER :: length               ! Length of input string

! Get length of string
length = LEN ( string )

! Now shift lowercase letters to uppercase.
DO i = 1, length
   IF ( LGE(string(i:i),'a') .AND. LLE(string(i:i),'z') ) THEN
      string(i:i) = ACHAR ( IACHAR ( string(i:i) ) - 32 )
```

(continued)

(concluded)

```
      END IF
   END DO

   END SUBROUTINE ucase

END MODULE btree

PROGRAM binary_tree
!
!   Purpose:
!     To read in a series of random names and phone numbers
!     and store them in a binary tree. After the values are
!     stored, they are written out in sorted order. Then the
!     user is prompted for a name to retrieve, and the program
!     recovers the data associated with that name.
!
!   Record of revisions:
!       Date          Programmer          Description of change
!       ====          ==========          =====================
!     12/24/06     S. J. Chapman          Original code
!
USE btree
IMPLICIT NONE

! Data dictionary: declare variable types & definitions
INTEGER :: error                   ! Error flag: 0=success
CHARACTER(len=20) :: filename      ! Input data file name
INTEGER :: istat                   ! Status: 0 for success
TYPE (node), POINTER :: root       ! Pointer to root node
TYPE (node), POINTER :: temp       ! Temp pointer to node

! Nullify new pointers
NULLIFY ( root, temp )

! Get the name of the file containing the input data.
WRITE (*,*) 'Enter the file name with the input data: '
READ (*,'(A20)') filename

! Open input data file. Status is OLD because the input data must
! already exist.
OPEN ( UNIT=9, FILE=filename, STATUS='OLD', ACTION='READ', &
       IOSTAT=istat )

! Was the OPEN successful?
fileopen: IF ( istat == 0 ) THEN              ! Open successful

   ! The file was opened successfully, allocate space for each
   ! node, read the data into that node, and insert it into the
   ! binary tree.
   input: DO
      ALLOCATE (temp,STAT=istat)              ! Allocate node
```

(continued)

(concluded)

```
        NULLIFY ( temp%before, temp%after)     ! Nullify pointers

        READ (9, 100, IOSTAT=istat) temp%last, temp%first, &
            temp%mi, temp%phone                ! Read data
        100 FORMAT (A10,1X,A10,1X,A1,1X,A16)
        IF ( istat /= 0 ) EXIT input           ! Exit on end of data
        CALL add_node(root, temp)              ! Add to binary tree
    END DO input


    ! Now, write out the sorted data.
    WRITE (*,'(/,1X,A)') 'The sorted data list is: '
    CALL write_node(root)

    ! Prompt for a name to search for in the tree.
    WRITE (*,'(/,1X,A)') 'Enter name to recover from tree:'
    WRITE (*,'(1X,A)',ADVANCE='NO') 'Last Name: '
    READ (*,'(A)') temp%last
    WRITE (*,'(1X,A)',ADVANCE='NO') 'First Name: '
    READ (*,'(A)') temp%first
    WRITE (*,'(1X,A)',ADVANCE='NO') 'Middle Initial: '
    READ (*,'(A)') temp%mi

    ! Locate record
    CALL find_node ( root, temp, error )
    check: IF ( error == 0 ) THEN
        WRITE (*,'(/,1X,A)') 'The record is:'
        WRITE (*,'(1X,7A)') temp%last, ', ', temp%first, ' ', &
                    temp%mi, ' ', temp%phone
    ELSE
        WRITE (*,'(/,1X,A)') 'Specified node not found!'
    END IF check

ELSE fileopen

    ! Else file open failed. Tell user.
    WRITE (*,'(1X,A,I6)') 'File open failed--status = ', istat

END IF fileopen

END PROGRAM binary_tree
```

5. **Test the resulting Fortran programs.**

To test this program, we will create an input data file containing names and telephone numbers, and we will execute the program with that data. The file "tree_in.dat" will be created containing the following data:

```
    Leroux      Hector      A (608) 555-1212
    Johnson     James       R (800) 800-1111
    Jackson     Andrew      D (713) 723-7777
    Romanoff    Alexi       N (212) 338-3030
```

15

```
Johnson     Jessie     R (800) 800-1111
Chapman     Stephen    J (713) 721-0901
Nachshon    Bini       M (618) 813-1234
Ziskend     Joseph     J (805) 238-7999
Johnson     Andrew     C (504) 388-3000
Chi         Shuchung   F (504) 388-3123
deBerry     Jonathan   S (703) 765-4321
Chapman     Rosa       P (713) 721-0901
Gomez       Jose       A (415) 555-1212
Rosenberg   Fred       R (617) 123-4567
```

We will execute the program twice. Once we will specify a valid name to look up, and once we will specify an invalid one, to test that the program is working properly in both cases. When the program is executed, the results are:

```
C:\book\chap15>binary_tree
Enter the file name with the input data:
tree_in.dat

The sorted data list is:
Chapman    , Rosa        P
Chapman    , Stephen     J
Chi        , Shuchung    F
deBerry    , Jonathan    S
Gomez      , Jose        A
Jackson    , Andrew      D
Johnson    , Andrew      C
Johnson    , James       R
Johnson    , Jessie      R
Leroux     , Hector      A
Nachshon   , Bini        M
Romanoff   , Alexi       N
Rosenberg  , Fred        R
Ziskend    , Joseph      J

Enter name to recover from tree:
Last Name:       Nachshon
First Name:      Bini
Middle Initial:  M

The record is:
Nachshon , Bini       M (618) 813-1234

C:\book\chap15>binary_tree
Enter the file name with the input data:
tree_in.dat

The sorted data list is:
Chapman    , Rosa        P
Chapman    , Stephen     J
Chi        , Shuchung    F
deBerry    , Jonathan    S
Gomez      , Jose        A
Jackson    , Andrew      D
```

```
Johnson    , Andrew    C
Johnson    , James     R
Johnson    , Jessie    R
Leroux     , Hector    A
Nachshon   , Bini      M
Romanoff   , Alexi     N
Rosenberg  , Fred      R
Ziskend    , Joseph    J

Enter name to recover from tree:
Last Name:      Johnson
First Name:     James
Middle Initial: A

Specified node not found!
```

The program appears to be working. Please note that it properly stored the data into the binary tree regardless of capitalization (deBerry is in the proper place).

Can you determine what the tree structure that the program created looks like? What is the maximum number of layers that the program must search through to find any particular data item in this tree?

▨ 15.10
SUMMARY

A pointer is a special type of variable that contains the *address* of another variable instead of containing a value. A pointer has a specified data type and (if it points to an array) rank, and it can point *only* to data items of that particular type and rank. Pointers are declared with the POINTER attribute in a type declaration statement or in a separate POINTER statement. The data item pointed to by a pointer is called a target. Only data items declared with the TARGET attribute in a type declaration statement or in a separate TARGET statement can be pointed to by pointers.

A pointer assignment statement places the address of a target in a pointer. The form of the statement is

```
pointer => target
pointer1 => pointer2
```

In the latter case, the address currently contained in *pointer2* is placed in *pointer1*, and both pointers independently point to the same target.

A pointer can have one of three possible association statuses: undefined, associated, or disassociated. When a pointer is first declared in a type declaration statement, its pointer association status is undefined. Once a pointer has been associated with a target by a pointer assignment statement, its association status becomes associated. If a pointer is later disassociated from its target and is not associated with any new target, then its association status becomes disassociated. A pointer should always be nullified or associated as soon as it is created. The function ASSOCIATED() can be used to determine the association status of a pointer.

15

Pointers can be used to dynamically create and destroy variables or arrays. Memory is allocated for data items in an ALLOCATE statement, and deallocated in a DEALLOCATE statement. The pointer in the ALLOCATE statement points to the data item that is created, and is the *only* way to access that data item. If that pointer is disassociated or is associated with another target before another pointer is set to point to the allocated memory, then the memory becomes inaccessible to the program. This is called a "memory leak."

When dynamic memory is deallocated in a DEALLOCATE statement, the pointer to the memory is automatically nullified. However, if there are other pointers pointing to that same memory, they must be manually nullified or reassigned. If not, the program might attempt to use them to read or write to the deallocated memory location, with potentially disastrous results.

Pointers may be used as components of derived data types, including the data type being defined. This feature permits us to create dynamic data structures such as linked lists and binary trees, where the pointers in one dynamically allocated data item point to the next item in the chain. This flexibility is extraordinarily useful in many problems.

It is not possible to declare an array of pointers, since the DIMENSION attribute in a pointer declaration refers to the dimension of the target, not the dimension of the pointer. When arrays of pointers are needed, they can be created by defining a derived data type containing only a pointer, and then creating an array of that derived data type.

Pointers may be passed to procedures as calling arguments, provided that the procedure has an explicit interface in the calling program. A dummy pointer argument must not have an INTENT attribute. It is also possible for a function to return a pointer value if the RESULT clause is used and the result variable is declared to be a pointer.

15.10.1 Summary of Good Programming Practice

The following guidelines should be adhered to when working with the pointers:

1. Always nullify or assign all pointers in a program unit as soon as they are created. This eliminates any possible ambiguities associated with the undefined allocation status.
2. In sorting or swapping large arrays or derived data types, it is more efficient to exchange pointers to the data than it is to manipulate the data itself.
3. Always nullify or reassign *all* pointers to a memory location when that memory is deallocated. One of them will be automatically nullified by the DEALLOCATE statement, and any others must be manually nullified in NULLIFY statements or reassigned in pointer assignment statements.
4. Always test the association status of any pointers passed to procedures as calling arguments. It is easy to make mistakes in a large program that result in an attempt to use an unassociated pointer, or an attempt to reallocate an already associated pointer (the latter case will produce a memory leak).

15

15.10.2 Summary of Fortran Statements and Structures

POINTER **Attribute:**

```
type, POINTER :: ptr1 [, ptr2, ... ]
```

Examples:

```
INTEGER, POINTER :: next_value
REAL, DIMENSION(:), POINTER :: array
```

Description:
The POINTER attribute declares the variables in the type definition statement to be pointers.

POINTER **Statement:**

```
POINTER :: ptr1 [, ptr2, ... ]
```

Example:

```
POINTER :: p1, p2, p3
```

Description:
The POINTER statement declares the variables in its list to be pointers. It is generally preferable to use the pointer attribute in a type declaration statement to declare a pointer instead of this statement.

TARGET **Attribute:**

```
type, TARGET :: var1 [, var2, ... ]
```

Examples:

```
INTEGER, TARGET :: num_values
REAL, DIMENSION(100), TARGET :: array
```

Description:
The TARGET attribute declares the variables in the type definition statement to be legal targets for pointers.

15

TARGET **Statement:**

```
TARGET :: var1 [, var2, ... ]
```

Examples:

```
TARGET :: my_data
```

Description:
The TARGET statement declares the variables in its list to be legal targets for pointers. It is generally preferable to use the target attribute in a type declaration statement to declare a target instead of this statement.

15.1.3 Exercises

15-1 What is the difference between a pointer variable and an ordinary variable?

15-2 How does a pointer assignment statement differ from an ordinary assignment statement? What happens in each of the two statements a = z and a => z below?

```
INTEGER :: x = 6, z = 8
INTEGER, POINTER == a
a => x
a = z
a => z
```

15-3 Is the program fragment shown below correct or incorrect? If it is incorrect, explain what is wrong with it. If it is correct, what does it do?

```
PROGRAM ex15_3
REAL, POINTER :: p1
REAL:: x1 = 11.
INTEGER, POINTER :: p2
INTEGER :: x2 = 12
p1 => x1
p2 => x2
WRITE (*,'(A,4G8.2)') ' p1, p2, x1, x2 = ', p1, p2, x1, x2
p1 => p2
p2 => x1
WRITE (*,'(A,4G8.2)') ' p1, p2, x1, x2 = ', p1, p2, x1, x2
END PROGRAM ex15_3
```

15-4 What are the possible association statuses of a pointer? How can you determine the association status of a given pointer?

15-5 Is the program fragment shown below correct or incorrect? If it is incorrect, explain what is wrong with it. If it is correct, what is printed out by the WRITE statement?

```
REAL, POINTER :: p1, p2
REAL, TARGET :: x1 = 11.1, x2 = -3.2
p1 => x1
WRITE (*,*) ASSOCIATED(p1), ASSOCIATED(p2), ASSOCIATED(p1,x2)
```

15-6 What is the purpose of the function NULL(), which was added to Fortran 95? What advantage does this function have over the nullify statement?

15-7 What are the proper Fortran statements to declare a pointer to an integer array, and then point that pointer to every tenth element in a 1000-element target array called my_data?

15-8 What is printed out by the program shown below?

```
PROGRAM ex15_8
IMPLICIT NONE
INTEGER :: i
REAL, DIMENSION(-25:25), TARGET :: info = (/ (2.1*i, i=-25,25) /)
REAL, DIMENSION(:), POINTER :: ptr1, ptr2, ptr3
ptr1 => info(-25:25:5)
ptr2 => ptr1(1::2)
ptr3 => ptr2(3:5)
WRITE (*,'(A,11F6.1)') ' ptr1 = ', ptr1
WRITE (*,'(A,11F6.1)') ' ptr2 = ', ptr2
WRITE (*,'(A,11F6.1)') ' ptr3 = ', ptr3
WRITE (*,'(A,11F6.1)') ' ave of ptr3 = ', SUM(ptr3)/SIZE(ptr3)
END PROGRAM ex15_8
```

15-9 How is dynamic memory allocated and deallocated by using pointers? How does memory allocation using pointers and differ from that using allocatable arrays?

15-10 What is a memory leak? Why is it a problem, and how can it be avoided?

15-11 Is the program shown below correct or incorrect? If it is incorrect, explain what is wrong with it. If it is correct, what is printed out by the WRITE statement?

```
MODULE my_sub
CONTAINS
   SUBROUTINE running_sum (sum, value)
   REAL, POINTER :: sum, value
   ALLOCATE (sum)
   sum = sum + value
   END SUBROUTINE running_sum
END MODULE my_subs

PROGRAM sum_values
USE my_sub
```

15

```
IMPLICIT NONE
INTEGER :: istat
REAL, POINTER :: sum, value
ALLOCATE (sum, value, STAT=istat)
WRITE (*,*) 'Enter values to add: '
DO
    READ (*,*,IOSTAT=istat) value
    IF ( istat /= 0 ) EXIT
    CALL running_sum (sum, value)
    WRITE (*,*) ' The sum is ', sum
END DO
END PROGRAM sum_values
```

15-12 Is the program shown below correct or incorrect? If it is incorrect, explain what is wrong with it. If it is correct, what is printed out by the WRITE statements? What happens when this program is compiled and executed on your computer?

```
PROGRAM ex15_12
IMPLICIT NONE
INTEGER :: i, istat
INTEGER, DIMENSION(:), POINTER :: ptr1, ptr2

ALLOCATE (ptr1(1:10), STAT=istat)
ptr1 = (/ (i, i = 1,10 ) /)
ptr2 => ptr1

WRITE (*,'(A,10I3)') ' ptr1 = ', ptr1
WRITE (*,'(A,10I3)') ' ptr2 = ', ptr2

DEALLOCATE(ptr1, STAT=istat)

ALLOCATE (ptr1(1:3), STAT=istat)
ptr1 = (/ -2, 0, 2 /)

WRITE (*,'(A,10I3)') ' ptr1 = ', ptr1
WRITE (*,'(A,10I3)') ' ptr2 = ', ptr2

END PROGRAM ex15_12
```

15-13 Create a version of the insertion sort program that will sort a set of input character values in a case-insensitive manner (that is, uppercase and lowercase are to be treated as equivalent). Ensure that the ASCII collating sequence is used regardless of the computer on which the program is executed.

15-14 Insertion Sort Using a Binary Tree versus a Linked List   (*a*) Create an insertion sort subroutine to sort an array of real data, using a linked list. This subroutine will be similar to the program in Example 15-2, except that the input data will be presented all at once in an array instead of being read one value at a time from the disk. (*b*) Create a set of subroutines to perform an insertion sort on an array of real data, using a binary tree structure. (*c*) Compare the two ways to perform insertion sorts by generating a set of 50,000 random numbers and sorting the list with both subroutines. Time both subroutines, using the elapsed time subroutines developed in Exercise 7-29. Which sorting algorithm was fastest?

15-15 How can an array of pointers be generated in Fortran 95/2003?

15-16 What is printed out by the following program?

```
PROGRAM ex15_16
TYPE :: ptr
   REAL, DIMENSION(:), POINTER :: p
END TYPE
TYPE (ptr), DIMENSION(4) :: p1
REAL, DIMENSION(4), TARGET :: a = (/ 1., 2., 3., 4. /)
REAL, DIMENSION(2), TARGET :: b = (/ 5., 6. /)
REAL, DIMENSION(3), TARGET :: c = (/ 7., 8., 9. /)
REAL, DIMENSION(5), TARGET :: d = (/ 10., 11., 12., 13., 14. /)
p1(1)%p => a
p1(2)%p => b
p1(3)%p => c
p1(4)%p => d

WRITE (*,'(F6.1,/)') p1(1)%p(2) + p1(4)%p(4) + p1(3)%p(3)

DO i = 1, 4
   WRITE (*,'(5F6.1)') p1(i)%p
END DO

END PROGRAM ex15_16
```

15-17 Write a function that accepts a real input array and returns a pointer to the largest value in the array.

15-18 Write a function that accepts a pointer to a real input array and returns a pointer to the largest value in the array.

15-19 **Linear Least-Squares Fit** Write a program that reads in an unknown number of real (x, y) pairs from a file, and stores them in a linked list. When all of the values have been read in, the list should be passed to a subroutine that will compute the linear least-squares fit of the data to a straight line. (The equations for the linear squares fit were introduced in Example 5-5.)

15-20 **Doubly Linked Lists** Linked lists have the limitation that, in order to find a particular element in the list, it is always necessary to search the list from the top down. There is no way to work backward up the list to find a particular item. For example, suppose that a program had examined the 1000th item in a list, and now wanted to examine the 999th item in the list. The only way to do so would be to go back to the top of the list and start over, working from item 1 down! We can get around this problem by creating a *doubly linked list*. A doubly linked list has pointers both to the next item in the list and to the previous item in the list, permitting searches to be conducted in either direction. Write a program that reads in an arbitrary number of real numbers, and adds them to a doubly linked list. Then, write out the numbers both in input order and in reverse input order

15

using the pointers. Test the program by creating 20 random values between -100.0 and 100.0 and processing them with the program.

15-21 Insertion Sort with Doubly Linked Lists   Write a version of the insertion sort program that inserts the real input values into a doubly linked list. Test the program by creating 50 random values between -1000.0 and 1000.0, and sorting them with the program. Print out the sorted values in both ascending and descending order.

15-22 Manually reconstruct the binary tree created by the program in Example 15-4 for the given test data set. How many layers are there in the tree? Is the tree regular or irregular?

16

Object-Oriented Programming in Fortran

OBJECTIVES

- Understand the basics of objects and object-oriented programming.
- Understand the relationship between an object and a class.
- Understand inheritance in an object-oriented methodology.
- Understand the structure of a Fortran class.
- Be able to use the CLASS keyword, and understand how it differs from the TYPE keyword.
- Know how to create a class, including how to create methods bound to the class.
- Know how to control access to instance variables and methods within a class, and know *why* you should control such access.
- Understand what a finalizer is and when it should be used.
- Understand how inheritance and polymorphism work.
- Understand what an abstract class is. Know how to declare one, and why you would wish to do so.

This chapter introduces the basic concepts of object-oriented programming (OOP) in Fortran. This entire chapter applies to Fortran 2003 only—there is no equivalent functionality in Fortran 95.

Fortran is not fundamentally an object-oriented language, but some of the new features introduced in Fortran 2003 allow (but do not require) a programmer to write code in an object-oriented style. We have already met most of the features needed for object-oriented programming: extended data types, access controls, and bound methods. We will introduce one new concept (the CLASS keyword), and then combine them properly to produce Fortran object-oriented programming.

This chapter begins with an introduction to the basic concepts of object-oriented programming, and then shows how Fortran 2003 can be adapted to that approach.

Throughout this chapter, we will be using the standard terms of object-oriented programming, such as classes, objects, fields, and methods. Most of these terms are not a part of the official Fortran 2003 standard, but the basic functionality is all there.

By using the standard terms, you will be better able to talk with and understand colleagues who were trained in object-oriented languages such as Java or C++.

16.1
AN INTRODUCTION TO OBJECT-ORIENTED PROGRAMMING

Object-oriented programming is the process of programming by modeling objects in software. The principal features of OOP are described in the following sections.

16.1.1 Objects

The physical world is full of objects: cars, pencils, trees, and so on. Any real object can be characterized by two different aspects: its *properties* and its *behavior.* For example, a car can be modeled as an object. A car has certain properties (color, speed, direction, fuel consumption) and certain behaviors (starting, stopping, turning, and so on).

In the software world, an **object** is a software component whose structure is like that of objects in the real world. Each object consists of a combination of data (called **properties**) and behaviors (called **methods).** The properties are variables describing the essential characteristics of the object, while the methods describe how the object behaves and how the properties of the object can be modified. Thus, an object is a software bundle of variables and related methods.

A software object is often represented as shown in Figure 16-1. The object can be thought of as a cell, with a central nucleus of variables (containing the object's properties) and an outer layer of methods that form an interface between the object's variables and the outside world. The nucleus of data is hidden from the outside world by the outer layer of methods. The object's variables are said to be *encapsulated* within the object, meaning that no code outside of the object can see or directly manipulate them. Any access to the object's data must be through calls to the object's methods.

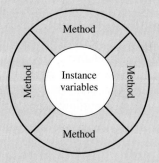

FIGURE 16-1
An object may be represented as a nucleus of data (instance variables) surrounded and protected by methods, which implement the object's behavior and form an interface between the variables and the outside world.

16

F-2003 ONLY

The variables and methods in an object are known as **instance variables** and **instance methods.** Each object of a given type has its own copies of the instance variables, but all of the objects share the same instance methods.

Typically, encapsulation is used to hide the implementation details of an object from other objects in the program. If the other objects in the program cannot see the internal state of an object, they cannot introduce bugs by accidentally modifying the object's state. In addition, changes to the internal operation of the object will not affect the operation of the other objects in a program. As long as the interface to the outer world is unchanged, the implementation details of an object can change at any time without affecting other parts of the program.

Encapsulation provides two primary benefits to software developers:

1. **Modularity.** An object can be written and maintained independently of the source code for other objects. Therefore, the object can be easily reused and passed around in the system.

2. **Information Hiding.** An object has a public interface (the calling sequence of its methods) that other objects can use to communicate with it. However, the object's instance variables are not directly accessible to other objects. Therefore, if the public interface is not changed, an object's variables and methods can be changed at any time without introducing side effects in the other objects that depend on it.

Good Programming Practice

Always make instance variables private, so that they are hidden within an object. Such encapsulation makes your programs more modular and easier to modify.

16.1.2 Messages

In an object-oriented programming model, objects communicate by passing *messages* back and forth among themselves. These messages are really just method calls. For example, if Object A wants Object B to perform some action for it, it sends a message to Object B requesting the object to execute one of its methods (see Figure 16-2). The message causes Object B to execute the specified method.

Each message has three components, which provide all of the information necessary for the receiving object to perform the desired action:

1. A reference pointing to the object to which the message is addressed.
2. The name of the method to perform on that object.
3. Any parameters needed by the method.

An object's behavior is expressed through its methods, so message passing supports all possible interactions between objects.

16

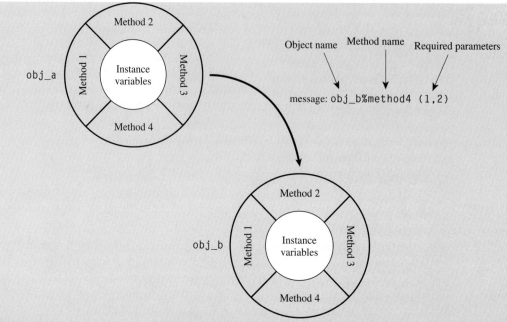

FIGURE 16-2
If object obj_a wants object obj_b to do some work for it, it sends a message to that object. The message contains three parts: a reference to the object to which it is addressed, the name of the method within the object that will do the work, and the required parameters. Note that the names of the object and the method are separated by a % sign.

F-2003 ONLY

16.1.3 Classes

In object-oriented programming, **classes** are the software blueprints from which objects are made. A class is a software construct that specifies the number and type of variables to be included in an object, and the methods that will be defined for the object. Each component of a class is known as a **member.** The two types of members are **fields,** which specify the data types defined by the class, and **methods,** which specify the operations on those fields. For example, suppose that we wish to create an object to represent a complex number. Such an object would have two instance variables, one for the real part of the number (re) and one for the imaginary part of the number (im). In addition, it would have methods describing how to add, subtract, multiply, divide, etc., with complex numbers. To create such objects, we would write a class complex_ob that defines the required fields re and im, together with their associated methods.

Note that a class is a *blueprint* for an object, not an object itself. The class describes what an object will look and behave like once it is created. Each object is created or *instantiated* in memory from the blueprint provided by a class, and many different objects can be instantiated from the same class. For example, Figure 16-3 shows a class complex_ob, together with three objects a, b, and c created from that class. Each of the three objects has its own copies of the instance variables re and im, while sharing a single set of methods to modify them.

16

F-2003
ONLY

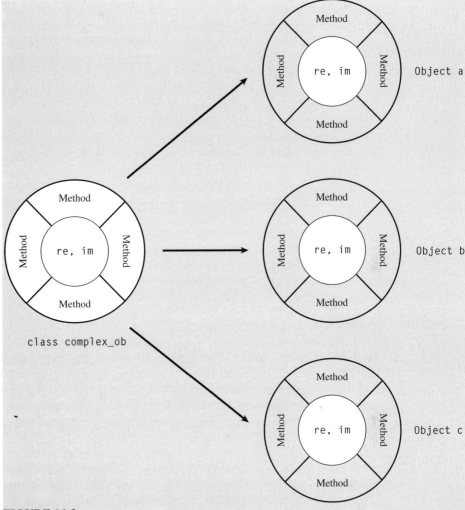

FIGURE 16-3
Many objects can be instantiated from a single class. In this example, three objects a, b, and c have been instantiated from class complex_ob.

16.1.4 Class Hierarchy and Inheritance

The classes in an object-oriented language are organized in a **class hierarchy,** with the highest-level classes being very general in behavior and lower-level ones becoming more specific. Each lower-level class is based on and derived from a higher-level class, and the lower-level classes *inherit both the instance variables and the instance methods* of the class from which they are derived. A new class starts with all of the instance variables and methods of the class on which it is based, and the programmer then adds the additional variables and methods necessary for the new class to perform its function.

The class on which a new class is based is referred to as a **superclass,** and the new class is referred to as a **subclass.** The new subclass can itself become the superclass for

16

another new subclass. A subclass normally adds instance variables and instance methods of its own, so a subclass is generally larger than its superclass. In addition, it can **override** some methods of its superclass, changing its behavior from that of its superclass. Because a subclass is more specific than its superclass, it represents a smaller group of objects.

For example, suppose that we define a class called vector_2d to contain two-dimensional vectors. Such a class would have two instance variables x and y to contain the x and y components of the two-dimensional (2D) vectors, and it would need methods to manipulate the vectors such as adding two vectors, subtracting two vectors, calculating the length of a vector, etc. Now suppose that we need to create a class called vector_3d to contain three-dimensional (3D) vectors. If this class is based on vector_2d, then it will automatically inherit instance variables x and y from its superclass, so the new class will only need to define a variable z (see Figure 16-4). The new class will also override the methods used to manipulate 2D vectors to allow them to work properly with 3D vectors.

The concepts of class hierarchy and inheritance are extremely important, since inheritance allows a programmer to define certain behaviors only once in a superclass, and to reuse those behaviors over and over again in many different subclasses. This reusability makes programming more efficient.

16.1.5 Object-Oriented Programming

Object-oriented programming (OOP) is the process of programming by modeling objects in software. In OOP, a programmer examines the problem to be solved and tries to break it down into identifiable objects, each of which contains certain data and specific methods by which that data is manipulated. Sometimes these objects will correspond to physical objects in nature, and sometimes that will be purely abstract software constructs.

Once the objects making up the problem have been identified, the programmer identifies the type of data to be stored as instance variables in each object, and the exact calling sequence of each method needed to manipulate the data.

The programmer can then develop and test the classes in the model one at a time. As long as the *interfaces* between the classes (the calling sequence of the methods) are unchanged, each class can be developed and tested without needing to change any other part of the program.

16.2
THE STRUCTURE OF A FORTRAN CLASS

The remainder of this chapter shows how to implement object-oriented programming in Fortran, starting with the structure of a Fortran class. The major components (class members) of a Fortran class are (see Figure 16-5):

1. **Fields.** Fields define the instance variables that will be created when an object is instantiated from a class. Instance variables are the data encapsulated inside an object. A new set of instance variables is created each time that an object is instantiated from the class.

16

F-2003 ONLY

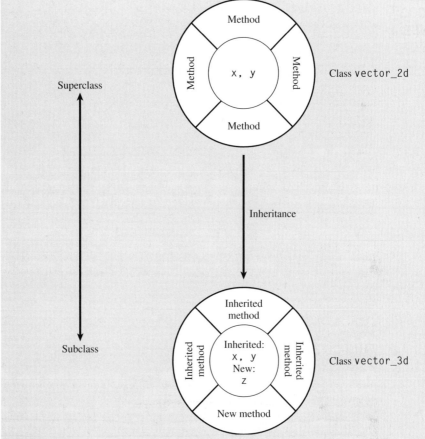

FIGURE 16-4
An example of inheritance. Class `vector_2d` has been defined to handle two-dimensional vectors. When class `vector_3d` is defined as a subclass of `vector_2d`, it inherits the instance variables x and y, as well as many methods. The programmer then adds a new instance variable z and new methods to the ones inherited from the superclass.

2. **Methods.** Methods implement the behaviors of a class. Some methods may be explicitly defined in a class, while other methods may be inherited from superclasses of the class.
3. **Constructor.** A constructor initializes the instance variables in an object when it is created. Fortran objects can be initialized either by using structure constructors, which were introduced in Section 12.1, or by special initializing methods.
4. **Finalizer.** Just before an object is destroyed, it makes a call to a special method called a **finalizer.** The method performs any necessary cleanup (releasing resources, etc.) before the object is destroyed. There can be at most one finalizer in a class, and many classes do not need a finalizer at all.

The members of a class, whether variables or methods, are accessed by referring to an object created from the class by using the **component selector,** the % symbol.

16

**F-2003
ONLY**

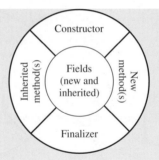

FIGURE 16-5
A class consists of fields (data), a constructor to initialize the data in an object, one or more methods to modify and manipulate the data, and up to one finalizer to clean up before the object is destroyed. Note that both fields and methods may be inherited from a superclass.

For example, suppose that a class `my_class` contains an instance variable `a` and a method `process_a()`. If an object of this class is named `my_obj`, then the instance variable in `my_obj` would be accessed as `my_obj%a`, and the method would be accessed as `my_obj%process_a()`.

16.3

THE `CLASS` KEYWORD

The `CLASS` keyword is a variant of the `TYPE` keyword that adds special properties important for object-oriented programming.

In an ordinary Fortran program, the type of each dummy argument in a procedure and the corresponding calling argument must match *exactly,* or there will be an error. Similarly, the type of a pointer and the corresponding target must match *exactly,* or there will be an error, and the type of an allocatable variable and the corresponding data must match *exactly,* or there will be an error.

The `CLASS` keyword relaxes this requirement in a special way. If an allocatable item, pointer, or dummy argument is declared with the `CLASS(type)` keyword, where `type` is a derived data type, then the item will match that data type *or any extension of that data type*.

For example, suppose that we declare the following two data types:

```
TYPE :: point
    REAL :: x
    REAL :: y
END TYPE

TYPE,EXTENDS(point) :: point_3d
    REAL :: z
END TYPE
```

Then a pointer declared as

```
TYPE(point),POINTER :: p
```

16

would accept only targets of type `point`, but a pointer declared as

```
CLASS(point),POINTER :: p
```

would accept targets of either type `point` or type `point_3d`, which is an extension of type `point`.

The type of a pointer or dummy argument declared with the `CLASS` keyword is known as the **declared type** of the pointer or dummy argument, and the type of the actual object assigned to the pointer or dummy argument at any time is known as the **dynamic type** of the pointer or dummy argument.

An item declared with the `CLASS` keyword is said to be **polymorphic** (meaning "many forms"), because it will match more than one data type.

Polymorphic pointers or dummy arguments have a special limitation: you can access only items of the *declared type* with them. Items defined in extensions are *not* accessible with the polymorphic pointer. For example, consider the following type definitions.

```
CLASS(point),POINTER :: p
TYPE(point),TARGET :: p1
TYPE(point_3d),TARGET :: p2
```

With these definitions, variables `p1` and `p2` can both be assigned to `p`, and the pointer `p` can be used to access components `x` and `y` within them. However, pointer `p` cannot be used to access component `z`, because that component is not defined in the declared type of the pointer.

To understand this more clearly, let's examine the code below. In line 1, pointer `p` is assigned to point to the target `p1`, and lines 2 and 3 access the components of `p` by using the original variable name and the pointer, respectively. This all works fine. In line 4 below, pointer `p` is assigned to point to the target `p2`, which is of type `point_3d`. Lines 5 and 6 access the components of `p` by using the original variable name and the pointer, respectively. Line 5 works fine, but line 6 produces an error, because we can't access component `z` by using a pointer of class `point`, since component `z` is not defined in that derived type.

```
1 p => p1
2 WRITE (*,*) p1%x, p1%y       ! These two lines produce the same output
3 WRITE (*,*) p%x, p%y         ! These two lines produce the same output
4 p => p2
5 WRITE (*,*) p2%x, p2%y, p2%z ! Legal
6 WRITE (*,*) p%x, p%y, p%z    ! Illegal-can't access z
```

There is a way around this limitation by using the `SELECT TYPE` construct, which we will meet later in the chapter.

It is also possible to define a pointer or dummy argument to be of `CLASS(*)`. Such a pointer or argument is said to be **unlimited polymorphic,** since it will match *any* derived type. However, you cannot directly access any components of the dynamic data type, since no components are defined in the declared type of the pointer or dummy argument.

16

16.4

IMPLEMENTING CLASSES AND OBJECTS IN FORTRAN

As we saw in Section 16.2, a Fortran class consists of instance variables, methods, a constructor, and possibly a finalizer. We will now learn how to create a simple Fortran class (without a finalizer), and how to instantiate objects from that class.

◑ Each Fortran class should be placed in a separate module, so that we can control access to its components, and so that we can have an explicit interface to the class via USE access.

16.4.1 Declaring Fields (Instance Variables)

The data fields (or instance variables) in a class are defined in a user-defined data type, and the name of that data type is the name of the class. In proper object-oriented programming, the data type should be declared with PUBLIC access, but the *components* of the data type should be declared PRIVATE. Thus it will be possible to create objects of this type outside of the module, but it will *not* be possible to read or modify the instance variables of the data type from outside of the module.

In actual object-oriented Fortran programs, we often do *not* declare the components of the data type to be PRIVATE. If a Fortran object is to have subclasses that inherit the data from the superclass, then that data must be declared with PUBLIC access, or the subclasses (which are defined in different modules) will not be able to access the data. Also, the Fortran language does not allow constructors to be used if the data fields are declared to be PRIVATE. This is a limitation of the Fortran implementation of object-oriented programming.

As an example, suppose that we are defining a simple complex number class named complex_ob. This class will contain two instance variables, re and im, for the real and the imaginary components of the complex number. This can be accomplished as follows:

```
MODULE complex_class
IMPLICIT NONE

! Type definition
TYPE,PUBLIC :: complex_ob    ! This will be the name we instantiate
   PRIVATE                   ! (Should be used, but might not be)
   REAL :: re                ! Real part
   REAL :: im                ! Imaginary part
END TYPE complex_ob

! Now add methods
CONTAINS

   (Insert methods here)

END MODULE complex_class
```

The constructor for this class can be used to initialize the instance variables if the fields in the class are declared PUBLIC. The constructor consists of the data type name followed by the initial values of the data elements, in parentheses. For example, if the fields in the class are declared PUBLIC, then the following code creates a complex object in which initial x and y values are 1 and 2, and assigns it to pointer p.

```
CLASS(complex_ob),POINTER :: p
p = complex_ob(1.,2.)
```

If the fields in the class are declared PRIVATE, then the programmer will have to write a special method to initialize the data in the class.

16.4.2 Creating Methods

Object-oriented methods differ from ordinary Fortran procedures in that they are *bound* to a particular class, and can only work with data from that class. How do we bind Fortran procedures to a particular class (i.e., a defined data type), and so create methods in Fortran?

As we saw in Chapter 12, **type-bound Fortran procedures** are created by adding a CONTAINS statement to the type definition, and declaring the bindings after that statement. For example, suppose that we wanted to include a subroutine to add two items of type complex_ob in our class. Then we would declare the type definition as follows:

```
MODULE complex_class
IMPLICIT NONE

! Type definition
TYPE,PUBLIC :: complex_ob   ! This will be the name we instantiate
   PRIVATE
   REAL :: re              ! Real part
   REAL :: im              ! Imaginary part
CONTAINS
   PROCEDURE::add => add_complex_to_complex
END TYPE complex_ob

! Declare access for methods
PRIVATE :: add_complex_to_complex

! Now add methods
CONTAINS

   ! Insert method add_complex_to_complex here:
   SUBROUTINE add_complex_to_complex( this, ... )
   CLASS(complex_ob) :: this
   ...
   END SUBROUTINE add_complex_to_complex

END MODULE complex_class
```

These statements declare that subroutine add_complex_to_complex is bound to this data type and only works with this data type, and that it will be accessed with the name add. The subroutine itself must have an item of the type definition as its *first* argument, because the PASS attribute is the default for bound procedures. This means that the object to which it is bound will always be passed as the first argument to the subroutine whenever it is called.

16

Bindings can also be generic, with multiple procedures bound to the same name, as long as the procedures can be distinguished by their calling arguments. For example, we might want to add either a complex number or a real number to the object. In that case, the binding could be as follows:

```
MODULE complex_class
IMPLICIT NONE

! Type definition
TYPE,PUBLIC :: complex_ob    ! This will be the name we instantiate
    PRIVATE
    REAL :: re                ! Real part
    REAL :: im                ! Imaginary part
CONTAINS
    PRIVATE
    PROCEDURE::ac => add_complex_to_complex
    PROCEDURE::ar => add_real_to_complex
    GENERIC,PUBLIC::add => ac,ar
END TYPE complex_ob

! Declare access for methods
PRIVATE :: add_complex_to_complex, add_real_to_complex

! Now add methods
CONTAINS

    ! Insert method add_complex_to_complex here:
    SUBROUTINE add_complex_to_complex( this, ... )
    CLASS(complex_ob) :: this
    ...
    END SUBROUTINE add_complex_to_complex

    ! Insert method add_real_to_complex here:
        SUBROUTINE add_real_to_complex( this, ... )
        CLASS(complex_ob) :: this
        ...
    END SUBROUTINE add_real_to_complex

END MODULE complex_class
```

This example defines a generic public binding add, and two private procedures ac and ar associated with the public binding. Note that ac and ar are mapped to subroutines with much longer names; the short forms are just for convenience. Also, note that ac, ar, add_complex_to_complex, and add_real_to_complex are all declared PRIVATE, so they cannot be accessed directly from outside the module.

As many methods as necessary can be created in this fashion, each one bound to the data object created from the class. All of the procedures would be accessed as obj%add(...), where obj is the name of an object created from this class. The particular method that is invoked will be determined by the arguments of the add method.

16.4.3 Creating (Instantiating) Objects from a Class

Objects of type complex_ob can be instantiated in another procedure by USEing module complex_class in the procedure, and then declaring the object by using the TYPE keyword.

16

```
USE complex_class
IMPLICIT NONE

TYPE(complex_ob) :: x, y, z
```

These statements have created (instantiated) three objects from the class complex_ob: x, y, and z. If the fields (instance variables) of the objects have *not* been declared PRIVATE, then they can also be initialized as they are created using constructors.

```
TYPE(complex_ob) :: x = complex_ob(1.,2.), y = complex_ob(3.,4.), z
```

Once they have been created, the methods in the objects can be accessed by using the object name and the component selector. For example, the method add could be accessed for object x as follows:

```
z = x%add(...)
```

16.5

FIRST EXAMPLE: A timer CLASS

In developing software, it is often useful to be able to determine how long a particular part of a program takes to execute. This measurement can help us locate the "hot spots" in the code, the places where the program is spending most of its time, so that we can try to optimize them. This is usually done with an *elapsed-time calculator*.

An elapsed-time calculator makes a great first object, because it is so simple. It is analogous to a physical stopwatch. A stopwatch is an object that measures the elapsed time between a push on a start button and a push on a stop button (often they are the same physical button). The basic actions (methods) performed on a physical stopwatch are:

1. A button push to reset and start the timer.
2. A button push to stop the timer and display the elapsed time.

Internally, the stopwatch must remember the time of the first button push in order to calculate the elapsed time.

Similarly, an elapsed-time class needs to contain the following components (members):

1. A method to store the start time of the timer (start_timer). This method will not require any input parameters from the calling program, and will not return any results to the calling program.
2. A method to return the elapsed time since the last start (elapsed_time). This method will not require any input parameters from the calling program, but it will return the elapsed time in seconds to the calling program.
3. A field (instance variable) to store the time that the timer started running, for use by the elapsed-time method.

This class will not need a finalizer.

The timer class must be able to determine the current time whenever one of its methods is called. Fortunately, the intrinsic subroutine date_and_time (see Appendix B)

16

provides this information. The optional argument `values` returns an array of eight integers, containing time information from the year all the way down to the current millisecond. These values can be turned into a current time in milliseconds since the start of the month as follows:

```
! Get time
CALL date_and_time ( VALUES=value )
time1 = 86400.D0 * value(3) + 3600.D0 * value(5) &
      + 60.D0 * value(6) + value(7) + 0.001D0 * value(8)
```

Be sure that variable `time1` is a 64-bit real, or there will not be enough precision to save all of the time information.

16.5.1 Implementing the `timer` Class

We will implement the `timer` class in a series of steps, defining the instance variables, constructor, and methods in succession.

1. **Define Instance Variables.** The `timer` class must contain a single instance variable called `saved_time`, which contains the last time at which `start_timer` method was called. It must be a 64-bit real value (`SELECTED_REAL_KIND(p=14)`), so that it can hold fractional parts of seconds.

   Instance variables are declared after the class definition, and before the constructors and methods. Therefore, class `timer` will begin as follows:

```
MODULE timer_class
IMPLICIT NONE

! Declare constants
INTEGER,PARAMETER :: DBL = SELECTED_REAL_KIND(p=14)

! Type definition
TYPE,PUBLIC :: timer    ! This will be the name we instantiate
   PRIVATE
   REAL(KIND=DBL) :: saved_time
END TYPE timer
```

   Note that we are declaring the field `saved_time` to be `PRIVATE`, so it will not be possible to initialize the data value by using a structure constructor. Instead, it must be initialized by using a user-defined method.

2. **Create the Methods.** The class must also include two methods to start the timer and to read the elapsed time. Method `start_timer()` simply resets the start time in the instance variable. Method `elapsed_time()` returns the elapsed time since the start of the timer in seconds. Both of these methods must be bound to the class.

   The dummy arguments of the `timer` type that are declared in these methods should use the `CLASS` keyword, so that they will also work with any extensions of the `timer` class that might be defined later.

**F-2003
ONLY**

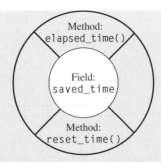

FIGURE 16-6
The timer class.

The resulting timer class is shown in Figure 16-6, and the source code for this class is shown in Figure 16-7.

FIGURE 16-7
The source code for the timer class.

```
MODULE timer_class
!
!   This module implements a timer class.
!
!   Record of revisions:
!      Date        Programmer          Description of change
!      ====        ==========          =====================
!   12/27/06    S. J. Chapman        Original code
!
IMPLICIT NONE

! Declare constants
INTEGER,PARAMETER :: DBL = SELECTED_REAL_KIND(p=14)

! Type definition
TYPE,PUBLIC :: timer   ! This will be the name we instantiate

   ! Instance variables
   PRIVATE
   REAL(KIND=DBL) :: saved_time         ! Saved time in ms

CONTAINS

   ! Bound procedures
   PROCEDURE,PUBLIC :: start_timer => start_timer_sub
   PROCEDURE,PUBLIC :: elapsed_time => elapsed_time_fn

END TYPE timer

! Restrict access to the actual subroutine names
PRIVATE :: start_timer_sub, elapsed_time_fn

! Now add subroutines
CONTAINS
```

(*continued*)

16

F-2003
ONLY

(concluded)

```
SUBROUTINE start_timer_sub(this)
!
! Subroutine to get and save the initial time
!
IMPLICIT NONE

! Declare calling arguments
CLASS(timer) :: this               ! Timer object

! Declare local variables
INTEGER,DIMENSION(8) :: value      ! Time value array

! Get time
CALL date_and_time ( VALUES=value )
this%saved_time = 86400.D0 * value(3) + 3600.D0 * value(5) &
               + 60.D0 * value(6) + value(7) + 0.001D0 * value(8)

END SUBROUTINE start_timer_sub

REAL FUNCTION elapsed_time_fn(this)
!
! Function to calculate elapsed time
!
IMPLICIT NONE

! Declare calling arguments
CLASS(timer) :: this               ! Timer object

! Declare local variables
INTEGER,DIMENSION(8) :: value      ! Time value array
REAL(KIND=DBL) :: current_time     ! Current time (ms)

! Get time
CALL date_and_time ( VALUES=value )
current_time = 86400.D0 * value(3) + 3600.D0 * value(5) &
            + 60.D0 * value(6) + value(7) + 0.001D0 * value(8)

! Get elapsed time in seconds
elapsed_time_fn = current_time - this%saved_time

END FUNCTION elapsed_time_fn
END MODULE timer_class
```

16.5.2 Using the timer Class

To use this class in a program, the programmer must first instantiate a timer object
with a statement like

```
TYPE(timer) :: t
```

This statement defines an object t of the timer class (see Figure 16-8). After this object
has been created, t is a timer object, and the methods in the object can be called by
using that reference: t%start_timer() and t%elapsed_time().

A program can reset the elapsed timer to zero at any time by calling
method start_timer(), and can get the elapsed time by executing method

F-2003 ONLY

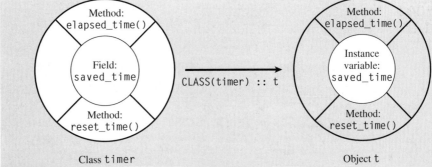

Class `timer`   Object `t`

FIGURE 16-8
The statement "CLASS(timer) :: t" creates (instantiates) a new `timer` object from the template provided by the class definition and gives it the name `t`. This object has its own unique copy of the instance variable `saved_time`.

`elapsed_time()`. An example program that uses the `timer` object is shown in Figure 16-9. The program tests this class by measuring the time required to perform 100,000,000 iterations of a pair of nested DO loops.

FIGURE 16-9
A program to test the `timer` class.

```
PROGRAM test_timer
!
!   This program tests the timer class.
!
!   Record of revisions:
!       Date        Programmer          Description of change
!       ====        ==========          =====================
!     12/27/06    S. J. Chapman         Original code
!
USE timer_class                         ! Import timer class
IMPLICIT NONE

! Declare local variables
INTEGER :: i, j                         ! Loop index
INTEGER :: k                            ! Scratch variable
TYPE(timer) :: t                        ! Timer object

! Reset the timer
CALL t%start_timer()

! Waste some time
DO i = 1, 10000
   DO j = 1, 10000
      k = i + j
   END DO
END DO

! Get the elapsed time
WRITE (*,'(A,F8.3,A)') 'Time =', t%elapsed_time(), ' s'

END PROGRAM test_timer
```

16

When this program is executed on my Pentium 4 1.6-GHz PC, the results are:

```
D:\book\chap16>test_timer
Time =   0.313 s
```

The measured time will of course differ on computers of different speeds.

16.5.3 Comments on the `timer` Class

This section contains a few notes about the operation of our `timer` class, and of classes in general.

First, note that the `timer` class saves its start time in the instance variable `saved_time`. Each time that an object is instantiated from a class, it receives its *own copy* of all instance variables defined in the class. Therefore, many `timer` objects could be instantiated and used simultaneously in a program, and *they will not interfere with each other,* because each timer has its own private copy of the instance variable `saved_time`.

Also, notice that each class member in Figure 16-7 is declared with either a PUBLIC or PRIVATE keyword. Any instance variable or method definition declared with the PUBLIC keyword can be accessed by USE association from other parts of the program. Any instance variable or method declared with the PRIVATE keyword is accessible only to methods of the object in which it is defined.[1]

In this case, the instance variable `saved_time` is declared PRIVATE, so it cannot be seen or modified by any method outside of the object in which it is defined. Since no part of the program outside of `timer` can see `saved_time`, it is not possible for some other part of the program to accidentally modify the value stored there and so mess up the elapsed-time measurement. The only way that a program can utilize the elapsed-time measurement is through the PUBLIC bound methods `start_timer()` and `elapsed_time()`. You should always declare all instance variables within your classes to be PRIVATE.

Also, note that the actual method names `start_timer_sub` and `elapsed_time_fn` are declared PRIVATE. This means that the actual methods cannot be called directly from another part of the program. The *only* way to execute these methods is by using the object name and the component selector (%).

16.6
CATEGORIES OF METHODS

Since instance variables are usually hidden within a class, the only way to work with them is through the interface formed by the class's methods. The methods are the public face of the class, providing a standard way to work with the information while hiding the unnecessary details of the implementation from the user.

---

[1] Actually, it is accessible to any other methods in the same module. Since we are putting each class in its own module, the PRIVATE keyword effectively restricts access to the object in which it is defined.

16

F-2003 ONLY

A class's methods must perform certain common "housekeeping" functions, as well as the specific actions required by the class. These housekeeping functions fall into a few broad categories, and they are common to most classes, regardless of their specific purpose. A class must usually provide a way to store data into its instance variables, read data from its instance variables, test the status of its instance variables, and manipulate the instance variables as required to solve problems.

Since the instance variables in a class cannot be used directly, classes must define methods to store data into the instance variables and to read data from them. By convention among object-oriented programmers, the names of methods that store data begin with `set` and are called **set methods,** while the names of methods that read data begin with `get` and are called **get methods.**

Set methods take information from the outside world and store the data into the class's instance variables. In the process, they *should also check the data for validity and consistency*. This checking prevents the instance variables of the class from being set into an illegal state.

For example, suppose that we have created a class `date` containing instance variables `day` (with a range of 1 to 31), `month` (with a range of 1 to 12), and `year` (with a range of 1900 to 2100). If these instance variables were declared `PUBLIC`, then any part of the program that `USE`s the class could modify them directly. For example, assume that a date object was declared as

```
USE date_class
. . .
TYPE(date) :: d1
```

With this declaration, any method in the program could directly set the day to an illegal value.

```
d1%day = 32;
```

Set methods and private instance variables prevent this sort of illegal behavior by testing the input parameters. If the parameters are valid, the method stores them in the appropriate instance variables. If the parameters are invalid, the method either modifies the inputs to be legal or provides some type of error message to the caller.

Good Programming Practice
Use `set` methods to check the validity and consistency of input data before it is stored in an object's instance variables.

`get` methods are used to retrieve information from the instance variables and to format it properly for presentation to the outside world. For example, our `date` class might include methods `get_day()`, `get_month()`, and `get_year()` to recover the day, month, and year, respectively.

Another category of method tests for the truth or falsity of some condition. These methods are called **predicate methods.** These methods typically begin with the word `is`, and they return a `LOGICAL` (true/false) result. For example, a `date` class might include a method `is_leap_year()`, which would return true if the specified year is a leap year, and false otherwise. In could also include methods like `is_equal()`, `is_earlier()`, and `is_later()` to compare two dates chronologically.

Good Programming Practice

Define predicate methods to test for the truth or falsity of conditions associated with any classes you create.

EXAMPLE 16-1

Creating a date *Class:*

We will illustrate the concepts described in this chapter by creating a date class designed to hold and manipulate dates on the Gregorian calendar.

This class should be able to hold the day, month, and year of a date in instance variables that are protected from outside access. The class must include set and get methods to change and retrieve the stored information, predicate methods to recover information about date objects and to allow two date objects to be compared, and a to_string method to allow the information in a date object to be displayed easily.

SOLUTION
The date class will need three instance variables, day, month, and year. They will be declared PRIVATE to protect them from direct manipulation by outside methods. The day variable should have a range of 1 to 31, corresponding to the days in a month. The month variable should have a range of 1 to 12, corresponding to the months in a year. The year variable will be greater than or equal to zero.

We will define a method `set_date(day,month,year)` to insert a new date into a date object, and three methods `get_day()`, `get_month()`, and `get_year()` to return the day, month, and year from a given date object.

The supported predicate methods will include `is_leap_year()` to test if a year is a leap year. This method will use the leap year test described in Example 4-3. In addition, we will create three methods `is_equal()`, `is_earlier()`, and `is_later()` to compare two date objects. Finally, method `to_string()` will format the date as a string in the normal U.S. style: mm/dd/yyyy.

The resulting class is shown in Figure 16-10. Notice that we took advantage of the renaming capability of the bindings to give each procedure a name that identified whether it is a subroutine or a function. This is *not* required in OOP, but I find it convenient to help me keep subroutines and functions straight.

FIGURE 16-10
The date class.

```
MODULE date_class
!
!    This module implements a date class, which stores
```

(*continued*)

16

**F-2003
ONLY**

```
(continued)
!     and manipulates dates on the Gregorian calendar.
!     It implements set methods, get methods, predicate
!     methods, and a "to_string" method for displays.
!
!  Record of revisions:
!     Date          Programmer           Description of change
!     ====          ==========           =====================
!   12/28/06     S. J. Chapman          Original code
!
IMPLICIT NONE

! Type definition
TYPE,PUBLIC :: date    ! This will be the name we instantiate

   ! Instance variables.  Note that the default
   ! date is January 1, 1900.
   PRIVATE
   INTEGER :: year = 1900    ! Year (0 - xxxx)
   INTEGER :: month = 1      ! Month (1-12)
   INTEGER :: day = 1        ! Day (1-31)

CONTAINS

   ! Bound procedures
   PROCEDURE,PUBLIC :: set_date => set_date_sub
   PROCEDURE,PUBLIC :: get_day => get_day_fn
   PROCEDURE,PUBLIC :: get_month => get_month_fn
   PROCEDURE,PUBLIC :: get_year => get_year_fn
   PROCEDURE,PUBLIC :: is_leap_year => is_leap_year_fn
   PROCEDURE,PUBLIC :: is_equal => is_equal_fn
   PROCEDURE,PUBLIC :: is_earlier_than => is_earlier_fn
   PROCEDURE,PUBLIC :: is_later_than => is_later_fn
   PROCEDURE,PUBLIC :: to_string => to_string_fn

END TYPE date

! Restrict access to the actual procedure names
PRIVATE :: set_date_sub, get_day_fn, get_month_fn, get_year_fn
PRIVATE :: is_leap_year_fn, is_equal_fn, is_earlier_fn
PRIVATE :: is_later_fn, to_string_fn

! Now add methods
CONTAINS

   SUBROUTINE set_date_sub(this, day, month, year)
   !
   ! Subroutine to set the initial date
   !
   IMPLICIT NONE

   ! Declare calling arguments
   CLASS(date) :: this                    ! Date object
   INTEGER,INTENT(IN) :: day              ! Day (1-31)
   INTEGER,INTENT(IN) :: month            ! Month (1-12)
   INTEGER,INTENT(IN) :: year             ! Year (0 - xxxx)

   ! Save date
   this%day   = day
```

16

(continued)

F-2003 ONLY

(continued)

```fortran
      this%month = month
      this%year  = year

      END SUBROUTINE set_date_sub

      INTEGER FUNCTION get_day_fn(this)
      !
      ! Function to return the day from this object
      !
      IMPLICIT NONE

      ! Declare calling arguments
      CLASS(date) :: this                ! Date object

      ! Get day
      get_day_fn = this%day

      END FUNCTION get_day_fn

      INTEGER FUNCTION get_month_fn(this)
      !
      ! Function to return the month from this object
      !
      IMPLICIT NONE

      ! Declare calling arguments
      CLASS(date) :: this                ! Date object

      ! Get month
      get_month_fn = this%month

      END FUNCTION get_month_fn

      INTEGER FUNCTION get_year_fn(this)
      !
      ! Function to return the year from this object
      !
      IMPLICIT NONE

      ! Declare calling arguments
      CLASS(date) :: this                ! Date object

      ! Get year
      get_year_fn = this%year

      END FUNCTION get_year_fn

      LOGICAL FUNCTION is_leap_year_fn(this)
      !
      ! Is this year a leap year?
      !
      IMPLICIT NONE

      ! Declare calling arguments
      CLASS(date) :: this                ! Date object

      ! Perform calculation
      IF ( MOD(this%year, 400) == 0 ) THEN
          is_leap_year_fn = .TRUE.
```

16

(continued)

```
(continued)
      ELSE IF ( MOD(this%year, 100) == 0 ) THEN
         is_leap_year_fn = .FALSE.
      ELSE IF ( MOD(this%year, 4) == 0 ) THEN
         is_leap_year_fn = .TRUE.
      ELSE
         is_leap_year_fn = .FALSE.
      END IF

      END FUNCTION is_leap_year_fn

      LOGICAL FUNCTION is_equal_fn(this,that)
      !
      ! Are these two dates equal?
      !
      IMPLICIT NONE

      ! Declare calling arguments
      CLASS(date) :: this              ! Date object
      CLASS(date) :: that              ! Another date for comparison

      ! Perform calculation
      IF ( (this%year == that%year) .AND. &
           (this%month == that%month) .AND. &
           (this%day == that%day) ) THEN
         is_equal_fn = .TRUE.
      ELSE
         is_equal_fn = .FALSE.
      END IF

      END FUNCTION is_equal_fn

      LOGICAL FUNCTION is_earlier_fn(this,that)
      !
      ! Is the date in "that" earlier than the date
      ! stored in the object?
      !
      IMPLICIT NONE

      ! Declare calling arguments
      CLASS(date) :: this              ! Date object
      CLASS(date) :: that              ! Another date for comparison

      ! Perform calculation
      IF ( that%year > this%year ) THEN
         is_earlier_fn = .FALSE.
      ELSE IF ( that%year < this%year ) THEN
         is_earlier_fn = .TRUE.
      ELSE
         IF ( that%month > this%month) THEN
            is_earlier_fn = .FALSE.
         ELSE IF ( that%month < this%month ) THEN
            is_earlier_fn = .TRUE.
         ELSE
            IF ( that%day >= this%day ) THEN
               is_earlier_fn = .FALSE.
            ELSE
```

16

(continued)

(continued)

```
            is_earlier_fn = .TRUE.
        END IF
    END IF
END IF

END FUNCTION is_earlier_fn

LOGICAL FUNCTION is_later_fn(this,that)
!
! Is the date in "that" later than the date
! stored in the object?
!
IMPLICIT NONE

! Declare calling arguments
CLASS(date) :: this                 ! Date object
CLASS(date) :: that                 ! Another date for comparison

! Perform calculation
IF ( that%year > this%year ) THEN
   is_later_fn = .TRUE.
ELSE IF ( that%year < this%year ) THEN
   is_later_fn = .FALSE.
ELSE
   IF ( that%month > this%month ) THEN
      is_later_fn = .TRUE.
   ELSE IF ( that%month < this%month ) THEN
      is_later_fn = .FALSE.
   ELSE
      IF ( that%day > this%day ) THEN
         is_later_fn = .TRUE.
      ELSE
         is_later_fn = .FALSE.
      END IF
   END IF
END IF

END FUNCTION is_later_fn

CHARACTER(len=10) FUNCTION to_string_fn(this)
!
! Represent the date as a string: MM/DD/YYYY.
!
IMPLICIT NONE

! Declare calling arguments
CLASS(date) :: this                 ! Date object

! Declare local variables
CHARACTER(len=2) :: dd              ! Day
CHARACTER(len=2) :: mm              ! Month
CHARACTER(len=4) :: yy              ! Year

! Get components
WRITE (dd,'(I2.2)') this%day
WRITE (mm,'(I2.2)') this%month
WRITE (yy,'(I4)') this%year
```

(continued)

F-2003
ONLY

(concluded)

```
   ! Return string
   to_string_fn = mm // '/' // dd // '/' // yy

   END FUNCTION to_string_fn

END MODULE date_class
```

We must create a program to test the date class. Such a program is shown in Figure 16-11. Program test_date instantiates four date objects, and initializes them. It then exercises all of the methods defined in the class.

FIGURE 16-11
Program test_date to test the date class.

```
PROGRAM test_date
!
!  This program tests the date class.
!
!  Record of revisions:
!       Date         Programmer           Description of change
!       ====         ==========           =====================
!     12/28/06     S. J. Chapman          Original code
!
USE date_class                        ! Import date class
IMPLICIT NONE

! Declare local variables
TYPE(date) :: d1                      ! Date 1
TYPE(date) :: d2                      ! Date 2
TYPE(date) :: d3                      ! Date 3
TYPE(date) :: d4                      ! Date 4
CHARACTER(len=10) :: str1             ! Date strings
CHARACTER(len=10) :: str2             ! Date strings
CHARACTER(len=10) :: str3             ! Date strings
CHARACTER(len=10) :: str4             ! Date strings

! Initialize dates d1, d2, and d3 (d4 defaults)
CALL d1%set_date(4,1,1996)
CALL d2%set_date(1,3,1998)
CALL d3%set_date(3,1,1996)

! Write out the dates
str1 = d1%to_string()
str2 = d2%to_string()
str3 = d3%to_string()
str4 = d4%to_string()
WRITE (*,'(A,A)') 'Date 1 = ', str1
WRITE (*,'(A,A)') 'Date 2 = ', str2
WRITE (*,'(A,A)') 'Date 3 = ', str3
WRITE (*,'(A,A)') 'Date 4 = ', str4

! Check for leap years
IF ( d1%is_leap_year() ) THEN
   WRITE (*,'(I4,A)') d1%get_year(), ' is a leap year.'
```

16

(continued)

F-2003 ONLY

(concluded)

```
ELSE
   WRITE (*,'(I4,A)') d1%get_year(), ' is a not leap year.'
END IF

IF ( d2%is_leap_year() ) THEN
   WRITE (*,'(I4,A)') d2%get_year(), ' is a leap year.'
ELSE
   WRITE (*,'(I4,A)') d2%get_year(), ' is a not leap year.'
END IF

! Check for equality
IF ( d1%is_equal(d3) ) THEN
   WRITE (*,'(3A)') str3, ' is equal to ', str1
ELSE
   WRITE (*,'(3A)') str3, ' is not equal to ', str1
END IF

! Check is_earlier
IF ( d1%is_earlier_than(d3) ) THEN
   WRITE (*,'(3A)') str3, ' is earlier than ', str1
ELSE
   WRITE (*,'(3A)') str3, ' is not earlier than ', str1
END IF

! Check is_later
IF ( d1%is_later_than(d3) ) THEN
   WRITE (*,'(3A)') str3, ' is later than ', str1
ELSE
   WRITE (*,'(3A)') str3, ' is not later than ', str1
END IF

END PROGRAM test_date
```

When this program is executed, the results are:

```
C:\book\chap16>test_date
Date 1 = 01/04/1996
Date 2 = 03/01/1998
Date 3 = 01/03/1996
Date 4 = 01/01/1900
1996 is a leap year.
1998 is a not leap year.
01/03/1996 is not equal to 01/04/1996
01/03/1996 is earlier than 01/04/1996
01/03/1996 is not later than 01/04/1996
```

Note that the date strings are being written out in the order month/day/year. From the test results, this class appears to be functioning correctly.

This class works, but it could be improved. For example, there is no validity checking performed on the input values in the set_date() method, and the to_string() method could be modified to produce dates with explicit month names such as "January 1, 1900." In addition, the U.S. order month/day/year is not used

16

everywhere in the world. It would be possible to customize the to_string() method so that it writes out date strings in different orders in different parts of the world. You will be asked to improve this class as an end-of-chapter exercise.

16.7
CONTROLLING ACCESS TO CLASS MEMBERS

The instance variables of a class are normally declared PRIVATE and the methods of a class are normally declared PUBLIC, so that the methods form an interface with the outside world, hiding the internal behavior of the class from any other parts of the program. This approach has many advantages, since it makes programs more modular. For example, suppose that we have written a program that makes extensive use of timer objects. If necessary, we could completely redesign the internal behavior of the timer class, and the program will continue to work properly as long as we have not changed the parameters or returned values from methods start_timer() and elapsed_time(). This **public interface** isolates the internals of the class from the rest of the program, making incremental modifications easier.

Good Programming Practice
The instance variables of a class should normally be declared PRIVATE, and the class methods should be used to provide a standard interface to the class.

There are some exceptions to this general rule. Many classes contain PRIVATE methods that perform specialized calculations in support of the PUBLIC methods of the class. These are called **utility methods,** and since they are not intended to be called directly by users, they are declared with the PRIVATE access modifier.

16.8
FINALIZERS

Just before an object is destroyed, it makes a call to a special method called a **finalizer,** if one is defined. A finalizer performs any necessary cleanup (releasing resources, closing files, etc.) before the object is destroyed. There can be more than one finalizer in a class, but most classes do not need a finalizer at all.

A finalizer is bound to a class by adding a FINAL keyword in the CONTAINS section of the type definition. For example, the following data type contains a pair of pointers to arrays of x and y data points. When an object of this data type is created and used, arrays will be allocated and data will be assigned to the pointer v.

```
TYPE,PUBLIC :: vector
   PRIVATE
   REAL,DIMENSION(:),POINTER :: v
   LOGICAL :: allocated = .FALSE.
END TYPE
```

F-2003 ONLY

If the object of this data type were later deleted, the pointers would go away, but the allocated memory would remain, and the program would have a memory leak.

Now suppose that we declare a final subroutine called `clean_vector` for this data type.

```
TYPE,PUBLIC :: vector
    PRIVALE
    REAL,DIMENSION(:),POINTER :: v
    LOGICAL :: v_allocated = .FALSE.
CONTAINS
    FINAL :: clean_vector
END TYPE
```

When an item of the data type is destroyed, the final subroutine `clean_vector` is automatically called with the object as an argument, just before it is destroyed. This subroutine can deallocate any memory allocated on x or y, and thus avoid a memory leak.

Final subroutines are also used to close files that might be open in an object, and to release similar system resources.

EXAMPLE 16-2

Using Finalizers:

To illustrate the use of finalizers, we will create a simple class capable of storing an arbitrary-length vector of real data. Since we don't know how long the vector will be, we will declare this vector by using a pointer, and allocate an array of the proper size on the pointer.

This class will contain a set method to place the vector into the object, a put method to retrieve the data, and a final method to deallocate the data when the object is destroyed.

The resulting class is shown in Figure 16-12.

FIGURE 16-12
The `vector` class.

```
MODULE vector_class
!
!    This module implements a vector class.  This initial
!    version of the class holds an arbitrary-length rank 1
!    REAL vector.  It includes procedures to put and get
!    the data, as well as a finalizer to deallocate the
!    data before an object of this type is destroyed.
!
!    Record of revisions:
!      Date          Programmer           Description of change
!      ====          ==========           =====================
!    12/29/06     S. J. Chapman           Original code
!
IMPLICIT NONE
```

(continued)

16

F-2003 ONLY

```
(continued)
! Type definition
TYPE,PUBLIC :: vector  ! This will be the name we instantiate

    ! Instance variables.
    PRIVATE
    REAL,DIMENSION(:),POINTER :: v
    LOGICAL :: v_allocated = .FALSE.

CONTAINS

    ! Bound procedures
    PROCEDURE,PUBLIC :: set_vector => set_vector_sub
    PROCEDURE,PUBLIC :: get_vector => get_vector_sub
    FINAL :: clean_vector

END TYPE vector

! Restrict access to the actual procedure names
PRIVATE :: set_vector_sub, get_vector_sub, clean_vector_sub

! Now add methods
CONTAINS

    SUBROUTINE set_vector_sub(this, array)
    !
    ! Subroutine to store data in the vector
    !
    IMPLICIT NONE

    ! Declare calling arguments
    CLASS(vector) :: this                 ! Vector object
    REAL,DIMENSION(:),INTENT(IN) :: array ! Input data

    ! Declare local variables
    INTEGER :: istat                      ! Allocate status

    ! Save data, for deleting any data that might have been
    ! stored in this object.
    IF ( this%v_allocated ) THEN
       DEALLOCATE(this%v,STAT=istat)
    END IF
    ALLOCATE(this%v(SIZE(array,1)),STAT=istat)
    this%v = array
    this%v_allocated = .TRUE.

    END SUBROUTINE set_vector_sub

    SUBROUTINE get_vector_sub(this, array)
    !
    ! Subroutine to get data in the vector
    !
    IMPLICIT NONE

    ! Declare calling arguments
    CLASS(vector) :: this                  ! Vector object
    REAL,DIMENSION(:),INTENT(OUT) :: array ! Output data
```

16

(continued)

F-2003 ONLY

(concluded)

```
! Declare local variables
INTEGER :: array_length            ! Length of array
INTEGER :: data_length             ! Length of data vector
INTEGER :: istat                   ! Allocate status

! Retrieve data.  If the size of the stored data does
! not match the array size, then return only a subset
! of the data or else pad the real data with zeros.
IF ( this%v_allocated ) THEN

   ! Return as much data as possible, truncating or
   ! zero padding as necessary.
   array_length = SIZE(array,1)
   data_length  = SIZE(this%v,1)
   IF ( array_length > data_length ) THEN
      array(1:data_length) = this%v
      array(data_length+1:array_length) = 0
   ELSE IF ( array_length == data_length ) THEN
      array = this%v
   ELSE
      array = this%v(1:array_length)
   END IF

ELSE
   ! No data--return zeros.
   array = 0

END IF

END SUBROUTINE get_vector_sub

SUBROUTINE clean_vector (this)
!
! Subroutine to finalize the vector
!
IMPLICIT NONE

! Declare calling arguments
CLASS(vector) :: this              ! Vector object

! Declare local variables
INTEGER :: istat                   ! Allocate status

! Debugging message
WRITE (*,*) 'In finalizer ...'

! Save data, for deleting any data that might have been
! stored in this object.
IF ( this%v_allocated ) THEN
   DEALLOCATE(this%v,STAT=istat)
END IF

END SUBROUTINE clean_vector

END MODULE vector_class
```

We must create a test driver program to test the vector class. Such a program is shown in Figure 16-13. This program creates a vector object by allocating it on a pointer. It stores and retrieves an array from the object, and then deallocates it. Note that when the object is deallocated, the final subroutine is automatically called to deallocate the instance variable v.

16

F-2003 ONLY

FIGURE 16-13
Test driver for the `vector` class.

```
PROGRAM test_vector
!
!  This program tests the vector class.
!
!  Record of revisions:
!     Date         Programmer          Description of change
!     ====         ==========          =====================
!    12/29/06    S. J. Chapman         Original code
!
USE vector_class                ! Import vector class
IMPLICIT NONE

! Declare variables
REAL,DIMENSION(6) :: array      ! Array of data to load / save
INTEGER :: istat                ! Allocate status
TYPE(vector),POINTER :: my_vec  ! Test object

! Create an object of type "vector" using the pointer
ALLOCATE( my_vec, STAT=istat )

! Save an array of data in this object.
array = (/ 1., 2., 3., 4., 5., 6. /)
CALL my_vec%set_vector(array)

! Retrieve the data from this vector.
array = 0
CALL my_vec%get_vector(array)
WRITE (*,'(A,6F6.1)') 'vector = ', array

! Destroy this object
WRITE (*,*) 'Deallocating vector object ...'
DEALLOCATE( my_vec, STAT=istat )

END PROGRAM test_vector
```

When this program was executed on my computer, the results were:

```
C:\book\chap16>test_vector
vector = 1.0 2.0 3.0 4.0 5.0 6.0
  Deallocating vector object ...
  In finalizer ...
```

Note that the data stored in the vector was recovered successfully. Also, note that the finalizer was called when the object was deallocated.

16.9

INHERITANCE AND POLYMORPHISM

In Section 16.1.4, we learned that classes could be organized in a class hierarchy, with lower-level classes inheriting instance variables and methods from the higher-level classes that they were based on.

Any class above a specific class in the class hierarchy is known as a superclass of that class. The class just above a specific class in the hierarchy is known as the

16

immediate superclass of the class. Any class below a specific class in the class hierarchy is known as a subclass of that class.

This section explains how inheritance allows Fortran to treat objects from different subclasses as a single unit by referring to them as objects of their common superclass. It also explains how, when working with a collection of superclass objects, Fortran is able to automatically apply the proper methods to each object, regardless of the subclass the object came from. This ability is known as **polymorphism.**

Inheritance is major advantage of object-oriented programming; once a behavior (method) is defined in a superclass, that behavior is automatically inherited by all subclasses unless it is explicitly overridden with a modified method. Thus behaviors only need to be coded *once*, and they can be used by all subclasses. A subclass need only provide methods to implement the *differences* between itself and its parent.

16.9.1 Superclasses and Subclasses

For example, suppose that we were to create a class `employee`, describing the characteristics of the employees of a company. This class would contain the name, social security number, address, etc. of the employee, together with pay information. However, most companies have two different types of employees, those on a salary and those paid by the hour. Therefore, we could create two subclasses of `employee`, `salaried_employee`, and `hourly_employee`, with different methods for calculating monthly pay. Both of these subclasses would inherit all of the common information and methods from `employee` (name, etc.), but would override the method used to calculate pay.

Figure 16-14 shows this inheritance hierarchy. In object-oriented programming, the relationship between superclasses and subclasses is shown with arrows pointing from a subclass to the parent class. Here, class `employee` is the parent of both class `salaried_employee` and class `hourly_employee`.

Objects of either the `salaried_employee` *or* `hourly_employee` *classes may be treated as objects of the* `employee` *class*, and so forth for any additional classes up the inheritance hierarchy. This fact is very important since objects of the two subclasses can be grouped together and treated as a *single* collection of objects of the superclass `employee`.

Objects of either the `salaried_employee` or `hourly_employee` classes inherit all of the `PUBLIC` instance variables and methods of the `employee` class. This means that if an object is to work with instance variables or override methods defined in the parent class, those instance variables and/or methods must have been declared with `PUBLIC` access.

16.9.2 Defining and Using Subclasses

A class is declared as a subclass of another class by including an `EXTENDS` attribute in the type definition. For example, suppose that the instance variables and methods of class `employee` were declared as follows:

F-2003
ONLY

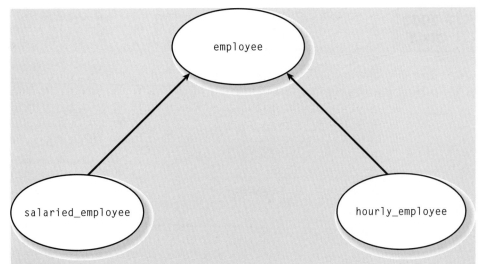

FIGURE 16-14
A simple inheritance hierarchy. Both `salaried_employee` and `hourly_employee` inherit
from `employee`, and an object of either of their classes is also an object of the `employee` class.

```
! Type definition
TYPE,PUBLIC :: employee ! This will be the name we instantiate

   ! Instance variables.
   CHARACTER(len=30) :: first_name    ! First name
   CHARACTER(len=30) :: last_name     ! Last name
   CHARACTER(len=11) :: ssn           ! Social security number
   REAL :: pay = 0                    ! Monthly pay

CONTAINS

   ! Bound procedures
   PROCEDURE,PUBLIC :: set_employee => set_employee_sub
   PROCEDURE,PUBLIC :: set_name => set_name_sub
   PROCEDURE,PUBLIC :: set_ssn => set_ssn_sub
   PROCEDURE,PUBLIC :: get_first_name => get_first_name_fn
   PROCEDURE,PUBLIC :: get_last_name => get_last_name_fn
   PROCEDURE,PUBLIC :: get_ssn => get_ssn_fn
   PROCEDURE,PUBLIC :: calc_pay => calc_pay_fn
END TYPE employee
```

Then a subclass `salaried_employee` could be declared using the `EXTENDS` attribute as
follows:

```
! Type definition
TYPE,PUBLIC,EXTENDS(employee) :: salaried_employee

   ! Additional instance variables.
   PRIVATE
   REAL :: salary = 0                 ! Monthlysalary
CONTAINS
```

16

```
        ! Bound procedures
        PROCEDURE,PUBLIC :: set_salary => set_salary_sub
        PROCEDURE,PUBLIC :: calc_pay => calc_pay_fn
     END TYPE employee
```

This new subclass *inherits* all of the instance variables from class employee, and adds a new instance variable salary of its own. It also inherits the methods of the parent class, except that it *overrides* (replaces) method calc_pay with a new version of it own. This overridden method calc_pay will be used instead of the one defined in class employee for objects of this subclass. It also adds a unique method set_salary that did not exist in the parent class.

A similar definition could be created for subclass hourly_employee.

```
        ! Type definition
        TYPE,PUBLIC,EXTENDS(employee) :: hourly_employee

           ! Additional instance variables.
           PRIVATE
           REAL :: rate = 0                      ! Hourly rate

        CONTAINS

           ! Bound procedures
           PUBLIC
           PROCEDURE::set_pay_rate => set_pay_rate_sub
           PROCEDURE::calc_pay => calc_pay_fn
        END TYPE employee
```

This class also extends employee. This new subclass inherits all of the instance variables from class employee, and adds a new instance variable rate of its own. It also inherits the methods of the parent class, except that it overrides method calc_pay with a new version of it own. This overridden method calc_pay will be used instead of the one defined in class employee for objects of this subclass. It also adds a unique method set_pay_rate that did not exist in the parent class.

For all practical purposes, any object of the subclass salaried_employee or subclass hourly_employee *is* an object of class employee. In object-oriented programming terms, we say that these classes have an "isa" relationship with employee, because an object of either class "is an" object of the parent class employee.

The Fortran code for the employee class is shown in Figure 16-15. This class includes four instance variables, first_name, last_name, ssn, and pay. The class also defines seven methods to manipulate the instance variables of the class.

FIGURE 16-15
The employee class.

```
MODULE employee_class
!
!    This module implements an employee class.
!
!    Record of revisions:
!       Date        Programmer          Description of change
!       ====        ==========          =====================
!    12/29/06    S. J. Chapman        Original code
```

(continued)

```
F-2003
ONLY
```

```
(continued)
!
IMPLICIT NONE

! Type definition
TYPE,PUBLIC :: employee  ! This will be the name we instantiate

   ! Instance variables.
   CHARACTER(len=30) :: first_name    ! First name
   CHARACTER(len=30) :: last_name     ! Last name
   CHARACTER(len=11) :: ssn           ! Social security number
   REAL :: pay = 0                    ! Monthly pay
CONTAINS

   ! Bound procedures
   PROCEDURE,PUBLIC :: set_employee => set_employee_sub
   PROCEDURE,PUBLIC :: set_name => set_name_sub
   PROCEDURE,PUBLIC :: set_ssn => set_ssn_sub
   PROCEDURE,PUBLIC :: get_first_name => get_first_name_fn
   PROCEDURE,PUBLIC :: get_last_name => get_last_name_fn
   PROCEDURE,PUBLIC :: get_ssn => get_ssn_fn
   PROCEDURE,PUBLIC :: calc_pay => calc_pay_fn

END TYPE employee

! Restrict access to the actual procedure names
PRIVATE :: set_employee_sub, set_name_sub, set_ssn_sub
PRIVATE :: get_first_name_fn, get_last_name_fn, get_ssn_fn
PRIVATE :: calc_pay_fn

! Now add methods
CONTAINS

   SUBROUTINE set_employee_sub(this, first, last, ssn)
   !
   ! Subroutine to initialize employee data.
   !
   IMPLICIT NONE

   ! Declare calling arguments
   CLASS(employee)  :: this           ! Employee object
   CHARACTER(len=*) :: first          ! First name
   CHARACTER(len=*) :: last           ! Last name
   CHARACTER(len=*) :: ssn            ! SSN

   ! Save data in this object.
   this%first_name = first
   this%last_name  = last
   this%ssn        = ssn
   this%pay        = 0

   END SUBROUTINE set_employee_sub


   SUBROUTINE set_name_sub(this, first, last)
   !
   ! Subroutine to initialize employee name.
   !
   IMPLICIT NONE
```

16

(continued)

F-2003 ONLY

(continued)

```fortran
! Declare calling arguments
CLASS(employee) :: this               ! Employee object
CHARACTER(len=*),INTENT(IN) :: first  ! First name
CHARACTER(len=*),INTENT(IN) :: last   ! Last name

! Save data in this object.
this%first_name = first
this%last_name  = last

END SUBROUTINE set_name_sub

SUBROUTINE set_ssn_sub(this, ssn)
!
! Subroutine to initialize employee SSN.
!
IMPLICIT NONE

! Declare calling arguments
CLASS(employee) :: this               ! Employee object
CHARACTER(len=*),INTENT(IN) :: ssn    ! SSN

! Save data in this object.
this%ssn = ssn

END SUBROUTINE set_ssn_sub

CHARACTER(len=30) FUNCTION get_first_name_fn(this)
!
! Function to return the first name.
!
IMPLICIT NONE

! Declare calling arguments
CLASS(employee) :: this               ! Employee object

! Return the first name
get_first_name_fn = this%first_name

END FUNCTION get_first_name_fn

CHARACTER(len=30) FUNCTION get_last_name_fn(this)
!
! Function to return the last name.
!
IMPLICIT NONE

! Declare calling arguments
CLASS(employee) :: this               ! Employee object

! Return the last name
get_last_name_fn = this%last_name

END FUNCTION get_last_name_fn

CHARACTER(len=30) FUNCTION get_ssn_fn(this)
!
```

16

(continued)

F-2003 ONLY

```
(concluded)
       ! Function to return the SSN.
       !
       IMPLICIT NONE

       ! Declare calling arguments
       CLASS(employee) :: this                ! Employee object

       ! Return the last name
       get_ssn_fn = this%ssn

       END FUNCTION get_ssn_fn


       REAL FUNCTION calc_pay_fn(this,hours)
       !
       ! Function to calculate the employee pay.  This
       ! function will be overridden by different subclasses.
       !
       IMPLICIT NONE

       ! Declare calling arguments
       CLASS(employee) :: this                ! Employee object
       REAL,INTENT(IN) :: hours               ! Hours worked

       ! Return pay
       calc_pay_fn = 0

       END FUNCTION calc_pay_fn
END MODULE employee_class
```

The method `calc_pay` in this class returns a zero instead of calculating a valid pay, since the method of calculating the pay will depend on the type of employee, and we don't know that information yet in this class.

Note that the calling arguments in each bound method include the object itself as the first parameter. This is necessary, because whenever a bound method with the `PASS` attribute is referenced by an object by using the format `obj%method()`; the object itself is passed to the method as its first argument. This allows the method to access or modify the contents of the object if necessary. Furthermore, note that the object is declared by using a `CLASS` keyword in each method call, for example:

```
       SUBROUTINE set_name_sub(this, first, last)
       !
       ! Subroutine to initialize employee name.
       !
       IMPLICIT NONE

       ! Declare calling arguments
       CLASS(employee)  :: this               ! Employee object
       CHARACTER(len=*) :: first              ! First name
       CHARACTER(len=*) :: last               ! Last name
```

The `CLASS` keyword in this list means that this subroutine will work with either an object of class `employee` or with an object of any subclass of `employee`. In Fortran terms, the **declared type** of the argument `this` is `employee`, but the **dynamic type** at runtime can be `employee` or any subclass of `employee`.

16

F-2003
ONLY

In contrast, if the calling argument were declared with a TYPE keyword instead

```
! Declare calling arguments
TYPE(employee) :: this                        ! Employee object
```

then it would only work with an object of the employee class, *not* with any of the subclasses. In this case the declared type and the dynamic type must be identical. To get polymorphic behavior, we must always declare the methods arguments with the CLASS keyword.

The Fortran code for the salaried_employee subclass is shown in Figure 16-16. This class *inherits* the four instance variables, first_name, last_name, ssn, and pay, and adds an additional instance variable salary. It also defines a new method set_salary, and overrides the method calc_pay from the superclass.

FIGURE 16-16
The salaried_employee class.

```
MODULE salaried_employee_class
!
!   This module implements a salaried employee class.
!
!   Record of revisions:
!      Date          Programmer            Description of change
!      ====          ==========            =====================
!   12/29/06      S. J. Chapman            Original code
!
USE employee_class                         ! USE parent class
IMPLICIT NONE

! Type definition
TYPE,PUBLIC,EXTENDS(employee) :: salaried_employee

    ! Additional instance variables.
    PRIVATE
    REAL :: salary = 0                     ! Monthly salary
CONTAINS

    ! Bound procedures
    PROCEDURE,PUBLIC :: set_salary  =>  set_salary_sub
    PROCEDURE,PUBLIC :: calc_pay  =>  calc_pay_fn
END TYPE salaried_employee

! Restrict access to the actual procedure names
PRIVATE :: calc_pay_fn, set_salary_sub

! Now add methods
CONTAINS

    SUBROUTINE set_salary_sub(this, salary)
    !
    ! Subroutine to initialize the salary of the salaried
    ! employee. This is a new method.
    !
    IMPLICIT NONE
```

(continued)

```
(concluded)
    ! Declare calling arguments
    CLASS(salaried_employee) :: this      ! Salaried employee object
    REAL,INTENT(IN) :: salary             ! Salary

    ! Save data in this object.
    this%pay    = salary
    this%salary = salary

    END SUBROUTINE set_salary_sub

    REAL FUNCTION calc_pay_fn(this,hours)
    !
    ! Function to calculate the salaried employee pay. This
    ! function overrides the one in the parent class.
    !
    IMPLICIT NONE

    ! Declare calling arguments
    CLASS(salaried_employee) :: this      ! Salaried employee object
    REAL,INTENT(IN) :: hours              ! Hours worked

    ! Return pay
    calc_pay_fn = this%salary

    END FUNCTION calc_pay_fn
END MODULE salaried_employee_class
```

A class is declared as a subclass of another class by including an EXTENDS attribute in the type definition. In this case, class salaried_employee is a subclass of class employee because of the EXTENDS(employee) attribute in the type definition. Therefore, this class inherits all of the PUBLIC instance variables and methods from class employee.

The class adds one new instance variable salary and one new method set_salary to the ones inherited from the parent class. In addition, the class *overrides* method calc_pay_fn, changing the meaning of this method for objects of type salaried_employee.

The Fortran code for the hourly_employee subclass is shown in Figure 16-17. This class *inherits* the four instance variables, first_name, last_name, ssn, and pay, and adds an additional instance variable rate. It also defines a new method set_rate, and overrides the method calc_pay from the superclass.

FIGURE 16-17
The hourly_employee class.

```
MODULE hourly_employee_class
!
!    This module implements an hourly employee class.
!
!    Record of revisions:
!        Date        Programmer          Description of change
!        ====        ==========          =====================
!      12/29/06    S. J. Chapman         Original code
```

16

(continued)

F-2003 ONLY

```
(concluded)
!
USE employee_class                        ! USE parent class
IMPLICIT NONE

! Type definition
TYPE,PUBLIC,EXTENDS(employee) :: hourly_employee

    ! Additional instance variables.
    PRIVATE
    REAL :: rate = 0                      ! Hourly rate

CONTAINS

    ! Bound procedures
    PROCEDURE,PUBLIC :: set_pay_rate  =>  set_pay_rate_sub
    PROCEDURE,PUBLIC :: calc_pay  =>  calc_pay_fn

END TYPE hourly_employee

! Restrict access to the actual procedure names
PRIVATE :: calc_pay_fn, set_pay_rate_sub

! Now add methods
CONTAINS

    SUBROUTINE set_pay_rate_sub(this, rate)
    !
    ! Subroutine to initialize the pay rate of the hourly
    ! employee. This is a new method.
    !
    IMPLICIT NONE

    ! Declare calling arguments
    CLASS(hourly_employee) :: this         ! Hourly employee object
    REAL,INTENT(IN) :: rate                ! Pay rate ($/hr)

    ! Save data in this object.
    this%rate = rate

    END SUBROUTINE set_pay_rate_sub


    REAL FUNCTION calc_pay_fn(this,hours)
    !
    ! Function to calculate the hourly employee pay. This
    ! function overrides the one in the parent class.
    !
    IMPLICIT NONE

    ! Declare calling arguments
    CLASS(hourly_employee) :: this         ! Hourly employee object
    REAL,INTENT(IN) :: hours               ! Hours worked

    ! Return pay
    this%pay = hours * this%rate
    calc_pay_fn = this%pay

    END FUNCTION calc_pay_fn

END MODULE hourly_employee_class
```

16

Class `hourly_employee` is a subclass of class `employee` because of the `EXTENDS(employee)` attribute in the type definition. Therefore, this class inherits all of the `PUBLIC` instance variables and methods from class `employee`.

The class adds one new instance variable `rate` and one new method `set_rate` to the ones inherited from the parent class. In addition, the class *overrides* method `calc_pay_fn`, changing the meaning of this method for objects of type `hourly_employee`.

16.9.3 The Relationship between Superclass Objects and Subclass Objects

An object of a subclass inherits all of the instance variables and methods of its superclass. In fact, *an object of any subclass may be treated as ("is") an object of its superclass*. This fact implies that we can manipulate objects with either pointers to the subclass or pointers to the superclass. Figure 16-18 illustrates this point.

FIGURE 16-18
A program that illustrates the manipulation of objects with superclass pointers.

```
PROGRAM test_employee
!
! This program tests the employee class and its subclasses.
!
! Record of revisions:
!       Date        Programmer           Description of change
!       ====        ==========           =====================
!     12/29/06    S. J. Chapman          Original code
!
USE hourly_employee_class           ! Import hourly employee class
USE salaried_employee_class         ! Import salaried employee class
IMPLICIT NONE

! Declare variables
CLASS(employee),POINTER :: emp1, emp2           ! Employees
TYPE(salaried_employee),POINTER :: sal_emp      ! Salaried employee
TYPE(hourly_employee),POINTER :: hourly_emp     ! Hourly employee
INTEGER :: istat                                ! Allocate status

! Create an object of type "salaried_employee"
ALLOCATE( sal_emp, STAT=istat )

! Initialize the data in this object
CALL sal_emp%set_employee('John','Jones','111-11-1111');
CALL sal_emp%set_salary(3000.00);

! Create an object of type "hourly_employee"
ALLOCATE( hourly_emp, STAT=istat )

! Initialize the data in this object
CALL hourly_emp%set_employee('Jane','Jones','222-22-2222');
CALL hourly_emp%set_pay_rate(12.50);
```

16

(continued)

F-2003 ONLY

```
(concluded)
! Now create pointers to "employees".
emp1 => sal_emp
emp2 => hourly_emp

! Calculate pay using subclass pointers
WRITE (*,'(A)') 'Pay using subclass pointers:'
WRITE (*,'(A,F6.1)') 'Emp 1 Pay = ', sal_emp%calc_pay(160.)
WRITE (*,'(A,F6.1)') 'Emp 2 Pay = ', hourly_emp%calc_pay(160.)

! Calculate pay using superclass pointers
WRITE (*,'(A)') 'Pay using superclass pointers:'
WRITE (*,'(A,F6.1)') 'Emp 1 Pay = ', emp1%calc_pay(160.)
WRITE (*,'(A,F6.1)') 'Emp 2 Pay = ', emp2%calc_pay(160.)

! List employee information using superclass pointers
WRITE (*,*) 'Employee information:'
WRITE (*,*) 'Emp1 Name / SSN = ', TRIM(emp1%get_first_name()) // &
            ' ' // TRIM(emp1%get_last_name()) // ' ', &
            TRIM(emp1%get_ssn())
WRITE (*,*) 'Emp 2 Name / SSN = ', TRIM(emp2%get_first_name()) // &
            ' ' // TRIM(emp2%get_last_name()) // ' ', &
            TRIM(emp2%get_ssn())
END PROGRAM test_employee
```

This test program creates one salaried_employee object and one hourly_employee object, and assigns them to pointers of the same types. Then it creates polymorphic pointers to employee objects, and assigns the two subtype objects to the employee pointers. Normally, it is illegal to assign an object of one type to a pointer of another type. However, it is OK here because *the objects of the subclasses* salaried_employee *and* hourly_employee *are also objects of the superclass* employee. The pointers were declared with the CLASS keyword, which allows them to match objects whose dynamic type is the declared type or any subclass of the declared type.

Once the program assigns the objects to the employee pointers, it uses both the original pointers and the employee pointers to access some methods. When this program executes, the results are:

```
D:\book\chap16>test_employee
Pay using subclass pointers:
Emp 1 Pay = 3000.0
Emp 2 Pay = 2000.0
Pay using superclass pointers:
Emp 1 Pay = 3000.0
Emp 2 Pay = 2000.0
 Employee information:
 Emp 1 Name / SSN = John Jones 111-11-1111
 Emp 2 Name / SSN = Jane Jones 222-22-2222
```

Notice that the pay calculated with the subclass pointers is identical to the pay calculated with the superclass pointers.

It is possible to freely assign an object of a subclass to a pointer of a superclass type, since the object of the subclass is also an object of the superclass. However, the converse is *not* true. An object of a superclass type is *not* an object of its subclass

16

F-2003 ONLY

types. Thus, if `e` is a pointer to `employee` and `s` is a pointer to `salaried_employee`, then the statement

$$e \Rightarrow s$$

is perfectly legal. In contrast, the statement

$$s \Rightarrow e$$

is illegal and will produce a compile time error.

16.9.4 Polymorphism

Let's look at the program in Figure 16-18 once more. Pay was calculated using super-class pointers, and employee information was displayed using superclass pointers. Note that the `calc_pay` method *differed* for `emp1` and `emp2`. The object referred to by `emp1` was really a `salaried_employee`, so Fortran used the `salaried_employee` version of `calc_pay()` to calculate the appropriate value for it. On the other hand, the object referred to by `emp2` was really an `hourly_employee`, so Fortran used the `hourly_employee` version of `calc_pay()` to calculate the appropriate value for it. The version of `calc_pay()` defined in class `employee` was never used at all.

Here, we were working with `employee` objects, but *this program automatically selected the proper method to apply to each given object on the basis of the subclass that it also belonged to.* This ability to automatically vary methods according to the subclass that an object belongs to is known as **polymorphism.**

Polymorphism is an incredibly powerful feature of object-oriented languages. It makes them very easy to change. For example, suppose that we wrote a program using arrays of `employees` to work out a company payroll, and then later the company wanted to add a new type of employee, one paid by the piece. We could define a new subclass called `piecework_employee` as a subclass of `employee`, overriding the `calc_pay()` method appropriately, and create employees of this type. *The rest of the program will not have to be changed,* since the program manipulates objects of class `employee`, and polymorphism allows Fortran to automatically select the proper version of a method to apply whenever an object belongs to a particular subclass.

Good Programming Practice
Polymorphism allows multiple objects of different subclasses to be treated as objects of a single superclass, while automatically selecting the proper methods to apply to a particular object based on the subclass that it belongs to.

Note that for polymorphism to work, the methods to be used must be *defined in the superclass and overridden in the various subclasses.* Polymorphism will *not* work if the method you want to use is defined only in the subclasses. Thus a polymorphic method call like `emp1.calc_pay()` is legal, because method `calc_pay()` is defined

16

in class `employee` and overridden in subclasses `salaried_employee` and `hourly_employee`. On the other hand, a method call like `emp1.set_rate()` is illegal, because method `set_rate()` is defined only in class `hourly_employee`, and we cannot use an `employee` pointer to refer to an `hourly_employee` method.

It *is* possible to access a subclass method or instance variable by using the `SELECT TYPE` construct, as we shall see in the next section.

Good Programming Practice

To create polymorphic behavior, declare all polymorphic methods in a common superclass, and then override the behavior of the methods in each subclass that inherits from the superclass.

16.9.5 The `SELECT TYPE` Construct

It is possible to explicitly determine which type of subclass a given object belongs to while it is being referenced with a superclass pointer. This is done by using a `SELECT TYPE` construct. Once that information is known, a program can access the additional instance variables and methods that are unique to the subclass.

The form of a `SELECT TYPE` construct is

```
[name:] SELECT TYPE (obj)
TYPE IS ( type_1 ) [name]

   Block 1

TYPE IS ( type_2 ) [name]

   Block 2

CLASS IS ( type_3 ) [name]

   Block 3

END SELECT [name]
```

The declared type of *obj* should be a superclass of the other types in the construct. If the input object *obj* has the dynamic type *type_1*, then the statements in Block 1 will be executed, and *the object pointer will be treated as being type_1 during the execution of the block*. This means that the program can access the instance variables and methods unique to subclass *type_1*, even though the declared type of *obj* is of a superclass type.

Similarly, if the input object *obj* has the dynamic type *type_2*, then the statements in Block 2 will be executed, and *the object pointer will be treated as being type_2 during the execution of the block*.

If the dynamic type of the input object *obj* does not exactly match any of the `TYPE IS` clauses, then the structure will look at the `CLASS IS` clauses, and it will execute the code in the block that provides the best match to the dynamic type of the input object.

16

**F-2003
ONLY**

The type of object will be treated as the type of the declared class during the execution of the statements in the block.

At most one block of statements will be executed by this construct. The rules for selecting the block to execute are:

1. If a TYPE IS block matches, execute it.
2. Otherwise, if a single CLASS IS block matches, execute it.
3. Otherwise, if several CLASS IS blocks match, one must be an extension of all the others, and it is executed.

An example program illustrating the use of this construct is shown in Figure 16-19. This program defines a 2D point type and two extensions of that type, one a 3D point and the other a 2D point with a temperature measurement. It then declares objects of each type and a pointer of class point, which can match any of the objects. In this case, the temperature point object is assigned to the pointer, and the SELECT TYPE construct will match the TYPE IS (point_temp) clause. The program will then treat the point pointer as though it were a point_temp pointer, allowing access to the instance variable temp that is only found in that type.

FIGURE 16-19
Example program illustrating the use of the SELECT TYPE construct.

```
PROGRAM test_select_type
!
!   This program tests the select type construct.
!
!   Record of revisions:
!      Date        Programmer         Description of change
!      ====        ==========         =====================
!    12/29/06    S. J. Chapman        Original code
!
IMPLICIT NONE

! Declare a 2D point type
TYPE :: point
    REAL :: x
    REAL :: y
END TYPE point

! Declare a 3D point type
TYPE,EXTENDS(point) :: point3d
    REAL :: z
END TYPE point3d

! Declare a 2D point with temperature data
TYPE,EXTENDS(point) :: point_temp
    REAL :: temp
END TYPE point_temp

! Declare variables
TYPE(point),TARGET :: p2
TYPE(point3d),TARGET :: p3
TYPE(point_temp),TARGET :: pt
CLASS(point),POINTER :: p
```

16

(*continued*)

F-2003 ONLY

(concluded)

```
! Initialize objects here...
p2%x = 1.
p2%y = 2.
p3%x = -1.
p3%y = 7.
p3%z = -2.
pt%x = 10.
pt%y = 0.
pt%temp = 700.

! Assign one of the objects to "p"
p => pt

! Now access the data in that object
SELECT TYPE (p)
TYPE IS ( point3d )
   WRITE (*,*) 'Type is point3d'
   WRITE (*,*) p%x, p%y, p%z
TYPE IS ( point_temp )
   WRITE (*,*) 'Type is point_temp'
   WRITE (*,*) p%x, p%y, p%temp
CLASS IS ( point )
   WRITE (*,*) 'Class is point'
   WRITE (*,*) p%x, p%y
END SELECT

END PROGRAM test_select_type
```

When this program is executed, the results are:

```
D:\book\chap16>test_select_type
Type is point_temp
  10.0000000    0.0000000    7.0000000E+02
```

16.10

PREVENTING METHODS FROM BEING OVERRIDDEN IN SUBCLASSES

It is sometimes desirable to ensure that one or more methods are *not* modified in subclasses of a given superclass. This can be done by declaring them in the binding with the NON_OVERRIDABLE attribute, as shown below:

```
TYPE :: point
   REAL :: x
   REAL :: y
CONTAINS
   PROCEDURE,NON_OVERRIDABLE :: my_proc
   ...
END TYPE
```

With this attribute, procedure my_proc would be declared in the definition of the point class, and could not be modified in any subclasses of the point class.

16

16.11
ABSTRACT CLASSES

Look at the `employee` class again. Note that we defined method `calc_pay()` in that class, but *the method is never used.* Since we instantiate only members of the subclasses `salaried_employee` and `hourly_employee`, this method is *always* overridden polymorphically by the corresponding method in the two subclasses. If this method is never going to be used, why did we bother to write it at all? The answer is that, in order for polymorphism to work, the polymorphic methods must be bound to the parent class, and therefore inherited in all of the subclasses.

However, the actual *methods* in the parent class will never be used if no objects are ever instantiated from that class, so Fortran allows us to declare the bindings and interface definitions only, without writing the actual methods. Such methods are called **abstract methods** or **deferred methods,** and types containing abstract methods are known as **abstract types,** as opposed to ordinary **concrete types.**

Abstract methods are declared by using the `DEFERRED` attribute in the type definition, together with an `ABSTRACT INTERFACE` to define the calling sequence for the method. Any type containing a deferred method must be declared with the `ABSTRACT` attribute. It is illegal to create any objects directly from an abstract type, but it is legal to create pointers of that type that can be used to manipulate objects of various subtypes.

A deferred method is declared with the following statement

```
PROCEDURE(CALC_PAYX),PUBLIC,DEFERRED :: calc_pay
```

In this statement, the name in parentheses after the `PROCEDURE` declaration (`CALC_PAYX` here) is the name of the abstract interface that applies to this method, and `calc_pay` is the actual name of the method.

An abstract version of the `Employee` class is shown in Figure 16-20.

FIGURE 16-20
An abstract `employee` class.

```
MODULE employee_class
!
!   This module implements an abstract employee class.
!
! Record of revisions:
!      Date        Programmer          Description of change
!      ====        ==========          =====================
!    12/30/06    S. J. Chapman        Original code
!
IMPLICIT NONE
! Type definition
TYPE,ABSTRACT,PUBLIC :: employee
   ! Instance variables.
   CHARACTER(len=30) :: first_name        ! First name
```

(continued)

16

F-2003 ONLY

(continued)

```fortran
    CHARACTER(len=30) :: last_name        ! Last name
    CHARACTER(len=11) :: ssn              ! Social security number
    REAL :: pay = 0                       ! Monthly pay

CONTAINS

    ! Bound procedures
    PROCEDURE,PUBLIC :: set_employee => set_employee_sub
    PROCEDURE,PUBLIC :: set_name => set_name_sub
    PROCEDURE,PUBLIC :: set_ssn => set_ssn_sub
    PROCEDURE,PUBLIC :: get_first_name => get_first_name_fn
    PROCEDURE,PUBLIC :: get_last_name => get_last_name_fn
    PROCEDURE,PUBLIC :: get_ssn => get_ssn_fn
    PROCEDURE(CALC_PAYX),PUBLIC,DEFERRED :: calc_pay

END TYPE employee

ABSTRACT INTERFACE

    REAL FUNCTION CALC_PAYX(this,hours)
    !
    ! Function to calculate the employee pay. This
    ! function will be overridden by different subclasses.
    !
    IMPLICIT NONE

    ! Declare calling arguments
    CLASS(employee) :: this               ! Employee object
    REAL,INTENT(IN) :: hours              ! Hours worked

    END FUNCTION CALC_PAYX

END INTERFACE

! Restrict access to the actual procedure names
PRIVATE :: set_employee_sub, set_name_sub, set_ssn_sub
PRIVATE :: get_first_name_fn, get_last_name_fn, get_ssn_fn

! Now add methods
CONTAINS

    ! All methods are the same as before, except that there is
    ! no implementation of method calc_pay...

    SUBROUTINE set_employee_sub(this, first, last, ssn)
    !
    ! Subroutine to initialize employee data.
    !
    IMPLICIT NONE

    ! Declare calling arguments
    CLASS(employee) :: this               ! Employee object
    CHARACTER(len=*) :: first             ! First name
    CHARACTER(len=*) :: last              ! Last name
    CHARACTER(len=*) :: ssn               ! SSN

    ! Save data in this object.
    this%first_name = first
```

16

(continued)

F-2003 ONLY

(*continued*)

```fortran
      this%last_name  = last
      this%ssn        = ssn
      this%pay        = 0

      END SUBROUTINE set_employee_sub

      SUBROUTINE set_name_sub(this, first, last)
      !
      ! Subroutine to initialize employee name.
      !
      IMPLICIT NONE

      ! Declare calling arguments
      CLASS(employee) :: this                ! Employee object
      CHARACTER(len=*),INTENT(IN) :: first   ! First name
      CHARACTER(len=*),INTENT(IN) :: last    ! Last name

      ! Save data in this object.
      this%first_name = first
      this%last_name = last

      END SUBROUTINE set_name_sub

      SUBROUTINE set_ssn_sub(this, ssn)
      !
      ! Subroutine to initialize employee SSN.
      !
      IMPLICIT NONE

      ! Declare calling arguments
      CLASS(employee) :: this                ! Employee object
      CHARACTER(len=*),INTENT(IN) :: ssn     ! SSN

      ! Save data in this object.
      this%ssn = ssn

      END SUBROUTINE set_ssn_sub

      CHARACTER(len=30) FUNCTION get_first_name_fn(this)
      !
      ! Function to return the first name.
      !
      IMPLICIT NONE

      ! Declare calling arguments
      CLASS(employee) :: this                ! Employee object

      ! Return the first name
      get_first_name_fn = this%first_name

      END FUNCTION get_first_name_fn

      CHARACTER(len=30) FUNCTION get_last_name_fn(this)
      !
      ! Function to return the last name.
      !
      IMPLICIT NONE
```

16

(*continued*)

F-2003
ONLY

(concluded)

```
    ! Declare calling arguments
    CLASS(employee) :: this                ! Employee object

    ! Return the last name
    get_last_name_fn = this%last_name

    END FUNCTION get_last_name_fn

    CHARACTER(len=30) FUNCTION get_ssn_fn(this)
    !
    ! Function to return the SSN.
    !
    IMPLICIT NONE

    ! Declare calling arguments
    CLASS(employee) :: this                ! Employee object

    ! Return the last name
    get_ssn_fn = this%ssn

    END FUNCTION get_ssn_fn
END MODULE employee_class
```

Abstract classes define the list of methods that will be available to subclasses of the class, and can provide partial implementations of those methods. For example, the abstract class employee in Figure 16-20 provides implementations of set_name and set_ssn that will be inherited by the subclasses of employee, but does *not* provide an implementation of calc_pay.

Any subclasses of an abstract class *must* override all abstract methods of the superclass, or they will be abstract themselves. Thus classes salaried_employee and hourly_employee must override method calc_pay, or they will be abstract themselves.

Unlike concrete classes, *no objects may be instantiated from an abstract class.* Since an abstract class does not provide a complete definition of the behavior of an object, no object may be created from it. The class serves as a template for concrete subclasses, and objects may be instantiated from those concrete subclasses. An abstract class defines the types of polymorphic behaviors that can be used with subclasses of the class, but does *not* define the details of those behaviors.

Programming Pitfalls

Objects may not be instantiated from an abstract class.

Abstract classes often appear at the top of an object-oriented programming class hierarchy, defining the broad types of actions possible with objects of all subclasses of the class. Concrete classes appear at lower levels in a hierarchy, providing implementation details for each subclass.

16

Good Programming Practice
Use abstract classes to define broad types of behaviors at the top of an object-oriented programming class hierarchy, and use concrete classes to provide implementation details in the subclasses of the abstract classes.

F-2003 ONLY

In summary, to create polymorphic behavior in a program:

1. **Create a parent class containing all methods that will be needed to solve the problem.** The methods that will change in different subclasses can be declared DEFERRED, if desired, and we will not have to write a method for them in the superclass—just an interface. Note that this makes the superclass ABSTRACT—no objects may be instantiated directly from it.
2. **Define subclasses for each type of object to be manipulated.** The subclasses must implement a specific method for each abstract method in the superclass definition.
3. **Create objects of the various subclasses, and refer to them using superclass pointers.** When a method call appears with a superclass pointer, Fortran automatically executes the method in the object's actual subclass.

The trick to getting polymorphism right is to determine what behaviors objects of the superclass must exhibit, and to make sure that there is a method to represent every behavior in the superclass definition.

EXAMPLE 16-3

Putting it All Together—A Shape Class Hierarchy:

To illustrate the object-oriented programming concepts introduced in this chapter, let's consider generic two-dimensional shapes. There are many types of shapes including circles, triangles, squares, rectangles, pentagons, and so forth. All of these shapes have certain characteristics in common, since they are closed two-dimensional shapes having an enclosed area and a perimeter of finite length.

Create a generic shape class having methods to determine the area and perimeter of a shape, and then create an appropriate class hierarchy for the following specific shapes: circles, equilateral triangles, squares, rectangles, and pentagons. Then, illustrate polymorphic behavior by creating shapes of each type and determining their area and perimeter using references to the generic shape class.

SOLUTION
To solve this problem, we should create a general shape class and a series of subclasses below it.

The listed shapes fall into a logical hierarchy based on their relationships. Circles, equilateral triangles, rectangles, and pentagons are all specific types of shapes, so they should be subclasses of our general shape class. A square is a special kind of rectangle, so it should be a subclass of the rectangle class. These relationships are shown in Figure 16-21.

16

F-2003 ONLY

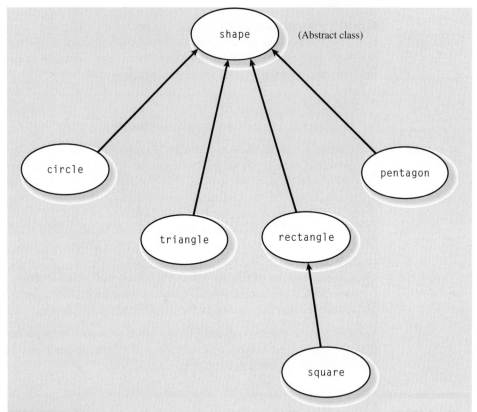

FIGURE 16-21
The shape class hierarchy.

A circle can be completely specified by it radius r, and the area A and perimeter (circumference) P of a circle can be calculated from the equations:

$$A = \pi r^2 \tag{16-1}$$

$$P = 2\pi r \tag{16-2}$$

An equilateral triangle can be completely specified by the length of one side s, and the area A and perimeter P of the equilateral triangle can be calculated from the equations:

$$A = \frac{\sqrt{3}}{4} s^2 \tag{16-3}$$

$$P = 3s \tag{16-4}$$

16

F-2003 ONLY

A rectangle can be completely specified by its length l and its width w, and the area A and perimeter P of the rectangle can be calculated from the equations:

$$A = lw \tag{16-5}$$

$$P = 2(l + w) \tag{16-6}$$

A square is a special rectangle whose length is equal to its width so it can be completely specified by setting the length and width of a rectangle to the same size s. The area A and perimeter P of the square can then be calculated from the Equations (9-5) and (9-6).

A pentagon can be completely specified by the length of one side s, and the area A and perimeter P of the pentagon can be calculated from the equations:

$$A = \frac{5}{4} s^2 \cot \frac{\pi}{5} \tag{16-7}$$

$$P = 5s \tag{16-8}$$

where cot is the cotangent, which is the reciprocal of the tangent.

1. **State the problem.**

Define and implement a class shape with methods to calculate the area and perimeter of a specified shape. Define and implement appropriate subclasses for circles, equilateral triangles, rectangles, squares, and pentagons, with the area and perimeter calculations appropriate for each shape.

2. **Define the inputs and outputs.**

The inputs to the various classes will be the radius r of the circles, the length of a side s for the equilateral triangles, the length l and width w for the rectangles, the length of a side s for the squares, and the length of a side s for the pentagons. The outputs will be the perimeters and areas of the various objects.

3. **Describe the algorithm.**

Each class will need methods capable of initializing the appropriate objects. For circles, the initializing method will need the radius r. For equilateral triangles, the initializing method will need the length of a side s. For rectangles, the initializing method will need the length l and width w. For squares, the initializing method will need the length of a side s. For pentagons, the initializing method will need the length of a side s.

Each of these classes will contain area, perimeter, and to_string methods, returning the area, perimeter, and a character representation of the shape respectively. They will also contain methods to retrieve the key parameters for each type of shape (radius etc.).

The classes required for this problem are shape, circle, triangle, rectangle, square, and pentagon. Class shape is a superclass representing

16

a closed, two-dimensional object with a finite area and perimeter. Classes circle, triangle, rectangle, and pentagon are special kinds of shapes, so they should be subclasses of shape. Class square is a special kind of rectangle, so it should be a subclass of rectangle. The methods in each class will be the class initializer, area, perimeter, to_string, and methods to recover the key parameters for the particular type of shape.

The pseudocode for the area() method in the circle class is:

```
get_area_fn = PI * this%r**2
```

The pseudocode for the perimeter() method in the circle class is:

```
get_perimeter_fn = 2.0 * PI * this%r
```

The pseudocode for the area() method in the triangle class is:

```
get_area_fn = SQRT(3.0) / 4.0 * this%s**2
```

The pseudocode for the perimeter() method in the triangle class is:

```
get_perimeter_fn = 3.0 * this%s
```

The pseudocode for the area() method in the rectangle class is:

```
get_area_fn = this%l * this%w
```

The pseudocode for the perimeter() method in the rectangle class is:

```
get_perimeter_fn = 2 * this%l + 2 * this%w
```

The pseudocode for the area() and perimeter() methods in the square class is the same as for the rectangle class. These methods may be directly inherited from the rectangle class.

The pseudocode for the area() method in the pentagon class is:

```
get_area_fn = 1.25 * this%s**2 / 0.72654253
```

The pseudocode for the perimeter() method in the pentagon class is:

```
get_perimeter_fn = 5.0 * this%s
```

4. **Turn the algorithm into Fortran statements.**
   The abstract class shape is shown in Figure 16-22. Note that this class defines abstract methods area(), perimeter(), and to_string(), so that all subclasses will be required to implement these methods, and they may be used polymorphically with objects of type shape.

FIGURE 16-22
The parent class shape.

```
MODULE shape_class
!
```

(continued)

F-2003 ONLY

```
(continued)
!    This module implements an abstract shape class.
!
!   Record of revisions:
!       Date          Programmer           Description of change
!       ====          ==========           =====================
!     12/31/06      S. J. Chapman          Original code
!
IMPLICIT NONE

! Type definition
TYPE,PUBLIC :: shape

   ! Instance variables.
   ! < none>

CONTAINS

   ! Bound procedures
   PROCEDURE,PUBLIC :: area => calc_area_fn
   PROCEDURE,PUBLIC :: perimeter => calc_perimeter_fn
   PROCEDURE,PUBLIC :: to_string => to_string_fn

END TYPE shape

! Restrict access to the actual procedure names
PRIVATE :: calc_area_fn, calc_perimeter_fn, to_string_fn

CONTAINS

   REAL FUNCTION calc_area_fn(this)
   !
   ! Return the area of this object.
   !
   IMPLICIT NONE

   ! Declare calling arguments
   CLASS(shape) :: this                  ! Shape object

   ! Return dummy area
   calc_area_fn = 0.

   END FUNCTION calc_area_fn

   REAL FUNCTION calc_perimeter_fn(this)
   !
   ! Return the perimeter of this object.
   !
   IMPLICIT NONE

   ! Declare calling arguments
   CLASS(shape) :: this                  ! Shape object

   ! Return dummy perimeter
   calc_perimeter_fn = 0.

   END FUNCTION calc_perimeter_fn

   CHARACTER(len=50) FUNCTION to_string_fn(this)
   !
```

(continued)

```
(concluded)
      ! Return a character description of this object.
      !
      IMPLICIT NONE

      ! Declare calling arguments
      CLASS(shape) :: this                  ! Shape object

      ! Return dummy string
      to_string_fn = ''

      END FUNCTION to_string_fn
END MODULE shape_class
```

The class circle is shown in Figure 16-23. This class defines an instance variable r for the radius of the circle, and provides concrete implementations of area(), perimeter(), and to_string(). It also defines a method initialize that is not inherited from the parent class.

FIGURE 16-23
Class circle.

```
MODULE circle_class
!
!     This module implements a circle class.
!
!     Record of revisions:
!        Date        Programmer            Description of change
!        ====        ==========            =====================
!     12/29/06    S. J. Chapman            Original code
!
USE shape_class                    ! USE parent class
IMPLICIT NONE

! Type definition
TYPE,PUBLIC,EXTENDS(shape) :: circle

   ! Additional instance variables.
   REAL :: r = 0                   ! Radius

CONTAINS

   ! Bound procedures
   PROCEDURE,PUBLIC :: initialize => initialize_sub
   PROCEDURE,PUBLIC :: area => get_area_fn
   PROCEDURE,PUBLIC :: perimeter => get_perimeter_fn
   PROCEDURE,PUBLIC :: to_string => to_string_fn

END TYPE circle

! Declare constant PI
REAL,PARAMETER :: PI = 3.141593

! Restrict access to the actual procedure names
PRIVATE :: initialize_sub, get_area_fn, get_perimeter_fn
PRIVATE :: to_string_fn

! Now add methods
CONTAINS
```

(continued)

F-2003 ONLY

(concluded)

```fortran
    SUBROUTINE initialize_sub(this,r)
    !
    ! Initialize the circle object.
    !
    IMPLICIT NONE

    ! Declare calling arguments
    CLASS(circle) :: this              ! Circle object
    REAL,INTENT(IN) :: r               ! Radius

    ! Initialize the circle
    this%r = r

    END SUBROUTINE initialize_sub

    REAL FUNCTION get_area_fn(this)
    !
    ! Return the area of this object.
    !
    IMPLICIT NONE

    ! Declare calling arguments
    CLASS(circle) :: this              ! Circle object

    ! Calculate area
    get_area_fn = PI * this%r**2

    END FUNCTION get_area_fn

    REAL FUNCTION get_perimeter_fn(this)
    !
    ! Return the perimeter of this object.
    !
    IMPLICIT NONE

    ! Declare calling arguments
    CLASS(circle) :: this              ! Circle object

    ! Calculate perimeter
    get_perimeter_fn = 2.0 * PI * this%r

    END FUNCTION get_perimeter_fn

    CHARACTER(len=50) FUNCTION to_string_fn(this)
    !
    ! Return a character description of this object.
    !
    IMPLICIT NONE

    ! Declare calling arguments
    CLASS(circle) :: this              ! Circle object

    ! Return description
    WRITE (to_string_fn,'(A,F6.2)') 'Circle of radius ', &
       this%r
    END FUNCTION to_string_fn
END MODULE circle_class
```

16

F-2003
ONLY

The class `triangle` is shown in Figure 16-24. This class defines an instance variable for the length of the side of the triangle, and provides concrete implementations of `area()`, `perimeter()`, and `to_string()`. It also defines a method `initialize` that is not inherited from the parent class.

FIGURE 16-24
Class `triangle`.

```
MODULE triangle_class
!
!   This module implements a triangle class.
!
!   Record of revisions:
!       Date         Programmer            Description of change
!       ====         ==========            =====================
!     12/29/06    S. J. Chapman            Original code
!
USE shape_class                           ! USE parent class
IMPLICIT NONE

! Type definition
TYPE,PUBLIC,EXTENDS(shape) :: triangle

    ! Additional instance variables.
    REAL :: s = 0                         ! Length of side

CONTAINS

    ! Bound procedures
    PROCEDURE,PUBLIC :: initialize => initialize_sub
    PROCEDURE,PUBLIC :: area => get_area_fn
    PROCEDURE,PUBLIC :: perimeter => get_perimeter_fn
    PROCEDURE,PUBLIC :: to_string => to_string_fn

END TYPE triangle

! Restrict access to the actual procedure names
PRIVATE :: initialize_sub, get_area_fn, get_perimeter_fn
PRIVATE :: to_string_fn

! Now add methods
CONTAINS

    SUBROUTINE initialize_sub(this,s)
    !
    ! Initialize the triangle object.
    !
    IMPLICIT NONE

    ! Declare calling arguments
    CLASS(triangle) :: this               ! Triangle object
    REAL,INTENT(IN) :: s                  ! Length of side

    ! Initialize the triangle
    this%s = s

    END SUBROUTINE initialize_sub
```

16

(*continued*)

F-2003
ONLY

(concluded)

```fortran
    REAL FUNCTION get_area_fn(this)
    !
    ! Return the area of this object.
    !
    IMPLICIT NONE

    ! Declare calling arguments
    CLASS(triangle) :: this              ! Triangle object

    ! Calculate area
    get_area_fn = SQRT(3.0) / 4.0 * this%s**2

    END FUNCTION get_area_fn

    REAL FUNCTION get_perimeter_fn(this)
    !
    ! Return the perimeter of this object.
    !
    IMPLICIT NONE

    ! Declare calling arguments
    CLASS(triangle) :: this              ! Triangle object

    ! Calculate perimeter
    get_perimeter_fn = 3.0 * this%s

    END FUNCTION get_perimeter_fn


    CHARACTER(len=50) FUNCTION to_string_fn(this)
    !
    ! Return a character description of this object.
    !
    IMPLICIT NONE

    ! Declare calling arguments
    CLASS(triangle) :: this              ! Triangle object

    ! Return description
    WRITE (to_string_fn,'(A,F6.2)') 'Equilateral triangle of side ', &
       this%s

    END FUNCTION to_string_fn
END MODULE triangle_class
```

The class `rectangle` is shown in Figure 16-25. This class defines instance variables `l` and `w` for the length and width of the rectangle, and provides concrete implementations of `area()`, `perimeter()`, and `to_string()`. It also defines a method `initialize` that is not inherited from the parent class.

FIGURE 16-25
Class `rectangle`.

```fortran
MODULE rectangle_class
!
!    This module implements a rectangle class.
!
```

16

(continued)

F-2003 ONLY

```
(continued)
!   Record of revisions:
!      Date      Programmer          Description of change
!      ====      ==========          =====================
!    12/29/06   S. J. Chapman        Original code
!
USE shape_class                                ! USE parent class
IMPLICIT NONE

! Type definition
TYPE,PUBLIC,EXTENDS(shape) :: rectangle

   ! Additional instance variables.
   REAL :: l = 0      ! Length
   REAL :: w = 0      ! Width

CONTAINS

   ! Bound procedures
   PROCEDURE,PUBLIC :: initialize => initialize_sub
   PROCEDURE,PUBLIC :: area => get_area_fn
   PROCEDURE,PUBLIC :: perimeter => get_perimeter_fn
   PROCEDURE,PUBLIC :: to_string => to_string_fn

END TYPE rectangle

! Restrict access to the actual procedure names
PRIVATE :: initialize_sub, get_area_fn, get_perimeter_fn
PRIVATE :: to_string_fn

! Now add methods
CONTAINS

   SUBROUTINE initialize_sub(this,l,w)
   !
   ! Initialize the rectangle object.
   !
   IMPLICIT NONE

   ! Declare calling arguments
   CLASS(rectangle) :: this                    ! Rectangle object
   REAL,INTENT(IN) :: l                        ! Length
   REAL,INTENT(IN) :: w                        ! Width

   ! Initialize the rectangle
   this%l = l
   this%w = w

   END SUBROUTINE initialize_sub

   REAL FUNCTION get_area_fn(this)
   !
   ! Return the area of this object.
   !
   IMPLICIT NONE

   ! Declare calling arguments
   CLASS(rectangle) :: this                           ! Rectangle object
```

(continued)

16

F-2003 ONLY

(concluded)

```
  ! Calculate area
  get_area_fn = this%l * this%w

  END FUNCTION get_area_fn


  REAL FUNCTION get_perimeter_fn(this)
  !
  ! Return the perimeter of this object.
  !
  IMPLICIT NONE

  ! Declare calling arguments
  CLASS(rectangle) :: this                ! Rectangle object

  ! Calculate perimeter
  get_perimeter_fn = 2 * this%l + 2 * this%w

  END FUNCTION get_perimeter_fn

  CHARACTER(len=50) FUNCTION to_string_fn(this)
  !
  ! Return a character description of this object.
  !
  IMPLICIT NONE

  ! Declare calling arguments
  CLASS(rectangle) :: this                ! Rectangle object

  ! Return description
  WRITE (to_string_fn,'(A,F6.2,A,F6.2)') 'Rectangle of length ', &
     this%l, ' and width ', this%w

  END FUNCTION to_string_fn
END MODULE rectangle_class
```

The class `square` is shown in Figure 16-26. Since a square is just a rectangle with its length equal to its width, this class *inherits* its instance variables l and w from class `rectangle`, as well as concrete implementations of `area()` and `perimeter()`. The class overrides method `to_string()`. It also defines a method `initialize` that is not inherited from the parent class.

FIGURE 16-26
Class `square`.

```
MODULE square_class
!
!   This module implements a square class.
!
!   Record of revisions:
!      Date        Programmer          Description of change
!      ====        ==========          =====================
!    12/29/06   S. J. Chapman          Original code
!
```

16

(continued)

```
(concluded)
USE rectangle_class                        ! USE parent class
IMPLICIT NONE

! Type definition
TYPE,PUBLIC,EXTENDS(rectangle) :: square

   ! Additional instance variables.
   !<none>

CONTAINS

   ! Bound procedures
   PROCEDURE,PUBLIC :: to_string => to_string_fn

END TYPE square

! Restrict access to the actual procedure names
PRIVATE :: to_string_fn

! Now add methods
CONTAINS

   CHARACTER(len=50) FUNCTION to_string_fn(this)
   !
   ! Return a character description of this object.
   !
   IMPLICIT NONE

   ! Declare calling arguments
   CLASS(square) :: this                   ! Square object

   ! Return description
   WRITE (to_string_fn,'(A,F6.2)') 'Square of length ', &
      this%l

   END FUNCTION to_string_fn

END MODULE square_class
```

The class pentagon is shown in Figure 16-27. This class defines an instance variable s for the length of the side of the pentagon, and provides concrete implementations of methods area(), perimeter(), and to_string(). It also defines a method initialize that is not inherited from the parent class.

FIGURE 16-27
Class pentagon.

```
MODULE pentagon_class
!
!   This module implements a pentagon class.
!
!   Record of revisions:
!      Date       Programmer          Description of change
!      ====       ==========          =====================
!   12/29/06    S. J. Chapman         Original code
!
```

(continued)

F-2003 ONLY

```
(continued)
USE shape_class                        ! USE parent class
IMPLICIT NONE

! Type definition
TYPE,PUBLIC,EXTENDS(shape) :: pentagon

   ! Additional instance variables.
   REAL :: s = 0              ! Length of side
CONTAINS

   ! Bound procedures
   PROCEDURE,PUBLIC :: initialize => initialize_sub
   PROCEDURE,PUBLIC :: area => get_area_fn
   PROCEDURE,PUBLIC :: perimeter => get_perimeter_fn
   PROCEDURE,PUBLIC :: to_string => to_string_fn

END TYPE pentagon

! Restrict access to the actual procedure names
PRIVATE :: initialize_sub, get_area_fn, get_perimeter_fn
PRIVATE :: to_string_fn

! Now add methods
CONTAINS

   SUBROUTINE initialize_sub(this,s)
   !
   ! Initialize the pentagon object.
   !
   IMPLICIT NONE

   ! Declare calling arguments
   CLASS(pentagon) :: this                  ! Pentagon object
   REAL,INTENT(IN) :: s                     ! Length of side

   ! Initialize the pentagon
   this%s = s

   END SUBROUTINE initialize_sub


   REAL FUNCTION get_area_fn(this)
   !
   ! Return the area of this object.
   !
   IMPLICIT NONE

   ! Declare calling arguments
   CLASS(pentagon) :: this                  ! Pentagon object

   ! Calculate area [0.72654253 is tan(PI/5)]
   get_area_fn = 1.25 * this%s**2 / 0.72654253

   END FUNCTION get_area_fn


   REAL FUNCTION get_perimeter_fn(this)
   !
```

16

(continued)

```
(concluded)
    ! Return the perimeter of this object.
    !
    IMPLICIT NONE

    ! Declare calling arguments
    CLASS(pentagon) :: this                ! Pentagon object

    ! Calculate perimeter
    get_perimeter_fn = 5.0 * this%s

    END FUNCTION get_perimeter_fn


    CHARACTER(len=50) FUNCTION to_string_fn(this)
    !
    ! Return a character description of this object.
    !
    IMPLICIT NONE

    ! Declare calling arguments
    CLASS(pentagon) :: this                ! Pentagon object

    ! Return description
    WRITE (to_string_fn,'(A,F6.2)') 'Pentagon of side ', &
        this%s

    END FUNCTION to_string_fn
END MODULE pentagon_class
```

5. Test the program.

To test this program, we will calculate the area and perimeter of several shapes by hand, and compare the results with those produced by a test driver program.

Shape	Area	Perimeter
Circle of radius 2:	$A = \pi r^2 = 12.5664$	$P = 2\pi r = 12.5664$
Triangle of side 2:	$A = \dfrac{\sqrt{3}}{4} s^2 = 1.732$	$P = 3s = 6$
Rectangle of length 2 and width 1:	$A = lw = 2$	$P = 2\,(l + w) = 6$
Square of side 2:	$A = lw = 2 \times 2 = 4$	$P = 2\,(l + w) = 8$
Pentagon of side 2:	$A = \dfrac{5}{4} s^2 \cot \dfrac{\pi}{5} = 6.8819$	$P = 5s = 10$

An appropriate test driver program is shown in Figure 16-28. Note that this program creates five objects of the various subclasses, and an array of pointers of type shape (as described in Section 15-6). It then assigns the objects to elements of the array. It then uses the methods to_string(), area(), and perimeter() on each object in the array shapes.

16

F-2003 ONLY

FIGURE 16-28
Program to test abstract class shape and its subclasses.

```fortran
PROGRAM test_shape
!
!   This program tests polymorphism using the shape class
!   and its subclasses.
!
! Record of revisions:
!      Date        Programmer          Description of change
!      ====        ==========          =====================
!   12/29/06     S. J. Chapman         Original code
!
USE circle_class                  ! Import circle class
USE square_class                  ! Import square class
USE rectangle_class               ! Import rectangle class
USE triangle_class                ! Import triangle class
USE pentagon_class                ! Import pentagon class
IMPLICIT NONE

! Declare variables
TYPE(circle),POINTER :: cir       ! Circle object
TYPE(square),POINTER :: squ       ! Square object
TYPE(rectangle),POINTER :: rec    ! Rectangle object
TYPE(triangle),POINTER :: tri     ! Triangle object
TYPE(pentagon),POINTER :: pen     ! Pentagon object
INTEGER :: i                      ! Loop index
CHARACTER(len=50) :: id_string    ! ID string
INTEGER :: istat                  ! Allocate status

! Create an array of shape pointers
TYPE :: shape_ptr
   CLASS(shape),POINTER :: p       ! Pointer to shapes
END TYPE shape_ptr
TYPE(shape_ptr),DIMENSION(5) :: shapes

! Create and initialize circle
ALLOCATE( cir, STAT=istat )
CALL cir%initialize(2.0)

! Create and initialize square
ALLOCATE( squ, STAT=istat )
CALL squ%initialize(2.0,2.0)

! Create and initialize rectangle
ALLOCATE( rec, STAT=istat )
CALL rec%initialize(2.0,1.0)

! Create and initialize triangle
ALLOCATE( tri, STAT=istat )
CALL tri%initialize(2.0)

! Create and initialize pentagon
ALLOCATE( pen, STAT=istat )
CALL pen%initialize(2.0)
```

16

(*continued*)

(concluded)

```
! Create the array of shape pointers
shapes(1)%p => cir
shapes(2)%p => squ
shapes(3)%p => rec
shapes(4)%p => tri
shapes(5)%p => pen

! Now display the results using the array of
! shape pointers.
DO i = 1, 5

   ! Get ID string
   id_string = shapes(i)%p%to_string()
   WRITE (*,'(/A)') id_string

   ! Get the area and perimeter
   WRITE (*,'(A,F8.4)') 'Area      = ', shapes(i)%p%area()
   WRITE (*,'(A,F8.4)') 'Perimeter = ', shapes(i)%p%perimeter()
END DO

END PROGRAM test_shape
```

When this program is executed, the results are:

```
C:\book\chap16>test_shape

Circle of radius 2.00
Area      = 12.5664
Perimeter = 12.5664

Square of length 2.00
Area      = 4.0000
Perimeter = 8.0000

Rectangle of length 2.00 and width 1.00
Area      = 2.0000
Perimeter = 6.0000

Equilateral triangle of side 2.00
Area      = 1.7321
Perimeter = 6.0000

Pentagon of side 2.00
Area      = 6.8819
Perimeter = 10.0000
```

The results of the program agree with our hand calculations to the number of significant digits that we performed the calculation. Note that the program called the correct polymorphic version of each method.

16

Quiz 16-1

This quiz provides a quick check to see if you have understood the concepts introduced in Sections 16.1 through 16.11. If you have trouble with the quiz, reread the section, ask your instructor, or discuss the material with a fellow student. The answers to this quiz are found in the back of the book.

1. What are the principal advantages of object-oriented programming?

2. Name the major components of a class, and describe their purposes.

3. What types of access modifiers may be defined in Fortran, and what access does each type give? What access modifier should normally be used for instance variables? for methods?

4. How are type-bound methods created in Fortran?

5. What is a finalizer? Why is a finalizer needed? How do you create one?

6. What is inheritance?

7. What is polymorphism?

8. What are abstract classes and abstract methods? Why would you wish to use abstract classes and methods in your programs?

16.12
SUMMARY

An object is a self-contained software component that consists of properties (variables) and methods. The properties (variables) are usually hidden from the outside world, and are modified only through the methods that are associated with them. Objects communicate with each other via messages (which are really method calls). An object uses a message to request another object to perform a task for it.

Classes are the software blueprints from which objects are made. The members of a class are instance variables, methods, and possibly a finalizer. The members of a class are accessed by using the object name and the access operator—the % operator.

A finalizer is a special method used to release resources just before an object is destroyed. A class can have at most one finalizer, but most classes do not need one.

When an object is instantiated from a class, a separate copy of each instance variable is created for the object. All objects derived from a given class share a single set of methods.

When a new class is created from some other class ("extends" the class), it inherits the instance variables and methods of its parent class. The class on which a new class is based is called the superclass of the new class, and the new class is a subclass of the class on which it is based. The subclass needs to provide only instance variables and methods to implement the *differences* between itself and its parent.

16

An object of a subclass may be treated as an object of its corresponding superclass. Thus an object of a subclass may be freely assigned to a superclass pointer.

Polymorphism is the ability to automatically vary methods according to the subclass that an object belongs to. To create polymorphic behavior, define all polymorphic methods in the common superclass, and override the behavior of the methods in each subclass that inherits from the superclass. All pointers and dummy arguments manipulating the objects must be declared to be the superclass type using the CLASS keyword.

An abstract method is a method whose interface is declared without an associated method being written. An abstract method is declared by adding the DEFERRED attribute to the binding, and by providing an abstract interface for the method. A class containing one or more abstract methods is called an abstract class. Each subclass of an abstract class must provide an implementation of all abstract methods, or the subclass will remain abstract.

16.12.1 Summary of Good Programming Practice

The following guidelines introduced in this chapter will help you to develop good programs:

1. Always make instance variables private, so that they are hidden within an object. Such encapsulation makes your programs more modular and easier to modify.
2. Use set methods to check the validity and consistency of input data before it is stored in an object's instance variables.
3. Define predicate methods to test for the truth or falsity of conditions associated with any classes you create.
4. The instance variables of a class should normally be declared PRIVATE, and the class methods should be used to provide a standard interface to the class.
5. Polymorphism allows multiple objects of different subclasses to be treated as objects of a single superclass, while automatically selecting the proper methods to apply to a particular object based on the subclass that it belongs to.
6. To create polymorphic behavior, declare all polymorphic methods in a common superclass, and then override the behavior of the methods in each subclass that inherits from the superclass.
7. Use abstract classes to define broad types of behaviors at the top of an object-oriented programming class hierarchy, and use concrete classes to provide implementation details in the subclasses of the abstract classes.

16.12.2 Summary of Fortran Statements and Structures

ABSTRACT **Attribute:**

TYPE,ABSTRACT :: *type_name*

16

(continued)

(concluded)

Examples:

```
TYPE,ABSTRACT :: test
    INTEGER :: a
    INTEGER :: b
CONTAINS
    PROCEDURE(ADD_PROC),DEFERRED :: add
END TYPE
```

Description:

The ABSTRACT attribute declares that a data type is abstract, meaning that no objects of this type can be created, because one or more of the bound methods are deferred.

ABSTRACT INTERFACE Construct:

```
ABSTRACT INTERFACE
```

Examples:

```
TYPE,ABSTRACT :: test
    INTEGER :: a
    INTEGER :: b
CONTAINS
    PROCEDURE(ADD_PROC),DEFERRED :: add
END TYPE
ABSTRACT INTERFACE
    SUBROUTINE add_proc (this, b)
    . . .
    END SUBROUTINE add_proc
END INTERFACE
```

Description:

The ABSTRACT INTERFACE construct declares the interface of a deferred procedure, so that the Fortran compiler will know the required calling sequence of the procedure.

CLASS Keyword:

```
CLASS(type_name) :: obj1, obj2, ...
```

Examples:

```
CLASS(point) :: my_point
CLASS(point),POINTER :: p1
```

16

(continued)

(concluded)

Description:
The CLASS keyword defines a pointer or dummy argument that can accept a target of the specified type, or of any type that extends the specified type. In other words, the pointer or dummy argument will work with targets of the specified class or of any subclass of the specified class.

DEFERRED **Attribute:**

```
PROCEDURE,DEFERRED :: proc_name
```

Examples:

```
TYPE,ABSTRACT :: test
    INTEGER :: a
    INTEGER :: b
CONTAINS
    PROCEDURE(ADD_PROC),DEFERRED :: add
END TYPE
```

Description:
The DEFERRED attribute declares that a procedure bound to a derived data type is not defined in the data type, making the type abstract. No object can be created with this data type. A concrete implementation must be defined in a subclass before objects of that type can be created.

EXTENDS **Attribute:**

```
TYPE,EXTENDS(parent_type) :: new_type
```

Example:

```
TYPE,EXTENDS(point2d) :: point3d
    REAL :: z
END TYPE
```

Description:
The EXTENDS attribute indicates that the new type being defined is an extension of the type specified in the EXTENDS attribute. The new type inherits all of the instance variables and methods of the original type, except for ones explicitly overridden in the type definition.

NON_OVERRIDABLE **Attribute:**

```
PROCEDURE,NON_OVERRIDABLE :: proc_name
```

16

(continued)

(*concluded*)

Example:

```
TYPE :: point
    REAL :: x
    REAL :: y
CONTAINS
    PROCEDURE,NON_OVERRIDABLE :: my_proc
END TYPE
```

Description:
The NON_OVERRIDABLE attribute indicates that a bound procedure can not be overridden in any subclasses derived from this class.

F-2003 ONLY

16.12.3 Exercises

16-1. List and describe the major components of a class.

16-2. Enhance the date class created in this chapter by adding:

(*a*) A method to calculate the day of year for the specified date.

(*b*) A method to calculate the number of days since January 1, 1900 for the specified date.

(*c*) A method to calculate the number of days between the date in the current date object and the date in another date object.

Also, convert the to_string method to generate the date string in the form Month dd, yyyy. Generate a test driver program to test all of the methods in the class.

16-3. Create a new class called salary_plus_employee as a subclass of the employee class created in this chapter. A salary-plus employee will receive a fixed salary for a normal work week, plus bonus overtime pay at an hourly rate for any hours greater than 42 in any given week. Override all of the necessary methods for this subclass. Then modify program test_employee to demonstrate the proper operation of all three subclasses of employee.

16-4. General Polygons Create a class called point, containing two instance variables x and y, representing the (*x, y*) location of a point on a Cartesian plane. Then, define a class polygon as a subclass of the shape class developed in Example 16-3. The polygon should be specified by an ordered series of (*x, y*) points denoting the ends of each line segment forming the polygon. For example, a triangle is specified by three (*x, y*) points, a quadrilateral is specified by three (*x, y*) points, and so forth.

The initializing method for this class should accept the number of points used to specify a particular polygon, and should allocate an array of point objects to hold the (*x, y*)

16

information. The class should implement `set` and `get` methods to allow the locations of each point to be set and retrieved, as well as area and perimeter calculations.

The area of a general polygon may be found from the equation

$$A = \frac{1}{2}\left(x_1y_2 + x_2y_3 + \cdots + x_{n-1}y_n + x_ny_1 - y_1x_2 - y_2x_3 - \cdots - y_{n-1}x_n - y_nx_1\right)$$

where x_i and y_i are (x, y) values of the ith point. The perimeter of the general polygon will be the sum of the lengths of each line segment, where the length of segment i is found from the equation:

$$Length = \sqrt{\left(x_{i+1} - x_i\right)^2 + \left(y_{i+1} - y_i\right)^2}$$

Once this class is created, write a test program that creates an array of `shapes` of various sorts, including general polygons, and sorts the shapes into ascending order of area.

16-5. Create an abstract class called `vec`, which includes instance variables `x` and `y`, and abstract methods to add and subtract two vectors. Create two subclasses, `vec2d` and `vec3d`, that implement these methods for two-dimensional and three-dimensional vectors, respectively. Class `vec3d` must also define the additional instance variable `z`. Write a test program to demonstrate that the proper methods are called polymorphically when `vec` objects are passed to the addition and subtraction methods.

16

Redundant, Obsolescent, and Deleted Fortran Features

OBJECTIVES

- Be able to look up and understand redundant, obsolescent, and deleted Fortran features when you encounter them.
- Understand that these features should *never* be used in any new program.

There are a number of odds and ends in the Fortran language that have not fit logically into our discussions in the previous chapters. These miscellaneous features of the language are described here.

Many of the features we will be describing in this chapter date from the early days of the Fortran language. They are the skeletons in Fortran's closet. For the most part, they are either incompatible with good structured programming or are obsolete and have been replaced by better methods. As such, *they should not be used in new programs that you write*. However, you may see them in existing programs that you are required to maintain or modify, so you should be familiar with them.

Many of these features are classified as either **obsolescent** or **deleted** in Fortran 95/2003. An *obsolescent* feature is one that has been declared undesirable, and that has been replaced in good usage by better methods. It is still supported by all compilers, but it should not be used in any new code. Obsolescent features are candidates for deletion in future versions of Fortran as their use declines. A *deleted* feature is one that has officially been removed from the Fortran language. It may be supported by your Fortran compiler for backward compatibility reasons, but there is no guarantee that it will work with all compilers.

Because the features described in this chapter are generally undesirable, there are no examples or quizzes featuring them. The contents of the chapter may be used as a cross-reference to help you understand (and possibly replace) older features found in existing programs.

▩ 17.1

PRE-FORTRAN 90 CHARACTER RESTRICTIONS

Before Fortran 90, the Fortran character set for naming variables officially included only the uppercase letters A to Z and the digits 0 to 9. The lowercase letters were undefined in the standard, but were usually made equivalent to the corresponding uppercase ones if they were supported at all by a particular compiler. In addition, the underscore character (_) was not legal in a variable name.

All Fortran names (procedure names, variable names, etc.) were restricted to a maximum of six characters. Because of these restrictions, you may encounter strange and hard-to-read names in older programs.

▩ 17.2

OBSOLESCENT SOURCE FORM

As we mentioned in Chapter 1, Fortran was one of the first major computer languages to be developed. It originated in the days before video displays and keyboards, when the punched card was the major form of input to the computer. Each punched card had a fixed length of 80 columns, and one character, number, or symbol could be typed in each column. The structure of statements in earlier versions of Fortran reflected this fixed limitation of 80 characters per line. By contrast, Fortran 90 and later versions were developed in the age of the video display and keyboard, so it allows free entry of statements in any column. For backward compatibility, Fortran 90/95/2003 also supports the old fixed form used by earlier versions of Fortran.

A fixed-source form Fortran statement still reflects the structure of the punched computer card. Each card has 80 columns. Figure 17-1 shows the use of these 80 columns in a fixed form Fortran statement.

Columns 1 through 5 are reserved for statement labels. A statement label may be located anywhere within columns 1 through 5, with either leading or trailing blanks. For example, the label 100 could be placed in columns 1 to 3, 2 to 4, or 3 to 5, and it would still be the same label.

A letter C or an asterisk (*) placed in column 1 indicates that the statement is a **comment.** The Fortran compiler completely ignores any statement beginning with these characters.

Column 6 is normally blank. If any character other than a blank or a zero is placed in that column, then the statement is interpreted as a continuation of the statement immediately preceding it.

Columns 7 to 72 contain the Fortran instructions that are interpreted by the compiler. The instructions may be freely placed anywhere within this area. Programmers typically take advantage of this freedom to indent certain instructions (loops and branches) to make their code more readable.

Columns 73 to 80 are sometimes called the **card identification field.** This field is totally ignored by the compiler, and may be used by the programmer for any desired purpose. In the days when programs were saved on decks of punched cards, this field was used to number the cards in consecutive order. If someone accidentally dropped

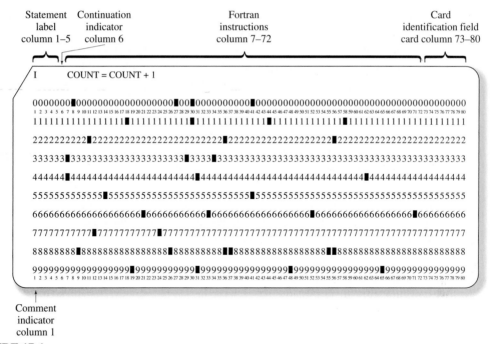

| Statement label column 1–5 | Continuation indicator column 6 | Fortran instructions column 7–72 | Card identification field card column 73–80 |

```
I          COUNT = COUNT + 1
```

FIGURE 17-1
The structure of a fixed-source form Fortran statement.

a numbered card deck, it was possible to reconstruct the order of the statements in the program from the numbers on the cards. Today, these columns are usually blank.

Figure 1-6 shows a sample Fortran program using the fixed-source form. Note that the statement label 100 falls in columns 1 to 5, and the Fortran instructions begin in column 7.

It is easy to convert a fixed-source form program into free-source form. A Fortran program to accomplish this conversion is freely available on the Internet. It was written by Michael Metcalf at CERN in Geneva, and is named `convert.f90`. It is freely available from many sources on the Internet.

The fixed-source form has been declared obsolescent in Fortran 95, which means that it is a candidate for deletion in future versions of Fortran. All new programs should use the free source form.

17.3

DANGER DO NOT USE

REDUNDANT DATA TYPE

In versions of Fortran before Fortran 90, there were two types of real variables: `REAL` and `DOUBLE PRECISION`. Double-precision variables were defined as having higher precision than real variables, but the exact precision and range of each data type varied from computer to computer. Thus, double precision on a VAX computer was a 64-bit variable, while double precision on a Cray supercomputer was a 128-bit variable. This

17

difference made programs that depended on having variables with a certain minimum range and precision inherently less portable.

These older data types have been replaced by the parameterized real data type, in which it is possible to explicitly specify the range and/or precision required for a given data item. The DOUBLE PRECISION data type should never be used in new Fortran programs.

17.4

OLDER, OBSOLESCENT, AND/OR UNDESIRABLE SPECIFICATION STATEMENTS

The syntax of many specification statements was different before Fortran 90. In addition, there are five obsolete and/or undesirable Fortran statements that may appear in the declaration section of a Fortran program. They are

1. The IMPLICIT statement
2. The DIMENSION statement
3. The EQUIVALENCE statement
4. The DATA statement
5. The PARAMETER statement

These statements are described below.

17.4.1 Pre-Fortran 90 Specification Statements

The form of many specification statements was different before Fortran 90. It was not possible to declare attributes in a type declaration statement, and the double colons (::) were not used. It was also not possible to initialize variables in a type declaration statement.

In addition, the lengths of character variables were declared by using an asterisk followed by the length in characters. The asterisk and length could be attached to either the CHARACTER statement, in which case it applied to all variables in the statement, or it could be attached to a specific variable name. If it were attached to a specific variable name, the length applied only to that variable.

Pre-Fortran 90 type specification statements took one of the following forms:

```
INTEGER list of integer variables
REAL list of real variables
DOUBLE PRECISION list of double precision variables
COMPLEX list of complex variables
LOGICAL list of logical variables
CHARACTER list of character variables
CHARACTER*<len> list of character variables
```

Examples of some pre-Fortran 90 type specification statements are shown below:

```
INTEGER I, J, K
DOUBLE PRECISION BIGVAL
CHARACTER*20 FILNM1, FILNM2, YN*1
```

The CHARACTER*<len> form of the character type declaration statement has been declared obsolescent in Fortran 95, which means that it is a candidate for deletion in future versions of Fortran.

17.4.2 The IMPLICIT Statement

By default, named constants and variables whose names begin with the letters I through N are integers, while all other named constants and variables are of type REAL. The IMPLICIT statement permits us to override these defaults.

The general form of the IMPLICIT statement is

```
IMPLICIT type1 (a₁,a₂,a₃,...), type2 (b₁,b₂,b₃,...), ...
```

where $type1$, $type2$, etc. are any legal data types: INTEGER, REAL, LOGICAL, CHARACTER, DOUBLE PRECISION, or COMPLEX. The letters a_1, a_2, a_3, etc. are the first letters whose type will be $type1$, and so forth for the other types. If a range of letters is to be declared as the same type, then the range may be indicated by the first and last letters separated by a dash (–). For example, the following statements declare that variables starting with the letters a, b, c, i, and z will be COMPLEX, and variables beginning with the letter d will be DOUBLE PRECISION. Variables beginning with other letters will retain their default types. Finally, the variables i1 and i2 are explicitly declared to be integers, overriding the IMPLICIT statement.

```
IMPLICIT COMPLEX (a-c, i, z), DOUBLE PRECISION d
INTEGER :: i1, i2
```

The IMPLICIT NONE statement was described in Chapter 2 and has been used throughout the book. It cancels all default types. When the IMPLICIT NONE statement is used in a program, every named constant, variable, and function name in the program must be declared explicitly. Since every named constant and variable in your program should be declared explicitly, there is no need for the standard IMPLICIT statement in any well-designed program. Only the IMPLICIT NONE statement should be used. However, you must be familiar with the IMPLICIT statement, since you will encounter it in older Fortran programs.

Good Programming Practice

Do not use IMPLICIT statements in your programs, except for IMPLICIT NONE. All of your programs should include the IMPLICIT NONE statement, and all named constants, variables, and functions in your programs should be explicitly typed.

17.4.3 The DIMENSION Statement

The DIMENSION statement is a declaration statement used to declare the *length* of arrays. The general form of a DIMENSION statement is

```
DIMENSION array( [i1:]i2, [j1:]j2, ... ), ...
```

17

where *array* is an array name, and i_1, i_2, j_1, j_2, etc. are the dimensions of the arrays. For example, a 6-element array `array1` could be declared with the following statement:

```
DIMENSION array1(6)
```

Notice that the `DIMENSION` statement declares the length of an array, but not its type. If `array1` is not included in any type specification statement, then its type will default to real because the name begins with the letter A. If we wish to declare both the type and the length of the array, then we would have to use one of the following sets of statements.

```
REAL, DIMENSION(6) :: array1
```

or

```
REAL :: array1
DIMENSION array1(6)
```

The `DIMENSION` statement is needed only when we declare the length of an array while using default typing. Since we never use default typing in good Fortran programs, there is no need to ever use this statement. It is a holdover from earlier versions of Fortran.

Good Programming Practice

Do not use `DIMENSION` statements in your programs. Since all variables and arrays in your programs will be explicitly typed, the lengths of the arrays can be declared in the type declaration statements with the `DIMENSION` attribute. There is never a need for `DIMENSION` statements in well-designed programs.

17.4.4 The `DATA` Statement

Before Fortran 90, it was not possible to initialize variables in a type declaration statement. Instead, the variables were initialized by a separate `DATA` statement, which took the form

```
DATA var_names/values/, var_names/values/, ...
```

where *var_names* is a list of variable names and *values* are the values to be assigned to those variables. There must be a one-to-one correspondence between the number of variables in the data statements and the number of values to initialize them. A single value could be repeated several times by preceding it with a repeat count followed by an asterisk. For example, the following statement initializes variables a1, b1, and c1 to 1.0, 0.0, and 0.0 respectively.

```
DATA a1, b1, c1 / 1.0, 2*0.0 /
```

Arrays may also be initialized in `DATA` statements. If an array is mentioned in a `DATA` statement, then there must be enough data values to initialize all of the elements in the array. The values are assigned to the array elements in *column order*. The following DATA statement initializes the 2 × 2 array a1.

```
REAL a1(2,2)
DATA a1 / 1., 2., 3., 4. /
```

Since values are assigned to the array elements in column order, this initializes a1(1,1) to 1.0, a1(2,1) to 2.0, a1(1,2) to 3.0, and a1(2,2) to 4.0.

It is possible to change the order in which values are assigned to array elements by using an implied DO loop. Thus the following DATA statement initializes the 2 × 2 array a2.

```
REAL a2(2,2)
DATA ((a2(i,j), j=1,2), i=1,2) / 1., 2., 3., 4. /
```

This implied DO loop initializes the array elements in the order a2(1,1), a2(1,2), a2(2,1), a2(2,2), so the values become a(1,1) = 1.0, a(1,2) = 2.0, a(2,1) = 3.0, and a(2,2) = 4.0.

The DATA statement is redundant, since data initializations can be made directly in type declaration statements. It should not be used in new programs.

Good Programming Practice

Do not use DATA statements in your programs. Instead, initialize your variables in their type declaration statements.

17.4.5 The PARAMETER Statement

The parameter or named constant was introduced in FORTRAN 77. At that time, parameters were declared in a PARAMETER statement of the form:

```
INTEGER SIZE
PARAMETER ( SIZE = 1000 )
```

The PARAMETER attribute was introduced in Fortran 90, so that the same parameter is now declared as

```
INTEGER, PARAMETER :: size = 1000
```

The older PARAMETER statement was retained for backward compatibility, but it should never be used. The syntax of that statement is not consistent with other Fortran statements, and it is simpler to declare a parameter value in its type declaration statement anyway.

Good Programming Practice

Do not use PARAMETER statements in your programs. Instead, use the PARAMETER attribute of a type declaration statement.

▪ 17.5

SHARING MEMORY LOCATIONS: COMMON AND EQUIVALENCE

Fortran includes two statements that permit different variables to physically share the same memory locations, either between program units or within a single program unit: the COMMON statement and the EQUIVALENCE statement. Both of these statements have been replaced by better methods in Fortran 90 and later versions.

17.5.1 COMMON Blocks

We saw in Chapter 7 that modules may be used to share data between program units. If a data item is defined in a module and has the PUBLIC attribute, then any program unit that uses the module can access the data item. This is the standard way to share data among program units in Fortran 90 and Fortran 95. However, modules did not exist before Fortran 90, and a totally different mechanism was used to share data.

Before Fortran 90, information was shared among program units through COMMON blocks. A COMMON block is a declaration of a region of computer memory that is accessible to every program unit containing the common block. The structure of a COMMON block is

```
COMMON / name / var1, var2, var3, ...
```

where *name* is the name of the COMMON block, and *var1*, *var2*, etc. are variables or arrays allocated in successive memory locations starting at the beginning of the block. Before Fortran 90, a COMMON block could contain any mixture of real, integer, and logical variables and arrays, or it could contain character data, but noncharacter and character data could not be mixed in the same COMMON block. This restriction was removed in Fortran 90.

A procedure can have as many COMMON blocks as the programmer wishes to declare, so it is possible to create separate COMMON blocks for logical groupings of data that need to be shared. Each separate COMMON block must have a unique name. The names have global scope, so they must be unique within the entire program.

When an array appears in a COMMON block, the size of the array may be declared in either the COMMON block or the type declaration statement, but *not* in both places. The following pairs of statements are legal and completely equivalent:

```
REAL, DIMENSION(10) :: a ! Preferred
COMMON / data1 / a


REAL :: a
COMMON / data1 / a(10)
```

while the following statements are illegal and will produce an error at compilation time:

```
REAL, DIMENSION(10) :: a
COMMON / data1 / a(10)
```

17

COMMON blocks permit procedures to share data by sharing a common region of memory. The Fortran compiler allocates all COMMON blocks with the same name in any program unit to the *same region of memory*, so that any data stored there by one procedure may be read and used by any of the other ones. The COMMON blocks with a given name do not all have to be the same length in every procedure, since the Fortran compiler and linker are smart enough to allocate enough memory to hold the largest block declared in any of the procedures.

A sample pair of routines with COMMON blocks are shown in Figure 17-2.

FIGURE 17-2
A main program and subroutine sharing data through a COMMON block.

```
PROGRAM main
IMPLICIT NONE
REAL :: a, b
REAL, DIMENSION(5) :: c
INTEGER :: i
COMMON / common1 / a, b, c, i
...
CALL sub11
END PROGRAM

SUBROUTINE sub11
REAL :: x
REAL,DIMENSION(5) :: y
INTEGER :: i, j
COMMON / common1 / x, y, i, j
...
END SUBROUTINE
```

Variables and arrays are allocated in a COMMON block in the order in which they are declared in the COMMON statement. In the main program, variable a occupies the first word in the block, variable b occupies the second word, etc. In the subroutine, variable x occupies the first word in the block, and array element y(1) occupies the second word, etc. Therefore, *variable a in the main program is really the same as variable x in the subroutine*. They are two different ways to refer to identically the same memory location. Note that the variables in the main program and the subroutine are related by their relative positions in their common blocks. This is known as **storage association,** because the variables are associated by sharing a single physical storage location.

Both COMMON blocks and modules are convenient ways to share large volumes of data between procedures. However, COMMON blocks must be used carefully to avoid problems, since they are subject to two types of errors that don't affect modules. Both of these errors are illustrated in Figure 17-3. Note that the 5-element array c in the main program and the corresponding 5-element array y in the subroutine are misaligned, because there is one fewer value declared in the block before the array in the subroutine than in the main program. Therefore, c(1) in the main program will be the same variable as y(2) in the subroutine. If arrays c and y are supposed to be the same,

Memory address	Program main	Subroutine sub1
0000	a	x
0001	b	y(1)
0002	c(1)	y(2)
0003	c(2)	y(3)
0004	c(3)	y(4)
0005	c(4)	y(5)
0006	c(5)	i
0007	i	j

FIGURE 17-3
Memory allocation in COMMON block /common1/, showing the misalignment between arrays c and y.

this misalignment will cause severe problems. Also, note that real array element c(5) in the main program is identical to integer variable i in the subroutine. It is extremely unlikely that the real variable stored in c(5) will be usable as an integer in subroutine sub1. This type mismatch must also be prevented. Neither the array misalignment nor the type mismatch can occur when modules are used to share data between program units, so modules are the best way to share data in all modern Fortran programs.

To properly use a COMMON block, we must ensure that all variables in the block appear *in the same order* and have *the same type and size* in every program unit containing the block. In addition, it is good programming practice to keep the *same names* for each of the variables in every program unit containing the block. The program will be much more understandable if the same names apply to the same variables in all procedures.

Good Programming Practice
Use modules rather than COMMON blocks to share data between program units. If you do use COMMON blocks, you should be sure to declare the blocks identically in every procedure containing them, so that the variables always have the same name, type, and order in each procedure.

17

17.5.2 Initializing Data in COMMON Blocks: The BLOCK DATA Subprogram

The DATA statement was introduced above. It may be used to initialize the values asso-ciated with local variables in a main program or subprogram. However, it may *not* be used in a main program or procedure to initialize variables in COMMON blocks. The reason for this restriction is illustrated in the following example program.

```
PROGRAM test
CALL sub1
CALL sub2
END PROGRAM

SUBROUTINE sub1
INTEGER ival1, ival2
COMMON / mydata / ival1, ival2
DATA ival1, ival2 /1, 2/
. . .
END SUBROUTINE sub1

SUBROUTINE sub2
INTEGER ival1, ival2
COMMON / mydata / ival1, ival2
DATA ival1, ival2 /3, 4/
. . .
END SUBROUTINE sub2
```

Here, COMMON block /mydata/ is exchanged between subroutines sub1 and sub2. Subroutine sub1 attempts to initialize ival1 and ival2 to 1 and 2 respectively, while subroutine sub2 attempts to initialize ival1 and ival2 to 3 and 4 respectively. And yet, they are the same two variables! How could the Fortran compiler possibly make sense of this situation? The simple answer is that it can't.

To guarantee that there is only one set of initial values for the variables in a COMMON block, the Fortran language prohibits the use of DATA statements with common variables in any Fortran main program or procedure. Instead, it includes a special type of program unit *whose only function is to initialize the variables in a* COMMON *block*: the BLOCK DATA subprogram. Since there is one and only one place where COMMON vari-ables may be initialized, there is no ambiguity about what values to assign to them.

A BLOCK DATA subprogram begins with a BLOCK DATA statement, and may contain any number of type definition statements, COMMON statements, and DATA statements. *It must not contain any executable statements.* An example BLOCK DATA subprogram is shown below:

```
BLOCK DATA initial
INTEGER ival1, ival2
COMMON / mydata / ival1, ival2
DATA ival1, ival2 /1, 2/
END BLOCK DATA
```

The name of this BLOCK DATA subprogram is initial. (BLOCK DATA names are optional: this subprogram would have worked equally well with no name.) The subprogram initializes the variables `ival1` and `ival2` in `COMMON` block `/mydata/` to 1 and 2 respectively.

17.5.3 The Unlabeled `COMMON` Statement

There is an alternative form of the `COMMON` statement, called the unlabeled `COMMON` statement. An unlabeled `COMMON` statement has the form

```
COMMON var1, var2, var3, ...
```

where `var1`, `var2`, etc. are variables or arrays allocated in successive memory locations starting at the beginning of the common block. The unlabeled `COMMON` statement is exactly like an ordinary `COMMON` block, except that this block has no name.

The unlabeled `COMMON` statement is a relic left over from earlier versions of Fortran. Before FORTRAN 66, it was possible to declare only one `COMMON` area in any given program. The unlabeled `COMMON` statement should never be used in any modern Fortran program.

17.5.4 The `EQUIVALENCE` Statement

In the past, it was sometimes useful to refer to a particular location in computer memory by more than one name. Computer memory was a limited and very expensive resource. Because computer memory was so expensive, it was common for large computer programs to reuse portions of memory for scratch calculations in different procedures within the program. Since dynamic memory allocation did not exist before Fortran 90, a single fixed block of scratch memory would be declared that would be large enough for any temporary calculations within the program. This block of memory would be used over and over wherever scratch memory was needed. The scratch memory would often be referred to by different names in different portions of the program, but the same physical memory would be used each time.

To support such applications, Fortran provided a mechanism for assigning two or more names to the same physical memory location: the `EQUIVALENCE` statement. The `EQUIVALENCE` statement appears in the declaration section of a program after all type declaration statements and before any `DATA` statements. The form of the `EQUIVALENCE` statement is

```
EQUIVALENCE ( var1, var2, var3, ...)
```

where `var1`, `var2`, etc. are variables or array elements. *Every variable appearing within the parentheses in an* `EQUIVALENCE` *statement is assigned to the same memory location by the Fortran compiler.* If some of the variables are array elements, then this statement also fixes the relative relationships of all elements within the arrays. Consider the following example:

```
INTEGER, DIMENSION(2,2) :: i1
INTEGER, DIMENSION(5) :: j1
EQUIVALENCE ( i1(2,1), j1(4) )
```

Memory address	Name 1	Name 2
001		j1(1)
002		j1(2)
003	i1(1,1)	j1(3)
004	i1(2,1)	j1(4)
005	i1(1,2)	j1(5)
006	i1(2,2)	
007		
008		

Effect of the statement

EQUIVALENCE (I1(2,1), J1(4))

on memory allocation in a Fortran program

FIGURE 17-4
The effect of the EQUIVALENCE statement on memory allocation in a Fortran program.
Because i1(2,1) and j1(4) must be the same physical location, arrays i1 and j1 will
overlap in the computer's memory.

Here, i1(2,1) and j1(4) occupy the same memory location. Because of the way
arrays are laid out in memory, i1(1,2) and j1(5) will also occupy a single memory
location (see Figure 17-4).

EQUIVALENCE statements are inherently quite dangerous. A common problem
occurs when we first perform some calculation using an equivalenced array under
one name (say array1) in a program, and then perform a different calculation using
the same equivalenced array under another name (say array2) in another part of the
program. If we then try to access values in array1, we will find that they have all been
destroyed by the operations on array2. This can be an especially big problem if the
program is being modified by some person other than the original programmer. Since
the data in array array1 has been destroyed without array1 ever appearing in an
assignment statement, it can be very hard to track down this bug.

Since computer memory has gotten both cheaper and more plentiful over the years,
the need for equivalencing arrays has decreased dramatically. You should not equivalence variable names in your programs unless you have a very good reason to do so. If
you need to reuse scratch memory arrays in your program, *it is better to use allocatable arrays or pointers to allocate and deallocate the scratch memory dynamically.*

17

Another use of the EQUIVALENCE statement was to assign the same memory address to variables of *different types* so that the same bit pattern could be examined in different ways. For example, a real variable and an integer variable could be assigned to the same location. When a real variable was stored in that location, the integer variable could be used to examine the bit patterns. If you have any older code that uses EQUIVALENCE statements in this fashion, it can be replaced by the TRANSFER intrinsic function. For example, the following code takes the exact bit pattern of real variable value and stores it in integer variable ivalue:

```
INTEGER :: ivalue
REAL :: value
...
ivalue = TRANSFER(value, 0)
```

Finally, note that the EQUIVALENCE statement effectively assigns two or more different names to the same *memory location*. From this statement, it follows that names must be associated with memory locations, or they may not be equivalenced. Names that are not associated with a specific memory location (for example, dummy argument names) may not be used in an EQUIVALENCE statement.

Good Programming Practice

Do not use EQUIVALENCE statements in your programs. If you need to reuse scratch memory arrays in your program, it is better to use allocate and deallocate them dynamically with allocatable arrays or pointers.

17.6

UNDESIRABLE SUBPROGRAM FEATURES

There are four subprogram features that are undesirable and should never be used in modern Fortran programs. They are:

1. Alternate subroutine returns
2. Alternate entry points
3. The statement function
4. Passing intrinsic functions as arguments

17.6.1 Alternate Subroutine Returns

When a Fortran program calls a normal subroutine, the subroutine is executed, and then control returns to the first executable statement following the subroutine call.

It is sometimes useful to execute different code in the calling procedure, depending on the results of the subroutine call. Earlier versions of Fortran supported such operations by providing alternate subroutine returns. Alternate subroutine returns are statement labels passed as calling arguments to the subroutine. When the subroutine executes, it can decide to return control to any of the statement labels specified in the argument list. Alternate subroutine returns are specified in the following manner:

1. The statement labels associated with all possible alternate returns are specified as arguments in the CALL statement by preceding each label with an asterisk:

```
CALL SUB1 (a, b, c, *n1, *n2, *n3)
```

where n1, n2, and n3 are the statement numbers to which execution may be transferred.

2. The alternate returns are specified in the SUBROUTINE statement by asterisks:

```
SUBROUTINE SUB1 (a, b, c, *, *, *)
```

where the asterisks correspond to the locations of the alternate returns in the calling statement.

3. The particular alternate return to be executed is specified by a parameter on the RETURN statement:

```
RETURN k
```

where k is the *position* of the alternate return to be executed. In the above example, there are three possible alternate returns, so k could take on a value from 1 to 3.

In the example in Figure 17-5, there are two possible returns. The first return is for normal completion, and the second one is for error conditions.

FIGURE 17-5
A program fragment illustrating the use of alternate subroutine returns.

```
CALL calc ( a1, a2, result, *100, *999 )

! Normal return--continue execution.
100 ...
...
STOP

! Error in subroutine call--process error and stop.
999 WRITE (*,*) 'Error in subroutine calc. Execution aborted.'
STOP 999
END PROGRAM

SUBROUTINE calc ( a1, a2, result, *, * )
REAL a1, a2, result, temp

IF ( a1 * a2 >= 0. ) THEN
   result = SQRT(a1 * a2)
ELSE
   RETURN 2
END IF

RETURN 1

END SUBROUTINE
```

17

Alternate subroutine returns should *never* be used in modern Fortran code. They make program maintenance and debugging much harder by making it difficult to follow the execution path through the program. They contribute to the "spaghetti code" so commonly found in older programs. There are other, much better ways to provide for different program execution paths depending on the results of a subroutine call. The simplest and best approach is to include a logical IF construct that tests the subroutine return parameters immediately after the subroutine call, and then takes action depending on the status returned by the subroutine.

Alternate subroutine returns have been declared obsolescent in Fortran 95, which means that they are a candidate for deletion in future versions of Fortran.

Good Programming Practice

Do not use alternate subroutine returns in your programs. They make programming debugging and maintenance much harder, and simple, structured alternatives are available.

17.6.2 Alternate Entry Points

The normal entry point for a Fortran procedure is the first executable statement in the procedure. However, it is possible to get program execution to start at a different point within the procedure if that point is specified with an ENTRY statement. An ENTRY statement has the form

```
ENTRY name ( arg1, arg2, ...)
```

where *name* is the name of the entry point, and *arg1, arg2*, etc. are the dummy arguments passed to the procedure at the entry point. When a subprogram is invoked by the name specified in the ENTRY statement, execution begins at the first executable statement following the ENTRY statement instead of the first executable statement in the subprogram.

A common use of the ENTRY statement occurred when a subprogram must be initialized the first time it is used but not thereafter. In that case, a special initialization entry point was sometimes included in the subprogram. For example, consider the subroutine in Figure 17-6, which evaluates a third order polynomial for a specific input value x. Before the polynomial can be evaluated, the coefficients of the polynomial must be specified. If the coefficients of the polynomial change infrequently, we could specify them in a special ENTRY to the subroutine.

FIGURE 17-6
A subroutine illustrating the use of multiple entry points.

```
PROGRAM test_entry
REAL :: a = 1., b = 2., c = 1., d = 2.
CALL init1 ( a, b, c, d )
DO I = 1, 10
```

```
      CALL eval3 ( REAL(i), result )
      WRITE (*,*) 'EVAL3(', i, ') = ', result
END DO
END PROGRAM

SUBROUTINE eval3 ( x, result )
!
!    Evaluates a third order polynomial of the form:
!       RESULT = A + B*X + C*X**2 + D*X**3
!
! Declare calling arguments
IMPLICIT NONE
REAL :: a1, b1, c1, d1, x, result

! Declare local variables
REAL, SAVE :: a, b, c, d

! Calculate result
result = a + b**x + c*x**2 + d*x**3

RETURN

! Entry INITL specifies the values of a, b, c, and d
! to be used when evaluating the polynomial.

ENTRY initl(a1, b1, c1, d1)
a = a1
b = b1
c = c1
d = d1

RETURN
END SUBROUTINE
```

Note from the above example that the various entry points in a subroutine do not have to have the same calling sequence. However, we must be sure to call each entry point with the proper argument list for that particular entry point.

The use of entry points should be discouraged. A major disadvantage of ENTRY statements occurs when we need to modify the code of a procedure containing multiple entry points. If there are any code segments or variables in common to the different entry points, we can get in serious trouble. In the process of changing the procedure to make one entry point work correctly, we can inadvertently screw up the operation of another entry point. After a procedure containing multiple entry points is modified, it must be tested *very* carefully, both the entry point being modified and all other entry points.

The original reason for using multiple entry points in a procedure was to share segments of code for multiple purposes, thus reducing the size of the completed program. This reason no longer makes sense today. As cheap as memory is now, there is no good reason to *ever* use an entry point. If you write separate procedure for each function you need, your code will be much more maintainable.

If you need to share data among multiple procedures, the data (and possibly the procedures themselves) should be placed in a module. The previous example can be rewritten without entry points as shown in Figure 17-7. Variables a, b, c, and d are made available to both subroutines eval3 and initl through host association, and the subroutines are made available to the main program through USE association.

17

FIGURE 17-7
The previous example program rewritten without multiple entry points.

```
MODULE evaluate
IMPLICIT NONE
PRIVATE
PUBLIC eval3, initl

! Declare shared data.
REAL, SAVE :: a, b, c, d

! Declare procedures
CONTAINS
   SUBROUTINE eval3 ( x, result )
   !
   !     Evaluates a third order polynomial of the form:
   !        RESULT = A + B*X + C*X**2 + D*X**3
   !
   ! Declare calling arguments
   REAL, INTENT(IN) :: x
   REAL, INTENT(OUT) :: result

   ! Calculate result
   result = a + b**x + c*x**2 + d*x**3

   END SUBROUTINE eval3

   SUBROUTINE initl (a1, b1, c1, d1 )
   !
   ! Subroutine INITL specifies the values of a, b, c, and d
   ! to be used when evaluating the polynomial.
   !
   REAL, INTENT(IN) :: a1, b1, c1, d1
   a = a1
   b = b1
   c = c1
   d = d1
   END SUBROUTINE initl
END MODULE evaluate

PROGRAM test_noentry
USE evaluate
REAL :: a = 1., b = 2., c = 1., d = 2.
CALL initl ( a, b, c, d )
DO i = 1, 10
   CALL eval3 ( REAL(i), result )
   WRITE (*,*) 'EVAL3(', i, ') = ', result
END DO
END PROGRAM test_noentry
```

Good Programming Practice

Avoid alternate entry points in your programs. There is no good reason to use them in a modern Fortran program.

17.6.3 The Statement Function

In Chapter 7, we introduced the external functions. An external function is a procedure that returns a single value to the invoking program unit. Its input values are passed via an argument list. An external function is invoked by being named as a part of a Fortran expression.

In Chapter 9, we introduced the internal functions. Internal functions are similar to external functions, except they are entirely contained within another program unit, and may be invoked only from that program unit.

There is a third type of Fortran function: the *statement function*. A statement function consists of a *single statement*. It must be defined in the declaration section of a Fortran program unit before the first executable statement in the program unit. An example of a statement function is shown in Figure 17-8.

FIGURE 17-8
A program using a statement function.

```
PROGRAM polyfn
!
! This program evaluates a third order polynomial
! of the form:
!     RES = A + B*X + C*X**2 + D*X**3
! using a statement function.

IMPLICIT NONE

! Declare local variables.
REAL :: a, b, c, d, x, y
INTEGER :: i

! Declare dummy arguments of the statement function.
REAL :: a1, b1, c1, d1, x1, res

! Declare statement function res.
res(a1,b1,c1,d1,x1) = a1 + b1**x1 + c1*x1**2 + d1*x1**3

! Set up coefficients of polynomial res.
a = 1.
b = 2.
c = 1.
d = 2.

! Evaluate polynomial for x values of 1 through 10.
C
DO i = 1, 10
   x = REAL(i)
   y = res(a,b,c,d,x)
   WRITE (*,*) 'y(',i,') = ', y
END DO
END PROGRAM polyfn
```

In this example, real statement function res is defined as

$$res(a1,b1,c1,d1,x1) = a1 + b1**x1 + c1*x1**2 + d1*x1**3$$

17

where a1, b1, c1, d1, and x1 are *dummy arguments*. The types of the function and its dummy arguments must all be declared or defaulted before the function is defined. The dummy arguments are placeholders for the actual values that are used when the function is executed later in the program. The dummy arguments must agree in type and number with the actual arguments that are used when the function is executed. At execution time, the value in the first argument of the function will be used instead of a1 wherever a1 appears in the statement function, and so forth for all other arguments.

If you take a close look, you will notice that a statement function looks exactly like an assignment statement that assigns a value to an array element. Since this is so, how can the Fortran compiler tell the difference between them? To make it possible to tell the difference between them, Fortran requires that *all statement functions must be defined in the declaration section of a program*, before the first executable statement.

Like internal functions, statement functions can be used only in the program unit in which they are declared. They are limited to functions that can be evaluated in a single expression with no branches or loops. In addition, the calling arguments must be variables, constants, or array elements. Unlike external or internal functions, it is not possible to pass whole arrays to a statement function.

Statement functions are a very old feature of Fortran, dating all the way back to Fortran 1 in 1954. They have been replaced by internal functions. Internal functions can do anything a statement function can do, and much more. There is no reason to ever use statement functions in your programs.

Statement functions have been declared obsolescent in Fortran 95, which means that they are a candidate for deletion in future versions of Fortran.

Good Programming Practice
Never use statement functions in your programs. Use internal functions instead.

17.6.4 Passing Intrinsic Functions as Arguments

It is possible to pass a **specific intrinsic function** as a calling argument to another procedure. If the name of a specific intrinsic function is included as an actual argument in a procedure call, then a pointer to that function is passed to the procedure. If the corresponding dummy argument in the procedure is used as a function, then when the procedure is executed, the intrinsic function in the calling argument list will be used in place of the dummy function in the procedure. *Generic intrinsic functions may not be used as calling arguments*—only specific intrinsic functions may be used.

Before it can be used as a calling argument to a procedure, a specific intrinsic function must be declared in an INTRINSIC statement in the calling program. The INTRINSIC statement is a specification statement of the form

```
INTRINSIC name1, name2, ...
```

It states that *name1, name2*, etc. are names of intrinsic functions. The INTRINSIC statement must appear in the declaration section of a procedure, before the first executable statement. The reason that an INTRINSIC statement is required is the same as the reason that an EXTERNAL statement is required: it permits the compiler to distinguish between a variable name and an intrinsic function of the same type.

An example program illustrating the passing of a specific intrinsic function as an argument is shown in Figure 17-9. This program is a modification of the test driver program in Figure 6-25. It calculates the average value of the intrinsic function SIN(X) over 101 samples in the interval $[0, 2\pi]$, and the result is printed out.

FIGURE 17-9
Program illustrating the passing of an intrinsic function as a calling argument.

```
PROGRAM test_ave_value2
!
!   Purpose:
!     To test function ave_value by calling it with the intrinsic
!     function sin.
!
!   Record of revisions:
!      Date        Programmer          Description of change
!      ====        ==========          =====================
!    12/31/06    S. J. Chapman         Original code
!
IMPLICIT NONE

! Declare functions:
REAL :: ave_value                    ! Average value of function
INTRINSIC sin                        ! Function to evaluate

! Declare parameters:
REAL, PARAMETER :: TWOPI = 6.283185 ! 2 * Pi

! Declare local variables:
REAL :: ave                          ! Average of my_function

! Call function with func=sin.
ave = ave_value ( sin, 0., TWOPI, 101 )
WRITE (*,1000) 'SIN', ave
1000 FORMAT (1X,'The average value of ',A,' between 0. and twopi is ', &
           F16.6,'.')
END PROGRAM test_ave_value2
```

When program test_ave_value2 is executed, the results are

```
C:\BOOK\F90\CHAP6>test_ave_value2
The average value of SIN between 0. and TWOPI is .000000.
```

The passing of intrinsic functions as calling arguments is very confusing, and is only possible for specific intrinsic functions. It should never be done in modern Fortran programs.

■ 17.7
MISCELLANEOUS EXECUTION CONTROL FEATURES

There are two statements that pause and stop the execution of a program: the PAUSE and STOP statements. The PAUSE statement is rarely used in a modern Fortran program, since the same function can be done more flexibly with a combination of WRITE and READ statements. The STOP statement is more common, but it is often not necessary either, since program execution will terminate when the END statement is reached. However, it is occasionally useful to have multiple stopping points in a program. In that case, each stopping point will need a STOP statement. If there are multiple STOP statements in a program, each one should be labeled with a unique argument (as explained below) so that the user can tell which STOP statement was executed.

Finally, there is an older form of the END statement to indicate the end of a separately compiled program unit.

17.7.1 The PAUSE Statement

When we write Fortran programs whose results are meant to be viewed from a terminal, it is necessary to pause the program at certain points while the user examines the results displayed on the terminal. Otherwise, the information may scroll off the top of the display before it can be read. After the user reads output data on the terminal, he or she can either continue the program or abort it.

Earlier versions of Fortran included a special statement designed to pause the execution of a program until the user starts it up again: the PAUSE statement. The general form of the PAUSE statement is

```
PAUSE prompt
```

where *prompt* is an optional value to be displayed when the PAUSE statement is executed. The prompt may be either a character constant or an integer between 0 and 99999. When the PAUSE statement is executed, the value of *prompt* is displayed on the terminal, and execution stops until the user restarts the program. When the program is restarted, execution will begin at the statement following the PAUSE statement.

The PAUSE statement was never particularly common, since it is possible to perform the same function with WRITE and READ statements with much more flexibility.

The PAUSE statement has been deleted in Fortran 95, which means that it is no longer an official part of the Fortran language.

17.7.2 Arguments Associated with the STOP Statement

As with the PAUSE statement described above, it is possible to include an argument with the STOP statement. The general form of the STOP statement is

```
STOP stop_value
```

17

where *stop_value* is an optional value to be displayed when the STOP statement is executed. The *stop_value* may be either a character constant or an integer between 0 and 99999. It is mainly used when there are multiple STOP statements in a program. If there are multiple STOP statements and a separate *stop_value* is associated with each one, then the programmer and user can tell which of the STOP statements was executed when the program quit.

If there are multiple STOP statements in a program, it is a good idea to use either a separate argument on each one or a separate WRITE statement before each one, so that a user can tell which STOP a program halted on. An example program with multiple STOP statements is shown in Figure 17-10. The first STOP occurs if the file specified by the user does not exist. It is clearly marked by the WRITE statement that occurs just before it. The second STOP occurs when the program completes normally. If this stop is executed, the message 'Normal Completion.' will be printed out when the program terminates.

FIGURE 17-10
A program to illustrate the use of multiple STOP statements in a single program unit.

```
PROGRAM stop_test
!
!   Purpose:
!     To illustrate multiple STOP statements in a program.
!
IMPLICIT NONE

! Declare parameters:
INTEGER, PARAMETER :: lu = 12      ! I/O unit

! Declare variables:
INTEGER :: error                   ! Error flag
CHARACTER(len=20) :: filename      ! File name

! Prompt user and get the name of the input file.
WRITE (*,*) 'Enter file name: '
READ (*,'(A)') filename

! Open the input file
OPEN (UNIT=lu,FILE=filename,STATUS='OLD',IOSTAT=error )

! Check to see of the OPEN failed.
IF ( error > 0 ) THEN
   WRITE (*,1020) filename
   1020 FORMAT (1X,'ERROR: File ',A,' does not exist!')
   STOP
END IF

! Normal processing...
...

! Close input file, and quit.
```

```
CLOSE (lu)

STOP 'Normal completion.'
END PROGRAM stop_test
```

As Fortran has improved over the years, the use of multiple STOP statements has declined. Modern structured techniques usually result in programs with a single starting point and a single stopping point. However, there are still occasions when multiple stopping points might occur in different error paths. If you do have multiple stopping points, be sure that each one is labeled distinctively so that they can be easily distinguished.

17.7.3 The END Statement

Before Fortran 90, all program units terminated with an END statement instead of separate END PROGRAM, END SUBROUTINE, END FUNCTION, END MODULE, or END BLOCK DATA statements. The END statement is still accepted for backward compatibility in independently compiled program units such as main programs, external subroutines, and external functions.

However, internal procedures and module procedures *must* end with an END SUBROUTINE or END FUNCTION statement—the older form won't work in these new types of procedures that did not exist before Fortran 90.

▨ 17.8

OBSOLETE BRANCHING AND LOOPING STRUCTURES

In Chapter 3, we described the logical IF structure and the CASE structure, which are the standard ways to implement branches in modern Fortran. In Chapter 4, we described the various forms of the DO loop, which are the standard iterative and while loops in modern Fortran. This section describes several additional ways to produce branches, and older forms of DO loops. They are all archaic survivals from earlier versions of Fortran that are still supported for backward compatibility. These features should *never* be used in any new Fortran program. However, you may run into them if you ever have to work with old Fortran programs. They are described here for possible future reference.

17.8.1 The Arithmetic IF Statement

The Arithmetic IF statement goes all the way back to the origins of Fortran in 1954. The structure of an arithmetic IF statement is

```
IF (arithmetic_expression) label1, label2, label3
```

where *arithmetic_expression* is any integer, real, or double-precision arithmetic expression, and *label1*, *label2*, and *label3* are labels of executable Fortran statements. When the arithmetic IF statement is executed, the arithmetic expression is evaluated. If the resulting value is negative, execution transfers to the statement at *label1*. If the value is zero, execution transfers to the statement at *label2*. If the value is positive, execution transfers to the statement at *label3*. An example statement is

```
       IF ( x - y ) 10, 20, 30
   10  (code for negative case)
       . . .
       GO TO 100
   20  (code for zero case)
       . . .
       GO TO 100
   40  (code for positive case)
       . . .
  100  CONTINUE
       . . .
```

The arithmetic IF should never be used in any modern Fortran program.

The arithmetic IF statement has been declared obsolescent in Fortran 95, which means that it is a candidate for deletion in future versions of Fortran.

Good Programming Practice

Never use arithmetic IF statement in your programs. Use the logical IF structure instead.

17.8.2 The Unconditional GO TO Statement

The GO TO statement has the form

```
   GO TO label
```

where *label* is the label of an executable Fortran statement. When this statement is executed, control jumps unconditionally to the statement with the specified label.

In the past, GO TO statements were often combined with IF statements to create loops and conditional branches. For example, a while loop could be implemented as

```
   10 CONTINUE
       . . .
       IF ( condition ) GO TO 20
       . . .
       GO TO 10
   20 . . .
```

There are better ways to create loops and branches in modern Fortran, so the GO TO statement is now rarely used. The excessive use of GO TO statements tends to lead to spaghetti code, so their use should be discouraged. However, there may be some rare occasions (such as exception handling) when the statement will prove useful.

Good Programming Practice

Avoid the use of GO TO statements whenever possible. Use structured loops and branches instead.

17.8.3 The Computed GO TO Statement

The computed GO TO statement has the form

```
GO TO (label1, label2, label3,..., labelk), int_expr
```

where *label1* through *labelk* are labels of executable Fortran statements, and the *int_expr* evaluates to an integer between 1 and k. If the integer expression evaluates to 1, then the statement at *label1* is executed. If the integer expression evaluates to 2, then the statement at *label2* is executed, and so forth up to k. If the integer expression is less than 1 or greater than k, this is an error condition, and the behavior of the statement will vary from processor to processor.

An example of a computed GO TO statement is shown below. In this example, the number 2 would be printed out when the program is executed.

```
PROGRAM test
i = 2
GO TO (10, 20), i
10 WRITE (*,*) '1'
GO TO 30
20 WRITE (*,*) '2'
30 STOP
END PROGRAM
```

The computed GO TO should never be used in any modern Fortran program. It has been entirely replaced by the CASE structure.

The computed GO TO statement has been declared obsolescent in Fortran 95, which means that it is a candidate for deletion in future versions of Fortran.

Good Programming Practice

Never use the computed GO TO statement in your programs. Use the CASE structure instead.

17

17.8.4 The Assigned GO TO Statement

The assigned GO TO statement has two possible forms:

```
GO TO integer variable, (label1, label2, label3,..., labelk)
```

or

```
GO TO integer variable
```

where *integer variable* contains the statement number of the statement to be executed next, and *label1* through *labelk* are labels of executable Fortran statements. Before this statement is executed, a statement label must be assigned to the integer variable by using the ASSIGN statement:

```
ASSIGN label TO integer variable
```

When the first form of the assigned GO TO is executed, the program checks the value of the integer variable against the list of statement labels. If the value of the variable is in the list, then execution branches to the statement with that label. If the value of the variable is not in the list, an error occurs.

When the second form of the assigned GO TO is executed, no error checking is done. If the value of the variable is a legal statement label in the program, control branches to the statement with that label. If the value of the variable is not a legal statement label, execution continues with the next executable statement after the assigned GO TO.

An example of an assigned GO TO statement is shown below. In this example, the number 1 would be printed out when the program is executed.

```
PROGRAM test
ASSIGN 10 TO i
GO TO i (10, 20)
10 WRITE (*,*) '1'
GO TO 30
20 WRITE (*,*) '2'
30 END PROGRAM
```

The assigned GO TO should never be used in any modern Fortran program.

The ASSIGN statement and the assigned GO TO statement have been deleted from Fortran 95, which means that they are no longer an official part of the Fortran language.

Good Programming Practice
Never use the assigned GO TO statement in your programs. Use the logical IF structure instead.

17

17.8.5 Older Forms of DO Loops

Before Fortran 90, DO loops had a different form than the one taught in this book. Modern counting DO loops have the structure

```
DO i = istart, iend, incr
   . . .
END DO
```

where istart is the starting value of the loop, iend is the ending value of the loop, and incr is the loop increment.

Early FORTRAN DO loops had the structure

```
DO 100 i = istart, iend, index
    . . .
100 . . .
```

A statement label is included in this form of the loop, and all of the code from the DO statement until the statement containing that statement label is included in the loop. An example of the earlier loop structure is:

```
DO 100 i = 1, 100
    a(i) = REAL(i)
100 b(i) = 2. * REAL(i)
```

This was the standard form of the DO loop used by most programmers from the beginning of FORTRAN until about the mid-1970s.

Because the end of this earlier form of the DO loop is so hard to recognize, many programmers developed the habit of always ending DO loops on a CONTINUE statement, which is a statement that does nothing. In addition, they indented all of the statements between the DO and the CONTINUE statement. An example of a "good" FORTRAN 77 DO loop is:

```
DO 200 i = 1, 100
    a(i) = REAL(i)
    b(i) = 2. * REAL(i)
200 CONTINUE
```

As you can see, this form of the loop is much easier to understand.

The termination of a DO loop on any statement other than an END DO or a CONTINUE has been declared obsolescent in Fortran 95, meaning that it is a candidate for deletion in future versions of the language.

Another feature of older DO loops was the ability to terminate more than one loop on a single statement. For example, in the following code, two DO loops terminate on a single statement.

```
DO 10 i = 1, 10
    DO 10 j = 1, 10
10 a(i,j) = REAL(i+j)
```

17

This sort of structure was terribly confusing, and it should not be used in any modern Fortran program.

The termination of more than one DO loop on a single statement has been declared obsolescent in Fortran 95, meaning that it is a candidate for deletion in future versions of the language.

Finally, FORTRAN 77 added the ability to use single-precision or double-precision real numbers as DO loop indices. This was a terrible decision, since the behavior of DO loops with real indices varied from processor to processor (this was explained in Chapter 4). Fortran 90 declared the use of real numbers as loop indices to be obsolescent.

The use of real numbers as DO loop indices has been deleted from Fortran 95, which means that it is no longer an official part of the Fortran language.

Good Programming Practice

Never use any of these older forms of the DO loop in any new program.

■ 17.9

REDUNDANT FEATURES OF I/O STATEMENTS

A number of features of I/O statements have become redundant and should not be used in modern Fortran programs. The END= and ERR= clauses in I/O statements have been largely replaced by the IOSTAT= clause. The IOSTAT= clause is more flexible and more compatible with modern structured programming techniques than the older clauses, and only the IOSTAT= clause should be used in new programs.

Similarly, three format descriptors have been made redundant and should no longer be used in modern Fortran programs. The H format descriptor was an old way to specify character strings in a FORMAT statement. It was briefly mentioned in Table 10-1. It has been completely replaced by the use of character strings surrounded by single or double quotes.

The H format descriptor has been deleted from Fortran 95, which means that it is no longer an official part of the Fortran language.

The P scale factor was used to shift the decimal point in data displayed with the E and F format descriptors. It has been made redundant by the introduction of the ES and EN format descriptors, and should never be used in any new programs.

The D format descriptor was used to input and output double-precision numbers in earlier versions of Fortran. It is now identical to the E descriptor, except that on output a D instead of an E may appear as the marker of the exponent. There is no need to ever use the D descriptor in a new program.

The BN and BZ format descriptors control the way blanks are interpreted in reading fields from card-image files. By default, Fortran 95/2003 ignores blanks in input fields. In FORTRAN 66 and earlier, blanks were treated as zeros. These descriptors

TABLE 17-1

Summary of older Fortran features

Feature	Status	Comment
Source form		
Fixed-source form	Obsolescent in Fortran 95	Use free form.
Specification statements		
CHARACTER*<len> statement	Obsolescent in Fortran 95	Use CHARACTER(len=<len>) form.
COMMON blocks	Redundant	Use modules to exchange data.
DATA statement	Redundant	Use initialization in type declaration statements.
DIMENSION statement	Redundant	Use dimension attribute in type declaration statements.
EQUIVALENCE statement	Unnecessary and confusing	Use dynamic memory allocation for temporary memory. Use the TRANSFER function to change the type of a particular data value.
IMPLICIT statement	Confusing but legal	*Do not use.* Always use IMPLICIT NONE and explicit type declaration statements.
PARAMETER statement	Redundant, and confusing syntax	Use parameter attribute in type declaration statements.
Unlabeled COMMON	Redundant	Use modules to exchange data.
Undesirable subprogram features		
Alternate entry points	Unnecessary and confusing	Share data between procedures in modules, and do not share code between procedures.
Alternate subroutine returns	Obsolescent in Fortran 95	Use status variable, and test status of variable after subroutine call.
Statement function	Obsolescent in Fortran 95	Use internal procedures.
Execution control statement		
PAUSE statement	Deleted in Fortran 95	Use WRITE statement followed by a READ statement.
Branching and looping control statements		
Arithmetic IF statement	Obsolescent in Fortran 95	Use logical IF.
Assigned GO TO statement	Deleted in Fortran 95	Use block IF or CASE construct.
Computed GO TO statement	Obsolescent in Fortran 95	Use CASE construct.
GO TO statement	Rarely needed	Largely replaced by IF, CASE, and DO constructs with CYCLE and EXIT statements.
DO 100 . . .	Redundant	Use DO . . .
100 CONTINUE		END DO
DO loops terminating on executable statement	Obsolescent in Fortran 95	Terminate loops on END DO statements.
Multiple DO loops terminating on same statement	Obsolescent in Fortran 95	Terminate loops on separate statements.
I/O features		
H format descriptor	Deleted in Fortran 95	Use single or double quotes to delimit strings.
D format descriptor	Redundant	Use E format descriptor.
P scale factor	Redundant and confusing	Use ES or EN format descriptors.
BN and BZ format descriptors	Unnecessary	Blanks should always be nulls, which is the default case.
S, SP, and SS format descriptors	Unnecessary	Processor's default behavior is acceptable.
ERR= clause	Redundant and confusing	Use IOSTAT= clause.
END= clause	Redundant and confusing	Use IOSTAT= clause.

are provided for backward compatibility with very early versions of Fortran; they should never be needed in any new program.

The S, SP, and SS format descriptors control the display of positive signs in a format descriptor. These descriptors are completely unnecessary and should never be used.

■ 17.10
SUMMARY

In this chapter, we introduced a variety of miscellaneous Fortran features. Most of these features are either redundant, obsolescent, or incompatible with modern structured programming. They are maintained for backward compatibility with older versions of Fortran.

None of the features described here should be used in any new programs, except possibly for arguments on multiple STOP statements. Since modern programming practices greatly reduce the need for STOP statements, they will not be used very often. However, if you do write a program that contains multiple STOP statements, you should make sure that you use WRITE statements or arguments on STOP statements to distinguish each of the possible stopping points in the program.

COMMON blocks may occasionally be needed in procedures that must work with older Fortran code, but completely new programs should use modules for data sharing instead of COMMON blocks.

There may also be rare circumstances in which the unconditional GO TO statement is useful, such as for exception handling. Most of the traditional uses of the GO TO statement have been replaced by the modern IF, CASE, and DO constructs, so they will be very rare in any modern Fortran program.

Table 17-1 summarizes the features of Fortran that should not be used in new programs, and gives suggestions as to how to replace them if you run into them in older code.

17.10.1 Summary of Good Programming Practice

None of the features described in this chapter should be used in any new programs, except possibly for arguments on multiple STOP statements. Since modern programming practices greatly reduce the need for multiple STOP statements, they will not be used very often. However, if you do write a program that contains multiple STOP statements, you should make sure that you use WRITE statements or arguments on STOP statements to distinguish each of the possible stopping points in the program.

17

17.10.2 Summary of Fortran Statements and Structures

Arithmetic IF Statement:

        IF (*arithmetic expression*) *label1, label2, label3*

Example:

        IF (b**2-4.*a*c) 10, 20, 30

Description:

The arithmetic IF statement is an obsolete conditional branching statement. If the arithmetic expression is negative, control will be transferred to statement with label label1. If the arithmetic expression is zero, control will be transferred to statement with label label2, and if the arithmetic expression is positive, control will be transferred to statement with label label3.

The arithmetic IF statement has been declared obsolescent in Fortran 95.

Assigned GO TO Statement:

        ASSIGN *label* TO *int_var*
        GO TO *int_var*

or

        GO TO *int_var*, (*label1, label2, ... labelk*)

Example:

        ASSIGN 100 TO i

        . . .
        GO TO i
        . . .
    100 ... (execution continues here)

Description:

The assigned GO TO statement is an obsolete branching structure. A statement label is first assigned to an integer variable, using the ASSIGN statement. When the assigned GO TO statement is executed, control branches to the statement whose label was assigned to the integer variable.

The assigned GO TO statement has been deleted in Fortran 95.

COMMON Block:

        COMMON / *name* / *var1, var2, ...*
        COMMON *var1, var2, ...*

Example:

        COMMON / shared / a, b, c
        COMMON a, i(-3:3)

Description:
This statement defines a COMMON block. The variables declared in the block will be allocated consecutively starting at a specific memory location. They will be accessible to any program unit in which the COMMON block is declared. The COMMON block has been replaced by data values declared in modules.

Computed GO TO Statement:

```
GO TO (label1, label2, ... labelk), int_var
```

Example:

```
GO TO (100, 200, 300, 400), i
```

Description:
The computed GO TO statement is an obsolete branching structure. Control is transferred to one of the statements whose label is listed, depending on the value of the integer variable. If the variable is 1, then control is transferred to the first statement in the list, etc.

The computed GO TO statement has been declared obsolescent in Fortran 95.

CONTINUE **Statement:**

```
CONTINUE
```

Description:
This statement is a placeholder statement that does nothing. It is sometimes used to terminate DO loops, or as a location to attach a statement label.

DIMENSION **Statement:**

```
DIMENSION array( [i1:]i2, [j1:]j2, ... ), ...
```

Example:

```
DIMENSION a1(100), a2(-5:5), i(2)
```

Description:
This statement declares the size of an array but *not* its type. Either the type must be declared in a separate type declaration statement, or else it will be defaulted. DIMENSION statements are not required in well-written code, since type declaration statements will serve the same purpose.

17

DO **Loops (Old Versions):**

$$DO\ k\ index = istart,\ iend,\ incr$$
$$\ldots$$
$$k\quad CONTINUE$$

or

$$DO\ k\ index = istart,\ iend,\ incr$$
$$\ldots$$
$$k\quad Executable\ statement$$

Examples:

$$DO\ 100\ index = 1,\ 10,\ 3$$
$$\ldots$$
$$100\ CONTINUE$$

or

$$DO\ 200\ i = 1,\ 10$$
$$200\ a(i) = REAL(i**2)$$

Description:
These forms of the DO loop repeatedly execute the block of code from the statement immediately following the DO up to and including the statement whose label appears in the DO. The loop control parameters are the same in these loops as they are in modern DO constructs.

Only the versions of the DO loop that end in an END DO statement should be used in new programs. DO loops that terminate in a CONTINUE statement are legal but redundant, and should not be used. DO loops that terminate on other statements (such as the one in the second example) have been declared obsolescent in Fortran 95.

ENTRY **Statement:**

$$ENTRY\ name(\ arg1,\ arg2,\ \ldots\ )$$

Example:

$$ENTRY\ sorti\ (\ num,\ data1\ )$$

Description:
This statement declares an entry point into a Fortran subroutine or function subprogram. The entry point is executed with a CALL statement or function reference. The dummy arguments arg1, arg2, ... are placeholders for the calling arguments passed when the subprogram is executed. This statement should be avoided in modern programs.

17

EQUIVALENCE **Statement:**

> EQUIVALENCE (*var1, var2, ...*)

Example:

> EQUIVALENCE (scr1, iscr1)

Description:

The EQUIVALENCE statement is a specification statement that specifies that all of the variables in the parentheses occupy the same location in memory.

GO TO **Statement:**

> GO TO *label*

Example:

> GO TO 100

Description:

The GO TO statement transfers control unconditionally to the executable statement that has the specified statement label.

IMPLICIT **Statement:**

> IMPLICIT *type1* $(a_1, a_2, a_3, ...)$, *type2* $(b_1, b_2, b_3, ...)$, ...

Example:

> IMPLICIT COMPLEX (c,z), LOGICAL (l)

Description:

The IMPLICIT statement is a specification statement that overrides the default typing built into Fortran. It specifies the default type to assume for parameters and variables whose names begin with the specified letters. This statement should never be used in any modern program.

PAUSE **Statement:**

> PAUSE *prompt*

Example:

> PAUSE 12

Description:

The PAUSE statement is an executable statement that temporarily stops the execution of the Fortran program, until the user resumes it. The prompt is either an integer between 0 and 99999 or a character constant. It is displayed when the PAUSE statement is executed.

The PAUSE statement has been deleted in Fortran 95.

17

Statement Function:

```
name(arg1,arg2,...) = expression containing arg1, arg2, ...
```

Example:

Definition: `quad(a,b,c,x) = a * x**2 + b * x + c`
Use: `result = 2. * pi * quad(a1,b1,c1,1.5*t)`

Description:
The statement function is an older structure that has been replaced by the internal function. It is defined in the declaration section of a program, and may be used only within that program. The arguments `arg1`, `arg2`, etc., are dummy arguments that are replaced by actual values when the function is used.

Statement functions have been declared obsolescent in Fortran 95. They should never be used in any modern program.

ASCII and EBCDIC Coding Systems

Each character in the default Fortran character set is stored in one byte of memory, so there are 256 possible values for each character variable. The table shown below contains the characters corresponding to each possible decimal, octal, and hexadecimal value in both the ASCII and the EBCDIC coding systems. Where characters are blank, they either correspond to control characters or are not defined.

Decimal	Octal	Hex	ASCII Character	EBCDIC Character
0	0	0	NUL	NUL
...		...	...	...
32	40	20	space	
33	41	21	!	
34	42	22	"	
35	43	23	#	
36	44	24	$	
37	45	25	%	
38	46	26	&	
39	47	27	'	
40	50	28	(	
41	51	29	)	
42	52	2A	*	
43	53	2B	+	
44	54	2C	,	
45	55	2D	-	
46	56	2E	.	
47	57	2F	/	
48	60	30	0	
49	61	31	1	
50	62	32	2	
51	63	33	3	
52	64	34	4	
53	65	35	5	
54	66	36	6	

(*continued*)

Decimal	Octal	Hex	ASCII Character	EBCDIC Character
55	67	37	7	
56	70	38	8	
57	71	39	9	
58	72	3A	:	
59	73	3B	;	
60	74	3C	<	
61	75	3D	=	
62	76	3E	>	
63	77	3F	?	
64	100	40	@	blank
65	101	41	A	
66	102	42	B	
67	103	43	C	
68	104	44	D	
69	105	45	E	
70	106	46	F	
71	107	47	G	
72	110	48	H	
73	111	49	I	
74	112	4A	J	¢
75	113	4B	K	.
76	114	4C	L	<
77	115	4D	M	(
78	116	4E	N	+
79	117	4F	O		
80	120	50	P	&
81	121	51	Q	
82	122	52	R	
83	123	53	S	
84	124	54	T	
85	125	55	U	
86	126	56	V	
87	127	57	W	
88	130	58	X	
89	131	59	Y	
90	132	5A	Z	!
91	133	5B	[	$
92	134	5C	\	*
93	135	5D	]	)
94	136	5E	^ (or ↑)	;
95	137	5F	_	¬
96	140	60	`	-
97	141	61	a	/

(*continued*)

Decimal	Octal	Hex	ASCII Character	EBCDIC Character
98	142	62	b	
99	143	63	c	
100	144	64	d	
101	145	65	e	
102	146	66	f	
103	147	67	g	
104	150	68	h	
105	151	69	i	
106	152	6A	j	
107	153	6B	k	,
108	154	6C	l	%
109	155	6D	m	_
110	156	6E	n	>
111	157	6F	o	?
112	160	70	p	
113	161	71	q	
114	162	72	r	
115	163	73	s	
116	164	74	t	
117	165	75	u	
118	166	76	v	
119	167	77	w	
120	170	78	x	
121	171	79	y	
122	172	7A	z	:
123	173	7B	{	#
124	174	7C	|	@
125	175	7D	}	'
126	176	7E	~	=
127	177	7F	DEL	"
128	200	80		
129	201	81		a
130	202	82		b
131	203	83		c
132	204	84		d
133	205	85		e
134	206	86		f
135	207	87		g
136	210	88		h
137	211	89		i
...	...	...	...	...
145	221	91		j
146	222	92		k

(*continued*)

Decimal	Octal	Hex	ASCII Character	EBCDIC Character
147	223	93		l
148	224	94		m
149	225	95		n
150	226	96		o
151	227	97		p
152	230	98		q
153	231	99		r
...	...	...	...	...
162	242	A2		s
163	243	A3		t
164	244	A4		u
165	245	A5		v
166	246	A6		w
167	247	A7		x
168	250	A8		y
169	251	A9		z
...	...	...	...	...
192	300	C0		}
193	301	C1		A
194	302	C2		B
195	303	C3		C
196	304	C4		D
197	305	C5		E
198	306	C6		F
199	307	C7		G
200	310	C8		H
201	311	C9		I
...	...	...	...	...
208	320	D0		}
209	321	D1		J
210	322	D2		K
211	323	D3		L
212	324	D4		M
213	325	D5		N
214	326	D6		O
215	327	D7		P
216	330	D8		Q
217	331	D9		R
...	...	...	...	...
224	340	E0		\
225	341	E1		
226	342	E2		S
227	343	E3		T

(*continued*)

Decimal	Octal	Hex	ASCII Character	EBCDIC Character
228	344	E4		U
229	345	E5		V
230	346	E6		W
231	347	E7		X
232	350	E8		Y
233	351	E9		Z
...	...	...	...	...
240	360	F0		0
241	361	F1		1
242	362	F2		2
243	363	F3		3
244	364	F4		4
245	365	F5		5
246	366	F6		6
247	367	F7		7
248	370	F8		8
249	371	F9		9
...	...	...	...	...
255	377	FF		

Fortran 95/2003 Intrinsic Procedures

This appendix describes the intrinsic procedures built into the Fortran 95 and Fortran 2003 languages, and provides some suggestions for their proper use. All of the intrinsic procedures that are present in Fortran 95 are also present in Fortran 2003, although some have additional arguments. Those procedures that are only in Fortran 2003 and those procedures that have additional arguments in Fortran 2003 are highlighted in the tables and discussions below.

A majority of Fortran intrinsic procedures are functions, although there are a few intrinsic subroutines.

B.1
CLASSES OF INTRINSIC PROCEDURES

Fortran 95/2003 intrinsic procedures can be broken down into three classes: elemental, inquiry, or transformational. An **elemental function**[1] is one that is specified for scalar arguments, but which may also be applied to array arguments. If the argument of an elemental function is a scalar, then the result of the function will be a scalar. If the argument of the function is an array, then the result of the function will be an array of the same shape as the input argument. If there is more than one input argument, all of the arguments must have the same shape. If an elemental function is applied to an array, the result will be the same as if the function were applied to each element of the array on an element-by-element basis.

An **inquiry function** or **inquiry subroutine** is a procedure whose value depends on the properties of an object being investigated. For example, the function PRESENT(A) is an inquiry function that returns a true value if the optional argument A is present in a procedure call. Other inquiry functions can return properties of the system used to represent real numbers and integers on a particular processor.

A **transformational function** is a function that has one or more array-valued arguments or an array-valued result. Unlike elemental functions that operate on an element-by-element basis, transformational functions operate on arrays as a whole. The output of a transformational function will often not have the same shape as the input arguments. For example, the function DOT_PRODUCT has two vector input arguments of the same size, and produces a scalar output.

---

[1] One intrinsic subroutine is also elemental.

▪ B.2

ALPHABETICAL LIST OF INTRINSIC PROCEDURES

Table B-1 contains an alphabetical listing of the intrinsic procedures included in Fortran 95 and Fortran 2003. The table is organized into five columns. The first column of the table contains the *generic name* of each procedure, and its calling sequence. The calling sequence is represented by the keywords associated with each argument. Mandatory arguments are shown in roman type, and optional arguments are shown in italics. The use of keywords is optional, but they must be supplied for optional arguments if earlier optional arguments in the calling sequence are missing, or if the arguments are specified in a nondefault order (see Section 13.3). For example, the function SIN has one argument, and the keyword of the argument is X. This function can be invoked either with or without the keyword, so the following two statements are equivalent.

```
result = sin(X=3.141593)
result = sin(3.141593)
```

Another example is the function MAXVAL. This function has one required argument and two optional arguments:

```
MAVXAL ( ARRAY, DIM, MASK )
```

If all three calling values are specified in that order, then they may be simply included in the argument list without the keywords. However, if the MASK is to be specified without DIM, then keywords must be used.

```
value = MAVXAL ( array, MASK=mask )
```

The types of the most common argument keywords are as shown below (any kind of the specified type may be used):

A	Any
ARRAY	Any array
BACK	Logical
CHAR	Character
DIM	Integer
I	Integer
KIND	Integer
MASK	Logical
SCALAR	Any scalar
STRING	Character
X, Y	Numeric (integer, real, or complex)
Z	Complex

For the types of other keywords, refer to the detailed procedure descriptions below.

The second column contains the *specific name* of an intrinsic function, which is the name by which the function must be called if it is to appear in an INTRINSIC statement and be passed to another procedure as an actual argument. If this column is blank, then the procedure does not have a specific name, and so may not be used as a calling argument. The types of arguments used with the specific functions are:

c, c1, c2, . . .	Default complex
d, d1, d2, . . .	Double precision real
i, i1, i2, . . .	Default integer
r, r1, r2, . . .	Default real
l, l1, l2, . . .	Logical
str1, str2, . . .	Character

The third column contains the type of the value returned by the procedure if it is a function. Obviously, intrinsic subroutines do not have a type associated with them. The fourth column is a reference to the section of this Appendix in which the procedure is described, and the fifth column is for notes, which are found at the end of the Table.

Those procedures that are present only in Fortran 2003 are shown with a shaded background.

Table B-1:
Specific and generic names for all Fortran 95/2003 intrinsic procedures

Generic name, keyword(s), and calling sequence	Specific name	Function type	Section	Notes
ABS(A)		Argument type	B.3	
	ABS(r)	Default real		
	CABS(c)	Default real		2
	DABS(d)	Double precision		
	IABS(i)	Default integer		
ACHAR(I, *KIND*)		Character(1)	B.7	4
ACOS(X)		Argument type	B.3	
	ACOS(r)	Default real		
	DACOS(d)	Double precision		
ADJUSTL(STRING)		Character	B.7	
ADJUSTR(STRING)		Character	B.7	
AIMAG(Z)	AIMAG(c)	Real	B.3	
AINT(A, KIND)		Argument type	B.3	
	AINT(r)	Default real		
	DINT(d)	Double precision		
ALL(MASK, *DIM*)		Logical	B.8	
ALLOCATED(ARRAY or SCALAR)		Logical	B.9	5
ANINT(A, *KIND*)		Argument type	B.3	
	ANINT(r)	Real		
	DNINT(d)	Double precision		
ANY(MASK, *DIM*)		Logical	B.8	
ASIN(X)	ASIN(r)	Argument type		

(continued)

Generic name, keyword(s), and calling sequence	Specific name	Function type	Section	Notes
	ASIN(r)	Real		
	DASIN(d)	Double precision		
ASSOCIATED(POINTER,*TARGET*)		Logical	B.9	
ATAN(X)		Argument type	B.3	
	ATAN(r)	Real		
	DATAN(d)	Double precision		
ATAN2(Y,X)		Argument type	B.3	
	ATAN2(r2,r1)	Real		
	DATAN2(d2,d1)	Double precision		
BIT_SIZE(I)		Integer	B.4	
BTEST(I,POS)		Logical	B.6	
CEILING(A,*KIND*)		Integer	B.3	4
CHAR(I,*KIND*)		Character(1)	B.7	
CMPLX(X,Y,*KIND*)		Complex	B.3	
COMMAND_ARGUMENT_COUNT()		Integer	B.5	5
CONGJ(Z)	CONJG(c)	Complex	B.3	
COS(X)		Argument type	B.3	
	CCOS(c)	Complex		
	COS(r)	Real		
	DCOS(d)	Double precision		
COSH(X)		Argument type	B.3	
	COSH(r)	Real		
	DCOSH(d)	Double precision		
COUNT(MASK,*DIM*)		Integer	B.8	
CPU_TIME(TIME)		Subroutine	B.5	
CSHIFT(ARRAY,*SHIFT*,DIM)		Array type	B.8	
DATE_AND_TIME(*DATE*,*TIME*,*ZONE*, *VALUES*)		Subroutine	B.5	
DBLE(A)		Double precision	B.3	
DIGITS(X)		Integer	B.4	
DIM(X,Y)		Argument type	B.3	
	DDIM(d1,d2)	Double precision		
	DIM(r1,r2)	Real		
	IDIM(i1,i2)	Integer		
DOT_PRODUCT(VECTOR_A,VECTOR_B)		Argument type	B.3	
DPROD(X,Y)	DPROD(x1,x2)	Double precision	B.3	
EOSHIFT(ARRAY,SHIFT,*BOUNDARY*,DIM)		Array type	B.8	
EPSILON(X)		Real	B.4	
EXP(X)		Argument type	B.3	
	CEXP(c)	Complex		
	DEXP(d)	Double precision		

(continued)

Generic name, keyword(s), and calling sequence	Specific name	Function type	Section	Notes
	`EXP(r)`	Real		
`EXPONENT(X)`		Integer	B.4	
`FLOOR(A,KIND)`		Integer	B.3	4
`FRACTION(X)`		Real	B.4	
`GET_COMMAND(COMMAND,LENGTH,STATUS)`			B.5	5
`GET_COMMAND_ARGUMENT(NUMBER,` `COMMAND,LENGTH,STATUS)`			B.5	5
`GET_ENVIRONMENT_VARIABLE(NAME,` `VALUE,LENGTH,STATUS,TRIM_NAME)`			B.5	5
`HUGE(X)`		Argument type	B.4	
`IACHAR(C)`		Integer	B.7	
`IAND(I,J)`		Integer	B.6	
`IBCLR(I,POS)`		Argument type	B.6	
`IBITSI,POS,LEN)`		Argument type	B.6	
`IBSET(I,POS)`		Argument type	B.6	
`ICHAR(C)`		Integer	B.7	
`IEOR(I,J)`		Argument type	B.6	
`INDEX(STRING,SUBSTRING,BACK)`	`INDEX(str1,str2)`	Integer	B.7	
`INT(A,KIND)`		Integer	B.3	
	`IDINT(i)`	Integer		1
	`IFIX(r)`	Integer		1
`IOR(I,J)`		Argument type	B.6	
`IS_IOSTAT_END(I)`		Logical	B.5	5
`IS_IOSTAT_EOR(I)`		Logical	B.5	5
`ISHFT(I,SHIFT)`		Argument type	B.6	
`ISHFTC(I,SHIFT,SIZE)`		Argument type	B.6	
`KIND(X)`		Integer	B.4	
`LBOUND(ARRAY,DIM)`		Integer	B.8	
`LEN(STRING)`	`LEN(str)`	Integer	B.7	
`LEN_TRIM(STRING)`		Integer	B.7	
`LGE(STRING_A,STRING_B)`		Logical	B.7	
`LGT(STRING_A,STRING_B)`		Logical	B.7	
`LLE(STRING_A,STRING_B)`		Logical	B.7	
`LLT(STRING_A,STRING_B)`		Logical	B.7	
`LOG(X)`		Argument type	B.3	
	`ALOG(r)`	Real		
	`CLOG(c)`	Complex		
	`DLOG(d)`	Double precision		
`LOG10(X)`		Argument type	B.3	
	`ALOG10(r)`	Real		
	`DLOG10(d)`	Double precision		
`LOGICAL(L,KIND)`		Logical	B.3	
`MATMUL(MATRIX_A,MATRIX_B)`		Argument type	B.3	
`MAX(A1,A2,A3,...)`		Argument type	B.3	
	`AMAX0(i1,i2,...)`	Real		1
	`AMAX1(r1,r2,...)`	Real		1
	`DMAX1(d1,d2,...)`	Double precision		1

(continued)

Generic name, keyword(s), and calling sequence	Specific name	Function type	Section	Notes
	`MAX0(i1,i2,...)`	Integer		1
	`MAX1(r1,r2,...)`	Integer		1
`MAXEXPONENT(X)`		Integer	B.4	
`MAXLOC(ARRAY,DIM,MASK)`		Integer	B.8	
`MAXVAL(ARRAY,DIM,MASK)`		Argument type	B.8	
`MERGE(TSOURCE,FSOURCE,MASK)`		Argument type	B.8	
`MIN(A1,A2,A3,...)`		Argument type	B.3	
	`AMIN0(i1,i2,...)`	Real		1
	`AMIN1(r1,r2,...)`	Real		1
	`DMIN1(d1,d2,...)`	Double precision		1
	`MIN0(i1,i2,...)`	Integer		1
	`MIN1(r1,r2,...)`	Integer		1
`MINEXPONENT(X)`		Integer	B.4	
`MINLOC(ARRAY,DIM,MASK)`		Integer	B.8	
`MINVAL(ARRAY,DIM,MASK)`		Argument type	B.8	
`MOD(A,P)`		Argument type	B.3	
	`AMOD(r1,r2)`	Real		
	`MOD(i,j)`	Integer		
	`DMOD(d1,d2)`	Double precision		
`MODULO(A,P)`		Argument type	B.3	
`MOVE_ALLOC(FROM,TO)`		Subroutine	B.10	
`MVBITS(FROM,FROMPOS,LEN,TO,TOPOS)`		Subroutine	B.6	
`NEAREST(X,S)`		Real	B.3	
`NEW_LINE(CHAR)`		Character	B.7	
`NINT(A,KIND)`		Integer	B.3	
	`IDNINT(i)`	Integer		
	`NINT(x)`	Integer		
`NOT(I)`		Argument type	B.6	
`NULL(MOLD)`		Pointer	B.8	
`PACK(ARRAY,MASK,VECTOR)`		Argument type	B.8	
`PRECISION(X)`		Integer	B.4	
`PRESENT(A)`		Logical	B.9	
`PRODUCT(ARRAY,DIM,MASK)`		Argument type	B.8	
`RADIX(X)`		Integer	B.4	
`RANDOM_NUMBER(HARVEST)`		Subroutine	B.3	
`RANDOM_SEED(SIZE,PUT,GET)`		Subroutine	B.3	
`RANGE(X)`		Integer	B.4	
`REAL(A,KIND)`		Real	B.3	
	`FLOAT(i)`	Real		1
	`SNGL(d)`	Real		1
`REPEAT(STRING,NCOPIES)`		Character	B.7	
`RESHAPE(SOURCE,SHAPE,PAD,ORDER)`		Argument type	B.8	
`RRSPACING(X)`		Argument type	B.4	
`SCALE(X,I)`		Argument type	B.4	
`SCAN(STRING,SET,BACK)`		Integer	B.7	
`SELECTED_CHAR_KIND(NAME)`		Integer	B.4	5
`SELECTED_INT_KIND(R)`		Integer	B.4	

(continued)

Generic name, keyword(s), and calling sequence	Specific name	Function type	Section	Notes
`SELECTED_REAL_KIND(P,R)`		Integer	B.4	3
`SET_EXPONENT(X,I)`		Argument type	B.4	
`SHAPE(SOURCE)`		Integer	B.8	
`SIGN(A,B)`		Argument type	B.3	
	`DSIGN(d1,d2)`	Double precision		
	`ISIGN(i1,i2)`	Integer		
	`SIGN(r1,r2)`	Real		
`SIN(X)`		Argument type	B.3	
	`CSIN(c)`	Complex		
	`DSIN(d)`	Double precision		
	`SIN(r)`	Real		
`SINH(X)`		Argument type	B.3	
	`DSINH(d)`	Double precision		
	`SINH(r)`	Real		
`SIZE(ARRAY, DIM)`		Integer	B.8	
`SPACING(X)`		Argument type	B.4	
`SPREAD(SOURCE, DIM, NCOPIES)`		Argument type	B.8	
`SQRT(X)`		Argument type	B.3	
	`CSQRT(c)`	Complex		
	`DSQRT(d)`	Double precision		
	`SQRT(r)`	Real		
`SUM(ARRAY, DIM, MASK)`		Argument type	B.8	
`SYSTEM_CLOCK(COUNT, COUNT_RATE, COUNT_MAX)`		Subroutine	B.5	
`TAN(X)`		Argument type	B.3	
	`DTAN(d)`	Double precision		
	`TAN(r)`	Real		
`TANH(X)`		Argument type	B.3	
	`DTANH(d)`	Double precision		
	`TANH(r)`	Real		
`TINY(X)`		Real	B.4	
`TRANSFER(SOURCE, MOLD, SIZE)`		Argument type	B.8	
`TRANSPOSE(MATRIX)`		Argument type	B.8	
`TRIM(STRING)`		Character	B.7	
`UBOUND(ARRAY, DIM)`			B.8	
`UNPACK(VECTOR, MASK, FIELD)`		Argument type	B.8	
`VERIFY(STRING, SET, BACK)`		Integer	B.7	

1. These intrinsic functions cannot be passed to procedures as calling arguments.
2. The result of function `CABS` is real with the same kind as the input complex argument.
3. At least one of P and R must be specified in any given call.
4. Argument `KIND` is available only in Fortran 2003 for this function.
5. These procedures are available only in Fortran 2003.

These intrinsic procedures are divided into broad categories based on their functions. Refer to Table B-1 to determine which of the following sections will contain a description of any particular function of interest.

The following information applies to all of the intrinsic procedure descriptions:

1. All arguments of all intrinsic functions have INTENT(IN). In other words, all of the functions are pure. The intent of subroutine arguments are specified in the description of each subroutine.
2. Optional arguments are shown in italics in all calling sequences.
3. When a function has an optional KIND dummy argument, then the function result will be of the kind specified in that argument. If the KIND argument is missing, then the result will be of the default kind. If the KIND argument is specified, it must correspond to a legal kind on the specified processor, or the function will abort. The KIND argument is always an integer.
4. When a procedure is said to have two arguments of the same type, it is understood that they must also be of the same kind. If this is not true for a particular procedure, the fact will be explicitly mentioned in the procedure description.
5. The lengths of arrays and character strings will be shown by an appended number in parentheses. For example, the expression

    Integer(*m*)

implies that a particular argument is an integer array containing *m* values.

B.3
MATHEMATICAL AND TYPE CONVERSION INTRINSIC PROCEDURES

ABS(A)
- Elemental function of the same type and kind as A.
- Returns the absolute value of A, $|A|$.
- If A is complex, the function returns $\sqrt{\text{real}^2 + \text{imaginary}^2}$.

ACOS(X)
- Elemental function of the same type and kind as X.
- Returns the inverse cosine of X.
- Argument is real of any kind, with $|X| \leq 1.0$ and $0 \leq \text{ACOS}(X) \leq \pi$.

AIMAG(Z)
- Real elemental function of the same kind as Z.
- Returns the imaginary part of complex argument Z.

AINT(A,*KIND*)
- Real elemental function.
- Returns A truncated to a whole number. AINT(A) is the largest integer that is smaller than $|A|$, with the sign of A. For example, AINT(3.7) is 3.0, and AINT(-3.7) is −3.0.
- Argument A is real; optional argument *KIND* is integer.

`ANINT(A,KIND)`
- Real elemental function.
- Returns the nearest whole number to `A`. For example, `ANINT(3.7)` is 4.0, and `AINT(-3.7)` is −4.0.
- Argument `A` is real; optional argument `KIND` is integer.

`ASIN(X)`
- Elemental function of the same type and kind as `X`.
- Returns the inverse sine of `X`.
- Argument is real of any kind, with $|X| \leq 1.0$, and $-\pi/2 \leq ASIN(X) \leq \pi/2$.

`ATAN(X)`
- Elemental function of the same type and kind as `X`.
- Returns the inverse tangent of `X`.
- Argument is real of any kind, with $-\pi/2 \leq ATAN(X) \leq \pi/2$.

`ATAN2(Y,X)`
- Elemental function of the same type and kind as `X`.
- Returns the inverse tangent of `Y/X` in the range $-\pi <$ `ATAN2(Y,X)` $\leq \pi$.
- `X,Y` are real of any kind, and must be of same kind.
- Both `X` and `Y` cannot be simultaneously 0.

`CEILING(A,KIND)`
- Integer elemental function.
- Returns the smallest integer $\geq$ `A`. For example, `CEILING(3.7)` is 4, and `CEILING(-3.7)` is −3.
- Argument `A` is real of any kind; optional argument `KIND` is integer.

`CMPLX(X,Y,KIND)`
- Complex elemental function.
- Returns a complex value as follows:
  1. If `X` is complex, then `Y` must not exist, and the value of `X` is returned.
  2. If `X` is not complex, and `Y` doesn't exist, then the returned value is `(X,0)`.
  3. If `X` is not complex and `Y` exists, then the returned value is `(X,Y)`.
- `X` is complex, real, or integer, `Y` is real or integer, and `KIND` is an integer.

`CONJG(Z)`
- Complex elemental function of the same kind as `Z`.
- Returns the complex conjugate of `Z`.
- `Z` is complex.

`COS(X)`
- Elemental function of the same type and kind as `X`.
- Returns the cosine of `X`.
- `X` is real or complex.

`COSH(X)`
- Elemental function of the same type and kind as `X`.
- Returns the hyperbolic cosine of `X`.
- `X` is real.

DIM(X,Y)
- Elemental function of the same type and kind as X.
- Returns X-Y if > 0; otherwise returns 0.
- X and Y are integer or real; both must be of the same type and kind.

DBLE(A)
- Double-precision real elemental function.
- Converts value of A to double-precision real.
- A is numeric. If A is complex, then only the real part of A is converted.

DOT_PRODUCT(VECTOR_A,VECTOR_B)
- Transformational function of the same type as VECTOR_A.
- Returns the dot product of numeric or logical vectors.
- Arguments are numeric or logical vectors. Both vectors must be of the same type, kind, and length.

DPROD(X,Y)
- Double-precision real elemental function.
- Returns the double-precision product of X and Y.
- Arguments X and Y are default real.

EXP(X)
- Elemental function of the same type and kind as X.
- Returns e^x.
- X is real or complex.

FLOOR(A,*KIND*)
- Integer elemental function.
- Returns the largest integer ≤ A. For example, FLOOR(3.7) is 3 and FLOOR(-3.7) is −4.
- Argument A is real of any kind; optional argument *KIND* is integer.

INT(A,*KIND*)
- Integer elemental function.
- This function truncates A and converts it into an integer. If A is complex, only the real part is converted. If A is integer, this function changes the kind only.
- A is numeric; optional argument *KIND* is integer.

LOG(X)
- Elemental function of the same type and kind as X.
- Returns $\log_e(x)$.
- X is real or complex. If real, X > 0. If complex, X ≠ 0.

LOG10(X)
- Elemental function of the same type and kind as X.
- Returns $\log_{10}(x)$.
- X is real and positive.

LOGICAL(L,*KIND*)
- Logical elemental function.

- Converts the logical value L to the specified kind.
- L is logical, and *KIND* is integer.

MATMUL(MATRIX_A,MATRIX_B)
- Transformational function of the same type and kind as MATRIX_A.
- Returns the *matrix product* of numeric or logical matrices. The resulting matrix will have the same number of rows as MATRIX_A and the same number of columns as MATRIX_B.
- Arguments are numeric or logical matrices. Both matrices must be of the same type and kind, and of compatible sizes. The following constraints apply:
  1. In general, both matrices are of rank 2.
  2. MATRIX_A may be rank 1. If so, MATRIX_B must be rank 2 with only one column.
  3. In all cases, the number of columns in MATRIX_A must be the same as the number of rows in MATRIX_B.

MAX(A1,A2,A3,...)
- Elemental function of same kind as its arguments.
- Returns the maximum value of A1, A2, etc.
- Arguments may be real, integer, or character; all must be of the same type.

MIN(A1,A2,A3,...)
- Elemental function of same kind as its arguments.
- Returns the minimum value of A1, A2, etc.
- Arguments may be real or integer, or character; all must be of the same type.

MOD(A1,P)
- Elemental function of same kind as its arguments.
- Returns the value $MOD(A,P) = A - P*INT(A/P)$ if $P \neq 0$. Results are processor dependent if $P = 0$.
- Arguments may be real or integer; they must be of the same type.
- Examples:

Function	Result
MOD(5,3)	2
MOD(-5,3)	−2
MOD(5,-3)	2
MOD(-5,-3)	−2

MODULO(A1,P)
- Elemental function of same kind as its arguments.
- Returns the modulo of A with respect to P if $P \neq 0$. Results are processor dependent if $P = 0$.
- Arguments may be real or integer; they must be of the same type.
- If $P > 0$, then the function determines the positive difference between A and the next lowest multiple of P. If $P < 0$, then the function determines the negative difference between A and the next highest multiple of P.

- Results agree with the MOD function for two positive or two negative arguments; results disagree for arguments of mixed signs
- Examples:

Function	Result	Explanation
MODULO(5,3)	2	5 is 2 up from 3
MODULO(-5,3)	1	−5 is 1 up from −6
MODULO(5,-3)	−1	5 is 1 down from 6
MODULO(-5,-3)	−2	−5 is 2 down from −3

NEAREST(X,S)
- Real elemental function.
- Returns the nearest machine-representable number different from X in the direction of S. The returned value will be of the same kind as X.
- X and S are real, and S ≠ 0.

NINT(A,*KIND*)
- Integer elemental function.
- Returns the nearest integer to the real value A.
- A is real.

RANDOM_NUMBER(HARVEST)
- Intrinsic subroutine.
- Returns pseudorandom number(s) from a uniform distribution in the range $0 \le$ HARVEST < 1. HARVEST may be either a scalar or an array. If it is an array, then a separate random number will be returned in each element of the array.
- Arguments:

HARVEST	Real	OUT	Holds random numbers. May be scalar or array.

RANDOM_SEED(*SIZE*,PUT,*GET*)
- Intrinsic subroutine.
- Performs three functions: (1) restarts the pseudorandom number generator used by subroutine RANDOM_NUMBER, (2) gets information about the generator, and (3) puts a new seed into the generator.
- Arguments:

SIZE	Integer	OUT	Number of integers used to hold the seed (n).
PUT	Integer(m)	IN	Set the seed to the value in *PUT*. Note that $m \ge n$.
GET	Integer(m)	OUT	Get the current value of the seed. Note that $m \ge n$.

- *SIZE* is an integer, and *PUT* and *GET* are integer arrays. All arguments are optional, and at most one can be specified in any given call.

- Functions:
  1. If no argument is specified, the call to RANDOM_SEED restarts the pseudorandom number generator.
  2. If *SIZE* is specified, then the subroutine returns the number of integers used by the generator to hold the seed.
  3. If *GET* is specified, then the current random generator seed is returned to the user. The integer array associated with keyword *GET* must be at least as long as *SIZE*.
  4. If *PUT* is specified, then the value in the integer array associated with keyword *PUT* is set into the generator as a new seed. The integer array associated with keyword *PUT* must be at least as long as *SIZE*.

REAL(A,*KIND*)
- Real elemental function.
- This function converts A into a real value. If A is complex, it converts the real part of A only. If A is real, this function changes the kind only.
- A is numeric; *KIND* is integer.

SIGN(A,B)
- Elemental function of same kind as its arguments.
- Returns the value of A with the sign of B.
- Arguments may be real or integer; they must be of the same type.

SIN(X)
- Elemental function of the same type and kind as X.
- Returns the sine of X.
- X is real or complex.

SINH(X)
- Elemental function of the same type and kind as X.
- Returns the hyperbolic sine of X.
- X is real.

SQRT(X)
- Elemental function of the same type and kind as X.
- Returns the square root of X.
- X is real or complex.
- If X is real, X must be ≥ 0. If X is complex, then the real part of X must be ≥ 0. If X is purely imaginary, then the imaginary part of X must be ≥ 0.

TAN(X)
- Elemental function of the same type and kind as X.
- Returns the tangent of X.
- X is real.

TANH(X)
- Elemental function of the same type and kind as X.
- Returns the hyperbolic tangent of X.
- X is real.

▦ B.4

KIND AND NUMERIC PROCESSOR INTRINSIC FUNCTIONS

Many of the functions in this section are based on the Fortran models for integer and real data. These models must be understood in order to make sense of the values returned by the functions.

Fortran uses **numeric models** to insulate a programmer from the physical details of how bits are laid out in a particular computer. For example, some computers use two's complement representations for numbers while other computers use sign-magnitude representations for numbers. Approximately the same range of numbers can be represented in either case, but the bit patterns are different. The numeric models tell the programmer what range and precision can be represented by a given type and kind of numbers without requiring a knowledge of the physical bit layout on a particular machine.

The Fortran model for an integer i is

$$i = s \times \sum_{k=0}^{q-1} w_k \times r^k \tag{B-1}$$

where r is an integer exceeding 1, q is a positive integer, each w_k is a nonnegative integer less than r, and s is $+1$ or -1. The values of r and q determine the set of model integers for a processor. They are chosen to make the model fit as well as possible to the machine on which the program is executed. Note that this model is independent of the actual bit pattern used to store integers on a particular processor.

The value r in this model is the **radix** or base of the numbering system used to represent integers on a particular computer. Essentially all modern computers use a base 2 numbering system, so r is 2. If r is 2, then the value q is one less than the number of bits used to represent an integer (1 bit is used for the sign of the number). For a typical 32-bit integer on a base 2 computer, the model of an integer becomes

$$i = \pm \sum_{k=0}^{30} w_k \times 2^k \tag{B-2}$$

where each w_k is either 0 or 1.

The Fortran model for a real number x is

$$x = \begin{cases} 0 & \text{or} \\ s \times b^e \times \displaystyle\sum_{k=1}^{p} f_k \times b^{-k} \end{cases} \tag{B-3}$$

where b and p are integers exceeding 1, each f_k is a nonnegative integer less than b (and f_1 must not be zero), s is $+1$ or -1, and e is an integer that lies between some integer maximum e_{max} and some integer minimum e_{min}. The values of b, p, e_{min}, and e_{max} determine the set of model floating point numbers. They are chosen to make the model fit as well as possible to the machine on which the program is executed. This model is independent of the actual bit pattern used to store floating-point numbers on a particular processor.

The value b in this model is the **radix** or base of the numbering system used to represent real numbers on a particular computer. Essentially all modern computers use a base 2 numbering system, so b is 2, and each f_k must be either 0 or 1 (f_1 must be 1).

The bits that make up a real or floating-point number are divided into two separate fields, one for the mantissa (the fractional part of the number) and one for the exponent. For a base 2 system, p is the number of bits in the mantissa, and the value of e is stored in a field that is one less than the number of bits in the exponent.[2] Since the IEEE single-precision standard devotes 24 bits to the mantissa and 8 bits to the exponent, p is 24, $e_{max} = 2^7 = 127$, and $e_{min} = -126$. For a typical 32-bit single precision real number on a base 2 computer, the model of the number becomes

$$x = \begin{cases} 0 & \text{or} \\ \pm 2^e \times \left(\dfrac{1}{2} + \displaystyle\sum_{k=2}^{24} f_x \times 2^{-k} \right) & -126 \leq e \leq 127 \end{cases} \tag{B-4}$$

The inquiry functions DIGITS, EPSILON, HUGE, MAXEXPONENT, MINEXPONENT, PRE-CISION, RANGE, RADIX, and TINY all return values related to the model parameters for the type and kind associated with the calling arguments. Of these functions, only PRE-CISION and RANGE matter to most programmers.

BIT_SIZE(I)
- Integer inquiry function.
- Returns the number of bits in integer I.
- I must be integer.

DIGITS(X)
- Integer inquiry function.
- Returns the number of significant digits in X. (This function returns q from the integer model in Equation B-1, or p from the real model in Equation B-3.)
- X must be integer or real.
- **Caution:** This function returns the number of significant digits in the base of the numbering system used on the computer. For most modern computers, this is base 2, so this function returns the number of significant bits. If you want the number of significant decimal digits, use PRECISION(X) instead.

EPSILON(X)
- Integer inquiry function of the same type as X.
- Returns a positive number that is almost negligible compared to 1.0 of the same type and kind as X. (The returned value is b^{1-p} where b and p are defined in Equation B-3.)
- X must be real.

---

[2] It is one less than the number of bits in the exponent because 1 bit is reserved for the sign of the exponent.

- Essentially, EPSILON(X) is the number that, when added to 1.0, produces the next number representable by the given KIND of real number on a particular processor.

EXPONENT(X)

- Integer inquiry function of the same type as X. Returns the exponent of X in the base of the computer numbering system. (This is e from the real number model as defined in Equation B-3.)
- X must be real.

FRACTION(X)

- Real elemental function of same kind as X.
- Returns the mantissa or the fractional part of the model representation of X. (This function returns the summation term from Equation B-3.)
- X must be real.

HUGE(X)

- Integer inquiry function of the same type as X.
- Returns the largest number of the same type and kind as X.
- X must be integer or real.

KIND(X)

- Integer inquiry function.
- Returns the kind value of X.
- X may be any intrinsic type.

MAXEXPONENT(X)

- Integer inquiry function.
- Returns the maximum exponent of the same type and kind as X. (The returned value is e_{max} from the model in Equation B-3.)
- X must be real.
- **Caution:** This function returns the maximum exponent in the base of the numbering system used on the computer. For most modern computers, this is base 2, so this function returns the maximum exponent as a base 2 number. If you want the maximum exponent as a decimal value, use RANGE(X) instead.

MINEXPONENT(X)

- Integer inquiry function.
- Returns the minimum exponent of the same type and kind as X. (The returned value is e_{min} from the model in Equation B-3.)
- X must be real.

PRECISION(X)

- Integer inquiry function.
- Returns the number of significant *decimal digits* in values of the same type and kind as X.
- X must be real or complex.

RADIX(X)
- Integer inquiry function.
- Returns the base of the mathematical model for the type and kind of X. Since most modern computers work on a base 2 system, this number will almost always be 2. (This is r in Equation B-1, or b in Equation B-3.)
- X must be integer or real.

RANGE(X)
- Integer inquiry function.
- Returns the *decimal* exponent range for values of the same type and kind as X.
- X must be integer, real, or complex.

RRSPACING(X)
- Elemental function of the same type and kind as X.
- Returns the reciprocal of the relative spacing of the numbers near X. (The result has the value $|x \times b^{-e}| \times b^p$, where b, e, and p are defined as in Equation B-3.)
- X must be real.

SCALE(X,I)
- Elemental function of the same type and kind as X.
- Returns the value $x \times b^I$, where b is the base of the model used to represent X. The base b can be found with the RADIX(X) function; it is almost always 2.
- X must be real, and I must be integer.

SELECTED_CHAR_KIND(STRING)
- Integer transformational function.
- Returns the kind number associated with the character input argument.
- STRING must be character.
- Fortran 2003 only.

SELECTED_INT_KIND(R)
- Integer transformational function.
- Returns the kind number for the smallest integer kind that can represent all integers n whose values satisfy the condition ABS(n) < 10**R. If more than one kind satisfies this constraint, then the kind returned will be the one with the smallest decimal range. If no kind satisfies the requirement, the value -1 is returned.
- R must be integer.

SELECTED_REAL_KIND(P,R)
- Integer transformational function.
- Returns the kind number for the smallest real kind that has a decimal precision of at least P digits and an exponent range of at least R powers of 10. If more than one kind satisfies this constraint, then the kind returned will be the one with the smallest decimal precision.
- If no real kind satisfies the requirement, a -1 is returned if the requested precision was not available, a -2 is returned if the requested range was not available, and a -3 is returned if neither was available.
- P and R must be integers.

SET_EXPONENT(X,I)
- Elemental function of the same type as X.
- Returns the number whose fractional part is the fractional part of the number X, and whose exponent part is I. If X = 0, then the result is 0.
- X is real and I is integer.

SPACING(X)
- Elemental function of the same type and kind as X.
- Returns the absolute spacing of the numbers near X in the model used to represent real numbers. If the absolute spacing is out of range, then this function returns the same value as TINY(X). (This function returns the value b^{e-p}, where b, e, and p are as defined in Equation B-3, as long as that value is in range.)
- X must be real.
- The result of this function is useful for establishing convergence criteria in a processor-independent manner. For example, we might conclude that a root-solving algorithm has converged when the answer gets within 10 times the minimum representable spacing.

TINY(X)
- Elemental function of the same type and kind as X.
- Returns the smallest positive number of the same type and kind as X. (The returned value is $b^{e_{min}-1}$ where b and e_{min} are as defined in Equation B-3.)
- X must be real.

B.5

SYSTEM ENVIRONMENT PROCEDURES

COMMAND_ARGUMENT_COUNT()
- Intrinsic function.
- Returns the number of command line arguments.
- Arguments: None.
- The purpose of this is to return the number of command line arguments. Argument 0 is the name of the program being executed, and arguments 1 to n are the actual arguments on the command line.
- Fortran 2003 only.

CPU_TIME(TIME)
- Intrinsic subroutine.
- Returns processor time expended on current program in seconds.
- Arguments:
  TIME   Real   OUT   Processor time.
- The purpose of this subroutine is to time sections of code by comparing the processor time before and after the code is executed.

- The definition of the time returned by this subroutine is processor dependent. On most processors, it is the CPU time spent executing the current program.
- On computers with multiple CPUs, TIME may be implemented as an array containing the times associated with each processor.

DATE_AND_TIME(*DATE*,*TIME*,*ZONE*,*VALUE*)
- Intrinsic subroutine.
- Returns date and time.
- All arguments are optional, but at least one must be included:

DATE	Character(8)	OUT	Returns a string in the form CCYYMMDD, where CC is century, YY is year, MM is month, and DD is day.
TIME	Character(10)	OUT	Returns a string in the form HHMMSS.SSS, where HH is hour, MM is minute, SS is second, and SSS is millisecond.
ZONE	Character(5)	OUT	Returns a string in the form ±HHMM, where HHMM is the time difference between local time and Coordinated Universal Time (UCT, or GMT).
VALUES	Integer(8)	OUT	See table below for values.

- If a value is not available for *DATE*, *TIME*, or *ZONE*, then the string blanks.
- The information returned in array *VALUES* is:

VALUES(1)	Century and year (for example, 1996)
VALUES(2)	Month (1–12)
VALUES(3)	Day (1–31)
VALUES(4)	Time zone difference from UTC in minutes
VALUES(5)	Hour (0–23)
VALUES(6)	Minutes (0–59)
VALUES(7)	Seconds (0–60)
VALUES(8)	Milliseconds (0–999)

- If no information is available for one of the elements of array *VALUES*, that element is set to the most negative representable integer (-HUGE(0)).
- Note that the seconds field ranges from 0 to 60. The extra second is included to allow for leap seconds.

F-2003 ONLY

GET_COMMAND(COMMAND,*LENGTH*,*STATUS*)
- Intrinsic subroutine.
- Returns the entire command line used to start the program.
- Fortran 2003 only.
- All arguments are optional:

COMMAND	Character(*)	OUT	Returns a string containing the command line.

LENGTH	Integer	OUT	Returns the length of the command line.
STATUS	Integer	OUT	Status: 0=success; -1= command line present but *COMMAND* is too short to hold it all; other value= retrieval failed.

F-2003 ONLY

GET_COMMAND_ARGUMENT(NUMBER, *VALUE*, *LENGTH*, *STATUS*)
- Intrinsic subroutine.
- Returns a specified command argument.
- Fortran 2003 only.
- Argument list:

NUMBER	Integer	IN	Argument number to return, in the range 0 to COMMAND_ARGUMENT_COUNT().
VALUE	Character(*)	OUT	Returns the specified argument.
LENGTH	Integer	OUT	Returns the length of the argument.
STATUS	Integer	OUT	Status: 0=success; -1=command line present but *COMMAND* is too short to hold it all; other value = retrieval failed.

F-2003 ONLY

GET_ENVIRONMENT_VARIABLE(NAME, *VALUE*, *LENGTH*, *STATUS*, *TRIM_NAME*)
- Intrinsic subroutine.
- Returns a specified command argument.
- Fortran 2003 only.
- All arguments are optional:

NAME	Character(*)	IN	Name of environment variable to retrieve.
VALUE	Character(*)	OUT	Returns the value of the specified environment variable.
LENGTH	Integer	OUT	Returns the length of the value in characters.
STATUS	Integer	OUT	Status: 0=success; -1=command line present but *COMMAND* is too short to hold it all; 2=processor does not support environment variables; other value = retrieval failed.

TRIM_NAME	Logical	IN	If true, ignore trailing blanks in NAME when matching to an environment variable; otherwise, include the blanks. If this argument is missing, trailing blanks are ignored.

F-2003 ONLY

IS_IOSTAT_END(I)
- Intrinsic function.
- Returns true if the value of I is equal to the IOSTAT_END flag.
- Fortran 2003 only.
- Arguments:

I	Integer	IN	This is the result of a READ operation returned by the IOSTAT= clause.

- The purpose of this is to provide a simple way to test for the end-of-file condition during a read operation.

F-2003 ONLY

IS_IOSTAT_EOR(I)
- Intrinsic function.
- Returns true if the value of I is equal to the IOSTAT_EOR flag.
- Fortran 2003 only.
- Arguments:

I	Integer	IN	This is the result of a READ operation returned by the IOSTAT= clause.

- The purpose of this is to provide a simple way to test for the end-of-record condition during a read operation with ADVANCE='NO'.

SYSTEM_CLOCK(COUNT,COUNT_RATE,COUNT_MAX)
- Intrinsic subroutine.
- Returns raw counts from the processor's real-time clock. The value in COUNT is increased by one for each clock count until COUNT_MAX is reached. When COUNT_MAX is reached, the value in COUNT is reset to 0 on the next clock count. Variable COUNT_RATE specifies the number of real-time clock counts per second, so it tells how to interpret the count information.
- Arguments:

COUNT	Integer	OUT	Number of counts of the system clock. The starting count is arbitrary.
COUNT_RATE	Integer or real	OUT	Number of clock counts per second.
COUNT_MAX	Integer	OUT	The maximum value for COUNT.

- If there is no clock, COUNT and COUNT_RATE are set to -HUGE(0) and COUNT_MAX is set to 0.

■ B.6

BIT INTRINSIC PROCEDURES

The layout of bits within an integer varies from processor to processor. For example, some processors place the most significant bit of a value at the bottom of the memory representing that value, while other processors place the least significant bit of a value at the top of the memory representing that value. To insulate programmers from these machine dependencies, Fortran defines a bit to be a binary digit w located at position k of a nonnegative integer based on a model nonnegative integer defined by

$$j = \sum_{k=0}^{z-1} w_k \times 2^k \qquad (B\text{-}5)$$

where w_k can be either 0 or 1. Thus bit 0 is the coefficient of 2^0, bit 1 is the coefficient of 2^1, etc. In this model, z is the number of bits in the integer, and the bits are numbered $0, 1, \ldots, z - 1$, regardless of the physical layout of the integer. The least significant bit is considered to be at the right of the model and the most significant bit is considered to be at the left of the model, regardless of the actual physical implementation. Thus, shifting a bit left increases its value, and shifting a bit right decreases its value.

Fortran 95/2003 includes 10 elemental functions and 1 elemental subroutine that manipulate bits according to this model. Logical operations on bits are performed by the elemental functions IOR, IAND, NOT, and IEOR. Shift operations are performed by the elemental functions ISHFT and ISHFTC. Bit subfields may be referenced by the elemental function IBITS and the elemental subroutine MVBITS. Finally, single-bit processing is performed by the elemental functions BTEST, IBSET, and IBCLR.

BTEST(I,POS)
- Logical elemental function.
- Returns true if bit POS of I is 1, and false otherwise.
- I and POS must be integers, with $0 \le POS < BIT\_SIZE(I)$.

IAND(I,J)
- Elemental function of the same type and kind as I.
- Returns the bit-by-bit logical AND of I and J.
- I and J must be integers of the same kind.

IBCLR(I,POS)
- Elemental function of the same type and kind as I.
- Returns I with bit POS set to 0.
- I and POS must be integers, with $0 \le POS < BIT\_SIZE(I)$.

IBITS(I,POS,LEN)
- Elemental function of the same type and kind as I.
- Returns a right-adjusted sequence of bits extracted from I of length LEN starting at bit POS. All other bits are zero.
- I, POS, and LEN must be integers, with $POS + LEN < BIT\_SIZE(I)$.

IBSET(I,POS)
- Elemental function of the same type and kind as I.
- Returns I with bit POS set to 1.
- I and POS must be integers, with $0 \leq$ POS $<$ BIT_SIZE(I).

IEOR(I,J)
- Elemental function of the same type and kind as I.
- Returns the bit by bit exclusive OR of I and J.
- I and J must be integers of the same kind.

IOR(I,J)
- Elemental function of the same type and kind as I.
- Returns the bit-by-bit inclusive OR of I and J.
- I and J must be integers of the same kind.

ISHFT(I,SHIFT)
- Elemental function of the same type and kind as I.
- Returns I logically shifted to the left (if SHIFT is positive) or right (if SHIFT is negative). The empty bits are filled with zeros.
- I must be an integer.
- SHIFT must be an integer, with ABS(SHIFT) <= BIT_SIZE(I).
- A shift to the left implies moving the bit in position i to position $i + 1$, and a shift to the right implies moving the bit in position i to position $i - 1$.

ISHFTC(I,SHIFT,*SIZE*)
- Elemental function of the same type and kind as I.
- Returns the value obtained by shifting the *SIZE* rightmost bits of I circularly by SHIFT bits. If SHIFT is positive, the bits are shifted left, and if SHIFT is negative, the bits are shifted right. If the optional argument *SIZE* is missing, all BIT_SIZE(I) bits of I are shifted.
- I must be an integer.
- SHIFT must be an integer, with ABS(SHIFT) <= *SIZE*.
- *SIZE* must be a positive integer, with $0 <$ *SIZE* $<=$ BIT_SIZE(I).

MVBITS(FROM,FROMPOS,LEN,TO,TOPOS)
- Elemental subroutine.
- Copies a sequence of bits from integer FROM to integer TO. The subroutine copies a sequence of LEN bits starting at FROMPOS in integer FROM, and stores them starting at TOPOS in integer TO. All other bits in integer TO are undisturbed.
- Note that FROM and TO can be the same integer.
- Arguments:

FROM	Integer	IN	The object from which the bits are to be moved.
FROMPOS	Integer	IN	Starting bit to move; must be ≥ 0.
LEN	Integer	IN	Number of bits to move; FROMPOS+LEN must be $\leq$ BIT_SIZE(FROM).

| TO | Integer, same kind as FROM | INOUT | Destination object. |
| TOPOS | Integer | IN | Starting bit in destination; $0 \leq$ TOPOS+LEN$\leq$ BIT_SIZE(TO). |

NOT(I)
- Elemental function of the same type and kind as I.
- Returns the logical complement of the bits in I.
- I must be integer.

B.7
CHARACTER INTRINSIC FUNCTIONS

These functions produce, manipulate, or provide information about character strings.

ACHAR(I,*KIND*)
- Character(1) elemental function.
- Returns the character in position I of the ASCII collating sequence.
- If $0 \leq I \leq 127$, the result is the character in position I of the ASCII collating sequence. If $I \geq 128$, the results are processor dependent.
- I must be integer.
- The *KIND* argument is Fortran 2003 only.
- *KIND* must be an integer whose value is a legal kind of character for the particular computer; if it is absent, the default kind of character is assumed.
- IACHAR is the inverse function of ACHAR.

ADJUSTL(STRING)
- Character elemental function.
- Returns a character value of the same length as STRING, with the nonblank contents left-justified. That is, the leading blanks of STRING are removed and the same number of trailing blanks are added at the end.
- STRING must be character.

ADJUSTR(STRING)
- Character elemental function.
- Returns a character value of the same length as STRING, with the nonblank contents right justified. That is, the trailing blanks of STRING are removed and the same number of leading blanks are added at the beginning.
- STRING must be character.

CHAR(I,*KIND*)
- Character(1) elemental function.
- Returns the character in position I of the processor collating sequence associated with the specified kind.
- I must be an integer in the range $0 \leq I \leq n - 1$, where n is the number of characters in the processor-dependent collating sequence.

- *KIND* must be an integer whose value is a legal kind of character for the particular computer; if it is absent, the default kind of character is assumed.
- ICHAR is the inverse function of CHAR.

IACHAR(C)

- Integer elemental function.
- Returns the position of a character in the ASCII collating sequence. A processor-dependent value is returned if C is not in the collating sequence.
- C must be character(1).
- ACHAR is the inverse function of IACHAR.

ICHAR(C)

- Integer elemental function.
- Returns the position of a character in the processor collating sequence associated with the kind of the character.
- C must be character(1).
- The result is in the range $0 \leq \text{ICHAR(C)} \leq n - 1$, where n is the number of characters in the processor-dependent collating sequence.
- CHAR is the inverse function of ICHAR.

INDEX(STRING,SUBSTRING,*BACK*)

- Integer elemental function.
- Returns the starting position of a substring within a string.
- STRING and SUBSTRING must be character values of the same kind, and *BACK* must be logical.
- If the substring is longer than the string, the result is 0. If the length of the substring is 0, then the result is 1. Otherwise, if *BACK* is missing or false, the function returns the starting position of the *first* occurrence of the substring within the string, searching from left to right through the string. If *BACK* is true, the function returns the starting position of the *last* occurrence of the substring within the string.

LEN(STRING)

- Integer inquiry function.
- Returns the length of STRING in characters.
- STRING must be character.

LEN_TRIM(STRING)

- Integer inquiry function.
- Returns the length of STRING in characters, less any trailing blanks. If STRING is completely blank, then the result is 0.
- STRING must be character.

LGE(STRING_A,STRING_B)

- Logical elemental function.
- Returns true if $\text{STRING\_A} \geq \text{STRING\_B}$ in the ASCII collating sequence.
- STRING_A and STRING_B must be of type default character.
- The comparison process is similar to that used by the >= relational operator, except that the comparison always uses the ASCII collating sequence.

LGT(STRING_A,STRING_B)
- Logical elemental function.
- Returns true if STRING_A > STRING_B in the ASCII collating sequence.
- STRING_A and STRING_B must be of type default character.
- The comparison process is similar to that used by the > relational operator, except that the comparison always uses the ASCII collating sequence.

LLE(STRING_A,STRING_B)
- Logical elemental function.
- Returns true if STRING_A ≤ STRING_B in the ASCII collating sequence.
- STRING_A and STRING_B must be of type default character.
- The comparison process is similar to that used by the <= relational operator, except that the comparison always uses the ASCII collating sequence.

LLT(STRING_A,STRING_B)
- Logical elemental function.
- Returns true if STRING_A < STRING_B in the ASCII collating sequence.
- STRING_A and STRING_B must be of type default character.
- The comparison process is similar to that used by the < relational operator, except that the comparison always uses the ASCII collating sequence.

F-2003 ONLY

NEW_LINE(CHAR)
- Inquiry function.
- Returns the newline character for the KIND of the input character string.
- Fortran 2003 only.

REPEAT(STRING,NCOPIES)
- Character transformational function.
- Returns a character string formed by concatenating NCOPIES copies of STRING one after another. If STRING is zero length or if NCOPIES is 0, the function returns a zero length string.
- STRING must be of type character; NCOPIES must be a nonnegative integer.

SCAN(STRING,SET,*BACK*)
- Integer elemental function.
- Scans STRING for the first occurrence of any one of the characters in SET, and returns the position of that occurrence. If no character of STRING is in set, or if either STRING or SET is zero length, the function returns a zero.
- STRING and SET must be of type character and the same kind, and *BACK* must be of type logical.
- If *BACK* is missing or false, the function returns the position of the *first* occurrence (searching left to right) of any of the characters contained in SET. If *BACK* is true, the function returns the position of the *last* occurrence (searching right to left) of any of the characters contained in SET.

TRIM(STRING)
- Character transformational function.
- Returns STRING with trailing blanks removed. If STRING is completely blank, then a zero-length string is returned.
- STRING must be of type character.

`VERIFY(STRING,SET,BACK)`
- Integer elemental function.
- Scans `STRING` for the first occurrence of any one of the characters *not* in `SET`, and returns the position of that occurrence. If all characters of `STRING` are in `SET`, or if either `STRING` or `SET` is zero length, the function returns a zero.
- `STRING` and `SET` must be of type character and the same kind, and `BACK` must be of type logical.
- If `BACK` is missing or false, the function returns the position of the *first* occurrence (searching left to right) of any of the characters not contained in `SET`. If `BACK` is true, the function returns the position of the *last* occurrence (searching right to left) of any of the characters not in `SET`.

■ B.8
ARRAY AND POINTER INTRINSIC FUNCTIONS

This section describes the 24 standard array and pointer intrinsic functions. Because certain arguments appear in many of these functions, they will be described in detail before we examine the functions themselves.

1. The rank of an array is defined as the number of dimensions in the array. It is abbreviated as r throughout this section.
2. A scalar is defined to be an array of rank 0.
3. The optional argument `MASK` is used by some functions to select the elements of another argument to operate on. When present, `MASK` must be a logical array of the same size and shape as the target array; if an element of `MASK` is true, then the corresponding element of the target array will be operated on.
4. The optional argument `DIM` is used by some functions to determine the dimension of an array along which to operate. When supplied, `DIM` must be a number in the range $1 \le DIM \le r$.
5. In the functions `ALL`, `ANY`, `LBOUND`, `MAXVAL`, `MINVAL`, `PRODUCT`, `SUM`, and `UBOUND`, the optional argument `DIM` affects the type of argument returned by the function. If the argument is absent, then the function returns a scalar result. If the argument is present, then the function returns a vector result. Because the presence or absence of `DIM` affects the type of value returned by the function, the compiler must be able to determine whether or not the argument is present when the program is compiled. Therefore, *the actual argument corresponding to `DIM` must not be an optional dummy argument in the calling program unit.* If it were, the compiler would be unable to determine whether or not `DIM` is present at compilation time. This restriction does not apply to functions `CSHIFT`, `EOSHIFT`, `SIZE`, and `SPREAD`, since the argument `DIM` does not affect the type of value returned from these functions.

To illustrate the use of `MASK` and `DIM`, let's apply the function `MAXVAL` to a 2×3 real array `array1` ($r = 2$) and two masking arrays `mask1` and `mask2`, defined as follows:

$$\text{array1} = \begin{bmatrix} 1. & 2. & 3. \\ 4. & 5. & 6. \end{bmatrix}$$

$$mask1 = \begin{bmatrix} \text{.TRUE.} & \text{.TRUE.} & \text{.TRUE.} \\ \text{.TRUE.} & \text{.TRUE.} & \text{.TRUE.} \end{bmatrix}$$

$$mask2 = \begin{bmatrix} \text{.TRUE.} & \text{.TRUE.} & \text{.FALSE.} \\ \text{.TRUE.} & \text{.TRUE.} & \text{.FALSE.} \end{bmatrix}$$

The function MAXVAL returns the maximum values along the dimension *DIM* of an array corresponding to the true elements of *MASK*. It has the calling sequence

```
result = MAXVAL(ARRAY,DIM,MASK)
```

If *DIM* is not present, the function returns a scalar equal to the largest value in the array for which *MASK* is true. Therefore, the function

```
result = MAXVAL(array1,MASK=mask1)
```

will produce a value of 6, while the function

```
result = MAXVAL(array1,MASK=mask2)
```

will produce a value of 5. If *DIM* is present, then the function will return an array of rank $r - 1$ containing the maximum values along dimension *DIM* for which *MASK* is true. That is, the function will hold the subscript in the specified dimension constant while searching along all other dimensions to find the masked maximum value in that subarray, and then repeat the process for every other possible value of the specified dimension. Since there are three elements in each row of the array, the function

```
result = MAXVAL(array1,DIM=1,MASK=mask1)
```

will search along the *columns* of the array at each row position, and will produce the vector [4. 5. 6.], where 4. was the maximum value in column 1, 5. was the maximum value in column 2, and 6. was the maximum value in column 3. Similarly, there are two elements in each column of the array, so the function

```
result = MAXVAL(array1,DIM=2,MASK=mask1)
```

will search along the *rows* of the array at each column position, and will produce the vector [3. 6.], where 3. was the maximum value in row 1, and 6. was the maximum value in row 2.

ALL(MASK,*DIM*)
- Logical transformational function.
- Returns true if all MASK values are true along dimension *DIM*, or if MASK has zero size. Otherwise, it returns false.
- MASK is a logical array. *DIM* is an integer in the range $1 \le DIM \le r$. The corresponding actual argument must not be an optional argument in the calling procedure.
- The result is a scalar if *DIM* is absent. It is an array of rank $r - 1$ and shape $(d(1),d(2),...,d(DIM-1),d(DIM+1),...,d(r))$, where the shape of MASK

is `(d(1),d(2),...,d(r))`. In other words, the shape of the returned vector is the same as the shape of the original mask with dimension *DIM* deleted.

ANY(MASK,*DIM*)

- Logical transformational function.
- Returns true if any `MASK` value is true along dimension *DIM*. Otherwise, it returns false. If `MASK` has zero size, it returns false.
- `MASK` is a logical array. `DIM` is an integer in the range 1 # DIM # r. The corresponding actual argument must not be an optional argument in the calling procedure.
- The result is a scalar if *DIM* is absent. It is an array of rank $r - 1$ and shape `(d(1),d(2),...,d(DIM-1),d(DIM+1),...,d(r))` where the shape of `MASK` is `(d(1),d(2),...,d(r))`. In other words, the shape of the returned vector is the same as the shape of the original mask with dimension *DIM* deleted.

COUNT(MASK,*DIM*)

- Logical transformational function.
- Returns the number of true elements of `MASK` along dimension *DIM*, and returns 0 if `MASK` has zero size.
- `MASK` is a logical array. *DIM* is an integer in the range $1 \leq DIM \leq r$. The corresponding actual argument must not be an optional argument in the calling procedure.
- The result is a scalar if *DIM* is absent. It is an array of rank $r - 1$ and shape `(d(1),d(2),...,d(DIM-1),d(DIM+1),...,d(r))`, where the shape of `MASK` is `(d(1),d(2),...,d(r))`. In other words, the shape of the returned vector is the same as the shape of the original mask with dimension *DIM* deleted.

CSHIFT(ARRAY,SHIFT,*DIM*)

- Transformational function of the same type as `ARRAY`.
- Performs a circular shift on an array expression of rank 1, or performs circular shifts on all the complete rank 1 sections along a given dimension of an array expression of rank 2 or greater. Elements shifted out at one end of a section are shifted in at the other end. Different sections may be shifted by different amounts and in different directions.
- `ARRAY` may be an array of any type and rank, but not a scalar. `SHIFT` is a scalar if `ARRAY` is rank 1. Otherwise, it is an array of rank $r - 1$ and of shape `(d(1),d(2),...,d(DIM-1),d(DIM+1),...,d(r))`, where the shape of `ARRAY` is `(d(1),d(2),...,d(r))`. *DIM* is an optional integer in the range $1 \leq DIM \leq r$. If *DIM* is missing, the function behaves as though *DIM* were present and equal to 1.

EOSHIFT(ARRAY,SHIFT,*DIM*)

- Transformational function of the same type as `ARRAY`.
- Performs an end-off shift on an array expression of rank 1, or performs end-off shifts on all the complete rank 1 sections along a given dimension of an array expression of rank 2 or greater. Elements are shifted off at one end of a section and copies of a boundary value are shifted in at the other end. Different sections may have different boundary values and may be shifted by different amounts and in different directions.

- ARRAY may be an array of any type and rank, but not a scalar. SHIFT is a scalar if ARRAY is rank 1. Otherwise, it is an array of rank $r - 1$ and of shape $(d(1),d(2),\ldots,d(DIM-1),d(DIM+1),\ldots,d(r))$, where the shape of ARRAY is $(d(1),d(2),\ldots,d(r))$. DIM is an optional integer in the range $1 \leq DIM \leq r$. If DIM is missing, the function behaves as though DIM were present and equal to 1.

LBOUND(ARRAY,DIM)

- Integer inquiry function.
- Returns all of the lower bounds or a specified lower bound of ARRAY.
- ARRAY is an array of any type. It must not be an unassociated pointer or an unallocated allocatable array. DIM is an integer in the range $1 \leq DIM \leq r$. The corresponding actual argument must not be an optional argument in the calling procedure.
- If DIM is present, the result is a scalar. If the actual argument corresponding to ARRAY is an array section or an array expression, or if dimension DIM has zero size, then the function will return 1. Otherwise, it will return the lower bound of that dimension of ARRAY. If DIM is not present, then the function will return an array whose ith element is LBOUND(ARRAY,i) for $i = 1, 2, \ldots, r$.

MAXLOC(ARRAY,DIM,MASK)

- Integer transformational function, returning a rank 1 array of size r.
- Returns the location of the maximum value of the elements in ARRAY along dimension DIM (if present) corresponding to the true elements of MASK (if present). If more than one element has the same maximum value, the location of the first one found is returned.
- ARRAY is an array of type integer, real, or character. DIM is an integer in the range $1 \leq DIM \leq r$. The corresponding actual argument must not be an optional argument in the calling procedure. MASK is a logical scalar or a logical array conformable with ARRAY.
- If DIM is not present and MASK is not present, the result is a rank 1 array containing the subscripts of the first element found in ARRAY having the maximum value. If DIM is not present and MASK is present, the search is restricted to those elements for which MASK is true. If DIM is present, the result is an array of rank $r - 1$ and of shape $(d(1),d(2),\ldots,d(DIM-1), d(DIM+1),\ldots,d(r))$, where the shape of ARRAY is $(d(1),d(2),\ldots,d(r))$. This array contains the subscripts of the largest values found along dimension DIM.
- For example, if

$$\text{ARRAY} = \begin{bmatrix} 1 & 3 & -9 \\ 2 & 2 & 6 \end{bmatrix}$$

and

$$\text{MASK} = \begin{bmatrix} \text{TRUE} & \text{FALSE} & \text{FALSE} \\ \text{TRUE} & \text{TRUE} & \text{FALSE} \end{bmatrix}$$

then the result of the function MAXLOC(ARRAY) is (/2,3/). The result of MAXLOC(ARRAY,MASK) is (/2,1/). The result of MAXLOC(ARRAY,DIM=1) is (/2,1,2/), and the result of MAXLOC(ARRAY,DIM=2) is (/2,3/).

MAXVAL(ARRAY,*DIM*,*MASK*)
- Transformational function of the same type as ARRAY.
- Returns the maximum value of the elements in ARRAY along dimension *DIM* (if present) corresponding to the true elements of *MASK* (if present). If ARRAY has zero size, or if all the elements of *MASK* are false, then the result is the largest possible negative number of the same type and kind as ARRAY.
- ARRAY is an array of type integer, real, or character. *DIM* is an integer in the range $1 \leq DIM \leq r$. The corresponding actual argument must not be an optional argument in the calling procedure. *MASK* is a logical scalar or a logical array conformable with ARRAY.
- If *DIM* is not present, the result is a scalar containing the maximum value found in the elements of ARRAY corresponding to true elements of *MASK*. If *MASK* is absent, the search is over all of the elements in ARRAY. If *DIM* is present, the result is an array of rank $r - 1$ and of shape (d(1),d(2),...,d(DIM-1), d(DIM+1),...,d(r)), where the shape of ARRAY is (d(1),d(2),...,d(r)).
- For example, if

$$ARRAY = \begin{bmatrix} 1 & 3 & -9 \\ 2 & 2 & 6 \end{bmatrix}$$

and

$$MASK = \begin{bmatrix} TRUE & FALSE & FALSE \\ TRUE & TRUE & FALSE \end{bmatrix}$$

then the result of the function MAXVAL(ARRAY) is 6. The result of MAXVAL(ARRAY,MASK) is 2. The result of MAXVAL(ARRAY,DIM=1) is (/2,3,6/), and the result of MAXLOC(ARRAY,DIM=2) is (/3,6/).

MERGE(TSOURCE,FSOURCE,MASK)
- Elemental function of the same type as TSOURCE.
- Selects one of two alternative values according to MASK. If a given element of MASK is true, then the corresponding element of the result comes from array TSOURCE. If a given element of MASK is false, then the corresponding element of the result comes from array FSOURCE. MASK may also be a scalar, in which case either all of TSOURCE or all of FSOURCE is selected. TSOURCE is any type of array; FSOURCE is the same type and kind as TSOURCE. MASK is a logical scalar, or a logical array conformable with TSOURCE.

MINLOC(ARRAY,*DIM*,*MASK*)
- Integer transformational function, returning a rank 1 array of size r.
- Returns the *location* of the minimum value of the elements in ARRAY along dimension *DIM* (if present) corresponding to the true elements of *MASK*

(if present). If more than one element has the same minimum value, the location of the first one found is returned. ARRAY is an array of type integer, real, or character. DIM is an integer in the range $1 \leq DIM \leq r$. The corresponding actual argument must not be an optional argument in the calling procedure. MASK is a logical scalar, or a logical array conformable with ARRAY.

- If DIM is not present and MASK is not present, the result is a rank 1 array containing the subscripts of the first element found in ARRAY having the minimum value. If DIM is not present and MASK is present, the search is restricted to those elements for which MASK is true. If DIM is present, the result is an array of rank r 1 and of shape (d(1),d(2),...,d(DIM-1), d(DIM+1),...,d(r)), where the shape of ARRAY is (d(1),d(2),...,d(r)). This array contains the subscripts of the smallest values found along dimension DIM.

- For example, if

$$ARRAY = \begin{bmatrix} 1 & 3 & -9 \\ 2 & 2 & 6 \end{bmatrix}$$

and

$$MASK = \begin{bmatrix} TRUE & FALSE & FALSE \\ TRUE & TRUE & FALSE \end{bmatrix}$$

then the result of the function MINLOC(ARRAY) is (/1,3/). The result of MINLOC(ARRAY,MASK) is (/1,1/). The result of MINLOC(ARRAY,DIM=1) is (/1,2,1/), and the result of MINLOC(ARRAY,DIM=2) is (/3,1/).

MINVAL(ARRAY,DIM,$MASK$)
- Transformational function of the same type as ARRAY.
- Returns the minimum value of the elements in ARRAY along dimension DIM (if present) corresponding to the true elements of MASK (if present). If ARRAY has zero size, or if all the elements of MASK are false, then the result is the largest possible positive number of the same type and kind as ARRAY.
- ARRAY is an array of type integer, real, or character. DIM is an integer in the range $1 \leq DIM \leq r$. The corresponding actual argument must not be an optional argument in the calling procedure. MASK is a logical scalar, or a logical array conformable with ARRAY.
- If DIM is not present, the result is a scalar containing the minimum value found in the elements of ARRAY corresponding to true elements of MASK. If MASK is absent, the search is over all of the elements in ARRAY. If DIM is present, the result is an array of rank $r - 1$ and of shape (d(1),d(2),...,d(DIM-1), d(DIM+1),...,d(r)), where the shape of ARRAY is (d(1),d(2),...,d(r)).
- For example, if

$$ARRAY = \begin{bmatrix} 1 & 3 & -9 \\ 2 & 2 & 6 \end{bmatrix}$$

and

$$MASK = \begin{bmatrix} TRUE & FALSE & FALSE \\ TRUE & TRUE & FALSE \end{bmatrix}$$

then the result of the function MINVAL(ARRAY) is -9. The result of MINVAL(ARRAY,MASK) is 1. The result of MINVAL(ARRAY,DIM=1) is $(/1,2,-9/)$, and the result of MINLOC(ARRAY,DIM=2) is $(/ -9,2/)$.

NULL(*MOLD*)
- Transformational function.
- Returns a disassociated pointer of the same type as *MOLD*, if present. If *MOLD* is not present, the pointer type is determined by context. (For example, if NULL() is being used to initialize an integer pointer, the returned value will be a disassociated integer pointer.)
- *MOLD* is a pointer of any type. Its pointer association status may be undefined, disassociated, or associated.
- This function is useful for initializing the status of a pointer at the time it is declared.

PACK(ARRAY,MASK,*VECTOR*)
- Transformational function of the same type as ARRAY.
- Packs an array into an array of rank 1 under the control of a mask.
- ARRAY is an array of any type. MASK is a logical scalar, or a logical array conformable with ARRAY. *VECTOR* is a rank 1 array of the same type as ARRAY. It must have at least as many elements as there are true values in the mask. If MASK is a true scalar with the value true, then it must have at least as many elements as there are in ARRAY.
- This function packs the elements of ARRAY into an array of rank 1 under the control of MASK. An element of ARRAY will be packed into the output vector if the corresponding element of MASK is true. If MASK is a true scalar value, then the entire input array will be packed into the output array. The packing is done in column order.
- If argument *VECTOR* is present, then the length of the function output will be the length of *VECTOR*. This length must be greater than or equal to the number of elements to be packed.
- For example, if

$$ARRAY = \begin{bmatrix} 1 & -3 \\ 4 & -2 \end{bmatrix}$$

and

$$MASK = \begin{bmatrix} FALSE & TRUE \\ TRUE & TRUE \end{bmatrix}$$

then the result of the function PACK(ARRAY,MASK) will be [4 -3 -2].

PRODUCT(ARRAY,*DIM*,MASK)
- Transformational function of the same type as ARRAY.
- Returns the product of the elements in ARRAY along dimension *DIM* (if present) corresponding to the true elements of *MASK* (if present). If ARRAY has zero size, or if all the elements of *MASK* are false, then the result has the value 1.
- ARRAY is an array of type integer, real, or complex. *DIM* is an integer in the range $1 \leq DIM \leq r$. The corresponding actual argument must not be an optional argument in the calling procedure. *MASK* is a logical scalar or a logical array conformable with ARRAY.
- If *DIM* is not present or if ARRAY has rank 1, the result is a scalar containing the product of all the elements of ARRAY corresponding to true elements of *MASK*. If *MASK* is also absent, the result is the product of all of the elements in ARRAY. If *DIM* is present, the result is an array of rank $r - 1$ and of shape (d(1),d(2),...,d(DIM-1),d(DIM+1),...,d(r)), where the shape of ARRAY is (d(1),d(2),...,d(r)).

RESHAPE(SOURCE,SHAPE,*PAD*,*ORDER*)
- Transformational function of the same type as SOURCE.
- Constructs an array of a specified shape from the elements of another array.
- SOURCE is an array of any type. SHAPE is a 1- to 7-element integer array containing the desired extent of each dimension of the output array. *PAD* is a rank 1 array of the same type as SOURCE. It contains elements to be used as a pad on the end if the output array if there are not enough elements in SOURCE. *ORDER* is an integer array of the same shape as SHAPE. It specifies the order in which dimensions are to be filled with elements from SOURCE.
- The result of this function is an array of shape SHAPE constructed from the elements of SOURCE. If SOURCE does not contain enough elements, the elements of *PAD* are used repeatedly to fill out the remainder of the output array. *ORDER* specifies the order in which the dimensions of the output array will be filled; by default they fill in the order $(1,2,...,n)$ where n is the size of SHAPE.
- For example, if SOURCE=[1 2 3 4 5 6], SHAPE=[2 5], and PAD=[0 0], then

$$\text{RESHAPE(SOURCE, SHAPE, PAD)} = \begin{bmatrix} 1 & 3 & 5 & 0 & 0 \\ 2 & 4 & 6 & 0 & 0 \end{bmatrix}$$

and

$$\text{RESHAPE(SOURCE, SHAPE, PAD, (/2, 1/))} = \begin{bmatrix} 1 & 2 & 3 & 4 & 5 \\ 6 & 0 & 0 & 0 & 0 \end{bmatrix}$$

SHAPE(SOURCE)
- Integer inquiry function.
- Returns the shape of SOURCE as a rank 1 array whose size is r and whose elements are the extents of the corresponding dimensions of SOURCE. If SOURCE is a scalar, a rank 1 array of size zero is returned.

- SOURCE is an array or scalar of any type. It must not be an unassociated pointer or an unallocated allocatable array.

SIZE(ARRAY,*DIM*)
- Integer inquiry function.
- Returns either the extent of ARRAY along a particular dimension if *DIM* is present; otherwise, it returns the total number of elements in the array.
- ARRAY is an array of any type. It must not be an unassociated pointer or an unallocated allocatable array. *DIM* is an integer in the range $1 \leq DIM \leq r$. If ARRAY is an assumed size array, *DIM* must be present, and must have a value less than r.

SPREAD(SOURCE,DIM,NCOPIES)
- Transformational function of the same type as SOURCE.
- Constructs an array of rank $r + 1$ by copying SOURCE along a specified dimension (as in forming a book from copies of a single page).
- SOURCE is an array or scalar of any type. The rank of SOURCE must be less than 7.
  - *DIM* is an integer specifying the dimension over which to copy SOURCE. It must satisfy the condition $1 \leq DIM \leq r + 1$.
- NCOPIES is the number of copies of SOURCE to make along dimension *DIM*. If NCOPIES is less than or equal to zero, a zero-sized array is produced.
- If SOURCE is a scalar, each element in the result has a value equal to SOURCE. If source is an array, the element in the result with subscripts $(s_1, s_2, \ldots, s_{n+1})$ has the value SOURCE($s_1, s_2, \ldots, s_{DIM-1}, s_{DIM+1}, \ldots, s_{n+1}$).
- For example, if SOURCE=[1 3 5], then the result of function SPREAD(SOURCE, DIM=1,NCOPIES=3) is the array

$$\begin{bmatrix} 1 & 3 & 5 \\ 1 & 3 & 5 \\ 1 & 3 & 5 \end{bmatrix}$$

SUM(ARRAY,*DIM*,*MASK*)
- Transformational function of the same type as ARRAY.
- Returns the sum of the elements in ARRAY along dimension *DIM* (if present) corresponding to the true elements of *MASK* (if present). If ARRAY has zero size, or if all the elements of *MASK* are false, then the result has the value zero.
- ARRAY is an array of type integer, real, or complex. *DIM* is an integer in the range $1 \leq DIM \leq r$. The corresponding actual argument must not be an optional argument in the calling procedure. *MASK* is a logical scalar or a logical array conformable with ARRAY.
- If *DIM* is not present or if ARRAY has rank 1, the result is a scalar containing the sum of all the elements of ARRAY corresponding to true elements of *MASK*. If *MASK* is also absent, the result is the sum of all of the elements in ARRAY. If *DIM* is present, the result is an array of rank $r - 1$ and of shape (d(1),d(2),...,d(DIM-1),d(DIM+1),...,d(r)) where the shape of ARRAY is (d(1),d(2),...,d(r)).

TRANSFER(SOURCE,MOLD,*SIZE*)
- Transformational function of the same type as MOLD.
- Returns either a scalar or a rank 1 array with a physical representation identical to that of SOURCE, but interpreted with the type and kind of MOLD. Effectively, this function takes the bit patterns in SOURCE and interprets them as though they were of the type and kind of MOLD.
- SOURCE is an array or scalar of any type. MOLD is an array or scalar of any type. *SIZE* is a scalar integer value. The corresponding actual argument must not be an optional argument in the calling procedure.
- If MOLD is a scalar and *SIZE* is absent, the result is a scalar. If MOLD is an array and *SIZE* is absent, the result has the smallest possible size that makes use of all of the bits in SOURCE. If *SIZE* is present, the result is a rank 1 array of length *SIZE*. If the number of bits in the result and in SOURCE are not the same, then bits will be truncated or extra bits will be added in an undefined, processor-dependent manner.
- Example 1: TRANSFER(4.0,0) has the integer value 1082130432 on a PC using IEEE Standard floating-point numbers, because the bit representations of a floating-point 4.0 and an integer 1082130432 are identical. The transfer function has caused the bit associated with the floating-point 4.0 to be reinterpreted as an integer.
- Example 2: In the function TRANSFER((/1.1,2.2,3.3/),(/(0.,0.)/)), the SOURCE is three real values long. The MOLD is a rank 1 array containing a complex number, which is two real values long. Therefore, the output will be a complex rank 1 array. In order to use all of the bits in SOURCE, the result of the function is a complex rank 1 array with two elements. The first element in the output array is (1.1,2.2), and the second element has a real part of 3.3 together with an unknown imaginary part.
- Example 3: In the function TRANSFER((/1.1,2.2,3.3/),(/(0.,0.)/),1), the SOURCE is three real values long. The MOLD is a rank 1 array containing a complex number, which is two real values long. Therefore, the output will be a complex rank 1 array. Since the *SIZE* is specified to be 1, only one complex value is produced. The result of the function is a complex rank 1 array with one element: (1.1,2.2).

TRANSPOSE(MATRIX)
- Transformational function of the same type as MATRIX.
- Transposes a matrix of rank 2. Element (i, j) of the output has the value of MATRIX(j,i).
- MATRIX is a rank 2 matrix of any type.

UBOUND(ARRAY,*DIM*)
- Integer inquiry function.
- Returns all of the upper bounds or a specified upper bound of ARRAY.
- ARRAY is an array of any type. It must not be an unassociated pointer or an unallocated allocatable array. *DIM* is an integer in the range $1 \le DIM \le r$. The corresponding actual argument must not be an optional argument in the calling procedure.

- If *DIM* is present, the result is a scalar. If the actual argument corresponding to ARRAY is an array section or an array expression, or if dimension *DIM* has zero size, then the function will return 1. Otherwise, it will return the upper bound of that dimension of ARRAY. If *DIM* is not present, then the function will return an array whose *i*th element is UBOUND(ARRAY,i) for $i=1, 2, \ldots, r$.

UPACK(VECTOR,MASK,FIELD)

- Transformational function of the same type as VECTOR.
- Unpacks a rank 1 array into an array under the control of a mask. The result is an array of the same type and type parameters as VECTOR and the same shape as MASK.
- VECTOR is a rank 1 array of any type. It must be at least as large as the number of true elements in MASK. MASK is a logical array. FIELD is of the same type as VECTOR and conformable with MASK.
- This function produces an array with the shape of MASK. The first element of the VECTOR is placed in the location corresponding to the first true value in MASK, the second element of VECTOR is placed in the location corresponding to the second true value in MASK, etc. If a location in MASK is false, then the corresponding element from FIELD is placed in the output array. If FIELD is a scalar, the same value is placed in the output array for all false locations.
- This function is the inverse of the PACK function.
- For example, suppose that V=[1 2 3],

$$M = \begin{bmatrix} TRUE & FALSE & FALSE \\ FALSE & FALSE & FALSE \\ TRUE & FALSE & TRUE \end{bmatrix}$$

and

$$F = \begin{bmatrix} 0 & 0 & 0 \\ 1 & 1 & 1 \\ 0 & 0 & 0 \end{bmatrix}$$

Then the function UNPACK(V,MASK=M,FIELD=0) would have the value

$$\begin{bmatrix} 1 & 0 & 0 \\ 1 & 1 & 1 \\ 2 & 0 & 3 \end{bmatrix}$$

and the function UNPACK(V,MASK=M,FIELD=F) would have the value

$$\begin{bmatrix} 1 & 0 & 0 \\ 1 & 1 & 1 \\ 2 & 0 & 3 \end{bmatrix}$$

B.9
MISCELLANEOUS INQUIRY FUNCTIONS

ALLOCATED(ARRAY)
- Logical inquiry function.
- Returns true if ARRAY is currently allocated, and false if ARRAY is not currently allocated. The result is undefined if the allocation status of ARRAY is undefined.
- ARRAY is any type of allocatable array.

ASSOCIATED(POINTER, *TARGET*)
- Logical inquiry function.
- There are three possible cases for this function:
  1. If *TARGET* is not present, this function returns true if POINTER is associated, and false otherwise.
  2. If *TARGET* is present and is a target, the result is true if TARGET does not have size zero and POINTER is currently associated with TARGET. Otherwise, the result is false.
  3. If *TARGET* is present and is a pointer, the result is true if both POINTER and TARGET are currently associated with the same non-zero-sized target. Otherwise, the result is false.
- POINTER is any type of pointer whose pointer association status is not undefined. *TARGET* is any type of pointer or target. If it is a pointer, its pointer association status must not be undefined.

PRESENT(A)
- Logical inquiry function.
- Returns true if optional argument A is present, and false otherwise.
- A is any optional argument.

B.10
MISCELLANEOUS PROCEDURE

MOVE_ALLOC(FROM,TO)
- Pure subroutine.
- Arguments:

| FROM | Any | INOUT | Allocatable scalar or array of any type and rank. |
| TO | Same as FROM | OUT | Allocatable scalar or array compatible with the FROM argument. |

- Transfers the current allocation from the FROM object to the TO object.
- The FROM object will be unallocated at the end of this subroutine.
- If the FROM object is unallocated at the time of the call, the TO object becomes unallocated.

F-2003 ONLY

- If the FROM object is allocated at the time of the call, the TO object becomes allocated with the type, type parameters, array bounds, and value originally in the FROM object.
- If the TO object has the TARGET attribute, then any pointers that used to point to the FROM object will now point to the TO object.
- If the TO object does not have the TARGET attribute, then any pointers that used to point to the FROM object will become undefined.
- Fortran 2003 only.

Order of Statements in a Fortran 95/2003 Program

Fortran programs consist of one or more program units, each of which contains at least two legal Fortran statements. Any number and type of program units may be included in the program, with the exception that one and only one main program may be included.

All Fortran statements may be grouped into one of 17 possible categories, which are listed below. (In this list, all undesirable, obsolescent, or deleted Fortran statements are shown in small type.)

1. Initial statements (PROGRAM, SUBROUTINE, FUNCTION, MODULE, and BLOCK DATA)
2. Comments
3. USE statements
4. IMPLICIT NONE statement
5. Other IMPLICIT statements
6. PARAMETER statements
7. DATA statements
8. Derived type definitions
9. Type declaration statements
10. Interface blocks
11. Statement function declarations
12. Other specification statements (PUBLIC, PRIVATE, SAVE, etc.)
13. FORMAT statements
14. ENTRY statements
15. Executable statements and constructs
16. CONTAINS statement
17. END statements (END PROGRAM, END FUNCTION, etc.)

The order in which these statements may appear in a program unit is specified in Table C-1. In this table, horizontal lines indicate varieties of statements that may not be mixed, while vertical lines indicate types of statements that may be interspersed.

Note from this table that nonexecutable statements generally precede executable statements in a program unit. The only nonexecutable statements that may be legally mixed with executable statements are FORMAT statements, ENTRY *statements*, and DATA *statements*. (The mixing of DATA statements among executable statements has been declared obsolescent as of Fortran 95.)

Table C-1
Requirements on Statement Ordering

PROGRAM, FUNCTION, MODULE, SUBROUTINE, or BLOCK DATA statement		
USE statements		
IMPORT statements		
IMPLICIT NONE statement		
FORMAT and ENTRY statements	PARAMETER statements	IMPLICIT statements
	PARAMETER and DATA statements	Derived type definitions, interface blocks, type declaration statements, enumeration definitions, procedure declarations, specification statements, and statement function statements
	DATA statements	Executable statements and constructs
CONTAINS statement		
Internal subprograms or module subprograms		
END statement		

In addition to the above constraints, not every type of Fortran statement may appear in every type of Fortran scoping unit. Table C-2 shows which types of Fortran statements are allowed in which scoping units.

Table C-2
Statements Allowed in Scoping Units

Kind of scoping unit:	Main program	Module	Block Data	External subprog	Module subprog	Internal subprog	Interface Body
USE statement	Yes	Yes	Yes	Yes	Yes	Yes	Yes
ENTRY statement	No	No	No	Yes	Yes	No	No
FORMAT statement	Yes	No	No	Yes	Yes	Yes	No
Miscellaneous declarations (see notes)	Yes	Yes	Yes	Yes	Yes	Yes	Yes
DATA statement	Yes	Yes	Yes	Yes	Yes	Yes	No
Derived-type definition	Yes	Yes	Yes	Yes	Yes	Yes	Yes
Interface block	Yes	Yes	No	Yes	Yes	Yes	Yes
Executable statement	Yes	No	No	Yes	Yes	Yes	No
CONTAINS statement	Yes	Yes	No	Yes	Yes	No	No
Statement function statement	Yes	No	No	Yes	Yes	Yes	No

Notes:

1. Miscellaneous declarations are PARAMETER statements, IMPLICIT statements, type declaration statements, and specification statements such as PUBLIC, SAVE, etc.
2. Derived type definitions are also scoping units, but they do not contain any of the above statements, and so have not been listed in the table.
3. The scoping unit of a module does not include any module subprograms that the module contains.

Glossary

This appendix contains a glossary of Fortran terms. Many of the definitions here are paraphrased from the definitions of terms in the Fortran 95 and 2003 Standards, ISO/IEC 1539: 1996 and ISO/IEC 1539: 2004.

abstract type   A derived type that has the ABSTRACT attribute. It can only be used as a basis for type extension—no objects of this type can be defined.

actual argument   An expression, variable, or procedure that is specified in a procedure invocation (a subroutine call or a function reference). It is associated with the dummy argument in the corresponding position of procedure definition, unless keywords are used to change the order of arguments.

algorithm   The "formula" or sequence of steps used to solve a specific problem.

allocatable array   An array specified as ALLOCATABLE with a certain type and rank. It can be allocated a certain extent with the ALLOCATE statement. The array cannot be referenced or defined until it has been allocated. When no longer needed, the corresponding storage area can be released with the DEALLOCATE statement.

allocatable variable   A variable, either intrinsic or user defined, specified as ALLOCATABLE. It can be allocated with the ALLOCATE statement. The variable cannot be referenced or defined until it has been allocated. When no longer needed, the corresponding storage area can be released with the DEALLOCATE statement.

allocation statement   A statement that allocates memory for an allocatable array or a pointer.

allocation status   A logical value indicating whether or not an allocatable array is currently allocated. It can be examined by using the ALLOCATED intrinsic function.

alpha release   The first completed version of a large program. The alpha release is normally tested by the programmers themselves and a few others very close to them, in order to discover the most serious bugs present in the program.

argument   A placeholder for a value or variable name that will be passed to a procedure when it is invoked (a dummy argument), or the value or variable name that is actually passed to the procedure when it is invoked (an actual argument). Arguments appear in parentheses after a procedure name both when the procedure is declared and when the procedure is invoked.

argument association   The relationship between an actual argument and a dummy argument during the execution of a procedure reference. Argument association is performed either by the relative position of actual and dummy arguments in the procedure reference and the procedure definition, or by means of argument keywords.

argument keyword   A dummy argument name. It may be used in a procedure reference followed by the equals symbol provided the procedure has an explicit interface.

argument list   A list of values and variables that are passed to a procedure when it is invoked. Argument lists appear in parentheses after a procedure name both when the procedure is declared and when the procedure is invoked.

array   A set of data items, all of the same type and kind, that are referred to by the same name. Individual elements within an array are accessed by using the array name followed by one or more subscripts.

array constructor   An array-valued constant.

array element   An individual data item within an array.

array element order   The order in which the elements of an array appear to be stored. The physical storage arrangement within a computer's memory may be different, but any reference to the array will make the elements appear to be in this order.

array overflow   An attempt to use an array element with an index outside the valid range for the array; an out-of-bounds reference.

array pointer   A pointer to an array.

array section   A subset of an array, which can be used and manipulated as an array in its own right.

array specification   A means of defining the name, shape, and size of an array in a type declaration statement.

array variable   An array-valued variable.

array-valued   Having the property of being an array.

array-valued function   A function whose result is an array.

ASCII   The American Standard Code for Information Interchange (ANSI X3.4 1977), a widely used internal character coding set. This set is also known as ISO 646 (International Reference Version).

ASCII collating sequence   The collating sequence of the ASCII character set.

assignment   Storing the value of an expression into a variable.

assignment operator   The equal (=) sign, which indicates that the value of the expression to the right of the equal sign should be assigned to the variable named on the left of the sign.

assignment statement   A Fortran statement that causes the value of an expression to be stored into a variable. The form of an assignment statement is "variable=expression".

associated   A pointer is associated with a target if it currently points to that target.

association status   A logical value indicating whether or not a pointer is currently associated with a target. The possible pointer association status values are: undefined, associated, and unassociated. It can be examined using the ASSOCIATED intrinsic function.

assumed-length character declaration   The declaration of a character dummy argument with an asterisk for its length. The actual length is determined from the corresponding actual argument when the procedure is invoked. For example:

```
CHARACTER(len=*) :: string
```

assumed-length character function   A character function whose *return length* is specified with an asterisk. These functions must have an explicit interface. They have been declared obsolescent in Fortran 95. In the example below, my_fun is an assumed length character function:

```
FUNCTION my_fun ( str1, str2 )
CHARACTER(len=*), INTENT(IN) :: str1, str2
CHARACTER(len=*) :: my_fun
```

assumed-shape array   A dummy array argument whose bounds in each dimension are represented by colons, with the actual bounds being obtained from the corresponding actual argument when the procedure is invoked. An assumed-shape array has a declared data type and rank, but its size is unknown until the procedure is actually executed. It may be used only in procedures with explicit interfaces. For example:

```
SUBROUTINE test( a, ... )
REAL, DIMENSION(:,:) :: a
```

assumed-size array   An older pre-Fortran 90 mechanism for declaring dummy arrays in procedures. In an assumed-size array, all of the dimensions of a dummy array are explicitly declared except for the last dimension, which is declared with an asterisk. Assumed-size arrays have been superseded by assumed-shape arrays.

F-2003 ONLY

asynchronous input/output   Input or output operations that can occur simultaneously with other Fortran statement executions. (Fortran 2003 only)

attribute   A property of a variable or constant that may be declared in a type declaration statement. Examples are PARAMETER, DIMENSION, SAVE, ALLOCATABLE, ASYNCHRONOUS, VOLATILE, and POINTER.

automatic array   An explicit-shape array that is local to a procedure, some or all of whose bounds are provided when the procedure is invoked. The array can have a different size and shape each time the procedure is invoked. When the procedure is invoked, the array is automatically allocated with the proper size, and when the procedure terminates, the array is automatically deallocated. In the example below, scratch is an automatic array:

```
SUBROUTINE my_sub ( a, rows, cols )
INTEGER :: rows, cols
...
REAL, DIMENSION(rows,cols) :: scratch
```

automatic length character function   A character function whose return length is specified when the function is invoked either by a dummy argument or by a value in a module or COMMON block. These functions must have an explicit interface. In the example below, my_fun is an automatic length character function:

```
FUNCTION my_fun ( str1, str2, n )
INTEGER, INTENT(IN) :: n
CHARACTER(len=*), INTENT(IN) :: str1, str2
CHARACTER(len=n) :: my_fun
```

automatic character variable   A local character variable in a procedure whose length is specified when the procedure is invoked either by a dummy argument or by a value in a module or COMMON block. When the procedure is invoked, the variable is automatically created with the proper size, and when the procedure terminates, the variable is automatically destroyed. In the example below, temp is an automatic character variable:

```
SUBROUTINE my_sub ( str1, str2, n )
CHARACTER(len=*) :: str1, str2
...
CHARACTER(len=n) :: temp
```

beta release   The second completed version of a large program. The beta release is normally given to "friendly" outside users who have a need for the program in their day-to-day jobs. These users exercise the program under many different conditions and with many different input data sets, and they report any bugs that they find to the program developers.

binary digit   A 0 or 1, the two possible digits in a base 2 system.

binary operator   An operator that is written between two operands. Examples include +, -, *, /, >, <, .AND, etc.

binary tree   A tree structure that splits into two branches at each node.

bit   A binary digit.

binding   The process of associating a procedure with a particular derived data type.

block   A sequence of executable statements embedded in an executable construct, bounded by statements that are particular to the construct, and treated as an integral unit. For example, the statements between IF and END IF below are a block.

```
IF ( x > 0. ) THEN
   ...
   (code block)
   ...
END IF
```

BLOCK DATA **program unit**   A program unit that provides initial values for variables in named COMMON blocks.

block IF **construct**   A program unit in which the execution of one or more blocks of statements is controlled by an IF statement, and optionally by one or more ELSE IF statements and up to one ELSE statement.

bound   An upper bound or a lower bound; the maximum or minimum value permitted for a subscript in an array.

F-2003 ONLY

bound procedure   A procedure that is bound to a derived data type, and that is accessible through the component selection syntax (i.e., using a variable name followed by the % component selector: a%proc()). (Fortran 2003 only)

bounds checking   The process of checking each array reference before it is executed to ensure that the specified subscripts are within the declared bounds of the array.

branch   (*a*) A transfer of control within a program, as in an IF or CASE structure. (*b*) A linked list that forms part of a binary tree.

bug   A programming error that causes a program to behave improperly.

byte   A group of 8 bits.

card identification field   Columns 73-80 of a fixed source form line. These columns are ignored by the compiler. In the past, these columns were used to number the individual cards in a source card deck.

central processing unit   The part of the computer that carries out the main data processing functions. It usually consists of one or more *control units* to select the data and the operations to be performed on it, and *arithmetic logic units* to perform arithmetic calculations.

character   (*a*) A letter, digit, or other symbol. (*b*) An intrinsic data type used to represent characters.

character constant edit descriptor   An edit descriptor that takes the form of a character constant in an output format. For example, in the statement

```
100 FORMAT (" X = ", x)
```

the "X = " is a character constant edit descriptor.

character context   Characters that form a part of a character literal constant or a character constant edit descriptor. Any legal character in a computer's character set may be used in a character context, not just those in the Fortran character set.

character data type   An intrinsic data type used to represent characters

character length parameter   The type parameter that specifies the number of characters for an entity of type character.

character operator   An operator that operates on character data.

character set   A collection of letters, numbers, and symbols that may be used in character strings. Three common characters sets are ASCII, EBCDIC, and Unicode.

character storage unit   The unit of storage that can hold a single character of the default type.

character string   A sequence of one or more characters.

character variable   A variable that can be used to store one or more characters.

F-2003 ONLY

child   A derived data type extended from a parent. It is defined with an EXTENDS clause.

class   The set of defined data types all extended from a single prototype, which is declared with the CLASS statement instead of the TYPE statement.

close   The process of terminating the link between a file and an input/output unit.

collating sequence   The order in which a particular character set is sorted by relational operators.

combinational operator   An operator whose operands are logical values, and whose result is a logical value. Examples include .AND., .OR., .NOT., etc.

comment   Text within a program unit that is ignored by a compiler, but provides information for the programmer. In free source form, comments begin with the first exclamation point (!) on a line that is not in a character context, and continue to the end of the line. In fixed source form, comments begin with a C or * in column 1, and continue to the end of the line.

COMMON block   A block of physical storage that may be accessed by any of the scoping units in a program. The data in the block is identified by its relative position, regardless of the name and type of the variable in that position.

compilation error   An error that is detected by a Fortran compiler during compilation.

compiler   A computer program that translates a program written in a computer language such as Fortran into the machine code used by a particular computer. The compiler usually translates the code into an intermediate form call object code, which is then prepared for execution by a separate linker.

complex   An intrinsic data type used to represent complex numbers.

complex constant   A constant of the complex type, written as an ordered pair of real values enclosed in parentheses. For example, (3.,-4.) is a complex constant.

complex number   A number consisting of a real part and an imaginary part.

component   One of the elements of a derived data type.

component order   The order of components in a derived data type.

component selector   The method of addressing a specific component within a structure. It consists of the structure name and the component name, separated by a percent (%) sign. For example, student%age.

computer   A device that stores both information (data) and instructions for modifying that information (programs). The computer executes programs to manipulate its data in useful ways.

concatenation   The process of attaching one character string to the end of another one, by means of a concatenation operator.

concatenation operator   An operator (//) that combines two characters strings to form a single character string.

conformable   Two arrays are said to be conformable if they have the same shape. A scalar is conformable with any array. Intrinsic operations are defined only for conformable data items.

constant   A data object whose value is unchanged throughout the execution of a program. Constants may be named (i.e., parameters) or unnamed.

construct   A sequence of statements starting with a DO, IF, SELECT CASE, FORALL, AS-SOCIATE, or WHERE statement and ending with the corresponding terminal statement.

construct association   The association between the selector of an ASSOCIATE or SELECT TYPE construct and the associated construct entity.

control character   The first character in an output buffer, which is used to control the vertical spacing for the current line.

control mask   In a WHERE statement or construct, an array of type logical whose value determines which elements of an array will be operated on. This definition also applies to the MASK argument in many array intrinsic functions.

counting loop   A DO loop that executes a specified number of times, based on the loop control parameters (also known as an iterative loop).

CPU   See central processing unit.

data   Information to be processed by a computer.

data abstraction   The ability to create new data types, together with associated operators, and to hide the internal structure and operations from the user.

data dictionary   A list of the names and definitions of all named variables and constants used in a program unit. The definitions should include both a description of the contents of the item and the units in which it is measured.

data hiding   The idea that some items in a program unit may not be accessible to other program units. Local data items in a procedure are hidden from any program unit that invokes the procedure. Access to the data items and procedures in a module may be controlled by using PUBLIC and PRIVATE statements.

data object   A constant or a variable.

data type   A named category of data that is characterized by a set of values, together with a way to denote these values and a collection of operations that interpret and manipulate the values.

deallocation statement   A statement that frees memory previously allocated for an allocatable array or a pointer.

debugging   Locating and eliminating bugs from a program.

decimal symbol   The character that separates the whole and fractional parts of a real number. This is a period in the United States, United Kingdom, and many other countries, and a comma in Spain, France, and some other parts of Europe.

default character set   The set of characters available for use by programs on a particular computer if no special action is taken to select another character set.

default complex   The kind of complex value used when no kind type parameter is specified.

default integer   The kind of integer value used when no kind type parameter is specified.

default kind   The kind type parameter used for a specific data type when no kind is explicitly specified. The default kinds of each data type are known as default integer, default real, default complex, etc. Default kinds vary from processor to processor.

default real   The kind of real value used when no kind type parameter is specified.

default typing   The type assigned to a variable when no type declaration statement is present in a program unit, based on the first letter of the variable name.

deferred-shape array   An allocatable array or a pointer array. The type and rank of these arrays are declared in type declaration statements, but the shape of the array is not determined until memory is allocated in an ALLOCATE statement.

defined assignment   A user-defined assignment that involves a derived data type. This is done with the INTERFACE ASSIGNMENT construct.

defined operation   A user-defined operation that either extends an intrinsic operation for use with derived types or defines a new operation for use with either intrinsic types or derived types. This is done with the INTERFACE OPERATOR construct.

deleted feature A feature of older versions of Fortran that has been deleted from later versions of the language. An example is the Hollerith (H) format descriptor.

dereferencing The process of accessing the corresponding target when a reference to a pointer appears in an operation or assignment statement.

derived type (or **derived data type**) A user-defined data type consisting of components, each of which is either of intrinsic type or of another derived type.

dimension attribute An attribute of a type declaration statement used to specify the number of subscripts in an array, and the characteristics of those subscripts such as their bounds and extent. This information can also be specified in a separate DIMENSION statement.

direct access Reading or writing the contents of a file in arbitrary order.

direct access file A form of file in which the individual records can be written and read in any order. Direct access files must have records of fixed length so that the location of any particular record can be quickly calculated.

disassociated A pointer is disassociated if it is not associated with a target. A pointer can be disassociated by using the NULLIFY() statement or the null() intrinsic function.

DO **construct** A loop that begins with a DO statement and ends with an END DO statement.

DO **loop** A loop that is controlled by a DO statement.

DO **loop index** The variable that is used to control the number of times the loop is executed in an iterative DO loop.

double precision A method of storing floating-point numbers on a computer that uses twice as much memory as single precision, resulting in more significant digits and (usually) a greater range in the representation of the numbers. Before Fortran 90, double precision variables were declared with a DOUBLE PRECISION type declaration statement. In Fortran 95 / 2003, they are just another kind of the real data type.

dummy argument An argument used in a procedure definition that will be associated with an actual argument when the procedure is invoked.

dynamic memory allocation Allocating memory for variables or arrays at execution time, as opposed to static memory allocation, which occurs at compilation time.

dynamic type The type of a data entity during execution. For polymorphic entities, it well be of the parent data type or a child of the parent type. For nonpolymorphic entities, it is the same as the declared data type.

dynamic variable A variable that is created when it is needed during the course of a program's execution, and that is destroyed when it is no longer needed. Examples are automatic arrays and character variables, allocatable arrays, and allocated pointer targets.

EBCDIC Extended Binary Coded Decimal Interchange Code. This is an internal character coding scheme used by IBM mainframes.

edit descriptor An item in a format that specifies the conversion between the internal and external representations of a data item. (Identical to format descriptor.)

elemental An adjective applied to an operation, procedure, or assignment that is applied independently to the elements of an array or corresponding elements of a set of conformable arrays and scalars. Elemental operations, procedures, or assignments may be easily partitioned among many processors in a parallel computer.

elemental function A function that is elemental.

elemental intrinsic procedure An intrinsic procedure that is defined for scalar inputs and outputs, but that can accept an array-valued argument or arguments and will deliver an array-valued result obtained by applying the procedure to the corresponding elements of the argument arrays in turn.

elemental procedure (user defined) A user-defined procedure that is defined with only scalar dummy arguments (no pointers or procedures) and with a scalar result (not a pointer). An elemental function must have no side effects, meaning that all arguments are INTENT(IN).

An elemental subroutine must have no side effects except for arguments explicitly specified with INTENT(OUT) or INTENT(INOUT). If the procedure is declared with the ELEMENTAL prefix, it will be able to accept an array-valued argument or arguments and will deliver an array-valued result obtained by applying the procedure to the corresponding elements of the argument arrays in turn. User-defined elemental procedures are available in Fortran 95 only.

end-of-file condition   A condition set when an endfile record is read from a file, which can be detected by an IOSTAT clause in a READ statement.

endfile record   A special record that occurs only at the end of a sequential file. It can be written by an ENDFILE statement.

error flag   A variable returned from a subroutine to indicate the status of the operation performed by the subroutine.

executable statement   A statement that causes the computer to perform some action during the execution of a program.

execution error   An error that occurs during the execution of a program (also called a runtime error).

explicit interface   A procedure interface that is known to the program unit that will invoke the procedure. An explicit interface to an external procedure may be created by an interface block, or by placing the external procedures in modules and then accessing them by USE association. An explicit interface is automatically created for any internal procedures, or for recursive procedures referencing themselves. (Compare with implicit interface, below.)

explicit-shape array   A named array that is declared with explicit bounds in every dimension.

explicit typing   Explicitly declaring the type of a variable in a type declaration statement (as opposed to default typing).

exponent   (*a*) In a binary representation, the power of 2 by which the mantissa is multiplied to produce a complete floating-point number. (*b*) In a decimal representation, the power of 10 by which the mantissa is multiplied to produce a complete floating-point number.

exponential notation   Representing real or floating-point numbers as a mantissa multiplied by a power of 10.

expression   A sequence of operands, operators, and parentheses where the operands may be variables, constants, or function references.

extent   The number of elements in a particular dimension of an array.

external file   A file that is stored on some external medium. This contrasts with an internal file, which is a character variable within a program.

external function   A function that is not an intrinsic function or an internal function.

external procedure   A function subprogram or a subroutine subprogram that is not a part of any other program unit.

external unit   An i/o unit that can be connected to an external file. External units are represented by numbers in Fortran I/O statements.

field width   The number of characters available for displaying an output formatted value or reading an input formatted value.

file   A unit of data that is held on some medium outside the memory of the computer. It is organized into records, which can be accessed individually by using READ and WRITE statements.

file storage unit   The basic unit of storage for an unformatted or stream file.

final subroutine   A subroutine that is called automatically by the processor during the finalization of a derived data entity.

finalizable   A derived data type that has final subroutine, or that has a finalizable component. Also, any object of a finalizable type.

finalization   The process of calling a final subroutine before an object is destroyed.

fixed source form   An obsolescent method of writing Fortran programs in which fixed columns were reserved for specific purposes. (Compare with free source form.)

floating point   A method of representing numbers in which the memory associated with the number is divided into separate fields for a mantissa (fractional part) and an exponent.

format   A sequence of edit descriptors that determines the interpretation of an input data record, or that specifies the form of an output data record. A format may be found in a FORMAT statement, or in a character constant or variable.

format descriptor   An item in a format that specifies the conversion between the internal and external representations of a data item. (Identical to edit descriptor.)

format statement   A labeled statement that defines a format.

formatted file   A file containing data stored as recognizable numbers, characters, etc.

formatted output statement   A formatted WRITE statement or PRINT statement.

formatted READ statement   A READ statement that uses format descriptors to specify how to translate the data in the input buffer as it is read.

formatted WRITE statement   A WRITE statement that uses format descriptors to specify how to format the output data as it is displayed.

F-2003 ONLY

Fortran Character Set   The 86 characters (97 in Fortran 2003) that can be used to write a Fortran program.

free format   List-directed I/O statements that do not require formats for either input or output.

free source form   The newer and preferred method of writing Fortran programs, in which any character position in a line can be used for any purpose. (Compare with fixed source form.)

function   A procedure that is invoked in an expression, and that computes a single result that is then used in evaluating the expression.

function reference   The use of a function name in an expression that invokes (executes) the function to carry out some calculation, and returns the result for use in evaluating the expression. A function is invoked or executed by naming it in an expression.

function subprogram   A program unit that begins with a FUNCTION statement and ends with an END FUNCTION statement.

function value   The value that is returned when the function executes.

generic function   A function that can be called with different types of arguments. For example, the intrinsic function ABS is a generic function, since it can be invoked with integer, real, or complex arguments.

generic interface block   A form of interface block used to define a generic name for a set of procedures

generic name   A name that is used to identify two or more procedures, with the required procedure being determined by the compiler at each invocation from the types of the nonoptional arguments in the procedure invocation. A generic name is defined for a set of procedures in a generic interface block.

global accessibility   The ability to directly access data and derived type definitions from any program unit. This capability is provided by USE association of modules.

global entity   An entity whose scope is that of the whole program. It may be a program unit, a common block, or an external procedure.

global storage   A block of memory accessible from any program unit—a COMMON block. Global storage in COMMON blocks has largely been replaced by global accessibility through modules.

guard digits   Extra digits in a mathematical calculation that are beyond the precision of the kind of real values used in the calculation. They are used to minimize truncation and roundoff errors.

head   The first item in a linked list.

hexadecimal   The base 16 number system, in which the legal digits are 0 through 9 and A through F.

host   A main program or subprogram that contains an internal subprogram is called the host of the internal subprogram. A module that contains a module subprogram is called the host of the module subprogram.

host association   The process by which data entities in a host scoping unit are made available to an inner scoping unit.

host scoping unit   A scoping unit that surrounds another scoping unit.

ill-conditioned system   A system of equations whose solution is highly sensitive to small changes in the values of its coefficients, or to truncation and roundoff errors.

imaginary part   The second of the two numbers that make up a COMPLEX data value.

implicit type declaration   Determining the type of a variable from the first letter of its name. Implicit type declaration should never be used in any modern Fortran program.

implicit interface   A procedure interface that is not fully known to the program unit that invokes the procedure. A Fortran program cannot detect type, size, or similar mismatches between actual arguments and dummy arguments when an implicit interface is used, so some programming errors will not be caught by the compiler. All pre-Fortran 90 interfaces were implicit. (Compare with explicit interface, above.)

implied DO loop   A shorthand loop structure used in input/output statements, array constructors, and DATA statements that specifies the order in which the elements of an array are used in that statement.

implied DO variable   A variable used to control an implied DO loop.

index array   An array containing indices to other arrays. Index arrays are often used in sorting to avoid swapping large chunks of data.

Inf   Infinite value returned by IEEE 754 arithmetic. It represents an infinite result.

infinite loop   A loop that never terminates, typically because of a programming error.

initial statement   The first statement of a program unit: a PROGRAM, SUBROUTINE, FUNCTION, MODULE, or BLOCK DATA statement.

initialization expression   A restricted form of constant expression that can appear as an initial value in a declaration statement. For example, the initialization expression in the following type declaration statement initializes pi to 3.141592.

```
REAL :: pi = 3.141592
```

input buffer   A section of memory used to hold a line of input data as it is entered from an input device such as a keyboard. When the entire line has been input, the input buffer is made available for processing by the computer.

input device   A device used to enter data into a computer. A common example is a keyboard.

input format   A format used in a formatted input statement.

input list   The list of variable, array, and/or array element names in a READ statement into which data is to be read.

input statement   A READ statement.

input/output unit   A number, asterisk, or name in an input/output statement referring to either an external unit or an internal unit. A number is used to refer to an external file unit, which may be connected to a specific file by using an OPEN statement and disconnected by using a CLOSE statement. An asterisk is used to refer to the standard input and output devices for a processor. A name is used to refer to an internal file unit that is just a character variable in the program's memory.

inquiry intrinsic function   An intrinsic function whose result depends on properties of the principal argument other than the value of the argument.

integer   An intrinsic data type used to represent whole numbers.

integer arithmetic   Mathematical operations involving only data of the integer data type.

integer division   Division of one integer by another integer. In integer division, the fractional part of the result is lost. Thus the result of dividing the integer 7 by the integer 4 is 1.

interface   The name of a procedure, the names and characteristics of its dummy arguments, and (for functions) the characteristics of the result variable.

interface assignment block   An interface block used to extend the meaning of the assignment operator (=).

interface block   (*a*) A means of making an interface to a procedure explicit. (*b*) A means of defining a generic procedure, operator, or assignment.

interface body   A sequence of statements in an interface block from a FUNCTION or SUB-ROUTINE statement to the corresponding END statement. The body specifies the calling sequence of the function or subroutine.

interface function   A function used to isolate calls to processor-specific procedures from the main portion of a program.

interface operator block   An interface block used to define a new operator or to extend the meaning of a standard Fortran operator (+, -, *, /, >, etc.).

internal file   A character variable that can be read from and written to by normal formatted READ and WRITE statements.

internal function   An internal procedure that is a function.

internal procedure   A subroutine or function that is contained within another program unit, and that can be invoked only from within that program unit.

intrinsic data type   One of the predefined data types in Fortran: integer, real, double precision, logical, complex, and character.

intrinsic function   An intrinsic procedure that is a function.

intrinsic module   A module that is defined as a part of the standard Fortran language.

intrinsic procedure   A procedure that is defined as a part of the standard Fortran language (see Appendix B).

intrinsic subroutine   An intrinsic procedure that is a subroutine.

iterative DO loop   A DO loop that executes a specified number of times, based on the loop control parameters (also known as a counting loop).

i/o unit   See input/output unit.

invoke   To CALL a subroutine, or to reference a function in an expression.

iteration count   The number of times that an iterative DO loop is executed.

iterative DO loop   A DO loop that executes a specified number of times, based on the loop control parameters (also known as a counting loop).

keyword   A word that has a defined meaning in the Fortran language.

keyword argument   A method of specifying the association between dummy arguments and actual arguments of the form: "DUMMY_ARGUMENT=actual_argument". Keyword arguments permit arguments to be specified in any order when a procedure is invoked, and are especially useful with optional arguments. Keyword arguments may only be used in procedures with explicit interfaces. An example of the use of a keyword argument is:

```
kind_value = SELECTED_REAL_KIND(r=100)
```

kind   All intrinsic data types except for DOUBLE PRECISION may have more than one, processor-dependent, representation. Each representation is known as a different kind of that type, and is identified by a processor-dependent integer called a kind type parameter.

kind selector   The means of specifying the kind type parameter of a variable or named constant.

kind type parameter   An integer value used to identify the kind of an intrinsic data type.

language extension   The ability to use the features of a language to extend the language for other purposes. The principal language extension features of Fortran are derived types, user-defined operations, and data hiding.

lexical functions   Intrinsic functions used to compare two character strings in a character-set-independent manner

librarian   A program that creates and maintains libraries of compiled object files.

library   A collection of procedures that are made available for use by a program. They may be in the form of modules or separately linked object libraries.

line printer   A type of printer used to print Fortran programs and output on large computer systems. It got its name from the fact that large line printers print an entire line at a time.

link   The process of combining object modules produced from program units to form an executable program.

linked list   A data structure in which each element contains a pointer that points to the next element in the structure. (It sometimes contains a pointer to the previous element as well.)

list-directed input   A special type of formatted input in which the format used to interpret the input data is selected by the processor in accordance with the type of the data items in the input list.

list-directed I/O statement   An input or output statement that uses list-directed input or output.

list-directed output   A special type of formatted output in which the format used to display the output data is selected by the processor in accordance with the type of the data items in the output list.

literal constant   A constant whose value is written directly, as opposed to a named constant. For example, 14.4 is a literal constant.

local entity   An entity defined within a single scoping unit.

local variable   A variable declared within a program unit, which is not also in a COMMON block. Such variables are local to that scoping unit.

logical   A data type that can have only two possible values: TRUE or FALSE.

logical constant   A constant with a logical value: TRUE or FALSE.

logical error   A bug or error in a program caused by a mistake in program design (improper branching, looping, etc.).

logical expression   An expression whose result is either TRUE or FALSE.

logical IF statement   A statement in which a logical expression controls whether or not the rest of the statement is executed.

logical operator   An operator whose result is a logical value. There are two types of logical operators: combinational (.AND., .OR., .NOT., etc.) and relational (>, <, ==, etc.).

logical variable   A variable of type LOGICAL.

loop   A sequence of statements repeated multiple times, and usually controlled by a DO statement.

loop index   An integer variable that is incremented or decremented each time an iterative DO loop is executed.

lower bound   The minimum value permitted for a subscript of an array.

machine language   The collection of binary instructions (also called op codes) actually understood and executed by a particular processor.

main memory   The computer memory used to store programs that are currently being executed and the data associated with them. This is typically semiconductor memory.

Main memory is typically much faster than secondary memory, but it is also much more expensive.

main program   A program unit that starts with a PROGRAM statement. Execution begins here when a program is started. There can be only one main program unit in any program.

mantissa   (*a*) In a binary representation, the fractional part of a floating-point number which, when multiplied by a power of two, produces the complete number. The power of two required is known as the exponent of the number. The value of the mantissa is always between 0.5 and 1.0. (*b*) In a decimal representation, the fractional part of a floating-point number that, when multiplied by a power of 10, produces the complete number. The power of 10 required is known as the exponent of the number. The value of the mantissa is always between 0.0 and 1.0.

many-one array section   An array section with a vector subscript having two or more elements with the same value. Such an array section cannot appear on the left side of an assignment statement.

mask   (*a*) A logical expression that is used to control assignment of array elements in a masked array assignment (a WHERE statement or a WHERE construct). (*b*) A logical argument in several array intrinsic functions that determines which array elements will be included in the operation.

masked array assignment   An array assignment statement whose operation is controlled by a logical MASK that is the same shape as the array. The operation specified in the assignment statement is applied only to those elements of the array corresponding to true elements of the MASK. Masked array assignments are implemented as WHERE statements or WHERE constructs.

matrix   A rank 2 array.

mixed-mode expression   An arithmetic expression involving operands of different types. For example, the addition of a real value and an integer is a mixed-mode expression.

module   A program unit that allows other program units to access constants, variables, derived type definitions, interfaces, and procedures declared within it by USE association.

module procedure   A procedure contained within a module.

name   A lexical token consisting of a letter followed by up to 30 alphanumeric characters (letters, digits, and underscores). The named entity could be a variable, a named constant, a pointer, or a program unit.

name association   Argument association, USE association, host association, or construct association.

named constant   A constant that has been named by a PARAMETER attribute in a type declaration statement, or by a PARAMETER statement.

NAMELIST **input/output**   A form of input or output in which the values in the data are accompanied by the names of the corresponding variables, in the form "NAME=*value*". NAMELISTs are defined once in each program unit, and can be used repeatedly in many I/O statements. NAMELIST input statements can be used to update only a portion of the variables listed in the NAMELIST.

NaN   Not-a-number value returned by IEEE 754 arithmetic. It represents an undefined value or the result of an illegal operation.

nested   The inclusion of one program construct as a part of another program construct, such as nested DO loops or nested block IF constructs.

node   An element in a linked list or binary tree.

nonadvancing input/output   A method of formatted I/O in which each READ, WRITE, or PRINT statement does not necessarily begin a new record.

nonexecutable statement   A statement used to configure the program environment in which computational actions take place. Examples include the `IMPLICIT NONE` statement and type declaration statements.

numeric type   Integer, real, or complex data type.

object   A data object.

object designator   A designator for a data object.

object module   The file output by most compilers. Multiple object modules are combined with libraries in a linker to produce the final executable program.

obsolescent feature   A feature from earlier versions of Fortran that is considered to be redundant but that is still in frequent use. Obsolescent features have been replaced by better methods in later versions of Fortran. An example is the fixed source form, which has been replaced by free form. Obsolescent features are candidates for deletion in future versions of Fortran as their use declines.

octal   The base 8 number system, in which the legal digits are 0 through 7.

one-dimensional array   A rank 1 array, or vector.

operand   An expression that precedes or follows an operator.

operation   A computation involving one or two operands.

operator   A character or sequence of characters that defines an operation. There are two kinds: unary operators, which have one operand, and binary operators, which have two operands.

optional argument   A dummy argument in a procedure that does not need to have a corresponding actual argument every time that the procedure is invoked. Optional arguments may exist only in procedures with an explicit interface.

out-of-bounds reference   A reference to an array using a subscript either smaller than the lower bound or larger than the upper bound of the corresponding array dimension.

output buffer   A section of memory used to hold a line of output data before it is sent to an output device.

output device   A device used to output data from a computer. Common examples are printers and cathode-ray tube (CRT) displays.

output format   A format used in a formatted output statement.

output statement   A statement that sends formatted or unformatted data to an output device or file.

parameter attribute   An attribute in a type declaration statement that specifies that the named item is a constant instead of a variable.

parameterized variable   A variable whose kind is explicitly specified.

F-2003 ONLY

parent   The type being extended in an extended derived data type. This type appears in the parentheses after the `EXTENDS(parent_type)` clause.

pass-by-reference   A scheme in which arguments are exchanged between procedures by passing the memory locations of the arguments, instead of the values of the arguments.

pointer   A variable that has the `POINTER` attribute. A pointer may not be referenced or defined unless it is a pointer associated with a target. If it is an array, it does not have a shape until it is associated, although it does have a rank. When a pointer is associated with a target, it contains the memory address of the target, and thus "points" to it.

pointer array   An array that is declared with the `POINTER` attribute. Its rank is determined in the type declaration statement, but its shape and size are not known until memory is allocated for the array in an `ALLOCATE` statement.

pointer assignment statement   A statement that associates a pointer with a target. Pointer assignment statements take the form `pointer => target`.

pointer association   The process by which a pointer becomes associated with a target. The association status of a pointer can be checked with the ASSOCIATED intrinsic function.

pointer attribute   An attribute in a type declaration statement that specifies that the named item is a pointer instead of a variable.

polymorphic   Able to be of different types during program execution. A derived data type declared with the CLASS keyword is polymorphic.

pre-connected   An input or output unit that is automatically connected to the program and does not require an OPEN statement. Examples are the standard input and standard output units.

precision   The number of significant decimal digits that can be represented in a floating-point number.

present   A dummy argument is present in a procedure invocation if it is associated with an actual argument, and the corresponding actual argument is present in the invoking program unit. The presence of a dummy argument can be checked with the PRESENT intrinsic function.

printer control character   The first character of each output buffer. When it is sent to the printer, it controls the vertical movement of the paper before the line is written.

private   An entity in a module that is not accessible outside the module by USE association; declared by a PRIVATE attribute or in a PRIVATE statement.

procedure   A subroutine or function.

procedure interface   The characteristics of a procedure, the name of the procedure, the name of each dummy argument, and the generic identifiers (if any) by which it may be referenced.

processor   A processor is the combination of a specific computer with a specific compiler. Processor-dependent items can vary from computer to computer, or from compiler to compiler on the same computer.

program   A sequence of instructions on a computer that causes the computer to carry out some specific function.

program unit   A main program, a subroutine, a function, a module, or a block data subprogram. Each of these units is separately compiled.

pseudocode   A set of English statements structured in a Fortran-like manner, and used to outline the approach to be taken in solving a problem without getting buried in the details of Fortran syntax.

public   An entity in a module that is accessible outside the module by USE association; declared by a PUBLIC attribute or in a PUBLIC statement. An entity in a module is public by default.

pure procedure   A pure procedure is a procedure without side effects. A pure function must not modify its dummy arguments in any fashion, and all arguments must be INTENT(IN). A pure subroutine must have no side effects except for arguments explicitly specified with INTENT(OUT) or INTENT(INOUT). Such a procedure is declared with a PURE prefix, and pure functions may be used in specification expressions to initialize data in type declaration statements. Note that all elemental procedures are also pure.

random access   Reading or writing the contents of a file in arbitrary order.

random access file   Another name for a direct access file: a form of file in which the individual records can be written and read in any order. Direct access files must have records of fixed length so that the location of any particular record can be quickly calculated.

random access memory (RAM)   The semiconductor memory used to store the programs and data that are actually being executed by a computer at a particular time.

range   The difference between the largest and smallest numbers that can be represented on a computer with a given data type and kind. For example, on most computers a single-precision real number has a range of 10^{-38} to 10^{38}, 0, and -10^{-38} to -10^{38}.

rank   The number of dimensions of an array. The rank of a scalar is zero. The maximum rank of a Fortran array is 7.

rank 1 array   An array having only one dimension, where each array element is addressed with a single subscript.

rank 2 array   An array having two dimensions, where each array element is addressed with two subscripts.

rank *n* array   An array having *n* dimensions, where each array element is addressed with *n* subscripts.

real   An intrinsic data type used to represent numbers with a floating-point representation.

real number   A number of the REAL data type.

real part   The first of the two numbers that make up a COMPLEX data value.

record   A sequence of values or characters that is treated as a unit within a file. (A record is a "line" or unit of data from a file.)

record number   The index number of a record in a direct access (or random access) file.

recursion   The invocation of a procedure by itself, either directly or indirectly. Recursion is allowed only if the procedure is declared with the RECURSIVE keyword.

recursive   Capable of being invoked recursively.

reference   The appearance of a data object name in a context requiring the value at that point during execution, the appearance of a procedure name, its operator symbol, or a defined assignment statement in a context requiring execution of the procedure at that point, or the appearance of a module name in a USE statement. Neither the act of defining a variable nor the appearance of the name of a procedure as an actual argument is regarded as a reference.

relational expression   A logical expression in which two nonlogical operands are compared by a relational operator to give a logical value for the expressions.

relational operator   An operator that compares two nonlogical operands and returns a TRUE or FALSE result. Examples include $>$, $>=$, $<$, $<=$, $==$, and $/=$.

repeat count   The number before a format descriptor or a group of format descriptors that specifies the number of times that they are to be repeated. For example, the descriptor 4F10.4 is used 4 times.

root   (*a*) The solution to an equation of the form $f(x) = 0$; (*b*) The node from which a binary tree grows.

round-off error   The cumulative error that occurs during floating-point operations when the result of each calculation is rounded off to the nearest value representable with a particular kind of real value.

result variable   The variable that returns the value of a function.

runtime error   An error that manifests itself only when a program is executed.

SAVE attribute   An attribute in the type declaration statement of a local variable in a procedure that specifies that value of the named item is to be preserved between invocations of the procedure. This attribute can also be specified in a separate SAVE statement.

scalar variable   A variable that is not an array variable. The variable name refers to a single item of an intrinsic or derived type, and no subscripts are used with the name.

scope   The part of a program in which a name or entity has a specified interpretation. There are three possible scopes in Fortran: global scope, local scope, and statement scope.

scoping unit   A scoping unit is a single region of local scope within a Fortran program. All local variables have a single interpretation throughout a scoping unit. The scoping units in Fortran are: (1) a derived type definition, (2) an interface body, excluding any derived-type definitions and interface bodies within it, and (3) a program unit or subprogram, excluding derived-type definitions, interface bodies, and subprograms within it.

scratch file   A temporary file that is used by a program during execution, and that is automatically deleted when it is closed. A scratch file may not be given a name.

secondary memory   The computer memory used to store programs that are not currently being executed and the data that is not currently needed. This is typically a disk. Secondary memory is typical much slower than main memory, but it is also much cheaper.

sequential access   Reading or writing the contents of a file in sequential order.

sequential file   A form of file in which each record is read or written in sequential order. Sequential files do not require a fixed record length. They are the default file type in Fortran.

shape   The rank and extent of an array in each of its dimensions. The shape can be stored in a rank 1 array, with each element of the array containing the extent of one dimension.

side effects   The modification by a function of the variables in its input argument list, or variables in modules made available by USE association, or variables in COMMON blocks.

single-precision   A method of storing floating-point numbers on a computer that uses less memory than double precision, resulting in fewer significant digits and (usually) a smaller range in the representation of the numbers. Single-precision numbers are the "default real" type, the type of real number that results if no kind is specified.

size   The total number of elements in an array.

source form   The style in which a Fortran program is written—either free form or fixed form.

specific function   A function that must always be called with a single type of argument. For example, the intrinsic function IABS is a specific function, while the intrinsic function ABS is a generic function.

specification expression   A restricted form of scalar integer constant expression that can appear in a type specification statement as a bound in an array declaration or as the length in a character declaration.

specifier   An item in a control list that provides additional information for the input/output statement in which it appears. Examples are the input/output unit number and the format specification for READ and WRITE statements.

statement entity   An entity whose scope is a single statement or part of a statement, such as the index variable in the implied DO loop of an array constructor.

statement label   A number preceding a statement that can be used to refer to that statement.

static memory allocation   Allocating memory for variables or arrays at compilation time, as opposed to dynamic memory allocation, which occurs during program execution.

static variable   A variable allocated at compilation time, and remaining in existence throughout the execution of a program.

storage association   A method of associating two or more variables or arrays by aligning their physical storage in a computer's memory. This was commonly achieved with COMMON blocks and EQUIVALENCE statements, but is not recommended for new programs.

stride   The increment specified in a subscript triplet.

structure   (1) An item of a derived data type. (2) An organized, standard way to describe an algorithm.

structure constructor   An unnamed (or literal) constant of a derived type. It consists of the name of the type followed by the components of the type in parentheses. The components appear in the order in which they were declared in the definition of the derived type. For example the following line declares a constant of type `person`:

```
john = person('John', 'R', 'Jones', '323-6439',21, 'M', '123-45-6789')
```

structure component   A part of an object of derived type that may be referenced by a component selector. A component selector consists of the object's name followed by the component's name, separated by a percent sign (%).

subroutine   A procedure that is invoked by a `CALL` statement, and that returns its result through its arguments.

subscript   One of the integer values in parentheses following an array name, which are used to identify a particular element of the array. There is one subscript value for each dimension of the array.

subscript triplet   A method of specifying one dimension of an array section by means of the initial and final values and a stride. The three components of the subscript triplet are written separated by colons, and some of them may be defaulted. For example, the following array section contains two subscript triplets: `array(1:3:2,2:4)`.

substring   A contiguous portion of a scalar character string.

substring specification   The specification of a substring of a character string. The specification takes the form `char_var(istart:iend)`, where `char_var` is the name of a character variable, `istart` is the first character in `char_var` to include in the substring, and `iend` is the first character in `char_var` to include in the substring.

syntax error   An error in the syntax of a Fortran statement, detected by the compiler during compilation.

tail   The last item in a linked list.·

target   A variable that has the `TARGET` attribute, and that can be the destination of a pointer.

test driver program   A small program that is written specifically to invoke a procedure for the purpose of testing it.

top-down design   The process of analyzing a problem by starting with the major steps, and successively refining each step until all of the small steps are easy to implement in Fortran code.

transformational intrinsic function   An intrinsic function that is neither an elemental function nor an inquiry function. It usually has array arguments and an array result whose elements have values that depend on the values of many of the elements of the arguments.

tree   A form of linked list in which each node points to two or more other nodes. If each node points to two other nodes, the structure is a binary tree.

truncation   (*a*) The process in which the fractional part of a real number is discarded before the number is assigned to an integer variable. (*b*) The process in which excess characters are removed from the right-hand side of a character string before it is assigned to a character variable of shorter length.

truncation error   (*a*) The error caused by terminating a calculation before it is complete. (*b*) The cumulative error that occurs during floating-point operations when the result of each calculation is truncated to the next lower value representable with a particular kind of real values.

truth table   A table showing the result of a combinational logic expression for all possible combinations of operand values.

two-dimensional array   A rank 2 array.

type declaration statement   A statement that specifies the type and optionally the attributes of one or more variables or constants: An INTEGER, REAL, DOUBLE PRECISION, COMPLEX, CHARACTER, LOGICAL, or TYPE (type-name) statement.

type parameter   A parameter of an intrinsic data type. KIND and LEN are the type parameters.

ultimate type   A structure component that is of intrinsic type. Structure components of derived data types are *not* ultimate types.

unary operator   An operator that has only one operand, such as .NOT. and the unary minus.

undefined   A data entity that does not have a defined value.

unformatted file   A file containing data stored in a sequence of bit patterns that are a direct copy of a portion of the computer's memory. Unformatted files are processor dependent, and can be produced only by unformatted WRITE statements and read by unformatted READ statements on the particular type of processor that produced them.

unformatted input statement   An unformatted READ statement.

unformatted output statement   An unformatted WRITE statement.

unformatted READ statement   A READ statement that does not contain a format specifier. Unformatted READ statements transfer bit patterns directly from an external device into memory without interpretation.

unformatted record   A record consisting of a sequence of bit patterns that are a direct copy of a portion of the computer's memory. Unformatted records are processor dependent, and can be produced only by unformatted WRITE statements and read by unformatted READ statements on the particular type of processor that produced them.

unformatted WRITE statement   A WRITE statement that does not contain a format specifier. Unformatted WRITE statements transfer bit patterns directly from a processor's memory to an external device without interpretation.

unicode   An internal character coding scheme that uses two bytes to represent each character. The unicode system can represent 65,536 possible different characters. The first 128 unicode characters are identical to the ASCII character set, and other blocks of characters are devoted to various languages such as Chinese, Japanese, Hebrew, Arabic, and Hindi.

uninitialized array   An array, some or all of whose elements have not been initialized.

uninitialized variable   A variable that has been defined in a type declaration statement, but for which no initial value has been assigned.

unit   An input/output unit.

unit specifier   A specifier that specifies the unit on which input or output is to occur.

unit testing   The process of testing individual procedures separately and independently before they are combined into a final program.

upper bound   The maximum value permitted for a subscript of an array.

USE association   The manner in which the contents of a module are made available for use in a program unit.

USE statement   A statement that references a module in order to make the contents of the module available for use in the program unit containing it.

value separator   A comma, a space, a slash, or end of record that separates two data values in a list-directed input.

variable   A data object whose value may be changed during program execution.

variable declaration   The declaration of the type and, optionally, the attributes of a variable.

varying string   A form of character data in which the length is not fixed at the time of the declaration of the character variable, but may vary during the execution of the program. Varying strings are not a part of the Fortran 95/2003 standard, but are included in a Fortran auxiliary standard.

vector   A rank 1 array.

vector subscript   A method of specifying an array section by a rank 1 array containing the subscripts of the elements to include in the array section.

well-conditioned system   A system of equations whose solution is relatively insensitive to small changes in the values of its coefficients, or to truncation and round-off errors.

while loop   A loop that executes indefinitely until some specified condition is satisfied.

whole array   An array that has a name.

WHERE **construct**   The construct used in a masked array assignment.

word   The fundamental unit of memory on a particular computer. The size of a word varies from processor to processor, but it typically is either 16, 32, or 64 bits.

work array   A temporary array used for the storage of intermediate results. This can be implemented as an automatic array in Fortran 95/2003.

Answers to Quizzes

QUIZ 1–1

1. (a) 11011_2 (b) 1011_2 (c) 100011_2 (d) 1111111_2
2. (a) 14_{10} (b) 85_{10} (c) 9_{10}
3. (a) 162655_8 or $E5AD_{16}$ (b) 1675_8 or $3BD_{16}$ (c) 113477_8 or $973F_{16}$
4. $131_{10} = 10000011_2$, so the fourth bit is a zero.
5. (a) ASCII: M; EBCDIC: ((b) ASCII: {; EBCDIC: # (c) ASCII: (unused); EBCDIC: 9
6. (a) –32768 (b) 32767
7. Yes, a 4-byte variable of the real data type can be used to store larger numbers than a 4-byte variable of the integer data type. The 8 bits of exponent in a real variable can represent values as large as 10^{38}. A 4-byte integer can represent only values as large as 2,147,483,647 (about 10^9). To do this, the real variable is restricted to 6 or 7 decimal digits of precision, while the integer variable has 9 or 10 decimal digits of precision.

QUIZ 2–1

1. Valid integer constant.
2. Invalid—Commas not permitted within constants.
3. Invalid—Real constants must have a decimal point.
4. Invalid—Single quotes within a character string delimited by single quotes must be doubled. Correct forms are: `'That"s ok! '` or `"That's ok! "`.
5. Valid integer constant.
6. Valid real constant.
7. Valid character constant.
8. Valid character constant.
9. Invalid—Character constants must be enclosed by symmetrical single or double quotes.
10. Valid character constant.
11. Valid real constant.
12. Invalid—real exponents are expressed using the E symbol instead of ^.
13. Same
14. Same
15. Different
16. Different
17. Valid program name.
18. Invalid—Program name must begin with a letter.
19. Valid integer variable.
20. Valid real variable.

21. Invalid—Name must begin with a letter.
22. Valid real variable.
23. Invalid—Name must begin with a letter.
24. Invalid—no double colons (: :) present.
25. Valid.

QUIZ 2–2

1. The order is (1) exponentials, working from right to left; (2) multiplications and divisions, working from left to right; (3) additions and subtractions, working from left to right. Parentheses modify this order—terms in parentheses are evaluated first, starting from the innermost parentheses and working outward.
2. (a) Legal: Result = 12; (b) Legal: Result = 42; (c) Legal: Result = 2; (d) Legal: Result = 2; (e) Illegal: Division by 0; (f) Legal: Result = –40.5; note that this result is legal because exponentiation precedes negation in operator precedence. It is equivalent to the expression: `-(3.**(4./2.))`, and does *not* involve taking the real power of a negative number.; (g) Legal: Result = 0.111111; (h) Illegal: two adjacent operators.
3. (a) 7; (b) −21; (c) 7; (d) 9
4. (a) Legal: Result = 256; (b) Legal: Result = 0.25; (c) Legal: Result = 4; (d) Illegal: negative real number raised to a real power; (e) Legal: Result = 0.25; (f) Legal: Result = −0.125
5. The statements are illegal, because they try to assign a value to named constant `k`.
6. `Result = 43.5`
7. `a = 3.0; b = 3.333333; n = 3`

QUIZ 2–3

1. `r_eq = r1 + r2 + r3 + r4`
2. `r_eq = 1. / ( 1./r1 + 1./r2 + 1./r3 + 1./r4 )`
3. `t = 2. * pi * SQRT( l / g )`
4. `v = v_max * EXP( - alpha * t ) * COS( omega * t )`
5. $d = \frac{1}{2}at^2 + v_0 t + x_0$
6. $f = \dfrac{1}{2\pi\sqrt{LC}}$
7. $E = \frac{1}{2}Li^2$
8. The results are
   `126      5.000000E-02`
   Make sure that you can explain why `a` is equal to 0.05!
9. The results are shown below. Can you explain why each value was assigned to a given variable by the `READ` statements?
   `1    3    180    2.000000    30.000000    3.4899499E-02`

QUIZ 3–1

1. (*a*) Legal: Result = `.FALSE.`; (*b*) Illegal: `.NOT.` works only with logical values; (*c*) Legal: Result = `.TRUE.`; (*d*) Legal: Result = `.TRUE.`; (*e*) Legal: Result = `.TRUE.`; (*f*) Legal: Result = `.TRUE.`; (*g*) Legal: Result = `.FALSE.`; (*h*) Illegal: `.OR.` works only with logical values.
2. An `F` (for false) will be printed, because `i + j` = 4 while `k` = 2, so that the expression `i + j == k` evaluates to be false.

QUIZ 3–2

1.
```
IF ( x >= 0. ) THEN
    sqrt_x = SQRT( x )
    WRITE (*,*) 'The square root of x is ', sqrt_x
ELSE
    WRITE (*,*) 'Error--x < 0!'
    sqrt_x = 0.
END IF
```

2.
```
IF ( ABS(denominator) < 1.0E-10 ) THEN
    WRITE (*,*) 'Divide by zero error!'
ELSE
    fun = numerator / denominator
    WRITE (*,*) 'FUN = ', fun
END IF
```

3.
```
IF ( distance > 300. ) THEN
    cost = 70. + 0.20 * ( distance - 300. )
ELSE IF ( distance > 100. ) THEN
    cost = 30. + 0.20 * ( distance - 100. )
ELSE
    cost = 0.30 * distance
END IF
average_cost = cost / distance
```

4. These statements are incorrect. There is no `ELSE` in front of `IF (VOLTS < 105.)`.
5. These statements are correct. They will print out the warning because `warn` is true, even though the speed limit is not exceeded.
6. These statements are incorrect, since a real value is used to control the operation of a `CASE` statement.
7. These statements are correct. They will print out the message `'Prepare to stop.'`.
8. These statements are technically correct, but they are unlikely to do what the user intended. If the temperature is greater than 100°, then the user probably wants `'Boiling point of water exceeded'` to be printed out. Instead, the message `'Human body temperature exceeded'` will be printed out, since the `IF` structure executes the first true branch that it comes to. If the temperature is greater than 100°, it is also greater than 37°.

QUIZ 4–1

1. 6
2. 0
3. 1
4. 7
5. 6
6. 0
7. ires = 10
8. ires = 55
9. ires = 10 (Note that once ires = 10, the loop will begin to cycle, and ires will never be updated again no matter how many times the loop executes!)
10. ires = 100
11. ires = 60
12. Invalid: These statements redefine DO loop index i within the loop.
13. Valid.
14. Illegal: DO loops overlap.

QUIZ 4–2

1. (a) Legal: Result = .FALSE. (b) Legal: Result = .TRUE. (c) Legal: Result = 'Hello there' (d) Legal: Result = 'Hellothere'
2. (a) Legal: Result = 'bcd' (b) Legal: Result = 'ABCd' (c) Legal: Result = .FALSE. (d) Legal: Result = .TRUE. (e) Illegal: can't compare character strings and integers (f) Legal: Result = .TRUE. (g) Legal: Result = .FALSE.
3. The length of str3 is 20, so the first WRITE statement produces a 20. The contents of str3 are 'Hello World' (with 5 blanks in the middle), so the trimmed length of the string is 15. After the next set of manipulations, the contents of str3 are 'HelloWorld', so the third WRITE statement prints out 20 and the fourth one prints out 10.

QUIZ 5–1

Note: There is more than one way to write each of the FORMAT statements in this quiz. Each of the answers shown below represents one of many possible correct answers to these questions.

1. WRITE (*,100)
   100 FORMAT ('1',24X,'This is a test!')
2. WRITE (*,110) i, j, data1
   100 FORMAT ('0',2I10,F10.2)
3. WRITE (*,110) result
   110 FORMAT ('1',T13,'The result .is ',ES12.4)
4.
```
    -.0001**********    3.1416
----|----|----|----|----|----|
    5   10   15   20   25   30
```
5.
```
      .000    .602E+24    3.14159
----|----|----|----|----|----|
    5   10   15   20   25   30
```

6. `********** 6.0200E+23    3.1416`
```
----|----|----|----|----|----|
    5   10   15   20   25   30
```
7. `32767`
`   24`
`*****`
```
----|----|----|----|----|----|
    5   10   15   20   25   30
```
8. `   32767 00000024 -1010101`
```
----|----|----|----|----|----|
    5   10   15   20   25   30
```
9. `ABCDEFGHIJ      12345`
```
----|----|----|----|----|----|
    5   10   15   20   25   30
```
10. `                    ABC12345IJ`
```
----|----|----|----|----|----|
    5   10   15   20   25   30
```
11. `ABCDE   12345`
```
----|----|----|----|----|----|
    5   10   15   20   25   30
```
12. Correct—all format descriptors match variable types.

13. Incorrect. Format descriptors do not match variable types for `test` and `ierror`.

14. This program skips to the top of a page, and writes the following data.

```
            Output Data
            ===========

POINT( 1) =      1.200000      2.400000
POINT( 2) =      2.400000      4.800000

----|----|----|----|----|----|----|----|
    5   10   15   20   25   30   35   40
```

QUIZ 5–2

Note: There is more than one way to write each of the FORMAT statements in this quiz. Each of the answers shown below represents one of many possible correct answers to these questions.

1. `READ (*,100) amplitude, count, identity`
   `100 FORMAT (9X,F11.2,T30,I6,T60,A13)`
2. `READ (*,110) title, i1, i2, i3, i4, i5`
   `110 FORMAT (T10,A25,/(4X,I8))`
3. `READ (*,120) string, number`
   `120 FORMAT (T11,A10,///,T11,I10)`
4. $a = 1.65 \times 10^{-10}$, b = 17., c = -11.7
5. a = -3.141593, b = 2.718282, c = 37.55
6. i = -35, j = 6705, k = 3687
7. string1 = 'FGHIJ', string2 = 'KLMNOPQRST', string3 = 'UVWXYZ0123 ',
   string4 = ' _TEST_ 1'

8. Correct.

9. Correct. These statements read integer junk from columns 60 to 74 of one line, and then read real variable scratch from columns 1 to 15 of the next line.

10. Incorrect. Real variable elevation will be read with an I6 format descriptor.

QUIZ 5–3

1.
```
OPEN (UNIT=25,FILE='INO52691',ACTION='READ',IOSTAT=istat)
IF ( istat /= 0 ) THEN
   WRITE (*,'(1X,A,I6)') 'Open error on file. IOSTAT = ', istat
ELSE
   ...
END IF
```

2.
```
OPEN (UNIT=4,FILE=out_name, STATUS='NEW',ACTION='WRITE', &
      IOSTAT=istat)
```

3. `CLOSE (UNIT=24)`

4.
```
READ (8,*,IOSTAT=istat) first, last
IF ( istat < 0 ) THEN
   WRITE (*,*) 'End of file encountered on unit 8.'
END IF
```

5.
```
DO i = 1, 8
   BACKSPACE (UNIT=13)
END DO
```

6. Incorrect. File data1 has been replaced, so there is no data to read.

7. Incorrect. You cannot specify a file name with a scratch file.

8. Incorrect. There is nothing in the scratch file to read, since the file was created when it was opened.

9. Incorrect. You cannot use a real value as an i/o unit number.

10. Correct.

QUIZ 6–1

1. 15

2. 256

3. 41

4. Valid. The array will be initialized with the values in the array constructor.

5. Valid. All 10 values in the array will be initialized to 0.

6. Valid. Every tenth value in the array will be initialized to 1000, and all other values will be initialized to zero. The values will then be written out.

7. Invalid. The arrays are not conformable, since array1 is 11 elements long and array2 is 10 elements long.

8. Valid. Every tenth element of array in will be initialized to 10, 20, 30, etc. All other elements will be zero. The 10-element array sub1 will be initialized to 10, 20, 30, ... , 100, and the 10-element array sub2 will be initialized to 1, 2, 3, ... , 10. The multiplication will work because arrays sub1 and sub2 are conformable.

9. Mostly valid. The values in array error will be printed out. However, since error(0) was never initialized, we don't know what will be printed out, or even whether printing that array element will cause an I/O error.

10. Valid. Array `ivec1` will be initialized to 1, 2, ... , 10, and array `ivec2` will be initialized to 10, 9, ... , 1. Array `data1` will be initialized to 1., 4., 9., ... , 100. The `WRITE` statement will print out 100., 81., 64., ... , 1., because of the vector subscript.

11. Probably invalid. These statements will compile correctly, but they probably do *not* do what the programmer intended. A 10-element integer array `mydata` will be created. Each `READ` statement reads values into the entire array, so array `mydata` will be initialized 10 times over (using up 100 input values!). The user probably intended for each array element to be initialized only once.

QUIZ 7–1

1. The call to `ave_sd` is incorrect. The second argument is declared as an integer in the calling program, but it is a real within the subroutine.

2. These statements are valid. When the subroutine finishes executing, `string2` contains the mirror image of the characters in `string1`.

3. These statements are incorrect. Subroutine `sub3` uses 30 elements in array `iarray`, but there are only 25 values in the array passed from the calling program. Also, the subroutine uses an assumed-size dummy array, which should not be used in any new programs.

QUIZ 7–2

1. If data values are defined in a module, and then two or more procedures USE that module, they can all see and share the data. This is a convenient way to share private data among a group of related procedures, such as `random0` and `seed` in Example 7-4.

2. If procedures are placed in a module and accessed by USE association, then they will have explicit interfaces, allowing the compiler to catch many errors in calling sequence.

3. There is no error in this program. The main program and the subroutine share data by using module `mydata`. The output from the program is `a(5) = 5.0`.

4. This program is invalid. Subroutine `sub2` is called with a constant in as the second argument, which is declared to be `INTENT(OUT)` in the subroutine. The compiler will catch this error because the subroutine is inside a module accessed by USE association.

QUIZ 7–3

1.
```
REAL FUNCTION f2(x)
IMPLICIT NONE
REAL, INTENT(IN) :: x
f2 = (x -1.) / (x + 1.)
END FUNCTION f2
```

2.
```
REAL FUNCTION tanh(x)
IMPLICIT NONE
REAL, INTENT(IN) :: x
tanh = (EXP(x)-EXP(-x)) / (EXP(x)+EXP(-x))
END FUNCTION tanh
```

3.
```
FUNCTION fact(n)
IMPLICIT NONE
INTEGER, INTENT(IN) :: n
```

```
INTEGER :: fact
INTEGER :: i
fact = 1.
DO i = n, 1, -1
   fact = fact * i
END DO
END FUNCTION fact
```

4.
```
LOGICAL FUNCTION compare(x,y)
IMPLICIT NONE
REAL, INTENT(IN) :: x, y
compare = (x**2 + y**2) > 1.0
END FUNCTION compare
```

5. This function is incorrect because sum is never initialized. The sum must be set to zero before the DO loop is executed.

6. This function is invalid. Argument a is INTENT(IN), but its value is modified in the function.

7. This function is valid.

QUIZ 8–1

1. 645 elements. The valid range is data_input(-64,0) to data_input(64,4).

2. 210 elements. The valid range is filenm(1,1) to filenm(3,70).

3. 294 elements. The valid range is in(-3,-3,1) to in(3,3,6).

4. Invalid. The array constructor is not conformable with array dist.

5. Valid. dist will be initialized with the values in the array constructor.

6. Valid. Arrays data1, data2, and data_out are all conformable, so this addition is valid. The first WRITE statement prints the five values: 1., 11., 11., 11., 11., and the second WRITE statement prints the two values: 11., 11.

7. Valid. These statements initialize the array, and then select the subset specified by list1 = (/1,4,2,2/) and list2 = (/1,2,3/). The resulting array section is

$$\text{array(list1,list2)} = \begin{bmatrix} \text{array(1,1)} & \text{array(1,2)} & \text{array(1,3)} \\ \text{array(4,1)} & \text{array(4,2)} & \text{array(4,3)} \\ \text{array(2,1)} & \text{array(2,2)} & \text{array(2,3)} \\ \text{array(2,1)} & \text{array(2,2)} & \text{array(2,3)} \end{bmatrix}$$

$$\text{array(list1,list2)} = \begin{bmatrix} 11 & 21 & 31 \\ 14 & 24 & 34 \\ 12 & 22 & 32 \\ 12 & 22 & 32 \end{bmatrix}$$

8. Invalid. There is a many-one array section of the left-hand side of an assignment statement.

9. The data on the first three lines would be read into array input. However, the data is read in column order, so mydata(1,1) = 11.2, mydata(2,1) = 16.5, mydata(3,1) = 31.3, etc. mydata(2,4) = 15.0.

10. The data on the first three lines would be read into array input. The data is read in column order, so mydata(0,2) = 11.2, mydata(1,2) = 16.5, mydata(2,2) = 31.3, etc. mydata(2,4) = 17.1.

11. The data on the first three lines would be read into array input. This time, the data is read in row order, so mydata(1,1) = 11.2, mydata(1,2) = 16.5, mydata(1,3) = 31.3, etc. mydata(2,4) = 17.1.

12. The data on the first three lines would be read into array input. The data is read in row order, but only the first five values on each line are read by each READ statement. The next READ statement begins with the first value on the next input line. Therefore, mydata(2,4) = 11.0.

13. −9.0

14. The rank of array mydata is 2.

15. The shape of array mydata is 3 × 5.

16. The extent of the first dimension of array data_input is 129.

17. 7

QUIZ 8–2

1. LBOUND(values,1) = -3, UBOUND(values,2) = 50, SIZE(values,1) = 7, SIZE(values) = 357, SHAPE(values) = 7,51

2. UBOUND(values,2) = 4, SIZE(values) = 60, SHAPE(values) = 3,4,5

3. MAXVAL(input1) = 9.0, MAXLOC(input1) = 5,5

4. SUM(arr1) = 5.0, PRODUCT(arr1) = 0.0, PRODUCT(arr1, MASK=arr1 /= 0.) = -45.0, ANY(arr1>0) = T, ALL(arr1>0) = F

5. The values printed out are: SUM(arr2, MASK=arr2 > 0.) = 20.0

6. REAL, DIMENSION(5,5) :: input1
   FORALL (i=1:5, j=1:5)
       input1(i,j) = i+j-1
   END FORALL
   WRITE (*,*) MAXVAL(input1)
   WRITE (*,*) MAXLOC(input1)

7. Invalid. The control mask for the WHERE construct (time > 0.) is not the same shape as the array dist in the body of the WHERE construct.

8. Invalid. Array time must be allocated before it is initialized.

9. Valid. The resulting output array is:

$$
data1 = \begin{bmatrix} 1 & 0 & 0 & 0 & 0 \\ 0 & 0 & 0 & 0 & 0 \\ 3 & 2 & 1 & 0 & 0 \\ 0 & 0 & 0 & 0 & 0 \\ 5 & 4 & 3 & 2 & 1 \end{bmatrix}
$$

10. Valid. Since the array is not allocated, the result of the ALLOCATED function is FALSE, and output of the WRITE statement is F.

QUIZ 9–1

1. The SAVE statement or the SAVE attribute should be used in any procedure that depends on local data values being unchanged between invocations of the procedure. All local variables that must remain constant between invocations should be declared with the SAVE attribute.

2. An automatic array is a local array in a procedure whose extent is specified by variables passed to the procedure when it is invoked. The array is automatically created each time procedure is invoked, and is automatically destroyed each time the procedure exits. Automatic arrays should be used for temporary storage within a procedure. An allocatable array is an array declared with the ALLOCATABLE attribute, and allocated with an ALLOCATE statement. It is more general and flexible than an automatic array, since it may appear in either main programs or procedures. Allocatable arrays can create memory leaks if misused. Allocatable arrays should be used to allocate memory in main programs.

3. Assumed-shape dummy arrays have the advantage (compared to assumed-size arrays) that they can be used with whole array operations, array intrinsic functions, and array sections. They are simpler than explicit-shape dummy arrays because the bounds of each array do not have to be passed to the procedure. The only disadvantage associated with them is that they must be used with an explicit interface.

4. This program will work on many processors, but it has two potentially serious problems. First, the value of variable isum is never initialized. Second, isum is not saved between calls to sub1. When it works, it will initialize the values of the array to 1, 2, ... , 10.

5. This program will work. When array b is written out, it will contain the values:

$$b = \begin{bmatrix} 2. & 8. & 18. \\ 32. & 50. & 72. \\ 98. & 128. & 162. \end{bmatrix}$$

6. This program is invalid. Subroutine sub4 uses assumed-shape arrays but does not have an explicit interface.

QUIZ 10–1

1. False for ASCII, and true for EBCDIC.
2. False for both ASCII and EBCDIC.
3. False.
4. These statements are legal.
5. This function is legal, provided that it has an explicit interface. Automatic length character functions must have an explicit interface.
6. Variable name will contain the string:
   'JOHNSON   ,JAMES   R'
7. a = '123'; b = 'ABCD23 IJKL'
8. ipos1 = 17, ipos2 = 0, ipos3 = 14, ipos4 = 37

QUIZ 10–2

1. Valid. The result is `-1234`, because `buff1(10:10)` is `'J'`, not `'K'`.
2. Valid. After these statements `outbuf` contains
   ```
   '        123         0      -11           '
   ```
3. The statements are valid. `ival1 = 456789`, `ival2 = 234`, `rval3 = 5678.90`.

QUIZ 11–1

1. This answer to this question is processor dependent. You must consult the manuals for your particular compiler.
2. `(-1.980198E-02,-1.980198E-01)`
3.
```
PROGRAM complex_math
!
! Purpose:
!   To perform the complex calculation:
!       D = ( A + B ) / C
!   where A = ( 1., -1.)
!         B = (-1., -1.)
!         C = (10.,  1.)
!   without using the COMPLEX data type.
!
IMPLICIT NONE
!
REAL :: ar = 1., ai = -1.
REAL :: br = -1., bi = -1.
REAL :: cr = 10., ci = 1.
REAL :: dr, di
REAL :: tempr, tempi

CALL complex_add ( ar, ai, br, bi, tempr, tempi )
CALL complex_divide ( tempr, tempi, cr, ci, dr, di )

WRITE (*,100) dr, di
100 FORMAT (1X,'D = (',F10.5,',',F10.5,')' )

END PROGRAM

SUBROUTINE complex_add ( x1, y1, x2, y2, x3, y3 )
!
! Purpose:
!   Subroutine to add two complex numbers (x1, y1) and
!   (x2, y2), and store the result in (x3, y3).
!
IMPLICIT NONE

REAL, INTENT(IN) :: x1, y1, x2, y2
REAL, INTENT(OUT) :: x3, y3
```

```
x3 = x1 + x2
y3 = y1 + y2

END SUBROUTINE complex_add

SUBROUTINE complex_divide ( x1, y1, x2, y2, x3, y3 )
!
!  Purpose:
!    Subroutine to divide two complex numbers (x1, y1) and
!    (x2, y2), and store the result in (x3, y3).
!
IMPLICIT NONE

REAL, INTENT(IN) :: x1, y1, x2, y2
REAL, INTENT(OUT) :: x3, y3
REAL :: denom

denom = x2**2 + y2**2
x3 = (x1 * x2 + y1 * y2) / denom
y3 = (y1 * x2 - x1 * y2) / denom

END SUBROUTINE complex_divide
```

It is much easier to use the complex data type to solve the problem than it is to use the definitions of complex operations and real numbers.

QUIZ 12–1

1.
```
    WRITE (*,100) points(7)%plot_time%day, points(7)%plot_time%month, &
                  points(7)%plot_time%year, points(7)%plot_time%hour, &
                  points(7)%plot_time%minute, points(7)%plot_time%second
100 FORMAT (1X,I2.2,'/',I2.2,'/',I4.4,' ',I2.2,':',I2.2,':',I2.2)
```
2.
```
    WRITE (*,110) points(7)%plot_position%x, &
                  points(7)%plot_position%y, &
                  points(7)%plot_position%z
110 FORMAT (1X,' x = ',F12.4, ' y = ',F12.4, ' z = ',F12.4 )
```
3. To calculate the time difference, we must subtract the times associated with the two points, taking into account the different scales associated with hours, minutes, seconds, etc. The code below converts the times to seconds before subtracting them, and also assumes that both points occur on the same day, month, and year. (It is easy to extend this calculation to handle arbitrary days, months, and years as well, but double precision real arithmetic must be used for the calculations.) To calculate the position difference, we use the equation

$$dpos = \sqrt{(x_2 - x_1)^2 + (y_2 - y_1)^2 + (z_2 - z_1)^2}$$

```
time1 = points(2)%plot_time%second + 60.*points(2)%plot_time%minute &
      + 3600.*points(2)%plot_time%hour
time2 = points(3)%plot_time%second + 60.*points(3)%plot_time%minute &
      + 3600.*points(3)%plot_time%hour
dtime = time2 - time1

dpos = SQRT ( &
          (points(3)%plot_position%x - points(2)%plot_position%x )**2 &
        + (points(3)%plot_position%y - points(2)%plot_position%y )**2 &
        + (points(3)%plot_position%z - points(2)%plot_position%z )**2 )

rate = dpos / dtime
```

4. Valid. This statement prints out all of the components of the first element of array points.
5. Invalid. The format descriptors do not match the order of the data in points(4).
6. Invalid. Intrinsic operations are not defined for derived data types, and component plot_position is a derived data type.

QUIZ 13–1

1. The scope of an object is the portion of a Fortran program over which the object is defined. The three levels of scope are global, local, and statement.
2. Host association is the process by which data entities in a host scoping unit are made available to an inner scoping unit. If variables and constants are defined in a host scoping unit, then those variables and constants are inherited by any inner scoping units *unless* another object with the same name is explicitly defined in the inner scoping unit.
3. When this program is executed $z = 3.666667$. Initially, z is set to 10.0, and then function fun1(z) is invoked. The function is an internal function, so it inherits the values of derived type variable xyz by host association. Since $xyz\%x = 1.0$ and $xyz\%z = 3.0$, the function evaluates to $(10. + 1.)/3. = 3.666667$. This function result is then stored in variable z.
4. $i = 20$. The first executable statement changes i to 27, and the fourth executable statement subtracts 7 from it to produce the final answer. (The i in the third statement has statement scope only, and so does not affect the value of i in the main program.)
5. This program is illegal. The program name abc must be unique within the program.
6. Recursive procedures are procedures that can call themselves. They are declared by using the RECURSIVE keyword in SUBROUTINE or FUNCTION statements. If the recursive procedure is a function, then the FUNCTION statement should also include a RESULT clause.
7. Keyword arguments are calling arguments of the form KEYWORD=value, where KEYWORD is the name used to declare the dummy argument in the procedure definition, and value is the value to be passed to that dummy argument when the procedure is invoked. Keyword arguments may be used only if the procedure being invoked has an explicit interface. Keyword arguments may be used to allow calling arguments to be specified in a different order, or to specify only certain optional arguments.
8. Optional arguments are arguments that do not have to be present when a procedure is invoked, but that will be used if they are present. Optional arguments may be used only if the procedure being invoked has an explicit interface. They may be used for input or output data that is not needed every time a procedure is invoked.

QUIZ 13–2

1. An interface block is a way to specify an explicit interface for a separately compiled external procedure. It consists of an INTERFACE statement and an END INTERFACE statement. Between these two statements are statements declaring the calling sequence of the procedure, including the order, type, and intent of each argument. Interface blocks may be placed in the declaration section of an invoking program unit, or else they may be placed in a module, and that module may be accessed by the invoking program unit via USE association.

2. A programmer might choose to create an interface block for a procedure because the procedure may be written in a language other than Fortran, or because the procedure must work with both Fortran 90/95/2003 and older FORTRAN 77 applications.

3. The interface body contains a SUBROUTINE or FUNCTION statement declaring the name of the procedure and its dummy arguments, followed by type declaration statements for each of the dummy arguments. It concludes with an END SUBROUTINE or END FUNCTION statement.

4. This program is valid. The multiple definitions for x1 and x2 do not interfere with each other because they are in different scoping units. When the program is executed, the results are:
   ```
   This is a test.      613.000        248.000
   ```

5. A generic procedure is defined by using a named interface block. The name of the generic procedure is specified in the INTERFACE statement, and the calling sequences of all possible specific procedures are specified in the body of the interface block. Each specific procedure must be distinguishable from all of the other specific procedures by some combination of its non-optional calling arguments. If the generic interface block appears in a module and the corresponding specific procedures are also defined in the module, then they are specified as being a part of the generic procedure with MODULE PROCEDURE statements.

6. A generic bound procedure is defined by using a GENERIC statement in the type definition. The GENERIC statement will declare the generic name of the procedure, followed by the list of specific procedures associated with it:

   ```
   TYPE :: point
      REAL :: x
      REAL :: y
   CONTAINS
      GENERIC :: add = >  point_plus_point, point_plus_scalar
   END TYPE point
   ```

7. This generic interface is illegal, because the number, types, and order of the dummy arguments for the two specific procedures are identical. There must be a difference between the two sets of dummy arguments so that the compiler can determine which one to use.

8. A MODULE PROCEDURE statement is used to specify that a specific procedure is a part of a generic procedure (or operator definition) when both the specific procedure and the generic procedure (or operator definition) appear within the same module. It is used because any procedure in a module automatically has an explicit interface. Respecifying the interface in a generic interface block would involve declaring the explicit interface of the procedure twice, which is illegal.

9. A user-defined operator is declared by using the INTERFACE OPERATOR block, while a user-defined assignment is declared by using the INTERFACE ASSIGNMENT block.

A user-defined operator is implemented by a one- or two-argument function (for unary and binary operators respectively). The arguments of the function must have INTENT(IN), and the result of the function is the result of the operation. A user-defined assignment is implemented by using a two-argument subroutine. The first argument must be INTENT(OUT) or INTENT(INOUT), and the second argument must be INTENT(IN). The first argument is the result of the assignment operation.

F-2003 ONLY

10. Access to the contents of a module may be controlled using PUBLIC, PRIVATE, and PROTECTED statements or attributes. It might be desirable to restrict access to the internal components of some user-defined data types, or to restrict direct access to procedures used to implement user-defined operators or assignments, so these items can be declared to be PRIVATE. The PROTECTED access allows a variable to be used but not modified, so it is effective read-only outside of the module in which it is defined.

F-2003 ONLY

11. The default type of access for items in a module is PUBLIC.

12. A program unit accessing items in a module by USE association can limit the items in the module that it accesses by using the ONLY clause in the USE statement. A programmer might wish to limit access in this manner to avoid conflicts if a public item in the module has the same name as a local item in the programming unit.

13. A program unit accessing items in a module by USE association can rename the items in the module that it accesses by using the => option in the USE statement. A programmer might wish to rename an item in order to avoid conflicts if an item in the module has the same name as a local item in the programming unit.

F-2003 ONLY

14. This program is illegal, because the program attempts to modify the protected value t1%z.

QUIZ 14–1

```
1.     4096.1  4096.07  .40961E+04  4096.1        4096.
  ---|----|----|----|----|----|----|----|----|----|----|----|
     5   10   15   20   25   30   35   40   45   50   55   60
2.     Data1( 1) = -17.2000,      Data1( 2) =   4.0000,
       Data1( 3) =   4.0000,      Data1( 4) =    .3000,
       Data1( 5) =  -2.2200
  ---|----|----|----|----|----|----|----|----|----|----|----|
     5   10   15   20   25   30   35   40   45   50   55   60
3.  12.200000E-06 12.345600E+06
     1.220000E-05  1.234560E+07
  ---|----|----|----|----|----|
     5   10   15   20   25   30
4.  i =     -2002 j =      -1001 k =         -3
  ---|----|----|----|----|----|----|----|----|
     5   10   15   20   25   30   35   40   45
```

QUIZ 14–2

1. A formatted file contains information stored as ASCII or EBCDIC characters. The information in a formatted file can be read with a text editor. By contrast, an unformatted file contains information stored in a form that is an exact copy of the bit patterns in the computer's memory. Its contents can not be easily examined. Formatted files are portable

between processors, but they occupy a relatively large amount of space and require extra processor time to perform the translations on input and output. Unformatted files are more compact and more efficient to read and write, but they are not portable between processors of different types.

2. A direct access file is a file whose records can be read and written in any arbitrary order. A sequential access file is a file whose records must be read and written sequentially. Direct access files are more efficient for accessing data in random order, but every record in a direct access file must be the same length. Sequential access files are efficient for reading and writing data in sequential order, but are very poor for random access. However, the records in a sequential access file may have variable lengths.

3. The `INQUIRE` statement is used to retrieve information about a file. The information may be retrieved by (1) file name or (2) i/o unit number. The third form of the `INQUIRE` statement is the `IOLENGTH` form. It calculates the length of a record in an unformatted direct access file in processor-dependent units.

4. Invalid. It is illegal to use a file name with a scratch file.

5. Invalid. The `RECL=` clause must be specified when a direct access file is opened.

6. Invalid. By default, direct access files are opened unformatted. Formatted I/O cannot be performed on unformatted files.

7. Invalid. By default, sequential access files are opened formatted. Unformatted I/O cannot be performed on formatted files.

8. Invalid. Either a file name or an i/o unit may be specified in an `INQUIRE` statement, but not both.

9. The contents of file `'out.dat'` will be:

```
&LOCAL_DATA
A =      -200.000000    -17.000000 0.000000E+00    100.000000 30.000000
B =          -37.000000
C =       0.000000E+00
/
```

QUIZ 15–1

1. A pointer is a Fortran variable that contains the *address* of another Fortran variable or array. A target is an ordinary Fortran variable or array that has been declared with the `TARGET` attribute, so that a pointer can point to it. The difference between a pointer and an ordinary variable is that a pointer contains the address of another Fortran variable or array, while an ordinary Fortran variable contains data.

2. A pointer assignment statement assigns the address of a target to a pointer. The difference between a pointer assignment statement and an ordinary assignment statement is that a pointer assignment statement assigns the address of a Fortran variable or array to a pointer, while an ordinary assignment statement assigns the value of an expression to the target pointed to by the pointer.

```
ptr1 => var      ! Assigns address of var to ptr1
ptr1 = var       ! Assigns value of var to target of ptr1
```

3. The possible association statuses of a pointer are: associated, disassociated, and undefined. When a pointer is first declared, its status is undefined. It may be associated with a target by using a pointer assignment statement or an `ALLOCATE` statement. The

pointer may be disassociated from a target by the NULLIFY statement, the DEALLOCATE statement, by assigning a null pointer to it in a pointer assignment statement, or by using the NULL() function.

4. Dereferencing is the process of accessing the corresponding target when a reference to a pointer appears in an operation or assignment statement.

5. Memory may be dynamically allocated with pointers by using the ALLOCATE statement. Memory may be deallocated by using the DEALLOCATE statement.

6. Invalid. This is an attempt to use ptr2 before it is associated with a target.

7. Valid. This statement assigns the address of the target variable value to pointer ptr2.

8. Invalid. A pointer must be of the same type as its target.

9. Valid. This statement assigns the address of the target array array to pointer ptr4. It illustrates the use of POINTER and TARGET statements.

10. Valid, but with a memory leak. The first WRITE statement will print out an F, because pointer ptr is not associated. The second WRITE statement will print out a T followed by the value 137, because a memory location was allocated by using the pointer, and the value 137 was assigned to that location. The final statement nullifies the pointer, leaving the allocated memory location inaccessible.

11. Invalid. These statements allocate a 10-element array using ptr1 and assign values to it. The address of the array is assigned to ptr2, and then the array is deallocated by using ptr1. This leaves ptr2 pointing to an invalid memory location. When the WRITE statement is executed, the results are unpredictable.

12. Valid. These statements define a derived data type containing a pointer, and then declare an array of that derived data type. The pointer contained in each element of the array is then used to allocate an array, and each array is initialized. Finally, the entire array pointed to by the pointer in the fourth element is printed out, and the first element of the array pointed to by the pointer in the seventh element is printed out. The resulting output is:
31 32 33 34 35 36 37 38 39 40
61

QUIZ 16–1

1. Object oriented programming provides a number of advantages:
   - **Encapsulation and data hiding.** Data inside an object cannot be accidentally or deliberately modified by other programming modules. The other modules can communicate with the object only through the defined interfaces, which are the object's public method calls. This allows a user to modify the internals of an object without affecting any other part of the code, as long as the interfaces are not changed.
   - **Reuse.** Since objects are self-contained, it is easy to reuse them in other projects.
   - **Reduced Effort.** Methods and behaviors can be coded only once in a superclass and inherited by all subclasses of that superclass. Each subclass has to code only the *differences* between it and its parent class.

2. The principal components of a class are:
   - **Fields.** Fields define the instance variables that will be created when an object is instantiated from a class. Instance variables are the data encapsulated inside an object. A new set of instance variables is created each time that an object is instantiated from the class.
   - **Methods.** Methods implement the behaviors of a class. Some methods may be explicitly defined in a class, while other methods may be inherited from superclasses of the class.

- **Finalizer.** Just before an object is destroyed, it makes a call to a special method called a **finalizer**. The method performs any necessary cleanup (releasing resources, etc.) before the object is destroyed. There can be at most one finalizer in a class, and many classes do not need a finalizer at all.

3. The three types of access modifiers are PUBLIC, PRIVATE, and PROTECTED. PUBLIC instance variables and methods may be accessed from any procedure that USEs the module containing the definitions. PRIVATE instance variables and methods may *not* be accessed from any procedure that USEs the module containing the definitions. PROTECTED instance variables may be read but not written from any procedure that USEs the module containing the definitions. The PRIVATE access modifier should normally be used for instance variables, so that they are not visible from outside the class. The PUBLIC access modifier should normally be used for methods, so that they can be used from outside the class.

4. Type-bound methods are created by using the CONTAINS clause in a derived type definition.

5. A finalizer is a special method that is called just before an object is destroyed. A finalizer performs any necessary cleanup (releasing resources, etc.) before the object is destroyed. There can be more than one finalizer in a class, but most classes do not need a finalizer at all. A finalizer is declared by adding a FINAL keyword in the CONTAINS section of the type definition.

6. Inheritance is the process by which a subclass receives all of the instance variables and bound methods from its parent class. If a new class extends an existing class, then all of the instance variables and bound methods from its parent class will automatically be included in the child class.

7. Polymorphism is the ability to work with objects of many different subclasses as though they were all objects of a common superclass. When a bound method is called on one of the objects, the program will automatically pick the proper version of the method for an object of that particular subclass.

8. Abstract methods are methods whose interface is declared in a superclass, but whose implementation is deferred until subclasses are derived from the superclass. Abstract methods can be used where you want to achieve polymorphic behavior, but the specific method will always be overridden in subclasses derived from the method. Any class with one or more abstract methods will be an abstract class. No objects can be derived from an abstract class, but pointers and dummy arguments can be of that type.

E

Index

X

Z

BARBEQUE BREAD
(6 - 8 PORTIONS)

175ml	milk
350ml	maize flour/mealie-meal
50ml	butter
25ml	chopped red pepper
1	medium onion, grated
200ml	carrots, grated
3	eggs, beaten
175ml	plain Gero yoghurt
250ml	cake flour
15ml	mustard powder
50ml	sugar
10ml	salt

1. Bring milk to the boil, add maize flour/mealie-meal and 30 ml butter, mix and allow to cool.
2. Saute onion, red pepper and carrots in 20 ml butter and leave to cool.
3. Beat eggs and add yoghurt, mix with cooled milk mixture and fried vegetables.
4. Add the remaining ingredients and mix lightly.
5. Pour into greased bread-pan and bake in pre-heated oven at 200°C for 60 minutes.
   Serve with butter.